CLARIFY YOUR MEANING— IN SECONDS!

At last there is a contemporary thesaurus designed for writers and business users, not just literary scholars. Avoiding archaic meanings and including the most up-to-date language, *The Pocket Word Finder® Thesaurus* provides word power you can really use. Each of the 15,000 main entries includes an average of fifteen synonyms—but some entries feature over 100!

As *The Pocket Word Finder® Thesaurus* helps you make yourself clear, you'll discover what a short step it is from "clear" to "explicit" to "unambiguous" to "eloquent." Whether you want to tone up a statement or tone it down, you'll find the right word in this indispensable guide.

THE POCKET WORD FINDER® THESAURUS

The Pocket Word Finder® Thesaurus **data:**

Mike Weiner, Editor
Dr. Roger Schlobin, Lexicographer
Joy Moncrief, Associate Editor
Taeyung Surh, Associate Editor

THE
POCKET
WORD
FINDER®
THESAURUS

Prepared by Microlytics, Inc.

POCKET BOOKS

New York   London   Toronto   Sydney   Tokyo   Singapore

Based on the Word Finder® Thesaurus software originally developed for the IBM PC and Apple Macintosh by Microlytics and Selfware, Inc.

An *Original* Publication of POCKET BOOKS

 POCKET BOOKS, a division of Simon & Schuster Inc.
1230 Avenue of the Americas, New York, NY 10020

ISBN: 0-671-68613-5

First Pocket Books printing February 1990

10 9 8 7 6 5 4 3 2

POCKET and colophon are registered trademarks of
Simon & Schuster Inc.

Printed in the U.S.A.

Preface

It has been said that there is no such thing as a true synonym in the English language. No two words mean exactly the same thing. Words have their own nuance and tone, even when expressing the same concept. Besides, many words have several meanings, so one word may be far more appropriate than another, depending on the particular context in which it is used.

The adjective *clear,* for example, can mean many things, from "bare," "legible," "understandable," "explicit," "unambiguous," and "eloquent" to "sunny." All this—and more—before we consider its use as a verb, where, among other things, it expedites, fades, empties, pardons, repays, and explains.

Thus the creation of a book of synonyms tends to be more art than science, for the presentation of alternative words should be more than a mere listing of very close, almost clinically exact substitutes. Writers and speakers of a language, any language, often search for a word on the far reaches of the one they have in mind, way out on the tip of the tongue, waiting to be found. Or they may be on the lookout for just a cat's-hair variation in meaning, barely enough to tone a statement up or down a trifle.

The creators of *The Pocket Word Finder® Thesaurus* had today's speakers and writers of English very much in mind. Their objective was to produce as contemporary a book of synonyms as possible without sacrificing the variety and nuance of the language. In assembling the 15,000 entries and 220,000 synonyms, they drew on the Word Finder® Thesaurus software for the IBM PC and Macintosh, which was developed by Microlytics and Selfware, Inc.

This reference book, then, is designed to give you maximum power of expression. When you have difficulty recalling the precise word to match a thought, turn to a main entry word with more or less the same meaning, and there you are likely to find the elusive alternative. And when you are in search of creative ideas, scan the book, for in it you will find new insights and perspectives. Indeed, not only will *The Pocket Word Finder® Thesaurus* increase your productivity, but it will add variety and spice to your speech and writing.

How to Use
The Pocket Word Finder® Thesaurus

1. The main entry words, or headwords, appear in strict alphabetical order, according to the system followed by most dictionaries. For example:

down
downfall
downgrade
downpour
downside
down-to-earth
downturn

2. Italics are used for foreign words and phrases encountered with some frequency in English speech and writing but not completely naturalized. This typographic device signals the user that such terms are ordinarily italicized in print and underscored in handwritten or typewritten material. One such main entry

word is the popular word *ciao,* an informal expression of farewell borrowed from Italian.

3. Each main entry word is followed by one or more of these part-of-speech labels, as appropriate: *adj* (adjective), *adv* (adverb), *conj* (conjunction), *n* (noun), *prep* (preposition), *v* (verb).

4. If a main entry word conveys more than one sense, or meaning, separate numbered lists of synonyms differentiate the various senses. For ease of reference, the lists are grouped by part of speech. For example, the entry for **hurt** includes two adjective lists, five noun lists, and seven verb lists.

5. Cross-references call attention to one or more groups of synonyms related to a particular word. If a main entry word to which the user is being directed has several senses, the cross-reference identifies them by number as well as by part of speech. For example, in the **move** entry the second noun item is "see: MANEU-VER *n* **2**." This indicates that for additional synonyms the reader should look at the second noun listing under the main entry word **maneuver**.

THE
POCKET
WORD
FINDER®
THESAURUS

a *adj* a few, any, at least one, each, every, individual, one, several, some

abandon *n* departure, desertion, evacuation, exit, going, leaving, pullback, pullout, removal, retreat, withdrawal

v 1 discard, dispose of, dump, eliminate, empty, quit, reject, scrap, unload

v 2 acquiesce, cede, give up, hand over, leave, relinquish, resign, submit, surrender, waive, yield

v 3 break up, cast off, chuck, defect, desert, disavow, discard, disenfranchise, disown, ditch, dump, forsake, jilt, junk, leave, quit, reject, renounce, spurn, strand, throw out

abandoned *adj* depraved, derelict, deserted, desolate, forsaken, secluded, solitary, uninhabited

abandonment *n* relaxation

abase *v* abash, belittle, cast down, cheapen, debase, defile, deflate, degrade, demean, depreciate, derogate, devalue, dishonor, embarrass, humble, humiliate, lower, mortify, put down, shame, sink

abash *v* 1 see: BELITTLE *v* 1

v 2 see: FRIGHTEN *v* 2

abashed *adj* ashamed, chagrined, embarrassed, humiliated, mortified, shamed

abate *v* 1 allay, assuage, mitigate, moderate, quench, satiate, satisfy

v 2 decline, deteriorate, fade, fail, flag, impair, languish, wane, weaken, wither, worsen

v 3 cease, decline, decrease, die down, diminish, drain, dwindle, ease, ebb, fall, lessen, let up, lull, recede, reduce, relax, relent, shrink, slacken, soften, stop, subside, taper off, wane, waste away, weaken

v 4 see: TERMINATE *v* 8

abatement *n* 1 alleviation, comfort, correction, cure, help, relief, remedy, respite, solace, solution

n 2 diminishing, easing, letup, loosening, relaxation, slackening

abbé *n* abbot, ascetic, friar, hermit, monk, recluse

abbey *n* cloister, monastery, priory

abbot *n* abbé, ascetic, friar, hermit, monk, recluse

abbreviate *v* abridge, condense, curtail, cut, cut back, diminish, edit, lessen, reduce, restrict, shorten, slash

abbreviated *adj* brief, compressed, concise, crisp, curt, laconic, pithy, short, succinct, terse, to the point

abdicate *v* quit, relinquish, renounce, resign, step down, vacate

abdication *n* departure, resignation, retirement

abdomen *n* belly, gut, midriff, paunch, stomach, tummy, tum-tum

abduct *v* carry away, grab, kidnap, seize, shanghai, steal

aberrant *adj* 1 see: IRREGULAR *adj* 2

adj 2 see: STRANGE *adj* 5

aberration *n* 1 apparition, delusion, fantasy, figment, ghost, hallucination, illusion, image, mirage, phantasm, specter, vision

n 2 abnormality, craziness, delusion, dementia, derangement, distraction, eccentricity, fugue, hallucination, insanity, irregularity, lunacy, madness, mania, psychosis, unbalance

abet *v* see: HELP *v* 4

abettor *n* accessory, accomplice, coconspirator, confederate, conspirator, partner, supporter

abeyance *n* 1 cease-fire, respite, timeout, truce

n 2 cessation, halt, impasse, moratorium, standstill, stay, stop, stopping, suspension

n 3 dormancy, inaction, inactivity, limbo, lull, pause, suspension

abhor *v* 1 abominate, bristle, desecrate, despise, detest, disdain, dislike, hate, loathe, reject, revile, scorn

v 2 disgust, nauseate, repel, repulse, revolt, sicken

abhorrent *adj* 1 despicable, repulsive, revolting, ugly

adj 2 base, gross, invidious, obnoxious, offensive, repellent, repugnant, repulsive, revulsive

adj 3 abominable, appalling, detestable, disgusting, dreadful, evil, frightful, ghastly, hateful, horrible, horrid, loathsome, odious, repulsive, revolting, shocking

abide *v* 1 await, bide, linger, loiter, remain, stay, stick around, tarry, wait

v 2 continue, endure, last, outlast, persevere, persist, prevail, remain, stay, stick to, stick with, survive

v 3 accept, acquiesce, allow, authorize, bear, concede, condone, digest, endure, experience, have, let, permit, put up with, stand, stomach, suffer, sustain, swallow, take, tolerate, undergo

abiding *adj* enduring, firm, never-failing, steadfast, sure, unfaltering, unshakable, unwavering

ability *n* adequacy, adroitness, aptitude, art, caliber, calling, capability, capacity, command, competence, craft, dexterity, experience, expertise, familiarity, forte, knack, know-how, knowledge, mastery, proficiency, prowess, qualification, savvy, skill, specialty, strength, talent, training, workmanship

abject *adj* 1 base, contemptible, debasing, despicable, false, servile

adj 2 common, groveling, humble, ingratiating, lowly, menial, obeisant, obsequious, servile, slavish, subservient

abjure *v* deny, disavow, disclaim, disown, forswear, reject, renounce, repudiate

ablaze *adj* afire, aflame, aglow, alight, blazing, burning, conflagrant, fiery, flaming, glowing

able *adj* 1 safe, solvent, sound

adj 2 accomplished, adept, apt, capable, competent, deft, dexterous, expert, fit, gifted, masterful, professional, proficient, proper, qualified, skillful, talented

ablutions *n* cleansing

abnormal *adj* 1 depressing, dismal, funereal, ghastly, gloomy, gruesome, macabre, morbid, sepulchral

adj 2 aberrant, anomalous, artificial, atypical, contrived, deviant, disparate, divergent, incongruous, irregular, off-key, uncharacteristic, unnatural

adj 3 see: SUPERFLUOUS *adj* 3

abnormality *n* 1 eccentricity, habit, idiosyncrasy, oddity, peculiarity, quirk, trademark

n 2 aberration, craziness, delusion, dementia, derangement, distraction, eccentricity, fugue, hallucination, insanity, irregularity, lunacy, madness, mania, psychosis, unbalance

abode *n* 1 barn, bungalow, cabin, coop, cottage, hatch, hovel, hut, lodge, shack, shanty

n 2 castle, domicile, dwelling, estate, home, house, mansion, palace, residence

abolish *v* 1 see: KILL *v* 3, 5

v 2 see: TERMINATE *v* 8

abominable *adj* abhorrent, appalling, detestable, disgusting, dreadful, evil, frightful, ghastly, hateful, horrible, horrid, loathsome, odious, repulsive, revolting, shocking

abominate *v* abhor, bristle, desecrate, despise, detest, disdain, dislike, hate, loathe, reject, revile, scorn

abomination *n* blasphemy, curse word, expletive, imprecation, obscenity, profanity, swearing

aboriginal *adj* 1 endemic, indigenous, native, primitive

adj 2 ancient, early, former, original, prehistoric, primeval, primitive, primordial, rudimentary

aborigine *n* barbarian, native, primitive, savage

abort *v* erase, kill, sever, stop, terminate

abortive *adj* fruitless, futile, ineffective, ineffectual, nonproductive, unavailing, unproductive, unsuccessful, unyielding, useless, vain, worthless

abound *v* increase, multiply, overrun, proliferate, propagate, teem

abounding *adj* see: PLENTIFUL *adj* 1

about *adv* almost, approximately, around, close to, more or less, nearly, not quite

prep apropos, as to, concerning, re, regarding, respecting, with respect to

above *adv* aloft, greater, more, on top of, over, overhead, superior

aboveboard *adj* candid, equitable, fair, forthright, honest, legitimate, plaindealing, straight, straightforward, trustworthy, upright

abrasion *n* cut, hurt, itch, scrape, scratch, sore

abrasive *adj* aggravating, annoying, caustic, cutting, grating, irritating

abreast *adj* acquainted, aware, conversant, familiar, informed, knowledgeable, up, versed

abridge *v* abbreviate, condense, curtail, cut, cut back, diminish, edit, lessen, reduce, restrict, shorten, slash

abridgement *n* abstract, brief, compendium, condensation, digest, essence, example, outline, review, sketch, summary, syllabus, synopsis

abroad *adv* overseas

abrogate *v* 1 see: CANCEL *v* 3

v 2 see: TERMINATE *v* 8

abrupt *adj* 1 audacious, desperate, headstrong, rash, reckless

adj 2 hasty, headlong, hurried, impetuous, impulsive, precipitant, precipitate, quick, rapid, rash, reckless, rushing, sudden

adj 3 bluff, blunt, brash, brusque, cheeky, crusty, curt, flip, flippant, gruff, harsh, impertinent, impudent, irritable, nasty, quick, rude, sarcastic, sassy, short, snippy, snotty, surly, testy, wisenheimer

abruptly *adv* fast, hastily, immediately, instantaneously, instantly, quick, quickly, short, suddenly, swiftly

abruptness *n* brevity, briefness, conciseness, curtness, quickness, shortness, transience

abscess *n* boil, carbuncle, pimple, ulcer

abscond v **1** bolt, break, depart, elude, escape, flee, fly, hightail it, lose, run, sneak away, split

v **2** see: LEAVE v 4

absence n error, disregard, neglect, omission, oversight, slip-up

absent adj away, gone, lacking, missing, omitted, truant, wanting

absentee n hooky player, nonattender, no-show, truant

absent-minded adj abstracted, bemused, careless, dazed, dizzy, groggy, inattentive, lost, mindless, oblivious, preoccupied, silly, spaced, vapid

absolute adj **1** firm, fixed, resolute, steadfast, unconditional, unreserved

adj **2** complete, flawless, good, intact, perfect, sound, unblemished, unbroken, undamaged, unimpaired, uninjured, unmarred, untouched, whole

adj **3** chief, complete, consummate, dominant, godlike, leading, main, perfect, principal, pure, ranking, sheer, supreme, total, unsurpassed, utter, whole

adj **4** agreed, bounded, categorical, clear, decided, definite, emphatic, established, exact, finite, fixed, guaranteed, limited, positive, specific, unequivocal, unmistakable, vested

adj **5** actual, authentic, bona fide, certain, definite, existent, factual, genuine, hard, inarguable, incontestable, incontrovertible, indisputable, indubitable, irrefutable, positive, real, sure, true, undeniable, undisputable, undoubtable, undoubted, unequivocal, unquestionable, veritable, viable

absolutely adv certainly, decidedly, definitely, entirely, incontrovertibly, indeed, indubitably, positively, surely, truly, unequivocally, unquestionably, verily, well, without doubt

absolution n amnesty, discharge, disengagement, dispensation, freedom, moratorium, pardon, release, relief, reprieve, respite, stay, suspension

absolve v **1** clean, purify, sanctify

v **2** acquit, cover up, exonerate, extenuate, mitigate, whitewash

v **3** acquit, clear, condone, exculpate, excuse, exempt, exonerate, forgive, free, pardon, remit, reprieve, vindicate

absorb v blot, consume, engross, engulf, occupy, soak up

absorbed adj **1** curious, drawn, engrossed, interested, involved

adj **2** agog, concentrated, deep, determined, distracted, engaged, engrossed, enraptured, entranced, fascinated, immersed, intent, preoccupied, rapt, wrapped up

absorbent adj spongy

absorber n agent, broker, catalyst, distributor, go-between, intermediary, mediator, middleman, negotiator

abstain v **1** forbear, keep, refrain, withhold

v **2** avoid, constrain, curb, deny, forgo, govern, hold back, refrain, resist, restrict, stop, tame

v **3** cast, decline, drop, eschew, forbear, forfeit, forgo, give up, lose, pass, reject, renounce, sacrifice, surrender, turn down, waive

v **4** see: STOP v 8, 10

abstinence n continence, moderation, restraint, self-restraint, sobriety, temperance

abstinent adj celibate, chaste, continent, maidenly, pure, virginal, virtuous

abstract adj conjectural, general, hypothetical, ideal, illustrative, speculative, symbolic, theoretical

n abridgement, brief, compendium, condensation, digest, essence, example, outline, review, sketch, summary, syllabus, synopsis

abstracted adj absent-minded, bemused, careless, dazed, dizzy, groggy, inattentive, lost, mindless, oblivious, preoccupied, silly, spaced, vapid

abstruse adj deep, esoteric, heartfelt, heavy, hermetic, insightful, mysterious, obscure, occult, penetrating, profound, recondite

absurd adj **1** chancy, debatable, doubtful, dubious, iffy, implausible, improbable, incredible, moot, preposterous, questionable, theoretical, unbelievable, uncertain, unlikely

adj **2** balmy, bizarre, crazy, emotional, foolish, frivolous, goofy, illogical, impossible, inane, insane, irrational, loony, lunatic, mad, muddled, nuts, preposterous, ridiculous, silly, touched, wacky, zany

adj **3** see: FUNNY adj 3

adj **4** see: SILLY adj 2, 3

abundance n **1** glut, great deal, lot, mass, much, ton

n **2** affluence, bounty, comfort, cornucopia, elegance, glut, good fortune, grandeur, luxury, opulence, plenty, prosperity, success, wealth

n **3** profusion

n **4** torrent

abundant adj **1** ample, countless, numerous

adj 2 elaborate, flamboyant, luscious, ornate, replete

adj 3 fattening, heavy, rich, sweet, thick

adj 4 abounding, ample, bounteous, bountiful, copious, enough, galore, generous, liberal, overflowing, plentiful, plenty, prodigal, profuse, teeming

adj 5 see: EXTRAVAGANT *adj* 4

adj 6 see: MANY *adj* 2

abuse *n* 1 defamation, mistreatment, scurrility

n 2 assault, attack, rape, sack, violation

v 1 corrupt, ill-use, misapply, misemploy, mishandle, misuse, pervert, prostitute

v 2 brutalize, exploit, harm, ill-treat, injure, maltreat, mistreat, molest, persecute, victimize, wrong

v 3 blemish, damage, hamper, harm, hurt, impair, injure, mar, obstruct, ruin, sabotage, scuttle, spoil, tarnish, vandalize

v 4 asperse, bad-mouth, belittle, condemn, damage, decry, defame, degrade, denigrate, denounce, deprecate, detract, diminish, discount, disparage, insult, knock, malign, put down, revile, run down, slander, take away, vilify

abusive *adj* 1 contemptuous, derisive, disrespectful, insulting, nasty, offensive, slighting

adj 2 hard, harsh, severe, stern, stiff, strict, tough, uncaring, unsympathetic

abutting *adj* adjacent, adjoining, alongside, bordering, close-by, connected, contiguous, juxtaposed, local, near-at-hand, nearby, neighboring, outlining, regional, touching, verging on

abyss *n* 1 canyon, chasm, cleft, crack, depth, fissure, gorge, gulch, pass, ravine

n 2 hades, hell, inferno

academic *adj* 1 educational, enlightening, eye-opening, illuminating, informative, instructive, revealing, scholastic

adj 2 conventional

adj 3 educated, educational, erudite, intellectual, learned, literary, literate, pedantic, scholarly, scholastic, well-read

academician *n* 1 educator, instructor, intern, professor, teacher

n 2 see: INTELLECTUAL *n*

academy *n* college, institute, lyceum, school, seminary, university

accede *v* acquiesce, bend, bow, buckle, capitulate, cave, comply, concede, cry uncle, defer, give in, give up, relent, submit, succumb, surrender, twist, yield

accelerate *v* 1 aid, assist, expedite, facilitate

v 2 expedite, hasten, hurry, quicken, rush, shake up, speed, step up

acceleration *n* achievement, advance, advancement, betterment, breakthrough, furtherance, growth, headway, improvement, increment, pickup, proficiency, progress, promotion, strengthening, upgrade

accent *n* 1 brogue, dialect, patois, speech, tongue

n 2 elocution, enunciation, inflection, intonation, manner, pronunciation

n 3 emphasis, highlighting, importance, priority, significance, stress, weight

v accentuate, amplify, concentrate, emphasize, feature, flag, focus, heighten, highlight, italicize, mark, punctuate, spotlight, stress, underline, underscore

accentuate *v* accent, amplify, concentrate, emphasize, feature, flag, focus, heighten, highlight, italicize, mark, punctuate, spotlight, stress, underline, underscore

accept *v* 1 believe, buy, swallow

v 2 agree, allow, approve, assent, comply, concur, consent, endorse, sign up, subscribe

v 3 approbate, approve, authorize, certify, condone, confirm, countenance, endorse, favor, pass, ratify, sanction, validate

v 4 see: TOLERATE *v*

acceptability *n* adequacy, competency, sufficiency

acceptable *adj* 1 allowable, eligible, fitting, qualified, suitable

adj 2 defensible, justifiable, legitimate, proper, reasonable, valid

adj 3 adequate, competent, decent, enough, fair, good, mediocre, passable, reasonable, respectable, satisfactory, sufficient, tolerable

acceptably *adv* adequately, amply, appropriately, correctly, properly, right, satisfactorily, suitably, well

acceptance *n* accord, agreement, approval, assent, compliance, concurrence, consent, go-ahead, nod, sympathy

accepted *adj* 1 established, proven, sound, standard, traditional

adj 2 implied, presumed, supposed, tacit, understood

adj 3 accustomed, chronic, common, constant, continual, customary, daily, everyday, familiar, frequent, habitual, inured, often, recurring, regular, routine, traditional, usual

accepting *adj* see: CHARITABLE *adj* 1

access *n* 1 entry

n **2** aperture, approach, entrance, inlet, mouth, opening, passage

n **3** approach, artery, avenue, boulevard, channel, drag, highway, pass, path, promenade, road, roadway, route, strait, street, thoroughfare, trail, way

n **4** approach

v accomplish, achieve, attain, derive, earn, fulfill, gain, get, merit, net, obtain, perform, profit, rack up, reach, realize, score, win

accessible *adj* available, close, convenient, feasible, functional, handy, helpful, multipurpose, nearby, open, practical, public, reachable, ready, serviceable, suitable, unrestricted, usable, useful, utilitarian, well-suited, within reach, working

accession *n* attainment

accessory *adj* adjunct, ancillary, assisting, auxiliary, subsidiary, supporting

n abettor, accomplice, coconspirator, confederate, conspirator, partner, supporter

accident *n* **1** collision, crackup, crash, destruction, mishap, pileup, smash, smashup, wreck, wreckage

n **2** see: MISTAKE *n* **2**

accidental *adj* **1** sudden, surprising, unanticipated, unexpected, unforeseen

adj **2** aimless, arbitrary, casual, chance, chaotic, haphazard, hit or miss, indiscriminate, irregular, random, unaimed, uncontrolled, unplanned

adj **3** casual, chance, chancy, circumstantial, coincidental, contingent, eventful, fluky, fortuitous, freak, incidental, lucky, odd, serendipitous, synchronous

adj **4** careless, caustic, heedless, inadvertent, inconsiderate, nonchalant, selfish, sharp, short, tactless, thoughtless, uncaring, unceremonious, ungracious, unheeding, unintended, unintentional, unreflective, unthinking

acclaim *n* applause, boost, citation, commendation, compliment, eulogy, plaudit, praise, rave, tribute

v **1** applaud, charm, cheer, commend, compliment, flatter, greet, hail, laud, praise, recognize, salute, stroke

v **2** see: LAUD *v* **1, 2**

acclaimed *adj* see: FAMOUS *adj*

acclimate *v* harden, season, toughen

accolade *n* award, commendation, credit, decoration, distinction, honor, kudos, laurels, medal, note, praise, recognition, reputation, reward, tribute

accommodate *v* **1** contain

v **2** convenience, favor, help, oblige, please, provide, serve

v **3** comply, conform, follow, keep, mind, obey, observe, submit

v **4** adjust, attune, conform, coordinate, harmonize, integrate, proportion, reconcile, reconciliate, tune

v **5** baby, cater, coddle, gratify, humor, indulge, overindulge, pamper, pander, placate, satisfy, spoil

accommodating *adj* agreeing, amenable, disposed, eager, glad, inclined, pleased, pliant, responsive, willing

accompanist *n* artiste, conductor, instrumentalist, musician, performer, virtuoso

accompany *v* **1** direct, escort, guide, lead, usher

v **2** accord, coexist, coincide, concur, co-ordinate, synchronize

v **3** associate, attend, bear, chaperon, conduct, consort with, convoy, escort

v **4** band, coincide, collaborate, collude, combine, concur, cooperate, pool, unite

accomplice *n* **1** abettor, accessory, coconspirator, confederate, conspirator, partner, supporter

n **2** see: FRIEND *n* **1**

accomplish *v* **1** behave, contend, cope, make do, manage, persevere

v **2** achieve, attain, consummate, execute, fulfill, perform, produce, pull off, realize, succeed, triumph, win

v **3** access, achieve, attain, derive, earn, fulfill, gain, get, merit, net, obtain, perform, profit, rack up, reach, realize, score, win

v **4** complete, consummate, execute, fulfill, implement, perform, realize

accomplished *adj* **1** experienced, proficient, schooled, trained, versed

adj **2** complete, concluded, done, ended, finished, over, performed, terminated, through, wrapped up

adj **3** see: QUALIFIED *adj* **4**

accomplishment *n* **1** legacy, masterpiece, monument

n **2** action, conduct, deed, delivery, demonstration, execution, performance, talent

n **3** achievement, arrival, attainment, completion, fruition, fulfillment, realization, satisfaction, success, triumph, victory

n **4** achievement, acquirement, act, action, battle, deed, doing, event, exploit, feat, stunt, thing, trick

n **5** achievement, conquest, success, triumph, victory, win, winner

accord *n* 1 calm, harmony, peace, serenity, stillness, tranquillity

n 2 acceptance, agreement, approval, assent, compliance, concurrence, consent, go-ahead, nod, sympathy

n 3 affinity, agreement, assent, concert, concord, congruence, cooperation, empathy, harmony, rapport, synergy, teamwork, unity

v 1 accompany, coexist, coincide, concur, coordinate, synchronize

v 2 agree, check, coalesce, coincide, comply with, concur, conform, consent, consist, correspond, fit in, harmonize, jibe, square, suit, tally

v 3 see: GIVE *v* 8

account *n* 1 admiration, consideration, esteem, favor, regard, respect

n 2 balance sheet, book, credit, ledger, score, statement, tab

n 3 budget, capital, cash, fund, money, savings, stock

n 4 diary, digest, journal, log, memoir, minutes, notation, notes, proceedings, record, recording, report

n 5 advantage, applicability, appropriateness, aptness, avail, benefit, decorum, expediency, fitness, manners, opportunism, pertinence, profit, propriety, relevance, rightness, service, suitability, use, usefulness, utility

n 6 amount, catalog, enumeration, inventory, itemization, list, litany, repertoire, supply, tally

n 7 advantage, behalf, benefit, betterment, gain, good, happiness, interest, prosperity, sake, welfare, well-being

v 1 delineate, report, specify

v 2 explain, explain away, justify, rationalize

v 3 calculate, consider, deem, judge, reckon, regard, surmise, view

accountability *n* blame, burden, culpability, fault, guilt, onus, responsibility, shame, stigma

accountable *adj* see: REPUTABLE *adj*

accountant *n* actuary, auditor, bookkeeper, comptroller

accouter *v* apparel, array, attire, clad, clothe, dress, garb, gear, outfit

accoutrements *n* apparel, attire, clothes, clothing, dress, garments, gear, togs

accredit *v* 1 apply, ascribe, assign, attribute, charge, credit, refer

v 2 authorize, certify, commission, empower, enable, entitle, facilitate, invest, license, permit, sanction, validate

accrue *v* accumulate, acquire, amass, assemble, collect, garner, gather, grow, hoard, save, squirrel, stash, stockpile, store up

accumulate *v* 1 bank, deposit, hoard, save, squirrel away, stockpile, store

v 2 accrue, acquire, amass, assemble, collect, garner, gather, grow, hoard, save, squirrel, stash, stockpile, store up

accumulation *n* fund, reservoir, source, store, supply

accurate *adj* 1 deadly, effective, sure

adj 2 correct, exact, precise, proper, right, valid

adj 3 certain, distinct, explicit, incontestable, infallible, perfect, unerring

adj 4 authentic, believable, certain, convincing, credible, dependable, faithful, real, reliable, safe, sure, tenable, true, trustworthy, trusty

accurately *adv* 1 carefully

adv 2 exactly, just so, precisely, right, sharp, smack, square, squarely

accusation *n* 1 charge, complaint, incrimination, inculpation, indictment

n 2 aspersion, defamation, libel, remark, slander, slur, smear

n 3 allegation, assertion, charge, comment, declaration, deposition, pronouncement, statement

accuse *v* 1 blame, charge, complain, condemn, criticize, fault, indict, reproach

v 2 allege, arraign, assert, charge, cite, impeach, imply, impute, incriminate, indict, litigate, prosecute, sue, try

v 3 see: IMPLICATE *v*

accused *n* con, convict, criminal, crook, culprit, delinquent, felon, guilty party, inmate, lawbreaker, offender, perpetrator, prisoner, scofflaw, suspect, swindler, transgressor, wrongdoer

accuser *n* betrayer, double-crosser, fink, informer, reptile, snake, sneak, stooge, traitor

accustomed *adj* accepted, chronic, common, constant, continual, customary, daily, everyday, familiar, frequent, habitual, inured, often, recurring, regular, routine, traditional, usual

ace *n* champion, expert, master, wizard

acedia *n* apathy, disinterest, disregard, indifference, lassitude, lethargy, listlessness

acerbic *adj* 1 acid, biting, curt, dry, pungent, sharp, sour, tart

adj 2 acrid, biting, bitter, caustic, corrosive, critical, pungent, sarcastic

acetate *n* overhead, slide, transparency

ache *n* 1 affliction, agony, anguish, hurt,

injury, pain, punishment, suffering, torture

n 2 agony, angina, burn, cramp, crick, heartache, hurt, pain, pang, soreness, spasm, sting, twinge

v 1 commiserate, empathize, feel for, pity, sympathize with

v 2 despair, grieve, hurt, pain, suffer

v 3 see: CRAVE *v* 4

achievable *adj* capable, doable, feasible, possible, practical, viable, workable

achieve *v* 1 do, execute, perform

v 2 answer, execute, fill, finish, fulfill, meet, realize, satisfy

v 3 cease, complete, conclude, consummate, end, finish, halt, perfect, terminate, wind up, wrap up

v 4 accomplish, attain, consummate, execute, fulfill, perform, produce, pull off, realize, succeed, triumph, win

v 5 see: PERFORM *v* 4, 5

achievement *n* 1 distinction, prestige, rank, recognition, stance, stature, status

n 2 accomplishment, arrival, attainment, completion, fruition, fulfillment, realization, satisfaction, success, triumph, victory

n 3 accomplishment, acquirement, act, action, battle, deed, doing, event, exploit, feat, stunt, thing, trick

n 4 accomplishment, conquest, success, triumph, victory, win, winner

n 5 acceleration, advance, advancement, betterment, breakthrough, furtherance, growth, headway, improvement, increment, pickup, proficiency, progress, promotion, strengthening, upgrade

achiever *n* performer

acid *adj* acerbic, biting, curt, dry, pungent, sharp, sour, tart

acidic *adj* caustic, corrosive, reactive

acknowledge *v* 1 admit, agree, recognize

v 2 applaud, appreciate, approve, clap, recognize, show gratitude, thank

v 3 admit, allow, avow, concede, confess, fess up, grant, own, own up

v 4 answer, come back, react, rejoin, reply, respond, retort, return

acknowledgment *n* answer, credit, recognition

acme *n* apex, apogee, climax, crescendo, crest, crown, culmination, epitome, height, noon, peak, pinnacle, point, prime, summit, tip, top, ultimate, utmost, zenith

acoustic *adj* auditory

acquaint *v* 1 advise, apprise, fill in, inform, notify, post, tell, update

v 2 announce, delineate, depict, introduce, present, reflect, represent, show

acquaintance *n* see: FRIEND *n* 1

acquainted *adj* abreast, aware, conversant, familiar, informed, knowledgeable, up, versed

acquiesce *v* 1 accede, bend, bow, buckle, capitulate, cave, comply, concede, cry uncle, defer, give in, give up, relent, submit, succumb, surrender, twist, yield

v 2 see: SURRENDER *v* 1, 3

v 3 see: TOLERATE *v*

acquiescence *n* compliance, dependence, obedience, subjection, submission

acquiescent *adj* compliant, docile, easy, meek, mild, nonresistant, obedient, passive, resigned, submissive, tame, tolerant, unassertive, yielding

acquire *v* 1 receive

v 2 arouse, commit, contract, engage, enlist, incur, induce

v 3 accrue, accumulate, amass, assemble, collect, garner, gather, grow, hoard, save, squirrel, stash, stockpile, store up

v 4 annex, buy, capture, gain, get, have, land, obtain, pick up, procure, purchase, requisition, secure, solicit, win

v 5 earn, make, obtain, procure

acquirement *n* accomplishment, achievement, act, action, battle, deed, doing, event, exploit, feat, stunt, thing, trick

acquisition *n* asset, buy, gain, merchandise, property, purchase

acquisitive *adj* avaricious, covetous, craving, desirous, eager, grabby, grasping, greedy, hungry, longing, miserly, selfish, wishful, yearning

acquit *v* 1 absolve, cover up, exonerate, extenuate, mitigate, whitewash

v 2 absolve, clear, condone, exculpate, excuse, exempt, exonerate, forgive, free, pardon, remit, reprieve, vindicate

acreage *n* domain, estate, grounds, holdings, land, property, real estate

acrid *adj* acerbic, biting, bitter, caustic, corrosive, critical, pungent, sarcastic

acrimony *n* see: HATE *n*

acrobat *n* gymnast

acrobatics *n* athletics, calisthenics, gymnastics

acrylic *n* art, canvas, depiction, drawing, etching, illustration, landscape, lithograph, mural, oil, painting, pastel, pen and ink, picture, portrait, print, seascape, sketch, still life, watercolor

act *n* 1 law, legislation, measure, ruling, statute

n 2 farce, make-believe, parody, performance, show, sketch, skit

n 3 accomplishment, achievement, acquirement, action, battle, deed, doing, event, exploit, feat, stunt, thing, trick

v 1 function, go, perform, run, work

v 2 bear, behave, carry, comport, conduct, demean, rule

v 3 assume, bluff, counterfeit, fabricate, fake, feign, imitate, invent, make believe, play, pretend, put on, sham

v 4 see: MIMIC *v*

action *n* 1 maneuver, measure, method, step

n 2 apparatus, gear, machinery, workings, works

n 3 bearing, behavior, conduct, demeanor, deportment, manners

n 4 battle, engagement, fray, gesture, movement, operation, proceeding

n 5 case, indictment, lawsuit, litigation, proceeding, prosecution, suit

n 6 accomplishment, conduct, deed, delivery, demonstration, execution, performance, talent

n 7 accomplishment, achievement, acquirement, act, battle, deed, doing, event, exploit, feat, stunt, thing, trick

n 8 see: ACTIVITY *n* 3

activate *v* 1 cause, elicit, generate, prompt, provoke, spark, trigger

v 2 charge, electrify, energize, enliven, excite, ignite, start, turn on, vitalize

v 3 begin, cause, commence, constitute, create, embark, enter, establish, inaugurate, induct, initiate, install, instigate, instill, institute, introduce, kick off, launch, lead off, open, originate, precipitate, preface, set up, start, tee off, usher in, venture forth

v 4 see: MOVE *v* 5

active *adj* 1 alive, functioning, live, operative, running, working

adj 2 alive, dynamic, energetic, sound, spirited, strong, vibrant, vigorous, vital

adj 3 bustling, busy, creative, driving, energetic, enterprising, inventive, lively, resourceful

adj 4 agile, astir, brisk, catty, energetic, lively, nimble, quick, sprightly, spry, zippy

activity *n* 1 discipline, drill, practice

n 2 business, endeavor, enterprise, exercise, project, undertaking, venture

n 3 action, ado, animation, bedlam, bother, bustle, chaos, commotion, excitement, flurry, fluster, fuss, hum, liveliness, mad-

house, movement, stir, to-do, tumult, turmoil, whirlpool, whirlwind

actor *n* actress, artist, entertainer, hero, heroine, lead, movie star, performer, player, protagonist, star, thespian, tragedian

actress *n* actor, artist, entertainer, hero, heroine, lead, movie star, performer, player, protagonist, star, thespian, tragedian

acts *n* bag of tricks, repertoire, résumé, skills, talents

actual *adj* absolute, authentic, bona fide, certain, definite, existent, factual, genuine, hard, inarguable, incontestable, incontrovertible, indisputable, indubitable, irrefutable, positive, real, sure, true, undeniable, undisputable, undoubtable, undoubted, unequivocal, unquestionable, veritable, viable

actuality *n* 1 fact, given, specific, statistic, truth

n 2 being, existence, fact, life, presence, reality, truth, vitality

actually *adv* exactly, genuinely, precisely, really, sincerely, truly, verifiably, veritably, very

actuary *n* accountant, auditor, bookkeeper, comptroller

actuate *v* 1 commit, do, enact, execute, perform, perpetrate

v 2 bring about, cause, create, draw on, effect, execute, invoke, make, produce, secure

v 3 activate, compel, drive, force, goad, impel, induce, mobilize, motivate, move, persuade, press, propel, push, spur, start, turn on

acumen *n* astuteness, awareness, cleverness, discernment, discrimination, insight, intellect, intuition, keenness, perception, sagacity, sensitivity, shrewdness, understanding, wit

acute *adj* 1 piercing, sharp, shooting, stabbing

adj 2 annoying, grating, high, loud, piercing, piping, sharp, shrill

adj 3 see: IMPORTANT *adj* 5

adj 4 see: QUICK *adj* 5

ad *n* advertisement, commercial, plug, promo, promotion, sponsorship, spot

adage *n* axiom, byword, cliché, dictum, maxim, motto, proverb, saying, slogan, talk

adamant *adj* 1 persistent, tenacious, unrelenting

adj 2 firm, resolute, steadfast, stern, strict

adj **3** cold, cruel, fierce, relentless, vindictive

adj **4** ceaseless, dedicated, determined, firm, immovable, inexhaustible, inexorable, inflexible, narrow-minded, obstinate, relentless, resolute, resolved, rigid, single-minded, steadfast, stubborn, unbendable, unbending, uncompromising, unswayable, unyielding

adapt *v* **1** prepare, process, ready, treat

v **2** conform, convert, cut, fashion, fit, measure, modify, rig, shape, suit, tailor

v **3** see: SERVICE *v*

adaptable *adj* adjustable, changeable, flexible, limber, malleable, maneuverable, moldable, plastic, pliable, pliant, responsive, soft, supple, swayed, versatile, yielding

adaptation *n* agreement, compliance, conformation, modification

adaptive *adj* bold, canny, clever, daring, enterprising, resourceful, venturesome

add *v* **1** append, attach, increase, join

v **2** contain, enclose, include, incorporate, insert

v **3** comment, declare, note, remark, say, state

added *adj* see: ADDITIONAL *adj* 2

addendum *n* addition, appendix, insert, rider, supplement

addition *n* **1** increase

n **2** addendum, appendix, insert, rider, supplement

n **3** adjunct, annex, annexation, branch, extension, section, wing

n **4** advancement, advantage, betterment, enhancement, gain, growth, improvement, plus

additional *adj* **1** covert, hidden, secondary, secret, ulterior, undeclared

adj **2** added, another, auxiliary, extra, further, incremental, more, one more, other, spare, supplemental, supplementary, surplus

additionally *adv* **1** beyond, farther, further, furthermore

adv **2** also, and, as well, as well as, besides, further, furthermore, in addition, likewise, moreover, plus, too

addle *v* confuse, daze, foul up, fumble, jumble, mix up, muddle, snarl up

address *n* **1** destination, direction, identification, location, zone

n **2** bow, greeting, honor, nod, recognition, salute

n **3** apartment, condo, condominium, domicile, dwelling, flat, home, house, location, pad, place, property, residence, site

n **4** lecture, speech, talk

v **1** deliver, lecture, preach, proclaim, speak, talk

v **2** aim, cast, direct, level, point, train, zero in

v **3** call to, embrace, greet, hail, meet, salute, summon, welcome

v **4** channel, consign, dispatch, export, forward, mail, post, remit, route, send, ship, transmit, transport

addressee *n* citizen, dweller, inhabitant, occupant, owner, resident, tenant

adduce *v* see: GIVE *v* 8

adept *adj* **1** dexterous, handy, mechanical, proficient, skilled

adj **2** experienced, practiced, proficient, seasoned, versed, veteran

adj **3** able, accomplished, apt, capable, competent, deft, dexterous, expert, fit, gifted, masterful, professional, proficient, proper, qualified, skillful, talented

adequacy *n* **1** ability, adroitness, aptitude, art, caliber, calling, capability, capacity, command, competence, craft, dexterity, experience, expertise, familiarity, forte, knack, know-how, knowledge, mastery, proficiency, prowess, qualification, savvy, skill, specialty, strength, talent, training, workmanship

n **2** acceptability, competency, sufficiency

adequate *adj* **1** capable, competent, effective, efficacious, efficient, proficient, successful, sufficient

adj **2** acceptable, competent, decent, enough, fair, good, mediocre, passable, reasonable, respectable, satisfactory, sufficient, tolerable

adequately *adv* **1** acceptably, amply, appropriately, correctly, properly, right, satisfactorily, suitably, well

adv **2** amply, enough, equitably, fairly, justly, moderately, passably, rather, satisfactorily, tolerably

adv **3** altogether, assiduously, completely, earnestly, entirely, exhaustively, fully, hard, intensely, intensively, painstakingly, perfectly, quite, sufficiently, thoroughly, totally, unremittingly, utterly, wholly

adhere *v* bond, cleave, cling, cohere, hold, join, stick

adhesion *n* friction, pulling, tension, traction

adhesive *adj* cohesive, gluey, gummy, sticky, tacky

n **1** cement, glue, paste

n **2** band, cellophane tape, strip, tape

adieu *n* adios, aloha, *arrivederci, auf Wiedersehen*, au revoir, bon voyage, bye, cheerio, *ciao*, farewell, goodbye, good day, *sayonara*, shalom, so long

adios *n* adieu, aloha, *arrivederci, auf Wiedersehen*, au revoir, bon voyage, bye, cheerio, *ciao*, farewell, goodbye, good day, *sayonara*, shalom, so long

adjacent *adj* abutting, adjoining, alongside, bordering, close by, connected, contiguous, juxtaposed, local, near at hand, nearby, neighboring, outlining, regional, touching, verging on

adjacently *adv* around, aside, atop, beside, by, near, nearby

adjoining *adj* abutting, adjacent, alongside, bordering, close by, connected, contiguous, juxtaposed, local, near at hand, nearby, neighboring, outlining, regional, touching, verging on

adjourn *v* 1 cap, climax, complete, conclude, consummate, crown, culminate, dissolve, end, finalize, finish, terminate, wind up, wrap up
v 2 see: DELAY *v* 4

adjudge *v* condemn, convict, discipline, imprison, penalize, punish, sentence

adjudicate *v* 1 arbitrate, judge, mediate, referee, try, umpire
v 2 conclude, decide, determine, establish, resolve, rule, settle, will

adjudication *n* 1 arbitration, facilitation, intercession, intervention, mediation
n 2 decision, decree, finding, judgment, ruling, sentence, verdict
n 3 award, determination, judgment, opinion, ruling, sentence, verdict

adjunct *adj* accessory, ancillary, assisting, auxiliary, subsidiary, supporting
n 1 annex, fitting, fixture, part, piece, unit
n 2 addition, annex, annexation, branch, extension, section, wing
n 3 see: FRIEND *n* 1

adjust *v* 1 factor
v 2 convert, prorate, regulate, scale
v 3 refund, reimburse, repay, return
v 4 agree, arrange, compromise, settle
v 5 align, dial, select, tune
v 6 finesse, fine-tune, modify, tweak, vary
v 7 conform, equalize, level, regulate, set policy, standardize
v 8 alter, catalyze, change, modify, mutate, refashion, vary
v 9 arrange, calibrate, decide, determine, establish, fix, resolve, set
v 10 balance, compensate, make equal, make up, offset, outweigh, redeem, set off

v 11 correct, cure, fix, heal, make well, mend, remedy, repair, restore
v 12 amend, correct, fix, improve, mend, modify, position, rectify, remedy, restore, right, straighten
v 13 adapt, balance, fit, fix, inspect, maintain, overhaul, recondition, refurbish, regulate, repair, service, support, tune up
v 14 align
v 15 accommodate, attune, conform, coordinate, harmonize, integrate, proportion, reconciliate, reconcile, tune

adjustable *adj* adaptable, changeable, flexible, limber, malleable, maneuverable, moldable, plastic, pliable, pliant, responsive, soft, supple, swayed, versatile, yielding

adjustment *n* alteration, anomaly, change, deviation, modification, mutation, permutation, shift, variation

administer *v* 1 construct, dispense, move along, plan, prepare, process, treat
v 2 apportion, deal, disburse, dispense, disperse, distribute, dole, expend, give
v 3 administrate, carry out, deliver, do, execute, give, present, render, submit
v 4 boss, command, direct, guide, manage, oversee, regulate, steer, supervise

administrate *v* administer, carry out, deliver, do, execute, give, present, render, submit

administration *n* 1 dominion, government, monarchy, power, regime, reign, rule, sovereignty
n 2 care, charge, conduct, handling, intendance, management, overseeing, running, supervision
n 3 administrators, authorities, bureaucracy, civil service, commission, department, direction, forces, government, management, ministry, officials, power, powers, rule, rulers

administrators *n* see: ADMINISTRATION *n* 3

admirable *adj* 1 appreciable, respectable, worthy
adj 2 commendable, excellent, fine, laudable, praiseworthy, worthwhile
adj 3 beautiful, delightful, glorious, good, magnificent, peachy, splendid, terrific, wonderful

admiration *n* 1 adoration, glory, praise, worship
n 2 account, consideration, esteem, favor, regard, respect

admire *v* 1 appreciate, cherish, delight, enjoy, relish, revel, savor *v* 2 adore, cherish, dote on, idolize, love, respect, revere, venerate, worship

v 3 see: APPRECIATE *v* 3

admired *adj* honored, praised, prized, respected, valued

admirer *n* buff, devotee, disciple, enthusiast, fan, follower, groupie

admission *n* 1 confession

n 2 entry

n 3 cover charge, entrance fee, fee, pass, ticket

admit *v* 1 acknowledge, agree, recognize

v 2 confront, face, realize

v 3 enroll, matriculate, receive, register

v 4 acknowledge, allow, avow, concede, confess, fess up, grant, own, own up

admonish *v* berate, blame, censure, chide, condemn, disapprove, lay into, punish, rebuke, reprimand, reproach, reprove, scold, warn

admonishment *n* admonition, blast, chewing out, chiding, criticism, denunciation, diatribe, harangue, hassle, libel, outburst, rap, rebuke, reprimand, reproach, reproof, scolding, slander, tirade

admonition *n* admonishment, blast, chewing out, chiding, criticism, denunciation, diatribe, harangue, hassle, libel, outburst, rap, rebuke, reprimand, reproach, reproof, scolding, slander, tirade

ado *n* action, activity, animation, bedlam, bother, bustle, chaos, commotion, excitement, flurry, fluster, fuss, hum, liveliness, madhouse, movement, stir, to-do, tumult, turmoil, whirlpool, whirlwind

adolescence *n* childhood, puberty, youth

adolescent *adj* fresh, green, immature, juvenile, precocious, undeveloped, unfledged, unready, young, youthful

n boy, child, girl, juvenile, kid, minor, teenager, teeny-bopper, youngster, youth

adopt *v* borrow, embrace, foster, subscribe, take on, take up, utilize

adorable *adj* charming, cute, dainty, delectable, delightful

adoration *n* admiration, glory, praise, worship

adore *v* 1 admire, cherish, dote on, idolize, love, respect, revere, venerate, worship

v 2 admire, appreciate, cherish, consider, covet, esteem, honor, idolize, love, prize, regard, respect, treasure, value

adored *adj* beloved, cherished, dear, esteemed, loved, precious, respected, revered, treasured, venerable, worshiped

adorn *v* 1 pique, plume, preen, pride, primp, stroke

v 2 beautify, bedeck, deck, decorate, dress up, embellish, enhance, garnish, glamorize, grace, ornament, polish, trim

adornment *n* decoration, embellishment, ornament

adroit *adj* 1 artful, cagey, canny, crafty, cunning, evasive, foxy, serpentine, sly

adj 2 apt, canny, clever, cunning, deft, handy, ingenious, nimble, skilled, skillful, sly, wily

adroitness *n* see: SKILL *n* 3

adulation *n* flattery

adult *adj* full-grown, grown, grown-up, mature, matured, ripened

adulterate *v* corrupt, debase, debauch, defile, demoralize, dishonor, pervert, ruin, seduce, taint

adultery *n* 1 congress, copulation, fooling around, fornication, intimacy, procreation, sex

n 2 see: AFFAIR *n* 3

advance *v* 1 approach, come, near

v 2 lease, lend, let, loan

v 3 benefit, gain, improve, profit, reward

v 4 cultivate, elevate, enhance, enrich, improve, refine, upgrade

v 5 begin again, continue, cycle, depart, get along, get on, go, leave, march, move, move forward, overture, part, proceed, progress, push on, recommence, reembark, restart, wend

v 6 abet, aid, ameliorate, amend, assist, avail, benefit, better, boost, cultivate, do for, ease, egg on, encourage, enhance, forward, foster, further, help, improve, nurture, prefer, promote, rev, serve, spur on, support

v 7 ascend, bloom, climb, develop, do well, excel, expand, flourish, flower, get ahead, grow, improve, progress, prosper, rise, strive, survive, thrive

n 1 prepayment

n 2 acceleration, achievement, advancement, betterment, breakthrough, furtherance, growth, headway, improvement, increment, pickup, proficiency, progress, promotion, strengthening, upgrade

advanced *adj* 1 bright, gifted, intelligent, precocious, promising, talented

adj 2 broad, broad-minded, liberal, progressive, radical, tolerant, unbiased

adj 3 early, first, hasty, premature, previous, soon, too soon, untimely

advancement *n* 1 addition, advantage, betterment, enhancement, gain, growth, improvement, plus

n 2 acceleration, achievement, advance, betterment, breakthrough, furtherance, growth, headway, improvement, increment, pickup, proficiency, progress, promotion, strengthening, upgrade

advancing *adj* approaching, forthcoming, imminent, looming, nearing, oncoming, pending

advantage *n* 1 lead

n 2 precedence, prerogative, priority, privilege, rank, seniority

n 3 addition, advancement, betterment, enhancement, gain, growth, improvement, plus

n 4 birthright, claim, edge, enablement, perquisite, prerogative, privilege, right, title

n 5 account, applicability, appropriateness, aptness, avail, benefit, decorum, expediency, fitness, manners, opportunism, pertinence, profit, propriety, relevance, rightness, service, suitability, use, usefulness, utility

n 6 account, behalf, benefit, betterment, gain, good, happiness, interest, prosperity, sake, welfare, well-being

advantageous *adj* better, desirable, enjoyable, preferable, superior, worthier, worthwhile

advent *n* approach, arrival, coming, entrance

adventure *n* 1 escapade, fantasy, saga, story

n 2 encounter, event, experience, hazard, ordeal, peril, risk

n 3 antic, caper, escapade, joke, lark, mischief, prank, trick

n 4 air travel, cruise, excursion, expedition, flight, journey, passage, safari, sally, tour, travel, trek, trip, venture, voyage

adversary *n* 1 antagonist, anti, challenger, competitor, con, contender, enemy, foe, match, opponent, rival

n 2 antagonist, naysayer, obstructionist, schmuck, shnook

adverse *adj* 1 antagonistic, anti, contrary, opposed, opposing

adj 2 deleterious, detrimental, harmful, injurious, negative, unfavorable

adj 3 bad, evil, harmful, ill, unfavorable, unlucky

adj 4 antagonistic, bellicose, hostile, ill, inimical, nasty, spiteful, unfriendly

adversity *n* 1 difficulty, discipline, discomfort, hardness, rigor, severity, strictness, stringency, uneasiness

n 2 affliction, blow, burden, calamity, difficulty, distress, hardship, mischance, misfortune, mishap, relapse, reversal, setback, suffering, tragedy, trouble

advertent *adj* alert, attentive, careful, conscientious, heedful, observant

advertise *v* 1 announce, blaze, broadcast, circulate, declare, disperse, disseminate, proclaim, promulgate, publish

v 2 air, boom, boost, drum up, endorse, pitch, plug, promote, publicize, push, rave, sell, tout

advertisement *n* 1 championship, praise, promotion, publicity, salesmanship

n 2 ad, commercial, plug, promo, promotion, sponsorship, spot

advice *n* counsel, opinion, recommendation, suggestion

advisable *adj* expedient, politic, prudent, recommended, suggested, wise

advise *v* 1 caution, counsel, evaluate, recommend, reprove

v 2 acquaint, apprise, fill in, inform, notify, post, tell, update

v 3 communicate, confer, consult, discuss, group, huddle, parley, powwow

v 4 authorize, command, decree, designate, dictate, direct, mandate, ordain, order, rule

advised *adj* calculated, careful, considered, contrived, deliberate, forewarned, measured, planned, premeditated, studied, studious

advisement *n* care, conference, consultation, counsel

adviser *n* see: EXPERT *n* 4

advocate *n* 1 attorney, barrister, counsel, counselor, intercessor, lawyer, mediator, solicitor

n 2 ally, angel, backer, benefactor, booster, champion, cheerleader, donor, friend, guarantor, helper, ombudsman, partner, patron, promoter, proponent, sponsor, supporter

n 3 see: LEADER *n* 3

v 1 defend

v 2 back, champion, endorse, guarantee, promote, sanction, side, support, uphold

v 3 countenance, encourage, favor

v 4 affirm, assure, avouch, avow, commit, devote, guarantee, pledge, promise, ratify, swear, vow

aeon *n* see: PERIOD *n* 2

aerobics *n* bodybuilding, calisthenics, exercise, jazzercise, slimnastics, workout

aesthete *n* connoisseur, critic, expert, virtuoso

aesthetic *adj* 1 empathetic, intuitive, sensitive

adj 2 artistic, classy, elegant, refined, stylish, tasteful, well-chosen

affable *adj* 1 amiable, approachable, cordial, friendly, genial, gentle, gracious, likable, lovable, peaceful, pleasant, serene *adj* 2 amenable, amiable, amicable, congenial, empathetic, friendly, gregarious, hospitable, neighborly, outgoing, receptive, sociable, social, sympathetic

affair *n* 1 business, concern, issue, matter
n 2 association, communication, friendship, intimacy, liaison, rapport, relationship, union
n 3 adultery, cheating, dalliance, entanglement, fling, flirtation, fooling around, infatuation, intimacy, intrigue, liaison, love affair, playing around, rendezvous, romance, tryst

affect *v* 1 feign, pretend, profess, purport
v 2 bother, burden, concern, daunt, disturb, faze, intimidate, oppress, upset, worry
v 3 assure, convince, impel, induce, influence, inspire, instigate, motivate, move, persuade, pressure, prompt, stir, sway, talk into, touch, win over

affectation *n* 1 haughtiness
n 2 airs, mannerism, peculiarity, pose, posturing, pretense, trait

affected *adj* 1 artificial, assumed, feigned, fictitious, put on, spurious
adj 2 effeminate, genteel, phony, pretentious

affecting *adj* 1 heartbreaking, impressive, moving, poignant, sad, touching
adj 2 see: PATHETIC *adj*

affection *n* 1 emotion, feeling, passion, regard, sensation, sense, sensibility, sentiment, tenderness
n 2 affinity, attachment, attraction, compassion, concern, devotion, fondness, heart, kinship, love, warmth

affectionate *adj* 1 amorous, attached, caring, devoted, enamored, fond, loving, romantic, tender
adj 2 see: TENDER *adj* **8, 9**

affective *adj* cognitive, emotional, mental, psychic, psychological, subconscious, subjective

affidavit *n* attestation, deposition, statement, testimony

affiliated *adj* akin, aligned, allied, associated, fraternal, friendly, kindred, parallel, related

affiliation *n* 1 allegiance, association, connection, obligation, tie
n 2 belief, church, creed, denomination, faith, persuasion, religion, rite, seat, theology
n 3 see: ALLIANCE *n*

affinity *n* 1 appreciation, attraction, fondness, liking, taste
n 2 compassion, empathy, kindness, mercy, pity, rue, sympathy, tenderness, understanding
n 3 analogy, approximation, comparison, likeness, match, metaphor, resemblance, semblance, similarity, simile
n 4 affection, attachment, attraction, compassion, concern, devotion, fondness, heart, kinship, love, warmth
n 5 accord, agreement, assent, concert, concord, congruence, cooperation, empathy, harmony, rapport, synergy, teamwork, unity
n 6 allure, appeal, attraction, attractiveness, aura, beguilement, enchantment, charisma, charm, enticement, fascination, glamour, infatuation, magnetism, sex appeal, spell

affirm *v* 1 bear witness, declare, depose, profess, swear, testify
v 2 attest, avow, contend, promise, say, swear, vouch, warrant
v 3 assert, attest, avow, confirm, declare, depose, predicate, profess, protest
v 4 advocate, assure, avouch, avow, commit, devote, guarantee, pledge, promise, ratify, swear, vow

affirmation *n* confirmation, documentation, evidence, proof, verification

affirmative *adj* agreeing, optimistic, positive

affix *v* 1 attach, bind, clip, connect, fasten, fix, rivet, weld
v 2 bind, bond, cement, fasten, fuse, glue, join, lock, paste, seal, secure, stick, unite

afflict *v* aggrieve, bother, burden, distress, grieve, hurt, injure, pain

affliction *n* 1 blight, impediment, pestilence, scourge
n 2 calamity, disability, flaw, handicap, impairment, limitation
n 3 ache, agony, anguish, hurt, injury, pain, punishment, suffering, torture
n 4 ailment, complaint, condition, disease, disorder, evil, harm, ill, illness, infirmity, malady, sickness
n 5 anguish, care, catastrophe, despair, disaster, dole, grief, heartache, mishap, pain, regret, remorse, rue, sickness, sorrow, woe
n 6 adversity, blow, burden, calamity, difficulty, distress, hardship, mischance, misfortune, mishap, relapse, reversal, setback, suffering, tragedy, trouble
n 7 see: FEAR *n* 3

affluence *n* abundance, bounty, comfort, cornucopia, elegance, glut, good fortune, grandeur, luxury, opulence, plenty, prosperity, success, wealth

affluent *adj* 1 comfortable, excessive, rich, superfluous

adj 2 booming, prosperous, successful, thriving, wealthy

adj 3 copious, leisure class, loaded, moneyed, opulent, rich, wealthy, well-to-do

affray *n* battle, brawl, brush, clash, conflict, difference, disagreement, dispute, encounter, fight, fracas, melee, quarrel, ruin, scrimmage, skirmish, spat, touch

affront *n* aspersion, attack, barb, caustic remark, crack, cut, denunciation, despite, dig, disparagement, disrespect, gibe, implication, indignity, innuendo, insult, invective, knock, reflection, sarcasm, scorn, slap, slight, slur, spike, tongue-lashing, verbal jab

v encounter, face, insult, offend, outrage, slight

afire *adj* ablaze, aflame, aglow, alight, blazing, burning, conflagrant, fiery, flaming, glowing

aflame *adj* ablaze, afire, aglow, alight, blazing, burning, conflagrant, fiery, flaming, glowing

aforementioned *adj* ancient, antecedent, anterior, archaic, earlier, foregoing, former, past, preceding, previous, prior, recent

afoul *adj* amiss, awry, bad, bum, improper, out of kilter, poor, rotten, unsatisfactory, wrong

afraid *adj* 1 averse, disinclined, hesitant, indisposed, loath, opposed, recalcitrant, reluctant, shy, timid, uneager, unwilling

adj 2 aghast, anxious, apprehensive, concerned, discerning, fearful, frightened, nervous, paranoid, scared, scary, terrified, worried

afresh *adv* anew, lately, new, newly, of late, recently

aft *adj* back, backward, dorsal, posterior, rear, tail

adv astern

after *adv* anon, behind, following, in pursuit, later, post, subsequently

adj beyond, ensuing, following, subsequent, succeeding, successive

aftermath *n* consequence, corollary, effect, eventuality, outcome, reaction, repercussion, result, reverberation, reward, upshot

afterward *adv* later, subsequently, successively, thereafter

again *adv* 1 ditto

adv 2 anew, once more, one more time

against *prep* 1 alongside, next to

prep 2 adverse to, antagonistic to, contrary to, in opposition to

age *n* aeon, cycle, decade, eon, epoch, era, eternity, forever, long time, millennium, period, reign, span, stage, time, years

v develop, grow, grow up, mature, mellow, progress, ripen

aged *adj* 1 grown old, matured, mellow, ripe, ripened

adj 2 age-old, ancient, antique, elderly, gray, grizzled, old, olden, senior, timeworn, venerable, vintage, worn

ageless *adj* see: PERPETUAL *adj* 2

agency *n* agent, channel, conduit, instrument, means, mechanism, medium, mode, vehicle

agenda *n* appointments, calendar, itinerary, list, plan, schedule

agent *n* 1 alternate, dummy, proxy, substitute, representative

n 2 ambassador, consul, delegate, deputy, diplomat, emissary, envoy

n 3 absorber, broker, catalyst, distributor, go-between, intermediary, mediator, middleman, negotiator

n 4 alternate, backup, contingency, part-timer, replacement, representative, standby, substitute, surrogate

n 5 agency, channel, conduit, instrument, means, mechanism, medium, mode, vehicle

n 6 realtor

n 7 catalyst, factor, force, power

n 8 custodian, janitor, manager, steward

age-old *adj* see: OLD *adj* 2

agglomerate *n* agglomeration, aggregate, conglomerate, mass, total

agglomeration *n* agglomeration, aggregate, conglomerate, mass, total

aggravate *v* 1 baffle, balk, bewilder, circumvent, confuse, dash, elude, foil, frustrate, hamper, impede, negate, nullify, perplex, thwart

v 2 anger, annoy, bother, bug, enrage, exasperate, frazzle, gall, grate, hassle, incense, inflame, infuriate, irk, irritate, madden, miff, nettle, outrage, peeve, pester, pique, provoke, rile, upset, vex

v 3 annoy, badger, bait, bedevil, beleaguer, bother, bug, harass, harry, hassle, heckle, hound, hurt, intimidate, jeer, nag, needle, persecute, pester, plague, provoke, ride, spite, taunt, tease, threaten, torment, worry

aggravated *adj* angry, annoyed, cross, enraged, excited, fuming, furious, hot, incensed, indignant, irate, irritable, mad, provoked, teed off, upset

aggravating *adj* abrasive, annoying, caustic, cutting, grating, irritating

aggravation *n* annoyance, disturbance, irritant, irritation

aggregate *adj* collective, common, communal, joint, mutual, public, shared
n 1 amount, body, budget, bulk, count, number, quantity, tally, total
n 2 all, entirety, gross, revenue, sales, sum, sum total, total, totality, whole
n 3 agglomerate, agglomeration, conglomerate, mass, total
v amount, number, plus, sum, total

aggression *n* 1 assault, attack, incursion, inroad, offense, offensive, onset, onslaught
n 2 aggressiveness, attack, bellicosity, belligerence, combativeness, fight, pugnacity

aggressive *adj* 1 defiant, insubordinate, rambunctious, restless, stubborn, unruly
adj 2 coercive, compelling, forceful, hard-sell, high-pressure, intensive, persuasive, pushy
adj 3 ambitious, assertive, assured, compelling, compulsive, confident, decided, dogmatic, driven, emphatic, energetic, insistent, militant, positive, pushing, pushy, self-assertive, sure, urging
adj 4 dominant, durable, firm, forceful, hardy, hearty, mighty, powerful, robust, rugged, stalwart, stout, strong, sturdy, tenacious, tough

aggressiveness *n* aggression, attack, bellicosity, belligerence, combativeness, fight, pugnacity

aggrieve *v* 1 exploit, oppress, persecute, torture
v 2 afflict, bother, burden, distress, grieve, hurt, injure, pain

aghast *adj* afraid, anxious, apprehensive, concerned, discerning, fearful, frightened, nervous, paranoid, scared, scary, terrified, worried

agile *adj* 1 deft, dexterous, skillful, subtle
adj 2 limber, lissome, lithe, lithesome, supple
adj 3 active, astir, brisk, catty, energetic, lively, nimble, quick, sprightly, spry, zippy

agitate *v* 1 derange, disorder, disturb, fluster, rock, ruffle, shake, sicken, unhinge, unsettle, upset
v 2 bake, boil, bubble, burn, churn, ferment, foam, fume, roast, seethe, simmer, smolder
v 3 anger, arouse, encourage, foment, ignite, incite, induce, inflame, inspire, instigate, invoke, motivate, muster, prod, propel, provoke, raise, set, set on, spur, stimulate, stir, urge

agitated *adj* see: TURBULENT *adj*

agitation *n* craze, excitement, frenzy, furor, fury, fuss, outrage, passion, tumult, uproar, wrath

agitator *n* 1 initiator, instigator, organizer, rabble-rouser, spark plug, troublemaker
n 2 see: REBEL *n*

aglow *adj* ablaze, afire, aflame, alight, blazing, burning, conflagrant, fiery, flaming, glowing

agnostic *n* 1 infidel, nonbeliever, skeptic
n 2 atheist, gentile, heathen, heretic, infidel, pagan, unbeliever

agog *adj* see: ENGROSSED *adj* 2

agonizingly *adv* painfully

agony *n* 1 ache, affliction, anguish, hurt, injury, pain, punishment, suffering, torture
n 2 anguish, bale, concern, distress, misery, nightmare, pain, sadness, sorrow, suffering, torment, travail, tribulation, trouble, woe, worry
n 3 see: PAIN *n* 2, 3, 4

agree *v* 1 acknowledge, admit, recognize
v 2 contract, covenant, pledge, promise
v 3 adjust, arrange, compromise, settle
v 4 accept, allow, approve, assent, comply, concur, consent, endorse, sign up, subscribe
v 5 accord, check, coalesce, coincide, comply with, concur, conform, consent, consist, correspond, fit in, harmonize, jibe, square, suit, tally

agreeable *adj* 1 gratifying, pleasant, pleasing, satisfying
adj 2 compatible, concurrent, congruent, harmonious, parallel
adj 3 bright, fine, good, nice, pleasant, sunny
adj 4 congenial, favorable, good, grateful, gratifying, nice, pleasant, pleasing, pleasurable, welcome

agreed *adj* absolute, bounded, categorical, clear, decided, definite, emphatic, established, exact, finite, fixed, guaranteed, limited, positive, specific, unequivocal, unmistakable, vested

agreeing *adj* 1 affirmative, optimistic, positive
adj 2 concerted, harmonious, unanimous, uncontested, undivided, unified
adj 3 accommodating, amenable, disposed, eager, glad, inclined, pleased, pliant, responsive, willing

agreement *n* 1 adaptation, compliance, conformation, modification *n* 2 arrangement, compromise, concession, decision, determination, franchise, settlement

n 3 clause, condition, provision, proviso, requirement, reservation, specification, stipulation, string, terms

n 4 acceptance, accord, approval, assent, compliance, concurrence, consent, go-ahead, nod, sympathy

n 5 accord, affinity, assent, concert, concord, congruence, cooperation, empathy, harmony, rapport, synergy, teamwork, unity

n 6 bargain, bond, compact, contract, convention, covenant, deal, pact, pledge, promise, transaction, treaty, understanding

ahead *adv* before, beyond, forward, in front, onward

aid *n* assistance, benefit, comfort, cure, hand, help, lift, nurture, relief, remedy, succor, support

v 1 accelerate, assist, expedite, facilitate

v 2 endow, finance, fund, subsidize, underwrite

v 3 comfort, cure, relieve, soothe, strengthen, support

v 4 baby, care for, help, nurse, nurture, pamper, succor

v 5 abet, advance, ameliorate, amend, assist, avail, benefit, better, boost, cultivate, do for, ease, egg on, encourage, enhance, forward, foster, further, help, improve, nurture, prefer, promote, rev, serve, spur on, support

aide *n* 1 aide-de-camp, assistant, attendant, employee, hand, helper, hired hand, laborer, servant, supporter, worker

n 2 assistant, clerk, recorder, scribe, secretary, stenographer

aide-de-camp *n* see: HELPER *n*

ailing *adj* delicate, diseased, down, frail, ill, impaired, indisposed, sick, sickly, suffering, unhealthy, unsound, unwell, weak

ailment *n* affliction, complaint, condition, disease, disorder, evil, harm, ill, illness, infirmity, malady, sickness

aim *n* 1 cause, consideration, goal, motive, purpose, reason

n 2 goal, mission, motive, objective, purpose, reason, sake, target, task

v 1 aspire, hope, strive, wish

v 2 establish, focus, point, set, shoot at, target

v 3 contemplate, design, intend, mean, plan, propose

v 4 address, cast, direct, level, point, train, zero in

aimless *adj* see: RANDOM *adj* 2

air *n* 1 affectation

n 2 harmony, measure, medley, melody, music, strain, tune

n 3 blow, breath, breeze, current, draft, gust, puff, wind

n 4 ambience, atmosphere, aura, emanation, feel, feeling, mood, semblance, spirit

n 5 call, carol, cry, lullaby, melody, note, rhapsody, song, tune

n 6 breath, breathing, inhalation

n 7 attitude, bearing, calmness, carriage, demeanor, disposition, poise, pose, posture, presence, set, stance

v 1 broadcast, relay, telecast, televise, transmit

v 2 bring up, broach, communicate, discuss, expose, express, give, introduce, open, put, reveal, state, tap, tell, vent, ventilate, verbalize

v 3 evaporate

v 4 advertise, boom, boost, drum up, endorse, pitch, plug, promote, publicize, push, rave, sell, tout

airborne *n* army, battalion, brigade, cavalry, company, footmen, guard, horsemen, infantry, legion, marines, militia, minutemen, paratroops, platoon, reserve, storm troopers

aircraft *n* 1 division, formation, squadron, wing

n 2 airliner, airplane, glider, jet, plane

airing *n* expression, utterance, venting

airliner *n* aircraft, airplane, glider, jet, plane

airman *n* aviator, barnstormer, flier, operator, pilot

airplane *n* aircraft, airliner, glider, jet, plane

airs *n* 1 affectation, mannerism, peculiarity, pose, posturing, pretense, trait

n 2 arrogance, cockiness, conceit, condescension, disdain, egotism, haughtiness, image, loftiness, narcissism, pride, self-esteem, self-image, vanity

airship *n* balloon, blimp, dirigible

airy *adj* 1 light

adj 2 breezy, brisk, drafty, gusty, lofty, open, windy

ajar *adj* cracked, open, unshut

akin *adj* 1 affiliated, aligned, allied, associated, fraternal, friendly, kindred, parallel, related

adj 2 alike, analogous, comparable, corresponding, equivalent, identical, kindred, like, matching, parallel, related, same, similar, such, uniform

alacrity *n* **1** cheerfulness, eagerness, sprightliness

n **2** dispatch, expedition, haste, hastiness, hurry, hustle, precipitance, precipitation, quickness, rush, rustle, speed, swiftness

n **3** cadence, celerity, dispatch, gait, pace, quickness, rapidity, rate, speed, step, stride, swiftness, trot, velocity, walk

n **4** see: PASSION *n* 7

alarm *n* **1** alert, SOS, warning

n **2** bell, buzzer, chime, gong, signal, siren

n **3** call, hail, shout, signal, whoop, yell

n **4** affliction, anxiety, apprehension, care, consternation, dismay, dread, fear, fright, horror, ordeal, panic, terror, trepidation, trial, trouble, worry

v **1** abash, awe, cow, daunt, frighten, horrify, intimidate, panic, scare, shock, spook, startle, terrify, terrorize, unnerve

v **2** see: INTIMIDATE *v* 2, 3

albeit *conj* although, even if, even though, notwithstanding, whereas, while, whilst

alchemy *n* alteration, changeover, conversion, revision, transformation

alcohol *n* booze, drinks, grog, liquor, moonshine, spirits, whiskey

alcove *n* chamber, room, ward

ale *n* beer, bock, brew, lager, Pilsner, stout, suds

alert *adj* **1** aware, mindful, wise

adj **2** apt, prompt, quick, ready

adj **3** advertent, attentive, careful, conscientious, heedful, observant

adj **4** careful, heedful, leery, prudent, suspicious, vigilant, wary, watchful

adj **5** careful, cautious, open-eyed, unsleeping, vigilant, wakeful, wary, watchful, wide-awake

adj **6** acute, astute, cagey, canny, clever, cunning, deft, keen, knowing, penetrating, perceptive, piercing, quick, quick-sighted, quick-witted, receptive, responsive, sagacious, savvy, sensitive, sharp, sharp-witted, shrewd, slick, smart, street-smart, wise

adj **7** see: INTELLIGENT *adj* 4

adj **8** see: LIVELY *adj* 8

n alarm, SOS, warning

v **1** divulge, tip, tip off, warn

v **2** augur, caution, flag, forebode, forewarn, indicate, inform, motion, notify, signal, warn, wave

alfresco *adj* open-air, outdoor, outside

alias *n* **1** anonym, nom de plume, pen name, pseudonym

n **2** designation, handle, moniker, name, nickname, title

alibi *n* **1** con, deception, lie, pretext, ruse, subterfuge, trick

n **2** defense, excuse, explanation, justification, plea, pretext, rationalization, reason, ruse

alien *adj* **1** extraneous, extraterrestrial, extrinsic, foreign

adj **2** foreign, remote, separate, unrelated

adj **3** exotic, foreign, strange, unfamiliar

n foreigner, newcomer, outsider, stranger

alienate *v* estrange, fend off, rebuff, repel, repulse, snub

alienated *adj* **1** disaffected, disunited, estranged, separated, weaned

adj **2** angry, bitter, emotional, hurt, jealous, offended, provoked, resentful

adj **3** see: ALONE *adj* 3

alight *adj* ablaze, afire, aflame, aglow, blazing, burning, conflagrant, fiery, flaming, glowing

v come down, descend, dismount, get off, land, settle

align *v* **1** adjust, dial, select, tune

v **2** adjust

v **3** arrange, array, assort, catalog, categorize, class, classify, cluster, compile, file, format, grade, group, lay out, line up, list, order, organize, outline, pigeonhole, place, position, prioritize, program, rank, rate, sort, stack, tabulate

aligned *adj* **1** neat, ordered, proper, straight

adj **2** affiliated, akin, allied, associated, fraternal, friendly, kindred, parallel, related

alike *adj* akin, analogous, comparable, corresponding, equivalent, identical, kindred, like, matching, parallel, related, same, similar, such, uniform

alimony *n* **1** allowance, annuity, payment, residual, stipend

n **2** compensation, fee, honorarium, payment, remuneration, reward, stipend

alive *adj* **1** developing, living, prospering, viable

adj **2** animate, animated, living, viable, vital

adj **3** active, functioning, live, operative, running, working

adj **4** active, dynamic, energetic, sound, spirited, strong, vibrant, vigorous, vital

adj **5** ample, overflowing, replete, rife, swarming, teeming

adj **6** attentive, awake, aware, cognizant, conscious, conversant, knowing, responsive, sentient, thinking

all *adj* all-out, complete, entire, full-blown, gross, integral, integrated, outright, total, unlimited, whole

n aggregate, entirety, gross, revenue, sales, sum, sum total, total, totality, whole

allay *v* **1** abate, assuage, mitigate, moderate, quench, satiate, satisfy

v **2** alleviate, assuage, attenuate, diminish, ease, extenuate, lessen, lighten, minimize, mitigate, moderate, mollify, reduce, relieve

v **3** see: APPEASE *v* 2

allegation *n* accusation, assertion, charge, comment, declaration, deposition, pronouncement, statement

allege *v* **1** assert, avow, claim, maintain, say, state

v **2** accuse, arraign, assert, charge, cite, impeach, imply, impute, incriminate, indict, litigate, prosecute, sue, try

allegiance *n* **1** affiliation, association, connection, obligation, tie

n **2** ardor, devotion, faithfulness, fidelity, loyalty

allegory *n* fable, fantasy, fiction, legend, lesson, lore, myth, mythology, parable, story, tale

allergy *n* hay fever, hives, rash, reaction, spots

alleviate *v* allay, assuage, attenuate, diminish, ease, extenuate, lessen, lighten, minimize, mitigate, moderate, mollify, reduce, relieve

alleviation *n* abatement, comfort, correction, cure, help, relief, remedy, respite, solace, solution

alleyway *n* passageway

alliance *n* affiliation, association, axis, bloc, coalition, concord, confederation, consolidation, faction, federation, joint venture, league, merger, organization, partnership, relationship, treaty, union

allied *adj* affiliated, akin, aligned, associated, fraternal, friendly, kindred, parallel, related

allocate *v* **1** appropriate, budget, plan

v **2** appoint, assign, establish, implement, institute, set

v **3** allot, allow, apportion, assign, designate, distribute, divide, divvy, earmark, give, measure, parcel, partition, portion, prorate, quota, ration, section, share, slice

allocation *n* distribution, marketing, merchandising, selling, share, sharing

allot *v* allocate, allow, apportion, assign, designate, distribute, divide, divvy, earmark, give, measure, parcel, partition, portion, prorate, quota, ration, section, share, slice

allotment *n* allowance, apportionment, budget, dispensation, dispersion, lot, measure, part, percentage, portion, quota, ration, share, slice

all-out *adj* all, complete, entire, full-blown, gross, integral, integrated, outright, total, unlimited, whole

allow *v* **1** acknowledge, admit, avow, concede, confess, fess up, grant, own, own up

v **2** accept, agree, approve, assent, comply, concur, consent, endorse, sign up, subscribe

v **3** see: ALLOCATE *v* 3

v **4** see: TOLERATE *v*

allowable *adj* **1** bearable, endurable, sustainable, tolerable

adj **2** acceptable, eligible, fitting, qualified, suitable

adj **3** authorized, lawful, legal, legitimate, permissible, rightful, valid

allowance *n* **1** alimony, annuity, payment, residual, stipend

n **2** allotment, apportionment, budget, dispensation, dispersion, lot, measure, part, percentage, portion, quota, ration, share, slice

allude *v* **1** bring up, hint, point out, recommend, refer

v **2** denote, indicate, mention, point out, refer to, reveal, show, speak of, specify, suggest, tell

v **3** see: SUGGEST *v* 4, 6

allure *n* affinity, appeal, attraction, attractiveness, aura, beguilement, charisma, charm, enchantment, enticement, fascination, glamour, infatuation, magnetism, sex appeal, spell

v **1** attract, bedevil, beguile, bewitch, captivate, charm, conjure, delight, draw, enchant, enthrall, fascinate, lure, magnetize, mesmerize, tempt, wile

v **2** see: TEASE *v* 2

alluring *adj* **1** compelling, desirable, irresistible, overpowering, seductive, tantalizing

adj **2** attractive, desirable, erotic, exciting, seductive, sexy, tantalizing, tempting

adj **3** attractive, becoming, coy, cute, enchanting, enticing, fascinating, foxy, inviting, pleasing, ravishing, seductive, sexy

adj **4** see: APPEALING *adj* 2

adj **5** see: BEAUTIFUL *adj* 2

adj **6** see: FASCINATING *adj* 1, 2

allusion *n* connotation, hint, implication,

innuendo, insinuation, notation, reference, suggestion

ally n 1 advocate, angel, backer, benefactor, booster, champion, cheerleader, donor, friend, guarantor, helper, ombudsman, partner, patron, promoter, proponent, sponsor, supporter

n 2 accomplice, acquaintance, adjunct, associate, buddy, chum, cohort, colleague, companion, compatriot, comrade, confidant, confrere, connection, copartner, counterpart, co-worker, crony, equal, fellow, follower, friend, intimate, mate, pal, partner, peer, relative, supporter

almanac n calendar

almost adv about, approximately, around, close to, more or less, nearly, not quite

alms n assistance, charity, contributions, dole, donations, oblation, offering

aloft adv above, greater, more, on top of, over, overhead, superior

adj elevated, high, lofty, overhead, soaring, tall

aloha n adieu, adios, *arrivederci, auf Wiedersehen,* au revoir, bon voyage, bye, cheerio, *ciao,* farewell, goodbye, good day, *sayonara,* shalom, so long

alone adj 1 lone, lonely, lonesome, single, singular, solitary, solo, unaccompanied

adj 2 incomparable, matchless, only, peerless, unequaled, unique, unmatched, unpaired, unparalleled, unrivaled

adj 3 alienated, apart, detached, hidden, isolated, private, removed, secluded, separated, sequestered, severed

alongside prep against, next to

adj see: ADJACENT adj

aloof adj 1 conservative, poised, reserved

adj 2 blasé, calm, careless, casual, composed, cool, detached, diffident, disinterested, distant, indifferent, informal, inhibited, nonchalant, numb, remote, reserved, shy, unconcerned, unfriendly, uninterested, withdrawn

aloofness n detachment, indifference, preoccupation, separation

alp n hill, mountaintop, peak, summit

also adv additionally, and, as well, as well as, besides, further, furthermore, in addition, likewise, moreover, plus, too

alter v 1 assort, diversify, mix, modify, vary

v 2 effect, impact, impress, influence, modify

v 3 adjust, catalyze, change, modify, mutate, refashion, vary

v 4 change, commute, convert, evolve,

further, improve, metamorphose, modernize, modify, mutate, revolutionize, transfer, transfigure, transform, transmute, vary

alterable adj 1 impressionable, inexperienced, malleable, naive, sensitive, susceptible

adj 2 elastic, flexible, movable, pliable, resilient, springy, supple

alteration n 1 alchemy, changeover, conversion, revision, transformation

n 2 adjustment, anomaly, change, deviation, modification, mutation, permutation, shift, variation

altercate v see: QUARREL v

altercation n argument, battle, brawl, challenge, combat, controversy, disagreement, discord, dispute, feud, fight, fracas, fray, hassle, melee, quarrel, rancor, rift, row, ruckus, scrap, scuffle, skirmish, spat, squabble, struggle, tiff, war

alternate adj 1 alternative, equivalent, substitute

adj 2 cyclic, cyclical, intermittent, periodic, periodical, recurrent, recurring, repeated, repetitive, sporadic

adj 3 another, certain, different, discrete, disparate, dissimilar, distinct, diverse, numerous, other, separate, several, some, unlike, various, varying

n 1 agent, dummy, proxy, representative, substitute

n 2 equivalent, exchange, replacement, substitute, substitution

n 3 agent, backup, contingency, part-timer, replacement, representative, standby, substitute, surrogate

v 1 fluctuate, oscillate, pendulate, sway, swing, vacillate, wave

v 2 change, cycle, lap, oscillate, rotate, shift, switch

alternation n circuit, circulation, gyration, revolution, rotation, round, sequence, spinning, succession, turn, whirl

alternative adj alternate, equivalent, substitute

n choice, decision, druthers, election, option, pick, preference, rathers, selection, vote

alternatives n options, possibilities, potential

although conj albeit, even if, even though, notwithstanding, whereas, while, whilst

altitude n 1 ascent, elevation, height

n 2 ceiling, limits, maximum, restraint

altogether adv adequately, assiduously, completely, earnestly, entirely, exhaustively, fully, hard, intensely, intensively, painstakingly, perfectly, quite, sufficiently, thoroughly, totally, unremittingly, utterly, wholly

altruism *n* charity, generosity, goodness, goodwill, grace, humanity, kindness, mercy

altruistic *adj* benevolent, bountiful, caring, charitable, Christian, compassionate, generous, giving, good, humane, humanitarian, kind, lenient, merciful, philanthropic, tender

always *adv* ad infinitum, all the time, constantly, continually, endlessly, eternally, forever, perpetually, timelessly, unceasingly

amalgamate *v* band, blend, coalesce, combine, compound, consolidate, fuse, intermingle, league, lump, meld, merge, mingle, mix, unify, unite

amass *v* **1** collect, gather, heap, pile, rake, take in
v **2** accrue, accumulate, acquire, assemble, collect, garner, gather, grow, hoard, save, squirrel, stash, stockpile, store up

amateur *n* beginner, dabbler, dilettante, hobbyist, layman, neophyte, nonprofessional, novice, part-timer
adj inexperienced, lay, nonprofessional, unprofessional

amateurish *adj* incompetent, inept, unprofessional

amaze *v* **1** astonish, astound, awe, delight, floor, impress, overwhelm, wow
v **2** daze, electrify, horrify, offend, outrage, overwhelm, scandalize, shock, stun
v **3** befog, bewilder, boggle, confound, confuse, daze, perplex, puzzle, stumble, stump
v **4** astonish, astound, awe, boggle, confound, dazzle, dumbfound, flabbergast, nonplus, stagger, stun, surprise

amazement *n* **1** astonishment, awe, bewilderment, shock, surprise, wonder
n **2** awe, consternation, dread, fear, respect, reverence, wonder

amazing *adj* **1** exaggerated, fabulous, questionable
adj **2** astounding, bizarre, remarkable, strange
adj **3** extraordinary, fantastic, inconceivable, incredible, unbelievable
adj **4** see: EXTRAORDINARY *adj* 2, 4

ambassador *n* agent, consul, delegate, deputy, diplomat, emissary, envoy

ambience *n* air, atmosphere, aura, emanation, feel, feeling, mood, semblance, spirit

ambiguous *adj* **1** cryptic, enigmatic, mystifying, occult, puzzling, vague
adj **2** bleary, confused, fuzzy, hazy, misty, mixed up, nebulous, unclear
adj **3** imperceptible, imprecise, indecisive, indefinite, indeterminate, indistinct, inexact, loose, vague, wishy-washy
adj **4** borderline, clouded, doubtful, dubious, equivocal, garbled, illogical, inarticulate, incalculable, incoherent, inexplicit, muddled, muffled, murky, obscure, precarious, questionable, shaky, suspect, suspicious, uncertain, unclear, uneasy, unintelligible, unsure, vague, wary

ambition *n* **1** aspiration, desire, goal, hope, will, wish
n **2** drive, enterprise, initiative, lead, leadership, push, thrust, volition
n **3** bent, design, goal, intent, intention, meaning, objective, plan, purpose

ambitious *adj* **1** aspiring, rising, striving
adj **2** assiduous, diligent, energetic, hardworking, industrious, persevering, persistent, resolute, sedulous, zealous
adj **3** aggressive, assertive, assured, compelling, compulsive, confident, decided, dogmatic, driven, emphatic, energetic, insistent, militant, positive, pushing, pushy, self-assertive, sure, urging
adj **4** see: FLAMBOYANT *adj* 2

ambivalent *adj* conflicting, equivocal, paradoxical, uncertain

amble *v* **1** flaunt, prance, stride, strut, swagger
v **2** hike, journey, march, pace, parade, plod, saunter, step, stride, stroll, strut, tramp, tread, trek, walk

ambrosial *adj* delightful, heavenly, scrumptious

ambulatory *adj* **1** locomotive, mobile, moving
adj **2** gypsy, itinerant, movable, nomadic, perambulatory, roving, transient, vagrant, wandering, wayfaring

ambush *n* assault, sneak attack, surprise
v assail, assault, attack, beset, invade, raid, storm, strike, trap, waylay

ameliorate *v* **1** convalesce, gain, heal, improve, loop up, mend, perk, rally, recover, recuperate, rehabilitate, revive
v **2** see: HELP *v* 3

amenable *adj* **1** complaisant, compliant, cooperative, obedient, submissive, subservient, tractable, willing
adj **2** accommodating, agreeing, disposed, eager, glad, inclined, pleased, pliant, responsive, willing
adj **3** affable, amiable, amicable, conge-

nial, empathetic, friendly, gregarious, hospitable, neighborly, outgoing, receptive, sociable, social, sympathetic

amend v 1 adjust, correct, fix, improve, mend, modify, position, rectify, remedy, restore, right, straighten

v 2 see: HELP v 3

amends n compensation, damages, indemnity, redress, reparation, restitution, restoration

American n Yankee

amethyst adj lavender, lilac, mauve, orchid, plum, purple, violet

amiable adj 1 benign, genial, kind, kindly, mild, nonmalignant

adj 2 complaisant, easy, good-humored, good-natured, lenient, mild, obliging

adj 3 affable, approachable, cordial, friendly, genial, gentle, gracious, likable, lovable, peaceful, pleasant, serene

adj 4 affable, amenable, amicable, congenial, empathetic, friendly, gregarious, hospitable, neighborly, outgoing, receptive, sociable, social, sympathetic

amicable adj affable, amenable, amiable, congenial, empathetic, friendly, gregarious, hospitable, neighborly, outgoing, receptive, sociable, social, sympathetic

amid prep among, inside, inside of, mid, midst, with, within

amidst prep among, atwixt, between, betwixt, halfway to, mid, midway, 'twixt

amiss adj 1 crude, defective, faulty, flawed, imperfect, incomplete, short, unfulfilled

adj 2 afoul, awry, bad, bum, improper, out of kilter, poor, rotten, unsatisfactory, wrong

ammo n ammunition, armor, arms, equipment, guns, machinery, munitions, ordnance, weapons

ammunition n ammo, armor, arms, equipment, guns, machinery, munitions, ordnance, weapons

amnesty n absolution, discharge, disengagement, dispensation, freedom, moratorium, pardon, release, relief, reprieve, respite, stay, suspension

among prep 1 amid, inside, inside of, mid, midst, with, within

prep 2 amidst, atwixt, between, betwixt, halfway to, mid, midway, 'twixt

amorous adj 1 affectionate, attached, caring, devoted, enamored, fond, loving, romantic, tender

adj 2 ardent, aroused, carnal, earthy, erotic, fervent, fleshly, horny, hot, impassioned, lascivious, lecherous, lewd, licentious, lustful, passionate, provocative, randy, raunchy, romantic, sensual, sexual, sexy, sultry, titillated, torrid, turned on, voluptuous, wanton

adj 3 aroused, horny, in heat, in the mood, lustful, passionate, stimulated

amorousness n amour, love, passion

amount n 1 dose, portion, prescription

n 2 balance, count, result, sum, total

n 3 amplitude, dimensions, magnitude, proportions, quantity, scope, size, volume

n 4 aggregate, body, budget, bulk, count, number, quantity, tally, total

n 5 account, catalog, enumeration, inventory, itemization, list, litany, repertoire, supply, tally

v 1 aggregate, number, plus, sum, total

v 2 approach, correspond to, equal, match,

amour n amorousness, love, passion

amphitheater n arena, bowl, coliseum, dome, hippodrome, scene, stadium

amphora n pot, urn, vase, vessel

ample adj 1 abundant, countless, numerous

adj 2 decent, generous, respectable, sizable, substantial

adj 3 broad, expansive, extended, extensive, ranging, vast, wide

adj 4 big, capacious, comfortable, commodious, open, roomy, spacious, vast, wide

adj 5 big, considerable, enormous, extensive, grand, hefty, huge, jumbo, large, major, sizable, spacious, vast

adj 6 abounding, abundant, bounteous, bountiful, copious, enough, galore, generous, liberal, overflowing, plentiful, plenty, prodigal, profuse, teeming

adj 7 alive, overflowing, replete, rife, swarming, teeming

amplify v 1 construct, develop, devise, elaborate, enhance, enlarge, expand, expound, increase, refine

v 2 bolster, encourage, enhance, enhearten, hearten, increase, inspire, reassure, strengthen, support

v 3 bloat, dilate, distend, enlarge, expand, fatten, grow, increase, inflate, magnify, stretch, swell, widen

v 4 accent, accentuate, concentrate, emphasize, feature, flag, focus, heighten, highlight, italicize, mark, punctuate, spotlight, stress, underline, underscore

v 5 append, augment, boost, build, enlarge, expand, extend, grow, heighten, increase, intensify, magnify, multiply, run up, snowball, supplement, upsurge, wax

amplitude *n* **1** caliber, concentration, magnitude, potency, strength

n **2** amount, dimensions, magnitude, proportions, quantity, scope, size, volume

amply *adv* **1** acceptably, adequately, appropriately, correctly, properly, right, satisfactorily, suitably, well

adv **2** adequately, enough, equitably, fairly, justly, moderately, passably, rather, satisfactorily, tolerably

amulet *n* charm, fetish, talisman

amuse *v* **1** delight, please, tickle

v **2** charm, divert, entertain, interest, please, recreate, stimulate

amusement *n* **1** game, knickknack, plaything, toy, trinket

n **2** distraction, diversion, enjoyment, entertainment, frolic, fun, game, hobby, pastime, play, recreation, sport

n **3** see: MERRIMENT *n*

amusing *adj* diverting, enjoyable, entertaining, fun, humorous, joking, playful

analgesic *n* balm, emollient, salve

analogize *v* associate, compare, correlate, explain, rank, relate

analogous *adj* akin, alike, comparable, corresponding, equivalent, identical, kindred, like, matching, parallel, related, same, similar, such, uniform

analogy *n* affinity, approximation, comparison, likeness, match, metaphor, resemblance, semblance, similarity, simile

analysis *n* **1** assay, examination, experiment, observation, test

n **2** digging, experimentation, exploration, inquiry, inquisition, investigation, research, study, testing, trial

n **3** assessment, commentary, criticism, critique, evaluation, examination, judgment, notion, opinion, review, ruling

n **4** see: CONSIDERATION *n* **5**

analytical *adj* **1** logical, probing, subtle

adj **2** cerebral, highbrow, intellectual, intelligent

analyze *v* **1** brief, condense, evaluate, outline, retrace, review, study, summarize, synopsize, update

v **2** assess, determine, diagnose, estimate, examine, penetrate, probe, scope, solve, survey, understand, unravel

v **3** annotate, clarify, define, detail, elucidate, explain, expound, express, interpret, narrate, spell out, state, understand

v **4** see: DEDUCE *v* **3**

anarchy *n* **1** rebellion

n **2** see: COMMOTION *n* **1**

anathema *n* condemnation, curse, execration, imprecation, malediction, voodoo

anatomy *n* body, build, figure, form, frame, physique, shape

ancestor *n* antecedent, ascendant, elder, forebear, forefather, forerunner, founder, grandparent, parent, patriarch, predecessor, progenitor

ancestry *n* blood, bloodline, descent, family, genealogy, heritage, line, lineage, origin, pedigree, stock, strain

anchor *v* **1** establish, moor, plant, root

v **2** catch, fasten, fix, moor, secure

ancient *adj* **1** aboriginal, early, former, original, prehistoric, primeval, primitive, primordial, rudimentary

adj **2** aged, age-old, antique, elderly, gray, grizzled, old, olden, senior, timeworn, venerable, vintage, worn

adj **3** see: OBSOLETE *adj*

adj **4** see: PRECEDING *adj*

ancillary *adj* **1** accessory, adjunct, assisting, auxiliary, subsidiary, supporting

adj **2** auxiliary, incidental, minor, related, secondary, side, subordinate

adj **3** conditional, contingent, dependent, indefinite, provisional, relative, reliant, temporary, uncertain

adj **4** assistant, collateral, complementary, dependent, lesser, minor, secondary, sub, subject, subordinate, subsidiary, substitute, supporter, tributary, worker

and *conj* see: ALSO *adv*

android *n* automaton, droid, robot

anecdote *n* description, fantasy, fiction, invention, myth, narration, narrative, novel, sketch, story, tale, yarn

anemic *adj* bloodless, gaunt, haggard, lifeless, pale, pallid, passionless, spiritless, watery, weak

anew *adv* **1** afresh, lately, new, newly, of late, recently

adv **2** again, once more, one more time

angel *n* **1** idol, model, prince, saint

n **2** archangel, cherub, spirit

n **3** advocate, ally, backer, benefactor, booster, champion, cheerleader, donor, friend, guarantor, helper, ombudsman, partner, patron, promoter, proponent, sponsor, supporter

anger *n* **1** animosity, hostility, huff, indignation, miff, offense, pique, resentment

n **2** dander, fit, frenzy, fury, indignation, ire, outrage, paroxysm, rage, tantrum, wrath

v **1** blow up, boil, boil over, brew, bristle, burn, flare up, fume, rage, seethe, simmer, smoke, steam, storm *v* 2 agitate, arouse, encourage, foment, ignite, incite, induce, inflame, inspire, instigate, invoke, motivate, muster, prod, propel, provoke, raise, set, set on, spur, stimulate, stir, urge

v 3 aggravate, annoy, bother, bug, enrage, exasperate, frazzle, gall, grate, hassle, incense, inflame, infuriate, irk, irritate, madden, miff, nettle, outrage, peeve, pester, pique, provoke, rile, upset, vex

angina *n* see: PAIN *n* 3

angle *n* 1 bearing, degree, heading, position, setting

n 2 grade, gradient, incline, pitch, ramp, rise, slant, slope, tilt

n 3 aspect, facet, hand, mien, opinion, perspective, phase, side, slant, view

n 4 bend, bow, detour, deviation, double, shift, tack, turn, turning, yaw

n 5 see: TECHNIQUE *n* 3

v 1 confuse, deceive, distort, falsify, garble, incline, misconstrue, misinterpret, misquote, misread, misrepresent, misunderstand, mix up, mumble, slant, slope, taint, twist

v 2 connive, fish, hint

v 3 arch, bend, bow, curve, flex, ply, round, tilt, tip, turn, twist, vault

angler *n* fisherman

angry *adj* 1 alienated, bitter, emotional, hurt, jealous, offended, provoked, resentful

adj 2 bellicose, belligerent, combative, contentious, hostile, militant, pugnacious, quarrelsome, warlike

adj 3 ferocious, fierce, furious, heated, intense, savage, severe, terrible, vehement, vicious, violent

adj 4 aggravated, annoyed, cross, enraged, excited, fuming, furious, hot, incensed, indignant, irate, irritable, mad, provoked, teed off, upset

adj 5 see: HOT-TEMPERED *adj*

anguish *n* 1 ache, affliction, agony, hurt, injury, pain, punishment, suffering, torture

n 2 affliction, care, catastrophe, despair, disaster, dole, grief, heartache, mishap, pain, regret, remorse, rue, sickness, sorrow, woe

n 3 agony, bale, concern, distress, misery, nightmare, pain, sadness, sorrow, suffering, torment, travail, tribulation, trouble, woe, worry

angular *adj* bony, emaciated, gaunt, lanky, lean, meager, scraggly, scrawny, skinny, slender, thin

anile *adj* absurd, asinine, brainless, childish, fatuous, foolish, idiotic, inept, meaningless, mindless, senseless, silly, simple, thoughtless, unintelligent, witless

animal *n* beast, being, brute, creature, monster, ogre

animate *adj* alive, animated, living, viable, vital

v brighten, cheer up, enliven, incite, inspire, liven, quicken, resuscitate, vivify

animated *adj* 1 alive, animate, living, viable, vital

adj 2 see: LIVELY *adj* 8

animation *n* 1 see: ACTIVITY *n* 3

n 2 see: VIGOR *n* 2

animosity *n* 1 anger, hostility, huff, indignation, miff, offense, pique, resentment

n 2 acrimony, antagonism, antipathy, aversion, bitterness, dislike, enmity, gall, hate, hatred, hostility, ill will, malice, rancor, spite, venom, vindictiveness

anklet *n* band, bangle, bracelet, brooch, earring, jewelry, medal, medallion, necklace, pin, ring

annex *n* 1 adjunct, fitting, fixture, part, piece, unit

n 2 addition, adjunct, annexation, branch, extension, section, wing

v 1 appropriate, commandeer, confiscate, expropriate, grab, impound, plunder, preempt, repossess, seize, sequester, shanghai, take

v 2 acquire, buy, capture, gain, get, have, land, obtain, pick up, procure, purchase, requisition, secure, solicit, win

annexation *n* addition, adjunct, annex, branch, extension, section, wing

annihilate *v* 1 decimate, demolish, destroy, destruct, devastate, dismantle, overturn, pulverize, raze, rub out, ruin, shatter, smash, tear down, undo, wreck

v 2 abolish, assassinate, bump off, butcher, decimate, destroy, dispatch, execute, exterminate, hang, hit, kill, knock off, liquidate, massacre, murder, put away, rub out, slaughter, slay, wipe out

v 3 crush, demolish, extinguish, put down, quash, quell, quench, repress, squash, stamp out, suppress

v 4 abate, abolish, abrogate, annul, call off, cancel, cease, delete, destroy, efface, erase, excise, expunge, invalidate, kill, negate, nullify, obliterate, omit, quash, remove, stop, terminate, wipe out

anniversary *n* birthday

annotate *v* 1 compile, correct, denote, edit, modify, polish, proofread, revise

v 2 see: ELUCIDATE *v* 1

announce *v* 1 call, hail, page, summon

v 2 acquaint, delineate, depict, introduce, present, reflect, represent, show

v 3 advertise, blaze, broadcast, circulate, declare, disperse, disseminate, proclaim, promulgate, publish

v 4 see: VERBALIZE *v* 2

announcement *n* 1 notice, placard, post, poster, proclamation, sign

n 2 see: CLICHÉ *n* 3

annoy *v* 1 antagonize, argue, bother, bug, concern, distress, disturb, goad, harass, hassle, inconvenience, irk, irritate, pain, perturb, strain, stress, taunt, trouble, try, upset, worry

v 2 aggravate, anger, bother, bug, enrage, exasperate, frazzle, gall, grate, hassle, incense, inflame, infuriate, irk, irritate, madden, miff, nettle, outrage, peeve, pester, pique, provoke, rile, upset, vex

v 3 aggravate, badger, bait, bedevil, beleaguer, bother, bug, harass, harry, hassle, heckle, hound, hurt, intimidate, jeer, nag, needle, persecute, pester, plague, provoke, ride, spite, taunt, tease, threaten, torment, worry

annoyance *n* 1 aggravation, disturbance, irritant, irritation

n 2 anxiety, apprehension, bother, care, concern, disquiet, disquietude, doubt, irritation, misgiving, reservation, restlessness, restraint, skepticism, trouble, uneasiness, vexation, worry

n 3 bother, conflict, contention, difference, discord, disharmony, dispute, dissension, dissent, dissidence, dissonance, disunity, division, hassle, inconvenience, mischief, nuisance, strife, trouble, variance

annoyed *adj* aggravated, angry, cross, enraged, excited, fuming, furious, hot, incensed, indignant, irate, irritable, mad, provoked, teed off, upset

annoying *adj* 1 abrasive, aggravating, caustic, cutting, grating, irritating

adj 2 acute, grating, high, loud, piercing, piping, sharp, shrill

adj 3 difficult, hurt, irksome, irritated, irritating, painful, sensitive, sore

adj 4 bad, difficult, disagreeable, displeasing, nasty, objectionable, offensive, rotten, sour, unhappy, unpleasant, upsetting

adj 5 anxious, bothersome, chafing, crabby, edgy, fretful, galling, impatient, irritating, jittery, nagging, on edge, restless, touchy, unsettling

adj 6 bothersome, glaring, harassing, irksome, irritating, mean, onerous, painful, pesky, troublesome, ugly, unwelcome, vexatious, wicked

annuity *n* alimony, allowance, payment, residual, stipend

annul *v* 1 abrogate, cancel, contradict, discharge, dismantle, dissolve, dwindle, fade, negate, nullify, quash, recall, repeal, rescind, reverse, revoke, set aside, vacate, void

v 2 abate, abolish, abrogate, annihilate, call off, cancel, cease, delete, destroy, efface, erase, excise, expunge, invalidate, kill, negate, nullify, obliterate, omit, quash, remove, stop, terminate, wipe out

annulment *n* dissolution, divorce, separation, split

anoint *v* 1 baptize, bless, consecrate, dedicate, devote, enshrine, exalt, hallow, purify, sanctify

v 2 salve

anomalous *adj* aberrant, abnormal, artificial, atypical, contrived, deviant, disparate, divergent, incongruous, irregular, off-key, uncharacteristic, unnatural

anomaly *n* adjustment, alteration, change, deviation, modification, mutation, permutation, shift, variation

anon *adv* 1 after, behind, following, in pursuit, later, post, subsequently

adv 2 see: IMMEDIATELY *adv* 3

anonym *n* alias, nom de plume, pen name, pseudonym

anonymous *adj* nameless, obscure, uncelebrated, unfamed, unheard-of, unknown, unnamed, unrenowned

another *adj* 1 added, additional, auxiliary, extra, further, incremental, more, one more, other, spare, supplemental, supplementary, surplus

adj 2 alternate, certain, different, discrete, disparate, dissimilar, distinct, diverse, numerous, other, separate, several, some, unlike, various, varying

answer *n* 1 acknowledgment, credit, recognition

n 2 explanation, key, result, secret, solution

n 3 comeback, put-down, quip, reaction, rejoinder, reply, response, retort, return

v 1 explain, resolve, solve, unravel

v 2 react, recur, respond, return, revert, turn back

v 3 do, fulfill, meet, qualify, satisfy, suffice, work

v 4 achieve, execute, fill, finish, fulfill, meet, realize, satisfy *v* 5 acknowledge, come back, react, rejoin, reply, respond, retort, return

answerable *adj* see: REPUTABLE *adj*

antagonism *n* 1 antithesis, con, opposition

n 2 conflict, discord, disharmony, friction

n 3 see: HATE *n*

antagonist *n* 1 adversary, anti, challenger, competitor, con, contender, enemy, foe, match, opponent, rival

n 2 adversary, naysayer, obstructionist, schmuck, shnook

antagonistic *adj* 1 adverse, anti, contrary, opposed, opposing

adj 2 adverse, bellicose, hostile, ill, inimical, nasty, spiteful, unfriendly

antagonize *v* annoy, argue, bother, bug, concern, distress, disturb, goad, harass, hassle, inconvenience, irk, irritate, pain, perturb, strain, stress, taunt, trouble, try, upset, worry

ante *n* see: REWARD *n* 8

antecedent *adj* aforementioned, ancient, anterior, archaic, earlier, foregoing, former, past, preceding, previous, prior, recent

n ancestor, ascendant, elder, forebear, forefather, forerunner, founder, grandparent, parent, patriarch, predecessor, progenitor

antedate *v* come before, forego, pioneer, precede, preface, spearhead

anterior *adj* aforementioned, ancient, antecedent, archaic, earlier, foregoing, former, past, preceding, previous, prior, recent

anteroom *n* approach, atrium, court, doorway, entrance hall, entry, foyer, hall, hallway, lobby, portal, vestibule

anti *adj* adverse, against, antagonistic, contrary, opposed, opposing

n see: ENEMY *n*

antibody *n* antidote, antigen, antitoxin, defense, serum, vaccine

antic *n* 1 adventure, caper, escapade, joke, lark, mischief, prank, trick

n 2 see: MANEUVER *n* 2

anticipate *v* 1 await, believe, count on, expect, hope, keep the faith, look, look forward to, wish

v 2 see: PREDICT *v* 2

anticipated *adj* contingent, hoped for, iffy, planned, probable, proposed, tentative

anticipation *n* 1 anxiety, apprehension, strain, stress, suspense, tension

n 2 caution, deterrent, precaution, preclusion, preparation, prevention, safeguard

n 3 expectation, hope, premonition

antidote *n* 1 cure, medication, medicine, panacea, prescription, remedy, serum, therapy, treatment

n 2 antibody, antigen, antitoxin, defense, serum, vaccine

antigen *n* antibody, antidote, antitoxin, defense, serum, vaccine

antipathy *n* acrimony, animosity, antagonism, aversion, bitterness, dislike, enmity, gall, hate, hatred, hostility, ill will, malice, rancor, spite, venom, vindictiveness

antiquated *adj* ancient, archaic, bygone, dated, dead, extinct, noncurrent, obsolete, old, outdated, outmoded, passé, past, worn

antique *adj* aged, age-old, ancient, elderly, gray, grizzled, old, olden, senior, timeworn, venerable, vintage, worn

n 1 bric-a-brac, curio, curiosity, novelty, objet d'art, oddity, rarity, treasure, wonder

n 2 gift, heirloom, keepsake, memento, memorial, relic, remembrance, reminder, souvenir, token, trophy

antisocial *adj* introverted, reclusive, standoffish

antithesis *n* 1 antagonism, con, opposition

n 2 converse, opposite, reverse

antitoxin *n* antibody, antidote, antigen, defense, serum, vaccine

antsy *adj* edgy, excitable, fidgety, highstrung, irritable, jittery, jumpy, moody, nervous, nervy, restless, shaky, skittish, temperamental

anxiety *n* 1 apprehension, distress, stress, sweat, worry

n 2 anticipation, apprehension, strain, stress, suspense, tension

n 3 burden, frustration, pressure, strain, stress, tension

n 4 annoyance, apprehension, bother, care, concern, disquiet, disquietude, doubt, irritation, misgiving, reservation, restlessness, restraint, skepticism, trouble, uneasiness, vexation, worry

n 5 see: FEAR *n* 3

anxious *adj* 1 insecure, nervous, precarious, threatened, uncertain, vulnerable

adj 2 careworn, distracted, distraught, distressed, frantic, harassed, tormented, troubled, upset, worried

adj 3 afraid, aghast, apprehensive, concerned, discerning, fearful, frightened, nervous, paranoid, scared, scary, terrified, worried

adj 4 ardent, avid, breathless, desirous, eager, enthusiastic, excited, fain, impatient, impetuous, keen, passionate, raring, zealous

adj 5 annoying, bothersome, chafing, crabby, edgy, fretful, galling, impatient, irritating, jittery, nagging, on edge, restless, touchy, unsettling

adj 6 edgy, fidgety, impatient, nervous, nervy, queasy, restive, restless, tense, troubled, uncomfortable, uneasy, uptight, worried

any *adj* a, a few, at least one, each, every, individual, one, several, some

apart *adj* alienated, alone, detached, hidden, isolated, private, removed, secluded, separated, sequestered, severed

apartheid *n* discrimination, racism, segregation

apartment *n* 1 address, condo, condominium, domicile, dwelling, flat, home, house, location, pad, place, property, residence, site

n 2 dorm, housing, lodging, room, shelter, suite

apathetic *adj* 1 dispassionate, unemotional, unresponsive

adj 2 indifferent, languid, passive, torpid

apathy *n* 1 dullness, indifference, insensibility, stoicism

n 2 impotence, inaction, inactivity, inertia, paralysis

n 3 boredom, dreariness, dullness, ennui, malaise, monotony, tedium

n 4 boredom, depression, doldrums, inertia, languor

n 5 acedia, disinterest, disregard, indifference, lassitude, lethargy, listlessness

n 6 coma, doze, ennui, grogginess, inertia, languor, lassitude, lethargy, nod, sleep, slumber, stupor

ape *v* act, copy, emulate, follow, imitate, lip-synch, mime, mimic, mock, model, mouth, pantomime, parody, pattern, take off

n gorilla, monkey, primate, simian

aperture *n* access, approach, entrance, inlet, mouth, opening, passage

apex *n* acme, apogee, climax, crescendo, crest, crown, culmination, epitome, height, noon, peak, pinnacle, point, prime, summit, tip, top, ultimate, utmost, zenith

aphorism *n* announcement, axiom, cliché, declaration, decree, dictum, edict, gospel, homily, maxim, moral, precept, pronouncement, rule, saying, teaching, truism, truth, verity

aplomb *n* assurance, confidence, esteem, nerve, poise, presence, savoir-faire, self-assurance, self-confidence

apocalypse *n* oracle, prophecy, revelation, vision

apogee *n* acme, apex, climax, crescendo, crest, crown, culmination, epitome, height, noon, peak, pinnacle, point, prime, summit, tip, top, ultimate, utmost, zenith

apologetic *adj* contrite, penitent, remorseful, repentant, sorry

apologize *v* excuse, regret, repent, seek penance

apology *n* excuse, explanation, regret

appall *v* daunt, discourage, dismay, horrify, panic, petrify, scare, shock, terrify, unnerve

appalling *adj* 1 abhorrent, abominable, detestable, disgusting, dreadful, evil, frightful, ghastly, hateful, horrible, horrid, loathsome, odious, repulsive, revolting, shocking

adj 2 awful, dire, dreadful, fearful, formidable, frightening, frightful, ghastly, horrendous, horrible, offensive, ominous, portentous, scary, shocking, spooky, terrible, terrifying, unpleasant

apparatus *n* 1 action, gear, machinery, workings, works

n 2 appliance, contraption, contrivance, device, doodad, doohickey, gadget, gimmick, gizmo, implement, instrument, invention, machine, mechanism, thingumajig, tool, utensil, widget

apparel *n* accoutrements, attire, clothes, clothing, dress, garments, gear, togs

v accouter, array, attire, clad, clothe, dress, garb, gear, outfit

apparent *adj* 1 illusive, illusory, ostensible, quasi, seeming, specious, superficial

adj 2 clear, conspicuous, distinct, evident, given, indisputable, indubitable, manifest, obvious, patent, plain, presumed, self-evident, straightforward, true, unambiguous, unequivocal, unmistakable

apparently *adv* presumably, seemingly, supposedly

apparition *n* aberration, delusion, fantasy, figment, ghost, hallucination, illusion, image, mirage, phantasm, specter, vision

appeal *n* 1 affinity, allure, attraction, attractiveness, aura, beguilement, charisma, charm, enchantment, enticement, fascination, glamour, infatuation, magnetism, sex appeal, spell

n 2 desire, favor, petition, plea, request, solicitation, wish *v* 1 apply, attack, file suit, go to court, litigate, petition, plead, prosecute, solicit, sue

v 2 arouse, attract, excite, fascinate, fire, interest, intrigue, lead on, lure, seduce, stir, tantalize

v 3 ask, beg, beseech, conjure, crave, desire, entreat, grovel, implore, indicate, invoke, plead, pray, request, seek, solicit, supplicate, whine

appealing *adj* 1 colorful, entertaining, interesting, lively, stimulating, varied

adj 2 alluring, attractive, charming, coquettish, coy, fast, fetching, flirtatious, seductive, sexy, tempting, winsome

appear *v* 1 indicate, look, portend, seem, sound

v 2 arise, ascend, come forth, emanate, emerge, form, issue, loom

v 3 arise, befall, break, come, come about, develop, do, ensue, evolve, fall out, happen, manifest, materialize, occur, pass, rise, take place, transpire, turn up

appearance *n* 1 aspect, cast, countenance, expression, face, look, visage

n 2 cover, facade, face, facet, factor, front, look, surface, veneer

appease *v* 1 comfort, comply, content, delight, elate, gratify, please, relieve, satisfy, suit

v 2 allay, assuage, balm, becalm, calm, compose, conciliate, ease, lull, mollify, pacify, placate, propitiate, quell, quiet, reconcile, satiate, settle, soften, soothe, still, sweeten, tranquilize

append *v* 1 add, attach, increase, join

v 2 see: INCREASE *v* 1, 8

appendage *n* arm, extremity, leg, limb, member, part

appendix *n* addendum, addition, insert, rider, supplement

appetite *n* 1 enjoyment, liking, relish, taste

n 2 craving, desire, eroticism, hankering, hunger, itch, longing, lust, passion, urge, yearning, yen

appetizing *adj* delectable, delicious, exquisite, luscious, palatable, savory, sweet, tasty

applaud *v* 1 acknowledge, appreciate, approve, clap, recognize, show gratitude, thank

v 2 acclaim, charm, cheer, commend, compliment, flatter, greet, hail, laud, praise, recognize, salute, stroke

v 3 see: LAUD *v* 1, 2

applause *n* 1 cheers, compliments, congratulations, kudos, plaudits, praise

n 2 acclaim, boost, citation, commenda-

tion, compliment, eulogy, plaudit, praise, rave, tribute

appliance *n* 1 application, employment, form, method, operation, play, technique, use, utilization

n 2 apparatus, contraption, contrivance, device, doodad, doohickey, gadget, gimmick, gizmo, implement, instrument, invention, machine, mechanism, thingumajig, tool, utensil, widget

applicability *n* account, advantage, appropriateness, aptness, avail, benefit, decorum, expediency, fitness, manners, opportunism, pertinence, profit, propriety, relevance, rightness, service, suitability, use, usefulness, utility

applicable *adj* appropriate, apropos, apt, befitting, convenient, desirable, felicitous, fit, fitting, germane, good, handy, just, material, meet, necessary, pertinent, proper, relevant, right, shipshape, suitable, suited, timely, useful

application *n* appliance, employment, form, method, operation, play, technique, use, utilization

apply *v* 1 exercise, resort, use, utilize

v 2 augment, capitalize on, enlarge, increase, parlay, use

v 3 bear, concern, pertain, refer, regard, relate

v 4 claim, enroll, file, petition, request, sign up

v 5 accredit, ascribe, assign, attribute, charge, credit, refer

v 6 bestow, employ, exercise, exploit, handle, use, utilize

v 7 focus

v 8 massage, rub, spread

v 9 appeal, attack, file suit, go to court, litigate, petition, plead, prosecute, solicit, sue

appoint *v* 1 allocate, assign, establish, implement, institute, set

v 2 declare, designate, name, nominate, propose, select, specify

v 3 ballot, choose, elect, nominate, opt, select, vote

v 4 arm, equip, fortify, furnish, gear, man, outfit, rig, set up, supply, turn out

appointment *n* 1 booking, date, engagement, listing, reservation, schedule

n 2 connection, duty, function, job, office, position, post, situation

appointments *n* agenda, calendar, itinerary, list, plan, schedule

apportion *v* 1 administer, deal, disburse, dispense, disperse, distribute, dole, expend, give *v* 2 allocate, allot, allow, assign, designate, distribute, divide, divvy, earmark, give, measure, parcel, partition, portion, pro-rate, quota, ration, section, share, slice

apportionment *n* 1 division, partition, segmentation, segregation, separation, subdivision

n 2 allotment, allowance, budget, dispensation, dispersion, lot, measure, part, percentage, portion, quota, ration, share, slice

appraisal *n* assessment, estimate, estimation, evaluation, valuation

appraise *v* assay, assess, charge, estimate, evaluate, levy, price, rank, rate, set at, survey, tax, valuate, value

appreciable *adj* 1 admirable, respectable, worthy

adj 2 cognizant, concrete, detectable, discernible, noticeable, observable, palpable, perceptible, sensible, tangible, visible

appreciate *v* 1 acknowledge, applaud, approve, clap, recognize, show gratitude, thank

v 2 admire, cherish, delight, enjoy, relish, revel, savor

v 3 admire, adore, cherish, consider, covet, esteem, honor, idolize, love, prize, regard, respect, treasure, value

appreciation *n* 1 gratitude, recognition, thankfulness

n 2 affinity, attraction, fondness, liking, taste

appreciative *adj* grateful, indebted, obligated, obliged, thankful

apprehend *v* arrest, bag, book, bust, capture, catch, collar, detain, get, grab, lock up, nail, nab, pick up, pinch, pull in, run in, secure, seize, take

apprehension *n* 1 anxiety, distress, stress, sweat, worry

n 2 anticipation, anxiety, strain, stress, suspense, tension

n 3 distrust, doubt, fear, hesitation, misbelief, mistrust, suspicion, wariness

n 4 foreboding, forewarning, harbinger, intuition, omen, premonition, presage, sign, warning

n 5 annoyance, anxiety, bother, care, concern, disquiet, disquietude, doubt, irritation, misgiving, reservation, restlessness, restraint, skepticism, trouble, uneasiness, vexation, worry

n 6 see: FEAR *n* 2, 3

apprehensive *adj* see: AFRAID *adj* 2

apprentice *n* beginner, disciple, freshman, intern, neophyte, newcomer, novice, no-

vitiate, pupil, recruit, rookie, student, tenderfoot, trainee

apprenticed *adj* articled, bound, indentured

apprise *v* acquaint, advise, fill in, inform, notify, post, tell, update

approach *n* 1 advent, arrival, coming, entrance

n 2 come-on, offer, overture, proposal, proposition, suggestion

n 3 access, aperture, entrance, inlet, mouth, opening, passage

n 4 anteroom, atrium, court, doorway, entrance hall, entry, foyer, hall, hallway, lobby, portal, vestibule

n 5 angle, code, delivery, execution, expression, fashion, manner, method, mode, organization, process, program, style, system, technique, way

n 6 access, artery, avenue, boulevard, channel, drag, highway, pass, path, promenade, road, roadway, route, strait, street, thoroughfare, trail, way

n 7 access

v 1 advance, come, near

v 2 border, bound, define, edge, hem, limit, outline, skirt, verge

v 3 amount, correspond to, equal, match

approachable *adj* affable, amiable, cordial, friendly, genial, gentle, gracious, likable, lovable, peaceful, pleasant, serene

approaching *adj* 1 advancing, forthcoming, imminent, looming, nearing, oncoming, pending

adj 2 eventual, expected, future, imminent, impending, next, prospective, subsequent

approbate *v* accept, approve, authorize, certify, condone, confirm, countenance, endorse, favor, pass, ratify, sanction, validate

approbative *adj* approbatory, approving, favorable, supporting, sustaining

approbatory *adj* approbative, approving, favorable, supporting, sustaining

appropriate *adj* 1 correct, deserved, due, fitting, just, merited, proper, rightful, suitable, warranted

adj 2 applicable, apropos, apt, befitting, convenient, desirable, felicitous, fit, fitting, germane, good, handy, just, material, meet, necessary, pertinent, proper, relevant, right, shipshape, suitable, suited, timely, useful

v 1 allocate, budget, plan

v 2 annex, commandeer, confiscate, expropriate, grab, impound, plunder, preempt, repossess, seize, sequester, shanghai, take

v 3 see: STEAL *v* 2

appropriately *adv* acceptably, adequately, amply, correctly, properly, right, satisfactorily, suitably, well

appropriateness *n* account, advantage, applicability, aptness, avail, benefit, decorum, expediency, fitness, manners, opportunism, pertinence, profit, propriety, relevance, rightness, service, suitability, use, usefulness, utility

approval *n* 1 authorization, consent, leave, license, permission, sanction

n 2 autograph, endorsement, John Hancock, mark, name, signature

n 3 confirmation, doctrine, enactment, evidence, passage, proof, testament, testimony, witness

n 4 acceptance, assent, accord, agreement, compliance, concurrence, consent, go-ahead, nod, sympathy

approve *v* 1 acknowledge, applaud, appreciate, clap, recognize, show gratitude, thank

v 2 authorize, decree, enact, legalize, legislate, ordain, pass, ratify, sanction

v 3 accept, agree, allow, assent, comply, concur, consent, endorse, sign up, subscribe

v 4 accept, approbate, authorize, certify, condone, confirm, countenance, endorse, favor, pass, ratify, sanction, validate

approving *adj* 1 commending, complimentary, congratulatory, extolling, flattering, praising

adj 2 approbative, approbatory, favorable, supporting, sustaining

approximate *adj* crude, estimated, proximate, rough, rounded

v 1 complement, correspond, equal, parallel

v 2 call, estimate, judge, place, put, reckon

approximately *adv* about, almost, around, close to, more or less, nearly, not quite

approximation *n* 1 estimation, extrapolation, guess, speculation

n 2 affinity, analogy, comparison, likeness, match, metaphor, resemblance, semblance, similarity, simile

apricot *adj* coral, orange, salmon, tangerine

apropos *adj* applicable, appropriate, apt, befitting, convenient, desirable, felicitous, fit, fitting, germane, good, handy, just, material, meet, necessary, pertinent, proper, relevant, right, shipshape, suitable, suited, timely, useful

prep about, as to, concerning, re, regarding, respecting, with respect to

apt *adj* 1 alert, prompt, quick, ready

adj 2 inclined, liable, likely, partial, prone

adj 3 adroit, canny, clever, cunning, deft, handy, ingenious, nimble, skilled, skillful, sly, wily

adj 4 applicable, appropriate, apropos, befitting, convenient, desirable, felicitous, fit, fitting, germane, good, handy, just, material, meet, necessary, pertinent, proper, relevant, right, shipshape, suitable, suited, timely, useful

adj 5 see: QUALIFIED *adj* 4

aptitude *n* 1 see: PERSONALITY *n* 4

n 2 see: SKILL *n* 3

aptness *n* see: UTILITY *n*

aqua *adj* azure, blue, cobalt, indigo, navy, Prussian, sapphire, turquoise

aquarium *n* aviary, menagerie, terrarium, zoo

arbiter *n* arbitrator, judge, mediator, moderator, referee, umpire

arbitrary *adj* 1 accidental, aimless, casual, chance, chaotic, haphazard, hit-or-miss, indiscriminate, irregular, random, unaimed, uncontrolled, unplanned

adj 2 capricious, changeable, erratic, fickle, flighty, inconsistent, inconstant, mercurial, uncertain, unsteady, unstable, variable, volatile, wavering, wayward

arbitrate *v* 1 adjudicate, judge, mediate, referee, try, umpire

v 2 intercede, interfere, interpose, intervene, intrude, mediate, settle, step in

arbitration *n* adjudication, facilitation, intercession, intervention, mediation

arbitrator *n* arbiter, judge, mediator, moderator, referee, umpire

arc *n* arch, bend, bow, coil, crook, curvature, curve, hook, round, spiral

arcane *adj* hermetic, impenetrable, impervious, mysterious, mystic, obscure, puzzling, secret, unexaminable, unknown, unseen

arch *n* arc, bend, bow, coil, crook, curvature, curve, hook, round, spiral

v angle, bend, bow, curve, flex, ply, round, tilt, tip, turn, twist, vault

archaic *adj* 1 ancient, antiquated, bygone, dated, dead, extinct, noncurrent, obsolete, old, outdated, outmoded, passé, past, worn

adj 2 see: PRECEDING *adj*

archangel *n* angel, cherub, spirit

arched *adj* bent, bowed, curved, curvilinear, flexed, rounded, unstraight

architect *n* designer, draftsperson, engineer, inventor, manager, operator, plotter, schemer, surveyor

archive *n* gallery, museum, treasury

archives *n* athenaeum, bibliotheca, books, library

arctic *adj* chilly, cold, cool, freezing, frigid, frosty, glacial, icy, nippy, wintry

ardent *adj* 1 decisive, determined, emphatic, extreme, forceful, intense, potent, powerful, severe, strong

adj 2 constant, dedicated, dependable, devoted, faithful, loyal, resolute, staunch, steadfast, steady, true, trusty

adj 3 enthusiastic, excitable, fervent, fiery, flaming, hot-blooded, impassioned, intense, passionate, stirring, sweaty, torrid, zealous

adj 4 anxious, avid, breathless, desirous, eager, enthusiastic, excited, fain, impatient, impetuous, keen, passionate, raring, zealous

adj 5 amorous, aroused, carnal, earthy, erotic, fervent, fleshly, horny, hot, impassioned, lascivious, lecherous, lewd, licentious, lustful, passionate, provocative, randy, raunchy, romantic, sensual, sexual, sexy, sultry, titillated, torrid, turned on, voluptuous, wanton

ardor *n* 1 allegiance, devotion, faithfulness, fidelity, loyalty

n 2 alacrity, delight, devotion, diligence, enjoyment, enthusiasm, excitement, fervor, fire, flame, gaiety, gusto, passion, relish, savor, thrill, zeal, zest

n 3 see: VIGOR *n* 3

arduous *adj* 1 formidable, herculean, heroic, superhuman, tremendous

adj 2 burdensome, demanding, exacting, grievous, onerous, oppressive, taxing, tough, trying

adj 3 demanding, difficult, formidable, hard, heavy, labored, laborious, rocky, rough, rugged, serious, severe, strenuous, tough, trying, uphill

arduously *adv* difficultly, laboriously, onerously, painfully

area *n* 1 divot, land, patch, sod, space, turf

n 2 country, entity, government, nation, province, state

n 3 locale, location, locus, place, point, property, scene, site, spot

n 4 arena, belt, field, realm, region, section, space, territory, tract, turf, zone

n 5 see: WARD *n* 2

arena *n* 1 locale, scene, site, theater

n 2 amphitheater, bowl, coliseum, dome, hippodrome, scene, stadium

n 3 see: REGION *n* 1

argue *v* 1 bargain, barter, dicker, haggle, negotiate, wrangle

v 2 assert, believe, claim, contend, defend, justify, know, maintain, state, think, vindicate, warrant

v 3 confer, contest, contradict, contrast, debate, dialogue, differ, disagree, discord, discuss, dispute, dissent, divide, oppose, vary

v 4 altercate, battle, bicker, brawl, clash, conflict, dispute, engage, equivocate, feud, fight, fray, haggle, hassle, quarrel, quibble, row, scrap, spar, squabble, wrangle

v 5 see: ANNOY *v* 1

argument *n* 1 demonstration, proof, representation, thesis

n 2 contention, controversy, debate, dialogue, discussion, dispute

n 3 grounds, justification, proof, reason, wherefore, why

n 4 controversy, issue, item, matter, motif, motive, point, proposition, question, subject, text, theme, topic

n 5 see: QUARREL *n* 2

argumentative *adj* cantankerous, contentious, controversial, debatable, disputatious, ill-natured, litigious, ornery

arguments *n* see: PRINCIPLE *n* 4

aria *n* arietta, solo, song

arid *adj* 1 dry, parched, thirsty, waterless

adj 2 see: DULL *adj* 7

arietta *n* aria, solo, song

arise *v* 1 ascend, aspire, go up, lift, mount, rise, soar

v 2 appear, ascend, come forth, emanate, emerge, form, issue, loom

v 3 come from, derive, emanate, flow, head, issue, originate, spring, stem

v 4 appear, befall, break, come, come about, develop, do, ensue, evolve, fall out, happen, manifest, materialize, occur, pass, rise, take place, transpire, turn up

aristocracy *n* blue blood, cream, elite, gentry, nobility, royalty, upper class

aristocratic *adj* 1 blue-blooded, imperial, kingly, majestic, noble, regal, royal, stately, well-bred

adj 2 see: AUTHORITATIVE *adj* 2

arm *n* 1 branch, division, limb, service, subsidiary, tributary

n 2 appendage, extremity, leg, limb, member, part

n 3 bay, cove, estuary, fiord, gulf, inlet, narrows, sound, strait *v* appoint, equip, fortify, furnish, gear, man, outfit, rig, set up, supply, turn out

armada *n* assembly, boats, convoy, fleet, flotilla, grouping, navy, ships, squadron

armoire *n* bureau, chest, dresser

armor *n* **1** ammo, ammunition, arms, equipment, guns, machinery, munitions, ordnance, weapons

n **2** covering, plate, protection, shell, shield

arms *n* ammo, ammunition, armor, equipment, guns, machinery, munitions, ordnance, weapons

army *n* **1** battalion, brigade, company, force, gang, men, power, soldiers, troops

n **2** airborne, battalion, brigade, cavalry, company, footmen, guard, horsemen, infantry, legion, marines, militia, minutemen, paratroops, platoon, reserve, storm troopers

aroma *n* **1** fragrance, odor, scent, smell

n **2** balm, bouquet, fragrance, incense, perfume, scent, spice

aromatic *adj* lively, peppery, piquant, poignant, pungent, racy, snappy, spicy, spirited, vigorous, zesty

around *adv* **1** about, almost, approximately, close to, more or less, nearly, not quite

adv **2** adjacently, aside, atop, beside, by, near, nearby

prep see: AT *prep*

arouse *v* **1** acquire, commit, contract, engage, enlist, incur, induce

v **2** awaken, challenge, excite, kindle, rally, rouse, stir, wake, waken

v **3** appeal, attract, excite, fascinate, fire, interest, intrigue, lead on, lure, seduce, stir, tantalize

v **4** awaken, excite, induce, instill, motivate, move, pique, prime, provoke, quicken, rouse, roust, spark, start, stimulate, titillate, urge

v **5** electrify, excite, fire, incite, inspire, rouse, spark, stimulate, tantalize, thrill, titillate, turn on, whet

v **6** agitate, anger, encourage, foment, ignite, incite, induce, inflame, inspire, instigate, invoke, motivate, muster, prod, propel, provoke, raise, set, set on, spur, stimulate, stir, urge

aroused *adj* **1** amorous, ardent, carnal, earthy, erotic, fervent, fleshly, horny, hot, impassioned, lascivious, lecherous, lewd, licentious, lustful, passionate, provocative, randy, raunchy, romantic, sensual, sexual, sexy, sultry, titillated, torrid, turned on, voluptuous, wanton

adj **2** amorous, horny, in heat, in the mood, lustful, passionate, stimulated

adj **3** ebullient, elated, euphoric, excited, exhilarated, happy, intoxicated, joyful, sparked, stimulated, turned on

arousing *adj* **1** awesome, breathtaking, exciting, magnificent, stimulating, stirring, stunning

adj **2** exciting, intriguing, provocative, seductive, sexy, stimulating, suggestive, tantalizing

arraign *v* accuse, allege, assert, charge, cite, impeach, imply, impute, incriminate, indict, litigate, prosecute, sue, try

arrange *v* **1** adjust, agree, compromise, settle

v **2** array, dispose, marshal, order, organize, systemize

v **3** adjust, calibrate, decide, determine, establish, fix, resolve, set

v **4** bespeak, book, engage, organize, plan, program, reserve, schedule, slate

v **5** blend, combine, compound, concoct, harmonize, integrate, make one, orchestrate, synthesize, unify

v **6** blueprint, cast, chart, design, devise, draft, draw, engineer, fashion, layout, map, outline, plan, plot, project, set out, sketch

v **7** align, array, assort, catalog, categorize, class, classify, cluster, compile, file, format, grade, group, lay out, line up, list, order, organize, outline, pigeonhole, place, position, prioritize, program, rank, rate, sort, stack, tabulate

v **8** conceive, conceptualize, organize, structure

v **9** neaten, organize, pick up, tidy

v **10** cater, deliver, dish out, dispense, feed, furnish, give, hand, nourish, nurture, organize, provide, purvey, serve, supply, sustain

arrangement *n* **1** design, form, plan, prearrangement, preparation, provision

n **2** array, format, lay out, outline, plan, style

n **3** agreement, compromise, concession, decision, determination, franchise, settlement

n **4** blueprint, method, order, orderliness, outline, pattern, plan, system

n **5** bouquet, bunch, corsage, flowers

n **6** disposal, disposition, distribution, grouping, ordering, sequence

arrangements *n* business, commerce, dealings, enterprise, industry, intercourse, negotiations, trade, traffic

arrant *adj* barefaced, blatant, brassy, brazen, extreme, impudent, notorious, obtrusive, shameless, unabashed

array *n* 1 arrangement, format, layout, outline, plan, style

n 2 blare, display, exhibit, exhibition, fanfare, fuss, parade, performance, presentation, procession, publicity, show, showing

n 3 bale, batch, battery, body, bunch, bundle, clump, cluster, group, lot, pack, parcel, quantity, set

v 1 arrange, dispose, marshal, order, organize, systemize

v 2 accouter, apparel, attire, clad, clothe, dress, garb, gear, outfit

v 3 see: CLASSIFY *v* 2

arrest *n* 1 custody, detention, imprisonment

n 2 confinement, detention, imprisonment, incarceration

v 1 block, check, freeze, halt, impede, interrupt, stall, stay, stop

v 2 apprehend, bag, book, bust, capture, catch, collar, detain, get, grab, lock up, nab, nail, pick up, pinch, pull in, run in, secure, seize, take

arresting *adj* astonishing, astounding, conspicuous, eye-catching, marked, noticeable, obvious, pointed, prominent, salient, sensational, striking, stunning

arrival *n* 1 advent, approach, coming, entrance

n 2 debarkation, docking, landing, mooring

n 3 see: ACHIEVEMENT *n* 2

arrive *v* 1 come

v 2 flourish, go, make out, prosper, score, succeed, thrive

arrivederci *n* adieu, adios, aloha, *auf Wiedersehen*, au revoir, bon voyage, bye, cheerio, *ciao*, farewell, goodbye, good day, *sayonara*, shalom, so long

arrogance *n* 1 airs, cockiness, conceit, condescension, disdain, egotism, haughtiness, image, loftiness, narcissism, pride, self-esteem, self-image, vanity

n 2 assurance, audacity, boldness, brashness, brass, cheek, chutzpah, condescension, confidence, crust, effrontery, face, gall, haughtiness, insolence, nerve, patronage, presumption, ridicule, sass, stamina, temerity

arrogant *adj* 1 condescending, haughty, patronizing, pretentious, snobbish

adj 2 audacious, conspicuous, flagrant, glaring, obvious

adj 3 cocky, disrespectful, flip, flippant, impertinent, impudent, wise

adj 4 cocky, conceited, haughty, narcissistic, self-assured, smug, stuck-up, vain

adj 5 aristocratic, authoritarian, authoritative, autocratic, belligerent, bossy, despotic, dictatorial, dogmatic, domineering, haughty, imperial, imperious, masterful, militaristic, opinionated, oppressive, overbearing, peremptory, pushy, stubborn

adj 6 cavalier, conceited, contemptuous, curt, dictatorial, disdainful, grandiose, haughty, huffy, insolent, lofty, lordly, moody, obtrusive, overbearing, patronizing, proud, scornful, snooty, stuck-up, supercilious, superior, vain

art *n* 1 acrylic, canvas, depiction, drawing, etching, illustration, landscape, lithograph, mural, oil, painting, pastel, pen and ink, picture, portrait, print, seascape, sketch, still life, watercolor

n 2 avocation, business, calling, career, discipline, employment, field, gig, job, labor, line, livelihood, occupation, office, profession, pursuit, role, schtick, situation, specialty, task, thing, trade, vocation, work

n 3 ability, adequacy, adroitness, aptitude, caliber, calling, capability, capacity, command, competence, craft, dexterity, experience, expertise, familiarity, forte, knack, know-how, knowledge, mastery, proficiency, prowess, qualification, savvy, skill, specialty, strength, talent, training, workmanship

artery *n* 1 access, approach, avenue, boulevard, channel, drag, highway, pass, path, promenade, road, roadway, route, strait, street, thoroughfare, trail, way

n 2 blood vessel, capillary, vein, vessel

artful *adj* adroit, cagey, canny, crafty, cunning, evasive, foxy, serpentine, sly

article *n* 1 element, entity, item, object, piece, thing

n 2 bulletin, byline, column, communication, dispatch, editorial, feature, headline, item, newsletter, report, story, vignette

n 3 composition, discourse, dissertation, essay, manuscript, memoir, monograph, paper, report, study, theme, thesis, tract, treatise, work

articled *adj* apprenticed, bound, indentured

articles *n* see: GOODS *n* 2

articulate *adj* 1 expressive, fluent, glib, perspicuous

adj 2 communicative, expressive, talkative, vocal

adj 3 clear, cogent, eloquent, fluent, persuasive, well-spoken

v announce, assert, couch, describe, dictate, draft, enunciate, express, intonate, orate, phrase, proclaim, pronounce, say, speak, state, stress, talk, utter, verbalize, vocalize, voice, word

artificial *adj* 1 awkward, formal, stiff, stilted, stuffy

adj 2 corny, exaggerated, pretentious, staged, theatrical

adj 3 affected, assumed, feigned, fictitious, put-on, spurious

adj 4 bogus, counterfeit, ersatz, fake, false, imitation, mock, phony, pseudo, sham, simulated, spurious, substitute, unreal

adj 5 counterfeit, fake, false, man-made, manufactured, plastic, synthetic

adj 6 aberrant, abnormal, anomalous, atypical, contrived, deviant, disparate, divergent, incongruous, irregular, off-key, uncharacteristic, unnatural

artisan *n* craftsman

artist *n* 1 artisan

n 2 adviser, authority, expert, guru, master, official, pro, professional, specialist, veteran, virtuoso, wizard

n 3 see: ACTOR *n*

artiste *n* accompanist, conductor, instrumentalist, musician, performer, virtuoso

artistic *adj* 1 creative, skilled, skillful, talented,

adj 2 aesthetic, classy, elegant, refined, stylish, tasteful, well-chosen

artless *adj* candid, frank, guileless, ingenuous, innocent, naive, natural, open, plain, simple, simple-hearted, unadorned, unaffected, unsophisticated, unstudied, untutored, unworldly

as *conj* because, since, whereas, while, whilst

ascend *v* 1 climb, increase, rise, soar, speed, zoom

v 2 climb, escalate, intensify, mount, scale, surmount

v 3 flit, flutter, fly, sail, soar, sweep, wing

v 4 arise, aspire, go up, lift, mount, rise, soar

v 5 appear, arise, come forth, emanate, emerge, form, issue, loom

v 6 come up, rise, surface

v 7 advance, bloom, climb, develop, do well, excel, expand, flourish, flower, get ahead, grow, improve, progress, prosper, rise, strive, survive, thrive

ascendant *n* ancestor, antecedent, elder, forebear, forefather, forerunner, founder,

grandparent, parent, patriarch, predecessor, progenitor

ascent *n* 1 altitude, elevation, height

n 2 escalation, climb, rise

ascertain *v* 1 catch on, determine, discover, find out, hear, learn, listen, uncover, unearth

v 2 catch, descry, detect, discover, encounter, espy, ferret, find, locate, spot, turn up, uncover

ascetic *adj* astringent, austere, chaste, rigid, simple, spartan, stern, stoic

n abbé, abbot, friar, hermit, monk, recluse

ascot *n* cravat, necktie, tie

ascribe *v* accredit, apply, assign, attribute, charge, credit, refer

ashamed *adj* 1 guilty, penitent, repentant

adj 2 abashed, chagrined, embarrassed, humiliated, mortified, shamed

ashen *adj* ashy, blanched, colorless, pale, pallid, sallow, sickly, sooty, wan, waxen, yellow

ashy *adj* ashen, blanched, colorless, pale, pallid, sallow, sickly, sooty, wan, waxen, yellow

aside *adv* adjacently, around, atop, beside, by, near, nearby

asinine *adj* absurd, anile, brainless, childish, fatuous, foolish, idiotic, inept, meaningless, mindless, senseless, silly, simple, thoughtless, unintelligent, witless

ask *v* 1 bid, encourage, invite, request, solicit

v 2 call, crave, demand, necessitate, require, take

v 3 cross-examine, examine, grill, inquire, interrogate, investigate, probe, pump, query, question, quiz

v 4 appeal, beg, beseech, conjure, crave, desire, entreat, grovel, implore, indicate, invoke, plead, pray, request, seek, solicit, supplicate, whine

askew *adj* awry, crooked, lopsided, off-center

asleep *adj* dormant, idle, immobile, inactive, inanimate, inert, inoperative, laid-back, motionless, nodding, passive, quiet, sleepy, slumbering, stable, stagnant, still

aspect *n* 1 appearance, cast, countenance, expression, face, look, visage

n 2 angle, facet, hand, mien, opinion, perspective, phase, side, slant, view

asperse *v* see: ABUSE *v* 4

aspersion *n* 1 accusation, defamation, libel, remark, slander, slur, smear

n 2 contempt, derision, disdain, irony, mockery, ridicule, sarcasm, satire, scorn *n* 3 affront, attack, barb, caustic remark, crack, cut, denunciation, despite, dig, disparagement, disrespect, gibe, implication, indignity, innuendo, insult, invective, knock, reflection, sarcasm, scorn, slap, slight, slur, spike, tongue-lashing, verbal jab

asphyxiate *v* choke, constrict, gag, garrote, muffle, quash, repress, smother, stifle, strangle, suffocate, suppress

aspirant *n* candidate, contestant, entrant, hopeful, nominee

aspiration *n* ambition, desire, goal, hope, will, wish

aspire *v* 1 aim, hope, strive, wish

v 2 arise, ascend, go up, lift, mount, rise, soar

aspiring *adj* ambitious, rising, striving

ass *n* 1 backside, base, behind, bottom, bucket, buns, butt, buttocks, derrière, end, fanny, hindquarters, posterior, rump, seat, stub, stump, tip, tush

assail *v* 1 ambush, assault, attack, beset, invade, raid, storm, strike, trap, waylay

v 2 attack, batter, beat, birch, buffet, flagellate, flog, hammer, lambaste, lash, lather, pelt, pound, pummel, punish, scourge, thrash, tromp, wallop, whip

assassin *n* executioner, killer, murderer

assassinate *v* abolish, annihilate, bump off, butcher, decimate, destroy, dispatch, execute, exterminate, hang, hit, kill, knock off, liquidate, massacre, murder, put away, rub out, slaughter, slay, wipe out

assassination *n* foul play, homicide, killing, manslaughter, murder

assault *n* 1 ambush, sneak attack, surprise,

n 2 attack, blitz, bombardment, onslaught, raid, strike

n 3 aggression, attack, incursion, inroad, offense, offensive, onset, onslaught

n 4 abuse, attack, rape, sack, violation

v 1 jump, leap, pounce, strike, surprise, swoop

v 2 attack, force, pillage, rape, ravish, sack, violate

v 3 ambush, assail, attack, beset, invade, raid, storm, strike, trap, waylay

assay *n* analysis, examination, experiment, observation, test

v 1 attempt, endeavor, essay, offer, quest, seek, strive, struggle, try, undertake

v 2 appraise, assess, charge, estimate, evaluate, levy, price, rank, rate, set at, survey, tax, valuate, value

assemblage *n* assembly, caucus, conference, congregation, convention, council,

crowd, gathering, group, meeting, rally, symposium

assemble *v* 1 build, construct, erect, establish, fabricate, forge, form, make, manufacture, mold, produce, trailblaze

v 2 accrue, accumulate, acquire, amass, collect, garner, gather, grow, hoard, save, squirrel, stash, stockpile, store up

v 3 associate, call, cluster, collect, concentrate, congregate, convene, flock, gather, group, lump, marshal, mass, mingle, mobilize, muster, order, rally, rendezvous, round up, send for, summon

assembly *n* 1 armada, boats, convoy, fleet, flotilla, grouping, navy, ships, squadron

n 2 clinic, congress, council, court, diet, forum, hearing, meeting, parliament, seminar, symposium

n 3 assemblage, caucus, conference, congregation, convention, council, crowd, gathering, group, meeting, rally, symposium

n 4 association, band, bevy, brood, bunch, camp, clique, cluster, collection, covey, crew, flock, group, organization, party, team, unit

assemblyman *n* congressman, councilman, lawmaker, legislator, representative, senator

assent *n* 1 acceptance, accord, agreement, approval, compliance, concurrence, consent, go-ahead, nod, sympathy

n 2 attainment

n 3 accord, affinity, agreement, concert, concord, congruence, cooperation, empathy, harmony, rapport, synergy, teamwork, unity

v 1 accept, agree, allow, approve, comply, concur, consent, endorse, sign up, subscribe

assert *v* 1 allege, avow, claim, maintain, say, state

v 2 demand, emphasize, force, insist, persist, require, urge

v 3 affirm, attest, avow, confirm, declare, depose, predicate, profess, protest

v 4 argue, believe, claim, contend, defend, justify, know, maintain, state, think, vindicate, warrant

v 5 accuse, allege, arraign, charge, cite, impeach, imply, impute, incriminate, indict, litigate, prosecute, sue, try

v 6 see: VERBALIZE *v* 2

assertion *n* accusation, allegation, charge, comment, declaration, deposition, pronouncement, statement

assertive *adj* aggressive, ambitious, assured, compelling, compulsive, confident, decided, dogmatic, driven, emphatic, energetic, insistent, militant, positive, pushing, pushy, self-assertive, sure, urging

assess *v* 1 analyze, determine, diagnose, estimate, examine, penetrate, probe, scope, solve, survey, understand, unravel
v 2 appraise, assay, charge, estimate, evaluate, levy, price, rank, rate, set at, survey, tax, valuate, value

assessment *n* 1 damages, fine, penalty, punishment, tax
n 2 examination, inquiry, review, scope, search, study, survey
n 3 analysis, commentary, criticism, critique, evaluation, examination, judgment, notion, opinion, review, ruling
n 4 cost, duty, expense, fee, impost, levy, offering, penalty, price, sacrifice, tariff, tax, toll, trade-off
n 5 impression, interpretation, reading, understanding
n 6 appraisal, estimate, estimation, evaluation, valuation

asset *n* 1 credit, resource, treasure, valuable
n 2 acquisition, buy, gain, merchandise, property, purchase
n 3 excess, inventory, overage, overstock, oversupply, plus, surplus

assets *n* 1 capacity, means, reserves, resources, wherewithal
n 2 belongings, equity, estate, fortune, goods, holdings, inheritance, money, ownership, possessions, property, prosperity, riches, treasure, wealth
n 3 bills, capital, cash, coffers, currency, dinero, dollars, estate, funds, goods, income, lucre, means, money, notes, pelf, pesos, property, resources, revenue, riches, rubles, shekels, sum, wealth
n 4 see: PROFITS *n*

assiduous *adj* ambitious, diligent, energetic, hard-working, industrious, persevering, persistent, resolute, sedulous, zealous
assiduously *adv* see: COMPLETELY *adv*
assign *v* 1 delegate, detail, task
v 2 cede, convey, deed, designate, transfer
v 3 allocate, appoint, establish, implement, institute, set
v 4 authorize, delegate, designate, empower, entrust, pass along
v 5 accredit, apply, ascribe, attribute, charge, credit, refer
v 6 allocate, allot, allow, apportion, designate, distribute, divide, divvy, earmark, give, measure, parcel, partition, portion, prorate, quota, ration, section, share, slice

assignment *n* 1 authorization, commission, warrant
n 2 chore, duty, effort, job, mission, responsibility, stint, task
n 3 diatribe, discourse, exercise, homily, lecture, lesson, preaching, sermon
n 4 direction, instruction, reference, referral

assist *v* 1 associate, collaborate, cooperate, join
v 2 accelerate, expedite, facilitate
v 3 keep up, maintain, provide, support, sustain, uphold
v 4 abet, advance, aid, ameliorate, amend, avail, benefit, better, boost, cultivate, do for, ease, egg on, encourage, enhance, forward, foster, further, help, improve, nurture, prefer, promote, rev, serve, spur on, support

assistance *n* 1 alms, charity, contributions, dole, donations, oblation, offering
n 2 aid, benefit, comfort, cure, hand, help, lift, nurture, relief, remedy, succor, support

assistant *adj* ancillary, collateral, complementary, dependent, lesser, minor, secondary, sub, subject, subordinate, subsidiary, substitute, supporter, tributary, worker
n 1 dependent, employee, subordinate, underling
n 2 aide, aide-de-camp, attendant, employee, hand, helper, hired hand, laborer, servant, supporter, worker
n 3 aide, clerk, recorder, secretary, scribe, stenographer

assisting *adj* accessory, adjunct, ancillary, auxiliary, subsidiary, supporting
associate *n* 1 collaborator, individual, member, participant, party, person, registrant
n 2 accomplice, acquaintance, adjunct, ally, buddy, chum, cohort, colleague, companion, compatriot, comrade, confidant, confrere, connection, copartner, counterpart, co-worker, crony, equal, fellow, follower, friend, intimate, mate, pal, partner, peer, relative, supporter
v 1 assist, collaborate, cooperate, join
v 2 analogize, compare, correlate, explain, rank, relate
v 3 accompany, attend, bear, chaperon, conduct, consort with, convoy, escort
v 4 blend, bond, coalesce, combine, compound, connect, couple, fasten, fuse, join,

link, marry, mate, meet, merge, pair, unite, wed

v 5 see: ASSEMBLE *v* 3

v 6 see: IMPLICATE *v*

associated *adj* affiliated, akin, aligned, allied, fraternal, friendly, kindred, parallel, related

associates *n* constituency, constituents, members, membership, personnel

association *n* 1 connection, linkage, nexus

n 2 closeness, contact, nearness, proximity

n 3 affiliation, allegiance, connection, obligation, tie

n 4 institute, institution, organization, society, union

n 5 combination, corporation, establishment, fellowship, foundation, institution, league, union

n 6 affair, communication, friendship, intimacy, liaison, rapport, relationship, union

n 7 body, club, company, contingent, delegation, fellowship, fraternity, group, guild, organization, society, union

n 8 see: ALLIANCE *n*

n 9 see: GROUP *n* 3, 5

assort *v* 1 alter, diversify, mix, modify, vary

v 2 see: CLASSIFY *v* 2

assorted *adj* 1 diverse, miscellaneous, mixed, motley, varied

adj 2 abundant, copious, diverse, extensive, legion, many, multifarious, multitudinous, myriad, numerous, plentiful, populous, prolific, sundry, various, voluminous

assortment *n* 1 hodgepodge, jumble, medley, mixture

n 2 bunch, collection, mixture, selection, spectrum, variety

assuage *v* 1 abate, allay, mitigate, moderate, quench, satiate, satisfy

v 2 allay, alleviate, attenuate, diminish, ease, extenuate, lessen, lighten, minimize, mitigate, moderate, mollify, reduce, relieve

v 3 see: APPEASE *v* 2

assume *v* 1 attack, attempt, tackle, take on, try

v 2 expect, posit, postulate, premise, presume, presuppose, propose

v 3 act, bluff, counterfeit, fabricate, fake, feign, imitate, invent, make believe, play, pretend, put on, sham

v 4 allude, extend, hypothesize, imagine, offer, pose, present, presume, propose,

speculate, suggest, suppose, surmise, theorize

v 5 believe, comprehend, conceive, estimate, expect, fathom, gather, grasp, guess, imagine, infer, know, presume, suppose, surmise, suspect, think, trust, understand

assumed *adj* affected, artificial, feigned, fictitious, put-on, spurious

assumption *n* 1 conjecture, deduction, opinion, supposition, surmise

n 2 foundation, ground rule, postulate, premise, proposition, supposition, theorem

n 3 conclusion, conjecture, discretion, estimate, guess, judgment, notion, presumption, theorization

n 4 conjecture, deduction, explanation, guess, hypothesis, inference, postulate, presumption, proposition, speculation, supposition, theory

assurance *n* 1 certainty, certitude, confidence, conviction, declaration

n 2 declaration, oath, pledge, promise, vow, word

n 3 exemption, guarantee, immunity, impunity, protection, release, safety, security

n 4 aplomb, confidence, esteem, nerve, poise, presence, savoir-faire, self-assurance, self-confidence

n 5 bond, commitment, earnest, guarantee, obligation, pawn, pledge, security, surety, token, warrant

n 6 arrogance, audacity, boldness, brashness, brass, cheek, chutzpah, condescension, confidence, crust, effrontery, face, gall, haughtiness, insolence, nerve, patronage, presumption, ridicule, sass, stamina, temerity

assure *v* 1 confirm, determine, establish

v 2 certify, contract, endorse, guarantee, pledge, sanction, underwrite, vouch, warrant

v 3 advocate, affirm, avouch, avow, commit, devote, guarantee, pledge, promise, ratify, swear, vow

v 4 affect, convince, impel, induce, influence, inspire, instigate, motivate, move, persuade, pressure, prompt, stir, sway, talk into, touch, win over

assured *adj* 1 confident, poised, sanguine, secure, self-assured, self-confident

adj 2 see: ASSERTIVE *adj*

astern *adv* aft

astir *adj* see: AGILE *adj* 3

astonish *v* 1 amaze, astound, awe, delight, floor, impress, overwhelm, wow *v* 2 amaze, astound, awe, boggle, confound, dazzle, dumbfound, flabbergast, nonplus, stagger, stun, surprise

astonishing *adj* 1 exceptional, incredible, remarkable, uncanny

adj 2 see: PROMINENT *adj* 2

astonishment *n* amazement, awe, bewilderment, shock, surprise, wonder

astound *v* 1 amaze, astonish, awe, delight, floor, impress, overwhelm, wow

v 2 amaze, astonish, awe, boggle, confound, dazzle, dumbfound, flabbergast, nonplus, stagger, stun, surprise

astounding *adj* 1 amazing, bizarre, remarkable, strange

adj 2 see: PROMINENT *adj* 2

astral *adj* celestial, heavenly, stellar

astringent *adj* ascetic, austere, chaste, rigid, simple, spartan, stern, stoic

astrologer *n* augur, fortuneteller, oracle, predictor, prophet, psychic, seer, soothsayer, visionary

astute *adj* 1 calculating, crafty, cunning, foxy, guileful, insidious, sharp, shrewd, sly, smart, subtle, tricky, wily, wise

adj 2 acute, alert, cagey, canny, clever, cunning, deft, keen, knowing, penetrating, perceptive, piercing, quick, quick-sighted, quick-witted, receptive, responsive, sagacious, savvy, sensitive, sharp, sharp-witted, shrewd, slick, smart, streetsmart, wise

adj 3 see: INTELLIGENT *adj* 4

adj 4 see: SENSIBLE *adj* 5

astuteness *n* acumen, awareness, cleverness, discernment, discrimination, insight, intellect, intuition, keenness, perception, sagacity, sensitivity, shrewdness, understanding, wit

asylum *n* 1 booby hatch, funny farm, institution, loony bin, madhouse

n 2 clinic, dispensary, hospital, infirmary, institution

n 3 cover, harbor, haven, oasis, port, preserve, protection, refuge, reserve, retreat, safety, sanctuary, seaport, security, shelter

at *prep* adjacent to, around, atop, beside, by, near, on

atheist *n* agnostic, gentile, heathen, heretic, infidel, pagan, unbeliever

athenaeum *n* archives, bibliotheca, books, library

athlete *n* jock, letterman, player, sportsman

athletic *adj* brawny, burly, husky, massive, muscular, ponderous, powerful, robust, stocky, stout, strapping, strong

athletics *n* acrobatics, calisthenics, gymnastics

atlas *n* compendium, directory, guide, guidebook, handbook, list, listing, manual, phone book, textbook, Yellow Pages

atmosphere *n* 1 climate, condition, mood, temperature, trend

n 2 climate, conditions, environment, habitat, niche, perimeter, settings, surroundings

n 3 air, ambience, aura, emanation, feel, feeling, mood, semblance, spirit

atoll *n* isle, cay, island, key

atom *n* see: DOT *n*

atonement *n* attrition, contrition, penance, penitence, reconciliation, remorse

atop *adv* adjacently, around, aside, beside, by, near, nearby

prep see: AT *prep*

atrium *n* anteroom, approach, court, doorway, entrance hall, entry, foyer, hall, hallway, lobby, portal, vestibule

atrocious *adj* 1 calamitous, dreadful, grievous, heinous, severe

adj 2 awful, crying, desperate, disgraceful, ghastly, grizzly, heinous, monstrous, notorious, odious, offensive, outrageous, scandalous, shocking, tasteless, wicked

atrophy *n* decay, degeneration, deterioration, shrinkage, wasting

v decay, deteriorate, dry up, dwindle, mummify, shrink, shrivel, waste away, welter, wilt, wither, wizen

attach *v* 1 add, append, increase, join

v 2 clip, fasten, nail, pin, staple, tack

v 3 affix, bind, clip, connect, fasten, fix, rivet, weld

v 4 bind, bond, cord, fasten, hitch, join, link, marry, tether, tie, tie up

attached *adj* 1 affectionate, amorous, caring, devoted, enamored, fond, loving, romantic, tender

adj 2 fast, firm, fixed, rigid, secure, set, taut, tense, tight

attachment *n* affection, affinity, attraction, compassion, concern, devotion, fondness, heart, kinship, love, warmth

attack *n* 1 attempt, blockade, bout, campaign, offensive, siege

n 2 assault, blitz, bombardment, onslaught, raid, strike

n 3 conquest, defeat, foray, inroad, intrusion, invasion, trespass

n 4 aggression, assault, incursion, inroad, offense, offensive, onset, onslaught

n 5 approach

n 6 abuse, assault, rape, sack, violation

n 7 aggression, aggressiveness, bellicosity,

belligerence, combativeness, fight, pugnacity

n 8 affront, aspersion, barb, caustic remark, crack, cut, denunciation, despite, dig, disparagement, disrespect, gibe, implication, indignity, innuendo, insult, invective, knock, reflection, sarcasm, scorn, slap, slight, slur, spike, tongue-lashing, verbal jab

v 1 beat, oppress, scourge, smite

v 2 foray, invade, overrun, raid

v 3 assume, attempt, tackle, take on, try

v 4 challenge, contradict, deny, impugn, oppose, rebut

v 5 battle, combat, contend, fight, oppose, struggle, war

v 6 encroach, entrench, infringe, intrude, invade, trespass, violate

v 7 assault, force, pillage, rape, ravish, sack, violate

v 8 ambush, assail, assault, beset, invade, raid, storm, strike, trap, waylay

v 9 butt, drive, knock, lunge, pass, plunge, ram, sink, stab, stick, thrust

v 10 appeal, apply, file suit, go to court, litigate, petition, plead, prosecute, solicit, sue

v 11 alarm, bully, club, coerce, frighten, harass, intimidate, menace, strong-arm, terrorize, threaten

v 12 assail, batter, beat, birch, buffet, flagellate, flog, hammer, lambaste, lash, lather, pelt, pound, pummel, punish, scourge, thrash, tromp, wallop, whip

attain *v* 1 accomplish, achieve, consummate, execute, fulfill, perform, produce, pull off, realize, succeed, triumph, win

v 2 access, accomplish, achieve, derive, earn, fulfill, gain, get, merit, net, obtain, perform, profit, rack up, reach, realize, score, win

v 3 earn

attainment *n* 1 accomplishment, achievement, arrival, completion, fruition, fulfillment, realization, satisfaction, success, triumph, victory

n 2 accession

attempt *n* 1 chance, spin, try, turn

n 2 attack, blockade, bout, campaign, offensive, siege

n 3 effort, endeavor, speculation, struggle, trial, try, undertaking, venture

n 4 chance, effort, fling, go, guess, heave, lob, pop, shot, slap, sling, stab, throw, toss, try, whirl

v 1 assume, attack, tackle, take on, try

v 2 bring about, cultivate, perpetuate, practice, proceed, pursue

v 3 assay, endeavor, essay, offer, quest, seek, strive, struggle, try, undertake

v 4 see: BET *v*

attend *v* 1 help, serve, wait

v 2 accompany, associate, bear, chaperon, conduct, consort with, convoy, escort

v 3 frequent, hang around, hang out, haunt, obsess, patronize, resort to, visit

attendant *n* 1 aide, aide-de-camp, assistant, employee, hand, helper, hired hand, laborer, servant, supporter, worker

n 2 escort, guide, usher

n 3 medic, nurse, orderly, therapist

attention *n* 1 center, crux, feature, focus, highlight, key, spotlight

n 2 awareness, care, carefulness, cognizance, concern, consciousness, consideration, heed, intimacy, knowing, knowledge, mark, note, notice, observance, observation, perception, recognition, regard, remark, sense

attentive *adj* 1 considerate, generous, kind, thoughtful, unselfish

adj 2 advertent, alert, careful, conscientious, heedful, observant

adj 3 alive, awake, aware, cognizant, conscious, conversant, knowing, responsive, sentient, thinking

attenuate *v* 1 dilute, diminish, lessen, purify, rarefy, reduce, refine, shorten, thin out, weaken

v 2 allay, alleviate, assuage, diminish, ease, extenuate, lessen, lighten, minimize, mitigate, moderate, mollify, reduce, relieve

adj diminished, lessened, rarefied, subtle, tenuous, thin

attest *v* 1 affirm, avow, contend, promise, say, swear, vouch, warrant

v 2 affirm, assert, avow, confirm, declare, depose, predicate, profess, protest

v 3 authenticate, certify, confirm, corroborate, justify, notarize, prove, ratify, sanction, substantiate, support, validate, verify, vouch, witness

attestation *n* affidavit, deposition, statement, testimony

attic *n* loft

attire *n* accoutrements, apparel, clothes, clothing, dress, garments, gear, togs

v accouter, apparel, array, clad, clothe, dress, garb, gear, outfit

attired *adj* clad, clothed, ensconced

attitude *n* 1 belief, point of view, position, stance, stand

n 2 disposition, feeling, humor, mind, mood, spirit, temper, timbre, tone, vein

n 3 belief, bias, conviction, feeling, inducement, leaning, mind, opinion, persuasion, sentiment, slant, view

n 4 air, bearing, calmness, carriage, demeanor, disposition, poise, pose, posture, presence, set, stance

attorney *n* advocate, barrister, counsel, counselor, intercessor, lawyer, mediator, solicitor

attract *v* 1 cajole, disarm, flatter, ingratiate

v 2 draw, elicit, induce, solicit

v 3 bait, decoy, entice, entrap, lure, tantalize

v 4 court, encourage, flirt, invite, lure, pursue, romance, solicit, tempt, woo

v 5 appeal, arouse, excite, fascinate, fire, interest, intrigue, lead on, lure, seduce, stir, tantalize

v 6 allure, bedevil, beguile, bewitch, captivate, charm, conjure, delight, draw, enchant, enthrall, fascinate, lure, magnetize, mesmerize, tempt, wile

attraction *n* 1 affinity, appreciation, fondness, liking, taste

n 2 affection, affinity, attachment, compassion, concern, devotion, fondness, heart, kinship, love, warmth

n 3 bait, come-on, decoy, enticement, lure, magnet, ruse, seduction, snare, temptation, trap, wile

n 4 see: CHARISMA *n* 2

attractive *adj* 1 alluring, desirable, erotic, exciting, seductive, sexy, tantalizing, tempting

adj 2 alluring, appealing, charming, coquettish, coy, fast, fetching, flirtatious, seductive, sexy, tempting, winsome

adj 3 alluring, becoming, coy, cute, enchanting, enticing, fascinating, foxy, inviting, pleasing, ravishing, seductive, sexy

adj 4 alluring, beautiful, breathtaking, comely, cute, fair, fine, foxy, gorgeous, lovely, luscious, magnificent, pretty, shapely, stunning

adj 5 becoming, comely, exquisite, fair, good-looking, gorgeous, handsome, pleasing, radiant, stately

attractiveness *n* 1 charm, decorum, elegance, grace, refinement

n 2 aura, beauty, comeliness, loveliness, pulchritude, radiance

n 3 see: CHARISMA *n* 2

attribute *n* character, characteristic, feature, highlight, mark, peculiarity, property, quality, trait, virtue

v 1 credit, honor, recognize, reward

v 2 accredit, apply, ascribe, assign, charge, credit, refer

attrition *n* atonement, contrition, penance, penitence, reconciliation, remorse

attune *v* accommodate, adjust, conform, coordinate, harmonize, integrate, proportion, reconcile, reconciliate, tune

atwixt *prep* amidst, among, between, betwixt, halfway to, mid, midway, 'twixt

atypical *adj* aberrant, abnormal, anomalous, artificial, contrived, deviant, disparate, divergent, incongruous, irregular, off-key, uncharacteristic, unnatural

auction *n* sale

audacious *adj* 1 arrogant, conspicuous, flagrant, glaring, obvious

adj 2 abrupt, desperate, headstrong, rash, reckless

adj 3 bold, brave, courageous, daring, dauntless, fearless, gallant, game, gutsy, heroic, intrepid, stalwart, unafraid, undaunted, valiant, valorous

adj 4 bold, brash, brazen, cheeky, daring, disrespectful, forward, fresh, impertinent, impudent, insolent, irreverent, nervy, pert, rude, sassy, saucy

adj 5 free, liberated, licentious, loose, rampant, unbridled, unconfined, uncontrolled, uncurbed, ungoverned, unhampered, uninhibited, unrestrained, unsecured, unshackled, untied, wild

adj 6 boorish, discourteous, disrespectful, ill-behaved, ill-bred, ill-mannered, impertinent, impolite, insolent, rude, surly, uncalled for, uncivil, uncivilized, uncouth, uncultured, unpolished, unrefined

audacity *n* arrogance, assurance, boldness, brashness, brass, cheek, chutzpah, condescension, confidence, crust, effrontery, face, gall, haughtiness, insolence, nerve, patronage, presumption, ridicule, sass, stamina, temerity

audience *n* patrons, spectators, witnesses

audit *v* balance, check, examine, inspect, verify

auditor *n* accountant, actuary, bookkeeper, comptroller

auditorium *n* assembly hall, hall, playhouse, theater

auditory *adj* acoustic

auger *v* bore, drill, pierce, ream, tool

augment *v* 1 enhance, magnify, maximize, optimize, utilize

v 2 apply, capitalize on, enlarge, increase, parlay, use

v 3 buttress, fortify, harden, intensify, invigorate, reinforce, strengthen

v 4 amplify, append, boost, build, enlarge, expand, extend, grow, heighten, increase, intensify, magnify, multiply, run up, snowball, supplement, upsurge, wax

augur *n* astrologer, fortuneteller, oracle, predictor, prophet, psychic, seer, soothsayer, visionary

v 1 anticipate, bode, budget, call, divine, estimate, forecast, foreshadow, foresee, foretell, guess, harbinger, herald, judge, plan, portend, preannounce, predict, presage, proclaim, prognosticate, project, prophesy, signify, soothsay

v 2 see: NOTIFY *v* 4

august *adj* baronial, exalted, grand, grandiose, haughty, imperial, imposing, impressive, lofty, lordly, magisterial, magnificent, magestic, noble, portly, princely, regal, royal, stately

aura *n* 1 attractiveness, beauty, comeliness, loveliness, pulchritude, radiance

n 2 air, ambience, atmosphere, emanation, feel, feeling, mood, semblance, spirit

n 3 see: CHARISMA *n* 2

aural *adj* auditory

auspices *n* authorization, backing, command, confirmation, endorsement, fiat, patronage, sanction, sponsorship, support

auspicious *adj* 1 favorable, opportune, propitious, seasonable, timely

adj 2 favorable, fortunate, happy, lucky, providential, serendipitous

adj 3 bright, confident, favorable, hopeful, promising, rosy, sunny, utopian

adj 4 cheerful, confident, encouraging, hopeful, optimistic, promising, sanguine, upbeat

adj 5 favorable, fortunate, propitious

austere *adj* 1 economical, sparse, spartan, terse

adj 2 ascetic, astringent, chaste, rigid, simple, spartan, stern, stoic

adj 3 narrow, narrow-minded, prim, prudish, puritanical, rigid, severe, strict

adj 4 see: NASTY *adj* 7

austerity *n* oppression, rigidity, severity, tyranny

authentic *adj* 1 certified, confirmed, demonstrated, proved, tested, tried, verified

adj 2 accurate, believable, certain, convincing, credible, dependable, faithful, real, reliable, safe, sure, tenable, trustworthy, true, trusty

adj 3 absolute, actual, bona fide, certain, definite, existent, factual, genuine, hard, inarguable, incontestable, incontrovertible, indisputable, indubitable, irrefutable, positive, real, sure, true, undeniable,

undisputable, undoubtable, undoubted, unequivocal, unquestionable, veritable, viable

authenticate *v* attest, certify, confirm, corroborate, justify, notarize, prove, ratify, sanction, substantiate, support, validate, verify, vouch, witness

author *n* 1 bard, composer, folk singer, muse, narrator, poet, storyteller, troubadour

n 2 creator, founder, initiator, instigator, inventor, maker, originator, parent, pioneer, seed, source

n 3 authoress, biographer, creator, dramatist, essayist, journalist, novelist, playwright, reporter, screenwriter, writer

v compose, create, draft, pen, prepare, type, write

authoress *n* author, biographer, creator, dramatist, essayist, journalist, novelist, playwright, reporter, screenwriter, writer

authoritarian *adj* 1 authoritative, autocratic, controlled, despotic, disciplined, firm, harsh, inflexible, ironhanded, restrictive, rigid, rigorous, ruthless, severe, solid, stern, strict, stringent, strong, tough, tyrannical

adj 2 see: AUTHORITATIVE *adj* 2

n 1 autocrat, dictator, disciplinarian, enforcer

n 2 autocrat, despot, dictator, fascist, tsar, tyrant

authoritative *adj* 1 dependable, due, faithful, legitimate, rightful, strict, true, trustworthy, undistorted, veracious

adj 2 aristocratic, arrogant, authoritarian, autocratic, belligerent, bossy, despotic, dictatorial, dogmatic, domineering, haughty, imperial, imperious, masterful, militaristic, opinionated, oppressive, overbearing, peremptory, pushy, stubborn

adj 3 see: RESTRICTIVE *adj*

authorities *n* 1 administration, administrators, bureaucracy, civil service, commission, department, direction, forces, government, management, ministry, officials, power, powers, rule, rulers

n 2 bobbies, constabulary, cops, gendarmes, highway patrol, military police, police, troopers

authority *n* 1 dictionary, encyclopedia, reference, source

n 2 brass, elders, leaders, management, officers

n 3 clout, control, in, influence, leverage, power, prestige, pull, weight *n* 4 expert, guide, guru, leader, master, mentor, pundit, teacher, wise man

n 5 command, commission, control, direction, domination, jurisdiction, management, mastery, might, power, rule

n 6 adviser, artist, expert, guru, master, official, pro, professional, specialist, veteran, virtuoso, wizard

authorization *n* 1 assignment, commission, warrant

n 2 approval, consent, leave, license, permission, sanction

n 3 auspices, backing, command, confirmation, endorsement, fiat, patronage, sanction, sponsorship, support

authorize *v* 1 assign, delegate, designate, empower, entrust, pass along

v 2 approve, decree, enact, legalize, legislate, ordain, pass, ratify, sanction

v 3 accredit, certify, commission, empower, enable, entitle, facilitate, invest, license, permit, sanction, validate

v 4 accept, approbate, approve, certify, condone, confirm, countenance, endorse, favor, pass, ratify, sanction, validate

v 5 see: MANDATE *v*

v 6 see: TOLERATE *v*

authorized *adj* 1 conventional, customary, established, set

adj 2 allowable, lawful, legal, legitimate, permissible, rightful, valid

auto *adj* automatic, cybernetic, robotic, self-steering

n automobile, bus, car, carriage, chariot, coach, jeep, motorcar, omnibus, sedan, truck, van, vehicle, wagon

v ride

autobiography *n* biography, compendium, profile, résumé, sketch, vita

autocracy *n* despotism, dictatorship, tyranny

autocrat *n* 1 authoritarian, dictator, disciplinarian, enforcer

n 2 authoritarian, despot, dictator, fascist, tsar, tyrant

n 3 chief, commander, despot, dictator, governor, head, king, leader, lord, master, monarch, potentate, ruler

autocratic *adj* 1 authoritarian, authoritative, controlled, despotic, disciplined, firm, harsh, inflexible, ironhanded, restrictive, rigid, rigorous, ruthless, severe, solid, stern, strict, stringent, strong, tough, tyrannical

adj 2 see: AUTHORITATIVE *adj* 2

autograph *n* approval, endorsement, John Hancock, mark, name, signature

v ink, sign, subscribe

automat *n* cafe, cafeteria, canteen, diner, grill, luncheonette, lunchroom, restaurant, tearoom

automated *adj* automatic, habitual, mechanical, robotic, routine

automatic *adj* 1 auto, cybernetic, robotic, self-steering

adj 2 automated, habitual, mechanical, robotic, routine

adj 3 deep, gut, innate, instinctive, intuitive, visceral

adj 4 impulsive, instinctive, involuntary, natural, rash, reflex, spontaneous, unconscious, unforced, unpremeditated, unprompted

n firearm, gun, handgun, heater, iron, luger, piece, pistol, revolver, rod

automaton *n* android, droid, robot

automobile *n* auto, bus, car, carriage, chariot, coach, jeep, motorcar, omnibus, sedan, truck, van, vehicle, wagon

autonomous *adj* 1 democratic, independent, self-governing

adj 2 distinct, free, independent, lone, separate, sovereign, unconnected

autonomy *n* freedom, independence, liberty, license

auxiliary *adj* 1 accessory, adjunct, ancillary, assisting, subsidiary, supporting

adj 2 ancillary, incidental, minor, related, secondary, side, subordinate

adj 3 added, additional, another, extra, further, incremental, more, one more, other, spare, supplemental, supplementary, surplus

avail *n* account, advantage, applicability, appropriateness, aptness, benefit, decorum, expediency, fitness, manners, opportunism, pertinence, profit, propriety, relevance, rightness, service, suitability, use, usefulness, utility

v abet, advance, aid, ameliorate, amend, assist, benefit, better, boost, cultivate, do for, ease, egg on, encourage, enhance, forward, foster, further, help, improve, nurture, prefer, promote, rev, serve, spur on, support

available *adj* 1 close by, convenient, near, nearby

adj 2 accessible, close, convenient, feasible, functional, handy, helpful, multipurpose, nearby, open, practical, public, reachable, ready, serviceable, suitable, unrestricted, usable, useful, utilitarian, well-suited, within reach, working

avarice *n* covetousness, craving, desire, greed, selfishness, yearning

avaricious *adj* 1 covetous, endless, insatiable, ravenous, unquenchable, voracious
adj 2 acquisitive, covetous, craving, desirous, eager, grabby, grasping, greedy, hungry, longing, miserly, selfish, wishful, yearning

avenge *v* see: PAY *v* 2

avenue *n* access, approach, artery, boulevard, channel, drag, highway, pass, path, promenade, road, roadway, route, strait, street, thoroughfare, trail, way

average *adj* 1 common, intermediate, mediocre, medium, middle, normal, ordinary, regular, standard, unimpressive
adj 2 common, commonplace, daily, everyday, general, mundane, natural, normal, ordinary, plain, prevalent, regular, routine, typical, unexceptional, unremarkable, usual, workaday
n 1 grade, marks, score
n 2 mean, median, medium, middle, norm, par, rule, standard

averse *adj* see: UNWILLING *adj*

aversion *n* 1 contempt, disgust, distaste, horror, loathing, nausea, repugnance, repulsion, revulsion
n 2 disfavor, dislike, displeasure, dissatisfaction, distaste, opposition
n 3 acrimony, animosity, antagonism, antipathy, bitterness, dislike, enmity, gall, hate, hatred, hostility, ill will, malice, rancor, spite, venom, vindictiveness

avert *v* 1 caution, deter, discourage, dissuade, distract, divert
v 2 bar, deter, eliminate, foil, forestall, hinder, hold off, inhibit, preclude, prevent, stave off, thwart, turn back, ward off
v 3 see: SKEW *v* 3

aviary *n* aquarium, menagerie, terrarium, zoo

aviator *n* airman, barnstormer, flier, operator, pilot

avid *adj* anxious, ardent, breathless, desirous, eager, enthusiastic, excited, fain, impatient, impetuous, keen, passionate, raring, zealous

avocation *n* 1 distraction, diversion, hobby, moonlighting, pastime, sideline
n 2 art, business, calling, career, discipline, employment, field, gig, job, labor, line, livelihood, occupation, office, profession, pursuit, role, schtick, situation, specialty, task, thing, trade, vocation, work

avoid *v* 1 bypass, circumvent, detour, evade
v 2 duck, elude, escape, eschew, evade, recoil, shun, shy

v 3 dodge, equivocate, evade, fence, hedge, shift, shuffle, sidestep
v 4 circumvent, deflect, detour, dodge, duck, evade, hedge, parry, shirk, sidestep, skirt, ward off
v 5 abstain, constrain, curb, deny, forgo, govern, hold back, refrain, resist, restrict, stop, tame
v 6 see: DELAY *v* 4

avoidance *n* deceit, diversion, dodging, escape, evasion, runaround

avouch *v* advocate, affirm, assure, avow, commit, devote, guarantee, pledge, promise, ratify, swear, vow

avow *v* 1 allege, assert, claim, maintain, say, state
v 2 affirm, attest, contend, promise, say, swear, vouch, warrant
v 3 affirm, assert, attest, confirm, declare, depose, predicate, profess, protest
v 4 acknowledge, admit, allow, concede, confess, fess up, grant, own, own up
v 5 see: ASSURE *v* 3

await *v* 1 anticipate, believe, count on, expect, hope, keep the faith, look, look forward to, wish
v 2 abide, bide, linger, loiter, remain, stay, stick around, tarry, wait

awaiting *adj* contingent, impending, pending, unfinished, unsettled

awake *adj* 1 fitful, fretful, restless, sleepless
adj 2 alive, attentive, aware, cognizant, conscious, conversant, knowing, responsive, sentient, thinking

awaken *v* 1 arouse, challenge, excite, kindle, rally, rouse, stir, wake, waken
v 2 see: PROVOKE *v* 2

award *n* 1 honor, medal, prize, trophy
n 2 bequest, endowment, gift, grant, reward, scholarship
n 3 adjudication, determination, judgment, opinion, ruling, sentence, verdict
n 4 ante, bonus, booty, cash, commission, dividend, donation, fee, gift, gratuity, largess, money, percentage, perquisite, perk, premium, prize, profit, purse, reward, sharing, stake, stipend, tip, winnings
n 5 see: COMMENDATION *n* 2
v accord, adduce, bequeath, bestow, concede, confer, contribute, deliver, devote, donate, endow, extend, fund, give, give away, grant, hand down, hand out, impart, offer, pose, present, proffer, provide, supply, tender, volunteer

aware *adj* 1 alert, mindful, wise
adj 2 abreast, acquainted, conversant, familiar, informed, knowledgeable, up, versed

adj 3 alive, attentive, awake, cognizant, conscious, conversant, knowing, responsive, sentient, thinking

awareness *n* 1 acumen, astuteness, cleverness, discernment, discrimination, insight, intellect, intuition, keenness, perception, sagacity, sensitivity, shrewdness, understanding, wit

n 2 attention, care, carefulness, cognizance, concern, consciousness, consideration, heed, intimacy, knowing, knowledge, mark, note, notice, observance, observation, perception, recognition, regard, remark, sense

n 3 emotion, faculty, feel, feeling, intuition, perception, reaction, response, sensation, sense

away *adj* absent, gone, lacking, missing, omitted, truant, wanting

awe *n* 1 amazement, astonishment, bewilderment, shock, surprise, wonder

n 2 amazement, consternation, dread, fear, respect, reverence, wonder

v 1 amaze, astonish, astound, delight, floor, impress, overwhelm, wow

v 2 see: FRIGHTEN *v* 2

v 3 see: SURPRISE *v* 2

awesome *adj* arousing, breathtaking, exciting, magnificent, stimulating, stirring, stunning

awful *adj* 1 contemptible, dreadful, lousy, mean

adj 2 frightful, grim, grisly, gruesome, hideous, lurid, repulsive, sensational, shocking, terrible, ugly, violent

adj 3 atrocious, crying, desperate, disgraceful, ghastly, grizzly, heinous, monstrous, notorious, odious, offensive, outrageous, scandalous, shocking, tasteless, wicked

adj 4 appalling, dire, dreadful, fearful, formidable, frightening, frightful, ghastly, horrendous, horrible, offensive, ominous, portentous, scary, shocking, spooky, terrible, terrifying, unpleasant

awfully *adv* dreadfully, eminently, endlessly, exceedingly, exceptionally, extremely, greatly, highly, mightily, notably, quite, remarkably, terribly, thoroughly, very

awkward *adj* 1 delicate, difficult, embarrassing, sticky, tricky

adj 2 artificial, formal, stiff, stilted, stuffy

adj 3 bumbling, clumsy, faltering, gauche, gawky, halting, hesitant, inept, lumbering, maladroit, ungainly, ungraceful

awry *adj* 1 askew, crooked, lopsided, off-center

adj 2 afoul, amiss, bad, bum, improper, out of kilter, poor, rotten, unsatisfactory, wrong

ax *v* 1 boot, bounce, can, discharge, dismiss, drop, fire, impeach, let go, sack, terminate

v 2 carve, chip, chop, cleave, cut, dissect, fell, hack, hew, mangle, mutilate, notch, pulverize, rend, saw, sever, slice, sliver, snip, split, sunder, whittle

v 3 cut down, fell, knock down, raze, topple

n hatchet

axiom *n* 1 announcement, aphorism, cliché, declaration, decree, dictum, edict, gospel, homily, maxim, moral, precept, pronouncement, rule, saying, teaching, truism, truth, verity

n 2 adage, byword, cliché, dictum, maxim, motto, proverb, saying, slogan, talk

axis *n* 1 axle, pin, pivot, pole, rod, shaft, spindle

n 2 center, focal point, focus, heart, hub, nerve center, target

n 3 affiliation, alliance, association, bloc, coalition, concord, confederation, consolidation, faction, federation, joint venture, league, merger, organization, partnership, relationship, treaty, union

n 4 plane

axle *n* axis, pin, pivot, pole, rod, shaft, spindle

azure *adj* aqua, blue, cobalt, indigo, navy, Prussian, sapphire, turquoise

B

babble *v* blab, blurt, burble, chatter, gossip, murmur, prattle, talk, tattle

n babbling, burble, chatter, gibber, murmur, prattle, rattle

babbling *adj* confused, incoherent, irrational, rambling, wild

n babble, burble, chatter, gibber, murmur, prattle, rattle

babe *n* baby, child, infant, newborn, tot, tyke

baby *n* babe, child, infant, newborn, tot, tyke

v 1 aid, care for, help, nurse, nurture, pamper, succor

v 2 accommodate, cater, coddle, gratify, humor, indulge, overindulge, pamper, pander, placate, satisfy, spoil

babyish *adj* callow, childish, immature, infantile, sophomoric

baby sitter *n* governess, nanny, nursemaid

bachelor *n* 1 chap, dude, fellow, gent,

gentleman, guy, male, man, mister, widower

n 2 single

back *adj 1* frontier, outlandish, remote, unsettled

adj 2 aft, backward, dorsal, posterior, rear, tail

v 1 advocate, champion, endorse, guarantee, promote, sanction, side, support, uphold

v 2 disavow, fall back, recall, recant, recede, renege, rescind, retract, retreat, retrograde, take back

backbone *n 1* spinal column, spine, vertebrae

n 2 see: PERSISTENCE *n 3*

backdrop *n* curtain, environment, scene, scenery, set, setting, stage set, stage setting, surroundings

backer *n* advocate, ally, angel, benefactor, booster, champion, cheerleader, donor, friend, guarantor, helper, ombudsman, partner, patron, promoter, proponent, sponsor, supporter

backfire *v 1* echo, repeat, resonate, resound, reverberate, vibrate

v 2 boomerang, bounce, brush, glance, graze, rebound, ricochet, skim, skip, touch

background *n 1* breeding, culture, development, education, environment, experience, past, schooling, training, upbringing

n 2 credentials, education, qualifications, training

backing *n* auspices, authorization, command, confirmation, endorsement, fiat, patronage, sanction, sponsorship, support

backlog *n* cache, hoard, holdings, inventory, nest egg, pile, reserve, reservoir, stash, stock, stockpile, store, supply

backside *n* ass, base, behind, bottom, bucket, buns, butt, buttocks, derrière, end, fanny, hindquarters, posterior, rump, seat, stub, stump, tip, tush

backsliding *n* lapse

backup *n* agent, alternate, contingency, part-timer, replacement, representative, standby, substitute, surrogate

backward *adj 1* converse, counter, reverse

adj 2 aft, back, dorsal, posterior, rear, tail

adj 3 bashful, coy, demure, diffident, innocent, modest, quiet, reserved, retiring, shy, staid, timid, unassured

adj 4 blunt, deficient, dense, dimwitted, dull, dumb, feebleminded, idiotic, moronic, obtuse, retarded, simple, simple-minded, slow, stupid, thick, uneducated, unintelligent

bad *adj 1* disobedient, ill-behaved, misbehaving, mischievous, naughty

adj 2 adverse, evil, harmful, ill, unfavorable, unlucky

adj 3 decayed, putrid, rancid, rotten, sharp, sour, spoiled

adj 4 defective, futile, inadequate, incorrect, inferior, invalid, malfunctioning, poor, void

adj 5 afoul, amiss, awry, bum, improper, out of kilter, poor, rotten, unsatisfactory, wrong

adj 6 baleful, corrupt, cunning, forbidding, harmful, hurtful, malevolent, malignant, menacing, ominous, sinister, sneaky

adj 7 annoying, difficult, disagreeable, displeasing, nasty, objectionable, offensive, rotten, sour, unhappy, unpleasant, upsetting

adj 8 mean, rough, tough

adj 9 corrupt, crooked, deceitful, dishonest, evil, fraudulent, immoral, iniquitous, lying, Machiavellian, manipulative, mercenary, reprobate, roguish, scheming, shady, shifty, sinful, unethical, unfair, unprincipled, unscrupulous, untruthful, venal, vile, wicked, wrong

badge *n 1* emblem

n 2 card, label, pass, tag, ticket, voucher

badger *v* aggravate, annoy, bait, bedevil, beleaguer, bother, bug, harass, harry, hassle, heckle, hound, hurt, intimidate, jeer, nag, needle, persecute, pester, plague, provoke, ride, spite, taunt, tease, threaten, torment, worry

badly *adv* harshly, imperfectly, improperly, inadequately, inappropriately, painfully, poorly, unsatisfactorily

baffle *v 1* confound, confuse, frustrate, perplex, stymie, thwart

v 2 aggravate, balk, bewilder, circumvent, confuse, dash, elude, foil, frustrate, hamper, impede, negate, nullify, perplex, thwart

baffling *adj* elusive, frustrating, mysterious, puzzling, subtle

bag *n 1* booty, catch, prize, spoils

n 2 field, hobby, interest, job, specialty

n 3 baggage, case, equipment, gear, grip, kit, luggage, pack, pouch, purse, sack, suitcase, valise, wallet

v 1 capture, catch, ensnare, entangle, entrap, hook, snag, snare, snarl, tangle, trap, trick

v 2 apprehend, arrest, book, bust, capture,

catch, collar, detain, get, grab, lock up, nab, nail, pick up, pinch, pull in, run in, secure, seize, take

baggage n bag, case, equipment, gear, grip, kit, luggage, pack, pouch, purse, sack, suitcase, valise, wallet

bait n 1 attraction, come-on, decoy, enticement, lure, magnet, ruse, seduction, snare, temptation, trap, wile

n 2 gear, hooks, lures, tackle

v 1 attract, decoy, entice, entrap, lure, tantalize

v 2 aggravate, annoy, badger, bedevil, beleaguer, bother, bug, harass, harry, hassle, heckle, hound, hurt, intimidate, jeer, nag, needle, persecute, pester, plague, provoke, ride, spite, taunt, tease, threaten, torment, worry

bake v 1 broil, burn, char, cook, melt, parch, roast, scorch, sear, singe, swelter, toast, warm

v 2 see: SEETHE v 2

baking adj blistering, boiling, broiling, burning, fiery, hot, scalding, scorching, sizzling, sultry, sweltering, torrid

balance n 1 equilibrium, poise, stability

n 2 harmony, symmetry, uniformity

n 3 amount, count, result, sum, total

v 1 audit, check, examine, inspect, verify

v 2 equal, equalize, equate, even, smooth

v 3 brace, calm, fix, steady, still

v 4 adjust, compensate, make equal, make up, offset, outweigh, redeem, set off

v 5 see: SERVICE v

balanced adj commensurate, equal, proportional, symmetrical

balcony n gallery

bald adj hairless

bale n 1 see: BUNCH n 2

n 2 see: PAIN n 4

baleful adj see: SINISTER

balk v 1 boggle, demur, desist, gag

v 2 see: THWART v 4

balking adj see: DISAGREEABLE adj 2

balky adj see: DISAGREEABLE adj 2

ball n 1 balloon, globe, orb, sphere

n 2 cotillion, dance, hop, party, prom

v gather up

ballerina n choreographer, chorine, dancer, gypsy, hoofer

ballet n cha-cha, dance, fox trot, hula, jitterbug, polka, tap, twist, waltz

balloon n 1 ball, globe, marble, orb, sphere

n 2 airship, blimp, dirigible

ballot n choice, franchise, option, preference, say, selection, vote

v appoint, choose, elect, nominate, opt, select, vote

ballyhoo n embellishment, exaggeration, hoopla, hype, hyperbole, overstatement, promotion, public relations

balm n 1 aroma, bouquet, fragrance, incense, perfume, scent, spice

n 2 analgesic, emollient, salve

v allay, appease, assuage, becalm, calm, compose, conciliate, ease, lull, mollify, pacify, placate, propitiate, quell, quiet, reconcile, satiate, settle, soften, soothe, still, sweeten, tranquilize

balmy adj 1 bright, clear, fair, pleasant, serene

adj 2 bland, faint, gentle, mild, pleasant, smooth, soft, weak

adj 3 see: ABSURD adj 2

baloney n bilge, bosh, bull, bunk, drivel, fiddlesticks, foolishness, junk, malarkey, nonsense, nothing, poppycock, rot, rubbish, schlock, silliness, trivia

bamboozle v see: CHEAT v 1

ban n 1 disapproval, refusal, rejection, thumbs down, turndown, veto

n 2 blockage, boycott, curtailment, embargo, prohibition, restriction, stoppage

n 3 bar, constraint, interdiction, prohibition, restriction, taboo

v bar, confine, enjoin, forbid, inhibit, nix, outlaw, prevent, prohibit, stop, suppress, veto

banal adj 1 commonplace, conventional, ordinary, trite, undistinguished

adj 2 bland, dull, flat, innocuous, insipid, tasteless, unexciting

adj 3 boring, clichéd, commonplace, corny, dull, hackneyed, musty, redundant, repetitious, repetitive, stale, tedious, threadbare, timeworn, tired, tiresome, trite, worn out

banality n cliché, commonplace, platitude, triteness

band n 1 coil, crown, garland, loop, ring, spiral, wreath

n 2 body, company, corps, group, outfit, party, troop, troupe

n 3 cabal, camp, circle, clan, clique, coterie, coven, cult, faction, family, gang, group, mob, ring, school, sect, tribe

n 4 assembly, association, bevy, brood, bunch, camp, clique, cluster, collection, covey, crew, flock, group, organization, party, team, unit

n 5 bunch, crew, crowd, drove, flock, following, gaggle, gang, herd, huddle, mass, mob, pack, rabble, riffraff, swarm, team, throng

n 6 cuff

n 7 ensemble, orchestra, strings

n 8 banding, ribbon, strip

n 9 adhesive, cellophane tape, strip, tape

n 10 gang, mob, posse, vigilantes

n 11 anklet, bangle, bracelet, brooch, earring, jewelry, medal, medallion, necklace, pin, ring

v 1 belt, bind, corset, fasten, gird, girdle, lash, strap, tie

v 2 accompany, coincide, collaborate, collude, combine, concur, cooperate, pool, unite

v 3 amalgamate, blend, coalesce, combine, compound, consolidate, fuse, intermingle, league, lump, meld, merge, mingle, mix, unify, unite

bandanna *n* mantilla, muffler, scarf, shawl

banding *n* band, ribbon, strip

bandit *n* brigand, burglar, cheat, con artist, con man, criminal, crook, embezzler, gyp, highwayman, looter, mugger, outlaw, robber, swindler, thief

bane *n* curse, disease, evil, misfortune, pestilence, plague, scourge

baneful *adj* deadly, fatal, lethal, mortal, noxious, pernicious, pestilent, ruinous

bang *n* 1 blare, blast, boom, discharge, explosion, noise, pop, report, roar

n 2 blow, box, bump, chop, clap, conk, crack, crash, cuff, hit, impact, jar, jolt, knock, lick, punch, rap, slap, slug, smack, smash, swat, swipe, tap, wallop, whack

n 3 bell ringer, bull's-eye, gong, hit, slam, smash, strike

n 4 boom, clang, clap, crash, resound, roar, rumble, shake, thunder

v 1 bump, collide, crash, hit, smash

v 2 beat, bludgeon, clobber, club, hit, pound, strike, whack

v 3 crack, pop, snap, thump

v 4 dent, dimple, hollow, indent

v 5 blow, bump, cuff, hit, knock, punch, strike

bangle *n* anklet, band, bracelet, brooch, earring, jewelry, medal, medallion, necklace, pin, ring

banish *v* 1 cast out, deport, dispel, displace, exile, expatriate, expel, extradite, ostracize, oust, relegate, remove

v 2 bar, blackball, cut, debar, dismiss, eliminate, except, exclude, ignore, leave out, omit, suspend

bank *n* 1 depository, lender, receptacle, repository

n 2 drift, heap, hill, mass, mound, mountain, pile, stack, stockpile

n 3 beach, coast, seashore, shoal, shore

v 1 drift, heap, mound, pile, stack

v 2 bend, incline, lean, pitch, slant, slope

v 3 accumulate, deposit, hoard, save, squirrel away, stockpile, store

v 4 hoard, lay aside, lay away, lay by, lay in, lay up, put by, salt away, save, spare

banker *n* cashier, money-changer, paymaster, purser, teller

banking *n* economics, finance, numbers, statistics

bankroll *v* capitalize, finance, fund, stake, subsidize

bankrupt *adj* broke, busted, destitute, dissolved, insolvent, out of business, penniless, ruined

v 1 break, bust, decay, do in, fold up, impoverish, ruin

v 2 deplete, drain, draw, draw down, exhaust, impoverish, use up

bankruptcy *n* poverty

banned *adj* forbidden, prohibited, taboo

banner *n* headline, placard, poster, sign

banquet *n* buffet, dinner, feast, lunch, meal, repast, smorgasbord, supper

bantam *adj* dainty, diminutive, dwarfish, Lilliputian, little, micro, microscopic, midget, mini, miniature, minuscule, minute, petite, pygmy, slight, small, tiny, wee

banter *n* 1 chatter

n 2 comedy, crack, funniness, gag, humor, jest, joke, quip, small talk, wisecrack, wit, witticism

v deride, gibe, jeer, joke, knock, mock, needle, rib, ridicule, roast, tease

baptize *v* 1 anoint, bless, consecrate, dedicate, devote, enshrine, exalt, hallow, purify, sanctify

v 2 bestow, call, christen, confer, designate, dub, entitle, name, nickname, tag, term, title

bar *n* 1 ingot, pole, rod, stick, strip

n 2 barricade, barrier, block, blockade, fence, obstacle, roadblock, stop, wall

n 3 barrier, bottleneck, crimp, dead end, deadlock, difficulty, encumbrance, hurdle, impasse, impediment, obstacle, obstruction, snag, stumbling block

n 4 barroom, cocktail lounge, den, dive, dump, gin mill, hangout, haunt, joint, lounge, pub, rathskeller, saloon, tavern, watering hole

n 5 bistro, cabaret, cafe, casino, discothèque, nightclub

n 6 ban, constraint, interdiction, prohibition, restriction, taboo

v 1 banish, blackball, cut, debar, dismiss, eliminate, except, exclude, ignore, leave out, omit, suspend

v 2 ban, confine, enjoin, forbid, inhibit, nix, outlaw, prevent, prohibit, stop, suppress, veto

v 3 block, brake, choke, clog, dam, deter, detract, encumber, frustrate, halt, hamper, hesitate, hinder, impair, impede, inhibit, jam, obstruct, prevent, repress, restrain, retard, slow, stay, stop, stop up, throttle

v 4 avert, deter, eliminate, foil, forestall, hinder, hold off, inhibit, preclude, prevent, stave off, thwart, turn back, ward off

barb *n* affront, aspersion, attack, caustic remark, crack, cut, denunciation, despite, dig, disparagement, disrespect, gibe, implication, indignity, innuendo, insult, invective, knock, reflection, sarcasm, scorn, slap, slight, slur, spike, tongue-lashing, verbal jab

barbarian *adj* barbaric, savage, uncivil, uncivilized, uncultivated, wild

n aborigine, native, primitive, savage

barbaric *adj* barbarian, savage, uncivil, uncivilized, uncultivated, wild

barbarous *adj* monstrous, outrageous, uncivilized, unconscionable, unethical, ungodly, unholy, wicked

barbecue *n* clambake, cookout, outing, picnic

bard *n* author, composer, folk singer, muse, narrator, poet, storyteller, troubadour

bare *adj* 1 blank, dull, empty, lifeless, unfilled

adj 2 barren, bleak, desolate, dismal, gaunt, grim

adj 3 barren, clear, empty, stark, vacant, vacuous, void

adj 4 exposed, in the raw, naked, nude, open, peeled, stripped, unclothed, uncovered, visible

adj 5 bald

adj 6 deficient, few, inadequate, inferior, insufficient, little, meager, paltry, petty, poor, scant, scanty, skimpy, spare, sparse

v 1 deprive, dismantle, divest, strip

v 2 expose, lay open, strip, subject, uncover

v 3 denude, discard, disrobe, doff, flash, remove, reveal, shed, strip, take off, unclothe, undress

barefaced *adj* arrant, blatant, brassy, brazen, extreme, impudent, notorious, obtrusive, shameless, unabashed

barely *adv* a tad, hardly, just about, least, minimally, not much, not quite, scarce, scarcely

bargain *n* 1 buy, deal, discount, promotion, reduction, sale, special, steal

n 2 agreement, bond, compact, contract, convention, covenant, deal, pact, pledge, promise, transaction, treaty, understanding

v 1 argue, barter, dicker, haggle, negotiate, wrangle

v 2 barter, convert, deal, exchange, swap, trade, traffic

barge *n* boat, canoe, craft, dory, ferry, float, kayak, raft, scow, skiff, tender

bark *n* 1 case, coating, crust, husk, peel, rind, shell, shuck, skin

n 2 bellow, blare, holler, roar, scream, shout, shriek, thunder, yell

v 1 gnarl, growl, grumble, rumble, snarl

v 2 bay, cry, growl, howl, shout, snap, woof, yap, yelp

v 3 see: SCREAM *v*

barn *n* 1 abode, bungalow, cabin, coop, cottage, hatch, hovel, hut, lodge, shack, shanty

n 2 coop, enclosure, hatch, lean-to, paddock, pen, pound, shack, shed, shelter, stable, stall, sty

barnacle *n* dependent, freeloader, hanger-on, leech, parasite, remora, sponge, vine

barnstormer *n* airman, aviator, flier, operator, pilot

baron *n* see: CAPITALIST *n*

baronial *adj* august, exalted, grand, grandiose, haughty, imperial, imposing, impressive, lofty, lordly, magisterial, magnificent, majestic, noble, portly, princely, regal, royal, stately

barracks *n* camp

barrage *n* burst, fusillade, round, shot, volley

barrel *n* bucket, cask, drum, keg, tub, vat, vessel

v see: RUSH *v* 3

barren *adj* 1 bare, bleak, desolate, dismal, gaunt, grim

adj 2 bare, clear, empty, stark, vacant, vacuous, void

adj 3 effete, frigid, impotent, infertile, spent, sterile, unbearing, unfertile, unfruitful, unproductive

n desert, waste, wasteland, wild, wilderness

barricade n bar, barrier, block, blockade, fence, obstacle, roadblock, stop, wall
v enclose, fortify, protect

barrier n 1 border, boundary, buffer, fence, hedge

n 2 mesh, netting, protection, screen, shield

n 3 bar, barricade, block, blockade, fence, obstacle, roadblock, stop, wall

n 4 bar, bottleneck, crimp, dead end, deadlock, difficulty, encumbrance, hurdle, impasse, impediment, obstacle, obstruction, snag, stumbling block

n 5 breaker, cape, harbor, head, jetty, neck, point, sea wall

barring prep aside from, except, excluding, save, unless

barrister n advocate, attorney, counsel, counselor, intercessor, lawyer, mediator, solicitor

barroom n bar, cocktail lounge, den, dive, dump, gin mill, hangout, haunt, joint, lounge, pub, rathskeller, saloon, tavern, watering hole

barter v 1 cajole, coax, con, urge

v 2 exchange, swap, switch, trade

v 3 argue, bargain, dicker, haggle, negotiate, wrangle

v 4 bargain, convert, deal, exchange, swap, trade, traffic

v 5 distribute, market, merchandise, peddle, retail, sell, vend, wholesale

base adj 1 cheap, common, sleazy, trashy

adj 2 abject, contemptible, debasing, despicable, false, servile

adj 3 common, humble, ignoble, knavish, low, lowly, mean, plebeian

adj 4 abhorrent, gross, invidious, obnoxious, offensive, repellent, repugnant, revulsive

adj 5 beneath, despicable, ignoble, inferior, low, lowdown, sordid, squalid, unworthy, vile, vulgar, wretched

adj 6 see: VICIOUS adj 3

n 1 seat

n 2 bottom, floor, ground, minimum

n 3 basis, bedrock, footing, foundation, ground, root

n 4 brace, buttress, column, footing, foundation, prop, shore, stay, support, underpinning

n 5 ass, backside, behind, bottom, bucket, buns, butt, buttocks, derrière, end, fanny, hindquarters, posterior, rump, seat, stub, stump, tip, tush

baseless adj erroneous, fallacious, groundless, invalid, unfounded, unsubstantiated

basement n cellar, underground, vault

bash n bender, binge, do, fling, orgy, party, spree

bashful adj backward, coy, demure, diffident, innocent, modest, quiet, reserved, retiring, shy, staid, timid, unassured

basic adj 1 conventional, established, official, standard

adj 2 creative, formative, fundamental, initiatory, productive, seminal

adj 3 crude, plain, primitive, rough, simple, undeveloped

adj 4 businesslike, down-to-earth, efficient, hardheaded, practical, pragmatic, sensible

adj 5 dominant, elementary, first, foremost, fundamental, head, highest, leading, main, outstanding, paramount, preeminent, premier, primary, rudimentary, supreme, top

adj 6 early, elementary, embryonic, essential, fundamental, initial, intrinsic, original, rudimentary, underlying

adj 7 congenital, genetic, inborn, indigenous, ingrained, inherent, inherited, innate, instinctive, intrinsic, natal, native, natural

n element, essential, foundation, fundamental, principle, rudiment

basics n see: GOODS n 2

basilica n cathedral, chapel, church, house of god, mosque, sanctuary, synagogue, tabernacle, temple

basin n 1 hollow

n 2 tub

n 3 sink, washbowl, washstand

n 4 lagoon, lake, loch, pond, pool, spring

basis n 1 beginning, essence, kernel, seed

n 2 base, bedrock, footing, foundation, ground, root

n 3 arguments, cause, explanation, foundation, grounds, principle, rationale, reason, rudiments, source

n 4 see: SUBSTANCE n 9

bask v 1 delight, enjoy, like, loaf, luxuriate, relax, relish, rest, savor, wallow

v 2 sun, sunbathe, tan

basket n box, crate, housing

bastard adj fatherless, illegitimate, misbegotten, orphaned, spurious, unauthentic, ungenuine

n deception, fake, fraud, hoax, put-on, sham

bastion n bulwark, defense, embankment, fort, fortification, rampart, wall

bat v clout, hit, nail, pop, smite, sock, strike, swat, whack *n* blackjack, boomerang, club, cudgel, cue, mallet, nightstick, stave, stick

batch *n* 1 catch, collection, haul, heap, take

n 2 array, bale, battery, body, bunch, bundle, clump, cluster, group, lot, pack, parcel, quantity, set

v lump, send, ship together

bath *n* tub

bathe *v* clean, cleanse, clean up, dip, flush, immerse, launder, rinse, rub, scour, scrape, scrub, shower, wash

bathrobe *n* gown, housecoat, negligee, nightgown, robe

bathroom *n* can, head, john, latrine, lavatory, loo, potty, powder room, toilet, water closet, wc

baton *n* rod, scepter, staff, wand

battalion *n* 1 army, brigade, company, force, gang, men, power, soldiers, troops

n 2 airborne, army, brigade, cavalry, company, footmen, guard, horsemen, infantry, legion, marines, militia, minutemen, paratroops, platoon, reserve, storm troopers

batter *v* assail, attack, beat, birch, buffet, flagellate, flog, hammer, lambaste, lash, lather, pelt, pound, pummel, punish, scourge, thrash, tromp, wallop, whip

battery *n* array, bale, batch, body, bunch, bundle, clump, cluster, group, lot, pack, parcel, quantity, set

battle *n* 1 combat, conflagration, dispute, encounter, fight, struggle, war

n 2 action, engagement, fray, gesture, movement, operation, proceeding

n 3 clash, competition, conflict, contest, discord, duel, fight, fighting, rivalry, strife, struggle, war, warfare

n 4 affray, brawl, brush, clash, conflict, difference, disagreement, dispute, encounter, fight, fracas, melee, quarrel, run-in, scrimmage, skirmish, spat, touch

n 5 altercation, argument, brawl, challenge, combat, controversy, disagreement, discord, dispute, feud, fight, fracas, fray, hassle, melee, quarrel, rancor, rift, row, ruckus, scrap, scuffle, skirmish, spat, squabble, struggle, tiff, war

n 6 see: ACCOMPLISHMENT *n* 4

v 1 attack, combat, contend, fight, oppose, struggle, war

v 2 see: QUARREL *v*

bauble *n* delicacy, frill, luxury, treat

bawdy *adj* coarse, crude, dirty, erotic, filthy, foul, gamy, gross, improper, indecent, lascivious, lewd, licentious, nasty, obscene, off-color, pornographic, profane, prurient, racy, rank, raunchy, rib-

ald, risqué, scandalous, smutty, suggestive, tainted, uncouth, vulgar, x-rated

bawl *v* bemoan, cry, grieve, groan, lament, moan, mourn, sigh, snivel, sob, wail, weep, whimper, whine

bay *v* bark, cry, growl, howl, shout, snap, woof, yap, yelp

n arm, cove, estuary, fiord, gulf, inlet, narrows, sound, strait

bayou *n* brook, creek, river, stream, tributary

bazaar *n* carnival, circus, fair, market

be *v* endure, exist, last, live, persist, prevail, survive

beach *v* land

n bank, coast, seashore, shoal, shore

beacon *n* 1 buoy

n 2 light, lighthouse, signal warning

bead *n* 1 circle, mark, spot

n 2 blob, bubble, drib, drop, droplet, globule, lump, sphere

n 3 atom, dab, dash, dot, drop, grain, iota, molecule, morsel, particle, pea, pellet, smidgen, speck, tad

beak *n* bill, muzzle, nib, nose, proboscis, prow, snout, trunk

beam *n* 1 glow, grin, simper, smile, smirk

n 2 flicker, glimmer, hint, light, ray, sliver, spark, trace

n 3 board, boom, girder, log, plank, rafter, spar, support, timber

v 1 burn, disperse, emit, gleam, glisten, radiate, shed, shine, transmit

v 2 smile

beaming *adj* see: BRIGHT *adj* 6

bear *v* 1 carry, have, possess

v 2 birth, bring forth, deliver

v 3 produce, turn out, yield

v 4 apply, concern, pertain, refer, regard, relate

v 5 act, behave, carry, comport, conduct, demean, rule

v 6 accompany, associate, attend, chaperon, conduct, consort with, convoy, escort

v 7 abide, accept, acquiesce, allow, authorize, concede, condone, digest, endure, experience, have, let, permit, put up with, stand, stomach, suffer, sustain, swallow, take, tolerate, undergo

v 8 see: BEGET *v*

v 9 see: CARRY *v* 1, 4

bearable *adj* allowable, endurable, sustainable, tolerable

bearing *n* 1 angle, degree, heading, position, setting

n 2 action, behavior, conduct, demeanor, deportment, manners

n 3 air, attitude, calmness, carriage, demeanor, disposition, poise, pose, posture, presence, set, stance

bearings n course, direction, heading, location, position

beast n animal, being, brute, creature, monster, ogre

beat adj burnt out, bushed, careworn, drawn, emaciated, exhausted, expended, fatigued, frazzled, haggard, jaded, pinched, pooped, run-down, shot, spent, tired, wearied, weary, worn, worn down, worn-out

n cadence, cycle, lilt, pulse, rate, rhythm, tempo, time

v 1 attack, oppress, scourge, smite

v 2 belabor, rehash, reiterate, repeat

v 3 blend, mingle, mix, stir, toss, whip

v 4 bang, bludgeon, clobber, club, hit, pound, strike, whack

v 5 flutter, palpitate, pulsate, pulse, quiver, throb, tremble, vibrate

v 6 best, better, cap, dwarf, eclipse, exceed, excel, go beyond, outdo, outgo, outshine, outstrip, overshadow, pass, surpass, top, transcend

v 7 belittle, blast, clobber, conquer, cream, defeat, dust, lambaste, lick, overrun, overwhelm, rout, shellac, smear, thrash, wallop, whip

v 8 assail, attack, batter, birch, buffet, flagellate, flog, hammer, lambaste, lash, lather, pelt, pound, pummel, punish, scourge, thrash, tromp, wallop, whip

v 9 see: CHEAT v 1

beaten adj clobbered, defeated, dejected, depressed, discouraged, licked, whipped

beau n boyfriend, date, escort, fiancé, lover, mate, paramour, suitor

beautiful adj 1 admirable, delightful, glorious, good, magnificent, peachy, splendid, terrific, wonderful

adj 2 alluring, attractive, breathtaking, comely, cute, fair, fine, foxy, gorgeous, lovely, luscious, magnificent, pretty, shapely, stunning

beautify v adorn, bedeck, deck, decorate, dress up, embellish, enhance, garnish, glamorize, grace, ornament, polish, trim

beauty n attractiveness, aura, comeliness, loveliness, pulchritude, radiance

becalm v see: APPEASE v 2

because conj as a result of, by reason of, due to, in view of, on account of, thanks to

beckon v gesture, motion, nod, signal

becloud v see: OBSCURE v

becoming adj 1 alluring, attractive, coy, cute, enchanting, enticing, fascinating,

foxy, inviting, pleasing, ravishing, seductive, sexy

adj 2 attractive, comely, exquisite, fair, good-looking, gorgeous, handsome, pleasing, radiant, stately

bed n berth, bunk, cot, couch, cradle, crib, stall

bedeck v see: DECORATE v

bedevil v 1 see: ANNOY v 3

v 2 see: ATTRACT v 6

bedim v see: OBSCURE v

bedlam n see: ACTIVITY n 3

bedrock n base, basis, footing, foundation, ground, root

beef n 1 guts, meat, substance

n 2 complaint, criticism, grievance, gripe, objection, protest

n 3 ardor, brawn, drive, energy, force, intensity, lustiness, might, muscle, pep, potency, power, punch, steam, strength, verve, vigor, vim, virility, vitality

beer n ale, bock, brew, lager, Pilsner, stout, suds

befall v appear, arise, break, come, come about, develop, do, ensue, evolve, fall out, happen, manifest, materialize, occur, pass, rise, take place, transpire, turn up

befitting adj see: APPLICABLE adj

befog v 1 see: BEWILDER v 1

v 2 see: OBSCURE v

before adv 1 desirably, preferably, rather

adv 2 ahead, beyond, forward, in front, onward

adv 3 earlier, first, formerly, heretofore, hitherto, once, previously, prior to

befoul v 1 catch, ensnare, entangle, foul, hang

v 2 besmirch, blacken, darken, defame, disparage, injure, libel, malign, revile, scandalize, slander, slur, smear, soil, tear down, traduce

befriend v patronize

befuddle v see: BEWILDER v 2

befuddlement n 1 bewilderment, complication, confusion, perplexity

n 2 daze, fog, haze, maze, muddledness, muddleheadedness

beg v appeal, ask, beseech, conjure, crave, desire, entreat, grovel, implore, indicate, invoke, plead, pray, request, seek, solicit, supplicate, whine

beget v bear, breed, come into, create, effect, engender, father, generate, hatch, impregnate, make, mate, multiply, originate, parent, procreate, promulgate, propagate, reproduce, sire, spawn

beggar n bum, derelict, drifter, hobo, loafer, mendicant, panhandler, pauper, tramp, vagabond, vagrant

begin v 1 activate, cause, commence, constitute, create, embark, enter, establish, inaugurate, induct, initiate, install, instigate, instill, institute, introduce, kick off, launch, lead off, open, originate, precipitate, preface, set up, start, tee off, usher in, venture forth

v 2 see: INVENT v 3

beginner n 1 amateur, dabbler, dilettante, hobbyist, layman, neophyte, nonprofessional, novice, part-timer

n 2 apprentice, disciple, freshman, intern, neophyte, newcomer, novice, novitiate, pupil, recruit, rookie, student, tenderfoot, trainee

beginning adj 1 budding, callow, embryonic

adj 2 introductory, opening, preliminary, preparatory, prior

adj 3 embryonic, founding, incipient, initial, introductory, nascent, rudimentary, starting

n 1 basis, essence, kernel, seed

n 2 briefing, commencement, debut, inauguration, induction, initiation, unveiling

n 3 birth, debut, delivery, inception, kindling, onset, outset, start

n 4 foreword, intro, introduction, overture, preamble, preface, prelude, prologue, start

n 5 conception, cradle, derivation, fountainhead, inception, infancy, mother, origin, root, seed, source, stem

begrudge v covet, envy, resent

begrudging adj petty, small-minded, spiteful

beguile v 1 see: ATTRACT v 6

v 2 see: CHEAT v 1

beguilement n see: CHARISMA n 2

beguiling adj see: FASCINATING adj 2

behalf n account, advantage, benefit, betterment, gain, good, happiness, interest, prosperity, sake, welfare, well-being

behave v 1 behave towards, handle, manage, treat

v 2 accomplish, contend, cope, make do, manage, persevere

v 3 act, bear, carry, comport, conduct, demean, rule

behavior n 1 conduct, handling, treatment

n 2 action, bearing, conduct, demeanor, deportment, manners

behest n see: COMMAND n 3

behind adv after, anon, following, in pursuit, later, post, subsequently

n ass, backside, base, bottom, bucket, buns, butt, buttocks, derrière, end, fanny, hindquarters, posterior, rump, seat, stub, stump, tip, tush

behold v 1 glimpse, look, mind, see, sight, spot, watch, witness

v 2 see: UNDERSTAND v 6

beige adj brown, chestnut, chocolate, hazel, mahogany, tan

being n 1 animal, beast, brute, creature, monster, ogre

n 2 entity, object, organism, sum, system, thing, totality, whole

n 3 actuality, existence, fact, life, presence, reality, truth, vitality

n 4 citizen, creature, entity, Homo sapiens, human, human being, individual, man, person, woman

belabor v beat, rehash, reiterate, repeat

belated adj delayed, late, overdue, slow, tardy, unpunctual

beleaguer v 1 beset, besiege, invest, surround

v 2 aggravate, annoy, badger, bait, bedevil, bother, bug, harass, harry, hassle, heckle, hound, hurt, intimidate, jeer, nag, needle, persecute, pester, plague, provoke, ride, spite, taunt, tease, threaten, torment, worry

belfry n spire, steeple, tower, turret

belief n 1 notion, superstition, tradition

n 2 attitude, point of view, position, stance, stand

n 3 custom, doctrine, mores, relic, rite, ritual, throwback, tradition

n 4 affiliation, church, creed, denomination, faith, persuasion, religion, rite, seat, theology

n 5 confidence, contingency, credence, credit, creed, dependence, desire, faith, hope, religion, trust

n 6 attitude, bias, conviction, feeling, inducement, leaning, mind, opinion, persuasion, sentiment, slant, view

n 7 canon, code, conviction, creed, doctrine, dogma, law, opinion, principle, rule, tenet, theory

beliefs n code, doctrine, ethics, outlook, philosophy, rites, values

believable adj accurate, authentic, certain, convincing, credible, dependable, faithful, real, reliable, safe, sure, tenable, true, trustworthy, trusty

believe v 1 accept, buy, swallow

v 2 anticipate, await, count on, expect, hope, keep the faith, look, look forward to, wish

v 3 argue, assert, claim, contend, defend,

justify, know, maintain, state, think, vindicate, warrant

v 4 assume, comprehend, conceive, estimate, expect, fathom, gather, grasp, guess, imagine, infer, know, presume, suppose, surmise, suspect, think, trust, understand

believer *n* convert, disciple, follower, zealot

believing *adj* credulous, easy, gullible, innocent, naive, susceptible, trustful

belittle *v* 1 abase, abash, cast down, cheapen, debase, defile, deflate, degrade, demean, depreciate, derogate, devalue, dishonor, embarrass, humble, humiliate, lower, mortify, put down, shame, sink

v 2 deprecate, disapprove, disfavor, disparage, frown upon, object

v 3 deride, flaunt, jab, jeer, jest, mock, quip, razz, ridicule, scoff, scorn, sneer, taunt, tease

v 4 beat, blast, clobber, conquer, cream, defeat, dust, lambaste, lick, overrun, overwhelm, rout, shellac, thrash, smear, wallop, whip

v 5 abuse, asperse, bad-mouth, condemn, damage, decry, defame, degrade, denigrate, denounce, deprecate, detract, diminish, discount, disparage, insult, knock, malign, put down, revile, run down, slander, take away, vilify

bell *n* alarm, buzzer, chime, gong, signal, siren

bellicose *adj* 1 brawling, difficult, feisty, quarrelsome, scrappy, spirited

adj 2 adverse, antagonistic, hostile, ill, inimical, nasty, spiteful, unfriendly

adj 3 angry, belligerent, combative, contentious, hostile, militant, pugnacious, quarrelsome, warlike

bellicosity *n* aggression, aggressiveness, attack, belligerence, combativeness, fight, pugnacity

belligerence *n* aggression, aggressiveness, attack, bellicosity, combativeness, fight, pugnacity

belligerent *adj* 1 forthright, outright, outspoken

adj 2 extroverted, free, intimidating, loud, outspoken, vocal, vociferous

adj 3 angry, bellicose, combative, contentious, hostile, militant, pugnacious, quarrelsome, warlike

adj 4 see: AUTHORITATIVE *adj* 2

bellow *n* bark, blare, holler, roar, scream, shout, shriek, thunder, yell

v 1 see: SCOLD *v* 4

v 2 see: SCREAM *v*

belly *n* abdomen, gut, midriff, paunch, stomach, tummy, tum-tum

bellyacher *n* crank, grouch, grump, sorehead, sourpuss

belongings *n* 1 assets, equity, estate, fortune, goods, holdings, inheritance, money, ownership, possessions, property, prosperity, riches, treasure, wealth

n 2 property, stuff, things

beloved *adj* adored, cherished, dear, esteemed, loved, precious, respected, revered, treasured, venerable, worshiped

below *prep* beneath, lower than, under, underneath

belt *n* area, arena, field, realm, region, section, space, territory, tract, turf, zone

v 1 band, bind, corset, fasten, gird, girdle, lash, strap, tie

v 2 hit

bemoan *v* 1 deplore, lament, regret, repent, rue

v 2 see: CRY *v* 3

bemused *adj* absent-minded, abstracted, careless, dazed, dizzy, groggy, inattentive, lost, mindless, oblivious, preoccupied, silly, spaced, vapid

bench *n* 1 court

n 2 chair, pew, seat, stool

benchmark *n* 1 criterion, guideline, measure, test

n 2 criterion, gauge, measure, observation, rule, standard, yardstick

bend *n* 1 crimp, kink, snarl, tangle, twist

n 2 arc, arch, bow, coil, crook, curvature, curve, hook, round, spiral

n 3 angle, bow, detour, deviation, double, shift, tack, turn, turning, yaw

v 1 contort, twist, warp

v 2 curve, meander, veer, wind, zigzag

v 3 connect, encircle, join, loop, twist

v 4 bank, incline, lean, pitch, slant, slope

v 5 bow, droop, duck, lower, slouch, slump, stoop

v 6 angle, arch, bow, curve, flex, ply, round, tilt, tip, turn, twist, vault

v 7 turn

v 8 bias, brainwash, compel, convert, indoctrinate, influence, predispose, prejudice, proselytize, slant, sway

v 9 accede, acquiesce, bow, buckle, capitulate, cave, comply, concede, cry uncle, defer, give in, give up, relent, submit, succumb, surrender, twist, yield

bender *n* bash, binge, do, fling, orgy, party, spree

bending *n* deflection

beneath *adj* base, despicable, ignoble, inferior, low, lowdown, sordid, squalid, un-worthy, vile, vulgar, wretched

prep below, lower than, under, under-neath

benediction *n* blessing

benefactor *n* advocate, ally, angel, backer, booster, champion, cheerleader, donor, friend, guarantor, helper, ombudsman, partner, patron, promoter, proponent, sponsor, supporter

beneficial *adj* 1 gainful, lucrative, profit-able, rewarding

adj 2 good, helpful, salutary, useful

adj 3 fulfilling, gratifying, pleasing, re-warding, worthwhile

benefit *n* 1 aid, assistance, comfort, cure, hand, help, lift, nurture, relief, remedy, succor, support

n 2 account, advantage, applicability, ap-propriateness, aptness, avail, decorum, expediency, fitness, manners, opportun-ism, pertinence, profit, propriety, rele-vance, rightness, service, suitability, use, usefulness, utility

n 3 account, advantage, behalf, better-ment, gain, good, happiness, interest, prosperity, sake, welfare, well-being

v 1 advance, gain, improve, profit, reward

v 2 experience, have, partake, profit, touch, use

v 3 abet, advance, aid, ameliorate, amend, assist, avail, better, boost, culti-vate, do for, ease, egg on, encourage, enhance, forward, foster, further, help, improve, nurture, prefer, promote, rev, serve, spur on, support

benevolence *n* boon, contribution, dona-tion, favor, gift, grant, largess, present

benevolent *adj* 1 big, chivalrous, consider-ate, generous, grandiose, lofty, magnani-mous, noble

adj 2 altruistic, bountiful, caring, charita-ble, Christian, compassionate, generous, giving, good, humane, humanitarian, kind, lenient, merciful, philanthropic, tender

benign *adj* 1 amiable, genial, kind, kindly, mild, non-malignant

adj 2 harmless, innocent, innocuous, in-offensive, mild, naive, pure, safe, unof-fending, unoffensive

bent *adj* 1 arched, bowed, curved, curvilin-ear, flexed, rounded, unstraight

adj 2 dedicated, determined, committed, fixed, intentional, purposeful, resolute, resolved, set, tenacious

n 1 ambition, design, goal, intent, inten-tion, meaning, objective, plan, purpose

n 2 disposition, fancy, fondness, idea, inclination, liking, mind, notion, plea-sure, propensity, yen

n 3 brains, brilliance, faculty, flair, ge-nius, gift, head, intelligence, knack, mind, nose, prowess, talent

n 4 bias, drift, habit, inclination, leaning, partiality, penchant, predilection, prefer-ence, priority, proclivity, propensity, tal-ent, taste, tendency

bequeath *v* 1 bestow, devise, impart, leave, will

v 2 endow, give, remember, reward, tip

v 3 accord, adduce, award, bestow, con-cede, confer, contribute, deliver, devote, donate, endow, extend, fund, give, give away, grant, hand down, hand out, im-part, offer, pose, present, proffer, provide, supply, tender, volunteer

bequest *n* award, endowment, gift, grant, reward, scholarship

berate *v* 1 lambaste, rebuke, scold

v 2 admonish, blame, censure, chide, con-demn, disapprove, lay into, punish, re-buke, reprimand, reproach, reprove, scold, warn

v 3 bawl out, bellow, chew out, mock, rail, rant, rave, revile, roar, scold, tell off, tongue-lash, upbraid, yell

v 4 see: SCOLD *v*

bereft *adj* deprived, destitute, lacking, wanting

beret *n* cap, derby, hat, helmet

berserk *adj* amok, crazy, frenzied, mania-cal, out of control, rushed about, violent

berth *n* 1 bed, bunk, cot, couch, cradle, crib, stall

n 2 billet, housing, quarters, shelter, space

beseech *v* appeal, ask, beg, conjure, crave, desire, entreat, grovel, implore, indicate, invoke, plead, pray, request, seek, solicit, supplicate, whine

beset *v* 1 ambush, assail, assault, attack, invade, raid, storm, strike, trap, waylay

v 2 beleaguer, besiege, invest, surround

beside *prep* adjacent to, around, at, atop, by, near, on

besides *adv* see: ALSO *adv*

besiege *v* beleaguer, beset, invest, surround

besmirch *v* see: DEFAME *v* 1

bespeak *v* arrange, book, engage, organize, plan, program, reserve, schedule, slate

best *adj* 1 optimum, prime, select, superi-or, top

adj 2 biggest, finest, greatest, largest, max-imum, most, number one, prime, select, superior, top, top-notch

adj 3 see: SUPERB *adj* 4

n choice, elite, favorite, finest, optimum, pick, pride, select

v 1 defeat, down, outdo, outmaneuver, outsmart, outwit

v 2 conquer, defeat, master, overcome, prevail, succeed, triumph, win

v 3 beat, better, cap, dwarf, eclipse, exceed, excel, go beyond, outdo, outgo, outshine, outstrip, overshadow, pass, surpass, top, transcend

bestow *v* 1 deluge, lavish, overwhelm, shower

v 2 bequeath, devise, impart, leave, will

v 3 apply, employ, exercise, exploit, handle, use, utilize

v 4 baptize, call, christen, confer, designate, dub, entitle, name, nickname, tag, term, title

v 5 accord, adduce, award, bequeath, concede, confer, contribute, deliver, devote, donate, endow, extend, fund, give, give away, grant, hand down, hand out, impart, offer, pose, present, proffer, provide, supply, tender, volunteer

best-selling *adj* popular, favorite, hot

bet *n* chance, fortune, gamble, hazard, luck, risk, stake

v attempt, chance, dare, gamble, hazard, play, risk, speculate, stake, venture, wager

betray *v* cross, divulge, double cross, reveal, sell out

betrayal *n* 1 deception, perfidy, subversion, treachery, trickery

n 2 insurrection, mutiny, revolt, sedition, subversion, treason, uprising

betrayer *n* accuser, double-crosser, fink, informer, reptile, snake, sneak, stooge, traitor

betrothal *n* engagement

betrothed *adj* committed, engaged, pledged, promised

better *adj* 1 favored, partial, preferential, select, special

adj 2 advantageous, desirable, enjoyable, preferable, superior, worthier, worthwhile

v 1 correct, improve, reform, modify, rehabilitate

v 2 elevate, enhance, enrich, fortify, improve, strengthen

v 3 beat, best, cap, dwarf, eclipse, exceed, excel, go beyond, outdo, outgo, outshine, outstrip, overshadow, pass, surpass, top, transcend

v 4 abet, advance, aid, ameliorate, amend, assist, avail, benefit, boost, cultivate, do for, ease, egg on, encourage,

enhance, forward, foster, further, help, improve, nurture, prefer, promote, rev, serve, spur on, support

betterment *n* 1 addition, advancement, advantage, enhancement, gain, growth, improvement, plus

n 2 account, advantage, behalf, benefit, gain, good, happiness, interest, prosperity, sake, welfare, well-being

n 3 acceleration, achievement, advance, advancement, breakthrough, furtherance, growth, headway, improvement, increment, pickup, proficiency, progress, promotion, strengthening, upgrade

between *prep* amidst, among, atwixt, betwixt, halfway to, mid, midway, 'twixt

betwixt *prep* amidst, among, atwixt, between, halfway to, mid, midway, 'twixt

bevy *n* assembly, association, band, brood, bunch, camp, clique, cluster, collection, covey, crew, flock, group, organization, party, team, unit

beware *v* look out for, mind, take caution, watch

bewilder *v* 1 amaze, befog, boggle, confound, confuse, daze, perplex, puzzle, stumble, stump

v 2 befuddle, confuse, daze, distract, dizzy, trick, embarrass, fluster, mix up, muddle, rattle, ruffle, unglue, unhinge

v 3 aggravate, baffle, balk, circumvent, confuse, dash, elude, foil, frustrate, hamper, impede, negate, nullify, perplex, thwart

bewildered *adj* confused, foggy, mixed up

bewilderment *n* 1 befuddlement, complication, confusion, perplexity

n 2 amazement, astonishment, awe, shock, surprise, wonder

bewitch *v* 1 allure, attract, bedevil, beguile, captivate, charm, conjure, delight, draw, enchant, enthrall, fascinate, lure, magnetize, mesmerize, tempt, wile

bewitching *adj* see: FASCINATING *adj* 2

bewitchment *n* enchantment, incantation, magic, occultism, sorcery, spell, voodoo, witchcraft, wizardry

beyond *adv* 1 additionally, farther, further, furthermore

adv 2 farther than, outside, past, yonder

adv 3 ahead, before, forward, in front, onward

adv 4 after, ensuing, following, subsequent, succeeding, successive

bias *n* 1 favoritism, nepotism, patronage

n 2 discrimination, prejudice, bigotry,

chauvinism, intolerance, parochialism, partiality, provincialism, racism, sexism

n 3 see: INCLINATION *n* 2

n 4 see: OPINION *n* 8

v 1 color, distort, embellish, exaggerate, influence, slant

v 2 corrupt, distort, misrepresent, pervert, skew, slant, warp

v 3 bend, brainwash, compel, convert, indoctrinate, influence, predispose, prejudice, proselytize, slant, sway

biased *adj* 1 emotional, partial, predisposed, prejudiced, subjective

adj 2 inequitable, partial, uneven, unfair, unjust, unrighteous, wrongful

Bible *n* gospel, manual, scripture

biblical *adj* scriptural

bibliotheca *n* archives, athenaeum, books, library

bibulate *v* booze, consume, drink, gulp, guzzle, imbibe, nip, partake, polish off, put away, put down, sample, savor, sip, suck, swig, swill, taste

bicker *v* altercate, argue, battle, brawl, clash, conflict, dispute, engage, equivocate, feud, fight, fray, haggle, hassle, quarrel, quibble, row, scrap, spar, squabble, wrangle

bid *n* expectation, hope, inducement, invitation, motion, offer, proffer, proposal, proposition, recommendation, request, suggestion

v 1 ask, encourage, invite, request, solicit

v 2 charge, claim, command, demand, direct, enjoin, instruct, order

v 3 counsel, endorse, offer, pose, present, proffer, propose, proposition, put forth, recommend, suggest, urge

bidding *n* see: COMMAND *n* 3

bide *v* abide, await, linger, loiter, remain, stay, stick around, tarry, wait

big *adj* 1 benevolent, chivalrous, considerate, generous, grandiose, lofty, magnanimous, noble

adj 2 ample, capacious, comfortable, commodious, open, roomy, spacious, vast, wide

adj 3 extra-large, fat, grand, great, huge, husky, immense, jumbo, large, obese, oversize, tremendous

adj 4 large, ample, considerable, enormous, extensive, grand, hefty, huge, jumbo, major, sizable, spacious, vast

biggest *adj* best, finest, greatest, largest, maximum, most, number one, prime, select, superior, top, top-notch

bigot *n* racist, segregationist, supremacist

bigotry *n* bias, chauvinism, discrimination, intolerance, parochialism, partiality, prejudice, provincialism, racism, sexism

bike *v* pedal, propel, push

bilge *n* baloney, bosh, bull, bunk, drivel, fiddlesticks, foolishness, junk, malarkey, nonsense, nothing, poppycock, rot, schlock, rubbish, silliness, trivia

bilk *v* see: CHEAT *v* 1

bill *n* 1 receipt

n 2 charge, check, debt, fee, invoice, note, tab

n 3 beak, muzzle, nib, nose, proboscis, prow, snout, trunk

n 4 bonus, charge, commission, compensation, consideration, earnings, fee, gross, income, pay, revenue, salary, stipend, wage

v charge, debit, dun, invoice, notice, render, solicit

billet *n* berth, housing, quarters, shelter, space

bills *n* assets, capital, cash, coffers, currency, dinero, dollars, estate, funds, goods, income, lucre, means, money, notes, pelf, pesos, property, resources, revenue, riches, rubles, shekels, sum, wealth

bind *n* box, corner, difficulty, dilemma, fix, impasse, jam, mess, pinch, plight, predicament, quandary, scrape, spot, trap, trouble

v 1 commit, contract, engage, pledge

v 2 chain, fasten, link, shackle

v 3 affix, attach, clip, connect, fasten, fix, rivet, weld

v 4 band, belt, corset, fasten, gird, girdle, lash, strap, tie

v 5 attach, bond, cord, fasten, hitch, join, link, marry, tether, tie, tie up

v 6 affix, bond, cement, fasten, fuse, glue, join, lock, paste, seal, secure, stick, unite

v 7 clog, confine, curb, fetter, hamper, handcuff, hold, leash, limit, restrain, restrict, shackle, tie, tie up

binder *n* 1 capsule, case, casing, cover, envelope, holder, sheath, skin, wrapper

n 2 file, record, folder, portfolio

binding *adj* committed, compelling, obligatory, unalterable

binge *n* bash, bender, do, fling, orgy, party, spree

binoculars *n* eye, field glass, glass, lens, magnifying glass, microscope, mirror, periscope, scope, spyglass, telescope

biographer *n* author, authoress, creator, dramatist, essayist, journalist, novelist, playwright, reporter, screenwriter, writer

biography *n* autobiography, compendium, profile, résumé, sketch, vita

birch *n* cane, club, pole, rod, shaft, staff, stake, stave, stick

v see: BATTER *v*

bird *n* bum, cad, fink, heel, jerk, rat, turkey

birth *n* 1 creation, conception, formulation, genesis, procreation

n 2 creation, fountain, genesis, origin, parent, root, source

n 3 beginning, debut, delivery, inception, kindling, onset, outset, start

v bear, bring forth, deliver

birthday *n* anniversary

birthright *n* 1 endowment, entitlement, estate, heritage, inheritance, legacy, patrimony

n 2 advantage, claim, edge, enablement, perquisite, prerogative, privilege, right, title

bisect *v* crisscross, cross, impede, intersect

bisexual *n* gay, homosexual, lesbian

bistro *n* bar, cabaret, cafe, casino, discothèque, nightclub

bit *n* 1 chip, dent, flake, fragment, mark, piece

n 2 clipping, cut, division, lot, member, parcel, part, piece, portion, sample, section, segment, slice

n 3 dab, end, fragment, iota, minutia, mite, morsel, particle, piece, pinch, portion, scrap, shred, speck, spot, strip, tidbit, trifle

bite *v* 1 burn, smart, sting

v 2 chew, crunch, gnaw, gulp, guzzle, munch, nibble, rend, wolf

n snack, morsel, nip, piece, quick meal

biting *adj* 1 caustic, cutting, incisive, penetrating, pointed, trenchant

adj 2 acerbic, acid, curt, dry, pungent, sharp, sour, tart

adj 3 acerbic, acrid, bitter, caustic, corrosive, critical, pungent, sarcastic

adj 4 hot, nippy, pungent, seasoned, sharp, spicy, tangy, tart

bitter *adj* 1 acerbic, acrid, biting, caustic, corrosive, critical, pungent, sarcastic

adj 2 alienated, angry, emotional, hurt, jealous, offended, provoked, resentful

adj 3 brutal, cruel, fierce, hard, harsh, inclement, intemperate, pitiless, rigorous, rough, rugged, severe, stern, strong, unkind, violent

bitterness *n see:* HATE *n*

bittersweet *adj* maudlin, poignant, sad, sentimental, sorrowful

bivouac *v* camp, dwell, lodge, nest, quarter, station

n barracks

bizarre *adj* 1 fantastic

adj 2 amazing, astounding, remarkable, strange

adj 3 bohemian, offbeat, unconventional, unorthodox

adj 4 eerie, ghostly, incredible, metaphysical, mystical, odd, ominous, spooky, strange, supernatural, uncanny, unearthly, weird

adj 5 aberrant, eccentric, erratic, odd, oddball, outlandish, peculiar, quaint, queer, singular, strange, uncanny, unconventional, unusual, weird

adj 6 absurd, balmy, crazy, emotional, foolish, frivolous, goofy, illogical, impossible, inane, insane, irrational, loony, lunatic, mad, muddled, nuts, preposterous, ridiculous, silly, touched, wacky, zany

blab *v* 1 divulge, gossip, inform, tell, reveal

v 2 babble, blurt, burble, chatter, gossip, murmur, prattle, talk, tattle

black *adj* 1 ebony, jet, sable

adj 2 charcoal, dark, pitch-black, shadowy

adj 3 dark, dingy, dirty, filthy, foul, grimy, grubby, mucky, murky, polluted, seedy, shabby, sooty, squalid, stained, unclean, unlit, unwashed

adj 4 see: GLOOMY *adj* 5

blackball *v* 1 boycott, cut, ignore, ostracize, rebuff, snub, spurn

v 2 bar, exclude, banish, cut, debar, dismiss, eliminate, except, ignore, leave out, omit, suspend

blacken *v see:* DEFAME *v* 1

blackjack *n* bat, boomerang, club, cudgel, cue, mallet, nightstick, stave, stick

blade *n* cutlass, dagger, knife, pocketknife, rapier, saber, scimitar, switchblade, sword

blah *adj* boring, commonplace, dim, dreary, dull, flat, humdrum, monotonous, ordinary, pedestrian, stodgy, tedious, tiresome

blamable *adj* condemned, convicted, culpable, guilty, responsible

blame *n* accountability, burden, culpability, fault, guilt, onus, responsibility, shame, stigma

v 1 accuse, charge, complain, condemn, criticize, fault, indict, reproach

v 2 see: BERATE *v* 2

v 3 see: IMPLICATE *v*

blameless *adj* commendable, exemplary,

exonerated, guiltless, innocent, irreproachable, pure, righteous, virtuous

blameworthy *adj* criminal, culpable, felonious, guilty, remiss, reprehensible

blanch *v* 1 fade, pale, whiten

v 2 cringe, flinch, jump, recoil, shrink,
start, startle, wince

blanched *adj* ashen, ashy, colorless, pale,
pallid, sallow, sickly, sooty, wan, waxen,
yellow

bland *adj* 1 banal, dull, flat, innocuous,
insipid, tasteless, unexciting

adj 2 balmy, faint, gentle, mild, pleasant,
smooth, soft, weak

adj 3 arid, bleak, boring, colorless, dead,
desolate, drab, dreary, dull, flat, lackluster, lifeless, lusterless, monotonous,
muted, somber, trite, unexciting, uninteresting

blandishment *n* adulation

blank *adj* bare, dull, empty, lifeless, unfilled

n cavity, crack, depression, emptiness,
gap, hole, hollow, nook, opening, space,
void

blanket *adj* comprehensive, expansive, extensive, sweeping, universal

n comforter, cover, quilt, warmer

blare *n* 1 bang, blast, boom, discharge,
explosion, noise, pop, report, roar

n 2 bark, bellow, holler, roar, scream,
shout, shriek, thunder, yell

n 3 see: EXHIBITION *n*

v 1 blaze, burn, flame, flare, glare, glow,
ignite, redden

v 2 bark, bellow, call, cry, holler, howl,
roar, scream, screech, shout, shriek,
shrill, squeal, thunder, wail, yell

blasé *adj* see: INDIFFERENT *adj* 4

blasphemous *adj* disrespectful, heretical,
irreverent, sacrilegious

blasphemy *n* 1 desecration, heresy, impiety, irreverence, sacrilege, violation

n 2 abomination, curse word, expletive,
imprecation, obscenity, profanity, swearing

blast *n* 1 bang, blare, boom, discharge,
explosion, noise, pop, report, roar

n 2 blizzard, blow, gale, gust, hurricane,
northeaster, snowstorm, squall, storm,
tempest, typhoon, wind

n 3 admonishment, admonition, chewing
out, chiding, criticism, denunciation, diatribe, harangue, hassle, libel, outburst,
rap, rebuke, reprimand, reproach, reproof, scolding, slander, tirade

v 1 blight, dash, decompose, nip, wither

v 2 thrash, wallop, beat, belittle, clobber,

conquer, cream, defeat, dust, lambaste,
lick, overrun, overwhelm, rout, shellac,
smear, whip

blatant *adj* 1 arrant, barefaced, brassy,
brazen, extreme, impudent, notorious,
obtrusive, shameless, unabashed

adj 2 see: NOISY *adj*

adj 3 see: OSTENTATIOUS *adj* 1

blaze *n* 1 fire

n 2 eruption, flare-up, outburst

n 3 light

v 1 blare, burn, flame, flare, glare, glow,
ignite, redden

v 2 advertise, announce, broadcast, circulate, declare, disperse, disseminate, proclaim, promulgate, publish

blazing *adj* ablaze, afire, aflame, aglow,
alight, burning, conflagrant, fiery, flaming, glowing

bleak *adj* 1 bare, barren, desolate, dismal,
gaunt, grim

adj 2 arid, bland, boring, colorless, dead,
desolate, drab, dreary, dull, flat, lackluster, lifeless, lusterless, monotonous,
muted, somber, trite, unexciting, uninteresting

adj 3 see: GLOOMY *adj* 5

bleary *adj* ambiguous, confused, fuzzy,
hazy, misty, mixed up, nebulous, unclear

n 1 blot, blur, smear, smudge, spot, stain

n 2 defect, failing, fault, flaw, imperfection, scar, shortcoming, weakness

v abuse, damage, hamper, harm, hurt,
impair, injure, mar, obstruct, ruin, sabotage, scuttle, spoil, tarnish, vandalize

blend *n* 1 combination, fusion, intermingling, joining, merging, mixture, union

n 2 brew, combination, composite, compound, concoction, ferment, mix, mixture

v 1 beat, mingle, mix, stir, toss, whip

v 2 arrange, combine, compound, concoct, harmonize, integrate, make one, orchestrate, synthesize, unify

v 3 amalgamate, band, coalesce, combine,
compound, consolidate, fuse, intermingle, league, lump, meld, merge, mingle,
mix, unify, unite

v 4 associate, bond, coalesce, combine,
compound, connect, couple, fasten, fuse,
join, link, marry, mate, meet, merge,
pair, unite, wed

v 5 shade

bless *v* anoint, baptize, consecrate, dedicate, devote, enshrine, exalt, hallow, purify, sanctify

blessed *adj* 1 glorious, golden, great, precious, splendid, superb

adj 2 celestial, consecrated, divine, godly, hallowed, holy, pure, sacred, sanctified, spiritual

blessing *n* 1 benediction

n 2 bonanza, boon, fortune, gain, godsend, luck, miracle, serendipity, stroke of luck, windfall

blight *n* affliction, impediment, pestilence, scourge

v blast, dash, decompose, nip, wither

blimp *n* airship, balloon, dirigible

blind *adj* 1 conscientious, loyal, meticulous, religious, strict, zealous

adj 2 sightless, unsighted, visionless

n 1 decoy

n 2 shade

v 1 dazzle

v 2 prevent seeing

blink *v* flash, flicker, glimmer, twinkle, wink

blip *n* catch, glitch, gotcha, hangup, hitch, showstopper, slip, snag

bliss *n* delight, ecstasy, Eden, elation, enchantment, heaven, joy, nirvana, paradise, pleasure, rapture, rhapsody

blister *n* fester, inflammation, lesion, sore, swelling, welt

v bubble, fester, ulcerate

blistering *adj* baking, boiling, broiling, burning, fiery, hot, scalding, scorching, sizzling, sultry, sweltering, torrid

blithe *adj* cheerful, cheery, lightsome, merry, sunny

blitz *n* assault, attack, bombardment, onslaught, raid, strike

v bomb, bombard, cannonade, shell

blizzard *n* blast, blow, gale, gust, hurricane, squall, storm, tempest, typhoon, wind

bloat *v* see: EXPAND *v* 4

bloated *adj* distended, inflated, puffy, swollen, tumescent, tumid, turgid

blob *n* bead, bubble, drib, drop, droplet, globule, lump, sphere

bloc *n* affiliation, alliance, association, axis, coalition, concord, confederation, consolidation, faction, federation, joint venture, league, merger, organization, partnership, relationship, treaty, union

block *n* 1 chunk, plank, slab

n 2 check, curb, hangup, inhibition, repression, restraint, reticence

n 3 bar, barricade, barrier, blockade, fence, obstacle, roadblock, stop, wall

v 1 close, obstruct, occlude, plug, shut, stop

v 2 catch, cut off, detain, hinder, intercept, obstruct, stop

v 3 arrest, check, freeze, halt, impede, interrupt, stall, stay, stop

v 4 bar, brake, choke, clog, dam, deter, detract, encumber, frustrate, halt, hamper, hesitate, hinder, impair, impede, inhibit, jam, obstruct, prevent, repress, restrain, retard, slow, stay, stop, stop up, throttle

blockade *n* 1 attack, attempt, bout, campaign, offensive, siege

n 2 bar, barricade, barrier, block, fence, obstacle, roadblock, stop, wall

blockage *n* 1 ban, boycott, curtailment, embargo, prohibition, restriction, stoppage

n 2 bottleneck, catch, flaw, hitch, impediment, jam, obstacle, obstruction, snag

blockhead *n* see: IDIOT *n*

blond *adj* fair, flaxen, light

blood *n* 1 gore

n 2 plasma, sap, serum

n 3 descent, kinship, lineage, relationship, stock

n 4 see: ANCESTRY *n*

bloodbath *n* bloodshed, butchery, carnage, extermination, genocide, holocaust, killing, massacre, pogrom, shambles, slaughter

bloodless *adj* anemic, gaunt, haggard, lifeless, pale, pallid, passionless, spiritless, watery, weak

bloodline *n* see: ANCESTRY *n*

bloodshed *n* bloodbath, butchery, carnage, extermination, genocide, holocaust, killing, massacre, pogrom, shambles, slaughter

bloodsucker *n* leech, sucker, vampire

bloom *v* 1 blossom, bud, develop, ferment, flourish, flower, germinate, grow, sprout

v 2 advance, ascend, climb, develop, do well, excel, expand, flourish, flower, get ahead, grow, improve, progress, prosper, rise, strive, survive, thrive

n blossom

blooper *n* accident, blunder, bungle, confusion, error, faux pas, foul-up, lapse, misreading, mistake, misunderstanding, slip, slip-up

blossom *v* bloom, bud, develop, ferment, flourish, flower, germinate, grow, sprout

n bloom

blot *n* blemish, blur, smear, smudge, spot, stain

v 1 smear, smudge, soil, stain, stigmatize

v 2 absorb, consume, engross, engulf, occupy, soak up

blow *n* 1 boot, kick, stroke

n 2 jerk, jolt, jump, shock, start, surprise

n 3 disturbance, jolt, shock, trauma, upheaval, upset

n 4 air, breath, breeze, current, draft,
gust, puff, wind

n 5 adversity, affliction, burden, calamity,
difficulty, distress, hardship, mischance,
misfortune, mishap, relapse, reversal, setback, suffering, tragedy, trouble

n 6 blast, blizzard, gale, gust, hurricane,
northeaster, snowstorm, squall, storm,
tempest, typhoon, wind

n 7 bang, box, bump, chop, clap, conk,
crack, crash, cuff, hit, impact, jar, jolt,
knock, lick, punch, rap, slap, slug, smash,
smack, swat, swipe, tap, wallop, whack

v 1 blunder, botch, bungle, butcher, damage, err, foul up, goof, hash, hurt, jeopardize, jumble, mess up, queer, ruin, screw
up

v 2 bang, bump, cuff, hit, knock, punch,
strike

bludgeon *v* bang, beat, clobber, club, hit,
pound, strike, whack

blue *adj* 1 aqua, azure, cobalt, indigo,
navy, Prussian, sapphire, turquoise

adj 2 black, bleak, cheerless, dejected,
depressed, desperate, despondent, discouraging, disheartening, distressing,
down, forlorn, gloomy, hopeless, joyless,
melancholy, moody, mournful, oppressive, prostrate, sad, somber, sorry, unhappy

blue-blooded *adj* aristocratic, imperial,
kingly, majestic, noble, regal, royal, stately, well-bred

blue-collar *adj* manual, menial, physical

blueprint *n* 1 chart, diagram, draft, map,
outline, plan, sketch

n 2 design, game plan, plan, project,
proposal, scheme, strategy

n 3 arrangement, method, order, orderliness, outline, pattern, plan, system

v arrange, cast, chart, design, devise,
draft, draw, engineer, fashion, lay out,
map, outline, plan, plot, project, set out,
sketch

blues *n* classical, country, folk, jazz, music,
ragtime, rock-and-roll, soul, swing

bluff *adj* abrupt, blunt, brash, brusque,
cheeky, crusty, curt, flip, flippant, gruff,
harsh, impertinent, impudent, irritable,
nasty, quick, rude, sarcastic, sassy, short,
snippy, snotty, surly, testy, wisenheimer

n cliff, hill, incline, slant, slope, steep
bank

v act, assume, counterfeit, fabricate, fake,
feign, imitate, invent, make believe, play,
pretend, put on, sham

blunder *n* 1 folly, impropriety, indiscretion, mistake, slip

n 2 accident, blooper, bungle, confusion,
error, faux pas, foul-up, lapse, misreading, mistake, misunderstanding, slip,
slip-up

v blow, botch, bungle, butcher, damage,
err, foul up, goof, hash, hurt, jeopardize,
jumble, mess up, queer, ruin, screw up

blunt *adj* 1 abrupt, bluff, brash, brusque,
cheeky, crusty, curt, flip, flippant, gruff,
harsh, impertinent, impudent, irritable,
nasty, quick, rude, sarcastic, sassy, short,
snippy, snotty, surly, testy, wisenheimer

adj 2 see: DUMB *adj* 2

adj 3 see: EXPLICIT *adj* 3

v dull, stupefy, weaken

blur *n* blemish, blot, smear, smudge, spot,
stain

v becloud, bedim, befog, cloud, confuse,
darken, dim, diminish, dull, eclipse, fade,
muddy, obscure, overshadow, pale,
shade, shadow, tarnish

blurt *v* 1 babble, blab, burble, chatter,
gossip, murmur, prattle, talk, tattle

v 2 cackle, cry, ejaculate, exclaim, shout,
spill, sputter, tattle, utter

blush *n* color, fever, flush, glow, warmth

v flush

blustery *adj* squally, stormy, tempestuous,
windy

board *n* 1 body, cabinet, commission, committee, council, directorship

n 2 beam, boom, girder, log, plank, rafter,
spar, support, timber

n 3 desk, secretary, table

v host, house, put up, shelter

boast *v* brag, crow, exult, flaunt, gloat,
revel, show off, strut, vaunt

boastful *adj* proud, smug, triumphant

boat *n* barge, canoe, craft, dory, ferry,
float, kayak, raft, scow, skiff, tender

boats *n* armada, assembly, convoy, fleet,
flotilla, grouping, navy, ships, squadron

bob *n* hairdo

v 1 heave, pitch, rock, roll, sway, swing,
toss

v 2 bound, hop, jaunt, jump, leap, lope,
prance, skip, spring, sprint, trip

bobber *n* float

bobbies *n* authorities, constabulary, cops,
gendarme, highway patrol, military police, police, troopers

bock *n* ale, beer, brew, lager, Pilsner, stout,
suds

bode *v* see: PREDICT *v* 2

bodiless *adj* see: SPIRITUAL *adj* 2

bodily *adj* carnal, corporeal, fleshly

body n 1 cadaver, carcass, corpse, remains, shell, stiff

n 2 board, cabinet, commission, committee, council, directorship

n 3 anatomy, build, figure, form, frame, physique, shape

n 4 band, company, corps, group, outfit, party, troop, troupe

n 5 aggregate, amount, budget, bulk, count, number, quantity, tally, total

n 6 association, club, company, contingent, delegation, fellowship, fraternity, group, guild, organization, society, union

n 7 array, bale, batch, battery, bunch, bundle, clump, cluster, group, lot, pack, parcel, quantity, set

n 8 basis, bulk, core, essence, essentials, gist, heart, import, mass, nucleus, object, staple, substance, volume

bodybuilding n aerobics, calisthenics, exercise, jazzercise, slimnastics, workout

bodyguard n chaperon, companion, escort, guide, retinue, scout

bog v delay, detain, hang up, impede, mire, retard, set back, slacken, slow

n marsh, mire, moor, swamp

boggle v 1 balk, demur, desist, gag

v 2 bewilder, puzzle, amaze, befog, confound, confuse, daze, perplex, stumble, stump

v 3 see: SURPRISE v 2

bogus adj artificial, counterfeit, ersatz, fake, false, imitation, mock, phony, pseudo, sham, simulated, spurious, substitute, unreal

bohemian adj bizarre, offbeat, unconventional, unorthodox

boil v 1 heat, overheat, parboil, seethe, simmer, stew

v 2 agitate, bake, bubble, burn, churn, ferment, foam, fume, roast, seethe, simmer, smolder

v 3 anger, blow up, boil over, brew, bristle, burn, flare up, fume, rage, seethe, simmer, smoke, steam, storm

n abscess, carbuncle, pimple, ulcer

boiling adj baking, blistering, broiling, burning, fiery, hot, scalding, scorching, sizzling, sultry, sweltering, torrid

boisterous adj blatant, clamorous, disturbing, loud, loudmouthed, noisy, obstreperous, raucous, rowdy, tumultuous, vociferous

bold adj 1 adaptive, canny, clever, daring, enterprising, resourceful, venturesome

adj 2 audacious, brave, courageous, daring, dauntless, fearless, gallant, game, gutsy, heroic, intrepid, stalwart, unafraid, undaunted, valiant, valorous

adj 3 see: RUDE adj 3

boldness n 1 bravery, courage, daring, fortitude, heart, heroism, spirit, strength, valor

n 2 arrogance, assurance, audacity, brashness, brass, cheek, chutzpah, condescension, confidence, crust, effrontery, face, gall, haughtiness, insolence, nerve, patronage, presumption, ridicule, sass, stamina, temerity

Bolshevik n communist, comrade, pinko, red

bolster v 1 buoy, cheer, comfort, console, gladden, solace, soothe, support, uplift, upraise

v 2 amplify, encourage, enhance, enhearten, hearten, increase, inspire, reassure, strengthen, support

v 3 bear up, brace, build up, buoy, buttress, carry, fortify, harden, nourish, nurture, prop, reinforce, shore, strengthen, support, sustain, toughen, uphold

bolt n 1 clamp, clasp, deadbolt, lock, padlock

n 2 brad, nut, peg, pin, rivet, spike, staple, stud, weld

n 3 fireball, flash, lightning, thunderbolt

v 1 close, latch, lock, seal, secure, shut, slam

v 2 abscond, break, depart, elude, escape, flee, fly, hightail it, lose, run, sneak away, split

v 3 jump, spring, start, startle

v 4 abscond, defect, depart, exit, fall back, flee, get away, give back, go, leave, move, pull away, pull out, push off, retreat, run along, secede, show off, take off, vacate, withdraw

bomb n 1 bust, disaster, dud, failure, fiasco, flop, turkey

n 2 bombshell, explosive, mine, missile, payload, rocket, rocketry, warhead

v 1 fail, flop, stumble, trip

v 2 blitz, bombard, cannonade, shell

bombard v 1 detonate, discharge, fire, shoot

v 2 blitz, bomb, cannonade, shell

bombardment n assault, attack, blitz, onslaught, raid, strike

bombastic adj 1 chatty, diffuse, garrulous, long-winded, loquacious, redundant, repetitious, superfluous, talkative, verbose, wordy

adj 2 see: FLAMBOYANT adj 2

bombed adj crocked, doped up, drunk, drunken, high, inebriated, intoxicated, juiced, loaded, looped, messed up, plastered, polluted, sloshed, smashed, stoned, tight, tipsy, turned on, wasted, wired

bombshell n bomb, explosive, mine, missile, payload, rocket, rocketry, warhead

bonanza n blessing, boon, fortune, gain, godsend, luck, miracle, serendipity, stroke of luck, windfall

bond n 1 cohesion, connection, fusion, solidarity, togetherness, union

n 2 chain, fetter, handcuff, iron, manacle, shackle, tie

n 3 assurance, commitment, earnest, guarantee, obligation, pawn, pledge, security, surety, token, warrant

n 4 agreement, bargain, compact, contract, convention, covenant, deal, pact, pledge, promise, transaction, treaty, understanding

n 5 see: LIMIT n 1

v 1 adhere, cleave, cling, cohere, hold, join, stick

v 2 attach, bind, cord, fasten, hitch, join, link, marry, tether, tie, tie up

v 3 affix, bind, cement, fasten, fuse, glue, join, lock, paste, seal, secure, stick, unite

v 4 associate, blend, coalesce, combine, compound, connect, couple, fasten, fuse, join, link, marry, mate, meet, merge, pair, unite, wed

bondage n enslavement, imprisonment, indenture, serfdom, servility, servitude, slavery

bonds n holdings, investments, securities, stocks

bone n fossil, remains, skeleton

bonus n 1 incentive, motivation, consideration, goal, inducement, motive, reason, reward, stimulus

n 2 ante, award, booty, cash, commission, dividend, donation, fee, gift, gratuity, largess, money, percentage, perquisite, perk, premium, prize, profit, purse, reward, sharing, stake, stipend, tip, winnings

n 3 see: SALARY n

bony adj angular, emaciated, gaunt, lanky, lean, meager, scraggly, scrawny, skinny, slender, thin

book n 1 account, balance sheet, credit, ledger, score, statement, tab

n 2 correspondence, edition, folio, issue, manuscript, monograph, opus, paperback, printing, publication, text, tome, volume, work, writing

v 1 arrange, bespeak, engage, organize, plan, program, reserve, schedule, slate

v 2 see: ARREST v 2

booking n appointment, engagement, date, listing, reservation, schedule

bookkeeper n accountant, actuary, auditor, comptroller

booklet n gazette, journal, magazine, monthly, periodical, publication, quarterly, weekly

books n archives, athenaeum, library

boom n 1 beam, board, girder, log, plank, rafter, spar, support, timber

n 2 bang, blare, blast, discharge, explosion, noise, pop, report, roar

n 3 bang, clang, clap, crash, resound, roar, rumble, shake, thunder

v 1 blow up, burst, detonate, explode

v 2 chime, clang, peal, resonate, resound, reverberate, ring, sound, toll

v 3 advertise, air, boost, drum up, endorse, pitch, plug, promote, publicize, push, rave, sell, tout

boomerang v backfire, bounce, brush, glance, graze, rebound, ricochet, skim, skip, touch

n bat, blackjack, club, cudgel, cue, mallet, nightstick, stave, stick

booming adj affluent, prosperous, successful, thriving, wealthy

boon n 1 benevolence, contribution, donation, favor, gift, grant, largess, present

n 2 blessing, bonanza, fortune, gain, godsend, luck, miracle, serendipity, stroke of luck, windfall

boor n see: IDIOT n

boorish adj audacious, discourteous, disrespectful, ill-behaved, ill-bred, ill-mannered, impertinent, impolite, insolent, rude, surly, uncalled for, uncivil, uncivilized, uncouth, uncultured, unpolished, unrefined

boost n acclaim, applause, citation, commendation, compliment, eulogy, plaudit, praise, rave, tribute

v 1 hike, increase, jack up, jump, put up, raise, up

v 2 budge, drive, force, impel, nudge, propel, push, shove, thrust

v 3 advertise, air, boom, drum up, endorse, pitch, plug, promote, publicize, push, rave, sell, tout

v 4 amplify, append, augment, build, enlarge, expand, extend, grow, heighten, increase, intensify, magnify, multiply, run up, snowball, supplement, upsurge, wax

v 5 see: HELP v 4

booster n 1 advocate, ally, angel, backer, benefactor, champion, cheerleader, donor, friend, guarantor, helper, ombudsman, partner, patron, promoter, proponent, sponsor, supporter

n 2 injection, inoculation, shot

boot *n* 1 blow, kick, stroke

n 2 brogan, chukka, footwear, moccasin, sandal, shoe, slipper, thong

v ax, bounce, can, discharge, dismiss, drop, fire, impeach, let go, sack, terminate

booty *n* 1 bag, catch, prize, spoils

n 2 bounty, gifts, largess, plenty, plunder, presents, reward

n 3 bounty, fortune, kitty, loot, money, plunder, pot, prize, spoils, swag, treasure, trove

n 4 see: REWARD *n* 4, 8

booze *v* bibulate, consume, drink, gulp, guzzle, imbibe, nip, partake, polish off, put away, put down, sample, savor, sip, swill, suck, swig, taste

n alcohol, drinks, grog, liquor, moonshine, spirits, whiskey

border *n* 1 barrier, boundary, buffer, fence, hedge

n 2 boundary, casing, form, frame, shape

n 3 boundary, bounds, brim, brink, curb, edge, fringe, limits, lip, margin, outskirt, perimeter, periphery, rim, side, skirt, verge

n 4 extreme, extremity, limit, periphery

v approach, bound, define, edge, hem, limit, outline, skirt, verge

bordering *adj* abutting, adjacent, adjoining, alongside, close by, connected, contiguous, juxtaposed, local, near at hand, nearby, neighboring, outlining, regional, touching, verging on

borderline *adj* 1 casual, frivolous, insignificant, light, lightweight, little, marginal, meager, minor, minute, negligible, nonessential, off, outside, petty, remote, secondary, slender, slight, slim, small, tenuous, trivial, unimportant

adj 2 ambiguous, clouded, doubtful, dubious, equivocal, garbled, illogical, inarticulate, incalculable, incoherent, inexplicit, muddled, muffled, murky, obscure, precarious, questionable, shaky, suspect, suspicious, uncertain, unclear, uneasy, unintelligible, unsure, vague, wary

n boundary, bounds, demarcation, periphery

bore *n* caliber, circle, diameter, radius

v 1 auger, drill, pierce, ream, tool

v 2 pall, tire, weary

bored *adj* disgusted, jaded, sick, tired, weary

boredom *n* 1 apathy, dreariness, dullness, ennui, malaise, monotony, tedium

n 2 apathy, depression, doldrums, inertia, languor

boring *adj* 1 dull, formal, pompous, stodgy, stuffy

adj 2 blah, commonplace, dim, dreary, dull, flat, humdrum, monotonous, ordinary, pedestrian, stodgy, tedious, tiresome

adj 3 arid, bland, bleak, colorless, dead, desolate, drab, dreary, dull, flat, lackluster, lifeless, lusterless, monotonous, muted, somber, trite, unexciting, uninteresting

adj 4 see: STALE *adj* 3

borough *n* 1 city, megalopolis, metropolis, municipality, suburb, town

n 2 burgh, community, hamlet, settlement, township, village

borrow *v* 1 hock, mortgage, pawn

v 2 adopt, embrace, foster, subscribe, take on, take up, utilize

bosh *n* see: NONSENSE *n* 2

bosom *n* breast, bust, chest

boss *n* chief, foreman, head, overseer, owner, superior, supervisor

v 1 administer, command, direct, guide, manage, oversee, regulate, steer, supervise

v 2 command, control, direct, dominate, govern, handle, influence, lead, manage, manipulate, order, supervise, sway

bossy *adj* aristocratic, arrogant, authoritarian, authoritative, autocratic, belligerent, despotic, dictatorial, dogmatic, domineering, haughty, imperial, imperious, masterful, militaristic, opinionated, oppressive, overbearing, peremptory, pushy, stubborn

botch *v* blow, blunder, bungle, butcher, damage, err, foul up, goof, hash, hurt, jeopardize, jumble, mess up, queer, ruin, screw up

botching *adj* bungling, goofing, helpless, ill-adapted, ill-suited, ill-timed, improper, inadequate, inappropriate, incapable, incongruous, incorrect, ineligible, inept, malapropos, unable, unbecoming, unbefitting, unequipped, unfit, unqualified, unseemly, unskilled, unsuitable, unsuited

bother *n* 1 annoyance, anxiety, apprehension, care, concern, disquiet, disquietude, doubt, irritation, misgiving, reservation, restlessness, restraint, skepticism, trouble, uneasiness, vexation, worry

n 2 annoyance, conflict, contention, difference, discord, disharmony, dispute, dissension, dissent, dissidence, dissonance, disunity, division, hassle, inconvenience, mischief, nuisance, strife, trouble, variance

n 3 see: ACTIVITY *n* 3

v 1 burden, encroach, impose, intrude, presume, saddle

v 2 afflict, aggrieve, burden, distress, grieve, hurt, injure, pain

v 3 affect, burden, concern, daunt, disturb, faze, intimidate, oppress, upset, worry

v 4 annoy, antagonize, argue, bug, concern, distress, disturb, goad, harass, hassle, inconvenience, irk, irritate, pain, perturb, strain, stress, taunt, trouble, try, upset, worry

v 5 aggravate, anger, annoy, bug, enrage, exasperate, frazzle, gall, grate, hassle, incense, inflame, infuriate, irk, irritate, madden, miff, nettle, outrage, peeve, pester, pique, provoke, rile, upset, vex

v 6 see: ANNOY *v* 1, 2, 3

bothersome *adj* 1 annoying, anxious, chafing, crabby, edgy, fretful, galling, impatient, irritating, jittery, nagging, on edge, restless, touchy, unsettling

adj 2 annoying, glaring, harassing, irksome, irritating, mean, onerous, painful, pesky, troublesome, ugly, unwelcome, vexatious, wicked

bottle *n* bucket, caddy, can, canister, jar, pail, shell, tin, vessel

bottleneck *n* 1 deadlock, draw, hung jury, impasse, stalemate, standoff, standstill, tie

n 2 blockage, catch, flaw, hitch, impediment, jam, obstacle, obstruction, snag

n 3 bar, barrier, crimp, dead end, deadlock, difficulty, encumbrance, hurdle, impasse, impediment, obstacle, obstruction, snag, stumbling block

bottom *n* 1 base, floor, ground, minimum

n 2 ass, backside, base, behind, bucket, buns, butt, buttocks, derrière, end, fanny, hindquarters, posterior, rump, seat, stub, stump, tip, tush

bough *n* branch, limb, twig

boulder *n* detritus, fragments, gravel, pebble, rock, stone

boulevard *n* access, approach, artery, avenue, channel, drag, highway, pass, path, promenade, road, roadway, route, strait, street, thoroughfare, trail, way

bounce *n* elasticity, resilience, spring

v 1 bump, jostle, skip, throw, volley

v 2 backfire, boomerang, brush, glance, graze, rebound, ricochet, skim, skip, touch

v 3 ax, boot, can, discharge, dismiss, drop, fire, impeach, let go, sack, terminate

v 4 reflect

bouncy *adj* 1 elastic, expansive, malleable, plastic, resilient

adj 2 bumpy, craggy, irregular, jagged, jolting, rough, rugged, scraggy, uneven, unsmooth

adj 3 alert, animated, bright, brisk, buoyant, chipper, dashing, dynamic, ebullient, energetic, enthusiastic, exuberant, frisky, frolicsome, gay, jumpy, kinetic, lively, peppy, pert, playful, rousing, scintillating, spirited, sprightly, spry, vivacious

bound *adj* 1 certain, headed for, sure

adj 2 committed, liable, obligated, required

adj 3 apprenticed, indentured

n hop, jump, leap, vault

v 1 confine, cramp, demarcate, limit, restrict

v 2 compass, encircle, enclose, encompass, enfold, envelop, surround

v 3 limit, restrict, scrimp, short, skimp, spare, stint

v 4 approach, border, define, edge, hem, limit, outline, skirt, verge

v 5 bob, hop, jaunt, jump, leap, lope, prance, skip, spring, sprint, trip

boundaries *n* form, framework, outline, pattern, structure

boundary *n* 1 borderline, bounds, demarcation, periphery

n 2 barrier, border, buffer, fence, hedge

n 3 border, casing, frame, form, shape

n 4 circuit, circumference, compass, perimeter, periphery

n 5 extent, field, matter, range, reach, scope, vicinity

n 6 bond, bridle, check, constraint, control, curb, damper, harness, leash, limit, rein, restraint, restriction

n 7 see: EDGE *n* 4

bounded *adj* absolute, agreed, categorical, clear, decided, definite, emphatic, established, exact, finite, fixed, guaranteed, limited, positive, specific, unequivocal, unmistakable, vested

boundless *adj* see: PERPETUAL *adj* 2

bounds *n* 1 borderline, boundary, demarcation, periphery

n 2 see: EDGE *n* 4

bounteous *adj* 1 bountiful, free, generous, handsome, liberal, openhanded, unsparing

adj 2 abounding, abundant, ample, bountiful, copious, enough, galore, generous, liberal, overflowing, plentiful, plenty, prodigal, profuse, teeming

bountiful *adj* 1 bounteous, free, generous, handsome, liberal, openhanded, unsparing

adj 2 abounding, abundant, ample, bounteous, copious, enough, galore, generous, liberal, overflowing, plentiful, plenty, prodigal, profuse, teeming

adj 3 altruistic, benevolent, caring, charitable, Christian, compassionate, generous, giving, good, humane, humanitarian, kind, lenient, merciful, philanthropic, tender

bounty *n* 1 booty, gifts, largess, plenty, plunder, presents, reward

n 2 booty, fortune, kitty, loot, money, plunder, pot, prize, spoils, swag, treasure, trove

n 3 abundance, affluence, comfort, cornucopia, elegance, glut, good fortune, grandeur, luxury, opulence, plenty, prosperity, success, wealth

bouquet *n* 1 aroma, balm, fragrance, incense, perfume, scent, spice

n 2 arrangement, bunch, corsage, flowers

bout *n* 1 attack, attempt, blockade, campaign, offensive, siege

n 2 competition, conflict, contest, event, game, marathon, match, meet, meeting, race, regatta, round robin, run, tournament, tourney

bow *n* 1 curtsy

n 2 address, greeting, honor, nod, recognition, salute

n 3 crown, fore, front, head, prow, stem, top

n 4 arc, arch, bend, coil, crook, curvature, curve, hook, round, spiral

n 5 angle, bend, detour, deviation, double, shift, tack, turn, turning, yaw

v 1 cringe, genuflect, grovel, kneel, kowtow, prostrate, scrape

v 2 bend, droop, duck, lower, slouch, slump, stoop

v 3 angle, arch, bend, curve, flex, ply, round, tilt, tip, turn, twist, vault

v 4 see: YIELD *v* 6

bowed *adj* arched, bent, curved, curvilinear, flexed, rounded, unstraight

bowl *n* amphitheater, arena, coliseum, dome, hippodrome, scene, stadium

box *n* 1 carton, case, chest, container, crate, receptacle

n 2 bind, corner, difficulty, dilemma, fix, impasse, jam, mess, pinch, plight, predic-

ament, quandary, scrape, spot, trap, trouble

n 3 basket, crate, housing

n 4 bang, blow, bump, chop, clap, conk, crack, crash, cuff, hit, impact, jar, jolt, knock, lick, punch, rap, slap, slug, smack, smash, swat, swipe, tap, wallop, whack

v 1 bundle, crate, pack, stow

v 2 clap, cuff, knock, punch, slap, smack, spank, strike, tap, whack

boy *n* 1 child, cub, junior, lad, son, young man

n 2 adolescent, child, juvenile, kid, minor, teenager, teeny-bopper, youngster, youth

boycott *n* 1 dispute, picket, strike, walkout

n 2 ban, blockage, curtailment, embargo, prohibition, restriction, stoppage

v blackball, cut, ignore, ostracize, rebuff, snub, spurn

boyfriend *n* beau, date, escort, fiancé, lover, mate, paramour, suitor

brace *n* base, buttress, column, footing, foundation, prop, shore, stay, support, underpinning

v 1 balance, calm, fix, steady, still

v 2 bear up, bolster, build up, buoy, buttress, carry, fortify, harden, nourish, nurture, prop, reinforce, shore, strengthen, support, sustain, toughen, uphold

bracelet *n* anklet, band, bangle, brooch, earring, jewelry, medal, medallion, necklace, pin, ring

bracket *v* collate, compare, contrast, correlate, equate, liken, match, relate, sort

n 1 parenthesis

n 2 breed, cast, category, class, division, family, genre, genus, group, grouping, ilk, kind, lot, mold, nature, order, persuasion, section, sector, set, sort, species, style, type, variety

brackish *adj* briny, foul, nasty, salty, stagnant, undrinkable

brad *n* bolt, nut, peg, pin, rivet, spike, staple, stud, weld

brag *v* boast, crow, exult, flaunt, gloat, revel, show off, strut, vaunt

brain *n* 1 cerebrum, head, mind, wit

n 2 Einstein, genius, intellect, prodigy, wizard

brainless *adj* absurd, anile, asinine, childish, fatuous, foolish, idiotic, inept, meaningless, mindless, senseless, silly, simple, thoughtless, unintelligent, witless

brains *n* see: TALENT *n* 2

brainwash *v* 1 convert, inculcate, indoctrinate, persuade, preach, proselytize

v 2 bend, bias, compel, convert, indoctrinate, influence, predispose, prejudice, proselytize, slant, sway

brainy *adj* alert, astute, bright, brilliant, clever, discerning, discriminating, educated, insightful, intellectual, intelligent, knowing, knowledgeable, perceptive, quick, sagacious, sage, sharp, smart, swift

brake *v* 1 bar, block, choke, clog, dam, deter, detract, encumber, frustrate, halt, hamper, hesitate, hinder, impair, impede, inhibit, jam, obstruct, prevent, repress, restrain, retard, slow, stay, stop, stop up, throttle

v 2 see: RESTRAIN *v* 5

branch *n* 1 department, division, office, unit

n 2 bypass, detour, deviation, diversion

n 3 arm, division, limb, service, subsidiary, tributary

n 4 addition, adjunct, annex, annexation, extension, section, wing

n 5 bough, limb, twig

n 6 growth, shoot, sprout

brand *n* cachet, emblem, imprint, logo, logotype, mark, seal, stamp, trademark

brash *adj* 1 audacious, bold, brazen, cheeky, daring, disrespectful, forward, fresh, impertinent, impudent, insolent, irreverent, nervy, pert, rude, sassy, saucy

adj 2 see: BLUNT *adj* 1

brashness *n* see: AUDACITY *n*

brass *n* 1 authority, elders, leaders, management, officers

n 2 see: AUDACITY *n*

brassy *adj* arrant, barefaced, blatant, brazen, extreme, impudent, notorious, obtrusive, shameless, unabashed

brat *n* imp

brave *adj* 1 audacious, bold, courageous, daring, dauntless, fearless, gallant, game, gutsy, heroic, intrepid, stalwart, unafraid, undaunted, valiant, valorous

adj 2 see: MASCULINE *adj*

v challenge, confront, dare, defy, face, mutiny, rebel, resist

bravery *n* boldness, courage, daring, fortitude, heart, heroism, spirit, strength, valor

brawl *n* 1 altercation, argument, battle, challenge, combat, controversy, disagreement, discord, dispute, feud, fight, fracas, fray, hassle, melee, quarrel, rancor, rift, row, ruckus, scrap, scuffle, skirmish, spat, squabble, struggle, tiff, war

n 2 see: CLASH *n* 2

v see: QUARREL *v*

brawling *adj* bellicose, difficult, feisty, quarrelsome, scrappy, spirited

brawn *n* see: VIGOR *n* 3

brawny *adj* athletic, burly, husky, massive, muscular, ponderous, powerful, robust, stocky, stout, strapping, strong

brazen *adj* 1 certain, cocksure, convinced, confident, positive, sure

adj 2 arrant, barefaced, blatant, brassy, extreme, impudent, notorious, obtrusive, shameless, unabashed

adj 3 audacious, bold, brash, cheeky, daring, disrespectful, forward, fresh, impudent, impertinent, insolent, irreverent, nervy, pert, rude, sassy, saucy

adj 4 see: OSTENTATIOUS *adj* 1

breach *n* 1 disclosure, leak, revelation

n 2 default, infraction, misdemeanor, trespass, violation

n 3 break, crack, fracture, gap, opening, space, split

v see: SEPARATE *v* 7

bread *n* 1 buck, cash, dollar, dough, money, moolah

n 2 breakfast, brunch, chow, cuisine, diet, dinner, dish, edibles, entree, fare, food, grub, lunch, meals, nosh, nutrition, provisions, rations, snack, supper, victuals, vittles

breadth *n* depth, dimensions, range, scope, span, width

break *n* 1 cavity, puncture, slot

n 2 breach, crack, fracture, gap, opening, space, split

n 3 delay, distraction, disturbance, diversion, holdup, interference, interruption, pause

n 4 disagreement, dissension, fight, misunderstanding, quarrel, rift, separation, spat

n 5 breath, breather, breathing space, intermission, pause, reprieve, respite, rest

n 6 cessation, delay, gap, interim, interval, lapse, lull, pause, stop

n 7 chance, crack, gap, occasion, opening, opportunity, shot, show, stroke of luck, time

v 1 break down, collapse, come apart, snap

v 2 chip, crack, fracture, gap, sever, smash, split

v 3 bankrupt, bust, decay, do in, fold up, impoverish, ruin

v 4 bump, bust, degrade, demerit, demote, downgrade, put down, reduce

v 5 confound, confute, contend, contradict, deny, disprove, dispute, rebut, refute *v* 6 burst, erupt, explode, fragment, rupture, shatter, smash, smatter, splinter

v 7 abscond, bolt, depart, elude, escape, flee, fly, hightail it, lose, run, sneak away, split

v 8 see: OCCUR *v* 2

breakable *adj* 1 brittle, crisp, crumbly, crunchy, fragile

adj 2 decrepit, delicate, dilapidated, feeble, flimsy, fragile, frail, jerry-built, jury-rigged, puny, Rube Goldberg, shoddy, sickly, thin, tinny, unsound, worn-out

breakdown *n* catastrophe, crash, crisis, death, destruction, doom, failure, finish, ruin

breaker *n* 1 ripple, roller, swell, wave, whitecap

n 2 barrier, cape, harbor, head, jetty, neck, point, sea wall

breakfast *n* bread, brunch, chow, cuisine, diet, dinner, dish, edibles, entree, fare, food, grub, lunch, meals, nosh, nutrition, provisions, rations, snack, supper, victuals, vittles

breakneck *adj* 1 expeditious, explosive, fast, fleet, hasty, impulsive, instant, lightning, mercurial, meteoric, precipitous, quick, rapid, spectacular, speedy, sudden, swift

adj 2 see: HAZARDOUS *adj* 1

breakout *n* escape, flight, getaway, lam, slip

breakthrough *n* 1 creation, innovation, invention

n 2 disclosure, discovery, exposition, find, revelation, unearthing

n 3 acceleration, achievement, advance, advancement, betterment, furtherance, growth, headway, improvement, increment, pickup, proficiency, progress, promotion, strengthening, upgrade

breast *n* 1 bosom, bust, chest

n 2 nipple, teat, udder

breath *n* 1 break, breather, breathing space, intermission, pause, reprieve, respite, rest

n 2 air, blow, breeze, current, draft, gust, puff, wind

n 3 clue, dash, glimmer, hint, insinuation, lick, shade, smell, smidgen, spice, sprinkling, suggestion, suspicion, tinge, tip, touch, trace, trifle, whiff, whisper, wisp

n 4 air, breathing, inhalation

breathe *v* 1 confide, divulge, share, tell, whisper

v 2 exhale, gasp, inhale

breather *n* break, breath, breathing space, intermission, pause, reprieve, respite, rest

breathing *n* air, breath, inhalation

breathless *adj* 1 gasping, panting, winded

adj 2 anxious, ardent, avid, desirous, eager, enthusiastic, excited, fain, impatient, impetuous, keen, passionate, raring, zealous

breathtaking *adj* 1 arousing, awesome, exciting, magnificent, stimulating, stirring, stunning

adj 2 alluring, attractive, beautiful, comely, cute, fair, fine, foxy, gorgeous, lovely, luscious, magnificent, pretty, shapely, stunning

breed *n* 1 clan, class, family, household, people, race, relatives, stock, tribe

n 2 bracket, cast, category, class, division, family, genre, genus, group, grouping, ilk, kind, lot, mold, nature, order, persuasion, section, sector, set, sort, species, style, type, variety

v see: BEGET *v*

breeding *n* 1 background, culture, development, education, environment, experience, past, schooling, training, upbringing

n 2 gentility

breeze *n* 1 cinch, dash, ease, snap, waltz, zip

n 2 air, blow, breath, current, draft, gust, puff, wind

breezy *adj* airy, brisk, drafty, gusty, lofty, open, windy

brevity *n* abruptness, briefness, conciseness, curtness, quickness, shortness, transience

brew *n* 1 blend, combination, composite, compound, concoction, ferment, mix, mixture

n 2 ale, beer, bock, lager, Pilsner, stout, suds

v 1 concoct, construe, contrive, create, devise, engineer, fabricate, formulate, hatch, invent, make up, plot, scheme

v 2 anger, blow up, boil, boil over, bristle, burn, flare up, fume, rage, seethe, simmer, smoke, steam, storm

bribe *n* payment, payoff, payola, ransom

v buy

bric-a-brac *n* antique, curio, curiosity, novelty, objet d'art, oddity, rarity, treasure, wonder

bride *n* cohabitant, consort, mate, spouse, squaw, wife, woman

bridegroom *n* groom, hubby, husband, man, master, mate, mister, spouse

bridge *n* overpass, trestle, viaduct

bridle n 1 check, cord, leash, restraint, rope, tether

n 2 bond, boundary, check, constraint, control, curb, damper, harness, leash, limit, rein, restraint, restriction

v check, constrain, control, crimp, curb, hold back, hold down, inhibit, leash, rein, restrain, restrict, withhold

brief adj 1 crude, cursory, hasty, rough, shallow, sketchy, superficial, uncritical

adj 2 ephemeral, fleeting, impermanent, momentary, passing, short, temporary, transient, transitory, volatile

adj 3 abbreviated, compressed, concise, crisp, curt, laconic, pithy, short, succinct, terse, to the point

adj 4 fleeting, passing, short, swift, transient

n abridgement, abstract, compendium, condensation, digest, essence, example, outline, review, sketch, summary, syllabus, synopsis

v 1 analyze, condense, evaluate, outline, retrace, review, study, summarize, synopsize, update

v 2 communicate, convey, declare, describe, disclose, divulge, explain, impart, inform, narrate, orate, portray, read, recite, recount, relate, report, retell, reveal, share, state, tattle, tell, transmit

briefing n beginning, commencement, debut, inauguration, induction, initiation, unveiling

briefness n abruptness, brevity, conciseness, curtness, quickness, shortness, transience

brig n see: JAIL n

brigade n 1 army, battalion, company, force, gang, men, power, soldiers, troops

n 2 airborne, army, battalion, cavalry, company, footmen, guard, horsemen, infantry, legion, marines, militia, minutemen, paratroops, platoon, reserve, storm troopers

brigand n see: CROOK n 2

bright adj 1 balmy, clear, fair, pleasant, serene

adj 2 agreeable, fine, good, nice, pleasant, sunny

adj 3 advanced, gifted, intelligent, precocious, promising, talented

adj 4 auspicious, confident, favorable, hopeful, promising, rosy, sunny, utopian

adj 5 contemporary, fresh, high-tech, modern, modernistic, new, novel, recent, up-to-date

adj 6 beaming, brilliant, burnished, emitting, glistening, glossy, lucid, luminous, lustrous, polished, radiant, shining, shiny

adj 7 alert, astute, brainy, brilliant, clever, discerning, discriminating, educated, insightful, intellectual, intelligent, knowing, knowledgeable, perceptive, quick, sagacious, sage, sharp, smart, swift

adj 8 see: LIVELY adj 8

adj 9 see: MERRY adj 2

brighten v 1 glow, illuminate, irradiate, light up, radiate, spotlight

v 2 animate, cheer up, enliven, incite, inspire, liven, quicken, resuscitate, vivify

brilliance n 1 see: PROMINENCE n

n 2 see: TALENT n 2

brilliant adj 1 clever, dazzling, good, irrepressible, scintillating, smart, sparkling, sprightly, witty

adj 2 beaming, bright, burnished, emitting, glistening, glossy, lucid, luminous, lustrous, polished, radiant, shining, shiny

adj 3 alert, astute, brainy, bright, clever, discerning, discriminating, educated, insightful, intellectual, intelligent, knowledgeable, knowing, perceptive, quick, sagacious, sage, sharp, smart, swift

adj 4 splendid

adj 5 amazing, exceptional, extraordinary, noteworthy, phenomenal, rare, remarkable, significant, singular, stunning, super, uncommon, uncustomary, unique, unusual

brim n border, boundary, bounds, brink, curb, edge, fringe, limits, lip, margin, outskirt, perimeter, periphery, rim, side, skirt, verge

bring v 1 carry, deliver, take

v 2 cause, convert, lead, move, persuade

v 3 fetch

brink n border, boundary, bounds, brim, curb, edge, fringe, limits, lip, margin, outskirt, perimeter, periphery, rim, side, skirt, verge

briny adj brackish, foul, nasty, salty, stagnant, undrinkable

brisk adj 1 curt, lively, quick, snappy

adj 2 heavy, intense, powerful, stiff, strong

adj 3 airy, breezy, drafty, gusty, lofty, open, windy

adj 4 active, agile, astir, catty, energetic, lively, nimble, quick, sprightly, spry, zippy

adj 5 see: LIVELY adj 2, 8

bristle v 1 anger, blow up, boil, boil over, brew, burn, flare up, fume, rage, seethe, simmer, smoke, steam, storm

v 2 see: HATE v

brittle *adj* breakable, crisp, crumbly, crunchy, fragile

broach *v* air, bring up, communicate, discuss, expose, express, give, introduce, open, put, reveal, state, tap, tell, vent, ventilate, verbalize

broad *adj* 1 ample, expansive, extended, extensive, ranging, vast, wide

adj 2 advanced, broad-minded, liberal, progressive, radical, tolerant, unbiased

adj 3 general, global, planetary, universal, urban, widespread, worldwide

broadcast *v* 1 air, relay, telecast, televise, transmit

v 2 advertise, announce, blaze, circulate, declare, disperse, disseminate, proclaim, promulgate, publish

v 3 disseminate, dissipate, distribute, scatter, sow, spread, strew, transmit

broaden *v* enlarge, flare, open, spread, widen

broad-minded *adj* advanced, broad, liberal, progressive, radical, tolerant, unbiased

Broadway *n* comedy, drama, extravaganza, musical, production, stage, theater

brochure *n* circular, flier, handbill, handout, leaflet, pamphlet, sheet

brogan *n* boot, chukka, footwear, moccasin, sandal, shoe, slipper, thong

brogue *n* accent, dialect, patois, speech, tongue

broil *v* bake, burn, char, cook, melt, parch, roast, scorch, sear, singe, swelter, toast, warm

broiling *adj* burning, baking, blistering, boiling, hot, fiery, scalding, scorching, sizzling, sultry, sweltering, torrid

broke *adj* 1 bankrupt, busted, destitute, dissolved, insolvent, out of business, penniless, ruined

adj 2 destitute, dirt poor, down and out, impoverished, indigent, needy, penniless, poor, poverty stricken, strapped, unprosperous

broken *adj* 1 cracked, damaged, fractured, out of order

adj 2 humbled

broker *n* 1 absorber, agent, catalyst, distributor, go-between, intermediary, mediator, middleman, negotiator

n 2 agent

brooch *n* anklet, band, bangle, bracelet, earring, jewelry, medallion, medal, necklace, pin, ring

brood *n* 1 clutch

n 2 litter, pups, young

n 3 children, descendants, offspring, posterity, progeny

n 4 assembly, association, band, bevy, bunch, camp, clique, cluster, collection, covey, crew, flock, group, organization, party, team, unit

v 1 fret, fuss, stew, worry

v 2 grieve, lament, languish, mourn, sorrow

v 3 crab, grouch, moan, mope, pout, scowl, sulk

brooding *adj* crabby, dour, gloomy, glum, moody, morose, sour, sulky, sullen, surly, ugly

brook *n* bayou, creek, river, stream, tributary

brotherhood *n* camaraderie, community, esprit de corps, fellowship, fraternity, lodge

brouhaha *n* see: CLAMOR *n*

brown *adj* tan, beige, chestnut, chocolate, hazel, mahogany

browse *v* 1 glance at, look through, peruse, scan, skim

v 2 graze

bruise *n* hurt, injury, pain, sprain, strain, wound

v 1 hurt, injure, lacerate, mangle, wound

v 2 crush, mash, mush up, pulp, squash

bruised *adj* irritated, painful, sore, tender

brunch *n* bread, breakfast, chow, cuisine, diet, dinner, dish, edibles, entree, fare, food, grub, lunch, meals, nosh, nutrition, provisions, rations, snack, supper, victuals, vittles

brush *n* 1 chalk, crayon, marker, pen, pencil, quill

n 2 affray, battle, brawl, clash, conflict, difference, disagreement, dispute, encounter, fight, fracas, melee, quarrel, run-in, scrimmage, skirmish, spat, touch

v 1 backfire, boomerang, bounce, glance, graze, rebound, ricochet, skim, skip, touch

v 2 clean

v 3 comb, paint, sweep

v 4 clean, polish, rub, wipe

v 5 graze, scrape, scratch, shave, skim, touch

brusque *adj* abrupt, bluff, blunt, brash, cheeky, crusty, curt, flip, flippant, gruff, harsh, impertinent, impudent, irritable, nasty, quick, rude, sarcastic, sassy, short, snippy, snotty, surly, testy, wisenheimer

brutal *adj* 1 bitter, cruel, fierce, hard, harsh, inclement, intemperate, pitiless, rigorous, rough, rugged, severe, stern, strong, unkind, violent

adj 2 austere, callous, coldblooded, compassionless, cruel, ferocious, fierce, hardened, hardhearted, heartless, indifferent, inhuman, inhumane, malicious, mean, merciless, nasty, obdurate, pitiless, ruthless, savage, spiteful, stony, tough, uncaring, unemotional, unfeeling, unkind, unmerciful, unpitying, unrelenting, unsympathetic, vicious

brutality n destructiveness, ferocity, force, frenzy, fury, rage, violence

brutalize v abuse, exploit, harm, ill-treat, injure, maltreat, mistreat, molest, persecute, victimize, wrong

brute n 1 animal, beast, being, creature, monster, ogre

n 2 demon, devil, fiend, rogue, satan, villain, wretch

bubble n bead, blob, drib, drop, droplet, globule, lump, sphere

v 1 blister, fester, ulcerate

v 2 crackle, hiss, sizzle, spit, sputter

v 3 agitate, bake, boil, burn, churn, ferment, foam, fume, roast, seethe, simmer, smolder

bubbly adj effervescent, giddy, sparkling

buck n 1 bread, cash, dollar, dough, money, moolah

n 2 Casanova, Don Juan, flirt, gallant, ladies' man, lecher, lover, philanderer, playboy, Romeo, stud

v pitch, throw, unseat

bucket n 1 barrel, cask, drum, keg, tub, vat, vessel

n 2 vessel, canister, bottle, caddy, can, jar, pail, shell, tin

n 3 ladle, scoop, shovel

n 4 ass, backside, base, behind, bottom, buns, butt, buttocks, derrière, end, fanny, hindquarters, posterior, rump, seat, stub, stump, tip, tush

buckle v 1 clasp, clinch, fasten, hook

v 2 accede, acquiesce, bend, bow, capitulate, cave, comply, concede, cry uncle, defer, give in, give up, relent, submit, succumb, surrender, twist, yield

n catch, clasp, clip, fastener, latch, pin, snap, zipper

buckshot n bullet, lead, missile, projectile, shell, shot, slug

bucolic adj country, garden, outland, pastoral, peaceful, provincial, rural, rustic, suburban, wooded

bud n egg, embryo, fetus, ovum, seed, zygote

v 1 bloom, blossom, develop, ferment, flourish, flower, germinate, grow, sprout

v 2 implant, graft, crossbreed

budding adj beginning, callow, embryonic

buddy n accomplice, acquaintance, adjunct, ally, associate, chum, cohort, colleague, companion, compatriot, comrade, confidant, confrere, connection, copartner, counterpart, co-worker, crony, equal, fellow, follower, friend, intimate, mate, pal, partner, peer, relative, supporter

budge v boost, drive, force, impel, nudge, push, propel, shove, thrust

budget n 1 forecast, estimate, plan, prediction, projection, quota

n 2 account, capital, cash, fund, money, savings, stock

n 3 aggregate, amount, body, bulk, count, number, quantity, tally, total

n 4 see: ALLOWANCE n 2

v 1 allocate, appropriate, plan

v 2 see: PREDICT v 2

buff n admirer, devotee, disciple, enthusiast, fan, follower, groupie

v burnish, furbish, glaze, glimmer, gloss, polish, renovate, rub, shine

buffer n 1 defense, protection, shield

n 2 barrier, border, boundary, fence, hedge

buffet n banquet, dinner, feast, lunch, meal, repast, smorgasbord, supper

v see: BATTER v

buffoon n comedian, comedienne, comic, fool, stand-up, zany

buffoonery n see: SATIRE n 2

bug n 1 defect, error, fault, glitch

n 2 insect

n 3 crusader, enthusiast, fanatic, fiend, freak, hobbyist, maniac, monomaniac, nut, radical, zealot

v 1 check, eavesdrop, monitor, observe, oversee, snoop, spy, wiretap

v 2 aggravate, anger, annoy, bother, enrage, exasperate, frazzle, gall, grate, hassle, incense, inflame, infuriate, irk, irritate, madden, miff, nettle, outrage, peeve, pester, pique, provoke, rile, upset, vex

v 3 annoy, antagonize, argue, bother, concern, distress, disturb, goad, harass, hassle, inconvenience, irk, irritate, pain, perturb, strain, stress, taunt, trouble, try, upset, worry

v 4 aggravate, annoy, badger, bait, bedevil, beleaguer, bother, harass, harry, hassle, heckle, hound, hurt, intimidate, jeer, nag, needle, persecute, pester, plague, provoke, ride, spite, taunt, tease, threaten, torment, worry

buggy n carriage, coach, rig, surrey, vehicle

build n anatomy, body, figure, form, frame, physique, shape *v* 1 conceive, construct, devise, frame, shape, surround

v 2 constitute, construct, create, erect, establish, found, initiate, institute, launch, set up, start

v 3 assemble, construct, erect, establish, fabricate, forge, form, make, manufacture, mold, produce, trail blaze

v 4 amplify, append, augment, boost, enlarge, expand, extend, grow, heighten, increase, intensify, magnify, multiply, run up, snowball, supplement, upsurge, wax

builder *n* maker, manufacturer, producer

building *n* 1 facility, office, place, service

n 2 edifice, erection, foundation, house, pile, store, structure, warehouse

bulge *n* jut, lump, projection, protrusion, swelling

v jut, overhang, overlap, overlay, poke, pop, project, protrude, protuberate, rise, stand out, stick out, swell

bulk *n* 1 greater part, majority, mass, preponderance

n 2 aggregate, amount, body, budget, count, number, quantity, tally, total

n 3 basis, body, core, essentials, essence, gist, heart, import, mass, nucleus, object, staple, substance, volume

bull *n* 1 falsehood, lie, misstatement, overstatement, untruth

n 2 baloney, bilge, bosh, bunk, drivel, fiddlesticks, foolishness, junk, malarkey, nonsense, nothing, poppycock, rot, rubbish, schlock, silliness, trivia

n 3 calf, cow, heifer, ox, steer

bulldoze *v* elbow, hustle, jostle, press, push, shoulder, shove

bullet *n* buckshot, lead, missile, projectile, shell, shot, slug

v barrel, expedite, fly, hasten, hurry, hustle, rocket, rush, speed, whisk, zip

bulletin *n* 1 daily, journal, newsletter, newspaper, organ, publication, review

n 2 article, byline, column, communication, dispatch, editorial, feature, headline, item, newsletter, report, story, vignette

bullheaded *adj* closed-minded, deaf, firm, hardheaded, hard-line, inelastic, inflexible, intractable, intransigent, obstinate, perverse, pigheaded, refractory, resolute, rigid, stiff, stubborn, tough, unbending, uncompromising,unpliable, unpliant, unwieldy, unyielding, willful

bully *v* 1 dominate, domineer, prevail, reign, rule

v 2 alarm, attack, club, coerce, frighten,

harass, intimidate, menace, strong-arm, terrorize, threaten

bullying *adj* coercive, forceful, menacing, strong-arm, threatening

bulwark *n* bastion, defense, embankment, fort, fortification, rampart, wall

v cover, defend, fend, fortify, guard, hide, protect, safeguard, screen, secure, shield

bum *adj* afoul, amiss, awry, bad, improper, out of kilter, poor, rotten, unsatisfactory, wrong

n 1 bird, cad, fink, heel, jerk, rat, turkey

n 2 beggar, derelict, drifter, hobo, loafer, mendicant, panhandler, pauper, tramp, vagabond, vagrant

bumble *v* falter, flounder, fumble, get stuck, grope, hesitate, stagger, stumble, waffle, waver

bumbling *adj* awkward, clumsy, faltering, gauche, gawky, halting, hesitant, inept, lumbering, maladroit, ungainly, ungraceful

bump *n* see: HIT *n* 1

v 1 bang, collide, crash, hit, smash

v 2 bounce, jostle, skip, throw, volley

v 3 jar, jolt, jostle, rattle, shake, shock, startle

v 4 break, bust, degrade, demerit, demote, downgrade, put down, reduce

v 5 bang, blow, cuff, hit, knock, punch, strike

bumpy *adj* bouncy, craggy, irregular, jagged, jolting, rough, rugged, scraggy, uneven, unsmooth

bunch *n* 1 assortment, collection, mixture, selection, spectrum, variety

n 2 array, bale, batch, battery, body, bundle, clump, cluster, group, lot, pack, parcel, quantity, set

n 3 assembly, association, band, bevy, brood, camp, clique, cluster, collection, covey, crew, flock, group, organization, party, team, unit

n 4 band, crew, crowd, drove, flock, following, gaggle, gang, herd, huddle, mass, mob, pack, rabble, riffraff, swarm, team, throng

n 5 arrangement, bouquet, corsage, flowers

bundle *n* array, bale, batch, battery, body, bunch, clump, cluster, group, lot, pack, parcel, quantity, set

v 1 box, crate, pack, stow

v 2 cover, enclose, envelop, package, wrap

bungalow *n* abode, barn, cabin, coop, cottage, hatch, hovel, hut, lodge, shack, shanty

bungle *n* accident, blooper, blunder, confusion, error, faux pas, foul-up, lapse, misreading, mistake, misunderstanding, slip, slip-up

v blow, blunder, botch, butcher, damage, err, foul up, goof, hash, hurt, jeopardize, jumble, mess up, queer, ruin, screw up

bungler *n* clod

bungling *adj* see: INADEQUATE *adj* 5

bunk *n* 1 bed, berth, cot, couch, cradle, crib, stall

n 2 baloney, bilge, bosh, bull, drivel, fiddlesticks, foolishness, junk, malarkey, nonsense, nothing, poppycock, rot, rubbish, schlock, silliness, trivia

buns *n* ass, backside, base, behind, bottom, bucket, butt, buttocks, derrière, end, fanny, hindquarters, posterior, rump, seat, stub, stump, tip, tush

buoy *n* floater

v 1 bolster, cheer, comfort, console, gladden, solace, soothe, support, uplift, upraise

v 2 bear up, bolster, brace, build up, buttress, carry, fortify, harden, nourish, nurture, prop, reinforce, shore, strengthen, support, sustain, toughen, uphold

buoyant *adj* 1 cheerful, ecstatic, elated, enthusiastic, exuberant, positive

adj 2 see: LIVELY *adj* 8

burble *v* babble, blab, blurt, chatter, gossip, murmur, prattle, talk, tattle

n babble, babbling, chatter, gibber, murmur, prattle, rattle

burden *n* 1 commitments, costs, expenditures, expenses, overhead

n 2 charge, commitment, duty, obligation, onus, responsibility

n 3 anxiety, frustration, pressure, strain, stress, tension

n 4 accountability, blame, culpability, fault, guilt, onus, responsibility, shame, stigma

n 5 cargo, consignment, freight, lading, load, payload, shipment, transportation, truck

n 6 adversity, affliction, blow, calamity, difficulty, distress, hardship, mischance, misfortune, mishap, relapse, reversal, setback, suffering, tragedy, trouble

v 1 impose, strain, tax

v 2 bother, encroach, impose, intrude, presume, saddle

v 3 afflict, aggrieve, bother, distress, grieve, hurt, injure, pain

v 4 check, encumber, hamper, hinder, impede, obstruct, restrain, restrict, retard

v 5 encumber, hamper, load, oppress, overdo, overload, saddle, strain, tax

v 6 affect, bother, concern, daunt, disturb, faze, intimidate, oppress, upset, worry

v 7 demand, encumber, force, prescribe

v 8 deject, depress, dishearten, grieve, hurt, lament, sadden, weigh down, wound

burdened *adj* encumbered, fraught, harried, laden, loaded, pressured

burdensome *adj* arduous, demanding, exacting, grievous, onerous, oppressive, taxing, tough, trying

bureau *n* armoire, chest, dresser

bureaucracy *n* 1 officialdom, red tape, regulations

n 2 administration, administrators, authorities, civil service, commission, department, direction, forces, government, management, ministry, officials, power, powers, rule, rulers

bureaucrat *n* civil servant, clerk, official, pen-pusher

burgh *n* borough, community, hamlet, settlement, township, village

burglar *n* bandit, brigand, cheat, con artist, con man, criminal, crook, embezzler, gyp, highwayman, looter, mugger, outlaw, robber, swindler, thief

burglarize *v* appropriate, defraud, embezzle, filch, heist, lift, misappropriate, pilfer, pillage, pinch, plunder, pocket, purloin, rip off, rob, snake, snitch, steal, swindle, swipe, take, thieve

burglary *n* larceny, looting, plagiarism, robbery, theft, thievery

burgundy *n* chablis, champagne, chianti, claret, port, sauterne, sherry, wine

burial *n* 1 catacomb, cenotaph, crypt, grave, mausoleum, memorial, monument, pit, sepulcher, tomb, vault

n 2 entombment

buried *adj* secluded, secret, sequestered, withdrawn

burlesque *n* buffoonery, caricature, comedy, farce, humor, imitation, joke, lampoon, mockery, parody, satire, spoof, takeoff, travesty

burly *adj* athletic, brawny, husky, massive, muscular, ponderous, powerful, robust, stocky, stout, strapping, strong

burn *n* pain, ache, agony, angina, cramp, crick, heartache, hurt, pang, soreness, spasm, sting, twinge

v 1 erupt, explode, flare

v 2 bite, smart, sting

v 3 cremate, destroy, incinerate, oxidize

v 4 enkindle, fire, ignite, inflame, kindle, light, spark

v 5 blare, blaze, flame, flare, glare, glow, ignite, redden

v 6 beam, disperse, emit, gleam, glisten, radiate, shed, shine, transmit

v 7 agitate, bake, boil, bubble, churn, ferment, foam, fume, roast, seethe, simmer, smolder

v 8 bake, broil, char, cook, melt, parch, roast, scorch, sear, singe, swelter, toast, warm

v 9 anger, blow up, boil, boil over, brew, bristle, flare up, fume, rage, seethe, simmer, smoke, steam, storm

v 10 bamboozle, beat, beguile, bilk, cajole, cheat, chicane, chisel, con, cross, deceive, defraud, dupe, embezzle, fleece, flimflam, fob, foist, fool, gyp, hoax, hoodwink, hustle, inveigle, screw, shaft, sham, swindle, trick, victimize

burning *adj* 1 ablaze, afire, aflame, aglow, alight, blazing, conflagrant, fiery, flaming, glowing

adj 2 acute, critical, crucial, desperate, dire, grave, heavy, important, major, momentous, ponderous, pressing, profound, serious, severe, solemn, somber, urgent, vital

adj 3 baking, blistering, boiling, broiling, fiery, hot, scalding, scorching, sizzling, sultry, sweltering, torrid

burnish *v* buff, furbish, glaze, glimmer, gloss, polish, renovate, rub, shine

burnished *adj* beaming, bright, brilliant, emitting, glistening, glossy, lucid, luminous, lustrous, polished, radiant, shining, shiny

burnt *adj* parched, scorched, shriveled

burrow *n* cave, den, grotto, lair, recess, tunnel

v 1 dig, furrow, root out, tunnel

v 2 dig, excavate, gouge, mine, scoop, shovel, unearth

burst *n* barrage, fusillade, round, shot, volley

v 1 blow up, boom, detonate, explode

v 2 discharge, erupt, explode, gush, spew, spout

v 3 break, erupt, explode, fragment, rupture, shatter, smash, smatter, splinter

bursting *adj* chock-full, crowded, filled up, full, jammed, jampacked, loaded, packed, rending, replete, stuffed

bury *v* 1 entomb

v 2 drown, engulf, flood, inundate, overflow, swamp, wash over

v 3 cache, cloister, conceal, cover, ditch, ensconce, hide, plant, secrete, sequester, stash

bus *n* auto, automobile, car, carriage, chariot, coach, jeep, motorcar, omnibus, sedan, truck, van, vehicle, wagon

bush *n* grass, hedge, plant, sapling, shrub, tree, vegetation, vine, weed

bushed *adj* beat, burnt out, careworn, drawn, emaciated, exhausted, expended, fatigued, frazzled, haggard, jaded, pinched, pooped, run-down, shot, spent, tired, wearied, weary, worn, worn down, worn-out

business *adj* commercial, mercantile, trade, trading

n 1 affair, concern, issue, matter

n 2 activity, endeavor, enterprise, exercise, project, undertaking, venture

n 3 arrangements, commerce, dealings, enterprise, industry, intercourse, negotiations, trade, traffic

n 4 company, concern, corporation, enterprise, establishment, firm, house, organization, partnership

n 5 department store, mall, market, mart, shop, store, supermarket

n 6 art, avocation, calling, career, discipline, employment, field, gig, job, labor, line, livelihood, occupation, office, profession, pursuit, role, schtick, situation, specialty, task, thing, trade, vocation, work

businesslike *adj* 1 basic, down-to-earth, efficient, hardheaded, practical, pragmatic, sensible

adj 2 enterprising, entrepreneurial, gumptious, up-and-coming

businessman *n* see: CAPITALIST *n*

businessperson *n* baron, big shot, businessman, businesswoman, capitalist, entrepreneur, executive, financier, industrialist, magnate, mogul, plutocrat, tycoon, VIP

businesswoman *n* see: CAPITALIST *n*

bust *n* 1 bomb, disaster, dud, failure, fiasco, flop, turkey

n 2 figure, icon, idol, image, sculpture, statue, statuette, symbol

n 3 breast, chest

v 1 bankrupt, break, decay, do in, fold up, impoverish, ruin

v 2 break, bump, degrade, demerit, demote, downgrade, put down, reduce

v 3 apprehend, arrest, bag, book, capture, catch, collar, detain, get, grab, lock up, nab, nail, pick up, pinch, pull in, run in, secure, seize, take

busted *adj* bankrupt, broke, destitute, dissolved, insolvent, out of business, penniless, ruined

bustle *n* action, activity, ado, animation, bedlam, bother, chaos, commotion, excitement, flurry, fluster, fuss, hum, liveliness, madhouse, movement, stir, to-do, tumult, turmoil, whirlpool, whirlwind

bustling *adj* active, busy, creative, driving, energetic, enterprising, inventive, lively, resourceful

busy *adj* 1 impertinent, intrusive, meddlesome, obtrusive, officious
adj 2 employed, engaged, functional, in use, occupied, working
adj 3 active, bustling, creative, driving, energetic, enterprising, inventive, lively, resourceful

busybody *n* gossip, interloper, intruder, kibitzer, meddler, snoop, yenta

but *adv* 1 except that, further, however, just, merely, nevertheless, only, simply, solely, yet
adv 2 at any rate, however, moreover, nevertheless, nonetheless, notwithstanding, still, though, yet

butcher *v* 1 blow, blunder, botch, bungle, damage, err, foul up, goof, hash, hurt, jeopardize, jumble, mess up, queer, ruin, screw up
v 2 abolish, annihilate, assassinate, bump off, decimate, destroy, dispatch, execute, exterminate, hang, hit, kill, knock off, liquidate, massacre, murder, put away, rub out, slaughter, slay, wipe out

butchery *n* bloodbath, bloodshed, carnage, extermination, genocide, holocaust, killing, massacre, pogrom, shambles, slaughter

butt *n* 1 casualty, object, prey, subject, sufferer, target, victim
n 2 ass, backside, base, behind, bottom, bucket, buns, buttocks, derrière, end, fanny, hindquarters, posterior, rump, seat, stub, stump, tip, tush
v attack, drive, knock, lunge, pass, plunge, ram, sink, stab, stick, thrust

buttocks *n* ass, backside, base, behind, bottom, bucket, buns, butt, derrière, end, fanny, hindquarters, posterior, rump, seat, stub, stump, tip, tush

buttress *n* base, brace, column, footing, foundation, prop, shore, stay, support, underpinning
v 1 augment, fortify, harden, intensify, invigorate, reinforce, strengthen
v 2 bear up, bolster, brace, build up, buoy, carry, fortify, harden, nourish, nurture, prop, reinforce, shore, strengthen, support, sustain, toughen, uphold

buy *n* 1 acquisition, asset, gain, merchandise, property, purchase
n 2 bargain, deal, discount, promotion, reduction, sale, special, steal
v 1 bribe
v 2 accept, believe, swallow
v 3 examine, procure, purchase, shop
v 4 convert, ransom, reclaim, redeem, recover, save
v 5 see: OBTAIN *v* 1

buyer *n* client, consumer, customer, end user, patron, purchaser, shopper, user

buzz *v* call, communicate, contact, phone, ring, telephone, touch

buzzer *n* alarm, bell, chime, gong, signal, siren

buzzwords *n* jargon, lexicons, lingo, nomenclature, terminology, terms, vocabulary

by *prep* adjacent to, around, at, atop, beside, near, on

bye *n* adieu, adios, aloha, *arrivederci, auf Wiedersehen,* au revoir, bon voyage, cheerio, *ciao,* farewell, goodbye, good day, *sayonara,* shalom, so long

bygone *adj* 1 erstwhile, former, late, old, once, onetime, past, sometime
adj 2 dead, defunct, departed, extinct, forgotten, gone, lost, vanished
adj 3 ancient, antiquated, archaic, dated, dead, extinct, noncurrent, obsolete, old, outdated, outmoded, passé, past, worn

byline *n* see: ARTICLE *n* 2

bypass *n* branch, detour, deviation, diversion
v 1 jump, pass over, skip
v 2 avoid, circumvent, detour, evade

by-product *n* see: PRODUCT *n* 1

byword *n* adage, axiom, cliché, dictum, maxim, motto, proverb, saying, slogan, talk

C

cab *n* hack, jitney, rickshaw, taxi, taxicab

cabal *n* 1 collusion, conspiracy, intrigue, junta, machination, plot, scheme, secret
n 2 band, camp, circle, clan, clique, coterie, coven, cult, faction, family, gang, group, mob, ring, school, sect, tribe

cabaret *n* bar, bistro, cafe, casino, discothèque, nightclub

cabin *n* abode, barn, bungalow, coop, cottage, hatch, hovel, hut, lodge, shack, shanty

cabinet *n* 1 case, enclosure, housing
n 2 board, body, commission, committee, council, directorship

n 3 chest, closet, compartment, cubby, locker, nook, wardrobe

n 4 console

cable *n* 1 hawser, rigging, wire

n 2 cord, fiber, hemp, lanyard, line, rope, strand, string, thread, twine, yarn

n 3 boob tube, channel, station, teevee, television, tube, TV, video

v notify, radio, telegraph, telex, wire

cache *n* 1 repository, stockroom, storehouse, warehouse

n 2 backlog, hoard, holdings, inventory, nest egg, pile, reserve, reservoir, stash, stock, stockpile, store, supply

v bury, cloister, conceal, cover, ditch, ensconce, hide, plant, secrete, sequester, stash

cachet *n* brand, mark, emblem, imprint, logo, logotype, seal, stamp, trademark

cackle *v* 1 chat, gab, gossip, talk, yak

v 2 blurt, cry, ejaculate, exclaim, shout, spill, sputter, tattle, utter

cacophony *n* brouhaha, chaos, clamor, confusion, din, discord, disorder, hubbub, mayhem, noise, pandemonium, racket, tumult, uproar

cad *n* 1 bird, bum, fink, heel, jerk, rat, turkey

n 2 cheat, knave, lecher, louse, rake, rascal, reprobate, rogue, scoundrel

cadaver *n* body, carcass, corpse, remains, shell, stiff

caddy *n* bottle, bucket, can, canister, jar, pail, shell, tin, vessel

cadence *n* 1 beat, cycle, lilt, pulse, rate, rhythm, tempo, time

n 2 alacrity, celerity, dispatch, gait, pace, quickness, rapidity, rate, speed, step, stride, swiftness, trot, velocity, walk

cadre *n* center, core, framework, infrastructure, nucleus

cafe *n* 1 bar, bistro, cabaret, casino, discothèque, nightclub

n 2 automat, cafeteria, canteen, diner, grill, luncheonette, lunchroom, restaurant, tearoom

cafeteria *n* automat, cafe, canteen, diner, grill, luncheonette, lunchroom, restaurant, tearoom

cage *n* brig, cell, cooler, coop, hoosegow, jail, pen, penitentiary, pokey, prison, reformatory, slammer, stir, stockade, tower

v confine, coop, detain, enclose, impound, imprison, incarcerate, intern, jail, lock up, restrain, trap

cagey *adj* 1 adroit, artful, canny, crafty, cunning, evasive, foxy, serpentine, sly

adj 2 see: QUICK *adj* 5

cajole *v* 1 barter, coax, con, urge

v 2 attract, disarm, flatter, ingratiate

v 3 see: CHEAT *v* 1

calamitous *adj* 1 atrocious, dreadful, grievous, heinous, severe

adj 2 cataclysmic, catastrophic, critical, crucial, devastating, disastrous, fatal, fateful, momentous, ruinous, vital

calamity *n* 1 affliction, disability, flaw, handicap, impairment, limitation

n 2 cataclysm, catastrophe, debacle, disaster, misfortune, tragedy, upheaval

n 3 adversity, affliction, blow, burden, difficulty, distress, hardship, mischance, misfortune, mishap, relapse, reversal, setback, suffering, tragedy, trouble

calculate *v* 1 adjust

v 2 cipher, code, compute, estimate, figure, reckon

v 3 cite, count, enumerate, itemize, list, number, numerate, tally

v 4 account, consider, deem, judge, reckon, regard, surmise, view

calculated *adj* 1 conscious, contrived, deliberate, intentional, planned, plotted, premeditated

adj 2 advised, careful, considered, contrived, deliberate, forewarned, measured, planned, premeditated, studied, studious

calculating *adj* 1 see: CAREFUL *adj* 7

adj 2 see: SLY *adj* 3

calculation *n* 1 forecast

n 2 count, number, summation

calendar *n* 1 almanac

n 2 agenda, appointments, itinerary, list, plan, schedule

calf *n* bull, cow, heifer, ox, steer

caliber *n* 1 class, grade, quality, rating

n 2 amplitude, concentration, magnitude, potency, strength

n 3 excellence, goodness, merit, quality, stature, value, worth

n 4 bore, circle, diameter, radius

n 5 ability, adequacy, adroitness, aptitude, art, calling, capability, capacity, command, competence, craft, dexterity, experience, expertise, familiarity, forte, knack, know-how, knowledge, mastery, proficiency, prowess, qualification, savvy, skill, specialty, strength, talent, training, workmanship

calibrate *v* 1 grade, graduate, measure

v 2 gauge, measure, range, rank, size

v 3 adjust, arrange, decide, determine, establish, fix, resolve, set

v 4 see: INSTALL *v* 1

calibration *n* scale

calisthenics *n* 1 acrobatics, athletics, gymnastics

n 2 aerobics, bodybuilding, exercise, jazzercise, slimnastics, workout

call *n* 1 cause, necessity, obligation, occasion

n 2 alarm, hail, shout, signal, whoop, yell

n 3 air, carol, cry, lullaby, melody, note, rhapsody, song, tune

v 1 announce, hail, page, summon

v 2 cite, evoke, serve, subpoena, summon

v 3 approximate, estimate, judge, place, put, reckon

v 4 define, designate, entitle, label, name, term

v 5 ask, crave, demand, necessitate, require, take

v 6 buzz, communicate, contact, phone, ring, telephone, touch

v 7 conscript, draft, enroll, force, impress, induct, select, shanghai

v 8 challenge, claim, demand, exact, need, postulate, require, requisition, solicit

v 9 baptize, bestow, christen, confer, designate, dub, entitle, name, nickname, tag, term, title

v 10 anticipate, augur, bode, budget, divine, estimate, forecast, foresee, foreshadow, foretell, guess, harbinger, herald, judge, plan, portend, preannounce, predict, presage, proclaim, prognosticate, project, prophesy, signify, soothsay

v 11 see: ASSEMBLE *v* 3

v 12 see: SCREAM *v*

caller *n* company, guest, visitor

calling *n* 1 art, avocation, business, career, discipline, employment, field, gig, job, labor, line, livelihood, occupation, office, profession, pursuit, role, schtick, situation, specialty, task, thing, trade, vocation, work

n 2 see: SKILL *n* 3

callous *adj* austere, brutal, coldblooded, compassionless, cruel, ferocious, fierce, hardened, hardhearted, heartless, indifferent, inhuman, inhumane, malicious, mean, merciless, nasty, obdurate, pitiless, ruthless, savage, spiteful, stony, tough, uncaring, unemotional, unfeeling, unkind, unmerciful, unpitying, unrelenting, unsympathetic, vicious

callow *adj* 1 beginning, budding, embryonic

adj 2 babyish, childish, immature, infantile, sophomoric

calm *adj* 1 coolheaded, nonaggressive, nonviolent, pacifist, passive, peaceful

adj 2 collected, composed, cool, demure, dormant, easy, gentle, hushed, idle, imperturbable, motionless, nonchalant, peaceful, placid, poised, quiet, relaxed, restful, sedate, self-composed, self-possessed, serene, soft, steady, still, tranquil, unflappable, unruffled, untroubled

adj 3 see: INDIFFERENT *adj* 4

n 1 peace, serenity, accord, harmony, stillness, tranquillity

n 2 peace, tranquillity, hush, lull, peacefulness, quiet, repose, respite, rest, siesta, silence, sleep, stillness

v 1 drug, sedate, tranquilize

v 2 balance, brace, fix, steady, still

v 3 lessen, muffle, quiet, reduce, soften, subdue

v 4 allay, appease, assuage, balm, becalm, compose, conciliate, ease, lull, mollify, pacify, placate, propitiate, quell, quiet, reconcile, satiate, settle, soften, soothe, still, sweeten, tranquilize

calmness *n* 1 composure, equanimity, harmony, peacefulness, self-possession, serenity, tranquillity

n 2 air, attitude, bearing, carriage, demeanor, disposition, poise, pose, posture, presence, set, stance

camaraderie *n* brotherhood, community, esprit de corps, fellowship, fraternity, lodge

camouflage *n* 1 cloak, costume, cover, curtain, disguise, mask, pretense, shield, shroud, veil

n 2 cover, incognito, privacy, secrecy, stealth

v cloak, conceal, cover, darken, disguise, envelop, hide, mask, occult, seclude, shield, shroud, veil

camp *n* 1 band, cabal, circle, clan, clique, coterie, coven, cult, faction, family, gang, group, mob, ring, school, sect, tribe

n 2 barracks

n 3 assembly, association, band, bevy, brood, bunch, clique, cluster, collection, covey, crew, flock, group, organization, party, team, unit

v bivouac, dwell, lodge, nest, quarter, station

campaign *n* 1 crusade, drive, effort, expedition, push

n 2 attack, attempt, blockade, bout, offensive, siege

v 1 canvass, influence, lobby, persuade, strive, support

v 2 canvass, drum, drum up, poll, prospect, seek, solicit

can *n* 1 bottle, bucket, caddy, canister, jar, pail, shell, tin, vessel

n 2 bathroom, head, john, latrine, lavatory, loo, potty, powder room, toilet, water closet, wc

v ax, boot, bounce, discharge, dismiss, drop, fire, impeach, let go, sack, terminate

canal *n* channel, conduit, crevice, curb, cut, ditch, duct, furrow, gorge, groove, gully, gutter, passageway, ravine, rut, trench, trough

canary *adj* jasmine, lemon, saffron, yellow

cancel *v* 1 end, halt, kill, stop

v 2 contradict, deny, disallow, forbid, negate, nix, nullify, override, overrule, reject, renege, repeal, revoke, torpedo, veto, void

v 3 abrogate, annul, contradict, discharge, dismantle, dissolve, dwindle, fade, negate, nullify, quash, recall, repeal, rescind, reverse, revoke, set aside, vacate, void

v 4 see: TERMINATE *v* 8

cancellation *n* recall, repeal, reversal, revocation

cancer *n* corruption, decay, evil, infection, malignancy, poison, rot, toxin, venom

candid *adj* 1 aboveboard, equitable, fair, forthright, honest, legitimate, plain-dealing, straight, straightforward, trustworthy, upright

adj 2 dispassionate, equal, equitable, fair, impartial, impersonal, indifferent, just, neutral, objective, open-minded, square, unbiased, uncolored, unprejudiced

adj 3 artless, frank, guileless, ingenuous, innocent, naive, natural, open, plain, simple, simple-hearted, unadorned, unaffected, unsophisticated, unstudied, untutored, unworldly

adj 4 see: SINCERE *adj*

candidate *n* aspirant, contestant, entrant, hopeful, nominee

candor *n* 1 frankness, honesty, sincerity, truthfulness

n 2 honesty, integrity, truth, truthfulness, veracity

cane *n* birch, club, pole, rod, shaft, staff, stake, stave, stick

canine *n* dog, hound, mongrel, mutt, pooch, pup, puppy

canister *n* bottle, bucket, caddy, can, jar, pail, shell, tin, vessel

cannonade *v* blitz, bomb, bombard, shell

canny *adj* 1 adaptive, bold, clever, daring, enterprising, resourceful, venturesome

adj 2 adroit, artful, cagey, crafty, cunning, evasive, foxy, serpentine, sly

adj 3 conservative, economical, frugal, provident, sparing, spartan, stewardly, thrifty, unwasteful

adj 4 adroit, apt, clever, cunning, deft, handy, ingenious, nimble, skilled, skillful, sly, wily

adj 5 see: QUICK *adj* 5

canoe *n* barge, boat, craft, dory, ferry, float, kayak, raft, scow, skiff, tender

canon *n* 1 belief, code, conviction, creed, doctrine, dogma, law, opinion, principle, rule, tenet, theory

n 2 behest, bidding, charge, command, criterion, decree, dictate, direction, edict, fiat, guideline, injunction, institution, law, mandate, order, ordinance, precept, prescript, prescription, regulation, rite, rule, ruling, statute, word

cant *v* careen, heel, incline, list, rear, roll, tilt

cantankerous *adj* argumentative, contentious, controversial, debatable, disputatious, ill-natured, litigious, ornery

canteen *n* automat, cafe, cafeteria, diner, grill, luncheonette, lunchroom, restaurant, tearoom

canvas *n* 1 tarpaulin

n 2 acrylic, art, depiction, drawing, etching, illustration, landscape, lithograph, mural, oil, painting, pastel, pen and ink, picture, portrait, print, seascape, sketch, still life, watercolor

canvass *v* 1 campaign, influence, lobby, persuade, strive, support

v 2 campaign, drum, drum up, poll, prospect, seek, solicit

v 3 case, check, examine, glance over, inspect, observe, peruse, pore over, regard, scrutinize, study, survey, watch

canyon *n* abyss, chasm, cleft, crack, depth, fissure, gorge, gulch, pass, ravine

cap *v* 1 adjourn, climax, complete, conclude, consummate, crown, culminate, dissolve, end, finalize, finish, terminate, wind up, wrap up

v 2 beat, best, better, dwarf, eclipse, exceed, excel, go beyond, outdo, outgo, outshine, outstrip, overshadow, pass, surpass, top, transcend

n 1 beret, derby, hat, helmet

n 2 cork, cover, lid, plate, plug, top

capability n ability, adequacy, adroitness, aptitude, art, caliber, calling, capacity, command, competence, craft, dexterity, experience, expertise, familiarity, forte, knack, know-how, knowledge, mastery, proficiency, prowess, qualification, savvy, skill, specialty, strength, talent, training, workmanship

capable adj 1 achievable, doable, feasible, possible, practical, viable, workable
adj 2 adequate, competent, effective, efficacious, efficient, proficient, successful, sufficient
adj 3 able, accomplished, adept, apt, competent, deft, dexterous, expert, fit, gifted, masterful, professional, proficient, proper, qualified, skillful, talented

capacious adj ample, big, comfortable, commodious, open, roomy, spacious, vast, wide

capacity n 1 content, measure, volume
n 2 elbowroom, leeway, room, space
n 3 assets, means, reserves, resources, wherewithal
n 4 grade, office, place, position, post, quality, rank, situation, spot, standing, state, station, status
n 5 potential
n 6 ability, adequacy, adroitness, aptitude, art, caliber, calling, capability, command, competence, craft, dexterity, experience, expertise, familiarity, forte, knack, know-how, knowledge, mastery, proficiency, prowess, qualification, savvy, skill, specialty, strength, talent, training, workmanship

cape n 1 isthmus, peninsula, point, promontory
n 2 cloak, coat, mantle, shawl, wrap
n 3 barrier, breaker, harbor, head, jetty, neck, point, sea wall

caper n adventure, antic, escapade, joke, lark, mischief, prank, trick
v cavort, frisk, frolic, gambol, play, prance, rollick, romp, skip

capillary n artery, blood vessel, vein, vessel

capital n 1 account, budget, cash, fund, money, savings, stock
n 2 assets, bills, cash, coffers, currency, dinero, dollars, estate, funds, goods, income, lucre, means, money, notes, pelf, pesos, property, resources, sum, revenue, riches, rubles, shekels, wealth

capitalist n baron, big shot, businessman, businessperson, businesswoman, entrepreneur, executive, financier, industrialist, magnate, mogul, plutocrat, tycoon, VIP

capitalize v 1 bankroll, finance, fund, stake, subsidize
v 2 benefit from, gain, profit

capitol n house, legislature, senate

capitulate v accede, acquiesce, bend, bow, buckle, cave, comply, concede, cry uncle, defer, give in, give up, relent, submit, succumb, surrender, twist, yield

capitulation n compliance, release, submission, subordination, subservience, surrender

caprice n fancy, humor, impulse, notion, vagary, whim, whimsy

capricious adj 1 careless, immature, irresponsible, undependable, unpredictable, untrustworthy
adj 2 dizzy, flighty, frivolous, giddy, irresponsible, scatterbrained, silly
adj 3 arbitrary, changeable, erratic, fickle, flighty, inconsistent, inconstant, mercurial, uncertain, unstable, unsteady, variable, volatile, wavering, wayward

capsize v 1 overturn, roll, tip over, upset
v 2 collapse, defeat, dislodge, knock over, overthrow, overturn, tip over, topple, tumble, turn over, upset

capsule n binder, case, casing, cover, envelope, holder, sheath, skin, wrapper

captious adj carping, censorious, critical, cutting, disparaging, faultfinding, hairsplitting, nit-picking

captivate v 1 charm, delight, engross, enrapture, enravish, enthrall, entrance, hypnotize, mesmerize, move, ravish, transport
v 2 allure, attract, bedevil, beguile, bewitch, charm, conjure, delight, draw, enchant, enthrall, fascinate, lure, magnetize, mesmerize, tempt, wile

captivated adj enamored, fascinated, infatuated, in love

captivating adj alluring, beguiling, bewitching, catchy, charming, dazzling, dynamic, enchanting, engaging, enthralling, enticing, fascinating, glamorous, intriguing, mesmerizing, riveting, spectacular, spellbinding

captive n hostage, prisoner, victim

capture v 1 bag, catch, ensnare, entangle, entrap, hook, snag, snare, snarl, tangle, trap, trick
v 2 chart, denote, enter, itemize, jot, list, log, note, preserve, record, register, take notes, tally, tape, write down
v 3 apprehend, arrest, bag, book, bust, catch, collar, detain, get, grab, lock up,

nab, nail, pick up, pinch, pull in, run in, secure, seize, take

v 4 see: OBTAIN *v* 1

car *n* auto, automobile, bus, carriage, chariot, coach, jeep, motorcar, omnibus, sedan, truck, van, vehicle, wagon

caravan *n* convoy, motorcade, procession

carbine *n* firearm, flintlock, gun, musket, rifle, shotgun

carbon *n* carbon copy, copy, duplicate, facsimile, replica, reproduction, telecopy, Xerox copy

carbuncle *n* abscess, boil, pimple, ulcer

carcass *n* body, cadaver, corpse, remains, shell, stiff

card *n* 1 badge, label, pass, tag, ticket, voucher

n 2 character, eccentric, kook, lunatic, nut, oddball, weirdo

cardinal *adj* 1 essential, fundamental, primary, prime, principal

adj 2 crimson, red, ruby, scarlet, vermilion

care *n* 1 advisement, conference, consultation, counsel

n 2 charge, custody, protection, safekeeping

n 3 administration, charge, conduct, handling, intendance, management, overseeing, running, supervision

n 4 affliction, anguish, catastrophe, despair, disaster, dole, grief, heartache, mishap, pain, regret, remorse, rue, sickness, sorrow, woe

n 5 annoyance, anxiety, apprehension, bother, concern, disquiet, disquietude, doubt, irritation, misgiving, reservation, restlessness, restraint, skepticism, trouble, uneasiness, vexation, worry

n 6 attention, awareness, carefulness, cognizance, concern, consciousness, consideration, heed, intimacy, knowing, knowledge, mark, note, notice, observance, observation, perception, recognition, regard, remark, sense

n 7 see: FEAR *n* 3

v 1 mind

v 2 manage, oversee, supervise

v 3 consider, heed, listen, mind, review

v 4 cherish, foster, mother, nourish, nurse, nurture, parent, protect, raise, rear, suckle

careen *v* 1 cant, heel, incline, list, rear, roll, tilt

v 2 lurch, pitch, reel, stagger, sway, toss, totter, wheel

career *n* 1 diary, events, experience, history, performance, record, résumé, track record, vita

n 2 see: TRADE *n* 3

careful *adj* 1 diligent, rigorous, studious, thorough

adj 2 advertent, alert, attentive, conscientious, heedful, observant

adj 3 alert, heedful, leery, prudent, suspicious, vigilant, wary, watchful

adj 4 alert, cautious, open-eyed, unsleeping, vigilant, wakeful, wary, watchful, wide-awake

adj 5 advised, calculated, considered, contrived, deliberate, forewarned, measured, planned, premeditated, studied, studious

adj 6 carping, cautious, conscientious, ethical, exacting, fussy, heedful, meticulous, painstaking, punctilious, scrupulous, unrelenting

adj 7 calculating, cautious, circumspect, considerate, discreet, gingerly, guarded, heedful, judicious, provident, prudent, restrained, reticent, safe, shrewd, wary

adj 8 see: CHOOSY *adj*

carefully *adv* accurately

carefulness *n* attention, awareness, care, cognizance, concern, consciousness, consideration, heed, intimacy, knowing, knowledge, mark, note, notice, observance, observation, perception, recognition, regard, remark, sense

careless *adj* 1 capricious, immature, undependable, irresponsible, unpredictable, untrustworthy

adj 2 foolish, impulsive, irresponsible, myopic, not smart, reckless, risky, shortsighted, unthinking, unwise

adj 3 defiant, delinquent, derelict, heedless, inattentive, lax, neglectful, negligent, reckless, sloppy

adj 4 disheveled, messy, scruffy, slatternly, slipshod, sloppy, sloven, slovenly, tacky, uncombed, unkempt, untidy

adj 5 accidental, caustic, heedless, inadvertent, inconsiderate, nonchalant, selfish, sharp, short, tactless, thoughtless, uncaring, unceremonious, ungracious, unheeding, unintended, unintentional, unreflective, unthinking

adj 6 see: INDIFFERENT *adj* 4

adj 7 see: PREOCCUPIED *adj* 1

caress *n* embrace, fondling, hug, kiss, squeeze, touch

v 1 clutch, embrace, grasp, hold

v 2 cradle, cuddle, embrace, feel, fondle, fool around, hold, hug, love, make out, neck, nuzzle, pet, snuggle, stroke

careworn adj 1 anxious, distracted, distraught, distressed, frantic, harassed, tormented, troubled, upset, worried

adj 2 see: WEARY adj 1

cargo n burden, consignment, freight, lading, load, payload, shipment, transportation, truck

caricature n buffoonery, burlesque, comedy, farce, humor, imitation, joke, lampoon, mockery, parody, satire, spoof, takeoff, travesty

caring adj 1 affectionate, amorous, attached, devoted, enamored, fond, loving, romantic, tender

adj 2 see: BENEVOLENT adj 2

carnage n 1 death, demise, fatality, mortality, ruin

n 2 bloodbath, bloodshed, butchery, extermination, genocide, holocaust, killing, massacre, pogrom, shambles, slaughter

carnal adj 1 worldly

adj 2 bodily, corporeal, fleshly

adj 3 intimate, physical, sexual

adj 4 delicious, enticing, erotic, hedonistic, luscious, lush, lusty, luxurious, pleasure-seeking, sensual, sensualistic, sensuous, sexual, voluptuous

adj 5 erogenous, erotic, genital, procreative, reproductive, sexual

adj 6 amorous, ardent, aroused, earthy, erotic, fervent, fleshly, horny, hot, impassioned, lascivious, lecherous, lewd, licentious, lustful, passionate, provocative, randy, raunchy, romantic, sensual, sexual, sexy, sultry, titillated, torrid, turned on, voluptuous, wanton

carnival n bazaar, circus, fair, market

carol n air, call, cry, lullaby, melody, note, rhapsody, song, tune

v chant, harmonize, hum, lilt, sing, yodel

carouse v celebrate, drink, frolic, make merry, party, revel, romp

carp v berate, cavil, criticize, find fault, flay, fuss, henpeck, nag, nit-pick, nudge, peck, quibble, scold

carpet n mat, mattress, pad, rug

carping adj 1 captious, censorious, critical, cutting, disparaging, faultfinding, hairsplitting, nit-picking

adj 2 see: CONSCIENTIOUS adj 3

carriage n 1 buggy, coach, rig, surrey, vehicle

n 2 air, attitude, bearing, calmness, demeanor, disposition, poise, pose, posture, presence, set, stance

n 3 auto, automobile, bus, car, chariot, coach, jeep, motorcar, omnibus, sedan, truck, van, vehicle, wagon

carrier n courier, delivery person, envoy, herald, messenger, runner

carry v 1 bear, have, possess

v 2 bring, deliver, take

v 3 change, modify

v 4 act, bear, behave, comport, conduct, demean, rule

v 5 channel, conduct, convey, funnel, pass, pipe, siphon, transmit

v 6 cart, drag, draw, haul, lug, pull, tow, truck, tug

v 7 bear, convey, crate, ferry, haul, lift, lug, pack, shoulder, shuttle, tote, traffic, transport, truck

v 8 see: STRENGTHEN v 5

carryable adj compact, lightweight, luggable, movable, pocket-size, portable, small, transportable

cart v carry, drag, draw, haul, lug, pull, tow, tug, truck

n handcart, pushcart, truck, wagon, wheelbarrow

cartel n chain, coalition, collaboration, combine, conglomerate, consortium, federation, group, partnership, pool, syndicate, trust

carton n box, case, chest, container, crate, receptacle

cartoons n docudrama, documentary, game shows, mini-series, movies, news, programs, series, sitcom, soap opera, soaps, talk shows, television, variety shows

carve v 1 cut, engrave, etch, inscribe

v 2 chisel, craft, cut, define, design, fashion, form, mold, sculpt, sculpture, shape, steer

v 3 ax, chip, chop, cleave, cut, dissect, fell, hack, hew, mangle, mutilate, notch, pulverize, rend, saw, sever, slice, sliver, snip, split, sunder, whittle

Casanova n buck, Don Juan, flirt, gallant, ladies' man, lecher, lover, philanderer, playboy, Romeo, stud

cascade v decant, emit, flood, inundate, overflow, plunge, pour, rain, shower, spill, swamp, tumble

case n 1 cabinet, enclosure, housing

n 2 event, eventuality, occurrence

n 3 condition, repair, shape, state

n 4 box, carton, chest, container, crate, receptacle

n 5 coat, cover, enclosure, folder, jacket, skin

n 6 action, indictment, lawsuit, litigation, proceeding, prosecution, suit

n 7 binder, capsule, casing, cover, envelope, holder, sheath, skin, wrapper *n* 8 bark, coating, crust, husk, peel, rind, shell, shuck, skin

n 9 case history, clarification, example, explanation, illumination, illustration, instance, representative, sample, sampling, specimen

n 10 bag, baggage, equipment, gear, grip, kit, luggage, pack, pouch, purse, sack, suitcase, valise, wallet

v canvass, check, examine, glance over, inspect, observe, peruse, pore over, regard, scrutinize, study, survey, watch

cash *n* 1 bread, buck, dollar, dough, money, moolah

n 2 account, budget, capital, fund, money, savings, stock

n 3 assets, bills, capital, coffers, currency, dinero, dollars, estate, funds, goods, income, lucre, means, money, notes, pelf, pesos, property, resources, revenue, riches, rubles, shekels, sum, wealth

n 4 see: PROFITS *n*

n 5 see: REWARD *n* 8

v convert, dissolve, exchange, liquidate, tender

cashier *n* banker, money-changer, paymaster, purser, teller

casing *n* 1 border, boundary, form, frame, shape

n 2 binder, capsule, case, cover, envelope, holder, sheath, skin, wrapper

casino *n* bar, bistro, cabaret, cafe, discothèque, nightclub

cask *n* barrel, bucket, drum, keg, tub, vat, vessel

cast *n* 1 color, hue, shade, tinge, tint, tone

n 2 configuration, conformation, figure, form, shape, structure

n 3 appearance, aspect, countenance, expression, face, look, visage

n 4 bracket, breed, category, class, division, family, genre, genus, group, grouping, ilk, kind, lot, mold, nature, order, persuasion, section, sector, set, sort, species, style, type, variety

v 1 address, aim, direct, level, point, train, zero in

v 2 flick, fling, flip, heave, hurl, launch, pitch, propel, sling, toss, throw

v 3 see: DESIGN *v* 4

v 4 see: FORFEIT *v*

castaway *n* émigré, escapee, evacuee, exile, expatriate, refugee

caste *n* 1 layer, ply, rank, row, stratum, tier

n 2 class, degree, echelon, estate, hierarchy, level, position, rank, status

castigate *v* chasten, chastise, correct, discipline, punish, torment

castle *n* abode, domicile, dwelling, estate, home, house, mansion, palace, residence

castrate *v* debilitate, dismember, emasculate, enervate, geld, unman, unnerve

casual *adj* 1 coming along, developing, easy, effortless, flowing, fluent, laid-back, running, smooth

adj 2 cavalier, colloquial, familiar, informal, ordinary, regular, relaxed, unceremonious, unconstrained, unofficial, usual, vernacular

adj 3 accidental, chance, chancy, circumstantial, coincidental, contingent, eventful, fluky, fortuitous, freak, incidental, lucky, odd, serendipitous, synchronous

adj 4 easy, fast, immoral, incontinent, indiscriminate, lax, lecherous, lewd, licentious, light, loose, promiscuous, unchaste, wanton, whorish

adj 5 aloof, blasé, calm, careless, composed, cool, detached, diffident, disinterested, distant, indifferent, informal, inhibited, nonchalant, numb, remote, reserved, shy, unconcerned, unfriendly, uninterested, withdrawn

adj 6 see: RANDOM *adj* 2

adj 7 see: TRIVIAL *adj* 2

casualty *n* 1 fatality, loss, victim

n 2 butt, object, prey, subject, sufferer, target, victim

cat *n* feline, kit, kitten, kitty, puss, pussy, tabby, tiger

cataclysm *n* calamity, catastrophe, debacle, disaster, misfortune, tragedy, upheaval

cataclysmic *adj* calamitous, catastrophic, critical, crucial, devastating, disastrous, fatal, fateful, momentous, ruinous, vital

catacomb *n* burial, cenotaph, crypt, grave, mausoleum, memorial, monument, pit, sepulcher, tomb, vault

catalog *n* 1 index, list, register, roster, schedule

n 2 account, amount, enumeration, inventory, itemization, list, litany, repertoire, supply, tally

v 1 check, inventory, itemize, tally

v 2 align, arrange, array, assort, categorize, class, classify, cluster, compile, file, format, grade, group, lay out, line up, list, order, organize, outline, pigeonhole, place, position, prioritize, program, rank, rate, sort, stack, tabulate

v 3 enroll, inscribe, list, register, sign up, write

catalyst *n* 1 absorber, agent, broker, distributor, go-between, intermediary, mediator, middleman, negotiator

n 2 enzyme

n 3 agent, factor, force, power

catalyze *v* adjust, alter, change, modify, mutate, refashion, vary

catastrophe *n 1* calamity, cataclysm, debacle, disaster, misfortune, tragedy, upheaval

n 2 breakdown, crash, crisis, death, destruction, doom, failure, finish, ruin

n 3 see: ANGUISH *n 2*

catastrophic *adj* calamitous, cataclysmic, critical, crucial, devastating, disastrous, fatal, fateful, momentous, ruinous, vital

catch *n 1* bag, booty, prize, spoils

n 2 batch, collection, haul, heap, take

n 3 blip, glitch, gotcha, hangup, hitch, showstopper, slip, snag

n 4 blockage, bottleneck, flaw, hitch, impediment, jam, obstacle, obstruction, snag

n 5 clincher, hook, snag

n 6 game, prey, quarry, target

n 7 buckle, clasp, clip, fastener, latch, pin, snap, zipper

v 1 anchor, fasten, fix, moor, secure

v 2 block, cut off, detain, hinder, intercept, obstruct, stop

v 3 clasp, clutch, grab, grapple, grasp, grip, hold, nab, nail, seize, snatch, take

v 4 ascertain, descry, detect, discover, encounter, espy, ferret, find, locate, spot, turn up, uncover

v 5 bag, capture, ensnare, entangle, entrap, hook, snag, snare, snarl, tangle, trap, trick

v 6 earn

v 7 befoul, ensnare, entangle, foul, hang

v 8 apprehend, arrest, bag, book, bust, capture, collar, detain, get, grab, lock up, nab, nail, pick up, pinch, pull in, run in, secure, seize, take

v 9 behold, comprehend, conjure, descry, digest, discern, distinguish, espy, fathom, grasp, know, look at, notice, observe, perceive, realize, recognize, savvy, see, sight, take in, understand, view

catching *adj* communicable, contagious, contaminative, epidemic, infectious, spreading, transmittable

catchy *adj* see: FASCINATING *adj 2*

categorical *adj* absolute, agreed, bounded, clear, decided, definite, emphatic, established, exact, finite, fixed, guaranteed, limited, positive, specific, unequivocal, unmistakable, vested

categorize *v* align, arrange, array, assort,

catalog, class, classify, cluster, compile, file, format, grade, group, lay out, line up, list, order, organize, outline, pigeonhole, place, position, prioritize, program, rank, rate, sort, stack, tabulate

category *n* bracket, breed, cast, class, division, family, genre, genus, group, grouping, ilk, kind, lot, mold, nature, order, persuasion, section, sector, set, sort, species, style, type, variety

cater *v 1* accommodate, baby, coddle, gratify, humor, indulge, overindulge, pamper, pander, placate, satisfy, spoil

v 2 arrange, deliver, dish out, dispense, feed, furnish, give, hand, nourish, nurture, organize, provide, purvey, serve, supply, sustain

cathedral *n* basilica, chapel, church, house of god, mosque, sanctuary, synagogue, tabernacle, temple

catlike *adj* cattish, catty, feline, furtive, skulking, stealthy

cattish *adj* catlike, catty, feline, furtive, skulking, stealthy

catty *adj 1* hostile, malevolent, malicious, resentful, spiteful, treacherous

adj 2 active, agile, astir, brisk, energetic, lively, nimble, quick, sprightly, spry, zippy

adj 3 catlike, cattish, feline, furtive, skulking, stealthy

caucus *n 1* assemblage, assembly, conference, congregation, convention, council, crowd, gathering, group, meeting, rally, symposium

n 2 chat, colloquy, conference, conversation, debate, dialogue, discourse, discussion, exchange, forum, interchange, intercourse, interlocution, meeting, talk

cauldron *n* cistern, container, jug, reservoir, tank, vat

causal *adj* causative, germinal, inducing, originative

causative *adj* causal, germinal, inducing, originative

cause *n 1* call, necessity, obligation, occasion

n 2 excuse, motive, purpose, rationale, reason, why

n 3 aim, consideration, goal, motive, purpose, reason

n 4 arguments, basis, explanation, foundation, grounds, principle, rationale, reason, rudiments, source

n 5 issue, situation, thing

v 1 generate, induce, muster, occasion, produce

v 2 bring, convert, lead, move, persuade

v 3 activate, elicit, generate, prompt, provoke, spark, trigger

v 4 actuate, bring about, create, draw on, effect, execute, invoke, make, produce, secure

v 5 activate, begin, commence, constitute, create, embark, enter, establish, inaugurate, induct, initiate, install, instigate, instill, institute, introduce, kick off, launch, lead off, open, originate, precipitate, preface, set up, start, tee off, usher in, venture forth

caustic *adj* 1 abrasive, aggravating, annoying, cutting, grating, irritating

adj 2 biting, cutting, incisive, penetrating, pointed, trenchant

adj 3 acerbic, acrid, biting, bitter, corrosive, critical, pungent, sarcastic

adj 4 inconsiderate, selfish, sharp, short, tactless, thoughtless, unceremonious, ungracious

adj 5 harsh, grating, guttural, hoarse, husky, rasping, raucous, rough, strident

adj 6 coarse, cutting, obscene, salty, scathing, scorching, sharp, spicy, trenchant, vulgar, witty

adj 7 accidental, careless, heedless, inadvertent, inconsiderate, nonchalant, selfish, sharp, short, tactless, thoughtless, uncaring, unceremonious, ungracious, unheeding, unintended, unintentional, unreflective, unthinking

adj 8 corrosive, reactive

caution *n* 1 warning

n 2 defense, precaution, protection, safeguard

n 3 anticipation, deterrent, precaution, preclusion, preparation, prevention, safeguard

v 1 advise, counsel, evaluate, recommend, reprove

v 2 avert, deter, discourage, dissuade, distract, divert

v 3 see: NOTIFY *v* 4

cautious *adj* 1 alert, careful, open-eyed, unsleeping, vigilant, wakeful, wary, watchful, wide-awake

adj 2 careful, carping, conscientious, ethical, exacting, fussy, heedful, meticulous, painstaking, punctilious, scrupulous, unrelenting

adj 3 calculating, careful, circumspect, considerate, discreet, gingerly, guarded, heedful, judicious, provident, prudent, restrained, reticent, safe, shrewd, wary

adj 4 see: CHOOSY *adj*

cavalier *adj* 1 casual, colloquial, familiar, informal, ordinary, regular, relaxed, unceremonious, unconstrained, unofficial, usual, vernacular

adj 2 arrogant, conceited, contemptuous, curt, dictatorial, disdainful, grandiose, haughty, huffy, insolent, lofty, lordly, moody, obtrusive, overbearing, patronizing, proud, scornful, snooty, stuck-up, supercilious, superior, vain

cavalry *n* airborne, army, battalion, brigade, company, footmen, guard, horsemen, infantry, legion, marines, militia, minutemen, paratroops, platoon, reserve, storm troopers

cave *n* burrow, den, grotto, lair, recess, tunnel

v see: YIELD *v* 6

caveat *n* 1 limitation, qualification, requisite, restriction, stipulation

n 2 foresight, forethought, providence, prudence, vigilance, vision, wariness

cavernous *adj* echo-filled, gaping, hollow, reverberant, spacious, vast

cavil *v* see: SCOLD *v* 2

cavity *n* 1 break, puncture, slot

n 2 blank, crack, depression, emptiness, gap, hole, hollow, nook, opening, space, void

cavort *v* caper, frisk, frolic, gambol, play, prance, rollick, romp, skip

cay *n* atoll, island, isle, key

cease *v* 1 die, elapse, expire, lapse, pass, pass away, perish, succumb, terminate

v 2 achieve, complete, conclude, consummate, end, finish, halt, perfect, terminate, wind up, wrap up

v 3 abstain, conclude, desist, discontinue, end, finish, forbear, freeze, halt, knock off, quit, refrain, sever, stop, terminate

v 4 see: SUBSIDE *v* 2

v 5 see: TERMINATE *v* 3, 4, 7, 8

cease-fire *n* abeyance, respite, timeout, truce

ceaseless *adj* 1 ageless, boundless, constant, continual, continuous, endless, eternal, everlasting, incessant, infinite, interminable, limitless, never-ending, ongoing, perpetual, persistent, relentless, timeless, unceasing, unending, uninterrupted, unremitting

adj 2 see: STUBBORN *adj* 6

ceasing *n* cessation, close, closure, conclusion, end, finale, finis, finish, stop, termination

cede *v* 1 assign, convey, deed, designate, transfer

v 2 abandon, acquiesce, give up, hand over, leave, relinquish, resign, submit, surrender, waive, yield

ceiling n 1 altitude, limits, maximum, restraint

n 2 roof

celebrate v 1 commemorate, keep, memorialize, observe, solemnize

v 2 carouse, drink, frolic, make merry, party, revel, romp

v 3 acclaim, applaud, commend, eulogize, exalt, extol, glorify, hail, honor, laud, praise, resound, salute, toast, tout, worship

celebrated adj acclaimed, distinguished, eminent, esteemed, excellent, famed, famous, foremost, illustrious, notable, outstanding, prominent, prestigious, renowned, well-known

celebration n ceremony, commemoration, festival, festivity, fiesta, gala, holiday, observance, party, revelry

celebrity n 1 dignitary, luminary, movie star, name, notable, personality, star

n 2 brilliance, distinction, excellence, fame, glory, halo, honor, luster, note, popularity, prominence, renown, repute, splendor

celerity n alacrity, cadence, dispatch, gait, pace, quickness, rapidity, rate, speed, step, stride, swiftness, trot, velocity, walk

celestial adj 1 astral, heavenly, stellar

adj 2 blessed, consecrated, divine, godly, hallowed, holy, pure, sacred, sanctified, spiritual

adj 3 bodiless, disembodied, ethereal, heavenly, incorporeal, insubstantial, intangible, metaphysical, nonmaterial, spiritual, unearthly, unreal, unsubstantial

celibate adj 1 abstinent, chaste, continent, maidenly, pure, virginal, virtuous

adj 2 see: PURE adj 1, 7

n virgin

cell n brig, cage, cooler, coop, hoosegow, jail, pen, penitentiary, pokey, prison, reformatory, slammer, stir, stockade, tower

cellar n basement, underground, vault

cement v affix, bind, bond, fasten, fuse, glue, join, lock, paste, seal, secure, stick, unite

n adhesive, glue, paste

cenotaph n burial, catacomb, crypt, grave, mausoleum, memorial, monument, pit, sepulcher, tomb, vault

censor v see: STIFLE v 3

censorious adj captious, carping, critical, cutting, disparaging, faultfinding, hairsplitting, nit-picking

censure n 1 disapproval, rejection, repudiation

n 2 see: HUMILIATION n

v 1 condemn, denounce, disparage, inveigh

v 2 admonish, berate, blame, chide, condemn, disapprove, lay into, punish, rebuke, reprimand, reproach, reprove, scold, warn

center adj centermost, equidistant, halfway, median, mid, middle, middlemost, midmost

n 1 cadre, core, framework, infrastructure, nucleus

n 2 core, hub, middle, midpoint, midst

n 3 core, gist, kernel, keynote, theme

n 4 attention, crux, feature, focus, highlight, key, spotlight

n 5 axis, focal point, focus, heart, hub, nerve center, target

n 6 core, crux, essence, gist, heart, life, marrow, nature, nucleus, pith, quick, quintessence, root, spirit, substance

v align

centermost adj center, equidistant, halfway, median, mid, middle, middlemost, midmost

central adj 1 middle

adj 2 crucial, dominant, pivotal

adj 3 chief, distinguished, dominant, famed, great, key, leading, main, major, number one, outstanding, predominant, preeminent, primary, prime, principal, prominent, star, successful, superior, top

centralization n concentration, consolidation, focus

centralize v concentrate, consolidate, focus, integrate, merge

cerebral adj analytical, highbrow, intellectual, intelligent

cerebrate v chew, consider, contemplate, deliberate, digest, meditate, mull, muse, ponder, reason, reflect, ruminate, see, speculate, study, think, weigh

cerebrum n brain, head, mind, wit

ceremonial n ceremony, formality, liturgy, observance, rite, ritual, service

ceremony n 1 ceremonial, formality, liturgy, observance, rite, ritual, service

n 2 celebration, commemoration, festival, festivity, fiesta, gala, holiday, observance, party, revelry

certain adj 1 bound, headed for, sure

adj 2 brazen, cocksure, confident, convinced, positive, sure

adj 3 accurate, distinct, explicit, incontestable, infallible, perfect, unerring

adj 4 explicit, expressed, firm, fixed, formal, mandated, set, settled, spoken, stated, stipulated

adj 5 alternate, another, different, discrete, disparate, dissimilar, distinct, diverse, numerous, other, separate, several, some, unlike, various, varying

adj 6 absolute, actual, authentic, bona fide, definite, existent, factual, genuine, hard, inarguable, incontestable, incontrovertible, indisputable, indubitable, irrefutable, positive, real, sure, true, undeniable, undisputable, undoubtable, undoubted, unequivocal, unquestionable, veritable, viable

adj 7 see: AUTHENTIC *adj* 2, 3

certainly *adv* absolutely, decidedly, definitely, entirely, incontrovertibly, indeed, indubitably, positively, surely, truly, unequivocally, unquestionably, verily, well, without doubt

certainty *n* assurance, certitude, confidence, conviction, declaration

certificate *n* 1 credential, document, instrument, license, pass, permit

n 2 credential, degree, diploma, sheepskin

certification *n* commencement, graduation, initiation, promotion

certified *adj* authentic, confirmed, demonstrated, proved, tested, tried, verified

certify *v* 1 assure, contract, endorse, guarantee, pledge, sanction, underwrite, vouch, warrant

v 2 accept, approbate, approve, authorize, condone, confirm, countenance, endorse, favor, pass, ratify, sanction, validate

v 3 attest, authenticate, confirm, corroborate, justify, notarize, prove, ratify, sanction, substantiate, support, validate, verify, vouch, witness

v 4 see: AUTHORIZE *v* 3, 4

certitude *n* assurance, certainty, confidence, conviction, declaration

cessation *n* 1 break, delay, gap, interim, interval, lapse, lull, pause, stop

n 2 abeyance, halt, impasse, moratorium, standstill, stay, stop, stopping, suspension

n 3 ceasing, close, closure, conclusion, end, finale, finis, finish, stop, termination

chablis *n* burgundy, champagne, chianti, claret, port, sauterne, sherry, wine

cha-cha *n* ballet, dance, foxtrot, hula, jitterbug, polka, tap, twist, waltz

chafe *v* irritate, rub, scrape

chafing *adj* annoying, anxious, bothersome, crabby, edgy, fretful, galling, impatient, irritating, jittery, nagging, on edge, restless, touchy, unsettling

chagrined *adj* abashed, ashamed, embarrassed, humiliated, mortified, shamed

chain *n* 1 bond, fetter, handcuff, iron, manacle, shackle, tie

n 2 course, lineup, order, progression, row, run, sequence, series, string, succession, train

n 3 cartel, coalition, collaboration, combine, conglomerate, consortium, federation, group, partnership, pool, syndicate, trust

v bind, fasten, link, shackle

chair *n* bench, pew, seat, stool

v head, lead, moderate, preside

chalice *n* container, cup, dish, Dixie cup, glass, goblet, mug, shot glass, stein, tumbler, vessel, wineglass

chalk *n* brush, crayon, marker, pen, pencil, quill

v dust, powder, sprinkle

chalky *adj* ivory, milky, snowy, white

challenge *v* 1 dispute, doubt, mistrust, query, question

v 2 attack, contradict, deny, impugn, oppose, rebut

v 3 brave, confront, dare, defy, face, mutiny, rebel, resist

v 4 arouse, awaken, excite, kindle, rally, rouse, stir, wake, waken

v 5 call, claim, demand, exact, need, postulate, require, requisition, solicit

n 1 demur, difficulty, hindrance, hurdle, objection, obstacle, problem, protest, question, snag

n 2 altercation, argument, battle, brawl, combat, controversy, disagreement, discord, dispute, feud, fight, fracas, fray, hassle, melee, quarrel, rancor, rift, row, ruckus, scrap, scuffle, skirmish, spat, squabble, struggle, tiff, war

challenger *n* adversary, antagonist, anti, competitor, con, contender, enemy, foe, match, opponent, rival

challenging *adj* difficult, hairy, tricky

chamber *n* alcove, room, ward

champagne *n* burgundy, chablis, chianti, claret, port, sauterne, sherry, wine

champion *adj* excellent, fine, first-class, first-rate, foremost, good, grade a, leading, number one, prime, principal, prominent, quality, select, stellar, superb, superior, top, top-drawer, top-notch, tops

n 1 standout

n 2 ace, expert, master, wizard

n 3 advocate, conqueror, hero, heroine, lead, leader, master, principal, protagonist, star, trailblazer, victor, winner

n 4 see: ADVOCATE *n* 2

v advocate, back, endorse, guarantee, promote, sanction, side, support, uphold

championship *n* advertisement, praise, promotion, publicity, salesmanship

chance *adj* 1 accidental, aimless, arbitrary, casual, chaotic, haphazard, hit or miss, indiscriminate, irregular, random, unaimed, uncontrolled, unplanned
adj 2 see: ACCIDENTAL *adj* 2, 3
n 1 attempt, spin, try, turn
n 2 freedom, latitude, opportunity, room
n 3 coincidence, good fortune, happenstance, luck, serendipity
n 4 expectation, likelihood, possibility, probability, prospect
n 5 bet, fortune, gamble, hazard, luck, risk, stake
n 6 break, crack, gap, occasion, opening, opportunity, shot, show, stroke of luck, time
n 7 attempt, effort, fling, go, guess, heave, lob, pop, shot, slap, sling, stab, throw, toss, try, whirl
v 1 discover, encounter, find, happen, hit, luck, meet, stumble
v 2 attempt, bet, dare, gamble, hazard, play, risk, speculate, stake, venture, wager

chancy *adj* 1 accidental, casual, chance, circumstantial, coincidental, contingent, eventful, fluky, fortuitous, freak, incidental, lucky, odd, serendipitous, synchronous
adj 2 see: PREPOSTEROUS *adj* 2

change *n* 1 move, reversal, shift, turnabout
n 2 adjustment, alteration, anomaly, deviation, modification, mutation, permutation, shift, variation
n 3 current, drift, flow, flux, gush, motion, movement, rush, stream, tide, transition
v 1 shift
v 2 bring about, carry, modify
v 3 invert, reverse, revert, transpose, turn
v 4 adjust, alter, catalyze, modify, mutate, refashion, vary
v 5 alternate, cycle, lap, oscillate, rotate, shift, switch
v 6 alter, commute, convert, evolve, further, improve, metamorphose, modernize, modify, mutate, revolutionize, transfer, transfigure, transform, transmute, vary

changeable *adj* 1 arbitrary, capricious, erratic, fickle, flighty, inconsistent, inconstant, mercurial, uncertain, unstable, unsteady, variable, volatile, wavering, wayward
adj 2 see: PLASTIC *adj* 2

changeover *n* alchemy, alteration, conversion, revision, transformation

channel *n* 1 conduit, cylinder, duct, pipe, tube
n 2 agency, agent, conduit, instrument, means, mechanism, medium, mode, vehicle
n 3 canal, conduit, crevice, curb, cut, ditch, duct, furrow, gorge, groove, gully, gutter, passageway, ravine, rut, trench, trough
n 4 access, approach, artery, avenue, boulevard, drag, highway, pass, path, promenade, road, roadway, route, strait, street, thoroughfare, trail, way
n 5 boob tube, cable, station, teevee, television, tube, TV, video
v 1 carry, conduct, convey, funnel, pass, pipe, siphon, transmit
v 2 address, consign, dispatch, export, forward, mail, post, remit, route, send, ship, transmit, transport

chant *v* carol, harmonize, hum, lilt, sing, yodel

chaos *n* 1 frenzy, hysteria, panic, riot
n 2 anarchy, commotion, confusion, disorder, disturbance, fracas, fray, outbreak, riot, ruckus, storm, tempest
n 3 brouhaha, cacophony, clamor, confusion, din, discord, disorder, hubbub, mayhem, noise, pandemonium, racket, tumult, uproar
n 4 damage, destruction, devastation, disaster, disorder, harm, havoc, hurt, injury, loss, mayhem, ruin, ruination, tort
n 5 clutter, confusion, derangement, disarray, disorder, jumble, mayhem, mess, mix-up, muddle, predicament, snafu, snarl, tangle, tumult, turmoil
n 6 see: ACTIVITY *n* 3

chaotic *adj* 1 fervent, fervid, feverish, frenetic, frenzied, hectic, jittery
adj 2 accidental, aimless, arbitrary, casual, chance, haphazard, hit or miss, indiscriminate, irregular, random, unaimed, uncontrolled, unplanned

chap *n* bachelor, dude, fellow, gent, gentleman, guy, male, man, mister, widower

chapel *n* basilica, cathedral, church, house of god, mosque, sanctuary, synagogue, tabernacle, temple

chaperon *n* bodyguard, companion, escort, guide, retinue, scout
v accompany, associate, attend, bear, conduct, consort with, convoy, escort

chaplain *n* clergyman, cleric, father, guru, minister, padre, parson, pastor, priest, rabbi, reverend

chapter *n* paragraph, passage, stanza, verse

char *v* bake, broil, burn, cook, melt, parch,

roast, scorch, sear, singe, swelter, toast, warm

character n 1 constitution, fiber, makeup, nature, quality, substance

n 2 card, eccentric, kook, lunatic, nut, oddball, weirdo

n 3 attribute, characteristic, feature, highlight, mark, peculiarity, property, quality, trait, virtue

n 4 emblem, example, icon, letter, logo, mark, model, representation, sign, symbol, token

n 5 aptitude, complexion, disposition, distinctiveness, heart, humor, identity, inclination, individuality, makeup, nature, personality, quality, spirit, state, temperament, tendency

n 6 part, portrayal, role

characteristic adj 1 classic, exemplary, ideal, model, representative, typical

adj 2 differentiating, distinctive, lone, one, particular, peculiar, select, single, solitary, special, unique, unusual

n 1 difference, distinction, feature, peculiarity

n 2 attribute, character, feature, highlight, mark, peculiarity, property, quality, trait, virtue

n 3 flavor, impression, nature, property, quality, ring, sound, tendency, tone, type

characterization n delineation, depiction, expression, portrayal, representation

charcoal adj black, dark, pitch-black, shadowy

charge n 1 care, custody, protection, safekeeping

n 2 accusation, complaint, incrimination, inculpation, indictment

n 3 burden, commitment, duty, obligation, onus, responsibility

n 4 bill, check, debt, fee, invoice, note, tab

n 5 accusation, allegation, assertion, comment, declaration, deposition, pronouncement, statement

n 6 cost, expense, fare, outlay, payment, price, rate, value, worth

n 7 administration, care, conduct, handling, intendance, management, overseeing, running, supervision

n 8 bill, bonus, commission, compensation, consideration, earnings, fee, gross, income, pay, revenue, salary, stipend, wage

n 9 see: COMMAND n 3

v 1 entrust

v 2 accredit, apply, ascribe, assign, attribute, credit, refer

v 3 bill, debit, dun, invoice, notice, render, solicit

v 4 bid, claim, command, demand, direct, enjoin, instruct, order

v 5 accuse, blame, complain, condemn, criticize, fault, indict, reproach

v 6 activate, electrify, energize, enliven, excite, ignite, start, turn on, vitalize

v 7 accuse, allege, arraign, assert, cite, impeach, imply, impute, incriminate, indict, litigate, prosecute, sue, try

v 8 see: APPRAISE v

chariot n auto, automobile, bus, car, carriage, coach, jeep, motorcar, omnibus, sedan, truck, van, vehicle, wagon

charisma n 1 dominance, influence, leadership, magnetism, personality, power, strength

n 2 affinity, allure, appeal, attraction, attractiveness, aura, beguilement, charm, enchantment, enticement, fascination, glamour, infatuation, magnetism, sex appeal, spell

charitable adj 1 accepting, easy, forbearing, indulgent, lenient, merciful, patient, restrained, sympathetic, tolerant

adj 2 altruistic, benevolent, bountiful, caring, Christian, compassionate, generous, giving, good, humane, humanitarian, kind, lenient, merciful, philanthropic, tender

charity n 1 alms, assistance, contributions, dole, donations, oblation, offering

n 2 altruism, generosity, goodness, goodwill, grace, humanity, kindness, mercy

charlatan n 1 cheat, fake, fraud, hypocrite, quack

n 2 counterfeit, fake, faker, fraud, hypocrite, impostor, liar, phony, pretender

charm n 1 amulet, fetish, talisman

n 2 attractiveness, decorum, elegance, grace, refinement

n 3 affinity, allure, appeal, attraction, attractiveness, aura, beguilement, charisma, enchantment, enticement, fascination, glamour, infatuation, magnetism, sex appeal, spell

v 1 disarm, entice, sway

v 2 amuse, divert, entertain, interest, please, recreate, stimulate

v 3 captivate, delight, engross, enrapture, enravish, enthrall, entrance, hypnotize, mesmerize, move, ravish, transport

v 4 allure, come on to, dally, flirt, fool, jest, kid, lead on, make eyes, make out, pick up, string along, tease, toy, trifle

v 5 allure, attract, bedevil, beguile, bewitch, captivate, conjure, delight, draw, enchant, enthrall, fascinate, lure, magnetize, mesmerize, tempt, wile

v 6 see: RECOGNIZE *v* 5

charming *adj* 1 slick, smooth, sophisticated, suave

adj 2 adorable, cute, dainty, delectable, delightful

adj 3 alluring, appealing, attractive, coquettish, coy, fast, fetching, flirtatious, seductive, sexy, tempting, winsome

adj 4 funny, odd, old-fashioned, picturesque, peculiar, puzzling, quaint, remarkable, special, uncommon, unusual, whimsical

adj 5 see: FASCINATING *adj* 2

chart *n* 1 blueprint, diagram, draft, map, outline, plan, sketch

n 2 bar graph, diagram, distribution, figure, flowchart, graph, histogram, outline, pie chart, plot, table

v 1 arrange, blueprint, cast, design, devise, draft, draw, engineer, fashion, lay out, map, outline, plan, plot, project, set out, sketch

v 2 see: RECORD *v* 2

charter *v* 1 commission, engage, lease

v 2 franchise, hire, lease, let, permit, rent, sublet

chartreuse *adj* emerald, green, jade, kelly

chase *n* exploration, hunt, pursuit, quest, search, undertaking, venture

v follow, hunt, pursue, seek, shadow, shoot for, tail, trace, track, trail

chasm *n* abyss, cleft, canyon, crack, depth, fissure, gorge, gulch, pass, ravine

chassis *n* framework, infrastructure, skeleton

chaste *adj* 1 abstinent, celibate, continent, maidenly, pure, virginal, virtuous

adj 2 austere, ascetic, astringent, rigid, simple, spartan, stern, stoic

adj 3 celibate, clean, decent, decorous, immaculate, modest, moral, pristine, proper, pure, spotless, stainless, stuffy, taintless, unadulterated, unblemished, undefiled, upstanding, virginal, wholesome

chasten *v* castigate, chastise, correct, discipline, punish, torment

chastise *v* 1 castigate, chasten, correct, discipline, punish, torment

v 2 dock, fine, penalize, punish, sentence, tariff, tax

chat *n* 1 caucus, colloquy, conference, conversation, debate, dialogue, discourse, discussion, exchange, forum, intercourse, interchange, interlocution, meeting, talk

n 2 chatter, talk, gab, gossip, rap

v 1 cackle, gab, gossip, talk, yak

v 2 converse, chatter, discuss, parley, speak, talk, visit

chattel *n* pauper, peasant, peon, serf, slave, vassal

chatter *n* 1 banter

n 2 chat, gab, gossip, rap, talk

n 3 babble, babbling, burble, gibber, murmur, prattle, rattle

v 1 chat, converse, discuss, parley, speak, talk, visit

v 2 babble, blab, blurt, burble, gossip, murmur, prattle, talk, tattle

chatty *adj* see: VERBOSE *adj*

chauvinism *n* bias, bigotry, discrimination, intolerance, parochialism, partiality, prejudice, provincialism, racism, sexism

cheap *adj* 1 base, common, sleazy, trashy

adj 2 economical, inexpensive, low, low-cost, moderate, reasonable

adj 3 close, greedy, mean, miserly, niggardly, parsimonious, penny-pinching, stingy, tight, tightfisted, ungenerous, ungiving

adj 4 chintzy, ragged, seedy

cheapen *v* 1 depreciate, devalue, diminish, downgrade, dwindle, lower, mark down, reduce, underrate, undervalue

v 2 abash, abase, belittle, cast down, debase, degrade, defile, deflate, demean, depreciate, derogate, devalue, dishonor, embarrass, humble, humiliate, lower, mortify, put down, shame, sink

cheat *n* 1 charlatan, fraud, fake, hypocrite, quack

n 2 cad, knave, lecher, louse, rake, rascal, reprobate, scoundrel, rogue

n 3 bandit, brigand, burglar, con artist, con man, criminal, crook, embezzler, gyp, highwayman, looter, mugger, outlaw, robber, swindler, thief

v 1 bamboozle, beat, beguile, bilk, burn, cajole, chicane, chisel, con, cross, deceive, defraud, dupe, embezzle, fleece, flimflam, fob, foist, fool, gyp, hoax, hoodwink, hustle, inveigle, screw, shaft, sham, swindle, trick, victimize

v 2 copy, crib, plagiarize

cheating *adj* see: TREACHEROUS *adj* 2

n 1 deceit, deception, dishonesty, fraud, hoax, lie, sham, subterfuge, trickery

n 2 see: AFFAIR *n* 3

check *n* 1 bridle, cord, leash, restraint, rope, tether *n* 2 bill, charge, debt, fee, invoice, note, tab

n 3 block, curb, hang-up, inhibition, repression, restraint, reticence

n 4 bond, boundary, bridle, constraint, control, curb, damper, harness, leash, limit, rein, restraint, restriction

v 1 catalog, inventory, itemize, tally

v 2 audit, balance, examine, inspect, verify

v 3 cramp, curtail, impede, shorten, stunt, throttle

v 4 oppose, resist, stanch, stem, stop, weather, withstand

v 5 bug, eavesdrop, monitor, observe, oversee, snoop, spy, wiretap

v 6 burden, encumber, hamper, hinder, impede, obstruct, restrain, restrict, retard

v 7 arrest, block, freeze, halt, impede, interrupt, stall, stay, stop

v 8 bridle, constrain, control, crimp, curb, hold back, hold down, inhibit, leash, rein, restrain, restrict, withhold

v 9 canvass, case, examine, glance over, inspect, observe, peruse, pore over, regard, scrutinize, study, survey, watch

v 10 see: AGREE *v* 5

cheek *n* see: AUDACITY *n*

cheeky *adj* 1 see: BLUNT *adj* 1

adj 2 see: RUDE *adj* 3

cheer *v* 1 bolster, buoy, comfort, console, gladden, solace, soothe, support, uplift, upraise

v 2 acclaim, applaud, charm, commend, compliment, flatter, greet, hail, laud, praise, recognize, salute, stroke

cheerful *adj* 1 blithe, cheery, lightsome, merry, sunny

adj 2 buoyant, ecstatic, elated, enthusiastic, exuberant, positive

adj 3 auspicious, confident, encouraging, hopeful, optimistic, promising, sanguine, upbeat

adj 4 see: MERRY *adj* 1, 2

cheerfulness *n* eagerness, sprightliness

cheerio *n* adieu, adios, aloha, *arrivederci, auf Wiedersehen,* au revoir, bon voyage, bye, *ciao,* farewell, goodbye, good day, *sayonara,* shalom, so long

cheerleader *n* see: ADVOCATE *n* 2

cheerless *adj* 1 cloudy, dim, dismal, drab, dull, gray, overcast

adj 2 see: GLOOMY *adj* 5

cheers *n* applause, compliments, congratulations, kudos, plaudits, praise

cheery *adj* 1 blithe, cheerful, lightsome, merry, sunny

adj 2 see: MERRY *adj* 1, 2

chemical *n* catalyst

chemicals *n* elements, material, matter, substance

cherish *v* 1 admire, appreciate, delight, enjoy, relish, revel, savor

v 2 admire, adore, dote on, idolize, love, respect, revere, venerate, worship

v 3 care, foster, mother, nourish, nurse, nurture, parent, protect, raise, rear, suckle

v 4 admire, adore, appreciate, consider, covet, esteem, honor, idolize, love, prize, regard, respect, treasure, value

cherished *adj* 1 favorite, pet, special

adj 2 adored, beloved, dear, esteemed, loved, precious, respected, revered, treasured, venerable, worshiped

cherub *n* angel, spirit

chessman *n* front, instrument, pawn, peon, puppet, stooge, tool

chest *n* 1 coffer, safe, strongbox, treasury, vault

n 2 box, carton, case, container, crate, receptacle

n 3 cabinet, closet, compartment, cubby, locker, nook, wardrobe

n 4 bosom, breast, bust

n 5 bureau, dresser

chestnut *adj* beige, brown, chocolate, hazel, mahogany, tan

chew *v* 1 bite, crunch, gnaw, gulp, guzzle, munch, nibble, rend, wolf

v 2 see: PONDER *v*

chianti *n* burgundy, chablis, champagne, claret, port, sauterne, sherry, wine

chic *adj* 1 current, fashionable, hip, in, smart, stylish, trendy, vogue

adj 2 dapper, dashing, debonair, jaunty, natty, neat, rakish, sleek, smart, snazzy, spiffy, suave, trim

n 1 class, flair, style

n 2 craze, fad, fashion, mode, rage, style, thing, trend, vogue

chicane *v* see: CHEAT *v* 1

chicken *adj* cowardly, fearful, gutless, spineless, timid, yellow

chide *v* admonish, berate, blame, censure, condemn, disapprove, lay into, punish, rebuke, reprimand, reproach, reprove, scold, warn

chiding *n* admonishment, admonition, blast, chewing out, criticism, denunciation, diatribe, harangue, hassle, libel, outburst, rap, rebuke, reprimand, reproach, reproof, scolding, slander, tirade

chief adj 1 crucial, key, salient, vital

adj 2 first, foremost, head, inaugural, initial, lead, leading, premier, prime

adj 3 central, distinguished, dominant, famed, great, key, leading, main, major, number one, outstanding, predominant, preeminent, primary, prime, principal, prominent, star, successful, superior, top

adj 4 see: UTTER adj

n 1 higher ranked, senior, superior, veteran

n 2 boss, foreman, head, overseer, owner, superior, supervisor

n 3 autocrat, commander, despot, dictator, governor, head, king, leader, lord, master, monarch, potentate, ruler

chiefly adv especially, notably, particularly, primarily, specifically

child n 1 descendant, heir, offspring, progeny, scion

n 2 babe, baby, infant, newborn, tot, tyke

n 3 boy, cub, junior, lad, son, young man

n 4 coed, daughter, debutante, girl, lass, miss, young lady, young woman

n 5 adolescent, boy, girl, juvenile, kid, minor, teenager, teeny-bopper, youngster, youth

childhood n adolescence, puberty, youth

childish adj 1 babyish, callow, immature, infantile, sophomoric

adj 2 see: SILLY adj 2

children n brood, descendants, offspring, posterity, progeny

chill v 1 cool, freeze, ice, refrigerate

v 2 deject, demoralize, depress, discourage, dishearten, disparage

chilly adj arctic, cold, cool, freezing, frigid, frosty, glacial, icy, nippy, wintry

chime n alarm, bell, buzzer, gong, signal, siren

v boom, clang, peal, resonate, resound, reverberate, ring, sound, toll

chink n cleft, crack, crevice, division, fissure, rent, rift, rupture, split

chintzy adj cheap, ragged, seedy

chip n 1 bit, dent, flake, fragment, mark, piece

n 2 grudge, ill will, malevolence, malice, maliciousness, malignancy, resentment, spite

v 1 break, crack, fracture, gap, sever, smash, split

v 2 ax, carve, chop, cleave, cut, dissect, fell, hack, hew, mangle, mutilate, notch,

pulverize, rend, saw, sever, slice, sliver, snip, split, sunder, whittle

chipper adj see: LIVELY adj 8

chisel v 1 carve, craft, cut, define, design, fashion, form, mold, sculpt, sculpture, shape, steer

v 2 bamboozle, beat, beguile, bilk, burn, cajole, cheat, chicane, con, cross, deceive, defraud, dupe, embezzle, fleece, flimflam, fob, foist, fool, gyp, hoax, hoodwink, hustle, inveigle, screw, shaft, sham, swindle, trick, victimize

chit n 1 letter, memo, memorandum, notandum, notation, note, record, reminder

chivalrous adj 1 benevolent, big, considerate, generous, grandiose, lofty, magnanimous, noble

adj 2 civil, civilized, cordial, courteous, courtly, decent, dignified, gallant, genteel, gentlemanly, gracious, mannerly, noble, polite, well-mannered

chocolate adj beige, brown, chestnut, hazel, mahogany, tan

choice adj 1 dainty, delicate, elegant, exquisite, fine, favorite, preferred, rare, select

adj 2 deluxe, elegant, first class, grand, luxuriant, luxurious, opulent, ornate, palatial, plush, posh, rich, soft, stately, sumptuous, thick

adj 3 favorite, preferred, select

n 1 means, option, recourse, remedy

n 2 ballot, franchise, option, preference, say, selection, vote

n 3 best, finest, favorite, elite, optimum, pick, pride, select

n 4 alternative, decision, druthers, election, option, pick, preference, rathers, selection, vote

choke n throttle

v 1 clog, congest, crowd, glut, jam

v 2 asphyxiate, constrict, gag, garrote, muffle, quash, repress, smother, suffocate, stifle, strangle, suppress

v 3 bar, block, brake, clog, dam, deter, detract, encumber, frustrate, halt, hamper, hesitate, hinder, impair, impede, inhibit, jam, obstruct, prevent, repress, restrain, retard, slow, stay, stop, stop up, throttle

v 4 cough, disgorge, gag, throw up, vomit

choose v 1 desire, elect, favor, prefer, select

v 2 elect, like, pick, will, wish

v 3 appoint, ballot, elect, nominate, opt, select, vote

v 4 covet, crave, desire, envy, fancy, lust, want, wish

v 5 cull, elect, pick, remove, select, separate, sift, single out, sort

choosy *adj* careful, cautious, discriminating, fastidious, finicky, fussy, meticulous, nit picking, particular, persnickety, picky, selective

chop *n* see: HIT *n* 1

v 1 mince

v 2 ax, carve, chip, cleave, cut, dissect, fell, hack, hew, mangle, mutilate, notch, pulverize, rend, saw, sever, slice, sliver, snip, split, sunder, whittle

choppy *adj* nasty, sloppy, rainy, rough, wet

choral *adj* euphonious, harmonious, lyric, mellow, melodic, melodious, musical, orchestral, philharmonic, rhythmical, symphonic, tuneful, vocal

chore *n* 1 assignment, duty, effort, job, mission, responsibility, stint, task

n 2 drudgery, grind, labor, slavery, sweat, tedium, toil, travail, work

choreographer *n* ballerina, chorine, dancer, gypsy, hoofer

chorine *n* dancer, ballerina, choreographer, gypsy, hoofer

chortle *v* chuckle, giggle, guffaw, laugh, roar, smile, snicker, snigger

chosen *adj* designated, elected, picked, select, selected

chow *n* bread, breakfast, brunch, cuisine, diet, dinner, dish, edibles, entree, fare, food, grub, lunch, meals, nosh, nutrition, provisions, rations, snack, supper, victuals, vittles

christen *v* baptize, bestow, call, confer, designate, dub, entitle, name, nickname, tag, term, title

Christian *adj* see: BENEVOLENT *adj* 2

chronic *adj* 1 incessant, prolonged, severe

adj 2 extended, incurable, persistent, protracted, refractory, stubborn

adj 3 accepted, accustomed, common, constant, continual, customary, daily, everyday, familiar, frequent, habitual, inured, often, recurring, regular, routine, traditional, usual

chronicle *n* epic, legend, opus, saga, story, tale

chronological *adj* consecutive, continuous, progressive, sequential, serial, successive

chronometer *n* clock, hourglass, stopwatch, timepiece, timer, watch

chubby *adj* fat, chunky, corpulent, fleshy, gross, heavy, hefty, meaty, obese, overweight, plump, portly, pudgy, rotund, stocky, stout

chuck *v* see: ABANDON *v* 3

chuckle *n* grin, laugh, laughter, smile, snigger

v chortle, giggle, guffaw, laugh, roar, smile, snicker, snigger

chukka *n* boot, brogan, footwear, moccasin, sandal, shoe, slipper, thong

chum *n* accomplice, acquaintance, adjunct, ally, associate, buddy, cohort, colleague, companion, compatriot, comrade, confidant, confrere, connection, copartner, counterpart, co-worker, crony, equal, fellow, follower, friend, intimate, mate, pal, partner, peer, relative, supporter

chump *n* dupe, mark, pushover, stooge, sucker, victim

chunk *n* block, plank, slab

chunky *adj* see: FAT *adj* 1

church *n* 1 basilica, cathedral, chapel, house of god, mosque, sanctuary, synagogue, tabernacle, temple

n 2 see: RELIGION *n* 2

churn *v* agitate, bake, boil, bubble, burn, ferment, foam, fume, roast, seethe, simmer, smolder

chutzpah *n* 1 arrogance, assurance, audacity, boldness, brashness, brass, cheek, condescension, confidence, crust, effrontery, face, gall, haughtiness, insolence, nerve, patronage, presumption, ridicule, sass, stamina, temerity

n 2 see: PERSISTENCE *n* 3

ciao *n* adieu, adios, aloha, *arrivederci, auf Wiedersehen,* au revoir, bon voyage, bye, cheerio, farewell, goodbye, good day, *sayonara,* shalom, so long

cinch *n* breeze, dash, ease, snap, waltz, zip

cinema *n* film, flick, motion picture, movie

cipher *n* digit, integer, number, numeral

v calculate, code, compute, estimate, figure, reckon

circle *n* 1 bead, mark, spot

n 2 band, cabal, camp, clan, clique, coterie, coven, cult, faction, family, gang, group, mob, ring, school, sect, tribe

n 3 bore, diameter, radius

n 4 compass, confines, dimension, distance, extension, extent, length, limit, orbit, purview, range, reach, realm, scope, size, spectrum, sweep, width

v gyrate, revolve, roll, rotate, spin, turn

circuit *n* 1 boundary, circumference, compass, perimeter, periphery

n 2 alternation, circulation, gyration, revolution, rotation, round, sequence, spinning, succession, turn, whirl

n 3 course, itinerary, journey, line,

means, passage, path, road, route, trip, voyage, way

circuitous adj circular, deviate, diagonal, indirect, oblique, round, roundabout

circular adj 1 globular, global, rotund, round, sphere-like, spherical

adj 2 indirect, circuitous, deviate, diagonal, oblique, round, roundabout

n brochure, flier, handbill, handout, leaflet, pamphlet, sheet

circulate v 1 pass around, revolve, route, travel

v 2 announce, advertise, blaze, broadcast, declare, disperse, disseminate, proclaim, promulgate, publish

circulation n alternation, circuit, gyration, revolution, rotation, round, sequence, spinning, succession, turn, whirl

circumference n boundary, circuit, compass, perimeter, periphery

circumspect adj calculating, careful, cautious, considerate, discreet, gingerly, guarded, heedful, judicious, provident, prudent, restrained, reticent, safe, shrewd, wary

circumstance n 1 context, environment, setting, situation

n 2 episode, event, happening, incident, occasion, occurrence, scene, thing

circumstantial adj 1 contingent, iffy, uncertain, vague

adj 2 accidental, casual, chancy, chance, coincidental, contingent, eventful, fluke, fortuitous, freak, incidental, lucky, odd, serendipitous, synchronous

circumvent v 1 avoid, bypass, detour, evade

v 2 avoid, deflect, detour, dodge, duck, evade, hedge, parry, shirk, sidestep, skirt, ward off

v 3 aggravate, baffle, balk, bewilder, confuse, dash, elude, foil, frustrate, hamper, impede, negate, nullify, perplex, thwart

circus n bazaar, carnival, fair, market

cistern n cauldron, container, jug, reservoir, tank, vat

citadel n fortress

citation n 1 notification, subpoena, summons, ticket, warrant, writ

n 2 acclaim, applause, boost, commendation, compliment, eulogy, plaudit, praise, rave, tribute

n 3 clipping, excerpt, extract, mention, passage, portion, quotation, quote, reference, section

cite v 1 paraphrase, quote, repeat, restate

v 2 call, evoke, serve, subpoena, summon

v 3 calculate, count, enumerate, itemize, list, number, numerate, tally

v 4 see: ACCUSE v 2

citizen n 1 countryman, indigene, inhabitant, national, native, subject

n 2 addressee, dweller, inhabitant, occupant, owner, resident, tenant

n 3 see: HUMAN n

citizens n civilization, colony, community, crowd, culture, folks, group, human beings, individuals, laity, masses, men and women, neighbors, people, persons, populace, population, public, settlement, society, staff, tribe

city n borough, megalopolis, metropolis, municipality, suburb, town

civic adj civil, municipal, national, public

civil adj 1 chivalrous, civilized, cordial, courteous, courtly, decent, dignified, gallant, genteel, gentlemanly, gracious, mannerly, noble, polite, well-mannered

adj 2 civic, municipal, national, public

civilization n citizens, colony, community, crowd, culture, folks, group, human beings, individuals, laity, masses, men and women, neighbors, people, persons, populace, population, public, settlement, society, staff, tribe

civilized adj 1 chivalrous, civil, cordial, courteous, courtly, decent, dignified, gallant, genteel, gentlemanly, gracious, mannerly, noble, polite, well-mannered

adj 2 see: SOPHISTICATED adj 2

clack v click

clad v accouter, apparel, array, attire, clothe, dress, garb, gear, outfit

adj attired, clothed, ensconced

claim n 1 interest, share, stake

n 2 demand, mandate, requirement, ultimatum

n 3 advantage, birthright, edge, enablement, perquisite, prerogative, privilege, right, title

v 1 copyright, patent, protect, register, trademark

v 2 allege, assert, avow, maintain, say, state

v 3 apply, enroll, file, petition, request, sign up

v 4 bid, charge, command, demand, direct, enjoin, instruct, order

v 5 call, challenge, demand, exact, need, postulate, require, requisition, solicit

v 6 argue, assert, believe, contend, defend, justify, know, maintain, state, think, vindicate, warrant

clairvoyant adj intuitive, mediumistic, prescient, psychic *n* medium, psychic, soothsayer, spiritualist

clam *n* cockle, crab, crustacean, mollusk, mussel, shellfish, shrimp, prawn, snail

clambake *n* barbecue, cookout, outing, picnic

clamor *n* brouhaha, cacophony, chaos, confusion, din, discord, disorder, hubbub, mayhem, noise, pandemonium, racket, tumult, uproar

clamorous *adj* blatant, boisterous, disturbing, loud, loudmouthed, noisy, obstreperous, raucous, rowdy, tumultuous, vociferous

clamp *n* 1 bolt, clasp, deadbolt, lock, padlock

n 2 see: HOLD *n* 2

clan *n* 1 breed, class, family, household, people, race, relatives, stock, tribe

n 2 band, cabal, camp, circle, clique, coterie, coven, cult, faction, family, gang, group, mob, ring, school, sect, tribe

clandestine *adj* 1 confidential, classified, concealed, covert, hidden, off the record, private, privileged, secret, sensitive, sub rosa

adj 2 covert, concealed, crafty, deceitful, devious, evasive, foxy, furtive, guileful, indirect, privy, secret, shifty, sly, sneaky, surreptitious, tricky, underground, underhand, underhanded, wily

clandestinely *adv* covertly, furtively, hush-hush, mystically, secretly, sneakily, stealthily, surreptitiously, under cover

clang *n* bang, boom, clap, crash, resound, roar, rumble, shake, thunder

v boom, chime, peal, resonate, resound, reverberate, ring, sound, toll

clap *n* 1 bang, boom, clang, crash, resound, roar, rumble, shake, thunder

n 2 bang, blow, box, bump, chop, conk, crack, crash, cuff, hit, impact, jar, jolt, knock, lick, punch, rap, slap, slug, smack, smash, swat, swipe, tap, wallop, whack

v 1 acknowledge, applaud, appreciate, approve, recognize, show gratitude, thank

v 2 box, cuff, knock, punch, slap, smack, spank, strike, tap, whack

claret *n* burgundy, chablis, champagne, chianti, port, sauterne, sherry, wine

clarification *n* 1 definition, denotation, explanation, meaning, translation

n 2 case, case history, example, explanation, illumination, illustration, instance, representative, sample, sampling, specimen

clarify *v* 1 disclose, explain, relate, reveal, unfold

v 2 depict, interpret, render, rephrase, represent, translate

v 3 analyze, annotate, define, detail, elucidate, explain, expound, express, interpret, narrate, spell out, state, understand

v 4 clear, clear up, delineate, depict, explain, elucidate, illuminate, illustrate, picture, portray, reveal

clarity *n* clearness, distinctness, exactness, freshness, lucidity, plainness, purity

clash *n* 1 battle, competition, conflict, contest, discord, duel, fight, fighting, rivalry, strife, struggle, war, warfare

n 2 affray, battle, brawl, brush, conflict, difference, disagreement, dispute, encounter, fight, fracas, melee, quarrel, run-in, scrimmage, skirmish, spat, touch

v 1 conflict, crash, discord, jangle, jar, mismatch

v 2 altercate, argue, battle, bicker, brawl, conflict, dispute, engage, equivocate, feud, fight, fray, haggle, hassle, quarrel, quibble, row, scrap, spar, squabble, wrangle

clashing *adj* conflicting

clasp *n* 1 bolt, clamp, deadbolt, lock, padlock

n 2 clamp, clench, clinch, clutch, command, control, grapple, grasp, grip, hold, influence

n 3 buckle, catch, clip, fastener, latch, pin, snap, zipper

v 1 buckle, clinch, fasten, hook

v 2 clinch, cuddle, embrace, enfold, hold, hug, press, squeeze

v 3 catch, clutch, grab, grapple, grasp, grip, hold, nab, nail, seize, snatch, take

class *n* 1 chic, flair, style

n 2 caliber, grade, quality, rating

n 3 breed, clan, family, household, people, race, relatives, stock, tribe

n 4 caste, degree, echelon, estate, hierarchy, level, position, rank, status

n 5 degree, grade, interval, level, mark, notch, position, rank, rate, step

n 6 bracket, breed, cast, category, division, family, genre, genus, group, grouping, ilk, kind, lot, mold, nature, order, persuasion, section, sector, set, sort, species, style, type, variety

v align, arrange, array, assort, catalog, categorize, classify, cluster, compile, file, format, grade, group, lay out, line up, list, order, organize, outline, pigeonhole, place, position, prioritize, program, rank, rate, sort, stack, tabulate

classic *adj* characteristic, exemplary, ideal, model, representative, typical

classical *n* blues, country, folk, jazz, music, ragtime, rock-and-roll, soul, swing

classification *n* 1 rating

n 2 sex

classified *adj* clandestine, concealed, confidential, covert, hidden, off the record, private, privileged, secret, sensitive, sub rosa

classify *v* 1 define, differentiate, discriminate, distinguish, isolate, separate

v 2 align, arrange, array, assort, catalog, categorize, class, cluster, compile, file, format, grade, group, lay out, line up, list, order, organize, outline, pigeonhole, place, position, prioritize, program, rank, rate, sort, stack, tabulate

classy *adj* aesthetic, artistic, elegant, refined, stylish, tasteful, well chosen

clause *n* agreement, condition, provision, proviso, requirement, reservation, specification, stipulation, string, terms

claw *n* hook, spur, talon

v cleave, disrupt, divide, rend, rip, rive, scratch, split, tear

clay *n* earth, dirt, dry land, dust, ground, land, loam, marl, soil, *terra,* terra firma

clean *adj* 1 healthy, hygienic, immaculate, sanitary, sterile

adj 2 equal, equitable, even, fair, honest, just, sportsmanlike, straight, upright

adj 3 celibate, chaste, decent, decorous, immaculate, modest, moral, pristine, proper, pure, spotless, stainless, stuffy, taintless, unadulterated, unblemished, undefiled, upstanding, virginal, wholesome

adj 4 immaculate, pristine, pure, spotless, taintless, unsoiled, unspoiled, unsullied, untouched, virgin

v 1 absolve, purify, sanctify

v 2 cleanse, filter, purify, refine, sterilize, wash

v 3 bathe, cleanse, clean up, dip, flush, immerse, launder, rinse, rub, scour, scrape, scrub, shower, wash

v 4 dust

v 5 brush, polish, rub, wipe

v 6 disembowel, dress, eviscerate, fillet, gut

cleanse *v* 1 eliminate, eradicate, erase, purge, remove

v 2 discharge, eliminate, empty, evacuate, excrete, void

v 3 clean, filter, purify, refine, sterilize, wash

v 4 bathe, clean, clean up, dip, flush,

immerse, launder, rinse, rub, scour, scrape, scrub, shower, wash

cleansing *n* 1 washing

n 2 enema, laxative, physic, purge

clear *adj* 1 descriptive, effective, graphic, precise

adj 2 distinct, legible, readable, understandable

adj 3 balmy, bright, fair, pleasant, serene

adj 4 cloudless, fair, pleasant, sunny, unclouded

adj 5 articulate, cogent, eloquent, fluent, persuasive, well-spoken

adj 6 effective, explicit, forceful, strong, trenchant, vigorous

adj 7 bare, barren, empty, stark, vacant, vacuous, void

adj 8 clear-cut, crystal, limpid, lucid, translucent, transparent, unambiguous, unblurred

adj 9 coherent, direct, easy, elementary, intelligible, logical, lucid, simple, understandable

adj 10 blunt, clear-cut, concise, decisive, definite, definitive, distinct, exact, explicit, precise, specific, unambiguous

adj 11 apparent, conspicuous, distinct, evident, given, indisputable, indubitable, manifest, obvious, patent, plain, presumed, self-evident, straightforward, true, unambiguous, unequivocal, unmistakable

adj 12 see: EXACT *adj* 5, 6

v 1 ease, expedite, facilitate, smooth

v 2 hurdle, leap, negotiate, surmount, vault

v 3 disappear, depart, evaporate, fade, vanish

v 4 deplete, drain, empty, evacuate, take out, vacate

v 5 absolve, acquit, condone, exculpate, excuse, exempt, exonerate, forgive, free, pardon, remit, reprieve, vindicate

v 6 clear off, discharge, liquidate, pay up, repay, satisfy, settle, square

v 7 clarify, clear up, delineate, depict, elucidate, explain, illuminate, illustrate, picture, portray, reveal

clear-cut *adj* 1 clear, crystal, limpid, lucid, translucent, transparent, unambiguous, unblurred

adj 2 see: EXPLICIT *adj* 3

clearly *adv* evidently, obviously, plainly, undoubtedly, unquestionably

clearness *n* clarity, distinctness, exactness, freshness, lucidity, plainness, purity

cleave *v* 1 adhere, bond, cling, cohere, hold, join, stick *v* 2 claw, disrupt, divide, rend, rip, rive, scratch, split, tear

v 3 ax, carve, chip, chop, cut, dissect, fell, hack, hew, mangle, mutilate, notch, pulverize, rend, saw, sever, slice, sliver, snip, split, sunder, whittle

v 4 see: SEPARATE *v* 7

cleft *n* 1 chink, crack, crevice, division, fissure, rent, rift, rupture, split

n 2 abyss, canyon, chasm, crack, depth, fissure, gorge, gulch, pass, ravine

clemency *n* forbearance, indulgence, lenience, leniency, mercifulness, mercy, tolerance, toleration

clench *n* clamp, clasp, clinch, clutch, command, control, grapple, grasp, grip, hold, influence

clergyman *n* chaplain, cleric, father, guru, minister, padre, parson, pastor, priest, rabbi, reverend

cleric *n* chaplain, clergyman, father, guru, minister, padre, parson, pastor, priest, rabbi, reverend

clerk *n* 1 bureaucrat, civil servant, official, pen pusher

n 2 aide, assistant, recorder, scribe, secretary, stenographer

n 3 representative, salesman, salesperson, saleswoman, shopkeeper, vendor

clever *adj* 1 gifted, handy, ingenious, inventive, talented, versatile

adj 2 adaptive, bold, canny, daring, enterprising, resourceful, venturesome

adj 3 brilliant, dazzling, good, irrepressible, scintillating, smart, sparkling, sprightly, witty

adj 4 creative, deft, enterprising, fertile, imaginative, ingenious, inventive, resourceful, skillful, talented

adj 5 adroit, apt, canny, cunning, deft, handy, ingenious, nimble, skilled, skillful, sly, wily

adj 6 alert, astute, brainy, bright, brilliant, discerning, discriminating, educated, insightful, intellectual, intelligent, knowing, knowledgeable, perceptive, quick, sagacious, sage, sharp, smart, swift

adj 7 acute, alert, astute, cagey, canny, cunning, deft, keen, knowing, penetrating, perceptive, piercing, quick, quicksighted, quick-witted, receptive, responsive, sagacious, savvy, sensitive, sharp, sharp-witted, shrewd, slick, smart, streetsmart, wise

cleverness *n* acumen, astuteness, awareness, discernment, discrimination, insight, intellect, intuition, keenness,

perception, sagacity, sensitivity, shrewdness, understanding, wit

cliché *n* 1 banality, commonplace, platitude, triteness

n 2 diction, expression, parlance, phrase, saying, slogan, style, term, wording

n 3 announcement, aphorism, axiom, declaration, decree, dictum, edict, gospel, homily, maxim, moral, precept, pronouncement, rule, saying, teaching, truism, truth, verity

n 4 adage, axiom, byword, dictum, maxim, motto, proverb, saying, slogan, talk

clichéd *adj* see: STALE *adj* 3

click *v* 1 clack

v 2 come off, go, go over, pan out, prove out, succeed

client *n* buyer, consumer, customer, end user, patron, purchaser, shopper, user

cliff *n* bluff, hill, incline, slant, slope, steep bank

cliff-hanger *n* melodrama, soap opera, thriller

climate *n* 1 atmosphere, condition, mood, temperature, trend

n 2 atmosphere, conditions, environment, habitat, niche, perimeter, settings, surroundings

climax *n* 1 outcome, payoff, result, return, reward

n 2 crisis, crux, dilemma, emergency, juncture, point, predicament

n 3 acme, apex, apogee, crescendo, crest, crown, culmination, epitome, height, noon, peak, pinnacle, point, prime, summit, tip, top, ultimate, utmost, zenith

v adjourn, cap, complete, conclude, consummate, crown, culminate, dissolve, end, finalize, finish, terminate, wind up, wrap up

climb *n* escalation, rise

v 1 ascend, increase, rise, soar, speed, zoom

v 2 ascend, escalate, intensify, mount, scale, surmount

v 3 crest, increase, jump, mount, rise, surge

v 4 see: FLOURISH *v* 3

clinch *n* clamp, clasp, clench, clutch, command, control, grapple, grasp, grip, hold, influence

v 1 confirm, fasten, secure

v 2 buckle, clasp, fasten, hook

v 3 clasp, cuddle, embrace, enfold, hold, hug, press, squeeze

clincher *n* catch, hook, snag

cling *v* adhere, bond, cleave, cohere, hold, join, stick

clinic *n* **1** asylum, dispensary, hospital, infirmary, institution

n **2** see: ASSEMBLY *n* 2

clinical *adj* detached, impersonal, scientific, systematic, technical

clip *n* buckle, catch, clasp, fastener, latch, pin, snap, zipper

v **1** attach, fasten, nail, pin, staple, tack

v **2** affix, attach, bind, connect, fasten, fix, rivet, weld

v **3** cut, cut back, cut down, lower, mark down, reduce, shave, slash

v **4** crop, cut, lop, pare, prune, shave, shear, snip, trim, whittle

clipping *n* **1** citation, excerpt, extract, mention, passage, portion, quotation, quote, reference, section

n **2** see: SECTION *n* 2, 4

clique *n* **1** band, cabal, camp, circle, clan, coterie, coven, cult, faction, family, gang, group, mob, ring, school, sect, tribe

n **2** assembly, association, band, bevy, brood, bunch, camp, cluster, collection, covey, crew, flock, group, organization, party, team, unit

cloak *n* **1** camouflage, costume, cover, curtain, disguise, mask, pretense, shield, shroud, veil

n **2** coat, cape, mantle, shawl, wrap

v camouflage, conceal, cover, darken, disguise, envelop, hide, mask, occult, seclude, shield, shroud, veil

clobber *v* **1** bang, beat, bludgeon, club, hit, pound, strike, whack

v **2** beat, belittle, blast, conquer, cream, defeat, dust, lambaste, lick, overrun, overwhelm, rout, shellac, smear, thrash, wallop, whip

clobbered *adj* beaten, defeated, dejected, depressed, discouraged, licked, whipped

clock *n* chronometer, hourglass, stopwatch, timepiece, timer, watch

clod *n* **1** bungler

n **2** see: IDIOT *n*

clog *v* **1** choke, congest, crowd, glut, jam

v **2** clot, coagulate, condense, congeal, curdle, dry, gel, harden, intensify, jell, pack, set, solidify, thicken

v **3** see: BIND *v* 7

v **4** see: HINDER *v* 5

cloister *n* abbey, monastery, priory

v bury, cache, conceal, cover, ditch, ensconce, hide, plant, secrete, sequester, stash

clone *n* see: REPLICA *n* 2

v copy, duplicate, image, imitate, mirror, print, re-create, redo, reduplicate, re-

make, replicate, reprint, reproduce, simulate

close *adj* **1** cramped, restricted, uncomfortable

adj **2** humid, stagnant, stuffy

adj **3** familiar, intimate, near, personal

adj **4** crowded, compact, dense, solid, thick, tight

adj **5** immediate, near, near at hand, nigh, proximate, virtual

adj **6** cheap, greedy, mean, miserly, niggardly, parsimonious, penny-pinching, stingy, tight, tightfisted, ungenerous, ungiving

adj **7** accessible, available, convenient, feasible, functional, handy, helpful, multipurpose, nearby, open, practical, public, reachable, ready, serviceable, suitable, unrestricted, usable, useful, utilitarian, well-suited, within reach, working

adv near, nearby, nigh

n ceasing, cessation, closure, conclusion, end, finale, finis, finish, stop, termination

v **1** block, obstruct, occlude, plug, shut, stop

v **2** bolt, latch, lock, seal, secure, shut, slam

v **3** package, seal, tape, wrap

close by *adj* see: ADJACENT *adj*

closed *adj* diffident, introverted, laconic, reserved, restrained, reticent, secretive, shy, subdued, taciturn, timid, timorous, uncommunicative, undaring

closed-minded *adj* bullheaded, deaf, firm, hardheaded, hard-line, inelastic, inflexible, intractable, intransigent, obstinate, perverse, pigheaded, refractory, resolute, rigid, stiff, stubborn, tough, unbending, uncompromising, unpliable, unpliant, unwieldy, unyielding, willful

closeness *n* **1** nearness, proximity, vicinity

n **2** association, contact, nearness, proximity

n **3** companionship, familiarity, fraternity, friendship, intimacy

closest *adj* nearest

closet *n* cabinet, chest, compartment, cubby, locker, nook, wardrobe

closing *adj* decisive, definitive, eventual, final, inevitable, last, latest

closure *n* see: CONCLUSION *n* 5

clot *n* coagulation, lump, mass

v clog, coagulate, condense, congeal, curdle, dry, gel, harden, intensify, jell, pack, set, solidify, thicken

cloth *n* fabric

clothe *v* **1** fit, furnish, outfit, provide, supply

v 2 accouter, apparel, array, attire, clad, dress, garb, gear, outfit

clothed *adj* attired, clad, ensconced

clothes *n* accoutrements, apparel, attire, clothing, dress, garments, gear, togs

clothing *n* accoutrements, apparel, attire, clothes, dress, garments, gear, togs

cloud *n* 1 fog, haze, mist, steam, vapor

n 2 cloudiness

v becloud, bedim, befog, blur, confuse, darken, dim, diminish, dull, eclipse, fade, muddy, obscure, overshadow, pale, shade, shadow, tarnish

cloudburst *n* deluge, downpour, drizzle, hail, precipitation, rain, shower, sprinkle

clouded *adj* ambiguous, borderline, doubtful, dubious, equivocal, garbled, illogical, inarticulate, incalculable, incoherent, inexplicit, muddled, muffled, murky, obscure, precarious, questionable, shaky, suspect, suspicious, uncertain, unclear, uneasy, unintelligible, unsure, vague, wary

cloudiness *n* cloud

cloudless *adj* clear, fair, pleasant, sunny, unclouded

cloudy *adj* 1 cheerless, dim, dismal, drab, dull, gray, overcast

adj 2 dismal, foggy, gray, hazy, murky, overcast, steamy, vaporous, vapory

clout *n* authority, control, in, influence, leverage, power, prestige, pull, weight

v bat, hit, nail, pop, smite, sock, strike, swat, whack

club *n* 1 birch, cane, pole, rod, shaft, staff, stake, stave, stick

n 2 association, body, company, contingent, delegation, fellowship, fraternity, group, guild, organization, society, union

n 3 hotel, inn, lodge, resort, spa

n 4 bat, blackjack, boomerang, cudgel, cue, mallet, nightstick, stave, stick

v 1 bang, beat, bludgeon, clobber, hit, pound, strike, whack

v 2 alarm, attack, bully, coerce, frighten, harass, intimidate, menace, strong-arm, terrorize, threaten

clue *n* 1 example, illustration, indication, manifestation, proof, sign

n 2 cue, guide, hint, indication, indicator, inkling, intimation, key, lead, mark, notion, pointer, sign, signal, tip, trace

n 3 see: TRACE *n* 4

clump *n* array, bale, batch, battery, body, bunch, bundle, cluster, group, lot, pack, parcel, quantity, set

v see: JOIN *v* 7

clumsy *adj* 1 heavy-handed, ponderous, slow

adj 2 gauche, indiscreet, insensitive, rude, tactless, thoughtless

adj 3 awkward, bumbling, faltering, gauche, gawky, halting, hesitant, inept, lumbering, maladroit, ungainly, ungraceful

cluster *n* 1 array, bale, batch, battery, body, bunch, bundle, clump, group, lot, pack, parcel, quantity, set

n 2 assembly, association, band, bevy, brood, bunch, camp, clique, collection, covey, crew, flock, group, organization, party, team, unit

v 1 mass, swarm, teem

v 2 see: ASSEMBLE *v* 3

v 3 see: CLASSIFY *v* 2

clutch *n* 1 brood

n 2 clamp, clasp, clench, clinch, command, control, grapple, grasp, grip, hold, influence

v 1 caress, embrace, grasp, hold

v 2 catch, clasp, grab, grapple, grasp, grip, hold, nab, nail, seize, snatch, take

clutter *n* see: CHAOS *n* 5

coach *n* 1 carriage, buggy, rig, surrey, vehicle

n 2 educator, instructor, leader, mentor, schoolteacher, teacher, trainer, tutor

n 3 auto, automobile, bus, car, carriage, chariot, jeep, motorcar, omnibus, sedan, truck, van, vehicle, wagon

v see: EDUCATE *v*

coagulate *v* clog, clot, condense, congeal, curdle, dry, gel, harden, intensify, jell, pack, set, solidify, thicken

coagulated *adj* thick

coagulation *n* lump, mass

coalesce *v* 1 accord, agree, check, coincide, comply with, concur, conform, consent, consist, correspond, fit in, harmonize, jibe, square, suit, tally

v 2 associate, blend, bond, combine, compound, connect, couple, fasten, fuse, join, link, marry, mate, meet, merge, pair, unite, wed

v 3 see: COMBINE *v* 3, 4

coalition *n* 1 cartel, chain, collaboration, combine, conglomerate, consortium, federation, group, partnership, pool, syndicate, trust

n 2 affiliation, alliance, association, axis, bloc, concord, confederation, consolidation, faction, federation, joint venture, league, merger, organization, partnership, relationship, treaty, union

coarse *adj* **1** grainy, granular, gritty, powdery, sandy

adj **2** caustic, cutting, obscene, salty, scathing, scorching, sharp, spicy, trenchant, vulgar, witty

adj **3** crass, crude, flagrant, glaring, gross, obscene, rough, shocking, uncouth, uncultured, unrefined

adj **4** see: VULGAR *adj* 2

coast *n* bank, beach, seashore, shoal, shore

v **1** drift, float, fly, glide, sail, slide, soar

v **2** cruise, explore, go, journey, migrate, proceed, sail, survey, tour, travel, trek, voyage

v **3** crawl, creep, glide, prowl, skate, skim, skulk, slick, slide, slink, slip, slither, snake, sneak, steal, wiggle, wriggle, writhe

coat *n* **1** case, cover, enclosure, folder, jacket, skin

n **2** cape, cloak, mantle, shawl, wrap

n **3** fur, hide, jacket, pelt, skin, stole

v electroplate, laminate, plate

coating *n* **1** covering, film, layer, membrane, sheet, tissue

n **2** gloss, glow, luster, patina, polish, radiance, sheen, shimmer, shine

n **3** bark, case, crust, husk, peel, rind, shell, shuck, skin

n **4** covering, scale, skin

coax *v* barter, cajole, con, urge

cobalt *adj* aqua, azure, blue, indigo, navy, Prussian, sapphire, turquoise

cock *n* faucet, nozzle, spigot, spout, tap, valve

cockiness *n* see: VANITY *n*

cockle *n* clam, crab, crustacean, mollusk, mussel, prawn, shellfish, shrimp, snail

cocksure *adj* brazen, certain, confident, convinced, positive, sure

cocky *adj* **1** arrogant, disrespectful, flip, flippant, impertinent, impudent, wise

adj **2** arrogant, conceited, haughty, narcissistic, self-assured, smug, stuck up, vain

coconspirator *n* abettor, accessory, accomplice, confederate, conspirator, partner, supporter

coddle *v* accommodate, baby, cater, gratify, humor, indulge, overindulge, pamper, pander, placate, satisfy, spoil

code *n* **1** beliefs, doctrine, ethics, outlook, philosophy, rites, values

n **2** see: PRINCIPLE *n* 5

n **3** see: TECHNIQUE *n* 3

v **1** program

v **2** calculate, cipher, compute, estimate, figure, reckon

coed *n* **1** child, daughter, debutante, girl, lass, miss, young lady, young woman

n **2** collegian, pupil, scholar, schoolmate, student, undergraduate

coerce *v* **1** compel, constrain, force, make, overpower, propel, push

v **2** exact, extort, gouge, shake down, squeeze, wrench, wrest, wring

v **3** alarm, attack, bully, club, frighten, harass, intimidate, menace, strong-arm, terrorize, threaten

coercion *n* compulsion, constraint, duress, force, violence

coercive *adj* **1** compelling, compulsory, unavoidable

adj **2** bullying, forceful, menacing, strong-arm, threatening

adj **3** aggressive, compelling, forceful, hard-sell, high-pressure, intensive, persuasive, pushy

adj **4** see: VIGOROUS *adj* 3

coexist *v* accompany, accord, coincide, concur, coordinate, synchronize

coexistent *adj* coexisting, coincident, concurrent, contemporary, simultaneous, synchronous

coexisting *adj* coexistent, coincident, concurrent, contemporary, simultaneous, synchronous

coffer *n* chest, safe, strongbox, treasury, vault

coffers *n* see: MONEY *n* 4

cogent *adj* **1** correct, logical, rational, sound

adj **2** articulate, clear, eloquent, fluent, persuasive, well-spoken

adj **3** compelling, convincing, effective, forceful, influential, persuasive, revealing, satisfactory, satisfying, solid, sound, telling, valid

cogitate *v* collude, connive, conspire, contrive, devise, frame, intrigue, machinate, maneuver, orchestrate, plan, plot, scheme

cogitation *n* analysis, consideration, contemplation, deliberation, logic, meditation, reason, reasoning, reflection, speculation, study, thinking, thought

cognition *n* comprehension, grasp, insight, perception, recognition, understanding

cognitive *adj* affective, emotional, mental, psychic, psychological, subconscious, subjective

cognizance *n* attention, awareness, care, carefulness, concern, consciousness, consideration, heed, intimacy, knowing, knowledge, mark, note, notice, observance, observation, perception, recognition, regard, remark, sense

cognizant adj **1** alive, attentive, aware, awake, conscious, conversant, knowing, responsive, sentient, thinking

adj **2** appreciable, concrete, detectable, discernible, noticeable, observable, palpable, perceptible, sensible, tangible, visible

cohabitant n bride, consort, mate, spouse, squaw, wife, woman

cohere v adhere, bond, cleave, cling, hold, join, stick

coherent adj clear, direct, easy, elementary, intelligible, logical, lucid, simple, understandable

cohesion n bond, connection, fusion, solidarity, togetherness, union

cohesive adj adhesive, gluey, gummy, sticky, tacky

cohort n see: FRIEND n **1**

coiffure n hairdo

coil n **1** band, crown, garland, loop, ring, spiral, wreath

n **2** arc, arch, bend, bow, crook, curvature, curve, hook, round, spiral

v corkscrew, curl, distort, entwine, gnarl, spiral, twist, wind

coin v **1** mint, stamp, strike

v **2** begin, conceive, craft, create, define, develop, devise, formulate, innovate, invent, make, originate, start

coincide v **1** accompany, accord, coexist, concur, coordinate, synchronize

v **2** accompany, band, collaborate, collude, combine, concur, cooperate, pool, unite

v **3** accord, agree, check, coalesce, comply with, concur, conform, consent, consist, correspond, fit in, harmonize, jibe, square, suit, tally

coincidence n chance, good fortune, happenstance, luck, serendipity

coincident adj coexistent, coexisting, concurrent, contemporary, simultaneous, synchronous

coincidental adj **1** curious, ironic, odd, strange, unexpected

adj **2** accidental, casual, chance, chancy, circumstantial, contingent, eventful, fluky, fortuitous, freak, incidental, lucky, odd, serendipitous, synchronous

coitus n conjugation, copulation, fooling around, foreplay, fornication, intercourse, mating, reproduction, sex, union

colander n sieve, sifter, strainer

cold adj **1** comatose, insensible, senseless, unconscious

adj **2** adamant, cruel, fierce, relentless, vindictive

adj **3** dead, deceased, defunct, departed, lifeless, spiritless

adj **4** arctic, chilly, cool, freezing, frigid, frosty, glacial, icy, nippy, wintry

adj **5** coldhearted, distant, emotionless, frigid, glacial, icy, impersonal, indifferent, unemotional, unfriendly

adj **6** dry, dull, impassive, laid-back, matter-of-fact, phlegmatic, poker-faced, reserved, stoic, stolid, unaffected, unemotional, unfeeling, unmoved, untouched

adj **7** frigid, inhibited, passionless, repressed, restrained, reticent, unresponsive

n illness, infection, virus

coldblooded adj see: NASTY adj **7**

coldhearted adj cold, distant, emotionless, frigid, glacial, icy, impersonal, indifferent, unemotional, unfriendly

coliseum n amphitheater, arena, bowl, dome, hippodrome, scene, stadium

collaborate v **1** assist, associate, cooperate, join

v **2** accompany, band, coincide, collude, combine, concur, cooperate, pool, unite

collaboration n see: SYNDICATE n

collaborator n associate, individual, member, participant, party, person, registrant

collapse n downfall, failure, fall, overthrow, ruin, upset

v **1** fail

v **2** faint, pass out, swoon

v **3** break, break down, come apart, snap

v **4** contract, crumple, deflate, shrink

v **5** cave in, disintegrate, drop, fall, go down, keel over, pitch, plunge, slump, spill, topple, tumble

v **6** capsize, defeat, dislodge, knock over, overthrow, tip over, topple, tumble, overturn, turn over, upset

collar v **1** bottle up, corner, tree

v **2** apprehend, arrest, bag, book, bust, capture, catch, detain, get, grab, lock up, nab, nail, pick up, pinch, pull in, run in, secure, seize, take

collate v bracket, compare, contrast, correlate, equate, liken, match, relate, sort

collateral adj see: SUBORDINATE adj **4**

colleague n see: FRIEND n **1**

collect v **1** gather, grow, harvest

v **2** amass, gather, heap, pile, rake, take in

v **3** accrue, accumulate, acquire, amass, assemble, garner, gather, grow, hoard, save, squirrel, stash, stockpile, store up

v **4** assemble, associate, call, cluster, concentrate, congregate, convene, flock, gather, group, lump, marshal, mass, mingle, mobilize, muster, order, rally, rendezvous, round up, send for, summon

collected *adj* calm, composed, cool, demure, dormant, easy, gentle, hushed, idle, imperturbable, motionless, nonchalant, peaceful, placid, poised, quiet, relaxed, restful, sedate, self-composed, self-possessed, serene, soft, steady, still, tranquil, unflappable, unruffled, untroubled

collection *n* 1 batch, catch, haul, heap, take

n 2 epitome, paraphrase, recapitulation, summary, summation

n 3 assortment, bunch, mixture, selection, spectrum, variety

n 4 assembly, association, band, bevy, brood, bunch, camp, clique, cluster, covey, crew, flock, group, organization, party, team, unit

collective *adj* 1 common, group, organizational, public, social, societal

adj 2 cooperative, helpful, joint, participatory, unified, united

adj 3 aggregate, common, communal, joint, mutual, public, shared

collectively *adv* as one, in unison, jointly, mutually, together

college *n* academy, institute, lyceum, school, seminary, university

collegian *n* coed, pupil, scholar, schoolmate, student, undergraduate

collide *v* 1 crash, demolish, smash, wreck

v 2 bang, bump, crash, hit, smash

v 3 conflict, hinder, impinge, interfere, obstruct

collision *n* accident, crackup, crash, destruction, mishap, pileup, smash, smashup, wreck, wreckage

colloquial *adj* casual, cavalier, familiar, informal, ordinary, regular, relaxed, unceremonious, unconstrained, unofficial, usual, vernacular

colloquy *n* caucus, chat, conference, conversation, debate, dialogue, discourse, discussion, exchange, forum, interchange, intercourse, interlocution, meeting, talk

collude *v* 1 accompany, band, coincide, collaborate, combine, concur, cooperate, pool, unite

v 2 cogitate, connive, conspire, contrive, devise, frame, intrigue, machinate, maneuver, orchestrate, plan, plot, scheme

collusion *n* cabal, conspiracy, intrigue, junta, machination, plot, scheme, secret

colony *n* citizens, civilization, community, crowd, culture, folks, group, human beings, individuals, laity, masses, men and women, neighbors, people, persons, populace, population, public, settlement, society, staff, tribe

color *n* 1 blush, fever, flush, glow, warmth

n 2 cast, hue, shade, tinge, tint, tone

n 3 coloring, dye, paint, pigment, stain, tincture, tint

v 1 dye, paint, stain, tinge, tint

v 2 bias, distort, embellish, exaggerate, influence, slant

v 3 enhance, flavor, imbue, infuse, salt, season, spice

colorful *adj* 1 appealing, entertaining, interesting, lively, stimulating, varied

adj 2 expressive, graphic, impressive, intense, potent, powerful, striking, strong, unforgettable, vivid

coloring *n* color, dye, paint, pigment, stain, tincture, tint

colorless *adj* 1 arid, bland, bleak, boring, dead, desolate, drab, dreary, dull, flat, lackluster, lifeless, lusterless, monotonous, muted, somber, trite, unexciting, uninteresting

adj 2 dull, flat, sterile

adj 3 ashen, ashy, blanched, pale, pallid, sallow, sickly, sooty, wan, waxen, yellow

colossal *adj* enormous, fantastic, Gargantuan, giant, gigantic, Goliath, great, huge, immense, jumbo, leviathan, mammoth, massive, mighty, monstrous, monumental, overwhelming, phenomenal, prodigious, Promethean, stupendous, Titanic, towering, tremendous, unfathomed, untold, vast, walloping, whopping

colt *n* equine, filly, foal, gelding, horse, mare, mount, nag, pony, steed, yearling

column *n* 1 list

n 2 pillar, pole, post, stake

n 3 base, brace, buttress, footing, foundation, prop, shore, stay, support, underpinning

n 4 article, bulletin, byline, communication, dispatch, editorial, feature, headline, item, newsletter, report, story, vignette

columnist *n* commentator, correspondent, editor, interviewer, journalist, newspaperman, publicist, writer

coma *n* apathy, doze, ennui, grogginess, inertia, languor, lassitude, lethargy, nod, sleep, slumber, stupor

comatose *adj* cold, insensible, senseless, unconscious

comb *v* 1 loot, ransack, rifle, scour, search, separate, sift, sort

v 2 brush, paint, sweep

combat *n* **1** battle, conflagration, dispute, encounter, fight, struggle, war
n **2** see: QUARREL *n* 2
v **1** attack, battle, contend, fight, oppose, struggle, war
v **2** contend, duel, fight, grapple, spar, struggle, wrestle
v **3** conflict, contend, contest, engage, scuffle, skirmish, struggle, tussle
v **4** see: COMPETE *v*

combative *adj* angry, bellicose, belligerent, contentious, hostile, militant, pugnacious, quarrelsome, warlike

combativeness *n* aggression, aggressiveness, attack, bellicosity, belligerence, fight, pugnacity

combination *n* **1** blend, fusion, intermingling, joining, merging, mixture, union
n **2** association, corporation, establishment, fellowship, foundation, institution, league, union
n **3** blend, brew, composite, compound, concoction, ferment, mix, mixture

combine *n* cartel, chain, coalition, collaboration, conglomerate, consortium, federation, group, partnership, pool, syndicate, trust
v **1** accompany, band, coincide, collaborate, collude, concur, cooperate, pool, unite
v **2** arrange, blend, compound, concoct, harmonize, integrate, make one, orchestrate, synthesize, unify
v **3** amalgamate, band, blend, coalesce, compound, consolidate, fuse, intermingle, league, lump, meld, merge, mingle, mix, unify, unite
v **4** associate, blend, bond, coalesce, compound, connect, couple, fasten, fuse, join, link, marry, mate, meet, merge, pair, unite, wed

combustible *adj* explosive, flammable, inflammable

come *v* **1** arrive
v **2** advance, approach, near
v **3** see: OCCUR *v* 2

comeback *n* **1** improvement, rally, reappearance, recovery, renewal, resurrection, return, revival
n **2** answer, put-down, quip, reaction, rejoinder, reply, response, retort, return

comedian *n* buffoon, comedienne, comic, fool, stand-up, zany

comedienne *n* buffoon, comedian, comic, fool, stand-up, zany

comedown *n* decline, decrease, descent, dive, drop, failure, fall, plunge, regression, setback, slide, tumble

comedy *n* **1** banter, crack, funniness, gag, humor, jest, joke, quip, small talk, wisecrack, wit, witticism
n **2** broadway, drama, extravaganza, musical, production, stage, theater
n **3** buffoonery, burlesque, caricature, farce, humor, imitation, joke, lampoon, mockery, parody, satire, spoof, takeoff, travesty

comeliness *n* attractiveness, aura, beauty, loveliness, pulchritude, radiance

comely *adj* **1** alluring, attractive, beautiful, breathtaking, cute, fair, fine, foxy, gorgeous, lovely, luscious, magnificent, pretty, shapely, stunning
adj **2** attractive, becoming, exquisite, fair, good-looking, gorgeous, handsome, pleasing, radiant, stately

come-on *n* attraction, bait, decoy, enticement, lure, magnet, ruse, seduction, snare, temptation, trap, wile

comfort *n* **1** ease, effortlessness, freedom, leisure, liberty
n **2** abatement, alleviation, correction, cure, help, relief, remedy, respite, solace, solution
n **3** aid, assistance, benefit, cure, hand, help, lift, nurture, relief, remedy, succor, support
n **4** see: WEALTH *n* 1
v **1** aid, cure, relieve, soothe, strengthen, support
v **2** bolster, buoy, cheer, console, gladden, solace, soothe, support, uplift, upraise
v **3** appease, comply, content, delight, elate, gratify, please, relieve, satisfy, suit

comfortable *adj* **1** desirable, genial, lively, warm
adj **2** affluent, excessive, rich, superfluous
adj **3** comfy, contented, cozy, cushy, homey, secure, snug, soft, warm
adj **4** ample, big, capacious, commodious, open, roomy, spacious, vast, wide

comforter *n* blanket, cover, quilt, warmer

comfy *adj* comfortable, contented, cozy, cushy, homey, secure, snug, soft, warm

comic *adj* see: FUNNY *adj* 3
n buffoon, comedian, comedienne, fool, stand-up, zany

comical *adj* **1** facetious, funny, humorous, jesting, jocular, joking, kidding, sarcastic, witty
adj **2** absurd, comic, crazy, droll, farcical, foolish, funny, hilarious, humorous, laughable, ludicrous, outrageous, ridiculous, silly

coming *n* advent, arrival, entrance

command *n* **1** backing, auspices, authorization, confirmation, endorsement, fiat, patronage, sanction, sponsorship, support

n 2 authority, commission, control, direction, domination, jurisdiction, management, mastery, might, power, rule

n 3 behest, bidding, canon, charge, criterion, decree, dictate, direction, edict, fiat, guideline, injunction, institution, law, mandate, order, ordinance, precept, prescript, prescription, regulation, rite, rule, ruling, statute, word

n 4 see: HOLD *n* 2

n 5 see: SKILL *n* 3

v 1 bid, charge, claim, demand, direct, enjoin, instruct, order

v 2 administer, boss, direct, guide, manage, oversee, regulate, steer, supervise

v 3 advise, authorize, decree, designate, dictate, direct, mandate, ordain, order, rule

v 4 boss, control, direct, dominate, govern, handle, influence, lead, manage, manipulate, order, supervise, sway

commandeer *v* annex, appropriate, confiscate, expropriate, grab, impound, plunder, preempt, repossess, seize, sequester, shanghai, take

commander *n* see: LEADER *n* 4

commanding *adj* compelling, forceful, important, influential, powerful

commemorate *v* 1 keep in mind, note, remember

v 2 celebrate, keep, memorialize, observe, solemnize

commemoration *n* 1 celebration, ceremony, festival, festivity, fiesta, gala, holiday, observance, party, revelry

n 2 drink, salutation, toast

commence *v* activate, begin, cause, constitute, create, embark, enter, establish, inaugurate, induct, initiate, install, instigate, instill, institute, introduce, kick off, launch, lead off, open, originate, precipitate, preface, set up, start, tee off, usher in, venture forth

commencement *n* 1 beginning, briefing, debut, inauguration, induction, initiation, unveiling

n 2 certification, graduation, initiation, promotion

commend *v* 1 commit, confide, consign, entrust, hand over, relegate, turn over

v 2 acclaim, applaud, charm, cheer, compliment, flatter, greet, hail, laud, praise, recognize, salute, stroke

v 3 see: LAUD *v* 1, 2

commendable *adj* 1 admirable, excellent, fine, laudable, praiseworthy, worthwhile

adj 2 blameless, exemplary, exonerated, guiltless, innocent, irreproachable, pure, righteous, virtuous

commendation *n* 1 acclaim, applause, boost, citation, compliment, eulogy, plaudit, praise, rave, tribute

n 2 accolade, award, credit, decoration, distinction, honor, kudos, laurels, medal, note, praise, recognition, reputation, reward, tribute

commending *adj* approving, flattering, complimentary, congratulatory, extolling, praising

commensurate *adj* balanced, equal, proportional, symmetrical

comment *n* 1 commentary, note, observation, remark, statement

n 2 accusation, allegation, assertion, charge, declaration, deposition, pronouncement, statement

v add, declare, note, remark, say, state

commentary *n* 1 comment, note, observation, remark, statement

n 2 analysis, assessment, criticism, critique, evaluation, examination, judgment, notion, opinion, review, ruling

commentator *n* 1 critic, evaluator, judge, reviewer

n 2 columnist, correspondent, editor, interviewer, journalist, newspaperman, publicist, writer

commerce *n* arrangements, business, dealings, enterprise, industry, intercourse, negotiations, trade, traffic

commercial *adj* 1 business, mercantile, trade, trading

adj 2 marketable, salable, vendible, wanted

n ad, advertisement, plug, promo, promotion, sponsorship, spot

commiserate *v* ache, empathize, feel for, pity, sympathize with

commission *n* 1 assignment, authorization, warrant

n 2 delegation, embassy, mission

n 3 board, body, cabinet, committee, council, directorship

n 4 authority, command, control, direction, domination, jurisdiction, management, mastery, might, power, rule

n 5 bill, bonus, charge, compensation, consideration, earnings, fee, gross, income, pay, revenue, salary, stipend, wage

n 6 ante, award, bonus, booty, cash, dividend, donation, fee, gift, gratuity, largess, money, percentage, perk, perquisite, pre-

mium, prize, profit, purse, reward, sharing, stake, stipend, tip, winnings

n 7 see: ADMINISTRATION *n* 3

v 1 charter, engage, lease

v 2 accredit, authorize, certify, empower,
enable, entitle, facilitate, invest, license,
permit, sanction, validate

commit *v* 1 plunge

v 2 bind, contract, engage, pledge

v 3 continue, extend, maintain, perpetuate, prolong, pull

v 4 actuate, do, enact, execute, perform,
perpetrate

v 5 acquire, arouse, contract, engage, enlist, incur, induce

v 6 commend, confide, consign, entrust,
hand over, relegate, turn over

v 7 advocate, affirm, assure, avouch,
avow, devote, guarantee, pledge, promise,
ratify, swear, vow

commitment *n* 1 love, passion, religion

n 2 guarantee, obligation, pledge, promise

n 3 burden, charge, duty, obligation,
onus, responsibility

n 4 assurance, bond, earnest, guarantee,
obligation, pawn, pledge, security, surety,
token, warrant

commitments *n* burden, costs, expenditures, expenses, overhead

committed *adj* 1 betrothed, engaged,
pledged, promised

adj 2 concerned, dedicated, interested,
involved

adj 3 binding, compelling, obligatory, unalterable

adj 4 bound, liable, obligated, required

adj 5 determined, fixed, focused, limited,
narrow, obsessive, one-track

adj 6 bent, dedicated, determined, fixed,
intentional, purposeful, resolute, resolved, set, tenacious

committee *n* board, body, cabinet, commission, council, directorship

commodious *adj* ample, big, capacious,
comfortable, open, roomy, spacious, vast,
wide

commodities *n* articles, basics, essentials,
goods, inventory, line, materials, merchandise, products, properties, staples,
stock, wares

common *adj* 1 general, generic, universal

adj 2 base, cheap, sleazy, trashy

adj 3 group, collective, organizational,
public, social, societal

adj 4 commonplace, dull, ordinary, pedestrian, prosaic, uneventful, unexceptional

adj 5 aggregate, collective, communal,
joint, mutual, public, shared

adj 6 earthly, earthy, mundane, pedestrian, terrestrial, uncelestial, worldly

adj 7 base, humble, ignoble, knavish, low,
lowly, mean, plebeian

adj 8 average, intermediate, mediocre,
medium, middle, normal, ordinary, regular, standard, unimpressive

adj 9 abject, groveling, humble, ingratiating, lowly, menial, obeisant, obsequious,
servile, slavish, subservient

adj 10 accepted, accustomed, chronic,
constant, continual, customary, daily,
everyday, familiar, frequent, habitual, inured, often, recurring, regular, routine,
traditional, usual

adj 11 omnipresent, ubiquitous, widespread

adj 12 average, commonplace, daily,
everyday, general, mundane, natural,
normal, ordinary, plain, prevalent, regular, routine, typical, unexceptional, unremarkable, usual, workaday

n green, park, plaza, square

commoner *n* common man, countryman,
peasant, plebeian, proletarian

commonplace *adj* 1 banal, conventional,
ordinary, trite, undistinguished

adj 2 common, dull, ordinary, pedestrian,
prosaic, uneventful, unexceptional

adj 3 see: MONOTONOUS *adj* 1

adj 4 see: STALE *adj* 3

adj 5 see: TYPICAL *adj* 2

n banality, cliché, platitude, triteness

commotion *n* 1 anarchy, chaos, confusion,
disorder, disturbance, fracas, fray, outbreak, riot, ruckus, storm, tempest

n 2 action, activity, ado, animation, bedlam, bother, bustle, chaos, excitement,
flurry, fluster, fuss, hum, liveliness, madhouse, movement, stir, to-do, tumult, turmoil, whirlpool, whirlwind

communal *adj* aggregate, collective, common, joint, mutual, public, shared

communicable *adj* catching, contagious,
contaminative, epidemic, infectious,
spreading, transmittable

communicate *v* 1 buzz, call, contact, phone,
ring, telephone, touch

v 2 advise, confer, consult, discuss, group,
huddle, parley, powwow

v 3 disclose, display, divulge, exhibit,
inform, notify, open, reveal, uncover, unveil

v 4 air, bring up, broach, discuss, expose,
express, give, introduce, open, put, re-

veal, state, tap, tell, vent, ventilate, verbalize

v 5 brief, convey, declare, describe, disclose, divulge, explain, impart, inform, narrate, orate, portray, read, recite, recount, relate, report, retell, reveal, share, state, tattle, tell, transmit

v 6 see: EDUCATE *v*

communication *n* 1 affair, association, friendship, intimacy, liaison, rapport, relationship, union

n 2 data, disclosure, exchange, expression, facts, information, intelligence, knowledge, news, notification

n 3 see: ARTICLE *n* 2

communicative *adj* articulate, expressive, talkative, vocal

communist *n* Bolshevik, comrade, pinko, red

community *n* 1 brotherhood, camaraderie, esprit de corps, fellowship, fraternity, lodge

n 2 citizens, civilization, colony, crowd, culture, folks, group, human beings, individuals, laity, masses, men and women, neighbors, people, persons, populace, population, public, settlement, society, staff, tribe

n 3 borough, burgh, hamlet, settlement, township, village

commute *v* 1 alter, change, convert, evolve, further, improve, metamorphose, modernize, modify, mutate, revolutionize, transfer, transfigure, transform, transmute, vary

v 2 drive, ride, travel

commuter *n* passenger, rider, traveler

compact *adj* 1 definitive, meaty, pithy, seminal, tight

adj 2 close, crowded, dense, solid, thick, tight

adj 3 carryable, lightweight, luggable, movable, pocket-size, portable, small, transportable

adj 4 firm, hard, hardened, rigid, secure, solid, sound, specific, stable, stiff, tight

n agreement, bargain, bond, contract, convention, covenant, deal, pact, pledge, promise, transaction, treaty, understanding

v compress, constrain, crowd, crush, jam, mash, pack, press, push, squash, squeeze

compactness *n* density, firmness, hardness, solidity, strength, tensile strength

companion *n* 1 bodyguard, chaperon, escort, guide, retinue, scout

n 2 accomplice, acquaintance, adjunct, ally, associate, buddy, chum, cohort, colleague, compatriot, comrade, confidant, confrere, connection, copartner, counterpart, co-worker, crony, equal, fellow, friend, follower, intimate, mate, pal, partner, peer, relative, supporter

companionship *n* closeness, familiarity, fraternity, friendship, intimacy

company *n* 1 guest, visitor

n 2 band, body, corps, group, outfit, party, troop, troupe

n 3 army, battalion, brigade, force, gang, men, power, soldiers, troops

n 4 business, concern, corporation, enterprise, establishment, firm, house, organization, partnership

n 5 association, body, club, contingent, delegation, fellowship, fraternity, group, guild, organization, society, union

n 6 airborne, army, battalion, brigade, cavalry, footmen, guard, horsemen, infantry, legion, marines, militia, minutemen, paratroops, platoon, reserve, storm troopers

comparable *adj* akin, alike, analogous, corresponding, equivalent, identical, kindred, like, matching, parallel, related, same, similar, such, uniform

comparative *adj* relative

compare *v* 1 analogize, associate, correlate, explain, rank, relate

v 2 bracket, collate, contrast, correlate, equate, liken, match, relate, sort

comparison *n* 1 percentage, proportion, ratio, relation, share

n 2 affinity, analogy, approximation, likeness, match, metaphor, resemblance, semblance, similarity, simile

compartment *n* cabinet, chest, closet, cubby, locker, nook, wardrobe

compass *n* 1 boundary, circuit, perimeter, periphery

n 2 see: REACH *n* 3

v bound, encircle, enclose, encompass, enfold, envelop, surround

compassion *n* 1 affinity, empathy, kindness, mercy, pity, rue, sympathy, tenderness, understanding

n 2 affection, affinity, attachment, attraction, concern, devotion, fondness, heart, kinship, love, warmth

compassionate *adj* 1 affectionate, considerate, empathetic, empathic, gentle, humane, kind, kindhearted, responsive, softhearted, sympathetic, tender, warm, warmhearted

adj 2 altruistic, benevolent, bountiful, caring, charitable, Christian, generous, giving, good, humane, humanitarian, kind, lenient, merciful, philanthropic, tender

compassionless adj see: NASTY adj 7

compatible adj 1 agreeable, concurrent, congruent, harmonious, parallel

adj 2 congenial, congruous, kindred, like, suitable

compatriot n see: FRIEND n 1

compel v 1 coerce, constrain, force, make, overpower, propel, push

v 2 see: MOVE v 5

v 3 see: SWAY v 6

compelling adj 1 compulsory, unavoidable

adj 2 binding, committed, obligatory, unalterable

adj 3 commanding, forceful, important, influential, powerful

adj 4 alluring, desirable, irresistible, overpowering, seductive, tantalizing

adj 5 aggressive, coercive, forceful, hardsell, high-pressure, intensive, persuasive, pushy

adj 6 cogent, convincing, effective, forceful, influential, persuasive, revealing, satisfactory, satisfying, solid, sound, telling, valid

adj 7 see: ASSERTIVE adj

adj 8 see: VIGOROUS adj 3

compendium n 1 autobiography, biography, profile, résumé, sketch, vita

n 2 atlas, directory, guide, guidebook, handbook, list, listing, manual, phone book, textbook, Yellow Pages

n 3 abridgement, abstract, brief, condensation, digest, essence, example, outline, review, sketch, summary, syllabus, synopsis

compensate v 1 adjust, balance, make equal, make up, offset, outweigh, redeem, set off

v 2 avenge, cover, disburse, indemnify, pay, reciprocate, redress, reimburse, remedy, remunerate, repair, repay, requite, retaliate, revenge, settle, vindicate

compensation n 1 earnings, gain, reward, wages

n 2 alimony, fee, honorarium, payment, remuneration, reward, stipend

n 3 amends, damages, indemnity, redress, reparation, restitution, restoration

n 4 see: SALARY n

compete v combat, contend, contest, counter, dispute, duel, fight, match, oppose, parry, pit, play, repel, resist, rival, strive, struggle, vie

competence n ability, adequacy, adroitness, aptitude, art, caliber, calling, capability, capacity, command, craft, dexterity, experience, expertise, familiarity, forte, knack, know-how, knowledge, mastery, proficiency, prowess, qualification, savvy, skill, specialty, strength, talent, training, workmanship

competency n adequacy, sufficiency

competent adj 1 adequate, capable, effective, efficacious, efficient, proficient, successful, sufficient

adj 2 acceptable, adequate, decent, enough, fair, good, mediocre, passable, reasonable, respectable, satisfactory, sufficient, tolerable

adj 3 able, accomplished, adept, apt, capable, deft, dexterous, expert, fit, gifted, masterful, professional, proficient, proper, qualified, skillful, talented

competing adj opposing, rival, vying

competition n 1 battle, clash, conflict, contest, discord, duel, fight, fighting, rivalry, strife, struggle, war, warfare

n 2 bout, conflict, contest, event, game, marathon, match, meet, meeting, race, regatta, round robin, run, tournament, tourney

competitor n 1 contestant, participant, player, team member

n 2 adversary, antagonist, anti, challenger, con, contender, enemy, foe, match, opponent, rival

compile v 1 annotate, correct, denote, edit, modify, polish, proofread, revise

v 2 align, arrange, array, assort, catalog, categorize, class, classify, cluster, file, format, grade, group, lay out, line up, list, order, organize, outline, pigeonhole, place, position, prioritize, program, rank, rate, sort, stack, tabulate

complain v 1 accuse, blame, charge, condemn, criticize, fault, indict, reproach

v 2 crab, criticize, grieve, gripe, grumble, mutter, nag, object, protest, whine

complaint n 1 accusation, charge, incrimination, inculpation, indictment

n 2 grievance, hardship, injury, injustice, wrong

n 3 beef, criticism, grievance, gripe, objection, protest

n 4 see: ILLNESS n 1

complaisant adj 1 amiable, easy, good-humored, good-natured, lenient, mild, obliging

adj 2 amenable, compliant, cooperative, obedient, submissive, subservient, tractable, willing

complement n counterpart, equal, equivalent, like, match, parallel, peer *v* 1 approximate, correspond, equal, parallel

v 2 complete, fulfill, round out, supplement

complementary *adj* see: SUBORDINATE *adj* 4

complete *adj* 1 comprehensive, exhaustive, thorough, unabridged

adj 2 accomplished, concluded, done, ended, finished, over, performed, terminated, through, wrapped up

adj 3 all, all-out, entire, full-blown, gross, integral, integrated, outright, total, unlimited, whole

adj 4 absolute, flawless, good, intact, perfect, sound, unblemished, unbroken, undamaged, unimpaired, uninjured, unmarred, untouched, whole

adj 5 absolute, chief, consummate, dominant, godlike, leading, main, perfect, principal, pure, ranking, sheer, supreme, total, unsurpassed, utter, whole

v 1 fulfill, redeem, satisfy

v 2 complement, fulfill, round out, supplement

v 3 achieve, cease, conclude, consummate, end, finish, halt, perfect, terminate, wind up, wrap up

v 4 adjourn, cap, climax, conclude, consummate, crown, culminate, dissolve, end, finalize, finish, terminate, wind up, wrap up

v 5 accomplish, consummate, execute, fulfill, implement, perform, realize

completely *adv* adequately, altogether, assiduously, earnestly, entirely, exhaustively, fully, hard, intensely, intensively, painstakingly, perfectly, quite, sufficiently, thoroughly, totally, unremittingly, utterly, wholly

completion *n* 1 conclusion, culmination, end, finale, finish, windup

n 2 accomplishment, achievement, arrival, attainment, fruition, fulfillment, realization, satisfaction, success, triumph, victory

complex *adj* 1 diverse, manifold, multifarious, multifold

adj 2 complicated, elaborate, enigmatic, intricate, involved, knotty, mysterious, tangled

adj 3 composite, compound, mixed

n infrastructure, maze, network, organization, system

complexion *n* aptitude, character, disposition, distinctiveness, heart, humor, identity, inclination, individuality, makeup, nature, personality, quality, spirit, state, temperament, tendency

complexity *n* convolution, intricacy, involution, involvement

compliance *n* 1 adaptation, agreement, conformation, modification

n 2 acquiescence, dependence, obedience, subjection, submission

n 3 acceptance, accord, agreement, approval, assent, concurrence, consent, go-ahead, nod, sympathy

n 4 capitulation, release, submission, subordination, subservience, surrender

compliant *adj* 1 willing

adj 2 amenable, complaisant, cooperative, obedient, submissive, subservient, tractable, willing

adj 3 acquiescent, docile, easy, meek, mild, nonresistant, obedient, passive, resigned, submissive, tame, tolerant, unassertive, yielding

complicate *v* confound, confuse, entangle, mix, mix up, snarl

complicated *adj* complex, elaborate, enigmatic, intricate, involved, knotty, mysterious, tangled

complication *n* 1 befuddlement, confusion, perplexity

n 2 cramp, crick, difficulty, kink

n 3 difficulty, dilemma, obstacle, plight, predicament, problem, quandary, situation, snag

complicity *n* connivance, conspiracy, participation

compliment *n* acclaim, applause, boost, citation, commendation, eulogy, plaudit, praise, rave, tribute

v acclaim, applaud, charm, cheer, commend, flatter, greet, hail, laud, praise, recognize, salute, stroke

complimentary *adj* 1 free, gratis, gratuitous

adj 2 approving, commending, congratulatory, extolling, flattering, praising

compliments *n* applause, cheers, congratulations, kudos, plaudits, praise

comply *v* 1 accommodate, conform, follow, keep, mind, obey, observe, submit

v 2 accept, agree, allow, approve, assent, concur, consent, endorse, sign up, subscribe

v 3 appease, comfort, content, delight, elate, gratify, please, relieve, satisfy, suit

v 4 see: YIELD *v* 6

component *n* 1 part, module, unit

n 2 installment, part, portion, segment

n 3 constituent, element, factor, ingredient, item, part, segment

comport *v* act, bear, behave, carry, conduct, demean, rule

compose *v* 1 constitute, construct, form

v 2 author, create, draft, pen, prepare, type, write

v 3 see: APPEASE *v* 2

composed *adj* 1 calm, collected, cool, demure, dormant, easy, gentle, hushed, idle, imperturbable, motionless, nonchalant, peaceful, placid, poised, quiet, relaxed, restful, sedate, self-composed, self-possessed, serene, soft, steady, still, tranquil, unflappable, unruffled, untroubled

adj 2 see: INDIFFERENT *adj* 4

composer *n* author, bard, folk singer, muse, narrator, poet, storyteller, troubadour

composite *n* blend, brew, combination, compound, concoction, ferment, mix, mixture

adj complex, compound, mixed

composition *n* 1 creation

n 2 article, discourse, dissertation, essay, manuscript, memoir, monograph, paper, report, study, theme, thesis, tract, treatise, work

composure *n* 1 equilibrium

n 2 calmness, equanimity, harmony, peacefulness, self-possession, serenity, tranquillity

compound *n* 1 drug, elixir, formula, medicine, narcotic, painkiller, pharmaceutical, prescription

n 2 blend, brew, combination, composite, concoction, ferment, mix, mixture

v 1 arrange, blend, combine, concoct, harmonize, integrate, make one, orchestrate, synthesize, unify

v 2 amalgamate, band, blend, coalesce, combine, consolidate, fuse, intermingle, league, lump, meld, merge, mingle, mix, unify, unite

v 3 associate, blend, bond, coalesce, combine, connect, couple, fasten, fuse, join, link, marry, mate, meet, merge, pair, unite, wed

adj composite, mixed

comprehend *v* 1 decipher, decode, infer, interpret, peruse, read, study, understand

v 2 comprise, contain, embody, embrace, encompass, have, include, incorporate, involve, take in

v 3 assume, believe, conceive, estimate, expect, fathom, gather, grasp, guess, imagine, infer, know, presume, suppose, surmise, suspect, think, trust, understand

v 4 behold, catch, conjure, descry, digest, discern, distinguish, espy, fathom, grasp, know, look at, notice, observe, perceive, realize, recognize, savvy, see, sight, take in, understand, view

comprehension *n* 1 intellect, mind, reason, understanding

n 2 cognition, grasp, insight, perception, recognition, understanding

comprehensive *adj* 1 complete, exhaustive, thorough, unabridged

adj 2 extensive, indiscriminate, large-scale, sweeping, wholesale

adj 3 blanket, expansive, extensive, sweeping, universal

compress *v* 1 condense, distill, express, extract, purify, refine

v 2 compact, constrain, crowd, crush, jam, mash, pack, press, push, squash, squeeze

v 3 concentrate, condense, constrict, contract, reduce, shrink

compressed *adj* abbreviated, brief, concise, crisp, curt, laconic, pithy, short, succinct, terse, to the point

comprise *v* comprehend, contain, embody, embrace, encompass, have, include, incorporate, involve, take in

compromise *n* agreement, arrangement, concession, decision, determination, franchise, settlement

v adjust, agree, settle

comptroller *n* accountant, actuary, bookkeeper

compulsion *n* coercion, constraint, duress, force, violence

compulsive *adj* see: ASSERTIVE *adj*

compulsory *adj* 1 coercive, compelling, unavoidable

adj 2 imperative, mandatory, must do, necessary, obligatory, prerequisite, required

compunction *n* conscience, pang, qualm, regret, reservation, restraint, scruple, twinge

compute *v* calculate, cipher, code, estimate, figure, reckon

comrade *n* 1 accomplice, acquaintance, adjunct, ally, associate, buddy, chum, cohort, colleague, companion, compatriot, confidant, confrere, connection, copartner, counterpart, co-worker, crony, equal, fellow, follower, friend, intimate, mate, pal, partner, peer, relative, supporter

n 2 Bolshevik, communist, pinko, red

con *n* 1 antagonism, opposition

n 2 alibi, deception, lie, pretext, ruse, subterfuge, trick

n 3 crime, graft, hustle, racket, rip-off, scam, scheme, sting, swindle

n 4 see: CRIMINAL *n* 2

n 5 see: ENEMY *n*

v 1 barter, cajole, coax, urge

v 2 bamboozle, beat, beguile, bilk, burn, cajole, cheat, chicane, chisel, cross, deceive, defraud, dupe, embezzle, fleece, flimflam, fob, foist, fool, gyp, hoax, hoodwink, hustle, inveigle, screw, shaft, sham, swindle, trick, victimize

conceal *v* 1 harbor, hide, house, keep, protect, safeguard, shelter, shield

v 2 bury, cache, cloister, cover, ditch, ensconce, hide, plant, secrete, sequester, stash

v 3 camouflage, cloak, cover, darken, disguise, envelop, hide, mask, occult, seclude, shield, shroud, veil

concealed *adj* 1 covert, invisible, obscure, unseen, veiled

adj 2 clandestine, classified, confidential, covert, hidden, off the record, private, privileged, secret, sensitive, sub rosa

adj 3 see: DECEITFUL *adj* 1

concede *v* 1 acknowledge, admit, allow, avow, confess, fess up, grant, own, own up

v 2 accede, acquiesce, bend, bow, buckle, capitulate, cave, comply, cry uncle, defer, give in, give up, relent, submit, succumb, surrender, twist, yield

v 3 see: GIVE *v* 8

v 4 see: TOLERATE *v*

conceit *n* airs, arrogance, cockiness, condescension, disdain, egotism, haughtiness, image, loftiness, narcissism, pride, self-esteem, self-image, vanity

conceited *adj* 1 arrogant, cocky, haughty, narcissistic, self-assured, smug, stuck up, vain

adj 2 see: VAIN *adj* 3, 5

conceivable *adj* likely, ostensible, plausible, possible, probable

conceive *v* 1 build, construct, devise, frame, shape, surround

v 2 conjecture, conjure up, create, envision, fancy, image, imagine, invent, project, realize, think, visualize

v 3 assume, believe, comprehend, estimate, expect, fathom, gather, grasp, guess, imagine, infer, know, presume, suppose, surmise, suspect, think, trust, understand

v 4 arrange, conceptualize, organize, structure

v 5 begin, coin, craft, create, define, develop, devise, formulate, innovate, invent, make, originate, start

conceived *adj* conjured, created, fancied, fanciful, fantastic, fictional, fictitious, illusory, imaginary, imagined, invented, make-believe, nonexistent, notional, unreal, whimsical

concentrate *n* essence, extract, juice

v 1 fix, fixate, focus, rivet

v 2 centralize, consolidate, focus, integrate, merge

v 3 compress, condense, constrict, contract, reduce, shrink

v 4 accent, accentuate, amplify, emphasize, feature, flag, focus, heighten, highlight, italicize, mark, punctuate, spotlight, stress, underline, underscore

v 5 assemble, associate, call, cluster, collect, congregate, convene, flock, gather, group, lump, marshal, mass, mingle, mobilize, muster, order, rally, rendezvous, round up, send for, summon

concentrated *adj* 1 crowded, populous, teeming

adj 2 exclusive, fixed, undistracted, undivided, unswerving, whole

adj 3 hearty, heavy-duty, lusty, potent, powerful, robust, stalwart, stout, strong, sturdy

adj 4 absorbed, agog, deep, determined, distracted, engaged, engrossed, enraptured, entranced, fascinated, immersed, intent, preoccupied, rapt, wrapped up

concentration *n* 1 centralization, consolidation, focus

n 2 amplitude, caliber, magnitude, potency, strength

n 3 depth, energy, intensity, profundity, strength, substance, vigor

concept *n* conception, hunch, idea, image, impression, notion, perception, recollection, thought, view

conception *n* 1 formulation, ideation, imagination

n 2 birth, creation, formulation, genesis, procreation

n 3 concept, hunch, idea, image, impression, notion, perception, recollection, thought, view

n 4 beginning, cradle, derivation, fountainhead, inception, infancy, mother, origin, root, seed, source, stem

n 5 fertilization, insemination, propagation, reproduction, spawning

conceptualize *v* arrange, conceive, organize, structure

concern *n* 1 affair, business, issue, matter

n 2 curiosity, inquisitiveness, interest, regard

n 3 emphasis, gravity, import, importance, significance, stress, weight

n 4 business, company, corporation, enterprise, establishment, firm, house, organization, partnership

n **5** doubt, dubiety, incertitude, indecision, mistrust, query, question, skepticism, suspicion, uncertainty, wonder

n **6** annoyance, anxiety, apprehension, bother, care, disquiet, disquietude, doubt, irritation, misgiving, reservation, restlessness, restraint, skepticism, trouble, uneasiness, vexation, worry

n **7** attention, awareness, care, carefulness, cognizance, consciousness, consideration, heed, intimacy, knowing, knowledge, mark, note, notice, observance, observation, perception, recognition, regard, remark, sense

n **8** see: LOVE *n* 2

n **9** see: PAIN *n* 4

v **1** influence, interest, involve

v **2** apply, bear, pertain, refer, regard, relate

v **3** affect, bother, burden, daunt, disturb, faze, intimidate, oppress, upset, worry

v **4** see: ANNOY *v* 1

concerned *adj* **1** committed, dedicated, interested, involved

adj **2** see: AFRAID *adj* 2

concerning *prep* about, apropos, as to, re, regarding, respecting, with respect to

concert *n* **1** concerto, étude, fugue, program, recital, serenade, sonata, symphony

n **2** accord, affinity, agreement, assent, concord, congruence, cooperation, empathy, harmony, rapport, synergy, teamwork, unity

concerted *adj* agreeing, harmonious, unanimous, uncontested, undivided, unified

concerto *n* concert, étude, fugue, program, recital, serenade, sonata, symphony

concession *n* agreement, arrangement, compromise, decision, determination, franchise, settlement

conciliate *v* see: APPEASE *v* 2

concise *adj* **1** abbreviated, brief, compressed, crisp, curt, laconic, pithy, short, succinct, terse, to the point

adj **2** see: EXPLICIT *adj* 3

conciseness *n* abruptness, brevity, briefness, curtness, quickness, shortness, transience

conclude *v* **1** bring about, end, generate, result in, yield

v **2** adjudicate, decide, determine, establish, resolve, rule, settle, will

v **3** achieve, cease, complete, consummate, end, finish, halt, perfect, terminate, wind up, wrap up

v **4** analyze, construe, deduce, derive, draw, educe, gather, glean, guess, infer, interpret, presume, surmise

v **5** adjourn, cap, climax, complete, consummate, crown, culminate, dissolve, end, finalize, finish, terminate, wind up, wrap up

v **6** abstain, cease, desist, discontinue, end, finish, forbear, freeze, halt, knock off, quit, refrain, sever, stop, terminate

concluded *adj* accomplished, complete, done, ended, finished, over, performed, terminated, through, wrapped up

concluding *adj* conclusive, final, last, terminal, ultimate

conclusion *n* **1** deduction, guess, inference, reasoning, summation

n **2** completion, culmination, end, finale, finish, windup

n **3** culmination, denouement, outcome, resolution, result, solution

n **4** assumption, conjecture, discretion, estimate, guess, judgment, notion, presumption, theorization

n **5** ceasing, cessation, close, closure, end, finale, finis, finish, stop, termination

conclusive *adj* **1** definitive

adj **2** concluding, final, last, terminal, ultimate

concoct *v* **1** deceive, equivocate, fabricate, falsify, fib, invent, lie, misstate, perjure

v **2** arrange, blend, combine, compound, harmonize, integrate, make one, orchestrate, synthesize, unify

v **3** brew, construe, contrive, create, devise, engineer, fabricate, formulate, hatch, invent, make up, plot, scheme

concoction *n* **1** creation, fabrication, fantasy, fiction, figment, invention

n **2** blend, brew, combination, composite, compound, ferment, mix, mixture

concord *n* **1** see: AGREEMENT *n* 5

n **2** see: ALLIANCE *n*

concrete *adj* **1** corporeal, material, objective, physical, real, sensible, substantial, tactile, tangible

adj **2** appreciable, cognizant, detectable, discernible, noticeable, observable, palpable, perceptible, sensible, tangible, visible

concubine *n* lover, mistress, trifle

concur *v* **1** accompany, accord, coexist, coordinate, synchronize

v **2** accompany, band, coincide, collaborate, collude, combine, cooperate, pool, unite

v **3** accept, agree, allow, approve, assent,

comply, consent, endorse, sign up, subscribe

v 4 see: AGREE *v* 4, 5

concurrence *n* acceptance, accord, agreement, approval, assent, compliance, consent, go-ahead, nod, sympathy

concurrent *adj* 1 agreeable, compatible, congruent, harmonious, parallel

adj 2 coexistent, coexisting, coincident, contemporary, simultaneous, synchronous

concurrently *adv* 1 side by side, simultaneously, together

adv 2 in the interim, in the interval, meantime, meanwhile

condemn *v* 1 damn

v 2 censure, denounce, disparage, inveigh

v 3 adjudge, convict, discipline, imprison, penalize, punish, sentence

v 4 curse, damn, denounce, molest, profane, swear, vex

v 5 accuse, blame, charge, complain, criticize, fault, indict, reproach

v 6 see: ABUSE *v* 4

v 7 see: BERATE *v* 2

v 8 see: DISMISS *v* 3

condemnation *n* anathema, curse, execration, imprecation, malediction, voodoo

condemned *adj* blamable, convicted, culpable, guilty, responsible

condensation *n* abridgement, abstract, brief, compendium, digest, essence, example, outline, review, sketch, summary, syllabus, synopsis

condense *v* 1 compress, distill, express, extract, purify, refine

v 2 analyze, brief, evaluate, outline, retrace, review, study, summarize, synopsize, update

v 3 abbreviate, abridge, curtail, cut, cut back, diminish, edit, lessen, reduce, restrict, shorten, slash

v 4 clog, clot, coagulate, congeal, curdle, dry, gel, harden, intensify, jell, pack, set, solidify, thicken

v 5 compress, concentrate, constrict, contract, reduce, shrink

condescend *v* deign, kowtow, patronize, stoop

condescending *adj* arrogant, haughty, patronizing, pretentious, snobbish

condescension *n* 1 arrogance, assurance, audacity, boldness, brashness, brass, cheek, chutzpah, confidence, crust, effrontery, face, gall, haughtiness, insolence, nerve, patronage, presumption, ridicule, sass, stamina, temerity

n 2 see: VANITY *n*

condition *n* 1 case, repair, shape, state

n 2 atmosphere, climate, mood, temperature, trend

n 3 level, phase, stage, state, step

n 4 habit, impulse, reaction, reflex, response

n 5 essential, must, necessity, precondition, prerequisite, requirement

n 6 agreement, clause, provision, proviso, requirement, reservation, specification, stipulation, string, terms

n 7 affliction, ailment, complaint, disease, disorder, evil, harm, ill, illness, infirmity, malady, sickness

n 8 fitness, kilter, repair, shape, trim

n 9 mode, perspective, posture, situation, state, status, update

v coach, communicate, convey, cultivate, develop, discipline, drill, edify, educate, enlighten, exercise, explain, groom, imbue, impart, implant, improve, inculcate, indoctrinate, inform, infuse, inseminate, inspire, instill, instruct, perfect, practice, prepare, ready, school, teach, train, tutor

conditional *adj* ancillary, contingent, dependent, indefinite, provisional, relative, reliant, temporary, uncertain

conditionally *adv* maybe, perchance, perhaps, possibly, tentatively

conditions *n* atmosphere, climate, environment, habitat, niche, perimeter, settings, surroundings

condo *n* see: RESIDENCE *n* 1

condominium *n* address, apartment, condo, domicile, dwelling, flat, home, house, location, pad, place, property, residence, site

condone *v* 1 absolve, acquit, clear, exculpate, excuse, exempt, exonerate, forgive, free, pardon, remit, reprieve, vindicate

v 2 see: APPROVE *v* 4

v 3 see: TOLERATE *v*

conduct *n* 1 behavior, handling, treatment

n 2 action, bearing, behavior, demeanor, deportment, manners

n 3 accomplishment, action, deed, delivery, demonstration, execution, performance, talent

n 4 course, guidelines, plan, policy, procedures, program, rules, scheme

n 5 administration, care, charge, handling, intendance, management, overseeing, running, supervision

v 1 proceed with, pursue, undertake, wage

v 2 act, bear, behave, carry, comport, demean, rule

v 3 accompany, associate, attend, bear, chaperon, consort with, convoy, escort

v 4 carry, channel, convey, funnel, pass, pipe, siphon, transmit

v 5 carry on, direct, keep, manage, operate, ordain, oversee, pilot, run

v 6 control, develop, direct, drive, guide, lead, operate, pilot, route, shepherd, show, steer

conductor *n* accompanist, artiste, instrumentalist, musician, performer, virtuoso

conduit *n* 1 channel, cylinder, duct, pipe, tube

n 2 agency, agent, channel, instrument, means, mechanism, medium, mode, vehicle

n 3 passageway, pathway, shaft, subway, tube, tunnel

n 4 canal, channel, crevice, curb, cut, ditch, duct, furrow, gorge, groove, gully, gutter, passageway, ravine, rut, trench, trough

confederate *n* abettor, accessory, accomplice, coconspirator, conspirator, partner, supporter

confederation *n* see: ALLIANCE *n*

confer *v* 1 discuss, interview, meet

v 2 advise, communicate, consult, discuss, group, huddle, parley, powwow

v 3 baptize, bestow, call, christen, designate, dub, entitle, name, nickname, tag, term, title

v 4 argue, contest, contradict, contrast, debate, dialogue, differ, disagree, discord, discuss, dispute, dissent, divide, oppose, vary

v 5 see: GIVE *v* 8

conference *n* 1 advisement, care, consultation, counsel

n 2 discourse, discussion, interview, meeting, query

n 3 meeting, parley, powwow, talk, tête-à-tête

n 4 assemblage, assembly, caucus, congregation, convention, council, crowd, gathering, group, meeting, rally, symposium

n 5 caucus, chat, colloquy, conversation, debate, dialogue, discourse, discussion, exchange, forum, interchange, intercourse, interlocution, meeting, talk

confess *v* acknowledge, admit, allow, avow, concede, fess up, grant, own, own up

confession *n* admission

confidant *n* see: FRIEND *n* 1

confide *v* 1 breathe, divulge, share, tell, whisper

v 2 commend, commit, consign, entrust, hand over, relegate, turn over

confidence *n* 1 enigma, intrigue, mystery, secret

n 2 assurance, certainty, certitude, conviction, declaration

n 3 disposition, feeling, frame of mind, mentality, mood, morale, outlook, state

n 4 aplomb, assurance, esteem, nerve, poise, presence, savoir-faire, self-assurance, self-confidence

n 5 belief, contingency, credence, credit, creed, dependence, desire, faith, hope, religion, trust

n 6 see: AUDACITY *n*

confident *adj* 1 assured, poised, sanguine, secure, self-assured, self-confident

adj 2 brazen, certain, cocksure, convinced, positive, sure

adj 3 auspicious, bright, favorable, hopeful, promising, rosy, sunny, utopian

adj 4 auspicious, cheerful, encouraging, hopeful, optimistic, promising, sanguine, upbeat

adj 5 see: ASSERTIVE *adj*

confidential *adj* clandestine, classified, concealed, covert, hidden, off the record, private, privileged, secret, sensitive, sub rosa

configuration *n* cast, conformation, figure, form, shape, structure

confine *v* 1 bound, cramp, demarcate, limit, restrict

v 2 cage, coop, detain, enclose, impound, imprison, incarcerate, intern, jail, lock up, restrain, trap

v 3 brake, contain, control, curb, drag, govern, hamper, hem, hold back, impede, repress, restrain, retard

v 4 bind, clog, curb, fetter, hamper, handcuff, hold, leash, limit, restrain, restrict, shackle, tie, tie up

v 5 see: PROHIBIT *v*

confined *adj* controlled, ignorant, limited, narrow, parochial, provincial, unsophisticated

confinement *n* arrest, detention, imprisonment, incarceration

confines *n* circle, compass, dimension, distance, extension, extent, length, limit, orbit, purview, range, reach, realm, scope, size, spectrum, sweep, width

confirm *v* 1 assure, determine, establish

v 2 clinch, fasten, secure

v 3 affirm, assert, attest, avow, declare, depose, predicate, profess, protest *v* 4 accept, approbate, approve, authorize, certify, condone, countenance, endorse, favor, pass, ratify, sanction, validate

v 5 attest, authenticate, certify, corroborate, justify, notarize, prove, ratify, sanction, substantiate, support, validate, verify, vouch, witness

confirmation *n* 1 affirmation, documentation, evidence, proof, verification

n 2 approval, doctrine, enactment, evidence, passage, proof, testament, testimony, witness

n 3 auspices, authorization, backing, command, endorsement, fiat, patronage, sanction, sponsorship, support

n 4 bar mitzvah

confirmed *adj* authentic, certified, demonstrated, proved, tested, tried, verified

confiscate *v* annex, appropriate, commandeer, expropriate, grab, impound, plunder, preempt, repossess, seize, sequester, shanghai, take

conflagrant *adj* ablaze, afire, aflame, aglow, alight, blazing, burning, fiery, flaming, glowing

conflagration *n* 1 fire

n 2 battle, combat, dispute, encounter, fight, struggle, war

conflict *n* 1 antagonism, discord, disharmony, friction

n 2 battle, clash, competition, contest, discord, duel, fight, fighting, rivalry, strife, struggle, war, warfare

n 3 affray, battle, brawl, brush, clash, difference, disagreement, dispute, encounter, fight, fracas, melee, quarrel, run-in, scrimmage, skirmish, spat, touch

n 4 annoyance, bother, contention, difference, discord, disharmony, dispute, dissension, dissent, dissidence, dissonance, disunity, division, hassle, inconvenience, mischief, nuisance, strife, trouble, variance

n 5 see: COMPETITION *n* 1, 2

v 1 collide, hinder, impinge, interfere, obstruct

v 2 combat, contend, contest, engage, scuffle, skirmish, struggle, tussle

v 3 altercate, argue, battle, bicker, brawl, clash, dispute, engage, equivocate, feud, fight, fray, haggle, hassle, quarrel, quibble, row, scrap, spar, squabble, wrangle

v 4 clash, crash, discord, jangle, jar, mismatch

conflicting *adj* 1 ambivalent, equivocal, paradoxical, uncertain

adj 2 contradictory, contrary, converse, counter, diametric, inverse, opposed, opposing, opposite, polar, reverse

adj 3 clashing

conform *v* 1 adjust, equalize, level, regulate, set policy, standardize

v 2 accommodate, comply, follow, keep, mind, obey, observe, submit

v 3 accommodate, adjust, attune, coordinate, harmonize, integrate, proportion, reconcile, reconciliate, tune

v 4 accord, agree, check, coalesce, coincide, comply with, concur, consent, consist, correspond, fit in, harmonize, jibe, square, suit, tally

v 5 see: ADAPT *v* 2

conformation *n* 1 adaptation, agreement, compliance, modification

n 2 cast, configuration, figure, form, shape, structure

confound *v* 1 complicate, confuse, entangle, mix, mix up, snarl

v 2 baffle, confuse, frustrate, perplex, stymie, thwart

v 3 break, confute, contend, contradict, deny, disprove, dispute, rebut, refute

v 4 amaze, befog, bewilder, boggle, confuse, daze, perplex, puzzle, stumble, stump

v 5 amaze, astonish, astound, awe, boggle, dazzle, dumbfound, flabbergast, nonplus, stagger, stun, surprise

confrere *n* see: FRIEND *n* 1

confront *v* 1 face, realize

v 2 brave, challenge, dare, defy, face, mutiny, rebel, resist

confrontation *n* encounter, gathering, meeting

confuse *v* 1 disorder, jostle, mix, scramble, shuffle

v 2 complicate, confound, entangle, mix, mix up, snarl

v 3 baffle, confound, frustrate, perplex, stymie, thwart

v 4 addle, daze, foul up, fumble, jumble, mix up, muddle, snarl up

v 5 amaze, befog, bewilder, boggle, confound, daze, perplex, puzzle, stumble, stump

v 6 befuddle, bewilder, daze, distract, dizzy, embarrass, fluster, mix up, muddle, rattle, ruffle, trick, unglue, unhinge

v 7 aggravate, baffle, balk, bewilder, circumvent, dash, elude, foil, frustrate, hamper, impede, negate, nullify, perplex, thwart

v **8** see: IMPLICATE *v*

v **9** see: MISREPRESENT *v* 2

v **10** see: OBSCURE *v*

confused *adj* **1** bewildered, foggy, mixed up

adj **2** babbling, incoherent, irrational, rambling, wild

adj **3** dizzy, faint, foggy, giddy, light-headed, reeling

adj **4** daffy, daft, dazed, dizzy, groggy, punchy, stunned

adj **5** ambiguous, bleary, fuzzy, hazy, misty, mixed up, nebulous, unclear

confusion *n* **1** befuddlement, bewilderment, complication, perplexity

n **2** chaos, clutter, derangement, disarray, disorder, jumble, mayhem, mess, mix-up, muddle, predicament, snafu, snarl, tangle, tumult, turmoil

n **3** see: CLAMOR *n*

n **4** see: COMMOTION *n* 1

n **5** see: ENIGMA *n* 2

n **6** see: MISTAKE *n* 2

confute *v* break, confound, contend, contradict, deny, disprove, dispute, rebut, refute

congeal *v* clog, clot, coagulate, condense, curdle, dry, gel, harden, intensify, jell, pack, set, solidify, thicken

congenial *adj* **1** compatible, congruous, kindred, like, suitable

adj **2** agreeable, favorable, good, grateful, gratifying, nice, pleasant, pleasing, pleasurable, welcome

adj **3** affable, amenable, amiable, amicable, empathetic, friendly, gregarious, hospitable, neighborly, outgoing, receptive, sociable, social, sympathetic

congenital *adj* basic, genetic, inborn, indigenous, ingrained, inherent, inherited, innate, instinctive, intrinsic, natal, native, natural

congest *v* choke, clog, crowd, glut, jam

conglomerate *n* **1** cartel, chain, coalition, collaboration, combine, consortium, federation, group, partnership, pool, syndicate, trust

n **2** agglomerate, agglomeration, aggregate, mass, total

congratulations *n* applause, cheers, compliments, kudos, plaudits, praise

congratulatory *adj* approving, commending, complimentary, extolling, flattering, praising

congregate *v* assemble, associate, call, cluster, collect, concentrate, convene, flock, gather, group, lump, marshal, mass, mingle, mobilize, muster, order, rally, rendezvous, round up, send for, summon

congregation *n* **1** devotees, flock, fold, followers, laity, members, parishioners

n **2** see: ASSEMBLY *n* 3

congress *n* **1** adultery, copulation, fooling around, fornication, intimacy, procreation, sex

n **2** assembly, clinic, council, court, diet, forum, hearing, meeting, parliament, seminar, symposium

congressman *n* assemblyman, councilman, lawmaker, legislator, representative, senator

congresswoman *n* assemblywoman, councilwoman, lawmaker, legislator, representative, senator

congruence *n* accord, affinity, agreement, assent, concert, concord, cooperation, empathy, harmony, rapport, synergy, teamwork, unity

congruent *adj* agreeable, compatible, concurrent, harmonious, parallel

congruous *adj* compatible, congenial, kindred, like, suitable

conjectural *adj* abstract, general, hypothetical, ideal, illustrative, speculative, symbolic, theoretical

conjecture *n* **1** assumption, deduction, opinion, supposition, surmise

n **2** assumption, conclusion, discretion, estimate, guess, judgment, notion, presumption, theorization

n **3** assumption, deduction, explanation, guess, hypothesis, inference, postulate, presumption, proposition, speculation, supposition, theory

v see: VISUALIZE *v*

conjugal *adj* matrimonial

conjugation *n* coitus, copulation, fooling around, foreplay, fornication, intercourse, mating, reproduction, sex, union

conjuration *n* invocation

conjure *v* **1** appeal, ask, beg, beseech, crave, desire, entreat, grovel, implore, indicate, invoke, plead, pray, request, seek, solicit, supplicate, whine

v **2** behold, catch, comprehend, descry, digest, discern, distinguish, espy, fathom, grasp, know, look at, notice, observe, perceive, realize, recognize, savvy, see, sight, take in, understand, view

v **3** see: ATTRACT *v* 6

conjured *adj* conceived, created, fancied, fanciful, fantastic, fictional, fictitious, illusory, imaginary, imagined, invented, make-believe, nonexistent, notional, unreal, whimsical

conjurer *n* diviner, magician, soothsayer, sorcerer, wizard

conk *n* see: HIT *n* 1

connect *v* 1 correlate

v 2 engage, hook up, interlock, mesh, network

v 3 join, nail, peg, pin, tack

v 4 bend, encircle, join, loop, twist

v 5 affix, attach, bind, clip, fasten, fix, rivet, weld

v 6 associate, blend, bond, coalesce, combine, compound, couple, fasten, fuse, join, link, marry, mate, meet, merge, pair, unite, wed

v 7 see: IMPLICATE *v*

connected *adj* abutting, adjacent, adjoining, alongside, bordering, close by, contiguous, juxtaposed, local, near at hand, nearby, neighboring, outlining, regional, touching, verging on

connection *n* 1 association, linkage, nexus

n 2 affiliation, allegiance, association, obligation, tie

n 3 groove, joining, joint, link, seam

n 4 bond, cohesion, fusion, solidarity, togetherness, union

n 5 appointment, duty, function, job, office, position, post, situation

n 6 see: FRIEND *n* 1

connivance *n* complicity, conspiracy, participation

connive *v* 1 cogitate, collude, conspire, contrive, devise, frame, intrigue, machinate, maneuver, orchestrate, plan, plot, scheme

v 2 fish, hint

conniving *adj* see: TREACHEROUS *adj* 2

connoisseur *n* aesthete, critic, expert, virtuoso

connotation *n* allusion, hint, implication, innuendo, insinuation, notation, reference, suggestion

connote *v* 1 hint, implant, imply, infer, insinuate, lead, offer, put forth, seed

v 2 add up to, convey, denote, identify, import, indicate, intend, mean, show, signify, symbolize

connubial *adj* matrimonial

conquer *v* 1 best, defeat, master, overcome, prevail, succeed, triumph, win

v 2 crush, defeat, destroy, down, hurdle, lick, overcome, overthrow, surmount

v 3 bear down, beat down, crush, defeat, dominate, enslave, exploit, overpower, quash, reduce, subdue, subjugate, suppress, vanquish

v 4 see: THRASH *v* 1

conquering *adj* successful, triumphant, undefeated, victorious, winning

conqueror *n* advocate, champion, hero, heroine, lead, leader, master, principal, protagonist, star, trailblazer, victor, winner

conquest *n* 1 attack, defeat, foray, inroad, intrusion, invasion, trespass

n 2 accomplishment, achievement, success, triumph, victory, win, winner

conscience *n* compunction, pang, qualm, regret, reservation, restraint, scruple, twinge

conscientious *adj* 1 advertent, alert, attentive, careful, heedful, observant

adj 2 blind, loyal, meticulous, religious, strict, zealous

adj 3 careful, carping, cautious, ethical, exacting, fussy, heedful, meticulous, painstaking, punctilious, scrupulous, unrelenting

adj 4 ethical, honest, honorable, moral, noble, principled, proper, respectable, right, righteous, scrupulous, sound, true, trustworthy, upright, virtuous

conscious *adj* 1 calculated, contrived, deliberate, intentional, planned, plotted, premeditated

adj 2 alive, attentive, awake, aware, cognizant, conversant, knowing, responsive, sentient, thinking

consciousness *n* attention, awareness, care, carefulness, cognizance, concern, consideration, heed, intimacy, knowing, knowledge, mark, note, notice, observance, observation, perception, recognition, regard, remark, sense

conscript *v* call, draft, enroll, force, impress, induct, select, shanghai

consecrate *v* anoint, baptize, bless, dedicate, devote, enshrine, exalt, hallow, purify, sanctify

consecrated *adj* 1 intact, inviolable, inviolate, protected, pure, sacred, sacrosanct

adj 2 blessed, celestial, divine, godly, hallowed, holy, pure, sacred, sanctified, spiritual

consecutive *adj* chronological, continuous, progressive, sequential, serial, successive

consensus *n* feeling, flavor, opinion, sense

consent *n* 1 approval, authorization, leave, license, permission, sanction

n 2 acceptance, accord, agreement, approval, assent, compliance, concurrence, go-ahead, nod, sympathy

v 1 accept, agree, allow, approve, assent,

comply, concur, endorse, sign up, subscribe

v 2 see: AGREE *v* 4

consequence *n* 1 development, progression, ramification, result

n 2 end, issue, outcome, result

n 3 import, importance, magnitude, moment, significance, substance, weight

n 4 aftermath, corollary, effect, eventuality, outcome, reaction, repercussion, result, reverberation, reward, upshot

consequent *adj* see: SENSIBLE *adj* 5

consequential *adj* considerable, critical, crucial, important, material, meaningful, momentous, prominent, significant, substantial, vital, weighty

conservative *adj* 1 aloof, poised, reserved

adj 2 dim, inconspicuous, quiet, restrained, subdued, tasteful, unassuming, unobtrusive

adj 3 canny, economical, frugal, provident, sparing, spartan, stewardly, thrifty, unwasteful

conserve *v* 1 economize, husband, safeguard, store

v 2 maintain, preserve, protect, save

consider *v* 1 care, heed, listen, mind, review

v 2 cerebrate, chew, contemplate, deliberate, digest, meditate, mull, muse, ponder, reason, reflect, ruminate, see, speculate, study, think, weigh

v 3 account, calculate, deem, judge, reckon, regard, surmise, view

v 4 admire, adore, appreciate, cherish, covet, esteem, honor, idolize, love, prize, regard, respect, treasure, value

considerable *adj* 1 consequential, critical, crucial, important, material, meaningful, momentous, prominent, significant, substantial, vital, weighty

adj 2 ample, big, enormous, extensive, grand, hefty, huge, jumbo, large, major, sizable, spacious, vast

considerably *adv* dramatically, far, quite, rather, significantly, very, well

considerate *adj* 1 attentive, generous, kind, thoughtful, unselfish

adj 2 benevolent, big, chivalrous, generous, grandiose, lofty, magnanimous, noble

adj 3 affectionate, compassionate, empathetic, empathic, gentle, humane, kind, kindhearted, responsive, softhearted, sympathetic, tender, warm, warmhearted

adj 4 calculating, careful, cautious, circumspect, discreet, gingerly, guarded, heedful, judicious, provident, prudent, restrained, reticent, safe, shrewd, wary

consideration *n* 1 aim, cause, goal, motive, purpose, reason

n 2 account, admiration, esteem, favor, regard, respect

n 3 diplomacy, discretion, poise, regard, savoir-faire, tact, tactfulness, thoughtfulness

n 4 bonus, goal, incentive, inducement, motivation, motive, reason, reward, stimulus

n 5 analysis, cogitation, contemplation, deliberation, logic, meditation, reason, reasoning, reflection, speculation, study, thinking, thought

n 6 attention, awareness, care, carefulness, cognizance, concern, consciousness, heed, intimacy, knowing, knowledge, mark, note, notice, observance, observation, perception, recognition, regard, remark, sense

n 7 courtesy, dispensation, favor, indulgence, kindness, privilege, respect, service

n 8 bill, bonus, charge, commission, compensation, earnings, fee, gross, income, pay, revenue, salary, stipend, wage

considered *adj* advised, calculated, careful, contrived, deliberate, forewarned, measured, planned, premeditated, studied, studious

consign *v* 1 commend, commit, confide, entrust, hand over, relegate, turn over

v 2 address, channel, dispatch, export, forward, mail, post, remit, route, send, ship, transmit, transport

consignment *n* 1 burden, cargo, freight, lading, load, payload, shipment, transportation, truck

n 2 dismissal, dispatch, forwarding, sending

consist *v* accord, agree, check, coalesce, coincide, comply with, concur, conform, consent, correspond, fit in, harmonize, jibe, square, suit, tally

consistent *adj* 1 homogeneous, plain, pure, straight, unadulterated, undiluted, unmixed

adj 2 constant, continuing, endless, equable, established, even, invariable, reliable, routine, same, serene, stable, steady, unchanging, unfailing, unfluctuating, uniform, unvarying

console *n* 1 CRT, display, monitor, screen, terminal

n 2 control panel

n 3 cabinet

v bolster, buoy, cheer, comfort, gladden, solace, soothe, support, uplift, upraise

consolidate v 1 centralize, concentrate, focus, integrate, merge

v 2 amalgamate, band, blend, coalesce, combine, compound, fuse, intermingle, league, lump, meld, merge, mingle, mix, unify, unite

consolidation n 1 centralization, concentration, focus

n 2 see: ALLIANCE n

consort n bride, cohabitant, mate, spouse, squaw, wife, woman

consortium n cartel, chain, coalition, collaboration, combine, conglomerate, federation, group, partnership, pool, syndicate, trust

conspicuous adj 1 arrogant, audacious, flagrant, glaring, obvious

adj 2 arresting, astonishing, astounding, eye-catching, marked, noticeable, obvious, pointed, prominent, salient, sensational, striking, stunning

adj 3 blatant, brazen, flagrant, flashy, garish, gaudy, glaring, loud, ostentatious, showy, tacky, tasteless, tawdry, tinsel

adj 4 apparent, clear, distinct, evident, given, indisputable, indubitable, manifest, obvious, patent, plain, presumed, self-evident, straightforward, true, unambiguous, unequivocal, unmistakable

conspiracy n 1 complicity, connivance, participation

n 2 cabal, collusion, intrigue, junta, machination, plot, scheme, secret

conspirator n abettor, accessory, accomplice, coconspirator, confederate, partner, supporter

conspire v cogitate, collude, connive, contrive, devise, frame, intrigue, machinate, maneuver, orchestrate, plan, plot, scheme

constabulary n authorities, bobbies, cops, gendarmes, highway patrol, military police, police, troopers

constant adj 1 continuing, durable, enduring, eternal, lasting, ongoing, permanent, stable

adj 2 ardent, dedicated, dependable, devoted, faithful, loyal, resolute, staunch, steadfast, steady, true, trusty

adj 3 determinate, firm, fixed, hard, immutable, inflexible, invariable, ironclad, resolute, stable, unalterable, unchangeable, unmovable

adj 4 accepted, accustomed, chronic, common, continual, customary, daily, everyday, familiar, frequent, habitual, inured, often, recurring, regular, routine, traditional, usual

adj 5 ageless, boundless, ceaseless, continual, continuous, endless, eternal, everlasting, incessant, infinite, interminable, limitless, never-ending, ongoing, perpetual, persistent, relentless, timeless, unceasing, unending, uninterrupted, unremitting

adj 6 consistent, continuing, endless, equable, established, even, invariable, reliable, routine, same, serene, stable, steady, unchanging, unfailing, unfluctuating, uniform, unvarying

constantly adv ad infinitum, all the time, always, continually, endlessly, eternally, forever, perpetually, timelessly, unceasingly

consternation n 1 amazement, awe, dread, fear, respect, reverence, wonder

n 2 affliction, alarm, anxiety, apprehension, care, dismay, dread, fear, fright, horror, ordeal, panic, terror, trepidation, trial, trouble, worry

constituency n associates, constituents, members, membership, personnel

constituent n 1 component, element, factor, ingredient, item, part, segment

n 2 member

constituents n associates, constituency, members, membership, personnel

constitute v 1 form, make up, produce

v 2 compose, construct, form

v 3 build, construct, create, erect, establish, found, initiate, institute, launch, set up, start

v 4 see: INITIATE v 1, 2

constitution n character, fiber, makeup, nature, quality, substance

constrain v 1 coerce, compel, force, make, overpower, propel, push

v 2 compact, compress, crowd, crush, jam, mash, pack, press, push, squash, squeeze

v 3 abstain, avoid, curb, deny, forgo, govern, hold back, refrain, resist, restrict, stop, tame

v 4 bridle, check, control, crimp, curb, hold back, hold down, inhibit, leash, rein, restrain, restrict, withhold

constrained adj noncommittal, reserved, restrained

constraint n 1 coercion, compulsion, duress, force, violence

n 2 ban, bar, interdiction, prohibition, restriction, taboo

n 3 bond, boundary, bridle, check, control, curb, damper, harness, leash, limit, rein, restraint, restriction

constrict v 1 compress, concentrate, condense, contract, reduce, shrink

v 2 asphyxiate, choke, gag, garrote, muffle, quash, repress, smother, stifle, strangle, suffocate, suppress

construct v 1 compose, constitute, form

v 2 build, conceive, devise, frame, shape, surround

v 3 administer, dispense, move along, plan, prepare, process, treat

v 4 amplify, develop, devise, elaborate, enhance, enlarge, expand, expound, increase, refine

v 5 build, constitute, create, erect, establish, found, initiate, institute, launch, set up, start

v 6 assemble, build, erect, establish, fabricate, forge, form, make, manufacture, mold, produce, trailblaze

constructive adj favorable, fruitful, helpful, positive, productive, useful, worthwhile

construe v 1 see: DEDUCE v 3

v 2 see: FORMULATE v 2

consul n agent, ambassador, delegate, deputy, diplomat, emissary, envoy

consult v advise, communicate, confer, discuss, group, huddle, parley, powwow

consultation n advisement, care, conference, counsel

consume v 1 demolish, destroy, ravage

v 2 absorb, blot, engross, engulf, occupy, soak up

v 3 eat, devour, digest, ingest, masticate, swallow

v 4 cast away, dissipate, drivel, empty, fritter, lavish, squander, throw away, use up, waste

v 5 deplete, exhaust, expend, finish, go, lessen, run through, spend, use up, waste, weaken

v 6 see: DRINK v 2

consumer n buyer, client, customer, end user, patron, purchaser, shopper, user

consummate adj absolute, chief, complete, dominant, godlike, leading, main, perfect, principal, pure, ranking, sheer, supreme, total, unsurpassed, utter, whole

v 1 achieve, cease, complete, conclude, end, finish, halt, perfect, terminate, wind up, wrap up

v 2 accomplish, achieve, attain, execute, fulfill, perform, produce, pull off, realize, succeed, triumph, win

v 3 adjourn, cap, climax, complete, conclude, crown, culminate, dissolve, end,

finalize, finish, terminate, wind up, wrap up

v 4 accomplish, complete, execute, fulfill, implement, perform, realize

contact n 1 handling

n 2 association, closeness, nearness, proximity

v 1 extend, get, reach

v 2 buzz, call, communicate, phone, ring, telephone, touch

contagious adj catching, communicable, contaminative, epidemic, infectious, spreading, transmittable

contain v 1 accommodate

v 2 add, enclose, include, incorporate, insert

v 3 comprehend, comprise, embody, embrace, encompass, have, include, incorporate, involve, take in

v 4 brake, confine, control, curb, drag, govern, hamper, hem, hold back, impede, repress, restrain, retard

container n 1 box, carton, case, chest, crate, receptacle

n 2 cauldron, cistern, jug, reservoir, tank, vat

n 3 chalice, cup, dish, Dixie cup, glass, goblet, mug, shot glass, stein, tumbler, vessel, wineglass

contaminant n defect, impurity, pollutant

contaminate v 1 dirty, foul, infect, poison, pollute

v 2 debase, degrade, desecrate, pervert, profane

contamination n corruption, decay, impurity, poison, taint

contaminative adj catching, communicable, contagious, epidemic, infectious, spreading, transmittable

contemplate v 1 aim, design, intend, mean, plan, propose

v 2 cerebrate, chew, consider, deliberate, digest, meditate, mull, muse, ponder, reason, reflect, ruminate, see, speculate, study, think, weigh

contemplation n analysis, cogitation, consideration, deliberation, logic, meditation, reason, reasoning, reflection, speculation, study, thinking, thought

contemporary adj 1 current, existent, instant, living, present

adj 2 coexistent, coexisting, coincident, concurrent, simultaneous, synchronous

adj 3 bright, fresh, high-tech, modern, modernistic, new, novel, recent, up-to-date

contempt n 1 aspersion, derision, disdain,

irony, mockery, ridicule, sarcasm, satire, scorn

n 2 aversion, disgust, distaste, horror, loathing, nausea, repugnance, repulsion, revulsion

n 3 censure, discredit, disfavor, disgrace, dishonor, disparagement, disrepute, humiliation, infamy, notoriety, scandal, shame

contemptible *adj* 1 awful, dreadful, lousy, mean

adj 2 abject, base, debasing, despicable, false, servile

contemptuous *adj* 1 abusive, derisive, disrespectful, insulting, nasty, offensive, slighting

adj 2 cynical, derisive, ironic, mocking, sarcastic, sardonic, scornful, skeptical, wry

adj 3 see: VAIN *adj* 5

contend *v* 1 accomplish, behave, cope, make do, manage, persevere

v 2 attack, battle, combat, fight, oppose, struggle, war

v 3 combat, duel, fight, grapple, spar, struggle, wrestle

v 4 affirm, attest, avow, promise, say, swear, vouch, warrant

v 5 combat, conflict, contest, engage, scuffle, skirmish, struggle, tussle

v 6 break, confound, confute, contradict, deny, disprove, dispute, rebut, refute

v 7 argue, assert, believe, claim, defend, justify, know, maintain, state, think, vindicate, warrant

v 8 combat, compete, contest, counter, dispute, duel, fight, match, oppose, parry, pit, play, repel, resist, rival, strive, struggle, vie

contender *n* adversary, antagonist, anti, challenger, competitor, con, enemy, foe, match, opponent, rival

content *n* 1 capacity, measure, volume

n 2 gist, meaning, significance

n 3 material, matter, property, substance, stuff

v appease, comfort, comply, delight, elate, gratify, please, relieve, satisfy, suit

adj see: MERRY *adj* 2

contented *adj* comfortable, comfy, cozy, cushy, homey, secure, snug, soft, warm

contention *n* 1 argument, controversy, debate, dialogue, discussion, dispute

n 2 annoyance, bother, conflict, difference, discord, disharmony, dispute, dissension, dissent, dissidence, dissonance, disunity, division, hassle, inconvenience,

mischief, nuisance, strife, trouble, variance

contentious *adj* 1 argumentative, cantankerous, controversial, debatable, disputatious, ill-natured, litigious, ornery

adj 2 angry, bellicose, belligerent, combative, hostile, militant, pugnacious, quarrelsome, warlike

contents *n* junk, objects, scrap, stuff, substance, things

contest *n* 1 battle, clash, competition, conflict, discord, duel, fight, fighting, rivalry, strife, struggle, war, warfare

n 2 bout, competition, conflict, event, game, marathon, match, meet, meeting, race, regatta, round robin, run, tournament, tourney

n 3 encounter, scramble, skirmish, struggle

v 1 combat, conflict, contend, engage, scuffle, skirmish, struggle, tussle

v 2 argue, confer, contradict, contrast, debate, dialogue, differ, disagree, discord, discuss, dispute, dissent, divide, oppose, vary

v 3 combat, compete, contend, counter, dispute, duel, fight, match, oppose, parry, pit, play, repel, resist, rival, strive, struggle, vie

contestant *n* 1 competitor, participant, player, team member

n 2 aspirant, candidate, entrant, hopeful, nominee

context *n* circumstance, environment, setting, situation

contiguous *adj* 1 continental

adj 2 current, direct, immediate, instant, nearby, primary, prompt, sudden, timely

adj 3 abutting, adjacent, adjoining, alongside, bordering, close by, connected, juxtaposed, local, near at hand, nearby, neighboring, outlining, regional, touching, verging on

continence *n* abstinence, moderation, restraint, self-restraint, sobriety, temperance

continent *adj* abstinent, celibate, chaste, maidenly, pure, virginal, virtuous

continental *adj* mainland

contingency *n* 1 agent, alternate, backup, part-timer, replacement, representative, standby, substitute, surrogate

n 2 belief, confidence, credence, credit, creed, dependence, desire, faith, hope, religion, trust

contingent *adj* 1 dependent, incidental, linked

adj 2 circumstantial, iffy, uncertain, vague

adj 3 awaiting, impending, pending, unfinished, unsettled

adj 4 anticipated, hoped for, iffy, planned, probable, proposed, tentative

adj 5 ancillary, conditional, dependent, indefinite, provisional, relative, reliant, temporary, uncertain

adj 6 accidental, casual, chance, chancy, circumstantial, coincidental, eventful, fluky, fortuitous, freak, incidental, lucky, odd, serendipitous, synchronous

n association, body, club, company, delegation, fellowship, fraternity, group, guild, organization, society, union

continual *adj* 1 continuing, gradual, increasing, incremental, intensifying, measured, moderate, progressive, successive

adj 2 accepted, accustomed, chronic, common, constant, customary, daily, everyday, familiar, frequent, habitual, inured, often, recurring, regular, routine, traditional, usual

adj 3 ageless, boundless, ceaseless, constant, continuous, endless, eternal, everlasting, incessant, infinite, interminable, limitless, never-ending, ongoing, perpetual, persistent, relentless, timeless, unceasing, unending, uninterrupted, unremitting

continually *adv* ad infinitum, all the time, always, constantly, endlessly, eternally, forever, perpetually, timelessly, unceasingly

continuation *n* 1 corollary, epilogue, outgrowth, sequel, supplement

n 2 duration, endurance, existence, life, span, subsistence, survival, term

continue *v* 1 commit, extend, maintain, perpetuate, prolong, pull

v 2 drag out, draw, elongate, extend, lengthen, prolong, protract, stretch

v 3 abide, endure, last, outlast, persevere, persist, prevail, remain, stay, stick to, stick with, survive

v 4 advance, begin again, cycle, depart, get along, get on, go, leave, march, move, move forward, overture, part, proceed, progress, push on, recommence, reembark, restart, wend

continuing *adj* 1 current, going, ongoing

adj 2 constant, durable, enduring, eternal, lasting, ongoing, permanent, stable

adj 3 continual, gradual, increasing, incremental, intensifying, measured, moderate, progressive, successive

adj 4 enduring, inveterate, lifelong, longlasting, long-lived, old, ongoing, perennial

adj 5 consistent, constant, endless, equable, established, even, invariable, reliable, routine, same, serene, stable, steady, unchanging, unfailing, unfluctuating, uniform, unvarying

continuous *adj* 1 chronological, consecutive, progressive, sequential, serial, successive

adj 2 ageless, boundless, ceaseless, constant, continual, endless, eternal, everlasting, incessant, infinite, interminable, limitless, never-ending, ongoing, perpetual, persistent, relentless, timeless, unceasing, unending, uninterrupted, unremitting

contort *v* bend, twist, warp

contorted *adj* grotesque, gruesome, hideous, ill-favored, ugly, uncomely, unsightly

contour *n* form, outline, profile, shape

contract *n* 1 order, purchase order, requisition, sale

n 2 agreement, bargain, bond, compact, convention, covenant, deal, pact, pledge, promise, transaction, treaty, understanding

v 1 bind, commit, engage, pledge

v 2 agree, covenant, pledge, promise

v 3 collapse, crumple, deflate, shrink

v 4 acquire, arouse, commit, engage, enlist, incur, induce

v 5 assure, certify, endorse, guarantee, pledge, sanction, underwrite, vouch, warrant

v 6 compress, concentrate, condense, constrict, reduce, shrink

contradict *v* 1 attack, challenge, deny, impugn, oppose, rebut

v 2 cross, deny, disaffirm, disagree, impugn, negate, rebut, traverse

v 3 break, confound, confute, contend, deny, disprove, dispute, rebut, refute

v 4 cancel, deny, disallow, forbid, negate, nix, nullify, override, overrule, reject, renege, repeal, revoke, torpedo, veto, void

v 5 abrogate, annul, cancel, discharge, dismantle, dissolve, dwindle, fade, negate, nullify, quash, recall, repeal, rescind, reverse, revoke, set aside, vacate, void

v 6 see: DISAGREE *v* 2, 3

contradiction *n* 1 difference, disparity, dissimilarity, gap, inconsistency

n 2 disagreement, discrepancy, hypocrisy, incongruity, inconsistency, paradox, variance

contradictory *adj* conflicting, contrary, converse, counter, diametric, inverse, opposed, opposing, opposite, polar, reverse

contraption *n* apparatus, appliance, contrivance, device, doodad, doohickey, gadget, gimmick, gizmo, implement, instrument, invention, machine, mechanism, thingumajig, tool, utensil, widget

contrary *adj* 1 adverse, antagonistic, anti, opposed, opposing

adj 2 conflicting, contradictory, converse, counter, diametric, inverse, opposed, opposing, opposite, polar, reverse

adj 3 balking, balky, cranky, disagreeable, irascible, mean, obstinate, ornery, perverse, wayward

contrast *n* difference, dissimilarity, distinction, diversion, opposition

v 1 bracket, collate, compare, correlate, equate, liken, match, relate, sort

v 2 see: DISAGREE *v* 3

contribute *v* accord, adduce, award, bequeath, bestow, concede, confer, deliver, devote, donate, endow, extend, fund, give, give away, grant, hand down, hand out, impart, offer, pose, present, proffer, provide, supply, tender, volunteer

contribution *n* benevolence, boon, donation, favor, gift, grant, largess, present

contributions *n* alms, assistance, charity, dole, donations, oblation, offering

contrite *adj* apologetic, penitent, remorseful, repentant, sorry

contrition *n* atonement, attrition, penance, penitence, reconciliation, remorse

contrivance *n* apparatus, appliance, contraption, device, doodad, doohickey, gadget, gimmick, gizmo, implement, instrument, invention, machine, mechanism, thingumajig, tool, utensil, widget

contrive *v* 1 brew, concoct, construe, create, devise, engineer, fabricate, formulate, hatch, invent, make up, plot, scheme

v 2 cogitate, collude, connive, conspire, devise, frame, intrigue, machinate, maneuver, orchestrate, plan, plot, scheme

contrived *adj* 1 fake, phony, seeming

adj 2 calculated, conscious, deliberate, intentional, planned, plotted, premeditated

adj 3 advised, calculated, careful, considered, deliberate, forewarned, measured, planned, premeditated, studied, studious

adj 4 see: IRREGULAR *adj* 2

control *n* 1 influence, predominance, preponderance, supremacy

n 2 authority, clout, in, influence, leverage, power, prestige, pull, weight

n 3 authority, command, commission, direction, domination, jurisdiction, management, mastery, might, power, rule

n 4 bond, boundary, bridle, check, constraint, curb, damper, harness, leash, limit, rein, restraint, restriction

n 5 pedal

n 6 clamp, clasp, clench, clinch, clutch, command, grapple, grasp, grip, hold, influence

v 1 corner, dominate, monopolize

v 2 govern, overrule, reign, rule

v 3 deploy, direct, maneuver, manipulate, use

v 4 brake, confine, contain, curb, drag, govern, hamper, hem, hold back, impede, repress, restrain, retard

v 5 conduct, develop, direct, drive, guide, lead, operate, pilot, route, shepherd, show, steer

v 6 bridle, check, constrain, crimp, curb, hold back, hold down, inhibit, leash, rein, restrain, restrict, withhold

v 7 boss, command, direct, dominate, govern, handle, influence, lead, manage, manipulate, order, supervise, sway

controllable *adj* docile, manageable, maneuverable, pliable, yielding

controlled *adj* 1 confined, ignorant, limited, narrow, parochial, provincial, unsophisticated

adj 2 see: RESTRICTIVE *adj*

controversial *adj* 1 forensic, judicial, legal

adj 2 argumentative, cantankerous, contentious, debatable, disputatious, ill-natured, litigious, ornery

controversy *n* 1 argument, contention, debate, dialogue, discussion, dispute

n 2 altercation, argument, battle, brawl, challenge, combat, disagreement, discord, dispute, feud, fight, fracas, fray, hassle, melee, quarrel, rancor, rift, row, ruckus, scrap, scuffle, skirmish, spat, squabble, struggle, tiff, war

n 3 see: SUBJECT *n* 4

conundrum *n* confusion, difficulty, dilemma, enigma, mystery, obstacle, paradox, perplexity, problem, puzzle, quandary, question, riddle, secret

convalesce *v* ameliorate, gain, heal, improve, loop up, mend, perk, rally, recover, recuperate, rehabilitate, revive

convalescent *n* invalid, patient, shut-in

convene *v* assemble, associate, call, cluster, collect, concentrate, congregate, flock, gather, group, lump, marshal, mass, mingle, mobilize, muster, order, rally, rendezvous, round up, send for, summon

convenience *v* accommodate, favor, help, oblige, please, provide, serve

convenient *adj* 1 available, close by, near, nearby

adj 2 accessible, available, close, feasible, functional, handy, helpful, multipurpose, nearby, open, practical, public, reachable, ready, serviceable, suitable, unrestricted, usable, useful, utilitarian, well-suited, within reach, working

adj 3 see: APPLICABLE *adj*

convention *n* 1 usage

n 2 custom, decorum, etiquette, formality, good form, manners, propriety, protocol, rites

n 3 assemblage, assembly, caucus, conference, congregation, council, crowd, gathering, group, meeting, rally, symposium

n 4 see: PACT *n*

conventional *adj* 1 customary, habitual, normal

adj 2 authorized, customary, established, set

adj 3 basic, established, official, standard

adj 4 banal, commonplace, ordinary, trite, undistinguished

adj 5 correct, decorous, fitting, nice, orthodox, polite, proper, right, suitable, well

adj 6 academic

converge *v* meet

conversant *adj* 1 abreast, acquainted, aware, familiar, informed, knowledgeable, up, versed

adj 2 alive, attentive, awake, aware, cognizant, conscious, knowing, responsive, sentient, thinking

conversation *n* caucus, chat, colloquy, conference, debate, dialogue, discourse, discussion, exchange, forum, interchange, intercourse, interlocution, meeting, talk

converse *adj* 1 backward, counter, reverse

adj 2 conflicting, contradictory, contrary, counter, diametric, inverse, opposed, opposing, opposite, polar, reverse

n opposite, reverse

v chat, chatter, discuss, parley, speak, talk, visit

conversion *n* alchemy, alteration, changeover, revision, transformation

convert *n* believer, disciple, follower, zealot

v 1 adjust, prorate, regulate, scale

v 2 cash, dissolve, exchange, liquidate, tender

v 3 bring, cause, lead, move, persuade

v 4 buy, ransom, reclaim, recover, redeem, save

v 5 brainwash, inculcate, indoctrinate, persuade, preach, proselytize

v 6 bargain, barter, deal, exchange, swap, trade, traffic

v 7 adapt, conform, cut, fashion, fit, measure, modify, rig, shape, suit, tailor

v 8 bend, bias, brainwash, compel, indoctrinate, influence, predispose, prejudice, proselytize, slant, sway

v 9 alter, change, commute, evolve, further, improve, metamorphose, modernize, modify, mutate, revolutionize, transfer, transfigure, transform, transmute, vary

convey *v* 1 reach

v 2 assign, cede, deed, designate, transfer

v 3 carry, channel, conduct, funnel, pass, pipe, siphon, transmit

v 4 express, hint, impart, imply, indicate, purport, say, suggest

v 5 add up to, connote, denote, identify, import, indicate, intend, mean, show, signify, symbolize

v 6 bear, carry, crate, ferry, haul, lift, lug, pack, shoulder, shuttle, tote, traffic, transport, truck

v 7 brief, communicate, declare, describe, disclose, divulge, explain, impart, inform, narrate, orate, portray, read, recite, recount, relate, report, retell, reveal, share, state, tattle, tell, transmit

v 8 see: EDUCATE *v*

convict *v* adjudge, condemn, discipline, imprison, penalize, punish, sentence

n see: CRIMINAL *n* 2

convicted *adj* blamable, condemned, culpable, guilty, responsible

conviction *n* 1 assurance, certainty, certitude, confidence, declaration

n 2 attitude, belief, bias, feeling, inducement, leaning, mind, opinion, persuasion, sentiment, slant, view

n 3 see: PRINCIPLE *n* 5

convince *v* affect, assure, impel, induce, influence, inspire, instigate, motivate, move, persuade, pressure, prompt, stir, sway, talk into, touch, win over

convinced *adj* brazen, certain, cocksure, confident, positive, sure

convincing *adj* 1 conclusive

adj 2 effective, forcible, impressive, inspiring, profound, striking

adj 3 cogent, compelling, effective, forceful, influential, persuasive, revealing, satisfactory, satisfying, solid, sound, telling, valid

adj 4 see: AUTHENTIC *adj* 2

convolution *n* complexity, intricacy, involution, involvement

convoy *n* 1 caravan, motorcade, procession

n 2 armada, assembly, boats, fleet, flotilla, grouping, navy, ships, squadron

v accompany, associate, attend, bear, chaperon, conduct, escort

convulsion *n* jerk, seizure, spasm, twitch

cook *v* bake, broil, burn, char, melt, parch, roast, scorch, sear, singe, swelter, toast, warm

cookout *n* barbecue, clambake, outing, picnic

cool *adj* 1 arctic, chilly, cold, freezing, frigid, frosty, glacial, icy, nippy, wintry

adj 2 calm, collected, composed, demure, dormant, easy, gentle, hushed, idle, imperturbable, motionless, nonchalant, peaceful, placid, poised, quiet, relaxed, restful, sedate, self-composed, self-possessed, serene, soft, steady, still, tranquil, unflappable, unruffled, untroubled

adj 3 see: INDIFFERENT *adj* 4

v chill, freeze, ice, refrigerate

cooler *n* brig, cage, cell, coop, hoosegow, jail, pen, penitentiary, pokey, prison, reformatory, slammer, stir, stockade, tower

coolheaded *adj* calm, nonaggressive, nonviolent, pacifist, passive, peaceful

coolness *n* distance, reserve, restraint, reticence

coop *n* 1 abode, barn, bungalow, cabin, cottage, hatch, hovel, hut, lodge, shack, shanty

n 2 barn, enclosure, hatch, lean-to, paddock, pen, pound, shack, shed, shelter, stable, stall, sty

n 3 brig, cage, cell, cooler, hoosegow, jail, pen, penitentiary, pokey, prison, reformatory, slammer, stir, stockade, tower

v see: IMPRISON *v* 2

cooperate *v* 1 assist, associate, collaborate, join

v 2 accompany, band, coincide, collaborate, collude, combine, concur, pool, unite

cooperation *n* accord, affinity, agreement, assent, concert, concord, congruence, empathy, harmony, rapport, synergy, teamwork, unity

cooperative *adj* 1 collective, helpful, joint, participatory, unified, united

adj 2 amenable, complaisant, compliant, obedient, submissive, subservient, tractable, willing

coordinate *v* 1 accompany, accord, coexist, coincide, concur, synchronize

v 2 accommodate, adjust, attune, conform, harmonize, integrate, proportion, reconcile, reconciliate, tune

copartner *n* see: FRIEND *n* 1

cope *v* accomplish, behave, contend, make do, manage, persevere

copied *adj* imitated, pseudo, simulated, unoriginal

copious *adj* 1 creative, fecund, fertile, fruitful, productive, prolific

adj 2 affluent, leisure class, loaded, moneyed, opulent, rich, wealthy, well-to-do

adj 3 abounding, abundant, ample, bounteous, bountiful, enough, galore, generous, liberal, overflowing, plentiful, plenty, prodigal, profuse, teeming

adj 4 see: MANY *adj* 2

cops *n* authorities, bobbies, constabulary, gendarmes, highway patrol, military police, police, troopers

copse *n* grove, shrubbery, thicket

copulation *n* 1 adultery, congress, fooling around, fornication, intimacy, procreation, sex

n 2 coitus, conjugation, fooling around, foreplay, fornication, intercourse, mating, reproduction, sex, union

copy *n* 1 carbon, carbon copy, duplicate, facsimile, replica, reproduction, telecopy, Xerox copy

n 2 impression, imprint, indent, indentation, mark, notch, print, stamp, tab

n 3 clone, counterfeit, duplicate, duplication, image, imitation, likeness, mock-up, model, print, replica, replication, representation, reproduction, resemblance, simulation

v 1 draw

v 2 paraphrase, plagiarize, rephrase, reword

v 3 note, record, summarize, transcribe, type, write

v 4 clone, duplicate, image, imitate, mirror, print, re-create, redo, reduplicate, remake, replicate, reprint, reproduce, simulate

v 5 act, ape, emulate, follow, imitate, lip-synch, mimic, mime, mock, model, mouth, pantomime, parody, pattern, take off

v 6 cheat, crib, plagiarize

copyright *v* claim, patent, protect, register, trademark

coquette *n* flirt, harlot, nymphomaniac, seductress, siren, tart, tease, temptress, vamp, wanton woman

coquettish *adj* alluring, appealing, attractive, charming, coy, fast, fetching, flirtatious, seductive, sexy, tempting, winsome

coral *adj* apricot, orange, salmon, tangerine

cord *n* 1 bridle, check, leash, restraint, rope, tether

n 2 cable, fiber, hemp, lanyard, line, rope, strand, string, thread, twine, yarn

v see: HITCH *v* 1

cordial *adj* 1 affable, amiable, approachable, friendly, genial, gentle, gracious, likable, lovable, peaceful, pleasant, serene

adj 2 see: POLITE *adj* 2

core *n* 1 cadre, center, framework, infrastructure, nucleus

n 2 center, hub, middle, midpoint, midst

n 3 center, gist, kernel, keynote, theme

n 4 basis, body, bulk, essence, essentials, gist, heart, import, mass, nucleus, object, staple, substance, volume

n 5 center, crux, essence, gist, heart, life, marrow, nature, nucleus, pith, quick, quintessence, root, spirit, substance

cork *n* cap, cover, lid, plate, plug, top

corkscrew *v* coil, curl, distort, entwine, gnarl, spiral, twist, wind

corner *n* 1 bind, box, difficulty, dilemma, fix, impasse, jam, mess, pinch, plight, predicament, quandary, scrape, spot, trap, trouble

n 2 exclusive, lock, monopoly, restraint

v 1 bottle up, collar, tree

v 2 dominate, monopolize

cornucopia *n* see: WEALTH *n* 1

cornucopian *adj* see: EXTRAVAGANT *adj* 4

corny *adj* 1 sentimental

adj 2 artificial, exaggerated, pretentious, staged, theatrical

adj 3 see: STALE *adj* 3

corollary *n* 1 continuation, epilogue, outgrowth, sequel, supplement

n 2 aftermath, consequence, effect, eventuality, outcome, reaction, repercussion, result, reverberation, reward, upshot

corporation *n* 1 association, combination, establishment, fellowship, foundation, institution, league, union

n 2 business, company, concern, enterprise, establishment, firm, house, organization, partnership

corporeal *adj* 1 bodily, carnal, fleshly

adj 2 concrete, material, objective, physical, real, sensible, substantial, tactile, tangible

corps *n* band, body, company, group, outfit, party, troop, troupe

corpse *n* body, cadaver, carcass, remains, shell, stiff

corpulent *adj* chubby, chunky, fat, fleshy, gross, heavy, hefty, meaty, obese, overweight, plump, portly, pudgy, rotund, stocky, stout

correct *adj* 1 cogent, logical, rational, sound

adj 2 accurate, exact, precise, proper, right, valid

adj 3 conventional, decorous, fitting, nice, orthodox, polite, proper, right, suitable, well

adj 4 appropriate, deserved, due, fitting, just, merited, proper, rightful, suitable, warranted

v 1 rectify, remedy, repair

v 2 better, improve, modify, reform, rehabilitate

v 3 castigate, chasten, chastise, discipline, punish, torment

v 4 annotate, compile, denote, edit, modify, polish, proofread, revise

v 5 adjust, cure, fix, heal, make well, mend, remedy, repair, restore

v 6 adjust, amend, fix, improve, mend, modify, position, rectify, remedy, restore, right, straighten

correction *n* 1 improvement, progress, reform

n 2 abatement, alleviation, comfort, cure, help, relief, remedy, respite, solace, solution

correctly *adv* acceptably, adequately, amply, appropriately, properly, right, satisfactorily, suitably, well

correctness *n* 1 justice, lawfulness, legality, truth, validity

n 2 flawlessness, perfection, precision

correlate *v* 1 connect

v 2 analogize, associate, compare, explain, rank, relate

v 3 bracket, collate, compare, contrast, equate, liken, match, relate, sort

correspond *v* 1 approximate, complement, equal, parallel

v 2 accord, agree, check, coalesce, coincide, comply with, concur, conform, consent, consist, fit in, harmonize, jibe, square, suit, tally

correspondence *n* see: BOOK *n* 2

correspondent *n* columnist, commentator, editor, interviewer, journalist, newspaperman, publicist, writer

corresponding *adj* akin, alike, analogous, comparable, equivalent, identical, kindred, like, matching, parallel, related, same, similar, such, uniform

corridor *n* passageway

corroborate *v* attest, authenticate, certify, confirm, justify, notarize, prove, ratify, sanction, substantiate, support, validate, verify, vouch, witness

corrode v deteriorate, eat, erode, gnaw, oxidize, rust, wear

corrosive adj 1 acerbic, acrid, biting, bitter, caustic, critical, pungent, sarcastic
adj 2 acidic, caustic, reactive

corrupt adj 1 bad, crooked, deceitful, dishonest, evil, fraudulent, immoral, iniquitous, lying, Machiavellian, manipulative, mercenary, reprobate, roguish, scheming, shady, shifty, sinful, unethical, unfair, unprincipled, unscrupulous, untruthful, venal, vile, wicked, wrong
adj 2 see: SINISTER adj 2
adj 3 see: VICIOUS adj 3
v 1 bribe
v 2 bias, distort, misrepresent, pervert, skew, slant, warp
v 3 abuse, ill-use, misapply, misemploy, mishandle, misuse, pervert, prostitute
v 4 adulterate, debase, debauch, defile, demoralize, dishonor, pervert, ruin, seduce, taint
v 5 see: DISINTEGRATE v 2

corruption n 1 crime, disgrace, exposé, outrage, scandal
n 2 contamination, decay, impurity, poison, taint
n 3 depravity, dishonesty, immorality, impurity, vice, wickedness, wrong
n 4 cancer, decay, evil, infection, malignancy, poison, rot, toxin, venom

corsage n arrangement, bouquet, bunch, flowers

corset n band, belt, bind, fasten, gird, girdle, lash, strap, tie

cosmopolitan adj see: SOPHISTICATED adj 2

cosmos n creation, firmament, grand scale, macrocosm, nature, solar system, universe, vast, world

cost n 1 damage, deficit, loss, penalty, suffering
n 2 charge, expense, fare, outlay, payment, price, rate, value, worth
n 3 see: FEE n 5

costly adj 1 dear, expensive, precious, valuable
adj 2 dear, excessive, exorbitant, expensive, high, overpriced, prohibitive, steep, stiff

costs n burden, commitments, expenditures, expenses, overhead

costume n 1 camouflage, cloak, cover, curtain, disguise, mask, pretense, shield, shroud, veil
n 2 dress, gown, kilt, skirt

cot n bed, berth, bunk, couch, cradle, crib, stall

coterie n band, cabal, camp, circle, clan, clique, coven, cult, faction, family, gang, group, mob, ring, school, sect, tribe

cotillion n ball, dance, hop, party, prom

cottage n abode, barn, bungalow, cabin, coop, hatch, hovel, hut, lodge, shack, shanty

cottony adj satiny, silky, slippery, smooth, soft, supple, velvety

couch n 1 bed, berth, bunk, cot, cradle, crib, stall
n 2 divan, lounge, settee, sofa
v announce, articulate, assert, describe, dictate, draft, enunciate, express, intonate, orate, phrase, proclaim, pronounce, say, speak, state, stress, talk, utter, verbalize, vocalize, voice, word

cough v choke, disgorge, gag, throw up, vomit

council n 1 board, body, cabinet, commission, committee, directorship
n 2 assembly, clinic, congress, court, diet, forum, hearing, meeting, parliament, seminar, symposium
n 3 assemblage, assembly, caucus, conference, congregation, convention, crowd, gathering, group, meeting, rally, symposium

councilman n assemblyman, congressman, lawmaker, legislator, representative, senator

counsel n 1 advisement, care, consultation
n 2 advice, opinion, recommendation, suggestion
n 3 advocate, attorney, barrister, counselor, intercessor, lawyer, mediator, solicitor
v 1 advise, caution, evaluate, recommend, reprove
v 2 bid, endorse, offer, pose, present, proffer, propose, proposition, put forth, recommend, suggest, urge

counselor n advocate, attorney, barrister, counsel, intercessor, lawyer, mediator, solicitor

count n 1 calculation, number, summation
n 2 record, score, tally, total
n 3 amount, balance, result, sum, total
n 4 aggregate, amount, body, budget, bulk, number, quantity, tally, total
v 1 gain, score, tally, win
v 2 calculate, cite, enumerate, itemize, list, number, numerate, tally

countenance n 1 face, features, kisser, mug
n 2 appearance, aspect, cast, expression, face, look, visage
v 1 advocate, encourage, favor

v 2 accept, approbate, approve, authorize, certify, condone, confirm, endorse, favor, pass, ratify, sanction, validate

counter *adj* 1 backward, reverse

adj 2 conflicting, contradictory, contrary, converse, diametric, inverse, opposed, opposing, opposite, polar, reverse

v 1 counterbalance, negate, neutralize, nullify, offset, thwart

v 2 combat, compete, contend, contest, dispute, duel, fight, match, oppose, parry, pit, play, repel, resist, rival, strive, struggle, vie

counterbalance *v* counter, negate, neutralize, nullify, offset, thwart

counterfeit *adj* 1 artificial, bogus, ersatz, fake, false, imitation, mock, phony, pseudo, sham, simulated, spurious, substitute, unreal

adj 2 artificial, fake, false, man-made, manufactured, plastic, synthetic

n 1 charlatan, fake, faker, fraud, hypocrite, impostor, liar, phony, pretender

n 2 clone, copy, duplicate, duplication, image, imitation, likeness, mock-up, model, print, replica, replication, representation, reproduction, resemblance, simulation

v act, assume, bluff, fabricate, fake, feign, imitate, invent, make believe, play, pretend, put on, sham

counterpart *n* 1 double, duplicate, match, mate, twin

n 2 complement, equal, equivalent, like, match, parallel, peer

n 3 see: FRIEND *n* 1

countless *adj* 1 abundant, numerous

adj 2 immeasurable, incalculable, infinite, innumerable, innumerous, legion, many, numberless, uncountable, unlimited, untold

country *adj* bucolic, garden, outland, pastoral, peaceful, provincial, rural, rustic, suburban, wooded

n 1 area, entity, government, nation, province, state

n 2 fatherland, home, homeland, land, motherland, soil

n 3 blues, classical, folk, jazz, music, ragtime, rock-and-roll, soul, swing

countryman *n* 1 commoner, common man, peasant, plebeian, proletarian

n 2 citizen, indigene, inhabitant, national, native, subject

county *n* district, jurisdiction, municipality, parish, precinct, township, ward

couple *v* associate, blend, bond, coalesce, combine, compound, connect, fasten, fuse, join, link, marry, mate, meet, merge, pair, unite, wed

n duet, duo, pair, set, twins, twosome

coupling *n* 1 crossing, interchange, joining, junction, juncture, linking, merger

n 2 liaison, linking, marriage, matrimony, union, wedlock

courage *n* boldness, bravery, daring, fortitude, heart, heroism, spirit, strength, valor

courageous *adj* 1 audacious, bold, brave, daring, dauntless, fearless, gallant, game, gutsy, heroic, intrepid, stalwart, unafraid, undaunted, valiant, valorous

adj 2 see: MASCULINE *adj*

courier *n* carrier, delivery person, envoy, herald, messenger, runner

course *n* 1 bearings, direction, heading, location, position

n 2 determination, plan, purpose, resolution, resolve

n 3 conduct, guidelines, plan, policy, procedures, program, rules, scheme

n 4 direction, drift, path, strategy, tack, tactic, tendency, tenor, trend

n 5 chain, lineup, order, progression, row, run, sequence, series, string, succession, train

n 6 circuit, itinerary, journey, line, means, passage, path, road, route, trip, voyage, way

n 7 discipline, study, subject

court *n* 1 judge, justice, magistrate

n 2 assembly, clinic, congress, council, diet, forum, hearing, meeting, parliament, seminar, symposium

n 3 anteroom, approach, atrium, doorway, entrance hall, entry, foyer, hall, hallway, lobby, portal, vestibule

n 4 courtroom

v 1 date, entertain, go out, meet

v 2 attract, encourage, flirt, invite, lure, pursue, romance, solicit, tempt, woo

courteous *adj* chivalrous, civil, civilized, cordial, courtly, decent, dignified, gallant, genteel, gentlemanly, gracious, mannerly, noble, polite, well-mannered

courtesy *n* consideration, dispensation, favor, indulgence, kindness, privilege, respect, service

courtly *adj* chivalrous, civil, civilized, cordial, courteous, decent, dignified, gallant, genteel, gentlemanly, gracious, mannerly, noble, polite, well-mannered

courtroom *n* court

cove *n* arm, bay, estuary, fiord, gulf, inlet, narrows, sound, strait

coven *n* band, cabal, camp, circle, clan,

clique, coterie, cult, faction, family, gang, group, mob, ring, school, sect, tribe

covenant *n* 1 coverage, guarantee, indemnity, insurance, pledge, policy, promise, warranty

n 2 agreement, bargain, bond, compact, contract, convention, deal, pact, pledge, promise, transaction, treaty, understanding

v agree, pledge, promise

cover *n* 1 case, coat, enclosure, folder, jacket, skin

n 2 binder, capsule, case, casing, envelope, holder, sheath, skin, wrapper

n 3 appearance, facade, face, facet, factor, front, look, surface, veneer

n 4 camouflage, cloak, costume, curtain, disguise, mask, pretense, shield, shroud, veil

n 5 asylum, harbor, haven, oasis, port, preserve, protection, refuge, reserve, retreat, safety, sanctuary, seaport, security, shelter

n 6 blanket, comforter, quilt, warmer

n 7 camouflage, incognito, privacy, secrecy, stealth

n 8 cap, cork, lid, plate, plug, top

v 1 fix, overlay, patch, repair

v 2 bundle, enclose, envelop, package, wrap

v 3 bulwark, defend, fend, fortify, guard, hide, protect, safeguard, screen, secure, shield

v 4 bury, cache, cloister, conceal, ditch, ensconce, hide, plant, secrete, sequester, stash

v 5 camouflage, cloak, conceal, darken, disguise, envelop, hide, mask, occult, seclude, shield, shroud, veil

v 6 avenge, compensate, disburse, indemnify, pay, reciprocate, redress, reimburse, remedy, remunerate, repair, repay, requite, retaliate, revenge, settle, vindicate

coverage *n* 1 journalism, news, press, reporting

n 2 covenant, guarantee, indemnity, insurance, pledge, policy, promise, warranty

covering *n* 1 coating, film, layer, membrane, sheet, tissue

n 2 coating, scale, skin

n 3 armor, plate, protection, shell, shield

covert *adj* 1 concealed, invisible, obscure, unseen, veiled

adj 2 additional, hidden, secondary, secret, ulterior, undeclared

adj 3 clandestine, classified, concealed, confidential, hidden, off the record, private, privileged, secret, sensitive, sub rosa

adj 4 clandestine, concealed, crafty, deceitful, devious, evasive, foxy, furtive, guileful, indirect, privy, secret, shifty, sly, sneaky, surreptitious, tricky, underground, underhand, underhanded, wily

covertly *adv* clandestinely, furtively, hush-hush, mystically, secretly, sneakily, stealthily, surreptitiously, under cover

coverup *n* excuse, snow job, whitewash

covet *v* 1 begrudge, envy, resent

v 2 choose, crave, desire, envy, fancy, lust, want, wish

v 3 see: APPRECIATE *v* 3

v 4 see: CRAVE *v* 3, 4

covetous *adj* 1 distrusting, envious, jealous, resentful, suspicious

adj 2 avaricious, endless, insatiable, ravenous, unquenchable, voracious

adj 3 acquisitive, avaricious, craving, desirous, eager, grabby, grasping, greedy, hungry, longing, miserly, selfish, wishful, yearning

covetousness *n* avarice, craving, desire, greed, selfishness, yearning

covey *n* see: GROUP *n* 5

cow *n* bull, calf, heifer, ox, steer

v abash, alarm, awe, daunt, frighten, horrify, intimidate, panic, scare, shock, spook, startle, terrify, terrorize, unnerve

cowardly *adj* chicken, fearful, gutless, spineless, timid, yellow

cowboy *n* pioneer, rustic, yokel

cower *v* cringe, flinch, grovel, quail, recoil, shrink, sneak

co-worker *n* see: FRIEND *n* 1

coy *adj* 1 alluring, appealing, attractive, charming, coquettish, fast, fetching, flirtatious, seductive, sexy, tempting, winsome

adj 2 backward, bashful, demure, diffident, innocent, modest, quiet, reserved, retiring, shy, staid, timid, unassured

adj 3 see: ATTRACTIVE *adj* 2, 3

cozy *adj* comfortable, comfy, contented, cushy, homey, secure, snug, soft, warm

crab *v* 1 brood, grouch, moan, mope, pout, scowl, sulk

v 2 complain, criticize, grieve, gripe, grumble, mutter, nag, object, protest, whine

n clam, cockle, crustacean, mollusk, mussel, prawn, shellfish, shrimp, snail

crabby *adj* 1 brooding, dour, gloomy, glum, moody, morose, sour, sulky, sullen, surly, ugly

adj 2 annoying, anxious, bothersome,

chafing, edgy, fretful, galling, impatient, irritating, jittery, nagging, on edge, restless, touchy, unsettling

crack *n* 1 hole, leak, opening, puncture

n 2 cut, gash, opening, rent, slit, trench

n 3 breach, break, fracture, gap, opening, space, split

n 4 gibe, jeer, put-down, quip, shot, sneer, torment

n 5 chink, cleft, crevice, division, fissure, rent, rift, rupture, split

n 6 abyss, canyon, chasm, cleft, depth, fissure, gorge, gulch, pass, ravine

n 7 blink of an eye, flash, instant, jiffy, minute, moment, second, shake, twinkling, wink

n 8 break, chance, gap, occasion, opening, opportunity, shot, show, stroke of luck, time

n 9 blank, cavity, depression, emptiness, gap, hole, hollow, nook, opening, space, void

n 10 banter, comedy, funniness, gag, humor, jest, joke, quip, small talk, wisecrack, wit, witticism

n 11 affront, aspersion, attack, barb, caustic remark, cut, denunciation, despite, dig, disparagement, disrespect, gibe, implication, indignity, innuendo, insult, invective, knock, reflection, sarcasm, scorn, slap, slight, slur, spike, tongue-lashing, verbal jab

n 12 see: HIT *n* 1

v 1 husk, open, peel, remove, shell

v 2 break, chip, fracture, gap, sever, smash, split

v 3 bang, pop, snap, thump

cracked *adj* 1 broken, damaged, fractured, out of order

adj 2 ajar, open, unshut

crackle *v* bubble, hiss, sizzle, spit, sputter

crackup *n* accident, collision, crash, destruction, mishap, pileup, smash, smashup, wreck, wreckage

cradle *n* 1 bed, berth, bunk, cot, couch, crib, stall

n 2 beginning, conception, derivation, fountainhead, inception, infancy, mother, origin, root, seed, source, stem

v caress, cuddle, embrace, feel, fondle, fool around, hold, hug, love, make out, neck, nuzzle, pet, snuggle, stroke

craft *n* 1 barge, boat, canoe, dory, ferry, float, kayak, raft, scow, skiff, tender

n 2 cruiser, freighter, frigate, ketch, liner, ocean liner, sailboat, schooner, ship, steamship, vessel, yacht

n 3 ability, adequacy, adroitness, aptitude, art, caliber, calling, capability, capacity, command, competence, dexterity, experience, expertise, familiarity, forte, knack, know-how, knowledge, mastery, proficiency, prowess, qualification, savvy, skill, specialty, strength, talent, training, workmanship

v 1 define, develop, formulate, list, make, process, specify, synthesize

v 2 carve, chisel, cut, define, design, fashion, form, mold, sculpt, sculpture, shape, steer

v 3 begin, coin, conceive, create, define, develop, devise, formulate, innovate, invent, make, originate, start

craftsman *n* artisan

crafty *adj* 1 adroit, artful, cagey, canny, cunning, evasive, foxy, serpentine, sly

adj 2 astute, calculating, cunning, foxy, guileful, insidious, sharp, shrewd, sly, smart, subtle, tricky, wily, wise

adj 3 clandestine, concealed, covert, deceitful, devious, evasive, foxy, furtive, guileful, indirect, privy, secret, shifty, sly, sneaky, surreptitious, tricky, underground, underhand, underhanded, wily

craggy *adj* bouncy, bumpy, irregular, jagged, jolting, rough, rugged, scraggy, uneven, unsmooth

cram *v* 1 study

v 2 crush, force, gorge, insert, jam, pack, press, ram, stuff

cramp *n* 1 complication, crick, difficulty, kink

n 2 ache, agony, angina, burn, crick, heartache, hurt, pain, pang, soreness, spasm, sting, twinge

n 3 injury, sprain, strain

v 1 bound, confine, demarcate, limit, restrict

v 2 check, curtail, impede, shorten, stunt, throttle

cramped *adj* close, restricted, uncomfortable

crank *n* bellyacher, grouch, grump, sorehead, sourpuss

cranky *adj* 1 balking, balky, contrary, disagreeable, irascible, mean, obstinate, ornery, perverse, wayward

adj 2 angry, cross, feisty, grouchy, hot-tempered, irascible, ireful, peppery, quick-tempered, short-fused, sullen, testy, touchy

crap *n* crud, debris, detritus, dirt, garbage, junk, litter, refuse, rubbish, rubble, sweepings, trash, waste

crash *n* 1 breakdown, catastrophe, crisis,

death, destruction, doom, failure, finish, ruin

n 2 accident, collision, crackup, destruction, mishap, pileup, smash, smashup, wreck, wreckage

n 3 bang, boom, clang, clap, resound, roar, rumble, shake, thunder

n 4 bang, blow, box, bump, chop, clap, conk, crack, cuff, hit, impact, jar, jolt, knock, lick, punch, rap, slap, slug, smack, smash, swat, swipe, tap, wallop, whack

v 1 collide, demolish, smash, wreck

v 2 bang, bump, collide, hit, smash

v 3 fail, flop, flunk

v 4 clash, conflict, discord, jangle, jar, mismatch

crass adj coarse, crude, flagrant, glaring, gross, obscene, rough, shocking, uncouth, uncultured, unrefined

crate n 1 box, carton, case, chest, container, receptacle

n 2 basket, box, housing

v 1 box, bundle, pack, stow

v 2 bear, carry, convey, ferry, haul, lift, lug, pack, shoulder, shuttle, tote, traffic, transport, truck

cravat n ascot, necktie, tie

crave v 1 like, relish, savor, taste

v 2 ask, call, demand, necessitate, require, take

v 3 choose, covet, desire, envy, fancy, lust, want, wish

v 4 ache, covet, desire, hanker, hunger, itch, long, lust, need, pine, thirst, want, yearn

v 5 see: PLEAD v 2

craving n 1 appetite, desire, eroticism, hankering, hunger, itch, longing, lust, passion, urge, yearning, yen

n 2 avarice, covetousness, desire, greed, selfishness, yearning

adj see: GREEDY adj 1

crawl v coast, creep, glide, prowl, skate, skim, skulk, slick, slide, slink, slip, slither, snake, sneak, steal, wiggle, wriggle, writhe

crayon n brush, chalk, marker, pen, pencil, quill

craze n 1 chic, fad, fashion, mode, rage, style, thing, trend, vogue

n 2 agitation, excitement, frenzy, furor, fury, fuss, outrage, passion, tumult, uproar, wrath

craziness n 1 folly, foolishness, frivolity, insanity, lunacy, madness, mania, nonsense, senselessness

n 2 aberration, abnormality, delusion, dementia, derangement, distraction, ec-

centricity, fugue, hallucination, insanity, irregularity, lunacy, madness, mania, psychosis, unbalance

crazy adj 1 amok, berserk, frenzied, maniacal, out of control, rushed about, violent

adj 2 absurd, balmy, bizarre, emotional, foolish, frivolous, goofy, illogical, impossible, inane, insane, irrational, loony, lunatic, mad, muddled, nuts, preposterous, ridiculous, silly, touched, wacky, zany

adj 3 eccentric, kooky, off-center

adj 4 absurd, comic, comical, droll, farcical, foolish, funny, hilarious, humorous, laughable, ludicrous, outrageous, ridiculous, silly

cream n aristocracy, blue blood, elite, gentry, nobility, royalty, upper class

v beat, belittle, blast, clobber, conquer, defeat, dust, lambaste, lick, overrun, overwhelm, rout, shellac, smear, thrash, wallop, whip

crease v 1 fold, muss, pleat, rumple, wrinkle

v 2 fold

n fold, pleat, rumple, wrinkle

create v 1 author, compose, draft, pen, prepare, type, write

v 2 actuate, bring about, cause, draw on, effect, execute, invoke, make, produce, secure

v 3 build, constitute, construct, erect, establish, found, initiate, institute, launch, set up, start

v 4 brew, concoct, construe, contrive, devise, engineer, fabricate, formulate, hatch, invent, make up, plot, scheme

v 5 begin, coin, conceive, craft, define, develop, devise, formulate, innovate, invent, make, originate, start

v 6 bear, beget, breed, come into, effect, engender, father, generate, hatch, impregnate, make, mate, multiply, originate, parent, procreate, promulgate, propagate, reproduce, sire, spawn

v 7 see: INITIATE v 1, 2

v 8 see: VISUALIZE v

created adj see: FICTITIOUS adj 3

creation n 1 composition

n 2 innovation, invention

n 3 birth, conception, formulation, genesis, procreation

n 4 concoction, fabrication, fantasy, fiction, figment, invention

n 5 birth, fountain, genesis, origin, parent, root, source

n 6 cosmos, firmament, grand scale, macrocosm, nature, solar system, universe, vast, world

creative *adj* 1 artistic, skilled, skillful, talented

adj 2 basic, formative, fundamental, initiatory, productive, seminal

adj 3 copious, fecund, fertile, fruitful, productive, prolific

adj 4 active, bustling, busy, driving, energetic, enterprising, inventive, lively, resourceful

adj 5 clever, deft, enterprising, fertile, imaginative, ingenious, inventive, resourceful, skillful, talented

creativity *n* 1 innovation

n 2 fancy, fantasy, image, imagination, ingenuity, inspiration, invention, resourcefulness, whimsy

creator *n* 1 author, founder, initiator, instigator, inventor, maker, originator, parent, pioneer, seed, source

n 2 see: WRITER *n* 2

creature *n* 1 animal, beast, being, brute, monster, ogre

n 2 being, citizen, entity, Homo sapiens, human, human being, individual, man, person, woman

credence *n* belief, confidence, contingency, credit, creed, dependence, desire, faith, hope, religion, trust

credential *n* 1 certificate, document, instrument, license, pass, permit

n 2 certificate, degree, diploma, sheepskin

credentials *n* background, education, qualifications, training

credible *adj* accurate, authentic, believable, certain, convincing, dependable, faithful, real, reliable, safe, sure, tenable, true, trustworthy, trusty

credit *n* 1 acknowledgment, recognition

n 2 asset, resource, treasure, valuable

n 3 account, balance sheet, book, ledger, score, statement, tab

n 4 belief, confidence, contingency, credence, creed, dependence, desire, faith, hope, religion, trust

n 5 accolade, award, commendation, decoration, distinction, honor, kudos, laurels, medal, note, praise, recognition, reputation, reward, tribute

v 1 attribute, honor, recognize, reward

v 2 accredit, apply, ascribe, assign, attribute, charge, refer

credulous *adj* 1 gullible, ingenuous, trusting, trustworthy

adj 2 believing, easy, gullible, innocent, naive, susceptible, trustful

creed *n* 1 affiliation, belief, church, denomination, faith, persuasion, religion, rite, seat, theology

n 2 belief, confidence, contingency, credence, credit, dependence, desire, faith, hope, religion, trust

n 3 belief, canon, code, conviction, doctrine, dogma, law, opinion, principle, rule, tenet, theory

creek *n* bayou, brook, river, stream, tributary

creep *n* blockhead, boor, clod, cretin, dimwit, dolt, dope, dullard, dumbbell, dummy, dunce, fool, goof, idiot, imbecile, jerk, nerd, nincompoop, numskull, oaf, pain, schlemiel, schmuck, simpleton, stooge, turkey

v coast, crawl, glide, prowl, skate, skim, skulk, slick, slide, slink, slip, slither, snake, sneak, steal, wiggle, wriggle, writhe

cremate *v* burn, destroy, incinerate, oxidize

crescendo *n* see: APEX *n*

crest *n* acme, apex, apogee, climax, crescendo, crown, culmination, epitome, height, noon, peak, pinnacle, point, prime, summit, tip, top, ultimate, utmost, zenith

v 1 crown, peak, top

v 2 climb, increase, jump, mount, rise, surge

cretin *n* blockhead, boor, clod, creep, dimwit, dolt, dope, dullard, dumbbell, dummy, dunce, fool, goof, idiot, imbecile, jerk, nerd, nincompoop, numskull, oaf, pain, schlemiel, schmuck, simpleton, stooge, turkey

crevice *n* 1 chink, cleft, crack, division, fissure, rent, rift, rupture, split

n 2 see: CHANNEL *n* 3

crew *n* 1 employees, faculty, help, people, personnel, staff, workers

n 2 assembly, association, band, bevy, brood, bunch, camp, clique, cluster, collection, covey, flock, group, organization, party, team, unit

n 3 see: CROWD *n* 1

crib *n* bed, berth, bunk, cot, couch, cradle, stall

v copy, plagiarize

crick *n* 1 complication, cramp, difficulty, kink

n 2 ache, agony, angina, burn, cramp, heartache, hurt, pain, pang, soreness, spasm, sting, twinge

crime *n* 1 corruption, disgrace, exposé, outrage, scandal

n 2 con, graft, hustle, racket, rip-off, scam, scheme, sting, swindle *n* 3 dishonor, disobedience, evil, fault, felony, infamy, infraction, iniquity, injury, lawbreaking, misdeed, misdemeanor, offense, outrage, sin, transgression, trespass, vice, violation, wrong, wrongdoing

criminal *adj* 1 blameworthy, culpable, felonious, guilty, remiss, reprehensible

adj 2 disgraceful, felonious, illegal, illegitimate, illicit, lawless, prohibited, unlawful, wrong, wrongful

n 1 bandit, brigand, burglar, cheat, con artist, con man, crook, embezzler, gyp, highwayman, looter, mugger, outlaw, robber, swindler, thief

n 2 accused, con, convict, crook, culprit, delinquent, felon, guilty party, inmate, lawbreaker, offender, perpetrator, prisoner, scofflaw, suspect, swindler, transgressor, wrongdoer

crimp *n* 1 bend, kink, snarl, tangle, twist

n 2 bar, barrier, bottleneck, dead end, deadlock, difficulty, encumbrance, hurdle, impasse, impediment, obstacle, obstruction, snag, stumbling block

v bridle, check, constrain, control, curb, hold back, hold down, inhibit, leash, rein, restrain, restrict, withhold

crimson *adj* cardinal, red, ruby, scarlet, vermilion

cringe *v* 1 bow, genuflect, grovel, kneel, kowtow, prostrate, scrape

v 2 cower, flinch, grovel, quail, recoil, shrink, sneak

v 3 blanch, flinch, jump, recoil, shrink, start, startle, wince

cripple *v* 1 dismember, maim, mangle, mutilate

v 2 debilitate, disable, drain, enfeeble, exhaust, sap, undermine, weaken

v 3 disable, disarm, encumber, freeze, halt, handcuff, immobilize, incapacitate, paralyze, prostrate, stop, stun

crippled *adj* disabled, lame, limping

crisis *n* 1 climax, crux, dilemma, emergency, juncture, point, predicament

n 2 breakdown, catastrophe, crash, death, destruction, doom, failure, finish, ruin

crisp *adj* 1 breakable, brittle, crumbly, crunchy, fragile

adj 2 abbreviated, brief, compressed, concise, curt, laconic, pithy, short, succinct, terse, to the point

crisscross *v* bisect, cross, impede, intersect

criterion *n* 1 requirement

n 2 benchmark, guideline, measure, test

n 3 benchmark, gauge, measure, observation, rule, standard, yardstick

n 4 behest, bidding, canon, charge, command, decree, dictate, direction, edict, fiat, guideline, injunction, institution, law, mandate, order, ordinance, precept, prescript, prescription, regulation, rite, rule, ruling, statute, word

critic *n* 1 commentator, evaluator, judge, reviewer

n 2 aesthete, connoisseur, expert, virtuoso

n 3 cynic, detractor, hatchet man, naysayer, pessimist, skeptic

critical *adj* 1 essential, integral, necessary, significant, strategic

adj 2 acerbic, acrid, biting, bitter, caustic, corrosive, pungent, sarcastic

adj 3 captious, carping, censorious, cutting, disparaging, faultfinding, hairsplitting, nit-picking

adj 4 essential, imperative, indispensable, mandatory, necessary, needed, prerequisite, required, vital

adj 5 breakneck, dangerous, harmful, hazardous, perilous, precarious, risky, serious, unsafe, venturesome

adj 6 acute, burning, crucial, desperate, dire, grave, heavy, important, major, momentous, ponderous, pressing, profound, serious, severe, solemn, somber, urgent, vital

adj 7 see: DISASTROUS *adj* 2

adj 8 see: SUBSTANTIAL *adj* 4

criticism *n* 1 beef, complaint, grievance, gripe, objection, protest

n 2 analysis, assessment, commentary, critique, evaluation, examination, judgment, notion, opinion, review, ruling

n 3 admonishment, admonition, blast, chewing out, chiding, denunciation, diatribe, harangue, hassle, libel, outburst, rap, rebuke, reprimand, reproach, reproof, scolding, slander, tirade

criticize *v* 1 accuse, blame, charge, complain, condemn, fault, indict, reproach

v 2 complain, crab, grieve, gripe, grumble, mutter, nag, object, protest, whine

v 3 berate, carp, cavil, find fault, flay, fuss, henpeck, nag, nit-pick, nudge, peck, quibble, scold

critique *n* analysis, assessment, commentary, criticism, evaluation, examination, judgment, notion, opinion, review, ruling

crocked *adj* bombed, doped up, drunk, drunken, high, inebriated, intoxicated, juiced, loaded, looped, messed up, plastered, polluted, sloshed, smashed, stoned, tight, tipsy, turned on, wasted, wired

crony *n* accomplice, acquaintance, adjunct, ally, associate, buddy, chum, cohort, colleague, companion, compatriot, comrade, confidant, confrere, connection, copartner, counterpart, co-worker, equal, fellow, follower, friend, intimate, mate, pal, partner, peer, relative, supporter

crook n 1 arc, arch, bend, bow, coil, curvature, curve, hook, round, spiral

n 2 bandit, brigand, burglar, cheat, con artist, con man, criminal, embezzler, gyp, highwayman, looter, mugger, outlaw, robber, swindler, thief

n 3 see: CRIMINAL n 2

crooked adj 1 askew, awry, lopsided, off-center

adj 2 meandering, serpentine, sinuous, spiral, turning, twisting, winding, zigzagging

adj 3 see: EVIL adj 4

crop v clip, cut, lop, pare, prune, shave, shear, snip, trim, whittle

n fruits, grain, harvest, produce, yield

cross adj 1 angry, cranky, feisty, grouchy, hot-tempered, irascible, ireful, peppery, quick-tempered, short-fused, sullen, testy, touchy

adj 2 see: ANGRY adj 4

n 1 emblem

n 2 monument

v 1 bisect, crisscross, impede, intersect

v 2 betray, divulge, double-cross, reveal, sell out

v 3 cruise, fly, sail, traverse, voyage

v 4 contradict, deny, disaffirm, disagree, impugn, negate, rebut, traverse

v 5 interbreed

v 6 bamboozle, beat, beguile, bilk, burn, cajole, cheat, chicane, chisel, con, deceive, defraud, dupe, embezzle, fleece, flimflam, fob, foist, fool, gyp, hoax, hoodwink, hustle, inveigle, screw, shaft, sham, swindle, trick, victimize

crossbreed v graft, implant

cross-examine v ask, examine, grill, inquire, interrogate, investigate, probe, pump, query, question, quiz

crossing n 1 coupling, interchange, joining, junction, juncture, linking, merger

n 2 crossroad, intersection, passageway

crossroad n crossing, intersection, passageway

crow v boast, brag, exult, flaunt, gloat, revel, show off, strut, vaunt

crowd n 1 band, bunch, crew, drove, flock, following, gaggle, gang, herd, huddle,

mass, mob, pack, rabble, riffraff, swarm, team, throng

n 2 see: ASSEMBLY n 3

n 3 see: SOCIETY n 3

v 1 choke, clog, congest, glut, jam

v 2 herd, jam, mob, press, push, swarm, teem, throng

v 3 compact, compress, constrain, crush, jam, mash, pack, press, push, squash, squeeze

crowded adj 1 concentrated, populous, teeming

adj 2 close, compact, dense, solid, thick, tight

adj 3 bursting, chock-full, filled up, full, jammed, jampacked, loaded, packed, rending, replete, stuffed

crown n 1 bow, fore, front, head, prow, stem, top

n 2 band, coil, garland, loop, ring, spiral, wreath

n 3 acme, apex, apogee, climax, crescendo, crest, culmination, epitome, height, noon, peak, pinnacle, point, prime, summit, tip, top, ultimate, utmost, zenith

v 1 crest, peak, top

v 2 adjourn, cap, climax, complete, conclude, consummate, culminate, dissolve, end, finalize, finish, terminate, wind up, wrap up

CRT n console, display, monitor, screen, terminal

crucial adj 1 central, dominant, pivotal

adj 2 chief, key, salient, vital

adj 3 acute, burning, critical, desperate, dire, grave, heavy, important, major, momentous, ponderous, pressing, profound, serious, severe, solemn, somber, urgent, vital

adj 4 see: DISASTROUS adj 2

adj 5 see: SUBSTANTIAL adj 4

crud n crap, debris, detritus, dirt, garbage, junk, litter, refuse, rubbish, rubble, sweepings, trash, waste

crude adj 1 approximate, estimated, proximate, rough, rounded

adj 2 basic, plain, primitive, rough, simple, undeveloped

adj 3 amiss, defective, faulty, flawed, imperfect, incomplete, short, unfulfilled

adj 4 brief, cursory, hasty, rough, shallow, sketchy, superficial, uncritical

adj 5 raw, rough, rude, undressed, unfashioned, unfinished, unhewn, unpolished

adj 6 coarse, crass, flagrant, glaring, gross,

obscene, rough, shocking, uncouth, uncultured, unrefined

adj 7 see: VULGAR *adj 2*

cruel *adj* **1** adamant, cold, fierce, relentless,
vindictive

adj **2** bitter, brutal, fierce, hard, harsh,
inclement, intemperate, pitiless, rigorous,
rough, rugged, severe, stern, strong, unkind, violent

adj **3** austere, brutal, callous, cold-
blooded, compassionless, ferocious, fierce,
hardened, hardhearted, heartless, indifferent, inhuman, inhumane, malicious,
mean, merciless, nasty, obdurate, pitiless,
ruthless, savage, spiteful, stony, tough,
uncaring, unemotional, unfeeling, unkind, unmerciful, unpitying, unrelenting,
unsympathetic, vicious

cruise *v* **1** cross, fly, sail, traverse, voyage

v **2** coast, explore, go, journey, migrate,
proceed, sail, survey, tour, travel, trek,
voyage

n see: JOURNEY *n* **2**

cruiser *n* craft, freighter, frigate, ketch,
liner, ocean liner, sailboat, schooner,
ship, steamship, vessel, yacht

crumble *v* corrupt, decay, decompose, degenerate, deteriorate, disintegrate, perish,
putrefy, rot, smell, spoil, taint, wane,
weaken, wither

crumbled *adj* decaying, decrepit, dilapidated, run-down

crumbly *adj* breakable, brittle, crisp,
crunchy, fragile

crumple *v* collapse, contract, deflate,
shrink

crunch *v* bite, chew, gnaw, gulp, guzzle,
munch, nibble, rend, wolf

crunchy *adj* breakable, brittle, crisp, crumbly, fragile

crusade *n* campaign, drive, effort, expedition, push

crusader *n* **1** evangelist, missionary, proselytizer

n **2** *see:* ENTHUSIAST *n* **2**

crush *n* dozens, horde, host, legion, many,
multitude, numerousness, oodles, press,
push, scores, squash, swarm

v **1** grind, pound, powder, pulverize

v **2** defeat, drown, overpower, overwhelm,
stifle

v **3** squash, stomp, tramp, trample, tread,
tromp

v **4** cram, force, gorge, insert, jam, pack,
press, ram, stuff

v **5** compact, compress, constrain, crowd,
jam, mash, pack, press, push, squash,
squeeze

v **6** bear down, beat down, conquer, defeat, dominate, enslave, exploit, overpower, quash, reduce, subdue, subjugate,
suppress, vanquish

v **7** bruise, mash, mush up, pulp, squash

v **8** conquer, defeat, destroy, down, hurdle, lick, overcome, overthrow, surmount

v **9** annihilate, demolish, extinguish, put
down, quash, quell, quench, repress,
squash, stamp out, suppress

crushed *adj* **1** defeated, distraught, emotional, overcome, subdued

adj **2** humbled

crushing *adj* devastating, overpowering,
overwhelming

crust *n* **1** bark, case, coating, husk, peel,
rind, shell, shuck, skin

n **2** *see:* AUDACITY *n*

crustacean *n* clam, cockle, crab, mollusk,
mussel, prawn, shellfish, shrimp, snail

crusty *adj see:* BLUNT *adj* **1**

crux *n* **1** climax, crisis, dilemma, emergency, juncture, point, predicament

n **2** attention, center, feature, focus, highlight, key, spotlight

n **3** center, core, essence, gist, heart, life,
marrow, nature, nucleus, pith, quick,
quintessence, root, spirit, substance

cry *n* **1** dirge, funeral hymn, lament

n **2** air, call, carol, lullaby, melody, note,
rhapsody, song, tune

v **1** bark, bay, growl, howl, shout, snap,
woof, yap, yelp

v **2** blurt, cackle, ejaculate, exclaim,
shout, spill, sputter, tattle, utter

v **3** bawl, bemoan, grieve, groan, lament,
moan, mourn, sigh, snivel, sob, wail,
weep, whimper, whine

v **4** bark, bellow, blare, call, holler, howl,
roar, scream, screech, shout, shriek,
shrill, squeal, thunder, wail, yell

crying *adj see:* MONSTROUS *adj* **2**

crypt *n* burial, catacomb, cenotaph, grave,
mausoleum, memorial, monument, pit,
sepulcher, tomb, vault

cryptic *adj* ambiguous, enigmatic, mystifying, occult, puzzling, vague

crystal *adj* clear, clear-cut, limpid, lucid,
translucent, transparent, unambiguous,
unblurred

crystallize *v* come together, develop, form,
jell, materialize, shape up

cub *n* boy, child, junior, lad, son, young
man

cubby *n* cabinet, chest, closet, compartment, locker, nook, wardrobe

cuddle *v* **1** clasp, clinch, embrace, enfold,
hold, hug, press, squeeze

v 2 caress, cradle, embrace, feel, fondle, fool around, hold, hug, love, make out, neck, nuzzle, pet, snuggle, stroke

cudgel *n* bat, blackjack, boomerang, club, cue, mallet, nightstick, stave, stick

cue *n* 1 clue, guide, hint, indication, indicator, inkling, intimation, key, lead, mark, notion, pointer, sign, signal, tip, trace

n 2 bat, blackjack, boomerang, club, cudgel, mallet, nightstick, stave, stick

v jog, nudge, prompt, push, remind, stimulate, stir, suggest

cuff *v* 1 box, clap, knock, punch, slap, smack, spank, strike, tap, whack

v 2 bang, blow, bump, hit, knock, punch, strike

n 1 band

n 2 bang, blow, box, bump, chop, clap, conk, crack, crash, hit, impact, jar, jolt, knock, lick, punch, rap, slap, slug, smack, smash, swat, swipe, tap, wallop, whack

cuisine *n* bread, breakfast, brunch, chow, diet, dinner, dish, edibles, entree, fare, food, grub, lunch, meals, nosh, nutrition, provisions, rations, snack, supper, victuals, vittles

cul-de-sac *n* dead end

cull *v* choose, elect, pick, remove, select, separate, sift, single out, sort

culminate *v* adjourn, cap, climax, complete, conclude, consummate, crown, dissolve, end, finalize, finish, terminate, wind up, wrap up

culmination *n* 1 completion, conclusion, end, finale, finish, windup

n 2 conclusion, denouement, outcome, resolution, result, solution

n 3 see: APEX *n*

culpability *n* accountability, blame, burden, fault, guilt, onus, responsibility, shame, stigma

culpable *adj* 1 blamable, condemned, convicted, guilty, responsible

adj 2 blameworthy, criminal, felonious, guilty, remiss, reprehensible

culprit *n* 1 accused, con, convict, criminal, crook, delinquent, felon, guilty party, inmate, lawbreaker, offender, perpetrator, prisoner, scofflaw, suspect, swindler, transgressor, wrongdoer

cult *n* 1 followers, following

n 2 band, cabal, camp, circle, clan, clique, coterie, coven, faction, family, gang, group, mob, ring, school, sect, tribe

cultivate *v* 1 befriend

v 2 attempt, bring about, perpetuate, practice, proceed, pursue

v 3 develop, encourage, foster, further, grow, promote

v 4 advance, elevate, enhance, enrich, improve, refine, upgrade

v 5 farm, grow, harvest, plant, plow, produce, raise, till

v 6 see: EDUCATE *v*

v 7 see: HELP *v* 4

cultivated *adj* see: SOPHISTICATED *adj* 2

culture *n* 1 customs, habits, mores, traditions

n 2 education, enrichment, erudition, learnedness, learning, wisdom

n 3 background, breeding, development, education, environment, experience, past, schooling, training, upbringing

n 4 citizens, civilization, colony, community, crowd, folks, group, human beings, individuals, laity, masses, men and women, neighbors, people, persons, populace, population, public, settlement, society, staff, tribe

n 5 gentility

cultured *adj* civilized, cosmopolitan, cultivated, elegant, genteel, ingratiating, poised, polished, refined, smooth, sophisticated, suave, urbane, well-bred

cunning *adj* 1 adroit, artful, cagey, canny, crafty, evasive, foxy, serpentine, sly

adj 2 adroit, apt, canny, clever, deft, handy, ingenious, nimble, skilled, skillful, sly, wily

adj 3 astute, calculating, crafty, foxy, guileful, insidious, sharp, shrewd, sly, smart, subtle, tricky, wily, wise

adj 4 see: QUICK *adj* 5

adj 5 see: SINISTER *adj* 2

cup *n* chalice, container, dish, Dixie cup, glass, goblet, mug, shot glass, stein, tumbler, vessel, wineglass

curative *adj* healing, medical, medicinal, therapeutic

curb *n* 1 block, check, hangup, inhibition, repression, restraint, reticence

n 2 bond, boundary, bridle, check, constraint, control, damper, harness, leash, limit, rein, restraint, restriction

n 3 see: CHANNEL *n* 3

n 4 see: EDGE *n* 4

v 1 discipline, govern, limit, regulate, restrain, retard

v 2 abstain, avoid, constrain, deny, forgo, govern, hold back, refrain, resist, restrict, stop, tame

v 3 bridle, check, constrain, control, crimp, hold back, hold down, inhibit, leash, rein, restrain, restrict, withhold

v 4 brake, confine, contain, control, drag,

govern, hamper, hem, hold back, impede, repress, restrain, retard

v 5 see: BIND *v* 7

v 6 see: STIFLE *v* 3

curdle *v* clog, clot, coagulate, condense, congeal, dry, gel, harden, intensify, jell, pack, set, solidify, thicken

cure *n* 1 antidote, medication, medicine, panacea, prescription, remedy, serum, therapy, treatment

n 2 abatement, alleviation, comfort, correction, help, relief, remedy, respite, solace, solution

n 3 aid, assistance, benefit, comfort, hand, help, lift, nurture, relief, remedy, succor, support

n 4 rehabilitation, therapy, treatment

v 1 aid, comfort, relieve, soothe, strengthen, support

v 2 adjust, correct, fix, heal, make well, mend, remedy, repair, restore

curio *n* antique, bric-a-brac, curiosity, novelty, objet d'art, oddity, rarity, treasure, wonder

curiosity *n* 1 concern, inquisitiveness, interest, regard

n 2 antique, bric-a-brac, curio, novelty, objet d'art, oddity, rarity, treasure, wonder

curious *adj* 1 absorbed, drawn, engrossed, interested, involved

adj 2 coincidental, ironic, odd, strange, unexpected

adj 3 inquiring, inquisitive, investigative, nosy, probing, prying, questioning, snooping

adj 4 exotic, far-out, fascinating, intriguing, kinky, marvelous, mysterious, new, novel, odd, outlandish, strange, ultra, unaccustomed, unexplored, unfamiliar, unique, unknown, unusual, weird

curl *n* loop, revolution, ring, roll, rotation, spin, spiral, twirl, twist, turn

v coil, corkscrew, distort, entwine, gnarl, spiral, twist, wind

currency *n* assets, bills, capital, cash, coffers, dinero, dollars, estate, funds, goods, income, lucre, means, money, notes, pelf, pesos, property, resources, revenue, riches, rubles, shekels, sum, wealth

current *adj* 1 continuing, going, ongoing

adj 2 extant, remaining, surviving, visible

adj 3 contemporary, existent, instant, living, present

adj 4 chic, fashionable, hip, in, smart, stylish, trendy, vogue

adj 5 contiguous, direct, immediate, instant, nearby, primary, prompt, sudden, timely

adj 6 democratic, dominant, extensive, fashionable, general, in vogue, popular, prevailing, prevalent, rampant, rife, sought after, well-liked, widespread

n 1 drift, pattern, run, series, succession, tendency, trend

n 2 air, blow, breath, breeze, draft, gust, puff, wind

n 3 change, drift, flow, flux, gush, motion, movement, rush, stream, tide, transition

n 4 electricity, juice, power

currently *adv* presently, promptly, today

curse *n* 1 anathema, condemnation, execration, imprecation, malediction, voodoo

n 2 bane, disease, evil, misfortune, pestilence, plague, scourge

v condemn, damn, denounce, molest, profane, swear, vex

cursed *adj* damned, doomed, hapless, hopeless, ill-fated, jinxed, luckless, unfortunate, unhappy, unlucky, untoward

cursory *adj* brief, crude, hasty, rough, shallow, sketchy, superficial, uncritical

curt *adj* 1 brisk, lively, quick, snappy

adj 2 acerbic, acid, biting, dry, pungent, sharp, sour, tart

adj 3 abrupt, bluff, blunt, brash, brusque, cheeky, crusty, flip, flippant, gruff, harsh, impertinent, impudent, irritable, nasty, quick, rude, sarcastic, sassy, short, snippy, snotty, surly, testy, wisenheimer

adj 4 see: CONCISE *adj* 1

adj 5 see: VAIN *adj* 5

curtail *v* 1 check, cramp, impede, shorten, stunt, throttle

v 2 abbreviate, abridge, condense, cut, cut back, diminish, edit, lessen, reduce, restrict, shorten, slash

curtailment *n* 1 ban, blockage, boycott, embargo, prohibition, restriction, stoppage

n 2 erosion

curtain *n* 1 backdrop, environment, scene, scenery, set, setting, stage set, stage setting, surroundings

n 2 camouflage, cloak, costume, cover, disguise, mask, pretense, shield, shroud, veil

n 3 divider, panel, partition, wall

curtness *n* abruptness, brevity, briefness, conciseness, quickness, shortness, transience

curtsy *n* bow

curvature n arc, arch, bend, bow, coil, crook, curve, hook, round, spiral

curve n 1 flight path, orbit, trajectory

n 2 arc, arch, bend, bow, coil, crook, curvature, hook, round, spiral

v 1 bend, meander, veer, wind, zigzag

v 2 angle, arch, bend, bow, flex, ply, round, tilt, tip, turn, twist, vault

curved adj arched, bent, bowed, curvilinear, flexed, rounded, unstraight

curvilinear adj arched, bent, bowed, curved, flexed, rounded, unstraight

cushy adj comfortable, comfy, contented, cozy, homey, secure, snug, soft, warm

custodian n 1 father, guardian, mother, parent, trustee

n 2 agent, janitor, manager, steward

custody n 1 possession

n 2 detention, imprisonment

n 3 care, charge, protection, safekeeping

custom n 1 belief, doctrine, mores, relic, rite, ritual, throwback, tradition

n 2 convention, decorum, etiquette, formality, good form, manners, propriety, protocol, rites

n 3 fashion, formality, habit, manner, mores, observance, practice, routine, tradition, usage, use, way, wont

customarily adv as a rule, frequently, generally, mainly, most, mostly, most often, normally, ordinarily, primarily, principally, usually

customary adj 1 conventional, habitual, normal

adj 2 authorized, conventional, established, set

adj 3 accepted, accustomed, chronic, common, constant, continual, daily, everyday, familiar, frequent, habitual, inured, often, recurring, regular, routine, traditional, usual

customer n buyer, client, consumer, end user, patron, purchaser, shopper, user

customs n culture, habits, mores, traditions

cut n 1 abrasion, hurt, itch, scrape, scratch, sore

n 2 crack, gash, opening, rent, slit, trench

n 3 gash, incision, nick, pierce, prick, puncture, slit, wound

n 4 bit, clipping, division, lot, member, parcel, part, piece, portion, sample, section, segment, slice

n 5 canal, channel, conduit, crevice, curb, ditch, duct, furrow, gorge, groove, gully, gutter, passageway, ravine, rut, trench, trough

n 6 affront, aspersion, attack, barb, caustic remark, crack, denunciation, despite, dig, disparagement, disrespect, gibe, implication, indignity, innuendo, insult, invective, knock, reflection, sarcasm, scorn, slap, slight, slur, spike, tongue-lashing, verbal jab

n 7 gouge, groove, scoop

v 1 carve, engrave, etch, inscribe

v 2 gibe, insult, remark, taunt

v 3 clip, cut back, cut down, lower, mark down, reduce, shave, slash

v 4 clip, crop, lop, pare, prune, shave, shear, snip, trim, whittle

v 5 adapt, conform, convert, fashion, fit, measure, modify, rig, shape, suit, tailor

v 6 abbreviate, abridge, condense, curtail, cut back, diminish, edit, lessen, reduce, restrict, shorten, slash

v 7 ax, carve, chip, chop, cleave, dissect, fell, hack, hew, mangle, mutilate, notch, pulverize, rend, saw, sever, slice, sliver, snip, split, sunder, whittle

v 8 blackball, boycott, ignore, ostracize, rebuff, snub, spurn

v 9 gash, incise, penetrate, pierce, punch, slash, slice, slit

v 10 detach, disconnect, disengage, dissociate, separate, sever, uncouple, unfasten, unhook, unyoke

v 11 banish, bar, blackball, debar, dismiss, eliminate, except, exclude, ignore, leave out, omit, suspend

v 12 carve, chisel, craft, define, design, fashion, form, mold, sculpt, sculpture, shape, steer

cutback n reduction

cute adj 1 adorable, charming, dainty, delectable, delightful

adj 2 see: ATTRACTIVE adj 3, 4

adj 3 see: BEAUTIFUL adj 2

cutlass n blade, dagger, knife, pocketknife, rapier, saber, scimitar, switchblade, sword

cutting adj 1 abrasive, aggravating, annoying, caustic, grating, irritating

adj 2 biting, caustic, incisive, penetrating, pointed, trenchant

adj 3 captious, carping, censorious, critical, disparaging, faultfinding, hairsplitting, nit-picking

adj 4 caustic, coarse, obscene, salty, scathing, scorching, sharp, spicy, trenchant, vulgar, witty

cybernetic adj automatic, robotic, self-steering

cycle n 1 beat, cadence, lilt, pulse, rate, rhythm, tempo, time *n* 2 duration, interval, period, season, span, spell, stage, stretch, term, time

n 3 see: PERIOD *n* 1, 2

v 1 alternate, change, lap, oscillate, rotate, shift, switch

v 2 see: PROCEED *v* 2

cyclic *adj* see: RECURRENT *adj*

cyclical *adj* alternate, cyclic, intermittent, periodic, periodical, recurrent, recurring, repeated, repetitive, sporadic

cylinder *n* channel, conduit, duct, pipe, tube

cynic *n* critic, detractor, hatchet man, naysayer, pessimist, skeptic

cynical *adj* 1 depressed, gloomy, glum, grim, negative, pessimistic

adj 2 contemptuous, derisive, ironic, mocking, sarcastic, sardonic, scornful, skeptical, wry

adj 3 distrustful, doubtful, dubious, incredulous, leery, questionable, shy, skeptical, skittish, suspicious, uncertain, unsure

D

dab *n* 1 atom, bead, dash, dot, drop, grain, iota, molecule, morsel, particle, pea, pellet, smidgen, speck, tad

n 2 see: FRAGMENT *n* 3

v paint, pat, tap, touch

dabble *v* dally, diddle, fiddle, fool, monkey, piddle, play, poke about, putter, tinker, toy, trifle

dabbler *n* amateur, beginner, dilettante, hobbyist, layman, neophyte, nonprofessional, novice, part-timer

dad *n* dada, daddy, father, pa, papa, pappy, parent, pater, patriarch, pop, poppa

dada *n* dad, daddy, father, pa, papa, pappy, parent, pater, patriarch, pop, poppa

daddy *n* dad, dada, father, pa, papa, pappy, parent, pater, patriarch, pop, poppa

daffy *adj* confused, daft, dazed, dizzy, groggy, punchy, stunned

daft *adj* confused, daffy, dazed, dizzy, groggy, punchy, stunned

dagger *n* blade, cutlass, knife, pocketknife, rapier, saber, scimitar, switchblade, sword

daily *adj* 1 everyday

adj 2 accepted, accustomed, chronic, common, constant, continual, customary, everyday, familiar, frequent, habitual, inured, often, recurring, regular, routine, traditional, usual

adj 3 see: TYPICAL *adj* 2

n bulletin, journal, newsletter, newspaper, organ, publication, review

dainty *adj* 1 adorable, charming, cute, delectable, delightful

adj 2 delicate, fine, gentle, nice, refined, subtle

adj 3 choice, delicate, elegant, exquisite, favorite, fine, preferred, rare, select

adj 4 see: TINY *adj* 1

dais *n* desk, lectern, podium, pulpit, rostrum, soapbox, stage, stand

dalliance *n* adultery, affair, cheating, entanglement, fling, flirtation, fooling around, infatuation, intimacy, intrigue, liaison, love affair, playing around, rendezvous, romance, tryst

dallier *n* dawdler, laggard, slowpoke

dally *v* 1 dabble, diddle, fiddle, fool, monkey, piddle, play, poke about, putter, tinker, toy, trifle

v 2 dawdle, delay, diddle, goof off, idle, lag, loaf, loiter, loll, lounge, malinger, poke, put off, putter, shirk, tarry

v 3 see: TEASE *v* 2

dam *v* bar, block, brake, choke, clog, deter, detract, encumber, frustrate, halt, hamper, hesitate, hinder, impair, impede, inhibit, jam, obstruct, prevent, repress, restrain, retard, slow, stay, stop, stop up, throttle

damage *n* 1 cost, deficit, loss, penalty, suffering

n 2 chaos, destruction, devastation, disaster, disorder, harm, havoc, hurt, injury, loss, mayhem, ruin, ruination, tort

v 1 abuse, blemish, hamper, harm, hurt, impair, injure, mar, obstruct, ruin, sabotage, scuttle, spoil, tarnish, vandalize

v 2 blow, blunder, botch, bungle, butcher, err, foul up, goof, hash, hurt, jeopardize, jumble, mess up, queer, ruin, screw up

v 3 abuse, asperse, bad-mouth, belittle, condemn, decry, defame, degrade, denigrate, denounce, deprecate, detract, diminish, discount, disparage, insult, knock, malign, put down, revile, run down, slander, take away, vilify

damaged *adj* broken, cracked, fractured, out of order

damages *n* 1 assessment, fine, penalty, punishment, tax

n 2 amends, compensation, indemnity, redress, reparation, restitution, restoration

damaging *adj* dangerous, deleterious, harmful, hurting, injurious, ruinous, unhealthy

dame *n* female, gentlewoman, lady, matron, miss, mistress, spinster, widow, woman

damn v 1 condemn

v 2 condemn, curse, denounce, molest, profane, swear, vex

damned adj cursed, doomed, hapless, hopeless, ill-fated, jinxed, luckless, unfortunate, unhappy, unlucky, untoward

damp adj 1 dank, drizzly, foggy, humid, misty, moist, wet

adj 2 fluid, juicy, liquefied, liquid, moist, watery, wet

adj 3 drenched, dripping, humid, moist, mucky, muggy, soaked, soggy, sopping, sticky, sultry, sweaty, wet

damper n see: LIMIT n 1

dampness n humidity, moisture, sogginess, wetness

damsel n girl, maid, maiden, wench

dance v flap, flicker, flitter, flutter, oscillate, prance, sparkle, sway, twinkle, undulate, wave

n 1 ball, cotillion, hop, party, prom

n 2 ballet, cha-cha, fox trot, hula, jitterbug, polka, tap, twist, waltz

dancer n ballerina, choreographer, chorine, gypsy, hoofer

dander n anger, fit, frenzy, fury, indignation, ire, outrage, paroxysm, rage, tantrum, wrath

danger n downside, exposure, hazard, jeopardy, liability, menace, peril, risk, threat

dangerous adj 1 damaging, deleterious, harmful, hurting, injurious, ruinous, unhealthy

adj 2 breakneck, critical, harmful, hazardous, perilous, precarious, risky, serious, unsafe, venturesome

adj 3 see: DELICATE adj 7

dangle v hang, suspend, swing

dank adj damp, drizzly, foggy, humid, misty, moist, wet

dapper adj chic, dashing, debonair, jaunty, natty, neat, rakish, sleek, smart, snazzy, spiffy, suave, trim

dare v 1 brave, challenge, confront, defy, face, mutiny, rebel, resist

v 2 attempt, bet, chance, gamble, hazard, play, risk, speculate, stake, venture, wager

daring adj 1 adaptive, bold, canny, clever, enterprising, resourceful, venturesome

adj 2 audacious, bold, brave, courageous, dauntless, fearless, gallant, game, gutsy, heroic, intrepid, stalwart, unafraid, undaunted, valiant, valorous

adj 3 see: RUDE adj 3

n boldness, bravery, courage, fortitude, heart, heroism, spirit, strength, valor

dark adj 1 black, charcoal, pitch-black, shadowy

adj 2 dim, dusky, gloomy, lightless, murky, obscure, shadowy, somber, tenebrous, unilluminated

adj 3 see: DIRTY adj 2

n evening, night, nighttime, wee hours

darken v 1 becloud, bedim, befog, blur, cloud, confuse, dim, diminish, dull, eclipse, fade, muddy, obscure, overshadow, pale, shade, shadow, tarnish

v 2 see: DEFAME v 1

v 3 see: DISGUISE v 2

dart n missile

v 1 gallop, jog, run, trot

v 2 dash, hasten, scamper, scoot, scurry, sprint

v 3 dash, fly, skim

dash n 1 breeze, cinch, ease, snap, waltz, zip

n 2 breath, clue, glimmer, hint, insinuation, lick, shade, smell, smidgen, spice, sprinkling, suggestion, suspicion, tinge, tip, touch, trace, trifle, whiff, whisper, wisp

n 3 see: DOT n 1

v 1 sally

v 2 blast, blight, decompose, nip, wither

v 3 dart, hasten, scamper, scoot, scurry, sprint

v 4 gallop, jog, race, run, speed, sprint

v 5 dart, fly, skim

v 6 aggravate, baffle, balk, bewilder, circumvent, confuse, elude, foil, frustrate, hamper, impede, negate, nullify, perplex, thwart

dashing adj 1 chic, dapper, debonair, jaunty, natty, neat, rakish, sleek, smart, snazzy, spiffy, suave, trim

adj 2 see: LIVELY adj 8

data n 1 details, dope, facts, information, report, scoop

n 2 discipline, facts, information, knowledge, lore, news, science, wisdom

n 3 communication, disclosure, exchange, expression, facts, information, intelligence, knowledge, news, notification

date n 1 appointment, booking, engagement, listing, reservation, schedule

n 2 fiancée, girlfriend, love

n 3 beau, boyfriend, escort, fiancé, lover, mate, paramour, suitor

v court, entertain, go out, meet

dated adj see: OBSOLETE adj

daughter n child, coed, debutante, girl, lass, miss, young lady, young woman

daunt v 1 affect, bother, burden, concern, disturb, faze, intimidate, oppress, upset, worry

v 2 appall, discourage, dismay, horrify, panic, petrify, scare, shock, terrify, unnerve

v 3 see: FRIGHTEN v 2

dauntless adj see: BRAVE adj 1

dawdle v dally, delay, diddle, goof off, idle, lag, linger, loaf, loiter, loll, lounge, malinger, poke, put off, putter, shirk, tarry

dawdler n dallier, laggard, slowpoke

dawn n daybreak, daylight, first light, morning, sunrise, sunup

dawning adj frontier, new, unexplored, unknown

day n daytime

daybreak n dawn, daylight, first light, morning, sunrise, sunup

daydream n 1 daze, spell, trance

n 2 dream, fancy, fantasy, musing, reverie, vision

daylight n 1 day

n 2 dawn, daybreak, first light, morning, sunrise, sunup

daytime n day

daze n 1 daydream, spell, trance

n 2 befuddlement, fog, haze, maze, muddledness, muddleheadedness

v 1 paralyze, shock, stun, stupefy

v 2 addle, confuse, foul up, fumble, jumble, mix up, muddle, snarl up

v 3 amaze, electrify, horrify, offend, outrage, overwhelm, scandalize, shock, stun

v 4 befuddle, bewilder, confuse, distract, dizzy, embarrass, fluster, mix up, muddle, rattle, ruffle, trick, unglue, unhinge

v 5 amaze, befog, bewilder, boggle, confound, confuse, perplex, puzzle, stumble, stump

dazed adj 1 insensible, numb, senseless, unconscious

adj 2 confused, daffy, daft, dizzy, groggy, punchy, stunned

adj 3 see: PREOCCUPIED adj 1

dazzle v 1 amaze, astonish, astound, awe, boggle, confound, dumbfound, flabbergast, nonplus, stagger, stun, surprise

v 2 blind

dazzling adj 1 brilliant, clever, good, irrepressible, scintillating, smart, sparkling, sprightly, witty

adj 2 alluring, beguiling, bewitching, captivating, catchy, charming, dynamic, enchanting, engaging, enthralling, enticing, fascinating, glamorous, intriguing, mesmerizing, riveting, spectacular, spellbinding

dead adj 1 cold, deceased, defunct, departed, lifeless, spiritless

adj 2 bygone, defunct, departed, extinct, forgotten, gone, lost, vanished

adj 3 hush, inanimate, inert, lifeless, noiseless, quiet, silent, soundless, still

adj 4 ancient, antiquated, archaic, bygone, dated, extinct, noncurrent, obsolete, old, outdated, outmoded, passé, past, worn

adj 5 see: DULL adj 7

deadbolt n bolt, clamp, clasp, lock, padlock

deadlock n 1 bottleneck, draw, hung jury, impasse, stalemate, standoff, standstill, tie

n 2 bar, barrier, bottleneck, crimp, dead end, difficulty, encumbrance, hurdle, impasse, impediment, obstacle, obstruction, snag, stumbling block

deadly adj 1 effective, sure

adj 2 baneful, fatal, lethal, mortal, noxious, pernicious, pestilent, ruinous

adj 3 see: VICIOUS adj 3

deaf adj bullheaded, closed-minded, firm, hardheaded, hard-line, inelastic, inflexible, intractable, intransigent, obstinate, perverse, pigheaded, refractory, resolute, rigid, stiff, stubborn, tough, unbending, uncompromising, unpliable, unpliant, unwieldy, unyielding, willful

deal n 1 exchange, sale, trade, transaction, transfer

n 2 bargain, buy, discount, promotion, reduction, sale, special, steal

n 3 agreement, bargain, bond, compact, contract, convention, covenant, pact, pledge, promise, transaction, treaty, understanding

v 1 bargain, barter, convert, exchange, swap, trade, traffic

v 2 hawk, horse-trade, huckster, hustle, monger, peddle, push, sell, swap

v 3 administer, apportion, disburse, dispense, disperse, distribute, dole, expend, give

dealer n marketer, merchant, monger, purveyor, seller, trader, vendor

dealings n arrangements, business, commerce, enterprise, industry, intercourse, negotiations, trade, traffic

dear adj 1 costly, expensive, precious, valuable

adj 2 costly, excessive, exorbitant, expensive, high, overpriced, prohibitive, steep, stiff

adj 3 adored, beloved, cherished, esteemed, loved, precious, respected, revered, treasured, venerable, worshiped

dearth *n* deficiency, deficit, drought, famine, lack, rarity, scarcity, shortage, sparseness, undersupply, want

death *n* 1 decease, departure, expiration, passing

n 2 carnage, demise, fatality, mortality, ruin

n 3 breakdown, catastrophe, crash, crisis, destruction, doom, failure, finish, ruin

debacle *n* 1 calamity, cataclysm, catastrophe, disaster, misfortune, tragedy, upheaval

n 2 defeat, disaster, downfall, overthrow, rout, ruination, thrashing, trouncing, undoing, vanquishment

debar *v* banish, bar, blackball, cut, dismiss, eliminate, except, exclude, ignore, leave out, omit, suspend

debarkation *n* arrival, docking, landing, mooring

debase *v* 1 contaminate, degrade, desecrate, pervert, profane

v 2 adulterate, corrupt, debauch, defile, demoralize, dishonor, pervert, ruin, seduce, taint

v 3 see: BELITTLE *v* 1

debasement *n* decline, deterioration, dip, downturn, drop, ebb, erosion, fall, involution, plunge, sag, slide, slip, slump, wane, weakening

debasing *adj* abject, base, contemptible, despicable, false, servile

debatable *adj* 1 argumentative, cantankerous, contentious, controversial, disputatious, ill-natured, litigious, ornery

adj 2 see: PREPOSTEROUS *adj* 2

debate *n* 1 argument, contention, controversy, dialogue, discussion, dispute

n 2 see: DISCUSSION *n* 3, 4

v argue, confer, contest, contradict, contrast, dialogue, differ, disagree, discord, discuss, dispute, dissent, divide, oppose, vary

debauch *v* 1 adulterate, corrupt, debase, defile, demoralize, dishonor, pervert, ruin, seduce, taint

v 2 deflower, deprave, ravish, seduce

debaucher *n* deviant, deviate, pervert, weirdo

debilitate *v* 1 castrate, dismember, emasculate, enervate, geld, unman, unnerve

v 2 cripple, disable, drain, enfeeble, exhaust, sap, undermine, weaken

debit *v* bill, charge, dun, invoice, notice, render, solicit

debonair *adj* chic, dapper, dashing, jaunty, natty, neat, rakish, sleek, smart, snazzy, spiffy, suave, trim

debris *n* 1 fragment, hulk, remains, rubbish, rubble, shell, trash, wreck, wreckage

n 2 crap, crud, detritus, dirt, garbage, junk, litter, refuse, rubbish, rubble, sweepings, trash, waste

debt *n* 1 loan, obligation, promise, responsibility

n 2 bill, charge, check, fee, invoice, note, tab

debunk *v* 1 discover, expose, show up, uncloak, unmask, unshroud

v 2 discredit, disprove, explode

debut *n* 1 beginning, briefing, commencement, inauguration, induction, initiation, unveiling

n 2 beginning, birth, delivery, inception, kindling, onset, outset, start

debutante *n* child, coed, daughter, girl, lass, miss, young lady, young woman

decade *n* aeon, age, cycle, eon, epoch, era, eternity, forever, long time, millennium, period, reign, span, stage, time, years

decadence *n* decay, decline, degeneration, weakening

decant *v* see: POUR *v* 2

decay *n* 1 decadence, decline, degeneration, weakening

n 2 atrophy, degeneration, deterioration, shrinkage, wasting

n 3 contamination, corruption, impurity, poison, taint

n 4 cancer, corruption, evil, infection, malignancy, poison, rot, toxin, venom

n 5 fungus, germ, mold

v 1 bankrupt, break, bust, do in, fold up, impoverish, ruin

v 2 atrophy, deteriorate, dry up, dwindle, mummify, shrink, shrivel, waste away, welter, wilt, wither, wizen

v 3 corrupt, crumble, decompose, degenerate, deteriorate, disintegrate, perish, putrefy, rot, smell, spoil, taint, wane, weaken, wither

decayed *adj* bad, putrid, rancid, rotten, sharp, sour, spoiled

decaying *adj* 1 crumbled, decrepit, dilapidated, run-down

adj 2 see: FOUL *adj* 3

decease *n* death, departure, expiration, passing

deceased *adj* cold, dead, defunct, departed, lifeless, spiritless

deceit *n* 1 avoidance, diversion, dodging, escape, evasion, runaround

n 2 cheating, deception, dishonesty, fraud, hoax, lie, sham, subterfuge, trickery

n 3 deception, fabrication, falsehood,

fraud, fraudulence, hypocrisy, lying, perjury, trickery, untruth

deceitful adj 1 clandestine, concealed, covert, crafty, devious, evasive, foxy, furtive, guileful, indirect, privy, secret, shifty, sly, sneaky, surreptitious, tricky, underground, underhand, underhanded, wily

adj 2 see: EVIL adj 4

adj 3 see: TREACHEROUS adj 2

deceive v 1 concoct, equivocate, fabricate, falsify, fib, invent, lie, misstate, perjure

v 2 angle, confuse, distort, falsify, garble, incline, misconstrue, misinterpret, misquote, misread, misrepresent, misunderstand, mix up, mumble, slant, slope, taint, twist

v 3 bamboozle, beat, beguile, bilk, burn, cajole, cheat, chicane, chisel, con, cross, defraud, dupe, embezzle, fleece, flimflam, fob, foist, fool, gyp, hoax, hoodwink, hustle, inveigle, screw, shaft, sham, swindle, trick, victimize

decent adj 1 ample, generous, respectable, sizable, substantial

adj 2 acceptable, adequate, competent, enough, fair, good, mediocre, passable, reasonable, respectable, satisfactory, sufficient, tolerable

adj 3 chivalrous, civil, civilized, cordial, courteous, courtly, dignified, gallant, genteel, gentlemanly, gracious, mannerly, noble, polite, well-mannered

adj 4 celibate, chaste, clean, decorous, immaculate, modest, moral, pristine, proper, pure, spotless, stainless, stuffy, taintless, unadulterated, unblemished, undefiled, upstanding, virginal, wholesome

deception n 1 error, fallacy, flaw, illusion, inaccuracy

n 2 betrayal, perfidy, subversion, treachery, trickery

n 3 alibi, con, lie, pretext, ruse, subterfuge, trick

n 4 cheating, deceit, dishonesty, fraud, hoax, lie, sham, subterfuge, trickery

n 5 deceit, fabrication, falsehood, fraud, fraudulence, hypocrisy, lying, perjury, trickery, untruth

n 6 fake, fraud, hoax, put-on, sham

deceptive adj 1 false, illusive, illusory, misleading, sham, unreal

adj 2 cheating, conniving, deceitful, dishonest, disloyal, faithless, false, insidious, manipulative, perfidious, sneaky, traitorous, treacherous, unfaithful, untrue, untrustworthy

decide v 1 adjust, arrange, calibrate, determine, establish, fix, resolve, set

v 2 adjudicate, conclude, determine, establish, resolve, rule, settle, will

decided adj 1 see: ASSERTIVE adj

adj 2 see: EXACT adj 6

decidedly adv absolutely, certainly, definitely, entirely, incontrovertibly, indeed, indubitably, positively, surely, truly, unequivocally, unquestionably, verily, well, without doubt

decimate v 1 annihilate, demolish, destroy, destruct, devastate, dismantle, overturn, pulverize, raze, rub out, ruin, shatter, smash, tear down, undo, wreck

v 2 see: KILL v 3

decipher v comprehend, decode, infer, interpret, peruse, read, study, understand

decision n 1 agreement, arrangement, compromise, concession, determination, franchise, settlement

n 2 adjudication, decree, finding, judgment, ruling, sentence, verdict

n 3 see: SELECTION n 3

decisive adj 1 closing, definitive, eventual, final, inevitable, last, latest

adj 2 ardent, determined, emphatic, extreme, forceful, intense, potent, powerful, severe, strong

adj 3 blunt, clear, clear-cut, concise, definite, definitive, distinct, exact, explicit, precise, specific, unambiguous

deck n forecastle, platform, quarterdeck

v adorn, beautify, bedeck, decorate, dress up, embellish, enhance, garnish, glamorize, grace, ornament, polish, trim

declaration n 1 assurance, certainty, certitude, confidence

n 2 assurance, oath, pledge, promise, vow, word

n 3 accusation, allegation, assertion, charge, comment, deposition, pronouncement, statement

n 4 see: CLICHÉ n 3

declare v 1 add, comment, note, remark, say, state

v 2 affirm, bear witness, depose, profess, swear, testify

v 3 appoint, designate, name, nominate, propose, select, specify

v 4 affirm, assert, attest, avow, confirm, depose, predicate, profess, protest

v 5 advertise, announce, blaze, broadcast, circulate, disperse, disseminate, proclaim, promulgate, publish

v 6 brief, communicate, convey, describe, disclose, divulge, explain, impart, inform, narrate, orate, portray, read, recite, recount, relate, report, retell, reveal, share, state, tattle, tell, transmit

decline *n* 1 decadence, decay, degeneration, weakening

n 2 comedown, decrease, descent, dive, drop, failure, fall, plunge, regression, setback, slide, tumble

n 3 debasement, deterioration, dip, downturn, drop, ebb, erosion, fall, involution, plunge, sag, slide, slip, slump, wane, weakening

n 4 decrease, decrement, lessening, reduction, weakening

v 1 delay, demur, disagree, object

v 2 descend, incline, skew, slant, slope, veer

v 3 die down, diminish, dip, settle, sink, slide, slip, subside

v 4 condemn, disapprove, dismiss, exile, object, refuse, reject, reprobate, repudiate, spurn, turn down

v 5 abate, deteriorate, fade, fail, flag, impair, languish, wane, weaken, wither, worsen

v 6 abstain, cast, drop, eschew, forbear, forfeit, forgo, give up, lose, pass, reject, renounce, sacrifice, surrender, turn down, waive

v 7 abate, cease, decrease, die down, diminish, drain, dwindle, ease, ebb, fall, lessen, let up, lull, recede, reduce, relax, relent, shrink, slacken, soften, stop, subside, taper off, wane, waste away, weaken

decode *v* comprehend, decipher, infer, interpret, peruse, read, study, understand

decompose *v* 1 blast, blight, dash, nip, wither

v 2 corrupt, crumble, decay, degenerate, deteriorate, disintegrate, perish, putrefy, rot, smell, spoil, taint, wane, weaken, wither

decorate *v* adorn, beautify, bedeck, deck, dress up, embellish, enhance, garnish, glamorize, grace, ornament, polish, trim

decoration *n* 1 adornment, embellishment, ornament

n 2 see: COMMENDATION *n* 2

decorous *adj* 1 conventional, correct, fitting, nice, orthodox, polite, proper, right, suitable, well

adj 2 celibate, chaste, clean, decent, immaculate, modest, moral, pristine, proper, pure, spotless, stainless, stuffy, taintless, unadulterated, unblemished, undefiled, upstanding, virginal, wholesome

decorum *n* 1 attractiveness, charm, elegance, grace, refinement

n 2 convention, custom, etiquette, formality, good form, manners, propriety, protocol, rites

n 3 see: UTILITY *n*

decoy *n* 1 attraction, bait, come-on, enticement, lure, magnet, ruse, seduction, snare, temptation, trap, wile

n 2 blind

v attract, bait, entice, entrap, lure, tantalize

decrease *n* 1 comedown, decline, descent, dive, drop, failure, fall, plunge, regression, setback, slide, tumble

n 2 decline, decrement, lessening, reduction, weakening

v abate, cease, decline, die down, diminish, drain, dwindle, ease, ebb, fall, lessen, let up, lull, recede, reduce, relax, relent, shrink, slacken, soften, stop, subside, taper off, wane, waste away, weaken

decree *n* 1 adjudication, decision, finding, judgment, ruling, sentence, verdict

n 2 announcement, aphorism, axiom, cliché, declaration, dictum, edict, gospel, homily, maxim, moral, precept, pronouncement, rule, saying, teaching, truism, truth, verity

n 3 behest, bidding, canon, charge, command, criterion, dictate, direction, edict, fiat, guideline, injunction, institution, law, mandate, order, ordinance, precept, prescript, prescription, regulation, rite, rule, ruling, statute, word

v 1 approve, authorize, enact, legalize, legislate, ordain, pass, ratify, sanction

v 2 advise, authorize, command, designate, dictate, direct, mandate, ordain, order, rule

decrement *n* decline, decrease, lessening, reduction, weakening

decrepit *adj* 1 crumbled, decaying, dilapidated, run-down

adj 2 breakable, delicate, dilapidated, feeble, flimsy, fragile, frail, jerry-built, jury-rigged, puny, Rube Goldberg, shoddy, sickly, thin, tinny, unsound, worn-out

decry *v* see: ABUSE *v* 4

dedicate *v* 1 apply

v 2 anoint, baptize, bless, consecrate, devote, enshrine, exalt, hallow, purify, sanctify

dedicated *adj* 1 deferential, devout, obeisant, respectful

adj 2 committed, concerned, interested, involved

adj 3 bent, committed, determined, fixed,

intentional, purposeful, resolute, resolved, set, tenacious

adj 4 see: FAITHFUL *adj* 3

adj 5 see: STUBBORN *adj* 6

deduce *v* 1 determine, discern, glean, learn

v 2 derive, draw, educe, elicit, evince, evoke, extract

v 3 analyze, conclude, construe, derive, draw, educe, gather, glean, guess, infer, interpret, presume, surmise

deduct *v* diminish, lessen, minus, reduce, subtract, take away

deduction *n* 1 assumption, conjecture, opinion, supposition, surmise

n 2 conclusion, guess, inference, reasoning, summation

n 3 assumption, conjecture, explanation, guess, hypothesis, inference, postulate, presumption, proposition, speculation, supposition, theory

deed *n* 1 document, paper, title

n 2 accomplishment, action, conduct, delivery, demonstration, execution, performance, talent

n 3 accomplishment, achievement, acquirement, act, action, battle, doing, event, exploit, feat, stunt, thing, trick

v assign, cede, convey, designate, transfer

deem *v* account, calculate, consider, judge, reckon, regard, surmise, view

deep *adj* 1 meaty, profound, rich, stimulating

adj 2 automatic, gut, innate, instinctive, intuitive, visceral

adj 3 abstruse, esoteric, heartfelt, heavy, hermetic, insightful, mysterious, obscure, occult, penetrating, profound, recondite

adj 4 absorbed, agog, concentrated, determined, distracted, engaged, engrossed, enraptured, entranced, fascinated, immersed, intent, preoccupied, rapt, wrapped up

defamation *n* 1 abuse, mistreatment, scurrility

n 2 accusation, aspersion, libel, remark, slander, slur, smear

defame *v* 1 befoul, besmirch, blacken, darken, disparage, injure, libel, malign, revile, scandalize, slander, slur, smear, soil, tear down, traduce

v 2 abuse, asperse, bad-mouth, belittle, condemn, damage, decry, degrade, denigrate, denounce, deprecate, detract, diminish, discount, disparage, insult, knock, malign, put down, revile, run down, slander, take away, vilify

default *n* breach, infraction, misdemeanor, trespass, violation

defeat *n* 1 attack, conquest, foray, inroad, intrusion, invasion, trespass

n 2 debacle, disaster, downfall, overthrow, rout, ruination, thrashing, trouncing, undoing, vanquishment

v 1 crush, drown, overpower, overwhelm, stifle

v 2 best, down, outdo, outmaneuver, outsmart, outwit

v 3 best, conquer, master, overcome, prevail, succeed, triumph, win

v 4 conquer, crush, destroy, down, hurdle, lick, overcome, overthrow, surmount

v 5 capsize, collapse, dislodge, knock over, overthrow, overturn, tip over, topple, tumble, turn over, upset

v 6 bear down, beat down, conquer, crush, dominate, enslave, exploit, overpower, quash, reduce, subdue, subjugate, suppress, vanquish

v 7 beat, belittle, blast, clobber, conquer, cream, dust, lambaste, lick, overrun, overwhelm, rout, shellac, smear, thrash, wallop, whip

defeated *adj* 1 crushed, distraught, emotional, overcome, subdued

adj 2 beaten, clobbered, dejected, depressed, discouraged, licked, whipped

defect *n* 1 impurity, pollutant

n 2 bug, error, fault, glitch

n 3 blemish, failing, fault, flaw, imperfection, scar, shortcoming, weakness

n 4 deficiency, demerit, fault, flaw, imperfection, inadequacy, lack, need, shortcoming, want

v 1 abscond, bolt, depart, exit, fall back, flee, get away, give back, go, leave, move, pull away, pull out, push off, retreat, run along, secede, shove off, take off, vacate, withdraw

v 2 see: ABANDON *v* 3

defective *adj* 1 amiss, crude, faulty, flawed, imperfect, incomplete, short, unfulfilled

adj 2 bad, futile, inadequate, incorrect, inferior, invalid, malfunctioning, poor, void

defector *n* see: REBEL *n*

defend *v* 1 advocate

v 2 guard, oversee, patrol, police, protect, regulate, safeguard, watch

v 3 bulwark, cover, fend, fortify, guard, hide, protect, safeguard, screen, secure, shield

v 4 argue, assert, believe, claim, contend, justify, know, maintain, state, think, vindicate, warrant

defense *n* 1 buffer, protection, shield

n **2** caution, precaution, protection, safeguard

n **3** bastion, bulwark, embankment, fort, fortification, rampart, wall

n **4** alibi, excuse, explanation, justification, plea, pretext, rationalization, reason, ruse

n **5** antibody, antidote, antigen, antitoxin, serum, vaccine

defenseless *adj* dependent, disarmed, exposed, helpless, powerless, susceptible, unprotected, vulnerable, weak

defensible *adj* acceptable, justifiable, legitimate, proper, reasonable, valid

defer *v* **1** adjourn, avoid, delay, hold, hold up, interrupt, lay over, postpone, procrastinate, prolong, put off, remit, reschedule, set aside, shelve, stay, suspend, table, wait, waive

v **2** see: YIELD *v* **6**

deference *n* devotion, esteem, homage, honor, just due, regard, respect, reverence

deferential *adj* dedicated, devout, obeisant, respectful

defiance *n* refusal

defiant *adj* **1** aggressive, insubordinate, rambunctious, restless, stubborn, unruly

adj **2** disobedient, insubordinate, insurgent, mutinous, rebellious, seditious

adj **3** careless, delinquent, derelict, heedless, inattentive, lax, neglectful, negligent, reckless, sloppy

deficiency *n* **1** defect, demerit, fault, flaw, imperfection, inadequacy, lack, need, shortcoming, want

n **2** deprivation, destitution, inadequacy, indigence, lack, need, poverty, privation, scarcity, want

n **3** dearth, deficit, drought, famine, lack, rarity, scarcity, shortage, sparseness, undersupply, want

deficient *adj* **1** inferior, meaner, not as good, poorer, worse

adj **2** inept, out of practice, rusty, stale, unpracticed, unprepared

adj **3** failing, inadequate, inferior, insufficient, scant, scarce, scrimpy, short, shy, wanting

adj **4** bare, few, inadequate, inferior, insufficient, little, meager, paltry, petty, poor, scant, scanty, skimpy, spare, sparse

adj **5** backward, blunt, dense, dimwitted, dull, dumb, feebleminded, idiotic, moronic, obtuse, retarded, simple, simpleminded, slow, stupid, thick, uneducated, unintelligent

deficit *n* **1** cost, damage, loss, penalty, suffering

n **2** dearth, deficiency, drought, famine, lack, rarity, scarcity, shortage, sparseness, undersupply, want

defile *v* **1** dirty, discolor, smear, soil, stain, sully, taint, tarnish

v **2** adulterate, corrupt, debase, debauch, demoralize, dishonor, pervert, ruin, seduce, taint

v **3** abase, abash, belittle, cast down, cheapen, debase, deflate, degrade, demean, depreciate, derogate, devalue, dishonor, embarrass, humble, humiliate, lower, mortify, put down, shame, sink

define *v* **1** specify

v **2** classify, differentiate, discriminate, distinguish, isolate, separate

v **3** call, designate, entitle, label, name, term

v **4** craft, develop, formulate, list, make, process, specify, synthesize

v **5** approach, border, bound, edge, hem, limit, outline, skirt, verge

v **6** carve, chisel, craft, cut, design, fashion, form, mold, sculpt, sculpture, shape, steer

v **7** analyze, annotate, clarify, detail, elucidate, explain, expound, express, interpret, narrate, spell out, state, understand

v **8** begin, coin, conceive, craft, create, develop, devise, formulate, innovate, invent, make, originate, start

definite *adj* **1** determinate, exclusive, fixed, limited, narrow, precise, restricted, segregated, specific

adj **2** determined, fixed, foregone, inevitable, inexorable, irrevocable, ordained, predestined, unalterable, unavoidable, unchangeable

adj **3** blunt, clear, clear-cut, concise, decisive, definitive, distinct, exact, explicit, precise, specific, unambiguous

adj **4** absolute, actual, authentic, bona fide, certain, existent, factual, genuine, hard, inarguable, incontestable, incontrovertible, indisputable, indubitable, irrefutable, positive, real, sure, true, undeniable, undisputable, undoubtable, undoubted, unequivocal, unquestionable, veritable, viable

adj **5** see: EXACT *adj* **5, 6**

definitely *adv* absolutely, certainly, decidedly, entirely, incontrovertibly, indeed, indubitably, positively, surely, truly, unequivocally, unquestionably, verily, well, without doubt

definition *n* **1** clarification, denotation, explanation, meaning, translation *n* 2 design, distinctness, outline, precision, specificity

definitive *adj* 1 conclusive

adj 2 compact, meaty, pithy, seminal, tight

adj 3 closing, decisive, eventual, inevitable, final, last, latest

adj 4 blunt, clear, clear-cut, concise, decisive, definite, distinct, exact, explicit, precise, specific, unambiguous

deflate *v* 1 collapse, contract, shrink

v 2 abase, abash, belittle, cast down, cheapen, debase, defile, degrade, demean, depreciate, derogate, devalue, dishonor, embarrass, humble, humiliate, lower, mortify, put down, shame, sink

deflect *v* 1 deviate, divert, drift, slip, stray, turn

v 2 see: AVOID *v* 4

v 3 see: SKEW *v* 3

deflection *n* bending

deflower *v* 1 desecrate, despoil, devastate, devour, loot, maraud, pillage, plunder, ravage, sack, scourge, spoil, strip, violate

v 2 debauch, deprave, seduce, ravish

deform *v* distort, misshape, torture, warp

defraud *v* 1 deprive, rob, swindle, take, usurp

v 2 bamboozle, beat, beguile, bilk, burn, cajole, cheat, chicane, chisel, con, cross, deceive, dupe, embezzle, fleece, flimflam, fob, foist, fool, gyp, hoax, hoodwink, hustle, inveigle, screw, shaft, sham, swindle, trick, victimize

v 3 see: STEAL *v* 2

deft *adj* 1 agile, dexterous, skillful, subtle

adj 2 adroit, apt, canny, clever, cunning, handy, ingenious, nimble, skilled, skillful, sly, wily

adj 3 able, accomplished, adept, apt, capable, competent, dexterous, expert, fit, gifted, masterful, professional, proficient, proper, qualified, skillful, talented

adj 4 see: QUICK *adj* 5

adj 5 see: RESOURCEFUL *adj* 3

defunct *adj* 1 cold, dead, deceased, departed, lifeless, spiritless

adj 2 bygone, dead, departed, extinct, forgotten, gone, lost, vanished

defy *v* 1 brave, challenge, confront, dare, face, mutiny, rebel, resist

v 2 disobey, ignore, infringe, obstruct, oppose, rebel, resist, violate

v 3 see: DISREGARD *v*

degenerate *adj* base, corrupt, deadly, depraved, deviant, evil, immoral, infamous, kinky, nefarious, perverse, putrid, rotten, ruthless, savage, vicious, villainous, wicked, wild

v corrupt, crumble, decay, decompose, deteriorate, disintegrate, perish, putrefy, rot, smell, spoil, taint, wane, weaken, wither

degeneration *n* 1 decadence, decay, decline, weakening

n 2 atrophy, decay, deterioration, shrinkage, wasting

degrade *v* 1 contaminate, debase, desecrate, pervert, profane

v 2 break, bump, bust, demerit, demote, downgrade, put down, reduce

v 3 abase, abash, belittle, cast down, cheapen, debase, defile, deflate, demean, depreciate, derogate, devalue, dishonor, embarrass, humble, humiliate, lower, mortify, put down, shame, sink

v 4 see: ABUSE *v* 4

degree *n* 1 extent, intensity, measure, ratio, scope

n 2 angle, bearing, heading, position, setting

n 3 distinction, enhancement, nuance, shade, subtlety, touch, trace, variation

n 4 caste, class, echelon, estate, hierarchy, level, position, rank, status

n 5 class, grade, interval, level, mark, notch, position, rank, rate, step

n 6 certificate, credential, diploma, sheepskin

deign *v* condescend, kowtow, patronize, stoop

deity *n* divinity, god, goddess, idol

deject *v* 1 chill, demoralize, depress, discourage, dishearten, disparage

v 2 burden, depress, dishearten, grieve, hurt, lament, sadden, weigh down, wound

dejected *adj* 1 beaten, clobbered, defeated, depressed, discouraged, licked, whipped

adj 2 black, bleak, blue, cheerless, depressed, desperate, despondent, discouraging, disheartening, distressing, down, forlorn, gloomy, hopeless, joyless, melancholy, moody, mournful, oppressive, prostrate, sad, somber, sorry, unhappy

delay *n* 1 interim, interval, lag, pause

n 2 interruption, postponement, reprieve, stay, stop, suspension

n 3 break, distraction, disturbance, diversion, holdup, interference, interruption, pause

n 4 break, cessation, gap, interim, interval, lapse, lull, pause, stop

n 5 interval, lull, pause, stay, suspension, wait

v 1 decline, demur, disagree, object

v 2 bog, detain, hang up, impede, mire, retard, set back, slacken, slow

v 3 dally, dawdle, diddle, goof off, idle, lag, linger, loaf, loiter, loll, lounge, malinger, poke, put off, putter, shirk, tarry

v 4 adjourn, avoid, defer, hold, hold up, interrupt, lay over, postpone, procrastinate, prolong, put off, remit, reschedule, set aside, shelve, stay, suspend, table, wait, waive

v 5 falter, halt, hesitate, pause, stagger, stall, vacillate, waver

delayed *adj* belated, late, overdue, slow, tardy, unpunctual

delectable *adj* 1 adorable, charming, cute, delightful

adj 2 appetizing, delicious, exquisite, luscious, palatable, savory, sweet, tasty

delegate *n* agent, ambassador, consul, deputy, diplomat, emissary, envoy

v 1 assign, detail, task

v 2 assign, authorize, designate, empower, entrust, pass along

delegation *n* 1 commission, embassy, mission

n 2 see: ORGANIZATION *n* 4

delete *v* abate, abolish, abrogate, annihilate, annul, call off, cancel, cease, destroy, efface, erase, excise, expunge, invalidate, kill, negate, nullify, obliterate, omit, quash, remove, stop, terminate, wipe out

deleterious *adj* 1 adverse, detrimental, harmful, injurious, negative, unfavorable

adj 2 damaging, dangerous, harmful, hurting, injurious, ruinous, unhealthy

deletion *n* erasure, pullout, removal

deliberate *adj* 1 calculated, conscious, contrived, intentional, planned, plotted, premeditated

adj 2 free, intentional, optional, unforced, unprescribed, voluntary, willful, willing

adj 3 advised, calculated, careful, considered, contrived, forewarned, measured, planned, premeditated, studied, studious

adj 4 dilatory, diligent, leisurely, methodical, meticulous, painstaking, patient, procrastinating, slow, thorough, unhasty, unhurried

v cerebrate, chew, consider, contemplate, digest, meditate, mull, muse, ponder, reason, reflect, ruminate, see, speculate, study, think, weigh

deliberation *n* analysis, cogitation, consideration, contemplation, logic, medita-

tion, reason, reasoning, reflection, speculation, study, thinking, thought

delicacy *n* bauble, frill, luxury, treat

delicate *adj* 1 fragile, frail, soft, tender

adj 2 awkward, difficult, embarrassing, sticky, tricky

adj 3 feeble, flimsy, inadequate, light, slight

adj 4 filmy, fine, flimsy, sheer, thin, transparent

adj 5 dainty, fine, gentle, nice, refined, subtle

adj 6 choice, dainty, elegant, exquisite, favorite, fine, preferred, rare, select

adj 7 dangerous, fluctuating, hazardous, precarious, rickety, risky, rocky, sensitive, shaky, tender, ticklish, touchy, tricky, unpredictable, unstable, wobbly

adj 8 breakable, decrepit, dilapidated, feeble, flimsy, fragile, frail, jerry-built, jury-rigged, puny, Rube Goldberg, shoddy, sickly, thin, tinny, unsound, worn-out

adj 9 see: ILL *adj* 3

delicious *adj* 1 appetizing, delectable, exquisite, luscious, palatable, savory, sweet, tasty

adj 2 see: SENSUAL *adj* 1

delight *n* 1 enjoyment, joy, pleasure, satisfaction

n 2 bliss, ecstasy, Eden, elation, enchantment, heaven, joy, nirvana, paradise, pleasure, rapture, rhapsody

n 3 see: PASSION *n* 7

v 1 amuse, please, tickle

v 2 admire, appreciate, cherish, enjoy, relish, revel, savor

v 3 amaze, astonish, astound, awe, floor, impress, overwhelm, wow

v 4 bask, enjoy, like, loaf, luxuriate, relax, relish, rest, savor, wallow

v 5 appease, comfort, comply, content, elate, gratify, please, relieve, satisfy, suit

v 6 captivate, charm, engross, enrapture, enravish, enthrall, entrance, hypnotize, mesmerize, move, ravish, transport

v 7 encourage, enjoy, gladden, hearten, inspire, please

v 8 allure, attract, bedevil, beguile, bewitch, captivate, charm, conjure, draw, enchant, enthrall, fascinate, lure, magnetize, mesmerize, tempt, wile

delighted *adj* 1 glad, honored, pleased, proud

adj 2 ecstatic, elated, enchanted, overjoyed, thrilled

delightful *adj* 1 adorable, charming, cute, dainty, delectable

adj 2 admirable, beautiful, glorious, good,

magnificent, peachy, splendid, terrific, wonderful

adj 3 ambrosial, heavenly, scrumptious

delineate *v* 1 account, report, specify

v 2 depict, illustrate, picture, portray, represent, sketch

v 3 acquaint, announce, depict, introduce, present, reflect, represent, show

v 4 clarify, clear, clear up, depict, elucidate, explain, illuminate, illustrate, picture, portray, reveal

delineation *n* characterization, depiction, expression, portrayal, representation

delinquent *adj* careless, defiant, derelict, heedless, inattentive, lax, neglectful, negligent, reckless, sloppy

n accused, con, convict, criminal, crook, culprit, felon, guilty party, inmate, lawbreaker, offender, perpetrator, prisoner, scofflaw, suspect, swindler, transgressor, wrongdoer

delirious *adj* deranged, fantasizing, frenzied, hallucinating, maniacal, raving

deliver *v* 1 bear, birth

v 2 bring, carry, take

v 3 address, lecture, preach, proclaim, speak, talk

v 4 administer, administrate, carry out, do, execute, give, present, render, submit

v 5 arrange, cater, dish out, dispense, feed, furnish, give, hand, nourish, nurture, organize, provide, purvey, serve, supply, sustain

v 6 express, give forth, impart

v 7 free, liberate, release, rescue, save

v 8 accord, adduce, award, bequeath, bestow, concede, confer, contribute, devote, donate, endow, extend, fund, give, give away, grant, hand down, hand out, impart, offer, pose, present, proffer, provide, supply, tender, volunteer

deliverance *n* extrication, freeing, recovery, release, rescue, saving

deliverer *n* liberator, messiah, rescuer, salvation, savior

delivery *n* 1 mail, package, parcel

n 2 beginning, birth, debut, inception, kindling, onset, outset, start

n 3 accomplishment, action, conduct, deed, demonstration, execution, performance, talent

n 4 see: TECHNIQUE *n* 3

deluge *n* 1 flood, overflow, submersion, surge, torrent

n 2 cloudburst, downpour, drizzle, hail, precipitation, rain, shower, sprinkle

n 3 excess, fat, glut, overabundance, overflow, overkill, plethora, redundancy, surfeit, surplus

v 1 bestow, lavish, overwhelm, shower

v 2 douse, drench, drown, dunk, flood, inundate, irrigate, overload, saturate, slosh, soak, sop, souse, swamp, swill, tax, wet

v 3 drizzle, fall, pour, rain, shower, sprinkle

delusion *n* 1 fallacy, illusion, myth, old wives' tale, superstition

n 2 aberration, apparition, fantasy, figment, ghost, hallucination, illusion, image, mirage, phantasm, specter, vision

n 3 aberration, abnormality, craziness, dementia, derangement, distraction, eccentricity, fugue, hallucination, insanity, irregularity, lunacy, madness, mania, psychosis, unbalance

deluxe *adj* choice, elegant, first-class, grand, luxuriant, luxurious, opulent, ornate, palatial, plush, posh, rich, soft, stately, sumptuous, thick

delve *v* dig, examine, explore, feel out, grope, hunt, inquire, investigate, look, observe, peer, probe, pursue, research, scan, scrutinize, search, seek, sound, study, test

demand *n* 1 need

n 2 claim, mandate, requirement, ultimatum

n 3 exigency, necessity, need, pressure, requirement, stress, urgency

v 1 expect, levy, require, want, wish

v 2 designate, indicate, insist, require, specify, stipulate

v 3 ask, call, crave, necessitate, require, take

v 4 assert, emphasize, force, insist, persist, require, urge

v 5 bid, charge, claim, command, direct, enjoin, instruct, order

v 6 call, challenge, claim, exact, need, postulate, require, requisition, solicit

v 7 burden, encumber, force, prescribe

demanding *adj* 1 arduous, burdensome, exacting, grievous, onerous, oppressive, taxing, tough, trying

adj 2 see: HARD *adj* 5

demarcate *v* bound, confine, cramp, limit, restrict

demarcation *n* borderline, boundary, bounds, periphery

demean *v* 1 act, bear, behave, carry, comport, conduct, rule

v 2 see: BELITTLE *v* 1

demeanor *n* 1 action, bearing, behavior, conduct, deportment, manners *n* **2** air, attitude, bearing, calmness, carriage, disposition, poise, pose, posture, presence, set, stance

demented *adj* deranged, distraught, insane, mentally ill, psychotic

dementia *n* aberration, abnormality, craziness, delusion, derangement, distraction, eccentricity, fugue, hallucination, insanity, irregularity, lunacy, madness, mania, psychosis, unbalance

demerit *n* defect, deficiency, fault, flaw, imperfection, inadequacy, lack, need, shortcoming, want

v break, bump, bust, degrade, demote, downgrade, put down, reduce

demilitarize *v* disarm

demise *n* carnage, death, fatality, mortality, ruin

demo *n* example, first, forerunner, model, prototype, sample, test

democratic *adj* **1** independent, self-governing

adj **2** see: POPULAR *adj* 2

demolish *v* **1** consume, destroy, ravage

v **2** collide, crash, smash, wreck

v **3** annihilate, decimate, destroy, destruct, devastate, dismantle, overturn, pulverize, raze, rub out, ruin, shatter, smash, tear down, undo, wreck

v **4** annihilate, crush, extinguish, put down, quash, quell, quench, repress, squash, stamp out, suppress

demon *n* brute, devil, fiend, rogue, Satan, villain, wretch

demoniac *adj* devilish, diabolic, fiendish, wicked

demonstrate *v* **1** determine, establish, evidence, prove, reveal, show

v **2** describe, display, draw, establish, examine, exhibit, explain, present, prove, show, sketch, tell

demonstrated *adj* authentic, certified, confirmed, proved, tested, tried, verified

demonstration *n* **1** argument, proof, representation, thesis

n **2** accomplishment, action, conduct, deed, delivery, execution, performance, talent

demoralize *v* **1** adulterate, corrupt, debase, debauch, defile, dishonor, pervert, ruin, seduce, taint

v **2** chill, deject, depress, discourage, dishearten, disparage

demote *v* break, bump, bust, degrade, demerit, downgrade, put down, reduce

demur *v* **1** balk, boggle, desist, gag

v **2** decline, delay, disagree, object

v **3** halt, hold up, interrupt, pause, rest, stop, suspend

n challenge, difficulty, hindrance, hurdle, objection, obstacle, problem, protest, question, snag

demure *adj* **1** backward, bashful, coy, diffident, innocent, modest, quiet, reserved, retiring, shy, staid, timid, unassured

adj **2** calm, collected, composed, cool, dormant, easy, gentle, hushed, idle, imperturbable, motionless, nonchalant, peaceful, placid, poised, quiet, relaxed, restful, sedate, self-composed, self-possessed, serene, soft, steady, still, tranquil, unflappable, unruffled, untroubled

den *n* **1** burrow, cave, grotto, lair, recess, tunnel

n **2** bar, barroom, cocktail lounge, dive, dump, gin mill, hangout, haunt, joint, lounge, pub, rathskeller, saloon, tavern, watering hole

n **3** study

denial *n* refusal

denigrate *v* abuse, asperse, bad-mouth, belittle, condemn, damage, decry, defame, degrade, denounce, deprecate, detract, diminish, discount, disparage, insult, knock, malign, put down, revile, run down, slander, take away, vilify

denomination *n* **1** group, persuasion, sect

n **2** affiliation, belief, church, creed, faith, persuasion, religion, rite, seat, theology

denotation *n* clarification, definition, explanation, meaning, translation

denote *v* **1** annotate, compile, correct, edit, modify, polish, proofread, revise

v **2** allude, indicate, mention, point out, refer to, reveal, show, speak of, specify, suggest, tell

v **3** add up to, connote, convey, identify, import, indicate, intend, mean, show, signify, symbolize

v **4** flag, mark, star

v **5** depict, express, illustrate, imply, mean, represent, speak for, symbolize

v **6** capture, chart, enter, itemize, jot, list, log, note, preserve, record, register, take notes, tally, tape, write down

denouement *n* conclusion, culmination, outcome, resolution, result, solution

denounce *v* **1** censure, condemn, disparage, inveigh

v **2** condemn, curse, damn, molest, profane, swear, vex

v **3** see: ABUSE *v* 4

dense *adj* **1** ignorant, oblivious, obtuse

adj 2 close, compact, crowded, solid, thick, tight

adj 3 see: DUMB *adj* 2

density *n* compactness, firmness, hardness, solidity, strength, tensile strength

dent *n* 1 bit, chip, flake, fragment, mark, piece

n 2 groove, indentation, nick, notch

v bang, dimple, hollow, indent

denude *v* bare, discard, disrobe, doff, flash, remove, reveal, shed, strip, take off, unclothe, undress

denunciation *n* 1 see: INSULT *n*

n 2 see: REPRIMAND *n*

deny *v* 1 disallow, refuse, reject, withhold

v 2 attack, challenge, contradict, impugn, oppose, rebut

v 3 contradict, cross, disaffirm, disagree, impugn, negate, rebut, traverse

v 4 abjure, disavow, disclaim, disown, forswear, reject, renounce, repudiate

v 5 break, confound, confute, contend, contradict, disprove, dispute, rebut, refute

v 6 abstain, avoid, constrain, curb, forgo, govern, hold back, refrain, resist, restrict, stop, tame

v 7 see: REJECT *v* 2, 3, 7

depart *v* 1 clear, disappear, evaporate, fade, vanish

v 2 abscond, bolt, break, elude, escape, flee, fly, hightail it, lose, run, sneak away, split

v 3 abscond, bolt, defect, exit, fall back, flee, get away, give back, go, leave, move, pull away, pull out, push off, retreat, run along, secede, shove off, take off, vacate, withdraw

v 4 see: PROCEED *v* 2

departed *adj* 1 cold, dead, deceased, defunct, lifeless, spiritless

adj 2 bygone, dead, defunct, extinct, forgotten, gone, lost, vanished

department *n* 1 branch, division, office, unit

n 2 faculty, instructors, professors, staff, teachers

n 3 see: ADMINISTRATION *n* 3

departure *n* 1 death, decease, expiration, passing

n 2 exit, farewell, leaving, parting, passing

n 3 abandon, desertion, evacuation, exit, going, leaving, pullback, pullout, removal, retreat, withdrawal

n 4 abdication, resignation, retirement

depend *v* bank on, build on, count on, need, rely, trust

dependable *adj* 1 fail-safe, infallible, reliable, sure, tested, tried

adj 2 observant, on time, precise, prompt, punctual, reliable, timely

adj 3 authoritative, due, faithful, legitimate, rightful, strict, true, trustworthy, undistorted, veracious

adj 4 accurate, authentic, believable, certain, convincing, credible, faithful, real, reliable, safe, sure, tenable, true, trustworthy, trusty

adj 5 accountable, answerable, honorable, honored, liable, reliable, respectable, respected, responsible, secure, solid, trusted, trustworthy, trusty, upstanding

adj 6 see: FAITHFUL *adj* 2, 3, 4

dependence *n* 1 acquiescence, compliance, obedience, subjection, submission

n 2 belief, confidence, contingency, credence, credit, creed, desire, faith, hope, religion, trust

dependent *adj* 1 contingent, incidental, linked

adj 2 lesser, subordinate, subservient

adj 3 ancillary, conditional, contingent, indefinite, provisional, relative, reliant, temporary, uncertain

adj 4 defenseless, disarmed, exposed, helpless, powerless, susceptible, unprotected, vulnerable, weak

adj 5 ancillary, assistant, collateral, complementary, lesser, minor, secondary, sub, subject, subordinate, subsidiary, substitute, supporter, tributary, worker

n 1 follower, satellite, sycophant

n 2 assistant, employee, subordinate, underling

n 3 barnacle, freeloader, hanger-on, leech, parasite, remora, sponge, vine

depict *v* 1 design, draw, paint, represent, sketch

v 2 delineate, illustrate, picture, portray, represent, sketch

v 3 clarify, interpret, render, rephrase, represent, translate

v 4 acquaint, announce, delineate, introduce, present, reflect, represent, show

v 5 denote, express, illustrate, imply, mean, represent, speak for, symbolize

v 6 clarify, clear, clear up, delineate, elucidate, explain, illuminate, illustrate, picture, portray, reveal

depiction *n* 1 characterization, delineation, expression, portrayal, representation

n 2 description, explanation, illustration, narration, report, sketch, story, verbalization

n 3 acrylic, art, canvas, drawing, etching,

illustration, landscape, lithograph, mural, oil, painting, pastel, pen and ink, picture, portrait, print, seascape, sketch, still life, watercolor

deplete v 1 clear, drain, empty, evacuate, take out, vacate

v 2 consume, exhaust, expend, finish, go, lessen, run through, spend, use up, waste, weaken

v 3 bankrupt, drain, draw, draw down, exhaust, impoverish, use up

deplorable adj affecting, lamentable, miserable, paltry, pathetic, pitiable, pitiful, poor, sad, unfortunate, woeful, wretched

deplore v bemoan, lament, regret, repent, rue

deploy v control, direct, maneuver, manipulate, use

deport v banish, cast out, dispel, displace, exile, expatriate, expel, extradite, ostracize, oust, relegate, remove

deportment n action, bearing, behavior, conduct, demeanor, manners

depose v 1 discharge, oust, remove, unseat

v 2 affirm, bear witness, declare, profess, swear, testify

v 3 affirm, assert, attest, avow, confirm, declare, predicate, profess, protest

deposit v accumulate, bank, hoard, save, squirrel away, stockpile, store

n muck, mud, sediment, silt, sludge

deposition n 1 affidavit, attestation, statement, testimony

n 2 accusation, allegation, assertion, charge, comment, declaration, pronouncement, statement

depository n bank, lender, receptacle, repository

depot n location, station, stop

deprave v debauch, deflower, ravish, seduce

depraved adj 1 abandoned, derelict, deserted, desolate, forsaken, secluded, solitary, uninhabited

adj 2 base, corrupt, deadly, degenerate, deviant, evil, immoral, infamous, kinky, nefarious, perverse, putrid, rotten, ruthless, savage, vicious, villainous, wicked, wild

depravity n corruption, dishonesty, immorality, impurity, vice, wickedness, wrong

deprecate v 1 minimize, play down, poohpooh

v 2 belittle, disapprove, disfavor, disparage, frown upon, object

v 3 abuse, asperse, bad-mouth, belittle, condemn, damage, decry, defame, degrade, denigrate, denounce, detract, diminish, discount, disparage, insult, knock,

malign, put down, revile, run down, slander, take away, vilify

depreciate v 1 cheapen, devalue, diminish, downgrade, dwindle, lower, mark down, reduce, underrate, undervalue

v 2 see: BELITTLE v 1

depress v 1 droop, flop, let down, lower, mire, sag, sink, wallow

v 2 chill, deject, demoralize, discourage, dishearten, disparage

v 3 burden, deject, dishearten, grieve, hurt, lament, sadden, weigh down, wound

depressed adj 1 cynical, gloomy, glum, grim, negative, pessimistic

adj 2 beaten, clobbered, defeated, dejected, discouraged, licked, whipped

adj 3 black, bleak, blue, cheerless, dejected, desperate, despondent, discouraging, disheartening, distressing, down, forlorn, gloomy, hopeless, joyless, melancholy, moody, mournful, oppressive, prostrate, sad, somber, sorry, unhappy

adj 4 sunken

depressing adj abnormal, dismal, funereal, ghastly, gloomy, gruesome, macabre, morbid, sepulchral

depression n 1 doldrums, down cycle, rut

n 2 blank, cavity, crack, emptiness, gap, hole, hollow, nook, opening, space, void

n 3 apathy, boredom, doldrums, inertia, languor

deprivation n deficiency, destitution, inadequacy, indigence, lack, need, poverty, privation, scarcity, want

deprive v 1 starve

v 2 bare, dismantle, divest, strip

v 3 defraud, rob, swindle, take, usurp

deprived adj bereft, destitute, lacking, wanting

depth n 1 breadth, dimensions, range, scope, span, width

n 2 concentration, energy, intensity, profundity, strength, substance, vigor

n 3 abyss, canyon, chasm, cleft, crack, fissure, gorge, gulch, pass, ravine

deputy n agent, ambassador, consul, delegate, diplomat, emissary, envoy

derange v agitate, disorder, disturb, fluster, rock, ruffle, shake, sicken, unhinge, unsettle, upset

deranged adj 1 demented, distraught, insane, mentally ill, psychotic

adj 2 delirious, fantasizing, frenzied, hallucinating, maniacal, raving

derangement n 1 aberration, abnormality, craziness, delusion, dementia, distraction, eccentricity, fugue, hallucination, insanity, irregularity, lunacy, madness, mania, psychosis, unbalance

n 2 see: CHAOS *n* 5

derby *n* beret, cap, hat, helmet

derelict *adj* 1 abandoned, depraved, deserted, desolate, forsaken, secluded, solitary, uninhabited

adj 2 careless, defiant, delinquent, heedless, inattentive, lax, neglectful, negligent, reckless, sloppy

n 1 beggar, bum, drifter, hobo, loafer, mendicant, panhandler, pauper, tramp, vagabond, vagrant

n 2 outcast, outsider, recluse

deride *v* 1 belittle, flaunt, jab, jeer, jest, mock, quip, razz, ridicule, scoff, scorn, sneer, taunt, tease

v 2 see: TEASE *v* 1

derision *n* aspersion, contempt, disdain, irony, mockery, ridicule, sarcasm, satire, scorn

derisive *adj* 1 abusive, contemptuous, disrespectful, insulting, nasty, offensive, slighting

adj 2 contemptuous, cynical, ironic, mocking, sarcastic, sardonic, scornful, skeptical, wry

derivation *n* beginning, conception, cradle, fountainhead, inception, infancy, mother, origin, root, seed, source, stem

derivative *adj* derived, secondary, stemming from

n by-product, end product, end result, growth, outgrowth, output, produce, product, production, productivity, result, yield

derive *v* 1 develop, evolve, mature, progress, unfold

v 2 gain, get, harvest, realize, reap

v 3 deduce, draw, educe, elicit, evince, evoke, extract

v 4 arise, come from, emanate, flow, head, issue, originate, spring, stem

v 5 analyze, conclude, construe, deduce, draw, educe, gather, glean, guess, infer, interpret, presume, surmise

v 6 access, accomplish, achieve, attain, earn, fulfill, gain, get, merit, net, obtain, perform, profit, rack up, reach, realize, score, win

derived *adj* derivative, secondary, stemming from

derogate *v* see: BELITTLE *v* 1

derogatory *adj* disparaging, insulting, malicious, nasty, sarcastic, snide

derrière *n* ass, backside, base, behind, bottom, bucket, buns, butt, buttocks, end,

fanny, hindquarters, posterior, rump, seat, stub, stump, tip, tush

descend *v* 1 grovel, sink, stoop, submit

v 2 decline, incline, skew, slant, slope, veer

v 3 alight, come down, dismount, get off, land, settle

v 4 dive, drop, fall, lapse, leap, lower, plummet, plunge, sink, swoop

descendant *n* child, heir, offspring, progeny, scion

descendants *n* brood, children, offspring, posterity, progeny

descent *n* 1 blood, kinship, lineage, relationship, stock

n 2 ancestry, blood, bloodline, family, genealogy, heritage, line, lineage, origin, pedigree, stock, strain

n 3 comedown, decline, decrease, dive, drop, failure, fall, plunge, regression, setback, slide, tumble

describe *v* 1 detail, itemize, list, specify

v 2 demonstrate, display, draw, establish, examine, exhibit, explain, present, prove, show, sketch, tell

v 3 brief, communicate, convey, declare, disclose, divulge, explain, impart, inform, narrate, orate, portray, read, recite, recount, relate, report, retell, reveal, share, state, tattle, tell, transmit

v 4 see: VERBALIZE *v* 2

description *n* 1 depiction, explanation, illustration, narration, report, sketch, story, verbalization

n 2 see: FICTION *n* 2

descriptive *adj* clear, effective, graphic, precise

descry *v* 1 see: DETECT *v* 2

v 2 see: UNDERSTAND *v* 6

desecrate *v* 1 contaminate, debase, degrade, pervert, profane

v 2 abhor, abominate, bristle, despise, detest, disdain, dislike, hate, loathe, reject, revile, scorn

v 3 deflower, despoil, devastate, devour, loot, maraud, pillage, plunder, ravage, sack, scourge, spoil, strip, violate

desecration *n* blasphemy, heresy, impiety, irreverence, sacrilege, violation

desegregate *v* integrate

desert *n* barren, waste, wasteland, wild, wilderness

v abandon, break up, cast off, chuck, defect, disavow, discard, disenfranchise, disown, ditch, dump, forsake, jilt, junk, leave, quit, reject, renounce, spurn, strand, throw out

deserted *adj* abandoned, depraved, derelict, desolate, forsaken, secluded, solitary, uninhabited

desertion *n* abandon, departure, evacuation, exit, going, leaving, pullback, pullout, removal, retreat, withdrawal

deserved *adj* appropriate, correct, due, fitting, just, merited, proper, rightful, suitable, warranted

deserving *adj* estimable, excellent, honorable, noble, precious, sterling, valuable, worthy

design *n* 1 device, figure, motif, motive, pattern
n 2 definition, distinctness, outline, precision, specificity
n 3 arrangement, form, plan, prearrangement, preparation, provision
n 4 blueprint, game plan, plan, project, proposal, scheme, strategy
n 5 ambition, bent, goal, intent, intention, meaning, objective, plan, purpose
v 1 depict, draw, paint, represent, sketch
v 2 aim, contemplate, intend, mean, plan, propose
v 3 carve, chisel, craft, cut, define, fashion, form, mold, sculpt, sculpture, shape, steer
v 4 arrange, blueprint, cast, chart, devise, draft, draw, engineer, fashion, lay out, map, outline, plan, plot, project, set out, sketch

designate *adj* chosen, elected, picked, select, selected
v 1 assign, cede, convey, deed, transfer
v 2 assign, authorize, delegate, empower, entrust, pass along
v 3 demand, indicate, insist, require, specify, stipulate
v 4 call, define, entitle, label, name, term
v 5 appoint, declare, name, nominate, propose, select, specify
v 6 advise, authorize, command, decree, dictate, direct, mandate, ordain, order, rule
v 7 baptize, bestow, call, christen, confer, dub, entitle, name, nickname, tag, term, title

designation *n* alias, handle, moniker, name, nickname, title

designer *n* architect, draftsperson, engineer, inventor, manager, operator, plotter, schemer, surveyor

desirable *adj* 1 comfortable, genial, lively, warm
adj 2 alluring, compelling, irresistible, overpowering, seductive, tantalizing
adj 3 advantageous, better, enjoyable, preferable, superior, worthier, worthwhile
adj 4 alluring, attractive, erotic, exciting, seductive, sexy, tantalizing, tempting
adj 5 see: APPLICABLE *adj*

desirably *adv* before, preferably, rather

desire *n* 1 ambition, aspiration, goal, hope, will, wish
n 2 appetite, craving, eroticism, hankering, hunger, itch, longing, lust, passion, urge, yearning, yen
n 3 avarice, covetousness, craving, greed, selfishness, yearning
n 4 appeal, favor, petition, plea, request, solicitation, wish
n 5 belief, confidence, contingency, credence, credit, creed, dependence, faith, hope, religion, trust
v 1 choose, elect, favor, prefer, select
v 2 choose, covet, crave, envy, fancy, lust, want, wish
v 3 ache, covet, crave, hanker, hunger, itch, long, lust, need, pine, thirst, want, yearn
v 4 appeal, ask, beg, beseech, conjure, crave, entreat, grovel, implore, indicate, invoke, plead, pray, request, seek, solicit, supplicate, whine

desirous *adj* 1 acquisitive, avaricious, covetous, craving, eager, grabby, grasping, greedy, hungry, longing, miserly, selfish, wishful, yearning
adj 2 see: EAGER *adj* 2

desist *v* 1 balk, boggle, demur, gag
v 2 abstain, cease, conclude, discontinue, end, finish, forbear, freeze, halt, knock off, quit, refrain, sever, stop, terminate

desk *n* 1 dais, lectern, podium, pulpit, rostrum, soapbox, stage, stand
n 2 board, secretary, table

desolate *adj* 1 bare, barren, bleak, dismal, gaunt, grim
adj 2 abandoned, depraved, derelict, deserted, forsaken, secluded, solitary, uninhabited
adj 3 see: DULL *adj* 7

despair *v* ache, grieve, hurt, pain, suffer
n see: anguish *n* 2

desperate *adj* 1 abrupt, audacious, headstrong, rash, reckless
adj 2 see: GLOOMY *adj* 5
adj 3 see: IMPORTANT *adj* 5
adj 4 see: MONSTROUS *adj* 2

despicable *adj* 1 abhorrent, repulsive, revolting, ugly
adj 2 abject, base, contemptible, debasing, false, servile

adj **3** infamous, notorious, offensive, scandalous, shady, unsavory, villainous

adj **4** base, beneath, ignoble, inferior, low, lowdown, sordid, squalid, unworthy, vile, vulgar, wretched

despise *v* abhor, abominate, bristle, desecrate, detest, disdain, dislike, hate, loathe, reject, revile, scorn

despite *adv* further, however, in spite of, regardless

n see: INSULT *n*

despoil *v* see: RAVAGE *v* 2

despondent *adj* see: GLOOMY *adj* 5

despot *n* **1** authoritarian, autocrat, dictator, fascist, tsar, tyrant

n **2** autocrat, chief, commander, dictator, governor, head, king, leader, lord, master, monarch, potentate, ruler

despotic *adj* **1** aristocratic, arrogant, authoritarian, authoritative, autocratic, belligerent, bossy, dictatorial, dogmatic, domineering, haughty, imperial, imperious, masterful, militaristic, opinionated, oppressive, overbearing, peremptory, pushy, stubborn

adj **2** authoritarian, authoritative, autocratic, controlled, disciplined, firm, harsh, inflexible, ironhanded, restrictive, rigid, rigorous, ruthless, severe, solid, stern, strict, stringent, strong, tough, tyrannical

despotism *n* autocracy, dictatorship, tyranny

destination *n* address, direction, identification, location, zone

destiny *n* fate, good fortune, karma, kismet, lot, luck, providence

destitute *adj* **1** bereft, deprived, lacking, wanting

adj **2** bankrupt, broke, busted, dissolved, insolvent, out of business, penniless, ruined

adj **3** broke, dirt-poor, down and out, impoverished, indigent, needy, penniless, poor, poverty-stricken, strapped, unprosperous

destitution *n* deficiency, deprivation, inadequacy, indigence, lack, need, poverty, privation, scarcity, want

destroy *v* **1** consume, demolish, ravage

v **2** burn, cremate, incinerate, oxidize

v **3** annihilate, decimate, demolish, destruct, devastate, dismantle, overturn, pulverize, raze, rub out, ruin, shatter, smash, tear down, undo, wreck

v **4** see: KILL *v* 3, 5

v **5** see: OVERCOME *v* 2

v **6** see: TERMINATE *v* 8

destruct *v* annihilate, decimate, demolish, destroy, devastate, dismantle, overturn, pulverize, raze, rub out, ruin, shatter, smash, tear down, undo, wreck

destruction *n* **1** downfall, infiltration, overthrow, ruin, subversion, upset

n **2** breakdown, catastrophe, crash, crisis, death, doom, failure, finish, ruin

n **3** accident, collision, crackup, crash, mishap, pileup, smash, smashup, wreck, wreckage

n **4** chaos, damage, devastation, disaster, disorder, harm, havoc, hurt, injury, loss, mayhem, ruin, ruination, tort

destructiveness *n* brutality, ferocity, force, frenzy, fury, rage, violence

detach *v* **1** insulate, isolate, seclude, separate, sequester

v **2** cut, disconnect, disengage, dissociate, separate, sever, uncouple, unfasten, unhook, unyoke

detached *adj* **1** clinical, impersonal, scientific, systematic, technical

adj **2** free, impartial, independent, neutral, nonpartisan, unattached, uncommitted, uninvolved

adj **3** alienated, alone, apart, hidden, isolated, private, removed, secluded, separated, sequestered, severed

adj **4** aloof, blasé, calm, careless, casual, composed, cool, diffident, disinterested, distant, indifferent, informal, inhibited, nonchalant, numb, remote, reserved, shy, unconcerned, unfriendly, uninterested, withdrawn

detachment *n* **1** aloofness, indifference, preoccupation, separation

n **2** isolation, privacy, quiet, seclusion, solitude

detail *n* feature, item, part, particular, specific

v **1** assign, task

v **2** describe, itemize, list, specify

v **3** analyze, annotate, clarify, define, elucidate, explain, expound, express, interpret, narrate, spell out, state, understand

detailed *adj* graphic, illustrative, photographic, pictorial, picturesque, visual, vivid

details *n* **1** minutiae, nuances, particulars, second level, trivia

n **2** data, dope, facts, information, report, scoop

detain *v* **1** block, catch, cut off, hinder, intercept, obstruct, stop

v **2** bog, delay, hang up, impede, mire, retard, set back, slacken, slow *v* 3 hold, hold back, keep, keep back, keep out, reserve, retain, set aside, withhold

v 4 cage, confine, coop, enclose, impound, imprison, incarcerate, intern, jail, lock up, restrain, trap

v 5 apprehend, arrest, bag, book, bust, capture, catch, collar, get, grab, lock up, nab, nail, pick up, pinch, pull in, run in, secure, seize, take

detect *v* 1 experience, feel, notice, perceive, sense

v 2 ascertain, catch, descry, discover, encounter, espy, ferret, find, locate, spot, turn up, uncover

detectable *adj* appreciable, cognizant, concrete, discernible, noticeable, observable, palpable, perceptible, sensible, tangible, visible

detection *n* discovery, finding, perception

detention *n* arrest, confinement, custody, imprisonment, incarceration

deter *v* 1 avert, caution, discourage, dissuade, distract, divert

v 2 avert, bar, eliminate, foil, forestall, hinder, hold off, inhibit, preclude, prevent, stave off, thwart, turn back, ward off

v 3 see: HINDER *v* 4, 5

deteriorate *v* 1 corrode, eat, erode, gnaw, oxidize, rust, wear

v 2 abate, decline, fade, fail, flag, impair, languish, wane, weaken, wither, worsen

v 3 atrophy, decay, dry up, dwindle, mummify, shrink, shrivel, waste away, welter, wilt, wither, wizen

v 4 corrupt, crumble, decay, decompose, degenerate, disintegrate, perish, putrefy, rot, smell, spoil, taint, wane, weaken, wither

deterioration *n* 1 atrophy, decay, degeneration, shrinkage, wasting

n 2 debasement, decline, dip, downturn, drop, ebb, erosion, fall, involution, plunge, sag, slide, slip, slump, wane, weakening

determinate *adj* 1 definite, exclusive, fixed, limited, narrow, precise, restricted, segregated, specific

adj 2 see: CONSTANT *adj* 3

determination *n* 1 course, plan, purpose, resolution, resolve

n 2 agreement, arrangement, compromise, concession, decision, franchise, settlement

n 3 adjudication, award, judgment, opinion, ruling, sentence, verdict

n 4 backbone, chutzpah, endurance, fortitude, grit, guts, moxie, nerve, persistence, pluck, resilience, spirit, spunk, stamina, strength, tenacity, tolerance, vigor, willpower

determine *v* 1 assure, confirm, establish

v 2 deduce, discern, glean, learn

v 3 evaluate, judge, test, try, verify

v 4 demonstrate, establish, evidence, prove, reveal, show

v 5 adjust, arrange, calibrate, decide, establish, fix, resolve, set

v 6 adjudicate, conclude, decide, establish, resolve, rule, settle, will

v 7 ascertain, catch on, discover, find out, hear, learn, listen, uncover, unearth

v 8 analyze, assess, diagnose, estimate, examine, penetrate, probe, scope, solve, survey, understand, unravel

determined *adj* 1 persistent, resolute, stubborn, tenacious

adj 2 committed, fixed, focused, limited, narrow, obsessive, one-track

adj 3 bent, committed, dedicated, fixed, intentional, purposeful, resolute, resolved, set, tenacious

adj 4 ardent, decisive, emphatic, extreme, forceful, intense, potent, powerful, severe, strong

adj 5 definite, fixed, foregone, inevitable, inexorable, irrevocable, ordained, predestined, unalterable, unavoidable, unchangeable

adj 6 adamant, ceaseless, dedicated, firm, immovable, inexhaustible, inexorable, inflexible, narrow-minded, obstinate, relentless, resolute, resolved, rigid, single-minded, steadfast, stubborn, unbendable, unbending, uncompromising, unswayable, unyielding

adj 7 see: ENGROSSED *adj* 2

deterrent *n* anticipation, caution, precaution, preclusion, preparation, prevention, safeguard

detest *v* abhor, abominate, bristle, desecrate, despise, disdain, dislike, hate, loathe, reject, revile, scorn

detestable *adj* abhorrent, abominable, appalling, disgusting, dreadful, evil, frightful, ghastly, hateful, horrible, horrid, loathsome, odious, repulsive, revolting, shocking

detonate *v* 1 blow up, boom, burst, explode

v 2 bombard, discharge, fire, shoot

detour *n* 1 branch, bypass, deviation, diversion

n 2 angle, bend, bow, deviation, double, shift, tack, turn, turning, yaw

v 1 avoid, bypass, circumvent, evade

v 2 deviate, differ, digress, diverge, meander, swerve

v **3** avoid, circumvent, deflect, dodge, duck, evade, hedge, parry, shirk, sidestep, skirt, ward off

detract *v* **1** see: ABUSE *v* **4**

v **2** see: HINDER *v* **5**

detractor *n* critic, cynic, hatchet man, naysayer, pessimist, skeptic

detrimental *adj* adverse, deleterious, harmful, injurious, negative, unfavorable

detritus *n* **1** crap, crud, debris, dirt, garbage, junk, litter, refuse, rubbish, rubble, sweepings, trash, waste

n **2** boulder, fragments, gravel, pebble, rock, stone

devalue *v* **1** cheapen, depreciate, diminish, downgrade, dwindle, lower, mark down, reduce, underrate, undervalue

v **2** see: BELITTLE *v* **1**

devastate *v* **1** deflower, desecrate, despoil, devour, loot, maraud, pillage, plunder, ravage, sack, scourge, spoil, strip, violate

v **2** annihilate, decimate, demolish, destroy, destruct, dishuman, overturn, pulverize, raze, rub out, ruin, shatter, smash, tear down, undo, wreck

devastating *adj* **1** crushing, overpowering, overwhelming

adj **2** calamitous, cataclysmic, catastrophic, critical, crucial, disastrous, fatal, fateful, momentous, ruinous, vital

devastation *n* chaos, damage, destruction, disaster, disorder, harm, havoc, hurt, injury, loss, mayhem, ruin, ruination, tort

develop *v* **1** derive, evolve, mature, progress, unfold

v **2** emerge, ensue, follow, happen, lead to, result

v **3** come together, crystallize, form, jell, materialize, shape up

v **4** cultivate, encourage, foster, further, grow, promote

v **5** age, grow, grow up, mature, mellow, progress, ripen

v **6** craft, define, formulate, list, make, process, specify, synthesize

v **7** bloom, blossom, bud, ferment, flourish, flower, germinate, grow, sprout

v **8** amplify, construct, devise, elaborate, enhance, enlarge, expand, expound, increase, refine

v **9** begin, coin, conceive, craft, create, define, devise, formulate, innovate, invent, make, originate, start

v **10** see: EDUCATE *v*

v **11** see: FLOURISH *v* **2, 3**

v **12** see: GUIDE *v* **3**

v **13** see: OCCUR *v* **2**

developing *adj* **1** alive, living, prospering, viable

adj **2** casual, coming along, easy, effortless, flowing, fluent, laid-back, running, smooth

development *n* **1** consequence, progression, ramification, result

n **2** background, breeding, culture, education, environment, experience, past, schooling, training, upbringing

developmental *adj* experimental, pilot, suggested, tentative, test, trial, untested

deviant *adj* **1** aberrant, abnormal, anomalous, artificial, atypical, contrived, disparate, divergent, incongruous, irregular, off-key, uncharacteristic, unnatural

adj **2** see: VICIOUS *adj* **3**

n debaucher, deviate, pervert, weirdo

deviate *adj* circuitous, circular, diagonal, indirect, oblique, round, roundabout

n debaucher, deviant, pervert, weirdo

v **1** detour, differ, digress, diverge, meander, swerve

v **2** deflect, divert, drift, slip, stray, turn

v **3** see: SKEW *v* **3**

deviation *n* **1** difference, distinction, variation

n **2** branch, bypass, detour, diversion

n **3** adjustment, alteration, anomaly, change, modification, mutation, permutation, shift, variation

n **4** angle, bend, bow, detour, double, shift, tack, turn, turning, yaw

device *n* **1** design, figure, motif, motive, pattern

n **2** engine, generator, machine, motor, turbine

n **3** apparatus, appliance, contraption, contrivance, doodad, doohickey, gadget, gimmick, gizmo, implement, instrument, invention, machine, mechanism, thingumajig, tool, utensil, widget

n **4** antic, diversion, gambit, gimmick, maneuver, mischief, move, plan, plot, ploy, prank, ruse, scheme, stratagem, strategy, tactic, trick, wile

devil *n* brute, demon, fiend, rogue, Satan, villain, wretch

devilish *adj* demoniac, diabolic, fiendish, wicked

devious *adj* clandestine, concealed, covert, crafty, deceitful, evasive, foxy, furtive, guileful, indirect, privy, secret, shifty, sly, sneaky, surreptitious, tricky, underground, underhand, underhanded, wily

devise *v* **1** bequeath, bestow, impart, leave, will

v 2 build, conceive, construct, frame, shape, surround

v 3 amplify, construct, develop, elaborate, enhance, enlarge, expand, expound, increase, refine

v 4 brew, concoct, construe, contrive, create, engineer, fabricate, formulate, hatch, invent, make up, plot, scheme

v 5 begin, coin, conceive, craft, create, define, develop, formulate, innovate, invent, make, originate, start

v 6 cogitate, collude, connive, conspire, contrive, frame, intrigue, machinate, maneuver, orchestrate, plan, plot, scheme

v 7 arrange, blueprint, cast, chart, design, draft, draw, engineer, fashion, lay out, map, outline, plan, plot, project, set out, sketch

devote *v* 1 see: ASSURE *v* 3

v 2 see: BLESS *v*

v 3 see: GIVE *v* 8

devoted *adj* 1 affectionate, amorous, attached, caring, enamored, fond, loving, romantic, tender

adj 2 see: FAITHFUL *adj* 3

devotee *n* admirer, buff, disciple, enthusiast, fan, follower, groupie

devotees *n* congregation, flock, fold, followers, laity, members, parishioners

devotion *n* 1 reverence, sanctity, worship

n 2 allegiance, ardor, faithfulness, fidelity, loyalty

n 3 affection, affinity, attachment, attraction, compassion, concern, fondness, heart, kinship, love, warmth

n 4 alacrity, ardor, delight, diligence, enjoyment, enthusiasm, excitement, fervor, fire, flame, gaiety, gusto, passion, relish, savor, thrill, zeal, zest

n 5 deference, esteem, homage, honor, just due, regard, respect, reverence

devour *v* 1 consume, digest, eat, ingest, masticate, swallow

v 2 see: RAVAGE *v* 2

devout *adj* 1 narrow, orthodox, strict, unquestioning

adj 2 dedicated, deferential, obeisant, respectful

adj 3 godly, holy, pious, prayerful, religious, reverent, sanctimonious

dexterity *n* ability, adequacy, adroitness, aptitude, art, caliber, calling, capability, capacity, command, competence, craft, experience, expertise, familiarity, forte, knack, know-how, knowledge, mastery, proficiency, prowess, qualification, savvy,

skill, specialty, strength, talent, training, workmanship

dexterous *adj* 1 agile, deft, skillful, subtle

adj 2 adept, handy, mechanical, proficient, skilled

adj 3 see: QUALIFIED *adj* 4

diabolic *adj* demoniac, devilish, fiendish, wicked

diagnose *v* 1 estimate, forecast, gauge, predetermine, predict, project

v 2 analyze, assess, determine, estimate, examine, penetrate, probe, scope, solve, survey, understand, unravel

diagnostician *n* doctor, healer, intern, physician, resident, specialist, surgeon

diagonal *adj* circuitous, circular, deviate, indirect, oblique, round, roundabout

diagram *n* 1 blueprint, chart, draft, map, outline, plan, sketch

n 2 bar graph, chart, distribution, figure, flowchart, graph, histogram, outline, pie chart, plot, table

dial *n* disk, display, gauge, indicator, measure, meter, pointer, selector

v adjust, align, select, tune

dialect *n* accent, brogue, patois, speech, tongue

dialogue *n* 1 bull session, discussion, rap, talk

n 2 argument, contention, controversy, debate, discussion, dispute

n 3 caucus, chat, colloquy, conference, conversation, debate, discourse, discussion, exchange, forum, interchange, intercourse, interlocution, meeting, talk

n 4 script

v argue, confer, contest, contradict, contrast, debate, differ, disagree, discord, discuss, dispute, dissent, divide, oppose, vary

diameter *n* bore, caliber, circle, radius

diametric *adj* conflicting, contradictory, contrary, converse, counter, inverse, opposed, opposing, opposite, polar, reverse

diary *n* 1 career, events, experience, history, performance, record, résumé, track record, vita

n 2 account, digest, journal, log, memoir, minutes, notation, notes, proceedings, record, recording, report

diatribe *n* 1 assignment, discourse, exercise, homily, lecture, lesson, preaching, sermon

n 2 see: REPRIMAND *n*

dicker *v* argue, bargain, barter, haggle, negotiate, wrangle

dictate *n* see: COMMAND *n* 3

v 1 advise, authorize, command, decree,

designate, direct, mandate, ordain, order, rule

v 2 see: VERBALIZE v 2

dictator n 1 authoritarian, autocrat, disciplinarian, enforcer

n 2 authoritarian, autocrat, despot, fascist, tsar, tyrant

n 3 autocrat, chief, commander, despot, governor, head, king, leader, lord, master, monarch, potentate, ruler

dictatorial adj 1 aristocratic, arrogant, authoritarian, authoritative, autocratic, belligerent, bossy, despotic, dogmatic, domineering, haughty, imperial, imperious, masterful, militaristic, opinionated, oppressive, overbearing, peremptory, pushy, stubborn

adj 2 see: VAIN adj 5

dictatorship n autocracy, despotism, tyranny

diction n cliché, expression, parlance, phrase, saying, slogan, style, term, wording

dictionary n 1 authority, encyclopedia, reference, source

n 2 glossary, lexicon, list, synonym finder, synonym listing, thesaurus, vocabulary, Word Finder®

dictum n 1 announcement, aphorism, axiom, cliché, declaration, decree, edict, gospel, homily, maxim, moral, precept, pronouncement, rule, saying, teaching, truism, truth, verity

n 2 adage, axiom, byword, cliché, maxim, motto, proverb, saying, slogan, talk

diddle v 1 dally, dawdle, delay, goof off, idle, lag, linger, loaf, loiter, loll, lounge, malinger, poke, put off, putter, shirk, tarry

v 2 see: TRIFLE v 1

die v cease, elapse, expire, lapse, pass, pass away, perish, succumb, terminate

n form, matrix, mold, punch

diet n 1 bread, breakfast, brunch, chow, cuisine, dinner, dish, edibles, entree, fare, food, grub, lunch, meals, nosh, nutrition, provisions, rations, snack, supper, victuals, vittles

n 2 see: ASSEMBLY n 2

v fast, lose weight, reduce, slenderize, slim, trim down

differ v 1 detour, deviate, digress, diverge, meander, swerve

v 2 argue, confer, contest, contradict, contrast, debate, dialogue, disagree, discord, discuss, dispute, dissent, divide, oppose, vary

difference n 1 distinction, variation

n 2 characteristic, distinction, feature, peculiarity

n 3 contrast, dissimilarity, distinction, diversion, opposition

n 4 contradiction, disparity, dissimilarity, gap, inconsistency

n 5 annoyance, bother, conflict, contention, discord, disharmony, dispute, dissension, dissent, dissidence, dissonance, disunity, division, hassle, inconvenience, mischief, nuisance, strife, trouble, variance

n 6 see: CLASH n 2

different adj 1 disparate, diverse, incongruous, opposite, unequal, unlike, unmatched, unrelated

adj 2 alternate, another, certain, discrete, disparate, dissimilar, distinct, diverse, numerous, other, separate, several, some, unlike, various, varying

differentiate v 1 classify, define, discriminate, distinguish, isolate, separate

v 2 discriminate, exclude, isolate, ostracize, segregate, separate, sequester

differentiating adj characteristic, distinctive, lone, one, particular, peculiar, select, single, solitary, special, unique, unusual

difficult adj 1 awkward, delicate, embarrassing, sticky, tricky

adj 2 bellicose, brawling, feisty, quarrelsome, scrappy, spirited

adj 3 annoying, hurt, irksome, irritated, irritating, painful, sensitive, sore

adj 4 annoying, bad, disagreeable, displeasing, nasty, objectionable, offensive, rotten, sour, unhappy, unpleasant, upsetting

adj 5 arduous, demanding, formidable, hard, heavy, labored, laborious, rocky, rough, rugged, serious, severe, strenuous, tough, trying, uphill

adj 6 challenging, hairy, tricky

difficultly adv arduously, laboriously, onerously, painfully

difficulty n 1 complication, cramp, crick, kink

n 2 adversity, discipline, discomfort, hardness, rigor, severity, strictness, stringency, uneasiness

n 3 complication, dilemma, obstacle, plight, predicament, problem, quandary, situation, snag

n 4 bar, barrier, bottleneck, crimp, dead end, deadlock, encumbrance, hurdle, impasse, impediment, obstacle, obstruction, snag, stumbling block

n 5 bind, box, corner, dilemma, fix, impasse, jam, mess, pinch, plight, predicament, quandary, scrape, spot, trap, trouble

n 6 adversity, affliction, blow, burden, calamity, distress, hardship, mischance, misfortune, mishap, relapse, reversal, setback, suffering, tragedy, trouble

n 7 challenge, demur, hindrance, hurdle, objection, obstacle, problem, protest, question, snag

n 8 confusion, conundrum, dilemma, enigma, mystery, obstacle, paradox, perplexity, problem, puzzle, quandary, question, riddle, secret

diffident *adj* 1 faltering, halting, hesitant, indecisive, reluctant, tentative, unsure, waffling, wavering

adj 2 backward, bashful, coy, demure, innocent, modest, quiet, reserved, retiring, shy, staid, timid, unassured

adj 3 closed, introverted, laconic, reserved, restrained, reticent, secretive, shy, subdued, taciturn, timid, timorous, uncommunicative, undaring

adj 4 aloof, blasé, calm, careless, casual, composed, cool, detached, disinterested, distant, indifferent, informal, inhibited, nonchalant, numb, remote, reserved, shy, unconcerned, unfriendly, uninterested, withdrawn

diffuse *adj* bombastic, chatty, garrulous, long-winded, loquacious, redundant, repetitious, superfluous, talkative, verbose, wordy

v disseminate, distribute, permeate, spread, sprinkle, strew

dig *n* 1 affront, aspersion, attack, barb, caustic remark, crack, cut, denunciation, despite, disparagement, disrespect, gibe, implication, indignity, innuendo, insult, invective, knock, reflection, sarcasm, scorn, slap, slight, slur, spike, tongue-lashing, verbal jab

n 2 excavation, lode, mine, quarry

v 1 burrow, furrow, root out, tunnel

v 2 burrow, excavate, gouge, mine, scoop, shovel, unearth

v 3 delve, examine, explore, feel out, grope, hunt, inquire, investigate, look, observe, peer, probe, pursue, research, scan, scrutinize, search, seek, sound, study, test

v 4 extract, grub, uproot, weed

digest *n* 1 account, diary, journal, log, memoir, minutes, notation, notes, proceedings, record, recording, report

n 2 abridgement, abstract, brief, compendium, condensation, essence, example,

outline, review, sketch, summary, syllabus, synopsis

v 1 consume, devour, eat, ingest, masticate, swallow

v 2 abide, accept, acquiesce, allow, authorize, bear, concede, condone, endure, experience, have, let, permit, put up with, stand, stomach, suffer, sustain, swallow, take, tolerate, undergo

v 3 see: PONDER *v*

v 4 see: UNDERSTAND *v* 6

digger *n* fang, gasher, molar, tooth, tush, tusk

digging *n* analysis, experimentation, exploration, inquiry, inquisition, investigation, research, study, testing, trial

digit *n* cipher, integer, number, numeral

dignified *adj* 1 see: POLITE *adj* 2

adj 2 see: SOLEMN *adj* 1

dignify *v* distinguish, elevate, exalt, glorify, grace, honor

dignitary *n* celebrity, luminary, movie star, name, notable, personality, star

dignity *n* ego, pride, self-esteem, self-regard, self-respect

digress *v* detour, deviate, differ, diverge, meander, swerve

dilapidated *adj* 1 crumbled, decaying, rundown

adj 2 breakable, decrepit, delicate, feeble, flimsy, fragile, frail, jerry-built, jury-rigged, puny, Rube Goldberg, shoddy, sickly, thin, tinny, unsound, worn-out

dilate *v* amplify, bloat, distend, enlarge, expand, fatten, grow, increase, inflate, magnify, stretch, swell, widen

dilatory *adj* 1 deliberate, diligent, leisurely, methodical, meticulous, painstaking, patient, procrastinating, slow, thorough, unhasty, unhurried

adj 2 easygoing, idle, indolent, inert, lackadaisical, laid-back, languid, lazy, lethargic, relaxed, slothful, sluggish, unconcerned

dilemma *n* 1 climax, crisis, crux, emergency, juncture, point, predicament

n 2 complication, difficulty, obstacle, plight, predicament, problem, quandary, situation, snag

n 3 confusion, conundrum, difficulty, enigma, mystery, obstacle, paradox, perplexity, problem, puzzle, quandary, question, riddle, secret

n 4 bind, box, corner, difficulty, fix, impasse, jam, mess, pinch, plight, predicament, quandary, scrape, spot, trap, trouble

dilettante *n* amateur, beginner, dabbler,

hobbyist, layman, neophyte, nonprofessional, novice, part-timer

diligence *n* see: PASSION *n* 7

diligent *adj* 1 careful, rigorous, studious, thorough

adj 2 ambitious, assiduous, energetic, hard-working, industrious, persevering, persistent, resolute, sedulous, zealous

adj 3 deliberate, dilatory, leisurely, methodical, meticulous, painstaking, patient, procrastinating, slow, thorough, unhasty, unhurried

dilute *v* attenuate, diminish, lessen, purify, rarefy, reduce, refine, shorten, thin out, weaken

diluted *adj* watery

dim *adj* 1 cheerless, cloudy, dismal, drab, dull, gray, overcast

adj 2 conservative, inconspicuous, quiet, restrained, subdued, tasteful, unassuming, unobtrusive

adj 3 dark, dusky, gloomy, lightless, murky, obscure, shadowy, somber, tenebrous, unilluminated

adj 4 blah, boring, commonplace, dreary, dull, flat, humdrum, monotonous, ordinary, pedestrian, stodgy, tedious, tiresome

v becloud, bedim, befog, blur, cloud, confuse, darken, diminish, dull, eclipse, fade, muddy, obscure, overshadow, pale, shade, shadow, tarnish

dimension *n* see: REACH *n* 3

dimensions *n* 1 breadth, depth, range, scope, span, width

n 2 amount, amplitude, magnitude, proportions, quantity, scope, size, volume

diminish *v* 1 lessen, repress, subject, subordinate, suppress, weaken

v 2 deduct, lessen, minus, reduce, subtract, take away

v 3 decline, die down, dip, settle, sink, slide, slip, subside

v 4 attenuate, dilute, lessen, purify, rarefy, reduce, refine, shorten, thin out, weaken

v 5 see: ABRIDGE *v*

v 6 see: ABUSE *v* 4

v 7 see: DEPRECIATE *v* 1

v 8 see: OBSCURE *v*

v 9 see: RELIEVE *v* 3

v 10 see: SUBSIDE *v* 1, 2

diminished *adj* 1 limited, modified, qualified, reduced

adj 2 attenuate, lessened, rarefied, subtle, tenuous, thin

diminishing *n* abatement, easing, letup, loosening, relaxation, slackening

diminutive *adj* bantam, dainty, dwarfish, Lilliputian, little, micro, microscopic, midget, mini, miniature, minuscule, minute, petite, pygmy, slight, small, tiny, wee

dimple *v* bang, dent, hollow, indent

dimwit *n* see: IDIOT *n*

dimwitted *adj* backward, blunt, deficient, dense, dull, dumb, feebleminded, idiotic, moronic, obtuse, retarded, simple, simple-minded, slow, stupid, thick, uneducated, unintelligent

din *n* brouhaha, cacophony, chaos, clamor, confusion, discord, disorder, hubbub, mayhem, noise, pandemonium, racket, tumult, uproar

diner *n* automat, cafe, cafeteria, canteen, grill, luncheonette, lunchroom, restaurant, tearoom

dinero *n* see: MONEY *n* 4

dingy *adj* see: DIRTY *adj* 2

dinner *n* 1 banquet, buffet, feast, lunch, meal, repast, smorgasbord, supper

n 2 bread, breakfast, brunch, chow, cuisine, diet, dish, edibles, entree, fare, food, grub, lunch, meals, nosh, nutrition, provisions, rations, snack, supper, victuals, vittles

dip *n* debasement, decline, deterioration, downturn, drop, ebb, erosion, fall, involution, plunge, sag, slide, slip, slump, wane, weakening

v 1 decline, die down, diminish, settle, sink, slide, slip, subside

v 2 bathe, clean, cleanse, clean up, flush, immerse, launder, rinse, rub, scour, scrape, scrub, shower

v 3 avert, deflect, deviate, divert, dodge, pivot, skew, swerve, swing, swivel, turn, veer, wheel, whip

diploma *n* certificate, credential, degree, sheepskin

diplomacy *n* 1 discretion, finesse, savvy, skill, subtlety, tact

n 2 consideration, discretion, poise, regard, savoir-faire, tact, tactfulness, thoughtfulness

diplomat *n* agent, ambassador, consul, delegate, deputy, emissary, envoy

dire *adj* 1 disastrous, dreadful, lamentable, pitiful, sorrowful, tragic

adj 2 appalling, awful, dreadful, fearful, formidable, frightening, frightful, ghastly, horrendous, horrible, offensive, ominous, portentous, scary, shocking, spooky, terrible, terrifying, unpleasant

adj 3 acute, burning, critical, crucial, desperate, grave, heavy, important, major, momentous, ponderous, pressing, profound, serious, severe, solemn, somber, urgent, vital

direct *adj* 1 linear, straight, straightforward, uninterrupted

adj 2 contiguous, current, immediate, instant, nearby, primary, prompt, sudden, timely

adj 3 clear, coherent, easy, elementary, intelligible, logical, lucid, simple, understandable

adj 4 see: SINCERE *adj*

v 1 accompany, escort, guide, lead, usher

v 2 give, implement, impose, inflict, strike

v 3 control, deploy, maneuver, manipulate, use

v 4 address, aim, cast, level, point, train, zero in

v 5 bid, charge, claim, command, demand, enjoin, instruct, order

v 6 carry on, conduct, keep, manage, operate, ordain, oversee, pilot, run

v 7 administer, boss, command, guide, manage, oversee, regulate, steer, supervise

v 8 conduct, control, develop, drive, guide, lead, operate, pilot, route, shepherd, show, steer

v 9 boss, command, control, dominate, govern, handle, influence, lead, manage, manipulate, order, supervise, sway

v 10 see: MANDATE *v*

direction *n* 1 bearings, course, heading, location, position

n 2 address, destination, identification, location, zone

n 3 directive, guideline, instruction, outline, policy, rule

n 4 course, drift, path, strategy, tack, tactic, tendency, tenor, trend

n 5 authority, command, commission, control, domination, jurisdiction, management, mastery, might, power, rule

n 6 administration, administrators, authorities, bureaucracy, civil service, commission, department, forces, government, management, ministry, officials, power, powers, rule, rulers

n 7 behest, bidding, canon, charge, command, criterion, decree, dictate, edict, fiat, guideline, injunction, institution, law, mandate, order, ordinance, precept, prescript, prescription, regulation, rite, rule, ruling, statute, word

n 8 assignment, instruction, reference, referral

directive *n* direction, guideline, instruction, outline, policy, rule

directly *adv* anon, any moment, at once, immediately, instantaneously, instantly, momentarily, now, presently, promptly, quickly, right now, shortly, soon, straightaway, *tout de suite*

director *n* manager

directorship *n* board, body, cabinet, committee, council

directory *n* atlas, compendium, guide, guidebook, handbook, list, listing, manual, phone book, textbook, Yellow Pages

dirge *n* cry, funeral hymn, lament

dirigible *n* balloon, blimp

dirt *n* 1 dung, filth, garbage, manure, muck, mud, slime, sludge

n 2 clay, dry land, dust, earth, ground, land, loam, marl, soil, *terra*, terra firma

n 3 crap, crud, debris, detritus, garbage, junk, litter, refuse, rubbish, rubble, sweepings, trash, waste

n 4 filth, grossness, indecency, obscenity, porn, pornography, ribaldry, smut, trash

dirty *adj* 1 disgusting, foul, lousy, nasty, putrid, rotten, sordid

adj 2 black, dark, dingy, filthy, foul, grimy, grubby, mucky, murky, polluted, seedy, shabby, sooty, squalid, stained, unclean, unlit, unwashed

adj 3 bawdy, coarse, crude, erotic, filthy, foul, gamy, gross, improper, indecent, lascivious, lewd, licentious, nasty, obscene, off-color, pornographic, profane, prurient, racy, rank, raunchy, ribald, risqué, scandalous, smutty, suggestive, tainted, uncouth, vulgar, x-rated

v 1 contaminate, foul, infect, poison, pollute

v 2 defile, discolor, smear, soil, stain, sully, taint, tarnish

disability *n* affliction, calamity, flaw, handicap, impairment, limitation

disable *v* 1 cripple, debilitate, drain, enfeeble, exhaust, sap, undermine, weaken

v 2 cripple, disarm, encumber, freeze, halt, handcuff, immobilize, incapacitate, paralyze, prostrate, stop, stun

disabled *adj* crippled, lame, limping

disabling *adj* disturbing, painful, shocking, traumatic, upsetting

disaffected *adj* alienated, disunited, estranged, separated, weaned

disaffirm *v* contradict, cross, deny, disagree, impugn, negate, rebut, traverse

disagree *v* 1 decline, delay, demur, object

v 2 contradict, cross, deny, disaffirm, impugn, negate, rebut, traverse

v 3 argue, confer, contest, contradict, contrast, debate, dialogue, differ, discord, discuss, dispute, dissent, divide, oppose, vary

disagreeable *adj* 1 distasteful, disturbing, sickening, unappetizing, undesirable, unpalatable, unsavory

adj 2 balking, balky, contrary, cranky, irascible, mean, obstinate, ornery, perverse, wayward

adj 3 annoying, bad, difficult, displeasing, nasty, objectionable, offensive, rotten, sour, unhappy, unpleasant, upsetting

disagreeing *adj* dissenting

disagreement *n* 1 contradiction, discrepancy, hypocrisy, incongruity, inconsistency, paradox, variance

n 2 break, dissension, fight, misunderstanding, quarrel, rift, separation, spat

n 3 altercation, argument, battle, brawl, challenge, combat, controversy, discord, dispute, feud, fight, fracas, fray, hassle, melee, quarrel, rancor, rift, row, ruckus, scrap, scuffle, skirmish, spat, squabble, struggle, tiff, war

n 4 see: CLASH *n* 2

disallow *v* 1 deny, refuse, reject, withhold

v 2 cancel, contradict, deny, forbid, negate, nix, nullify, override, overrule, reject, renege, repeal, revoke, torpedo, veto, void

disappear *v* clear, depart, evaporate, fade, vanish

disappoint *v* disenchant, disillusion, dissatisfy, fail, frustrate, let down

disapproval *n* 1 censure, rejection, repudiation

n 2 ban, refusal, rejection, thumbs down, turndown, veto

disapprove *v* 1 condemn, decline, dismiss, exile, object, refuse, reject, reprobate, repudiate, spurn, turn down

v 2 belittle, deprecate, disfavor, disparage, frown upon, object

v 3 admonish, berate, blame, censure, chide, condemn, lay into, punish, rebuke, reprimand, reproach, reprove, scold, warn

disarm *v* 1 demilitarize

v 2 charm, entice, sway

v 3 attract, flatter, ingratiate

v 4 cripple, disable, encumber, freeze, halt, handcuff, immobilize, incapacitate, paralyze, prostrate, stop, stun

disarmed *adj* defenseless, dependent, exposed, helpless, powerless, susceptible, unprotected, vulnerable, weak

disarray *n* chaos, clutter, confusion, derangement, disorder, jumble, mayhem, mess, mix-up, muddle, predicament, snafu, snarl, tangle, tumult, turmoil

v dislocate, disorder, disorganize, disrupt, disturb, interfere, interrupt, jumble, mess, mix up, muss, rummage, shuffle, sift through, unsettle

disaster *n* 1 calamity, cataclysm, catastrophe, debacle, misfortune, tragedy, upheaval

n 2 bomb, bust, dud, failure, fiasco, flop, turkey

n 3 chaos, damage, destruction, devastation, disorder, harm, havoc, hurt, injury, loss, mayhem, ruin, ruination, tort

n 4 see: ANGUISH *n* 2

n 5 see: ROUT *n*

disastrous *adj* 1 dire, dreadful, lamentable, pitiful, sorrowful, tragic

adj 2 calamitous, cataclysmic, catastrophic, critical, crucial, devastating, fatal, fateful, momentous, ruinous, vital

disavow *v* 1 abjure, deny, disclaim, disown, forswear, reject, renounce, repudiate

v 2 back, fall back, recall, recant, recede, renege, rescind, retract, retreat, retrograde, take back

v 3 see: ABANDON *v* 3

disband *v* disperse, dissipate, dissociate, dissolve, scatter, separate

disbelief *n* distrust, doubt, incredulity, skepticism, unbelief

disburse *v* 1 administer, apportion, deal, dispense, disperse, distribute, dole, expend, give

v 2 see: PAY *v* 2

discard *v* 1 abandon, dispose of, dump, eliminate, empty, quit, reject, scrap, unload

v 2 abandon, break up, cast off, chuck, defect, desert, disavow, disenfranchise, disown, ditch, dump, forsake, jilt, junk, leave, quit, reject, renounce, spurn, strand, throw out

v 3 bare, denude, disrobe, doff, flash, remove, reveal, shed, strip, take off, unclothe, undress

n failure, garbage, junk, reject, scrap, second

discern *v* 1 deduce, determine, glean, learn

v 2 behold, catch, comprehend, conjure, descry, digest, distinguish, espy, fathom, grasp, know, look at, notice, observe, perceive, realize, recognize, savvy, see, sight, take in, understand, view

discernible *adj* appreciable, cognizant, concrete, detectable, noticeable, observable, palpable, perceptible, sensible, tangible, visible

discerning *adj* **1** discreet, discriminating, keen, sensitive, subtle, tactful

adj **2** see: AFRAID *adj* 2

adj **3** see: INTELLIGENT *adj* 4

discernment *n* acumen, astuteness, awareness, cleverness, discrimination, insight, intellect, intuition, keenness, perception, sagacity, sensitivity, shrewdness, understanding, wit

discharge *n* **1** bang, blare, blast, boom, explosion, noise, pop, report, roar

n **2** excretion

n **3** absolution, amnesty, disengagement, dispensation, freedom, moratorium, pardon, release, relief, reprieve, respite, stay, suspension

v **1** ejaculate, shoot, spurt

v **2** bombard, detonate, fire, shoot

v **3** depose, oust, remove, unseat

v **4** cleanse, eliminate, empty, evacuate, excrete, void

v **5** burst, erupt, explode, gush, spew, spout

v **6** emit, fire, hurl, launch, project, shoot

v **7** emanate, emit, expel, project, radiate, release, send

v **8** emancipate, free, liberate, loosen, release, unbind, unchain, unshackle

v **9** drip, emit, exude, leak, ooze, secrete, seep, trickle

v **10** ax, boot, bounce, can, dismiss, drop, fire, impeach, let go, sack, terminate

v **11** clear, clear off, liquidate, pay up, repay, satisfy, settle, square

v **12** abrogate, annul, cancel, contradict, dismantle, dissolve, dwindle, fade, negate, nullify, quash, recall, repeal, rescind, reverse, revoke, set aside, vacate, void

disciple *n* **1** believer, convert, follower, zealot

n **2** admirer, buff, devotee, enthusiast, fan, follower, groupie

n **3** see: BEGINNER *n* 2

disciplinarian *n* authoritarian, autocrat, dictator, enforcer

discipline *n* **1** drill, practice

n **2** persistence, self-control, volition, will, willpower

n **3** dockage, fee, fine, loss, penalty, punishment

n **4** data, facts, information, knowledge, lore, news, science, wisdom

n **5** adversity, difficulty, discomfort, hardness, rigor, severity, strictness, stringency, uneasiness

n **6** study, subject

n **7** art, avocation, business, calling, career, employment, field, gig, job, labor, line, livelihood, occupation, office, profession, pursuit, role, schtick, situation, specialty, task, thing, trade, vocation, work

v **1** castigate, chasten, chastise, correct, punish, torment

v **2** curb, govern, limit, regulate, restrain, retard

v **3** adjudge, condemn, convict, imprison, penalize, punish, sentence

v **4** coach, communicate, condition, convey, cultivate, develop, drill, edify, educate, enlighten, exercise, explain, groom, imbue, impart, implant, improve, inculcate, indoctrinate, inform, infuse, inseminate, inspire, instill, instruct, perfect, practice, prepare, ready, school, teach, train, tutor

disciplined *adj* see: RESTRICTIVE *adj*

disclaim *v* abjure, deny, disavow, disown, forswear, reject, renounce, repudiate

disclose *v* **1** clarify, explain, relate, reveal, unfold

v **2** display, evince, express, imply, indicate, manifest, reflect, reveal, show

v **3** communicate, display, divulge, exhibit, inform, notify, open, reveal, uncover, unveil

v **4** brief, communicate, convey, declare, describe, divulge, explain, impart, inform, narrate, orate, portray, read, recite, recount, relate, report, retell, reveal, share, state, tattle, tell, transmit

disclosure *n* **1** breach, leak, revelation

n **2** breakthrough, discovery, exposition, find, revelation, unearthing

n **3** communication, data, exchange, expression, facts, information, intelligence, knowledge, news, notification

discolor *v* defile, dirty, smear, soil, stain, sully, taint, tarnish

discomfort *n* adversity, difficulty, discipline, hardness, rigor, severity, strictness, stringency, uneasiness

disconnect *v* cut, detach, disengage, dissociate, separate, sever, uncouple, unfasten, unhook, unyoke

discontent *n* dissatisfaction, regret, unhappiness, vexation

discontinue *v* abstain, cease, conclude, desist, end, finish, forbear, freeze, halt, knock off, quit, refrain, sever, stop, terminate

discord *n* **1** antagonism, conflict, disharmony, friction

n **2** battle, clash, competition, conflict,

contest, duel, fight, fighting, rivalry, strife, struggle, war, warfare

n 3 brouhaha, cacophony, chaos, clamor, confusion, din, disorder, hubbub, mayhem, noise, pandemonium, racket, tumult, uproar

n 4 annoyance, bother, conflict, contention, difference, disharmony, dispute, dissension, dissent, dissidence, dissonance, disunity, division, hassle, inconvenience, mischief, nuisance, strife, trouble, variance

n 5 see: QUARREL *n 2*

v 1 clash, conflict, crash, jangle, jar, mismatch

v 2 argue, confer, contest, contradict, contrast, debate, dialogue, differ, disagree, discuss, dispute, dissent, divide, oppose, vary

discotheque *n* bar, bistro, cabaret, cafe, casino, nightclub

discount *n 1* bargain price, cut rate, wholesale

n 2 bargain, buy, deal, promotion, reduction, sale, special, steal

v 1 promote, rebate, reduce

v 2 defy, disregard, exclude, forget, ignore, miss, neglect, omit, ostracize, overlook, overpass, pass, pass by, pass over, shun, skip, slight, snub

v 3 see: ABUSE *v 4*

discourage *v 1* avert, caution, deter, dissuade, distract, divert

v 2 chill, deject, demoralize, depress, dishearten, disparage

v 3 appall, daunt, dismay, horrify, panic, petrify, scare, shock, terrify, unnerve

discouraged *adj* beaten, clobbered, defeated, dejected, depressed, licked, whipped

discouraging *adj* see: GLOOMY *adj 5*

discourse *n 1* conference, discussion, interview, meeting, query

n 2 assignment, diatribe, exercise, homily, lecture, lesson, preaching, sermon

n 3 expression, speaking, speech, statement, talk, utterance, verbalization, word

n 4 caucus, chat, colloquy, conference, conversation, debate, dialogue, discussion, exchange, forum, interchange, intercourse, interlocution, meeting, talk

n 5 article, composition, dissertation, essay, manuscript, memoir, monograph, paper, report, study, theme, thesis, tract, treatise, work

v discuss, elaborate, expatiate, ramble, sermonize

discourteous *adj* audacious, boorish, disrespectful, ill-behaved, ill-bred, ill-mannered, impertinent, impolite, insolent, rude, surly, uncalled for, uncivil, uncivilized, uncouth, uncultured, unpolished, unrefined

discover *v 1* debunk, expose, show up, uncloak, unmask, unshroud

v 2 chance, encounter, find, happen, hit, luck, meet, stumble

v 3 ascertain, catch on, determine, find out, hear, learn, listen, uncover, unearth

v 4 ascertain, catch, descry, detect, encounter, espy, ferret, find, locate, spot, turn up, uncover

discovered *adj* found, located, uncovered

discovery *n 1* detection, finding, perception

n 2 breakthrough, disclosure, exposition, find, revelation, unearthing

discredit *n* censure, contempt, disfavor, disgrace, dishonor, disparagement, disrepute, humiliation, infamy, notoriety, scandal, shame

v debunk, disprove, explode

discreet *adj 1* off the record, private, quiet, secretive

adj 2 discerning, discriminating, keen, sensitive, subtle, tactful

adj 3 dry, homely, modest, plain, simple, unadorned, undecorated, unembellished, unembroidered, ungarnished, unpretentious

adj 4 calculating, careful, cautious, circumspect, considerate, gingerly, guarded, heedful, judicious, provident, prudent, restrained, reticent, safe, shrewd, wary

discrepancy *n* contradiction, disagreement, hypocrisy, incongruity, inconsistency, paradox, variance

discrete *adj* alternate, another, certain, different, disparate, dissimilar, distinct, diverse, numerous, other, separate, several, some, unlike, various, varying

discretion *n 1* diplomacy, finesse, savvy, skill, subtlety, tact

n 2 consideration, diplomacy, poise, regard, savoir-faire, tact, tactfulness, thoughtfulness

n 3 assumption, conclusion, conjecture, estimate, guess, judgment, notion, presumption, theorization

discretionary *adj* elective

discriminate *v 1* classify, define, differentiate, distinguish, isolate, separate

v 2 differentiate, exclude, isolate, ostracize, segregate, separate, sequester

discriminating *adj 1* discerning, discreet, keen, sensitive, subtle, tactful

adj 2 careful, cautious, choosy, fastidious,

finicky, fussy, meticulous, nit-picking, particular, persnickety, picky, selective
adj 3 see: INTELLIGENT *adj* 4

discrimination *n* 1 bias, bigotry, chauvinism, intolerance, parochialism, partiality, prejudice, provincialism, racism, sexism
n 2 acumen, astuteness, awareness, cleverness, discernment, insight, intellect, intuition, keenness, perception, sagacity, sensitivity, shrewdness, understanding, wit
n 3 apartheid, racism, segregation

discuss *v* 1 confer, interview, meet
v 2 discourse, elaborate, expatiate, ramble, sermonize
v 3 chat, chatter, converse, parley, speak, visit
v 4 advise, communicate, confer, consult, group, huddle, parley, powwow
v 5 see: COMMUNICATE *v* 2, 4
v 6 see: DISAGREE *v* 3

discussion *n* 1 bull session, dialogue, rap, talk
n 2 conference, discourse, interview, meeting, query
n 3 argument, contention, controversy, debate, dialogue, dispute
n 4 caucus, chat, colloquy, conference, conversation, debate, dialogue, discourse, exchange, forum, interchange, intercourse, interlocution, meeting, talk

disdain *n* 1 aspersion, contempt, derision, irony, mockery, ridicule, sarcasm, satire, scorn
n 2 see: VANITY *n*
v 1 frown, glare, gloom, glower, grimace, lower, pout, scowl, sulk
v 2 abhor, abominate, bristle, desecrate, despise, detest, dislike, hate, loathe, reject, revile, scorn

disdainful *adj* arrogant, cavalier, conceited, contemptuous, curt, dictatorial, grandiose, haughty, huffy, insolent, lofty, lordly, moody, obtrusive, overbearing, patronizing, proud, scornful, snooty, stuck up, supercilious, superior, vain

disease *n* 1 affliction, ailment, complaint, condition, disorder, evil, harm, ill, illness, infirmity, malady, sickness
n 2 bane, curse, evil, misfortune, pestilence, plague, scourge

diseased *adj* see: ILL *adj* 3

disembodied *adj* see: SPIRITUAL *adj* 2

disembowel *v* clean, dress, eviscerate, fillet, gut

disenchant *v* 1 disappoint, disillusion, dissatisfy, fail, frustrate, let down
v 2 disillusion

disenfranchise *v* see: ABANDON *v* 3

disengage *v* 1 cut, detach, disconnect, dissociate, separate, sever, uncouple, unfasten, unhook, unyoke
v 2 extricate, loosen, open, unbind, unclasp, undo, unfasten, unknot, unloose, unloosen, untie

disengagement *n* absolution, amnesty, discharge, dispensation, freedom, moratorium, pardon, release, relief, reprieve, respite, stay, suspension

disentangle *v* undo, unravel, untangle, unwind

disfavor *n* 1 censure, contempt, discredit, disgrace, dishonor, disparagement, disrepute, humiliation, infamy, notoriety, scandal, shame
n 2 aversion, dislike, displeasure, dissatisfaction, distaste, opposition
v 1 disgrace, dishonor, humiliate, reproach, shame, stain, tarnish
v 2 belittle, deprecate, disapprove, disparage, frown upon, slight

disgorge *v* choke, cough, gag, throw up, vomit

disgrace *n* 1 corruption, crime, exposé, outrage, scandal
n 2 censure, contempt, discredit, disfavor, dishonor, disparagement, disrepute, humiliation, infamy, notoriety, scandal, shame
v disfavor, dishonor, humiliate, reproach, shame, stain, tarnish

disgraceful *adj* 1 see: ILLICIT *adj*
adj 2 see: MONSTROUS *adj* 2

disguise *n* camouflage, cloak, costume, cover, curtain, mask, pretense, shield, shroud, veil
v 1 masquerade, pass, pose, posture, pretend
v 2 camouflage, cloak, conceal, cover, darken, envelop, hide, mask, occult, seclude, shield, shroud, veil

disguised *adj* hidden

disgust *n* aversion, contempt, distaste, horror, loathing, nausea, repugnance, repulsion, revulsion
v abhor, nauseate, repel, repulse, revolt, sicken

disgusted *adj* bored, jaded, sick, tired, weary

disgusting *adj* 1 dirty, foul, lousy, nasty, putrid, rotten, sordid
adj 2 abhorrent, abominable, appalling, detestable, dreadful, evil, frightful, ghast-

ly, hateful, horrible, horrid, loathsome, odious, repulsive, revolting, shocking

dish *n* 1 bread, breakfast, brunch, chow, cuisine, diet, dinner, edibles, entree, fare, food, grub, lunch, meals, nosh, nutrition, provisions, rations, snack, supper, victuals, vittles

n 2 plate, platter, saucer

n 3 chalice, container, cup, Dixie cup, glass, goblet, mug, shot glass, stein, tumbler, vessel, wineglass

disharmony *n* 1 antagonism, conflict, discord, friction

n 2 see: TROUBLE *n* 5

dishearten *v* 1 chill, deject, demoralize, depress, discourage, disparage

v 2 burden, deject, depress, grieve, hurt, lament, sadden, weigh down, wound

disheartening *adj* see: GLOOMY *adj* 5

disheveled *adj* careless, messy, scruffy, slatternly, slipshod, sloppy, sloven, slovenly, tacky, uncombed, unkempt, untidy

dishonest *adj* 1 cheating, conniving, deceitful, deceptive, disloyal, faithless, false, insidious, manipulative, perfidious, sneaky, traitorous, treacherous, unfaithful, untrue, untrustworthy

adj 2 see: EVIL *adj* 4

dishonesty *n* 1 corruption, depravity, immorality, impurity, vice, wickedness, wrong

n 2 cheating, deceit, deception, fraud, hoax, lie, sham, subterfuge, trickery

n 3 falsehood, mendacity, untruthfulness

dishonor *n* 1 censure, contempt, discredit, disfavor, disgrace, disparagement, disrepute, humiliation, infamy, notoriety, scandal, shame

n 2 see: CRIME *n* 3

v 1 disfavor, disgrace, humiliate, reproach, shame, stain, tarnish

v 2 adulterate, corrupt, debase, debauch, defile, demoralize, pervert, ruin, seduce, taint

v 3 see: BELITTLE *v* 1

disillusion *v* 1 disappoint, disenchant, dissatisfy, fail, frustrate, let down

v 2 disenchant

disinclined *adj* afraid, averse, hesitant, indisposed, loath, opposed, recalcitrant, reluctant, shy, timid, uneager, unwilling

disintegrate *v* 1 cave in, collapse, drop, fall, go down, keel over, pitch, plunge, slump, spill, topple, tumble

v 2 corrupt, crumble, decay, decompose, degenerate, deteriorate, perish, putrefy, rot, smell, spoil, taint, wane, weaken, wither

disinterest *n* acedia, apathy, disregard, indifference, lassitude, lethargy, listlessness

disinterested *adj* aloof, blasé, calm, careless, casual, composed, cool, detached, diffident, distant, indifferent, informal, inhibited, nonchalant, numb, remote, reserved, shy, unconcerned, unfriendly, uninterested, withdrawn

disjoin *v* breach, break up, cleave, dismember, disrupt, dissect, dissever, disunite, divide, divorce, part, polarize, rupture, separate, sever, split, sunder

disk *n* dial, display, gauge, indicator, measure, meter, pointer, selector

diskettes *n* bubble memory, floppy, hard disk, media, memory, RAM

dislike *n* 1 acrimony, animosity, antagonism, antipathy, aversion, bitterness, enmity, gall, hate, hatred, hostility, ill will, malice, rancor, spite, venom, vindictiveness

n 2 aversion, disfavor, displeasure, dissatisfaction, distaste, opposition

v abhor, abominate, bristle, desecrate, despise, detest, disdain, hate, loathe, reject, revile, scorn

dislocate *v* 1 dislodge, displace, disturb, move, oust, remove, shift, ship, transfer

v 2 disarray, disorder, disorganize, disrupt, disturb, interfere, interrupt, jumble, mess, mix up, muss, rummage, shuffle, sift through, unsettle

dislodge *v* 1 dislocate, displace, disturb, move, oust, remove, shift, ship, transfer

v 2 capsize, collapse, defeat, knock over, overthrow, overturn, tip over, topple, tumble, turn over, upset

disloyal *adj* cheating, conniving, deceitful, deceptive, dishonest, faithless, false, insidious, manipulative, perfidious, sneaky, traitorous, treacherous, unfaithful, untrue, untrustworthy

dismal *adj* 1 bare, barren, bleak, desolate, gaunt, grim

adj 2 cheerless, cloudy, dim, drab, dull, gray, overcast

adj 3 abnormal, depressing, funereal, ghastly, gloomy, gruesome, macabre, morbid, sepulchral

adj 4 cloudy, foggy, gray, hazy, misty, murky, overcast, steamy, vaporous, vapory

adj 5 doleful, gloomy, lamentable, melancholy, mournful, plaintive, regretful, regrettable, rueful, sorrowful, woeful

dismantle *v* 1 bare, deprive, divest, strip

v 2 annihilate, decimate, demolish, destroy, destruct, devastate, overturn, pulverize, raze, rub out, ruin, shatter, smash, tear down, undo, wreck

v 3 abrogate, annul, cancel, contradict, discharge, dissolve, dwindle, fade, negate, nullify, quash, recall, repeal, rescind, reverse, revoke, set aside, vacate, void

dismay *v* appall, daunt, discourage, horrify, panic, petrify, scare, shock, terrify, unnerve

n see: FEAR *n* 3

dismember *v* 1 cripple, maim, mangle, mutilate

v 2 castrate, debilitate, emasculate, enervate, geld, unman, unnerve

v 3 breach, break up, cleave, disjoin, disrupt, dissect, dissever, disunite, divide, divorce, part, polarize, rupture, separate, sever, split, sunder

dismiss *v* 1 pension, retire, superannuate

v 2 boot out, chuck out, eject, evacuate, evict, expel, kick out, throw out

v 3 condemn, decline, disapprove, exile, object, refuse, reject, reprobate, repudiate, spurn, turn down

v 4 ax, boot, bounce, can, discharge, drop, fire, impeach, let go, sack, terminate

v 5 see: BAR *v* 1

dismissal *n* 1 consignment, dispatch, forwarding, sending

n 2 ejection, expulsion, extraction, firing, impeachment, ouster, removal, termination

dismount *v* alight, come down, descend, get off, land, settle

disobedience *n* see: CRIME *n* 3

disobedient *adj* 1 bad, ill-behaved, misbehaving, mischievous, naughty

adj 2 defiant, insubordinate, insurgent, mutinous, rebellious, seditious

disobey *v* defy, ignore, infringe, obstruct, oppose, rebel, resist, violate

disorder *n* 1 affliction, ailment, complaint, condition, disease, evil, harm, ill, illness, infirmity, malady, sickness

n 2 chaos, damage, destruction, devastation, disaster, harm, havoc, hurt, injury, loss, mayhem, ruin, ruination, tort

n 3 chaos, clutter, confusion, derangement, disarray, jumble, mayhem, mess, mix-up, muddle, predicament, snafu, snarl, tangle, tumult, turmoil

n 4 see: CLAMOR *n*

n 5 see: COMMOTION *n* 1

v 1 confuse, jostle, mix, scramble, shuffle

v 2 agitate, derange, disturb, fluster, rock, ruffle, shake, sicken, unhinge, unsettle, upset

v 3 disarray, dislocate, disorganize, disrupt, disturb, interfere, interrupt, jumble, mess, mix up, muss, rummage, shuffle, sift through, unsettle

disorderly *adj* see: TURBULENT *adj*

disorganize *v* disarray, dislocate, disorder, disrupt, disturb, interfere, interrupt, jumble, mess, mix up, muss, rummage, shuffle, sift through, unsettle

disown *v* 1 abjure, deny, disavow, disclaim, forswear, reject, renounce, repudiate

v 2 see: ABANDON *v* 3

disparage *v* 1 censure, condemn, denounce, inveigh

v 2 befoul, besmirch, blacken, darken, defame, injure, libel, malign, revile, scandalize, slander, slur, smear, soil, tear down, traduce

v 3 chill, deject, demoralize, discourage, dishearten

v 4 belittle, deprecate, disapprove, disfavor, frown upon, object

v 5 abuse, asperse, bad-mouth, belittle, condemn, damage, decry, defame, degrade, denigrate, denounce, deprecate, detract, diminish, discount, insult, knock, malign, put down, revile, run down, slander, take away, vilify

disparagement *n* 1 see: HUMILIATION *n*

n 2 see: INSULT *n*

disparaging *adj* 1 derogatory, insulting, malicious, nasty, sarcastic, snide

adj 2 captious, carping, censorious, critical, cutting, faultfinding, hairsplitting, nit-picking

disparate *adj* 1 different, diverse, incongruous, opposite, unequal, unlike, unmatched, unrelated

adj 2 aberrant, abnormal, anomalous, artificial, atypical, contrived, deviant, divergent, incongruous, irregular, off-key, uncharacteristic, unnatural

adj 3 alternate, another, certain, different, discrete, dissimilar, distinct, diverse, numerous, other, separate, several, some, unlike, various, varying

disparity *n* 1 split

n 2 contradiction, difference, dissimilarity, gap, inconsistency

dispassionate *adj* 1 apathetic, unemotional, unresponsive

adj 2 see: FAIR *adj* 7

dispatch *n* 1 article, bulletin, byline, column, communication, editorial, feature, headline, item, newsletter, report, story, vignette

n 2 alacrity, expedition, haste, hastiness, hurry, hustle, precipitancy, precipitation, quickness, rush, rustle, speed, swiftness *n* 3 alacrity, cadence, celerity, gait, pace, quickness, rapidity, rate, speed, step, stride, swiftness, trot, velocity, walk

n 4 consignment, dismissal, forwarding, sending

v 1 address, channel, consign, export, forward, mail, post, remit, route, send, ship, transmit, transport

v 2 abolish, annihilate, assassinate, bump off, butcher, decimate, destroy, execute, exterminate, hang, hit, kill, knock off, liquidate, massacre, murder, put away, rub out, slaughter, slay, wipe out

dispel *v* 1 disperse, disseminate, dissipate, scatter, strew

v 2 see: BANISH *v* 1

dispensary *n* asylum, clinic, hospital, infirmary, institution

dispensation *n* 1 absolution, amnesty, discharge, disengagement, freedom, moratorium, pardon, release, relief, reprieve, respite, stay, suspension

n 2 consideration, courtesy, favor, indulgence, kindness, privilege, respect, service

n 3 allotment, allowance, apportionment, budget, dispersion, lot, measure, part, percentage, portion, quota, ration, share, slice

dispense *v* 1 handle, maneuver, manipulate, ply, swing, wield

v 2 administer, construct, move along, plan, prepare, process, treat

v 3 administer, apportion, deal, disburse, disperse, distribute, dole, expend, give

v 4 arrange, cater, deliver, dish out, feed, furnish, give, hand, nourish, nurture, organize, provide, purvey, serve, supply, sustain

disperse *v* 1 dispel, disseminate, dissipate, scatter, strew

v 2 administer, apportion, deal, disburse, dispense, distribute, dole, expend, give

v 3 beam, burn, emit, gleam, glisten, radiate, shed, shine, transmit

v 4 disband, dissipate, dissociate, dissolve, scatter, separate

v 5 advertise, announce, blaze, broadcast, circulate, declare, disseminate, proclaim, promulgate, publish

dispersion *n* see: ALLOWANCE *n* 2

displace *v* 1 cut out, supplant, usurp

v 2 dislocate, dislodge, disturb, move, oust, remove, shift, ship, transfer

v 3 banish, cast out, deport, dispel, exile, expatriate, expel, extradite, ostracize, oust, relegate, remove

v 4 lose

display *n* 1 console, CRT, monitor, screen, terminal

n 2 dial, disk, gauge, indicator, measure, meter, pointer, selector

n 3 array, blare, exhibit, exhibition, fanfare, fuss, parade, performance, presentation, procession, publicity, show, showing

v 1 exhibit, post, proclaim

v 2 exhibit, flaunt, manifest, parade, promenade

v 3 disclose, evince, express, imply, indicate, manifest, reflect, reveal, show

v 4 communicate, disclose, divulge, exhibit, inform, notify, open, reveal, uncover, unveil

v 5 demonstrate, describe, draw, establish, examine, exhibit, explain, present, prove, show, sketch, tell

displeasing *adj* annoying, bad, difficult, disagreeable, nasty, objectionable, offensive, rotten, sour, unhappy, unpleasant, upsetting

displeasure *n* aversion, disfavor, dislike, dissatisfaction, distaste, opposition

disposal *n* 1 sale

n 2 arrangement, disposition, distribution, grouping, ordering, sequence

dispose *v* arrange, array, marshal, order, organize, systemize

disposed *adj* accommodating, agreeing, amenable, eager, glad, inclined, pleased, pliant, responsive, willing

disposition *n* 1 confidence, feeling, frame of mind, mentality, mood, morale, outlook, state

n 2 attitude, feeling, humor, mind, mood, spirit, temper, timbre, tone, vein

n 3 bent, fancy, fondness, idea, inclination, liking, mind, notion, pleasure, propensity, yen

n 4 air, attitude, bearing, calmness, carriage, demeanor, poise, pose, posture, presence, set, stance

n 5 aptitude, character, complexion, distinctiveness, heart, humor, identity, inclination, individuality, makeup, nature, personality, quality, spirit, state, temperament, tendency

n 6 arrangement, disposal, distribution, grouping, ordering, sequence

disprove *v* 1 break, confound, confute, contend, contradict, deny, dispute, rebut, refute

v 2 debunk, discredit, explode

disputatious *adj* argumentative, cantankerous, contentious, controversial, debatable, ill-natured, litigious, ornery

dispute n 1 boycott, picket, strike, walkout

n 2 argument, contention, controversy, debate, dialogue

n 3 battle, combat, conflagration, encounter, fight, struggle, war

n 4 altercation, argument, battle, brawl, challenge, combat, controversy, disagreement, discord, feud, fight, fracas, fray, hassle, melee, quarrel, rancor, rift, row, ruckus, scrap, scuffle, skirmish, spat, squabble, struggle, tiff, war

n 5 see: CLASH n 2

n 6 see: TROUBLE n 5

v 1 challenge, doubt, mistrust, query, question

v 2 break, confound, confute, contend, contradict, deny, disprove, rebut, refute

v 3 argue, confer, contest, contradict, contrast, debate, dialogue, differ, disagree, discord, discuss, dissent, divide, oppose, vary

v 4 argue, altercate, battle, bicker, brawl, clash, conflict, engage, equivocate, feud, fight, fray, haggle, hassle, quarrel, quibble, row, scrap, spar, squabble, wrangle

v 5 see: COMPETE v

disquiet n annoyance, anxiety, apprehension, bother, care, concern, disquietude, doubt, irritation, misgiving, reservation, restlessness, restraint, skepticism, trouble, uneasiness, vexation, worry

disquietude n annoyance, anxiety, apprehension, bother, care, concern, disquiet, doubt, irritation, misgiving, reservation, restlessness, restraint, skepticism, trouble, uneasiness, vexation, worry

disregard n 1 absence, error, neglect, omission, oversight, slip-up

n 2 acedia, apathy, disinterest, indifference, lassitude, lethargy, listlessness

v defy, discount, exclude, forget, ignore, miss, neglect, omit, ostracize, overlook, overpass, pass, pass by, pass over, shun, skip, slight, snub

disrepute n see: HUMILIATION n

disrespect n see: INSULT n

disrespectful adj 1 blasphemous, heretical, irreverent, sacrilegious

adj 2 abusive, contemptuous, derisive, insulting, nasty, offensive, slighting

adj 3 arrogant, cocky, flip, flippant, impertinent, impudent, wise

adj 4 audacious, bold, brash, brazen, cheeky, daring, forward, fresh, impertinent, impudent, insolent, irreverent, nervy, pert, rude, sassy, saucy

adj 5 audacious, boorish, discourteous, ill-behaved, ill-bred, ill-mannered, impertinent, impolite, insolent, rude, surly, uncalled for, uncivil, uncivilized, uncouth, uncultured, unpolished, unrefined

disrobe v bare, denude, discard, doff, flash, remove, reveal, shed, strip, take off, unclothe, undress

disrupt v 1 claw, cleave, divide, rend, rip, rive, scratch, split, tear

v 2 disarray, dislocate, disorder, disorganize, disturb, interfere, interrupt, jumble, mess, mix up, muss, rummage, shuffle, sift through, unsettle

v 3 see: SEPARATE v 7

dissatisfaction n 1 discontent, regret, unhappiness, vexation

n 2 aversion, disfavor, dislike, displeasure, distaste, opposition

dissatisfy v disappoint, disenchant, disillusion, fail, frustrate, let down

dissect v 1 breach, break up, cleave, disjoin, dismember, disrupt, dissever, disunite, divide, divorce, part, polarize, rupture, separate, sever, split, sunder

v 2 examine

v 3 ax, carve, chip, chop, cleave, cut, fell, hack, hew, mangle, mutilate, notch, pulverize, rend, saw, sever, slice, sliver, snip, split, sunder, whittle

disseminate v 1 dispel, disperse, dissipate, scatter, strew

v 2 diffuse, distribute, permeate, spread, sprinkle, strew

v 3 broadcast, dissipate, distribute, scatter, sow, spread, strew, transmit

v 4 advertise, announce, blaze, broadcast, circulate, declare, disperse, proclaim, promulgate, publish

dissension n 1 break, disagreement, fight, misunderstanding, quarrel, rift, separation, spat

n 2 see: TROUBLE n 5

dissent v argue, confer, contest, contradict, contrast, debate, dialogue, differ, disagree, discord, discuss, dispute, divide, oppose, vary

n see: TROUBLE n 5

dissenting adj disagreeing

dissertation n article, composition, discourse, essay, manuscript, memoir, monograph, paper, report, study, theme, thesis, tract, treatise, work

dissever v see: SEPARATE v 7

dissidence n see: TROUBLE n 5

dissident adj dissenting

n agitator, defector, heretic, iconoclast, insurgent, malcontent, maverick, misfit, nonconformist, rebel, renegade, traitor, troublemaker, turncoat

dissimilar *adj* alternate, another, certain, different, discrete, disparate, distinct, diverse, numerous, other, separate, several, some, unlike, various, varying

dissimilarity *n* **1** contrast, difference, distinction, diversion, opposition

n **2** contradiction, difference, disparity, gap, inconsistency

dissipate *v* **1** dispel, disperse, disseminate, scatter, strew

v **2** cast away, consume, drivel, empty, fritter, lavish, squander, throw away, use up, waste

v **3** disband, disperse, dissociate, dissolve, scatter, separate

v **4** broadcast, disseminate, distribute, scatter, sow, spread, strew, transmit

dissociate *v* **1** disband, disperse, dissipate, dissolve, scatter, separate

v **2** cut, detach, disconnect, disengage, separate, sever, uncouple, unfasten, unhook, unyoke

dissolution *n* annulment, divorce, separation, split

dissolve *v* **1** cash, convert, exchange, liquidate, tender

v **2** flux, fuse, liquefy, melt, run, thaw

v **3** adjourn, cap, climax, complete, conclude, consummate, crown, culminate, end, finalize, finish, terminate, wind up, wrap up

v **4** disband, disperse, dissipate, dissociate, scatter, separate

v **5** abrogate, annul, cancel, contradict, discharge, dismantle, dwindle, fade, negate, nullify, quash, recall, repeal, rescind, reverse, revoke, set aside, vacate, void

dissolved *adj* bankrupt, broke, busted, destitute, insolvent, out of business, penniless, ruined

dissonance *n* see: TROUBLE *n* 5

dissuade *v* avert, caution, deter, discourage, distract, divert

distance *n* **1** reach, span, stretch

n **2** future, horizon, outlook, perspective, purview, vision, vista

n **3** coolness, reserve, restraint, reticence

n **4** circle, compass, confines, dimension, extension, extent, length, limit, orbit, purview, range, reach, realm, scope, size, spectrum, sweep, width

distant *adj* **1** forbidding, snobbish, unfriendly

adj **2** far, faraway, obscure, out-of-the-way, outlying, remote, removed

adj **3** cold, coldhearted, emotionless, frigid, glacial, icy, impersonal, indifferent, unemotional, unfriendly

adj **4** aloof, blasé, calm, careless, casual, composed, cool, detached, diffident, disinterested, indifferent, informal, inhibited, nonchalant, numb, remote, reserved, shy, unconcerned, unfriendly, uninterested, withdrawn

distaste *n* **1** aversion, contempt, disgust, horror, loathing, nausea, repugnance, repulsion, revulsion

n **2** aversion, disfavor, dislike, displeasure, dissatisfaction, opposition

distasteful *adj* disagreeable, disturbing, sickening, unappetizing, undesirable, unpalatable, unsavory

distend *v* amplify, bloat, dilate, enlarge, expand, fatten, grow, increase, inflate, magnify, stretch, swell, widen

distended *adj* bloated, inflated, puffy, swollen, tumescent, tumid, turgid

distill *v* compress, condense, express, extract, purify, refine

distinct *adj* **1** clear, legible, readable, understandable

adj **2** accurate, certain, explicit, incontestable, infallible, perfect, unerring

adj **3** autonomous, free, independent, lone, separate, sovereign, unconnected

adj **4** blunt, clear, clear-cut, concise, decisive, definite, definitive, exact, explicit, precise, specific, unambiguous

adj **5** alternate, another, certain, different, discrete, disparate, dissimilar, diverse, numerous, other, separate, several, some, unlike, various, varying

adj **6** apparent, clear, conspicuous, evident, given, indisputable, indubitable, manifest, obvious, patent, plain, presumed, self-evident, straightforward, true, unambiguous, unequivocal, unmistakable

distinction *n* **1** deviation, difference, variation

n **2** characteristic, difference, feature, peculiarity

n **3** contrast, difference, dissimilarity, diversion, opposition

n **4** achievement, prestige, rank, recognition, stance, stature, status

n **5** degree, enhancement, nuance, shade, subtlety, touch, trace, variation

n **6** brilliance, celebrity, excellence, fame, glory, halo, honor, luster, note, popularity, prominence, renown, repute, splendor

n **7** see: COMMENDATION *n* 2

distinctive *adj* characteristic, differentiating, lone, one, particular, peculiar, select, single, solitary, special, unique, unusual

distinctiveness *n* 1 individuality, oneness, singularity, singularness, unity

n 2 individuality, originality, uniqueness

n 3 aptitude, character, complexion, disposition, heart, humor, identity, inclination, individuality, makeup, nature, personality, quality, spirit, state, temperament, tendency

distinctness *n* 1 definition, design, outline, precision, specificity

n 2 clarity, clearness, exactness, freshness, lucidity, plainness, purity

distinguish *v* 1 identify, know, name, recognize, specify

v 2 classify, define, differentiate, discriminate, isolate, separate

v 3 dignify, elevate, exalt, glorify, grace, honor

v 4 behold, catch, comprehend, conjure, descry, digest, discern, espy, fathom, grasp, know, look at, notice, observe, perceive, realize, recognize, savvy, see, sight, take in, understand, view

distinguished *adj* 1 acclaimed, celebrated, eminent, esteemed, excellent, famed, famous, foremost, illustrious, notable, outstanding, prestigious, prominent, renowned, well-known

adj 2 central, chief, dominant, famed, great, key, leading, main, major, number one, outstanding, predominant, preeminent, primary, prime, principal, prominent, star, successful, superior, top

distort *v* 1 deform, misshape, torture, warp

v 2 bias, color, embellish, exaggerate, influence, slant

v 3 bias, corrupt, misrepresent, pervert, skew, slant, warp

v 4 coil, corkscrew, curl, entwine, gnarl, spiral, twist, wind

v 5 angle, confuse, deceive, falsify, garble, incline, misconstrue, misinterpret, misquote, misread, misrepresent, misunderstand, mix up, mumble, slant, slope, taint, twist

distract *v* 1 avert, caution, deter, discourage, divert

v 2 befuddle, bewilder, confuse, daze, dizzy, embarrass, fluster, mix up, muddle, rattle, ruffle, trick, unglue, unhinge

v 3 disturb, divert, interrupt

distracted *adj* 1 heedless, inattentive, unaware, unheeding, unnoticing, unobservant, unperceiving, unwatchful

adj 2 anxious, careworn, distraught, dis-

tressed, frantic, harassed, tormented, troubled, upset, worried

adj 3 see: ENGROSSED *adj* 2

distraction *n* 1 avocation, diversion, hobby, moonlighting, pastime, sideline

n 2 break, delay, disturbance, diversion, holdup, interference, interruption, pause

n 3 amusement, diversion, enjoyment, entertainment, frolic, fun, game, hobby, pastime, play, recreation, sport

n 4 aberration, abnormality, craziness, delusion, dementia, derangement, eccentricity, fugue, hallucination, insanity, irregularity, lunacy, madness, mania, psychosis, unbalance

distraught *adj* 1 crushed, defeated, emotional, overcome, subdued

adj 2 demented, deranged, insane, mentally ill, psychotic

adj 3 anxious, careworn, distracted, distressed, frantic, harassed, tormented, troubled, upset, worried

distress *n* 1 grief, melancholy, sadness, sorrow, suffering

n 2 anxiety, apprehension, stress, sweat, worry

n 3 adversity, affliction, blow, burden, calamity, difficulty, hardship, mischance, misfortune, mishap, relapse, reversal, setback, suffering, tragedy, trouble

n 4 agony, anguish, bale, concern, misery, nightmare, pain, sadness, sorrow, suffering, torment, travail, tribulation, trouble, woe, worry

v 1 disturb, move, rend, sadden, wring

v 2 afflict, aggrieve, bother, burden, grieve, hurt, injure, pain

v 3 see: ANNOY *v* 1

distressed *adj* anxious, careworn, distracted, distraught, frantic, harassed, tormented, troubled, upset, worried

distressing *adj* see: GLOOMY *adj* 5

distribute *v* 1 diffuse, disseminate, permeate, spread, sprinkle, strew

v 2 barter, market, merchandise, peddle, retail, sell, vend, wholesale

v 3 administer, apportion, deal, disburse, dispense, disperse, dole, expend, give

v 4 bring out, get out, give out, go to press, issue, print, publish, put out, reissue, reprint, set type

v 5 broadcast, disseminate, dissipate, scatter, sow, spread, strew, transmit

v 6 allocate, allot, allow, apportion, assign, designate, divide, divvy, earmark, give, measure, parcel, partition, portion, prorate, quota, ration, section, share, slice

distribution n 1 allocation, marketing, merchandising, selling, share, sharing

n 2 bar graph, chart, diagram, figure, flowchart, graph, histogram, outline, pie chart, plot, table

n 3 arrangement, disposal, disposition, grouping, ordering, sequence

distributor n see: MEDIATOR n 3

district n 1 area, domain, environs, jurisdiction, locality, neighborhood, parish, precinct, province, range, region, section, sphere, vicinity, ward, zone

n 2 county, jurisdiction, municipality, parish, precinct, township, ward

distrust n 1 disbelief, doubt, incredulity, skepticism, unbelief

n 2 apprehension, doubt, fear, hesitation, misbelief, mistrust, suspicion, wariness

v doubt, fear, mistrust, suspect

distrusted adj questionable, suspect, suspicious

distrustful adj cynical, doubtful, dubious, incredulous, leery, questionable, shy, skeptical, skittish, suspicious, uncertain, unsure

distrusting adj covetous, envious, jealous, resentful, suspicious

disturb v 1 distress, move, rend, sadden, wring

v 2 dislocate, dislodge, displace, move, oust, remove, shift, ship, transfer

v 3 affect, bother, burden, concern, daunt, faze, intimidate, oppress, upset, worry

v 4 agitate, derange, disorder, fluster, rock, ruffle, shake, sicken, unhinge, unsettle, upset

v 5 disarray, dislocate, disorder, disorganize, disrupt, interfere, interrupt, jumble, mess, mix up, muss, rummage, shuffle, sift through, unsettle

v 6 annoy, antagonize, argue, bother, bug, concern, distress, goad, harass, hassle, inconvenience, irk, irritate, pain, perturb, strain, stress, taunt, trouble, try, upset, worry

v 7 distract, divert, interrupt

disturbance n 1 aggravation, annoyance, irritant, irritation

n 2 blow, jolt, shock, trauma, upheaval, upset

n 3 break, delay, distraction, diversion, holdup, interference, interruption, pause

n 4 anarchy, chaos, commotion, confusion, disorder, fracas, fray, outbreak, riot, ruckus, storm, tempest

disturbing adj 1 disabling, painful, shocking, traumatic, upsetting

adj 2 disagreeable, distasteful, sickening, unappetizing, undesirable, unpalatable, unsavory

adj 3 see: NOISY adj

disunite v see: SEPARATE v 7

disunited adj alienated, disaffected, estranged, separated, weaned

disunity n see: TROUBLE n 5

ditch n canal, channel, conduit, crevice, curb, cut, duct, furrow, gorge, groove, gully, gutter, passageway, ravine, rut, trench, trough

v 1 abandon, break up, cast off, chuck, defect, desert, disavow, discard, disenfranchise, disown, dump, forsake, jilt, junk, leave, quit, reject, renounce, spurn, strand, throw out

v 2 see: HIDE v 3

ditto adv repeatedly

ditty n 1 limerick, lyric, madrigal, poem, poetry, rhyme, song, sonnet, verse

n 2 doggerel

diurnal adj daily

divan n couch, lounge, settee, sofa

dive n 1 comedown, decline, decrease, descent, drop, failure, fall, plunge, regression, setback, slide, tumble

n 2 bar, barroom, cocktail lounge, den, dump, gin mill, hangout, haunt, joint, lounge, pub, rathskeller, saloon, tavern, watering hole

v 1 descend, drop, fall, lapse, leap, lower, plummet, plunge, sink, swoop

v 2 lunge, lurch, pitch, plunge

diverge v detour, deviate, differ, digress, meander, swerve

divergent adj aberrant, abnormal, anomalous, artificial, atypical, contrived, deviant, disparate, incongruous, irregular, off-key, uncharacteristic, unnatural

diverse adj 1 complex, manifold, multifarious, multifold

adj 2 assorted, miscellaneous, mixed, motley, varied

adj 3 haphazard, jumbled, mixed, promiscuous, random

adj 4 different, disparate, incongruous, opposite, unequal, unlike, unmatched, unrelated

adj 5 alternate, another, certain, different, discrete, disparate, dissimilar, distinct, numerous, other, separate, several, some, unlike, various, varying

adj 6 abundant, assorted, copious, extensive, legion, many, multifarious, multitudinous, myriad, numerous, plentiful, populous, prolific, sundry, various, voluminous

diversify *v* alter, assort, mix, modify, vary

diversion *n* 1 branch, detour, deviation

n 2 contrast, difference, dissimilarity, distinction, opposition

n 3 avoidance, deceit, dodging, escape, evasion, runaround

n 4 avocation, distraction, hobby, moonlighting, pastime, sideline

n 5 break, delay, distraction, disturbance, holdup, interference, interruption, pause

n 6 amusement, distraction, enjoyment, entertainment, frolic, fun, game, hobby, pastime, play, recreation, sport

n 7 see: MANEUVER *n* 2

divert *v* 1 avert, caution, deter, discourage, dissuade, distract

v 2 deflect, deviate, drift, slip, stray, turn

v 3 amuse, charm, entertain, interest, please, recreate, stimulate

v 4 avert, deflect, deviate, dip, dodge, pivot, skew, swerve, swing, swivel, turn, veer, wheel, whip

v 5 distract, interrupt

v 6 redirect, refer, submit

diverting *adj* amusing, enjoyable, entertaining, fun, humorous, joking, playful

divest *v* bare, deprive, strip

divide *v* 1 claw, cleave, disrupt, rend, rip, rive, scratch, split, tear

v 2 breach, break up, cleave, disjoin, dismember, disrupt, dissect, dissever, disunite, divorce, part, polarize, rupture, separate, sever, split, sunder

v 3 allocate, allot, allow, apportion, assign, designate, distribute, divvy, earmark, give, measure, parcel, partition, portion, prorate, quota, ration, section, share, slice

v 4 see: DISAGREE *v* 3

dividend *n* ante, award, bonus, booty, cash, commission, donation, fee, gift, gratuity, largess, money, percentage, perk, perquisite, premium, prize, profit, purse, reward, sharing, stake, stipend, tip, winnings

divider *n* curtain, panel, partition, wall

divine *adj* blessed, celestial, consecrated, godly, hallowed, holy, pure, sacred, sanctified, spiritual

v see: PREDICT *v* 2

diviner *n* conjurer, magician, soothsayer, sorcerer, wizard

divinity *n* deity, god, goddess, idol

division *n* 1 branch, department, office, unit

n 2 arm, branch, limb, service, subsidiary, tributary

n 3 apportionment, partition, segmentation, segregation, separation, subdivision

n 4 chink, cleft, crack, crevice, fissure, rent, rift, rupture, split

n 5 bit, clipping, cut, lot, member, parcel, part, piece, portion, sample, section, segment, slice

n 6 aircraft, formation, squadron, wing

n 7 annoyance, bother, conflict, contention, difference, discord, disharmony, dispute, dissension, dissent, dissidence, dissonance, disunity, hassle, inconvenience, mischief, nuisance, strife, trouble, variance

n 8 bracket, breed, cast, category, class, family, genre, genus, group, grouping, ilk, kind, lot, mold, nature, order, persuasion, section, sector, set, sort, species, style, type, variety

divorce *n* annulment, dissolution, separation, split

v breach, break up, cleave, disjoin, dismember, disrupt, dissect, dissever, disunite, divide, part, polarize, rupture, separate, sever, split, sunder

divot *n* area, land, patch, sod, space, turf

divulge *v* 1 hint, leak, reveal

v 2 alert, tip, tip off, warn

v 3 betray, cross, double-cross, reveal, sell out

v 4 breathe, confide, share, tell, whisper

v 5 blab, gossip, inform, reveal, tell

v 6 communicate, disclose, display, exhibit, inform, notify, open, reveal, uncover, unveil

v 7 brief, communicate, convey, declare, describe, disclose, explain, impart, inform, narrate, orate, portray, read, recite, recount, relate, report, retell, reveal, share, state, tattle, tell, transmit

divvy *v* allocate, allot, allow, apportion, assign, designate, distribute, divide, earmark, give, measure, parcel, partition, portion, prorate, quota, ration, section, share, slice

dizzy *adj* 1 confused, faint, foggy, giddy, lightheaded, reeling

adj 2 capricious, flighty, frivolous, giddy, irresponsible, scatterbrained, silly

adj 3 confused, daffy, daft, dazed, groggy, punchy, stunned

adj 4 see: PREOCCUPIED *adj* 1

v befuddle, bewilder, confuse, daze, distract, embarrass, fluster, mix up, muddle, rattle, ruffle, trick, unglue, unhinge

do *n* bash, bender, binge, fling, orgy, party, spree

v 1 achieve, execute, perform

v 2 actuate, commit, enact, execute, perform, perpetrate

v 3 answer, fulfill, meet, qualify, satisfy, suffice, work

v 4 administer, administrate, carry out, deliver, execute, give, present, render, submit

v 5 fare, get along, get by, get on, make out, manage, muddle through, shift, stagger

v 6 see: OCCUR *v* 2

doable *adj* 1 justifiable, practical, realistic, tenable

adj 2 achievable, capable, feasible, possible, practical, viable, workable

docile *adj* 1 controllable, manageable, maneuverable, pliable, yielding

adj 2 acquiescent, compliant, easy, meek, mild, nonresistant, obedient, passive, resigned, submissive, tame, tolerant, unassertive, yielding

dock *v* chastise, fine, penalize, punish, sentence, tariff, tax

n jetty, landing, pier, wharf

dockage *n* discipline, fee, fine, loss, penalty, punishment

docking *n* arrival, debarkation, landing, mooring

doctor *n* diagnostician, healer, intern, physician, resident, specialist, surgeon

v fix, mend, overhaul, patch, rebuild, recondition, reconstruct, refit, renovate, repair, revamp

doctrine *n* 1 beliefs, code, ethics, outlook, philosophy, rites, values

n 2 belief, custom, mores, relic, rite, ritual, throwback, tradition

n 3 approval, confirmation, enactment, evidence, passage, proof, testament, testimony, witness

n 4 belief, canon, code, conviction, creed, dogma, law, opinion, principle, rule, tenet, theory

docudrama *n* cartoons, documentary, game shows, mini-series, movies, news, programs, series, sitcom, soap opera, soaps, talk shows, television, variety shows

document *n* 1 text

n 2 deed, paper, title

n 3 certificate, credential, instrument, license, pass, permit

documentary *n* cartoons, docudrama, game shows, mini-series, movies, news, programs, series, sitcom, soap opera, soaps, talk shows, television, variety shows

documentation *n* affirmation, confirmation, evidence, proof, verification

dodge *v* 1 avoid, equivocate, evade, fence, hedge, shift, shuffle, sidestep

v 2 avoid, circumvent, deflect, detour, duck, evade, hedge, parry, shirk, sidestep, skirt, ward off

v 3 avert, deflect, deviate, dip, divert, pivot, skew, swerve, swing, swivel, turn, veer, wheel, whip

dodging *n* avoidance, deceit, diversion, escape, evasion, runaround

doff *v* see: UNDRESS *v*

dog *n* canine, hound, mongrel, mutt, pooch, pup, puppy

doggerel *n* ditty

dogma *n* belief, canon, code, conviction, creed, doctrine, law, opinion, principle, rule, tenet, theory

dogmatic *adj* 1 aggressive, ambitious, assertive, assured, compelling, compulsive, confident, decided, driven, emphatic, energetic, insistent, militant, positive, pushing, pushy, self-assertive, sure, urging

adj 2 aristocratic, arrogant, authoritarian, authoritative, autocratic, belligerent, bossy, despotic, dictatorial, domineering, haughty, imperial, imperious, masterful, militaristic, opinionated, oppressive, overbearing, peremptory, pushy, stubborn

doing *n* accomplishment, achievement, acquirement, act, action, battle, deed, event, exploit, feat, stunt, thing, trick

doldrums *n* 1 depression, down cycle, rut

n 2 apathy, boredom, depression, inertia, languor

dole *n* 1 alms, assistance, charity, contributions, donations, oblation, offering

n 2 affliction, anguish, care, catastrophe, despair, disaster, grief, heartache, mishap, pain, regret, remorse, rue, sickness, sorrow, woe

v administer, apportion, deal, disburse, dispense, disperse, distribute, expend, give

doleful *adj* dismal, gloomy, lamentable, melancholy, mournful, plaintive, regretful, regrettable, rueful, sorrowful, woeful

doll *n* dummy, effigy, mannequin, replica

dollar *n* bread, buck, cash, dough, money, moolah

dollars *n* assets, bills, capital, cash, coffers, currency, dinero, estate, funds, goods, income, lucre, means, money, notes, pelf, pesos, property, resources, revenue, riches, rubles, shekels, sum, wealth

dolt n see: IDIOT n

domain n 1 dominion, field, kingdom, province, realm, sphere, territory

n 2 acreage, estate, grounds, holdings, land, property, real estate

n 3 area, district, environs, jurisdiction, locality, neighborhood, parish, precinct, province, range, region, section, sphere, vicinity, ward, zone

dome n amphitheater, arena, bowl, coliseum, hippodrome, scene, stadium

domestic adj 1 handcrafted, homemade, home-oriented, homespun

adj 2 endemic, folk, indigenous, local, native, traditional

domicile n 1 address, apartment, condo, condominium, dwelling, flat, home, house, location, pad, place, property, residence, site

n 2 abode, castle, dwelling, estate, home, house, mansion, palace, residence

v dwell, inhabit, live, occupy, reside, room, settle, stay

dominance n charisma, influence, leadership, magnetism, personality, power, strength

dominant adj 1 crucial, pivotal

adj 2 master, overbearing, overwhelming, paramount, predominant, preponderant, prevailing, prevalent, sovereign

adj 3 basic, elementary, first, foremost, fundamental, head, highest, leading, main, outstanding, paramount, preeminent, premier, primary, rudimentary, supreme, top

adj 4 absolute, chief, complete, consummate, godlike, leading, main, perfect, principal, pure, ranking, sheer, supreme, total, unsurpassed, utter, whole

adj 5 central, chief, distinguished, famed, great, key, leading, main, major, number one, outstanding, predominant, preeminent, primary, prime, principal, prominent, star, successful, superior, top

adj 6 aggressive, durable, firm, forceful, hardy, hearty, mighty, powerful, robust, rugged, stalwart, stout, strong, sturdy, tenacious, tough

adj 7 see: POPULAR adj 2

dominate v 1 tower

v 2 control, corner, monopolize

v 3 excel, lead, star

v 4 bully, domineer, prevail, reign, rule

v 5 boss, command, control, direct, govern, handle, influence, lead, manage, manipulate, order, supervise, sway

v 6 bear down, beat down, conquer, crush, defeat, enslave, exploit, overpower, quash, reduce, subdue, subjugate, suppress, vanquish

domination n authority, command, commission, control, direction, jurisdiction, management, mastery, might, power, rule

domineer v bully, dominate, prevail, reign, rule

domineering adj aristocratic, arrogant, authoritarian, authoritative, autocratic, belligerent, bossy, despotic, dictatorial, dogmatic, haughty, imperial, imperious, masterful, militaristic, opinionated, oppressive, overbearing, peremptory, pushy, stubborn

dominion n 1 domain, field, kingdom, province, realm, sphere, territory

n 2 administration, government, monarchy, power, regime, reign, rule, sovereignty

donate v accord, adduce, award, bequeath, bestow, concede, confer, contribute, deliver, devote, endow, extend, fund, give, give away, grant, hand down, hand out, impart, offer, pose, present, proffer, provide, supply, tender, volunteer

donation n 1 benevolence, boon, contribution, favor, gift, grant, largess, present

n 2 see: REWARD n 8

donations n alms, assistance, charity, contributions, dole, oblation, offering

done adj accomplished, complete, concluded, ended, finished, over, performed, terminated, through, wrapped up

donor n see: ADVOCATE n 2

doodad n see: DEVICE n 3

doodle v draw, jot, scratch, scrawl, scribble, sketch, write

doohickey n see: DEVICE n 3

doom n breakdown, catastrophe, crash, crisis, death, destruction, failure, finish, ruin

v condemn

doomed adj cursed, damned, hapless, hopeless, ill-fated, jinxed, luckless, unfortunate, unhappy, unlucky, untoward

doorway n 1 exit, gateway, outlet, portal

n 2 anteroom, approach, atrium, court, entrance hall, entry, foyer, hall, hallway, lobby, portal, vestibule

dope n 1 data, details, facts, information, report, scoop

n 2 drug, grass, marijuana, narcotic, pot

n 3 blockhead, boor, clod, creep, cretin, dimwit, dolt, dullard, dumbbell, dummy, dunce, fool, goof, idiot, imbecile, jerk, nerd, nincompoop, numskull, oaf, pain, schlemiel, schmuck, simpleton, stooge, turkey

dorm *n* apartment, housing, lodging, room, shelter, suite

dormancy *n* abeyance, inaction, inactivity, limbo, lull, pause, suspension

dormant *adj* 1 inert, lethargic, numb, sluggish, torpid
adj 2 inactive, inert, latent, on hold, passive, potential, quiet, suspended, unused
adj 3 asleep, idle, immobile, inactive, inanimate, inert, inoperative, laid-back, motionless, nodding, passive, quiet, sleepy, slumbering, stable, stagnant, still
adj 4 see: CALM *adj* 2

dorsal *adj* aft, back, backward, posterior, rear, tail

dory *n* barge, boat, canoe, craft, ferry, float, kayak, raft, scow, skiff, tender

dose *n* amount, portion, prescription

dot *n* 1 atom, bead, dab, dash, drop, grain, iota, molecule, morsel, particle, pea, pellet, smidgen, speck, tad
n 2 point

double *n* 1 counterpart, duplicate, match, mate, twin
n 2 angle, bend, bow, detour, deviation, shift, tack, turn, turning, yaw
v fold

double-crosser *n* accuser, betrayer, fink, informer, reptile, snake, sneak, stooge, traitor

doubt *n* 1 disbelief, distrust, incredulity, skepticism, unbelief
n 2 apprehension, distrust, fear, hesitation, misbelief, mistrust, suspicion, wariness
n 3 concern, dubiety, incertitude, indecision, mistrust, query, question, skepticism, suspicion, uncertainty, wonder
n 4 annoyance, anxiety, apprehension, bother, care, concern, disquiet, disquietude, irritation, misgiving, reservation, restlessness, restraint, skepticism, trouble, uneasiness, vexation, worry
v 1 distrust, fear, mistrust, suspect
v 2 challenge, dispute, mistrust, query, question

doubtful *adj* 1 cynical, distrustful, dubious, incredulous, leery, questionable, shy, skeptical, skittish, suspicious, uncertain, unsure
adj 2 absurd, chancy, debatable, dubious, iffy, implausible, improbable, incredible, moot, preposterous, questionable, theoretical, unbelievable, uncertain, unlikely
adj 3 ambiguous, borderline, clouded, dubious, equivocal, garbled, illogical, inarticulate, incalculable, incoherent, inexplicit, muddled, muffled, murky, obscure, precarious, questionable, shaky, suspect, suspicious, uncertain, unclear, uneasy, unintelligible, unsure, vague, wary

dough *n* bread, buck, cash, dollar, money, moolah

dour *adj* 1 firm, forbidding, grim, sad, serious, severe, sour, stern, unpleasant
adj 2 brooding, crabby, gloomy, glum, moody, morose, sour, sulky, sullen, surly, ugly

douse *v* 1 extinguish, put out, quench, out
v 2 deluge, drench, drown, dunk, flood, inundate, irrigate, overload, saturate, slosh, soak, sop, souse, swamp, swill, tax, wet

down *adj* 1 idle, lax, off, slack, slow, sluggish
adj 2 ailing, delicate, diseased, frail, ill, impaired, indisposed, sick, sickly, suffering, unhealthy, unsound, unwell, weak
adj 3 black, bleak, blue, cheerless, dejected, depressed, desperate, despondent, discouraging, disheartening, distressing, forlorn, gloomy, hopeless, joyless, melancholy, moody, mournful, oppressive, prostrate, sad, somber, sorry, unhappy
v 1 best, defeat, outdo, outmaneuver, outsmart, outwit
v 2 conquer, crush, defeat, destroy, hurdle, lick, overcome, overthrow, surmount

downfall *n* 1 collapse, failure, fall, overthrow, ruin, upset
n 2 destruction, infiltration, overthrow, ruin, subversion, upset
n 3 see: ROUT *n*

downgrade *v* 1 break, bump, bust, degrade, demerit, demote, put down, reduce
v 2 cheapen, depreciate, devalue, diminish, dwindle, lower, mark down, reduce, underrate, undervalue

downpour *n* cloudburst, deluge, drizzle, hail, precipitation, rain, shower, sprinkle

downside *n* danger, exposure, hazard, jeopardy, liability, menace, peril, risk, threat

down-to-earth *adj* basic, businesslike, efficient, hardheaded, practical, pragmatic, sensible

downturn *n* see: FALL *n* 3

doze *n* apathy, coma, ennui, grogginess, inertia, languor, lassitude, lethargy, nod, sleep, slumber, stupor
v nap, rest, sleep, snooze

dozens *n* see: HORDE *n*

dozing *adj* drowsy, lethargic, napping, nodding, sleepy, slumberous, snoozy, somnolent, tired

drab *adj* 1 cheerless, cloudy, dim, dismal, dull, gray, overcast

adj 2 arid, bland, bleak, boring, colorless, dead, desolate, dreary, dull, flat, lackluster, lifeless, lusterless, monotonous, muted, somber, trite, unexciting, uninteresting

draft *n* 1 blueprint, chart, diagram, map, outline, plan, sketch

n 2 air, blow, breath, breeze, current, gust, puff, wind

n 3 outline, skeleton, sketch

v 1 drain, draw, draw off, pump, siphon, suck, tap

v 2 author, compose, create, pen, prepare, type, write

v 3 call, conscript, enroll, force, impress, induct, select, shanghai

v 4 arrange, blueprint, cast, chart, design, devise, draw, engineer, fashion, lay out, map, outline, plan, plot, project, set out, sketch

v 5 announce, articulate, assert, couch, describe, dictate, enunciate, express, intonate, orate, phrase, proclaim, pronounce, say, speak, state, stress, talk, utter, verbalize, vocalize, voice, word

draftsperson *n* architect, designer, engineer, inventor, manager, operator, plotter, schemer, surveyor

drafty *adj* airy, breezy, brisk, gusty, lofty, open, windy

drag *n* 1 jerk, pluck, pull, tug, yank

n 2 access, approach, artery, avenue, boulevard, channel, highway, pass, path, promenade, road, roadway, route, strait, street, thoroughfare, trail, way

v 1 follow, lag, trail, traipse

v 2 carry, cart, draw, haul, lug, pull, tow, truck, tug

v 3 draw, inhale, puff, smoke

v 4 brake, confine, contain, control, curb, govern, hamper, hem, hold back, impede, repress, restrain, retard

drain *v* 1 extract, milk, squeeze

v 2 clear, deplete, empty, evacuate, take out, vacate

v 3 draft, draw, draw off, pump, siphon, suck, tap

v 4 cripple, debilitate, disable, enfeeble, exhaust, sap, undermine, weaken

v 5 bankrupt, deplete, drain, draw down, exhaust, impoverish, use up

v 6 exhaust, fatigue, jade, tire, wear down, wear out, weary

v 7 abate, cease, decline, decrease, die down, diminish, dwindle, ease, ebb, fall, lessen, let up, lull, recede, reduce, relax, relent, shrink, slacken, soften, stop, subside, taper off, wane, waste away, weaken

drama *n* 1 melodrama, mystery, theatrics, tragedy, tragicomedy

n 2 Broadway, comedy, extravaganza, musical, production, stage, theater

dramatic *adj* 1 melodramatic, sensational, theatrical, thrilling

adj 2 extraordinary, sensational, shocking, startling

adj 3 epic, grand, heroic, legendary, noble, stirring, vivid

dramatically *adv* considerably, far, quite, rather, significantly, very, well

dramatist *n* author, authoress, biographer, creator, essayist, journalist, novelist, playwright, reporter, screenwriter, writer

drastic *adj* excessive, extreme, intense, passionate, radical, severe, strong

draw *n* bottleneck, deadlock, hung jury, impasse, stalemate, standoff, standstill, tie

v 1 copy

v 2 attract, elicit, induce, solicit

v 3 depict, design, paint, represent, sketch

v 4 deduce, derive, educe, elicit, evince, evoke, extract

v 5 draft, drain, draw off, pump, siphon, suck, tap

v 6 doodle, jot, scratch, scrawl, scribble, sketch, write

v 7 flex, pull, strain, stretch, tense, tighten, twist

v 8 continue, drag out, elongate, extend, lengthen, prolong, protract, stretch

v 9 carry, cart, drag, haul, lug, pull, tow, truck, tug

v 10 analyze, conclude, construe, deduce, derive, educe, gather, glean, guess, infer, interpret, presume, surmise

v 11 allure, attract, bedevil, beguile, bewitch, captivate, charm, conjure, delight, enchant, enthrall, fascinate, lure, magnetize, mesmerize, tempt, wile

v 12 drag, inhale, puff, smoke

v 13 bankrupt, deplete, drain, draw down, exhaust, impoverish, use up

v 14 demonstrate, describe, display, establish, examine, exhibit, explain, present, prove, show, sketch, tell

v 15 arrange, blueprint, cast, chart, design, devise, draft, engineer, fashion, lay out, map, outline, plan, plot, project, set out, sketch

drawing *n* 1 icon, image, model, representation, simulation, symbol

n 2 acrylic, art, canvas, depiction, etching, illustration, landscape, lithograph, mural, oil, painting, pastel, pen and ink, picture, portrait, print, seascape, sketch, still life, watercolor

drawn adj 1 absorbed, curious, engrossed, interested, involved

adj 2 see: WEARY adj 1

drawn-out adj elongated, extended, lengthened, lengthy, long, prolonged, protracted, stretched, sustained

dread n 1 amazement, awe, consternation, fear, respect, reverence, wonder

n 2 affliction, alarm, anxiety, apprehension, care, consternation, dismay, fear, fright, horror, ordeal, panic, terror, trepidation, trial, trouble, worry

dreadful adj 1 awful, contemptible, lousy, mean

adj 2 atrocious, calamitous, grievous, heinous, severe

adj 3 dire, disastrous, lamentable, pitiful, sorrowful, tragic

adj 4 abhorrent, abominable, appalling, detestable, disgusting, evil, frightful, ghastly, hateful, horrible, horrid, loathsome, odious, repulsive, revolting, shocking

adj 5 appalling, awful, dire, fearful, formidable, frightening, frightful, ghastly, horrendous, horrible, offensive, ominous, portentous, scary, shocking, spooky, terrible, terrifying, unpleasant

dreadfully adv awfully, eminently, endlessly, exceedingly, exceptionally, extremely, greatly, highly, mightily, notably, quite, remarkably, terribly, thoroughly, very

dream n daydream, fancy, fantasy, musing, reverie, vision

v fantasize, imagine, muse, suppose

dreamer n idealist, romantic, utopian, visionary

dreariness n apathy, boredom, dullness, ennui, malaise, monotony, tedium

dreary adj 1 blah, boring, commonplace, dim, dull, flat, humdrum, monotonous, ordinary, pedestrian, stodgy, tedious, tiresome

adj 2 arid, bland, bleak, boring, colorless, dead, desolate, drab, dull, flat, lackluster, lifeless, lusterless, monotonous, muted, somber, trite, unexciting, uninteresting

dregs n leftovers, remainder, remains, remnant, residual, residue, rest, scrap, shred, silt

drench v deluge, douse, drown, dunk, flood, inundate, irrigate, overload, saturate, slosh, soak, sop, souse, swamp, swill, tax, wet

drenched adj 1 dripping, full, immersed, inundated, saturated, soaked, soaking, sodden, sopping, waterlogged, wet

adj 2 damp, dripping, humid, moist, mucky, muggy, soaked, soggy, sopping, sticky, sultry, sweaty, wet

dress n 1 accoutrements, apparel, attire, clothes, clothing, garments, gear, togs

n 2 costume, gown, kilt, skirt

v 1 equip, groom, spiff up, spruce

v 2 accouter, apparel, array, attire, clad, clothe, garb, gear, outfit

v 3 clean, disembowel, eviscerate, fillet, gut

dresser n armoire, bureau, chest

drib n bead, blob, bubble, drop, droplet, globule, lump, sphere

dribble v 1 drip, drop, leak, ooze, run, seep, trickle

v 2 drivel, drool, slobber

drift n 1 strain, subject, theme, thread

n 2 implication, intent, purport, substance, tenor

n 3 current, pattern, run, series, succession, tendency, trend

n 4 course, direction, path, strategy, tack, tactic, tendency, tenor, trend

n 5 bank, heap, hill, mass, mound, mountain, pile, stack, stockpile

n 6 change, current, flow, flux, gush, motion, movement, rush, stream, tide, transition

n 7 bent, bias, habit, inclination, leaning, partiality, penchant, predilection, preference, priority, proclivity, propensity, talent, taste, tendency

v 1 bank, heap, mound, pile, stack

v 2 deflect, deviate, divert, slip, stray, turn

v 3 coast, float, fly, glide, sail, slide, soar

v 4 float, ride, wash

drifter n 1 emigrant, itinerant, migrant, nomad, transient

n 2 beggar, bum, derelict, hobo, loafer, mendicant, panhandler, pauper, tramp, vagabond, vagrant

drill n 1 activity, discipline, practice

n 2 exercise, practice, rehearsal, training, workout

v 1 auger, bore, pierce, ream, tool

v 2 learn, perfect, practice, prepare, rehearse, repeat, review, study

v 3 see: EDUCATE v

drink v 1 carouse, celebrate, frolic, make merry, party, revel, romp

v 2 bibulate, booze, consume, gulp, guzzle, imbibe, nip, partake, polish off, put away, put down, sample, savor, sip, suck, swig, swill, taste

n salutation, toast

drinks *n* alcohol, booze, grog, liquor, moonshine, spirits, whiskey

drip *v* 1 dribble, drop, leak, ooze, run, seep, trickle

v 2 discharge, emit, exude, leak, ooze, secrete, seep, trickle

dripping *adj* 1 drenched, full, immersed, inundated, saturated, soaked, soaking, sodden, sopping, waterlogged, wet

adj 2 damp, drenched, humid, moist, mucky, muggy, soaked, soggy, sopping, sticky, sultry, sweaty, wet

drive *n* 1 campaign, crusade, effort, expedition, push

n 2 excursion, jaunt, journey, outing, ride, spin

n 3 ambition, enterprise, initiative, lead, leadership, push, thrust, volition

n 4 animation, élan, energy, enthusiasm, esprit de corps, go, gusto, pep, potency, sparkle, spirit, spunk, verve, vigor, vitality, vim, zing, zip

n 5 see: VIGOR *n* 2, 3

v 1 boost, budge, force, impel, nudge, propel, push, shove, thrust

v 2 attack, butt, knock, lunge, pass, plunge, ram, sink, stab, stick, thrust

v 3 activate, actuate, compel, force, goad, impel, induce, mobilize, motivate, move, persuade, press, propel, push, spur, start, turn on

v 4 commute, ride, travel

v 5 hammer, impress, imprint, mark, pound, press, print, stamp, strike, thump, whack

v 6 conduct, control, develop, direct, guide, lead, operate, pilot, route, shepherd, show, steer

drivel *n* baloney, bilge, bosh, bull, bunk, fiddlesticks, foolishness, junk, malarkey, nonsense, nothing, poppycock, rot, rubbish, schlock, silliness, trivia

v 1 cast away, consume, dissipate, empty, fritter, lavish, squander, throw away, use up, waste

v 2 dribble, drool, slobber

driven *adj* see: ASSERTIVE *adj*

driving *adj* active, bustling, busy, creative, energetic, enterprising, inventive, lively, resourceful

drizzle *n* cloudburst, deluge, downpour, hail, precipitation, rain, shower, sprinkle

v deluge, fall, pour, rain, shower, sprinkle

drizzly *adj* damp, dank, foggy, humid, misty, moist, wet

droid *n* robot, android

droll *adj* absurd, comic, comical, crazy, farcical, foolish, funny, hilarious, humorous, laughable, ludicrous, outrageous, ridiculous, silly

drool *v* dribble, drivel, slobber

droop *v* 1 sag

v 2 hunch, slouch, stoop

v 3 bend, bow, duck, lower, slouch, slump, stoop

v 4 depress, flop, let down, lower, mire, sag, sink, wallow

drop *n* 1 bead, blob, bubble, drib, droplet, globule, lump, sphere

n 2 comedown, decline, decrease, descent, dive, failure, fall, plunge, regression, setback, slide, tumble

n 3 atom, bead, dab, dash, dot, grain, iota, molecule, morsel, particle, pea, pellet, smidgen, speck, tad

n 4 debasement, decline, deterioration, dip, downturn, ebb, erosion, fall, involution, plunge, sag, slide, slip, slump, wane, weakening

v 1 litter, mess up, scatter

v 2 go, leave, quit, resign, retire, terminate

v 3 dribble, drip, leak, ooze, run, seep, trickle

v 4 descend, dive, fall, lapse, leap, lower, plummet, plunge, sink, swoop

v 5 ax, boot, bounce, can, discharge, dismiss, fire, impeach, let go, sack, terminate

v 6 cave in, collapse, disintegrate, fall, go down, keel over, pitch, plunge, slump, spill, topple, tumble

v 7 abstain, cast, decline, eschew, forbear, forfeit, forgo, give up, lose, pass, reject, renounce, sacrifice, surrender, turn down, waive

v 8 cast off, molt, peel, repel, shed

droplet *n* bead, blob, bubble, drib, drop, globule, lump, sphere

droppings *n* excrement, feces, stool, waste

drought *n* see: DEFICIT *n* 2

drove *n* band, bunch, crew, crowd, flock, following, gaggle, gang, herd, huddle, mass, mob, pack, rabble, riffraff, swarm, team, throng

droves *n* loads, lots, many, multitudes, plenty, scads, slew

drown *v* 1 crush, defeat, overpower, overwhelm, stifle

v 2 bury, engulf, flood, inundate, overflow, swamp, wash over

v 3 deluge, douse, drench, dunk, flood, inundate, irrigate, overload, saturate, slosh, soak, sop, souse, swamp, swill, tax, wet

drowsy *adj* dozing, lethargic, napping, nodding, sleepy, slumberous, snoozy, somnolent, tired

drudge v grub, hustle, labor, slave, strain, strive, sweat, toil, work

drudgery n chore, grind, labor, slavery, sweat, tedium, toil, travail, work

drug n 1 compound, elixir, formula, medicine, narcotic, painkiller, pharmaceutical, prescription

n 2 dope, grass, marijuana, narcotic, pot
v sedate, tranquilize

drum n barrel, bucket, cask, keg, tub, vat, vessel

v campaign, canvass, drum up, poll, prospect, seek, solicit

drunk adj bombed, crocked, doped up, drunken, high, inebriated, intoxicated, juiced, loaded, looped, messed up, plastered, polluted, sloshed, smashed, stoned, tight, tipsy, turned on, wasted, wired

drunken adj bombed, crocked, doped up, drunk, high, inebriated, intoxicated, juiced, loaded, looped, messed up, plastered, polluted, sloshed, smashed, stoned, tight, tipsy, turned on, wasted, wired

druthers n alternative, choice, decision, election, option, pick, preference, rathers, selection, vote

dry adj 1 arid, parched, thirsty, waterless
adj 2 acerbic, acid, biting, curt, pungent, sharp, sour, tart
adj 3 discreet, homely, modest, plain, simple, unadorned, undecorated, unembellished, unembroidered, ungarnished, unpretentious
adj 4 cold, dull, impassive, laid-back, matter-of-fact, phlegmatic, poker-faced, reserved, stoic, stolid, unaffected, unemotional, unfeeling, unmoved, untouched
v 1 evaporate
v 2 clog, clot, coagulate, condense, congeal, curdle, gel, harden, intensify, jell, pack, set, solidify, thicken

dub v baptize, bestow, call, christen, confer, designate, entitle, name, nickname, tag, term, title

dubiety n concern, doubt, incertitude, indecision, mistrust, query, question, skepticism, suspicion, uncertainty, wonder

dubious adj 1 cynical, distrustful, doubtful, incredulous, leery, questionable, shy, skeptical, skittish, suspicious, uncertain, unsure
adj 2 absurd, chancy, debatable, doubtful, iffy, implausible, improbable, incredible, moot, preposterous, questionable, theoretical, unbelievable, uncertain, unlikely
adj 3 ambiguous, borderline, clouded, doubtful, equivocal, garbled, illogical, inarticulate, incalculable, incoherent, inex-

plicit, muddled, muffled, murky, obscure, precarious, questionable, shaky, suspect, suspicious, uncertain, unclear, uneasy, unintelligible, unsure, vague, wary
adj 4 insecure, questionable, undependable, unreliable, unsure, untrustworthy

duck v 1 bend, bow, droop, lower, slouch, slump, stoop
v 2 avoid, elude, escape, eschew, evade, recoil, shun, shy
v 3 avoid, circumvent, deflect, detour, dodge, evade, hedge, parry, shirk, sidestep, skirt, ward off

duct n 1 channel, conduit, pipe, tube
n 2 see: CHANNEL n 1, 3

dud n bomb, bust, disaster, failure, fiasco, flop, turkey

dude n see: MAN n 2

due adj 1 open, outstanding, owed, payable, unpaid
adj 2 authoritative, dependable, faithful, legitimate, rightful, strict, true, trustworthy, undistorted, veracious
adj 3 appropriate, correct, deserved, fitting, just, merited, proper, rightful, suitable, warranted

duel n battle, clash, competition, conflict, contest, discord, fight, fighting, rivalry, strife, struggle, war, warfare
v 1 combat, contend, fight, grapple, spar, struggle, wrestle
v 2 combat, compete, contend, contest, counter, dispute, fight, match, oppose, parry, pit, play, repel, resist, rival, strive, struggle, vie

duet n couple, duo, pair, set, twins, twosome

dull adj 1 bare, blank, empty, lifeless, unfilled
adj 2 boring, formal, pompous, stodgy, stuffy
adj 3 banal, bland, flat, innocuous, insipid, tasteless, unexciting
adj 4 common, commonplace, ordinary, pedestrian, prosaic, uneventful, unexceptional
adj 5 cheerless, cloudy, dim, dismal, drab, gray, overcast
adj 6 blah, boring, commonplace, dim, dreary, flat, humdrum, monotonous, ordinary, pedestrian, stodgy, tedious, tiresome
adj 7 arid, bland, bleak, boring, colorless, dead, desolate, drab, dreary, flat, lackluster, lifeless, lusterless, monotonous, muted, somber, trite, unexciting, uninteresting
adj 8 colorless, flat, sterile

adj 9 cold, dry, impassive, laid-back, matter-of-fact, phlegmatic, poker-faced, reserved, stolid, unaffected, unemotional, unfeeling, unmoved, untouched

adj 10 backward, blunt, deficient, dense, dimwitted, dumb, feebleminded, idiotic, moronic, obtuse, retarded, simple, simple-minded, slow, stupid, thick, uneducated, unintelligent

adj 11 banal, boring, clichéd, commonplace, corny, hackneyed, musty, redundant, repetitious, repetitive, stale, tedious, threadbare, timeworn, tired, tiresome, trite, worn out

v 1 blunt, stupefy, weaken

v 2 becloud, bedim, befog, blur, cloud, confuse, darken, dim, diminish, eclipse, fade, muddy, obscure, overshadow, pale, shade, shadow, tarnish

dullard *n* see: IDIOT *n*

dullness *n* 1 apathy, indifference, insensibility, stoicism

n 2 apathy, boredom, dreariness, ennui, malaise, monotony, tedium

dumb *adj* 1 inarticulate, mute, reticent, silent, speechless, tacit, voiceless

adj 2 backward, blunt, deficient, dense, dimwitted, dull, feebleminded, idiotic, moronic, obtuse, retarded, simple, simple-minded, slow, stupid, thick, uneducated, unintelligent

dumbbell *n* see: IDIOT *n*

dumbfound *v* amaze, astonish, astound, awe, boggle, confound, dazzle, flabbergast, nonplus, stagger, stun, surprise

dummy *n* 1 agent, alternate, proxy, representative, substitute

n 2 doll, effigy, mannequin, replica

n 3 blockhead, boor, clod, creep, cretin, dimwit, dolt, dope, dullard, dumbbell, dunce, fool, goof, idiot, imbecile, jerk, nerd, nincompoop, numskull, oaf, pain, schlemiel, schmuck, simpleton, stooge, turkey

dump *n* bar, barroom, cocktail lounge, den, dive, gin mill, hangout, haunt, joint, lounge, pub, rathskeller, saloon, tavern, watering hole

v 1 abandon, discard, dispose of, eliminate, empty, quit, reject, scrap, unload

v 2 abandon, break up, cast off, chuck, defect, desert, disavow, discard, disenfranchise, disown, ditch, forsake, jilt, junk, leave, quit, reject, renounce, spurn, strand, throw out

dun *v* bill, charge, debit, invoice, notice, render, solicit

dunce *n* see: IDIOT *n*

dung *n* dirt, filth, garbage, manure, muck, mud, slime, sludge

dunk *v* see: SATURATE *v* 2

duo *n* couple, duet, pair, set, twins, twosome

dupe *n* chump, mark, pushover, stooge, sucker, victim

v bamboozle, beat, beguile, bilk, burn, cajole, cheat, chicane, chisel, con, cross, deceive, defraud, embezzle, fleece, flimflam, fob, foist, fool, gyp, hoax, hoodwink, hustle, inveigle, screw, shaft, sham, swindle, trick, victimize

duplicate *adj* equal, equivalent, identical, same, substitute, synonymous, tantamount

n 1 counterpart, double, match, mate, twin

n 2 carbon, carbon copy, copy, facsimile, replica, reproduction, telecopy, Xerox copy

n 3 clone, copy, counterfeit, duplication, image, imitation, likeness, mock-up, model, print, replica, replication, representation, reproduction, resemblance, simulation

v clone, copy, image, imitate, mirror, print, re-create, redo, reduplicate, remake, replicate, reprint, reproduce, simulate

duplication *n* see: REPLICA *n* 2

durable *adj* 1 constant, continuing, enduring, eternal, lasting, ongoing, permanent, stable

adj 2 aggressive, dominant, firm, forceful, hardy, hearty, mighty, powerful, robust, rugged, stalwart, stout, strong, sturdy, tenacious, tough

duration *n* 1 hold, interval, length, occupancy, tenure, term, time

n 2 continuation, endurance, existence, life, span, subsistence, survival, term

n 3 cycle, interval, period, season, span, spell, stage, stretch, term, time

duress *n* coercion, compulsion, constraint, force, violence

during *prep* at the time, in the course of, in the interval, throughout

dusk *n* nightfall, sundown, sunset, twilight

dusky *adj* dark, dim, gloomy, lightless, murky, obscure, shadowy, somber, tenebrous, unilluminated

dust *n* clay, dirt, dry land, earth, ground, land, loam, marl, soil, *terra*, terra firma

v 1 beat, belittle, blast, clobber, conquer, cream, defeat, lambaste, lick, overrun, overwhelm, rout, shellac, smear, thrash, wallop, whip

v 2 clean

v 3 chalk, powder, sprinkle

duty *n* 1 function, purpose, use

n 2 burden, charge, commitment, obligation, onus, responsibility

n 3 appointment, connection, function, job, office, position, post, situation

n 4 assignment, chore, effort, job, mission, responsibility, stint, task

n 5 assessment, cost, expense, fee, impost, levy, offering, penalty, price, sacrifice, tariff, tax, toll, trade-off

dwarf *n* Lilliputian, midget, mite, pygmy

v beat, best, better, cap, eclipse, exceed, excel, go beyond, outdo, outgo, outshine, outstrip, overshadow, pass, surpass, top, transcend

dwarfish *adj* see: TINY *adj* 1

dwell *v* 1 bivouac, camp, lodge, nest, quarter, station

v 2 domicile, inhabit, live, occupy, reside, room, settle, stay

dweller *n* addressee, citizen, inhabitant, occupant, owner, resident, tenant

dwelling *n* 1 address, apartment, condo, condominium, domicile, flat, home, house, location, pad, place, property, residence, site

n 2 abode, castle, domicile, estate, home, house, mansion, palace, residence

dwindle *v* 1 cheapen, depreciate, devalue, diminish, downgrade, lower, mark down, reduce, underrate, undervalue

v 2 see: CANCEL *v* 3

v 3 see: SUBSIDE *v* 2

v 4 see: WITHER *v* 4

dye *n* color, coloring, paint, pigment, stain, tincture, tint

v color, paint, stain, tinge, tint

dynamic *adj* 1 electrifying, exciting, inspiring, stimulating, thrilling

adj 2 alive, active, energetic, sound, spirited, strong, vibrant, vigorous, vital

adj 3 coercive, compelling, energetic, forceful, hardy, lusty, mighty, passionate, powerful, robust, strong, sturdy, vigorous

adj 4 alluring, beguiling, bewitching, captivating, catchy, charming, dazzling, enchanting, engaging, enthralling, enticing, fascinating, glamorous, intriguing, mesmerizing, riveting, spectacular, spellbinding

adj 5 see: LIVELY *adj* 8

dynamite *adj* excellent, extraordinary, great, out of sight, outstanding, phenome-

nal, premier, super, superb, superlative, tremendous, wonderful

E

each *adj* a, a few, any, at least one, every, individual, one, several, some

eager *adj* 1 accommodating, agreeing, amenable, disposed, glad, inclined, pleased, pliant, responsive, willing

adj 2 anxious, ardent, avid, breathless, desirous, enthusiastic, excited, fain, impatient, impetuous, keen, passionate, raring, zealous

adj 3 see: GREEDY *adj* 1

eagerness *n* alacrity, cheerfulness, sprightliness

earlier *adv* before, first, formerly, heretofore, hitherto, once, previously, prior to

adj see: PRECEDING *adj*

earliest *adj* first, founding, fundamental, initial, maiden, original, pioneer, primary, prime

early *adj* 1 advanced, first, hasty, premature, previous, soon, too soon, untimely

adj 2 aboriginal, ancient, former, original, prehistoric, primeval, primitive, primordial, rudimentary

adj 3 basic, elementary, embryonic, essential, fundamental, initial, intrinsic, original, rudimentary, underlying

earmark *v* allocate, allot, allow, apportion, assign, designate, distribute, divide, divvy, give, measure, parcel, partition, portion, prorate, quota, ration, section, share, slice

n flap, label, tab

earn *v* 1 access, accomplish, achieve, attain, derive, fulfill, gain, get, merit, net, obtain, perform, profit, rack up, reach, realize, score, win

v 2 catch

v 3 acquire, make, obtain, procure

earnest *adj* 1 candid, direct, forthright, frank, genuine, heartfelt, hearty, honest, no-holds-barred, open, real, sincere, straightforward, true, trustworthy, truthful, undesigning, unfeigned, unpretentious, wholehearted

adj 2 see: SOLEMN *adj* 1

n see: COMMITMENT *n* 4

earnestly *adv* see: COMPLETELY *adv*

earnings *n* 1 compensation, gain, reward, wages

n 2 assets, cash, gain, gross, haul, net, payback, proceeds, profits, receipts, return, revenue, take, yield

n 3 bill, bonus, charge, commission, compensation, consideration, fee, gross, income, pay, revenue, salary, stipend, wage

earring *n* anklet, band, bangle, bracelet, brooch, jewelry, medal, medallion, necklace, pin, ring

earth *n* 1 clay, dirt, dry land, dust, ground, land, loam, marl, soil, *terra,* terra firma

n 2 globe, home, the planet, world

earthly *adj* common, earthy, mundane, pedestrian, terrestrial, uncelestial, worldly

earthy *adj* 1 common, earthly, mundane, pedestrian, terrestrial, uncelestial, worldly

adj 2 see: EROTIC *adj* 3

ease *n* 1 comfort, effortlessness, freedom, leisure, liberty

n 2 breeze, cinch, dash, snap, waltz, zip

v 1 clear, expedite, facilitate, smooth

v 2 ease off, lax, loosen, mellow out, relax, slack, slacken

v 3 allay, alleviate, assuage, attenuate, diminish, extenuate, lessen, lighten, minimize, mitigate, moderate, mollify, reduce, relieve

v 4 abate, cease, decline, decrease, die down, diminish, drain, dwindle, ebb, fall, lessen, let up, lull, recede, reduce, relax, relent, shrink, slacken, soften, stop, subside, taper off, wane, waste away, weaken

v 5 see: APPEASE *v* 2

v 6 see: HELP *v* 4

easily *adv* effortlessly, lightly, naturally, readily, willingly

easing *n* abatement, diminishing, letup, loosening, relaxation, slackening

easy *adj* 1 amiable, complaisant, good-humored, good-natured, lenient, mild, obliging

adj 2 believing, credulous, gullible, innocent, naive, susceptible, trustful

adj 3 casual, coming along, developing, effortless, flowing, fluent, laid-back, running, smooth

adj 4 clear, coherent, direct, elementary, intelligible, logical, lucid, simple, understandable

adj 5 accepting, charitable, forbearing, indulgent, lenient, merciful, patient, restrained, sympathetic, tolerant

adj 6 acquiescent, compliant, docile, meek, mild, nonresistant, obedient, passive, resigned, submissive, tame, tolerant, unassertive, yielding

adj 7 see: CALM *adj* 2

adj 8 see: PROMISCUOUS *adj* 2

easygoing *adj* see: LAZY *adj*

eat *v* 1 consume, devour, digest, ingest, masticate, swallow

v 2 corrode, deteriorate, erode, gnaw, oxidize, rust, wear

eavesdrop *v* bug, check, monitor, observe, oversee, snoop, spy, wiretap

ebb *v* 1 go backwards, recede, regress, retrograde, retrogress, return, revert, throw back

v 2 see: SUBSIDE *v* 2

n see: FALL *n* 3

ebony *adj* black, jet, sable

ebullient *adj* 1 aroused, elated, euphoric, excited, exhilarated, happy, intoxicated, joyful, sparked, stimulated, turned on

adj 2 bright, cheerful, cheery, content, ecstatic, elated, exuberant, festive, gay, glad, happy, jovial, joyful, joyous, merry, mirthful, pleased, radiant, rejoicing

adj 3 alert, animated, bouncy, bright, brisk, buoyant, chipper, dashing, dynamic, energetic, enthusiastic, exuberant, frisky, frolicsome, gay, jumpy, kinetic, lively, peppy, pert, playful, rousing, scintillating, spirited, sprightly, spry, vivacious

eccentric *adj* 1 aberrant, bizarre, erratic, odd, oddball, outlandish, peculiar, quaint, queer, singular, strange, uncanny, unconventional, unusual, weird

adj 2 crazy, kooky, off-center

n card, character, kook, lunatic, nut, oddball, weirdo

eccentricity *n* 1 abnormality, habit, idiosyncrasy, oddity, peculiarity, quirk, trademark

n 2 aberration, abnormality, craziness, delusion, dementia, derangement, distraction, fugue, hallucination, insanity, irregularity, lunacy, madness, mania, psychosis, unbalance

echelon *n* caste, class, degree, estate, hierarchy, level, position, rank, status

echo *v* backfire, repeat, resonate, resound, reverberate, vibrate

echoing *n* reverberation

eclipse *v* 1 excel, outshine, surpass

v 2 becloud, bedim, befog, blur, cloud, confuse, darken, dim, diminish, dull, fade, muddy, obscure, overshadow, pale, shade, shadow, tarnish

v 3 see: SURPASS *v* 1, 2

economical *adj* 1 austere, sparse, spartan, terse

adj 2 cheap, inexpensive, low, low-cost, moderate, reasonable

adj 3 canny, conservative, frugal, provident, sparing, spartan, stewardly, thrifty, unwasteful

economics *n* banking, finance, numbers, statistics

economize *v* 1 conserve, husband, safeguard, store

v 2 save, scrape, scrimp, skimp

economy *n* frugality, moderation, prudence, thrift

ecstasy *n* 1 euphoria, high, rush

n 2 bliss, delight, Eden, elation, enchantment, heaven, joy, nirvana, paradise, pleasure, rapture, rhapsody

ecstatic *adj* 1 entranced, overjoyed, rapturous

adj 2 delighted, elated, enchanted, overjoyed, thrilled

adj 3 buoyant, cheerful, elated, enthusiastic, exuberant, positive

adj 4 bright, cheerful, cheery, content, ebullient, elated, exuberant, festive, gay, glad, happy, jovial, joyful, joyous, merry, mirthful, pleased, radiant, rejoicing

eddy *n* whirlpool

Eden *n* see: DELIGHT *n* 2

edge *n* 1 advantage

n 2 end, nib, nub, tip

n 3 advantage, birthright, claim, enablement, perquisite, prerogative, privilege, right, title

n 4 border, boundary, bounds, brim, brink, curb, fringe, limits, lip, margin, outskirt, perimeter, periphery, rim, side, skirt, verge

v 1 file, grind, hone, polish, sharpen, whet

v 2 approach, border, bound, define, hem, limit, outline, skirt, verge

edgy *adj* 1 antsy, excitable, fidgety, highstrung, irritable, jittery, jumpy, moody, nervous, nervy, restless, shaky, skittish, temperamental

adj 2 annoying, anxious, bothersome, chafing, crabby, fretful, galling, impatient, irritating, jittery, nagging, on edge, restless, touchy, unsettling

adj 3 anxious, fidgety, impatient, nervous, nervy, queasy, restive, restless, tense, troubled, uncomfortable, uneasy, uptight, worried

edibles *n* bread, breakfast, brunch, chow, cuisine, diet, dinner, dish, entree, fare, food, grub, lunch, meals, nosh, nutrition, provisions, rations, snack, supper, victuals, vittles

edict *n* 1 announcement, aphorism, axiom, cliché, declaration, decree, dictum, gospel, homily, maxim, moral, precept, pronouncement, rule, saying, teaching, truism, truth, verity

n 2 behest, bidding, canon, charge, command, criterion, decree, dictate, direction, fiat, guideline, injunction, institution, law, mandate, order, ordinance, precept, prescript, prescription, regulation, rite, rule, ruling, statute, word

edifice *n* building, erection, foundation, house, pile, store, structure, warehouse

edify *v* see: EDUCATE *v*

edit *v* 1 annotate, compile, correct, denote, modify, polish, proofread, revise

v 2 abbreviate, abridge, condense, curtail, cut, cut back, diminish, lessen, reduce, restrict, shorten, slash

v 3 modify, redraft, redraw, rehash, revamp, revise, rework, rewrite

edition *n* 1 version

n 2 book, correspondence, folio, issue, manuscript, monograph, opus, paperback, printing, publication, text, tome, volume, work, writing

editor *n* columnist, commentator, correspondent, interviewer, journalist, newspaperman, publicist, writer

editorial *n* article, bulletin, byline, column, communication, dispatch, feature, headline, item, newsletter, report, story, vignette

educate *v* coach, communicate, condition, convey, cultivate, develop, discipline, drill, edify, enlighten, exercise, explain, groom, imbue, impart, implant, improve, inculcate, indoctrinate, inform, infuse, inseminate, inspire, instill, instruct, perfect, practice, prepare, ready, school, teach, train, tutor

educated *adj* 1 academic, educational, erudite, intellectual, learned, literary, literate, pedantic, scholarly, scholastic, well-read

adj 2 see: INTELLIGENT *adj* 4

education *n* 1 experience, exposure, involvement, practice, skill

n 2 instruction, learning, research, scholarship, schooling, study

n 3 culture, enrichment, erudition, learnedness, learning, wisdom

n 4 background, breeding, culture, development, environment, experience, past, schooling, training, upbringing

n 5 background, credentials, qualifications, training

educational *adj* 1 academic, enlightening, eye-opening, illuminating, informative, instructive, revealing, scholastic

adj 2 see: EDUCATED *adj* 1

educator *n* 1 academician, instructor, intern, professor, teacher

n 2 coach, instructor, leader, mentor, school teacher, teacher, trainer, tutor

educe *v* 1 deduce, derive, draw, elicit, evince, evoke, extract

v 2 analyze, conclude, construe, deduce, derive, draw, gather, glean, guess, infer, interpret, presume, surmise

eerie *adj* bizarre, ghostly, incredible, metaphysical, mystical, odd, ominous, spooky, strange, supernatural, uncanny, unearthly, weird

efface *v* abate, abolish, abrogate, annihilate, annul, call off, cancel, cease, delete, destroy, erase, excise, expunge, invalidate, kill, negate, nullify, obliterate, omit, quash, remove, stop, terminate, wipe out

effect *n* aftermath, consequence, corollary, eventuality, outcome, reaction, repercussion, result, reverberation, reward, upshot

v 1 alter, impact, impress, influence, modify

v 2 actuate, bring about, cause, create, draw on, execute, invoke, make, produce, secure

v 3 bring off, carry out, carry through, effectuate

v 4 bear, beget, breed, come into, create, engender, father, generate, hatch, impregnate, make, mate, multiply, originate, parent, procreate, promulgate, propagate, reproduce, sire, spawn

effective *adj* 1 accurate, deadly, sure

adj 2 clear, descriptive, graphic, precise

adj 3 lively, potent, punchy, snappy, strong

adj 4 convincing, forcible, impressive, inspiring, profound, striking

adj 5 clear, explicit, forceful, strong, trenchant, vigorous

adj 6 adequate, capable, competent, efficacious, efficient, proficient, successful, sufficient

adj 7 see: SOLID *adj* 4

effectively *adv* by itself, essentially, intrinsically, per se, practically, virtually

effectiveness *n* see: POTENCY *n* 2

effectuate *v* bring off, carry out, carry through, effect

effeminate *adj* 1 affected, genteel, phony, pretentious

adj 2 effete, sissy, swishy, unmanly, wimpy

effervescent *adj* bubbly, giddy, sparkling

effete *adj* 1 barren, frigid, impotent, infertile, spent, sterile, unbearing, unfertile, unfruitful, unproductive

adj 2 effeminate, sissy, swishy, unmanly, wimpy

efficacious *adj* adequate, capable, competent, effective, efficient, proficient, successful, sufficient

efficient *adj* 1 basic, businesslike, down-to-earth, hardheaded, practical, pragmatic, sensible

adj 2 adequate, capable, competent, effective, efficacious, proficient, successful, sufficient

effigy *n* doll, dummy, mannequin, replica

effort *n* 1 campaign, crusade, drive, expedition, push

n 2 attempt, endeavor, speculation, struggle, trial, try, undertaking, venture

n 3 assignment, chore, duty, job, mission, responsibility, stint, task

n 4 elbow grease, exertion, labor, pains, strain, struggle, toil, trouble, try, work

n 5 attempt, chance, fling, go, guess, heave, lob, pop, shot, slap, sling, stab, throw, toss, try, whirl

effortless *adj* casual, coming along, developing, easy, flowing, fluent, laid-back, running, smooth

effortlessly *adv* easily, lightly, naturally, readily, willingly

effortlessness *n* comfort, ease, freedom, leisure, liberty

effrontery *n* arrogance, assurance, audacity, boldness, brashness, brass, cheek, chutzpah, condescension, confidence, crust, face, gall, haughtiness, insolence, nerve, patronage, presumption, ridicule, sass, stamina, temerity

effuse *v* emote, emotionalize, gush, slobber

egg *n* bud, embryo, fetus, ovum, seed, zygote

v encourage, exhort, goad, incite, persuade, prick, prod, prompt, propel, spur, urge

egghead *n* academician, highbrow, intellectual, philosopher, pundit, researcher, sage, savant, scholar, thinker, wise man

ego *n* 1 dignity, pride, self-esteem, self-regard, self-respect

n 2 id, individuality, mind, persona, personality, psyche, self, soul, spirit

egotism *n* airs, arrogance, cockiness, conceit, condescension, disdain, haughtiness, image, loftiness, narcissism, pride, self-esteem, self-image, vanity

Einstein *n* brain, genius, intellect, prodigy, wizard

ejaculate *v* 1 discharge, shoot, spurt

v 2 blurt, cackle, cry, exclaim, shout, spill, sputter, tattle, utter

eject *v* boot out, chuck out, dismiss, evacuate, evict, expel, kick out, throw out

ejection *n* dismissal, expulsion, extraction, firing, impeachment, ouster, removal, termination

elaborate *adj* 1 abundant, flamboyant, luscious, ornate, replete

adj 2 complex, complicated, enigmatic, intricate, involved, knotty, mysterious, tangled

v 1 discourse, discuss, expatiate, ramble, sermonize

v 2 amplify, construct, develop, devise, enhance, enlarge, expand, expound, increase, refine

élan *n* animation, drive, energy, enthusiasm, esprit de corps, go, gusto, pep, potency, sparkle, spirit, spunk, verve, vigor, vim, vitality, zing, zip

elapse *v* cease, die, expire, lapse, pass, pass away, perish, succumb, terminate

elastic *adj* 1 bouncy, expansive, malleable, plastic, resilient

adj 2 alterable, flexible, movable, pliable, resilient, springy, supple

elasticity *n* bounce, resilience, spring

elate *v* appease, comfort, comply, content, delight, gratify, please, relieve, satisfy, suit

elated *adj* 1 delighted, ecstatic, enchanted, overjoyed, thrilled

adj 2 buoyant, cheerful, ecstatic, enthusiastic, exuberant, positive

adj 3 aroused, ebullient, euphoric, excited, exhilarated, happy, intoxicated, joyful, sparked, stimulated, turned on

adj 4 see: MERRY *adj* 2

elation *n* 1 bliss, delight, ecstasy, Eden, enchantment, heaven, joy, nirvana, paradise, pleasure, rapture, rhapsody

n 2 see: MERRIMENT *n*

elbow *v* bulldoze, hustle, jostle, press, push, shoulder, shove

elbowroom *n* capacity, leeway, room, space

elder *adj* first, older, oldest, senior

n ancestor, antecedent, ascendant, forebear, forefather, forerunner, founder, grandparent, parent, patriarch, predecessor, progenitor

elderly *adj* 1 senior

adj 2 aged, age-old, ancient, antique, gray, grizzled, old, olden, senior, timeworn, venerable, vintage, worn

elders *n* authority, brass, leaders, management, officers

elect *v* 1 choose, desire, favor, prefer, select

v 2 choose, like, pick, will, wish

v 3 appoint, ballot, choose, nominate, opt, select, vote

v 4 choose, cull, pick, remove, select, separate, sift, single out, sort

elected *adj* chosen, designated, picked, select, selected

election *n* alternative, choice, decision, druthers, option, pick, preference, rathers, selection, vote

elective *adj* optional

electric *adj* 1 exciting, exhilarating, provocative, rousing, stimulating, stirring

adj 2 magnetic

electricity *n* current, juice, power

electrify *v* 1 activate, charge, energize, enliven, excite, ignite, start, turn on, vitalize

v 2 amaze, daze, horrify, offend, outrage, overwhelm, scandalize, shock, stun

v 3 arouse, excite, fire, incite, inspire, rouse, spark, stimulate, tantalize, thrill, titillate, turn on, whet

electrifying *adj* dynamic, exciting, inspiring, stimulating, thrilling

electroplate *v* laminate, plate

elegance *n* 1 finesse, polish, refinement, style

n 2 attractiveness, charm, decorum, grace, refinement

n 3 see: WEALTH *n* 1

elegant *adj* 1 aesthetic, artistic, classy, refined, stylish, tasteful, well-chosen

adj 2 choice, dainty, delicate, exquisite, favorite, fine, preferred, rare, select

adj 3 best, finest, gilt-edged, magnificent, majestic, outstanding, preeminent, sensational, splendid, superb, superior, superlative

adj 4 civilized, cosmopolitan, cultivated, cultured, genteel, ingratiating, poised, polished, refined, smooth, sophisticated, suave, well-bred

adj 5 choice, deluxe, first-class, grand, luxuriant, luxurious, opulent, ornate, palatial, plush, posh, rich, soft, stately, sumptuous, thick

element *n* 1 article, entity, item, object, piece, thing

n 2 basic, essential, foundation, fundamental, principle, rudiment

n 3 component, constituent, factor, ingredient, item, part, segment

elementary *adj* 1 clear, coherent, direct, easy, intelligible, logical, lucid, simple, understandable *adj* 2 basic, dominant, first, foremost, fundamental, head, highest, leading, main, outstanding, paramount, preeminent, premier, primary, rudimentary, supreme, top

adj 3 basic, early, embryonic, essential, fundamental, initial, intrinsic, original, rudimentary, underlying

elements *n* chemicals, material, matter, substance

elevate *v* 1 better, enhance, enrich, fortify, improve, strengthen

    v 2 dignify, distinguish, exalt, glorify, grace, honor

    v 3 heave, hoist, lift, pick up, raise, take up

    v 4 advance, cultivate, enhance, enrich, improve, refine, upgrade

elevated *adj* 1 exalted, excellent, grand, great, heavenly, high, lofty, magnificent, prominent, sublime, superb

    adj 2 ethical, high-minded, moral, noble

    adj 3 aloft, high, lofty, overhead, soaring, tall

elevation *n* altitude, ascent, height

elf *n* fairy, naiad, nymph, pixie, sprite

elicit *v* 1 attract, draw, induce, solicit

    v 2 activate, cause, generate, prompt, provoke, spark, trigger

    v 3 deduce, derive, draw, educe, evince, evoke, extract

eligible *adj* acceptable, allowable, fitting, qualified, suitable

eliminate *v* 1 cleanse, eradicate, erase, purge, remove

    v 2 cleanse, discharge, empty, evacuate, excrete, void

    v 3 dispose of, expel, flush, purge, remove, rid, vanquish

    v 4 abandon, discard, dispose of, dump, empty, quit, reject, scrap, unload

    v 5 banish, bar, blackball, cut, debar, dismiss, except, exclude, ignore, leave out, omit, suspend

    v 6 see: PREVENT *v* 2

elite *n* 1 aristocracy, blue blood, cream, gentry, nobility, royalty, upper class

    n 2 best, choice, favorite, finest, optimum, pick, pride, select

elixir *n* compound, drug, formula, medicine, narcotic, painkiller, pharmaceutical, prescription

elocution *n* 1 accent, enunciation, inflection, intonation, manner, pronunciation

    n 2 rhetoric

elongate *v* continue, drag out, draw, extend, lengthen, prolong, protract, stretch

elongated *adj* 1 drawn out, extended, lengthened, lengthy, long, prolonged, protracted, stretched, sustained

    adj 2 rectangular

eloquent *adj* 1 expressive, intelligible, meaningful

    adj 2 articulate, clear, cogent, fluent, persuasive, well-spoken

elucidate *v* 1 analyze, annotate, clarify, define, detail, explain, expound, express, interpret, narrate, spell out, state, understand

    v 2 clarify, clear, clear up, delineate, depict, explain, illuminate, illustrate, picture, portray, reveal

elude *v* 1 avoid, duck, escape, eschew, evade, recoil, shun, shy

    v 2 see: FLEE *v* 1

    v 3 see: THWART *v* 4

elusive *adj* 1 intangible

    adj 2 evasive, fleeting, slippery

    adj 3 baffling, frustrating, mysterious, puzzling, subtle

emaciated *adj* 1 angular, bony, gaunt, lanky, lean, meager, scraggly, scrawny, skinny, slender, thin

    adj 2 see: WEARY *adj* 1

emanate *v* 1 ensue, follow, result, succeed

    v 2 discharge, emit, expel, project, radiate, release, send

    v 3 appear, arise, ascend, come forth, emerge, form, issue, loom

    v 4 arise, come from, derive, flow, head, issue, originate, spring, stem

emanation *n* air, ambience, atmosphere, aura, feel, feeling, mood, semblance, spirit

emancipate *v* discharge, free, liberate, loosen, release, unbind, unchain, unshackle

emasculate *adj* impotent, inadequate, ineffective, ineffectual, spineless, weak

    v castrate, debilitate, dismember, enervate, geld, unman, unnerve

embankment *n* bastion, bulwark, defense, fort, fortification, rampart, wall

embargo *n* ban, blockage, boycott, curtailment, prohibition, restriction, stoppage

embark *v* see: INITIATE *v* 2

embarrass *v* 1 see: BELITTLE *v* 1

    v 2 see: BEWILDER *v* 2

embarrassed *adj* abashed, ashamed, chagrined, humiliated, mortified, shamed

embarrassing *adj* awkward, delicate, difficult, sticky, tricky

embassy *n* commission, delegation, mission

embellish *v* 1 bias, color, distort, exaggerate, influence, slant

    v 2 adorn, beautify, bedeck, deck, decorate, dress up, enhance, garnish, glamorize, grace, ornament, polish, trim

embellishment *n* 1 decoration, ornament

n 2 ballyhoo, exaggeration, hoopla, hype, hyperbole, overstatement, promotion, public relations

embezzle *v* 1 bamboozle, beat, beguile, bilk, burn, cajole, cheat, chicane, chisel, con, cross, deceive, defraud, dupe, fleece, flimflam, fob, foist, fool, gyp, hoax, hoodwink, hustle, inveigle, screw, shaft, sham, swindle, trick, victimize

v 2 see: STEAL *v* 2

embezzler *n* bandit, brigand, burglar, cheat, con artist, con man, criminal, crook, gyp, highwayman, looter, mugger, outlaw, robber, swindler, thief

emblem *n* 1 badge

n 2 brand, cachet, imprint, logo, logotype, mark, seal, stamp, trademark

n 3 character, example, icon, letter, logo, mark, model, representation, sign, symbol, token

embody *v* 1 incarnate

v 2 exemplify, express, personify, represent, symbolize, typify

v 3 comprehend, comprise, contain, embrace, encompass, have, include, incorporate, involve, take in

embrace *n* caress, fondling, hug, kiss, squeeze, touch

v 1 caress, clutch, grasp, hold

v 2 adopt, borrow, foster, subscribe, take on, take up, utilize

v 3 address, call to, greet, hail, meet, salute, summon, welcome

v 4 clasp, clinch, cuddle, enfold, hold, hug, press, squeeze

v 5 comprehend, comprise, contain, embody, encompass, have, include, incorporate, involve, take in

v 6 caress, cradle, cuddle, feel, fondle, fool around, hold, hug, love, make out, neck, nuzzle, pet, snuggle, stroke

embroil *v* accuse, associate, blame, confuse, connect, enmesh, ensnare, entangle, implicate, involve, mire, tangle

embryo *n* bud, egg, fetus, ovum, seed, zygote

embryonic *adj* 1 beginning, budding

adj 2 beginning, founding, incipient, initial, introductory, nascent, rudimentary, starting

adj 3 basic, early, elementary, essential, fundamental, initial, intrinsic, original, rudimentary, underlying

emerald *adj* chartreuse, green, jade, kelly

emerge *v* 1 develop, ensue, follow, happen, lead to, result

v 2 appear, arise, ascend, come forth, emanate, form, issue, loom

emergency *n* climax, crisis, crux, dilemma, juncture, point, predicament

emigrant *n* drifter, itinerant, migrant, nomad, transient

émigré *n* castaway, escapee, evacuee, exile, expatriate, refugee

eminent *adj* 1 great, important, outstanding, superior

adj 2 acclaimed, celebrated, distinguished, esteemed, excellent, famed, famous, foremost, illustrious, notable, outstanding, prestigious, prominent, renowned, well-known

eminently *adv* awfully, dreadfully, endlessly, exceedingly, exceptionally, extremely, greatly, highly, mightily, notably, quite, remarkably, terribly, thoroughly, very

emissary *n* agent, ambassador, consul, delegate, deputy, diplomat, envoy

emission *n* excretion

emit *v* 1 discharge, fire, hurl, launch, project, shoot

v 2 discharge, emanate, expel, project, radiate, release, send

v 3 discharge, drip, exude, leak, ooze, secrete, seep, trickle

v 4 beam, burn, disperse, gleam, glisten, radiate, shed, shine, transmit

v 5 see: POUR *v* 2

emitting *adj* see: BRIGHT *adj* 6

emollient *n* balm, salve

emote *v* effuse, emotionalize, gush, slobber

emotion *n* 1 affection, feeling, passion, regard, sensation, sense, sensibility, sentiment, tenderness

n 2 awareness, faculty, feel, feeling, intuition, perception, reaction, response, sensation, sense

emotional *adj* 1 flowery, gushy, melodramatic, sentimental

adj 2 biased, partial, predisposed, prejudiced, subjective

adj 3 crushed, defeated, distraught, overcome, subdued

adj 4 feeling, sensitive, sentient, susceptible, tender

adj 5 affective, cognitive, mental, psychic, psychological, subconscious, subjective

adj 6 alienated, angry, bitter, hurt, jealous, offended, provoked, resentful

adj 7 fervent, fiery, zealous

adj 8 absurd, balmy, bizarre, crazy, foolish, frivolous, goofy, illogical, impossible, inane, insane, irrational, loony, lunatic, mad, muddled, nuts, preposterous, ridiculous, silly, touched, wacky, zany

emotionalize v effuse, emote, gush, slobber

emotionless adj cold, coldhearted, distant, frigid, glacial, icy, impersonal, indifferent, unemotional, unfriendly

empathetic adj 1 intuitive, sensitive

adj 2 affectionate, compassionate, considerate, empathic, gentle, humane, kind, kindhearted, responsive, softhearted, sympathetic, tender, warm, warmhearted

adj 3 see: FRIENDLY adj 3

empathic adj affectionate, compassionate, considerate, empathetic, gentle, humane, kind, kindhearted, responsive, softhearted, sympathetic, tender, warm, warmhearted

empathize v ache, commiserate, feel for, pity, sympathize with

empathy n 1 affinity, compassion, kindness, mercy, pity, rue, sympathy, tenderness, understanding

n 2 accord, affinity, agreement, assent, concert, concord, congruence, cooperation, harmony, rapport, synergy, teamwork, unity

emphasis n 1 accent, highlighting, importance, priority, significance, stress, weight

n 2 concern, gravity, import, importance, significance, stress, weight

emphasize v 1 reiterate, repeat, reprise, resay, stress

v 2 iterate, reiterate, repeat, restate, stress

v 3 assert, demand, force, insist, persist, require, urge

v 4 accent, accentuate, amplify, concentrate, feature, flag, focus, heighten, highlight, italicize, mark, punctuate, spotlight, stress, underline, underscore

emphatic adj 1 ardent, decisive, determined, extreme, forceful, intense, potent, powerful, severe, strong

adj 2 see: ASSERTIVE adj

adj 3 see: EXACT adj 6

employ v 1 engage, hire, put on, recruit, retain, take on

v 2 apply, bestow, exercise, exploit, handle, use, utilize

employed adj busy, engaged, functional, in use, occupied, working

employee n 1 assistant, dependent, subordinate, underling

n 2 aide, aide-de-camp, assistant, attendant, hand, helper, hired hand, laborer, servant, supporter, worker

employees n crew, faculty, help, people, personnel, staff, workers

employment n 1 appliance, application, form, method, operation, play, technique, use, utilization

n 2 art, avocation, business, calling, career, discipline, field, gig, job, labor, line, livelihood, occupation, office, profession, pursuit, role, schtick, situation, specialty, task, thing, trade, vocation, work

n 3 engagement, engaging, hiring, recruitment

empower v 1 assign, authorize, delegate, designate, entrust, pass along

v 2 accredit, authorize, certify, commission, enable, entitle, facilitate, invest, license, permit, sanction, validate

emptiness n 1 nil, nothing, nothingness, oblivion, void

n 2 blank, cavity, crack, depression, gap, hole, hollow, nook, opening, space, void

empty adj 1 bare, blank, dull, lifeless, unfilled

adj 2 hollow, idle, insincere, meaningless, shallow, vain

adj 3 bare, barren, clear, stark, vacant, vacuous, void

v 1 clear, deplete, drain, evacuate, take out, vacate

v 2 cleanse, discharge, eliminate, evacuate, excrete, void

v 3 abandon, discard, dispose of, dump, eliminate, quit, reject, scrap, unload

v 4 cast away, consume, dissipate, drivel, fritter, lavish, squander, throw away, use up, waste

emulate v act, ape, copy, follow, imitate, lip-synch, mime, mimic, mock, model, mouth, pantomime, parody, pattern, take off

enable v accredit, authorize, certify, commission, empower, entitle, facilitate, invest, license, permit, sanction, validate

enablement n advantage, birthright, claim, edge, perquisite, prerogative, privilege, right, title

enact v 1 actuate, commit, do, execute, perform, perpetrate

v 2 approve, authorize, decree, legalize, legislate, ordain, pass, ratify, sanction

enactment n approval, confirmation, doctrine, evidence, passage, proof, testament, testimony, witness

enamored adj 1 captivated, fascinated, infatuated, in love

adj 2 affectionate, amorous, attached, caring, devoted, fond, loving, romantic, tender

enchant v allure, attract, bedevil, beguile, bewitch, captivate, charm, conjure, delight, draw, enthrall, fascinate, lure, magnetize, mesmerize, tempt, wile

enchanted *adj* delighted, ecstatic, elated, overjoyed, thrilled

enchanting *adj* **1** alluring, attractive, becoming, coy, cute, enticing, fascinating, foxy, inviting, pleasing, ravishing, seductive, sexy

adj **2** alluring, beguiling, bewitching, captivating, catchy, charming, dazzling, dynamic, engaging, enthralling, enticing, fascinating, glamorous, intriguing, mesmerizing, riveting, spectacular, spellbinding

enchantment *n* **1** bewitchment, incantation, magic, occultism, sorcery, spell, voodoo, witchcraft, wizardry

n **2** see: CHARISMA *n* 2

n **3** see: DELIGHT *n* 2

encircle *v* **1** bend, connect, join, loop, twist

v **2** bound, compass, enclose, encompass, enfold, envelop, surround

encircling *adj* around, enclosing, nearby, on all sides, surrounding

enclose *v* **1** barricade, fortify, protect

v **2** add, contain, include, incorporate, insert

v **3** bundle, cover, envelop, package, wrap

v **4** bound, compass, encircle, encompass, enfold, envelop, surround

v **5** see: IMPRISON *v* 2

enclosed *adj* hidden, inner, innermost, interior, internal, private, secret

enclosing *adj* around, encircling, nearby, on all sides, surrounding

enclosure *n* **1** case, housing

n **2** case, coat, cover, folder, jacket, skin

n **3** barn, coop, hatch, lean-to, paddock, pen, pound, shack, shelter, shed, stable, stall, sty

encode *v* program

encompass *v* **1** bound, compass, encircle, enclose, enfold, envelop, surround

v **2** comprehend, comprise, contain, embody, embrace, have, include, incorporate, involve, take in

encore *n* reappearance

encounter *n* **1** confrontation, gathering, meeting

n **2** adventure, event, experience, hazard, ordeal, peril, risk

n **3** battle, combat, conflagration, dispute, fight, struggle, war

n **4** contest, scramble, skirmish, struggle

n **5** affray, battle, brawl, brush, clash, conflict, difference, disagreement, dispute, fight, fracas, melee, quarrel, run-in, scrimmage, skirmish, spat, touch

v **1** endure, experience, know, realize, understand

v **2** greet, interview, meet, receive, see, visit

v **3** affront, face, insult, offend, outrage, slight

v **4** chance, discover, find, happen, hit, luck, meet, stumble

v **5** ascertain, catch, descry, detect, discover, espy, ferret, find, locate, spot, turn up, uncover

encourage *v* **1** egg on, lead on, maintain, string

v **2** ask, bid, invite, request, solicit

v **3** cultivate, develop, foster, further, grow, promote

v **4** amplify, bolster, enhance, enhearten, hearten, increase, inspire, reassure, strengthen, support

v **5** egg, exhort, goad, incite, persuade, prick, prod, prompt, propel, spur, urge

v **6** advocate, countenance, favor

v **7** delight, enjoy, gladden, hearten, inspire, please

v **8** attract, court, flirt, invite, lure, pursue, romance, solicit, tempt, woo

v **9** agitate, anger, arouse, foment, ignite, incite, induce, inflame, inspire, instigate, invoke, motivate, muster, prod, propel, provoke, raise, set, set on, spur, stimulate, stir, urge

v **10** abet, advance, aid, ameliorate, amend, assist, avail, benefit, better, boost, cultivate, do for, ease, egg on, enhance, forward, foster, further, help, improve, nurture, prefer, promote, rev, serve, spur on, support

encouragement *n* motivation

encouraging *adj* auspicious, cheerful, confident, hopeful, optimistic, promising, sanguine, upbeat

encroach *v* **1** bother, burden, impose, intrude, presume, saddle

v **2** attack, entrench, infringe, intrude, invade, trespass, violate

encumber *v* **1** burden, check, hamper, hinder, impede, obstruct, restrain, restrict, retard

v **2** burden, hamper, load, oppress, overdo, overload, saddle, strain, tax

v **3** burden, demand, force, prescribe

v **4** cripple, disable, disarm, freeze, halt, handcuff, immobilize, incapacitate, paralyze, prostrate, stop, stun

v **5** bar, block, brake, choke, clog, dam, deter, detract, frustrate, halt, hamper, hesitate, hinder, impair, impede, inhibit, jam, obstruct, prevent, repress, restrain, retard, slow, stay, stop, stop up, throttle

encumbered *adj* burdened, fraught, harried, laden, loaded, pressured

encumbrance *n* 1 indebtedness, liability, lien, mortgage, obligation, security

n 2 bar, barrier, bottleneck, crimp, dead end, deadlock, difficulty, hurdle, impasse, impediment, obstacle, obstruction, snag, stumbling block

encyclopedia *n* authority, dictionary, reference, source

end *n* 1 consequence, issue, outcome, result

n 2 edge, nib, nub, tip

n 3 completion, conclusion, culmination, finale, finish, windup

n 4 patch, piece, rag, scrap, shred, tatter

n 5 ceasing, cessation, close, closure, conclusion, finale, finis, finish, stop, termination

n 6 bit, dab, fragment, iota, minutia, mite, morsel, particle, piece, pinch, portion, scrap, shred, speck, spot, strip, tidbit, trifle

n 7 last, tail, trailing

n 8 ass, backside, base, behind, bottom, bucket, buns, butt, buttocks, derrière, fanny, hindquarters, posterior, rump, seat, stub, stump, tip, tush

v 1 cancel, halt, kill, stop

v 2 bring about, conclude, generate, result in, yield

v 3 achieve, cease, complete, conclude, consummate, finish, halt, perfect, terminate, wind up, wrap up

v 4 adjourn, cap, climax, complete, conclude, consummate, crown, culminate, dissolve, finalize, finish, terminate, wind up, wrap up

v 5 abstain, cease, conclude, desist, discontinue, finish, forbear, freeze, halt, knock off, quit, refrain, sever, stop, terminate

endeavor *n* 1 activity, business, enterprise, exercise, project, undertaking, venture

n 2 attempt, effort, speculation, struggle, trial, try, undertaking, venture

v assay, attempt, essay, offer, quest, seek, strive, struggle, try, undertake

ended *adj* accomplished, complete, concluded, done, finished, over, performed, terminated, through, wrapped up

endemic *adj* 1 aboriginal, indigenous, native, primitive

adj 2 domestic, folk, indigenous, local, native, traditional

endless *adj* 1 long, slow, tedious, tiresome

adj 2 eternal, immortal, infinite, perpetual, unceasing, undying

adj 3 avaricious, covetous, insatiable, ravenous, unquenchable, voracious

adj 4 ageless, boundless, ceaseless, constant, continual, continuous, eternal, everlasting, incessant, infinite, interminable, limitless, never-ending, ongoing, perpetual, persistent, relentless, timeless, unceasing, unending, uninterrupted, unremitting

adj 5 consistent, constant, continuing, equable, established, even, invariable, reliable, routine, same, serene, stable, steady, unchanging, unfailing, unfluctuating, uniform, unvarying

endlessly *adv* 1 awfully, dreadfully, eminently, exceedingly, exceptionally, extremely, greatly, highly, mightily, notably, quite, remarkably, terribly, thoroughly, very

adv 2 see: FOREVER *adv*

endorse *v* 1 promote, ratify, second, support

v 2 assure, certify, contract, guarantee, pledge, sanction, underwrite, vouch, warrant

v 3 advocate, back, champion, guarantee, promote, sanction, side, support, uphold

v 4 accept, agree, allow, approve, assent, comply, concur, consent, sign up, subscribe

v 5 accept, approbate, approve, authorize, certify, condone, confirm, countenance, favor, pass, ratify, sanction, validate

v 6 advertise, air, boom, boost, drum up, pitch, plug, promote, publicize, push, rave, sell, tout

v 7 see: PROPOSE *v* 4

endorsement *n* 1 approval, autograph, John Hancock, mark, name, signature

n 2 auspices, authorization, backing, command, confirmation, fiat, patronage, sanction, sponsorship, support

endow *v* 1 equip, furnish, give, provide

v 2 aid, finance, fund, subsidize, underwrite

v 3 bequeath, give, remember, reward, tip

v 4 accord, adduce, award, bequeath, bestow, concede, confer, contribute, deliver, devote, donate, extend, fund, give, give away, grant, hand down, hand out, impart, offer, pose, present, proffer, provide, supply, tender, volunteer

endowment *n* 1 award, bequest, gift, grant, reward, scholarship

n 2 birthright, entitlement, estate, heritage, inheritance, legacy, patrimony

endurable *adj* allowable, bearable, sustainable, tolerable

endurance *n* 1 forbearance, patience, perseverance, persistence, resignation, resolution, tenacity

n 2 continuation, duration, existence, life, span, subsistence, survival, term

n 3 backbone, chutzpah, determination, fortitude, grit, guts, moxie, nerve, persistence, pluck, resilience, spirit, spunk, stamina, strength, tenacity, tolerance, vigor, willpower

endure *v* 1 experience, subject, suffer

v 2 encounter, experience, know, realize, understand

v 3 be, exist, last, live, persist, prevail, survive

v 4 abide, continue, last, outlast, persevere, persist, prevail, remain, stay, stick to, stick with, survive

v 5 abide, accept, acquiesce, allow, authorize, bear, concede, condone, digest, experience, have, let, permit, put up with, stand, stomach, suffer, sustain, swallow, take, tolerate, undergo

enduring *adj* 1 continuing, constant, durable, eternal, lasting, ongoing, permanent, stable

adj 2 abiding, firm, never-failing, steadfast, sure, unfaltering, unshakable, unwavering

adj 3 continuing, inveterate, lifelong, long-lasting, long-lived, old, ongoing, perennial

enema *n* cleansing, laxative, physic, purge

enemy *n* adversary, antagonist, anti, challenger, competitor, con, contender, foe, match, opponent, rival

energetic *adj* 1 active, alive, dynamic, sound, spirited, strong, vibrant, vigorous, vital

adj 2 active, bustling, busy, creative, driving, enterprising, inventive, lively, resourceful

adj 3 coercive, compelling, dynamic, forceful, hardy, lusty, mighty, passionate, powerful, robust, strong, sturdy, vigorous

adj 4 aggressive, ambitious, assertive, assured, compelling, compulsive, confident, decided, dogmatic, driven, emphatic, insistent, militant, positive, pushing, pushy, self-assertive, sure, urging

adj 5 alert, animated, bouncy, bright, brisk, buoyant, chipper, dashing, dynamic, ebullient, enthusiastic, exuberant, frisky, frolicsome, gay, jumpy, kinetic, lively, peppy, pert, playful, rousing, scintillating, spirited, sprightly, spry, vivacious

adj 6 see: AGILE *adj* 3

adj 7 see: HARD-WORKING *adj*

energize *v* activate, charge, electrify, enliven, excite, ignite, start, turn on, vitalize

energizing *adj* exhilarating, fresh, invigorating, refreshing, stimulating

energy *n* 1 nourishment, provisions, rations, supply

n 2 concentration, depth, intensity, profundity, strength, substance, vigor

n 3 animation, drive, élan, enthusiasm, esprit de corps, go, gusto, pep, potency, sparkle, spirit, spunk, verve, vigor, vim, vitality, zing, zip

n 4 ardor, beef, brawn, drive, force, intensity, lustiness, might, muscle, pep, potency, power, punch, steam, strength, verve, vigor, vim, virility, vitality

n 5 fuel, gasoline, petrol, propellant

enervate *v* castrate, debilitate, dismember, emasculate, geld, unman, unnerve

enfeeble *v* cripple, debilitate, disable, drain, exhaust, sap, undermine, weaken

enfold *v* 1 bound, compass, enclose, encircle, encompass, envelop, surround

v 2 clasp, clinch, cuddle, embrace, hold, hug, press, squeeze

enforcer *n* authoritarian, autocrat, dictator

engage *v* 1 charter, commission, lease

v 2 bind, commit, contract, pledge

v 3 connect, hook up, interlock, mesh, network

v 4 employ, hire, put on, recruit, retain, take on

v 5 acquire, arouse, commit, contract, enlist, incur, induce

v 6 enlist, enroll, muster, recruit, register, secure, sign up

v 7 combat, conflict, contend, contest, scuffle, skirmish, struggle, tussle

v 8 arrange, bespeak, book, organize, plan, program, reserve, schedule, slate

v 9 altercate, argue, battle, bicker, brawl, clash, conflict, dispute, equivocate, feud, fight, fray, haggle, hassle, quarrel, quibble, row, scrap, spar, squabble, wrangle

engaged *adj* 1 betrothed, committed, pledged, promised

adj 2 busy, employed, functional, in use, occupied, working

adj 3 absorbed, agog, concentrated, deep, determined, distracted, engrossed, enraptured, entranced, fascinated, immersed, intent, preoccupied, rapt, wrapped up

engagement *n* 1 betrothal

n **2** appointment, booking, date, listing, reservation, schedule

n **3** action, battle, fray, gesture, movement, operation, proceeding

n **4** employment, engaging, hiring, recruitment

engaging *adj* see: FASCINATING *adj* 2

n employment, engagement, hiring, recruitment

engender *v* **1** father, fertilize, husband, impregnate, inseminate, sire

v **2** see: BEGET *v*

engine *n* device, generator, machine, motor, turbine

engineer *n* architect, designer, draftsperson, inventor, manager, operator, plotter, schemer, surveyor

v **1** arrange, blueprint, cast, chart, design, devise, draft, draw, fashion, lay out, map, outline, plan, plot, project, set out, sketch

v **2** see: FORMULATE *v* 2

engram *n* memory, recall, remembrance, retention, retentiveness, retrospection

engrave *v* **1** ingrain

v **2** carve, cut, etch, inscribe

engross *v* **1** absorb, blot, consume, engulf, occupy, soak up

v **2** captivate, charm, delight, enrapture, enravish, enthrall, entrance, hypnotize, mesmerize, move, ravish, transport

engrossed *adj* **1** absorbed, curious, drawn, interested, involved

adj **2** absorbed, agog, concentrated, deep, determined, distracted, engaged, enraptured, entranced, fascinated, immersed, intent, preoccupied, rapt, wrapped up

engulf *v* **1** absorb, blot, consume, engross, occupy, soak up

v **2** bury, drown, flood, inundate, overflow, swamp, wash over

enhance *v* **1** augment, magnify, maximize, optimize, utilize

v **2** better, elevate, enrich, fortify, improve, strengthen

v **3** advance, cultivate, elevate, enrich, improve, refine, upgrade

v **4** color, flavor, imbue, infuse, salt, season, spice

v **5** amplify, construct, develop, devise, elaborate, enlarge, expand, expound, increase, refine

v **6** amplify, bolster, encourage, enhearten, hearten, increase, inspire, reassure, strengthen, support

v **7** adorn, beautify, bedeck, deck, decorate, dress up, embellish, garnish, glamorize, grace, ornament, polish, trim

v **8** abet, advance, aid, ameliorate, amend, assist, avail, benefit, better, boost, cultivate, do for, ease, egg on, encourage, forward, foster, further, help, improve, nurture, prefer, promote, rev, serve, spur on, support

enhancement *n* **1** addition, advancement, advantage, betterment, gain, growth, improvement, plus

n **2** degree, distinction, nuance, shade, subtlety, touch, trace, variation

enhearten *v* amplify, bolster, encourage, enhance, hearten, increase, inspire, reassure, strengthen, support

enigma *n* **1** confidence, intrigue, mystery, secret

n **2** confusion, conundrum, difficulty, dilemma, mystery, obstacle, paradox, perplexity, problem, puzzle, quandary, question, riddle, secret

enigmatic *adj* **1** ambiguous, cryptic, mystifying, occult, puzzling, vague

adj **2** incomprehensible, inexplicable, inscrutable, mysterious, occult, puzzling

adj **3** complex, complicated, elaborate, intricate, involved, knotty, mysterious, tangled

enjoin *v* **1** bid, charge, claim, command, demand, direct, instruct, order

v **2** see: PROHIBIT *v*

enjoy *v* **1** admire, appreciate, cherish, delight, relish, revel, savor

v **2** bask, delight, like, loaf, luxuriate, relax, relish, rest, savor, wallow

v **3** delight, encourage, gladden, hearten, inspire, please

enjoyable *adj* **1** advantageous, better, desirable, preferable, superior, worthier, worthwhile

adj **2** amusing, diverting, entertaining, fun, humorous, joking, playful

enjoyment *n* **1** appetite, liking, relish, taste

n **2** delight, joy, pleasure, satisfaction

n **3** excitement, kicks, pleasure, stimulation, thrills

n **4** see: PASSION *n* 7

n **5** see: RECREATION *n* 2

enkindle *v* burn, fire, ignite, inflame, kindle, light, spark

enlarge *v* **1** broaden, flare, open, spread, widen

v **2** apply, augment, capitalize on, increase, parlay, use

v **3** amplify, construct, develop, devise, elaborate, enhance, expand, expound, increase, refine

v **4** amplify, bloat, dilate, distend, expand, fatten, grow, increase, inflate, magnify, stretch, swell, widen *v* **5** amplify, append, augment, boost, build, expand, extend, grow, heighten, increase, intensify, magnify, multiply, run up, snowball, supplement, upsurge, wax

v **6** focus

enlargement *n* growth, increase, rise, swell

enlighten *v* coach, communicate, condition, convey, cultivate, develop, discipline, drill, edify, educate, exercise, explain, groom, imbue, impart, implant, improve, inculcate, indoctrinate, inform, infuse, inseminate, inspire, instill, instruct, perfect, practice, prepare, ready, school, teach, train, tutor

enlightened *adj* see: WISE *adj* **4**

enlightening *adj* academic, educational, eye-opening, illuminating, informative, instructive, revealing, scholastic

enlist *v* **1** acquire, arouse, commit, contract, engage, incur, induce

v **2** engage, enroll, muster, recruit, register, secure, sign up

enliven *v* **1** animate, brighten, cheer up, incite, inspire, liven, quicken, resuscitate, vivify

v **2** activate, charge, electrify, energize, excite, ignite, start, turn on, vitalize

enmesh *v* accuse, associate, blame, confuse, connect, embroil, ensnare, entangle, implicate, involve, mire, tangle

enmity *n* see: HATE *n*

ennui *n* **1** apathy, boredom, dreariness, dullness, malaise, monotony, tedium

n **2** see: LETHARGY *n* **1**

enormous *adj* **1** colossal, fantastic, Gargantuan, giant, gigantic, Goliath, great, huge, immense, jumbo, leviathan, mammoth, massive, mighty, monstrous, monumental, overwhelming, phenomenal, prodigious, promethean, stupendous, titanic, towering, tremendous, unfathomed, untold, vast, walloping, whopping

adj **2** see: BIG *adj* **4**

enough *adj* **1** abounding, abundant, ample, bounteous, bountiful, copious, galore, generous, liberal, overflowing, plentiful, plenty, prodigal, profuse, teeming

adj **2** acceptable, adequate, competent, decent, fair, good, mediocre, passable, reasonable, respectable, satisfactory, sufficient, tolerable

adv adequately, amply, equitably, fairly, justly, moderately, passably, rather, satisfactorily, tolerably

enrage *v* see: BOTHER *v* **5**

enraged *adj* aggravated, angry, annoyed, cross, excited, fuming, furious, hot, in-

censed, indignant, irate, irritable, mad, provoked, teed off, upset

enrapture *v* captivate, charm, delight, engross, enravish, enthrall, entrance, hypnotize, mesmerize, move, ravish, transport

enraptured *adj* see: ENGROSSED *adj* **2**

enravish *v* captivate, charm, delight, engross, enrapture, enthrall, entrance, hypnotize, mesmerize, move, ravish, transport

enrich *v* **1** better, elevate, enhance, fortify, improve, strengthen

v **2** advance, cultivate, elevate, enhance, improve, refine, upgrade

v **3** fertilize

v **4** sweeten

enrichment *n* culture, education, eruditeness, erudition, learnedness, learning, wisdom

enroll *v* **1** admit, matriculate, receive, register

v **2** apply, claim, file, petition, request, sign up

v **3** engage, enlist, muster, recruit, register, secure, sign up

v **4** call, conscript, draft, force, impress, induct, select, shanghai

v **5** catalog, inscribe, list, register, sign up, write

ensconce *v* **1** harbor, nestle, settle, shelter, snuggle

v **2** bury, cache, cloister, conceal, cover, ditch, hide, plant, secrete, sequester, stash

ensconced *adj* **1** entrenched, established, fixed, fundamental, ingrained, intrinsic, inveterate, settled, sworn

adj **2** clad, clothed

ensemble *n* band, orchestra, strings

enshrine *v* anoint, baptize, bless, consecrate, dedicate, devote, exalt, hallow, purify, sanctify

enslave *v* bear down, beat down, conquer, crush, defeat, dominate, exploit, overpower, quash, reduce, subdue, subjugate, suppress, vanquish

enslavement *n* bondage, imprisonment, indenture, serfdom, servility, servitude, slavery

ensnare *v* **1** accuse, associate, blame, confuse, connect, embroil, enmesh, entangle, implicate, involve, mire, tangle

v **2** befoul, catch, entangle, foul, hang

v **3** bag, capture, catch, entangle, entrap, hook, snag, snare, snarl, tangle, trap, trick

ensue *v* **1** emanate, follow, result, succeed

v 2 develop, emerge, follow, happen, lead to, result

v 3 see: OCCUR *v* 2

ensuing *adj* 1 following, latter, next, subsequent, succeeding, successive

adj 2 after, beyond, following, subsequent, succeeding, successive

entangle *v* 1 complicate, confound, confuse, mix, mix up, snarl

v 2 accuse, associate, blame, confuse, connect, embroil, enmesh, ensnare, implicate, involve, mire, tangle

v 3 bag, capture, catch, ensnare, entrap, hook, snag, snare, snarl, tangle, trap, trick

v 4 befoul, catch, ensnare, foul, hang

entanglement *n* adultery, affair, cheating, dalliance, fling, flirtation, fooling around, infatuation, intimacy, intrigue, liaison, love affair, playing around, rendezvous, romance, tryst

enter *v* 1 infiltrate, infuse, penetrate, permeate, transfuse

v 2 capture, chart, denote, itemize, jot, list, log, note, preserve, record, register, take notes, tally, tape, write down

v 3 come in, go in, immigrate

v 4 log, record, register

v 5 activate, begin, cause, commence, constitute, create, embark, establish, inaugurate, induct, initiate, install, instigate, instill, institute, introduce, kick off, launch, lead off, open, originate, precipitate, preface, set up, start, tee off, usher in, venture forth

enterprise *n* 1 gumption, initiative, resourcefulness, spirit, spunk, volition

n 2 activity, business, endeavor, exercise, project, undertaking, venture

n 3 ambition, drive, initiative, lead, leadership, push, thrust, volition

n 4 arrangements, business, commerce, dealings, industry, intercourse, negotiations, trade, traffic

n 5 business, company, concern, corporation, establishment, firm, house, organization, partnership

enterprising *adj* 1 adaptive, bold, canny, clever, resourceful, venturesome

adj 2 active, bustling, busy, creative, driving, energetic, inventive, lively, resourceful

adj 3 clever, creative, deft, fertile, imaginative, ingenious, inventive, resourceful, skillful, talented

adj 4 businesslike, entrepreneurial, gumptious, up and coming

entertain *v* 1 court, date, go out, meet

v 2 amuse, charm, divert, interest, please, recreate, stimulate

entertainer *n* actor, actress, artist, hero, heroine, lead, movie star, performer, player, protagonist, star, thespian, tragedian

entertaining *adj* 1 appealing, colorful, interesting, lively, stimulating, varied

adj 2 amusing, diverting, enjoyable, fun, humorous, joking, playful

entertainment *n* amusement, distraction, diversion, enjoyment, frolic, fun, game, hobby, pastime, play, recreation, sport

enthrall *v* 1 captivate, charm, delight, engross, enrapture, enravish, entrance, hypnotize, mesmerize, move, ravish, transport

v 2 see: ATTRACT *v* 6

enthralling *adj* see: FASCINATING *adj* 2

enthusiasm *n* 1 alacrity, ardor, delight, devotion, diligence, enjoyment, excitement, fervor, fire, flame, gaiety, gusto, passion, relish, savor, thrill, zeal, zest

n 2 animation, drive, élan, energy, esprit de corps, go, gusto, pep, potency, sparkle, spirit, spunk, verve, vigor, vim, vitality, zing, zip

enthusiast *n* 1 admirer, buff, devotee, disciple, fan, follower, groupie

n 2 bug, crusader, fanatic, fiend, freak, hobbyist, maniac, monomaniac, nut, radical, zealot

enthusiastic *adj* 1 buoyant, cheerful, ecstatic, elated, exuberant, positive

adj 2 ardent, excitable, fervent, fiery, flaming, hot-blooded, impassioned, intense, passionate, stirring, sweaty, torrid, zealous

adj 3 anxious, ardent, avid, breathless, desirous, eager, excited, fain, impatient, impetuous, keen, passionate, raring, zealous

adj 4 alert, animated, bouncy, bright, brisk, buoyant, chipper, dashing, dynamic, ebullient, energetic, exuberant, frisky, frolicsome, gay, jumpy, kinetic, lively, peppy, pert, playful, rousing, scintillating, spirited, sprightly, spry, vivacious

entice *v* 1 charm, disarm, sway

v 2 attract, bait, decoy, entrap, lure, tantalize

enticement *n* 1 attraction, bait, come-on, decoy, lure, magnet, ruse, seduction, snare, temptation, trap, wile

n 2 see: CHARISMA *n* 2

enticing *adj* 1 alluring, attractive, becoming, coy, cute, enchanting, fascinating, foxy, inviting, pleasing, ravishing, seductive, sexy

adj 2 carnal, delicious, erotic, hedonistic, luscious, lush, lusty, luxurious, pleasure-seeking, sensual, sensualistic, sensuous, sexual, voluptuous

adj 3 alluring, beguiling, bewitching, captivating, catchy, charming, dazzling, dynamic, enchanting, engaging, enthralling, fascinating, glamorous, intriguing, mesmerizing, riveting, spectacular, spellbinding

entire *adj* all, all-out, complete, full-blown, gross, integral, integrated, outright, total, unlimited, whole

entirely *adv* 1 adequately, altogether, assiduously, completely, earnestly, exhaustively, fully, hard, intensely, intensively, painstakingly, perfectly, quite, sufficiently, thoroughly, totally, unremittingly, utterly, wholly

adv 2 see: DEFINITELY *adv*

entirety *n* aggregate, all, gross, revenue, sales, sum, sum total, total, totality, whole

entitle *v* 1 call, define, designate, label, name, term

v 2 baptize, bestow, call, christen, confer, designate, dub, name, nickname, tag, term, title

v 3 see: AUTHORIZE *v* 3

entitlement *n* birthright, endowment, estate, heritage, inheritance, legacy, patrimony

entity *n* 1 article, element, item, object, piece, thing

n 2 area, country, government, nation, province, state

n 3 being, object, organism, sum, system, thing, totality, whole

n 4 being, citizen, creature, Homo sapiens, human, human being, individual, man, person, woman

entomb *v* bury

entombment *n* burial

entrance *n* 1 advent, approach, arrival, coming

n 2 access, aperture, approach, inlet, mouth, opening, passage

v captivate, charm, delight, engross, enrapture, enravish, enthrall, hypnotize, mesmerize, move, ravish, transport

entranced *adj* 1 ecstatic, overjoyed, rapturous

adj 2 absorbed, agog, concentrated, deep, determined, distracted, engaged, engrossed, enraptured, fascinated, immersed, intent, preoccupied, rapt, wrapped up

entrant *n* aspirant, candidate, contestant, hopeful, nominee

entrap *v* 1 attract, bait, decoy, entice, lure, tantalize

v 2 bag, capture, catch, ensnare, entangle, hook, snag, snare, snarl, tangle, trap, trick

entreat *v* appeal, ask, beg, beseech, conjure, crave, desire, grovel, implore, indicate, invoke, plead, pray, request, seek, solicit, supplicate, whine

entree *n* bread, breakfast, brunch, chow, cuisine, diet, dinner, dish, edibles, fare, food, grub, lunch, meals, nosh, nutrition, provisions, rations, snack, supper, victuals, vittles

entrench *v* attack, encroach, infringe, intrude, invade, trespass, violate

entrenched *adj* ensconced, established, fixed, fundamental, ingrained, intrinsic, inveterate, settled, sworn

entrepreneur *n* baron, big shot, businessman, businessperson, businesswoman, capitalist, executive, financier, industrialist, magnate, mogul, plutocrat, tycoon, VIP

entrepreneurial *adj* businesslike, enterprising, gumptious, up and coming

entrust *v* 1 charge

v 2 assign, authorize, delegate, designate, empower, pass along

v 3 commend, commit, confide, consign, hand over, relegate, turn over

entry *n* 1 admission

n 2 anteroom, approach, atrium, court, doorway, entrance hall, foyer, hall, hallway, lobby, portal, vestibule

entwine *v* coil, corkscrew, curl, distort, gnarl, spiral, twist, wind

enumerate *v* calculate, cite, count, itemize, list, number, numerate, tally

enumeration *n* account, amount, catalog, inventory, itemization, list, litany, repertoire, supply, tally

enunciate *v* announce, articulate, assert, couch, describe, dictate, draft, express, intonate, orate, phrase, proclaim, pronounce, say, speak, state, stress, talk, utter, verbalize, vocalize, voice, word

enunciation *n* accent, elocution, inflection, intonation, manner, pronunciation

envelop *v* 1 bundle, cover, package, wrap

v 2 bound, compass, encircle, enclose, encompass, enfold, surround

v 3 see: DISGUISE *v* 2

envelope n **1** binder, capsule, case, casing, cover, holder, sheath, skin, wrapper

n **2** file, folder, mailer, sleeve

envious adj covetous, distrusting, jealous, resentful, suspicious

environment n **1** circumstance, context, setting, situation

n **2** atmosphere, climate, conditions, habitat, niche, perimeter, settings, surroundings

n **3** backdrop, curtain, scene, scenery, set, setting, stage set, stage setting, surroundings

n **4** background, breeding, culture, development, education, experience, past, schooling, training, upbringing

environs n see: WARD n 2

envision v conceive, conjecture, conjure up, create, fancy, image, imagine, invent, project, realize, think, visualize

envoy n **1** carrier, courier, delivery person, herald, messenger, runner

n **2** ambassador, agent, consul, delegate, deputy, diplomat

n **3** foregoer, forerunner, harbinger, herald, messenger, outrider, precursor, predictor, prophet

envy n greed, jealousy, rivalry

v **1** begrudge, resent

v **2** choose, covet, crave, desire, fancy, lust, want, wish

enzyme n catalyst

eon n see: PERIOD n 2

ephemeral adj brief, fleeting, impermanent, momentary, passing, short, temporary, transient, transitory, volatile

ephemeris n calendar

epic adj dramatic, grand, heroic, legendary, noble, stirring, vivid

n chronicle, legend, opus, saga, story, tale

epicure n bon vivant, gastronome, gourmand, gourmet

epidemic adj catching, communicable, contagious, contaminative, infectious, spreading, transmittable

epilogue n continuation, corollary, outgrowth, sequel, supplement

episode n circumstance, event, happening, incident, occasion, occurrence, scene, thing

epitome n **1** collection, paraphrase, recapitulation, summary, summation

n **2** example, exemplar, ideal, mirror, model, outline, paradigm, pattern, plan, prototype, rule of thumb, standard

n **3** acme, apex, apogee, climax, crescendo, crest, crown, culmination, height, noon, peak, pinnacle, point, prime, summit, tip, top, ultimate, utmost, zenith

epoch n **4** aeon, age, cycle, decade, eon, era, eternity, forever, long time, millennium, period, reign, span, stage, time, years

equable adj consistent, constant, continuing, endless, established, even, invariable, reliable, routine, same, serene, stable, steady, unchanging, unfailing, unfluctuating, uniform, unvarying

equal adj **1** balanced, commensurate, proportional, symmetrical

adj **2** duplicate, equivalent, identical, same, substitute, synonymous, tantamount

adj **3** clean, equitable, even, fair, honest, just, sportsmanlike, straight, upright

adj **4** candid, dispassionate, equitable, fair, impartial, impersonal, indifferent, just, neutral, objective, open-minded, square, unbiased, uncolored, unprejudiced

adj **5** par

n **1** complement, counterpart, equivalent, like, match, parallel, peer

n **2** accomplice, acquaintance, adjunct, ally, associate, buddy, chum, cohort, colleague, companion, compatriot, comrade, confidant, confrere, connection, copartner, counterpart, co-worker, crony, fellow, follower, friend, intimate, mate, pal, partner, peer, relative, supporter

v **1** approximate, complement, parallel

v **2** balance, equalize, equate, even, smooth

v **3** match, measure up, meet, rival, tie, touch

v **4** amount, approach, correspond to, match

equality n equilibrium, equity, equivalence, evenness, par, parity, similarity, symmetry

equalize v **1** balance, equal, equate, even, smooth

v **2** adjust, conform, level, regulate, set policy, standardize

equanimity n calmness, composure, harmony, peacefulness, self-possession, serenity, tranquillity

equate v **1** balance, equal, equalize, even, smooth

v **2** bracket, collate, compare, contrast, correlate, liken, match, relate, sort

equidistant adj center, centermost, halfway, median, mid, middle, middlemost, midmost

equilibrium n **1** composure

n **2** balance, poise, stability

n 3 equality, equity, equivalence, evenness, par, parity, similarity, symmetry

equine *n* colt, filly, foal, gelding, horse, mare, mount, nag, pony, steed, yearling

equip *v* 1 endow, furnish, give, provide

v 2 dress, groom, spiff up, spruce

v 3 appoint, arm, fortify, furnish, gear, man, outfit, rig, set up, supply, turn out

equipment *n* 1 paraphernalia

n 2 fixtures, furnishings, gear, materials, provisions, supplies

n 3 ammo, ammunition, armor, arms, guns, machinery, munitions, ordnance, weapons

n 4 bag, baggage, case, gear, grip, kit, luggage, pack, pouch, purse, sack, suitcase, valise, wallet

equitable *adj* 1 clean, equal, even, fair, honest, just, sportsmanlike, straight, upright

adj 2 candid, dispassionate, equal, fair, impartial, impersonal, indifferent, just, neutral, objective, open-minded, square, unbiased, uncolored, unprejudiced

adj 3 see: HONEST *adj* 2, 3

equitably *adv* adequately, amply, enough, fairly, justly, moderately, passably, rather, satisfactorily, tolerably

equity *n* 1 fairness, impartiality, justice, objectivity

n 2 equality, equilibrium, equivalence, evenness, par, parity, similarity, symmetry

n 3 see: BELONGINGS *n* 1

equivalence *n* equality, equilibrium, equity, evenness, par, parity, similarity, symmetry

equivalent *adj* 1 alternate, substitute

adj 2 duplicate, equal, identical, same, substitute, synonymous, tantamount

adj 3 akin, alike, analogous, comparable, corresponding, identical, kindred, like, matching, parallel, related, same, similar, such, uniform

n 1 alternate, exchange, replacement, substitute, substitution

n 2 complement, counterpart, equal, like, match, parallel, peer

equivocal *adj* 1 ambivalent, conflicting, paradoxical, uncertain

adj 2 see: VAGUE *adj* 6

equivocate *v* 1 avoid, dodge, evade, fence, hedge, shift, shuffle, sidestep

v 2 concoct, deceive, fabricate, falsify, fib, invent, lie, misstate, perjure

v 3 altercate, argue, battle, bicker, brawl, clash, conflict, dispute, engage, feud,

fight, fray, haggle, hassle, quarrel, quibble, row, scrap, spar, squabble, wrangle

era *n* aeon, age, cycle, decade, eon, epoch, eternity, forever, long time, millennium, period, reign, span, stage, time, years

eradicate *v* cleanse, eliminate, erase, purge, remove

erase *v* 1 cleanse, eliminate, eradicate, purge, remove

v 2 abort, kill, sever, stop, terminate

v 3 abate, abolish, abrogate, annihilate, annul, call off, cancel, cease, delete, destroy, efface, excise, expunge, invalidate, kill, negate, nullify, obliterate, omit, quash, remove, stop, terminate, wipe out

erasure *n* deletion, pullout, removal

erect *v* 1 build, constitute, construct, create, establish, found, initiate, institute, launch, set up, start

v 2 assemble, build, construct, establish, fabricate, forge, form, make, manufacture, mold, produce, trailblaze

erection *n* building, edifice, foundation, house, pile, store, structure, warehouse

erode *v* corrode, deteriorate, eat, gnaw, oxidize, rust, wear

erogenous *adj* carnal, erotic, genital, procreative, reproductive, sexual

erosion *n* 1 curtailment

n 2 debasement, decline, deterioration, dip, downturn, drop, ebb, fall, involution, plunge, sag, slide, slip, slump, wane, weakening

erotic *adj* 1 alluring, attractive, desirable, exciting, seductive, sexy, tantalizing, tempting

adj 2 carnal, delicious, enticing, hedonistic, luscious, lush, lusty, luxurious, pleasure-seeking, sensual, sensualistic, sensuous, sexual, voluptuous

adj 3 amorous, ardent, aroused, carnal, earthy, fervent, fleshly, horny, hot, impassioned, lascivious, lecherous, lewd, licentious, lustful, passionate, provocative, randy, raunchy, romantic, sensual, sexual, sexy, sultry, titillated, torrid, turned on, voluptuous, wanton

adj 4 improper, indecent, racy, suggestive, unbecoming

adj 5 carnal, erogenous, genital, procreative, reproductive, sexual

adj 6 bawdy, coarse, crude, dirty, filthy, foul, gamy, gross, improper, indecent, lascivious, lewd, licentious, nasty, obscene, off-color, pornographic, profane, prurient, racy, rank, raunchy, ribald, risqué, scandalous, smutty, suggestive, tainted, uncouth, vulgar, x-rated

eroticism *n* see: DESIRE *n* 2

err *v* 1 miscalculate, misconstrue, misinterpret, misjudge, underestimate

v 2 fall, offend, sin, transgress, trespass, violate

v 3 blow, blunder, botch, bungle, butcher, damage, foul up, goof, hash, hurt, jeopardize, jumble, mess up, queer, ruin, screw up

erratic *adj* 1 flaky, unbalanced, unsound

adj 2 arbitrary, capricious, changeable, fickle, flighty, inconsistent, inconstant, mercurial, uncertain, unstable, unsteady, variable, volatile, wavering, wayward

adj 3 see: STRANGE *adj* 5

erroneous *adj* 1 baseless, fallacious, groundless, invalid, unfounded, unsubstantiated

adj 2 false, faulty, imprecise, inaccurate, incorrect, inexact, mistaken, specious, untrue, wrong

error *n* 1 bug, defect, fault, glitch

n 2 deception, fallacy, flaw, illusion, inaccuracy

n 3 absence, disregard, neglect, omission, oversight, slip-up

n 4 malfeasance, malpractice, misbehavior, misdeed, mismanagement, offense, transgression, wrong, wrongdoing

n 5 accident, blooper, blunder, bungle, confusion, faux pas, foul-up, lapse, misreading, mistake, misunderstanding, slip, slip-up

errorless *adj* see: EXQUISITE *adj* 3

ersatz *adj* artificial, bogus, counterfeit, fake, false, imitation, mock, phony, pseudo, sham, simulated, spurious, substitute, unreal

erstwhile *adj* bygone, former, late, old, once, onetime, past, sometime

erudite *adj* academic, educated, educational, intellectual, learned, literary, literate, pedantic, scholarly, scholastic, well-read

erudition *n* culture, education, enrichment, learnedness, learning, wisdom

erupt *v* 1 burn, explode, flare

v 2 burst, discharge, explode, gush, spew, spout

v 3 break, burst, explode, fragment, rupture, shatter, smash, smatter, splinter

eruption *n* blaze, flare-up, outburst

escalate *v* ascend, climb, intensify, mount, scale, surmount

escalation *n* ascent, climb, rise

escapade *n* 1 adventure, fantasy, saga, story

n 2 adventure, antic, caper, joke, lark, mischief, prank, trick

escape *n* 1 breakout, flight, getaway, lam, slip

n 2 avoidance, deceit, diversion, dodging, evasion, runaround

v 1 avoid, duck, elude, eschew, evade, recoil, shun, shy

v 2 abscond, bolt, break, depart, elude, flee, fly, hightail it, lose, run, sneak away, split

escapee *n* 1 fugitive, outlaw, runaway

n 2 castaway, émigré, evacuee, exile, expatriate, refugee

eschew *v* 1 avoid, duck, elude, escape, evade, recoil, shun, shy

v 2 see: FORFEIT *v*

escort *n* 1 bodyguard, chaperon, companion, guide, retinue, scout

n 2 attendant, guide, usher

n 3 beau, boyfriend, date, fiancé, lover, mate, paramour, suitor

v 1 accompany, direct, guide, lead, usher

v 2 accompany, associate, attend, bear, chaperon, conduct, consort with, convoy

esoteric *adj* abstruse, deep, heartfelt, heavy, hermetic, insightful, mysterious, obscure, occult, penetrating, profound, recondite

especially *adv* chiefly, notably, particularly, primarily, specifically

espionage *n* observation, reconnaissance, surveillance

esprit *n* humor, spirit, wit

espy *v* 1 see: DETECT *v* 2

v 2 see: UNDERSTAND *v* 6

essay *n* article, composition, discourse, dissertation, manuscript, memoir, monograph, paper, report, study, theme, thesis, tract, treatise, work

v assay, attempt, endeavor, offer, quest, seek, strive, struggle, try, undertake

essayist *n* author, authoress, biographer, creator, dramatist, journalist, novelist, playwright, reporter, screenwriter, writer

essence *n* 1 basis, beginning, kernel, seed

n 2 basis, body, bulk, core, essentials, gist, heart, import, mass, nucleus, object, staple, substance, volume

n 3 center, core, crux, gist, heart, life, marrow, nature, nucleus, pith, quick, quintessence, root, spirit, substance

n 4 concentrate, extract, juice

n 5 abridgement, abstract, brief, compendium, condensation, digest, example, outline, review, sketch, summary, syllabus, synopsis

essential *adj* **1** critical, integral, necessary, significant, strategic

adj **2** cardinal, fundamental, primary, prime, principal

adj **3** critical, imperative, indispensable, mandatory, necessary, needed, prerequisite, required, vital

adj **4** basic, early, elementary, embryonic, fundamental, initial, intrinsic, original, rudimentary, underlying

n **1** condition, must, necessity, precondition, prerequisite, requirement

n **2** basic, element, foundation, fundamental, principle, rudiment

essentially *adv* by itself, effectively, intrinsically, per se, practically, virtually

essentials *n* **1** basis, body, bulk, core, essence, gist, heart, import, mass, nucleus, object, staple, substance, volume

n **2** see: GOODS *n* **2**

establish *v* **1** correlate

v **2** assure, confirm

v **3** anchor, moor, plant, root

v **4** aim, focus, point, set, shoot at, target

v **5** allocate, appoint, assign, implement, institute, set

v **6** demonstrate, determine, evidence, prove, reveal, show

v **7** adjust, arrange, calibrate, decide, determine, fix, resolve, set

v **8** adjudicate, conclude, decide, determine, resolve, rule, settle, will

v **9** build, constitute, construct, create, erect, found, initiate, institute, launch, set up, start

v **10** calibrate, fix, insert, install, lay, locate, place, plant, position, put, set, settle, situate, station

v **11** predicate

v **12** assemble, build, construct, erect, fabricate, forge, form, make, manufacture, mold, produce, trailblaze

v **13** demonstrate, describe, display, draw, examine, exhibit, explain, present, prove, show, sketch, tell

v **14** activate, begin, cause, commence, constitute, create, embark, enter, inaugurate, induct, initiate, install, instigate, instill, institute, introduce, kick off, launch, lead off, open, originate, precipitate, preface, set up, start, tee off, usher in, venture forth

established *adj* **1** authorized, conventional, customary, set

adj **2** normal, regular, standard, uniform

adj **3** basic, conventional, official, standard

adj **4** accepted, proven, sound, standard, traditional

adj **5** ensconced, entrenched, fixed, fundamental, ingrained, intrinsic, inveterate, settled, sworn

adj **6** consistent, constant, continuing, endless, equable, even, invariable, reliable, routine, same, serene, stable, steady, unchanging, unfailing, unfluctuating, uniform, unvarying

adj **7** see: EXACT *adj* **6**

establishment *n* **1** association, combination, corporation, fellowship, foundation, institution, league, union

n **2** business, company, concern, corporation, enterprise, firm, house, organization, partnership

estate *n* **1** birthright, endowment, entitlement, heritage, inheritance, legacy, patrimony

n **2** acreage, domain, grounds, holdings, land, property, real estate

n **3** caste, class, degree, echelon, hierarchy, level, position, rank, status

n **4** assets, belongings, equity, fortune, goods, holdings, inheritance, money, ownership, possessions, property, prosperity, riches, treasure, wealth

n **5** abode, castle, domicile, dwelling, home, house, mansion, palace, residence

n **6** assets, bills, capital, cash, coffers, currency, dinero, dollars, funds, goods, income, lucre, means, money, notes, pelf, pesos, property, resources, revenue, riches, rubles, shekels, sum, wealth

esteem *n* **1** account, admiration, consideration, favor, regard, respect

n **2** fame, good standing, name, perception, regard, reputation, stature

n **3** aplomb, assurance, confidence, nerve, poise, presence, savoir-faire, self-assurance, self-confidence

n **4** deference, devotion, homage, honor, just due, regard, respect, reverence

v admire, adore, appreciate, cherish, consider, covet, honor, idolize, love, prize, regard, respect, treasure, value

esteemed *adj* **1** adored, beloved, cherished, dear, loved, precious, respected, revered, treasured, venerable, worshiped

adj **2** see: FAMOUS *adj*

estimable *adj* deserving, excellent, honorable, noble, precious, sterling, valuable, worthy

estimate *n* **1** budget, forecast, plan, prediction, projection, quota

n **2** assumption, conclusion, conjecture,

discretion, guess, judgment, notion, presumption, theorization

n 3 appraisal, assessment, estimation, evaluation, valuation

v 1 calculate, cipher, code, compute, figure, reckon

v 2 approximate, call, judge, place, put, reckon

v 3 diagnose, forecast, gauge, predetermine, predict, project

v 4 appraise, assay, assess, charge, evaluate, levy, price, rank, rate, set at, survey, tax, valuate, value

v 5 assume, believe, comprehend, conceive, expect, fathom, gather, grasp, guess, imagine, infer, know, presume, suppose, surmise, suspect, think, trust, understand

v 6 analyze, assess, determine, diagnose, examine, penetrate, probe, scope, solve, survey, understand, unravel

v 7 anticipate, augur, bode, budget, call, divine, forecast, foresee, foreshadow, foretell, guess, harbinger, herald, judge, plan, portend, preannounce, predict, presage, proclaim, prognosticate, project, prophesy, signify, soothsay

estimated *adj* approximate, crude, proximate, rough, rounded

estimation *n* 1 approximation, extrapolation, guess, speculation

n 2 appraisal, assessment, estimate, evaluation, valuation

estrange *v* alienate, fend off, rebuff, repel, repulse, snub

estranged *adj* alienated, disaffected, disunited, separated, weaned

estuary *n* arm, bay, cove, fiord, gulf, inlet, narrows, sound, strait

etch *v* carve, cut, inscribe

etching *n* acrylic, art, canvas, depiction, drawing, illustration, landscape, lithograph, mural, oil, painting, pastel, pen and ink, picture, portrait, print, seascape, sketch, still life, watercolor

eternal *adj* 1 endless, immortal, infinite, perpetual, unceasing, undying

adj 2 constant, continuing, durable, enduring, lasting, ongoing, permanent, stable

adj 3 ageless, boundless, ceaseless, constant, continual, continuous, endless, everlasting, incessant, infinite, interminable, limitless, never-ending, ongoing, perpetual, persistent, relentless, timeless, unceasing, unending, uninterrupted, unremitting

eternally *adv* ad infinitum, all the time,

always, constantly, continually, endlessly, forever, perpetually, timelessly, unceasingly

eternity *n* see: PERIOD *n* 2

ethereal *adj* bodiless, celestial, disembodied, heavenly, incorporeal, insubstantial, intangible, metaphysical, nonmaterial, spiritual, unearthly, unreal, unsubstantial

ethical *adj* 1 lucid, moral, rational, responsible, sane, stable

adj 2 careful, carping, cautious, conscientious, exacting, fussy, heedful, meticulous, painstaking, punctilious, scrupulous, unrelenting

adj 3 conscientious, honest, honorable, moral, noble, principled, proper, respectable, right, righteous, scrupulous, sound, true, trustworthy, upright, virtuous

adj 4 elevated, high-minded, moral, noble

ethics *n* 1 code of conduct, morals, principles

n 2 beliefs, code, doctrine, outlook, philosophy, rites, values

ethnic *adj* national, racial, tribal

etiquette *n* convention, custom, decorum, formality, good form, manners, propriety, protocol, rites

étude *n* concert, concerto, fugue, program, recital, serenade, sonata, symphony

eulogize *v* acclaim, applaud, celebrate, commend, exalt, extol, glorify, hail, honor, laud, praise, resound, salute, toast, tout, worship

eulogy *n* acclaim, applause, boost, citation, commendation, compliment, plaudit, praise, rave, tribute

euphonious *adj* choral, harmonious, lyric, mellow, melodic, melodious, musical, orchestral, philharmonic, rhythmical, symphonic, tuneful, vocal

euphoria *n* ecstasy, high, rush

euphoric *adj* aroused, ebullient, elated, excited, exhilarated, happy, intoxicated, joyful, sparked, stimulated, turned on

evacuate *v* 1 clear, deplete, drain, empty, take out, vacate

v 2 cleanse, discharge, eliminate, empty, excrete, void

v 3 boot out, chuck out, dismiss, eject, evict, expel, kick out, throw out

evacuation *n* abandon, departure, desertion, exit, going, leaving, pullback, pullout, removal, retreat, withdrawal

evacuee *n* castaway, émigré, escapee, exile, expatriate, refugee

evade *v* 1 avoid, circumvent, detour

v 2 avoid, duck, elude, escape, eschew, recoil, shun, shy

v 3 avoid, dodge, equivocate, fence, hedge, shift, shuffle, sidestep

v 4 avoid, circumvent, deflect, detour, dodge, duck, hedge, parry, shirk, side-step, skirt, ward off

evaluate *v* 1 grade, mark, rate, score

v 2 advise, caution, counsel, recommend, reprove

v 3 determine, judge, test, try, verify

v 4 analyze, brief, condense, outline, retrace, review, study, summarize, synopsize, update

v 5 appraise, assay, assess, charge, estimate, levy, price, rank, rate, set at, survey, tax, valuate, value

evaluation *n* 1 rating

n 2 analysis, assessment, commentary, criticism, critique, examination, judgment, notion, opinion, review, ruling

n 3 appraisal, assessment, estimate, estimation, valuation

evaluator *n* commentator, critic, judge, reviewer

evangelist *n* crusader, missionary, proselytizer

evaporate *v* 1 clear, depart, disappear, fade, vanish

v 2 dry

evasion *n* avoidance, deceit, diversion, dodging, escape, runaround

evasive *adj* 1 elusive, fleeting, slippery

adj 2 adroit, artful, cagey, canny, crafty, cunning, foxy, serpentine, sly

adj 3 see: DECEITFUL *adj* 1

even *adj* 1 exact, square, tie

adj 2 flat, flush, level, plane, smooth

adj 3 clean, equal, equitable, fair, honest, just, sportsmanlike, straight, upright

adj 4 consistent, constant, continuing, endless, equable, established, invariable, reliable, routine, same, serene, stable, steady, unchanging, unfailing, unfluctuating, uniform, unvarying

v 1 balance, equal, equalize, equate, smooth

v 2 flatten, flush, grade, lay, level, plane, smooth, tamp

evening *n* dark, night, nighttime, wee hours

evenness *n* equality, equilibrium, equivalence, equity, par, parity, similarity, symmetry

event *n* 1 milepost, milestone, occasion

n 2 case, eventuality, occurrence

n 3 adventure, encounter, experience, hazard, ordeal, peril, risk

n 4 circumstance, episode, happening, incident, occasion, occurrence, scene, thing

n 5 bout, competition, conflict, contest, game, marathon, match, meet, meeting, race, regatta, round robin, run, tournament, tourney

n 6 see: ACCOMPLISHMENT *n* 4

eventful *adj* see: ACCIDENTAL *adj* 3

events *n* career, diary, experience, history, performance, record, résumé, track record, vita

eventual *adj* 1 closing, decisive, definitive, final, inevitable, last, latest

adj 2 approaching, expected, future, imminent, impending, next, prospective, subsequent

eventuality *n* 1 case, event, occurrence

n 2 aftermath, consequence, corollary, effect, outcome, reaction, repercussion, result, reverberation, reward, upshot

eventually *adv* at last, finally, lastly, ultimately

everlasting *adj* ageless, boundless, ceaseless, constant, continual, continuous, endless, eternal, incessant, infinite, interminable, limitless, never-ending, ongoing, perpetual, persistent, relentless, timeless, unceasing, unending, uninterrupted, unremitting

every *adj* a, a few, any, at least one, each, individual, one, several, some

everyday *adj* 1 daily

adj 2 accepted, accustomed, chronic, common, constant, continual, customary, daily, familiar, frequent, habitual, inured, often, recurring, regular, routine, traditional, usual

adj 3 see: TYPICAL *adj* 2

evict *v* boot out, chuck out, dismiss, eject, evacuate, expel, kick out, throw out

evidence *n* 1 affirmation, confirmation, documentation, proof, verification

n 2 approval, confirmation, doctrine, enactment, passage, proof, testament, testimony, witness

v demonstrate, determine, establish, prove, reveal, show

evident *adj* apparent, clear, conspicuous, distinct, given, indisputable, indubitable, manifest, obvious, patent, plain, presumed, self-evident, straightforward, true, unambiguous, unequivocal, unmistakable

evidently *adv* clearly, obviously, plainly, undoubtedly, unquestionably

evil *adj* 1 adverse, bad, harmful, ill, unfavorable, unlucky

adj 2 abhorrent, abominable, appalling,

detestable, disgusting, dreadful, frightful, ghastly, hateful, horrible, horrid, loathsome, odious, repulsive, revolting, shocking

adj 3 base, corrupt, deadly, degenerate, depraved, deviant, immoral, infamous, kinky, nefarious, perverse, putrid, rotten, ruthless, savage, vicious, villainous, wicked, wild

adj 4 bad, corrupt, crooked, deceitful, dishonest, fraudulent, immoral, iniquitous, lying, Machiavellian, manipulative, mercenary, reprobate, roguish, scheming, shady, shifty, sinful, unethical, unfair, unprincipled, unscrupulous, untruthful, venal, vile, wicked, wrong

n 1 cancer, corruption, decay, infection, malignancy, poison, rot, toxin, venom

n 2 crime, dishonor, disobedience, fault, felony, infamy, infraction, iniquity, injury, lawbreaking, misdeed, misdemeanor, offense, outrage, sin, transgression, trespass, vice, violation, wrong, wrongdoing

n 3 bane, curse, disease, misfortune, pestilence, plague, scourge

n 4 affliction, ailment, complaint, condition, disease, disorder, harm, ill, illness, infirmity, malady, sickness

evince *v* 1 deduce, derive, draw, educe, elicit, evoke, extract

v 2 disclose, display, express, imply, indicate, manifest, reflect, reveal, show

eviscerate *v* clean, disembowel, fillet, gut

evoke *v* 1 call, cite, serve, subpoena, summon

v 2 deduce, derive, draw, educe, elicit, evince, extract

evolve *v* 1 derive, develop, mature, progress, unfold

v 2 alter, change, commute, convert, further, improve, metamorphose, modernize, modify, mutate, revolutionize, transfer, transfigure, transform, transmute, vary

v 3 appear, arise, befall, break, come, come about, develop, do, ensue, fall out, happen, manifest, materialize, occur, pass, rise, take place, transpire, turn up

exact *adj* 1 even, square, tie

adj 2 identical, precise, same, very

adj 3 accurate, correct, precise, proper, right, valid

adj 4 faithful, literal, precise, strict, true, verbatim, word for word

adj 5 blunt, clear, clear-cut, concise, decisive, definite, definitive, distinct, explicit, precise, specific, unambiguous

adj 6 absolute, agreed, bounded, categorical, clear, decided, definite, emphatic, established, finite, fixed, guaranteed, limited, positive, specific, unequivocal, unmistakable, vested

v 1 coerce, extort, gouge, shake down, squeeze, wrench, wrest, wring

v 2 call, challenge, claim, demand, need, postulate, require, requisition, solicit

exacting *adj* 1 fastidious, finicky, meticulous, picky, precise, rigid, strict

adj 2 arduous, burdensome, demanding, grievous, onerous, oppressive, taxing, tough, trying

adj 3 careful, carping, cautious, conscientious, ethical, fussy, heedful, meticulous, painstaking, punctilious, scrupulous, unrelenting

exactly *adv* 1 just, perfectly, precisely

adv 2 accurately, just so, precisely, right, sharp, smack, square, squarely

adv 3 actually, genuinely, precisely, really, sincerely, truly, verifiably, veritably, very

exactness *n* clarity, clearness, distinctness, freshness, lucidity, plainness, purity

exaggerate *v* 1 expand, inflate, oversell, overstate, stretch

v 2 bias, color, distort, embellish, influence, slant

exaggerated *adj* 1 amazing, fabulous, questionable

adj 2 artificial, corny, pretentious, staged, theatrical

exaggeration *n* 1 ballyhoo, embellishment, hoopla, hype, hyperbole, overstatement, promotion, public relations

n 2 fabrication, falsehood, falsity, fib, invention, lie, misstatement, story, tale

exalt *v* 1 dignify, distinguish, elevate, glorify, grace, honor

v 2 anoint, baptize, bless, consecrate, dedicate, devote, enshrine, hallow, purify, sanctify

v 3 see: LAUD *v* 2

exalted *adj* 1 elevated, excellent, grand, great, heavenly, high, lofty, magnificent, prominent, sublime, superb

adj 2 see: GRAND *adj* 2, 5

exam *n* examination, final, inquiry, oral, questionnaire, quiz, test

examination *n* 1 analysis, assay, experiment, observation, test

n 2 exam, final, inquiry, oral, questionnaire, quiz, test

n 3 inquiry, inspection, probing, scrutiny, search, study, survey

n 4 assessment, inquiry, review, scope, search, study, survey *n* **5** analysis, assessment, commentary, criticism, critique, evaluation, judgment, notion, opinion, review, ruling

examine *v* **1** buy, procure, purchase, shop

v **2** focus, highlight, spotlight, target

v **3** inspect, observe, peruse, scan

v **4** audit, balance, check, inspect, verify

v **5** explore, investigate, scout, spy, survey

v **6** feel, finger, fondle, grope, handle, manipulate, maul, palpate, paw, probe, touch

v **7** ask, cross-examine, grill, inquire, interrogate, investigate, probe, pump, query, question, quiz

v **8** analyze, assess, determine, diagnose, estimate, penetrate, probe, scope, solve, survey, understand, unravel

v **9** canvass, case, check, glance over, inspect, observe, peruse, pore over, regard, scrutinize, study, survey, watch

v **10** dissect

v **11** demonstrate, describe, display, draw, establish, exhibit, explain, present, prove, show, sketch, tell

v **12** delve, dig, explore, feel out, grope, hunt, inquire, investigate, look, observe, peer, probe, pursue, research, scan, scrutinize, search, seek, sound, study, test

example *n* **1** clue, illustration, indication, manifestation, proof, sign

n **2** demo, first, forerunner, model, prototype, sample, test

n **3** case, case history, clarification, explanation, illumination, illustration, instance, representative, sample, sampling, specimen

n **4** character, emblem, icon, letter, logo, mark, model, representation, sign, symbol, token

n **5** epitome, exemplar, ideal, mirror, model, outline, paradigm, pattern, plan, prototype, rule of thumb, standard

n **6** see: SUMMARY *n* 2

exasperate *v* see: BOTHER *v* 5

excavate *v* burrow, dig, gouge, mine, scoop, shovel, unearth

excavation *n* dig, lode, mine, quarry

exceed *v* **1** cross the line, overstep, transgress, trespass

v **2** beat, best, better, cap, dwarf, eclipse, excel, go beyond, outdo, outgo, outshine, outstrip, overshadow, pass, surpass, top, transcend

exceedingly *adv* awfully, dreadfully, eminently, endlessly, exceptionally, extremely, greatly, highly, mightily, notably,

quite, remarkably, terribly, thoroughly, very

excel *v* **1** dominate, lead, star

v **2** outshine, surpass

v **3** beat, best, better, cap, dwarf, eclipse, exceed, go beyond, outdo, outgo, outshine, outstrip, overshadow, pass, surpass, top, transcend

v **4** advance, ascend, bloom, climb, develop, do well, expand, flourish, flower, get ahead, grow, improve, progress, prosper, rise, strive, survive, thrive

excellence *n* **1** caliber, goodness, merit, quality, stature, value, worth

n **2** see: PROMINENCE *n*

excellent *adj* **1** admirable, commendable, fine, laudable, praiseworthy, worthwhile

adj **2** deserving, estimable, honorable, noble, precious, sterling, valuable, worthy

adj **3** extraordinary, great, impressive, noteworthy, outstanding, shining, smashing, superb, wonderful

adj **4** errorless, exquisite, fastidious, faultless, flawless, ideal, immaculate, impeccable, irreproachable, perfect

adj **5** fabulous, fantastic, fine, good, great, marvelous, super, terrific, tremendous, wonderful

adj **6** champion, fine, first class, first rate, foremost, good, grade a, leading, number one, prime, principal, prominent, quality, select, stellar, superb, superior, top, top-drawer, top-notch, tops

adj **7** dynamite, extraordinary, great, out of sight, outstanding, phenomenal, premier, super, superb, superlative, tremendous, wonderful

adj **8** acclaimed, celebrated, distinguished, eminent, esteemed, famed, famous, foremost, illustrious, notable, outstanding, prestigious, prominent, renowned, well known

adj **9** see: GRAND *adj* 2

except *prep* aside from, barring, excluding, save, unless

v **1** inveigh, kick, object, protest, remonstrate

v **2** banish, bar, blackball, cut, debar, dismiss, eliminate, exclude, ignore, leave out, omit, suspend

exceptional *adj* **1** astonishing, incredible, remarkable, uncanny

adj **2** amazing, brilliant, extraordinary, noteworthy, phenomenal, rare, remarkable, significant, singular, stunning, super, uncommon, uncustomary, unique, unusual

exceptionally *adv* awfully, dreadfully, eminently, endlessly, exceedingly, extremely, greatly, highly, mightily, notably, quite, remarkably, terribly, thoroughly, very

excerpt *n* citation, clipping, extract, mention, passage, portion, quotation, quote, reference, section

excess *adj* leftover, remaining, residual, superfluous

n 1 give, leeway, margin, play, slack, stretch

n 2 asset, inventory, overage, overstock, oversupply, plus, surplus

n 3 expense

n 4 deluge, fat, glut, overabundance, overflow, overkill, plethora, redundancy, surfeit, surplus

excessive *adj* 1 affluent, comfortable, rich, superfluous

adj 2 drastic, extreme, intense, passionate, radical, severe, strong

adj 3 costly, dear, exorbitant, expensive, high, overpriced, prohibitive, steep, stiff

adj 4 gluttonous, immoderate, inordinate, intemperate, overindulgent, prodigious, unbridled, undue, unrestrained, voracious

adj 5 exorbitant, expensive, extravagant, extreme, ghastly, lavish, outlandish, overpriced, profuse, ultimate, unbelievable

exchange *n* 1 alternate, equivalent, replacement, substitute, substitution

n 2 deal, sale, trade, transaction, transfer

n 3 communication, data, disclosure, expression, facts, information, intelligence, knowledge, news, notification

n 4 caucus, chat, colloquy, conference, conversation, debate, dialogue, discourse, discussion, forum, interchange, intercourse, interlocution, meeting, talk

n 5 movement, traffic, travel

v 1 barter, swap, switch, trade

v 2 cash, convert, dissolve, liquidate, tender

v 3 replace, represent, return, substitute, supplant, swap, switch

v 4 bargain, barter, convert, deal, swap, trade, traffic

excise *v* see: TERMINATE *v* 8

excitable *adj* 1 see: PASSIONATE *adj* 2

adj 2 see: TEMPERAMENTAL *adj*

excite *v* 1 arouse, awaken, challenge, kindle, rally, rouse, stir, wake, waken

v 2 activate, charge, electrify, energize, enliven, ignite, start, turn on, vitalize

v 3 appeal, arouse, attract, fascinate, fire, interest, intrigue, lead on, lure, seduce, stir, tantalize

v 4 arouse, awaken, induce, instill, motivate, move, pique, prime, provoke, quicken, rouse, roust, spark, start, stimulate, titillate, urge

v 5 arouse, electrify, fire, incite, inspire, rouse, spark, stimulate, tantalize, thrill, titillate, turn on, whet

v 6 see: SPARKLE *v* 2

excited *adj* 1 aroused, ebullient, elated, euphoric, exhilarated, happy, intoxicated, joyful, sparked, stimulated, turned on

adj 2 anxious, ardent, avid, breathless, desirous, eager, enthusiastic, fain, impatient, impetuous, keen, passionate, raring, zealous

adj 3 see: ANGRY *adj* 4

adj 4 see: TURBULENT *adj*

excitement *n* 1 enjoyment, kicks, pleasure, stimulation, thrills

n 2 agitation, craze, frenzy, furor, fury, fuss, outrage, passion, tumult, uproar, wrath

n 3 see: ACTIVITY *n* 3

n 4 see: MERRIMENT *n*

n 5 see: PASSION *n* 5, 7

exciting *adj* 1 dynamic, electrifying, inspiring, stimulating, thrilling

adj 2 hot, sensational, sexy, spectacular, stirring

adj 3 electric, exhilarating, provocative, rousing, stimulating, stirring

adj 4 arousing, awesome, breathtaking, magnificent, stimulating, stirring, stunning

adj 5 exotic, inspiring, interesting, intriguing, provocative, stimulating, tingling, titillating

adj 6 arousing, intriguing, provocative, seductive, sexy, stimulating, suggestive, tantalizing

adj 7 alluring, attractive, desirable, erotic, seductive, sexy, tantalizing, tempting

exclaim *v* blurt, cackle, cry, ejaculate, shout, spill, sputter, tattle, utter

exclude *v* 1 fence, partition, restrict, separate

v 2 differentiate, discriminate, isolate, ostracize, segregate, separate, sequester

v 3 banish, bar, blackball, cut, debar, dismiss, eliminate, except, ignore, leave out, omit, suspend

v 4 defy, discount, disregard, forget, ignore, miss, neglect, omit, ostracize, overlook, overpass, pass, pass by, pass over, shun, skip, slight, snub

excluding *prep* aside from, barring, except, save, unless

exclusive *adj* 1 expensive, high class, luxurious

adj 2 nonpublic, private, restricted

adj 3 concentrated, fixed, undistracted, undivided, unswerving, whole

adj 4 individual, intimate, own, personal, private, secret, special

adj 5 definite, determinate, fixed, limited, narrow, precise, restricted, segregated, specific

adj 6 see: LONE *adj* 3

n corner, lock, monopoly, restraint

excrement *n* droppings, feces, stool, waste

excrete *v* cleanse, discharge, eliminate, empty, evacuate, void

excretion *n* discharge

excruciating *adj* intolerable, painful, unbearable, unendurable

exculpate *v* absolve, acquit, clear, condone, excuse, exempt, exonerate, forgive, free, pardon, remit, reprieve, vindicate

excursion *n* 1 drive, jaunt, journey, outing, ride, spin

n 2 adventure, air travel, cruise, expedition, flight, journey, passage, safari, sally, tour, travel, trek, trip, venture, voyage

excusable *adj* extenuating, justifying, mitigating, offsetting

excuse *n* 1 apology, explanation, regret

n 2 cause, motive, purpose, rationale, reason, why

n 3 alibi, defense, explanation, justification, plea, pretext, rationalization, reason, ruse

n 4 coverup, snow job, whitewash

v 1 apologize, regret, repent, seek penance

v 2 absolve, acquit, clear, condone, exculpate, exempt, exonerate, forgive, free, pardon, remit, reprieve, vindicate

execration *n* anathema, condemnation, curse, imprecation, malediction, voodoo

execute *v* 1 achieve, perform

v 2 actuate, commit, do, enact, perform, perpetrate

v 3 achieve, answer, fill, finish, fulfill, meet, realize, satisfy

v 4 administer, administrate, carry out, deliver, do, give, present, render, submit

v 5 actuate, bring about, cause, create, draw on, effect, invoke, make, produce, secure

v 6 accomplish, achieve, attain, consummate, fulfill, perform, produce, pull off, realize, succeed, triumph, win

v 7 abolish, annihilate, assassinate, bump off, butcher, decimate, destroy, dispatch, exterminate, hang, hit, kill, knock off,

liquidate, massacre, murder, put away, rub out, slaughter, slay, wipe out

v 8 hit, kill, shoot, wound

v 9 accomplish, complete, consummate, fulfill, implement, perform, realize

execution *n* 1 timing

n 2 exercise, implementation, practice, training

n 3 accomplishment, action, conduct, deed, delivery, demonstration, performance, talent

n 4 killing, slaying

n 5 angle, approach, code, delivery, expression, fashion, manner, method, mode, organization, process, program, style, system, technique, way

executioner *n* assassin, killer, murderer

executive *n* baron, big shot, businessman, businessperson, businesswoman, capitalist, entrepreneur, financier, industrialist, magnate, mogul, plutocrat, tycoon, VIP

exemplar *n* epitome, example, ideal, mirror, model, outline, paradigm, pattern, plan, prototype, rule of thumb, standard

exemplary *adj* 1 flawless, ideal, model, perfect, perfected

adj 2 characteristic, classic, ideal, model, representative, typical

adj 3 blameless, commendable, exonerated, guiltless, innocent, irreproachable, pure, righteous, virtuous

exemplify *v* embody, express, personify, represent, symbolize, typify

exempt *adj* guarded, immune, protected, safe, secure

v absolve, acquit, clear, condone, exculpate, excuse, exonerate, forgive, free, pardon, remit, reprieve, vindicate

exemption *n* 1 grant, patent, permission, right, safeguard

n 2 assurance, guarantee, immunity, impunity, protection, release, safety, security

exercise *n* 1 execution, implementation, practice, training

n 2 drill, practice, rehearsal, training, workout

n 3 activity, business, endeavor, enterprise, project, undertaking, venture

n 4 assignment, diatribe, discourse, homily, lecture, lesson, preaching, sermon

n 5 aerobics, bodybuilding, calisthenics, jazzercise, slimnastics, workout

v 1 apply, resort, use, utilize

v 2 apply, bestow, employ, exploit, handle, use, utilize

v 3 coach, communicate, condition, convey, cultivate, develop, discipline, drill, edify, educate, enlighten, explain, groom, imbue, impart, implant, improve, inculcate, indoctrinate, inform, infuse, inseminate, inspire, instill, instruct, perfect, practice, prepare, ready, school, teach, train, tutor

exertion n effort, elbow grease, labor, pains, strain, struggle, toil, trouble, try, work

exhale v 1 expire

v 2 breathe, gasp, inhale

exhaust n fume, gas, smoke

v 1 cripple, debilitate, disable, drain, enfeeble, sap, undermine, weaken

v 2 consume, deplete, expend, finish, go, lessen, run through, spend, use up, waste, weaken

v 3 bankrupt, deplete, drain, draw down, impoverish, use up

v 4 drain, fatigue, jade, tire, wear down, wear out, weary

exhausted adj beat, burnt out, bushed, careworn, drawn, emaciated, expended, fatigued, frazzled, haggard, jaded, pinched, pooped, run-down, shot, spent, tired, wearied, weary, worn, worn down, worn out

exhaustion n fatigue, lassitude, weariness

exhaustive adj complete, comprehensive, thorough, unabridged

exhaustively adv see: COMPLETELY adv

exhibit n array, blare, display, exhibition, fanfare, fuss, parade, performance, presentation, procession, publicity, show, showing

v 1 display, post, proclaim

v 2 display, flaunt, manifest, parade, promenade

v 3 communicate, disclose, display, divulge, inform, notify, open, reveal, uncover, unveil

v 4 demonstrate, describe, display, draw, establish, examine, explain, present, prove, show, sketch, tell

exhibition n array, blare, display, exhibit, fanfare, fuss, parade, performance, presentation, procession, publicity, show, showing

exhilarated adj aroused, ebullient, elated, euphoric, excited, happy, intoxicated, joyful, sparked, stimulated, turned on

exhilarating adj 1 electric, exciting, provocative, rousing, stimulating, stirring

adj 2 energizing, fresh, invigorating, refreshing, stimulating

exhilaration n see: MERRIMENT n

exhort v egg, encourage, goad, incite, persuade, prick, prod, prompt, propel, spur, urge

exigency n demand, necessity, need, pressure, requirement, stress, urgency

exile n 1 limbo

n 2 castaway, émigré, escapee, evacuee, expatriate, refugee

n 3 isolation, leisure, quarantine, relaxation, rest, retirement, retreat, seclusion, solitude, withdrawal

v 1 banish, cast out, deport, dispel, displace, expatriate, expel, extradite, ostracize, oust, relegate, remove

v 2 see: DISMISS v 3

exist v 1 occur

v 2 be, endure, last, live, persist, prevail, survive

existence n 1 continuation, duration, endurance, life, span, subsistence, survival, term

n 2 actuality, being, fact, life, presence, reality, truth, vitality

existent adj 1 contemporary, current, instant, living, present

adj 2 absolute, actual, authentic, bona fide, certain, definite, factual, genuine, hard, inarguable, incontestable, incontrovertible, indisputable, indubitable, irrefutable, positive, real, sure, true, undeniable, undisputable, undoubtable, undoubted, unequivocal, unquestionable, veritable, viable

exit n 1 doorway, gateway, outlet, portal

n 2 departure, farewell, leaving, parting, passing

n 3 abandon, departure, desertion, evacuation, going, leaving, pullback, pullout, removal, retreat, withdrawal

v abscond, bolt, defect, depart, fall back, flee, get away, give back, go, leave, move, pull away, pull out, push off, retreat, run along, secede, shove off, take off, vacate, withdraw

exonerate v 1 absolve, acquit, cover up, extenuate, mitigate, whitewash

v 2 absolve, acquit, clear, condone, exculpate, excuse, exempt, forgive, free, pardon, remit, reprieve, vindicate

exonerated adj blameless, commendable, exemplary, guiltless, innocent, irreproachable, pure, righteous, virtuous

exorbitant adj 1 costly, dear, excessive, expensive, high, overpriced, prohibitive, steep, stiff

adj 2 excessive, expensive, extravagant, extreme, ghastly, lavish, outlandish, overpriced, profuse, ultimate, unbelievable

exorcism n invocation

exotic *adj* 1 exciting, inspiring, interesting, intriguing, provocative, stimulating, tingling, titillating

adj 2 alien, foreign, strange, unfamiliar

adj 3 curious, far-out, fascinating, intriguing, kinky, marvelous, mysterious, new, novel, odd, outlandish, strange, ultra, unaccustomed, unexplored, unfamiliar, unique, unknown, unusual, weird

expand *v* 1 exaggerate, inflate, oversell, overstate, stretch

v 2 extend, fan, open, outstretch, spread, unfold

v 3 amplify, construct, develop, devise, elaborate, enhance, enlarge, expound, increase, refine

v 4 amplify, bloat, dilate, distend, enlarge, fatten, grow, increase, inflate, magnify, stretch, swell, widen

v 5 advance, ascend, bloom, climb, develop, do well, excel, flourish, flower, get ahead, grow, improve, progress, prosper, rise, strive, survive, thrive

v 6 see: INCREASE *v* 8, 9, 10

expansive *adj* 1 bouncy, elastic, malleable, plastic, resilient

adj 2 blanket, comprehensive, extensive, sweeping, universal

adj 3 ample, broad, extended, extensive, ranging, vast, wide

expatiate *v* discourse, discuss, elaborate, ramble, sermonize

expatriate *n* castaway, émigré, escapee, evacuee, exile, refugee

v banish, cast out, deport, dispel, displace, exile, expel, extradite, ostracize, oust, relegate, remove

expect *v* 1 demand, levy, require, want, wish

v 2 assume, posit, postulate, premise, presume, presuppose, propose

v 3 anticipate, await, believe, count on, hope, keep the faith, look, look forward to, wish

v 4 assume, believe, comprehend, conceive, estimate, fathom, gather, grasp, guess, imagine, infer, know, presume, suppose, surmise, suspect, think, trust, understand

expectation *n* 1 chance, likelihood, possibility, probability, prospect

n 2 bid, hope, inducement, invitation, motion, offer, proffer, proposal, proposition, recommendation, request, suggestion

n 3 anticipation, hope, premonition

expected *adj* approaching, eventual, future, imminent, impending, next, prospective, subsequent

expediency *n* see: UTILITY *n*

expedient *adj* advisable, politic, prudent, recommended, suggested, wise

n makeshift, means, measure, recourse, refuge, replacement, resort, stopgap, substitute, surrogate

expedite *v* 1 accelerate, aid, assist, facilitate

v 2 clear, ease, facilitate, smooth

v 3 accelerate, hasten, hurry, quicken, rush, shake up, speed, step up

v 4 barrel, bullet, fly, hasten, hurry, hustle, rocket, rush, speed, whisk, zip

expedition *n* 1 foray, sally, sortie

n 2 campaign, crusade, drive, effort, push

n 3 alacrity, dispatch, haste, hastiness, hurry, hustle, precipitance, precipitation, quickness, rush, rustle, speed, swiftness

n 4 adventure, air travel, cruise, excursion, flight, journey, passage, safari, sally, tour, travel, trek, trip, venture, voyage

expeditious *adj* breakneck, explosive, fast, fleet, hasty, impulsive, instant, lightning, mercurial, meteoric, precipitous, quick, rapid, spectacular, speedy, sudden, swift

expeditiously *adv* fast, full tilt, hastily, in a snap, lickety-split, promptly, pronto, quick, quickly, rapidly, right away, soon, speedily, swiftly, urgently

expel *v* 1 dispose of, eliminate, flush, purge, remove, rid, vanquish

v 2 discharge, emanate, emit, project, radiate, release, send

v 3 boot out, chuck out, dismiss, eject, evacuate, evict, kick out, throw out

v 4 banish, cast out, deport, dispel, displace, exile, expatriate, extradite, ostracize, oust, relegate, remove

v 5 exhale

expend *v* 1 administer, apportion, deal, disburse, dispense, disperse, distribute, dole, give

v 2 consume, deplete, exhaust, finish, go, lessen, run through, spend, use up, waste, weaken

expended *adj* see: WEARY *adj* 1

expenditures *n* burden, commitments, costs, expenses, overhead

expense *n* 1 charge, cost, fare, outlay, payment, price, rate, value, worth

n 2 excess

n 3 assessment, cost, duty, fee, impost, levy, offering, penalty, price, sacrifice, tariff, tax, toll, trade-off

expenses *n* burden, commitments, costs, expenditures, overhead

expensive *adj* 1 exclusive, high class, luxurious

adj 2 costly, precious, valuable

adj 3 costly, dear, excessive, exorbitant, high, overpriced, prohibitive, steep, stiff

adj 4 excessive, exorbitant, extravagant, extreme, ghastly, lavish, outlandish, overpriced, profuse, ultimate, unbelievable

experience *n* 1 education, exposure, involvement, practice, skill

n 2 adventure, encounter, event, hazard, ordeal, peril, risk

n 3 career, diary, events, history, performance, record, résumé, track record, vita

n 4 background, breeding, culture, development, education, environment, past, schooling, training, upbringing

n 5 see: SKILL *n* 1, 3

v 1 endure, subject, suffer

v 2 feel, sample, taste

v 3 detect, feel, notice, perceive, sense

v 4 encounter, endure, know, realize, understand

v 5 benefit, have, partake, profit, touch, use

v 6 see: TOLERATE *v*

experienced *adj* 1 accomplished, proficient, schooled, trained, versed

adj 2 adept, practiced, proficient, seasoned, versed, veteran

adj 3 expert, grizzled, hardened, mature, seasoned, trained, weathered

experiment *n* analysis, assay, examination, observation, test

experimental *adj* developmental, pilot, suggested, tentative, test, trial, untested

experimentation *n* analysis, digging, exploration, inquiry, inquisition, investigation, research, study, testing, trial

expert *adj* 1 experienced, grizzled, hardened, mature, seasoned, trained, weathered

adj 2 able, accomplished, adept, apt, capable, competent, deft, dexterous, fit, gifted, masterful, professional, proficient, proper, qualified, skillful, talented

n 1 ace, champion, master, wizard

n 2 aesthete, connoisseur, critic, virtuoso

n 3 authority, guide, guru, leader, master, mentor, pundit, teacher, wise man

n 4 adviser, artist, authority, guru, master, official, pro, professional, specialist, veteran, virtuoso, wizard

expertise *n* ability, adequacy, adroitness, aptitude, art, caliber, calling, capability, capacity, command, competence, craft, dexterity, experience, familiarity, forte, knack, know-how, knowledge, mastery,

proficiency, prowess, qualification, savvy, skill, specialty, strength, talent, training, workmanship

expiration *n* death, decease, departure, passing

expire *v* 1 cease, die, elapse, lapse, pass, pass away, perish, succumb, terminate

v 2 exhale

explain *v* 1 specify

v 2 answer, resolve, solve, unravel

v 3 account, explain away, justify, rationalize

v 4 clarify, disclose, relate, reveal, unfold

v 5 analogize, associate, compare, correlate, rank, relate

v 6 demonstrate, describe, display, draw, establish, examine, exhibit, present, prove, show, sketch, tell

v 7 analyze, annotate, clarify, define, detail, elucidate, expound, express, interpret, narrate, spell out, state, understand

v 8 brief, communicate, convey, declare, describe, disclose, divulge, impart, inform, narrate, orate, portray, read, recite, recount, relate, report, retell, reveal, share, state, tattle, tell, transmit

v 9 clarify, clear, clear up, delineate, depict, elucidate, illuminate, illustrate, picture, portray, reveal

v 10 coach, communicate, condition, convey, cultivate, develop, discipline, drill, edify, educate, enlighten, exercise, groom, imbue, impart, implant, improve, inculcate, indoctrinate, inform, infuse, inseminate, inspire, instill, instruct, perfect, practice, prepare, ready, school, teach, train, tutor

explanation *n* 1 apology, excuse, regret

n 2 clarification, definition, denotation, meaning, translation

n 3 answer, key, result, secret, solution

n 4 depiction, description, illustration, narration, report, sketch, story, verbalization

n 5 alibi, defense, excuse, justification, plea, pretext, rationalization, reason, ruse

n 6 arguments, basis, cause, foundation, grounds, principle, rationale, reason, rudiments, source

n 7 case, case history, clarification, example, illumination, illustration, instance, representative, sample, sampling, specimen

n 8 solution

n 9 assumption, conjecture, deduction, guess, hypothesis, inference, postulate, presumption, proposition, speculation, supposition, theory expletive *n* abomination, blasphemy, curse word, imprecation, obscenity, profanity, swearing

explicit *adj* 1 clear, effective, forceful, strong, trenchant, vigorous

adj 2 accurate, certain, distinct, incontestable, infallible, perfect, unerring

adj 3 blunt, clear, clear-cut, concise, decisive, definite, definitive, distinct, exact, precise, specific, unambiguous

adj 4 see: FIXED *adj* 9

explode *v* 1 burn, erupt, flare

v 2 blow up, burst, detonate

v 3 burst, discharge, erupt, gush, spew, spout

v 4 break, burst, erupt, fragment, rupture, shatter, smash, smatter, splinter

v 5 debunk, disprove

exploit *n* accomplishment, achievement, acquirement, act, action, battle, deed, doing, event, feat, stunt, thing, trick

v 1 milk

v 2 manipulate, misuse, take advantage

v 3 aggrieve, oppress, persecute, torture

v 4 apply, bestow, employ, exercise, handle, use, utilize

v 5 abuse, brutalize, harm, ill-treat, injure, maltreat, mistreat, molest, persecute, victimize, wrong

v 6 bear down, beat down, conquer, crush, defeat, dominate, enslave, overpower, quash, reduce, subdue, subjugate, suppress, vanquish

exploitation *n* misuse

exploration *n* 1 hunt, pursuit, quest, search

n 2 foray, infiltration, invasion, patrol, penetration, raid

n 3 feel, feeling, palpation, sensation, texture, touch

n 4 chase, hunt, pursuit, quest, search, undertaking, venture

n 5 analysis, digging, experimentation, inquiry, inquisition, investigation, research, study, testing, trial

explore *v* 1 frisk, search, seek

v 2 fathom, plumb, probe, sound

v 3 examine, investigate, scout, spy, survey

v 4 delve, dig, examine, feel out, grope, hunt, inquire, investigate, look, observe, peer, probe, pursue, research, scan, scrutinize, search, seek, sound, study, test

v 5 coast, cruise, go, journey, migrate, proceed, sail, survey, tour, travel, trek, voyage

explosion *n* bang, blare, blast, boom, discharge, noise, pop, report, roar

explosive *n* bomb, bombshell, mine, missile, payload, rocket, rocketry, warhead

adj 1 combustible, flammable, inflammable

adj 2 breakneck, expeditious, fast, fleet, hasty, impulsive, instant, lightning, mercurial, meteoric, precipitous, quick, rapid, spectacular, speedy, sudden, swift

export *v* see: SEND *v* 3

expose *v* 1 bare, lay open, strip, subject, uncover

v 2 debunk, discover, show up, uncloak, unmask, unshroud

v 3 see: COMMUNICATE *v* 4

exposé *n* corruption, crime, disgrace, outrage, scandal

exposed *adj* 1 liable, prone, subject, vulnerable

adj 2 bare, in the raw, naked, nude, open, peeled, stripped, unclothed, uncovered, visible

adj 3 defenseless, dependent, disarmed, helpless, powerless, susceptible, unprotected, vulnerable, weak

exposition *n* breakthrough, disclosure, discovery, find, revelation, unearthing

exposure *n* 1 education, experience, involvement, practice, skill

n 2 danger, downside, hazard, jeopardy, liability, menace, peril, risk, threat

expound *v* 1 amplify, construct, develop, devise, elaborate, enhance, enlarge, expand, increase, refine

v 2 analyze, annotate, clarify, define, detail, elucidate, explain, express, interpret, narrate, spell out, state, understand

express *v* 1 embody, exemplify, personify, represent, symbolize, typify

v 2 compress, condense, distill, extract, purify, refine

v 3 convey, hint, impart, imply, indicate, purport, say, suggest

v 4 disclose, display, evince, imply, indicate, manifest, reflect, reveal, show

v 5 analyze, annotate, clarify, define, detail, elucidate, explain, expound, interpret, narrate, spell out, state, understand

v 6 air, bring up, broach, communicate, discuss, expose, give, introduce, open, put, reveal, state, tap, tell, vent, ventilate, verbalize

v 7 announce, articulate, assert, couch, describe, dictate, draft, enunciate, intonate, orate, phrase, proclaim, pronounce, say, speak, state, stress, talk, utter, verbalize, vocalize, voice, word

v 8 deliver, give forth, impart

v 9 denote, depict, illustrate, imply, mean, represent, speak for, symbolize

adj fast, next-day, nonstop, quick, rapid, speedy, swift

expressed *adj* 1 oral, spoken, stated, unwritten, verbal, word-of-mouth

adj 2 certain, explicit, firm, fixed, formal, mandated, set, settled, spoken, stated, stipulated

expression *n* 1 opinion, say, say-so, voice

n 2 characterization, delineation, portrayal, representation

n 3 appearance, aspect, cast, countenance, face, look, visage

n 4 face, grimace, mouth, pout, scowl, smirk, sneer, visage

n 5 idiom, locution, name, phrase, saying, term, word, wording

n 6 formula, methodology, plan, procedure, recipe, scheme, system, theorem

n 7 discourse, speaking, speech, statement, talk, utterance, verbalization, word

n 8 cliché, diction, parlance, phrase, saying, slogan, style, term, wording

n 9 communication, data, disclosure, exchange, facts, information, intelligence, knowledge, news, notification

n 10 airing, utterance, venting

n 11 buzz words, idiom, jargon, language, lingo, parlance, verbiage, vernacular, vocabulary

n 12 angle, approach, code, delivery, execution, fashion, manner, method, mode, organization, process, program, style, system, technique, way

expressive *adj* 1 eloquent, intelligible, meaningful

adj 2 articulate, fluent, glib, perspicuous

adj 3 articulate, communicative, talkative, vocal

adj 4 colorful, graphic, impressive, intense, potent, powerful, striking, strong, unforgettable, vivid

expropriate *v* annex, appropriate, commandeer, confiscate, grab, impound, plunder, preempt, repossess, seize, sequester, shanghai, take

expulsion *n* dismissal, ejection, extraction, firing, impeachment, ouster, removal, termination

expunge *v* abate, abolish, abrogate, annihilate, annul, call off, cancel, cease, delete, destroy, efface, erase, excise, invalidate, kill, negate, nullify, obliterate, omit, quash, remove, stop, terminate, wipe out

exquisite *adj* 1 appetizing, delectable, delicious, luscious, palatable, savory, sweet, tasty

adj 2 choice, dainty, delicate, elegant, favorite, fine, preferred, rare, select

adj 3 errorless, excellent, fastidious, faultless, flawless, ideal, immaculate, impeccable, irreproachable, perfect

adj 4 attractive, becoming, comely, fair, good-looking, gorgeous, handsome, pleasing, radiant, stately

extant *adj* current, remaining, surviving, visible

extemporaneous *adj* ad lib, impromptu, improvised, instantaneous, invented, offhand, off the cuff, spontaneous, unrehearsed, unstudied

extend *v* 1 contact, get, reach

v 2 go, range, run, span, vary

v 3 expand, fan, open, outstretch, spread, unfold

v 4 commit, continue, maintain, perpetuate, prolong, pull

v 5 continue, drag out, draw, elongate, lengthen, prolong, protract, stretch

v 6 allude, assume, hypothesize, imagine, offer, pose, present, presume, propose, speculate, suggest, suppose, surmise, theorize

v 7 see: GIVE *v* 8

v 8 see: INCREASE *v* 8

extended *adj* 1 chronic, incurable, persistent, protracted, refractory, stubborn

adj 2 ample, broad, expansive, extensive, ranging, vast, wide

adj 3 drawn-out, elongated, lengthened, lengthy, long, prolonged, protracted, stretched, sustained

extension *n* 1 addition, adjunct, annex, annexation, branch, section, wing

n 2 circle, compass, confines, dimension, distance, extent, length, limit, orbit, purview, range, reach, realm, scope, size, spectrum, sweep, width

extensive *adj* 1 comprehensive, indiscriminate, large-scale, sweeping, wholesale

adj 2 blanket, comprehensive, expansive, sweeping, universal

adj 3 ample, broad, expansive, extended, ranging, vast, wide

adj 4 ample, big, considerable, enormous, grand, hefty, huge, jumbo, large, major, sizable, spacious, vast

adj 5 current, democratic, dominant, fashionable, general, in vogue, popular, prevailing, prevalent, rampant, rife, sought-after, well-liked, widespread

adj 6 see: MANY *adj* 2

extent *n* 1 degree, intensity, measure, ratio, scope

n 2 boundary, field, matter, range, reach, scope, vicinity

n 3 circle, compass, confines, dimension, distance, extension, length, limit, orbit, purview, range, reach, realm, scope, size, spectrum, sweep, width

extenuate *v* 1 absolve, acquit, cover up, exonerate, mitigate, whitewash

v 2 allay, alleviate, assuage, attenuate, diminish, ease, lessen, lighten, minimize, mitigate, moderate, mollify, reduce, relieve

extenuating *adj* excusable, justifying, mitigating, offsetting

exterior *adj* external, outside, superficial

n facade, outside, skin, surface

exterminate *v* abolish, annihilate, assassinate, bump off, butcher, decimate, destroy, dispatch, execute, hang, hit, kill, knock off, liquidate, massacre, murder, put away, rub out, slaughter, slay, wipe out

extermination *n* bloodbath, bloodshed, butchery, carnage, genocide, holocaust, killing, massacre, pogrom, shambles, slaughter

external *adj* exterior, outside, superficial

extinct *adj* 1 bygone, dead, defunct, departed, forgotten, gone, lost, vanished

adj 2 ancient, antiquated, archaic, bygone, dated, dead, noncurrent, obsolete, old, outdated, outmoded, passé, past, worn

extinguish *v* 1 douse, out, put out, quench

v 2 annihilate, crush, demolish, put down, quash, quell, quench, repress, squash, stamp out, suppress

extol *v* acclaim, applaud, celebrate, commend, eulogize, exalt, glorify, hail, honor, laud, praise, resound, salute, toast, tout, worship

extolling *adj* approving, commending, complimentary, congratulatory, flattering, praising

extort *v* coerce, exact, gouge, shake down, squeeze, wrench, wrest, wring

extra *adj* 1 added, additional, another, auxiliary, further, incremental, more, one more, other, spare, supplemental, supplementary, surplus

adj 2 see: SUPERFLUOUS *adj* 3

extract *v* 1 drain, milk, squeeze

v 2 purloin, remove, take out, withdraw

v 3 pull, remove, suck, tear, withdraw, yank

v 4 compress, condense, distill, express, purify, refine

v 5 deduce, derive, draw, educe, elicit, evince

v 6 dig, grub, uproot, weed

n 1 concentrate, essence, juice

n 2 citation, clipping, excerpt, mention, passage, portion, quotation, quote, reference, section

extraction *n* dismissal, ejection, expulsion, firing, impeachment, ouster, removal, termination

extradite *v* banish, cast out, deport, dispel, displace, exile, expatriate, expel, ostracize, oust, relegate, remove

extraneous *adj* 1 alien, extraterrestrial, extrinsic, foreign

adj 2 abnormal, extra, foreign, illogical, immaterial, insignificant, irregular, irrelevant, malapropos, nonessential, peripheral, superfluous, surplus, unimportant, unnecessary, unrelated

extraordinary *adj* 1 dramatic, sensational, shocking, startling

adj 2 amazing, fantastic, inconceivable, incredible, unbelievable

adj 3 excellent, great, impressive, noteworthy, outstanding, shining, smashing, superb, wonderful

adj 4 amazing, brilliant, exceptional, noteworthy, phenomenal, rare, remarkable, significant, singular, stunning, super, uncommon, uncustomary, unique, unusual

adj 5 dynamite, excellent, great, out of sight, outstanding, phenomenal, premier, super, superb, superlative, tremendous, wonderful

extrapolation *n* approximation, estimation, guess, speculation

extraterrestrial *adj* alien, extraneous, extrinsic, foreign

extravagant *adj* 1 fantastic, preposterous, wild

adj 2 intemperate, loose, reckless, unrestrained, wanton, wild

adj 3 excessive, exorbitant, expensive, extreme, ghastly, lavish, outlandish, overpriced, profuse, ultimate, unbelievable

adj 4 abundant, cornucopian, exuberant, garish, generous, lavish, lush, luxuriant, opulent, prodigal, profuse, rich, wasteful

extravaganza *n* Broadway, comedy, drama, musical, production, stage, theater

extreme *adj* 1 drastic, excessive, intense, passionate, radical, severe, strong

adj 2 extremist, fanatic, fanatical, rabid, radical, revolutionary, ultra, zealous

adj 3 arrant, barefaced, blatant, brassy,

brazen, impudent, notorious, obtrusive, shameless, unabashed

adj 4 ardent, decisive, determined, emphatic, forceful, intense, potent, powerful, severe, strong

adj 5 excessive, exorbitant, expensive, extravagant, ghastly, lavish, outlandish, overpriced, profuse, ultimate, unbelievable

adj 6 farthest, furthermost, furthest, hindmost, most distant, most remote, outermost, utmost

n border, extremity, limit, periphery

extremely *adv* awfully, dreadfully, eminently, endlessly, exceedingly, exceptionally, greatly, highly, mightily, notably, quite, remarkably, terribly, thoroughly, very

extremist *adj* extreme, fanatic, fanatical, rabid, radical, revolutionary, ultra, zealous

extremity *n* 1 border, extreme, limit, periphery

n 2 foot, hand, hoof, paw

n 3 appendage, arm, leg, limb, member, part

extricate *v* 1 free, liberate, release, remove, rescue

v 2 disengage, loosen, open, unbind, unclasp, undo, unfasten, unknot, unloose, unloosen, untie

extrication *n* deliverance, freeing, recovery, release, rescue, saving

extrinsic *adj* alien, extraneous, extraterrestrial, foreign

extroverted *adj* belligerent, free, intimidating, loud, outspoken, vocal, vociferous

exuberant *adj* 1 buoyant, cheerful, ecstatic, elated, enthusiastic, positive

adj 2 abundant, cornucopian, extravagant, garish, generous, lavish, lush, luxuriant, opulent, prodigal, profuse, rich, wasteful

adj 3 bright, cheerful, cheery, content, ebullient, ecstatic, elated, festive, gay, glad, happy, jovial, joyful, joyous, merry, mirthful, pleased, radiant, rejoicing

adj 4 alert, animated, bouncy, bright, brisk, buoyant, chipper, dashing, dynamic, ebullient, energetic, enthusiastic, frisky, frolicsome, gay, jumpy, kinetic, lively, peppy, pert, playful, rousing, scintillating, spirited, sprightly, spry, vivacious

exude *v* 1 perspire

v 2 discharge, drip, emit, leak, ooze, secrete, seep, trickle

exult *v* boast, brag, crow, flaunt, gloat, revel, show off, strut, vaunt

eye *v* 1 eyeball, gape, gawk, gaze, goggle, observe, ogle, peer, stare, study

v 2 glance, glimpse, look, peak

n binoculars, field glass, glass, lens, magnifying glass, microscope, mirror, periscope, scope, spyglass, telescope

eyeball *v* see: STARE *v* 2

eye-catching *adj* arresting, astonishing, astounding, conspicuous, marked, noticeable, obvious, pointed, prominent, salient, sensational, striking, stunning

eye-opening *adj* academic, educational, enlightening, illuminating, informative, instructive, revealing, scholastic

eyesight *n* perception, sight, vision

F

fable *n* allegory, fantasy, fiction, legend, lesson, lore, myth, mythology, parable, story, tale

fabric *n* 1 cloth

n 2 filling, weft, woof

fabricate *v* 1 concoct, deceive, equivocate, falsify, fib, invent, lie, misstate, perjure

v 2 assemble, build, construct, erect, establish, forge, form, make, manufacture, mold, produce, trailblaze

v 3 brew, concoct, construe, contrive, create, devise, engineer, formulate, hatch, invent, make up, plot, scheme

v 4 see: ACT *v* 3

fabrication *n* 1 concoction, creation, fantasy, fiction, figment, invention

n 2 exaggeration, falsehood, falsity, fib, invention, lie, misstatement, story, tale

n 3 deceit, deception, falsehood, fraud, fraudulence, hypocrisy, lying, perjury, trickery, untruth

fabulous *adj* 1 amazing, exaggerated, questionable

adj 2 excellent, fantastic, fine, good, great, marvelous, super, terrific, tremendous, wonderful

adj 3 legendary, mythical, mythological

facade *n* 1 exterior, outside, skin, surface

n 2 appearance, cover, face, facet, factor, front, look, surface, veneer

face *n* 1 countenance, features, kisser, mug

n 2 appearance, aspect, cast, countenance, expression, look, visage

n 3 expression, grimace, mouth, pout, scowl, smirk, sneer, visage

n 4 appearance, cover, facade, facet, factor, front, look, surface, veneer

n 5 side, siding, surface, wall

n 6 family, font, printwheel, size, style, type, typeface

n 7 arrogance, assurance, audacity, boldness, brashness, brass, cheek, chutzpah, condescension, confidence, crust, effrontery, gall, haughtiness, insolence, nerve, patronage, presumption, ridicule, sass, stamina, temerity

v 1 admit, confront, realize

v 2 affront, encounter, insult, offend, outrage, slight

v 3 brave, challenge, confront, dare, defy, mutiny, rebel, resist

v 4 front

facet *n* 1 appearance, cover, facade, face, factor, front, look, surface, veneer

n 2 angle, aspect, hand, mien, opinion, perspective, phase, side, slant, view

facetious *adj* comical, funny, humorous, jesting, jocular, joking, kidding, sarcastic, witty

facile *adj* light, simple, smooth

facilitate *v* 1 accelerate, aid, assist, expedite

v 2 clear, ease, expedite, smooth

v 3 accredit, authorize, certify, commission, empower, enable, entitle, invest, license, permit, sanction, validate

facilitation *n* adjudication, arbitration, intercession, intervention, mediation

facility *n* building, office, place, service

facsimile *n* carbon, carbon copy, copy, duplicate, replica, reproduction, telecopy, Xerox copy

fact *n* 1 actuality, given, specific, statistic, truth

n 2 actuality, being, existence, life, presence, reality, truth, vitality

faction *n* 1 band, cabal, camp, circle, clan, clique, coterie, coven, cult, family, gang, group, mob, ring, school, sect, tribe

n 2 see: ALLIANCE *n*

factor *n* 1 component, constituent, element, ingredient, item, part, segment

n 2 appearance, cover, facade, face, facet, front, look, surface, veneer

n 3 agent, catalyst, force, power

v adjust

facts *n* 1 data, details, dope, information, report, scoop

n 2 data, discipline, information, knowledge, lore, news, science, wisdom

n 3 communication, data, disclosure, exchange, expression, information, intelligence, knowledge, news, notification

factual *adj* 1 honest, trustworthy, truthful, veracious

adj 2 absolute, actual, authentic, bona fide, certain, definite, existent, genuine, hard, inarguable, incontestable, incontro-

vertible, indisputable, indubitable, irrefutable, positive, real, sure, true, undeniable, undisputable, undoubtable, undoubted, unequivocal, unquestionable, veritable, viable

faculty *n* 1 department, instructors, professors, staff, teachers

n 2 crew, employees, help, people, personnel, staff, workers

n 3 bent, brains, brilliance, flair, genius, gift, head, intelligence, knack, mind, nose, prowess, talent

n 4 common sense, good sense, gumption, horse sense, judgment, logic, sense, wisdom

n 5 awareness, emotion, feel, feeling, intuition, perception, reaction, response, sensation, sense

fad *n* chic, craze, fashion, mode, rage, style, thing, trend, vogue

fade *v* 1 blanch, pale, whiten

v 2 clear, depart, disappear, vanish

v 3 abate, decline, deteriorate, fail, flag, impair, languish, wane, weaken, wither, worsen

v 4 see: CANCEL *v* 3

v 5 see: OBSCURE *v*

faded *adj* frayed, poor, run-down, shabby, tattered, threadbare, worn

fail *v* 1 collapse

v 2 bomb, flop, stumble, trip

v 3 disappoint, disenchant, disillusion, dissatisfy, frustrate, let down

v 4 abate, decline, deteriorate, fade, flag, impair, languish, wane, weaken, wither, worsen

v 5 crash, flop, flunk

v 6 give out, lose, miss, run out

v 7 fizzle, miscarry, misfire, miss

failing *adj* deficient, inadequate, inferior, insufficient, scant, scarce, scrimpy, short, shy, wanting

n 1 fault, foible, frailty, limitation, shortcoming, vice, weakness

n 2 blemish, defect, fault, flaw, imperfection, scar, shortcoming, weakness

fail-safe *adj* dependable, infallible, reliable, sure, tested, tried

failure *n* 1 collapse, downfall, fall, overthrow, ruin, upset

n 2 bomb, bust, disaster, dud, fiasco, flop, turkey

n 3 breakdown, catastrophe, crash, crisis, death, destruction, doom, finish, ruin

n 4 comedown, decline, decrease, descent, dive, drop, fall, plunge, regression, setback, slide, tumble *n* 5 discard, garbage, junk, reject, scrap, second

fain *adj* see: EAGER *adj* 2

faint *adj* 1 dizzy, confused, foggy, giddy, lightheaded, reeling

adj 2 imperceptible, meager, remote, slight, subtle, vague

adj 3 balmy, bland, gentle, mild, pleasant, smooth, soft, weak

v collapse, pass out, swoon

fair *adj* 1 balmy, bright, clear, pleasant, serene

adj 2 clear, cloudless, pleasant, sunny, unclouded

adj 3 clean, equal, equitable, even, honest, just, sportsmanlike, straight, upright

adj 4 aboveboard, candid, equitable, forthright, honest, legitimate, plain-dealing, straight, straightforward, trustworthy, upright

adj 5 acceptable, adequate, competent, decent, enough, good, mediocre, passable, reasonable, respectable, satisfactory, sufficient, tolerable

adj 6 alluring, attractive, beautiful, breathtaking, comely, cute, fine, foxy, gorgeous, lovely, luscious, magnificent, pretty, shapely, stunning

adj 7 candid, dispassionate, equal, equitable, impartial, impersonal, indifferent, just, neutral, objective, open-minded, square, unbiased, uncolored, unprejudiced

adj 8 blond, flaxen, light

adj 9 attractive, becoming, comely, exquisite, good-looking, gorgeous, handsome, pleasing, radiant, stately

n bazaar, carnival, circus, market

fairly *adv* 1 moderately, pretty, reasonably, somewhat, so-so

adv 2 adequately, amply, enough, equitably, justly, moderately, passably, rather, satisfactorily, tolerably

fairness *n* equity, justice, impartiality, objectivity

fairy *n* elf, naiad, nymph, pixie, sprite

faith *n* 1 affiliation, belief, church, creed, denomination, persuasion, religion, rite, seat, theology

n 2 belief, confidence, contingency, credence, credit, creed, dependence, desire, hope, religion, trust

faithful *adj* 1 exact, literal, precise, strict, true, verbatim, word for word

adj 2 authoritative, dependable, due, legitimate, rightful, strict, true, trustworthy, undistorted, veracious

adj 3 ardent, constant, dedicated, dependable, devoted, loyal, resolute, staunch, steadfast, steady, true, trusty

adj 4 accurate, authentic, believable, certain, convincing, credible, dependable, real, reliable, safe, sure, tenable, true, trustworthy, trusty

faithfulness *n* allegiance, ardor, devotion, fidelity, loyalty

faithless *adj* cheating, conniving, deceitful, deceptive, dishonest, disloyal, false, insidious, manipulative, perfidious, sneaky, traitorous, treacherous, unfaithful, untrue, untrustworthy

fake *adj* 1 contrived, phony, seeming

adj 2 feigned, fictitious, mock, sham, simulated

adj 3 artificial, counterfeit, false, man-made, manufactured, plastic, synthetic

adj 4 artificial, bogus, counterfeit, ersatz, false, imitation, mock, phony, pseudo, sham, simulated, spurious, substitute, unreal

n 1 charlatan, cheat, fraud, hypocrite, quack

n 2 charlatan, counterfeit, faker, fraud, hypocrite, impostor, liar, phony, pretender

n 3 bastard, deception, fraud, hoax, put-on, sham

v act, assume, bluff, counterfeit, fabricate, feign, imitate, invent, make believe, play, pretend, put on, sham

faker *n* charlatan, counterfeit, fake, fraud, hypocrite, impostor, liar, phony, pretender

fall *n* 1 downfall, collapse, failure, overthrow, ruin, upset

n 2 comedown, decline, decrease, descent, dive, drop, failure, plunge, regression, setback, slide, tumble

n 3 debasement, decline, deterioration, dip, downturn, drop, ebb, erosion, involution, plunge, sag, slide, slip, slump, wane, weakening

v 1 lapse, sink, slip

v 2 err, offend, sin, transgress, trespass, violate

v 3 lurch, skid, skim, slide, slip, stumble, totter, trip, tumble

v 4 descend, dive, drop, lapse, leap, lower, plummet, plunge, sink, swoop

v 5 cave in, collapse, disintegrate, drop, go down, keel over, pitch, plunge, slump, spill, topple, tumble

v 6 abate, cease, decline, decrease, die down, diminish, drain, dwindle, ease, ebb, lessen, let up, lull, recede, reduce, relax, relent, shrink, slacken, soften, stop, subside, taper off, wane, waste away, weaken

v 7 deluge, drizzle, pour, rain, shower, sprinkle

v 8 give up, go under, submit, succumb, surrender, yield

fallacious *adj* baseless, erroneous, groundless, invalid, unfounded, unsubstantiated

fallacy *n* 1 deception, error, flaw, illusion, inaccuracy

n 2 delusion, illusion, myth, old wives' tale, superstition

fall in *v* line up, queue, wait

false *adj* 1 abject, base, contemptible, debasing, despicable, servile

adj 2 deceptive, illusive, illusory, misleading, sham, unreal

adj 3 erroneous, faulty, imprecise, inaccurate, incorrect, inexact, mistaken, specious, untrue, wrong

adj 4 artificial, bogus, counterfeit, ersatz, fake, imitation, mock, phony, pseudo, sham, simulated, spurious, substitute, unreal

adj 5 cheating, conniving, deceitful, deceptive, dishonest, disloyal, faithless, insidious, manipulative, perfidious, sneaky, traitorous, treacherous, unfaithful, untrue, untrustworthy

adj 6 artificial, counterfeit, fake, manmade, manufactured, plastic, synthetic

falsehood *n* 1 bull, lie, misstatement, overstatement, untruth

n 2 exaggeration, fabrication, falsity, fib, invention, lie, misstatement, story, tale

n 3 deceit, deception, fabrication, fraud, fraudulence, hypocrisy, lying, perjury, trickery, untruth

n 4 dishonesty, mendacity, untruthfulness

falsify *v* 1 concoct, deceive, equivocate, fabricate, fib, invent, lie, misstate, perjure

v 2 angle, confuse, deceive, distort, garble, incline, misconstrue, misinterpret, misquote, misread, misrepresent, misunderstand, mix up, mumble, slant, slope, taint, twist

falsity *n* exaggeration, fabrication, falsehood, fib, invention, lie, misstatement, story, tale

falter *v* 1 halt, hobble, limp

v 2 bumble, flounder, fumble, get stuck, grope, hesitate, stagger, stumble, waffle, waver

v 3 delay, halt, hesitate, pause, stagger, stall, vacillate, waver

faltering *adj* 1 diffident, halting, hesitant,

indecisive, reluctant, tentative, unsure, waffling, wavering

adj 2 see: AWKWARD *adj* 3

fame *n* 1 position, prestige, prosperity, station, status, success

n 2 esteem, good standing, name, perception, regard, reputation, stature

n 3 brilliance, celebrity, distinction, excellence, glory, halo, honor, luster, note, popularity, prominence, renown, repute, splendor

famed *adj* 1 acclaimed, celebrated, distinguished, eminent, esteemed, excellent, famous, foremost, illustrious, notable, outstanding, prestigious, prominent, renowned, well-known

adj 2 central, chief, distinguished, dominant, great, key, leading, main, major, number one, outstanding, predominant, preeminent, primary, prime, principal, prominent, star, successful, superior, top

familiar *adj* 1 close, intimate, near, personal

adj 2 abreast, acquainted, aware, conversant, informed, knowledgeable, up, versed

adj 3 casual, cavalier, colloquial, informal, ordinary, regular, relaxed, unceremonious, unconstrained, unofficial, usual, vernacular

adj 4 accepted, accustomed, chronic, common, constant, continual, customary, daily, everyday, frequent, habitual, inured, often, recurring, regular, routine, traditional, usual

familiarity *n* 1 fraternity, friendship, closeness, companionship, intimacy

n 2 see: SKILL *n* 3

family *n* 1 kin, people, relation, relative

n 2 breed, clan, class, household, people, race, relatives, stock, tribe

n 3 ancestry, blood, bloodline, descent, genealogy, heritage, line, lineage, origin, pedigree, stock, strain

n 4 band, cabal, camp, circle, clan, clique, coterie, coven, cult, faction, gang, group, mob, ring, school, sect, tribe

n 5 bracket, breed, cast, category, class, division, genre, genus, group, grouping, ilk, kind, lot, mold, nature, order, persuasion, section, sector, set, sort, species, style, type, variety

n 6 face, font, printwheel, size, style, type, typeface

famine *n* dearth, deficiency, deficit, drought, lack, rarity, scarcity, shortage, sparseness, undersupply, want

famish *v* fast, starve, wither

famished *adj* hungry, ravenous, starved, starving, voracious

famous *adj* acclaimed, celebrated, distinguished, eminent, esteemed, excellent, famed, foremost, illustrious, notable, outstanding, prestigious, prominent, renowned, well-known

fan *n* admirer, buff, devotee, disciple, enthusiast, follower, groupie

   v expand, extend, open, outstretch, spread, unfold

fanatic *adj* extreme, extremist, fanatical, rabid, radical, revolutionary, ultra, zealous

   n bug, crusader, enthusiast, fiend, freak, hobbyist, maniac, monomaniac, nut, radical, zealot

fanatical *adj* extreme, extremist, fanatic, rabid, radical, revolutionary, ultra, zealous

fancied *adj* see: FICTITIOUS *adj* 3

fanciful *adj* conceived, conjured, created, fancied, fantastic, fictional, fictitious, illusory, imaginary, imagined, invented, make-believe, nonexistent, notional, unreal, whimsical

fancy *n* 1 daydream, dream, fantasy, musing, reverie, vision

   n 2 caprice, humor, impulse, notion, vagary, whim, whimsy

   n 3 creativity, fantasy, image, imagination, ingenuity, inspiration, invention, resourcefulness, whimsy

   n 4 bent, disposition, fondness, idea, inclination, liking, mind, notion, pleasure, propensity, yen

   v 1 crave, choose, covet, desire, envy, lust, want, wish

   v 2 see: VISUALIZE *v*

fanfare *n* array, blare, display, exhibit, exhibition, fuss, parade, performance, presentation, procession, publicity, show, showing

fang *n* digger, gasher, molar, tooth, tush, tusk

fanny *n* backside, base, bottom, bucket, buns, butt, buttocks, behind, derrière, end, hindquarters, posterior, rump, seat, stub, stump, tip, tush

fantasize *v* dream, imagine, muse, suppose

fantasizing *adj* delirious, deranged, frenzied, hallucinating, maniacal, raving

fantastic *adj* 1 bizarre
   adj 2 extravagant, preposterous, wild
   adj 3 amazing, extraordinary, inconceivable, incredible, unbelievable

   adj 4 excellent, fabulous, fine, good, great, marvelous, super, terrific, tremendous, wonderful
   adj 5 see: FICTITIOUS *adj* 3
   adj 6 see: HUGE *adj* 3

fantasy *n* 1 adventure, escapade, saga, story

   n 2 daydream, dream, fancy, musing, reverie, vision

   n 3 concoction, creation, fabrication, fiction, figment, invention

   n 4 creativity, fancy, image, imagination, ingenuity, inspiration, invention, resourcefulness, whimsy

   n 5 allegory, fable, fiction, legend, lesson, lore, myth, mythology, parable, story, tale

   n 6 aberration, apparition, delusion, figment, ghost, hallucination, illusion, image, mirage, phantasm, specter, vision

   n 7 anecdote, description, fiction, invention, myth, narration, narrative, novel, sketch, story, tale, yarn

far *adv* considerably, dramatically, quite, rather, significantly, very, well

   adj distant, faraway, obscure, outlying, out-of-the-way, remote, removed

faraway *adj* distant, far, obscure, outlying, out-of-the-way, remote, removed

farce *n* 1 act, make-believe, parody, performance, show, sketch, skit

   n 2 buffoonery, burlesque, caricature, comedy, humor, imitation, joke, lampoon, mockery, parody, satire, spoof, takeoff, travesty

farcical *adj* absurd, comic, comical, crazy, droll, foolish, funny, hilarious, humorous, laughable, ludicrous, outrageous, ridiculous, silly

fare *n* 1 charge, cost, expense, outlay, payment, price, rate, value, worth

   n 2 bread, breakfast, brunch, chow, cuisine, diet, dinner, dish, edibles, entree, food, grub, lunch, meals, nosh, nutrition, provisions, rations, snack, supper, victuals, vittles

   v do, get along, get by, get on, make out, manage, muddle through, shift, stagger

farewell *n* 1 departure, exit, leaving, parting, passing

   n 2 adieu, adios, aloha, *arrivederci*, *auf Wiedersehen*, au revoir, bon voyage, bye, cheerio, *ciao*, goodbye, good day, *sayonara*, shalom, so long

far-fetched *adj* impractical, remote, unfeasible, unrealistic

farm *v* cultivate, grow, harvest, plant, plow, produce, raise, till
n ranch, range, spread

far-out *adj* see: UNUSUAL *adj* 4

farsighted *adj* longsighted

farther *adv* additionally, beyond, further, furthermore

farthest *adj* extreme, furthermost, furthest, hindmost, most distant, most remote, outermost, utmost

fascinate *v* 1 appeal, arouse, attract, excite, fire, interest, intrigue, lead on, lure, seduce, stir, tantalize
v 2 allure, attract, bedevil, beguile, bewitch, captivate, charm, conjure, delight, draw, enchant, enthrall, lure, magnetize, mesmerize, tempt, wile

fascinated *adj* 1 captivated, enamored, infatuated, in love
adj 2 see: ENGROSSED *adj* 2

fascinating *adj* 1 alluring, attractive, becoming, coy, cute, enchanting, enticing, foxy, inviting, pleasing, ravishing, seductive, sexy
adj 2 alluring, beguiling, bewitching, captivating, catchy, charming, dazzling, dynamic, enchanting, engaging, enthralling, enticing, glamorous, intriguing, mesmerizing, riveting, spectacular, spellbinding
adj 3 see: UNUSUAL *adj* 4

fascination *n* affinity, allure, appeal, attraction, attractiveness, aura, beguilement, charisma, charm, enchantment, enticement, glamour, infatuation, magnetism, sex appeal, spell

fascist *n* authoritarian, autocrat, despot, dictator, tsar, tyrant

fashion *n* 1 flavor, manner, mode, style, tone, vein
n 2 chic, craze, fad, mode, rage, style, thing, trend, vogue
n 3 custom, formality, habit, manner, mores, observance, practice, routine, tradition, usage, use, way, wont
n 4 angle, approach, code, delivery, execution, expression, manner, method, mode, organization, process, program, style, system, technique, way
v 1 adapt, conform, convert, cut, fit, measure, modify, rig, shape, suit, tailor
v 2 carve, chisel, craft, cut, define, design, form, mold, sculpt, sculpture, shape, steer
v 3 arrange, blueprint, cast, chart, design, devise, draft, draw, engineer, lay out, map, outline, plan, plot, project, set out, sketch

fashionable *adj* 1 chic, current, hip, in, smart, stylish, trendy, vogue
adj 2 current, democratic, dominant, extensive, general, in vogue, popular, prevailing, prevalent, rampant, rife, sought after, well-liked, widespread

fast *adv* 1 firm, firmly, hard, loyally, reliably, solidly, tight, tightly
adv 2 abruptly, hastily, immediately, instantaneously, instantly, quick, quickly, short, suddenly, swiftly
adv 3 expeditiously, full tilt, hastily, in a snap, lickety-split, promptly, pronto, quick, quickly, rapidly, right away, soon, speedily, swiftly, urgently
adj 1 attached, firm, fixed, rigid, secure, set, taut, tense, tight
adj 2 casual, easy, immoral, incontinent, indiscriminate, lax, lecherous, lewd, licentious, light, loose, promiscuous, unchaste, wanton, whorish
adj 3 breakneck, expeditious, explosive, fleet, hasty, impulsive, instant, lightning, mercurial, meteoric, precipitous, quick, rapid, spectacular, speedy, sudden, swift
adj 4 express, next-day, nonstop, quick, rapid, speedy, swift
adj 5 alluring, appealing, attractive, charming, coquettish, coy, fetching, flirtatious, seductive, sexy, tempting, winsome
v 1 famish, starve, wither
v 2 diet, lose weight, reduce, slenderize, slim, trim down

fasten *v* 1 clinch, secure
v 2 buckle, clasp, hook
v 3 bind, chain, link, shackle
v 4 anchor, catch, fix, moor, secure
v 5 attach, clip, nail, pin, staple, tack
v 6 affix, attach, bind, clip, connect, fix, rivet, weld
v 7 band, belt, bind, corset, gird, girdle, lash, strap, tie
v 8 attach, bind, bond, cord, hitch, join, link, marry, tether, tie, tie up
v 9 clump, hitch, join, knot, lace, lash, link, loop, rope, secure, tie, unite
v 10 affix, bind, bond, cement, fuse, glue, join, lock, paste, seal, secure, stick, unite
v 11 associate, blend, bond, coalesce, combine, compound, connect, couple, fuse, join, link, marry, mate, meet, merge, pair, unite, wed

fastened *adj* fixed, in position, motionless, permanent, set, solid, standing, static, stationary, still

fastener *n* buckle, catch, clasp, clip, latch, pin, snap, zipper

fastidious *adj* 1 exacting, finicky, meticulous, picky, precise, rigid, strict *adj* 2 errorless, excellent, exquisite, faultless, flawless, ideal, immaculate, impeccable, irreproachable, perfect

adj 3 careful, cautious, choosy, discriminating, finicky, fussy, meticulous, nitpicking, particular, persnickety, picky, selective

fat *adj* 1 chubby, chunky, corpulent, fleshy, gross, heavy, hefty, meaty, obese, overweight, plump, portly, pudgy, rotund, stocky, stout

adj 2 see: BIG *adj* 3

n deluge, excess, glut, overabundance, overflow, overkill, plethora, redundancy, surfeit, surplus

fatal *adj* 1 baneful, deadly, lethal, mortal, noxious, pernicious, pestilent, ruinous

adj 2 calamitous, cataclysmic, catastrophic, critical, crucial, devastating, disastrous, fateful, momentous, ruinous, vital

fatality *n* 1 casualty, loss, victim

n 2 carnage, death, demise, mortality, ruin

fate *n* destiny, good fortune, karma, kismet, lot, luck, providence

fateful *adj* calamitous, cataclysmic, catastrophic, critical, crucial, devastating, disastrous, fatal, momentous, ruinous, vital

father *n* 1 custodian, guardian, mother, parent, trustee

n 2 chaplain, clergyman, cleric, guru, minister, padre, parson, pastor, priest, rabbi, reverend

n 3 dad, dada, daddy, pa, papa, pappy, parent, pater, patriarch, pop, poppa

v 1 engender, fertilize, impregnate, inseminate, sire

v 2 bear, beget, breed, come into, create, effect, engender, generate, hatch, impregnate, make, mate, multiply, originate, parent, procreate, promulgate, propagate, reproduce, sire, spawn

fatherland *n* country, home, homeland, land, motherland, soil

fatherless *adj* bastard, illegitimate, misbegotten, orphaned, spurious, unauthentic, ungenuine

fathom *v* 1 explore, plumb, probe, sound

v 2 assume, believe, comprehend, conceive, estimate, expect, gather, grasp, guess, imagine, infer, know, presume, suppose, surmise, suspect, think, trust, understand

v 3 see: UNDERSTAND *v* 5, 6

fatigue *n* exhaustion, lassitude, weariness

v drain, exhaust, jade, tire, wear down, wear out, weary

fatigued *adj* beat, burnt out, bushed, careworn, drawn, emaciated, exhausted, expended, frazzled, haggard, jaded, pinched, pooped, run-down, shot, spent, tired, wearied, weary, worn, worn down, worn-out

fatten *v* see: EXPAND *v* 4

fattening *adj* abundant, heavy, rich, sweet, thick

fatuous *adj* absurd, anile, asinine, brainless, childish, foolish, idiotic, inept, meaningless, mindless, senseless, silly, simple, thoughtless, unintelligent, witless

faucet *n* cock, nozzle, spigot, spout, tap, valve

fault *n* 1 bug, defect, error, glitch

n 2 failing, foible, frailty, limitation, shortcoming, vice, weakness

n 3 blemish, defect, failing, flaw, imperfection, scar, shortcoming, weakness

n 4 accountability, blame, burden, culpability, guilt, onus, responsibility, shame, stigma

n 5 defect, deficiency, demerit, flaw, imperfection, inadequacy, lack, need, shortcoming, want

n 6 see: CRIME *n* 3

v accuse, blame, charge, complain, condemn, criticize, indict, reproach

faultfinding *adj* captious, carping, censorious, critical, cutting, disparaging, hairsplitting, nit-picking

faultless *adj* errorless, excellent, exquisite, fastidious, flawless, ideal, immaculate, impeccable, irreproachable, perfect

faulty *adj* 1 amiss, crude, defective, flawed, imperfect, incomplete, short, unfulfilled

adj 2 erroneous, false, imprecise, inaccurate, incorrect, inexact, mistaken, specious, untrue, wrong

favor *n* 1 account, admiration, consideration, esteem, regard, respect

n 2 benevolence, boon, contribution, donation, gift, grant, largess, present

n 3 appeal, desire, petition, plea, request, solicitation, wish

n 4 consideration, courtesy, dispensation, indulgence, kindness, privilege, respect, service

v 1 imitate, look like, resemble

v 2 choose, desire, elect, prefer, select

v 3 accommodate, convenience, help, oblige, please, provide, serve

v 4 advocate, encourage

v 5 accept, approbate, approve, authorize,

certify, condone, confirm, countenance, endorse, pass, ratify, sanction, validate

favorable adj 1 auspicious, opportune, propitious, seasonable, timely

adj 2 auspicious, fortunate, happy, lucky, providential, serendipitous

adj 3 constructive, fruitful, helpful, positive, productive, useful, worthwhile

adj 4 auspicious, bright, confident, hopeful, promising, rosy, sunny, utopian

adj 5 agreeable, congenial, good, grateful, gratifying, nice, pleasant, pleasing, pleasurable, welcome

adj 6 auspicious, fortunate, propitious

adj 7 glowing, healthy, rosy

adj 8 approbative, approbatory, approving, supporting, sustaining

favorably adv fortunately, happily, positively, successfully, well

favored adj better, partial, preferential, select, special

favorite adj 1 cherished, pet, special

adj 2 best-selling, hot, popular

adj 3 choice, dainty, delicate, elegant, exquisite, fine, preferred, rare, select

adj 4 choice, preferred, select

n 1 icon, idol, god, hero

n 2 best, choice, elite, finest, optimum, pick, pride

favoritism n bias, nepotism, patronage

faze v affect, bother, burden, concern, daunt, disturb, intimidate, oppress, upset, worry

fear n 1 amazement, awe, consternation, dread, respect, reverence, wonder

n 2 apprehension, distrust, doubt, hesitation, misbelief, mistrust, suspicion, wariness

n 3 affliction, alarm, anxiety, apprehension, care, consternation, dismay, dread, fright, horror, ordeal, panic, terror, trepidation, trial, trouble, worry

v distrust, doubt, mistrust, suspect

fearful adj 1 afraid, aghast, anxious, apprehensive, concerned, discerning, frightened, nervous, paranoid, scared, scary, terrified, worried

adj 2 chicken, cowardly, gutless, spineless, timid, yellow

adj 3 appalling, awful, dire, dreadful, formidable, frightening, frightful, ghastly, horrendous, horrible, offensive, ominous, portentous, scary, shocking, spooky, terrible, terrifying, unpleasant

fearless adj see: BRAVE adj 1

feasible adj 1 achievable, capable, doable, possible, practical, viable, workable

adj 2 accessible, available, close, convenient, functional, handy, helpful, multipurpose, nearby, open, practical, public, reachable, ready, serviceable, suitable, unrestricted, usable, useful, utilitarian, well-suited, within reach, working

feast n banquet, buffet, dinner, lunch, meal, repast, smorgasbord, supper

feat n accomplishment, achievement, acquirement, act, action, battle, deed, doing, event, exploit, stunt, thing, trick

feather n plume

feature n 1 characteristic, difference, distinction, peculiarity

n 2 detail, item, part, particular, specific

n 3 attention, center, crux, focus, highlight, key, spotlight

n 4 attribute, character, characteristic, highlight, mark, peculiarity, property, quality, trait, virtue

n 5 article, bulletin, byline, column, communication, dispatch, editorial, headline, item, newsletter, report, story, vignette

v see: ACCENTUATE v

features n countenance, face, kisser, mug

feces n droppings, excrement, stool, waste

fecund adj copious, creative, fertile, fruitful, productive, prolific

federation n 1 cartel, chain, coalition, collaboration, combine, conglomerate, consortium, group, partnership, pool, syndicate, trust

n 2 affiliation, alliance, association, axis, bloc, coalition, concord, confederation, consolidation, faction, joint venture, league, merger, organization, partnership, relationship, treaty, union

fee n 1 admission, cover charge, entrance fee, pass, ticket

n 2 discipline, dockage, fine, loss, penalty, punishment

n 3 bill, charge, check, debt, invoice, note, tab

n 4 alimony, compensation, honorarium, payment, remuneration, reward, stipend

n 5 assessment, cost, duty, expense, impost, levy, offering, penalty, price, sacrifice, tariff, tax, toll, trade-off

n 6 bill, bonus, charge, commission, compensation, consideration, earnings, gross, income, pay, revenue, salary, stipend, wage

n 7 ante, award, bonus, booty, cash, commission, dividend, donation, gift, gratuity, largess, money, percentage, perk, perquisite, premium, prize, profit, purse, reward, sharing, stake, stipend, tip, winnings

feeble *adj* **1** delicate, flimsy, inadequate, light, slight

adj **2** flimsy, frail, insubstantial, slight, tenuous, unsubstantial, weak

adj **3** flabby, flaccid, lax, limp, loose, pendulous, relaxed, slack

adj **4** breakable, decrepit, delicate, dilapidated, flimsy, fragile, frail, jerry-built, jury-rigged, puny, Rube Goldberg, shoddy, sickly, thin, tinny, unsound, worn-out

adj **5** helpless, impotent, inept, powerless, weak

feebleminded *adj* backward, blunt, deficient, dense, dim-witted, dull, dumb, idiotic, moronic, obtuse, retarded, simple, simple-minded, slow, stupid, thick, uneducated, unintelligent

feed *v* **1** fire, fuel, ignite, incite, kindle, light, nourish, propel, stoke, sustain

v **2** arrange, cater, deliver, dish out, dispense, furnish, give, hand, nourish, nurture, organize, provide, purvey, serve, supply, sustain

feel *n* **1** exploration, feeling, palpation, sensation, texture, touch

n **2** ambience, air, atmosphere, aura, emanation, feeling, mood, semblance, spirit

n **3** awareness, emotion, faculty, feeling, intuition, reaction, response, sensation, sense

v **1** experience, sample, taste

v **2** detect, experience, notice, perceive, sense

v **3** examine, finger, fondle, grope, handle, manipulate, maul, palpate, paw, probe, touch

v **4** caress, cradle, cuddle, embrace, fondle, fool around, hold, hug, love, make out, neck, nuzzle, pet, snuggle, stroke

feeling *adj* emotional, sensitive, sentient, susceptible, tender

n **1** consensus, flavor, opinion, sense

n **2** exploration, feel, palpation, sensation, texture, touch

n **3** confidence, disposition, frame of mind, mentality, mood, morale, outlook, state

n **4** foreboding, guess, hunch, instinct, intuition, premonition, sense, suspicion

n **5** affection, emotion, passion, regard, sensation, sense, sensibility, sentiment, tenderness

n **6** air, ambience, atmosphere, aura, emanation, feel, mood, semblance, spirit

n **7** attitude, disposition, humor, mind, mood, spirit, temper, timbre, tone, vein

n **8** attitude, belief, bias, conviction, inducement, leaning, mind, opinion, persuasion, sentiment, slant, view

n **9** awareness, emotion, faculty, feel, intuition, perception, reaction, response, sensation, sense

feign *v* **1** affect, pretend, profess, purport

v **2** act, assume, bluff, counterfeit, fabricate, fake, imitate, invent, make believe, play, pretend, put on, sham

feigned *adj* **1** fake, fictitious, mock, sham, simulated

adj **2** affected, artificial, assumed, fictitious, put-on, spurious

adj **3** partial, pseudo, quasi, semi, so-called, somewhat, unofficial

feisty *adj* **1** bellicose, brawling, difficult, quarrelsome, scrappy, spirited

adj **2** angry, cranky, cross, grouchy, hot-tempered, irascible, ireful, peppery, quick-tempered, short-fused, sullen, testy, touchy

felicitous *adj* see: APPLICABLE *adj*

feline *adj* catlike, cattish, catty, furtive, skulking, stealthy

n cat, kit, kitten, kitty, puss, pussy, tabby, tiger

fell *v* **1** ax, cut down, knock down, raze, topple

v **2** ax, carve, chip, chop, cleave, cut, dissect, hack, hew, mangle, mutilate, notch, pulverize, rend, saw, sever, slice, sliver, snip, split, sunder, whittle

fellow *n* **1** bachelor, chap, dude, gent, gentleman, guy, male, man, mister, widower

n **2** see: FRIEND *n* **1**

fellowship *n* **1** brotherhood, camaraderie, community, esprit de corps, fraternity, lodge

n **2** association, combination, corporation, establishment, foundation, institution, league, union

n **3** association, body, club, company, contingent, delegation, fraternity, group, guild, organization, society, union

felon *n* accused, con, convict, criminal, crook, culprit, delinquent, guilty party, inmate, lawbreaker, offender, perpetrator, prisoner, scofflaw, suspect, swindler, transgressor, wrongdoer

felonious *adj* **1** blameworthy, criminal, culpable, guilty, remiss, reprehensible

adj **2** criminal, disgraceful, illegal, illegitimate, illicit, lawless, prohibited, unlawful, wrong, wrongful

felony *n* crime, dishonor, disobedience, evil, fault, infamy, infraction, iniquity, injury, lawbreaking, misdemeanor, misdeed, offense, outrage, sin, transgression, trespass, vice, violation, wrong, wrongdoing

female *adj* feminine, gentle, ladylike, nurturing, tender, womanly

n dame, gentlewoman, lady, matron, miss, mistress, spinster, widow, woman

feminine *adj* female, gentle, ladylike, nurturing, tender, womanly

fence *n* 1 barrier, border, boundary, buffer, hedge

n 2 bar, barricade, barrier, block, blockade, obstacle, roadblock, stop, wall

v 1 exclude, partition, restrict, separate

v 2 avoid, dodge, equivocate, evade, hedge, shift, shuffle, sidestep

fend *v* bulwark, cover, defend, fortify, guard, hide, protect, safeguard, screen, secure, shield

ferment *n* 1 blend, brew, combination, composite, compound, concoction, mix, mixture

n 2 yeast

v 1 bloom, blossom, bud, develop, flourish, flower, germinate, grow, sprout

v 2 agitate, bake, boil, bubble, burn, churn, foam, fume, roast, seethe, simmer, smolder

ferocious *adj* 1 angry, fierce, furious, heated, intense, savage, severe, terrible, vehement, vicious, violent

adj 2 see: NASTY *adj* 7

ferocity *n* 1 frenzy, fury, intensity, rage

n 2 brutality, destructiveness, force, frenzy, fury, rage, violence

ferret *v* ascertain, catch, descry, detect, discover, encounter, espy, find, locate, spot, turn up, uncover

ferry *n* barge, boat, canoe, craft, dory, float, kayak, raft, scow, skiff, tender

v bear, carry, convey, crate, haul, lift, lug, pack, shoulder, shuttle, tote, traffic, transport, truck

fertile *adj* 1 copious, creative, fecund, fruitful, productive, prolific

adj 2 see: RESOURCEFUL *adj* 3

fertilization *n* conception, insemination, propagation, reproduction, spawning

fertilize *v* 1 engender, father, impregnate, inseminate, sire

v 2 enrich

fervent *adj* 1 chaotic, fervid, feverish, frenetic, frenzied, hectic, jittery

adj 2 ardent, enthusiastic, excitable, fiery, flaming, hot-blooded, impassioned, intense, passionate, stirring, sweaty, torrid, zealous

adj 3 amorous, ardent, aroused, carnal, earthy, erotic, fleshly, horny, hot, impassioned, lascivious, lecherous, lewd, licentious, lustful, passionate, provocative, randy, raunchy, romantic, sensual, sexual, sexy, sultry, titillated, torrid, turned on, voluptuous, wanton

adj 4 fiery, zealous

fervid *adj* chaotic, fervent, feverish, frenetic, frenzied, hectic, jittery

fervor *n* alacrity, ardor, delight, devotion, diligence, enjoyment, enthusiasm, excitement, fire, flame, gaiety, gusto, passion, relish, savor, thrill, zeal, zest

fester *n* blister, inflammation, lesion, sore, swelling, welt

v blister, bubble, ulcerate

festival *n* celebration, ceremony, commemoration, festivity, fiesta, gala, holiday, observance, party, revelry

festive *adj* bright, cheerful, cheery, content, ebullient, ecstatic, elated, exuberant, gay, glad, happy, jovial, joyful, joyous, merry, mirthful, pleased, radiant, rejoicing

festivity *n* celebration, ceremony, commemoration, festival, fiesta, gala, holiday, observance, party, revelry

fetch *v* bring

fetching *adj* alluring, appealing, attractive, charming, coquettish, coy, fast, flirtatious, seductive, sexy, tempting, winsome

fetid *adj* decaying, foul, gamy, malodorous, musty, putrid, rancid, rank, reeking, rotten, smelly, sour, spoiled, stale, stinking, tainted

fetish *n* 1 amulet, charm, talisman

n 2 fixation, infatuation, obsession, passion, preoccupation

fetter *n* bond, chain, handcuff, iron, manacle, shackle, tie

v see: BIND *v* 7

fetus *n* bud, egg, embryo, ovum, seed, zygote

feud *v* argue, altercate, battle, bicker, brawl, clash, conflict, dispute, engage, equivocate, fight, fray, haggle, hassle, quarrel, quibble, row, scrap, spar, squabble, wrangle

n see: QUARREL *n* 2

fever *n* blush, color, flush, glow, warmth

feverish *adj* 1 chaotic, fervent, fervid, frenetic, frenzied, hectic, jittery

adj 2 hot

few *adj* 1 lacking, limited, nonabundant, not many, scant, short, sparse

adj 2 infrequent, isolated, occasional, rare, scarce, seldom, sporadic, uncommon, unusual

adj 3 bare, deficient, inadequate, inferior,

insufficient, little, meager, paltry, petty, poor, scant, scanty, skimpy, spare, sparse

fiancé *n* beau, boyfriend, date, escort, lover, mate, paramour, suitor

fiancée *n* date, girlfriend, lover

fiasco *n* bomb, bust, disaster, dud, failure, flop, turkey

fiat *n* 1 auspices, authorization, backing, command, confirmation, endorsement, patronage, sanction, support, sponsorship

n 2 behest, bidding, canon, charge, command, criterion, decree, dictate, direction, edict, guideline, injunction, institution, law, mandate, order, ordinance, precept, prescript, prescription, regulation, rite, rule, ruling, statute, word

fib *n* exaggeration, fabrication, falsehood, falsity, invention, lie, misstatement, story, tale

v concoct, deceive, equivocate, fabricate, falsify, invent, lie, misstate, perjure

fiber *n* 1 character, constitution, makeup, nature, quality, substance

n 2 cable, cord, hemp, lanyard, line, rope, strand, string, thread, twine, yarn

fickle *adj* arbitrary, capricious, changeable, erratic, flighty, inconsistent, inconstant, mercurial, uncertain, unstable, unsteady, variable, volatile, wavering, wayward

fiction *n* 1 concoction, creation, fabrication, fantasy, figment, invention

n 2 anecdote, description, fantasy, invention, myth, narration, narrative, novel, sketch, story, tale, yarn

n 3 see: LEGEND *n* 3

fictional *adj* conceived, conjured, created, fancied, fanciful, fantastic, fictitious, illusory, imaginary, imagined, invented, make-believe, nonexistent, notional, unreal, whimsical

fictitious *adj* 1 fake, feigned, mock, sham, simulated

adj 2 affected, artificial, assumed, feigned, put-on, spurious

adj 3 conceived, conjured, created, fancied, fanciful, fantastic, fictional, illusory, imaginary, imagined, invented, make-believe, nonexistent, notional, unreal, whimsical

fiddle *v* 1 dabble, dally, diddle, fool, monkey, piddle, play, poke about, putter, tinker, toy, trifle

v 2 butt in, chisel in, cut in, horn in, interfere, interlope, intrude, meddle,

mess around, peek, peer, poke, pry, snoop, tamper with

fiddlesticks *n* see: NONSENSE *n* 2

fidelity *n* allegiance, ardor, devotion, faithfulness, loyalty

fidget *v* squirm, twitch, writhe

fidgety *adj* 1 antsy, edgy, excitable, high-strung, irritable, jittery, jumpy, moody, nervous, nervy, restless, shaky, skittish, temperamental

adj 2 anxious, edgy, impatient, nervous, nervy, queasy, restive, restless, tense, troubled, uncomfortable, uneasy, uptight, worried

field *n* 1 bag, hobby, interest, job, specialty

n 2 grass, green, grounds, lawn, plot, yard

n 3 domain, dominion, kingdom, province, realm, sphere, territory

n 4 boundary, extent, matter, range, reach, scope, vicinity

n 5 art, avocation, business, calling, career, discipline, employment, gig, job, labor, line, livelihood, occupation, office, profession, pursuit, role, schtick, situation, specialty, task, thing, trade, vocation, work

n 6 grassland, lea, meadow, pasture, plain, prairie

n 7 area, arena, belt, realm, region, section, space, territory, tract, turf, zone

fiend *n* 1 brute, demon, devil, rogue, Satan, villain, wretch

n 2 bug, crusader, enthusiast, fanatic, freak, hobbyist, maniac, monomaniac, nut, radical, zealot

fiendish *adj* demoniac, devilish, diabolic, wicked

fierce *adj* 1 adamant, cold, relentless, vindictive

adj 2 angry, ferocious, furious, heated, intense, savage, severe, terrible, vehement, vicious, violent

adj 3 agitated, disorderly, excited, frantic, frenzied, furious, mad, stormy, tumultuous, turbulent, violent, wild

adj 4 bitter, brutal, cruel, hard, harsh, inclement, intemperate, pitiless, rigorous, rough, rugged, severe, stern, strong, unkind, violent

adj 5 see: NASTY *adj* 7

fiery *adj* 1 ablaze, afire, aflame, aglow, alight, blazing, burning, conflagrant, flaming, glowing

adj 2 feverish

adj 3 emotional, fervent, zealous

adj 4 baking, blistering, boiling, broiling, burning, hot, scalding, scorching, sizzling, sultry, sweltering, torrid *adj* 5 ardent, enthusiastic, excitable, fervent, flaming, hot-blooded, impassioned, intense, passionate, stirring, sweaty, torrid, zealous

fiesta *n* celebration, ceremony, commemoration, festival, festivity, gala, holiday, observance, party, revelry

fight *n* 1 incident, outbreak, scene, spectacle, tantrum

n 2 battle, combat, conflagration, dispute, encounter, struggle, war

n 3 break, disagreement, dissension, misunderstanding, quarrel, rift, separation, spat

n 4 battle, clash, competition, conflict, contest, discord, duel, fighting, rivalry, strife, struggle, war, warfare

n 5 affray, battle, brawl, brush, clash, conflict, difference, disagreement, dispute, encounter, fracas, melee, quarrel, run-in, scrimmage, skirmish, spat, touch

n 6 aggression, aggressiveness, attack, bellicosity, belligerence, combativeness, pugnacity

n 7 altercation, argument, battle, brawl, challenge, combat, controversy, disagreement, discord, dispute, feud, fracas, fray, hassle, melee, quarrel, rancor, rift, row, ruckus, scrap, scuffle, skirmish, spat, squabble, struggle, tiff, war

v 1 attack, battle, combat, contend, oppose, struggle, war

v 2 combat, contend, duel, grapple, spar, struggle, wrestle

v 3 combat, compete, contend, contest, counter, dispute, duel, match, oppose, parry, pit, play, repel, resist, rival, strive, struggle, vie

v 4 altercate, argue, battle, bicker, brawl, clash, conflict, dispute, engage, equivocate, feud, fray, haggle, hassle, quarrel, quibble, row, scrap, spar, squabble, wrangle

fighting *n* battle, clash, competition, conflict, contest, discord, duel, fight, rivalry, strife, struggle, war, warfare

figment *n* 1 creation, concoction, fabrication, fantasy, fiction, invention

n 2 aberration, apparition, delusion, fantasy, ghost, hallucination, illusion, image, mirage, phantasm, specter, vision

figure *n* 1 design, device, motif, motive, pattern

n 2 cast, configuration, conformation, form, shape, structure

n 3 anatomy, body, build, form, frame, physique, shape

n 4 bust, icon, idol, image, sculpture, statue, statuette, symbol

n 5 bar graph, chart, diagram, distribution, flow chart, graph, histogram, outline, pie chart, plot, table

v calculate, cipher, code, compute, estimate, reckon

filch *v* see: STEAL *v* 2

file *v* 1 apply, claim, enroll, petition, request, sign up

v 2 edge, grind, hone, polish, sharpen, whet

v 3 align, arrange, array, assort, catalog, categorize, class, classify, cluster, compile, format, grade, group, lay out, line up, list, order, organize, outline, pigeonhole, place, position, prioritize, program, rank, rate, sort, stack, tabulate

v 4 grate, grind, grit, rasp, sand

n 1 envelope, folder, mailer, sleeve

n 2 binder, folder, portfolio, record

fill *v* 1 furnish, replenish, stock, store, supply

v 2 heap, load, pack, place, stack, stuff

v 3 glut, gorge, overeat, pig out, satiate, stuff, surfeit

v 4 achieve, answer, execute, finish, fulfill, meet, realize, satisfy

v 5 occupy

filled *adj* full, quenched, sated, satisfied, saturated

fillet *v* clean, disembowel, dress, eviscerate, gut

filling *n* fabric, weft, woof

filly *n* colt, equine, foal, gelding, horse, mare, mount, nag, pony, steed, yearling

film *n* 1 coating, covering, layer, membrane, sheet, tissue

n 2 cinema, flick, motion picture, movie

filmy *adj* delicate, fine, flimsy, sheer, thin, transparent

filter *v* 1 sift

v 2 process, screen, sift

v 3 clean, cleanse, purify, refine, sterilize, wash

filth *n* 1 dirt, dung, garbage, manure, muck, mud, slime, sludge

n 2 dirt, grossness, indecency, obscenity, porn, pornography, ribaldry, smut, trash

filthy *adj* 1 black, dark, dingy, dirty, foul, grimy, grubby, mucky, murky, polluted, seedy, shabby, sooty, squalid, stained, unclean, unlit, unwashed

adj 2 see: VULGAR *adj* 2

final *adj* 1 concluding, conclusive, last, terminal, ultimate

adj 2 closing, decisive, definitive, eventual, inevitable, last, latest *n* exam, examination, inquiry, oral, questionnaire, quiz, test

finale *n* 1 completion, conclusion, culmination, end, finish, windup

n 2 ceasing, cessation, close, closure, conclusion, end, finis, finish, stop, termination

finalize *v* adjourn, cap, climax, complete, conclude, consummate, crown, culminate, dissolve, end, finish, terminate, wind up, wrap up

finally *adv* at last, eventually, lastly, ultimately

finance *n* banking, economics, numbers, statistics

v 1 aid, endow, fund, subsidize, underwrite

v 2 bankroll, capitalize, fund, stake, subsidize

financial *adj* fiscal, monetary, pecuniary

financier *n* baron, big shot, businessman, businessperson, businesswoman, capitalist, entrepreneur, executive, industrialist, magnate, mogul, plutocrat, tycoon, VIP

find *n* breakthrough, disclosure, discovery, exposition, revelation, unearthing

v 1 chance, discover, encounter, happen, hit, luck, meet, stumble

v 2 ascertain, catch, descry, detect, discover, encounter, espy, ferret, locate, spot, turn up, uncover

finding *n* 1 detection, discovery, perception

n 2 adjudication, decision, decree, judgment, ruling, sentence, verdict

fine *adj* 1 admirable, commendable, excellent, laudable, praiseworthy, worthwhile

adj 2 agreeable, bright, good, nice, pleasant, sunny

adj 3 delicate, filmy, flimsy, sheer, thin, transparent

adj 4 dainty, delicate, gentle, nice, refined, subtle

adj 5 choice, dainty, delicate, elegant, exquisite, favorite, preferred, rare, select

adj 6 alluring, attractive, beautiful, breathtaking, comely, cute, fair, foxy, gorgeous, lovely, luscious, magnificent, pretty, shapely, stunning

adj 7 champion, excellent, first-class, first-rate, foremost, good, grade A, leading, number one, prime, principal, prominent, quality, select, stellar, superior, top, top-drawer, top-notch, tops

adj 8 ground, powdery, pulverized

adj 9 excellent, fabulous, fantastic, good, great, marvelous, super, terrific, tremendous, wonderful

n 1 assessment, damages, penalty, punishment, tax

n 2 discipline, dockage, fee, loss, penalty, punishment

v chastise, dock, penalize, punish, sentence, tariff, tax

finesse *n* 1 elegance, refinement, polish, style

n 2 diplomacy, discretion, savvy, skill, subtlety, tact

v adjust, fine-tune, modify, tweak, vary

finest *adj* 1 best, biggest, greatest, largest, maximum, most, number one, prime, select, superior, top, top-notch

adj 2 see: SUPERB *adj* 4

n best, choice, elite, favorite, optimum, pick, pride, select

finger *v* examine, feel, fondle, handle, grope, manipulate, maul, palpate, paw, probe, touch

fingers *n* hand, knuckles, palm

finicky *adj* 1 exacting, fastidious, meticulous, picky, precise, rigid, strict

adj 2 careful, cautious, choosy, discriminating, fastidious, fussy, meticulous, nitpicking, particular, persnickety, picky, selective

finis *n* ceasing, cessation, close, closure, conclusion, end, finale, finish, stop, termination

finish *n* 1 gloss, glaze, polish, shine

n 2 completion, conclusion, culmination, end, finale, windup

n 3 breakdown, catastrophe, crash, crisis, death, destruction, doom, failure, ruin

n 4 ceasing, cessation, close, closure, conclusion, end, finale, finis, stop, termination

v 1 achieve, answer, execute, fill, fulfill, meet, realize, satisfy

v 2 consume, deplete, exhaust, expend, go, lessen, run through, spend, use up, waste, weaken

v 3 achieve, cease, complete, conclude, consummate, end, halt, perfect, terminate, wind up, wrap up

v 4 adjourn, cap, climax, complete, conclude, consummate, crown, culminate, dissolve, end, finalize, terminate, wind up, wrap up

v 5 abstain, cease, conclude, desist, discontinue, end, forbear, freeze, halt, knock off, quit, refrain, sever, stop, terminate

finished *adj* accomplished, complete, concluded, done, ended, over, performed, terminated, through, wrapped up

finite *adj* absolute, agreed, bounded, categorical, clear, decided, definite, emphatic, established, exact, fixed, guaranteed, limited, positive, specific, unequivocal, unmistakable, vested

fink *n* 1 bird, bum, cad, heel, jerk, rat, turkey

n 2 accuser, betrayer, double-crosser, informer, reptile, snake, sneak, stooge, traitor

v inform, rat, sing, snitch, squeal, stool, tattle, tattletale

fiord *n* arm, bay, cove, estuary, gulf, inlet, narrows, sound, strait

fire *n* 1 blaze

n 2 alacrity, ardor, delight, devotion, diligence, enjoyment, enthusiasm, excitement, fervor, flame, gaiety, gusto, **passion**, relish, savor, thrill, zeal, zest

v 1 bombard, detonate, discharge, shoot

v 2 discharge, emit, hurl, launch, project, shoot

v 3 burn, enkindle, inflame, ignite, kindle, light, spark

v 4 feed, fuel, ignite, incite, kindle, light, nourish, propel, stoke, sustain

v 5 ax, boot, bounce, can, discharge, dismiss, drop, impeach, let go, sack, terminate

v 6 appeal, arouse, attract, excite, fascinate, interest, intrigue, lead on, lure, seduce, stir, tantalize

v 7 arouse, electrify, excite, incite, inspire, rouse, spark, stimulate, tantalize, thrill, titillate, turn on, whet

firearm *n* 1 carbine, flintlock, gun, musket, rifle, shotgun

n 2 automatic, gun, handgun, heater, iron, luger, piece, pistol, revolver, rod

fireball *n* bolt, flash, lightning, thunderbolt

firing *n* dismissal, ejection, expulsion, extraction, impeachment, ouster, removal, termination

firm *adv* fast, firmly, hard, loyally, reliably, solidly, tight, tightly

adj 1 indomitable, invincible, unconquerable, unyielding

adj 2 adamant, resolute, steadfast, stern, strict

adj 3 hard, stiff, taut, tense, tight

adj 4 absolute, fixed, resolute, steadfast, unconditional, unreserved

adj 5 abiding, enduring, never-failing, steadfast, sure, unfaltering, unshakable, unwavering

adj 6 dour, forbidding, grim, sad, serious, severe, sour, stern, unpleasant

adj 7 attached, fast, fixed, rigid, secure, set, taut, tense, tight

adj 8 certain, explicit, expressed, fixed,

formal, mandated, set, settled, spoken, stated, stipulated

adj 9 compact, hard, hardened, rigid, secure, solid, sound, specific, stable, stiff, tight

adj 10 constant, determinate, fixed, hard, immutable, inflexible, invariable, ironclad, resolute, stable, unalterable, unchangeable, unmovable

adj 11 adamant, ceaseless, dedicated, determined, immovable, inexhaustible, inexorable, inflexible, narrow-minded, obstinate, relentless, resolute, resolved, rigid, single-minded, steadfast, stubborn, unbendable, unbending, uncompromising, unswayable, unyielding

adj 12 bullheaded, closed-minded, deaf, hardheaded, hard-line, inelastic, inflexible, intractable, intransigent, obstinate, perverse, pigheaded, refractory, resolute, rigid, stiff, stubborn, tough, unbending, uncompromising, unpliable, unpliant, unwieldy, unyielding, willful

adj 13 aggressive, dominant, durable, forceful, hardy, hearty, mighty, powerful, robust, rugged, stalwart, stout, strong, sturdy, tenacious, tough

adj 14 authoritarian, authoritative, autocratic, controlled, despotic, disciplined, harsh, inflexible, ironhanded, restrictive, rigid, rigorous, ruthless, severe, solid, stern, strict, stringent, strong, tough, tyrannical

n business, company, concern, corporation, enterprise, establishment, house, organization, partnership

firmament *n* cosmos, creation, grand scale, macrocosm, nature, solar system, vast, universe, world

firmly *adv* fast, firm, hard, loyally, reliably, solidly, tight, tightly

firmness *n* compactness, density, hardness, solidity, strength, tensile strength

first *adj* 1 nearest

adj 2 elder, eldest, older, oldest, senior

adj 3 advanced, early, hasty, premature, previous, soon, too soon, untimely

adj 4 chief, foremost, head, inaugural, initial, lead, leading, premier, prime

adj 5 earliest, founding, fundamental, initial, maiden, original, pioneer, primary, prime

adj 6 basic, dominant, elementary, foremost, fundamental, head, highest, leading, main, outstanding, paramount, preeminent, premier, primary, rudimentary, supreme, top

adj 7 fore, foremost, forward, leading

adj 8 least, lowest, minimum, slightest, smallest, tiniest

n demo, example, forerunner, model, prototype, sample, test

adv before, earlier, formerly, heretofore, hitherto, once, previously, prior to

fiscal *adj* financial, monetary, pecuniary

fish *v* angle, connive, hint

fisherman *n* angler

fissure *n* 1 chink, cleft, crack, crevice, division, rent, rift, rupture, split

n 2 abyss, canyon, chasm, cleft, crack, depth, gorge, gulch, pass, ravine

fit *adj* 1 hardy, healthy, robust, rubicund, ruddy, sound, sturdy, well, wholesome

adj 2 applicable, appropriate, apropos, apt, befitting, convenient, desirable, felicitous, fitting, germane, good, handy, just, material, meet, necessary, pertinent, proper, relevant, right, shipshape, suitable, suited, timely, useful

adj 3 see: QUALIFIED *adj* 4

n 1 passion, rage, tantrum, temper

n 2 anger, dander, frenzy, fury, indignation, ire, outrage, paroxysm, rage, tantrum, wrath

v 1 clothe, furnish, outfit, provide, supply

v 2 adapt, conform, convert, cut, fashion, measure, modify, rig, shape, suit, tailor

v 3 see: service *v*

fitful *adj* awake, fretful, restless, sleepless

fitness *n* 1 account, advantage, applicability, appropriateness, aptness, avail, benefit, decorum, expediency, manners, opportunism, pertinence, profit, propriety, relevance, rightness, service, suitability, use, usefulness, utility

n 2 condition, kilter, repair, shape, trim

fitting *adj* 1 acceptable, allowable, eligible, qualified, suitable

adj 2 conventional, correct, decorous, nice, orthodox, polite, proper, right, suitable, well

adj 3 appropriate, correct, deserved, due, just, merited, proper, rightful, suitable, warranted

adj 4 see: APPLICABLE *adj*

n adjunct, annex, fixture, part, piece, unit

fix *n* bind, box, corner, difficulty, dilemma, impasse, jam, mess, pinch, plight, predicament, quandary, scrape, spot, trap, trouble

v 1 concentrate, fixate, focus, rivet

v 2 cover, overlay, patch, repair

v 3 anchor, catch, fasten, moor, secure

v 4 balance, brace, calm, steady, still

v 5 adjust, arrange, calibrate, decide, determine, establish, resolve, set

v 6 affix, attach, bind, clip, connect, fasten, rivet, weld

v 7 adjust, correct, cure, heal, make well, mend, remedy, repair, restore

v 8 doctor, mend, overhaul, patch, rebuild, recondition, reconstruct, refit, renovate, repair, revamp

v 9 adjust, amend, correct, improve, mend, modify, position, rectify, remedy, restore, right, straighten

v 10 calibrate, establish, insert, install, lay, locate, place, plant, position, put, set, settle, situate, station

v 11 adapt, adjust, balance, fit, inspect, maintain, overhaul, recondition, refurbish, regulate, repair, service, support, tune up

fixate *v* concentrate, fix, focus, rivet

fixation *n* fetish, infatuation, obsession, passion, preoccupation

fixed *adj* 1 absolute, firm, resolute, steadfast, unconditional, unreserved

adj 2 concentrated, exclusive, undistracted, undivided, unswerving, whole

adj 3 committed, determined, focused, limited, narrow, obsessive, one-track

adj 4 ensconced, entrenched, established, fundamental, ingrained, intrinsic, inveterate, settled, sworn

adj 5 attached, fast, firm, rigid, secure, set, taut, tense, tight

adj 6 definite, determinate, exclusive, limited, narrow, precise, restricted, segregated, specific

adj 7 bent, committed, dedicated, determined, intentional, purposeful, resolute, resolved, set, tenacious

adj 8 fastened, in position, motionless, permanent, set, solid, standing, static, stationary, still

adj 9 certain, explicit, expressed, firm, formal, mandated, set, settled, spoken, stated, stipulated

adj 10 definite, determined, foregone, inevitable, inexorable, irrevocable, ordained, predestined, unalterable, unavoidable, unchangeable

adj 11 constant, determinate, firm, hard, immutable, inflexible, invariable, ironclad, resolute, stable, unalterable, unchangeable, unmovable

adj 12 absolute, agreed, bounded, categorical, clear, decided, definite, emphatic, established, exact, finite, guaranteed, limited, positive, specific, unequivocal, unmistakable, vested

fixture *n* adjunct, annex, fitting, part, piece, unit

fixtures *n* equipment, furnishings, gear, materials, provisions, supplies

fizzle *v* fail, miscarry, misfire, miss

flabbergast *v* amaze, astonish, astound, awe, boggle, confound, dazzle, dumbfound, nonplus, stagger, stun, surprise

flabby *adj* feeble, flaccid, lax, limp, loose, pendulous, relaxed, slack

flaccid *adj* feeble, flabby, lax, limp, loose, pendulous, relaxed, slack

flag *n* 1 pennant
n 2 guideline, principle, rule, standard
v 1 abate, decline, deteriorate, fade, fail, impair, languish, wane, weaken, wither, worsen
v 2 alert, augur, caution, forebode, forewarn, indicate, inform, motion, notify, signal, warn, wave
v 3 denote, mark, star
v 4 accent, accentuate, amplify, concentrate, emphasize, feature, focus, heighten, highlight, italicize, mark, punctuate, spotlight, stress, underline, underscore

flagellate *v* assail, attack, batter, beat, birch, buffet, flog, hammer, lambaste, lash, lather, pelt, pound, pummel, punish, scourge, thrash, tromp, wallop, whip

flagrant *adj* 1 arrogant, audacious, conspicuous, glaring, obvious
adj 2 coarse, crass, crude, glaring, gross, obscene, rough, shocking, uncouth, uncultured, unrefined
adj 3 see: OSTENTATIOUS *adj* 1

flair *n* 1 chic, style
n 2 effectiveness, kick, pep, pizzazz, potency, punch, sizzle, snap, spark, verve, vigor, wallop
n 3 bent, brains, brilliance, faculty, genius, gift, head, intelligence, knack, mind, nose, prowess, talent

flake *n* bit, chip, dent, fragment, mark, piece

flaky *adj* erratic, unbalanced, unsound

flamboyant *adj* 1 abundant, elaborate, luscious, ornate, replete
adj 2 ambitious, bombastic, garish, grandiose, inflated, jaunty, lofty, ostentatious, pompous, portentous, pretentious, showy, splashy, splendid, utopian, visionary

flame *v* blare, blaze, burn, flare, glare, glow, ignite, redden
n see: PASSION *n* 7

flaming *adj* 1 ablaze, aflame, afire, aglow, alight, blazing, burning, conflagrant, fiery, glowing
adj 2 see: PASSIONATE *adj* 2

flammable *adj* combustible, explosive, inflammable

flap *v* dance, flicker, flitter, flutter, oscillate, prance, sparkle, sway, twinkle, undulate, wave
n earmark, label, tab

flare *v* 1 erupt, explode
v 2 broaden, enlarge, open, spread, widen
v 3 blare, blaze, burn, flame, glare, glow, ignite, redden
n flashlight, illumination, light

flare-up *n* blaze, eruption, outburst

flash *n* 1 blink of an eye, crack, instant, jiffy, minute, moment, second, shake, twinkling, wink
n 2 bolt, lightning, thunderbolt
n 3 gleam, glimmer, glitter, shimmer, shine, sparkle, twinkle
v 1 blink, flicker, glimmer, twinkle, wink
v 2 excite, gleam, glimmer, glint, glisten, glitter, scintillate, shimmer, shine, sparkle, twinkle
v 3 bare, denude, discard, disrobe, doff, remove, reveal, shed, strip, take off, unclothe, undress
v 4 race, speed, zoom

flashlight *n* illumination, light

flashy *adj* see: OSTENTATIOUS *adj*

flat *adj* 1 even, flush, level, plane, smooth
adj 2 banal, bland, dull, innocuous, insipid, tasteless, unexciting
adj 3 horizontal, lengthwise, longways, prone, prostrate, reclining, recumbent
adj 4 blah, boring, commonplace, dim, dreary, dull, humdrum, monotonous, ordinary, pedestrian, stodgy, tedious, tiresome
adj 5 colorless, dull, sterile
adj 6 arid, bland, bleak, boring, colorless, dead, desolate, drab, dreary, dull, lackluster, lifeless, lusterless, monotonous, muted, somber, trite, unexciting, uninteresting
n address, apartment, condo, condominium, domicile, dwelling, home, house, location, pad, place, property, residence, site

flatten *v* even, flush, grade, lay, level, plane, smooth, tamp

flatter *v* 1 attract, cajole, disarm, ingratiate
v 2 acclaim, applaud, charm, cheer, commend, compliment, greet, hail, laud, praise, recognize, salute, stroke

flattering *adj* approving, commending, complimentary, congratulatory, extolling, praising

flattery *n* adulation

flaunt *v* 1 display, exhibit, manifest, parade, promenade

v 2 amble, prance, stride, strut, swagger

v 3 boast, brag, crow, exult, gloat, revel, show off, strut, vaunt

v 4 belittle, deride, jab, jeer, jest, mock, quip, razz, ridicule, scoff, scorn, sneer, taunt, tease

flavor *n* 1 consensus, feeling, opinion, sense

n 2 palate, sample, savor, spice, tang, taste

n 3 fashion, manner, mode, style, tone, vein

n 4 characteristic, impression, nature, property, quality, ring, sound, tendency, tone, type

v color, enhance, imbue, infuse, salt, season, spice

flaw *n* 1 deception, error, fallacy, illusion, inaccuracy

n 2 affliction, calamity, disability, handicap, impairment, limitation

n 3 blemish, defect, failing, fault, imperfection, scar, shortcoming, weakness

n 4 blockage, bottleneck, catch, hitch, impediment, jam, obstacle, obstruction, snag

n 5 defect, deficiency, demerit, fault, imperfection, inadequacy, lack, need, shortcoming, want

flawed *adj* 1 amiss, crude, defective, faulty, imperfect, incomplete, short, unfulfilled

adj 2 flimsy, imperfect, inferior, lousy, mediocre, miserable, paltry, poor, second-rate, shabby, shoddy, sorry, so-so, tacky, unworthy, worthless

flawless *adj* 1 exemplary, ideal, model, perfect, perfected

adj 2 errorless, excellent, exquisite, fastidious, faultless, ideal, immaculate, impeccable, irreproachable, perfect

adj 3 absolute, complete, good, intact, perfect, sound, unblemished, unbroken, undamaged, unimpaired, uninjured, unmarred, untouched, whole

flawlessness *n* perfection, precision

flaxen *adj* blond, fair, light

flay *v* 1 peel, scale, skin, strip

v 2 berate, carp, cavil, criticize, find fault, fuss, henpeck, nag, nit-pick, nudge, peck, scold, quibble

flee *v* 1 abscond, bolt, break, depart, elude, escape, fly, hightail it, lose, run, sneak away, split

v 2 abscond, bolt, defect, depart, exit, fall back, get away, give back, go, leave, move, pull away, pull out, push off, retreat, run along, secede, shove off, take off, vacate, withdraw

fleece *v* see: CHEAT *v* 1

fleet *n* armada, assembly, boats, convoy, flotilla, grouping, navy, ships, squadron

adj see: RAPID *adj* 2

fleeting *adj* 1 elusive, slippery

adj 2 brief, ephemeral, impermanent, momentary, passing, short, temporary, transient, transitory, volatile

adj 3 brief, passing, short, swift, transient

fleshly *adj* 1 bodily, corporeal

adj 2 see: EROTIC *adj* 3

fleshy *adj* see: FAT *adj* 1

flex *v* 1 draw, pull, strain, stretch, tense, tighten, twist

v 2 angle, arch, bend, bow, curve, ply, round, tilt, tip, turn, twist, vault

flexed *adj* arched, bent, bowed, curved, curvilinear, rounded, unstraight

flexible *adj* 1 comparative

adj 2 alterable, elastic, movable, pliable, resilient, springy, supple

adj 3 adaptable, adjustable, changeable, limber, malleable, maneuverable, moldable, plastic, pliable, pliant, responsive, soft, supple, swayed, versatile, yielding

flick *n* cinema, film, motion picture, movie

v cast, fling, flip, heave, hurl, launch, pitch, propel, sling, throw, toss

flicker *n* beam, glimmer, hint, light, ray, sliver, spark, trace

v 1 blink, flash, glimmer, twinkle, wink

v 2 dance, flap, flitter, flutter, oscillate, prance, sparkle, sway, twinkle, undulate, wave

flier *n* 1 brochure, circular, handbill, handout, leaflet, pamphlet, sheet

n 2 aviator, airman, barnstormer, operator, pilot

flight *n* 1 breakout, escape, getaway, lam, slip

n 2 see: JOURNEY *n* 2

flighty *adj* 1 capricious, dizzy, frivolous, giddy, irresponsible, scatterbrained, silly

adj 2 see: INCONSISTENT *adj* 3

flimflam *v* see: CHEAT *v* 1

flimsy *adj* 1 delicate, feeble, inadequate, light, slight

adj 2 delicate, filmy, fine, sheer, thin, transparent

adj 3 feeble, frail, insubstantial, slight, tenuous, unsubstantial, weak

adj 4 insecure, jiggly, rickety, shaky, teetering, unstable, unsure, vacillating, wavering, weak, wobbly

adj 5 breakable, decrepit, delicate, dilapidated, feeble, fragile, frail, jerry-built,

jury-rigged, puny, Rube Goldberg, shoddy, sickly, thin, tinny, unsound, worn-out
adj 6 see: INFERIOR *adj* 6

flinch *v* 1 cower, cringe, grovel, quail, recoil, shrink, sneak
v 2 blanch, cringe, jump, recoil, shrink, start, startle, wince
v 3 see: QUIVER *v* 2

fling *n* 1 bash, bender, binge, do, orgy, party, spree
n 2 adultery, affair, cheating, dalliance, entanglement, flirtation, fooling around, infatuation, intimacy, intrigue, liaison, love affair, playing around, rendezvous, romance, tryst
n 3 attempt, chance, effort, go, guess, heave, lob, pop, shot, slap, sling, stab, throw, toss, try, whirl
v cast, flick, flip, heave, hurl, launch, pitch, propel, sling, throw, toss

flintlock *n* carbine, firearm, gun, musket, rifle, shotgun

flip *adj* 1 arrogant, cocky, disrespectful, flippant, impertinent, impudent, wise
adj 2 see: BLUNT *v* 1
v see: THROW *v* 2

flippant *adj* 1 light
adj 2 arrogant, cocky, disrespectful, flip, impertinent, impudent, wise
adj 3 abrupt, bluff, blunt, brash, brusque, cheeky, crusty, curt, flip, gruff, harsh, impertinent, impudent, irritable, nasty, quick, rude, sarcastic, sassy, short, snippy, snotty, surly, testy, wisenheimer

flirt *v* 1 attract, court, encourage, invite, lure, pursue, romance, solicit, tempt, woo
v 2 allure, charm, come onto, dally, fool, jest, kid, lead on, make eyes, make out, pick up, string along, tease, toy, trifle
n 1 coquette, harlot, nymphomaniac, seductress, siren, tart, tease, temptress, vamp, wanton woman
n 2 buck, Casanova, Don Juan, gallant, ladies' man, lecher, lover, philanderer, playboy, Romeo, stud

flirtation *n* adultery, affair, cheating, dalliance, entanglement, fling, fooling around, infatuation, intimacy, intrigue, liaison, love affair, playing around, rendezvous, romance, tryst

flirtatious *adj* alluring, appealing, attractive, charming, coquettish, coy, fast, fetching, seductive, sexy, tempting, winsome

flit *v* ascend, flutter, fly, sail, soar, sweep, wing

flitter *v* dance, flap, flicker, flutter, oscillate, prance, sparkle, sway, twinkle, undulate, wave

float *n* 1 barge, boat, canoe, craft, dory, ferry, kayak, raft, scow, skiff, tender
n 2 bobber
v 1 coast, drift, fly, glide, sail, slide, soar
v 2 drift, ride, wash

floater *n* buoy

flock *n* 1 congregation, devotees, fold, followers, laity, members, parishioners
n 2 see: CROWD *n* 1
n 3 see: GROUP *n* 5
v assemble, associate, call, cluster, collect, concentrate, congregate, convene, gather, group, lump, marshal, mass, mingle, mobilize, muster, order, rally, rendezvous, round up, send for, summon

flog *v* assail, attack, batter, beat, birch, buffet, flagellate, hammer, lambaste, lash, lather, pelt, pound, pummel, punish, scourge, thrash, tromp, wallop, whip

flood *n* deluge, overflow, submersion, surge, torrent
v 1 glut, overload, oversupply
v 2 bury, drown, engulf, inundate, overflow, swamp, wash over
v 3 flow, gush, peak, pour, rise, roll, spill, stream, surge, swell
v 4 cascade, emit, inundate, overflow, plunge, pour, rain, shower, spill, swamp, tumble
v 5 see: SATURATE *v* 2

floor *n* 1 bottom, base, ground, minimum
n 2 ground, level, story, tier
v amaze, astonish, astound, awe, delight, impress, overwhelm, wow

flop *n* bomb, bust, disaster, dud, fiasco, failure, turkey
v 1 bomb, fail, stumble, trip
v 2 depress, droop, let down, lower, mire, sag, sink, wallow
v 3 crash, flunk

floppy *n* bubble memory, diskette, hard disk, media, memory, RAM

flora *n* foliage, herb, plant, vegetable

florid *adj* flush, full-blooded, glowing, red, ruddy, sanguine

flotilla *n* armada, assembly, boats, convoy, fleet, grouping, navy, ships, squadron

flounder *v* bumble, falter, fumble, get stuck, grope, hesitate, stagger, stumble, waffle, waver

flourish *v* 1 arrive, go, make out, prosper, score, succeed, thrive
v 2 bloom, blossom, bud, develop, ferment, flower, germinate, grow, sprout
v 3 advance, ascend, bloom, climb, develop, do well, excel, expand, flower, get

ahead, grow, improve, progress, prosper, rise, strive, survive, thrive

flow n change, current, drift, flux, gush, motion, movement, rush, stream, tide, transition

v 1 gurgle, ooze, purl, spurt

v 2 gush, run, rush, stream

v 3 arise, come from, derive, emanate, head, issue, originate, spring, stem

v 4 flood, gush, peak, pour, rise, roll, spill, stream, surge, swell

flower v 1 bloom, blossom, bud, develop, ferment, flourish, germinate, grow, sprout

v 2 advance, ascend, bloom, climb, develop, do well, excel, expand, flourish, get ahead, grow, improve, progress, prosper, rise, strive, survive, thrive

flowering n bloom

flowers n arrangement, bouquet, bunch

flowery adj emotional, gushy, melodramatic, sentimental

flowing adj casual, coming along, developing, easy, effortless, fluent, laid-back, running, smooth

fluctuate v 1 alternate, oscillate, pendulate, sway, swing, vacillate, wave

v 2 oscillate, pulsate, surge, throb, undulate, vibrate

fluctuating adj see: DELICATE adj 7

fluent adj 1 articulate, expressive, glib, perspicuous

adj 2 articulate, clear, cogent, eloquent, persuasive, well-spoken

adj 3 casual, coming along, developing, easy, effortless, flowing, laid-back, running, smooth

fluid adj 1 graceful

adj 2 damp, juicy, liquefied, liquid, moist, watery, wet

n juice, liquid, sap, secretion, solution

fluky adj see: ACCIDENTAL adj 3

flunk v crash, fail, flop

flurry n action, activity, ado, animation, bedlam, bother, bustle, chaos, commotion, excitement, fluster, fuss, hum, liveliness, madhouse, movement, stir, to-do, tumult, turmoil, whirlpool, whirlwind

flush adj 1 even, flat, level, plane, smooth

adj 2 florid, full-blooded, glowing, red, ruddy, sanguine

n blush, color, fever, glow, warmth

v 1 dispose of, eliminate, expel, purge, remove, rid, vanquish

v 2 bathe, clean, cleanse, clean up, dip, immerse, launder, rinse, rub, scour, scrape, scrub, shower, wash

v 3 blush

v 4 even, flatten, grade, lay, level, plane, smooth, tamp

fluster v 1 agitate, derange, disorder, disturb, rock, ruffle, shake, sicken, unhinge, unsettle, upset

v 2 befuddle, bewilder, confuse, daze, distract, dizzy, embarrass, mix up, muddle, rattle, ruffle, trick, unglue, unhinge

n see: activity n 3

flutter v 1 ascend, flit, fly, sail, soar, sweep, wing

v 2 beat, palpitate, pulsate, pulse, quiver, throb, tremble, vibrate

v 3 dance, flap, flicker, flitter, oscillate, prance, sparkle, sway, twinkle, undulate, wave

v 4 flinch, jar, pulsate, quake, quaver, quiver, shake, shiver, shudder, tremble, twitch, twitter, vibrate

n quake, quiver, shiver, tingle, tremor

flux n change, current, drift, flow, gush, motion, movement, rush, stream, tide, transition

v dissolve, fuse, liquefy, run, melt, thaw

fly v 1 cross, cruise, sail, traverse, voyage

v 2 coast, drift, float, glide, sail, slide, soar

v 3 ascend, flit, flutter, sail, soar, sweep, wing

v 4 abscond, bolt, break, depart, elude, escape, flee, hightail it, lose, run, sneak away, split

v 5 dart, dash, skim

v 6 barrel, bullet, expedite, hasten, hurry, hustle, rocket, rush, speed, whisk, zip

foal n colt, equine, filly, gelding, horse, mare, mount, nag, pony, steed, yearling

foam v see: SEETHE v 2

fob v see: CHEAT v 1

focus n 1 concentration, consolidation

n 2 attention, center, crux, feature, highlight, key, spotlight

n 3 axis, center, focal point, heart, hub, nerve center, target

v 1 concentrate, fix, fixate, rivet

v 2 examine, highlight, spotlight, target

v 3 centralize, concentrate, consolidate, integrate, merge

v 4 aim, establish, point, set, shoot at, target

v 5 accent, accentuate, amplify, concentrate, emphasize, feature, flag, heighten, highlight, italicize, mark, punctuate, spotlight, stress, underline, underscore

v 6 apply

v 7 enlarge

focused adj committed, determined, fixed, limited, narrow, obsessive, one-track

foe n adversary, antagonist, anti, challenger, competitor, con, contender, enemy, match, opponent, rival

fog n 1 cloud, haze, mist, steam, vapor

n 2 befuddlement, daze, haze, maze, muddledness, muddleheadedness

foggy adj 1 confused, mixed up

adj 2 confused, dizzy, faint, giddy, light-headed, reeling

adj 3 damp, dank, drizzly, humid, misty, moist, wet

adj 4 cloudy, dismal, gray, hazy, misty, murky, overcast, steamy, vaporous, vapory

foible n failing, fault, frailty, limitation, shortcoming, vice, weakness

foil v 1 avert, bar, deter, eliminate, forestall, hinder, hold off, inhibit, preclude, prevent, stave off, thwart, turn back, ward off

v 2 aggravate, baffle, balk, bewilder, circumvent, confuse, dash, elude, frustrate, hamper, impede, negate, nullify, perplex, thwart

foist v 1 edge in, imbue, infiltrate, insinuate, penetrate, permeate, sneak in, work in, worm

v 2 see: CHEAT v 1

fold n 1 congregation, devotees, flock, followers, laity, members, parishioners

n 2 crease, pleat, rumple, wrinkle

v 1 collapse

v 2 crease, muss, pleat, rumple, wrinkle

v 3 crease

folder n 1 case, coat, cover, enclosure, jacket, skin

n 2 envelope, file, mailer, sleeve

n 3 binder, file, portfolio, record

foliage n flora, herb, plant, vegetable

folio n book, correspondence, edition, issue, manuscript, monograph, opus, paperback, printing, publication, text, tome, volume, work, writing

folk adj domestic, endemic, indigenous, local, native, traditional

n blues, classical, country, jazz, music, ragtime, rock-and-roll, soul, swing

folks n citizens, civilization, colony, community, crowd, culture, group, human beings, individuals, laity, masses, men and women, neighbors, people, persons, populace, population, public, settlement, society, staff, tribe

follies n musical, review, revue, song and dance, variety show, vaudeville

follow v 1 drag, lag, trail, traipse

v 2 emanate, ensue, result, succeed

v 3 develop, emerge, ensue, happen, lead to, result

v 4 accommodate, comply, conform, keep, mind, obey, observe, submit

v 5 chase, hunt, pursue, seek, shadow, shoot for, tail, trace, track, trail

v 6 act, ape, copy, emulate, imitate, lip-synch, mime, mimic, mock, model, mouth, pantomime, parody, pattern, take off

follower n 1 dependent, satellite, sycophant

n 2 believer, convert, disciple, zealot

n 3 admirer, buff, devotee, disciple, enthusiast, fan, groupie

n 4 see: FRIEND n 1

followers n 1 cult, following

n 2 congregation, devotees, flock, fold, laity, members, parishioners

following adj 1 ensuing, latter, next, subsequent, succeeding, successive

adj 2 after, beyond, ensuing, subsequent, succeeding, successive

n 1 cult, followers

n 2 see: CROWD n 1

folly n 1 blunder, impropriety, indiscretion, mistake, slip

n 2 craziness, foolishness, frivolity, insanity, lunacy, madness, mania, nonsense, senselessness

foment v agitate, anger, arouse, encourage, ignite, incite, induce, inflame, inspire, instigate, invoke, motivate, muster, prod, propel, provoke, raise, set, set on, spur, stimulate, stir, urge

fond adj affectionate, amorous, attached, caring, devoted, enamored, loving, romantic, tender

fondle v 1 examine, feel, finger, grope, handle, manipulate, maul, palpate, paw, probe, touch

v 2 caress, cradle, cuddle, embrace, feel, fool around, hold, hug, love, make out, neck, nuzzle, pet, snuggle, stroke

fondling n caress, embrace, hug, kiss, squeeze, touch

fondness n 1 affinity, appreciation, attraction, liking, taste

n 2 bent, disposition, fancy, idea, inclination, liking, mind, notion, pleasure, propensity, yen

n 3 affection, affinity, attachment, attraction, compassion, concern, devotion, heart, kinship, love, warmth

font n face, family, printwheel, size, style, type, typeface

food n 1 nourishment, nutriment, support, sustenance

n 2 bread, breakfast, brunch, chow, cuisine, diet, dinner, dish, edibles, entree, fare, grub, lunch, meals, nosh, nutrition, provisions, rations, snack, supper, victuals, vittles

fool *n 1* buffoon, comedian, comedienne, comic, stand-up, zany

n 2 blockhead, boor, clod, creep, cretin, dimwit, dolt, dope, dullard, dumbbell, dummy, dunce, goof, idiot, imbecile, jerk, nerd, nincompoop, numskull, oaf, pain, schlemiel, schmuck, simpleton, stooge, turkey

v 1 dabble, dally, diddle, fiddle, monkey, piddle, play, poke about, putter, tinker, trifle, toy

v 2 allure, charm, come onto, dally, flirt, jest, kid, lead on, make eyes, make out, pick up, string along, tease, toy, trifle

v 3 bamboozle, beat, beguile, bilk, burn, cajole, cheat, chicane, chisel, con, cross, deceive, defraud, dupe, embezzle, fleece, flimflam, fob, foist, gyp, hoax, hoodwink, hustle, inveigle, screw, shaft, sham, swindle, trick, victimize

foolish *adj 1* futile, ill-advised, profitless, pointless, stupid, vain

adj 2 careless, impulsive, irresponsible, myopic, not smart, reckless, risky, shortsighted, unthinking, unwise

adj 3 absurd, anile, asinine, brainless, childish, fatuous, idiotic, inept, meaningless, mindless, senseless, silly, simple, thoughtless, unintelligent, witless

adj 4 absurd, balmy, bizarre, crazy, emotional, frivolous, goofy, illogical, impossible, inane, insane, irrational, loony, lunatic, mad, muddled, nuts, preposterous, ridiculous, silly, touched, wacky, zany

adj 5 ill-advised, indiscreet, misdirected, misguided, mistaken, unwise

adj 6 absurd, comic, comical, crazy, droll, farcical, funny, hilarious, humorous, laughable, ludicrous, outrageous, ridiculous, silly

foolishness *n 1* craziness, folly, frivolity, insanity, lunacy, madness, mania, nonsense, senselessness

n 2 see: NONSENSE *n 1, 2*

foot *n* extremity, hand, hoof, paw

foothill *n* hill, hillock, hump, knoll, mound, mount, raise, rise, swelling

footing *n 1* base, basis, bedrock, foundation, ground, root

n 2 base, brace, buttress, column, foundation, prop, shore, stay, support, underpinning

n 3 foundation, standing, surface

footmen *n* airborne, army, battalion, brigade, cavalry, company, guard, horsemen, infantry, legion, marines, militia, minutemen, paratroops, platoon, reserve, storm troopers

footwear *n* boot, brogan, chukka, moccasin, sandal, shoe, slipper, thong

foray *n 1* expedition, sally, sortie

n 2 exploration, infiltration, invasion, patrol, penetration, raid

n 3 attack, conquest, defeat, inroad, intrusion, invasion, trespass

v attack, invade, overrun, raid

forbear *v 1* abstain, keep, refrain, withhold

v 2 see: FORFEIT *v*

v 3 see: STOP *v 10*

forbearance *n 1* endurance, patience, perseverance, persistence, resignation, resolution, tenacity

n 2 clemency, indulgence, lenience, leniency, mercifulness, mercy, tolerance, toleration

forbearing *adj* accepting, charitable, easy, indulgent, lenient, merciful, patient, restrained, sympathetic, tolerant

forbid *v 1* ban, bar, confine, enjoin, inhibit, nix, outlaw, prevent, prohibit, stop, suppress, veto

v 2 see: REJECT *v 7*

forbidden *adj* banned, prohibited, taboo

forbidding *adj 1* distant, snobbish, unfriendly

adj 2 frightening, hairy, scary, spooky

adj 3 dour, firm, grim, sad, serious, severe, sour, stern, unpleasant

adj 4 bad, baleful, corrupt, cunning, harmful, hurtful, malevolent, malignant, menacing, ominous, sinister, sneaky

force *n 1* coercion, compulsion, constraint, duress, violence

n 2 brutality, destructiveness, ferocity, frenzy, fury, rage, violence

n 3 army, battalion, brigade, company, gang, men, power, soldiers, troops

n 4 ardor, beef, brawn, drive, energy, intensity, lustiness, might, muscle, pep, potency, power, punch, steam, strength, verve, vigor, vim, virility, vitality

n 5 agent, catalyst, factor, power

v 1 frame

v 2 pull, seize, turn, twist, wrest

v 3 coerce, compel, constrain, make, overpower, propel, push

v 4 assert, demand, emphasize, insist, persist, require, urge

v 5 assault, attack, pillage, rape, ravish, sack, violate

v 6 call, conscript, draft, enroll, impress, induct, select, shanghai *v* **7** boost, budge, drive, impel, nudge, propel, push, shove, thrust

v **8** cram, crush, gorge, insert, jam, pack, press, ram, stuff

v **9** pry

v **10** burden, demand, encumber, prescribe

v **11** activate, actuate, compel, drive, goad, impel, induce, mobilize, motivate, move, persuade, press, propel, push, spur, start, turn on

forceful *adj* **1** commanding, compelling, important, influential, powerful

adj **2** bullying, coercive, menacing, strong-arm, threatening

adj **3** highhanded, important, intense, maximum, powerful, utmost

adj **4** clear, effective, explicit, strong, trenchant, vigorous

adj **5** aggressive, coercive, compelling, hard-sell, high-pressure, intensive, persuasive, pushy

adj **6** ardent, decisive, determined, emphatic, extreme, intense, potent, powerful, severe, strong

adj **7** cogent, compelling, convincing, effective, influential, persuasive, revealing, satisfactory, satisfying, solid, sound, telling, valid

adj **8** coercive, compelling, dynamic, energetic, hardy, lusty, mighty, passionate, powerful, robust, strong, sturdy, vigorous

adj **9** aggressive, dominant, durable, firm, hardy, hearty, mighty, powerful, robust, rugged, stalwart, stout, strong, sturdy, tenacious, tough

forces *n* see: ADMINISTRATION *n* 3

forcible *adj* convincing, effective, impressive, inspiring, profound, striking

fore *n* bow, crown, front, head, prow, stem, top

adj first, foremost, forward, leading

forebear *n* ancestor, antecedent, ascendant, elder, forefather, forerunner, founder, grandparent, parent, patriarch, predecessor, progenitor

forebode *v* see: NOTIFY *v* 4

foreboding *adj* imminent, impending, menacing, ominous, portentous, predictive, prophetic, sinister, threatening

n **1** feeling, guess, hunch, instinct, intuition, premonition, sense, suspicion

n **2** apprehension, forewarning, harbinger, intuition, omen, premonition, presage, sign, warning

forecast *n* **1** prognosis

n **2** prediction, prophecy, revelation, warning

n **3** budget, estimate, plan, prediction, projection, quota

v **1** diagnose, estimate, gauge, predetermine, predict, project

v **2** anticipate, augur, bode, budget, call, divine, estimate, foresee, foreshadow, foretell, guess, harbinger, herald, judge, plan, portend, preannounce, predict, presage, proclaim, prognosticate, project, prophesy, signify, soothsay

forecastle *n* deck, platform, quarterdeck

forefather *n* ancestor, antecedent, ascendant, elder, forebear, forerunner, founder, grandparent, parent, patriarch, predecessor, progenitor

forefront *n* front, head, lead, pioneer, spearhead, vanguard

forego *v* antedate, come before, pioneer, precede, preface, spearhead

foregoer *n* envoy, forerunner, harbinger, herald, messenger, outrider, precursor, predictor, prophet

foregoing *adj* aforementioned, ancient, antecedent, anterior, archaic, earlier, former, past, preceding, prior, previous, recent

foregone *adj* definite, determined, fixed, inevitable, inexorable, irrevocable, ordained, predestined, unalterable, unavoidable, unchangeable

foreign *adj* **1** alien, extraneous, extrinsic

adj **2** alien, remote, separate, unrelated

adj **3** abnormal, extra, extraneous, illogical, immaterial, insignificant, irregular, irrelevant, malapropos, nonessential, peripheral, superfluous, surplus, unimportant, unnecessary, unrelated

adj **4** imported, nondomestic, offshore

adj **5** alien, exotic, strange, unfamiliar

foreigner *n* alien, newcomer, outsider, stranger

foreman *n* boss, chief, head, overseer, owner, superior, supervisor

foremost *adj* **1** majority, maximum, most, optimal, top, unequaled

adj **2** chief, first, head, inaugural, initial, lead, leading, premier, prime

adj **3** basic, dominant, elementary, first, fundamental, head, highest, leading, main, outstanding, paramount, preeminent, premier, primary, rudimentary, supreme, top

adj **4** champion, excellent, fine, first-class, first-rate, good, grade A, leading, number one, prime, principal, prominent, quality, select, superb, superior, stellar, top, top-drawer, top-notch, tops

adj **5** first, fore, forward, leading

adj 6 acclaimed, celebrated, distinguished, eminent, esteemed, excellent, famed, famous, illustrious, notable, outstanding, prestigious, prominent, renowned, well-known

forensic *adj* judicial, legal

foreplay *n* coitus, conjugation, copulation, fooling around, fornication, intercourse, mating, fornication, sex, union

forerunner *n* 1 demo, example, first, model, prototype, sample, test

n 2 envoy, foregoer, harbinger, herald, messenger, outrider, precursor, predictor, prophet

n 3 see: ANCESTOR *n*

foresee *v* anticipate, augur, bode, budget, call, divine, estimate, forecast, foreshadow, foretell, guess, harbinger, herald, judge, plan, portend, preannounce, predict, presage, proclaim, prognosticate, project, prophesy, signify, soothsay

foreshadow *v* see: PREDICT *v* 2

foresight *n* caveat, forethought, providence, prudence, vigilance, vision, wariness

forest *n* 1 lumber, trees, wood

n 2 jungle, woodland, woods

forestall *v* avert, bar, deter, eliminate, foil, hinder, hold off, inhibit, preclude, prevent, stave off, thwart, turn back, ward off

foretell *v* anticipate, augur, bode, budget, call, divine, estimate, forecast, foresee, foreshadow, guess, harbinger, herald, judge, plan, portend, preannounce, predict, presage, proclaim, prognosticate, project, prophesy, signify, soothsay

forethought *n* caveat, foresight, providence, prudence, vigilance, vision, wariness

forever *adv* ad infinitum, all the time, always, constantly, continually, endlessly, eternally, perpetually, timelessly, unceasingly

n see: PERIOD *n* 2

forewarn *v* see: NOTIFY *v* 4

forewarned *adj* advised, calculated, careful, considered, contrived, deliberate, measured, planned, premeditated, studied, studious

forewarning *n* apprehension, foreboding, harbinger, intuition, omen, premonition, presage, sign, warning

foreword *n* see: INTRODUCTION *n*

forfeit *v* abstain, cast, decline, drop, eschew, forbear, forgo, give up, lose, pass, reject, renounce, sacrifice, surrender, turn down, waive

forge *v* see: BUILD *v* 3

forget *v* defy, discount, disregard, exclude, ignore, miss, neglect, omit, ostracize, overlook, overpass, pass, pass by, pass over, shun, skip, slight, snub

forgive *v* absolve, acquit, clear, condone, exculpate, excuse, exempt, exonerate, free, pardon, remit, reprieve, vindicate

forgo *v* 1 abstain, avoid, constrain, curb, deny, govern, hold back, refrain, resist, restrict, stop, tame

v 2 see: FORFEIT *v*

forgotten *adj* 1 gone, left behind, lost, once, past, suppressed, unremembered, vague

adj 2 bygone, dead, defunct, departed, extinct, gone, lost, vanished

forlorn *adj* see: GLOOMY *adj* 5

form *n* 1 usage

n 2 contour, outline, profile, shape

n 3 border, boundary, casing, frame, shape

n 4 boundaries, framework, outline, pattern, structure

n 5 arrangement, design, plan, prearrangement, preparation, provision

n 6 cast, configuration, conformation, figure, shape, structure

n 7 anatomy, body, build, figure, frame, physique, shape

n 8 appliance, application, employment, method, operation, play, technique, use, utilization

n 9 die, matrix, mold, punch

v 1 constitute, make up, produce

v 2 constitute, construct

v 3 come together, crystallize, develop, jell, materialize, shape up

v 4 appear, arise, ascend, come forth, emanate, emerge, issue, loom

v 5 assemble, build, construct, erect, establish, fabricate, forge, make, manufacture, mold, produce, trailblaze

v 6 carve, chisel, craft, cut, define, design, fashion, mold, sculpt, sculpture, shape, steer

formal *adj* 1 artificial, awkward, stiff, stilted, stuffy

adj 2 boring, dull, pompous, stodgy, stuffy

adj 3 certain, explicit, expressed, firm, fixed, mandated, set, settled, spoken, stated, stipulated

formality *n* 1 ceremonial, ceremony, liturgy, observance, rite, ritual, service

n 2 convention, custom, decorum, etiquette, good form, manners, propriety, protocol, rites

n 3 see: PRACTICE *n* 6

format *n* arrangement, array, layout, outline, plan, style

v 1 number, paginate, sequence

v 2 see: CLASSIFY *v* 2

formation *n* aircraft, division, squadron, wing

formative *adj* basic, creative, fundamental, initiatory, productive, seminal

former *adj* 1 bygone, erstwhile, late, old, once, onetime, past, sometime

adj 2 aboriginal, ancient, early, original, prehistoric, primeval, primitive, primordial, rudimentary

adj 3 aforementioned, ancient, antecedent, anterior, archaic, earlier, foregoing, past, preceding, previous, prior, recent

formerly *adv* before, earlier, first, heretofore, hitherto, once, previously, prior to

formidable *adj* 1 arduous, herculean, heroic, superhuman, tremendous

adj 2 huge, immense, impressive, intimidating, massive, significant, substantial

adj 3 arduous, demanding, difficult, hard, heavy, labored, laborious, rocky, rough, rugged, serious, severe, strenuous, tough, trying, uphill

adj 4 appalling, awful, dire, dreadful, fearful, frightening, frightful, ghastly, horrendous, horrible, offensive, ominous, portentous, scary, shocking, spooky, terrible, terrifying, unpleasant

formula *n* 1 compound, drug, elixir, medicine, narcotic, painkiller, pharmaceutical, prescription

n 2 expression, methodology, plan, procedure, recipe, scheme, system, theorem

formulate *v* 1 craft, define, develop, list, make, process, specify, synthesize

v 2 brew, concoct, construe, contrive, create, devise, engineer, fabricate, hatch, invent, make up, plot, scheme

v 3 begin, coin, conceive, craft, create, define, develop, devise, innovate, invent, make, originate, start

formulation *n* 1 conception, ideation, imagination

n 2 birth, conception, creation, genesis, procreation

fornication *n* 1 adultery, congress, copulation, fooling around, intimacy, procreation, sex

n 2 coitus, conjugation, copulation, fooling around, foreplay, intercourse, mating, reproduction, sex, union

forsake *v* abandon, break up, cast off, chuck, defect, desert, disavow, discard, disenfranchise, disown, ditch, dump, jilt, junk, leave, quit, reject, renounce, spurn, strand, throw out

forsaken *adj* abandoned, depraved, derelict, deserted, desolate, secluded, solitary, uninhabited

forswear *v* abjure, deny, disavow, disclaim, disown, reject, renounce, repudiate

fort *n* bastion, bulwark, defense, embankment, fortification, rampart, wall

forte *n* see: SKILL *n* 3

forthcoming *adj* advancing, approaching, imminent, looming, nearing, oncoming, pending

forthright *adj* 1 belligerent, outright, outspoken

adj 2 aboveboard, candid, equitable, fair, honest, legitimate, plain-dealing, straight, straightforward, trustworthy, upright

adj 3 candid, direct, earnest, frank, genuine, heartfelt, hearty, honest, no-holds-barred, open, real, sincere, straightforward, true, trustworthy, truthful, undesigning, unfeigned, unpretentious, wholehearted

forthwith *adv* at once, immediately, instantly, promptly, right now, this instant, *tout de suite*

fortification *n* bastion, bulwark, defense, embankment, fort, rampart, wall

fortify *v* 1 barricade, enclose, protect

v 2 better, elevate, enhance, enrich, improve, strengthen

v 3 augment, buttress, harden, intensify, invigorate, reinforce, strengthen

v 4 bulwark, cover, defend, fend, guard, hide, protect, safeguard, screen, secure, shield

v 5 appoint, arm, equip, furnish, gear, man, outfit, rig, set up, supply, turn out

v 6 bear up, bolster, brace, build up, buoy, buttress, carry, harden, nourish, nurture, prop, reinforce, shore, strengthen, support, sustain, toughen, uphold

fortitude *n* 1 boldness, bravery, courage, daring, heart, heroism, spirit, strength, valor

n 2 backbone, chutzpah, determination, endurance, grit, guts, moxie, nerve, persistence, pluck, resilience, spirit, spunk, stamina, strength, tenacity, tolerance, vigor, willpower

fortress *n* stronghold

fortuitous *adj* accidental, casual, chance, chancy, circumstantial, coincidental, contingent, eventful, fluky, freak, incidental, lucky, odd, serendipitous, synchronous

fortunate *adj* 1 auspicious, favorable, happy, lucky, providential, serendipitous

adj 2 auspicious, favorable, propitious

fortunately *adv* favorably, happily, positively, successfully, well

fortune *n* 1 bet, chance, gamble, hazard, luck, risk, stake

n 2 blessing, bonanza, boon, gain, godsend, luck, miracle, serendipity, stroke of luck, windfall

n 3 booty, bounty, kitty, loot, money, plunder, pot, prize, spoils, swag, treasure, trove

n 4 assets, belongings, equity, estate, goods, holdings, inheritance, money, ownership, possessions, property, prosperity, riches, treasure, wealth

n 5 heap, loads, mint, scads

fortuneteller *n* astrologer, augur, oracle, predictor, prophet, psychic, seer, soothsayer, visionary

forum *n* 1 assembly, clinic, congress, council, court, diet, hearing, meeting, parliament, seminar, symposium

n 2 see: DISCUSSION *n* 4

forward *adv* ahead, before, beyond, in front, onward

v 1 address, channel, consign, dispatch, export, mail, post, remit, route, send, ship, transmit, transport

v 2 abet, advance, aid, ameliorate, amend, assist, avail, benefit, better, boost, cultivate, do for, ease, egg on, encourage, enhance, foster, further, help, improve, nurture, prefer, promote, rev, serve, spur on, support

adj 1 first, fore, leading

adj 2 audacious, bold, brash, brazen, cheeky, daring, disrespectful, fresh, impertinent, impudent, insolent, irreverent, nervy, pert, rude, sassy, saucy

forwarding *n* consignment, dispatch, sending

fossil *n* remains, skeleton

foster *v* 1 cultivate, develop, encourage, further, grow, promote

v 2 adopt, borrow, embrace, subscribe, take on, take up, utilize

v 3 care, cherish, mother, nourish, nurse, nurture, parent, protect, raise, rear, suckle

v 4 see: HELP *v* 4

foul *adj* 1 brackish, briny, nasty, salty, stagnant, undrinkable

adj 2 dirty, disgusting, lousy, nasty, putrid, rotten, sordid

adj 3 decaying, fetid, gamy, malodorous, musty, putrid, rancid, rank, reeking, rotten, smelly, sour, spoiled, stale, stinking, tainted

adj 4 black, dark, dingy, dirty, filthy, grimy, grubby, mucky, murky, polluted, seedy, shabby, sooty, squalid, stained, unclean, unlit, unwashed

adj 5 see: VULGAR *adj* 2

v 1 contaminate, dirty, infect, poison, pollute

v 2 befoul, catch, ensnare, entangle, hang

foul-up *n* accident, blooper, blunder, bungle, confusion, error, faux pas, lapse, misreading, mistake, misunderstanding, slip, slip-up

found *adj* discovered, located, uncovered

v build, constitute, construct, create, erect, establish, initiate, institute, launch, set up, start

foundation *n* 1 base, basis, bedrock, footing, ground, root

n 2 basic, element, essential, fundamental, principle, rudiment

n 3 assumption, ground rule, postulate, premise, proposition, supposition, theorem

n 4 association, combination, corporation, establishment, fellowship, institution, league, union

n 5 building, edifice, erection, house, pile, store, structure, warehouse

n 6 base, brace, buttress, column, footing, prop, shore, stay, support, underpinning

n 7 arguments, basis, cause, explanation, grounds, principle, rationale, reason, rudiments, source

n 8 footing, standing, surface

founder *n* 1 author, creator, initiator, instigator, inventor, maker, originator, parent, pioneer, seed, source

n 2 ancestor, antecedent, ascendant, elder, forebear, forefather, forerunner, grandparent, parent, patriarch, predecessor, progenitor

founding *adj* 1 earliest, first, fundamental, initial, maiden, original, pioneer, primary, prime

adj 2 beginning, embryonic, incipient, initial, introductory, nascent, rudimentary, starting

fountain *n* birth, creation, genesis, origin, parent, root, source

fountainhead *n* beginning, conception, cradle, derivation, inception, infancy, mother, origin, root, seed, source, stem

fox trot *n* ballet, cha-cha, dance, hula, jitterbug, polka, tap, twist, waltz

foxy *adj* 1 adroit, artful, cagey, canny, crafty, cunning, evasive, serpentine, sly *adj* 2 alluring, attractive, becoming, coy, cute, enchanting, enticing, fascinating, inviting, pleasing, ravishing, seductive, sexy

adj 3 astute, calculating, crafty, cunning, guileful, insidious, sharp, shrewd, sly, smart, subtle, tricky, wily, wise

adj 4 see: BEAUTIFUL *adj* 2

adj 5 see: DECEITFUL *adj* 1

foyer *n* 1 anteroom, approach, atrium, court, doorway, entrance hall, entry, hall, hallway, lobby, portal, vestibule

n 2 family room, living room, parlor, salon

fracas *n* 1 anarchy, chaos, commotion, confusion, disorder, disturbance, fray, outbreak, riot, ruckus, storm, tempest

n 2 affray, battle, brawl, brush, clash, conflict, difference, disagreement, dispute, encounter, fight, melee, quarrel, run-in, scrimmage, skirmish, spat, touch

n 3 altercation, argument, battle, brawl, challenge, combat, controversy, disagreement, discord, dispute, feud, fight, fray, hassle, melee, quarrel, rancor, rift, row, ruckus, scrap, scuffle, skirmish, spat, squabble, struggle, tiff, war

fracture *n* breach, break, crack, gap, opening, space, split

v break, chip, crack, gap, sever, smash, split

fractured *adj* broken, cracked, damaged, out of order

fragile *adj* 1 delicate, frail, soft, tender

adj 2 breakable, brittle, crisp, crumbly

adj 3 breakable, decrepit, delicate, dilapidated, feeble, flimsy, frail, jerry-built, jury-rigged, puny, Rube Goldberg, shoddy, sickly, thin, tinny, unsound, worn-out

fragment *n* 1 bit, chip, dent, flake, mark, piece

n 2 debris, hulk, remains, rubbish, rubble, shell, trash, wreck, wreckage

n 3 bit, dab, end, iota, minutia, mite, morsel, particle, piece, pinch, portion, scrap, shred, speck, spot, strip, tidbit, trifle

n 4 shred, sliver, splinter

v break, burst, erupt, explode, rupture, shatter, smash, smatter, splinter

fragmentary *adj* halfway, incomplete, partial, unfinished

fragments *n* boulder, detritus, gravel, pebble, rock, stone

fragrance *n* 1 aroma, odor, scent, smell

n 2 aroma, balm, bouquet, incense, perfume, scent, spice

frail *adj* 1 delicate, fragile, soft, tender

adj 2 feeble, flimsy, insubstantial, slight, tenuous, unsubstantial, weak

adj 3 ailing, delicate, diseased, down, ill, impaired, indisposed, sick, sickly, suffering, unhealthy, unsound, unwell, weak

adj 4 breakable, decrepit, delicate, dilapidated, feeble, flimsy, fragile, jerry-built, jury-rigged, puny, Rube Goldberg, shoddy, sickly, thin, tinny, unsound, worn-out

frailty *n* failing, fault, foible, limitation, shortcoming, vice, weakness

frame *n* 1 border, boundary, casing, form, shape

n 2 anatomy, body, build, figure, form, physique, shape

v 1 force

v 2 build, conceive, construct, devise, shape, surround

v 3 see: PLOT *v* 1

framework *n* 1 chassis, infrastructure, skeleton

n 2 cadre, center, core, infrastructure, nucleus

n 3 boundaries, form, outline, pattern, structure

franchise *n* 1 agreement, arrangement, compromise, concession, decision, settlement

n 2 ballot, choice, option, preference, say, selection, vote

v charter, hire, lease, let, permit, rent, sublet

frank *adj* 1 artless, candid, guileless, ingenuous, innocent, naive, natural, open, plain, simple, simple-hearted, unadorned, unaffected, unsophisticated, unstudied, untutored, unworldly

adj 2 candid, direct, earnest, forthright, genuine, heartfelt, hearty, honest, no-holds-barred, open, real, sincere, straightforward, true, trustworthy, truthful, undesigning, unfeigned, unpretentious, wholehearted

frankness *n* candor, honesty, sincerity, truthfulness

frantic *adj* 1 anxious, careworn, distracted, distraught, distressed, harassed, tormented, troubled, upset, worried

adj 2 agitated, disorderly, excited, fierce, frenzied, furious, mad, stormy, tumultuous, turbulent, violent, wild

fraternal *adj* affiliated, akin, aligned, allied, associated, friendly, kindred, parallel, related

fraternity *n* 1 closeness, companionship, familiarity, friendship, intimacy *n* 2 brotherhood, camaraderie, community, esprit de corps, fellowship, lodge

n 3 see: ORGANIZATION *n* 4

fraud *n* 1 charlatan, cheat, fake, hypocrite, quack

n 2 cheating, deceit, deception, dishonesty, hoax, lie, sham, subterfuge, trickery

n 3 charlatan, counterfeit, fake, faker, hypocrite, impostor, liar, phony, pretender

n 4 deceit, deception, fabrication, falsehood, fraudulence, hypocrisy, lying, perjury, trickery, untruth

n 5 bastard, deception, fake, hoax, put-on, sham

fraudulence *n* deceit, deception, fabrication, falsehood, fraud, hypocrisy, lying, perjury, trickery, untruth

fraudulent *adj* bad, corrupt, crooked, deceitful, dishonest, evil, immoral, iniquitous, lying, Machiavellian, manipulative, mercenary, reprobate, roguish, scheming, shady, shifty, sinful, unethical, unfair, unprincipled, unscrupulous, untruthful, venal, vile, wicked, wrong

fraught *adj* burdened, encumbered, harried, laden, loaded, pressured

fray *n* 1 action, battle, engagement, gesture, movement, operation, proceeding

n 2 anarchy, chaos, commotion, confusion, disorder, disturbance, fracas, outbreak, riot, ruckus, storm, tempest

n 3 see: QUARREL *n* 2

v see: QUARREL *v*

frayed *adj* faded, poor, run-down, shabby, tattered, threadbare, worn

frazzle *v* aggravate, anger, annoy, bother, bug, enrage, exasperate, gall, grate, hassle, incense, inflame, infuriate, irk, irritate, madden, miff, nettle, outrage, peeve, pester, pique, provoke, rile, upset, vex

frazzled *adj* see: WEARY *adj* 2

freak *adj* see: ACCIDENTAL *adj* 3

n 1 monster

n 2 bug, crusader, enthusiast, fanatic, fiend, hobbyist, maniac, monomaniac, nut, radical, zealot

free *adj* 1 complimentary, gratis, gratuitous

adj 2 autonomous, distinct, independent, lone, separate, sovereign, unconnected

adj 3 bounteous, bountiful, generous, handsome, liberal, openhanded, unsparing

adj 4 belligerent, extroverted, intimidating, loud, outspoken, vocal, vociferous

adj 5 detached, impartial, independent,

neutral, nonpartisan, unattached, uncommitted, uninvolved

adj 6 deliberate, intentional, optional, unforced, unprescribed, voluntary, willful, willing

adj 7 audacious, liberated, licentious, loose, rampant, unbridled, unconfined, uncontrolled, uncurbed, ungoverned, unhampered, uninhibited, unrestrained, unsecured, unshackled, untied, wild

v 1 extricate, liberate, release, remove, rescue

v 2 discharge, emancipate, liberate, loosen, release, unbind, unchain, unshackle

v 3 absolve, acquit, clear, condone, exculpate, excuse, exempt, exonerate, forgive, pardon, remit, reprieve, vindicate

v 4 deliver, liberate, release, rescue, save

freedom *n* 1 chance, latitude, opportunity, room

n 2 autonomy, independence, liberty, license

n 3 comfort, ease, effortlessness, leisure, liberty

n 4 absolution, amnesty, discharge, disengagement, dispensation, moratorium, pardon, release, relief, reprieve, respite, stay, suspension

freeing *n* deliverance, extrication, recovery, release, rescue, saving

freeloader *n* barnacle, dependent, hanger-on, leech, parasite, remora, sponge, vine

freeze *v* 1 arrest, block, check, halt, impede, interrupt, stall, stay, stop

v 2 cripple, disable, disarm, encumber, halt, handcuff, immobilize, incapacitate, paralyze, prostrate, stop, stun

v 3 chill, cool, ice, refrigerate

v 4 abstain, end, cease, conclude, desist, discontinue, end, finish, forbear, halt, knock off, quit, refrain, sever, stop, terminate

freezing *adj* see: COLD *adj* 4

freight *n* burden, cargo, consignment, lading, load, payload, shipment, transportation, truck

freighter *n* craft, cruiser, frigate, ketch, liner, ocean liner, sailboat, schooner, ship, steamship, vessel, yacht

frenetic *adj* chaotic, fervent, fervid, feverish, frenzied, hectic, jittery

frenzied *adj* 1 delirious, deranged, fantasizing, hallucinating, maniacal, raving

adj 2 amok, berserk, crazy, maniacal, out of control, rushed about, violent

adj 3 chaotic, fervent, fervid, feverish, frenetic, hectic, jittery

adj 4 agitated, disorderly, excited, fierce,

frantic, furious, mad, stormy, tumultuous, turbulent, violent, wild

frenzy n 1 ferocity, fury, intensity, rage

n 2 chaos, hysteria, panic, riot

n 3 brutality, destructiveness, ferocity, force, fury, rage, violence

n 4 see: AGITATION n

n 5 see: ANGER n 2

v rage, rampage, rebel, revolt, riot, stampede, storm

frequency n level, pitch, sound, tone

frequent adj accepted, accustomed, chronic, common, constant, continual, customary, daily, everyday, familiar, habitual, inured, often, recurring, regular, routine, traditional, usual

v attend, hang around, hang out, haunt, obsess, patronize, resort to, visit

frequently adv 1 often, regularly, repeatedly, typically, usually

adv 2 see: USUALLY adv 1, 2

fresh adj 1 mint, new, unused

adj 2 bright, contemporary, high-tech, modern, modernistic, new, novel, recent, up-to-date

adj 3 refreshing

adj 4 rare, raw, uncooked

adj 5 energizing, exhilarating, invigorating, refreshing, stimulating

adj 6 adolescent, green, immature, juvenile, precocious, undeveloped, unfledged, unready, young, youthful

adj 7 audacious, bold, brash, brazen, cheeky, daring, disrespectful, forward, impertinent, impudent, insolent, irreverent, nervy, pert, rude, sassy, saucy

freshen v see: REJUVENATE v 2

freshman n see: BEGINNER n 2

freshness n clarity, clearness, distinctness, exactness, lucidity, plainness, purity

fret v brood, fuss, stew, worry

fretful adj 1 awake, fitful, restless, sleepless

adj 2 annoying, anxious, bothersome, chafing, crabby, edgy, galling, impatient, irritating, jittery, nagging, on edge, restless, touchy, unsettling

friar n abbé, abbot, ascetic, hermit, monk, recluse

friction n 1 adhesion, pulling, tension, traction

n 2 antagonism, conflict, discord

friend n 1 accomplice, acquaintance, adjunct, ally, associate, buddy, chum, cohort, colleague, companion, compatriot, comrade, confidant, confrere, connection, copartner, counterpart, co-worker, crony, equal, fellow, follower, intimate,

mate, pal, partner, peer, relative, supporter

n 2 see: ADVOCATE n 2

friendly adj 1 affiliated, akin, aligned, allied, associated, fraternal, kindred, parallel, related

adj 2 affable, amiable, approachable, cordial, genial, gentle, gracious, likable, lovable, peaceful, pleasant, serene

adj 3 affable, amenable, amiable, amicable, congenial, empathetic, gregarious, hospitable, neighborly, outgoing, receptive, sociable, social, sympathetic

friendship n 1 closeness, companionship, familiarity, fraternity, intimacy

n 2 association, affair, communication, intimacy, liaison, rapport, relationship, union

frigate n craft, cruiser, freighter, ketch, liner, ocean liner, sailboat, schooner, ship, steamship, vessel, yacht

fright n 1 affliction, alarm, anxiety, apprehension, care, consternation, dismay, dread, fear, horror, ordeal, panic, terror, trepidation, trial, trouble, worry

n 2 horror, scare, shock, start, terror

frighten v 1 alarm, attack, bully, club, coerce, harass, intimidate, menace, strong-arm, terrorize, threaten

v 2 abash, alarm, awe, cow, daunt, horrify, intimidate, panic, scare, shock, spook, startle, terrify, terrorize, unnerve

frightened adj afraid, aghast, anxious, apprehensive, concerned, discerning, fearful, nervous, paranoid, scared, scary, terrified, worried

frightening adj 1 forbidding, hairy, scary, spooky

adj 2 appalling, awful, dire, dreadful, fearful, formidable, frightful, ghastly, horrendous, horrible, offensive, ominous, portentous, scary, shocking, spooky, terrible, terrifying, unpleasant

frightful adj 1 awful, grim, grisly, gruesome, hideous, lurid, repulsive, sensational, shocking, terrible, ugly, violent

adj 2 abhorrent, abominable, appalling, detestable, disgusting, dreadful, evil, ghastly, hateful, horrible, horrid, loathsome, odious, repulsive, revolting, shocking

adj 3 appalling, awful, dire, dreadful, fearful, formidable, frightening, ghastly, horrendous, horrible, offensive, ominous, portentous, scary, shocking, spooky, terrible, terrifying, unpleasant

frigid adj 1 arctic, chilly, cold, cool, freezing, frosty, glacial, icy, nippy, wintry *adj* 2 cold, coldhearted, distant, emotionless, glacial, icy, impersonal, indifferent, unemotional, unfriendly

adj 3 cold, inhibited, passionless, repressed, restrained, reticent, unresponsive

adj 4 barren, effete, impotent, infertile, spent, sterile, unbearing, unfertile, unfruitful, unproductive

frill *n* bauble, luxury, treat

fringe *n* border, boundary, bounds, brim, brink, curb, edge, limits, lip, margin, outskirt, perimeter, periphery, rim, side, skirt, verge

frisk *v* 1 search, seek

v 2 caper, cavort, frolic, gambol, play, prance, rollick, romp, skip

frisky *adj* see: LIVELY *adj* 8

fritter *v* cast away, consume, dissipate, drivel, empty, lavish, squander, throw away, use up, waste

frivolity *n* 1 craziness, folly, foolishness, insanity, lunacy, madness, mania, nonsense, senselessness

n 2 amusement, elation, excitement, exhilaration, gaiety, glee, guffaws, happiness, hilarity, jocularity, jocundity, jollity, joviality, joy, laughter, levity, merriment, mirth

frivolous *adj* 1 capricious, dizzy, flighty, giddy, irresponsible, scatterbrained, silly

adj 2 borderline, casual, insignificant, light, lightweight, little, marginal, meager, minor, minute, negligible, nonessential, off, outside, petty, remote, secondary, slender, slight, slim, small, tenuous, trivial, unimportant

adj 3 see: ABSURD *adj* 2

frolic *v* 1 carouse, celebrate, drink, make merry, party, revel, romp

v 2 caper, cavort, frisk, gambol, play, prance, rollick, romp, skip

n see: RECREATION *n* 2

frolicsome *adj* see: LIVELY *adj* 8

front *n* 1 forefront, head, lead, pioneer, spearhead, vanguard

n 2 bow, crown, fore, head, prow, stem, top

n 3 chessman, instrument, pawn, peon, puppet, stooge, tool

n 4 appearance, cover, facade, face, facet, factor, look, surface, veneer
v face

frontier *adj* 1 back, outlandish, remote, unsettled

adj 2 dawning, new, unexplored, unknown

n hinterland, outback, outland, threshold

frosty *adj* arctic, chilly, cold, cool, freezing, frigid, glacial, icy, nippy, wintry

frown *v* disdain, glare, gloom, glower, grimace, lower, pout, scowl, sulk

frowning *adj* scowling

frugal *adj* canny, conservative, economical, provident, sparing, spartan, stewardly, thrifty, unwasteful

frugality *n* economy, moderation, prudence, thrift

fruit *n* harvest, product, result, reward

fruitful *adj* 1 copious, creative, fecund, fertile, productive, prolific

adj 2 constructive, favorable, helpful, positive, productive, useful, worthwhile

fruition *n* accomplishment, achievement, arrival, attainment, completion, fulfillment, realization, satisfaction, success, triumph, victory

fruitless *adj* abortive, futile, ineffective, ineffectual, nonproductive, unavailing, unproductive, unsuccessful, unyielding, useless, vain, worthless

fruits *n* crop, grain, harvest, produce, yield

frustrate *v* 1 baffle, confound, confuse, perplex, stymie, thwart

v 2 disappoint, disenchant, disillusion, dissatisfy, fail, let down

v 3 aggravate, baffle, balk, bewilder, circumvent, confuse, dash, elude, foil, hamper, impede, negate, nullify, perplex, thwart

v 4 see: HINDER *v* 5

frustrating *adj* baffling, elusive, mysterious, puzzling, subtle

frustration *n* anxiety, burden, pressure, strain, stress, tension

fuel *v* feed, fire, ignite, incite, kindle, light, nourish, propel, stoke, sustain

n energy, gasoline, petrol, propellant

fugitive *n* escapee, outlaw, runaway

fugue *n* 1 aberration, abnormality, craziness, delusion, dementia, derangement, distraction, eccentricity, hallucination, insanity, irregularity, lunacy, madness, mania, psychosis, unbalance

n 2 concert, concerto, étude, program, recital, serenade, sonata, symphony

fulfill *v* 1 complete, redeem, satisfy

v 2 complement, complete, round out, supplement

v 3 answer, do, meet, qualify, satisfy, suffice, work

v 4 achieve, answer, execute, fill, finish, meet, realize, satisfy

v 5 accomplish, complete, consummate, execute, implement, perform, realize

v 6 accomplish, achieve, attain, consummate, execute, perform, produce, pull off, realize, succeed, triumph, win

v 7 access, accomplish, achieve, attain, derive, earn, gain, get, merit, net, obtain, perform, profit, rack up, reach, realize, score, win

fulfilling *adj* beneficial, gratifying, pleasing, rewarding, worthwhile

fulfillment *n* accomplishment, achievement, arrival, attainment, completion, fruition, realization, satisfaction, success, triumph, victory

full *adj* 1 filled, quenched, sated, satisfied, saturated

adj 2 bursting, chock-full, crowded, filled up, jammed, jampacked, loaded, packed, rending, replete, stuffed

adj 3 drenched, dripping, immersed, inundated, saturated, soaked, soaking, sodden, sopping, waterlogged, wet

adj 4 sheer

full-blown *adj* all, all-out, complete, entire, gross, integral, integrated, outright, total, unlimited, whole

full-grown *adj* adult, grown, grown-up, mature, matured, ripened

fully *adv* adequately, altogether, assiduously, completely, earnestly, entirely, exhaustively, hard, intensely, intensively, painstakingly, perfectly, quite, sufficiently, thoroughly, totally, unremittingly, utterly, wholly

fulmination *n* harassment, intimidation, threat, warning

fumble *v* 1 addle, confuse, daze, foul up, jumble, mix up, muddle, snarl up

v 2 bumble, falter, flounder, get stuck, grope, hesitate, stagger, stumble, waffle, waver

fume *v* 1 agitate, bake, boil, bubble, burn, churn, ferment, foam, roast, seethe, simmer, smolder

v 2 anger, blow up, boil, boil over, brew, bristle, burn, flare up, rage, seethe, simmer, smoke, steam, storm

n exhaust, gas, smoke

fuming *adj* see: ANGRY *adj* 4

fun *adj* amusing, diverting, enjoyable, entertaining, humorous, joking, playful

n see: RECREATION *n* 2

function *n* 1 duty, purpose, use

n 2 appointment, connection, duty, job, office, position, post, situation

v act, go, perform, run, work

functional *adj* 1 busy, employed, engaged, in use, occupied, working

adj 2 accessible, available, close, convenient, feasible, handy, helpful, multipurpose, nearby, open, practical, public, reachable, ready, serviceable, suitable, unrestricted, usable, useful, utilitarian, well-suited, within reach, working

functioning *adj* active, alive, live, operative, running, working

fund *n* 1 accumulation, reservoir, source, store, supply

n 2 account, budget, capital, cash, money, savings, stock

v 1 aid, endow, finance, subsidize, underwrite

v 2 bankroll, capitalize, finance, stake, subsidize

v 3 accord, adduce, award, bequeath, bestow, concede, confer, contribute, deliver, devote, donate, endow, extend, give, give away, grant, hand down, hand out, impart, offer, pose, present, proffer, provide, supply, tender, volunteer

fundamental *adj* 1 cardinal, essential, primary, prime, principal

adj 2 basic, creative, formative, initiatory, productive, seminal

adj 3 ensconced, entrenched, established, fixed, ingrained, intrinsic, inveterate, settled, sworn

adj 4 earliest, first, founding, initial, maiden, original, pioneer, primary, prime

adj 5 basic, dominant, elementary, first, foremost, head, highest, leading, main, outstanding, paramount, preeminent, premier, primary, rudimentary, supreme, top

adj 6 basic, early, elementary, embryonic, essential, initial, intrinsic, original, rudimentary, underlying

n basic, element, essential, foundation, principle, rudiment

funds *n* assets, bills, capital, cash, coffers, currency, dinero, dollars, estate, goods, income, lucre, means, money, notes, pelf, pesos, property, resources, revenue, riches, rubles, shekels, sum, wealth

funeral *n* burial

funereal *adj* abnormal, depressing, dismal, ghastly, gloomy, gruesome, macabre, morbid, sepulchral

fungus *n* decay, germ, mold

funnel *v* carry, channel, conduct, convey, pass, pipe, siphon, transmit

funniness *n* banter, comedy, crack, gag, humor, jest, joke, quip, small talk, wisecrack, wit, witticism

funny *adj* 1 comical, facetious, humorous, jesting, jocular, joking, kidding, sarcastic, witty *adj* 2 charming, odd, old-fashioned, quaint, peculiar, picturesque, puzzling, remarkable, special, uncommon, unusual, whimsical

adj 3 absurd, comic, comical, crazy, droll, farcical, foolish, hilarious, humorous, laughable, ludicrous, outrageous, ridiculous, silly

fur *n* coat, hide, jacket, pelt, skin, stole

furbish *v* buff, burnish, glaze, glimmer, gloss, polish, renovate, rub, shine

furious *adj* 1 angry, ferocious, fierce, heated, intense, savage, severe, terrible, vehement, vicious, violent

adj 2 agitated, disorderly, excited, fierce, frantic, frenzied, mad, stormy, tumultuous, turbulent, violent, wild

adj 3 aggravated, angry, annoyed, cross, enraged, excited, fuming, hot, incensed, indignant, irate, irritable, mad, provoked, teed off, upset

furlough *n* day off, holiday, leave, respite, sabbatical, time off, vacation

furnish *v* 1 endow, equip, give, provide

v 2 fill, replenish, stock, store, supply

v 3 clothe, fit, outfit, provide, supply

v 4 appoint, arm, equip, fortify, gear, man, outfit, rig, set up, supply, turn out

v 5 arrange, cater, deliver, dish out, dispense, feed, give, hand, nourish, nurture, organize, provide, purvey, serve, supply, sustain

furnishings *n* equipment, fixtures, gear, materials, provisions, supplies

furor *n* see: AGITATION *n*

furrow *n* canal, channel, conduit, crevice, curb, cut, ditch, duct, gorge, groove, gully, gutter, passageway, ravine, rut, trench, trough

v burrow, dig, root out, tunnel

furry *adj* fuzzy, hairy, woolly

further *adv* 1 incidentally

adv 2 additionally, beyond, farther, furthermore

adv 3 despite, however, in spite of, regardless

adv 4 but, except that, however, just, merely, only, nevertheless, simply, solely, yet

adv 5 see: ALSO *adv*

v 1 cultivate, develop, encourage, foster, grow, promote

v 2 alter, change, commute, convert, evolve, improve, metamorphose, modernize, modify, mutate, revolutionize,

transfigure, transfer, transform, transmute, vary

v 3 see: HELP *v* 4

adj see: ADDITIONAL *adj* 2

furtherance *n* acceleration, achievement, advance, advancement, betterment, breakthrough, growth, headway, improvement, increment, pickup, proficiency, progress, promotion, strengthening, upgrade

furthermore *adv* 1 additionally, beyond, further

adv 2 additionally, also, and, as well, as well as, besides, further, in addition, likewise, moreover, plus, too

furthermost *adj* extreme, farthest, furthest, hindmost, most distant, most remote, outermost, utmost

furthest *adj* extreme, farthest, furthermost, hindmost, most distant, most remote, outermost, utmost

furtive *adj* 1 clandestine, concealed, covert, crafty, deceitful, devious, evasive, foxy, guileful, indirect, privy, secret, shifty, sly, sneaky, surreptitious, tricky, underground, underhand, underhanded, wily

adj 2 catlike, cattish, catty, feline, skulking, stealthy

furtively *adv* clandestinely, covertly, hush-hush, mystically, secretly, sneakily, stealthily, surreptitiously, under cover

fury *n* 1 ferocity, frenzy, intensity, rage

n 2 brutality, destructiveness, ferocity, force, frenzy, rage, violence

n 3 agitation, craze, excitement, frenzy, furor, fuss, outrage, passion, tumult, uproar, wrath

n 4 anger, dander, fit, frenzy, indignation, ire, outrage, paroxysm, rage, tantrum, wrath

fuse *v* 1 dissolve, flux, liquefy, melt, run, thaw

v 2 affix, bind, bond, cement, fasten, glue, join, lock, paste, seal, secure, stick, unite

v 3 amalgamate, band, blend, coalesce, combine, compound, consolidate, intermingle, league, lump, meld, merge, mingle, mix, unify, unite

v 4 associate, blend, bond, coalesce, combine, compound, connect, couple, fasten, join, link, marry, mate, meet, merge, pair, unite, wed

fusillade *n* barrage, burst, round, shot, volley

fusion *n* 1 bond, cohesion, connection, solidarity, togetherness, union *n* 2 blend, combination, intermingling, joining, merging, mixture, union

fuss *n* 1 objection

n 2 agitation, craze, excitement, frenzy, furor, fury, outrage, passion, tumult, uproar, wrath

n 3 action, activity, ado, animation, bedlam, bother, bustle, chaos, commotion, excitement, flurry, fluster, hum, liveliness, madhouse, movement, stir, to-do, tumult, turmoil, whirlpool, whirlwind

n 4 see: EXHIBITION *n*

v 1 brood, fret, stew, worry

v 2 berate, carp, cavil, criticize, find fault, flay, henpeck, nag, nit-pick, nudge, peck, quibble, scold

fusspot *n* nit-picker, perfectionist, purist, stickler

fussy *adj* 1 careful, cautious, choosy, discriminating, fastidious, finicky, meticulous, nit-picking, particular, persnickety, picky, selective

adj 2 careful, carping, cautious, conscientious, ethical, exacting, heedful, meticulous, painstaking, punctilious, scrupulous, unrelenting

futile *adj* 1 foolish, ill-advised, pointless, profitless, stupid, vain

adj 2 bad, defective, inadequate, incorrect, inferior, invalid, malfunctioning, poor, void

adj 3 abortive, fruitless, ineffective, ineffectual, nonproductive, unavailing, unproductive, unsuccessful, unyielding, useless, vain, worthless

future *adj* approaching, eventual, expected, imminent, impending, next, prospective, subsequent

n 1 distance, horizon, outlook, perspective, purview, vision, vista

n 2 outlook, posterity, tomorrow

fuzzy *adj* 1 ambiguous, bleary, confused, hazy, misty, mixed up, nebulous, unclear

adj 2 furry, hairy, woolly

G

gab *v* cackle, chat, gossip, talk, yak

n chat, chatter, gossip, rap, talk

gadget *n* apparatus, appliance, contraption, contrivance, device, doodad, doohickey, gimmick, gizmo, implement, instrument, invention, machine, mechanism, thingumajig, tool, utensil, widget

gag *n* banter, comedy, crack, funniness, humor, jest, joke, quip, small talk, wisecrack, wit, witticism

v 1 balk, demur, desist

v 2 asphyxiate, choke, constrict, garrote, muffle, quash, repress, smother, stifle, strangle, suffocate, suppress

v 3 choke, cough, disgorge, throw up, vomit

v 4 censor, curb, hush, inhibit, muffle, mute, quell, quiet, repress, restrain, silence, squelch, stifle, still, subdue, suppress, throttle, tone down

gaggle *n* see: CROWD *n* 1

gaiety *n* 1 amusement, elation, excitement, exhilaration, frivolity, glee, guffaws, happiness, hilarity, jocularity, jocundity, jollity, joviality, joy, laughter, levity, merriment, mirth

n 2 see: PASSION *n* 7

gain *n* 1 compensation, earnings, reward, wages

n 2 acquisition, asset, buy, merchandise, property, purchase

n 3 addition, advancement, advantage, betterment, enhancement, growth, improvement, plus

n 4 assets, cash, earnings, gross, haul, net, payback, proceeds, profits, receipts, return, revenue, take, yield

n 5 account, advantage, behalf, benefit, betterment, good, happiness, interest, prosperity, sake, welfare, well-being

n 6 see: FORTUNE *n* 2

v 1 count, score, tally, win

v 2 advance, benefit, improve, profit, reward

v 3 derive, get, harvest, realize, reap

v 4 acquire, annex, buy, capture, get, have, land, obtain, pick up, procure, purchase, requisition, secure, solicit, win

v 5 access, accomplish, achieve, attain, derive, earn, fulfill, get, merit, net, obtain, perform, profit, rack up, reach, realize, score, win

v 6 capitalize, profit

v 7 ameliorate, convalesce, heal, improve, loop up, mend, perk, rally, recover, recuperate, rehabilitate, revive

gainful *adj* beneficial, lucrative, profitable, rewarding

gait *n* 1 march, pace, shuffle, step, stride, walk

n 2 alacrity, cadence, celerity, dispatch, pace, quickness, rapidity, rate, speed, step, stride, swiftness, trot, velocity, walk

gala *n* see: CELEBRATION *n*

gale *n* blast, blizzard, blow, gust, hurricane, northeaster, snowstorm, squall, storm, tempest, typhoon, wind

gall *n* 1 arrogance, assurance, audacity, boldness, brashness, brass, cheek, chutzpah, condescension, confidence, crust, effrontery, face, haughtiness, insolence, nerve, patronage, presumption, ridicule, sass, stamina, temerity

n 2 see: HATE *n*

v see: BOTHER *v* 5

gallant *adj* 1 chivalrous, civil, civilized, cordial, courteous, courtly, decent, dignified, genteel, gentlemanly, gracious, mannerly, noble, polite, well-mannered

adj 2 audacious, bold, brave, courageous, daring, dauntless, fearless, game, gutsy, heroic, intrepid, stalwart, unafraid, undaunted, valiant, valorous

n buck, Casanova, Don Juan, flirt, ladies' man, lecher, lover, philanderer, playboy, Romeo, stud

gallery *n* 1 balcony

n 2 archive, museum, treasury

galling *adj* annoying, anxious, bothersome, chafing, crabby, edgy, fretful, impatient, irritating, jittery, nagging, on edge, restless, touchy, unsettling

gallop *v* 1 dart, jog, run, trot

v 2 dash, jog, race, run, speed, sprint

galore *adj* see: PLENTIFUL *adj* 1

gambit *n* antic, device, diversion, gimmick, maneuver, mischief, move, plan, plot, ploy, prank, ruse, scheme, stratagem, strategy, tactic, trick, wile

gamble *n* bet, chance, fortune, hazard, luck, risk, stake

v attempt, bet, chance, dare, hazard, play, risk, speculate, stake, venture, wager

gambol *v* caper, cavort, frisk, frolic, play, prance, rollick, romp, skip

game *adj* 1 prepared, primed, ready, ripe, set

adj 2 see: BRAVE *adj* 1

n 1 amusement, knickknack, plaything, toy, trinket

n 2 bout, competition, conflict, contest, event, marathon, match, meet, meeting, race, regatta, round robin, run, tournament, tourney

n 3 catch, quarry, prey, target

n 4 amusement, distraction, diversion, enjoyment, entertainment, frolic, fun, hobby, pastime, play, recreation, sport

gamesome *adj* lively, playful

gamy *adj* 1 see: FOUL *adj* 3

adj 2 see: VULGAR *adj* 2

gang *n* 1 army, battalion, brigade, company, force, men, power, soldiers, troops

n 2 band, cabal, camp, circle, clan, clique, coterie, coven, cult, faction, family, group, mob, ring, school, sect, tribe

n 3 band, mob, posse, vigilantes

n 4 band, bunch, crew, crowd, drove, flock, following, gaggle, herd, huddle, mass, mob, pack, rabble, riffraff, swarm, team, throng

gangster *n* mobster

gap *n* 1 contradiction, difference, disparity, dissimilarity, inconsistency

n 2 breach, break, crack, fracture, opening, space, split

n 3 break, cessation, delay, interim, interval, lapse, lull, pause, stop

n 4 break, chance, crack, occasion, opening, opportunity, shot, show, stroke of luck, time

n 5 blank, cavity, crack, depression, emptiness, hole, hollow, nook, opening, space, void

n 6 opening, portal, window

v break, chip, crack, fracture, sever, smash, split

gape *v* eye, eyeball, gawk, gaze, goggle, observe, ogle, peer, stare, study

gaping *adj* cavernous, echo-filled, hollow, reverberant, spacious, vast

garb *v* accouter, apparel, array, attire, clad, clothe, dress, gear, outfit

garbage *n* 1 dirt, dung, filth, manure, muck, mud, slime, sludge

n 2 crap, crud, debris, detritus, dirt, junk, litter, refuse, rubbish, rubble, sweepings, trash, waste

n 3 discard, failure, junk, reject, scrap, second

garble *v* 1 mumble, mutter, slur

v 2 see: MISREPRESENT *v* 2

garbled *adj* see: VAGUE *adj* 6

garden *adj* bucolic, country, outland, pastoral, peaceful, provincial, rural, rustic, suburban, wooded

Gargantuan *adj* colossal, enormous, fantastic, giant, gigantic, Goliath, great, huge, immense, jumbo, leviathan, mammoth, massive, mighty, monstrous, monumental, overwhelming, phenomenal, prodigious, Promethean, stupendous, Titanic, towering, tremendous, unfathomed, untold, vast, walloping, whopping

garish *adj* 1 abundant, cornucopian, extravagant, exuberant, generous, lavish, lush, luxuriant, opulent, prodigal, profuse, rich, wasteful

adj 2 blatant, brazen, conspicuous, flagrant, flashy, gaudy, glaring, loud, ostentatious, showy, tacky, tasteless, tawdry, tinsel

adj 3 ambitious, bombastic, flamboyant, grandiose, inflated, jaunty, lofty, ostentatious, pompous, portentous, pretentious, showy, splashy, splendid, utopian, visionary

garland n band, coil, crown, loop, ring, spiral, wreath

garments n apparel, accoutrements, attire, clothes, clothing, dress, gear, togs

garner v accrue, accumulate, acquire, amass, assemble, collect, gather, grow, hoard, save, squirrel, stash, stockpile, store up

garnish v adorn, beautify, bedeck, deck, decorate, dress up, embellish, enhance, glamorize, grace, ornament, polish, trim

garret n attic

garrote v see: SUFFOCATE v

garrulous adj bombastic, chatty, diffuse, long-winded, loquacious, redundant, repetitious, superfluous, talkative, verbose, wordy

gas n exhaust, fume, smoke

gash n 1 crack, cut, opening, rent, slit, trench

n 2 cut, incision, nick, pierce, prick, puncture, slit, wound

v cut, incise, penetrate, pierce, punch, slash, slice, slit

gasher n digger, fang, molar, tooth, tush, tusk

gasoline n energy, fuel, petrol, propellant

gasp v exhale, inhale

gasping adj breathless, panting, winded

gastronome n bon vivant, gourmand, gourmet

gateway n doorway, exit, outlet, portal

gather v 1 collect, grow, harvest

v 2 amass, collect, heap, pile, rake, take in

v 3 analyze, conclude, construe, deduce, derive, draw, educe, glean, guess, infer, interpret, presume, surmise

v 4 accrue, accumulate, acquire, amass, assemble, collect, garner, grow, hoard, save, squirrel, stash, stockpile, store up

v 5 assume, believe, comprehend, conceive, estimate, expect, fathom, grasp, guess, imagine, infer, know, presume, suppose, surmise, suspect, think, trust, understand

v 6 assemble, associate, call, cluster, collect, concentrate, congregate, convene, flock, group, lump, marshal, mass, mingle, mobilize, muster, order, rally, rendezvous, round up, send for, summon

gathering n 1 confrontation, encounter, meeting

n 2 assemblage, assembly, caucus, conference, congregation, convention, council, crowd, group, meeting, rally, symposium

gauche adj 1 clumsy, indiscreet, insensitive, rude, tactless, thoughtless

adj 2 awkward, bumbling, clumsy, faltering, gawky, halting, hesitant, inept, lumbering, maladroit, ungainly, ungraceful

gaudy adj blatant, brazen, conspicuous, flagrant, flashy, garish, glaring, loud, ostentatious, showy, tacky, tasteless, tawdry, tinsel

gauge n 1 benchmark, criterion, measure, observation, rule, standard, yardstick

n 2 dial, disk, display, indicator, measure, meter, pointer, selector

v 1 indicate, measure, meter

v 2 calibrate, measure, range, rank, size

v 3 diagnose, estimate, forecast, predetermine, predict, project

gaunt adj 1 bare, barren, bleak, desolate, dismal, grim

adj 2 anemic, bloodless, haggard, lifeless, pale, pallid, passionless, spiritless, watery, weak

adj 3 angular, bony, emaciated, lanky, lean, meager, scraggly, scrawny, skinny, slender, thin

gawk v eye, eyeball, gape, gaze, goggle, observe, ogle, peer, stare, study

gawky adj see: AWKWARD adj 3

gay adj 1 bright, cheerful, cheery, content, ebullient, ecstatic, elated, exuberant, festive, glad, happy, jovial, joyful, joyous, merry, mirthful, pleased, radiant, rejoicing

adj 2 see: LIVELY adj 8

n bisexual, homosexual, lesbian

gaze v eye, eyeball, gape, gawk, goggle, observe, ogle, peer, stare, study

gazette n booklet, journal, magazine, monthly, periodical, publication, quarterly, weekly

gear n 1 action, apparatus, machinery, workings, works

n 2 equipment, fixtures, furnishings, materials, provisions, supplies

n 3 accoutrements, apparel, attire, clothes, clothing, dress, garments, togs

n 4 bait, hooks, lures, tackle

n 5 bag, baggage, case, equipment, grip, kit, luggage, pack, pouch, purse, sack, suitcase, valise, wallet

v 1 accouter, apparel, array, attire, clad, clothe, dress, outfit

v 2 appoint, arm, equip, fortify, furnish, man, outfit, rig, set up, supply, turn out

gel v see: THICKEN v

gelatinous adj coagulated

geld v castrate, debilitate, dismember, emasculate, enervate, unman, unnerve

gelding *n* colt, equine, filly, foal, horse, mare, mount, nag, pony, steed, yearling

gem *n* jewel, paragon, treasure

gendarmes *n* authorities, bobbies, constabulary, cops, highway patrol, military police, police, troopers

gender *n* sex

genealogy *n* ancestry, blood, bloodline, descent, family, heritage, line, lineage, origin, pedigree, stock, strain

general *adj* 1 common, generic, universal
adj 2 broad, global, planetary, universal, urban, widespread, worldwide
adj 3 abstract, conjectural, hypothetical, ideal, illustrative, speculative, symbolic, theoretical
adj 4 average, common, commonplace, daily, everyday, mundane, natural, normal, ordinary, plain, prevalent, regular, routine, typical, unexceptional, unremarkable, usual, workaday
adj 5 see: POPULAR *adj* 2

generally *adv* as a rule, customarily, frequently, mainly, most, mostly, most often, normally, ordinarily, primarily, principally, usually

generate *v* 1 cause, induce, muster, occasion, produce
v 2 bring about, conclude, end, result in, yield
v 3 activate, cause, elicit, prompt, provoke, spark, trigger
v 4 bear, beget, breed, come into, create, effect, engender, father, hatch, impregnate, make, mate, multiply, originate, parent, procreate, promulgate, propagate, reproduce, sire, spawn

generator *n* device, engine, machine, motor, turbine

generic *adj* common, universal

generosity *n* altruism, charity, goodness, goodwill, grace, humanity, kindness, mercy

generous *adj* 1 ample, decent, respectable, sizable, substantial
adj 2 attentive, considerate, kind, thoughtful, unselfish
adj 3 bounteous, bountiful, free, handsome, liberal, openhanded, unsparing
adj 4 benevolent, big, chivalrous, considerate, grandiose, lofty, magnanimous, noble
adj 5 abounding, abundant, ample, bounteous, bountiful, copious, enough, galore, liberal, overflowing, plentiful, plenty, prodigal, profuse, teeming
adj 6 altruistic, benevolent, bountiful, caring, charitable, Christian, compassionate, giving, good, humane, humanitarian, kind, lenient, merciful, philanthropic, tender
adj 7 giving, selfless, unselfish
adj 8 abundant, cornucopian, extravagant, exuberant, garish, lavish, lush, luxuriant, opulent, prodigal, profuse, rich, wasteful

genesis *n* 1 birth, conception, creation, formulation, procreation
n 2 birth, creation, fountain, origin, parent, root, source

genetic *adj* basic, congenital, inborn, indigenous, ingrained, inherent, inherited, innate, instinctive, intrinsic, natal, native, natural

genial *adj* 1 comfortable, desirable, lively, warm
adj 2 amiable, benign, kind, kindly, mild, nonmalignant
adj 3 affable, amiable, approachable, cordial, friendly, gentle, gracious, likable, lovable, peaceful, pleasant, serene

genital *adj* carnal, erogenous, erotic, procreative, reproductive, sexual

genitalia *n* genitals, glands, gonads, organs

genitals *n* genitalia, glands, gonads, organs

genius *n* 1 brain, Einstein, intellect, prodigy, wizard
n 2 bent, brains, brilliance, faculty, flair, gift, head, intelligence, knack, mind, nose, prowess, talent

genocide *n* bloodbath, bloodshed, butchery, carnage, extermination, holocaust, killing, massacre, pogrom, shambles, slaughter

genre *n* bracket, breed, cast, category, class, division, family, genus, group, grouping, ilk, kind, lot, mold, nature, order, persuasion, section, sector, set, sort, species, style, type, variety

gent *n* bachelor, chap, dude, fellow, gentleman, guy, male, man, mister, widower

genteel *adj* 1 civilized, cosmopolitan, cultivated, cultured, elegant, ingratiating, poised, polished, refined, smooth, sophisticated, suave, urbane, well-bred
adj 2 chivalrous, civil, civilized, cordial, courteous, courtly, decent, dignified, gallant, gentlemanly, gracious, mannerly, noble, polite, well-mannered
adj 3 affected, phony, pretentious

gentile *n* agnostic, atheist, heathen, heretic, infidel, pagan, unbeliever

gentility *n* culture

gentle *adj* 1 female, feminine, ladylike, nurturing, tender, womanly *adj 2* dainty, delicate, fine, nice, refined, subtle

adj 3 balmy, bland, faint, mild, pleasant, smooth, soft, weak

adj 4 affable, amiable, approachable, cordial, friendly, genial, gracious, likable, lovable, peaceful, pleasant, serene

adj 5 affectionate, compassionate, considerate, empathetic, empathic, humane, kind, kindhearted, responsive, softhearted, sympathetic, tender, warm, warmhearted

adj 6 see: CALM *adj 2*

gentleman *n* bachelor, chap, dude, fellow, gent, guy, male, man, mister, widower

gentlemanly *adj* see: POLITE *adj 2*

gentlewoman *n* dame, female, lady, matron, miss, mistress, spinster, widow, woman

gentry *n* aristocracy, blue blood, cream, elite, nobility, royalty, upper class

genuflect *v* bow, cringe, grovel, kneel, kowtow, prostrate, scrape

genuine *adj 1* candid, direct, earnest, forthright, frank, heartfelt, hearty, honest, no-holds-barred, open, real, sincere, straightforward, true, trustworthy, truthful, undesigning, unfeigned, unpretentious, wholehearted

adj 2 absolute, actual, authentic, bona fide, certain, definite, existent, factual, hard, inarguable, incontestable, incontrovertible, indisputable, indubitable, irrefutable, positive, real, sure, true, undeniable, undisputable, undoubtable, undoubted, unequivocal, unquestionable, veritable, viable

genuinely *adv* actually, exactly, precisely, really, sincerely, truly, verifiably, veritably, very

genus *n* see: CATEGORY *n*

germ *n* fungus, mold

germane *adj* see: APPLICABLE *adj*

germinal *adj* causal, causative, inducing, originative

germinate *v* bloom, blossom, bud, develop, ferment, flourish, flower, grow, sprout

gesture *n* action, battle, engagement, fray, movement, operation, proceeding

v beckon, motion, nod, signal

get *v 1* contact, reach

v 2 derive, gain, harvest, realize, reap

v 3 learn, master, pick up, read, realize, study, understand

v 4 acquire, annex, buy, capture, gain, have, land, obtain, pick up, procure, purchase, requisition, secure, solicit, win

v 5 access, accomplish, achieve, attain, derive, earn, fulfill, gain, merit, net, obtain, perform, profit, rack up, reach, realize, score, win

v 6 see: ARREST *v 2*

getaway *n* breakout, escape, flight, lam, slip

ghastly *adj 1* abnormal, depressing, dismal, funereal, gloomy, gruesome, macabre, morbid, sepulchral

adj 2 abhorrent, abominable, appalling, detestable, disgusting, dreadful, evil, frightful, hateful, horrible, horrid, loathsome, odious, repulsive, revolting, shocking

adj 3 appalling, awful, dire, dreadful, fearful, formidable, frightening, frightful, horrendous, horrible, offensive, ominous, portentous, scary, shocking, spooky, terrible, terrifying, unpleasant

adj 4 see: EXTRAVAGANT *adj 3*

adj 5 see: MONSTROUS *adj 2*

ghost *n* aberration, apparition, delusion, fantasy, figment, hallucination, illusion, image, mirage, phantasm, specter, vision

ghostly *adj* see: WEIRD *adj 1*

giant *adj* see: HUGE *adj 3*

gibber *n* babble, babbling, burble, chatter, murmur, prattle, rattle

gibe *n 1* crack, jeer, put-down, quip, shot, sneer, torment

n 2 affront, aspersion, attack, barb, caustic remark, crack, cut, denunciation, despite, dig, disparagement, disrespect, implication, indignity, innuendo, insult, invective, knock, reflection, sarcasm, scorn, slap, slight, slur, spike, tongue-lashing, verbal jab

v 1 cut, insult, remark, taunt

v 2 banter, deride, jeer, joke, knock, mock, needle, rib, ridicule, roast, tease

giddy *adj 1* bubbly, effervescent, sparkling

adj 2 confused, dizzy, faint, foggy, light-headed, reeling

adj 3 capricious, dizzy, flighty, frivolous, irresponsible, scatterbrained, silly

gift *n 1* award, bequest, endowment, grant, reward, scholarship

n 2 benevolence, boon, contribution, donation, favor, grant, largess, present

n 3 antique, heirloom, keepsake, memento, memorial, relic, remembrance, reminder, souvenir, token, trophy

n 4 bent, brains, brilliance, faculty, flair, genius, head, intelligence, knack, mind, nose, prowess, talent

n 5 see: REWARD *n 8*

gifted *adj 1* clever, handy, ingenious, inventive, talented, versatile *adj* 2 advanced, bright, intelligent, precocious, promising, talented

adj 3 see: QUALIFIED *adj* 4

gifts *n* booty, bounty, largess, plenty, plunder, presents, reward

gig *n* see: TRADE *n* 3

gigantic *adj* colossal, enormous, fantastic, Gargantuan, giant, Goliath, great, huge, immense, jumbo, leviathan, mammoth, massive, mighty, monstrous, monumental, overwhelming, phenomenal, prodigious, Promethean, stupendous, Titanic, towering, tremendous, unfathomed, untold, vast, walloping, whopping

giggle *v* chortle, chuckle, guffaw, laugh, roar, smile, snicker, snigger

gilt-edged *adj* see: SUPERB *adj* 4

gimmick *n* 1 apparatus, appliance, contraption, contrivance, device, doodad, doohickey, gadget, gizmo, implement, instrument, invention, machine, mechanism, thingumajig, tool, utensil, widget

n 2 antic, device, diversion, gambit, maneuver, mischief, move, plan, plot, ploy, prank, ruse, scheme, stratagem, strategy, tactic, trick, wile

gingerly *adj* calculating, careful, cautious, circumspect, considerate, discreet, guarded, heedful, judicious, provident, prudent, restrained, reticent, safe, shrewd, wary

gird *v* band, belt, bind, corset, fasten, girdle, lash, strap, tie

girder *n* beam, board, boom, log, plank, rafter, spar, support, timber

girdle *v* band, belt, bind, corset, fasten, gird, lash, strap, tie

girl *n* 1 child, coed, daughter, debutante, lass, miss, young lady, young woman

n 2 adolescent, child, juvenile, kid, minor, teenager, teeny-bopper, youngster, youth

n 3 damsel, maid, maiden, wench

girlfriend *n* date, lover

gist *n* 1 content, meaning, significance

n 2 center, core, kernel, keynote, theme

n 3 basis, body, bulk, core, essence, essentials, heart, import, mass, nucleus, object, staple, substance, volume

n 4 center, core, crux, essence, heart, life, marrow, nature, nucleus, pith, quick, quintessence, root, spirit, substance

give *n* excess, leeway, margin, play, slack, stretch

v 1 yield

v 2 endow, furnish, provide

v 3 bequeath, endow, remember, reward, tip

v 4 direct, implement, impose, inflict, strike

v 5 administer, apportion, deal, disburse, dispense, disperse, distribute, dole

v 6 administer, administrate, carry out, deliver, do, execute, present, render, submit

v 7 arrange, cater, deliver, dish out, dispense, feed, furnish, hand, nourish, nurture, organize, provide, purvey, serve, supply, sustain

v 8 accord, adduce, award, bequeath, bestow, concede, confer, contribute, deliver, devote, donate, endow, extend, fund, give away, grant, hand down, hand out, impart, offer, pose, present, proffer, provide, supply, tender, volunteer

v 9 see: ALLOCATE *v* 3

v 10 see: COMMUNICATE *v* 4

given *n* actuality, fact, specific, statistic, truth

adj see: OBVIOUS *adj* 3

giving *adj* 1 generous, selfless, unselfish

adj 2 altruistic, benevolent, bountiful, caring, charitable, Christian, compassionate, generous, good, humane, humanitarian, kind, lenient, merciful, philanthropic, tender

gizmo *n* see: DEVICE *n* 3

glacial *adj* 1 arctic, chilly, cold, cool, freezing, frigid, frosty, icy, nippy, wintry

adj 2 see: UNEMOTIONAL *adj* 2

glad *adj* 1 delighted, honored, pleased, proud

adj 2 accommodating, agreeing, amenable, disposed, eager, inclined, pleased, pliant, responsive, willing

adj 3 bright, cheerful, cheery, content, ebullient, ecstatic, elated, exuberant, festive, gay, happy, jovial, joyful, joyous, merry, mirthful, pleased, radiant, rejoicing

gladden *v* 1 bolster, buoy, cheer, comfort, console, solace, soothe, support, uplift, upraise

v 2 delight, encourage, enjoy, hearten, inspire, please

glamorize *v* adorn, beautify, bedeck, deck, decorate, dress up, embellish, enhance, garnish, grace, ornament, polish, trim

glamorous *adj* see: FASCINATING *adj* 2

glamour *n* affinity, allure, appeal, attraction, attractiveness, aura, beguilement, charisma, charm, enchantment, enticement, fascination, infatuation, magnetism, sex appeal, spell

glance *n* glimpse, look, peek

v 1 backfire, boomerang, bounce, brush,

graze, rebound, ricochet, skim, skip, touch

v 2 eye, glimpse, look, peek

gland *n* genitalia, genitals, gonad, organ

glare *v* 1 blare, blaze, burn, flame, flare, glow, ignite, redden

v 2 disdain, frown, gloom, glower, grimace, lower, pout, scowl, sulk

n light

glaring *adj* 1 arrogant, audacious, conspicuous, flagrant, obvious

adj 2 frowning

adj 3 coarse, crass, crude, flagrant, gross, obscene, rough, shocking, uncouth, uncultured, unrefined

adj 4 blatant, brazen, conspicuous, flagrant, flashy, garish, gaudy, loud, ostentatious, showy, tacky, tasteless, tawdry, tinsel

adj 5 annoying, bothersome, harassing, irksome, irritating, mean, onerous, painful, pesky, troublesome, ugly, unwelcome, vexatious, wicked

glass *n* 1 binoculars, eye, field glass, lens, magnifying glass, microscope, mirror, periscope, scope, spyglass, telescope

n 2 chalice, container, cup, dish, Dixie cup, goblet, mug, shot glass, stein, tumbler, vessel, wineglass

glaze *n* finish, gloss, polish, shine

v buff, burnish, furbish, glimmer, gloss, polish, renovate, rub, shine

gleam *v* 1 beam, burn, disperse, emit, glisten, radiate, shed, shine, transmit

v 2 excite, flash, glimmer, glint, glisten, glitter, scintillate, shimmer, shine, sparkle, twinkle

n flash, glimmer, glitter, shimmer, shine, sparkle, twinkle

glean *v* 1 deduce, determine, discern, learn

v 2 analyze, conclude, construe, deduce, derive, draw, educe, gather, guess, infer, interpret, presume, surmise

glee *n* amusement, elation, excitement, exhilaration, frivolity, gaiety, guffaws, happiness, hilarity, jocularity, jocundity, jollity, joviality, joy, laughter, levity, merriment, mirth

glib *adj* articulate, expressive, fluent, perspicuous

glide *v* 1 coast, drift, float, fly, sail, slide, soar

v 2 see: SNEAK *v* 2

glider *n* aircraft, airliner, airplane, jet, plane

glimmer *n* 1 beam, flicker, hint, light, ray, sliver, spark, trace

n 2 flash, gleam, glitter, shimmer, shine, sparkle, twinkle

n 3 breath, clue, dash, hint, insinuation, lick, shade, smell, smidgen, spice, sprinkling, suggestion, suspicion, tinge, tip, touch, trace, trifle, whiff, whisper, wisp

v 1 blink, flash, flicker, twinkle, wink

v 2 buff, burnish, furbish, glaze, gloss, polish, renovate, rub, shine

v 3 excite, flash, gleam, glint, glisten, glitter, scintillate, shimmer, shine, sparkle, twinkle

glimpse *n* glance, look, peek

v 1 behold, look, mind, see, sight, spot, watch, witness

v 2 eye, glance, look, peek

glint *v* excite, flash, gleam, glimmer, glisten, glitter, scintillate, shimmer, shine, sparkle, twinkle

glisten *v* 1 beam, burn, disperse, emit, gleam, radiate, shed, shine, transmit

v 2 excite, flash, gleam, glimmer, glint, glitter, scintillate, shimmer, shine, sparkle, twinkle

glistening *adj* see: BRIGHT *adj* 6

glitch *n* 1 bug, defect, error

n 2 blip, catch, gotcha, hangup, hitch, showstopper, slip, snag

glitter *v* excite, flash, gleam, glimmer, glint, glisten, scintillate, shimmer, shine, sparkle, twinkle

n flash, gleam, glimmer, shimmer, shine, sparkle, twinkle

gloat *v* boast, brag, crow, exult, flaunt, revel, show off, strut, vaunt

global *adj* 1 circular, globular, rotund, round, sphere-like, spherical

adj 2 broad, general, planetary, universal, urban, widespread, worldwide

globe *n* 1 ball, balloon, marble, orb, sphere

n 2 earth, home, the planet, world

globular *adj* circular, global, rotund, round, sphere-like, spherical

globule *n* bead, blob, bubble, drib, drop, droplet, lump, sphere

gloom *n* grief, misery, pessimism, woe

v disdain, frown, glare, glower, grimace, lower, pout, scowl, sulk

gloomy *adj* 1 cynical, depressed, glum, grim, negative, pessimistic

adj 2 abnormal, depressing, dismal, funereal, ghastly, gruesome, macabre, morbid, sepulchral

adj 3 dark, dim, dusky, lightless, murky, obscure, shadowy, somber, tenebrous, unilluminated

adj 4 brooding, crabby, dour, glum,

moody, morose, sour, sulky, sullen, surly, ugly

adj 5 black, bleak, blue, cheerless, dejected, depressed, desperate, despondent, discouraging, disheartening, distressing, down, forlorn, hopeless, joyless, melancholy, moody, mournful, oppressive, prostrate, sad, somber, sorry, unhappy

adj 6 dismal, doleful, lamentable, melancholy, mournful, plaintive, regretful, regrettable, rueful, sorrowful, woeful

glorify *v 1* dignify, distinguish, elevate, exalt, grace, honor

v 2 acclaim, applaud, celebrate, commend, eulogize, exalt, extol, hail, honor, laud, praise, resound, salute, toast, tout, worship

glorious *adj 1* blessed, golden, great, precious, splendid, superb

adj 2 admirable, beautiful, delightful, good, magnificent, peachy, splendid, terrific, wonderful

glory *n 1* admiration, adoration, praise, worship

n 2 brilliance, celebrity, distinction, excellence, fame, halo, honor, luster, note, popularity, prominence, renown, repute, splendor

gloss *n 1* finish, glaze, polish, shine

n 2 coating, glow, luster, patina, polish, radiance, sheen, shimmer, shine

v buff, burnish, furbish, glaze, glimmer, polish, renovate, rub, shine

glossary *n* dictionary, lexicon, list, synonym finder, synonym listing, thesaurus, vocabulary, Word Finder®

glossy *adj 1* shiny, sleek, smooth

adj 2 beaming, bright, brilliant, burnished, emitting, glistening, lucid, luminous, lustrous, polished, radiant, shining, shiny

glow *n 1* heat, temperature, warmth

n 2 blush, color, fever, flush, warmth

n 3 beam, grin, simper, smile, smirk

n 4 coating, gloss, luster, patina, polish, radiance, sheen, shimmer, shine

v 1 brighten, illuminate, irradiate, light up, radiate, spotlight

v 2 blare, blaze, burn, flame, flare, glare, ignite, redden

glower *v* disdain, frown, glare, gloom, grimace, lower, pout, scowl, sulk

glowing *adj 1* florid, flush, full-blooded, red, ruddy, sanguine

adj 2 ablaze, afire, aflame, aglow, alight, blazing, burning, conflagrant, fiery

adj 3 favorable, healthy, rosy

adj 4 incandescent, luminous, moonlit, sunlit

glue *v* affix, bind, bond, cement, fasten, fuse, join, lock, paste, seal, secure, stick, unite

n adhesive, cement, paste

gluey *adj* adhesive, cohesive, gummy, sticky, tacky

glum *adj 1* cynical, depressed, gloomy, grim, negative, pessimistic

adj 2 brooding, crabby, dour, gloomy, moody, morose, sour, sulky, sullen, surly, ugly

glut *n 1* abundance, great deal, lot, mess, much, ton

n 2 abundance, affluence, bounty, comfort, cornucopia, elegance, good fortune, grandeur, luxury, opulence, plenty, prosperity, success, wealth

n 3 deluge, excess, fat, overabundance, overflow, overkill, plethora, redundancy, surfeit, surplus

v 1 flood, overload, oversupply

v 2 choke, clog, congest, crowd, jam

v 3 fill, gorge, overeat, pig out, satiate, stuff, surfeit

glutton *n* hog, overdoer, overeater, pig, swine

gluttonous *adj* excessive, immoderate, inordinate, intemperate, overindulgent, prodigious, unbridled, undue, unrestrained, voracious

gluttony *n* overindulgence

gnarl *v 1* bark, growl, grumble, rumble, snarl

v 2 coil, corkscrew, curl, distort, entwine, spiral, twist, wind

gnash *v* grate, grind, grit

gnaw *v 1* corrode, deteriorate, eat, erode, oxidize, rust, wear

v 2 bite, chew, crunch, gulp, guzzle, munch, nibble, rend, wolf

go *n 1* attempt, chance, effort, fling, guess, heave, lob, pop, shot, slap, sling, stab, throw, toss, try, whirl

n 2 see: VIGOR *n 2*

v 1 extend, range, run, span, vary

v 2 act, function, perform, run, work

v 3 drop, leave, quit, resign, retire, terminate

v 4 arrive, flourish, make out, prosper, score, succeed, thrive

v 5 advance, begin again, continue, cycle, depart, get along, get on, leave, march, move, move forward, overture, part, proceed, progress, push on, recommence, reembark, restart, wend

v 6 abscond, bolt, defect, depart, exit, fail

back, flee, get away, give back, leave, move, pull away, pull out, push off, retreat, run along, secede, shove off, take off, vacate, withdraw

v 7 click, come off, go over, pan out, prove out, succeed

v 8 consume, deplete, exhaust, expend, finish, lessen, run through, spend, use up, waste, weaken

v 9 coast, cruise, explore, journey, migrate, proceed, sail, survey, tour, travel, trek, voyage

goad *v* 1 egg, encourage, exhort, incite, persuade, prick, prod, prompt, propel, spur, urge

v 2 see: ANNOY *v* 1

v 3 see: MOVE *v* 5

goal *n* 1 ambition, aspiration, desire, hope, will, wish

n 2 aim, cause, consideration, motive, purpose, reason

n 3 bonus, consideration, incentive, inducement, motivation, motive, reason, reward, stimulus

n 4 ambition, bent, design, intent, intention, meaning, objective, plan, purpose

n 5 aim, mission, motive, objective, purpose, reason, sake, target, task

goblet *n* chalice, container, cup, dish, Dixie cup, glass, mug, shot glass, stein, tumbler, vessel, wineglass

god *n* 1 deity, divinity, goddess, idol

n 2 favorite, hero, icon, idol

goddess *n* deity, divinity, god, idol

godlike *adj* absolute, chief, complete, consummate, dominant, leading, main, perfect, principal, pure, ranking, sheer, supreme, total, unsurpassed, utter, whole

godly *adj* 1 devout, holy, pious, prayerful, religious, reverent, sanctimonious

adj 2 blessed, celestial, consecrated, divine, hallowed, holy, pure, sacred, sanctified, spiritual

godsend *n* blessing, bonanza, boon, fortune, gain, luck, miracle, serendipity, stroke of luck, windfall

go-getter *n* achiever

goggle *v* eye, eyeball, gape, gawk, gaze, observe, ogle, peer, stare, study

going *adj* continuing, ongoing

n abandon, departure, desertion, evacuation, exit, leaving, pullback, pullout, removal, retreat, withdrawal

golden *adj* blessed, glorious, great, precious, splendid, superb

Goliath *adj* colossal, enormous, fantastic, Gargantuan, giant, gigantic, great, huge, immense, jumbo, leviathan, mammoth, massive, mighty, monstrous, monumental, overwhelming, phenomenal, prodigious, Promethean, stupendous, Titanic, towering, tremendous, unfathomed, untold, vast, walloping, whopping

gonad *n* genitalia, genitals, gland, organ

gone *adj* 1 absent, away, lacking, omitted, missing, truant, wanting

adj 2 forgotten, left behind, lost, once, past, suppressed, unremembered, vague

adj 3 bygone, dead, defunct, departed, extinct, forgotten, lost, vanished

gong *n* 1 alarm, bell, buzzer, chime, signal, siren

n 2 bang, bell ringer, bull's-eye, hit, slam, smash, strike

good *adj* 1 beneficial, helpful, salutary, useful

adj 2 agreeable, bright, fine, nice, pleasant, sunny

adj 3 admirable, beautiful, delightful, glorious, magnificent, peachy, splendid, terrific, wonderful

adj 4 brilliant, clever, dazzling, irrepressible, scintillating, smart, sparkling, sprightly, witty

adj 5 agreeable, congenial, favorable, grateful, gratifying, nice, pleasant, pleasing, pleasurable, welcome

adj 6 champion, excellent, fine, first-class, first-rate, foremost, grade A, leading, number one, prime, principal, prominent, quality, select, stellar, superb, superior, top, top-drawer, top-notch, tops

adj 7 see: ADEQUATE *adj* 2

adj 8 see: APPLICABLE *adj*

adj 9 see: BENEVOLENT *adj* 2

adj 10 see: GREAT *adj* 4

adj 11 see: INTACT *adj* 2

n account, advantage, behalf, benefit, betterment, gain, happiness, interest, prosperity, sake, welfare, well-being

goodbye *n* adieu, adios, aloha, *arrivederci*, *auf Wiedersehen*, au revoir, bon voyage, bye, cheerio, *ciao*, farewell, good day, *sayonara*, shalom, so long

good-humored *adj* amiable, complaisant, easy, good-natured, lenient, mild, obliging

good-looking *adj* attractive, becoming, comely, exquisite, fair, gorgeous, handsome, pleasing, radiant, stately

good-natured *adj* amiable, complaisant, easy, good-humored, lenient, mild, obliging

goodness *n* 1 caliber, excellence, merit, quality, stature, value, worth *n* 2 altruism, charity, generosity, good-will, grace, humanity, kindness, mercy

n 3 morality, principle, probity, purity, rectitude, righteousness, uprightness, virtue

goods *n* 1 inventory, provisions, reserve, stock, store, supply

n 2 articles, basics, commodities, essentials, inventory, line, materials, merchandise, products, properties, staples, stock, wares

n 3 assets, belongings, equity, estate, fortune, holdings, inheritance, money, ownership, possessions, property, prosperity, riches, treasure, wealth

n 4 see: MONEY *n* 4

gooey *adj* sticky, tacky, thick

goof *v* blow, blunder, botch, bungle, butcher, damage, err, foul up, hash, hurt, jeopardize, jumble, mess up, queer, ruin, screw up

n see: IDIOT *n*

goofing *adj* see: INADEQUATE *adj* 5

goofy *adj* see: ABSURD *adj* 2

gore *n* blood

v impale, lance, penetrate, pierce, puncture, spear, stab

gorge *n* 1 abyss, canyon, chasm, cleft, crack, depth, fissure, gulch, pass, ravine

n 2 see: CHANNEL *n* 3

v 1 fill, glut, overeat, pig out, satiate, stuff, surfeit

v 2 cram, crush, force, insert, jam, pack, press, ram, stuff

gorgeous *adj* 1 alluring, attractive, beautiful, breathtaking, comely, cute, fair, fine, foxy, lovely, luscious, magnificent, pretty, shapely, stunning

adj 2 attractive, becoming, comely, exquisite, fair, good-looking, handsome, pleasing, radiant, stately

gorilla *n* 1 hoodlum, hooligan, punk, roughneck, rowdy, ruffian, thug, tough

n 2 ape, monkey, primate, simian

gospel *n* 1 Bible, manual, scripture

n 2 announcement, aphorism, axiom, cliché, declaration, decree, dictum, edict, homily, maxim, moral, precept, pronouncement, rule, teaching, truism, truth, verity

gossip *n* 1 grapevine, hearsay, murmur, report, rumble, rumor, scuttlebutt, story, talk, word

n 2 chat, chatter, gab, rap, talk

n 3 busybody, interloper, intruder, kibitzer, meddler, snoop, yenta

v 1 cackle, chat, gab, talk, yak

v 2 blab, divulge, inform, reveal, tell

v 3 babble, blab, blurt, burble, chatter, murmur, prattle, talk, tattle

gotcha *n* blip, catch, glitch, hangup, hitch, showstopper, slip, snag

gouge *v* 1 burrow, dig, excavate, mine, scoop, shovel, unearth

v 2 coerce, exact, extort, shake down, squeeze, wrench, wrest, wring

n cut, groove, scoop

gourmand *n* bon vivant, epicure, gastronome, gourmet

gourmet *n* bon vivant, epicure, gastronome, gourmand

govern *v* 1 control, overrule, reign, rule

v 2 curb, discipline, limit, regulate, restrain, retard

v 3 abstain, avoid, constrain, curb, deny, forgo, hold back, refrain, resist, restrict, stop, tame

v 4 boss, command, control, direct, dominate, handle, influence, lead, manage, manipulate, order, supervise, sway

v 5 see: RESTRAIN *v* 5

governess *n* babysitter, nanny, nursemaid

government *n* 1 area, country, entity, nation, province, state

n 2 administration, dominion, monarchy, power, regime, reign, rule, sovereignty

n 3 administration, administrators, authorities, bureaucracy, civil service, commission, department, direction, forces, management, ministry, officials, power, powers, rule, rulers

governor *n* autocrat, chief, commander, despot, dictator, head, king, leader, lord, master, monarch, potentate, ruler

gown *n* 1 costume, dress, kilt, skirt

n 2 bathrobe, housecoat, negligee, nightgown, robe

grab *v* 1 abduct, carry away, kidnap, seize, shanghai, steal

v 2 catch, clasp, clutch, grapple, grasp, grip, hold, nab, nail, seize, snatch, take

v 3 see: ARREST *v* 2

v 4 see: TAKE *v* 4, 5

grabby *adj* acquisitive, avaricious, covetous, craving, desirous, eager, grasping, greedy, hungry, longing, miserly, selfish, wishful, yearning

grace *n* 1 attractiveness, charm, decorum, elegance, refinement

n 2 altruism, charity, generosity, goodness, goodwill, humanity, kindness, mercy

v 1 dignify, distinguish, elevate, exalt, honor

v 2 adorn, beautify, bedeck, deck, decorate, dress up, embellish, enhance, garnish, glamorize, ornament, polish, trim

graceful *adj* fluid

gracious *adj* 1 see: AMIABLE *adj* 3
adj 2 see: POLITE *adj* 2

grade *n* 1 average, marks, score
n 2 caliber, class, quality, rating
n 3 angle, gradient, incline, pitch, ramp, rise, slant, slope, tilt
n 4 class, degree, interval, level, mark, notch, position, rank, rate, step
n 5 see: STANDING *n* 1
v 1 calibrate, graduate, measure
v 2 evaluate, mark, rate, score
v 3 even, flatten, flush, lay, level, plane, smooth, tamp
v 4 align, arrange, array, assort, catalog, categorize, class, classify, cluster, compile, file, format, group, lay out, line up, list, order, organize, outline, pigeonhole, place, position, prioritize, program, rank, rate, sort, stack, tabulate

gradient *n* angle, grade, incline, pitch, ramp, rise, slant, slope, tilt

gradual *adj* continual, continuing, increasing, incremental, intensifying, measured, moderate, progressive, successive

graduate *v* 1 calibrate, measure
v 2 shade

graduation *n* certification, commencement, initiation, promotion

graft *n* con, crime, hustle, racket, rip-off, scam, scheme, sting, swindle
v bud, crossbreed, implant

grain *n* 1 atom, bead, dab, dash, dot, drop, iota, molecule, morsel, particle, pea, pellet, smidgen, speck, tad
n 2 crop, fruits, harvest, produce, yield

grainy *adj* coarse, granular, gritty, powdery, sandy

grand *adj* 1 dramatic, epic, heroic, legendary, noble, stirring, vivid
adj 2 elevated, exalted, excellent, great, heavenly, high, lofty, magnificent, prominent, sublime, superb
adj 3 big, extra-large, fat, great, huge, husky, immense, jumbo, large, obese, oversize, tremendous
adj 4 ample, big, considerable, enormous, extensive, hefty, huge, jumbo, large, major, sizable, spacious, vast
adj 5 august, baronial, exalted, grandiose, haughty, imperial, imposing, impressive, lofty, lordly, magisterial, magnificent, majestic, noble, portly, princely, regal, royal, stately
adj 6 see: LUXURIOUS *adj* 2

grandeur *n* see: WEALTH *n* 1

grandiose *adj* 1 benevolent, big, chivalrous, considerate, generous, lofty, magnanimous, noble
adj 2 ambitious, bombastic, flamboyant, garish, inflated, jaunty, lofty, ostentatious, pompous, portentous, pretentious, showy, splashy, splendid, utopian, visionary
adj 3 august, baronial, exalted, grand, haughty, imperial, imposing, impressive, lofty, lordly, magisterial, magnificent, majestic, noble, portly, princely, regal, royal, stately
adj 4 see: VAIN *adj* 5

grandparent *n* see: ANCESTOR *n*

grant *n* 1 exemption, patent, permission, right, safeguard
n 2 award, bequest, endowment, gift, reward, scholarship
n 3 benevolence, boon, contribution, donation, favor, gift, largess, present
v 1 acknowledge, admit, allow, avow, concede, confess, fess up, own, own up
v 2 accord, adduce, award, bequeath, bestow, concede, confer, contribute, deliver, devote, donate, endow, extend, fund, give, give away, hand down, hand out, impart, offer, pose, present, proffer, provide, supply, tender, volunteer

granular *adj* coarse, grainy, gritty, powdery, sandy

grapevine *n* gossip, hearsay, murmur, report, rumble, rumor, scuttlebutt, story, talk, word

graph *n* bar graph, chart, diagram, distribution, figure, flow chart, histogram, outline, pie chart, plot, table

graphic *adj* 1 clear, descriptive, effective, precise
adj 2 detailed, illustrative, photographic, pictorial, picturesque, visual, vivid
adj 3 colorful, expressive, impressive, intense, potent, powerful, striking, strong, unforgettable, vivid

grapple *n* clamp, clasp, clench, clinch, clutch, command, control, grasp, grip, hold, influence
v 1 combat, contend, duel, fight, spar, struggle, wrestle
v 2 catch, clasp, clutch, grab, grasp, grip, hold, nab, nail, seize, snatch, take

grasp *n* 1 cognition, comprehension, insight, perception, recognition, understanding
n 2 clamp, clasp, clench, clinch, clutch, command, control, grapple, grip, hold, influence
v 1 caress, clutch, hold

v 2 assume, believe, comprehend, conceive, estimate, expect, fathom, gather, guess, imagine, infer, know, presume, suppose, surmise, suspect, think, trust, understand

v 3 behold, catch, comprehend, conjure, descry, digest, discern, distinguish, espy, fathom, know, look at, notice, observe, perceive, realize, recognize, savvy, see, sight, take in, understand, view

v 4 see: CATCH *v* 3

grasping *adj* acquisitive, avaricious, covetous, craving, desirous, eager, grabby, greedy, hungry, longing, miserly, selfish, wishful, yearning

grass *n* 1 field, green, grounds, lawn, plot, yard

n 2 bush, hedge, plant, sapling, shrub, tree, vegetation, vine, weed

n 3 dope, drug, marijuana, narcotic, pot

grassland *n* field, lea, meadow, pasture, plain, prairie

grate *v* 1 gnash, grind, grit

v 2 file, grind, grit, rasp, sand

v 3 aggravate, anger, annoy, bother, bug, enrage, exasperate, frazzle, gall, hassle, incense, inflame, infuriate, irk, irritate, madden, miff, nettle, outrage, peeve, pester, pique, provoke, rile, upset, vex

grateful *adj* 1 appreciative, indebted, obligated, obliged, thankful

adj 2 agreeable, congenial, favorable, good, gratifying, nice, pleasant, pleasing, pleasurable, welcome

gratify *v* 1 appease, comfort, comply, content, delight, elate, please, relieve, satisfy, suit

v 2 accommodate, baby, cater, coddle, humor, indulge, overindulge, pamper, pander, placate, satisfy, spoil

gratifying *adj* 1 agreeable, pleasant, pleasing, satisfying

adj 2 beneficial, fulfilling, pleasing, rewarding, worthwhile

adj 3 agreeable, congenial, favorable, good, grateful, nice, pleasant, pleasing, pleasurable, welcome

grating *adj* 1 abrasive, aggravating, annoying, caustic, irritating

adj 2 acute, annoying, high, loud, piercing, piping, sharp, shrill

adj 3 caustic, guttural, harsh, hoarse, husky, rasping, raucous, rough, strident

gratis *adj* complimentary, free, gratuitous

gratitude *n* appreciation, recognition, thankfulness

gratuitous *adj* complimentary, free

gratuity *n* ante, award, bonus, booty, cash, commission, dividend, donation, fee, gift, largess, money, percentage, perk, perquisite, premium, prize, profit, purse, reward, sharing, stake, stipend, tip, winnings

grave *adj* 1 dignified, earnest, pensive, sedate, serious, sober, solemn, somber, staid, stoic, unemotional, unflinching

adj 2 acute, burning, critical, crucial, desperate, dire, heavy, important, major, momentous, ponderous, pressing, profound, serious, severe, solemn, somber, urgent, vital

n burial, catacomb, cenotaph, crypt, mausoleum, memorial, monument, pit, sepulcher, tomb, vault

gravel *n* boulder, detritus, fragments, pebble, rock, stone

gravity *n* concern, emphasis, import, importance, significance, stress, weight

gray *adj* 1 cheerless, cloudy, dim, dismal, drab, dull, overcast

adj 2 cloudy, dismal, foggy, hazy, misty, murky, overcast, steamy, vaporous, vapory

adj 3 aged, age-old, ancient, antique, elderly, grizzled, old, olden, senior, timeworn, venerable, vintage, worn

graze *v* 1 backfire, boomerang, bounce, brush, glance, rebound, ricochet, skim, skip, touch

v 2 browse

v 3 brush, scrape, scratch, shave, skim, touch

greasy *adj* oily, sleek, slick, slippery, smooth, unctuous

great *adj* 1 eminent, important, outstanding, superior

adj 2 blessed, glorious, golden, precious, splendid, superb

adj 3 excellent, extraordinary, impressive, noteworthy, outstanding, shining, smashing, superb, wonderful

adj 4 excellent, fabulous, fantastic, fine, good, marvelous, super, terrific, tremendous, wonderful

adj 5 big, extra-large, fat, grand, huge, husky, immense, large, jumbo, obese, oversize, tremendous

adj 6 central, chief, distinguished, dominant, famed, key, leading, main, major, number one, outstanding, predominant, preeminent, primary, prime, principal, prominent, star, successful, superior, top

adj 7 dynamite, excellent, extraordinary, out of sight, outstanding, phenomenal, premier, super, superb, superlative, tremendous, wonderful *adj* 8 colossal, enormous, fantastic, Gargantuan, giant, gigantic, Goliath, huge, immense, jumbo, leviathan, mammoth, massive, mighty, monstrous, monumental, overwhelming, phenomenal, prodigious, Promethean, stupendous, Titanic, towering, tremendous, unfathomed, untold, vast, walloping, whopping

adj 9 see: GRAND *adj* 2, 3

greater *adv* above, aloft, on top of, over, overhead, more, superior

adj best, biggest, finest, greatest, larger, largest, maximum, most, number one, prime, select, superior, top, top-notch

greatest *adj* best, biggest, finest, greater, larger, largest, maximum, most, number one, prime, select, superior, top, top-notch

greatly *adv* awfully, dreadfully, eminently, endlessly, exceedingly, exceptionally, extremely, highly, mightily, notably, quite, remarkably, terribly, thoroughly, very

greed *n* 1 envy, jealousy, rivalry

n 2 avarice, covetousness, craving, desire, selfishness, yearning

greedy *adj* 1 acquisitive, avaricious, covetous, craving, desirous, eager, grabby, grasping, hungry, longing, miserly, selfish, wishful, yearning

adj 2 see: CHEAP *adj* 3

green *adj* 1 chartreuse, emerald, jade, kelly

adj 2 immature, inexperienced, naive, new, novice, raw, unsophisticated, virgin

adj 3 adolescent, fresh, juvenile, immature, precocious, undeveloped, unfledged, unready, young, youthful

n 1 field, grass, grounds, lawn, plot, yard

n 2 common, park, plaza, square

greet *v* 1 encounter, interview, meet, receive, see, visit

v 2 address, call to, embrace, hail, meet, salute, summon, welcome

v 3 see: RECOGNIZE *v* 5

greeting *n* 1 hospitality, salutation, welcome

n 2 address, bow, honor, nod, recognition, salute

greetings *n* regards, respects, salutations, salvo

gregarious *adj* see: FRIENDLY *adj* 3

grief *n* 1 gloom, misery, pessimism, woe

n 2 distress, melancholy, sadness, sorrow, suffering

n 3 affliction, anguish, care, catastrophe, despair, disaster, dole, heartache, mishap, pain, regret, remorse, rue, sickness, sorrow, woe

grievance *n* 1 complaint, hardship, injury, injustice, wrong

n 2 beef, complaint, criticism, gripe, objection, protest

grieve *v* 1 brood, lament, languish, mourn, sorrow

v 2 ache, despair, hurt, pain, suffer

v 3 afflict, aggrieve, bother, burden, distress, hurt, injure, pain

v 4 complain, crab, criticize, gripe, grumble, mutter, nag, object, protest, whine

v 5 burden, deject, depress, dishearten, hurt, lament, weigh down, sadden, wound

v 6 bawl, bemoan, cry, groan, lament, moan, mourn, sigh, snivel, sob, wail, weep, whimper, whine

grievous *adj* 1 atrocious, calamitous, dreadful, heinous, severe

adj 2 arduous, burdensome, demanding, exacting, onerous, oppressive, taxing, tough, trying

grill *v* ask, cross-examine, examine, inquire, interrogate, investigate, probe, pump, query, question, quiz

n automat, cafe, cafeteria, canteen, diner, luncheonette, lunchroom, restaurant, tearoom

grim *adj* 1 bare, barren, bleak, desolate, dismal

adj 2 cynical, depressed, gloomy, glum, negative, pessimistic

adj 3 dour, firm, forbidding, sad, serious, severe, sour, stern, unpleasant

adj 4 awful, frightful, grisly, gruesome, hideous, lurid, repulsive, sensational, shocking, terrible, ugly, violent

grimace *n* expression, face, mouth, pout, scowl, smirk, sneer, visage

v 1 leer, mock, ogle, scorn, smirk, sneer

v 2 disdain, frown, glare, gloom, glower, lower, pout, scowl, sulk

grimy *adj* black, dark, dingy, dirty, filthy, foul, grubby, mucky, murky, polluted, seedy, shabby, sooty, squalid, stained, unclean, unlit, unwashed

grin *n* 1 beam, glow, simper, smile, smirk

n 2 chuckle, laugh, laughter, smile, snigger

v smile

grind *n* chore, drudgery, labor, slavery, sweat, tedium, toil, travail, work

v 1 gnash, grate, grit

v 2 crush, pound, powder, pulverize

v 3 edge, file, hone, polish, sharpen, whet

v 4 file, grate, grit, rasp, sand

grip *n* 1 clamp, clasp, clench, clinch,

clutch, command, control, grapple, grasp, hold, influence

n 2 bag, baggage, case, equipment, gear, kit, luggage, pack, pouch, purse, sack, suitcase, valise, wallet

v catch, clasp, clutch, grab, grapple, grasp, hold, nab, nail, seize, snatch, take

gripe n beef, complaint, criticism, grievance, objection, protest

v complain, crab, criticize, grieve, grumble, mutter, nag, object, protest, whine

grisly adj awful, frightful, grim, gruesome, hideous, lurid, repulsive, sensational, shocking, terrible, ugly, violent

grit v 1 grate, grind

v 2 file, grate, grind, rasp, sand

n see: PERSISTENCE n 3

gritty adj coarse, grainy, granular, powdery, sandy

grizzled adj 1 experienced, expert, hardened, mature, seasoned, trained, weathered

adj 2 see: OLD adj 2

grizzly adj see: MONSTROUS adj 2

groan n moan, sigh, sob, wail

v bawl, bemoan, cry, grieve, lament, moan, mourn, sigh, snivel, sob, wail, weep, whimper, whine

grog n alcohol, booze, drinks, liquor, moonshine, spirits, whiskey

grogginess n apathy, coma, doze, ennui, inertia, languor, lassitude, lethargy, nod, sleep, slumber, stupor

groggy adj 1 confused, daffy, daft, dazed, dizzy, punchy, stunned

adj 2 see: PREOCCUPIED adj 1

groom v 1 dress, equip, spiff up, spruce

v 2 coach, communicate, condition, convey, cultivate, develop, discipline, drill, edify, educate, enlighten, exercise, explain, imbue, impart, implant, improve, inculcate, indoctrinate, inform, infuse, inseminate, inspire, instill, instruct, perfect, practice, prepare, ready, school, teach, train, tutor

n bridegroom, hubby, husband, man, master, mate, mister, spouse

groove n 1 notch, opening, slot

n 2 connection, joining, joint, link, seam

n 3 canal, channel, conduit, crevice, curb, cut, ditch, duct, furrow, gorge, gully, gutter, passageway, ravine, rut, trench, trough

n 4 cut, gouge, scoop

n 5 dent, indentation, nick, notch

grope v 1 examine, feel, finger, fondle,

handle, manipulate, maul, palpate, paw, probe, touch

v 2 see: PROBE v 2, 5

v 3 see: STUMBLE v 5

gross adj 1 abhorrent, base, invidious, obnoxious, offensive, repellent, repugnant, revulsive

adj 2 all, all-out, complete, entire, full-blown, integral, integrated, outright, total, unlimited, whole

adj 3 coarse, crass, crude, flagrant, glaring, obscene, rough, shocking, uncouth, uncultured, unrefined

adj 4 bawdy, coarse, crude, dirty, erotic, filthy, foul, gamy, improper, indecent, lascivious, lewd, licentious, nasty, obscene, off-color, pornographic, profane, prurient, racy, rank, raunchy, ribald, risqué, scandalous, smutty, suggestive, tainted, uncouth, vulgar, x-rated

adj 5 see: FAT adj 1

n 1 aggregate, all, entirety, revenue, sales, sum, sum total, total, totality, whole

n 2 assets, cash, earnings, gain, haul, net, payback, proceeds, profits, receipts, return, revenue, take, yield

n 3 see: SALARY n

grossness n dirt, filth, indecency, obscenity, porn, pornography, ribaldry, smut, trash

grotesque adj 1 bizarre

adj 2 contorted, gruesome, hideous, ill-favored, ugly, uncomely, unsightly

grotto n burrow, cave, den, lair, recess, tunnel

grouch v brood, crab, moan, mope, pout, scowl, sulk

n bellyacher, crank, grump, sorehead, sourpuss

grouchy adj angry, cranky, cross, feisty, hot-tempered, irascible, ireful, peppery, quick-tempered, short-fused, sullen, testy, touchy

ground n 1 base, bottom, floor, minimum

n 2 base, basis, bedrock, footing, foundation, root

n 3 clay, dirt, dry land, dust, earth, land, loam, marl, soil, terra, terra firma

n 4 pavement, paving, sidewalk, walkway

n 5 floor, level, story, tier

adj fine, powdery, pulverized

v establish

groundless adj baseless, erroneous, fallacious, invalid, unfounded, unsubstantiated

grounds n 1 argument, justification, proof, reason, wherefore, why

n 2 field, grass, green, lawn, plot, yard

n 3 acreage, domain, estate, holdings, land, property, real estate

n 4 arguments, basis, cause, explanation, foundation, principle, rationale, reason, rudiments, source

group *adj* collective, common, organizational, public, social, societal

n 1 denomination, persuasion, sect

n 2 band, body, company, corps, outfit, party, troop, troupe

n 3 association, body, club, company, contingent, delegation, fellowship, fraternity, guild, organization, society, union

n 4 band, cabal, camp, circle, clan, clique, coterie, coven, cult, faction, family, gang, mob, ring, school, sect, tribe

n 5 assembly, association, band, bevy, brood, bunch, camp, clique, cluster, collection, covey, crew, flock, organization, party, team, unit

n 6 citizens, civilization, colony, community, crowd, culture, folks, human beings, individuals, laity, masses, men and women, neighbors, people, persons, populace, population, public, settlement, society, staff, tribe

n 7 see: ASSEMBLY *n* 3, 4

n 8 see: BUNCH *n* 2, 3

n 9 see: CATEGORY *n*

n 10 see: SYNDICATE *n*

v 1 advise, communicate, confer, consult, discuss, huddle, parley, powwow

v 2 assemble, associate, call, cluster, collect, concentrate, congregate, convene, flock, gather, lump, marshal, mass, mingle, mobilize, muster, order, rally, rendezvous, round up, send for, summon

v 3 align, arrange, array, assort, catalog, categorize, class, classify, cluster, compile, file, format, grade, lay out, line up, list, order, organize, outline, pigeonhole, place, position, prioritize, program, rank, rate, sort, stack, tabulate

groupie *n* admirer, buff, devotee, disciple, enthusiast, fan

grouping *n* 1 armada, assembly, boats, convoy, fleet, flotilla, navy, ships, squadron

n 2 bracket, breed, cast, category, class, division, family, genre, genus, group, ilk, kind, lot, mold, nature, order, persuasion, section, sector, set, sort, species, style, type, variety

n 3 arrangement, disposal, disposition, distribution, ordering, sequence

grove *n* shrubbery, thicket

grovel *v* 1 descend, sink, stoop, submit

v 2 bow, cringe, genuflect, kneel, kowtow, prostrate, scrape

v 3 cower, cringe, flinch, quail, recoil, shrink, sneak

v 4 appeal, ask, beg, beseech, conjure, crave, desire, entreat, implore, indicate, invoke, plead, pray, request, seek, solicit, supplicate, whine

groveling *adj* abject, common, humble, ingratiating, lowly, menial, obeisant, obsequious, servile, slavish, subservient

grow *v* 1 gather, harvest

v 2 cultivate, develop, encourage, foster, promote

v 3 age, develop, grow up, mature, mellow, progress, ripen

v 4 cultivate, farm, harvest, plant, plow, produce, raise, till

v 5 bloom, blossom, bud, develop, ferment, flourish, flower, germinate, sprout

v 6 advance, ascend, bloom, climb, develop, do well, excel, expand, flourish, flower, get ahead, improve, progress, prosper, rise, strive, survive, thrive

v 7 see: ACCUMULATE *v* 2

v 8 see: EXPAND *v* 4, 5

v 9 see: INCREASE *v* 8, 10

growl *v* 1 bark, gnarl, grumble, rumble, snarl

v 2 bark, bay, cry, howl, shout, snap, woof, yap, yelp

grown *adj* adult, full-grown, grown-up, mature, matured, ripened

grown-up *adj* adult, full-grown, grown, mature, matured, ripened

growth *n* 1 addition, advancement, advantage, betterment, enhancement, gain, improvement, plus

n 2 by-product, derivative, end product, end result, outgrowth, output, produce, product, production, productivity, result, yield

n 3 shoot, sprout

n 4 enlargement, increase, rise, swell

n 5 acceleration, achievement, advance, advancement, betterment, breakthrough, furtherance, headway, improvement, increment, pickup, proficiency, progress, promotion, strengthening, upgrade

grub *n* bread, breakfast, brunch, chow, cuisine, diet, dinner, dish, edibles, entree, fare, food, lunch, meals, nosh, nutrition, provisions, rations, snack, supper, victuals, vittles

v 1 rummage, search, uncover

v 2 dig, extract, uproot, weed

v 3 drudge, hustle, labor, slave, strain, strive, sweat, toil, work

grubby *adj* black, dark, dingy, dirty, filthy, foul, grimy, mucky, murky, polluted, seedy, shabby, sooty, squalid, stained, unclean, unlit, unwashed

grudge *n* chip, ill will, malevolence, malice, maliciousness, malignancy, resentment, spite

gruesome *adj* 1 contorted, grotesque, hideous, ill-favored, ugly, uncomely, unsightly

adj 2 abnormal, depressing, dismal, funereal, ghastly, gloomy, macabre, morbid, sepulchral

adj 3 awful, frightful, grim, grisly, hideous, lurid, repulsive, sensational, shocking, terrible, ugly, violent

gruff *adj* abrupt, bluff, blunt, brash, brusque, cheeky, crusty, curt, flip, flippant, harsh, impertinent, impudent, irritable, nasty, quick, rude, sarcastic, sassy, short, snippy, snotty, surly, testy, wisenheimer

grumble *v* 1 bark, gnarl, growl, rumble, snarl

v 2 complain, crab, criticize, grieve, gripe, mutter, nag, object, protest, whine

grump *n* bellyacher, crank, grouch, sorehead, sourpuss

guarantee *n* 1 commitment, obligation, pledge, promise

n 2 assurance, exemption, immunity, impunity, protection, release, safety, security

n 3 covenant, coverage, indemnity, insurance, pledge, policy, promise, warranty

n 4 assurance, bond, commitment, earnest, obligation, pawn, pledge, security, surety, token, warrant

v 1 assure, certify, contract, endorse, pledge, sanction, underwrite, vouch, warrant

v 2 advocate, back, champion, endorse, promote, sanction, side, support, uphold

v 3 advocate, affirm, assure, avouch, avow, commit, devote, pledge, promise, ratify, swear, vow

guaranteed *adj* see: EXACT *adj* 6

guarantor *n* see: ADVOCATE *n* 2

guard *n* 1 lookout, picket, sentinel, sentry, ward, warden, watch, watchman

n 2 airborne, army, battalion, brigade, cavalry, company, footmen, horsemen, infantry, legion, marines, militia, minutemen, paratroops, platoon, reserve, storm troopers

v 1 defend, oversee, patrol, police, protect, regulate, safeguard, watch

v 2 bulwark, cover, defend, fend, fortify, hide, protect, safeguard, screen, secure, shield

guarded *adj* 1 exempt, immune, protected, safe, secure

adj 2 calculating, careful, cautious, circumspect, considerate, discreet, gingerly, heedful, judicious, provident, prudent, restrained, reticent, safe, shrewd, wary

guardian *n* custodian, father, mother, parent, trustee

guess *n* 1 approximation, estimation, extrapolation, speculation

n 2 conclusion, deduction, inference, reasoning, summation

n 3 feeling, foreboding, hunch, instinct, intuition, premonition, sense, suspicion

n 4 assumption, conclusion, conjecture, discretion, estimate, judgment, notion, presumption, theorization

n 5 assumption, conjecture, deduction, explanation, hypothesis, inference, postulate, presumption, proposition, speculation, supposition, theory

n 6 attempt, chance, effort, fling, go, heave, lob, pop, shot, slap, sling, stab, throw, toss, try, whirl

v 1 assume, believe, comprehend, conceive, estimate, expect, fathom, gather, grasp, imagine, infer, know, presume, suppose, surmise, suspect, think, trust, understand

v 2 see: DEDUCE *v* 3

v 3 see: PREDICT *v* 2

guest *n* caller, company, visitor

guffaw *v* chortle, chuckle, giggle, laugh, roar, smile, snicker, snigger

guffaws *n* see: MERRIMENT

guide *n* 1 bodyguard, chaperon, companion, escort, retinue, scout

n 2 authority, expert, guru, leader, master, mentor, pundit, teacher, wise man

n 3 atlas, compendium, directory, guidebook, handbook, list, listing, manual, phone book, textbook, Yellow Pages

n 4 attendant, escort, usher

n 5 clue, cue, hint, indication, indicator, inkling, intimation, key, lead, mark, notion, pointer, sign, signal, tip, trace

v 1 accompany, direct, escort, lead, usher

v 2 administer, boss, command, direct, manage, oversee, regulate, steer, supervise

v 3 conduct, control, develop, direct, drive, lead, operate, pilot, route, shepherd, show, steer

guidebook *n* atlas, compendium, directory, guide, handbook, list, listing, manual, phone book, textbook, Yellow Pages

guideline n 1 benchmark, criterion, measure, test

n 2 flag, principle, rule, standard

n 3 direction, directive, instruction, outline, policy, rule

n 4 see: COMMAND n 3

guidelines n conduct, course, plan, policy, procedures, program, rules, scheme

guild n association, body, club, company, contingent, delegation, fellowship, fraternity, group, organization, society, union

guileful adj 1 astute, calculating, crafty, cunning, foxy, insidious, sharp, shrewd, sly, smart, subtle, tricky, wily, wise

adj 2 see: DECEITFUL adj 1

guileless adj artless, candid, frank, ingenuous, innocent, naive, natural, open, plain, simple, simple-hearted, unadorned, unaffected, unsophisticated, unstudied, untutored, unworldly

guilt n 1 penitence, regret, remorse, repentance, sorrow

n 2 accountability, blame, burden, culpability, fault, onus, responsibility, shame, stigma

guiltless adj blameless, commendable, exemplary, exonerated, innocent, irreproachable, pure, righteous, virtuous

guilty adj 1 ashamed, penitent, repentant

adj 2 blamable, condemned, convicted, responsible

adj 3 blameworthy, criminal, culpable, felonious, remiss, reprehensible

gulch n abyss, canyon, chasm, cleft, crack, depth, fissure, gorge, pass, ravine

gulf n arm, bay, cove, estuary, fiord, inlet, narrows, sound, strait

gullet n mouth, opening, orifice

gullible adj 1 credulous, ingenuous, trusting, trustworthy

adj 2 believing, credulous, easy, innocent, naive, susceptible, trustful

gully n canal, channel, conduit, crevice, curb, cut, ditch, duct, furrow, gorge, groove, gutter, passageway, ravine, rut, trench, trough

gulp v 1 bite, chew, crunch, gnaw, guzzle, munch, nibble, rend, wolf

v 2 bibulate, booze, consume, drink, guzzle, imbibe, nip, partake, polish off, put away, put down, sample, savor, sip, suck, swig, swill, taste

gummy adj adhesive, cohesive, gluey, sticky, tacky

gumption n 1 enterprise, initiative, resourcefulness, spirit, spunk, volition

n 2 common sense, faculty, good sense, horse sense, judgment, logic, sense, wisdom

gumptious adj businesslike, enterprising, entrepreneurial, up-and-coming

gun n 1 carbine, firearm, flintlock, musket, rifle, shotgun

n 2 automatic, firearm, handgun, heater, iron, luger, piece, pistol, revolver, rod

v rev, speed, throttle

guns n ammo, ammunition, armor, arms, equipment, machinery, munitions, ordnance, weapons

gurgle v flow, ooze, purl, spurt

guru n 1 authority, expert, guide, leader, master, mentor, pundit, teacher, wise man

n 2 chaplain, clergyman, cleric, father, minister, padre, parson, pastor, priest, rabbi, reverend

n 3 adviser, artist, authority, expert, master, official, pro, professional, specialist, veteran, virtuoso, wizard

gush n 1 rush, surge, swell, wave

n 2 change, current, drift, flow, flux, motion, movement, rush, stream, tide, transition

v 1 effuse, emote, emotionalize, slobber

v 2 flow, run, rush, stream

v 3 burst, discharge, erupt, explode, spew, spout

v 4 flood, flow, peak, pour, rise, roll, spill, stream, surge, swell

gushy adj emotional, flowery, melodramatic, sentimental

gust n 1 air, blow, breath, breeze, current, draft, puff, wind

n 2 blast, blizzard, blow, gale, hurricane, northeaster, snowstorm, squall, storm, tempest, typhoon, wind

gusto n 1 alacrity, ardor, delight, devotion, diligence, enjoyment, enthusiasm, excitement, fervor, fire, flame, gaiety, passion, relish, savor, thrill, zeal, zest

n 2 see: VIGOR n 2

gusty adj airy, breezy, brisk, drafty, lofty, open, windy

gut adj automatic, deep, innate, instinctive, intuitive, visceral

n abdomen, belly, midriff, paunch, stomach, tummy, tum-tum

v clean, disembowel, dress, eviscerate, fillet

gutless *adj* chicken, cowardly, fearful, spineless, timid, yellow

guts *n* 1 gore

n 2 beef, meat, substance

n 3 see: PERSISTENCE *n* 3

gutsy *adj* see: BRAVE *adj* 1

gutter *n* see: CHANNEL *n* 3

guttural *adj* caustic, grating, harsh, hoarse, husky, rasping, raucous, rough, strident

guy *n* bachelor, chap, dude, fellow, gent, gentleman, male, man, mister, widower

guzzle *v* 1 bite, chew, crunch, gnaw, gulp, munch, nibble, rend, wolf

v 2 see: DRINK *v* 2

gymnast *n* acrobat

gymnastics *n* athletics, calisthenics

gyp *n* see: CROOK *n* 2

v see: CHEAT *v* 1

gypsy *adj* see: WANDERING *adj*

n ballerina, choreographer, chorine, dancer, hoofer

gyrate *v* 1 circle, revolve, roll, rotate, spin, turn

v 2 pirouette, purl, reel, spin, swim, turn, twirl, whirl

gyration *n* alternation, circuit, circulation, revolution, rotation, round, sequence, spinning, succession, turn, whirl

H

habit *n* 1 mechanization, repetition, rote, routine

n 2 method, mores, procedure, routine, system

n 3 condition, impulse, reaction, reflex, response

n 4 abnormality, eccentricity, idiosyncrasy, oddity, peculiarity, quirk, trademark

n 5 custom, fashion, formality, manner, mores, observance, practice, routine, tradition, usage, use, way, wont

n 6 see: INCLINATION *n* 2

habitat *n* atmosphere, climate, conditions, environment, niche, perimeter, settings, surroundings

habits *n* culture, customs, mores, traditions

habitual *adj* 1 conventional, normal

adj 2 automated, automatic, mechanical, robotic, routine

adj 3 accepted, accustomed, chronic, common, constant, continual, customary, daily, everyday, familiar, frequent, inured, often, recurring, regular, routine, traditional, usual

hack *n* cab, jitney, rickshaw, taxi, taxicab

v ax, carve, chip, chop, cleave, cut, dis-

sect, fell, hew, mangle, mutilate, notch, pulverize, rend, saw, sever, slice, sliver, snip, split, sunder, whittle

hacker *n* techie

hackneyed *adj* banal, boring, clichéd, commonplace, corny, dull, musty, redundant, repetitious, repetitive, stale, tedious, threadbare, timeworn, tired, tiresome, trite, worn-out

hades *n* abyss, hell, inferno

haggard *adj* 1 anemic, bloodless, gaunt, lifeless, pale, pallid, passionless, spiritless, watery, weak

adj 2 see: WEARY *adj* 1

haggle *v* 1 argue, bargain, barter, dicker, negotiate, wrangle

v 2 see: QUARREL *v*

hail *n* 1 alarm, call, shout, signal, whoop, yell

n 2 cloudburst, deluge, downpour, drizzle, precipitation, rain, shower, sprinkle

v 1 announce, call, page, summon

v 2 address, call to, embrace, greet, meet, salute, summon, welcome

v 3 see: LAUD *v* 1, 2

v 4 see: RECOGNIZE *v* 5

hairdo *n* coiffure

hairless *adj* bald

hairsplitting *adj* captious, carping, censorious, critical, cutting, disparaging, faultfinding, nit-picking

hairy *adj* 1 forbidding, frightening, scary, spooky

adj 2 challenging, difficult, tricky

adj 3 furry, fuzzy, woolly

halftone *n* photo, photograph, picture, slide, snapshot

halfway *adj* 1 intermediate, mean, middle

adj 2 fragmentary, incomplete, partial, unfinished

adj 3 center, centermost, equidistant, median, mid, middle, middlemost, midmost

hall *n* 1 anteroom, approach, atrium, court, doorway, entrance hall, entry, foyer, hallway, lobby, portal, vestibule

n 2 assembly hall, auditorium, playhouse, theater

hallow *v* anoint, baptize, bless, consecrate, dedicate, devote, enshrine, exalt, purify, sanctify

hallowed *adj* blessed, celestial, consecrated, divine, godly, holy, pure, sacred, sanctified, spiritual

hallucinating *adj* delirious, deranged, fantasizing, frenzied, maniacal, raving

hallucination *n* 1 aberration, apparition, delusion, fantasy, figment, ghost, illusion, image, mirage, phantasm, specter, vision *n* 2 aberration, abnormality, craziness, delusion, dementia, derangement, distraction, eccentricity, fugue, insanity, irregularity, lunacy, madness, mania, psychosis, unbalance

hallway *n* anteroom, approach, atrium, court, doorway, entrance hall, entry, foyer, hall, lobby, portal, vestibule

halo *n* see: PROMINENCE *n*

halt *n* abeyance, cessation, impasse, moratorium, standstill, stay, stop, stopping, suspension

v 1 falter, hobble, limp

v 2 cancel, end, kill, stop

v 3 demur, hold up, interrupt, pause, rest, stop, suspend

v 4 arrest, block, check, freeze, impede, interrupt, stall, stay, stop

v 5 achieve, cease, complete, conclude, consummate, end, finish, perfect, terminate, wind up, wrap up

v 6 cripple, disable, disarm, encumber, freeze, handcuff, immobilize, incapacitate, paralyze, prostrate, stop, stun

v 7 abstain, cease, conclude, desist, discontinue, end, finish, forbear, freeze, knock off, quit, refrain, sever, stop, terminate

v 8 delay, falter, hesitate, pause, stagger, stall, vacillate, waver

v 9 bar, block, brake, choke, clog, dam, deter, detract, encumber, frustrate, hamper, hesitate, hinder, impair, impede, inhibit, jam, obstruct, prevent, repress, restrain, retard, slow, stay, stop, stop up, throttle

halting *adj* 1 diffident, faltering, hesitant, indecisive, reluctant, tentative, unsure, waffling, wavering

adj 2 see: AWKWARD *adj* 3

hamlet *n* borough, burgh, community, settlement, township, village

hammer *v* 1 see: BATTER *v*

v 2 see: STAMP *v* 2

hamper *v* 1 burden, check, encumber, hinder, impede, obstruct, restrain, restrict, retard

v 2 burden, encumber, load, oppress, overdo, overload, saddle, strain, tax

v 3 brake, confine, contain, control, curb, drag, govern, hem, hold back, impede, repress, restrain, retard

v 4 bind, clog, confine, curb, fetter, handcuff, hold, leash, limit, restrain, restrict, shackle, tie, tie up

v 5 abuse, blemish, damage, harm, hurt, impair, injure, mar, obstruct, ruin, sabotage, scuttle, spoil, tarnish, vandalize

v 6 aggravate, baffle, balk, bewilder, circumvent, confuse, dash, elude, foil, frustrate, impede, negate, nullify, perplex, thwart

v 7 see: HINDER *v* 3, 5

hand *n* 1 angle, aspect, facet, mien, opinion, perspective, phase, side, slant, view

n 2 aide, aide-de-camp, assistant, attendant, employee, helper, hired hand, laborer, servant, supporter, worker

n 3 aid, assistance, benefit, comfort, cure, help, lift, nurture, relief, remedy, succor, support

n 4 fingers, knuckles, palm

n 5 extremity, foot, hoof, paw

v arrange, cater, deliver, dish out, dispense, feed, furnish, give, nourish, nurture, organize, provide, purvey, serve, supply, sustain

handbill *n* brochure, circular, flier, handout, leaflet, pamphlet, sheet

handbook *n* atlas, compendium, directory, guide, guidebook, list, listing, manual, phone book, textbook, Yellow Pages

handcart *n* cart, pushcart, truck, wagon, wheelbarrow

handcrafted *adj* domestic, homemade, home-oriented, homespun

handcuff *n* bond, chain, fetter, iron, manacle, shackle, tie

v 1 bind, clog, confine, curb, fetter, hamper, hold, leash, limit, restrain, restrict, shackle, tie, tie up

v 2 see: INCAPACITATE *v*

handgun *n* automatic, firearm, gun, heater, iron, luger, piece, pistol, revolver, rod

handicap *n* affliction, calamity, disability, flaw, impairment, limitation

handle *n* alias, designation, moniker, name, nickname, title

v 1 behave, behave towards, manage, treat

v 2 dispense, maneuver, manipulate, ply, swing, wield

v 3 apply, bestow, employ, exercise, exploit, use, utilize

v 4 examine, feel, finger, fondle, grope, manipulate, maul, palpate, paw, probe, touch

v 5 boss, command, control, direct, dominate, govern, influence, lead, manage, manipulate, order, supervise, sway

handling *n* 1 touch

n 2 behavior, conduct, treatment

n 3 administration, care, charge, conduct, intendance, management, overseeing, running, supervision

handout *n* brochure, circular, flier, handbill, leaflet, pamphlet, sheet

handsome *adj* **1** bounteous, bountiful, free, generous, liberal, openhanded, unsparing

adj **2** attractive, becoming, comely, exquisite, fair, good-looking, gorgeous, pleasing, radiant, stately

handwriting *n* penmanship, script, writing

handy *adj* **1** adept, dexterous, mechanical, proficient, skilled

adj **2** clever, gifted, ingenious, inventive, talented, versatile

adj **3** adroit, apt, canny, clever, cunning, deft, ingenious, nimble, skilled, skillful, sly, wily

adj **4** accessible, available, close, convenient, feasible, functional, helpful, multipurpose, nearby, open, practical, public, reachable, ready, serviceable, suitable, unrestricted, usable, useful, utilitarian, well-suited, within reach, working

adj **5** see: APPLICABLE *adj*

hang *v* **1** dangle, suspend, swing

v **2** befoul, catch, ensnare, entangle

v **3** abolish, annihilate, assassinate, bump off, butcher, decimate, destroy, dispatch, execute, exterminate, hit, kill, knock off, liquidate, massacre, murder, put away, rub out, slaughter, slay, wipe out

hanger-on *n* barnacle, dependent, freeloader, leech, parasite, remora, sponge, vine

hangout *n* bar, barroom, cocktail lounge, den, dive, dump, gin mill, haunt, joint, lounge, pub, rathskeller, saloon, tavern, watering hole

hangup *n* **1** block, check, curb, inhibition, repression, restraint, reticence

n **2** blip, catch, glitch, gotcha, hitch, showstopper, slip, snag

hanker *v* ache, covet, crave, desire, hunger, itch, long, lust, need, pine, thirst, want, yearn

hankering *n* appetite, craving, desire, eroticism, hunger, itch, longing, lust, passion, urge, yearning, yen

haphazard *adj* **1** diverse, jumbled, mixed, promiscuous, random

adj **2** accidental, aimless, arbitrary, casual, chance, chaotic, hit-or-miss, indiscriminate, irregular, random, unaimed, uncontrolled, unplanned

hapless *adj* cursed, damned, doomed, hopeless, ill-fated, jinxed, luckless, unfortunate, unhappy, unlucky, untoward

happen *v* **1** occur

v **2** develop, emerge, ensue, follow, lead to, result

v **3** chance, discover, encounter, find, hit, luck, meet, stumble

v **4** appear, arise, befall, break, come, come about, develop, do, ensue, evolve, fall out, manifest, materialize, occur, pass, rise, take place, transpire, turn up

happening *n* circumstance, episode, event, incident, occasion, occurrence, scene, thing

happenstance *n* chance, coincidence, good fortune, luck, serendipity

happily *adv* favorably, fortunately, positively, successfully, well

happiness *n* **1** amusement, elation, excitement, exhilaration, frivolity, gaiety, glee, guffaws, hilarity, jocularity, jocundity, jollity, joviality, joy, laughter, levity, merriment, mirth

n **2** account, advantage, behalf, benefit, betterment, gain, good, interest, prosperity, sake, welfare, well-being

happy *adj* **1** auspicious, favorable, fortunate, lucky, providential, serendipitous

adj **2** aroused, ebullient, elated, euphoric, excited, exhilarated, intoxicated, joyful, sparked, stimulated, turned on

adj **3** see: MERRY *adj* **2**

harangue *n* admonishment, admonition, blast, chewing out, chiding, criticism, denunciation, diatribe, hassle, libel, outburst, rap, rebuke, reprimand, reproach, reproof, scolding, slander, tirade

harass *v* **1** alarm, attack, bully, club, coerce, frighten, intimidate, menace, strong-arm, terrorize, threaten

v **2** annoy, antagonize, argue, bother, bug, concern, distress, disturb, goad, hassle, inconvenience, irk, irritate, pain, perturb, strain, stress, taunt, trouble, try, upset, worry

v **3** see: ANNOY *v* **1, 3**

harassed *adj* anxious, careworn, distracted, distraught, distressed, frantic, tormented, troubled, upset, worried

harassing *adj* annoying, bothersome, glaring, irksome, irritating, mean, onerous, painful, pesky, troublesome, ugly, unwelcome, vexatious, wicked

harassment *n* fulmination, intimidation, threat, warning

harbinger *n* **1** envoy, foregoer, forerunner, herald, messenger, outrider, precursor, predictor, prophet

n **2** apprehension, foreboding, forewarning, intuition, omen, premonition, presage, sign, warning

v see: PREDICT *v* **2**

harbor *n* **1** asylum, cover, haven, oasis, port, preserve, protection, refuge, reserve, retreat, safety, sanctuary, seaport, security, shelter *n* 2 barrier, breaker, cape, head, jetty, neck, point, sea wall

v 1 ensconce, nestle, settle, shelter, snuggle

v 2 conceal, hide, house, keep, protect, safeguard, shelter, shield

hard *adv* 1 fast, firm, firmly, loyally, reliably, solidly, tight, tightly

adv 2 see: COMPLETELY *adv*

adj 1 firm, stiff, taut, tense, tight

adj 2 abusive, harsh, severe, stern, stiff, strict, tough, uncaring, unsympathetic

adj 3 compact, firm, hardened, rigid, secure, solid, sound, specific, stable, stiff, tight

adj 4 constant, determinate, firm, fixed, immutable, inflexible, invariable, ironclad, resolute, stable, unalterable, unchangeable, unmovable

adj 5 arduous, demanding, difficult, formidable, heavy, labored, laborious, rocky, rough, rugged, serious, severe, strenuous, tough, trying, uphill

adj 6 bitter, brutal, cruel, fierce, harsh, inclement, intemperate, pitiless, rigorous, rough, rugged, severe, stern, strong, unkind, violent

adj 7 absolute, actual, authentic, bona fide, certain, definite, existent, factual, genuine, inarguable, incontestable, incontrovertible, indisputable, indubitable, irrefutable, positive, real, sure, true, undeniable, undisputable, undoubtable, undoubted, unequivocal, unquestionable, veritable, viable

harden *v* 1 augment, buttress, fortify, intensify, invigorate, reinforce, strengthen

v 2 acclimate, season, toughen

v 3 clog, clot, coagulate, congeal, curdle, condense, dry, gel, intensify, jell, pack, set, solidify, thicken

v 4 bear up, bolster, brace, build up, buoy, buttress, carry, fortify, nourish, nurture, prop, reinforce, shore, strengthen, support, sustain, toughen, uphold

hardened *adj* 1 experienced, expert, grizzled, mature, seasoned, trained, weathered

adj 2 compact, firm, hard, rigid, secure, solid, sound, specific, stable, stiff, tight

adj 3 see: NASTY *adj* 7

hardheaded *adj* 1 bullheaded, closed-minded, deaf, firm, hard-line, inelastic, inflexible, intractable, intransigent, obstinate, perverse, pigheaded, refractory, resolute, rigid, stiff, stubborn, tough, unbending, uncompromising, unpliable, unpliant, unwieldy, unyielding, willful

adj 2 basic, businesslike, down-to-earth, efficient, practical, pragmatic, sensible

hardhearted *adj* see: NASTY *adj* 7

hard-line *adj* bullheaded, closed-minded, deaf, firm, hardheaded, inelastic, inflexible, intractable, intransigent, obstinate, perverse, pigheaded, refractory, resolute, rigid, stiff, stubborn, tough, unbending, uncompromising, unpliable, unpliant, unwieldy, unyielding, willful

hardly *adv* a tad, barely, just about, least, minimally, not much, not quite, scarce, scarcely

hardness *n* 1 adversity, difficulty, discipline, discomfort, rigor, severity, strictness, stringency, uneasiness

n 2 compactness, density, firmness, solidity, strength, tensile strength

hardship *n* 1 complaint, grievance, injury, injustice, wrong

n 2 adversity, affliction, blow, burden, calamity, difficulty, distress, mischance, misfortune, mishap, relapse, reversal, setback, suffering, tragedy, trouble

hard-working *adj* ambitious, assiduous, diligent, energetic, industrious, persevering, persistent, resolute, sedulous, zealous

hardy *adj* 1 fit, healthy, robust, rubicund, ruddy, sound, sturdy, well, wholesome

adj 2 coercive, compelling, dynamic, energetic, forceful, lusty, mighty, passionate, powerful, robust, strong, sturdy, vigorous

adj 3 aggressive, dominant, durable, firm, forceful, hearty, mighty, powerful, robust, rugged, stalwart, stout, strong, sturdy, tenacious, tough

harlot *n* 1 coquette, flirt, nymphomaniac, seductress, siren, tart, tease, temptress, vamp, wanton woman

n 2 call girl, hooker, hussy, prostitute, slut, streetwalker, tart, tramp, trollop, wanton woman, wench, whore

harm *n* 1 chaos, damage, destruction, devastation, disaster, disorder, havoc, hurt, injury, loss, mayhem, ruin, ruination

n 2 see: ILLNESS *n* 1

v 1 abuse, brutalize, exploit, ill-treat, injure, maltreat, mistreat, molest, persecute, victimize, wrong

v 2 abuse, blemish, damage, hamper, hurt, impair, injure, mar, obstruct, ruin, sabotage, scuttle, spoil, tarnish, vandalize

harmful *adj* 1 noxious, poisonous, toxic, unhealthy

adj 2 adverse, deleterious, detrimental, injurious, negative, unfavorable *adj* 3 adverse, bad, evil, ill, unfavorable, unlucky

adj 4 damaging, dangerous, deleterious, hurting, injurious, ruinous, unhealthy

adj 5 breakneck, critical, dangerous, hazardous, perilous, precarious, risky, serious, unsafe, venturesome

adj 6 see: SINISTER *adj* 2

harmless *adj* benign, innocent, innocuous, inoffensive, mild, naive, pure, unoffending, unoffensive, safe

harmonious *adj* 1 agreeable, compatible, concurrent, congruent, parallel

adj 2 agreeing, concerted, unanimous, uncontested, undivided, unified

adj 3 choral, euphonious, lyric, mellow, melodic, melodious, musical, orchestral, philharmonic, rhythmical, symphonic, tuneful, vocal

harmonize *v* 1 carol, chant, hum, lilt, sing, yodel

v 2 accommodate, adjust, attune, conform, coordinate, integrate, proportion, reconcile, reconciliate, tune

v 3 arrange, blend, combine, compound, concoct, integrate, make one, orchestrate, synthesize, unify

v 4 accord, agree, check, coalesce, coincide, comply with, concur, conform, consent, consist, correspond, fit in, jibe, square, suit, tally

harmony *n* 1 balance, symmetry, uniformity

n 2 accord, calm, peace, serenity, stillness, tranquillity

n 3 air, measure, medley, melody, music, strain, tune

n 4 accord, affinity, agreement, assent, concert, concord, congruence, cooperation, empathy, rapport, synergy, teamwork, unity

n 5 calmness, composure, equanimity, peacefulness, self-possession, serenity, tranquillity

harness *n* bond, boundary, bridle, check, constraint, control, curb, damper, leash, limit, rein, restraint, restriction

harpy *n* nag, shrew

harried *adj* burdened, encumbered, fraught, laden, loaded, pressured

harry *v* see: ANNOY *v* 3

harsh *adj* 1 abusive, hard, severe, stern, stiff, strict, tough, uncaring, unsympathetic

adj 2 caustic, grating, guttural, hoarse, husky, rasping, raucous, rough, strident

adj 3 bitter, brutal, cruel, fierce, hard, inclement, intemperate, pitiless, rigorous,

rough, rugged, severe, stern, strong, unkind, violent

adj 4 authoritarian, authoritative, autocratic, controlled, despotic, disciplined, firm, inflexible, ironhanded, restrictive, rigid, rigorous, ruthless, severe, solid, stern, strict, stringent, strong, tough, tyrannical

adj 5 see: BLUNT *adj* 1

harshly *adv* badly, imperfectly, improperly, inadequately, inappropriately, painfully, poorly, unsatisfactorily

harvest *v* 1 collect, gather, grow

v 2 derive, gain, get, realize, reap

v 3 cultivate, farm, grow, plant, plow, produce, raise, till

n 1 fruit, product, result, reward

n 2 crop, fruits, grain, produce, yield

hash *v* 1 chop

v 2 see: BLUNDER *v*

hassle *n* 1 annoyance, bother, conflict, contention, difference, discord, disharmony, dispute, dissension, dissent, dissidence, dissonance, disunity, division, inconvenience, mischief, nuisance, strife, trouble, variance

n 2 see: QUARREL *n* 2

n 3 see: REPRIMAND *n*

v 1 annoy, antagonize, argue, bother, bug, concern, distress, disturb, goad, harass, inconvenience, irk, irritate, pain, perturb, strain, stress, taunt, trouble, try, upset, worry

v 2 aggravate, anger, annoy, bother, bug, enrage, exasperate, frazzle, gall, grate, incense, inflame, infuriate, irk, irritate, madden, miff, nettle, outrage, peeve, pester, pique, provoke, rile, upset, vex

v 3 see: ANNOY *v* 1, 2, 3

v 4 see: QUARREL

haste *n* alacrity, dispatch, expedition, hastiness, hurry, hustle, precipitance, precipitation, quickness, rush, rustle, speed, swiftness

hasten *v* 1 dart, dash, scamper, scoot, scurry, sprint

v 2 accelerate, expedite, hurry, quicken, rush, shake up, speed, step up

v 3 barrel, bullet, expedite, fly, hurry, hustle, rocket, rush, speed, whisk, zip

hastily *adv* 1 expeditiously, fast, full-tilt, in a snap, lickety-split, promptly, pronto, quick, quickly, rapidly, right away, soon, speedily, swiftly, urgently

adv 2 abruptly, fast, immediately, instantaneously, instantly, quick, quickly, short, suddenly, swiftly

hastiness *n* alacrity, dispatch, expedition,

haste, hurry, hustle, precipitance, precipitation, quickness, rush, rustle, speed, swiftness

hasty *adj* 1 inconsiderate, indiscreet, reckless, tactless, thoughtless

adj 2 advanced, early, first, premature, previous, soon, too soon, untimely

adj 3 brief, crude, cursory, rough, shallow, sketchy, superficial, uncritical

adj 4 abrupt, headlong, hurried, impetuous, impulsive, precipitant, precipitate, quick, rapid, rash, reckless, rushing, sudden

adj 5 breakneck, expeditious, explosive, fast, fleet, impulsive, instant, lightning, mercurial, meteoric, precipitous, quick, rapid, spectacular, speedy, sudden, swift

hat *n* beret, cap, derby, helmet

hatch *v* 1 brew, concoct, construe, contrive, create, devise, engineer, fabricate, formulate, invent, make up, plot, scheme

v 2 see: BEGET *v*

hatchet *n* ax

hate *n* acrimony, animosity, antagonism, antipathy, aversion, bitterness, dislike, enmity, gall, hatred, hostility, ill will, malice, rancor, spite, venom, vindictiveness

v abhor, abominate, bristle, desecrate, despise, detest, disdain, dislike, loathe, reject, revile, scorn

hateful *adj* abhorrent, abominable, appalling, detestable, disgusting, dreadful, evil, frightful, ghastly, horrible, horrid, loathsome, odious, repulsive, revolting, shocking

hatred *n* acrimony, animosity, antagonism, antipathy, aversion, bitterness, dislike, enmity, gall, hate, hostility, ill will, malice, rancor, spite, venom, vindictiveness

haughtiness *n* 1 affectation

n 2 see: AUDACITY *n*

n 3 see: VANITY *n*

haughty *adj* 1 arrogant, condescending, patronizing, pretentious, snobbish

adj 2 arrogant, cocky, conceited, narcissistic, self-assured, smug, stuck-up, vain

adj 3 arrogant, cavalier, conceited, contemptuous, curt, dictatorial, disdainful, grandiose, huffy, insolent, lofty, lordly, moody, obtrusive, overbearing, patronizing, proud, scornful, snooty, stuck-up, supercilious, superior, vain

adj 4 see: AUTHORITATIVE *adj* 2

adj 5 see: GRAND *adj* 5

haul *n* 1 batch, catch, collection, heap, take

n 2 see: PROFITS *n*

v 1 carry, cart, drag, draw, lug, pull, tow, truck, tug

v 2 bear, carry, convey, crate, ferry, lift, lug, pack, shoulder, shuttle, tote, traffic, transport, truck

haunt *n* bar, barroom, cocktail lounge, den, dive, dump, gin mill, hangout, joint, lounge, pub, rathskeller, saloon, tavern, watering hole

v attend, frequent, hang around, hang out, obsess, patronize, resort to, visit

have *v* 1 bear, carry, possess

v 2 hold, keep, own, possess, retain

v 3 benefit, experience, partake, profit, touch, use

v 4 comprehend, comprise, contain, embody, embrace, encompass, include, incorporate, involve, take in

v 5 acquire, annex, buy, capture, gain, get, land, obtain, pick up, procure, purchase, requisition, secure, solicit, win

v 6 see: TOLERATE *v*

haven *n* asylum, cover, harbor, oasis, port, preserve, protection, refuge, reserve, retreat, safety, sanctuary, seaport, security, shelter

havoc *n* chaos, damage, destruction, devastation, disaster, disorder, harm, hurt, injury, loss, mayhem, ruin, ruination

hawk *v* deal, horse-trade, huckster, hustle, monger, peddle, push, sell, swap

hawser *n* cable, rigging, wire

hazard *n* 1 adventure, encounter, event, experience, ordeal, peril, risk

n 2 bet, chance, fortune, gamble, luck, risk, stake

n 3 danger, downside, exposure, jeopardy, liability, menace, peril, risk, threat

v attempt, bet, chance, dare, gamble, play, risk, speculate, stake, venture, wager

hazardous *adj* 1 breakneck, critical, dangerous, harmful, perilous, precarious, risky, serious, unsafe, venturesome

adj 2 see: DELICATE *adj* 7

haze *n* 1 cloud, fog, mist, steam, vapor

n 2 befuddlement, daze, fog, maze, muddledness, muddleheadedness

hazel *adj* beige, brown, chestnut, chocolate, mahogany, tan

hazy *adj* 1 ambiguous, bleary, confused, fuzzy, misty, mixed up, nebulous, unclear

adj 2 cloudy, dismal, foggy, gray, misty, murky, overcast, steamy, vaporous, vapory

head *adj* 1 chief, first, foremost, inaugural, initial, lead, leading, premier, prime

adj 2 see: FOREMOST *adj* 2, 3

n 1 brain, cerebrum, mind, wit

n 2 forefront, front, lead, pioneer, spearhead, vanguard

n 3 bow, crown, fore, front, prow, stem, top

n 4 boss, chief, foreman, overseer, owner, superior, supervisor

n 5 autocrat, chief, commander, despot, dictator, governor, king, leader, lord, master, monarch, potentate, ruler

n 6 bent, brains, brilliance, faculty, flair, genius, gift, intelligence, knack, mind, nose, prowess, talent

n 7 barrier, breaker, cape, harbor, jetty, neck, point, sea wall

n 8 bathroom, can, john, latrine, lavatory, loo, potty, powder room, toilet, water closet, wc

v 1 chair, lead, moderate, preside

v 2 arise, come from, derive, emanate, flow, issue, originate, spring, stem

heading *n* 1 bearings, course, direction, location, position

n 2 angle, bearing, position, setting

headline *n* 1 banner, placard, poster, sign

n 2 article, bulletin, byline, column, communication, dispatch, editorial, feature, item, newsletter, report, story, vignette

headlong *adj* abrupt, hasty, hurried, impetuous, impulsive, precipitant, precipitate, quick, rapid, rash, reckless, rushing, sudden

headstrong *adj* abrupt, audacious, desperate, rash, reckless

headway *n* 1 locomotion, motion, movement, progress

n 2 acceleration, achievement, advance, advancement, betterment, breakthrough, furtherance, growth, improvement, increment, pickup, proficiency, progress, promotion, strengthening, upgrade

heal *v* 1 adjust, correct, cure, fix, make well, mend, remedy, repair, restore

v 2 ameliorate, convalesce, gain, improve, loop up, mend, perk, rally, recover, recuperate, rehabilitate, revive

healer *n* diagnostician, doctor, intern, physician, resident, specialist, surgeon

healing *adj* curative, medical, medicinal, therapeutic

healthy *adj* 1 clean, hygienic, immaculate, sanitary, sterile

adj 2 fit, hardy, robust, rubicund, ruddy, sound, sturdy, well, wholesome

adj 3 refreshing

adj 4 favorable, glowing, rosy

heap *n* 1 batch, catch, collection, haul, take

n 2 bank, drift, hill, mass, mound, mountain, pile, stack, stockpile

n 3 fortune, loads, mint, scads

v 1 bank, drift, mound, pile, stack

v 2 amass, collect, gather, pile, rake, take in

v 3 fill, load, pack, place, stack, stuff

hear *v* ascertain, catch on, determine, discover, find out, learn, listen, uncover, unearth

hearing *n* assembly, clinic, congress, council, court, diet, forum, meeting, parliament, seminar, symposium

hearsay *n* gossip, grapevine, murmur, report, rumble, rumor, scuttlebutt, story, talk, word

heart *n* 1 axis, center, focal point, focus, hub, nerve center, target

n 2 boldness, bravery, courage, daring, fortitude, heroism, spirit, strength, valor

n 3 basis, body, bulk, core, essence, essentials, gist, import, mass, nucleus, object, staple, substance, volume

n 4 center, core, crux, essence, gist, life, marrow, nature, nucleus, pith, quick, quintessence, root, spirit, substance

n 5 see: LOVE *n* 2

n 6 see: PERSONALITY

heartache *n* 1 affliction, anguish, care, catastrophe, despair, disaster, dole, grief, mishap, pain, regret, remorse, rue, sickness, sorrow, woe

n 2 see: PAIN *n* 3

heartbreaking *adj* affecting, impressive, moving, poignant, sad, touching

hearten *v* 1 amplify, bolster, encourage, enhance, enhearten, increase, inspire, reassure, strengthen, support

v 2 delight, encourage, enjoy, gladden, inspire, please

heartfelt *adj* 1 abstruse, deep, esoteric, heavy, hermetic, insightful, mysterious, obscure, occult, penetrating, profound, recondite

adj 2 candid, direct, earnest, forthright, frank, genuine, hearty, honest, no-holds-barred, open, real, sincere, straightforward, true, trustworthy, truthful, undesigning, unfeigned, unpretentious, wholehearted

heartless *adj* austere, brutal, callous, cold-blooded, compassionless, cruel, ferocious, fierce, hardened, hardhearted, indifferent, inhuman, inhumane, malicious, mean, merciless, nasty, obdurate, pitiless, ruthless, savage, spiteful, stony, tough, uncaring, unemotional, unfeeling, unkind, unmerciful, unpitying, unrelenting, unsympathetic, vicious

hearty *adj* **1** concentrated, heavy-duty, lusty, potent, powerful, robust, stalwart, stout, strong, sturdy

adj **2** aggressive, dominant, durable, firm, forceful, hardy, mighty, powerful, robust, rugged, stalwart, stout, strong, sturdy, tenacious, tough

adj **3** candid, direct, earnest, forthright, frank, genuine, heartfelt, honest, no-holds-barred, open, real, sincere, straightforward, true, trustworthy, truthful, undesigning, unfeigned, unpretentious, wholehearted

heat *n* glow, temperature, warmth

v boil, overheat, parboil, seethe, simmer, stew

heated *adj* **1** hot, lukewarm, tepid, warm

adj **2** angry, ferocious, fierce, furious, intense, savage, severe, terrible, vehement, vicious, violent

adj **3** liquefied, melted, molten

heater *n* automatic, firearm, gun, handgun, iron, luger, piece, pistol, revolver, rod

heathen *n* agnostic, atheist, gentile, heretic, infidel, pagan, unbeliever

heave *n* attempt, chance, effort, fling, go, guess, lob, pop, shot, slap, sling, stab, throw, toss, try, whirl

v **1** elevate, hoist, lift, pick up, raise, take up

v **2** bob, pitch, rock, roll, sway, swing, toss

v **3** cast, flick, fling, flip, hurl, launch, pitch, propel, sling, throw, toss

heaven *n* **1** palace, utopia, Zion

n **2** bliss, delight, ecstasy, Eden, elation, enchantment, joy, nirvana, paradise, pleasure, rapture, rhapsody

heavenly *adj* **1** astral, celestial, stellar

adj **2** elevated, exalted, excellent, grand, great, high, lofty, magnificent, prominent, sublime, superb

adj **3** bodiless, celestial, disembodied, ethereal, incorporeal, insubstantial, intangible, metaphysical, nonmaterial, spiritual, unearthly, unreal, unsubstantial

adj **4** delightful, scrumptious

heavy *adj* **1** abundant, fattening, rich, sweet, thick

adj **2** brisk, intense, powerful, stiff, strong

adj **3** abstruse, deep, esoteric, heartfelt, hermetic, insightful, mysterious, obscure, occult, penetrating, profound, recondite

adj **4** chubby, chunky, corpulent, fat, fleshy, gross, hefty, meaty, obese, plump, portly, pudgy, rotund, stocky, stout, overweight

adj **5** arduous, demanding, difficult, formidable, hard, labored, laborious, rocky, rough, rugged, serious, severe, strenuous, tough, trying, uphill

adj **6** acute, burning, critical, crucial, desperate, dire, grave, important, major, momentous, ponderous, pressing, profound, serious, severe, solemn, somber, urgent, vital

heavy-duty *adj* see: ROBUST *adj* **2**

heavy-handed *adj* clumsy, ponderous, slow

heckle *v* aggravate, annoy, badger, bait, bedevil, beleaguer, bother, bug, harass, harry, hassle, hound, hurt, intimidate, jeer, nag, needle, persecute, pester, plague, provoke, ride, spite, taunt, tease, threaten, torment, worry

hectic *adj* chaotic, fervent, fervid, feverish, frenetic, frenzied, jittery

hedge *n* **1** barrier, border, boundary, buffer

n **2** bush, grass, plant, sapling, shrub, tree, vegetation, vine, weed

v **1** avoid, dodge, equivocate, evade, fence, shift, shuffle, sidestep

v **2** avoid, circumvent, deflect, detour, dodge, duck, evade, parry, shirk, sidestep, skirt, ward off

hedonistic *adj* carnal, delicious, enticing, erotic, luscious, lush, lusty, luxurious, pleasure-seeking, sensual, sensualistic, sensuous, sexual, voluptuous

heed *n* attention, awareness, care, carefulness, cognizance, concern, consciousness, consideration, intimacy, knowing, knowledge, mark, note, notice, observance, observation, perception, recognition, regard, remark, sense

v care, consider, listen, mind, review

heedful *adj* **1** advertent, alert, attentive, careful, conscientious, observant

adj **2** alert, careful, leery, prudent, suspicious, vigilant, wary, watchful

adj **3** careful, carping, cautious, conscientious, ethical, exacting, fussy, meticulous, painstaking, punctilious, scrupulous, unrelenting

adj **4** see: CAREFUL *adj* **3, 6, 7**

heedless *adj* **1** distracted, inattentive, unaware, unheeding, unnoticing, unobservant, unperceiving, unwatchful

adj **2** accidental, careless, caustic, inadvertent, inconsiderate, nonchalant, selfish, sharp, short, tactless, thoughtless, uncaring, unceremonious, ungracious, unheeding, unintended, unintentional, unreflective, unthinking

adj **3** thankless, unappreciative, unaware, ungrateful

adj **4** careless, defiant, delinquent, derelict, inattentive, lax, neglectful, negligent, reckless, sloppy

heel *n* bird, bum, cad, fink, jerk, rat, turkey
v cant, careen, incline, list, rear, roll, tilt

hefty *adj* **1** see: BIG *adj* 4
adj **2** see: FAT *adj* 1

heifer *n* bull, calf, cow, ox, steer

height *n* **1** altitude, elevation
n **2** see: APEX *n*

heighten *v* **1** accent, accentuate, amplify, concentrate, emphasize, feature, flag, focus, highlight, italicize, mark, punctuate, spotlight, stress, underline, underscore
v **2** amplify, append, augment, boost, build, enlarge, expand, extend, grow, increase, intensify, magnify, multiply, run up, snowball, supplement, upsurge, wax

heinous *adj* **1** atrocious, calamitous, dreadful, grievous, severe
adj **2** atrocious, awful, crying, desperate, disgraceful, ghastly, grizzly, monstrous, notorious, odious, offensive, outrageous, scandalous, shocking, tasteless, wicked

heir *n* child, descendant, offspring, progeny, scion

heirloom *n* antique, gift, keepsake, memento, memorial, relic, remembrance, reminder, souvenir, token, trophy

heist *v* appropriate, burglarize, defraud, embezzle, filch, lift, misappropriate, pilfer, pillage, pinch, plunder, pocket, purloin, rip off, rob, snake, snitch, steal, swindle, swipe, take, thieve
n holdup, robbery, theft

hell *n* abyss, hades, inferno

helmet *n* cap, beret, hat

help *n* **1** crew, employees, faculty, people, personnel, staff, workers
n **2** abatement, alleviation, comfort, correction, cure, relief, remedy, respite, solace, solution
n **3** aid, assistance, benefit, comfort, cure, hand, lift, nurture, relief, remedy, succor, support
v **1** attend, serve, wait
v **2** accommodate, convenience, favor, oblige, please, provide, serve
v **3** aid, baby, care for, nurse, nurture, pamper, succor
v **4** abet, advance, aid, ameliorate, amend, assist, avail, benefit, better, boost, cultivate, do for, ease, egg on, encourage, enhance, forward, foster, further, improve, nurture, prefer, promote, rev, serve, spur on, support

helper *n* **1** aide, aide-de-camp, assistant, attendant, employee, hand, hired hand, laborer, servant, supporter, worker
n **2** see: ADVOCATE *n* 2

helpful *adj* **1** beneficial, good, salutary, useful
adj **2** collective, cooperative, joint, participatory, unified, united
adj **3** constructive, favorable, fruitful, positive, productive, useful, worthwhile
adj **4** see: PRACTICAL *adj* 4

helpless *adj* **1** feeble, impotent, inept, powerless, weak
adj **2** defenseless, dependent, disarmed, exposed, powerless, susceptible, unprotected, vulnerable, weak
adj **3** botching, bungling, goofing, ill-adapted, ill-suited, ill-timed, improper, inadequate, inappropriate, incapable, incongruous, incorrect, ineligible, inept, malapropos, unable, unbecoming, unbefitting, unequipped, unfit, unqualified, unseemly, unskilled, unsuitable, unsuited

hem *v* **1** approach, border, bound, define, edge, limit, outline, skirt, verge
v **2** see: RESTRAIN *v* 5

hemp *n* cable, cord, fiber, lanyard, line, rope, strand, string, thread, twine, yarn

henceforth *adv* hereafter

henpeck *v* berate, carp, cavil, criticize, find fault, flay, fuss, nag, nit-pick, nudge, peck, quibble, scold

herald *n* **1** carrier, courier, delivery person, envoy, messenger, runner
n **2** envoy, foregoer, forerunner, harbinger, messenger, outrider, precursor, predictor, prophet
v see: PREDICT *v* 2

herb *n* flora, foliage, plant, vegetable

herculean *adj* arduous, formidable, heroic, superhuman, tremendous

herd *n* band, bunch, crew, crowd, drove, flock, following, gaggle, gang, huddle, mass, mob, pack, rabble, riffraff, swarm, team, throng
v crowd, jam, mob, press, push, swarm, teem, throng

hereafter *adv* henceforth

heresy *n* blasphemy, desecration, impiety, irreverence, sacrilege, violation

heretic *n* **1** agnostic, atheist, gentile, heathen, infidel, pagan, unbeliever
n **2** agitator, defector, dissident, iconoclast, insurgent, malcontent, maverick, misfit, nonconformist, rebel, renegade, traitor, troublemaker, turncoat

heretical *adj* blasphemous, disrespectful, irreverent, sacrilegious

heretofore *adv* before, earlier, first, formerly, hitherto, once, previously, prior to

heritage *n* 1 birthright, endowment, entitlement, estate, inheritance, legacy, patrimony

n 2 ancestry, blood, bloodline, descent, family, genealogy, line, lineage, origin, pedigree, stock, strain

hermetic *adj* 1 arcane, impenetrable, impervious, mysterious, mystic, obscure, puzzling, secret, unexaminable, unknown, unseen

adj 2 abstruse, deep, esoteric, heartfelt, heavy, insightful, mysterious, obscure, occult, penetrating, profound, recondite

hermit *n* abbé, abbot, ascetic, friar, monk, recluse

hero *n* 1 favorite, icon, idol

n 2 actor, actress, artist, entertainer, heroine, lead, movie star, performer, player, protagonist, star, thespian, tragedian

n 3 advocate, champion, conqueror, heroine, lead, leader, master, principal, protagonist, star, trailblazer, victor, winner

heroic *adj* 1 arduous, formidable, herculean, superhuman, tremendous

adj 2 dramatic, epic, grand, legendary, noble, stirring, vivid

adj 3 audacious, bold, brave, courageous, daring, dauntless, fearless, gallant, game, gutsy, intrepid, stalwart, unafraid, undaunted, valiant, valorous

heroine *n* 1 actor, actress, artist, entertainer, hero, lead, movie star, performer, player, protagonist, star, thespian, tragedian

n 2 advocate, champion, conqueror, hero, lead, leader, master, principal, protagonist, star, trailblazer, victor, winner

heroism *n* boldness, bravery, courage, daring, fortitude, heart, spirit, strength, valor

hesitant *adj* 1 diffident, faltering, halting, indecisive, reluctant, tentative, unsure, waffling, wavering

adj 2 awkward, bumbling, clumsy, faltering, gauche, gawky, halting, inept, lumbering, maladroit, ungainly, ungraceful

adj 3 afraid, averse, disinclined, indisposed, loath, opposed, recalcitrant, reluctant, shy, timid, uneager, unwilling

hesitate *v* 1 bumble, falter, flounder, fumble, get stuck, grope, stagger, stumble, waffle, waver

v 2 delay, falter, halt, pause, stagger, stall, vacillate, waver

v 3 bar, block, brake, choke, clog, dam, deter, detract, encumber, frustrate, halt,

hamper, hinder, impair, impede, inhibit, jam, obstruct, prevent, repress, restrain, retard, slow, stay, stop, stop up, throttle

hesitation *n* apprehension, distrust, doubt, fear, misbelief, mistrust, suspicion, wariness

hew *v* ax, carve, chip, chop, cleave, cut, dissect, fell, hack, mangle, mutilate, notch, pulverize, rend, saw, sever, slice, sliver, snip, split, sunder, whittle

heyday *n* reign

hidden *adj* 1 disguised

adj 2 additional, covert, secondary, secret, ulterior, undeclared

adj 3 enclosed, inner, innermost, interior, internal, private, secret

adj 4 alienated, alone, apart, detached, isolated, private, removed, secluded, separated, sequestered, severed

adj 5 clandestine, classified, concealed, confidential, covert, off the record, private, privileged, secret, sensitive, sub rosa

hide *v* 1 protect, screen, shade, shadow

v 2 conceal, harbor, house, keep, protect, safeguard, shelter, shield

v 3 bury, cache, cloister, conceal, cover, ditch, ensconce, plant, secrete, sequester, stash

v 4 camouflage, cloak, conceal, cover, darken, disguise, envelop, mask, occult, seclude, shield, shroud, veil

v 5 bulwark, cover, defend, fend, fortify, guard, protect, safeguard, screen, secure, shield

n coat, fur, jacket, pelt, skin, stole

hideous *adj* 1 homely, plain, repulsive, ugly, unattractive

adj 2 contorted, grotesque, gruesome, ill-favored, ugly, uncomely, unsightly

adj 3 awful, frightful, grim, grisly, gruesome, lurid, repulsive, sensational, shocking, terrible, ugly, violent

hierarchy *n* 1 progression

n 2 caste, class, degree, echelon, estate, level, position, rank, status

high *adj* 1 acute, annoying, grating, loud, piercing, piping, sharp, shrill

adj 2 costly, dear, excessive, exorbitant, expensive, overpriced, prohibitive, steep, stiff

adj 3 elevated, exalted, excellent, grand, great, heavenly, lofty, magnificent, prominent, sublime, superb

adj 4 aloft, elevated, lofty, overhead, soaring, tall

adj 5 bombed, crocked, doped up, drunk, drunken, inebriated, intoxicated, juiced, loaded, looped, messed up, plastered, polluted, sloshed, smashed, stoned, tight, tipsy, turned on, wasted, wired

n ecstasy, euphoria, rush

highbrow *adj* analytical, cerebral, intellectual, intelligent

n academician, egghead, intellectual, philosopher, pundit, researcher, sage, savant, scholar, thinker, wise man

highest *adj* see: FOREMOST *adj 3*

highhanded *adj* forceful, important, intense, maximum, powerful, utmost

highlight *n* 1 benchmark, landmark, milestone

n 2 attention, center, crux, feature, focus, key, spotlight

n 3 attribute, character, characteristic, feature, mark, peculiarity, property, quality, trait, virtue

v 1 examine, focus, spotlight, target

v 2 accent, accentuate, amplify, concentrate, emphasize, feature, flag, focus, heighten, italicize, mark, punctuate, spotlight, stress, underline, underscore

highlighting *n* accent, emphasis, importance, priority, significance, stress, weight

highly *adv* awfully, dreadfully, eminently, endlessly, exceedingly, exceptionally, extremely, greatly, mightily, notably, quite, remarkably, terribly, thoroughly, very

high-pressure *adj* aggressive, coercive, compelling, forceful, hard-sell, intensive, persuasive, pushy

high-strung *adj* antsy, edgy, excitable, fidgety, irritable, jittery, jumpy, moody, nervous, nervy, restless, shaky, skittish, temperamental

high-tech *adj* bright, contemporary, fresh, modern, modernistic, new, novel, recent, up-to-date

highway *n* access, approach, artery, avenue, boulevard, channel, drag, pass, path, promenade, road, roadway, route, strait, street, thoroughfare, trail, way

highwayman *n* see: CROOK *n* 2

hike *n* march, stroll, tramp, trek, walk

v 1 boost, increase, jack up, jump, put up, raise, up

v 2 see: WALK *v* 1

hilarious *adj* absurd, comic, comical, crazy, droll, farcical, foolish, funny, humorous, laughable, ludicrous, outrageous, ridiculous, silly

hilarity *n* amusement, elation, excitement, exhilaration, frivolity, gaiety, glee, guffaws, happiness, jocularity, jocundity, jollity, joviality, joy, laughter, levity, merriment, mirth

hill *n* 1 bank, drift, heap, mass, mound, mountain, pile, stack, stockpile

n 2 alp, mountaintop, peak, summit

n 3 bluff, cliff, incline, slant, slope, steep bank

n 4 foothill, hillock, hump, knoll, mound, mount, raise, rise, swelling

hillock *n* foothill, hill, hump, knoll, mound, mount, raise, rise, swelling

hinder *v* 1 collide, conflict, impinge, interfere, obstruct

v 2 block, catch, cut off, detain, intercept, obstruct, stop

v 3 burden, check, encumber, hamper, impede, obstruct, restrain, restrict, retard

v 4 avert, bar, deter, eliminate, foil, forestall, hold off, inhibit, preclude, prevent, stave off, thwart, turn back, ward off

v 5 bar, block, brake, choke, clog, dam, deter, detract, encumber, frustrate, halt, hamper, hesitate, impair, impede, inhibit, jam, obstruct, prevent, repress, restrain, retard, slow, stay, stop, stop up, throttle

hindmost *adj* extreme, farthest, furthermost, furthest, most distant, most remote, outermost, utmost

hindquarters *n* ass, backside, base, behind, bottom, bucket, buns, butt, buttocks, derrière, end, fanny, posterior, rump, seat, stub, stump, tip, tush

hindrance *n* challenge, demur, difficulty, hurdle, objection, obstacle, problem, protest, question, snag

hint *n* 1 beam, flicker, glimmer, light, ray, sliver, spark, trace

n 2 allusion, connotation, implication, innuendo, insinuation, notation, reference, suggestion

n 3 clue, cue, guide, indication, indicator, inkling, intimation, key, lead, mark, notion, pointer, sign, signal, tip, trace

n 4 breath, clue, dash, glimmer, insinuation, lick, shade, smell, smidgen, spice, sprinkling, suggestion, suspicion, tinge, tip, touch, trace, trifle, whiff, whisper, wisp

v 1 divulge, leak, reveal

v 2 allude, bring up, point out, recommend, refer

v 3 convey, express, impart, imply, indicate, purport, say, suggest

v 4 connote, implant, imply, infer, insinuate, lead, offer, put forth, seed

v 5 angle, connive, fish

hinterland *n* frontier, outback, outland, threshold

hip *adj* chic, current, fashionable, in, smart, stylish, trendy, vogue

hippodrome *n* amphitheater, arena, bowl, coliseum, dome, scene, stadium

hire *v* 1 employ, engage, put on, recruit, retain, take on
v 2 charter, franchise, lease, let, permit, rent, sublet

hiring *n* employment, engagement, engaging, recruitment

hiss *v* bubble, crackle, sizzle, spit, sputter

histogram *n* bar graph, chart, diagram, distribution, figure, flowchart, graph, outline, pie chart, plot, table

history *n* career, diary, events, experience, performance, record, résumé, track record, vita

hit *n* 1 bang, blow, box, bump, chop, clap, conk, crack, crash, cuff, impact, jar, jolt, knock, lick, punch, rap, slap, slug, smack, smash, swat, swipe, tap, wallop, whack
n 2 bang, bell ringer, bull's-eye, gong, slam, smash, strike
v 1 bang, bump, collide, crash, smash
v 2 bang, beat, bludgeon, clobber, club, pound, strike, whack
v 3 chance, discover, encounter, find, happen, luck, meet, stumble
v 4 bat, clout, nail, pop, smite, sock, strike, swat, whack
v 5 belt
v 6 execute, kill, shoot, wound
v 7 bang, blow, bump, cuff, knock, punch, strike
v 8 abolish, annihilate, assassinate, bump off, butcher, decimate, destroy, dispatch, execute, exterminate, hang, kill, knock off, liquidate, massacre, murder, put away, rub out, slaughter, slay, wipe out

hitch *n* 1 blip, catch, glitch, gotcha, hang-up, showstopper, slip, snag
n 2 blockage, bottleneck, catch, flaw, impediment, jam, obstacle, obstruction, snag
v 1 attach, bind, bond, cord, fasten, join, link, marry, tether, tie, tie up
v 2 clump, fasten, join, knot, lace, lash, link, loop, rope, secure, tie, unite

hitherto *adv* before, earlier, first, formerly, heretofore, once, previously, prior to

hives *n* allergy, hay fever, rash, reaction, spots

hoard *n* backlog, cache, holdings, inventory, nest egg, pile, reserve, reservoir, stash, stock, stockpile, store, supply
v 1 accumulate, bank, deposit, save, squirrel away, stockpile, store

v 2 bank, lay aside, lay away, lay by, lay in, lay up, put by, salt away, save, spare
v 3 accrue, accumulate, acquire, amass, assemble, collect, garner, gather, grow, save, squirrel, stash, stockpile, store up

hoarse *adj* caustic, grating, guttural, harsh, husky, rasping, raucous, rough, strident

hoax *n* 1 cheating, deceit, deception, dishonesty, fraud, lie, sham, subterfuge, trickery
n 2 bastard, deception, fake, fraud, put-on, sham
v bamboozle, beat, beguile, bilk, burn, cajole, cheat, chicane, chisel, con, cross, deceive, defraud, dupe, embezzle, fleece, flimflam, fob, foist, fool, gyp, hoodwink, hustle, inveigle, screw, shaft, sham, swindle, trick, victimize

hobble *v* falter, halt, limp

hobby *n* 1 bag, field, interest, job, specialty
n 2 avocation, distraction, diversion, moonlighting, pastime, sideline
n 3 amusement, distraction, diversion, enjoyment, entertainment, frolic, fun, game, pastime, play, recreation, sport

hobbyist *n* 1 amateur, beginner, dabbler, dilettante, layman, neophyte, nonprofessional, novice, part-timer
n 2 bug, crusader, enthusiast, fanatic, fiend, freak, maniac, monomaniac, nut, radical, zealot

hobo *n* beggar, bum, derelict, drifter, loafer, mendicant, panhandler, pauper, tramp, vagabond, vagrant

hock *v* borrow, mortgage, pawn

hodgepodge *n* assortment, jumble, medley, mixture

hog *n* glutton, overdoer, overeater, pig, swine

hoist *v* elevate, heave, lift, pick up, raise, take up

hold *n* 1 duration, interval, length, occupancy, tenure, term, time
n 2 clamp, clasp, clench, clinch, clutch, command, control, grapple, grasp, grip, influence
v 1 accommodate
v 2 caress, clutch, embrace, grasp
v 3 have, keep, own, possess, retain
v 4 adhere, bond, cleave, cling, cohere, join, stick
v 5 clasp, clinch, cuddle, embrace, enfold, hug, press, squeeze
v 6 detain, hold back, keep, keep back, keep out, reserve, retain, set aside, withhold

v 7 catch, clasp, clutch, grab, grapple, grasp, grip, nab, nail, seize, snatch, take

v 8 see: BIND *v* 7

v 9 see: CARESS *v* 1, 2

v 10 see: DELAY *v* 4

holder *n* binder, capsule, case, casing, cover, envelope, sheath, skin, wrapper

holdings *n* 1 bonds, investments, securities, stocks

n 2 acreage, domain, estate, grounds, land, property, real estate

n 3 see: BELONGINGS *n* 1

n 4 see: STOCKPILE *n* 2

holdup *n* 1 break, delay, distraction, disturbance, diversion, interference, interruption, pause

n 2 robbery, theft

hole *n* 1 crack, leak, opening, puncture

n 2 blank, cavity, crack, depression, emptiness, gap, hollow, nook, opening, space, void

holiday *n* 1 day off, furlough, leave, respite, sabbatical, time off, vacation

n 2 celebration, ceremony, commemoration, festival, festivity, fiesta, gala, observance, party, revelry

holler *n* bark, bellow, blare, roar, scream, shout, shriek, thunder, yell

v see: SCREAM *v*

hollow *adj* 1 empty, idle, insincere, meaningless, shallow, vain

adj 2 cavernous, echo filled, gaping, reverberant, spacious, vast

adj 3 nominal, perfunctory, professed, representative, small, symbolic, token

adj 4 sunken

n 1 blank, cavity, crack, depression, emptiness, gap, hole, nook, opening, space, void

n 2 basin

v bang, dent, dimple, indent

holocaust *n* bloodbath, bloodshed, butchery, carnage, extermination, genocide, killing, massacre, pogrom, shambles, slaughter

holy *adj* 1 devout, godly, pious, prayerful, religious, reverent, sanctimonious

adj 2 blessed, celestial, consecrated, divine, godly, hallowed, pure, sacred, sanctified, spiritual

homage *n* deference, devotion, esteem, honor, just due, regard, respect, reverence

home *n* 1 address, apartment, condo, condominium, domicile, dwelling, flat, house, location, pad, place, property, residence, site

n 2 earth, globe, the planet, world

n 3 country, fatherland, homeland, land, motherland, soil

n 4 abode, castle, domicile, dwelling, estate, house, mansion, palace, residence

homeland *n* country, fatherland, home, land, motherland, soil

homely *adj* 1 hideous, plain, repulsive, ugly, unattractive

adj 2 discreet, dry, modest, plain, simple, unadorned, undecorated, unembellished, unembroidered, ungarnished, unpretentious

adj 3 plain, unalluring, unattractive, unbeauteous, uncomely, unpretty

homemade *adj* domestic, handcrafted, home-oriented, homespun

home-oriented *adj* domestic, handcrafted, homemade, homespun

homespun *adj* domestic, handcrafted, homemade, home-oriented

homey *adj* comfortable, comfy, contented, cozy, cushy, secure, snug, soft, warm

homicide *n* assassination, foul play, killing, manslaughter, murder

homily *n* 1 assignment, diatribe, discourse, exercise, lecture, lesson, preaching, sermon

n 2 see: CLICHÉ *n* 3

homogeneous *adj* consistent, plain, pure, straight, unadulterated, undiluted, unmixed

homosexual *n* bisexual, gay, lesbian

hone *v* edge, file, grind, polish, sharpen, whet

honed *adj* keen, pointed, razor sharp, sharp, unblunted, whetted

honest *adj* 1 factual, trustworthy, truthful, veracious

adj 2 clean, equal, equitable, even, fair, just, sportsmanlike, straight, upright

adj 3 aboveboard, candid, equitable, fair, forthright, legitimate, plain-dealing, straight, straightforward, trustworthy, upright

adj 4 conscientious, ethical, honorable, moral, noble, principled, proper, respectable, right, righteous, scrupulous, sound, true, trustworthy, upright, virtuous

adj 5 candid, direct, earnest, forthright, frank, genuine, heartfelt, hearty, no-holds-barred, open, real, sincere, straightforward, true, trustworthy, truthful, undesigning, unfeigned, unpretentious, wholehearted

honesty *n* 1 candor, frankness, sincerity, truthfulness

n 2 honor, integrity, principle, trustworthiness, virtue

n 3 candor, integrity, truth, truthfulness, veracity

honor *n* 1 award, medal, prize, trophy

n 2 honesty, integrity, principle, trustworthiness, virtue

n 3 address, bow, greeting, nod, recognition, salute

n 4 brilliance, celebrity, distinction, excellence, fame, glory, halo, luster, note, popularity, prominence, renown, repute, splendor

n 5 accolade, award, commendation, credit, decoration, distinction, kudos, laurels, medal, note, praise, recognition, reputation, reward, tribute

n 6 deference, devotion, esteem, homage, just due, regard, respect, reverence

v 1 attribute, credit, recognize, reward

v 2 dignify, distinguish, elevate, exalt, glorify, grace

v 3 admire, adore, appreciate, cherish, consider, covet, esteem, idolize, love, prize, regard, respect, treasure, value

v 4 acclaim, applaud, celebrate, commend, eulogize, exalt, extol, glorify, hail, laud, praise, resound, salute, toast, tout, worship

honorable *adj* 1 deserving, estimable, excellent, noble, precious, sterling, valuable, worthy

adj 2 accountable, answerable, dependable, honored, liable, reliable, reputable, respected, responsible, secure, solid, trusted, trustworthy, trusty, upstanding

adj 3 conscientious, ethical, honest, moral, noble, principled, proper, respectable, right, righteous, scrupulous, sound, true, trustworthy, upright, virtuous

honorarium *n* alimony, compensation, fee, payment, remuneration, reward, stipend

honored *adj* 1 delighted, glad, pleased, proud

adj 2 admired, praised, prized, respected, valued

adj 3 accountable, answerable, dependable, honorable, liable, reliable, reputable, respected, responsible, secure, solid, trusted, trustworthy, trusty, upstanding

hoodlum *n* gorilla, hooligan, punk, roughneck, rowdy, ruffian, thug, tough

hoodwink *v* see: cheat *v* 1

hoof *n* extremity, foot, hand, paw

hoofer *n* ballerina, choreographer, chorine, dancer

hook *n* 1 arc, arch, bend, bow, coil, crook, curvature, curve, round, spiral

n 2 catch, clincher, snag

n 3 claw, spur, talon

v 1 buckle, clasp, clinch, fasten

v 2 bag, capture, catch, ensnare, entangle, entrap, snag, snare, snarl, tangle, trap, trick

hooker *n* call girl, harlot, hussy, prostitute, slut, streetwalker, tart, tramp, trollop, wanton woman, wench, whore

hooks *n* bait, gear, lures, tackle

hooligan *n* gorilla, hoodlum, punk, roughneck, rowdy, ruffian, thug, tough

hoopla *n* ballyhoo, embellishment, exaggeration, hype, hyperbole, overstatement, promotion, public relations

hoosegow *n* see: JAIL *n*

hop *v* bob, bound, jaunt, jump, leap, lope, prance, skip, spring, sprint, trip

n 1 bound, jump, leap, vault

n 2 ball, cotillion, dance, party, prom

hope *n* 1 ambition, aspiration, desire, goal, will, wish

n 2 bid, expectation, inducement, invitation, motion, offer, proffer, proposal, proposition, recommendation, request, suggestion

n 3 anticipation, expectation, premonition

n 4 belief, confidence, contingency, credence, credit, creed, dependence, desire, faith, religion, trust

v 1 aim, aspire, strive, wish

v 2 anticipate, await, believe, count on, expect, keep the faith, look, look forward to, wish

hopeful *adj* 1 auspicious, bright, confident, favorable, promising, rosy, sunny, utopian

adj 2 auspicious, cheerful, confident, encouraging, optimistic, promising, sanguine, upbeat

n aspirant, candidate, contestant, entrant, nominee

hopeless *adj* 1 cursed, damned, doomed, hapless, ill-fated, jinxed, luckless, unhappy, unlucky, untoward

adj 2 impossible, incurable, irreparable, irresolvable, irrevocable, permanent, terminal, unalterable, uncorrectable, uncurable, unfixable

adj 3 see: GLOOMY *adj* 5

horde *n* crush, dozens, host, legion, many, multitude, numerousness, oodles, press, push, scores, squash, swarm

horizon *n* 1 lookout, outlook, perspective, prospect, vista *n* 2 distance, future, outlook, perspective, purview, vision, vista

horizontal *adj* flat, lengthwise, longways, prone, prostrate, reclining, recumbent
n plane

horny *adj* 1 amorous, aroused, in heat, in the mood, lustful, passionate, stimulated
adj 2 amorous, ardent, aroused, carnal, earthy, erotic, fervent, fleshly, hot, impassioned, lascivious, lecherous, lewd, licentious, lustful, passionate, provocative, randy, raunchy, romantic, sensual, sexual, sexy, sultry, titillated, torrid, turned on, voluptuous, wanton

horrendous *adj* appalling, awful, dire, dreadful, fearful, formidable, frightening, frightful, ghastly, horrible, offensive, ominous, portentous, scary, shocking, spooky, terrible, terrifying, unpleasant

horrible *adj* 1 abhorrent, abominable, appalling, detestable, disgusting, dreadful, evil, frightful, ghastly, hateful, horrid, loathsome, odious, repulsive, revolting, shocking
adj 2 appalling, awful, dire, dreadful, fearful, formidable, frightening, frightful, ghastly, horrendous, offensive, ominous, portentous, scary, shocking, spooky, terrible, terrifying, unpleasant

horrid *adj* abhorrent, abominable, appalling, detestable, disgusting, dreadful, evil, frightful, ghastly, hateful, horrible, loathsome, odious, repulsive, revolting, shocking

horrify *v* 1 amaze, daze, electrify, offend, outrage, overwhelm, scandalize, shock, stun
v 2 appall, daunt, discourage, dismay, panic, petrify, scare, shock, terrify, unnerve
v 3 abash, alarm, awe, cow, daunt, frighten, intimidate, panic, scare, shock, spook, startle, terrify, terrorize, unnerve

horror *n* 1 aversion, contempt, disgust, distaste, loathing, nausea, repugnance, repulsion, revulsion
n 2 affliction, alarm, anxiety, apprehension, care, consternation, dismay, dread, fear, fright, ordeal, panic, terror, trepidation, trial, trouble, worry
n 3 fright, scare, shock, start, terror

horse *n* colt, equine, filly, foal, gelding, mare, mount, nag, pony, steed, yearling

horsemen *n* airborne, army, battalion, brigade, cavalry, company, footmen, guard, infantry, legion, marines, militia, minutemen, paratroops, platoon, reserve, storm troopers

horse-trade *v* deal, hawk, huckster, hustle, monger, peddle, push, sell, swap

hospitable *adj* affable, amenable, amiable, amicable, congenial, empathetic, friendly, gregarious, neighborly, outgoing, receptive, sociable, social, sympathetic

hospital *n* asylum, clinic, dispensary, infirmary, institution

hospitality *n* greeting, salutation, welcome

host *n* crush, dozens, horde, legion, many, multitude, numerousness, oodles, press, push, scores, squash, swarm
v board, house, put up, shelter

hostage *n* captive, prisoner, victim

hostile *adj* 1 catty, malevolent, malicious, resentful, spiteful, treacherous
adj 2 adverse, antagonistic, bellicose, ill, inimical, nasty, spiteful, unfriendly
adj 3 angry, bellicose, belligerent, combative, contentious, militant, pugnacious, quarrelsome, warlike

hostility *n* 1 anger, animosity, huff, indignation, miff, offense, pique, resentment
n 2 acrimony, animosity, antagonism, antipathy, aversion, bitterness, dislike, enmity, gall, hate, hatred, ill will, malice, rancor, spite, venom, vindictiveness

hot *adj* 1 favorite, popular
adj 2 heated, lukewarm, tepid, warm
adj 3 exciting, sensational, sexy, spectacular, stirring
adj 4 humid, muggy, steamy, sticky, stifling, sunny, tropical
adj 5 biting, nippy, pungent, seasoned, sharp, spicy, tangy, tart
adj 6 feverish
adj 7 baking, blistering, boiling, broiling, burning, fiery, scalding, scorching, sizzling, sultry, sweltering, torrid
adj 8 aggravated, angry, annoyed, cross, enraged, excited, fuming, furious, incensed, indignant, irate, irritable, mad, provoked, teed off, upset
adj 9 amorous, ardent, aroused, carnal, earthy, erotic, fervent, fleshly, horny, impassioned, lascivious, lecherous, lewd, licentious, lustful, passionate, provocative, randy, raunchy, romantic, sensual, sexual, sexy, sultry, titillated, torrid, turned on, voluptuous, wanton

hot-blooded *adj* see: PASSIONATE *adj* 2

hotel *n* club, inn, lodge, resort, spa

hot-tempered *adj* angry, cranky, cross, feisty, grouchy, irascible, ireful, peppery, quick-tempered, short-fused, sullen, testy, touchy

hound *v* aggravate, annoy, badger, bait, bedevil, beleaguer, bother, bug, harass, harry, hassle, heckle, hurt, intimidate, jeer, nag, needle, persecute, pester, plague, provoke, ride, spite, taunt, tease, threaten, torment, worry

n canine, dog, mongrel, mutt, pooch, pup, puppy

hourglass *n* chronometer, clock, stopwatch, timepiece, timer, watch

house *n* 1 capitol, legislature, senate

n 2 building, edifice, erection, foundation, pile, store, structure, warehouse

n 3 business, company, concern, corporation, enterprise, establishment, firm, organization, partnership

n 4 address, apartment, condo, condominium, domicile, dwelling, flat, home, location, pad, place, property, residence, site

n 5 abode, castle, domicile, dwelling, estate, home, mansion, palace, residence

v 1 board, host, put up, shelter

v 2 conceal, harbor, hide, keep, protect, safeguard, shelter, shield

housecoat *n* bathrobe, gown, negligee, nightgown, robe

household *n* breed, clan, class, family, people, race, relatives, stock, tribe

housemother *n* mother, mother superior, superintendent

housing *n* 1 cabinet, case, enclosure

n 2 box, crate

n 3 berth, billet, quarters, shelter, space

n 4 apartment, dorm, lodging, room, shelter, suite

hovel *n* abode, barn, bungalow, cabin, coop, cottage, hut, lodge, shack, shanty

however *adv* 1 despite, further, in spite of, regardless

adv 2 but, except that, further, just, merely, nevertheless, only, simply, solely, yet

adv 3 at any rate, but, moreover, nevertheless, nonetheless, notwithstanding, still, though, yet

howl *v* 1 bark, bay, cry, growl, shout, snap, woof, yap, yelp

v 2 bark, bellow, blare, call, cry, holler, roar, scream, screech, shout, shriek, shrill, squeal, thunder, wail, yell

hub *n* 1 center, core, middle, midpoint, midst

n 2 axis, center, focal point, focus, heart, nerve center, target

hubbub *n* brouhaha, cacophony, chaos, clamor, confusion, din, discord, disorder, mayhem, noise, pandemonium, racket, tumult, uproar

hubby *n* bridegroom, groom, husband, man, master, mate, mister, spouse

huckster *v* deal, hawk, horse-trade, hustle, monger, peddle, push, sell, swap

huddle *n* band, bunch, crew, crowd, drove, flock, following, gaggle, gang, herd, mass, mob, pack, rabble, riffraff, swarm, team, throng

v advise, communicate, confer, consult, discuss, group, parley, powwow

hue *n* cast, color, shade, tinge, tint, tone

huff *n* anger, animosity, hostility, indignation, miff, offense, pique, resentment

huffy *adj* see: VAIN *adj* 5

hug *n* caress, embrace, fondling, kiss, squeeze, touch

v 1 clasp, clinch, cuddle, embrace, enfold, hold, press, squeeze

v 2 caress, cradle, cuddle, embrace, feel, fondle, fool around, hold, love, make out, neck, nuzzle, pet, snuggle, stroke

huge *adj* 1 formidable, immense, impressive, intimidating, massive, significant, substantial

adj 2 big, extra-large, fat, grand, great, husky, immense, jumbo, large, obese, oversize, tremendous

adj 3 colossal, enormous, fantastic, Gargantuan, giant, gigantic, Goliath, great, immense, jumbo, leviathan, mammoth, massive, mighty, monstrous, monumental, overwhelming, phenomenal, prodigious, Promethean, stupendous, Titanic, towering, tremendous, unfathomed, untold, vast, walloping, whopping

adj 4 see: BIG *adj* 3, 4

hula *n* cha-cha, ballet, dance, fox trot, jitterbug, polka, tap, twist, waltz

hulk *n* debris, fragment, remains, rubbish, rubble, shell, trash, wreck, wreckage

hum *v* carol, chant, harmonize, lilt, sing, yodel

n see: ACTIVITY *n* 3

human *adj* mortal

n being, citizen, creature, entity, Homo sapiens, human being, individual, man, person, woman

humane *adj* see: TENDER *adj* 9

humanitarian *adj* altruistic, benevolent, bountiful, caring, charitable, Christian, compassionate, generous, giving, good, humane, kind, lenient, merciful, philanthropic, tender

humanity *n* 1 humankind, human race, mankind, world

n 2 altruism, charity, generosity, goodness, goodwill, grace, kindness, mercy

humankind *n* humanity, human race, mankind, world

humble adj 1 lowly, meek, modest, unassuming, unpretentious

adj 2 base, common, ignoble, knavish, low, lowly, mean, plebeian

adj 3 see: SERVILE adj 2

v abase, abash, belittle, cast down, cheapen, debase, defile, deflate, degrade, demean, depreciate, derogate, devalue, dishonor, embarrass, humiliate, lower, mortify, put down, shame, sink

humbled adj broken

humdrum adj blah, boring, commonplace, dim, dreary, dull, flat, monotonous, ordinary, pedestrian, stodgy, tedious, tiresome

humid adj 1 stagnant, stuffy

adj 2 damp, dank, drizzly, foggy, misty, moist, wet

adj 3 hot, muggy, steamy, sticky, stifling, sunny, tropical

adj 4 damp, drenched, dripping, moist, mucky, muggy, soaked, soggy, sopping, sticky, sultry, sweaty, wet

humidity n dampness, moisture, sogginess, wetness

humiliate v 1 disfavor, disgrace, dishonor, reproach, shame, stain, tarnish

v 2 abase, abash, belittle, cast down, cheapen, debase, defile, deflate, degrade, demean, depreciate, derogate, devalue, dishonor, embarrass, humble, lower, mortify, put down, shame, sink

humiliated adj abashed, ashamed, chagrined, embarrassed, mortified, shamed

humiliation n censure, contempt, discredit, disfavor, disgrace, dishonor, disparagement, disrepute, infamy, notoriety, scandal, shame

humility n 1 modesty, reserve, shyness

n 2 modesty, propriety, virtue

humor n 1 esprit, spirit, wit

n 2 caprice, fancy, impulse, notion, vagary, whim, whimsy

n 3 attitude, disposition, feeling, mind, mood, spirit, temper, timbre, tone, vein

n 4 banter, comedy, crack, funniness, gag, jest, joke, quip, small talk, wisecrack, wit, witticism

n 5 aptitude, character, complexion, disposition, distinctiveness, heart, identity, inclination, individuality, makeup, nature, personality, quality, spirit, state, temperament, tendency

n 6 see: SATIRE n 2

v accommodate, baby, cater, coddle, gratify, indulge, overindulge, pamper, pander, placate, satisfy, spoil

humorous adj 1 amusing, diverting, enjoyable, entertaining, fun, joking, playful

adj 2 comical, facetious, funny, jesting, jocular, joking, kidding, sarcastic, witty

adj 3 absurd, comic, comical, crazy, droll, farcical, foolish, funny, hilarious, laughable, ludicrous, outrageous, ridiculous, silly

hump n foothill, hill, hillock, knoll, mound, mount, raise, rise, swelling

hunch n 1 feeling, foreboding, guess, instinct, intuition, premonition, sense, suspicion

n 2 concept, conception, idea, image, impression, notion, perception, recollection, thought, view

v droop, slouch, stoop

hunger n appetite, craving, desire, eroticism, hankering, itch, longing, lust, passion, urge, yearning, yen

v ache, crave, covet, desire, hanker, itch, long, lust, need, pine, thirst, want, yearn

hungry adj 1 famished, ravenous, starved, starving, voracious

adj 2 acquisitive, avaricious, covetous, craving, desirous, eager, grabby, grasping, greedy, longing, miserly, selfish, wishful, yearning

hunt n 1 exploration, pursuit, quest, search

n 2 chase, exploration, pursuit, quest, search, undertaking, venture

v 1 chase, follow, pursue, seek, shadow, shoot for, tail, trace, track, trail

v 2 delve, dig, examine, explore, feel out, grope, inquire, investigate, look, observe, peer, probe, pursue, research, scan, scrutinize, search, seek, sound, study, test

hurdle n 1 bar, barrier, bottleneck, crimp, dead end, deadlock, difficulty, encumbrance, impasse, impediment, obstacle, obstruction, snag, stumbling block

n 2 challenge, demur, difficulty, hindrance, objection, obstacle, problem, protest, question, snag

v 1 clear, leap, negotiate, surmount, vault

v 2 conquer, crush, defeat, destroy, down, lick, overcome, overthrow, surmount

hurl v 1 discharge, emit, fire, launch, project, shoot

v 2 cast, flick, fling, flip, heave, launch, pitch, propel, sling, throw, toss

hurricane n blast, blizzard, blow, gale, gust, northeaster, snowstorm, squall, storm, tempest, typhoon, wind

hurried adj abrupt, hasty, headlong, impetuous, impulsive, precipitant, precipitate, quick, rapid, rash, reckless, rushing, sudden

hurry *n* alacrity, dispatch, expedition, haste, hastiness, hustle, precipitance, precipitation, quickness, rush, rustle, speed, swiftness

v 1 accelerate, expedite, hasten, quicken, rush, shake up, speed, step up

v 2 barrel, bullet, expedite, fly, hasten, hustle, rocket, rush, speed, whisk, zip

hurt *adj* 1 alienated, angry, bitter, emotional, jealous, offended, provoked, resentful

adj 2 annoying, difficult, irksome, irritated, irritating, painful, sensitive, sore

n 1 bruise, injury, pain, sprain, strain, wound

n 2 abrasion, cut, itch, scrape, scratch, sore

n 3 ache, affliction, agony, anguish, injury, pain, punishment, suffering, torture

n 4 ache, agony, angina, burn, cramp, crick, heartache, pain, pang, soreness, spasm, sting, twinge

n 5 chaos, damage, destruction, devastation, disaster, disorder, harm, havoc, injury, loss, mayhem, ruin, ruination

v 1 ache, despair, grieve, pain, suffer

v 2 bruise, injure, lacerate, mangle, wound

v 3 afflict, aggrieve, bother, burden, distress, grieve, injure, pain

v 4 abuse, blemish, damage, hamper, harm, impair, injure, mar, obstruct, ruin, sabotage, scuttle, spoil, tarnish, vandalize

v 5 burden, deject, depress, dishearten, grieve, lament, sadden, weigh down, wound

v 6 blow, blunder, botch, bungle, butcher, damage, err, foul up, goof, hash, jeopardize, jumble, mess up, queer, ruin, screw up

v 7 aggravate, annoy, badger, bait, bedevil, beleaguer, bother, bug, harass, harry, hassle, heckle, hound, intimidate, jeer, nag, needle, persecute, pester, plague, provoke, ride, spite, taunt, tease, threaten, torment, worry

hurtful *adj* see: SINISTER *adj* 2

hurting *adj* damaging, dangerous, deleterious, harmful, injurious, ruinous, unhealthy

husband *v* conserve, economize, safeguard, store

n bridegroom, groom, hubby, man, master, mate, mister, spouse

hush *adj* dead, inanimate, inert, lifeless, noiseless, quiet, silent, soundless, still

n calm, lull, peace, peacefulness, quiet,

repose, respite, rest, siesta, silence, sleep, stillness, tranquillity

v censor, curb, gag, inhibit, muffle, mute, quell, quiet, repress, restrain, silence, squelch, stifle, still, subdue, suppress, throttle, tone down

hushed *adj* see: CALM *adj* 2

hush-hush *adv* clandestinely, covertly, furtively, mystically, secretly, sneakily, stealthily, surreptitiously, under cover

husk *n* bark, case, coating, crust, peel, rind, shell, shuck, skin

v crack, open, peel, remove, shell

husky *adj* 1 caustic, grating, guttural, harsh, hoarse, rasping, raucous, rough, strident

adj 2 athletic, brawny, burly, massive, muscular, ponderous, powerful, robust, stocky, stout, strapping, strong

adj 3 see: BIG *adj* 3

hussy *n* call girl, harlot, hooker, prostitute, slut, streetwalker, tart, tramp, trollop, wanton woman, wench, whore

hustle *n* 1 con, crime, graft, racket, rip-off, scam, scheme, sting, swindle

n 2 alacrity, dispatch, expedition, haste, hastiness, hurry, precipitance, precipitation, quickness, rush, rustle, speed, swiftness

v 1 bulldoze, elbow, jostle, press, push, shoulder, shove

v 2 deal, hawk, horse-trade, huckster, monger, peddle, push, sell, swap

v 3 barrel, bullet, expedite, fly, hasten, hurry, rocket, rush, speed, whisk, zip

v 4 drudge, grub, labor, slave, strain, strive, sweat, toil, work

v 5 bamboozle, beat, beguile, bilk, burn, cajole, cheat, chicane, chisel, con, cross, deceive, defraud, dupe, embezzle, fleece, flimflam, fob, foist, fool, gyp, hoax, hoodwink, inveigle, screw, shaft, sham, swindle, trick, victimize

hut *n* abode, barn, bungalow, cabin, coop, cottage, hovel, lodge, shack, shanty

hygienic *adj* clean, healthy, immaculate, sanitary, sterile

hymn *n* psalm

hype *n* ballyhoo, embellishment, exaggeration, hoopla, hyperbole, overstatement, promotion, public relations

hyperbole *n* ballyhoo, embellishment, exaggeration, hoopla, hype, overstatement, promotion, public relations

hyperopic *adj* farsighted

hypnotize *v* captivate, charm, delight, engross, enrapture, enravish, enthrall, entrance, mesmerize, move, ravish, transport

hypocrisy *n* 1 contradiction, disagreement, discrepancy, incongruity, inconsistency, paradox, variance

n 2 deceit, deception, fabrication, falsehood, fraud, fraudulence, lying, perjury, trickery, untruth

hypocrite *n* 1 charlatan, cheat, fake, fraud, quack

n 2 charlatan, counterfeit, fake, faker, fraud, impostor, liar, phony, pretender

hypothesis *n* assumption, conjecture, deduction, explanation, guess, inference, postulate, presumption, proposition, speculation, supposition, theory

hypothesize *v* allude, assume, extend, imagine, offer, pose, present, presume, propose, speculate, suggest, suppose, surmise, theorize

hypothetical *adj* abstract, conjectural, general, ideal, illustrative, speculative, symbolic, theoretical

hysteria *n* chaos, frenzy, panic, riot

I

ice *v* chill, cool, freeze, refrigerate

icon *n* 1 favorite, god, hero, idol

n 2 drawing, image, model, representation, simulation, symbol

n 3 bust, figure, idol, image, sculpture, statue, statuette, symbol

n 4 character, emblem, example, letter, logo, mark, model, representation, sign, symbol, token

iconoclast *n* agitator, defector, dissident, heretic, insurgent, malcontent, maverick, misfit, nonconformist, rebel, renegade, traitor, troublemaker, turncoat

icy *adj* 1 arctic, chilly, cold, cool, freezing, frigid, frosty, glacial, nippy, wintry

adj 2 cold, coldhearted, distant, emotionless, frigid, glacial, impersonal, indifferent, unemotional, unfriendly

id *n* ego, individuality, mind, persona, personality, psyche, self, soul, spirit

idea *n* 1 concept, conception, hunch, image, impression, notion, perception, recollection, thought, view

n 2 see: FONDNESS *n* 2

ideal *adj* 1 model, optimal, perfect, very

adj 2 exemplary, flawless, model, perfect, perfected

adj 3 characteristic, classic, exemplary, model, representative, typical

adj 4 abstract, conjectural, general, hypothetical, illustrative, speculative, symbolic, theoretical

adj 5 errorless, excellent, exquisite, fastidious, faultless, flawless, immaculate, impeccable, irreproachable, perfect

n epitome, example, exemplar, mirror, model, outline, paradigm, pattern, plan, prototype, rule of thumb, standard

idealist *n* dreamer, romantic, utopian, visionary

ideation *n* conception, formulation, imagination

identical *adj* 1 exact, precise, same, very

adj 2 duplicate, equal, equivalent, same, substitute, synonymous, tantamount

adj 3 see: ALIKE *adj*

identification *n* 1 address, destination, direction, location, zone

n 2 pass, passport, permit, ticket, visa

identify *v* 1 distinguish, know, name, recognize, specify

v 2 see: MEAN *v* 2

identity *n* see: PERSONALITY *n* 4

idiom *n* 1 expression, locution, name, phrase, saying, term, word, wording

n 2 see: LANGUAGE *n*

idiosyncrasy *n* abnormality, eccentricity, habit, oddity, peculiarity, quirk, trademark

idiot *n* blockhead, boor, clod, creep, cretin, dimwit, dolt, dope, dullard, dumbbell, dummy, dunce, fool, goof, imbecile, jerk, nerd, nincompoop, numskull, oaf, pain, schlemiel, schmuck, simpleton, stooge, turkey

idiotic *adj* 1 absurd, anile, asinine, brainless, childish, fatuous, foolish, inept, meaningless, mindless, senseless, silly, simple, thoughtless, unintelligent, witless

adj 2 backward, blunt, deficient, dense, dimwitted, dull, dumb, feebleminded, moronic, obtuse, retarded, simple, simple-minded, slow, stupid, thick, uneducated, unintelligent

idle *adj* 1 jobless, out of work, unemployed

adj 2 empty, hollow, insincere, meaningless, shallow, vain

adj 3 down, lax, off, slack, slow, sluggish

adj 4 asleep, dormant, immobile, inactive, inanimate, inert, inoperative, laid-back, motionless, nodding, passive, quiet, sleepy, slumbering, stable, stagnant, still

adj 5 vacant

adj 6 dilatory, easygoing, indolent, inert, lackadaisical, laid-back, languid, lazy, lethargic, relaxed, slothful, sluggish, unconcerned

adj 7 calm, collected, composed, cool,

demure, dormant, easy, gentle, hushed, imperturbable, motionless, nonchalant, peaceful, placid, poised, quiet, relaxed, restful, sedate, self-composed, self-possessed, serene, soft, steady, still, tranquil, unflappable, unruffled, untroubled

v dally, dawdle, delay, diddle, goof off, lag, linger, loaf, loiter, loll, lounge, malinger, poke, put off, putter, shirk, tarry

idol *n* 1 deity, divinity, god

n 2 favorite, god, hero, icon

n 3 angel, model, prince, saint

n 4 bust, figure, icon, image, sculpture, statue, statuette, symbol

idolize *v* 1 admire, adore, cherish, dote on, love, respect, revere, venerate, worship

v 2 see: APPRECIATE *v* 3

iffy *adj* 1 circumstantial, contingent, uncertain, vague

adj 2 anticipated, contingent, hoped for, planned, probable, proposed, tentative

adj 3 absurd, chancy, debatable, doubtful, dubious, implausible, improbable, incredible, moot, preposterous, questionable, theoretical, unbelievable, uncertain, unlikely

ignite *v* 1 burn, enkindle, fire, inflame, kindle, light, spark

v 2 blare, blaze, burn, flame, flare, glare, glow, redden

v 3 activate, charge, electrify, energize, enliven, excite, start, turn on, vitalize

v 4 feed, fire, fuel, incite, kindle, light, nourish, propel, stoke, sustain

v 5 see: INSTIGATE *v* 1

ignoble *adj* 1 base, common, humble, knavish, low, lowly, mean, plebeian

adj 2 base, beneath, despicable, inferior, low, lowdown, sordid, squalid, unworthy, vile, vulgar, wretched

ignorant *adj* 1 dense, oblivious, obtuse

adj 2 confined, controlled, limited, narrow, parochial, provincial, unsophisticated

adj 3 illiterate, uneducated, uninstructed, unlearned, unlettered, unschooled, untaught, untutored

ignore *v* 1 defy, disobey, infringe, obstruct, oppose, rebel, resist, violate

v 2 banish, bar, blackball, cut, debar, dismiss, eliminate, except, exclude, leave out, omit, suspend

v 3 defy, discount, disregard, exclude, forget, miss, neglect, omit, ostracize, overlook, overpass, pass, pass by, pass over, shun, skip, slight, snub

v 4 blackball, boycott, cut, ostracize, rebuff, snub, spurn

ilk *n* see: CATEGORY *n*

ill *adj* 1 adverse, bad, evil, harmful, unfavorable, unlucky

adj 2 adverse, antagonistic, bellicose, hostile, inimical, nasty, spiteful, unfriendly

adj 3 ailing, delicate, diseased, down, frail, impaired, indisposed, sick, sickly, suffering, unhealthy, unsound, unwell, weak

n affliction, ailment, complaint, condition, disease, disorder, evil, harm, illness, infirmity, malady, sickness

ill-adapted *adj* see: INADEQUATE *adj* 5

ill-advised *adj* 1 foolish, futile, pointless, profitless, stupid, vain

adj 2 foolish, indiscreet, misdirected, misguided, mistaken, unwise

ill-behaved *adj* 1 bad, disobedient, misbehaving, mischievous, naughty

adj 2 audacious, boorish, discourteous, disrespectful, ill-bred, ill-mannered, impertinent, impolite, insolent, rude, surly, uncalled for, uncivil, uncivilized, uncouth, uncultured, unpolished, unrefined

ill-bred *adj* audacious, boorish, discourteous, disrespectful, ill-behaved, ill-mannered, impertinent, impolite, insolent, rude, surly, uncalled for, uncivil, uncivilized, uncouth, uncultured, unpolished, unrefined

illegal *adj* criminal, disgraceful, felonious, illegitimate, illicit, lawless, prohibited, unlawful, wrong, wrongful

illegible *adj* 1 scribbled, unclear, undecipherable, unreadable

adj 2 incomprehensible, inconceivable, mysterious, unclear, unintelligible, unthinkable

illegitimate *adj* 1 criminal, disgraceful, felonious, illegal, illicit, lawless, prohibited, unlawful, wrong, wrongful

adj 2 bastard, fatherless, misbegotten, orphaned, spurious, unauthentic, ungenuine

ill-famed *adj* infamous, notorious, opprobrious

ill-fated *adj* cursed, damned, doomed, hapless, hopeless, jinxed, luckless, unfortunate, unhappy, unlucky, untoward

ill-favored *adj* 1 contorted, grotesque, gruesome, hideous, ugly, uncomely, unsightly

adj 2 inadmissible, objectionable, unacceptable, undesirable, unwanted, unwelcome

illicit *adj* criminal, disgraceful, felonious,

illegal, illegitimate, lawless, prohibited, unlawful, wrong, wrongful

illiterate *adj* ignorant, uneducated, uninstructed, unlearned, unlettered, unschooled, untaught, untutored

ill-mannered *adj* audacious, boorish, discourteous, disrespectful, ill-behaved, ill-bred, impertinent, impolite, insolent, rude, surly, uncalled for, uncivil, uncivilized, uncouth, uncultured, unpolished, unrefined

ill-natured *adj* argumentative, cantankerous, contentious, controversial, debatable, disputatious, litigious, ornery

illness *n* 1 affliction, ailment, complaint, condition, disease, disorder, evil, harm, ill, infirmity, malady, sickness
n 2 cold, infection, virus

illogical *adj* 1 inconclusive, indecisive, indefinite, open, unconvincing, unsettled, unverified
adj 2 abnormal, extra, extraneous, foreign, immaterial, insignificant, irregular, irrelevant, malapropos, nonessential, peripheral, superfluous, surplus, unimportant, unnecessary, unrelated
adj 3 absurd, balmy, bizarre, crazy, emotional, foolish, frivolous, goofy, impossible, inane, insane, irrational, loony, lunatic, mad, muddled, nuts, preposterous, ridiculous, silly, touched, wacky, zany
adj 4 ambiguous, borderline, clouded, doubtful, dubious, equivocal, garbled, inarticulate, incalculable, incoherent, inexplicit, muddled, muffled, murky, obscure, precarious, questionable, shaky, suspect, suspicious, uncertain, unclear, uneasy, unintelligible, unsure, vague, wary

ill-suited *adj* see: INADEQUATE *adj* 5

ill-timed *adj* see: INADEQUATE *adj* 5

ill-treat *v* see: HARM *v* 1

illuminate *v* 1 brighten, glow, irradiate, light up, radiate, spotlight
v 2 clarify, clear, clear up, delineate, depict, elucidate, explain, illustrate, picture, portray, reveal

illuminating *adj* academic, educational, enlightening, eye-opening, informative, instructive, revealing, scholastic

illumination *n* 1 case, case history, clarification, example, explanation, illustration, instance, representative, sample, sampling, specimen
n 2 flare, flashlight, light
n 3 lamps, lighting, lights, luminescence

ill-use *v* abuse, corrupt, misapply, misem-

ploy, mishandle, misuse, pervert, prostitute

illusion *n* 1 deception, error, fallacy, flaw, inaccuracy
n 2 delusion, fallacy, myth, old wives' tale, superstition
n 3 aberration, apparition, delusion, fantasy, figment, ghost, hallucination, image, mirage, phantasm, specter, vision

illusive *adj* 1 false, deceptive, illusory, misleading, sham, unreal
adj 2 apparent, illusory, ostensible, quasi, seeming, specious, superficial

illusory *adj* 1 false, deceptive, illusive, misleading, sham, unreal
adj 2 apparent, illusive, ostensible, quasi, seeming, specious, superficial
adj 3 conceived, conjured, created, fancied, fanciful, fantastic, fictional, fictitious, imaginary, imagined, invented, make-believe, nonexistent, notional, unreal, whimsical

illustrate *v* 1 delineate, depict, picture, portray, represent, sketch
v 2 denote, depict, express, imply, mean, represent, speak for, symbolize
v 3 clarify, clear, clear up, delineate, depict, elucidate, explain, illuminate, picture, portray, reveal

illustration *n* 1 clue, example, indication, manifestation, proof, sign
n 2 depiction, description, explanation, narration, report, sketch, story, verbalization
n 3 case, case history, clarification, example, explanation, illumination, instance, representative, sample, sampling, specimen
n 4 acrylic, art, canvas, depiction, drawing, etching, landscape, lithograph, mural, oil, painting, pastel, pen and ink, picture, portrait, print, seascape, sketch, still life, watercolor

illustrative *adj* 1 detailed, graphic, photographic, pictorial, picturesque, visual, vivid
adj 2 abstract, conjectural, general, hypothetical, ideal, speculative, symbolic, theoretical

illustrious *adj* acclaimed, celebrated, distinguished, eminent, esteemed, excellent, famed, famous, foremost, notable, outstanding, prestigious, prominent, renowned, well-known

ill will *n* acrimony, animosity, antagonism, antipathy, aversion, bitterness, dislike, enmity, gall, hate, hatred, hostility, malice, rancor, spite, venom, vindictiveness

image *n* 1 drawing, icon, model, representation, simulation, symbol

n 2 bust, figure, icon, idol, sculpture, statue, statuette, symbol

n 3 creativity, fancy, fantasy, imagination, ingenuity, inspiration, invention, resourcefulness, whimsy

n 4 concept, conception, hunch, idea, impression, notion, perception, recollection, thought, view

n 5 aberration, apparition, delusion, fantasy, figment, ghost, hallucination, illusion, mirage, phantasm, specter, vision

n 6 airs, arrogance, cockiness, conceit, condescension, disdain, egotism, haughtiness, loftiness, narcissism, pride, self-esteem, self-image, vanity

n 7 clone, copy, counterfeit, duplicate, duplication, imitation, likeness, mock-up, model, print, replica, replication, representation, reproduction, resemblance, simulation

v 1 see: DUPLICATE *v*

v 2 see: VISUALIZE *v*

imaginary *adj* conceived, conjured, created, fancied, fanciful, fantastic, fictional, fictitious, illusory, imagined, invented, make-believe, nonexistent, notional, unreal, whimsical

imagination *n* 1 conception, formulation

n 2 creativity, fancy, fantasy, image, ingenuity, inspiration, invention, resourcefulness, whimsy

imaginative *adj* clever, creative, deft, enterprising, fertile, ingenious, inventive, resourceful, skillful, talented

imagine *v* 1 dream, fantasize, muse, suppose

v 2 conceive, conjecture, conjure up, create, envision, fancy, image, invent, project, realize, think, visualize

v 3 assume, believe, comprehend, conceive, estimate, expect, fathom, gather, grasp, guess, infer, know, presume, suppose, surmise, suspect, think, trust, understand

v 4 see: SUGGEST *v* 6

imagined *adj* see: FICTITIOUS *adj* 3

imbecile *n* blockhead, boor, clod, creep, cretin, dimwit, dolt, dope, dullard, dumbbell, dummy, dunce, fool, goof, idiot, jerk, nerd, nincompoop, numskull, oaf, pain, schlemiel, schmuck, simpleton, stooge, turkey

imbibe *v* bibulate, booze, consume, drink, gulp, guzzle, nip, partake, polish off, put away, put down, sample, savor, sip, suck, swill, swig, taste

imbue *v* 1 impregnate, permeate, saturate, wet

v 2 color, enhance, flavor, infuse, salt, season, spice

v 3 edge in, foist, infiltrate, insinuate, penetrate, permeate, sneak in, work in, worm

v 4 impart, infuse, ingrain, inject, inoculate, instill, invest, penetrate, pervade, spread, steep, suffuse, teach, train

v 5 see: EDUCATE *v*

imitate *v* 1 favor, look like, resemble

v 2 copy, clone, duplicate, image, mirror, print, re-create, redo, reduplicate, remake, replicate, reprint, reproduce, simulate

v 3 act, ape, copy, emulate, follow, lip-synch, mime, mimic, mock, model, mouth, pantomime, parody, pattern, take off

v 4 see: ACT *v* 3

imitated *adj* copied, pseudo, simulated, unoriginal

imitation *adj* artificial, bogus, counterfeit, ersatz, fake, false, mock, phony, pseudo, sham, simulated, spurious, substitute, unreal

n 1 clone, copy, counterfeit, duplicate, duplication, image, likeness, mock up, model, print, replica, replication, representation, reproduction, resemblance, simulation

n 2 see: SATIRE *n* 2

immaculate *adj* 1 clean, healthy, hygienic, sanitary, sterile

adj 2 errorless, excellent, exquisite, fastidious, faultless, flawless, ideal, impeccable, irreproachable, perfect

adj 3 celibate, chaste, clean, decent, decorous, modest, moral, pristine, proper, pure, spotless, stainless, stuffy, taintless, unadulterated, unblemished, undefiled, upstanding, virginal, wholesome

adj 4 clean, pristine, pure, spotless, taintless, unsoiled, unspoiled, unsullied, untouched, virgin

immaterial *adj* 1 abnormal, extra, extraneous, foreign, illogical, insignificant, irregular, irrelevant, malapropos, nonessential, peripheral, superfluous, surplus, unimportant, unnecessary, unrelated

adj 2 see: TRIVIAL *adj* 1

immature *adj* 1 babyish, callow, childish, infantile, sophomoric

adj 2 careless, capricious, irresponsible, undependable, unpredictable, untrustworthy *adj* **3** green, inexperienced, naive, new, novice, raw, unsophisticated, virgin

adj **4** adolescent, fresh, green, juvenile, precocious, undeveloped, unfledged, unready, young, youthful

immeasurable *adj* countless, incalculable, infinite, innumerable, innumerous, legion, many, numberless, uncountable, unlimited, untold

immediate *adj* **1** instant, instantaneous, quick, rapid, swift, urgent

adj **2** close, near, near at hand, nigh, proximate, virtual

adj **3** any second, imminent, impending, looming, momentary, poised, threatening

adj **4** contiguous, current, direct, instant, nearby, primary, prompt, sudden, timely

immediately *adv* **1** at once, forthwith, instantly, promptly, right now, this instant, *tout de suite*

adv **2** abruptly, fast, hastily, instantaneously, instantly, quick, quickly, short, suddenly, swiftly

adv **3** anon, any moment, at once, directly, instantaneously, instantly, momentarily, now, presently, promptly, quickly, right now, shortly, soon, straightaway, *tout de suite*

immense *adj* **1** formidable, huge, impressive, intimidating, massive, significant, substantial

adj **2** big, extra-large, fat, grand, great, huge, husky, jumbo, large, obese, oversize, tremendous

adj **3** see: HUGE *adj* 1, 2, 3

immerse *v* bathe, clean, cleanse, clean up, dip, flush, launder, rinse, rub, scour, scrape, scrub, shower, wash

immersed *adj* **1** drenched, dripping, full, inundated, saturated, soaked, soaking, sodden, sopping, waterlogged, wet

adj **2** absorbed, agog, concentrated, deep, determined, distracted, engaged, engrossed, enraptured, entranced, fascinated, intent, preoccupied, rapt, wrapped up

immigrate *v* come in, enter, go in

imminent *adj* **1** advancing, approaching, forthcoming, looming, nearing, oncoming, pending

adj **2** any second, immediate, impending, looming, momentary, poised, threatening

adj **3** approaching, eventual, expected, future, impending, next, prospective, subsequent

adj **4** foreboding, impending, menacing,

ominous, portentous, predictive, prophetic, sinister, threatening

immobile *adj* see: INACTIVE *adj* 2

immobilize *v* cripple, disable, disarm, encumber, freeze, halt, handcuff, incapacitate, paralyze, prostrate, stop, stun

immoderate *adj* excessive, gluttonous, inordinate, intemperate, overindulgent, prodigious, unbridled, undue, unrestrained, voracious

immoral *adj* **1** casual, easy, fast, incontinent, indiscriminate, lax, lecherous, lewd, licentious, light, loose, promiscuous, unchaste, wanton, whorish

adj **2** see: EVIL *adj* 3, 4

adj **3** see: VICIOUS *adj* 3

immorality *n* corruption, depravity, dishonesty, impurity, vice, wickedness, wrong

immortal *adj* endless, eternal, infinite, perpetual, unceasing, undying

immovable *adj* adamant, ceaseless, dedicated, determined, firm, inexhaustible, inexorable, inflexible, narrow-minded, obstinate, relentless, resolute, resolved, rigid, single-minded, steadfast, stubborn, unbendable, unbending, uncompromising, unswayable, unyielding

immune *adj* exempt, guarded, protected, safe, secure

immunity *n* assurance, exemption, guarantee, impunity, protection, release, safety, security

immunize *v* inject, inoculate, vaccinate

immutable *adj* see: CONSTANT *adj* 3

imp *n* brat

impact *v* alter, effect, impress, influence, modify

n see: HIT *n* 1

impair *v* **1** abate, decline, deteriorate, fade, fail, flag, languish, wane, weaken, wither, worsen

v **2** abuse, blemish, damage, hamper, harm, hurt, injure, mar, obstruct, ruin, sabotage, scuttle, spoil, tarnish, vandalize

v **3** see: HINDER *v* 5

impaired *adj* ailing, delicate, diseased, down, frail, ill, indisposed, sick, sickly, suffering, unhealthy, unsound, unwell, weak

impairment *n* affliction, calamity, disability, flaw, handicap, limitation

impale *v* gore, lance, penetrate, pierce, puncture, spear, stab

impart *v* **1** bequeath, bestow, devise, leave, will

v **2** convey, express, hint, imply, indicate, purport, say, suggest *v* 3 imbue, infuse, ingrain, inject, inoculate, instill, invest, penetrate, pervade, spread, steep, suffuse, teach, train

v 4 brief, communicate, convey, declare, describe, disclose, divulge, explain, inform, narrate, orate, portray, read, recite, recount, relate, report, retell, reveal, share, state, tattle, tell, transmit

v 5 deliver, express, give forth

v 6 accord, adduce, award, bequeath, bestow, concede, confer, contribute, deliver, devote, donate, endow, extend, fund, give, give away, grant, hand down, hand out, offer, pose, present, proffer, provide, supply, tender, volunteer

v 7 coach, communicate, condition, convey, cultivate, develop, discipline, drill, edify, educate, enlighten, exercise, explain, groom, imbue, implant, improve, inculcate, indoctrinate, inform, infuse, inseminate, inspire, instill, instruct, perfect, practice, prepare, ready, school, teach, train, tutor

impartial *adj* 1 detached, free, independent, neutral, nonpartisan, unattached, uncommitted, uninvolved

adj 2 candid, dispassionate, equal, equitable, fair, impersonal, indifferent, just, neutral, objective, open-minded, square, unbiased, uncolored, unprejudiced

impartiality *n* equity, fairness, justice, objectivity

impasse *n* 1 bottleneck, deadlock, draw, hung jury, stalemate, standoff, standstill, tie

n 2 abeyance, cessation, halt, moratorium, standstill, stay, stop, stopping, suspension

n 3 bar, barrier, bottleneck, crimp, dead end, deadlock, difficulty, encumbrance, hurdle, impediment, obstacle, obstruction, snag, stumbling block

n 4 bind, box, corner, difficulty, dilemma, fix, jam, mess, pinch, plight, predicament, quandary, scrape, spot, trap, trouble

impassioned *adj* 1 ardent, enthusiastic, excitable, fervent, fiery, flaming, hot-blooded, intense, passionate, stirring, sweaty, torrid, zealous

adj 2 amorous, ardent, aroused, carnal, earthy, erotic, fervent, fleshly, horny, hot, lascivious, lecherous, lewd, licentious, lustful, passionate, provocative, randy, raunchy, romantic, sensual, sexual, sexy, sultry, titillated, torrid, turned on, voluptuous, wanton

impassive *adj* cold, dry, dull, laid-back,

matter-of-fact, phlegmatic, poker-faced, reserved, stoic, stolid, unaffected, unemotional, unfeeling, unmoved, untouched

impatient *adj* 1 annoying, anxious, bothersome, chafing, crabby, edgy, fretful, galling, irritating, jittery, nagging, on edge, restless, touchy, unsettling

adj 2 anxious, edgy, fidgety, nervous, nervy, queasy, restive, restless, tense, troubled, uncomfortable, uneasy, uptight, worried

adj 3 see: EAGER *adj* 2

v 1 see: ACCUSE *v* 2

v 2 see: FIRE *v* 5

impeachment *n* dismissal, ejection, expulsion, extraction, firing, ouster, removal, termination

impeccable *adj* errorless, excellent, exquisite, fastidious, faultless, flawless, ideal, immaculate, irreproachable, perfect

impede *v* 1 bisect, cross, intersect

v 2 check, cramp, curtail, shorten, stunt, throttle

v 3 burden, check, encumber, hamper, hinder, obstruct, restrain, restrict, retard

v 4 bog, delay, detain, hang up, mire, retard, set back, slacken, slow

v 5 arrest, block, check, freeze, halt, interrupt, stall, stay, stop

v 6 brake, confine, contain, control, curb, drag, govern, hamper, hem, hold back, repress, restrain, retard

v 7 bar, block, brake, choke, clog, dam, deter, detract, encumber, frustrate, halt, hamper, hesitate, hinder, impair, inhibit, jam, obstruct, prevent, repress, restrain, retard, slow, stay, stop, stop up, throttle

v 8 see: THWART *v* 4

impediment *n* 1 affliction, blight, pestilence, scourge

n 2 blockage, bottleneck, catch, flaw, hitch, jam, obstacle, obstruction, snag

n 3 bar, barrier, bottleneck, crimp, dead end, deadlock, difficulty, encumbrance, hurdle, impasse, obstacle, obstruction, snag, stumbling block

impel *v* 1 boost, budge, drive, force, nudge, propel, push, shove, thrust

v 2 activate, actuate, compel, drive, force, goad, induce, mobilize, motivate, move, persuade, press, propel, push, spur, start, turn on

v 3 see: CONVINCE *v*

impending *adj* 1 awaiting, contingent, pending, unfinished, unsettled

adj 2 any second, immediate, imminent, looming, momentary, poised, threatening

adj 3 approaching, eventual, expected,

future, imminent, next, prospective, sub-sequent

adj 4 foreboding, imminent, menacing, ominous, portentous, predictive, pro-phetic, sinister, threatening

impenetrable *adj* arcane, hermetic, imper-vious, mysterious, mystic, obscure, puz-zling, secret, unexaminable, unknown, unseen

imperative *adj* 1 compulsory, mandatory, must do, necessary, obligatory, prerequi-site, required

adj 2 critical, essential, indispensable, mandatory, necessary, needed, prerequi-site, required, vital

imperceptible *adj* 1 faint, meager, remote, slight, subtle, vague

adj 2 ambiguous, imprecise, indecisive, indefinite, indeterminate, indistinct, in-exact, loose, vague, wishy-washy

adj 3 imponderable, inappreciable, indis-cernible, insensible, intangible, invisible, minute, scant, unapparent, unobservable, weak

imperfect *adj* 1 amiss, crude, defective, faulty, flawed, incomplete, short, unful-filled

adj 2 flawed, flimsy, inferior, lousy, medi-ocre, miserable, paltry, poor, second-rate, shabby, shoddy, sorry, so-so, tacky, un-worthy, worthless

imperfection *n* 1 blemish, defect, failing, fault, flaw, scar, shortcoming, weakness

n 2 defect, deficiency, demerit, fault, flaw, inadequacy, lack, need, shortcoming, want

imperfectly *adv* badly, harshly, improperly, inadequately, inappropriately, painfully, poorly, unsatisfactorily

imperial *adj* 1 aristocratic, blue-blooded, kingly, majestic, noble, regal, royal, state-ly, well-bred

adj 2 august, baronial, exalted, grand, grandiose, haughty, imposing, impres-sive, lofty, lordly, majestic, magisterial, magnificent, noble, portly, princely, re-gal, royal, stately

adj 3 see: AUTHORITATIVE *adj* 2

imperious *adj* see: AUTHORITATIVE *adj* 2

impermanent *adj* brief, ephemeral, fleeting, momentary, passing, short, temporary, transient, transitory, volatile

impersonal *adj* 1 clinical, detached, scien-tific, systematic, technical

adj 2 cold, coldhearted, distant, emotion-less, frigid, glacial, icy, indifferent, un-emotional, unfriendly

adj 3 candid, dispassionate, equal, equi-table, fair, impartial, indifferent, just, neutral, objective, open-minded, square, unbiased, uncolored, unprejudiced

impertinent *adj* 1 busy, intrusive, meddle-some, obtrusive, officious

adj 2 arrogant, cocky, disrespectful, flip, flippant, impudent, wise

adj 3 audacious, bold, brash, brazen, cheeky, daring, disrespectful, forward, fresh, impudent, insolent, irreverent, nervy, pert, rude, sassy, saucy

adj 4 audacious, boorish, discourteous, disrespectful, ill-behaved, ill-bred, ill-mannered, impolite, insolent, rude, surly, uncalled for, uncivil, uncivilized, un-couth, uncultured, unpolished, unrefined

adj 5 see: BLUNT *adj* 1

imperturbable *adj* see: CALM *adj* 2

impervious *adj* arcane, hermetic, impene-trable, mysterious, mystic, obscure, puz-zling, secret, unexaminable, unknown, unseen

impetuous *adj* 1 abrupt, hasty, headlong, hurried, impulsive, precipitant, precipi-tate, quick, rapid, rash, reckless, rushing, sudden

adj 2 anxious, ardent, avid, breathless, desirous, eager, enthusiastic, excited, fain, impatient, keen, passionate, raring, zealous

impetus *n* impulse, stimulus, urge

impiety *n* blasphemy, desecration, heresy, irreverence, sacrilege, violation

impinge *v* collide, conflict, interfere, ob-struct

implant *v* 1 plant, root, seed, sow, strew

v 2 connote, hint, imply, infer, insinuate, lead, offer, put forth, seed

v 3 fill in, insert, insinuate, interject, interpolate, interpose, interrupt, intro-duce, throw in

v 4 bud, crossbreed, graft

v 5 coach, communicate, condition, con-vey, cultivate, develop, discipline, drill, edify, educate, enlighten, exercise, ex-plain, groom, imbue, impart, improve, inculcate, indoctrinate, inform, infuse, inseminate, inspire, instill, instruct, per-fect, practice, prepare, ready, school, teach, train, tutor

implausible *adj* absurd, chancy, debatable, doubtful, dubious, iffy, improbable, in-credible, moot, preposterous, question-able, theoretical, unbelievable, uncertain, unlikely

implement *v* 1 direct, give, impose, inflict, strike

v 2 allocate, appoint, assign, establish, institute, set

v 3 accomplish, complete, consummate, execute, fulfill, perform, realize

n see: DEVICE

implementation n execution, exercise, practice, training

implicate v accuse, associate, blame, confuse, connect, embroil, enmesh, ensnare, entangle, involve, mire, tangle

implication n 1 drift, intent, purport, substance, tenor

n 2 allusion, connotation, hint, innuendo, insinuation, notation, reference, suggestion

n 3 see: INSULT n

implicit adj implied, indicated, inferred, inherent, insinuated, intuitive, presumed, suggested, tacit, understood, unexpressed, unsaid, unspoken, wordless

implied adj 1 accepted, presumed, supposed, tacit, understood

adj 2 implicit, indicated, inferred, inherent, insinuated, intuitive, presumed, suggested, tacit, understood, unexpressed, unsaid, unspoken, wordless

implore v appeal, ask, beg, beseech, conjure, crave, desire, entreat, grovel, indicate, invoke, plead, pray, request, seek, solicit, supplicate, whine

imply v 1 resemble, savor, smack, smell, suggest, taste

v 2 convey, express, hint, impart, indicate, purport, say, suggest

v 3 disclose, display, evince, express, indicate, manifest, reflect, reveal, show

v 4 connote, hint, implant, infer, insinuate, lead, offer, put forth, seed

v 5 denote, depict, express, illustrate, mean, represent, speak for, symbolize

v 6 accuse, allege, arraign, assert, charge, cite, impeach, impute, incriminate, indict, litigate, prosecute, sue, try

impolite adj audacious, boorish, discourteous, disrespectful, ill-behaved, ill-bred, ill-mannered, impertinent, insolent, rude, surly, uncalled for, uncivil, uncivilized, uncouth, uncultured, unpolished, unrefined

imponderable adj imperceptible, inappreciable, indiscernible, insensible, intangible, invisible, minute, scant, unapparent, unobservable, weak

import n 1 concern, emphasis, gravity, importance, significance, stress, weight

n 2 consequence, importance, magnitude, moment, significance, substance, weight

n 3 intent, meaning, message, sense, significance, understanding

n 4 basis, body, bulk, core, essence, essentials, gist, heart, mass, nucleus, object, staple, substance, volume

v add up to, connote, convey, denote, identify, indicate, intend, mean, show, signify, symbolize

importance n 1 accent, emphasis, highlighting, priority, significance, stress, weight

n 2 concern, emphasis, gravity, import, significance, stress, weight

n 3 consequence, import, magnitude, moment, significance, substance, weight

important adj 1 eminent, great, outstanding, superior

adj 2 commanding, compelling, forceful, influential, powerful

adj 3 forceful, highhanded, intense, maximum, powerful, utmost

adj 4 consequential, considerable, critical, crucial, material, meaningful, momentous, prominent, significant, substantial, vital, weighty

adj 5 acute, burning, critical, crucial, desperate, dire, grave, heavy, major, momentous, ponderous, pressing, profound, serious, severe, solemn, somber, urgent, vital

imported adj foreign, nondomestic, offshore

impose v 1 burden, strain, tax

v 2 direct, give, implement, inflict, strike

v 3 bother, burden, encroach, intrude, presume, saddle

imposing adj see: GRAND adj 5

impossible adj 1 inconceivable, incredible, strange, unachievable, undoable, unthinkable

adj 2 hopeless, incurable, irreparable, irresolvable, irrevocable, permanent, terminal, unalterable, uncorrectable, uncurable, unfixable

adj 3 see: ABSURD adj 2

impost n assessment, cost, duty, expense, fee, levy, offering, penalty, price, sacrifice, tariff, tax, toll, trade-off

impostor n charlatan, counterfeit, fake, faker, fraud, hypocrite, liar, phony, pretender

impotence n apathy, inaction, inactivity, inertia, paralysis

impotent adj 1 emasculate, inadequate, ineffective, ineffectual, spineless, weak

adj 2 barren, effete, frigid, infertile, spent, sterile, unbearing, unfertile, unfruitful, unproductive *adj* 3 feeble, helpless, inept, powerless, weak

impound *v* 1 cage, confine, coop, detain, enclose, imprison, incarcerate, intern, jail, lock up, restrain, trap

v 2 annex, appropriate, commandeer, confiscate, expropriate, grab, plunder, preempt, repossess, seize, sequester, shanghai, take

impoverish *v* 1 bankrupt, break, bust, decay, do in, fold up, ruin

v 2 bankrupt, deplete, drain, draw, draw down, exhaust, use up

impoverished *adj* broke, destitute, dirt-poor, down and out, indigent, needy, penniless, poor, poverty-stricken, strapped, unprosperous

impractical *adj* 1 far-fetched, remote, unfeasible, unrealistic

adj 2 inoperable, undoable, unworkable

imprecation *n* 1 anathema, curse, condemnation, execration, malediction, voodoo

n 2 abomination, blasphemy, curse word, expletive, obscenity, profanity, swearing

imprecise *adj* 1 ambiguous, imperceptible, indecisive, indefinite, indeterminate, indistinct, inexact, loose, vague, wishy-washy

adj 2 see: FALSE *adj* 3

impregnable *adj* invulnerable, protected, safe, safeguarded, secure

impregnate *v* 1 imbue, permeate, saturate, wet

v 2 engender, father, fertilize, inseminate, sire

v 3 bear, beget, breed, come into, create, effect, engender, father, generate, hatch, make, mate, multiply, originate, parent, procreate, promulgate, propagate, reproduce, sire, spawn

impress *v* 1 ingrain

v 2 alter, effect, impact, influence, modify

v 3 amaze, astonish, astound, awe, delight, floor, overwhelm, wow

v 4 call, conscript, draft, enroll, force, induct, select, shanghai

v 5 drive, hammer, imprint, mark, pound, press, print, stamp, strike, thump, whack

v 6 register

impression *n* 1 copy, imprint, indent, indentation, mark, notch, print, stamp, tab

n 2 concept, conception, hunch, idea, image, notion, perception, recollection, thought, view

n 3 characteristic, flavor, nature, property, quality, ring, sound, tendency, tone, type

n 4 assessment, interpretation, reading, understanding

impressionable *adj* alterable, inexperienced, malleable, naive, sensitive, susceptible

impressive *adj* 1 convincing, effective, forcible, inspiring, profound, striking

adj 2 affecting, heartbreaking, moving, poignant, sad, touching

adj 3 formidable, huge, immense, intimidating, massive, significant, substantial

adj 4 excellent, extraordinary, great, noteworthy, outstanding, shining, smashing, superb, wonderful

adj 5 colorful, expressive, graphic, intense, potent, powerful, striking, strong, unforgettable, vivid

adj 6 see: GRAND *adj* 5

imprint *n* 1 brand, cachet, emblem, logo, logotype, mark, seal, stamp, trademark

n 2 copy, impression, indent, indentation, mark, notch, print, stamp, tab

v drive, hammer, impress, mark, pound, press, print, stamp, strike, thump, whack

imprison *v* 1 adjudge, condemn, convict, discipline, penalize, punish, sentence

v 2 cage, confine, coop, detain, enclose, impound, incarcerate, intern, jail, lock up, restrain, trap

imprisonment *n* 1 arrest, custody, detention

n 2 bondage, enslavement, indenture, serfdom, servility, servitude, slavery

n 3 arrest, confinement, detention, incarceration

improbable *adj* absurd, chancy, debatable, doubtful, dubious, iffy, implausible, incredible, moot, preposterous, questionable, theoretical, unbelievable, uncertain, unlikely

impromptu *adj* 1 makeshift, provisional, stopgap, temporary

adj 2 ad-lib, extemporaneous, improvised, instantaneous, invented, off the cuff, offhand, spontaneous, unrehearsed, unstudied

improper *adj* 1 afoul, amiss, awry, bad, bum, out of kilter, poor, rotten, unsatisfactory, wrong

adj 2 indecent, indelicate, lewd, malodorous, off-color, offensive, rough, scurrilous, suggestive, unbecoming, unseemly, untoward

adj 3 botching, bungling, goofing, helpless, ill-adapted, ill-suited, ill-timed, inadequate, inappropriate, incapable, incongruous, incorrect, ineligible, inept, malapropos, unable, unbecoming, unbefitting, unequipped, unfit, unqualified, unseemly, unskilled, unsuitable, unsuited

adj **4** bawdy, coarse, crude, dirty, erotic, filthy, foul, gamy, gross, indecent, lascivious, lewd, licentious, nasty, obscene, off-color, pornographic, profane, prurient, racy, rank, raunchy, ribald, risqué, scandalous, smutty, suggestive, tainted, uncouth, vulgar, x-rated

adj **5** see: EROTIC, indecent, racy, suggestive, unbecoming

improperly *adv* badly, harshly, imperfectly, inadequately, inappropriately, painfully, poorly, unsatisfactorily

impropriety *n* **1** blunder, folly, indiscretion, mistake, slip

n **2** exploitation

improve *v* **1** advance, benefit, gain, profit, reward

v **2** better, correct, modify, reform, rehabilitate

v **3** better, elevate, enhance, enrich, fortify, strengthen

v **4** advance, cultivate, elevate, enhance, enrich, refine, upgrade

v **5** adjust, amend, correct, fix, mend, modify, position, rectify, remedy, restore, right, straighten

v **6** ameliorate, convalesce, gain, heal, loop up, mend, perk, rally, recover, recuperate, rehabilitate, revive

v **7** alter, change, commute, convert, evolve, further, metamorphose, modernize, modify, mutate, revolutionize, transfer, transfigure, transform, transmute, vary

v **8** advance, ascend, bloom, climb, develop, do well, excel, expand, flourish, flower, get ahead, grow, progress, prosper, rise, strive, survive, thrive

v **9** see: EDUCATE *v*

v **10** see: HELP *v* **4**

improvement *n* **1** addition, advancement, advantage, betterment, enhancement, gain, growth, plus

n **2** comeback, rally, reappearance, recovery, renewal, resurrection, return, revival

n **3** correction, progress, reform

n **4** acceleration, achievement, advance, advancement, betterment, breakthrough, furtherance, growth, headway, increment, pickup, proficiency, progress, promotion, strengthening, upgrade

improvised *adj* ad-lib, extemporaneous, impromptu, instantaneous, invented, off the cuff, offhand, spontaneous, unrehearsed, unstudied

impudence *n* back talk, lip, rudeness, sass

impudent *adj* **1** arrogant, cocky, disrespectful, flip, flippant, impertinent, wise

adj **2** arrant, barefaced, blatant, brassy, brazen, extreme, notorious, obtrusive, shameless, unabashed

adj **3** audacious, bold, brash, brazen, cheeky, daring, disrespectful, forward, fresh, impertinent, insolent, irreverent, nervy, pert, rude, sassy, saucy

adj **4** see: BLUNT *adj* **1**

impugn *v* **1** attack, challenge, contradict, deny, oppose, rebut

v **2** contradict, cross, deny, disaffirm, disagree, negate, rebut, traverse

impulse *n* **1** impetus, stimulus, urge

n **2** condition, habit, reaction, reflex, response

n **3** caprice, fancy, humor, notion, vagary, whim, whimsy

impulsive *adj* **1** careless, foolish, irresponsible, myopic, not smart, reckless, risky, shortsighted, unthinking, unwise

adj **2** automatic, instinctive, involuntary, natural, rash, reflex, spontaneous, unconscious, unforced, unpremeditated, unprompted

adj **3** abrupt, hasty, headlong, hurried, impetuous, precipitant, precipitate, quick, rapid, rash, reckless, rushing, sudden

adj **4** see: RAPID *adj* **2, 4**

impunity *n* assurance, exemption, guarantee, immunity, protection, release, safety, security

impurity *n* **1** contaminant, defect, pollutant

n **2** contamination, corruption, decay, poison, taint

n **3** corruption, depravity, dishonesty, immorality, vice, wickedness, wrong

impute *v* see: ACCUSE *v*

in *adj* chic, current, fashionable, hip, smart, stylish, trendy, vogue

n authority, clout, control, influence, leverage, power, prestige, pull, weight

inability *n* incompetence, ineptitude, lack of skill

inaccuracy *n* deception, error, fallacy, illusion

inaccurate *adj* erroneous, false, faulty, imprecise, incorrect, inexact, mistaken, specious, untrue, wrong

inaction *n* **1** apathy, impotence, inactivity, inertia, paralysis

n **2** abeyance, dormancy, inactivity, limbo, lull, pause, suspension

inactive *adj* **1** dormant, inert, latent, on hold, passive, potential, quiet, suspended, unused *adj* 2 asleep, dormant, idle, immobile, inanimate, inert, inoperative, laid-back, motionless, nodding, passive, quiet, sleepy, slumbering, stable, stagnant, still

inactivity *n* 1 apathy, impotence, inaction, inertia, paralysis

n 2 slack

n 3 abeyance, dormancy, inaction, limbo, lull, pause, suspension

inadequacy *n* 1 deficiency, deprivation, destitution, indigence, lack, need, privation, poverty, scarcity, want

n 2 see: DEFECT *n* 4

inadequate *adj* 1 delicate, feeble, flimsy, light, slight

adj 2 emasculate, impotent, ineffective, ineffectual, spineless, weak

adj 3 bad, defective, futile, incorrect, inferior, invalid, malfunctioning, poor, void

adj 4 deficient, failing, inferior, insufficient, scant, scarce, scrimpy, short, shy, wanting

adj 5 botching, bungling, goofing, helpless, ill-adapted, ill-suited, ill-timed, improper, inappropriate, incapable, incongruous, incorrect, ineligible, inept, malapropos, unable, unbecoming, unbefitting, unequipped, unfit, unqualified, unseemly, unskilled, unsuitable, unsuited

adj 6 see: MEAGER *adj* 2

inadequately *adv* badly, harshly, imperfectly, improperly, inappropriately, painfully, poorly, unsatisfactorily

inadmissible *adj* ill-favored, objectionable, unacceptable, undesirable, unwanted, unwelcome

inadvertent *adj* accidental, careless, caustic, heedless, inconsiderate, nonchalant, selfish, sharp, tactless, thoughtless, uncaring, unceremonious, ungracious, unheeding, unintended, unintentional, unreflective, unthinking

inane *adj* see: ABSURD *adj* 2

inanimate *adj* 1 dead, hush, inert, lifeless, noiseless, quiet, silent, soundless, still

adj 2 asleep, dormant, idle, immobile, inactive, inert, inoperative, laid-back, motionless, nodding, passive, quiet, sleepy, slumbering, stable, stagnant, still

inapplicable *adj* inconsistent, irrelevant, spurious, unfitting

inappreciable *adj* imperceptible, imponderable, indiscernible, insensible, intangible, invisible, minute, scant, unapparent, unobservable, weak

inappropriate *adj* botching, bungling, goofing, helpless, ill-adapted, ill-suited, ill-timed, improper, inadequate, incapable, incongruous, incorrect, ineligible, inept, malapropos, unable, unbecoming, unbefitting, unequipped, unfit, unqualified, unseemly, unskilled, unsuitable, unsuited

inappropriately *adv* badly, harshly, imperfectly, improperly, inadequately, painfully, poorly, unsatisfactorily

inarguable *adj* absolute, actual, authentic, bona fide, certain, definite, existent, factual, genuine, hard, incontestable, incontrovertible, indisputable, indubitable, irrefutable, positive, real, sure, true, undeniable, undisputable, undoubtable, undoubted, unequivocal, unquestionable, veritable, viable

inarticulate *adj* 1 dumb, mute, reticent, silent, speechless, tacit, voiceless

adj 2 see: VAGUE *adj* 6

inattentive *adj* 1 distracted, heedless, unaware, unheeding, unnoticing, unobservant, unperceiving, unwatchful

adj 2 careless, defiant, delinquent, derelict, heedless, lax, neglectful, negligent, reckless, sloppy

adj 3 absent-minded, abstracted, bemused, careless, dazed, dizzy, groggy, lost, mindless, oblivious, preoccupied, silly, spaced, vapid

inaugural *adj* chief, first, foremost, head, initial, lead, leading, premier, prime

inaugurate *v* activate, begin, cause, commence, constitute, create, embark, enter, establish, induct, initiate, install, instigate, instill, institute, introduce, kick off, launch, lead off, open, originate, precipitate, preface, set up, start, tee off, usher in, venture forth

inauguration *n* beginning, briefing, commencement, debut, induction, initiation, unveiling

inborn *adj* basic, congenital, genetic, indigenous, ingrained, inherent, inherited, innate, instinctive, intrinsic, natal, native, natural

incalculable *adj* 1 countless, immeasurable, infinite, innumerable, innumerous, legion, many, numberless, uncountable, unlimited, untold

adj 2 see: VAGUE *adj* 6

incandescent *adj* glowing, luminous, moonlit, sunlit

incantation *n* bewitchment, enchantment, magic, occultism, sorcery, spell, voodoo, witchcraft, wizardry

incapable *adj* botching, bungling, goofing, helpless, ill-adapted, ill-suited, ill-timed, improper, inadequate, inappropriate, incongruous, incorrect, ineligible, inept, malapropos, unable, unbecoming, unbefitting, unequipped, unfit, unqualified, unseemly, unskilled, unsuitable, unsuited

incapacitate *v* cripple, disable, disarm, encumber, freeze, halt, handcuff, immobilize, paralyze, prostrate, stop, stun

incarcerate *v* cage, confine, coop, detain, enclose, impound, imprison, intern, jail, lock up, restrain, trap

incarceration *n* arrest, confinement, imprisonment

incarnate *v* embody

incense *n* aroma, balm, bouquet, fragrance, perfume, scent, spice

v see: BOTHER *v* 5

incensed *adj* aggravated, angry, annoyed, cross, enraged, excited, fuming, furious, hot, indignant, irate, irritable, mad, provoked, teed off, upset

incentive *n* bonus, consideration, goal, inducement, motivation, motive, reason, reward, stimulus

inception *n* 1 beginning, birth, debut, delivery, kindling, onset, outset, start

n 2 beginning, conception, cradle, derivation, fountainhead, infancy, mother, origin, root, seed, source, stem

incertitude *n* concern, doubt, dubiety, indecision, mistrust, question, query, skepticism, suspicion, uncertainty, wonder

incessant *adj* 1 chronic, prolonged, severe

adj 2 ageless, boundless, ceaseless, constant, continual, continuous, endless, eternal, everlasting, infinite, interminable, limitless, never-ending, ongoing, perpetual, persistent, relentless, timeless, unceasing, unending, uninterrupted, unremitting

incident *n* 1 fight, outbreak, scene, spectacle, tantrum

n 2 circumstance, episode, event, happening, occasion, occurrence, scene, thing

incidental *adj* 1 contingent, dependent, linked

adj 2 ancillary, auxiliary, minor, related, secondary, side, subordinate

adj 3 accidental, casual, chance, chancy, circumstantial, coincidental, contingent, eventful, fluky, fortuitous, freak, lucky, odd, serendipitous, synchronous

incidentally *adv* further

incinerate *v* burn, cremate, destroy, oxidize

incipient *adj* beginning, embryonic, founding, initial, introductory, nascent, rudimentary, starting

incise *v* cut, gash, penetrate, pierce, punch, slash, slice, slit

incision *n* cut, gash, nick, pierce, prick, puncture, slit, wound

incisive *adj* biting, caustic, cutting, penetrating, pointed, trenchant

incite *v* 1 animate, brighten, cheer up, enliven, inspire, liven, quicken, resuscitate, vivify

v 2 agitate, anger, arouse, encourage, foment, ignite, induce, inflame, inspire, instigate, invoke, motivate, muster, prod, propel, provoke, raise, set, set on, spur, stimulate, stir, urge

v 3 arouse, electrify, excite, fire, inspire, rouse, spark, stimulate, tantalize, thrill, titillate, turn on, whet

v 4 see: FIRE *v* 4, 7

v 5 see: URGE *v* 3

incitement *n* infection, infusion, inspiration, stimulation

inclement *adj* bitter, brutal, cruel, fierce, hard, harsh, intemperate, pitiless, rigorous, rough, rugged, severe, stern, strong, unkind, violent

inclination *n* 1 bent, disposition, fancy, fondness, idea, liking, mind, notion, pleasure, propensity, yen

n 2 bent, bias, drift, habit, leaning, partiality, penchant, predilection, preference, priority, proclivity, propensity, talent, taste, tendency

n 3 see: PERSONALITY *n* 4

incline *n* 1 angle, grade, gradient, pitch, ramp, rise, slant, slope, tilt

n 2 bluff, cliff, hill, slant, slope, steep bank

v 1 decline, descend, skew, slant, slope, veer

v 2 bank, bend, lean, pitch, slant, slope

v 3 cant, careen, heel, list, rear, roll, tilt

v 4 angle, confuse, deceive, distort, falsify, garble, misconstrue, misinterpret, misquote, misread, misrepresent, misunderstand, mix up, mumble, slant, slope, taint, twist

inclined *adj* 1 apt, liable, likely, partial, prone

adj 2 accommodating, agreeing, amenable, disposed, eager, glad, pleased, pliant, responsive, willing

include *v* 1 add, contain, enclose, incorporate, insert

v 2 comprehend, comprise, contain, embody, embrace, encompass, have, incorporate, involve, take in

incognito *adj* disguised

n camouflage, cover, privacy, secrecy, stealth

incoherent *adj* 1 babbling, confused, irrational, rambling, wild

adj 2 see: VAGUE *adj* 6

income *n* 1 bill, bonus, charge, commission, compensation, consideration, earnings, fee, gross, pay, revenue, salary, stipend, wage

n 2 see: MONEY *n* 4

incomparable *adj* alone, matchless, only, peerless, unequaled, unique, unmatched, unpaired, unparalleled, unrivaled

incompatible *adj* incongruous, inconsistent, irreconcilable

incompetence *n* inability, ineptitude, lack of skill

incompetent *adj* amateurish, inept, unprofessional

incomplete *adj* 1 fragmentary, halfway, partial, unfinished

adj 2 amiss, crude, defective, faulty, flawed, imperfect, short, unfulfilled

incomprehensible *adj* 1 enigmatic, inexplicable, inscrutable, mysterious, occult, puzzling

adj 2 illegible, inconceivable, mysterious, unclear, unintelligible, unthinkable

inconceivable *adj* 1 amazing, extraordinary, fantastic, incredible, unbelievable

adj 2 impossible, incredible, strange, unachievable, undoable, unthinkable

adj 3 illegible, incomprehensible, mysterious, unclear, unintelligible, unthinkable

inconclusive *adj* illogical, indecisive, indefinite, open, unconvincing, unsettled, unverified

incongruity *n* contradiction, disagreement, discrepancy, hypocrisy, inconsistency, paradox, variance

incongruous *adj* 1 incompatible, inconsistent, irreconcilable

adj 2 different, disparate, diverse, opposite, unequal, unlike, unmatched, unrelated

adj 3 aberrant, abnormal, anomalous, artificial, atypical, contrived, deviant, disparate, divergent, irregular, off-key, uncharacteristic, unnatural

adj 4 see: INADEQUATE *adj* 5

inconsequential *adj* see: TRIVIAL *adj* 1

inconsiderable *adj* see: TRIVIAL *adj* 1

inconsiderate *adj* 1 hasty, indiscreet, reckless, tactless, thoughtless

adj 2 caustic, selfish, sharp, short, tactless, thoughtless, unceremonious, ungracious

adj 3 accidental, careless, caustic, heedless, inadvertent, nonchalant, selfish, sharp, short, tactless, thoughtless, uncaring, unceremonious, ungracious, unheed-

ing, unintended, unintentional, unreflective, unthinking

inconsistency *n* 1 contradiction, difference, disparity, dissimilarity

n 2 contradiction, disagreement, discrepancy, hypocrisy, incongruity, paradox, variance

inconsistent *adj* 1 incompatible, incongruous, irreconcilable

adj 2 inapplicable, irrelevant, spurious, unfitting

adj 3 arbitrary, capricious, changeable, erratic, fickle, flighty, inconstant, mercurial, uncertain, unstable, unsteady, variable, volatile, wavering, wayward

inconspicuous *adj* conservative, dim, quiet, restrained, subdued, tasteful, unassuming, unobtrusive

inconstant *adj* arbitrary, capricious, changeable, erratic, fickle, flighty, inconsistent, mercurial, uncertain, unstable, unsteady, variable, volatile, wavering, wayward

incontestable *adj* 1 accurate, certain, distinct, explicit, infallible, perfect, unerring

adj 2 absolute, actual, authentic, bona fide, certain, definite, existent, factual, genuine, hard, inarguable, incontrovertible, indisputable, indubitable, irrefutable, positive, real, sure, true, undeniable, undisputable,. undoubtable, undoubted, unequivocal, unquestionable, veritable, viable

incontinent *adj* see: PROMISCUOUS *adj* 2

incontrovertible *adj* absolute, actual, authentic, bona fide, certain, definite, existent, factual, genuine, hard, inarguable, incontestable, indisputable, indubitable, irrefutable, positive, real, sure, true, undeniable, undisputable, undoubtable, undoubted, unequivocal, unquestionable, veritable, viable

incontrovertibly *adv* absolutely, certainly, decidedly, definitely, entirely, indeed, indubitably, positively, surely, truly, unequivocally, unquestionably, verily, well, without doubt

inconvenience *n* annoyance, bother, conflict, contention, difference, discord, disharmony, dispute, dissension, dissent, dissidence, dissonance, disunity, division, hassle, mischief, nuisance, strife, trouble, variance

v annoy, antagonize, argue, bother, bug, concern, distress, disturb, goad, harass, hassle, irk, irritate, pain, perturb, strain, stress, taunt, trouble, try, upset, worry

incorporate v 1 add, contain, enclose, include, insert

v 2 comprehend, comprise, contain, embody, embrace, encompass, have, include, involve, take in

incorporeal adj bodiless, celestial, disembodied, ethereal, heavenly, insubstantial, intangible, metaphysical, nonmaterial, spiritual, unearthly, unreal, unsubstantial

incorrect adj 1 bad, defective, futile, inadequate, inferior, invalid, malfunctioning, poor, void

adj 2 erroneous, false, faulty, imprecise, inaccurate, inexact, mistaken, specious, untrue, wrong

adj 3 botching, bungling, goofing, helpless, ill-adapted, ill-suited, ill-timed, improper, inadequate, inappropriate, incapable, incongruous, ineligible, inept, malapropos, unable, unbecoming, unbefitting, unequipped, unfit, unqualified, unseemly, unskilled, unsuitable, unsuited

increase n 1 addition

n 2 enlargement, growth, rise, swell

v 1 add, append, attach, join

v 2 apply, augment, capitalize on, enlarge, parlay, use

v 3 ascend, climb, rise, soar, speed, zoom

v 4 abound, multiply, overrun, proliferate, propagate, teem

v 5 climb, crest, jump, mount, rise, surge

v 6 boost, hike, jack up, jump, put up, raise, up

v 7 amplify, bolster, encourage, enhance, enhearten, hearten, inspire, reassure, strengthen, support

v 8 amplify, append, augment, boost, build, enlarge, expand, extend, grow, heighten, intensify, magnify, multiply, run up, snowball, supplement, upsurge, wax

v 9 amplify, construct, develop, devise, elaborate, enhance, enlarge, expand, expound, refine

v 10 amplify, bloat, dilate, distend, enlarge, expand, fatten, grow, inflate, magnify, stretch, swell, widen

increasing adj continual, continuing, gradual, incremental, intensifying, measured, moderate, progressive, successive

incredible adj 1 astonishing, exceptional, remarkable, uncanny

adj 2 amazing, extraordinary, fantastic, inconceivable, unbelievable

adj 3 impossible, inconceivable, strange, unachievable, undoable, unthinkable

adj 4 absurd, chancy, debatable, doubtful, dubious, iffy, implausible, improbable, moot, preposterous, questionable, theoretical, unbelievable, uncertain, unlikely

adj 5 see: WEIRD adj 1

incredulity n disbelief, distrust, doubt, skepticism, unbelief

incredulous adj see: DOUBTFUL adj 1

increment n 1 addition

n 2 acceleration, achievement, advance, advancement, betterment, breakthrough, furtherance, growth, headway, improvement, pickup, proficiency, progress, promotion, strengthening, upgrade

incremental adj 1 continual, continuing, gradual, increasing, intensifying, measured, moderate, progressive, successive

adj 2 added, additional, another, auxiliary, extra, further, more, one more, other, spare, supplementary, supplemental, surplus

incriminate v see: ACCUSE v 2

incrimination n accusation, charge, complaint, inculpation, indictment

inculcate v 1 brainwash, convert, indoctrinate, persuade, preach, proselytize

v 2 see: EDUCATE v

inculpation n accusation, charge, complaint, incrimination, indictment

incur v acquire, arouse, commit, contract, engage, enlist, induce

incurable adj 1 chronic, extended, persistent, protracted, refractory, stubborn

adj 2 hopeless, impossible, irreparable, irresolvable, irrevocable, permanent, terminal, unalterable, uncorrectable, uncurable, unfixable

incursion n aggression, assault, attack, inroad, offense, offensive, onset, onslaught

indebted adj appreciative, grateful, obligated, obliged, thankful

indebtedness n encumbrance, liability, lien, mortgage, obligation, security

indecency n dirt, filth, grossness, obscenity, porn, pornography, ribaldry, smut, trash

indecent adj 1 improper, indelicate, lewd, malodorous, off-color, offensive, rough, scurrilous, suggestive, unbecoming, unseemly, untoward

adj 2 bawdy, coarse, crude, dirty, erotic, filthy, foul, gamy, gross, improper, lascivious, lewd, licentious, nasty, obscene, off-color, pornographic, profane, prurient, racy, rank, raunchy, ribald, risqué, scandalous, smutty, suggestive, tainted, uncouth, vulgar, x-rated

adj 3 erotic, improper, racy, suggestive, unbecoming

indecision n see: UNCERTAINTY n

indecisive adj 1 diffident, faltering, halting,

hesitant, reluctant, tentative, unsure, wavering, waffling

adj **2** ambiguous, imperceptible, imprecise, indefinite, indeterminate, indistinct, inexact, loose, vague, wishy-washy

adj **3** illogical, inconclusive, indefinite, open, unconvincing, unsettled, unverified

indeed *adv* absolutely, certainly, decidedly, definitely, entirely, incontrovertibly, indubitably, positively, surely, truly, unequivocally, unquestionably, verily, well, without doubt

indefinite *adj* **1** ancillary, conditional, contingent, dependent, provisional, relative, reliant, temporary, uncertain

adj **2** ambiguous, imperceptible, imprecise, indecisive, indeterminate, indistinct, inexact, loose, vague, wishy-washy

adj **3** illogical, inconclusive, indecisive, open, unconvincing, unsettled, unverified

indelible *adj* **1** memorable, momentous, unforgettable

adj **2** permanent, unalterable, unerasable

indelicate *adj* improper, indecent, lewd, malodorous, off-color, offensive, rough, scurrilous, suggestive, unbecoming, unseemly, untoward

indemnified *adj* paid, paid off, reimbursed, remunerated, repaid, rewarded

indemnify *v* avenge, compensate, cover, disburse, pay, reciprocate, redress, reimburse, remedy, remunerate, repair, repay, requite, retaliate, revenge, settle, vindicate

indemnity *n* **1** amends, compensation, damages, redress, reparation, restitution, restoration

n **2** covenant, coverage, guarantee, insurance, pledge, policy, promise, warranty

indent *n* copy, impression, imprint, indentation, mark, notch, print, stamp, tab

v bang, dent, hollow

indentation *n* **1** copy, impression, imprint, indent, mark, notch, print, stamp, tab

n **2** dent, groove, nick, notch

indenture *n* bondage, enslavement, imprisonment, serfdom, servility, servitude, slavery

indentured *adj* apprenticed, articled, bound

independence *n* autonomy, freedom, liberty, license

independent *adj* **1** autonomous, democratic, self-governing

adj **2** autonomous, distinct, free, lone, separate, sovereign, unconnected

adj **3** detached, free, impartial, neutral, nonpartisan, unattached, uncommitted, uninvolved

n freelance, individualist, loner, maverick, nonconformist

indeterminate *adj* ambiguous, imperceptible, imprecise, indecisive, indefinite, indistinct, inexact, loose, vague, wishy-washy

index *n* catalog, list, register, roster, schedule

indicate *v* **1** embody

v **2** gauge, measure, meter

v **3** appear, look, portend, seem, sound

v **4** demand, designate, insist, require, specify, stipulate

v **5** convey, express, hint, impart, imply, purport, say, suggest

v **6** disclose, display, evince, express, imply, manifest, reflect, reveal, show

v **7** allude, denote, mention, point out, refer to, reveal, show, speak of, specify, suggest, tell

v **8** add up to, connote, convey, denote, identify, import, intend, mean, show, signify, symbolize

v **9** alert, augur, caution, flag, forebode, forewarn, inform, motion, notify, signal, warn, wave

v **10** see: PLEAD *v* **2**

indicated *adj* implicit, implied, inferred, inherent, insinuated, intuitive, presumed, suggested, tacit, understood, unexpressed, unsaid, unspoken, wordless

indication *n* **1** clue, example, illustration, manifestation, proof, sign

n **2** clue, cue, guide, hint, indicator, inkling, intimation, key, lead, mark, notion, pointer, sign, signal, tip, trace

indicator *n* **1** dial, disk, display, gauge, measure, meter, pointer, selector

n **2** clue, cue, guide, hint, indication, inkling, intimation, key, lead, mark, notion, pointer, sign, signal, tip, trace

indict *v* **1** accuse, blame, charge, complain, condemn, criticize, fault, reproach

v **2** accuse, allege, arraign, assert, charge, cite, impeach, imply, impute, incriminate, litigate, prosecute, sue, try

indictment *n* **1** accusation, charge, complaint, incrimination

n **2** action, case, lawsuit, litigation, proceeding, prosecution, suit

indifference *n* **1** aloofness, detachment, preoccupation, separation

n **2** apathy, dullness, insensibility, stoicism

n 3 apathy, acedia, disinterest, disregard, lassitude, lethargy, listlessness

indifferent *adj* 1 negative

adj 2 apathetic, languid, passive, torpid

adj 3 cold, coldhearted, distant, emotionless, frigid, glacial, icy, unemotional, unfriendly

adj 4 aloof, blasé, calm, careless, casual, composed, cool, detached, diffident, disinterested, distant, informal, inhibited, nonchalant, numb, remote, reserved, shy, unconcerned, unfriendly, uninterested, withdrawn

adj 5 see: FAIR *adj* 7

adj 6 see: NASTY *adj* 7

indigence *n* deficiency, deprivation, destitution, inadequacy, lack, need, poverty, privation, scarcity, want

indigene *n* citizen, countryman, inhabitant, national, native, subject

indigenous *adj* 1 aboriginal, endemic, native, primitive

adj 2 domestic, endemic, folk, local, native, traditional

adj 3 basic, congenital, genetic, inborn, ingrained, inherent, inherited, innate, instinctive, intrinsic, natal, native, natural

indigent *adj* broke, destitute, dirt-poor, down and out, impoverished, needy, penniless, poor, poverty-stricken, strapped, unprosperous

indignant *adj* aggravated, angry, annoyed, cross, enraged, excited, fuming, furious, hot, incensed, irate, irritable, mad, provoked, teed off, upset

indignation *n* 1 anger, animosity, hostility, huff, miff, offense, pique, resentment

n 2 anger, dander, fit, frenzy, fury, ire, outrage, paroxysm, rage, tantrum, wrath

indignity *n* see: INSULT *n*

indigo *adj* aqua, azure, blue, cobalt, navy, Prussian, sapphire, turquoise

indirect *adj* 1 by proxy, secondhand, surrogate, vicarious

adj 2 circuitous, circular, deviate, diagonal, oblique, round, roundabout

adj 3 see: DECEITFUL *adj* 1

indiscernible *adj* imperceptible, imponderable, inappreciable, insensible, intangible, invisible, minute, scant, unapparent, unobservable, weak

indiscreet *adj* 1 hasty, inconsiderate, reckless, tactless, thoughtless

adj 2 clumsy, gauche, insensitive, rude, tactless, thoughtless

adj 3 foolish, ill-advised, misdirected, misguided, mistaken, unwise

indiscretion *n* blunder, folly, impropriety, mistake, slip

indiscriminate *adj* 1 comprehensive, extensive, large-scale, sweeping, wholesale

adj 2 accidental, aimless, arbitrary, casual, chance, chaotic, haphazard, hit-or-miss, irregular, random, unaimed, uncontrolled, unplanned

adj 3 casual, easy, fast, immoral, incontinent, lax, lecherous, lewd, licentious, light, loose, promiscuous, unchaste, wanton, whorish

indispensable *adj* critical, essential, imperative, mandatory, necessary, needed, prerequisite, required, vital

indisposed *adj* 1 afraid, averse, disinclined, hesitant, loath, opposed, recalcitrant, reluctant, shy, timid, uneager, unwilling

adj 2 ailing, delicate, diseased, down, frail, ill, impaired, sick, sickly, suffering, unhealthy, unsound, unwell, weak

indisputable *adj* 1 absolute, actual, authentic, bona fide, certain, definite, existent, factual, genuine, hard, inarguable, incontestable, incontrovertible, indubitable, irrefutable, positive, real, sure, true, undeniable, undisputable, undoubtable, undoubted, unequivocal, unquestionable, veritable, viable

adj 2 see: OBVIOUS *adj* 3

indistinct *adj* see: INDECISIVE *adj* 2

individual *adj* 1 particular, personal, special, specific

adj 2 introspective, personal, private, subjective

adj 3 exclusive, intimate, own, personal, private, secret, special

adj 4 a, a few, any, at least one, each, every, one, several, some

adj 5 see: LONE

n 1 associate, collaborator, member, participant, party, person, registrant

n 2 being, citizen, creature, entity, Homo sapiens, human, human being, man, person, woman

individualist *n* freelance, independent, loner, maverick, nonconformist

individuality *n* 1 distinctiveness, oneness, singularity, singularness, unity

n 2 ego, id, mind, persona, personality, psyche, self, soul, spirit

n 3 aptitude, character, complexion, disposition, distinctiveness, heart, humor, identity, inclination, makeup, nature, personality, quality, spirit, state, temperament, tendency *n* **4** distinctiveness, originality, uniqueness

individually *adv* separately

individuals *n* citizens, civilization, colony, community, crowd, culture, folks, group, human beings, laity, masses, men and women, neighbors, people, persons, populace, population, public, settlement, society, staff, tribe

indoctrinate *v* **1** brainwash, convert, inculcate, persuade, preach, proselytize

v **2** bend, bias, brainwash, compel, convert, influence, predispose, prejudice, proselytize, slant, sway

v **3** coach, communicate, condition, convey, cultivate, develop, discipline, drill, edify, educate, enlighten, exercise, explain, groom, imbue, impart, implant, improve, inculcate, inform, infuse, inseminate, inspire, instill, instruct, perfect, practice, prepare, ready, school, teach, train, tutor

indolent *adj* see: LAZY *adj*

indomitable *adj* **1** firm, invincible, unconquerable, unyielding

adj **2** intractable, recalcitrant, stubborn, uncontrollable, undisciplined, unmanageable, unruly, untoward, wild

indubitable *adj* **1** absolute, actual, authentic, bona fide, certain, definite, existent, factual, genuine, hard, inarguable, incontestable, incontrovertible, indisputable, irrefutable, positive, real, sure, true, undeniable, undisputable, undoubtable, undoubted, unequivocal, unquestionable, veritable, viable

adj **2** see: OBVIOUS *adj* 3

indubitably *adv* see: DEFINITELY *adv*

induce *v* **1** attract, draw, solicit

v **2** cause, generate, muster, occasion, produce

v **3** acquire, arouse, commit, contract, engage, enlist

v **4** arouse, awaken, excite, instill, motivate, move, pique, prime, provoke, quicken, roust, rouse, spark, start, stimulate, titillate, urge

v **5** affect, assure, convince, impel, influence, inspire, instigate, motivate, move, persuade, pressure, prompt, stir, sway, talk into, touch, win over

v **6** agitate, anger, arouse, encourage, foment, ignite, incite, inflame, inspire, instigate, invoke, motivate, muster, prod, propel, provoke, raise, set, set on, spur, stimulate, stir, urge

v **7** see: MOVE *v* 5, 6

inducement *n* **1** bonus, consideration, goal, incentive, motivation, motive, reason, reward, stimulus

n **2** bid, expectation, hope, invitation, motion, offer, proffer, proposal, proposition, recommendation, request, suggestion

n **3** attitude, belief, bias, conviction, feeling, leaning, mind, opinion, persuasion, sentiment, slant, view

inducing *adj* causal, causative, germinal, originative

induct *v* **1** call, conscript, draft, enroll, force, impress, select, shanghai

v **2** see: INITIATE *v* 2

induction *n* beginning, briefing, commencement, debut, inauguration, initiation, unveiling

indulge *v* accommodate, baby, cater, coddle, gratify, humor, overindulge, pamper, pander, placate, satisfy, spoil

indulgence *n* **1** consideration, courtesy, dispensation, favor, kindness, privilege, respect, service

n **2** clemency, forbearance, lenience, leniency, mercifulness, mercy, tolerance, toleration

indulgent *adj* accepting, charitable, easy, forbearing, lenient, merciful, patient, restrained, sympathetic, tolerant

industrialist *n* baron, big shot, businessman, businessperson, businesswoman, capitalist, entrepreneur, executive, financier, magnate, mogul, plutocrat, tycoon, VIP

industrious *adj* ambitious, assiduous, diligent, energetic, hard-working, persevering, persistent, resolute, sedulous, zealous

industry *n* arrangements, business, commerce, dealings, enterprise, intercourse, negotiations, trade, traffic

inebriated *adj* bombed, crocked, doped up, drunk, drunken, high, intoxicated, juiced, loaded, looped, messed up, plastered, polluted, sloshed, smashed, stoned, tight, tipsy, turned on, wasted, wired

ineffective *adj* **1** emasculate, impotent, inadequate, ineffectual, spineless, weak

adj **2** abortive, fruitless, futile, ineffectual, nonproductive, unavailing, unproductive, unsuccessful, unyielding, useless, vain, worthless

ineffectual *adj* **1** emasculate, impotent, inadequate, ineffective, spineless, weak

adj **2** limited, little, mean, narrow, paltry, set, small

adj **3** abortive, fruitless, futile, ineffective, nonproductive, unavailing, unproductive, unsuccessful, unyielding, useless, vain, worthless

inelastic *adj* bullheaded, closed-minded, deaf, firm, hardheaded, hard-line, inflexible, intractable, intransigent, obstinate, perverse, pigheaded, refractory, resolute, rigid, stiff, stubborn, tough, unbending, uncompromising, unpliable, unpliant, unwieldy, unyielding, willful

ineligible *adj* botching, bungling, goofing, helpless, ill-adapted, ill-suited, ill-timed, improper, inadequate, inappropriate, incapable, incongruous, incorrect, inept, malapropos, unable, unbecoming, unbefitting, unequipped, unfit, unqualified, unseemly, unskilled, unsuitable, unsuited

inept *adj* 1 amateurish, incompetent, unprofessional

adj 2 deficient, out of practice, rusty, stale, unpracticed, unprepared

adj 3 awkward, bumbling, clumsy, faltering, gauche, gawky, halting, hesitant, lumbering, maladroit, ungainly, ungraceful

adj 4 botching, bungling, goofing, helpless, ill-adapted, ill-suited, ill-timed, improper, inadequate, inappropriate, incapable, incongruous, incorrect, ineligible, malapropos, unable, unbecoming, unbefitting, unequipped, unfit, unqualified, unseemly, unskilled, unsuitable, unsuited

adj 5 feeble, helpless, impotent, powerless, weak

adj 6 absurd, anile, asinine, brainless, childish, fatuous, foolish, idiotic, meaningless, mindless, senseless, silly, simple, thoughtless, unintelligent, witless

ineptitude *n* inability, incompetence, lack of skill

inequitable *adj* biased, partial, uneven, unfair, unjust, unrighteous, wrongful

inequity *n* injustice, prejudice, unfairness, wrong

inert *adj* 1 dormant, lethargic, numb, sluggish, torpid

adj 2 dormant, inactive, latent, on hold, passive, potential, quiet, suspended, unused

adj 3 dead, hush, inanimate, lifeless, noiseless, quiet, silent, soundless, still

adj 4 asleep, dormant, idle, immobile, inactive, inanimate, inoperative, laidback, motionless, nodding, passive, quiet, sleepy, slumbering, stable, stagnant, still

adj 5 see: LAZY *adj*

inertia *n* 1 apathy, impotence, inaction, inactivity, paralysis

n 2 apathy, boredom, depression, languor

n 3 apathy, coma, doze, ennui, grogginess, languor, lassitude, lethargy, nod, sleep, slumber, stupor

inevitable *adj* 1 closing, decisive, definitive, eventual, final, latest, last

adj 2 definite, determined, fixed, foregone, inexorable, irrevocable, ordained, predestined, unalterable, unavoidable, unchangeable

inexact *adj* 1 erroneous, false, faulty, imprecise, inaccurate, incorrect, mistaken, specious, untrue, wrong

adj 2 ambiguous, imperceptible, imprecise, indecisive, indefinite, indeterminate, indistinct, loose, vague, wishy-washy

inexhaustible *adj* see: STUBBORN *adj* 6

inexorable *adj* 1 definite, determined, fixed, foregone, inevitable, irrevocable, ordained, predestined, unalterable, unavoidable, unchangeable

adj 2 see: STUBBORN *adj* 6

inexpensive *adj* cheap, economical, low, low-cost, moderate, reasonable

inexperienced *adj* 1 alterable, impressionable, malleable, naive, sensitive, susceptible

adj 2 green, immature, naive, new, novice, raw, unsophisticated, virgin

adj 3 amateur, lay, nonprofessional, unprofessional

inexplicable *adj* enigmatic, incomprehensible, inscrutable, mysterious, occult, puzzling

inexplicit *adj* see: VAGUE *adj* 6

infallible *adj* 1 dependable, fail-safe, reliable, sure, tested, tried

adj 2 accurate, certain, distinct, explicit, incontestable, perfect, unerring

infamous *adj* 1 despicable, notorious, offensive, scandalous, shady, unsavory, villainous

adj 2 base, corrupt, deadly, degenerate, depraved, deviant, evil, immoral, kinky, nefarious, perverse, putrid, rotten, ruthless, savage, vicious, villainous, wicked, wild

adj 3 ill-famed, notorious, opprobrious

infamy *n* 1 censure, contempt, discredit, disfavor, disgrace, dishonor, disparagement, disrepute, humiliation, notoriety, scandal, shame

n 2 see: CRIME *n* 3

infancy *n* see: ORIGIN *n* 3

infant *n* babe, baby, child, newborn, tot, tyke

infantile *adj* babyish, callow, childish, immature, sophomoric

infantry *n* airborne, army, battalion, brigade, cavalry, company, footmen, guard, horsemen, legion, marines, militia, minutemen, paratroops, platoon, reserve, storm troopers

infatuated *adj* captivated, enamored, fascinated, in love

infatuation *n* 1 fetish, fixation, obsession, passion, preoccupation

n 2 adultery, affair, cheating, dalliance, entanglement, fling, flirtation, fooling around, intimacy, intrigue, liaison, love affair, playing around, rendezvous, romance, tryst

n 3 affinity, allure, appeal, attraction, attractiveness, aura, beguilement, charisma, charm, enchantment, enticement, fascination, glamour, magnetism, sex appeal, spell

infect *v* contaminate, dirty, foul, poison, pollute

infection *n* 1 cancer, corruption, decay, evil, malignancy, poison, rot, toxin, venom

n 2 cold, illness, virus

n 3 incitement, infusion, inspiration, stimulation

infectious *adj* catching, communicable, contagious, contaminative, epidemic, spreading, transmittable

infer *v* 1 comprehend, decipher, decode, interpret, peruse, read, study, understand

v 2 connote, hint, implant, imply, insinuate, lead, offer, put forth, seed

v 3 analyze, conclude, construe, draw, deduce, derive, educe, gather, glean, guess, interpret, presume, surmise

v 4 assume, believe, comprehend, conceive, estimate, expect, fathom, gather, grasp, guess, imagine, know, presume, suppose, surmise, suspect, think, trust, understand

inference *n* 1 conclusion, deduction, guess, reasoning, summation

n 2 assumption, conjecture, deduction, explanation, guess, hypothesis, postulate, presumption, proposition, speculation, supposition, theory

inferior *adj* 1 lesser, lower, subordinate, under

adj 2 deficient, meaner, not as good, poorer, worse

adj 3 bad, defective, futile, inadequate, incorrect, invalid, malfunctioning, poor, void

adj 4 base, beneath, despicable, ignoble, low, lowdown, sordid, squalid, unworthy, vile, vulgar, wretched

adj 5 bare, deficient, few, inadequate, insufficient, little, meager, paltry, petty, poor, scant, scanty, skimpy, spare, sparse

adj 6 flawed, flimsy, imperfect, lousy, mediocre, miserable, paltry, poor, second-rate, shabby, shoddy, sorry, so-so, tacky, unworthy, worthless

adj 7 see: DEFICIENT *adj* 3, 4

inferno *n* hades, hell

inferred *adj* implicit, implied, indicated, inherent, insinuated, intuitive, presumed, suggested, tacit, understood, unexpressed, unsaid, unspoken, wordless

infertile *adj* barren, effete, frigid, impotent, spent, sterile, unbearing, unfertile, unfruitful, unproductive

infest *v* invade, overrun, pervade, plague, swarm

infidel *n* 1 agnostic, nonbeliever, skeptic

n 2 agnostic, atheist, gentile, heathen, heretic, pagan, unbeliever

infiltrate *v* 1 enter, infuse, penetrate, permeate, transfuse

v 2 edge in, foist, imbue, insinuate, penetrate, permeate, sneak in, work in, worm

infiltration *n* 1 exploration, foray, invasion, patrol, penetration, raid

n 2 destruction, downfall, overthrow, ruin, subversion, upset

infinite *adj* 1 endless, eternal, immortal, perpetual, unceasing, undying

adj 2 countless, immeasurable, incalculable, innumerable, innumerous, legion, many, numberless, uncountable, unlimited, untold

adj 3 ageless, boundless, ceaseless, constant, continual, continuous, endless, eternal, everlasting, incessant, interminable, limitless, never-ending, ongoing, perpetual, persistent, relentless, timeless, unceasing, unending, uninterrupted, unremitting

infirmary *n* asylum, clinic, dispensary, hospital, institution

infirmity *n* affliction, ailment, complaint, condition, disease, disorder, evil, harm, ill, illness, malady, sickness

inflame *v* 1 burn, enkindle, fire, ignite, kindle, light, spark

v 2 see: BOTHER *v* 5

v 3 see: INSTIGATE *v* 1

inflammable *adj* combustible, flammable

inflammation *n* blister, fester, lesion, sore, swelling, welt

inflate *v* 1 exaggerate, expand, oversell, overstate, stretch

v 2 amplify, bloat, dilate, distend, enlarge, expand, fatten, grow, increase, magnify, stretch, swell, widen

inflated *adj* 1 bloated, distended, puffy, swollen, tumescent, tumid, turgid

adj 2 see: FLAMBOYANT *adj* 2

inflect *v* moderate, modify, modulate, regulate, restrain, temper

inflection *n* accent, elocution, enunciation, intonation, manner, pronunciation

inflexible *adj* 1 constant, determinate, firm, fixed, hard, immutable, invariable, ironclad, resolute, stable, unalterable, unchangeable, unmovable

adj 2 authoritarian, authoritative, autocratic, controlled, despotic, disciplined, firm, harsh, ironhanded, restrictive, rigid, rigorous, ruthless, severe, solid, stern, strict, stringent, strong, tough, tyrannical

adj 3 adamant, ceaseless, dedicated, determined, firm, immovable, inexhaustible, inexorable, narrow-minded, obstinate, relentless, resolute, resolved, rigid, single-minded, steadfast, stubborn, unbendable, unbending, uncompromising, unswayable, unyielding

adj 4 bullheaded, closed-minded, deaf, firm, hardheaded, hard-line, inelastic, intractable, intransigent, obstinate, perverse, pigheaded, refractory, resolute, rigid, stiff, stubborn, tough, unbending, uncompromising, unpliable, unpliant, unwieldy, unyielding, willful

inflict *v* direct, give, implement, impose, strike

influence *n* 1 control, predominance, preponderance, supremacy

n 2 charisma, dominance, leadership, magnetism, personality, power, strength

n 3 authority, clout, control, in, leverage, power, prestige, pull, weight

n 4 see: HOLD *n* 2

v 1 concern, interest, involve

v 2 alter, effect, impact, impress, modify

v 3 bias, color, distort, embellish, exaggerate, slant

v 4 campaign, canvass, lobby, persuade, strive, support

v 5 bend, bias, brainwash, compel, convert, indoctrinate, predispose, prejudice, proselytize, slant, sway

v 6 affect, assure, convince, impel, induce,

inspire, instigate, motivate, move, persuade, pressure, prompt, stir, sway, talk into, touch, win over

v 7 see: GOVERN *v* 4

influential *adj* 1 commanding, compelling, important, powerful

adj 2 see: SOLID

inform *v* 1 blab, divulge, reveal, tell

v 2 acquaint, advise, apprise, fill in, notify, post, tell, update

v 3 fink, rat, sing, snitch, squeal, stool, tattle, tattletale

v 4 communicate, disclose, display, divulge, exhibit, notify, open, reveal, uncover, unveil

v 5 alert, augur, caution, flag, forebode, forewarn, indicate, motion, notify, signal, warn, wave

v 6 brief, communicate, convey, declare, describe, disclose, divulge, explain, impart, narrate, orate, portray, read, recite, recount, relate, report, retell, reveal, share, state, tattle, tell, transmit

v 7 coach, communicate, condition, convey, cultivate, develop, discipline, drill, edify, educate, enlighten, exercise, explain, groom, imbue, impart, implant, improve, inculcate, indoctrinate, infuse, inseminate, inspire, instill, instruct, perfect, practice, prepare, ready, school, teach, train, tutor

informal *adj* 1 casual, cavalier, colloquial, familiar, ordinary, regular, relaxed, unceremonious, unconstrained, unofficial, usual, vernacular

adj 2 see: INDIFFERENT *adj* 4

information *n* 1 data, details, dope, facts, report, scoop

n 2 data, discipline, facts, knowledge, lore, news, science, wisdom

n 3 see: COMMUNICATION *n* 2

informative *adj* academic, educational, enlightening, eye-opening, illuminating, instructive, revealing, scholastic

informed *adj* abreast, acquainted, aware, conversant, familiar, knowledgeable, up, versed

informer *n* accuser, betrayer, double-crosser, fink, reptile, snake, sneak, stooge, traitor

infraction *n* 1 breach, default, misdemeanor, trespass, violation

n 2 crime, dishonor, disobedience, evil, fault, felony, infamy, iniquity, injury, lawbreaking, misdeed, misdemeanor, offense, outrage, sin, transgression, trespass, vice, violation, wrong, wrongdoing

infrastructure n 1 base

n 2 chassis, framework, skeleton

n 3 cadre, center, core, nucleus

n 4 complex, maze, network, organization, system

infrequent adj few, isolated, occasional, rare, scarce, seldom, sporadic, uncommon, unusual

infrequently adv now and then, once in a while, rarely, sporadically

infringe v 1 attack, encroach, entrench, intrude, invade, trespass, violate

v 2 defy, disobey, ignore, obstruct, oppose, rebel, resist, violate

infuriate v aggravate, anger, annoy, bother, bug, enrage, exasperate, frazzle, gall, grate, hassle, incense, inflame, irk, irritate, madden, miff, nettle, outrage, peeve, pester, pique, provoke, rile, upset, vex

infuse v 1 enter, infiltrate, penetrate, permeate, transfuse

v 2 color, enhance, flavor, imbue, salt, season, spice

v 3 imbue, impart, ingrain, inject, inoculate, instill, invest, penetrate, pervade, spread, steep, suffuse, teach, train

v 4 see: EDUCATE v

infusion n incitement, infection, inspiration, stimulation

ingenious adj 1 clever, gifted, handy, inventive, talented, versatile

adj 2 clever, creative, deft, enterprising, fertile, imaginative, inventive, resourceful, skillful, talented

adj 3 adroit, apt, canny, clever, cunning, deft, handy, nimble, skilled, skillful, sly, wily

ingenuity n creativity, fancy, fantasy, image, imagination, inspiration, invention, resourcefulness, whimsy

ingenuous adj 1 credulous, gullible, trusting, trustworthy

adj 2 artless, candid, frank, guileless, innocent, naive, natural, open, plain, simple, simple-hearted, unadorned, unaffected, unsophisticated, unstudied, untutored, unworldly

ingest v consume, devour, digest, eat, masticate, swallow

ingot n bar, pole, rod, stick, strip

ingrain v 1 engrave

v 2 imbue, impart, infuse, inject, inoculate, instill, invest, penetrate, pervade, spread, steep, suffuse, teach, train

ingrained adj 1 ensconced, entrenched, established, fixed, fundamental, intrinsic, inveterate, settled, sworn

adj 2 see: INSTINCTIVE adj 3

ingratiate v attract, cajole, disarm, flatter

ingratiating adj 1 abject, common, groveling, humble, lowly, menial, obeisant, obsequious, servile, slavish, subservient

adj 2 see: SOPHISTICATED adj 2

ingredient n component, constituent, element, factor, item, part, segment

ingredients n makings, potential, substance

inhabit v domicile, dwell, live, occupy, reside, room, settle, stay

inhabitant n 1 citizen, countryman, indigene, national, native, subject

n 2 lessee, occupant, renter, resident, squatter, tenant

n 3 addressee, citizen, dweller, occupant, owner, resident, tenant

inhalation n breath, breathing

inhale v 1 breathe, exhale, gasp

v 2 drag, draw, puff, smoke

inharmonious adj conflicting

inherent adj 1 latent, possible, potential, promising, realizable

adj 2 basic, congenital, genetic, inborn, indigenous, ingrained, inherited, innate, instinctive, intrinsic, natal, native, natural

adj 3 see: IMPLIED adj 2

inherit v acquire

inheritance n 1 birthright, endowment, entitlement, estate, heritage, legacy, patrimony

n 2 assets, belongings, equity, estate, fortune, goods, holdings, money, ownership, possessions, property, prosperity, riches, treasure, wealth

inherited adj see: INSTINCTIVE adj 3

inhibit v 1 ban, bar, confine, enjoin, forbid, nix, outlaw, prevent, prohibit, stop, suppress, veto

v 2 bridle, check, constrain, control, crimp, curb, hold back, hold down, leash, rein, restrain, restrict, withhold

v 3 avert, bar, deter, eliminate, foil, forestall, hinder, hold off, preclude, prevent, stave off, thwart, turn back, ward off

v 4 see: HINDER v 4, 5

v 5 see: STIFLE v 3

inhibited adj 1 cold, frigid, passionless, repressed, restrained, reticent, unresponsive

adj 2 aloof, blasé, calm, careless, casual, composed, cool, detached, diffident, disinterested, distant, indifferent, informal, nonchalant, numb, remote, reserved, shy, unconcerned, unfriendly, uninterested, withdrawn

inhibition *n* block, check, curb, hangup, repression, restraint, reticence

inhuman *adj* see: NASTY *adj* 7

inhumane *adj* see: NASTY *adj* 7

inimical *adj* adverse, antagonistic, bellicose, hostile, ill, nasty, spiteful, unfriendly

iniquitous *adj* bad, corrupt, crooked, deceitful, dishonest, evil, fraudulent, immoral, lying, Machiavellian, manipulative, mercenary, reprobate, roguish, scheming, shady, shifty, sinful, unethical, unfair, unprincipled, unscrupulous, untruthful, venal, vile, wicked, wrong

iniquity *n* crime, dishonor, disobedience, evil, fault, felony, infamy, infraction, injury, lawbreaking, misdeed, misdemeanor, offense, outrage, sin, transgression, trespass, vice, violation, wrong, wrongdoing

initial *adj* 1 chief, first, foremost, head, inaugural, lead, leading, premier, prime
adj 2 earliest, first, founding, fundamental, maiden, original, pioneer, primary, prime
adj 3 beginning, embryonic, founding, incipient, introductory, nascent, rudimentary, starting
adj 4 basic, early, elementary, embryonic, essential, fundamental, intrinsic, original, rudimentary, underlying

initiate *v* 1 build, constitute, construct, create, erect, establish, found, institute, launch, set up, start
v 2 activate, begin, cause, commence, constitute, create, embark, enter, establish, inaugurate, induct, install, instigate, instill, institute, introduce, kick off, launch, lead off, open, originate, precipitate, preface, set up, start, tee off, usher in, venture forth

initiation *n* 1 beginning, briefing, commencement, debut, inauguration, induction, unveiling
n 2 certification, commencement, graduation, promotion

initiative *n* 1 enterprise, gumption, resourcefulness, spirit, spunk, volition
n 2 ambition, drive, enterprise, lead, leadership, push, thrust, volition

initiator *n* 1 agitator, instigator, organizer, rabble-rouser, spark plug, troublemaker
n 2 author, creator, founder, instigator, inventor, maker, originator, parent, pioneer, seed, source

initiatory *adj* basic, creative, formative, fundamental, productive, seminal

inject *v* 1 imbue, impart, infuse, ingrain, inoculate, instill, invest, penetrate, pervade, spread, steep, suffuse, teach, train
v 2 inoculate, vaccinate

injection *n* booster, inoculation, shot

injunction *n* behest, bidding, canon, charge, command, criterion, decree, dictate, direction, edict, fiat, guideline, institution, law, mandate, order, ordinance, precept, prescript, prescription, regulation, rite, rule, ruling, statute, word

injure *v* 1 bruise, hurt, lacerate, mangle, wound
v 2 afflict, aggrieve, bother, burden, distress, grieve, hurt, pain
v 3 abuse, brutalize, exploit, harm, illtreat, maltreat, mistreat, molest, persecute, victimize, wrong
v 4 abuse, blemish, damage, hamper, harm, hurt, impair, mar, obstruct, ruin, sabotage, scuttle, spoil, tarnish, vandalize
v 5 see: DEFAME *v* 1

injurious *adj* 1 adverse, deleterious, detrimental, harmful, negative, unfavorable
adj 2 damaging, dangerous, deleterious, harmful, hurting, ruinous, unhealthy

injury *n* 1 complaint, hardship, grievance, injustice, wrong
n 2 bruise, hurt, pain, sprain, strain, wound
n 3 ache, affliction, agony, anguish, hurt, pain, punishment, suffering, torture
n 4 chaos, damage, destruction, devastation, disaster, disorder, harm, havoc, hurt, loss, mayhem, ruin, ruination
n 5 cramp, sprain, strain
n 6 crime, dishonor, disobedience, evil, fault, felony, infamy, infraction, iniquity, lawbreaking, misdeed, misdemeanor, offense, outrage, sin, transgression, trespass, vice, violation, wrong, wrongdoing

injustice *n* 1 inequity, prejudice, unfairness, wrong
n 2 complaint, grievance, hardship, wrong

ink *v* autograph, sign, subscribe

inkling *n* clue, cue, guide, hint, indication, indicator, intimation, key, lead, mark, notion, pointer, sign, signal, tip, trace

inlet *n* 1 access, aperture, approach, entrance, mouth, opening, passage
n 2 arm, bay, cove, estuary, fiord, gulf, narrows, sound, strait

inmate *n* see: CRIMINAL *n* 2

inn *n* club, hotel, lodge, resort, spa

innate *adj* **1** automatic, deep, gut, instinctive, intuitive, visceral

adj **2** basic, congenital, genetic, inborn, indigenous, ingrained, inherent, inherited, instinctive, intrinsic, natal, native, natural

inner *adj* enclosed, hidden, innermost, interior, internal, private, secret

innermost *adj* enclosed, hidden, inner, interior, internal, private, secret

innocent *adj* **1** believing, credulous, easy, gullible, naive, susceptible, trustful

adj **2** blameless, commendable, exemplary, exonerated, guiltless, irreproachable, pure, righteous, virtuous

adj **3** benign, harmless, innocuous, inoffensive, mild, naive, pure, safe, unoffending, unoffensive

adj **4** artless, candid, frank, guileless, ingenuous, naive, natural, open, plain, simple, simple-hearted, unadorned, unaffected, unsophisticated, unstudied, untutored, unworldly

adj **5** see: SHY *adj* **2**

n virgin

innocuous *adj* **1** banal, bland, dull, flat, insipid, tasteless, unexciting

adj **2** benign, harmless, innocent, inoffensive, mild, naive, pure, safe, unoffending, unoffensive

innovate *v* see: INVENT *v* **3**

innovation *n* **1** creativity

n **2** breakthrough, creation, invention

innovative *adj* new, novel, original, pioneering, trailblazing, unprecedented

innovators *n* leaders, pacesetters, pioneers, trendsetters, vanguard

innuendo *n* **1** allusion, connotation, hint, implication, insinuation, notation, reference, suggestion

n **2** affront, aspersion, attack, barb, caustic remark, crack, cut, denunciation, despite, dig, disparagement, disrespect, gibe, implication, indignity, insult, invective, knock, reflection, sarcasm, scorn, slap, slight, slur, spike, tongue-lashing, verbal jab

innumerable *adj* countless, immeasurable, incalculable, infinite, innumerous, legion, many, numberless, uncountable, unlimited, untold

innumerous *adj* countless, immeasurable, incalculable, infinite, innumerable, legion, many, numberless, uncountable, unlimited, untold

inoculate *v* **1** imbue, impart, infuse, ingrain, inject, instill, invest, penetrate, pervade, spread, steep, suffuse, teach, train

v **2** immunize, inject, vaccinate

inoculation *n* injection, shot

inoffensive *adj* benign, harmless, innocent, innocuous, mild, naive, pure, safe, unoffending, unoffensive

inoperable *adj* impractical, undoable, unworkable

inoperative *adj* see: INACTIVE *adj* **2**

inordinate *adj* excessive, gluttonous, immoderate, intemperate, overindulgent, prodigious, unbridled, undue, unrestrained, voracious

inquire *v* **1** ask, cross-examine, examine, grill, interrogate, investigate, probe, pump, query, question, quiz

v **2** delve, dig, examine, explore, feel out, grope, hunt, investigate, look, observe, peer, probe, pursue, research, scan, scrutinize, search, seek, sound, study, test

inquiring *adj* **1** keen, penetrating, piercing, probing, searching

adj **2** curious, inquisitive, investigative, nosy, probing, prying, questioning, snooping

inquiry *n* **1** exam, examination, final, oral, questionnaire, quiz, test

n **2** examination, inspection, probing, scrutiny, search, study, survey

n **3** assessment, examination, review, scope, search, study, survey

n **4** see: INVESTIGATION *n*

inquisition *n* see: INVESTIGATION *n*

inquisitive *adj* curious, inquiring, investigative, nosy, probing, prying, questioning, snooping

inquisitiveness *n* concern, curiosity, interest, regard

inroad *n* **1** attack, conquest, defeat, foray, intrusion, invasion, trespass

n **2** aggression, assault, attack, incursion, offense, offensive, onset, onslaught

insane *adj* **1** demented, deranged, distraught, mentally ill, psychotic

adj **2** absurd, balmy, bizarre, crazy, emotional, foolish, frivolous, goofy, illogical, impossible, inane, irrational, loony, lunatic, mad, muddled, nuts, preposterous, ridiculous, silly, touched, wacky, zany

insanity *n* **1** craziness, folly, foolishness, frivolity, lunacy, madness, mania, nonsense, senselessness

n **2** aberration, abnormality, craziness, delusion, dementia, derangement, distraction, eccentricity, fugue, hallucination, irregularity, lunacy, madness, mania, psychosis, unbalance

insatiable *adj* avaricious, covetous, endless, ravenous, unquenchable, voracious

inscribe *v* 1 carve, cut, engrave, etch

v 2 catalog, enroll, list, register, signup, write

inscription *n* legend

inscrutable *adj* enigmatic, incomprehensible, inexplicable, mysterious, occult, puzzling

insect *n* bug

insecure *adj* 1 anxious, nervous, precarious, threatened, uncertain, vulnerable

adj 2 flimsy, jiggly, rickety, shaky, teetering, unstable, unsure, vacillating, wavering, weak, wobbly

adj 3 dubious, questionable, undependable, unreliable, unsure, untrustworthy

inseminate *v* 1 engender, father, fertilize, impregnate, sire

v 2 see: EDUCATE *v*

insemination *n* conception, fertilization, propagation, reproduction, spawning

insensibility *n* apathy, dullness, indifference, stoicism

insensible *adj* 1 dazed, numb, senseless, unconscious

adj 2 cold, comatose, senseless, unconscious

adj 3 imperceptible, imponderable, inappreciable, indiscernible, intangible, invisible, minute, scant, unapparent, unobservable, weak

insensitive *adj* clumsy, gauche, indiscreet, rude, tactless, thoughtless

insert *n* addendum, addition, appendix, rider, supplement

v 1 add, contain, enclose, include

v 2 fill in, implant, insinuate, interject, interpolate, interpose, interrupt, introduce, throw in

v 3 cram, crush, force, gorge, jam, pack, press, ram, stuff

v 4 see: INSTALL *v* 1

inside *prep* amid, among, inside of, mid, midst, with, within

insidious *adj* 1 astute, calculating, crafty, cunning, foxy, guileful, sharp, shrewd, sly, smart, subtle, tricky, wily, wise

adj 2 see: TREACHEROUS *adj* 2

insight *n* 1 cognition, comprehension, grasp, perception, recognition, understanding

n 2 acumen, astuteness, awareness, cleverness, discernment, discrimination, intellect, intuition, keenness, perception,

sagacity, sensitivity, shrewdness, understanding, wit

insightful *adj* 1 see: ESOTERIC *adj*

adj 2 see: INTELLIGENT *adj* 4

insignificant *adj* 1 abnormal, extra, extraneous, foreign, illogical, immaterial, irregular, irrelevant, malapropos, nonessential, peripheral, superfluous, surplus, unimportant, unnecessary, unrelated

adj 2 immaterial, inconsequential, inconsiderable, little, low, meaningless, measly, minor, nominal, paltry, petty, picayune, picky, puny, skimpy, slight, small, tiny, trifling, trivial, unessential, unimportant, worthless

adj 3 borderline, casual, frivolous, light, lightweight, little, marginal, meager, minor, minute, negligible, nonessential, off, outside, petty, remote, secondary, slender, slight, slim, small, tenuous, trivial, unimportant

insincere *adj* empty, hollow, idle, meaningless, shallow, vain

insinuate *v* 1 connote, hint, implant, imply, infer, lead, offer, put forth, seed

v 2 edge in, foist, imbue, infiltrate, penetrate, permeate, sneak in, work in, worm

v 3 fill in, implant, insert, interject, interpolate, interpose, interrupt, introduce, throw in

insinuated *adj* implicit, implied, indicated, inferred, inherent, intuitive, presumed, suggested, tacit, understood, unexpressed, unsaid, unspoken, wordless

insinuation *n* 1 allusion, connotation, hint, implication, innuendo, notation, reference, suggestion

n 2 see: TRACE *n* 4

insipid *adj* banal, bland, dull, flat, innocuous, tasteless, unexciting

insist *v* 1 demand, designate, indicate, require, specify, stipulate

v 2 assert, demand, emphasize, force, persist, require, urge

insistent *adj* aggressive, ambitious, assertive, assured, compelling, compulsive, confident, decided, dogmatic, driven, emphatic, energetic, militant, positive, pushing, pushy, self-assertive, sure, urging

insolence *n* arrogance, assurance, audacity, boldness, brashness, brass, cheek, chutzpah, condescension, confidence, crust, effrontery, face, gall, haughtiness, nerve, patronage, presumption, ridicule, sass, stamina, temerity

insolent *adj* 1 audacious, bold, brash, brazen, cheeky, daring, disrespectful, forward, fresh, impertinent, impudent, irreverent, nervy, pert, rude, sassy, saucy

adj 2 audacious, boorish, discourteous, disrespectful, ill-behaved, ill-bred, ill-mannered, impertinent, impolite, rude, surly, uncalled for, uncivil, uncivilized, uncouth, uncultured, unpolished, unrefined

adj 3 arrogant, cavalier, conceited, contemptuous, curt, dictatorial, disdainful, grandiose, haughty, huffy, lofty, lordly, moody, obtrusive, overbearing, patronizing, proud, scornful, snooty, stuck up, supercilious, superior, vain

insolvency *n* poverty

insolvent *adj* bankrupt, broke, busted, destitute, dissolved, out of business, penniless, ruined

inspect *v* 1 examine, observe, peruse, scan

v 2 audit, balance, check, examine, verify

v 3 canvass, case, check, examine, glance over, observe, peruse, pore over, regard, scrutinize, study, survey, watch

v 4 adapt, adjust, balance, fit, fix, maintain, overhaul, recondition, refurbish, regulate, repair, service, support, tune up

inspection *n* examination, inquiry, probing, scrutiny, search, study, survey

inspiration *n* 1 creativity, fancy, fantasy, image, imagination, ingenuity, invention, resourcefulness, whimsy

n 2 motivation

n 3 incitement, infection, stimulation

inspire *v* 1 animate, brighten, cheer up, enliven, incite, liven, quicken, resuscitate, vivify

v 2 amplify, bolster, encourage, enhance, enhearten, hearten, increase, reassure, strengthen, support

v 3 agitate, anger, arouse, encourage, foment, ignite, incite, induce, inflame, instigate, invoke, motivate, muster, prod, propel, provoke, raise, set, set on, spur, stimulate, stir, urge

v 4 delight, encourage, enjoy, gladden, please

v 5 arouse, electrify, excite, fire, incite, rouse, spark, stimulate, tantalize, thrill, titillate, turn on, whet

v 6 affect, assure, convince, impel, induce, influence, instigate, motivate, move, persuade, pressure, prompt, stir, sway, talk into, touch, win over

v 7 coach, communicate, condition, convey, cultivate, develop, discipline, drill, edify, educate, enlighten, exercise, explain, groom, imbue, impart, implant, improve, inculcate, indoctrinate, inform,

infuse, inseminate, instill, instruct, perfect, practice, prepare, ready, school, teach, train, tutor

inspiring *adj* 1 dynamic, electrifying, exciting, stimulating, thrilling

adj 2 convincing, effective, forcible, impressive, profound, striking

adj 3 exciting, exotic, interesting, intriguing, provocative, stimulating, tingling, titillating

install *v* 1 calibrate, establish, fix, insert, lay, locate, place, plant, position, put, set, settle, situate, station

v 2 see: INITIATE *v* 2

installation *n* maintenance, repair, service, upkeep

installment *n* component, part, portion, segment

instance *n* case, case history, clarification, example, explanation, illumination, illustration, representative, sample, sampling, specimen

instant *adj* 1 contemporary, current, existent, living, present

adj 2 immediate, instantaneous, quick, rapid, swift, urgent

adj 3 contiguous, current, direct, immediate, nearby, primary, prompt, sudden, timely

adj 4 see: RAPID *adj* 1, 2

n 1 moment, occasion, time

n 2 blink of an eye, crack, flash, jiffy, minute, moment, second, shake, twinkling, wink

instantaneous *adj* 1 immediate, instant, quick, rapid, swift, urgent

adj 2 ad-lib, extemporaneous, impromptu, improvised, invented, offhand, off the cuff, spontaneous, unrehearsed, unstudied

instantaneously *adv* 1 abruptly, fast, hastily, immediately, instantly, quick, quickly, short, suddenly, swiftly

adv 2 see: IMMEDIATELY *adv* 2, 3

instantly *adv* 1 at once, forthwith, immediately, promptly, right now, this instant, *tout de suite*

adv 2 abruptly, fast, hastily, immediately, instantaneously, quick, quickly, short, suddenly, swiftly

adv 3 see: IMMEDIATELY *adv* 1, 2, 3

instigate *v* 1 agitate, anger, arouse, encourage, foment, ignite, incite, induce, inflame, inspire, invoke, motivate, muster, prod, provoke, raise, set, set on, spur, stimulate, stir, urge

v 2 see: CONVINCE *v*

v 3 see: INITIATE *v* 2

instigator *n* **1** agitator, initiator, organizer, rabble-rouser, spark plug, troublemaker

n **2** author, creator, founder, initiator, inventor, maker, originator, parent, pioneer, seed, source

instill *v* **1** imbue, impart, infuse, ingrain, inject, inoculate, invest, penetrate, pervade, spread, steep, suffuse, teach, train

v **2** see: EDUCATE *v*

v **3** see: INITIATE

v **4** see: PROVOKE *v* **2**

instinct *n* feeling, foreboding, guess, hunch, intuition, premonition, sense, suspicion

instinctive *adj* **1** automatic, deep, gut, innate, intuitive, visceral

adj **2** automatic, impulsive, involuntary, natural, rash, reflex, spontaneous, unconscious, unforced, unpremeditated, unprompted

adj **3** basic, congenital, genetic, inborn, indigenous, ingrained, inherent, inherited, innate, intrinsic, natal, native, natural

institute *n* **1** association, institution, organization, society, union

n **2** academy, college, lyceum, school, seminary, university

v **1** allocate, appoint, assign, establish, implement, set

v **2** build, constitute, construct, create, erect, establish, found, initiate, launch, set up, start

v **3** activate, begin, cause, commence, constitute, create, embark, enter, establish, inaugurate, induct, initiate, install, instigate, instill, introduce, kick off, launch, lead off, open, originate, precipitate, preface, set up, start, tee off, usher in, venture forth

institution *n* **1** asylum, booby hatch, funny farm, loony bin, madhouse

n **2** asylum, clinic, dispensary, hospital

n **3** association, institute, organization, society, union

n **4** association, combination, corporation, establishment, fellowship, foundation, league, union

n **5** see: COMMAND *n* **3**

instruct *v* **1** bid, charge, claim, command, demand, direct, order

v **2** coach, communicate, condition, convey, cultivate, develop, discipline, drill, edify, educate, enlighten, exercise, explain, groom, imbue, impart, implant, improve, inculcate, indoctrinate, inform, infuse, inseminate, inspire, instill, perfect, practice, prepare, ready, school, teach, train, tutor

instruction *n* **1** direction, directive, guideline, outline, policy, rule

n **2** education, learning, research, scholarship, schooling, study

n **3** assignment, direction, reference, referral

instructive *adj* academic, educational, enlightening, eye-opening, illuminating, informative, revealing, scholastic

instructor *n* **1** academician, educator, intern, professor, teacher

n **2** coach, educator, leader, mentor, schoolteacher, teacher, trainer, tutor

instructors *n* department, faculty, professors, staff, teachers

instrument *n* **1** certificate, credential, document, license, pass, permit

n **2** chessman, front, pawn, peon, puppet, stooge, tool

n **3** agency, agent, channel, conduit, means, mechanism, medium, mode, vehicle

n **4** see: DEVICE *n* **3**

instrumentalist *n* accompanist, artiste, conductor, musician, performer, virtuoso

insubordinate *adj* **1** aggressive, defiant, rambunctious, restless, stubborn, unruly

adj **2** defiant, disobedient, insurgent, mutinous, rebellious, seditious

insubstantial *adj* **1** feeble, flimsy, frail, slight, tenuous, unsubstantial, weak

adj **2** see: SPIRITUAL *adj* **2**

insufficient *adj* **1** deficient, failing, inadequate, inferior, scant, scarce, scrimpy, short, shy, wanting

adj **2** see: MEAGER *adj* **2**

insulate *v* detach, isolate, seclude, separate, sequester

insult *n* affront, aspersion, attack, barb, caustic remark, crack, cut, denunciation, despite, dig, disparagement, disrespect, gibe, implication, indignity, innuendo, invective, knock, reflection, sarcasm, scorn, slap, slight, slur, spike, tonguelashing, verbal jab

v **1** cut, gibe, remark, taunt

v **2** affront, encounter, face, offend, outrage, slight

v **3** abuse, asperse, bad-mouth, belittle, condemn, damage, decry, defame, degrade, denigrate, denounce, deprecate, detract, diminish, discount, disparage, knock, malign, put down, revile, run down, slander, take away, vilify

insulting *adj* **1** derogatory, disparaging, malicious, nasty, sarcastic, snide *adj* 2 abusive, contemptuous, derisive, disrespectful, nasty, offensive, slighting

insurance *n* covenant, coverage, guarantee, indemnity, pledge, policy, promise, warranty

insurgent *adj* defiant, disobedient, insubordinate, mutinous, rebellious, seditious
n agitator, defector, dissident, heretic, iconoclast, malcontent, maverick, misfit, nonconformist, rebel, renegade, traitor, troublemaker, turncoat

insurrect *v* mutiny, rebel, revolt, rise against

insurrection *n* betrayal, mutiny, revolt, sedition, subversion, treason, uprising

intact *adj* 1 consecrated, inviolable, inviolate, protected, pure, sacred, sacrosanct
adj 2 absolute, complete, flawless, good, perfect, sound, unblemished, unbroken, undamaged, unimpaired, uninjured, unmarred, untouched, whole

intangible *adj* 1 elusive
adj 2 imperceptible, imponderable, inappreciable, indiscernible, insensible, invisible, minute, scant, unapparent, unobservable, weak
adj 3 bodiless, celestial, disembodied, ethereal, heavenly, incorporeal, insubstantial, metaphysical, nonmaterial, spiritual, unearthly, unreal, unsubstantial

integer *n* cipher, digit, number, numeral

integral *adj* 1 critical, essential, necessary, significant, strategic
adj 2 all, all-out, complete, entire, full-blown, gross, integrated, outright, total, unlimited, whole

integrate *v* 1 centralize, concentrate, consolidate, focus, merge
v 2 accommodate, adjust, attune, conform, coordinate, harmonize, proportion, reconcile, reconciliate, tune
v 3 arrange, blend, combine, compound, concoct, harmonize, make one, orchestrate, synthesize, unify
v 4 desegregate

integrated *adj* 1 all, all-out, complete, entire, full-blown, gross, integral, outright, total, unlimited, whole
adj 2 mixed

integrity *n* 1 honesty, honor, principle, trustworthiness, virtue
n 2 candor, honesty, truth, truthfulness, veracity
n 3 purity

intellect *n* 1 comprehension, mind, reason, understanding
n 2 brain, Einstein, genius, prodigy, wizard

n 3 acumen, astuteness, awareness, cleverness, discernment, discrimination, insight, intuition, keenness, perception, sagacity, sensitivity, shrewdness, understanding, wit

intellectual *adj* 1 cerebral, analytical, highbrow, intelligent
adj 2 academic, educated, educational, erudite, learned, literary, literate, pedantic, scholarly, scholastic, well-read
adj 3 alert, astute, brainy, bright, brilliant, clever, discerning, discriminating, educated, insightful, intelligent, knowing, knowledgeable, perceptive, quick, sagacious, sage, sharp, smart, swift
n academician, egghead, highbrow, philosopher, pundit, researcher, sage, savant, scholar, thinker, wise man

intelligence *n* 1 communication, data, disclosure, exchange, expression, facts, information, knowledge, news, notification
n 2 see: TALENT *n* 2

intelligent *adj* 1 analytical, cerebral, intellectual
adj 2 advanced, bright, gifted, precocious, promising, talented
adj 3 astute, consequent, knowing, logical, perceptive, rational, reasonable, sane, sensible, shrewd, sober, sound, wise
adj 4 alert, astute, brainy, bright, brilliant, clever, discerning, discriminating, educated, insightful, intellectual, knowing, knowledgeable, perceptive, quick, sagacious, sage, sharp, smart, swift

intelligible *adj* 1 expressive, meaningful
adj 2 clear, coherent, direct, easy, elementary, logical, lucid, simple, understandable

intemperate *adj* 1 extravagant, loose, reckless, unrestrained, wanton, wild
adj 2 excessive, gluttonous, immoderate, inordinate, overindulgent, prodigious, unbridled, undue, unrestrained, voracious
adj 3 bitter, brutal, cruel, fierce, hard, harsh, inclement, pitiless, rigorous, rough, rugged, severe, stern, strong, unkind, violent

intend *v* 1 aim, contemplate, design, mean, plan, propose
v 2 add up to, connote, convey, denote, identify, import, indicate, mean, show, signify, symbolize

intendance *n* administration, care, charge, conduct, handling, management, overseeing, running, supervision

intense *adj* 1 brisk, heavy, powerful, stiff, strong

adj 2 forceful, highhanded, important, maximum, powerful, utmost

adj 3 drastic, excessive, extreme, passionate, radical, severe, strong

adj 4 ardent, decisive, determined, emphatic, extreme, forceful, potent, powerful, severe, strong

adj 5 colorful, expressive, graphic, impressive, potent, powerful, striking, strong, unforgettable, vivid

adj 6 angry, ferocious, fierce, furious, heated, savage, severe, terrible, vehement, vicious, violent

adj 7 ardent, enthusiastic, excitable, fervent, fiery, flaming, hot-blooded, impassioned, passionate, stirring, sweaty, torrid, zealous

intensely *adv* see: COMPLETELY *adv*

intensify *v* 1 ascend, climb, escalate, mount, scale, surmount

v 2 augment, buttress, fortify, harden, invigorate, reinforce, strengthen

v 3 clog, clot, coagulate, condense, congeal, curdle, dry, gel, harden, jell, pack, set, solidify, thicken

v 4 amplify, append, augment, boost, build, enlarge, expand, extend, grow, heighten, increase, magnify, multiply, run up, snowball, supplement, upsurge, wax

intensifying *adj* continual, continuing, gradual, increasing, incremental, measured, moderate, progressive, successive

intensity *n* 1 ferocity, frenzy, fury, rage

n 2 degree, extent, measure, ratio, scope

n 3 power, severity, tumult, turbulence, violence

n 4 concentration, depth, energy, profundity, strength, substance, vigor

n 5 see: VIGOR *n* 1, 3

intensive *adj* aggressive, coercive, compelling, forceful, hard-sell, high-pressure, persuasive, pushy

intensively *adv* see: COMPLETELY *adv*

intent *adj* absorbed, agog, concentrated, deep, determined, distracted, engaged, engrossed, enraptured, entranced, fascinated, immersed, preoccupied, rapt, wrapped up

n 1 drift, implication, purport, substance, tenor

n 2 ambition, bent, design, goal, intention, meaning, objective, plan, purpose

n 3 import, meaning, message, sense, significance, understanding

intention *n* ambition, bent, design, goal, intent, meaning, objective, plan, purpose

intentional *adj* 1 calculated, conscious, contrived, deliberate, planned, plotted, premeditated

adj 2 deliberate, free, optional, unforced, unprescribed, voluntary, willful, willing

adj 3 bent, committed, dedicated, determined, fixed, purposeful, resolute, resolved, set, tenacious

inter *v* bury

interbreed *v* cross

intercede *v* arbitrate, interfere, interpose, intervene, intrude, mediate, settle, step in

intercept *v* 1 tackle

v 2 block, catch, cut off, detain, hinder, obstruct, stop

intercession *n* arbitration, adjudication, facilitation, intervention, mediation

intercessor *n* advocate, attorney, barrister, counsel, counselor, lawyer, mediator, solicitor

interchange *n* 1 coupling, crossing, joining, junction, juncture, linking, merger

n 2 see: DISCUSSION *n* 4

intercourse *n* 1 arrangements, business, commerce, dealings, enterprise, industry, negotiations, trade, traffic

n 2 caucus, chat, colloquy, conference, conversation, debate, dialogue, discourse, discussion, exchange, forum, interchange, interlocution, meeting, talk

n 3 coitus, conjugation, copulation, fooling around, foreplay, fornication, mating, reproduction, sex, union

interdiction *n* ban, bar, constraint, prohibition, restriction, taboo

interest *n* 1 claim, share, stake

n 2 concern, curiosity, inquisitiveness, regard

n 3 bag, field, hobby, job, specialty

n 4 account, advantage, behalf, benefit, betterment, gain, good, happiness, prosperity, sake, welfare, well-being

v 1 concern, involve

v 2 amuse, charm, divert, entertain, please, recreate, stimulate

v 3 appeal, arouse, attract, excite, fascinate, fire, intrigue, lead on, lure, seduce, stir, tantalize

interested *adj* 1 committed, concerned, involved

adj 2 absorbed, curious, drawn, engrossed, involved

interesting *adj* 1 appealing, colorful, entertaining, lively, stimulating, varied

adj 2 exciting, exotic, inspiring, intriguing, provocative, stimulating, tingling, titillating

interfere *v* 1 collide, conflict, hinder, impinge, obstruct *v* **2** arbitrate, intercede, interpose, intervene, intrude, mediate, settle, step in

v **3** disarray, dislocate, disorder, disorganize, disrupt, disturb, interrupt, jumble, mess, mix up, muss, rummage, shuffle, sift through, unsettle

v **4** butt in, chisel in, cut in, fiddle, horn in, interlope, intrude, meddle, mess around, peek, peer, poke, pry, snoop, tamper with

interference *n* break, delay, distraction, disturbance, diversion, hold-up, interruption, pause

interim *n* **1** delay, interval, lag, pause

n **2** break, cessation, delay, gap, interval, lapse, lull, pause, stop

interior *adj* enclosed, hidden, inner, innermost, internal, private, secret

interject *v* fill in, implant, insert, insinuate, interpolate, interpose, interrupt, introduce, throw in

interlock *v* connect, engage, hook up, mesh, network

interlocution *n* see: DISCUSSION *n* **4**

interlope *v* butt in, chisel in, cut in, fiddle, horn in, interfere, intrude, meddle, mess around, peek, peer, poke, pry, snoop, tamper with

interloper *n* busybody, gossip, intruder, kibitzer, meddler, snoop, yenta

interlude *n* idle time, lull, recreation, relaxation, repose, rest, vacation

intermediary *n* absorber, agent, broker, catalyst, distributor, go-between, mediator, middleman, negotiator

intermediate *adj* **1** halfway, mean, middle

adj **2** average, common, mediocre, medium, middle, normal, ordinary, regular, standard, unimpressive

interminable *adj* see: PERPETUAL *adj* **2**

intermingle *v* amalgamate, band, blend, coalesce, combine, compound, consolidate, fuse, league, lump, meld, merge, mingle, mix, unify, unite

intermingling *n* blend, combination, fusion, joining, merging, mixture, union

intermission *n* break, breath, breather, breathing space, pause, reprieve, respite, rest

intermittent *adj* alternate, cyclic, cyclical, periodic, periodical, recurrent, recurring, repeated, repetitive, sporadic

intern *n* **1** academician, educator, instructor, professor, teacher

n **2** diagnostician, doctor, healer, physician, resident, specialist, surgeon

n **3** see: BEGINNER *n* **2**

v cage, confine, coop, detain, enclose,

impound, imprison, incarcerate, jail, lock up, restrain, trap

internal *adj* enclosed, hidden, inner, innermost, private, secret

international *adj* universal

interpolate *v* fill in, implant, insert, insinuate, interject, interpose, interrupt, introduce, throw in

interpose *v* **1** arbitrate, intercede, interfere, intervene, intrude, mediate, settle, step in

v **2** fill in, implant, insert, insinuate, interject, interpolate, interrupt, introduce, throw in

interpret *v* **1** clarify, depict, render, rephrase, represent, translate

v **2** comprehend, decipher, decode, infer, peruse, read, study, understand

v **3** analyze, conclude, construe, deduce, derive, draw, educe, gather, glean, guess, infer, presume, surmise

v **4** analyze, annotate, clarify, define, detail, elucidate, explain, expound, express, narrate, spell out, state, understand

interpretation *n* assessment, impression, reading, understanding

interrogate *v* ask, cross-examine, examine, grill, inquire, investigate, probe, pump, query, question, quiz

interrogatory *n* query

interrupt *v* **1** demur, halt, hold up, pause, rest, stop, suspend

v **2** fill in, implant, insert, insinuate, interject, interpolate, interpose, introduce, throw in

v **3** arrest, block, check, freeze, impede, halt, stall, stay, stop

v **4** disarray, dislocate, disorder, disorganize, disrupt, disturb, interfere, jumble, mess, mix up, muss, rummage, shuffle, sift through, unsettle

v **5** distract, disturb, divert

v **6** adjourn, avoid, defer, delay, hold, hold up, lay over, postpone, procrastinate, prolong, put off, remit, reschedule, set aside, shelve, stay, suspend, table, wait, waive

interruption *n* **1** delay, postponement, reprieve, stay, stop, suspension

n **2** break, delay, distraction, disturbance, diversion, hold-up, interference, pause

intersect *v* **1** meet

v **2** bisect, crisscross, cross, impede

intersection *n* crossing, crossroad, passageway

interval *n* **1** delay, interim, lag, pause

n **2** duration, hold, length, occupancy, tenure, term, time *n* **3** break, cessation, delay, gap, interim, lapse, lull, pause, stop

n **4** class, degree, grade, level, mark, notch, position, rank, rate, step

n **5** cycle, duration, period, season, span, spell, stage, stretch, term, time

n **6** delay, lull, pause, stay, suspension, wait

intervene *v* arbitrate, intercede, interfere, interpose, intrude, mediate, settle, step in

intervention *n* adjudication, arbitration, facilitation, mediation

interview *n* conference, discourse, discussion, meeting, query

v **1** discuss, meet

v **2** encounter, greet, meet, receive, see, visit

interviewer *n* columnist, commentator, correspondent, editor, journalist, newspaperman, publicist, writer

intimacy *n* **1** closeness, companionship, familiarity, friendship

n **2** adultery, congress, copulation, fooling around, fornication, procreation, sex

n **3** affair, association, communication, friendship, liaison, rapport, relationship, union

n **4** adultery, affair, cheating, dalliance, entanglement, fling, flirtation, fooling around, infatuation, intrigue, liaison, love affair, playing around, rendezvous, romance, tryst

n **5** attention, awareness, care, carefulness, cognizance, concern, consciousness, consideration, heed, knowledge, knowing, mark, note, notice, observance, observation, perception, recognition, regard, remark, sense

intimate *adj* **1** carnal, physical, sexual

adj **2** close, familiar, near, personal

adj **3** moving, romantic, tender, touching

adj **4** exclusive, individual, own, personal, private, secret, special

n see: FRIEND *n* 1

intimation *n* see: CLUE *n* 2

intimidate *v* **1** affect, bother, burden, concern, daunt, disturb, faze, oppress, upset, worry

v **2** alarm, attack, bully, club, coerce, frighten, harass, menace, strong-arm, terrorize, threaten

v **3** abash, alarm, awe, cow, daunt, frighten, horrify, panic, scare, shock, spook, startle, terrify, terrorize, unnerve

v **4** see: ANNOY *v* 3

intimidating *adj* **1** formidable, huge, immense, impressive, massive, significant, substantial

adj **2** belligerent, extroverted, free, loud, outspoken, vocal, vociferous

intimidation *n* fulmination, harassment, threat, warning

into *prep* to

intolerable *adj* excruciating, painful, unbearable, unendurable

intolerance *n* bias, bigotry, chauvinism, discrimination, parochialism, partiality, prejudice, provincialism, racism, sexism

intonate *v* announce, articulate, assert, couch, describe, dictate, draft, enunciate, express, orate, phrase, proclaim, pronounce, say, speak, state, stress, talk, utter, verbalize, vocalize, voice, word

intonation *n* accent, elocution, enunciation, inflection, manner, pronunciation

intoxicated *adj* **1** aroused, ebullient, elated, euphoric, excited, exhilarated, happy, joyful, sparked, stimulated, turned on

adj **2** bombed, crocked, doped up, drunk, drunken, high, inebriated, juiced, loaded, looped, messed up, plastered, polluted, sloshed, smashed, stoned, tight, tipsy, turned on, wasted, wired

intractable *adj* **1** indomitable, recalcitrant, stubborn, uncontrollable, undisciplined, unmanageable, unruly, untoward, wild

adj **2** bullheaded, closed-minded, deaf, firm, hardheaded, hard-line, inelastic, inflexible, intransigent, obstinate, perverse, pigheaded, refractory, resolute, rigid, stiff, stubborn, tough, unbending, uncompromising, unpliable, unpliant, unwieldy, unyielding, willful

intransigent *adj* bullheaded, closed-minded, deaf, firm, hardheaded, hard-line, inelastic, inflexible, intractable, obstinate, perverse, pigheaded, refractory, resolute, rigid, stiff, stubborn, tough, unbending, uncompromising, unpliable, unpliant, unwieldy, unyielding, willful

intrepid *adj* see: BRAVE *adj* 1

intricacy *n* complexity, convolution, involution, involvement

intricate *adj* complex, complicated, elaborate, enigmatic, involved, knotty, mysterious, tangled

intrigue *n* **1** confidence, mystery, secret

n **2** logistics, plotting, strategy, tactics

n **3** cabal, collusion, conspiracy, junta, machination, plot, scheme, secret

n **4** see: AFFAIR *n* 3

v **1** appeal, arouse, attract, excite, fascinate, fire, interest, lead on, lure, seduce, stir, tantalize

v **2** see: PLOT

intriguing *adj* **1** exciting, exotic, inspiring,

interesting, provocative, stimulating, tingling, titillating

adj 2 arousing, exciting, provocative, seductive, sexy, stimulating, suggestive, tantalizing

adj 3 alluring, beguiling, bewitching, captivating, catchy, charming, dazzling, dynamic, enchanting, engaging, enthralling, enticing, fascinating, glamorous, mesmerizing, riveting, spectacular, spellbinding

adj 4 curious, exotic, far-out, fascinating, kinky, marvelous, mysterious, new, novel, odd, outlandish, strange, ultra, unaccustomed, unexplored, unfamiliar, unique, unknown, unusual, weird

intrinsic *adj* 1 ensconced, entrenched, established, fixed, fundamental, ingrained, inveterate, settled, sworn

adj 2 basic, congenital, genetic, inborn, indigenous, ingrained, inherent, inherited, innate, instinctive, natal, native, natural

adj 3 basic, early, elementary, embryonic, essential, fundamental, initial, original, rudimentary, underlying

intrinsically *adv* by itself, effectively, essentially, per se, practically, virtually

intro *n* see: INTRODUCTION *n*

introduce *v* 1 acquaint, announce, delineate, depict, present, reflect, represent, show

v 2 fill in, implant, insert, insinuate, interject, interpolate, interpose, interrupt, throw in

v 3 activate, begin, cause, commence, constitute, create, embark, enter, establish, inaugurate, induct, initiate, install, instigate, instill, institute, kick off, launch, lead off, open, originate, precipitate, preface, set up, start, tee off, usher in, venture forth

v 4 see: COMMUNICATE *v* 4

introduction *n* beginning, foreword, intro, overture, preamble, preface, prelude, prologue, start

introductory *adj* 1 beginning, opening, preliminary, preparatory, prior

adj 2 beginning, embryonic, founding, incipient, initial, nascent, rudimentary, starting

introspective *adj* individual, personal, private, subjective

introverted *adj* 1 antisocial, reclusive, standoffish

adj 2 closed, diffident, laconic, reserved, restrained, reticent, secretive, shy, subdued, taciturn, timid, timorous, uncommunicative, undaring

intrude *v* 1 bother, burden, encroach, impose, presume, saddle

v 2 attack, encroach, entrench, infringe, invade, trespass, violate

v 3 arbitrate, intercede, interfere, interpose, intervene, mediate, settle, step in

v 4 butt in, chisel in, cut in, fiddle, horn in, interfere, interlope, meddle, mess around, peek, peer, poke, pry, snoop, tamper with

intruder *n* busybody, gossip, interloper, kibitzer, meddler, snoop, yenta

intrusion *n* attack, conquest, defeat, foray, inroad, invasion, trespass

intrusive *adj* busy, impertinent, meddlesome, obtrusive, officious

intuition *n* 1 feeling, foreboding, guess, hunch, instinct, premonition, sense, suspicion

n 2 apprehension, foreboding, forewarning, harbinger, omen, premonition, presage, sign, warning

n 3 acumen, astuteness, awareness, cleverness, discernment, discrimination, insight, intellect, keenness, perception, sagacity, sensitivity, shrewdness, understanding, wit

n 4 awareness, emotion, faculty, feel, feeling, perception, reaction, response, sensation, sense

intuitive *adj* 1 aesthetic, empathetic, sensitive

adj 2 clairvoyant, mediumistic, prescient, psychic

adj 3 automatic, deep, gut, innate, instinctive, visceral

adj 4 see: IMPLIED *adj* 2

inundate *v* 1 bury, drown, engulf, flood, overflow, swamp, wash over

v 2 cascade, emit, flood, overflow, plunge, pour, rain, shower, spill, swamp, tumble

v 3 deluge, douse, drench, drown, dunk, flood, irrigate, overload, saturate, slosh, soak, sop, souse, swamp, swill, tax, wet

inundated *adj* drenched, dripping, full, immersed, saturated, soaked, soaking, sodden, sopping, waterlogged, wet

inured *adj* accepted, accustomed, chronic, common, constant, continual, customary, daily, everyday, familiar, frequent, habitual, often, recurring, regular, routine, traditional, usual

invade *v* 1 attack, foray, overrun, raid

v 2 infest, overrun, pervade, plague, swarm

v 3 attack, encroach, entrench, infringe, intrude, trespass, violate

v 4 ambush, assail, assault, attack, beset, raid, storm, strike, trap, waylay

invalid *adj* 1 baseless, erroneous, fallacious, groundless, unfounded, unsubstantiated

adj 2 bad, defective, futile, inadequate, incorrect, inferior, malfunctioning, poor, void

n convalescent, patient, shut-in

invalidate *v* abate, abolish, abrogate, annihilate, annul, call off, cancel, cease, delete, destroy, efface, erase, excise, expunge, kill, negate, nullify, obliterate, omit, quash, remove, stop, terminate, wipe out

invaluable *adj* irreplaceable, precious, priceless, rare, unparalleled

invariable *adj* 1 consistent, constant, continuing, endless, equable, established, even, reliable, routine, same, serene, stable, steady, unchanging, unfailing, unfluctuating, uniform, unvarying

adj 2 see: CONSTANT *adj* 3, 6

invasion *n* 1 exploration, foray, infiltration, patrol, penetration, raid

n 2 attack, conquest, defeat, foray, inroad, intrusion, trespass

invective *n* see: INSULT *n*

inveigh *v* 1 censure, condemn, denounce

v 2 except, kick, object, protest, remonstrate

inveigle *v* see: CHEAT *v* 1

invent *v* 1 concoct, deceive, equivocate, fabricate, falsify, fib, lie, misstate, perjure

v 2 brew, concoct, construe, contrive, create, devise, engineer, fabricate, formulate, hatch, make up, plot, scheme

v 3 begin, coin, conceive, craft, create, define, develop, devise, formulate, innovate, make, originate, start

v 4 see: ACT

v 5 see: VISUALIZE *v*

invented *adj* 1 see: FICTITIOUS

adj 2 see: SPONTANEOUS *adj* 1

invention *n* 1 composition

n 2 breakthrough, creation, innovation

n 3 concoction, creation, fabrication, fantasy, fiction

n 4 creativity, fancy, fantasy, image, imagination, ingenuity, inspiration, resourcefulness, whimsy

n 5 exaggeration, fabrication, falsehood, falsity, fib, lie, misstatement, story, tale

n 6 apparatus, appliance, contraption, contrivance, device, doodad, doohickey, gadget, gimmick, gizmo, implement, instrument, machine, mechanism, thingumajig, tool, utensil, widget

n 7 see: FICTION *n* 1, 2

inventive *adj* 1 clever, gifted, handy, ingenious, talented, versatile

adj 2 active, bustling, busy, creative, driving, energetic, enterprising, lively, resourceful

adj 3 clever, creative, deft, enterprising, fertile, imaginative, ingenious, resourceful, skillful, talented

inventor *n* 1 architect, designer, draftsperson, engineer, manager, operator, plotter, schemer, surveyor

n 2 author, creator, founder, initiator, instigator, maker, originator, parent, pioneer, seed, source

inventory *n* 1 goods, provisions, reserve, stock, store, supply

n 2 asset, excess, overage, overstock, oversupply, plus, surplus

n 3 articles, basics, commodities, essentials, goods, line, materials, merchandise, products, properties, staples, stock, wares

n 4 backlog, cache, hoard, holdings, nest egg, pile, reserve, reservoir, stash, stock, stockpile, store, supply

n 5 account, amount, catalog, enumeration, itemization, list, litany, repertoire, supply, tally

v catalog, check, itemize, tally

inverse *adj* see: CONFLICTING *adj* 2

invert *v* change, reverse, revert, transpose, turn

invest *v* 1 imbue, impart, infuse, ingrain, inject, inoculate, instill, penetrate, pervade, spread, steep, suffuse, teach, train

v 2 beleaguer, besiege, surround

v 3 accredit, authorize, certify, commission, empower, enable, entitle, facilitate, license, permit, sanction, validate

investigate *v* 1 examine, explore, scout, spy, survey

v 2 ask, cross-examine, examine, grill, inquire, interrogate, probe, pump, query, question, quiz

v 3 delve, dig, examine, explore, feel out, grope, hunt, inquire, look, observe, peer, probe, pursue, research, scan, scrutinize, search, seek, sound, study, test

investigation *n* analysis, digging, experimentation, exploration, inquiry, inquisition, research, study, testing, trial

investigative *adj* curious, inquiring, inquisitive, nosy, probing, prying, questioning, snooping

investments *n* bonds, holdings, securities, stocks

inveterate *adj* **1** ensconced, entrenched, established, fixed, fundamental, ingrained, intrinsic, settled, sworn

adj **2** continuing, enduring, lifelong, long-lasting, long-lived, old, ongoing, perennial

invidious *adj* abhorrent, base, gross, obnoxious, offensive, repellent, repugnant, revulsive

invigorate *v* **1** augment, buttress, fortify, harden, intensify, reinforce, strengthen

v **2** reclaim, recondition, reconstruct, recover, recur, rehabilitate, rejuvenate, restore, resuscitate, retrain, revitalize, revive

invigorating *adj* energizing, exhilarating, fresh, refreshing, stimulating

invincible *adj* **1** firm, indomitable, unconquerable, unyielding

adj **2** mighty, omnipotent, powerful, supreme

inviolable *adj* consecrated, intact, inviolate, protected, pure, sacred, sacrosanct

inviolate *adj* consecrated, intact, inviolable, protected, pure, sacred, sacrosanct

invisible *adj* **1** concealed, covert, obscure, unseen, veiled

adj **2** imperceptible, imponderable, inappreciable, indiscernible, insensible, intangible, minute, scant, unapparent, unobservable, weak

invitation *n* bid, expectation, hope, inducement, motion, offer, proffer, proposal, proposition, recommendation, request, suggestion

invite *v* **1** ask, bid, encourage, request, solicit

v **2** attract, court, encourage, flirt, lure, pursue, romance, solicit, tempt, woo

inviting *adj* see: ATTRACTIVE *adj* **3**

invocation *n* **1** petition, plea, prayer, request

n **2** conjuration

invoice *n* bill, charge, check, debt, fee, note, tab

v bill, charge, debit, dun, notice, render, solicit

invoke *v* **1** actuate, bring about, cause, create, draw on, effect, execute, make, produce, secure

v **2** see: INSTIGATE *v* **1**

v **3** see: PLEAD *v* **2**

involuntary *adj* automatic, impulsive, instinctive, natural, rash, reflex, spontaneous, unconscious, unforced, unpremeditated, unprompted

involution *n* **1** complexity, convolution, intricacy, involvement

n **2** see: FALL *n* **3**

involve *v* **1** commit

v **2** concern, influence, interest

v **3** partake, participate, receive, share

v **4** accuse, associate, blame, confuse, connect, embroil, enmesh, ensnare, entangle, implicate, mire, tangle

v **5** see: COMPRISE *v*

involved *adj* **1** committed, concerned, dedicated, interested

adj **2** absorbed, curious, drawn, engrossed

adj **3** complex, complicated, elaborate, enigmatic, intricate, knotty, mysterious, tangled

involvement *n* **1** complexity, convolution, intricacy

n **2** education, experience, exposure, practice, skill

invulnerable *adj* impregnable, protected, safe, safeguarded, secure

iota *n* **1** bit, dab, end, fragment, minutia, mite, morsel, particle, piece, pinch, portion, scrap, shred, speck, spot, strip, tidbit, trifle

n **2** see: DOT *n* **1**

irascible *adj* **1** balking, balky, contrary, cranky, disagreeable, mean, obstinate, ornery, perverse, wayward

adj **2** angry, cranky, cross, feisty, grouchy, hot-tempered, ireful, peppery, quick-tempered, short-fused, sullen, testy, touchy

irate *adj* aggravated, angry, annoyed, cross, enraged, excited, fuming, furious, hot, incensed, indignant, irritable, mad, provoked, teed off, upset

ire *n* anger, dander, fit, frenzy, fury, indignation, outrage, paroxysm, rage, tantrum, wrath

ireful *adj* see: HOT-TEMPERED *adj*

irk *v* **1** aggravate, anger, annoy, bother, bug, enrage, exasperate, frazzle, gall, grate, hassle, incense, inflame, infuriate, irritate, madden, miff, nettle, outrage, peeve, pester, pique, provoke, rile, upset, vex

v **2** see: ANNOY *v* **1, 2**

irksome *adj* **1** annoying, difficult, hurt, irritated, irritating, painful, sensitive, sore

adj **2** annoying, bothersome, glaring, harassing, irritating, mean, onerous, painful, pesky, troublesome, ugly, unwelcome, vexatious, wicked

iron *n* **1** bond, chain, fetter, handcuff, manacle, shackle, tie *n* 2 automatic, firearm, gun, handgun, heater, luger, piece, pistol, revolver, rod

ironclad *adj* constant, determinate, firm, fixed, hard, immutable, inflexible, invariable, resolute, stable, unalterable, unchangeable, unmovable

ironhanded *adj* see: RESTRICTIVE *adj*

ironic *adj* 1 coincidental, curious, odd, strange, unexpected

adj 2 contemptuous, cynical, derisive, mocking, sarcastic, sardonic, scornful, skeptical, wry

irony *n* aspersion, contempt, derision, disdain, mockery, ridicule, sarcasm, satire, scorn

irradiate *v* brighten, glow, illuminate, light up, radiate, spotlight

irrational *adj* 1 babbling, confused, incoherent, rambling, wild

adj 2 absurd, balmy, bizarre, crazy, emotional, foolish, frivolous, goofy, illogical, impossible, inane, insane, loony, lunatic, mad, muddled, nuts, preposterous, ridiculous, silly, touched, wacky, zany

irreconcilable *adj* incompatible, incongruous

irrefutable *adj* absolute, actual, authentic, bona fide, certain, definite, existent, factual, genuine, hard, inarguable, incontestable, incontrovertible, indisputable, indubitable, positive, real, sure, true, undeniable, undisputable, undoubtable, undoubted, unequivocal, unquestionable, veritable, viable

irregular *adj* 1 bouncy, bumpy, craggy, jagged, jolting, rough, rugged, scraggy, uneven, unsmooth

adj 2 aberrant, abnormal, anomalous, artificial, atypical, contrived, deviant, disparate, divergent, incongruous, off-key, uncharacteristic, unnatural

adj 3 see: RANDOM *adj* 2

adj 4 see: SUPERFLUOUS *adj* 3

irregularity *n* aberration, abnormality, craziness, delusion, dementia, derangement, distraction, eccentricity, fugue, hallucination, insanity, lunacy, madness, mania, psychosis, unbalance

irrelevant *adj* 1 inapplicable, inconsistent, spurious, unfitting

adj 2 abnormal, extra, extraneous, foreign, illogical, immaterial, insignificant, irregular, malapropos, nonessential, peripheral, superfluous, surplus, unimportant, unnecessary, unrelated

irreparable *adj* hopeless, impossible, incurable, irresolvable, irrevocable, perma-

nent, terminal, unalterable, uncorrectable, uncurable, unfixable

irreplaceable *adj* invaluable, precious, priceless, rare, unparalleled

irrepressible *adj* brilliant, clever, dazzling, good, scintillating, smart, sparkling, sprightly, witty

irreproachable *adj* 1 blameless, commendable, exemplary, exonerated, guiltless, innocent, pure, righteous, virtuous

adj 2 errorless, excellent, exquisite, fastidious, faultless, flawless, ideal, immaculate, impeccable, perfect

irresistible *adj* alluring, compelling, desirable, overpowering, seductive, tantalizing

irresolvable *adj* hopeless, impossible, incurable, irreparable, irrevocable, permanent, terminal, unalterable, uncorrectable, uncurable, unfixable

irresponsible *adj* 1 capricious, careless, immature, undependable, unpredictable, untrustworthy

adj 2 capricious, dizzy, flighty, frivolous, giddy, scatterbrained, silly

adj 3 careless, foolish, impulsive, myopic, not smart, reckless, risky, shortsighted, unthinking, unwise

irreverence *n* blasphemy, desecration, heresy, impiety, sacrilege, violation

irreverent *adj* 1 blasphemous, disrespectful, sacrilegious

adj 2 audacious, bold, brash, brazen, cheeky, daring, disrespectful, forward, fresh, impertinent, impudent, insolent, nervy, pert, rude, sassy, saucy

irrevocable *adj* 1 permanent, noncancelable, nonrescindable, unalterable, uncancelable

adj 2 definite, determined, fixed, foregone, inevitable, inexorable, ordained, predestined, unalterable, unavoidable, unchangeable

adj 3 hopeless, impossible, incurable, irreparable, irresolvable, permanent, terminal, unalterable, uncorrectable, uncurable, unfixable

irrigate *v* see: SATURATE *v* 2

irritable *adj* 1 aggravated, angry, annoyed, cross, enraged, excited, fuming, furious, hot, incensed, indignant, irate, mad, provoked, teed off, upset

adj 2 abrupt, bluff, blunt, brash, brusque, cheeky, crusty, curt, flip, flippant, gruff, harsh, impertinent, impudent, nasty, quick, rude, sarcastic, sassy, short, snippy, snotty, surly, testy, wisenheimer

adj 3 see: TEMPERAMENTAL *adj*

irritant *n* aggravation, annoyance, irritation

irritate *v* 1 chafe, rub, scrape

v 2 annoy, antagonize, argue, bother, bug, concern, distress, disturb, goad, harass, hassle, inconvenience, irk, pain, perturb, strain, stress, taunt, trouble, try, upset, worry

v 3 aggravate, anger, annoy, bother, bug, enrage, exasperate, frazzle, gall, grate, hassle, incense, inflame, infuriate, irk, madden, miff, nettle, outrage, peeve, pester, pique, provoke, rile, upset, vex

irritated *adj* 1 bruised, painful, sore, tender

adj 2 annoying, difficult, hurt, irksome, irritating, painful, sensitive, sore

irritating *adj* 1 abrasive, aggravating, annoying, caustic, cutting, grating

adj 2 annoying, difficult, hurt, irksome, irritated, painful, sensitive, sore

adj 3 annoying, anxious, bothersome, chafing, crabby, edgy, fretful, galling, impatient, jittery, nagging, on edge, restless, touchy, unsettling

adj 4 annoying, bothersome, glaring, harassing, irksome, mean, onerous, painful, pesky, troublesome, ugly, unwelcome, vexatious, wicked

irritation *n* 1 aggravation, annoyance, disturbance, irritant

n 2 annoyance, anxiety, apprehension, bother, care, concern, disquiet, disquietude, doubt, misgiving, reservation, restlessness, restraint, skepticism, trouble, uneasiness, vexation, worry

island *n* atoll, cay, isle, key

isle *n* atoll, cay, island, key

isolate *v* 1 detach, insulate, seclude, separate, sequester

v 2 classify, define, differentiate, discriminate, distinguish, separate

v 3 differentiate, discriminate, exclude, ostracize, segregate, separate, sequester

isolated *adj* 1 few, infrequent, occasional, rare, scarce, seldom, sporadic, uncommon, unusual

adj 2 alienated, alone, apart, detached, hidden, private, removed, secluded, separated, sequestered, severed

isolation *n* 1 detachment, privacy, quiet, seclusion, solitude

n 2 exile, leisure, quarantine, relaxation, rest, retirement, retreat, seclusion, solitude, withdrawal

issue *n* 1 affair, business, concern, matter

n 2 consequence, end, outcome, result

n 3 argument, controversy, item, matter, motif, motive, point, proposition, question, subject, text, theme, topic

n 4 cause, situation, thing

n 5 book, correspondence, edition, folio, manuscript, monograph, opus, paperback, printing, publication, text, tome, volume, work, writing

v 1 appear, arise, ascend, come forth, emanate, emerge, form, loom

v 2 arise, come from, derive, emanate, flow, head, originate, spring, stem

v 3 bring out, distribute, get out, give out, go to press, print, publish, put out, reissue, reprint, set type

isthmus *n* cape, peninsula, point, promontory

italicize *v* accent, accentuate, amplify, concentrate, emphasize, feature, flag, focus, heighten, highlight, mark, punctuate, spotlight, stress, underline, underscore

itch *n* 1 abrasion, cut, hurt, scrape, scratch, sore

n 2 appetite, craving, desire, eroticism, hankering, hunger, longing, lust, passion, urge, yearning, yen

v ache, covet, crave, desire, hanker, hunger, long, lust, need, pine, thirst, want, yearn

item *n* 1 detail, feature, part, particular, specific

n 2 article, element, entity, object, piece, thing

n 3 component, constituent, element, factor, ingredient, part, segment

n 4 see: ARTICLE *n* 1, 2

n 5 see: SUBJECT *n* 4

itemization *n* account, amount, catalog, enumeration, inventory, list, litany, repertoire, supply, tally

itemize *v* 1 describe, detail, list, specify

v 2 catalog, check, tally

v 3 calculate, cite, count, enumerate, list, number, numerate, tally

v 4 see: RECORD *v* 2

iterate *v* emphasize, reiterate, repeat, restate, stress

itinerant *adj* ambulatory, gypsy, movable, nomadic, perambulatory, roving, transient, vagrant, wandering, wayfaring

n drifter, emigrant, migrant, nomad, transient

itinerary *n* 1 agenda, appointments, calendar, list, plan, schedule

n 2 circuit, course, journey, line, means,

passage, path, road, route, trip, voyage, way

n 3 schedule

itinerate *v* see: WANDER *v*

ivory *adj* chalky, milky, snowy, white

J

jab *v* 1 peck, pick, poke

v 2 belittle, deride, flaunt, jeer, jest, mock, quip, razz, ridicule, scoff, scorn, sneer, taunt, tease

n punch, swing, thrust

jacket *n* 1 case, coat, cover, enclosure, folder, skin

n 2 coat, fur, hide, pelt, skin, stole

jade *adj* chartreuse, emerald, green, Kelly

v drain, exhaust, fatigue, tire, wear down, wear out, weary

jaded *adj* 1 indifferent

adj 2 beat, burnt out, bushed, careworn, drawn, emaciated, exhausted, expended, fatigued, frazzled, haggard, pinched, pooped, run-down, shot, spent, tired, wearied, weary, worn, worn down, worn-out

adj 3 bored, disgusted, sick, tired, weary

jagged *adj* bouncy, bumpy, craggy, irregular, jolting, rough, rugged, scraggy, uneven, unsmooth

jail *n* brig, cage, cell, cooler, coop, hoosegow, pen, penitentiary, pokey, prison, reformatory, slammer, stir, stockade, tower

v cage, confine, coop, detain, enclose, impound, imprison, incarcerate, intern, lock up, restrain, trap

jam *n* 1 blockage, bottleneck, catch, flaw, hitch, impediment, obstacle, obstruction, snag

n 2 bind, box, corner, difficulty, dilemma, fix, impasse, mess, pinch, plight, predicament, quandary, scrape, spot, trap, trouble

v 1 choke, clog, congest, crowd

v 2 crowd, herd, mob, press, push, swarm, teem, throng

v 3 cram, crush, force, gorge, insert, pack, press, ram, stuff

v 4 compact, compress, constrain, crowd, crush, mash, pack, press, push, squash, squeeze

v 5 see: HINDER *v* 5

jammed *adj* bursting, chock-full, crowded, filled up, full, jampacked, loaded, packed, rending, replete, stuffed

jangle *v* clash, conflict, crash, discord, jar, mismatch

janitor *n* agent, custodian, manager, steward

jar *n* 1 bottle, bucket, caddy, can, canister, pail, shell, tin, vessel

n 2 see: HIT *n* 1

v 1 bump, jolt, jostle, rattle, shake, shock, startle

v 2 flinch, flutter, pulsate, quake, quaver, quiver, shake, shiver, shudder, tremble, twitch, twitter, vibrate

v 3 clash, conflict, crash, discord, jangle, mismatch

jargon *n* 1 buzzwords, lexicons, lingo, nomenclature, terminology, terms, vocabulary

n 2 buzzwords, expression, idiom, language, lingo, parlance, verbiage, vernacular, vocabulary

jasmine *adj* canary, lemon, saffron, yellow

jaunt *n* drive, excursion, journey, outing, ride, spin

v see: HOP *v*

jaunty *adj* 1 chic, dapper, dashing, debonair, natty, neat, rakish, sleek, smart, snazzy, spiffy, suave, trim

adj 2 see: FLAMBOYANT *adj* 2

jazz *n* blues, classical, country, folk, music, ragtime, rock-and-roll, soul, swing

jazzercise *n* aerobics, bodybuilding, calisthenics, exercise, slimnastics, workout

jealous *adj* 1 covetous, distrusting, envious, resentful, suspicious

adj 2 alienated, angry, bitter, emotional, hurt, offended, provoked, resentful

jealousy *n* envy, greed, rivalry

jeep *n* auto, automobile, bus, car, carriage, chariot, coach, motorcar, omnibus, sedan, truck, van, vehicle, wagon

jeer *n* crack, gibe, put-down, quip, shot, sneer, torment

v 1 belittle, deride, flaunt, jab, jest, mock, quip, razz, ridicule, scoff, scorn, sneer, taunt, tease

v 2 aggravate, annoy, badger, bait, bedevil, beleaguer, bother, bug, harass, harry, hassle, heckle, hound, hurt, intimidate, nag, needle, persecute, pester, plague, provoke, ride, spite, taunt, tease, threaten, torment, worry

v 3 see: TEASE *v* 1, 3, 4

jell *v* 1 come together, crystallize, develop, form, materialize, shape up

v 2 see: THICKEN *v*

jeopardize *v* blow, blunder, botch, bungle, butcher, damage, err, foul up, goof, hash, hurt, jumble, mess up, queer, ruin, screw up

n danger, downside, exposure, hazard, liability, menace, peril, risk, threat

jerk *n* 1 convulsion, seizure, spasm, twitch

n 2 drag, pluck, pull, tug, yank

n 3 blow, jolt, jump, shock, start, surprise

n 4 bird, bum, cad, fink, heel, rat, turkey

n 5 blockhead, boor, clod, creep, cretin, dimwit, dolt, dope, dullard, dumbbell, dummy, dunce, fool, goof, idiot, imbecile, nerd, nincompoop, numskull, oaf, pain, schlemiel, schmuck, simpleton, stooge, turkey

v pull, tear, tug, twist, wrench, wring, yank

jerry-built *adj* breakable, decrepit, delicate, dilapidated, feeble, flimsy, fragile, frail, jury-rigged, puny, Rube Goldberg, shoddy, sickly, thin, tinny, unsound, worn-out

jest *n* banter, comedy, crack, funniness, gag, humor, joke, quip, small talk, wisecrack, wit, witticism

v 1 allure, charm, come onto, dally, flirt, fool, kid, lead on, make eyes, make out, pick up, string along, tease, trifle, toy

v 2 belittle, deride, flaunt, jab, jeer, mock, quip, razz, ridicule, scoff, scorn, sneer, taunt, tease

jesting *adj* see: FUNNY *adj* 1

jet *adj* black, ebony, sable

n aircraft, airliner, airplane, glider, plane

v shoot, spew, spout, spritz, spurt, squirt, surge

jetty *n* 1 dock, landing, pier, wharf

n 2 barrier, breaker, cape, harbor, head, neck, point, sea wall

jewel *n* gem, paragon, treasure

jewelry *n* anklet, band, bangle, bracelet, brooch, earring, medal, medallion, necklace, pin, ring

jibe *v* accord, agree, check, coalesce, coincide, comply with, concur, conform, consent, consist, fit in, harmonize, square, suit, tally

jiffy *n* blink of an eye, crack, flash, instant, minute, moment, second, shake, twinkling, wink

jig *v* jiggle, joggle, jump, shake, twitch, wiggle

jiggle *v* jig, joggle, jump, shake, twitch, wiggle

jiggly *adj* flimsy, insecure, rickety, shaky, teetering, unstable, unsure, vacillating, wavering, weak, wobbly

jilt *v* abandon, break up, cast off, chuck, defect, desert, disavow, discard, disenfranchise, disown, ditch, dump, forsake, junk, leave, quit, reject, renounce, spurn, strand, throw out

jimmy *v* pry

jinxed *adj* cursed, damned, doomed, hapless, hopeless, ill-fated, luckless, unfortunate, unhappy, unlucky, untoward

jitney *n* cab, hack, rickshaw, taxi, taxicab

jitterbug *n* ballet, cha-cha, dance, fox trot, hula, polka, tap, twist, waltz

jittery *adj* 1 chaotic, fervent, fervid, feverish, frenetic, frenzied

adj 2 antsy, edgy, excitable, fidgety, highstrung, irritable, jumpy, moody, nervous, nervy, restless, shaky, skittish, temperamental

adj 3 annoying, anxious, bothersome, chafing, crabby, edgy, fretful, galling, impatient, irritating, nagging, on edge, restless, touchy, unsettling

job *n* 1 bag, field, hobby, specialty

n 2 appointment, connection, duty, function, office, position, post, situation

n 3 assignment, chore, duty, effort, mission, responsibility, stint, task

n 4 art, avocation, business, calling, career, discipline, employment, field, gig, labor, line, livelihood, occupation, office, profession, pursuit, role, schtick, situation, specialty, task, thing, trade, vocation, work

jobless *adj* idle, out of work, unemployed

jock *n* athlete, letterman, player, sportsman

jocular *adj* comical, facetious, funny, humorous, jesting, joking, kidding, sarcastic, witty

jocularity *n* see: MERRIMENT *n*

jocundity *n* see: MERRIMENT *n*

jog *v* 1 dart, gallop, run, trot

v 2 dash, gallop, race, run, speed, sprint

v 3 cue, nudge, prompt, push, remind, stimulate, stir, suggest

joggle *v* jig, jiggle, jump, shake, twitch, wiggle

john *n* bathroom, can, head, latrine, lavatory, loo, potty, powder room, toilet, water closet, wc

join *v* 1 add, append, attach

v 2 assist, collaborate, cooperate

v 3 connect, nail, peg, pin, tack

v 4 bend, connect, encircle, loop, twist

v 5 adhere, bond, cleave, cling, cohere, stick

v 6 attach, bind, bond, cord, fasten, hitch, link, marry, tether, tie, tie up

v 7 clump, fasten, hitch, knot, lace, lash, link, loop, rope, secure, tie, unite *v* 8 affix, bind, bond, cement, fasten, fuse, glue, lock, paste, seal, secure, stick, unite

v 9 associate, blend, bond, coalesce, combine, compound, connect, couple, fasten, fuse, link, marry, mate, meet, merge, pair, unite, wed

joining *n* 1 connection, groove, joint, link, seam

n 2 coupling, crossing, interchange, junction, juncture, linking, merger

n 3 blend, combination, fusion, intermingling, merging, mixture, union

joint *adj* aggregate, collective, common, communal, mutual, public, shared

n 1 connection, groove, joining, link, seam

n 2 bar, barroom, cocktail lounge, den, dive, dump, gin mill, hangout, haunt, lounge, pub, rathskeller, saloon, tavern, watering hole

n 3 juncture, pause, period

jointly *adv* 1 as one, collectively, in unison, mutually, together

adj 2 collectively, cooperatively, helpfully, together

joke *n* 1 banter

n 2 adventure, antic, caper, escapade, lark, mischief, prank, trick

n 3 banter, comedy, crack, funniness, gag, humor, jest, quip, small talk, wisecrack, wit, witticism

n 4 see: SATIRE *n* 2

v banter, deride, gibe, jeer, knock, mock, needle, rib, ridicule, roast, tease

joking *adj* 1 amusing, diverting, enjoyable, entertaining, fun, humorous, playful

adj 2 see: FUNNY *adj* 1

jollity *n* see: MERRIMENT *n*

jolt *n* 1 blow, jerk, jump, shock, start, surprise

n 2 blow, disturbance, shock, trauma, upheaval, upset

n 3 see: HIT *n* 1

v bump, jar, jostle, rattle, shake, shock, startle

jolting *adj* bouncy, bumpy, craggy, irregular, jagged, rough, rugged, scraggy, uneven, unsmooth

jostle *v* 1 confuse, disorder, mix, scramble, shuffle

v 2 bounce, bump, skip, throw, volley

v 3 bump, jar, jolt, rattle, shake, shock, startle

v 4 bulldoze, elbow, hustle, press, push, shoulder, shove

jot *v* 1 doodle, draw, scratch, scrawl, scribble, sketch, write

v 2 capture, chart, denote, enter, itemize, list, log, note, preserve, record, register, take notes, tally, tape, write down

journal *n* 1 bulletin, daily, newsletter, newspaper, organ, publication, review

n 2 booklet, gazette, magazine, monthly, periodical, publication, quarterly, weekly

n 3 account, diary, digest, log, memoir, minutes, notation, notes, proceedings, record, recording, report

journalism *n* coverage, news, press, reporting

journalist *n* 1 columnist, commentator, correspondent, editor, interviewer, newspaperman, publicist, writer

n 2 author, authoress, biographer, creator, dramatist, essayist, novelist, playwright, reporter, screenwriter, writer

journalists *n* media, press, reporters

journey *n* 1 drive, excursion, jaunt, outing, ride, spin

n 2 adventure, air travel, cruise, excursion, expedition, flight, passage, safari, sally, tour, travel, trek, trip, venture, voyage

n 3 see: PATH *n* 2

v 1 coast, cruise, explore, go, migrate, proceed, sail, survey, tour, travel, trek, voyage

v 2 amble, hike, march, pace, parade, plod, saunter, step, stride, stroll, strut, tramp, tread, trek, walk

jovial *adj* bright, cheerful, cheery, content, ebullient, ecstatic, elated, exuberant, festive, gay, glad, happy, joyful, joyous, merry, mirthful, pleased, radiant, rejoicing

joviality *n* amusement, elation, excitement, exhilaration, frivolity, gaiety, glee, guffaws, happiness, hilarity, jocularity, jocundity, jollity, joy, laughter, levity, merriment, mirth

joy *n* 1 delight, enjoyment, pleasure, satisfaction

n 2 bliss, delight, ecstasy, Eden, elation, enchantment, heaven, nirvana, paradise, pleasure, rapture, rhapsody

n 3 amusement, elation, excitement, exhilaration, frivolity, gaiety, glee, guffaws, happiness, hilarity, jocularity, jocundity, jollity, joviality, laughter, levity, merriment, mirth

joyful *adj* 1 aroused, ebullient, elated, eu-

phoric, excited, exhilarated, happy, intoxicated, sparked, stimulated, turned on
adj 2 see: MERRY *adj 2*

joyless *adj* see: GLOOMY *adj 5*

joyous *adj* see: MERRY *adj 2*

jubilee *n* anniversary

judge *n 1* court, justice, magistrate
n 2 commentator, critic, reviewer
n 3 arbiter, arbitrator, mediator, moderator, referee, umpire
v 1 determine, evaluate, test, try, verify
v 2 approximate, call, estimate, place, put, reckon
v 3 adjudicate, arbitrate, mediate, referee, try, umpire
v 4 account, calculate, consider, deem, reckon, regard, surmise, view
v 5 anticipate, augur, bode, budget, call, divine, estimate, forecast, foresee, foreshadow, foretell, guess, harbinger, herald, plan, portend, preannounce, predict, presage, proclaim, prognosticate, project, prophesy, signify, soothsay

judgmatical *adj* enlightened, judicious, just, lucid, prudent, rational, sage, sane, sapient, sensible, wise

judgment *n 1* adjudication, decision, decree, finding, ruling, sentence, verdict
n 2 adjudication, award, determination, opinion, ruling, sentence, verdict
n 3 assumption, conclusion, conjecture, discretion, estimate, guess, notion, presumption, theorization
n 4 analysis, assessment, commentary, criticism, critique, evaluation, examination, notion, opinion, review, ruling
n 5 common sense, faculty, good sense, gumption, horse sense, logic, sense, wisdom

judicial *adj* controversial, forensic, legal

judicious *adj 1* enlightened, judgmatical, just, lucid, prudent, rational, sage, sane, sapient, sensible, wise
adj 2 see: CAREFUL *adj 7*

jug *n* cauldron, cistern, container, reservoir, tank, vat

juice *n 1* electricity, power
n 2 concentrate, extract
n 3 fluid, liquid, sap, secretion, solution

juiced *adj* bombed, crocked, doped up, drunk, drunken, high, inebriated, intoxicated, loaded, looped, messed up, plastered, polluted, sloshed, smashed, stoned, tight, tipsy, turned on, wasted, wired

juicy *adj 1* moist, savory, succulent, tender
adj 2 damp, fluid, liquefied, liquid, moist, watery, wet

jumble *n 1* assortment, hodgepodge, medley, mixture
n 2 see: CHAOS *n 5*
v 1 addle, confuse, daze, foul up, fumble, mix up, muddle, snarl up
v 2 disarray, dislocate, disorder, disorganize, disrupt, disturb, interfere, interrupt, mess, mix up, muss, rummage, shuffle, sift through, unsettle
v 3 see: BLUNDER *v*

jumbled *adj* diverse, haphazard, mixed, promiscuous, random

jumbo *adj 1* big, extra-large, fat, grand, great, huge, husky, immense, large, obese, oversize, tremendous
adj 2 ample, big, considerable, enormous, extensive, grand, hefty, huge, large, major, sizable, spacious, vast
adj 3 see: HUGE *adj 2, 3*

jump *n 1* blow, jerk, jolt, shock, start, surprise
n 2 bound, hop, leap, vault
v 1 bypass, pass over, skip
v 2 assault, leap, pounce, strike, surprise, swoop
v 3 climb, crest, increase, mount, rise, surge
v 4 boost, hike, increase, jack up, put up, raise, up
v 5 blanch, cringe, flinch, recoil, shrink, start, startle, wince
v 6 bob, bound, hop, jaunt, leap, lope, prance, skip, spring, sprint, trip
v 7 bolt, spring, start, startle
v 8 jig, jiggle, joggle, shake, twitch, wiggle

jumpy *adj 1* antsy, edgy, excitable, fidgety, high-strung, irritable, jittery, moody, nervous, nervy, restless, shaky, skittish, temperamental
adj 2 see: LIVELY *adj 8*

junction *n* coupling, crossing, interchange, joining, juncture, linking, merger

juncture *n 1* climax, crisis, crux, dilemma, emergency, point, predicament
n 2 coupling, crossing, interchange, joining, junction, linking, merger
n 3 joint, pause, period

jungle *n* forest, woodland, woods

junior *n* boy, child, cub, lad, son, young man

junk *n 1* contents, objects, scrap, stuff, substance, things
n 2 crap, crud, debris, detritus, dirt, garbage, litter, refuse, rubbish, rubble, sweepings, trash, waste
n 3 discard, failure, garbage, reject, scrap, second
n 4 baloney, bilge, bosh, bull, bunk, driv-

el, fiddlesticks, foolishness, malarkey, nonsense, nothing, poppycock, rot, rubbish, schlock, silliness, trivia

v abandon, break up, cast off, chuck, defect, desert, disavow, discard, disenfranchise, disown, ditch, dump, forsake, jilt, leave, quit, reject, renounce, spurn, strand, throw out

junta *n* cabal, collusion, conspiracy, intrigue, machination, plot, scheme, secret

jurisdiction *n* **1** authority, command, commission, control, direction, domination, management, mastery, might, power, rule

n **2** area, district, domain, environs, locality, neighborhood, parish, precinct, province, range, region, section, sphere, vicinity, ward, zone

n **3** county, district, municipality, parish, precinct, township, ward

jury *n* panel

jury-rigged *adj* breakable, decrepit, delicate, dilapidated, feeble, flimsy, fragile, frail, jerry-built, puny, Rube Goldberg, shoddy, sickly, thin, tinny, unsound, worn-out

just *adv* **1** exactly, perfectly, precisely

adv **2** but, except that, further, however, merely, nevertheless, only, simply, solely, yet

adj **1** clean, equal, equitable, even, fair, honest, sportsmanlike, straight, upright

adj **2** appropriate, correct, deserved, due, fitting, merited, proper, rightful, suitable, warranted

adj **3** candid, dispassionate, equal, equitable, fair, impartial, impersonal, indifferent, neutral, objective, open-minded, square, unbiased, uncolored, unprejudiced

adj **4** see: APPLICABLE *adj*

adj **5** see: WISE *adj* **4**

justice *n* **1** judge, magistrate

n **2** equity, fairness, impartiality, objectivity

n **3** correctness, lawfulness, legality, truth, validity

justifiable *adj* **1** doable, practical, realistic, tenable

adj **2** acceptable, defensible, legitimate, proper, reasonable, valid

justification *n* **1** argument, grounds, proof, reason, wherefore, why

n **2** alibi, defense, excuse, explanation, plea, pretext, rationalization, reason, ruse

justify *v* **1** account, explain, rationalize

v **2** argue, assert, believe, claim, contend, defend, know, maintain, state, think, vindicate, warrant

v **3** attest, authenticate, certify, confirm, corroborate, notarize, prove, ratify, sanction, substantiate, support, validate, verify, vouch, witness

justifying *adj* excusable, extenuating, mitigating, offsetting

justly *adv* adequately, amply, enough, equitably, fairly, moderately, passably, rather, satisfactorily, tolerably

jut *n* bulge, lump, projection, protrusion, swelling

v bulge, overhang, overlap, overlay, poke, pop, project, protrude, protuberate, rise, stand out, stick out, swell

juvenile *adj* adolescent, fresh, green, immature, precocious, undeveloped, unfledged, unready, young, youthful

n adolescent, boy, child, girl, kid, minor, teenager, teeny-bopper, youngster, youth

juxtaposed *adj* abutting, adjacent, adjoining, alongside, bordering, close by, connected, contiguous, local, near at hand, nearby, neighboring, outlining, regional, touching, verging on

K

karma *n* destiny, fate, good fortune, kismet, lot, luck, providence

kayak *n* barge, boat, canoe, craft, dory, ferry, float, raft, scow, skiff, tender

keen *adj* **1** inquiring, penetrating, piercing, probing, searching

adj **2** discerning, discreet, discriminating, sensitive, subtle, tactful

adj **3** honed, pointed, razor sharp, sharp, unblunted, whetted

adj **4** anxious, ardent, avid, breathless, desirous, eager, enthusiastic, excited, fain, impatient, impetuous, passionate, raring, zealous

adj **5** see: QUICK *adj* **5**

keenness *n* acumen, astuteness, awareness, cleverness, discernment, discrimination, insight, intellect, intuition, perception, sagacity, sensitivity, shrewdness, understanding, wit

keep *v* **1** abstain, forbear, refrain, withhold

v **2** celebrate, commemorate, memorialize, observe, solemnize

v **3** have, hold, own, possess, retain

v **4** accommodate, comply, conform, follow, mind, obey, observe, submit

v **5** conceal, harbor, hide, house, protect, safeguard, shelter, shield

v **6** carry on, conduct, direct, manage, operate, ordain, oversee, pilot, run

v **7** detain, hold, hold back, keep back,

keep out, reserve, retain, set aside, with-hold

n livelihood, living, maintenance, minimum, subsistence, support, sustenance

keepsake *n* antique, gift, heirloom, memento, memorial, relic, remembrance, reminder, souvenir, token, trophy

keg *n* barrel, bucket, cask, drum, tub, vat, vessel

kelly *adj* chartreuse, emerald, green

kernel *n* 1 basis, beginning, essence, seed

n 2 center, core, gist, keynote, theme

ketch *n* craft, cruiser, freighter, frigate, liner, ocean liner, sailboat, schooner, ship, steamship, vessel, yacht

key *adj* 1 chief, crucial, salient, vital

adj 2 central, chief, distinguished, dominant, famed, great, leading, main, major, number one, outstanding, predominant, preeminent, primary, prime, principal, prominent, star, successful, superior, top

n 1 answer, explanation, result, secret, solution

n 2 attention, center, crux, feature, focus, highlight, spotlight

n 3 clue, cue, guide, hint, indication, indicator, inkling, intimation, lead, mark, notion, pointer, sign, signal, tip, trace

n 4 atoll, island, isle

keynote *n* center, core, gist, kernel, theme

kibitzer *n* busybody, gossip, interloper, intruder, meddler, snoop, yenta

kick *n* 1 blow, boot, stroke

n 2 effectiveness, flair, pep, pizzazz, potency, punch, sizzle, snap, spark, verve, vigor, wallop

v except, inveigh, object, protest, remonstrate

kicks *n* enjoyment, excitement, pleasure, stimulation, thrills

kid *n* adolescent, boy, child, girl, juvenile, minor, teenager, teeny-bopper, youngster, youth

v allure, charm, come onto, dally, flirt, fool, jest, lead on, make eyes, make out, pick up, string along, tease, toy, trifle

kidding *adj* see: FUNNY *adj* 1

kidnap *v* abduct, carry away, grab, seize, shanghai, steal

kill *v* 1 cancel, end, halt, stop

v 2 abort, erase, sever, stop, terminate

v 3 abolish, annihilate, assassinate, bump off, butcher, decimate, destroy, dispatch, execute, exterminate, hang, hit, knock off, liquidate, massacre, murder, put away, rub out, slaughter, slay, wipe out

v 4 execute, hit, shoot, wound

v 5 abate, abolish, abrogate, annihilate, annul, call off, cancel, cease, delete, destroy, efface, erase, excise, expunge, invalidate, negate, nullify, obliterate, omit, quash, remove, stop, terminate, wipe out

killer *n* assassin, executioner, murderer

killing *n* 1 assassination, foul play, homicide, manslaughter, murder

n 2 bloodbath, bloodshed, butchery, carnage, extermination, genocide, holocaust, massacre, pogrom, shambles, slaughter

n 3 death penalty, execution, slaying

kilt *n* costume, dress, gown, skirt

kilter *n* condition, fitness, repair, shape, trim

kin *n* family, people, relation, relative

kind *adj* 1 attentive, considerate, generous, thoughtful, unselfish

adj 2 amiable, benign, genial, kindly, mild, nonmalignant

adj 3 affectionate, compassionate, considerate, empathetic, empathic, gentle, humane, kindhearted, responsive, softhearted, sympathetic, tender, warm, warmhearted

adj 4 see: BENEVOLENT *adj* 2

n see: CATEGORY *n*

kindhearted *adj* see: TENDER *adj* 9

kindle *v* 1 burn, enkindle, fire, ignite, inflame, light, spark

v 2 arouse, awaken, challenge, excite, rally, rouse, stir, wake, waken

v 3 feed, fire, fuel, ignite, incite, light, nourish, propel, stoke, sustain

kindling *n* beginning, birth, debut, delivery, inception, onset, outset, start

kindly *adj* amiable, benign, genial, kind, mild, nonmalignant

kindness *n* 1 altruism, charity, generosity, goodness, goodwill, grace, humanity, mercy

n 2 affinity, compassion, empathy, mercy, pity, rue, sympathy, tenderness, understanding

n 3 consideration, courtesy, dispensation, favor, indulgence, privilege, respect, service

kindred *adj* 1 compatible, congenial, congruous, like, suitable

adj 2 affiliated, akin, aligned, allied, associated, fraternal, friendly, parallel, related

adj 3 see: ALIKE *adj*

kinetic *adj* alert, animated, bouncy, bright, brisk, buoyant, chipper, dashing, dynamic, ebullient, energetic, enthusiastic, exuberant, frisky, frolicsome, gay, jumpy, lively, peppy, pert, playful, rousing, scintillating, spirited, sprightly, spry, vivacious

king *n* autocrat, chief, commander, despot, dictator, governor, head, leader, lord, master, monarch, potentate, ruler

kingdom *n* domain, dominion, field, province, realm, sphere, territory

kingly *adj* aristocratic, blue-blooded, imperial, majestic, noble, regal, royal, stately, well-bred

kink *n* 1 complication, cramp, crick
n 2 bend, crimp, snarl, tangle, twist

kinky *adj* 1 see: UNUSUAL *adj* 4
adj 2 see: VICIOUS *adj* 3

kinship *n* 1 blood, descent, lineage, relationship, stock
n 2 affection, affinity, attachment, attraction, compassion, concern, devotion, fondness, heart, love, warmth

kismet *n* destiny, fate, good fortune, karma, lot, luck, providence

kiss *n* caress, embrace, fondling, hug, squeeze, touch

kisser *n* countenance, face, features, mug

kit *n* 1 cat, feline, kitten, kitty, puss, pussy, tabby, tiger
n 2 bag, baggage, case, equipment, gear, grip, luggage, pack, pouch, purse, sack, suitcase, valise, wallet

kitten *n* cat, feline, kit, kitty, puss, pussy, tabby, tiger

kitty *n* 1 cat, feline, kit, kitten, puss, pussy, tabby, tiger
n 2 booty, bounty, fortune, loot, money, plunder, pot, prize, spoils, swag, treasure, trove

knack *n* 1 bent, brains, brilliance, faculty, flair, genius, gift, head, intelligence, mind, nose, prowess, talent
n 2 see: SKILL *n* 3

knave *n* cad, cheat, lecher, louse, rake, rascal, reprobate, rogue, scoundrel

knavish *adj* base, common, humble, ignoble, low, lowly, mean, plebeian

knead *v* massage

kneel *v* bow, cringe, genuflect, grovel, kowtow, prostrate, scrape

knickknack *n* amusement, game, plaything, toy, trinket

knife *n* blade, cutlass, dagger, pocketknife, rapier, saber, scimitar, switchblade, sword

knock *n* 1 bang, blow, box, bump, chop, clap, conk, crack, crash, cuff, hit, impact, jar, jolt, lick, punch, rap, slap, slug, smack, smash, swat, swipe, tap, wallop, whack
n 2 affront, aspersion, attack, barb, caustic remark, crack, cut, denunciation, despite, dig, disparagement, disrespect, gibe, implication, indignity, innuendo, insult, invective, reflection, sarcasm, scorn, slap, slight, slur, spike, tongue-lashing, verbal jab

v 1 box, clap, cuff, punch, slap, smack, spank, strike, tap, whack
v 2 banter, deride, gibe, jeer, joke, **mock**, needle, rib, ridicule, roast, tease
v 3 attack, butt, drive, lunge, pass, plunge, ram, sink, stab, stick, thrust
v 4 bang, blow, bump, cuff, hit, punch, strike
v 5 abuse, asperse, bad-mouth, belittle, condemn, damage, decry, defame, degrade, denigrate, denounce, deprecate, detract, diminish, discount, disparage, insult, malign, put down, revile, run down, slander, take away, vilify

knoll *n* foothill, hill, hillock, hump, mound, mount, raise, rise, swelling

knot *v* clump, fasten, hitch, join, lace, lash, link, loop, rope, secure, tie, unite

knotty *adj* complex, complicated, elaborate, enigmatic, intricate, involved, mysterious, tangled

know *v* 1 distinguish, identify, name, recognize, specify
v 2 encounter, endure, experience, realize, understand
v 3 assume, believe, comprehend, conceive, estimate, expect, fathom, gather, grasp, guess, imagine, infer, presume, suppose, surmise, suspect, think, trust, understand
v 4 see: ARGUE *v* 2
v 5 see: UNDERSTAND *v* 1, 5, 6

know-how *n* see: SKILL *n* 3

knowing *adj* 1 alive, attentive, awake, aware, cognizant, conscious, conversant, responsive, sentient, thinking
adj 2 acute, alert, astute, cagey, canny, clever, cunning, deft, keen, penetrating, perceptive, piercing, quick, quick-sighted, quick-witted, receptive, responsive, sagacious, savvy, sensitive, sharp, sharp-witted, shrewd, slick, smart, street-smart, wise
adj 3 see: INTELLIGENT *adj* 3, 4
adj 4 see: SENSIBLE *adj* 5
n attention, awareness, care, carefulness, cognizance, concern, consciousness, consideration, heed, intimacy, knowledge, mark, note, notice, observance, observation, perception, recognition, regard, remark, sense

knowledge n 1 laws, philosophy, principles, thinking, wisdom

n 2 data, discipline, facts, information, lore, news, science, wisdom

n 3 communication, data, disclosure, exchange, expression, facts, information, intelligence, news, notification

n 4 attention, awareness, care, carefulness, cognizance, concern, consciousness, consideration, heed, intimacy, knowing, mark, note, notice, observance, observation, perception, regard, recognition, remark, sense

n 5 see: SKILL n 3

knowledgeable adj 1 abreast, acquainted, aware, conversant, familiar, informed, up, versed

adj 2 alert, astute, brainy, bright, brilliant, clever, discerning, discriminating, educated, insightful, intellectual, intelligent, knowing, perceptive, quick, sagacious, sage, sharp, smart, swift

knuckles n hand, palm

kook n card, character, eccentric, lunatic, nut, oddball, weirdo

kooky adj crazy, eccentric, off-center

kowtow v 1 condescend, patronize, stoop

v 2 bow, cringe, genuflect, grovel, kneel, prostrate, scrape

kudos n 1 applause, cheers, compliments, congratulations, plaudits, praise

n 2 accolade, award, commendation, credit, decoration, distinction, honor, laurels, medal, note, praise, recognition, reputation, reward, tribute

L

label n 1 badge, card, pass, tag, ticket, voucher

n 2 flap, tab

v call, define, designate, entitle, name, term

labor n 1 chore, drudgery, grind, slavery, sweat, tedium, toil, travail, work

n 2 effort, elbow grease, pains, exertion, strain, struggle, toil, trouble, try, work

n 3 see: TRADE n 3

v drudge, grub, hustle, slave, strain, strive, sweat, toil, work

labored adj arduous, demanding, difficult, formidable, hard, heavy, laborious, rocky, rough, rugged, serious, severe, strenuous, tough, trying, uphill

laborer n aide, aide-de-camp, assistant, attendant, employee, hand, helper, hired hand, servant, supporter, worker

laborious adj arduous, demanding, difficult, formidable, hard, heavy, labored, rocky, rough, rugged, serious, severe, strenuous, tough, trying, uphill

laboriously adv arduously, difficultly, onerously, painfully

lace v clump, fasten, hitch, join, knot, lash, link, loop, rope, secure, tie, unite

lacerate v bruise, hurt, injure, mangle, wound

lack n 1 defect, deficiency, demerit, fault, flaw, imperfection, inadequacy, need, shortcoming, want

n 2 deficiency, deprivation, destitution, inadequacy, indigence, need, poverty, privation, scarcity, want

n 3 dearth, deficiency, deficit, drought, famine, rarity, scarcity, shortage, sparseness, undersupply, want

v miss

lackadaisical adj dilatory, easygoing, idle, indolent, inert, laid-back, languid, lazy, lethargic, relaxed, slothful, sluggish, unconcerned

lacking adj 1 bereft, deprived, destitute, wanting

adj 2 absent, away, gone, missing, omitted, truant, wanting

adj 3 few, limited, nonabundant, not many, scant, short, sparse

lackluster adj see: DULL adj 7

laconic adj 1 abbreviated, brief, compressed, concise, crisp, curt, pithy, short, succinct, terse, to the point

adj 2 closed, diffident, introverted, reserved, restrained, reticent, secretive, shy, subdued, taciturn, timid, timorous, uncommunicative, undaring

lad n boy, child, cub, junior, son, young man

laden adj burdened, encumbered, fraught, harried, loaded, pressured

lading n burden, cargo, consignment, freight, load, payload, shipment, transportation, truck

ladle n scoop, shovel

lady n dame, female, gentlewoman, matron, miss, mistress, spinster, widow, woman

ladylike adj female, feminine, gentle, nurturing, tender, womanly

lag n delay, interim, interval, pause

v 1 drag, follow, trail, traipse

v 2 dally, dawdle, delay, diddle, goof off, idle, linger, loaf, loiter, loll, lounge, malinger, poke, put off, putter, shirk, tarry

lager *n* ale, beer, bock, brew, Pilsner, stout, suds

laggard *n* dallier, dawdler, slowpoke
adj slow, sluggish, tardy

lagoon *n* basin, lake, loch, pond, pool, spring

lair *n* burrow, cave, den, grotto, recess, tunnel

laity *n* 1 congregation, devotees, flock, fold, followers, members, parishioners
n 2 see: SOCIETY *n* 3

lake *n* basin, lagoon, loch, pond, pool, spring

lam *n* breakout, escape, flight, getaway, slip

lambaste *v* 1 berate, rebuke, scold
v 2 beat, belittle, blast, clobber, conquer, cream, defeat, dust, lick, overrun, overwhelm, rout, shellac, smear, thrash, wallop, whip
v 3 see: BATTER *v*

lame *adj* crippled, disabled, limping

lament *n* cry, dirge, funeral hymn
v 1 bemoan, deplore, regret, repent, rue
v 2 brood, grieve, languish, mourn, sorrow
v 3 bawl, bemoan, cry, grieve, groan, moan, mourn, sigh, snivel, sob, wail, weep, whimper, whine
v 4 burden, deject, depress, dishearten, grieve, hurt, sadden, weigh down, wound

lamentable *adj* 1 dire, disastrous, dreadful, pitiful, sorrowful, tragic
adj 2 affecting, deplorable, miserable, paltry, pathetic, pitiable, pitiful, poor, sad, unfortunate, woeful, wretched
adj 3 dismal, doleful, gloomy, melancholy, mournful, plaintive, regretful, regrettable, rueful, sorrowful, woeful

laminate *v* coat, electroplate, plate

lampoon *n* buffoonery, burlesque, caricature, comedy, farce, humor, imitation, joke, mockery, parody, satire, spoof, takeoff, travesty

lamps *n* illumination, lighting, lights, luminescence

lanai *n* patio, piazza, porch, terrace, veranda

lance *v* gore, impale, penetrate, pierce, puncture, spear, stab
n missile

land *n* 1 lot, parcel, plot, property, tract
n 2 area, divot, patch, sod, space, turf
n 3 acreage, domain, estate, grounds, holdings, property, real estate
n 4 clay, dirt, dry land, dust, earth, ground, loam, marl, soil, *terra*, terra firma
n 5 country, fatherland, home, homeland, motherland, soil
v 1 beach
v 2 alight, come down, descend, dismount, get off, settle
v 3 acquire, annex, buy, capture, gain, get, have, obtain, pick up, procure, purchase, requisition, secure, solicit, win

landing *n* 1 arrival, debarkation, docking, mooring
n 2 dock, jetty, pier, wharf

landlord *n* lessor, owner, possessor, proprietor, stockholder

landmark *n* benchmark, highlight, milestone

landscape *n* 1 outlook, scene, scenery, sight, view, vista
n 2 acrylic, art, canvas, depiction, drawing, etching, illustration, lithograph, mural, oil, painting, pastel, pen and ink, picture, portrait, print, seascape, sketch, still life, watercolor

language *n* buzzwords, expression, idiom, jargon, lingo, parlance, verbiage, vernacular, vocabulary

languid *adj* 1 apathetic, indifferent, passive, torpid
adj 2 dilatory, easygoing, idle, indolent, inert, lackadaisical, laid-back, lazy, lethargic, relaxed, slothful, sluggish, unconcerned

languish *v* 1 loll, lounge, recline, repose
v 2 brood, grieve, lament, mourn, sorrow
v 3 abate, decline, deteriorate, fade, fail, flag, impair, wane, weaken, wither, worsen

languor *n* 1 apathy, coma, doze, ennui, grogginess, inertia, lassitude, lethargy, nod, sleep, slumber, stupor
n 2 apathy, boredom, depression, doldrums, inertia

lank *adj* narrow, skinny, slender, slight, slim, tenuous, thin, veiled, wiry

lanky *adj* angular, bony, emaciated, gaunt, lean, meager, scraggly, scrawny, skinny, slender, thin

lanyard *n* cable, cord, fiber, hemp, line, rope, strand, string, thread, twine, yarn

lap *v* 1 alternate, change, cycle, oscillate, rotate, shift, switch
v 2 lick, moisten, tongue

lapse *n* 1 break, cessation, delay, gap, interim, interval, lull, pause, stop
n 2 accident, blooper, blunder, bungle, confusion, error, faux pas, foul-up, mis-

reading, mistake, misunderstanding, slip, slip-up

n 3 backsliding

v 1 fall, sink, slip

v 2 cease, die, elapse, expire, pass, pass away, perish, succumb, terminate

v 3 descend, dive, drop, fall, leap, lower, plummet, plunge, sink, swoop

larceny *n* burglary, looting, plagiarism, robbery, theft, thievery

large *adj* 1 big, extra-large, fat, grand, great, huge, husky, immense, jumbo, obese, oversize, tremendous

adj 2 ample, big, considerable, enormous, extensive, grand, hefty, huge, jumbo, major, sizable, spacious, vast

larger *adj* better, bigger, finer, greater, more, select, superior, top-notch

largess *n* 1 booty, bounty, gifts, plenty, plunder, presents, reward

n 2 benevolence, boon, contribution, donation, favor, gift, grant, present

n 3 see: REWARD *n* 4, 8

largest *adj* best, biggest, finest, greatest, maximum, most, number one, prime, select, superior, top, top-notch

lariat *n* rope

lark *n* adventure, antic, caper, escapade, joke, mischief, prank, trick

lascivious *adj* 1 amorous, ardent, aroused, carnal, earthy, erotic, fervent, fleshly, horny, hot, impassioned, lecherous, lewd, licentious, lustful, passionate, provocative, randy, raunchy, romantic, sensual, sexual, sexy, sultry, titillated, torrid, turned on, voluptuous, wanton

adj 2 bawdy, coarse, crude, dirty, erotic, filthy, foul, gamy, gross, improper, indecent, lewd, licentious, nasty, obscene, off-color, pornographic, profane, prurient, racy, rank, raunchy, ribald, risqué, scandalous, smutty, suggestive, tainted, uncouth, vulgar, x-rated

lash *v* 1 band, belt, bind, corset, fasten, gird, girdle, strap, tie

v 2 assail, attack, batter, beat, birch, buffet, flagellate, flog, hammer, lambaste, lather, pelt, pound, pummel, punish, scourge, thrash, tromp, wallop, whip

v 3 see: JOIN *v* 7

lass *n* child, coed, daughter, debutante, girl, miss, young lady, young woman

lassitude *n* 1 apathy, coma, doze, ennui, grogginess, inertia, languor, lethargy, nod, sleep, slumber, stupor

n 2 exhaustion, weariness

n 3 acedia, apathy, disinterest, disregard, indifference, lethargy, listlessness

lasso *n* rope

last *adj* 1 least, lowest, poorest, worst

adj 2 concluding, conclusive, final, terminal, ultimate

adj 3 closing, decisive, definitive, eventual, final, inevitable, latest

v 1 be, endure, exist, live, persist, prevail, survive

v 2 abide, continue, endure, outlast, persevere, persist, prevail, remain, stay, stick to, stick with, survive

n end, tail, trailing

lasting *adj* constant, continuing, durable, enduring, eternal, ongoing, permanent, stable

lastly *adv* at last, eventually, ultimately

latch *v* bolt, close, lock, seal, secure, shut, slam

n buckle, catch, clasp, clip, fastener, pin, snap, zipper

late *adj* 1 belated, delayed, overdue, slow, tardy, unpunctual

adj 2 bygone, erstwhile, former, old, once, onetime, past, sometime

lately *adv* afresh, anew, new, newly, of late, recently

latent *adj* 1 inherent, possible, potential, promising, realizable

adj 2 dormant, inactive, inert, on hold, passive, potential, quiet, suspended, unused

later *adv* 1 afterward, subsequently, successively, thereafter

adv 2 after, anon, behind, in pursuit, post, subsequent

latest *adj* closing, decisive, definitive, eventual, final, last

lather *v* see: BATTER *v*

latitude *n* chance, freedom, opportunity, room

latrine *n* bathroom, can, head, john, lavatory, loo, potty, powder room, toilet, water closet, wc

latter *adj* ensuing, following, next, subsequent, succeeding, successive

laud *v* 1 acclaim, applaud, charm, cheer, commend, compliment, flatter, greet, hail, praise, recognize, salute, stroke

v 2 acclaim, applaud, celebrate, commend, eulogize, exalt, extol, glorify, hail, honor, praise, resound, salute, toast, tout, worship

n hymn

laudable *adj* admirable, commendable, excellent, fine, praiseworthy, worthwhile

laugh v chortle, chuckle, giggle, guffaw, roar, smile, snicker, snigger

n chuckle, grin, laughter, smile, snigger

laughable adj absurd, comic, comical, crazy, droll, farcical, foolish, funny, hilarious, humorous, ludicrous, outrageous, ridiculous, silly

laughter n 1 chuckle, grin, laugh, smile, snigger

n 2 amusement, elation, excitement, exhilaration, frivolity, gaiety, glee, guffaws, happiness, hilarity, jocularity, jocundity, jollity, joviality, joy, levity, merriment, mirth

launch v 1 discharge, emit, fire, hurl, project, shoot

v 2 build, constitute, construct, create, erect, establish, found, initiate, institute, set up, start

v 3 cast, flick, fling, flip, heave, hurl, pitch, propel, sling, throw, toss

v 4 activate, begin, cause, commence, constitute, create, embark, enter, establish, inaugurate, induct, initiate, install, instigate, instill, institute, introduce, kick off, lead off, open, originate, precipitate, preface, set up, start, tee off, usher in, venture forth

launder v bathe, clean, cleanse, clean up, dip, flush, immerse, rinse, rub, scour, scrape, scrub, shower, wash

laurels n accolade, award, commendation, credit, decoration, distinction, honor, kudos, medal, note, praise, recognition, reputation, reward, tribute

lavatory n bathroom, can, head, john, latrine, loo, potty, powder room, toilet, water closet, wc

lavender adj amethyst, lilac, mauve, orchid, plum, purple, violet

lavish adj 1 excessive, exorbitant, expensive, extravagant, extreme, ghastly, outlandish, overpriced, profuse, ultimate, unbelievable

adj 2 abundant, cornucopian, extravagant, exuberant, garish, generous, lush, luxuriant, opulent, prodigal, profuse, rich, wasteful

v 1 bestow, deluge, overwhelm, shower

v 2 see: WASTE v 1

law n 1 act, legislation, measure, ruling, statute

n 2 belief, canon, code, conviction, creed, doctrine, dogma, opinion, principle, rule, tenet, theory

n 3 see: COMMAND n 3

lawbreaker n accused, con, convict, criminal, crook, culprit, delinquent, felon,

guilty party, inmate, offender, perpetrator, prisoner, scofflaw, suspect, swindler, transgressor, wrongdoer

lawbreaking n see: CRIME n 3

lawful adj allowable, authorized, legal, legitimate, permissible, rightful, valid

lawfulness n correctness, justice, legality, truth, validity

lawless adj see: ILLICIT adj

lawmaker n assemblyman, congressman, councilman, legislator, representative, senator

lawn n field, grass, green, grounds, plot, yard

laws n knowledge, philosophy, principles, thinking, wisdom

lawsuit n action, case, indictment, litigation, proceeding, prosecution, suit

lawyer n advocate, attorney, barrister, counsel, counselor, intercessor, mediator, solicitor

lax adj 1 down, idle, off, slack, slow, sluggish

adj 2 feeble, flabby, flaccid, limp, loose, pendulous, relaxed, slack

adj 3 careless, defiant, delinquent, derelict, heedless, inattentive, neglectful, negligent, reckless, sloppy

adj 4 casual, easy, fast, immoral, incontinent, indiscriminate, lecherous, lewd, licentious, light, loose, promiscuous, unchaste, wanton, whorish

v ease, ease off, loosen, mellow out, relax, slack, slacken

laxative n cleansing, enema, physic, purge

lay v 1 calibrate, establish, fix, insert, install, locate, place, plant, position, put, set, settle, situate, station

v 2 set

v 3 even, flatten, flush, grade, level, plane, smooth, tamp

adj amateur, inexperienced, nonprofessional, unprofessional

layer n 1 coating, covering, film, membrane, sheet, tissue

n 2 caste, ply, rank, row, stratum, tier

layman n amateur, beginner, dabbler, dilettante, hobbyist, neophyte, nonprofessional, novice, part-timer

layout n arrangement, array, format, outline, plan, style

lay out v see: CLASSIFY v 2

lazy adj dilatory, easygoing, idle, indolent, inert, lackadaisical, laid-back, languid, lethargic, relaxed, slothful, sluggish, unconcerned

lea n field, grassland, meadow, pasture, plain, prairie

lead *adj* **1** chief, first, foremost, head, inaugural, initial, leading, premier, prime

adj **2** principal, star, top-billed

n **1** advantage

n **2** prospect

n **3** forefront, front, head, pioneer, spearhead, vanguard

n **4** ambition, drive, enterprise, initiative, leadership, push, thrust, volition

n **5** buckshot, bullet, missile, projectile, shell, shot, slug

n **6** actor, actress, artist, entertainer, hero, heroine, movie star, performer, player, protagonist, star, thespian, tragedian

n **7** advocate, champion, conqueror, hero, heroine, leader, master, principal, protagonist, star, trailblazer, victor, winner

n **8** clue, cue, guide, hint, indication, indicator, inkling, intimation, key, mark, notion, pointer, sign, signal, tip, trace

v **1** dominate, excel, star

v **2** chair, head, moderate, preside

v **3** accompany, direct, escort, guide, usher

v **4** bring, cause, convert, move, persuade

v **5** connote, hint, implant, imply, infer, insinuate, offer, put forth, seed

v **6** conduct, control, develop, direct, drive, guide, operate, pilot, route, shepherd, show, steer

v **7** boss, command, control, direct, dominate, govern, handle, influence, manage, manipulate, order, supervise, sway

leader *n* **1** coach, educator, instructor, mentor, schoolteacher, teacher, trainer, tutor

n **2** authority, expert, guide, guru, master, mentor, pundit, teacher, wise man

n **3** advocate, champion, conqueror, hero, heroine, lead, master, principal, protagonist, star, trailblazer, victor, winner

n **4** autocrat, chief, commander, despot, dictator, governor, head, king, lord, master, monarch, ruler, potentate

n **5** manager

leaders *n* **1** authority, brass, elders, management, officers

n **2** innovators, pacesetters, pioneers, trendsetters, vanguard

leadership *n* **1** charisma, dominance, influence, magnetism, personality, power, strength

n **2** ambition, drive, enterprise, initiative, lead, push, thrust, volition

leading *adj* **1** chief, first, foremost, head, inaugural, initial, lead, premier, prime

adj **2** absolute, chief, complete, consummate, dominant, godlike, main, perfect, principal, pure, ranking, sheer, supreme, total, unsurpassed, utter, whole

adj **3** champion, excellent, fine, first-class, first-rate, foremost, good, grade A, number one, prime, principal, prominent, quality, select, stellar, superb, superior, top, top-drawer, top-notch, tops

adj **4** first, fore, foremost, forward

adj **5** basic, dominant, elementary, first, foremost, fundamental, head, highest, main, outstanding, paramount, preeminent, premier, primary, rudimentary, supreme, top

adj **6** central, chief, distinguished, dominant, famed, great, key, main, major, number one, outstanding, predominant, preeminent, primary, prime, principal, prominent, star, successful, superior, top

leaflet *n* brochure, circular, flier, handbill, handout, pamphlet, sheet

league *n* **1** association, combination, corporation, establishment, fellowship, foundation, institution, union

n **2** affiliation, alliance, association, axis, bloc, coalition, concord, confederation, consolidation, faction, federation, joint venture, merger, organization, partnership, relationship, treaty, union

v see: COMBINE *v* **3**

leak *n* **1** disclosure, revelation

n **2** crack, hole, opening, puncture

v **1** divulge, reveal

v **2** dribble, drip, drop, ooze, run, seep, trickle

v **3** discharge, drip, emit, exude, secrete, seep, ooze, trickle

lean *adj* angular, bony, emaciated, gaunt, lanky, meager, scraggly, scrawny, skinny, slender, thin

v bank, bend, incline, pitch, slant, slope

leaning *n* **1** bent, bias, drift, habit, inclination, partiality, penchant, predilection, preference, priority, proclivity, propensity, talent, taste, tendency

n **2** see: OPINION *n* **8**

lean-to *n* barn, coop, enclosure, hatch, paddock, pen, pound, shack, shed, shelter, stable, stall, sty

leap *v* **1** clear, hurdle, negotiate, surmount, vault

v **2** assault, jump, pounce, strike, surprise, swoop

v **3** bob, bound, hop, jaunt, jump, lope, prance, skip, spring, sprint, trip

v 4 descend, dive, drop, fall, lapse, lower, plummet, plunge, sink, swoop
n bound, hop, jump, vault

learn *v* 1 memorize, remember, retain
v 2 deduce, determine, discern
v 3 get, master, pick up, read, realize, study, understand
v 4 drill, perfect, practice, prepare, rehearse, repeat, review, study
v 5 ascertain, catch on, determine, discover, find out, hear, listen, uncover, unearth

learned *adj* academic, educated, educational, erudite, intellectual, literary, literate, pedantic, scholarly, scholastic, well-read

learnedness *n* culture, education, enrichment, erudition, learning, wisdom

learning *n* 1 education, instruction, research, scholarship, schooling, study
n 2 culture, education, enrichment, erudition, learnedness, wisdom

lease *v* 1 charter, commission
v 2 advance, lend, let, loan
v 3 charter, franchise, hire, let, permit, rent, sublet

leash *n* 1 bridle, check, cord, restraint, rope, tether
n 2 see: LIMIT *n* 1
v 1 bridle, check, constrain, control, crimp, curb, hold back, hold down, inhibit, rein, restrain, restrict, withhold
v 2 see: BIND *v* 7

least *adv* a tad, barely, hardly, just about, minimally, not much, not quite, scarce, scarcely
adj 1 last, lowest, poorest, worst
adj 2 first, lowest, minimum, slightest, smallest, tiniest

leave *n* 1 approval, authorization, consent, license, permission, sanction
n 2 day off, furlough, holiday, respite, sabbatical, time off, vacation
v 1 bequeath, bestow, devise, impart, will
v 2 drop, go, quit, resign, retire, terminate
v 3 abandon, acquiesce, cede, give up, hand over, relinquish, resign, submit, surrender, waive, yield
v 4 abscond, bolt, defect, depart, exit, fall back, flee, get away, give back, go, move, pull away, pull out, push off, retreat, run along, secede, shove off, take off, vacate, withdraw
v 5 see: ABANDON *v* 2, 3
v 6 see: PROCEED *v* 2

leaven *n* yeast

leaving *n* 1 departure, exit, farewell, parting, passing

n 2 abandon, departure, desertion, evacuation, exit, going, pullback, pullout, removal, retreat, withdrawal

lecher *n* 1 cad, cheat, knave, louse, rake, rascal, reprobate, rogue, scoundrel
n 2 buck, Casanova, Don Juan, flirt, gallant, ladies' man, lover, philanderer, playboy, Romeo, stud

lecherous *adj* 1 amorous, ardent, aroused, carnal, earthy, erotic, fervent, fleshly, horny, hot, impassioned, lascivious, lewd, licentious, lustful, passionate, provocative, randy, raunchy, romantic, sensual, sexual, sexy, sultry, titillated, torrid, turned on, voluptuous, wanton
adj 2 see: PROMISCUOUS *adj* 2

lectern *n* dais, desk, podium, pulpit, rostrum, soapbox, stage, stand

lecture *n* 1 assignment, diatribe, discourse, exercise, homily, lesson, preaching, sermon
n 2 address, speech, talk
v address, deliver, preach, proclaim, speak, talk

ledge *n* mantle, shelf, sill

ledger *n* account, balance sheet, book, credit, score, statement, tab

leech *n* 1 barnacle, dependent, freeloader, hanger-on, parasite, remora, sponge, vine
n 2 bloodsucker, sucker, vampire

leer *v* grimace, mock, ogle, scorn, smirk, sneer

leery *adj* 1 alert, careful, heedful, prudent, suspicious, vigilant, wary, watchful
adj 2 cynical, distrustful, doubtful, dubious, incredulous, questionable, shy, skeptical, skittish, suspicious, uncertain, unsure

leeway *n* 1 capacity, room, space
n 2 excess, give, margin, play, slack, stretch

leftover *adj* excess, remaining, residual, superfluous

leftovers *n* dregs, remainder, remains, remnant, residual, residue, rest, scrap, shred, silt

leg *n* appendage, arm, extremity, limb, member, part

legacy *n* 1 accomplishment, masterpiece, monument
n 2 birthright, endowment, entitlement, estate, heritage, inheritance, patrimony

legal *adj* 1 controversial, forensic, judicial
adj 2 allowable, authorized, lawful, legitimate, permissible, rightful, valid

legality *n* correctness, justice, lawfulness, truth, validity

legalize *v* approve, authorize, decree, enact, legislate, ordain, pass, ratify, sanction

legend *n* 1 inscription

n 2 chronicle, epic, opus, saga, story, tale

n 3 allegory, fable, fantasy, fiction, lesson, lore, myth, mythology, parable, story, tale

legendary *adj* 1 dramatic, epic, grand, heroic, noble, stirring, vivid

adj 2 fabulous, mythical, mythological

legible *adj* clear, distinct, readable, understandable

legion *adj* 1 countless, immeasurable, incalculable, infinite, innumerable, innumerous, many, numberless, uncountable, unlimited, untold

adj 2 abundant, assorted, copious, diverse, extensive, many, multifarious, multitudinous, myriad, numerous, plentiful, populous, prolific, sundry, various, voluminous

n 1 crush, dozens, horde, host, many, multitude, numerous, oodles, press, push, scores, squash, swarm

n 2 airborne, army, battalion, brigade, cavalry, company, footmen, guard, horsemen, infantry, marines, militia, minutemen, paratroops, platoon, reserve, storm troopers

legislate *v* approve, authorize, decree, enact, legalize, ordain, pass, ratify, sanction

legislation *n* act, law, measure, ruling, statute

legislator *n* assemblyman, congressman, councilman, lawmaker, representative, senator

legislature *n* capitol, house, senate

legitimate *adj* 1 acceptable, defensible, justifiable, proper, reasonable, valid

adj 2 allowable, authorized, lawful, legal, permissible, rightful, valid

adj 3 authoritative, dependable, due, faithful, rightful, strict, true, trustworthy, undistorted, veracious

adj 4 aboveboard, candid, equitable, fair, forthright, honest, plain-dealing, straight, straightforward, trustworthy, upright

leisure *n* 1 comfort, ease, effortlessness, freedom, liberty

n 2 exile, isolation, quarantine, relaxation, rest, retirement, retreat, seclusion, solitude, withdrawal

leisurely *adj* deliberate, dilatory, diligent, methodical, meticulous, painstaking, patient, procrastinating, slow, thorough, unhasty, unhurried

lemon *adj* canary, jasmine, saffron, yellow

lend *v* advance, lease, let, loan

lender *n* bank, depository, receptacle, repository

length *n* 1 duration, hold, interval, occupancy, tenure, term, time

n 2 measure, piece, strip

n 3 circle, compass, confines, dimension, distance, extension, extent, limit, orbit, purview, range, reach, realm, scope, size, spectrum, sweep, width

lengthen *v* continue, drag out, draw, elongate, extend, prolong, protract, stretch

lengthened *adj* drawn-out, elongated, extended, lengthy, long, prolonged, protracted, stretched, sustained

lengthwise *adj* flat, horizontal, longways, prone, prostrate, reclining, recumbent

lengthy *adj* drawn-out, elongated, extended, lengthened, long, prolonged, protracted, stretched, sustained

lenience *n* clemency, forbearance, indulgence, leniency, mercifulness, mercy, tolerance, toleration

leniency *n* clemency, forbearance, indulgence, lenience, mercifulness, mercy, tolerance, toleration

lenient *adj* 1 amiable, complaisant, easy, good-humored, good-natured, mild, obliging

adj 2 accepting, charitable, easy, forbearing, indulgent, merciful, patient, restrained, sympathetic, tolerant

adj 3 see: BENEVOLENT *adj* 2

lens *n* binoculars, eye, field glass, glass, magnifying glass, microscope, mirror, periscope, scope, spyglass, telescope

lesbian *n* gay, homosexual

lesion *n* blister, fester, inflammation, sore, swelling, welt

lessee *n* inhabitant, occupant, renter, resident, squatter, tenant

lessen *v* 1 diminish, repress, subject, subordinate, suppress, weaken

v 2 calm, muffle, quiet, reduce, soften, subdue

v 3 deduct, diminish, minus, reduce, subtract, take away

v 4 attenuate, dilute, diminish, purify, rarefy, reduce, refine, shorten, thin out, weaken

v 5 consume, deplete, exhaust, expend, finish, go, run through, spend, use up, waste, weaken

v 6 allay, alleviate, assuage, attenuate, diminish, ease, extenuate, lighten, minimize, mitigate, moderate, mollify, reduce, relieve

v 7 see: ABRIDGE *v*

v 8 see: SUBSIDE *v* 2

lessened *adj* attenuate, diminished, rarefied, subtle, tenuous, thin

lessening *n* decline, decrease, decrement, reduction, weakening

lesser *adj* 1 dependent, subordinate, subservient

adj 2 inferior, lower, subordinate, under

adj 3 see: SUBORDINATE *adj* 1, 2, 4

lesson *n* 1 assignment, diatribe, discourse, exercise, homily, lecture, preaching, sermon

n 2 allegory, fable, fantasy, fiction, legend, lore, myth, mythology, parable, story, tale

lessor *n* landlord, owner, possessor, proprietor, stockholder

let *v* 1 advance, lend, loan

v 2 charter, franchise, hire, lease, permit, rent, sublet

v 3 see: TOLERATE *v*

lethal *adj* baneful, deadly, fatal, mortal, noxious, pernicious, pestilent, ruinous

lethargic *adj* 1 dormant, inert, numb, sluggish, torpid

adj 2 dozing, drowsy, napping, nodding, sleepy, slumberous, snoozy, somnolent, tired

adj 3 dilatory, easygoing, idle, indolent, inert, lackadaisical, laid-back, languid, lazy, relaxed, slothful, sluggish, unconcerned

lethargy *n* 1 apathy, coma, doze, ennui, grogginess, inertia, languor, lassitude, nod, sleep, slumber, stupor

n 2 acedia, apathy, disinterest, disregard, indifference, lassitude, listlessness

letter *n* 1 chit, memo, memorandum, notandum, notation, note, record, reminder

n 2 see: SYMBOL *n* 4

letterhead *n* page, paper, papyrus, parchment, sheepskin, sheet, stationery, vellum

letterman *n* athlete, jock, player, sportsman

letup *n* abatement, diminishing, easing, loosening, relaxation, slackening

level *adj* even, flat, flush, plane, smooth

n 1 frequency, pitch, sound, tone

n 2 condition, phase, stage, state, step

n 3 caste, class, degree, echelon, estate, hierarchy, position, rank, status

n 4 class, degree, grade, interval, mark, notch, position, rank, rate, step

n 5 floor, ground, story, tier

v 1 adjust, conform, equalize, regulate, set policy, standardize

v 2 address, aim, cast, direct, point, train, zero in

v 3 even, flatten, flush, grade, lay, plane, smooth, tamp

levelheaded *adj* moderate, sober, temperate, unimpassioned

lever *n* pedal

leverage *n* authority, clout, control, in, influence, power, prestige, pull, weight

leviathan *adj* see: HUGE *adj* 3

levity *n* amusement, elation, excitement, exhilaration, frivolity, gaiety, glee, guffaws, happiness, hilarity, jocularity, jocundity, jollity, joviality, joy, merriment, mirth

levy *n* assessment, cost, duty, expense, fee, impost, offering, penalty, price, sacrifice, tariff, tax, toll, trade-off

v 1 demand, expect, require, want, wish

v 2 see: APPRAISE *v*

lewd *adj* 1 improper, indecent, indelicate, malodorous, off-color, offensive, rough, scurrilous, suggestive, unbecoming, unseemly, untoward

adj 2 casual, easy, fast, immoral, incontinent, indiscriminate, lax, lecherous, licentious, light, loose, promiscuous, unchaste, wanton, whorish

adj 3 bawdy, coarse, crude, dirty, erotic, filthy, foul, gamy, gross, improper, indecent, lascivious, licentious, nasty, obscene, off-color, pornographic, profane, prurient, racy, rank, raunchy, ribald, risqué, scandalous, smutty, suggestive, tainted, uncouth, vulgar, x-rated

adj 4 see: EROTIC *adj* 3, 6

lexicon *n* dictionary, glossary, list, synonym finder, synonym listing, thesaurus, vocabulary, Word Finder®

lexicons *n* buzzwords, jargon, lingo, nomenclature, terminology, terms, vocabulary

liability *n* 1 encumbrance, indebtedness, lien, mortgage, obligation, security

n 2 danger, downside, exposure, hazard, jeopardy, menace, peril, risk, threat

liable *adj* 1 susceptible

adj 2 bound, committed, obligated, required

adj 3 exposed, prone, subject, vulnerable

adj 4 apt, inclined, likely, partial, prone

adj 5 see: REPUTABLE *adj*

liaison *n* 1 affair, association, communication, friendship, intimacy, rapport, relationship, union

n 2 adultery, affair, cheating, dalliance, entanglement, fling, flirtation, fooling around, infatuation, intimacy, intrigue, love affair, playing around, rendezvous, romance, tryst *n* 3 coupling, linking, marriage, matrimony, union, wedlock

liar *n* charlatan, counterfeit, fake, faker, fraud, hypocrite, impostor, phony, pretender

libel *n* 1 accusation, aspersion, defamation, remark, slander, slur, smear

n 2 see: REPRIMAND *n*

v befoul, besmirch, blacken, darken, defame, disparage, injure, malign, revile, scandalize, slander, slur, smear, soil, tear down, traduce

liberal *adj* 1 bounteous, bountiful, free, generous, handsome, openhanded, unsparing

adj 2 advanced, broad, broad-minded, progressive, radical, tolerant, unbiased

adj 3 abounding, abundant, ample, bounteous, bountiful, copious, enough, galore, generous, overflowing, plentiful, plenty, prodigal, profuse, teeming

liberate *v* 1 extricate, free, release, remove, rescue

v 2 discharge, emancipate, free, loosen, release, unbind, unchain, unshackle

v 3 deliver, free, release, rescue, save

liberated *adj* audacious, free, licentious, loose, rampant, unbridled, unconfined, uncontrolled, uncurbed, ungoverned, unhampered, uninhibited, unrestrained, unsecured, unshackled, untied, wild

liberator *n* deliverer, messiah, rescuer, salvation, savior

liberty *n* 1 autonomy, freedom, independence, license

n 2 comfort, ease, effortlessness, freedom

library *n* archives, athenaeum, bibliotheca, books

libretto *n* musical, opera, operetta, score

license *n* 1 autonomy, freedom, liberty

n 2 certificate, credential, document, instrument, pass, permit

n 3 approval, authorization, consent, leave, permission, sanction

v accredit, authorize, certify, commission, empower, enable, entitle, facilitate, invest, permit, sanction, validate

licentious *adj* 1 casual, easy, fast, immoral, incontinent, indiscriminate, lax, lecherous, lewd, light, loose, promiscuous, unchaste, wanton, whorish

adj 2 audacious, free, liberated, loose, rampant, unbridled, unconfined, uncontrolled, uncurbed, ungoverned, unhampered, uninhibited, unrestrained, unsecured, unshackled, untied, wild

adj 3 amorous, ardent, aroused, carnal, earthy, erotic, fervent, fleshly, horny, hot,

impassioned, lascivious, lecherous, lewd, lustful, passionate, provocative, randy, raunchy, romantic, sensual, sexual, sexy, sultry, titillated, torrid, turned on, voluptuous, wanton

adj 4 bawdy, coarse, crude, dirty, erotic, filthy, foul, gamy, gross, improper, indecent, lascivious, lewd, nasty, obscene, off-color, pornographic, profane, prurient, racy, rank, raunchy, ribald, risqué, scandalous, smutty, suggestive, tainted, uncouth, vulgar, x-rated

lick *n* 1 breath, clue, dash, glimmer, hint, insinuation, shade, smell, smidgen, spice, sprinkling, suggestion, suspicion, tinge, tip, touch, trace, trifle, whisper, whiff, wisp

n 2 see: HIT *n* 1

v 1 conquer, crush, defeat, destroy, down, hurdle, overcome, overthrow, surmount

v 2 lap, moisten, tongue

v 3 beat, belittle, blast, clobber, conquer, cream, defeat, dust, lambaste, overrun, overwhelm, rout, shellac, smear, thrash, wallop, whip

licked *adj* beaten, clobbered, defeated, dejected, depressed, discouraged, whipped

lickety-split *adv* expeditiously, fast, full tilt, hastily, in a snap, promptly, pronto, quick, quickly, rapidly, right away, soon, speedily, swiftly, urgently

lid *n* cap, cork, cover, plate, plug, top

lie *n* 1 bull, falsehood, misstatement, overstatement, untruth

n 2 alibi, con, deception, pretext, ruse, subterfuge, trick

n 3 cheating, deceit, deception, dishonesty, fraud, hoax, sham, subterfuge, trickery

n 4 exaggeration, fabrication, falsehood, falsity, fib, invention, misstatement, story, tale

v concoct, deceive, equivocate, fabricate, falsify, fib, invent, misstate, perjure

lien *n* encumbrance, indebtedness, liability, mortgage, obligation, security

life *n* 1 continuation, duration, endurance, existence, span, subsistence, survival, term

n 2 see: ESSENCE *n* 3

n 3 see: EXISTENCE *n* 1, 2

lifeless *adj* 1 bare, blank, dull, empty, unfilled

adj 2 cold, dead, deceased, defunct, departed, spiritless

adj 3 dead, hush, inanimate, inert, noiseless, quiet, silent, soundless, still

adj 4 anemic, bloodless, gaunt, haggard,

pale, pallid, passionless, spiritless, watery, weak

adj 5 see: DULL *adj* 1, 7

lifelong *adj* continuing, enduring, inveterate, long-lasting, long-lived, old, ongoing, perennial

lift *n* aid, assistance, benefit, comfort, cure, hand, help, nurture, relief, remedy, succor, support

v 1 elevate, heave, hoist, pick up, raise, take up

v 2 arise, ascend, aspire, go up, mount, rise, soar

v 3 appropriate, burglarize, defraud, embezzle, filch, heist, misappropriate, pilfer, pillage, pinch, plunder, pocket, purloin, rip off, rob, snake, snitch, steal, swindle, swipe, take, thieve

v 4 see: CARRY *v* 7

light *adj* 1 airy

adj 2 facile, simple, smooth

adj 3 delicate, feeble, flimsy, inadequate, slight

adj 4 weightless

adj 5 blond, fair

adj 6 casual, easy, fast, immoral, incontinent, indiscriminate, lax, lecherous, lewd, licentious, loose, promiscuous, unchaste, wanton, whorish

adj 7 borderline, casual, frivolous, insignificant, lightweight, little, marginal, meager, minor, minute, negligible, nonessential, off, outside, petty, remote, secondary, slender, slight, slim, small, tenuous, trivial, unimportant

n 1 beam, flicker, glimmer, hint, ray, sliver, spark, trace

n 2 glare

n 3 beacon, lighthouse, signal warning

n 4 flare, flashlight, illumination

v 1 burn, enkindle, fire, ignite, inflame, kindle, spark

v 2 feed, fire, fuel, ignite, incite, kindle, nourish, propel, stoke, sustain

lighten *v* allay, alleviate, assuage, attenuate, diminish, ease, extenuate, lessen, minimize, mitigate, moderate, mollify, reduce, relieve

lightheaded *adj* confused, dizzy, faint, foggy, giddy, reeling

lighthouse *n* beacon, light, signal warning

lighting *n* illumination, lamps, lights, luminescence

lightless *adj* dark, dim, dusky, gloomy, murky, obscure, shadowy, somber, tenebrous, unilluminated

lightly *adv* easily, effortlessly, naturally, readily, willingly

lightning *adj* see: RAPID *adj* 2

n bolt, fireball, flash, thunderbolt

lights *n* illumination, lamps, lighting, luminescence

lightsome *adj* blithe, cheerful, cheery, merry, sunny

lightweight *adj* 1 carryable, compact, luggable, movable, pocket-size, portable, small, transportable

adj 2 borderline, casual, frivolous, insignificant, light, little, marginal, meager, minor, minute, negligible, nonessential, off, outside, petty, remote, secondary, slender, slight, slim, small, tenuous, trivial, unimportant

adj 3 light

likable *adj* affable, amiable, approachable, cordial, friendly, genial, gentle, gracious, lovable, peaceful, pleasant, serene

like *adj* 1 compatible, congenial, congruous, kindred, suitable

adj 2 akin, alike, analogous, comparable, corresponding, equivalent, identical, kindred, matching, parallel, related, same, similar, such, uniform

n complement, counterpart, equal, equivalent, match, parallel, peer

v 1 crave, relish, savor, taste

v 2 choose, elect, pick, will, wish

v 3 bask, delight, enjoy, loaf, luxuriate, relax, relish, rest, savor, wallow

likelihood *n* chance, expectation, possibility, probability, prospect

likely *adj* 1 apt, inclined, liable, partial, prone

adj 2 conceivable, ostensible, plausible, possible, probable

liken *v* bracket, collate, compare, contrast, correlate, equate, match, relate, sort

likeness *n* 1 affinity, analogy, approximation, comparison, match, metaphor, resemblance, semblance, similarity, simile

n 2 clone, copy, counterfeit, duplicate, duplication, image, imitation, mock-up, model, print, replica, replication, representation, reproduction, resemblance, simulation

likewise *adv* additionally, also, and, as well, as well as, besides, further, furthermore, in addition, moreover, plus, too

liking *n* 1 appetite, enjoyment, relish, taste

n 2 affinity, appreciation, fondness, taste

n 3 bent, disposition, fancy, fondness, idea, inclination, mind, notion, pleasure, propensity, yen

lilac *adj* amethyst, lavender, mauve, orchid, plum, purple, violet

Lilliputian *adj* bantam, dainty, diminutive, dwarfish, little, micro, microscopic, midget, mini, miniature, minuscule, minute, petite, pygmy, slight, small, tiny, wee
n dwarf, midget, mite, pygmy

lilt *n* beat, cadence, cycle, pulse, rate, rhythm, tempo, time
v carol, chant, harmonize, hum, sing, yodel

limb *n* 1 arm, branch, division, service, subsidiary, tributary
n 2 branch, twig
n 3 appendage, arm, extremity, leg, member, part

limber *adj* 1 agile, lissome, lithe, lithesome, supple
adj 2 adaptable, adjustable, changeable, flexible, malleable, maneuverable, moldable, plastic, pliable, pliant, responsive, soft, supple, swayed, versatile, yielding

limbo *n* 1 oblivion
n 2 abeyance, dormancy, inaction, inactivity, lull, pause, suspension

limerick *n* ditty, lyric, madrigal, poem, poetry, rhyme, song, sonnet, verse

limit *n* 1 bond, boundary, bridle, check, constraint, control, curb, damper, harness, leash, rein, restraint, restriction
n 2 circle, compass, confines, dimension, distance, extension, extent, length, orbit, purview, range, reach, realm, scope, size, spectrum, sweep, width
n 3 border, extreme, periphery
v 1 bound, confine, cramp, restrict
v 2 curb, discipline, govern, regulate, restrain, retard
v 3 bound, restrict, scrimp, short, skimp, spare, stint
v 4 approach, border, bound, define, edge, hem, outline, skirt, verge
v 5 bind, clog, confine, curb, fetter, hamper, handcuff, hold, leash, restrain, restrict, shackle, tie, tie up

limitation *n* 1 caveat, qualification, requisite, restriction, stipulation
n 2 affliction, calamity, disability, flaw, impairment
n 3 failing, fault, foible, frailty, shortcoming, vice, weakness

limited *adj* 1 diminished, modified, qualified, reduced
adj 2 few, lacking, nonabundant, not many, scant, short, sparse
adj 3 confined, controlled, ignorant, narrow, parochial, provincial, unsophisticated

adj 4 ineffectual, little, mean, narrow, paltry, set, small
adj 5 committed, determined, fixed, focused, narrow, obsessive, one-track
adj 6 definite, determinate, exclusive, fixed, narrow, precise, restricted, segregated, specific
adj 7 absolute, agreed, bounded, categorical, clear, decided, definite, emphatic, established, exact, finite, fixed, guaranteed, positive, specific, unequivocal, unmistakable, vested

limitless *adj* see: PERPETUAL *adj* 2

limits *n* 1 altitude, ceiling, maximum, restraint
n 2 see: EDGE *n* 4

limp *adj* feeble, flabby, flaccid, lax, loose, pendulous, relaxed, slack
v falter, hobble

limpid *adj* clear, clear-cut, crystal, lucid, translucent, transparent, unambiguous, unblurred

limping *adj* crippled, lame

line *n* 1 order, queue, rank
n 2 come-on, pitch, presentation, spiel, talk
n 3 order, priority, procession, sequence, succession, timing
n 4 cable, cord, fiber, hemp, lanyard, rope, strand, string, thread, twine, yarn
n 5 ancestry, blood, bloodline, descent, family, genealogy, heritage, lineage, origin, pedigree, stock, strain
n 6 circuit, course, itinerary, journey, means, passage, path, road, route, trip, voyage, way
n 7 articles, basics, commodities, essentials, goods, inventory, materials, merchandise, products, properties, staples, stock, wares
n 8 see: TRADE *n* 3

lineage *n* 1 blood, descent, kinship, relationship, stock
n 2 ancestry, blood, bloodline, descent, family, genealogy, heritage, line, origin, pedigree, stock, strain

linear *adj* direct, straight, straightforward, uninterrupted

liner *n* craft, cruiser, freighter, frigate, ketch, ocean liner, sailboat, schooner, ship, steamship, vessel, yacht

lines *n* script

lineup *n* see: SERIES *n* 2

line up *v* fall in, queue, wait

linger *v* 1 abide, await, bide, loiter, remain, stay, stick around, tarry, wait
v 2 dally, dawdle, delay, diddle, goof off,

idle, lag, loaf, loiter, loll, lounge, malinger, poke, put off, putter, shirk, tarry

lingo n **1** buzzwords, jargon, lexicons, nomenclature, terminology, terms, vocabulary

n **2** buzzwords, expression, idiom, jargon, language, parlance, verbiage, vernacular, vocabulary

linguist n morphologist, phonetician, semanticist

link n connection, groove, joint, seam
v **1** chain, bind, shackle
v **2** clump, fasten, hitch, join, knot, lace, lash, loop, rope, secure, tie, unite
v **3** associate, blend, bond, coalesce, combine, compound, connect, couple, fasten, fuse, join, marry, mate, meet, merge, pair, unite, wed
v **4** see: HITCH v **1, 2**

linkage n association, connection, nexus

linked adj contingent, dependent

linking n **1** coupling, crossing, interchange, joining, junction, juncture, merger
n **2** coupling, liaison, marriage, matrimony, union, wedlock

lip n **1** back talk, impudence, rudeness, sass
n **2** see: EDGE n **4**

liquefied adj **1** damp, fluid, juicy, liquid, moist, watery, wet
adj **2** melted, molten

liquefy v dissolve, flux, fuse, melt, run, thaw

liquid adj damp, fluid, juicy, liquefied, moist, watery, wet
n fluid, juice, sap, secretion, solution

liquidate v **1** cash, convert, dissolve, tender
v **2** clear, clear off, discharge, pay up, repay, satisfy, settle, square
v **3** abolish, annihilate, assassinate, bump off, butcher, decimate, destroy, dispatch, execute, exterminate, hang, hit, kill, knock off, massacre, murder, put away, rub out, slaughter, slay, wipe out

liquor n alcohol, booze, drinks, grog, moonshine, spirits, whiskey

lissome adj agile, limber, lithe, lithesome, supple

list n **1** table
n **2** catalog, index, register, roster, schedule
n **3** agenda, appointments, calendar, itinerary, plan, schedule
n **4** dictionary, glossary, lexicon, synonym finder, synonym listing, thesaurus, vocabulary, Word Finder®
n **5** atlas, compendium, directory, guide,

guidebook, handbook, listing, manual, phone book, textbook, Yellow Pages
n **6** account, amount, catalog, enumeration, inventory, itemization, litany, repertoire, supply, tally
v **1** describe, detail, itemize, specify
v **2** cant, careen, heel, incline, rear, roll, tilt
v **3** calculate, cite, count, enumerate, itemize, number, numerate, tally
v **4** craft, define, develop, formulate, make, process, specify, synthesize
v **5** capture, chart, denote, enter, itemize, jot, log, note, preserve, record, register, take notes, tally, tape, write down
v **6** catalog, enroll, inscribe, register, sign up, write
v **7** align, arrange, array, assort, catalog, categorize, class, classify, cluster, compile, file, format, grade, group, lay out, line up, order, organize, outline, pigeonhole, place, position, prioritize, program, rank, rate, sort, stack, tabulate

listen v **1** care, consider, heed, mind, review
v **2** ascertain, catch on, determine, discover, find out, hear, learn, uncover, unearth

listing n **1** appointment, booking, date, engagement, reservation, schedule
n **2** atlas, compendium, directory, guide, guidebook, handbook, list, manual, phone book, textbook, Yellow Pages

listlessness n acedia, apathy, disinterest, disregard, indifference, lethargy

litany n account, amount, catalog, enumeration, inventory, itemization, list, repertoire, supply, tally

literal adj exact, faithful, precise, strict, true, verbatim, word for word

literary adj academic, educated, educational, erudite, intellectual, learned, literate, pedantic, scholarly, scholastic, well-read

literate adj academic, educated, educational, erudite, intellectual, learned, literary, pedantic, scholarly, scholastic, well-read

lithe adj agile, limber, lissome, lithesome, supple

lithesome adj agile, limber, lithe, supple

lithograph n acrylic, art, canvas, depiction, drawing, etching, illustration, landscape, mural, oil, painting, pastel, pen and ink, picture, portrait, print, seascape, sketch, still life, watercolor

litigate v **1** appeal, apply, attack, file suit,

go to court, petition, plead, prosecute, solicit, sue

v 2 accuse, allege, arraign, assert, charge, cite, impeach, imply, impute, incriminate, indict, prosecute, sue, try

litigation *n* action, case, indictment, lawsuit, proceeding, prosecution, suit

litigious *adj* argumentative, cantankerous, contentious, controversial, debatable, disputatious, ill-natured, ornery

litter *n* 1 crap, crud, debris, detritus, dirt, garbage, junk, refuse, rubbish, rubble, sweepings, trash, waste

n 2 brood, pups, young

v drop, mess up, scatter

little *adj* 1 ineffectual, limited, mean, narrow, paltry, set, small

adj 2 bare, deficient, few, inadequate, inferior, insufficient, meager, paltry, petty, poor, scant, scanty, skimpy, spare, sparse

adj 3 bantam, dainty, diminutive, dwarfish, Lilliputian, micro, microscopic, midget, mini, miniature, minuscule, minute, petite, pygmy, slight, small, tiny, wee

adj 4 see: TRIVIAL *adj* 1, 2

liturgy *n* ceremonial, ceremony, formality, observance, rite, ritual, service

live *adj* active, alive, functioning, operative, running, working

v 1 be, endure, exist, last, persist, prevail, survive

v 2 domicile, dwell, inhabit, occupy, reside, room, settle, stay

livelihood *n* 1 keep, living, maintenance, minimum, subsistence, support, sustenance

n 2 art, avocation, business, calling, career, discipline, employment, field, gig, job, labor, line, occupation, office, profession, pursuit, role, schtick, situation, specialty, task, thing, trade, vocation, work

liveliness *n* see: ACTIVITY *n* 3

lively *adj* 1 fun-loving, gamesome, playful

adj 2 brisk, curt, quick, snappy

adj 3 comfortable, desirable, genial, warm

adj 4 effective, potent, punchy, snappy, strong

adj 5 appealing, colorful, entertaining, interesting, stimulating, varied

adj 6 active, bustling, busy, creative, driving, energetic, enterprising, resourceful

adj 7 active, agile, astir, brisk, catty, energetic, nimble, quick, sprightly, spry, zippy

adj 8 alert, animated, bouncy, bright, brisk, buoyant, chipper, dashing, dynamic, ebullient, energetic, enthusiastic, exuberant, frisky, frolicsome, gay, jumpy, kinetic, peppy, pert, playful, rousing, scintillating, spirited, sprightly, spry, vivacious

adj 9 see: ZESTY *adj*

liven *v* animate, brighten, cheer up, enliven, incite, inspire, quicken, resuscitate, vivify

living *adj* 1 human

adj 2 alive, developing, prospering, viable

adj 3 alive, animate, animated, viable, vital

adj 4 contemporary, current, existent, present

n keep, livelihood, maintenance, minimum, subsistence, support, sustenance

load *n* burden, cargo, consignment, freight, lading, payload, shipment, transportation, truck

v 1 fill, heap, pack, place, stack, stuff

v 2 burden, encumber, hamper, oppress, overdo, overload, saddle, strain, tax

loaded *adj* 1 burdened, encumbered, fraught, harried, pressured

adj 2 affluent, copious, leisure class, moneyed, opulent, rich, wealthy, well-to-do

adj 3 bursting, chock-full, crowded, filled up, full, jammed, jampacked, packed, rending, replete, stuffed

adj 4 bombed, crocked, doped up, drunk, drunken, high, inebriated, intoxicated, juiced, looped, messed up, plastered, polluted, sloshed, smashed, stoned, tight, tipsy, turned on, wasted, wired

loads *n* 1 fortune, heap, mint, scads

n 2 droves, lots, many, multitudes, plenty, scads, slew

loaf *v* 1 dally, dawdle, delay, diddle, goof off, idle, lag, linger, loiter, loll, lounge, malinger, poke, put off, putter, shirk, tarry

v 2 see: ENJOY *v* 2

loafer *n* beggar, bum, derelict, drifter, hobo, mendicant, panhandler, pauper, tramp, vagabond, vagrant

loam *n* clay, dirt, dry land, dust, earth, ground, land, marl, soil, *terra*, terra firma

loan *n* debt, obligation, promise, responsibility

v advance, lease, lend, let

loath *adj* afraid, averse, disinclined, hesitant, indisposed, opposed, recalcitrant, reluctant, shy, timid, uneager, unwilling

loathe *v* abhor, abominate, bristle, desecrate, despise, detest, disdain, dislike, hate, reject, revile, scorn

loathing *n* aversion, contempt, disgust, distaste, horror, nausea, repugnance, repulsion, revulsion

loathsome *adj* abhorrent, abominable, appalling, detestable, disgusting, dreadful, evil, frightful, ghastly, hateful, horrible, horrid, odious, repulsive, revolting, shocking

lob *n* attempt, chance, effort, fling, go, guess, heave, pop, shot, slap, sling, stab, throw, toss, try, whirl

lobby *n* anteroom, approach, atrium, court, doorway, entrance hall, entry, foyer, hall, hallway, portal, vestibule
v campaign, canvass, influence, persuade, strive, support

local *adj* 1 domestic, endemic, folk, indigenous, native, traditional
adj 2 see: ADJACENT *adj*

locale *n* 1 arena, scene, site, theater
n 2 area, location, locus, place, point, property, scene, site, spot

locality *n* area, district, domain, environs, jurisdiction, neighborhood, parish, precinct, province, range, region, section, sphere, vicinity, ward, zone

locate *v* 1 ascertain, catch, descry, detect, discover, encounter, espy, ferret, find, spot, turn up, uncover
v 2 see: INSTALL *v* 1

located *adj* found, uncovered

location *n* 1 bearings, course, direction, heading, position
n 2 address, destination, direction, identification, zone
n 3 area, locale, locus, place, point, property, scene, site, spot
n 4 address, apartment, condo, condominium, domicile, dwelling, flat, home, house, pad, place, property, residence, site
n 5 depot, station, stop

loch *n* basin, lagoon, lake, pond, pool, spring

lock *n* 1 bolt, clamp, clasp, deadbolt, padlock
n 2 corner, exclusive, monopoly, restraint
v 1 bolt, close, latch, seal, secure, shut, slam
v 2 affix, bind, bond, cement, fasten, fuse, glue, join, paste, seal, secure, stick, unite

locker *n* cabinet, chest, closet, compartment, cubby, nook, wardrobe

locomotion *n* headway, motion, movement, progress

locomotive *adj* mobile, moving

locus *n* area, locale, location, place, point, property, scene, site, spot

locution *n* expression, idiom, name, phrase, saying, term, word, wording

lode *n* dig, mine, quarry

lodge *n* 1 brotherhood, camaraderie, community, esprit de corps, fellowship
n 2 abode, barn, bungalow, cabin, coop, cottage, hovel, hut, shack, shanty
n 3 club, hotel, inn, resort, spa
v bivouac, camp, dwell, nest, quarter, station

lodging *n* apartment, dorm, housing, room, shelter, suite

loft *n* attic

loftiness *n* see: VANITY *n*

lofty *adj* 1 airy, breezy, brisk, drafty, gusty, open, windy
adj 2 benevolent, big, chivalrous, considerate, generous, grandiose, magnanimous, noble
adj 3 elevated, exalted, excellent, grand, great, heavenly, high, magnificent, prominent, sublime, superb
adj 4 ambitious, bombastic, flamboyant, garish, grandiose, inflated, jaunty, ostentatious, pompous, portentous, pretentious, showy, splendid, splashy, utopian, visionary
adj 5 aloft, elevated, high, overhead, soaring, tall
adj 6 august, baronial, exalted, grand, grandiose, haughty, imperial, imposing, impressive, lordly, magisterial, magnificent, majestic, noble, portly, princely, regal, royal, stately
adj 7 arrogant, cavalier, conceited, contemptuous, curt, dictatorial, disdainful, grandiose, haughty, huffy, insolent, lordly, moody, obtrusive, overbearing, patronizing, proud, scornful, snooty, stuck up, supercilious, superior, vain

log *n* 1 beam, board, boom, girder, plank, rafter, spar, support, timber
n 2 account, diary, digest, journal, memoir, minutes, notation, notes, proceedings, record, recording, report
v 1 capture, chart, denote, enter, itemize, jot, list, note, preserve, record, register, take notes, tally, tape, write down
v 2 enter, record, register

logic *n* 1 analysis, cogitation, consideration, contemplation, deliberation, meditation, reason, reasoning, reflection, speculation, study, thinking, thought
n 2 common sense, faculty, good sense, gumption, horse sense, sense, wisdom

logical *adj* 1 analytical, probing, subtle
adj 2 cogent, correct, rational, sound
adj 3 clear, coherent, direct, easy, elemen-

tary, intelligible, lucid, simple, understandable

adj 4 astute, consequent, intelligent, knowing, perceptive, rational, reasonable, sane, sensible, shrewd, sober, sound, wise

logistics n intrigue, plotting, strategy, tactics

logo n 1 brand, cachet, emblem, imprint, logotype, mark, seal, stamp, trademark

n 2 see: SYMBOL n 4

logotype n brand, cachet, emblem, imprint, logo, mark, seal, stamp, trademark

loiter v 1 abide, await, bide, linger, remain, stay, stick around, tarry, wait

v 2 see: DELAY v 3

loll v 1 languish, lounge, recline, repose

v 2 see: DELAY v 3

lone adj 1 autonomous, distinct, free, independent, separate, sovereign, unconnected

adj 2 alone, lonely, lonesome, single, singular, solitary, solo, unaccompanied

adj 3 exclusive, individual, odd, one, only, particular, separate, single, singular, sole, solitary, unique, unshared

adj 4 see: UNIQUE adj 2, 3

lonely adj alone, lone, lonesome, single, singular, solitary, solo, unaccompanied

loner n 1 freelance, independent, individualist, maverick, nonconformist

n 2 recluse

lonesome adj alone, lone, lonely, single, singular, solitary, solo, unaccompanied

long adj 1 endless, slow, tedious, tiresome

adj 2 drawn-out, elongated, extended, lengthened, lengthy, prolonged, protracted, stretched, sustained

v ache, covet, crave, desire, hanker, hunger, itch, lust, need, pine, thirst, want, yearn

longing adj see: GREEDY adj 1

n see: DESIRE n 2

long-lasting adj continuing, enduring, inveterate, lifelong, long-lived, old, ongoing, perennial

long-lived adj continuing, enduring, inveterate, lifelong, long-lasting, old, ongoing, perennial

longsighted adj farsighted

longways adj flat, horizontal, lengthwise, prone, prostrate, reclining, recumbent

long-winded adj bombastic, chatty, diffuse, garrulous, loquacious, redundant, repetitious, superfluous, talkative, verbose, wordy

loo n bathroom, can, head, john, latrine, lavatory, potty, powder room, toilet, water closet, wc

look n 1 glance, glimpse, peek

n 2 picture, sight, view

n 3 appearance, aspect, cast, countenance, expression, face, visage

n 4 appearance, cover, facade, face, facet, factor, front, surface, veneer

v 1 appear, indicate, portend, seem, sound

v 2 behold, glimpse, mind, see, sight, spot, watch, witness

v 3 anticipate, await, believe, count on, expect, hope, keep the faith, look forward to, wish

v 4 delve, dig, examine, explore, feel out, grope, hunt, inquire, investigate, observe, peer, probe, pursue, research, scan, scrutinize, search, seek, sound, study, test

v 5 face

v 6 eye, glance, glimpse, peek

lookout n 1 horizon, outlook, perspective, prospect, vista

n 2 guard, picket, sentinel, sentry, ward, warden, watch, watchman

n 3 observer, outrider, scout

loom v appear, arise, ascend, come forth, emanate, emerge, form

looming adj 1 advancing, approaching, forthcoming, imminent, nearing, oncoming, pending

adj 2 any second, immediate, imminent, impending, momentary, poised, threatening

loony adj see: ABSURD adj 2

loop n 1 band, coil, crown, garland, ring, spiral, wreath

n 2 curl, revolution, ring, roll, rotation, spin, spiral, turn, twirl, twist

v 1 bend, connect, encircle, join, twist

v 2 clump, fasten, hitch, join, knot, lace, lash, link, rope, secure, tie, unite

looped adj bombed, crocked, doped up, drunk, drunken, high, inebriated, intoxicated, juiced, loaded, messed up, plastered, polluted, sloshed, smashed, stoned, tight, tipsy, turned on, wasted, wired

loose adj 1 extravagant, intemperate, reckless, unrestrained, wanton, wild

adj 2 feeble, flabby, flaccid, lax, limp, pendulous, relaxed, slack

adj 3 ambiguous, imperceptible, imprecise, indecisive, indefinite, indeterminate, indistinct, inexact, vague, wishy-washy

adj 4 casual, easy, fast, immoral, incontinent, indiscriminate, lax, lecherous, lewd, licentious, light, promiscuous, unchaste, wanton, whorish

adj 5 audacious, free, liberated, licentious, rampant, unbridled, unconfined, uncontrolled, uncurbed, ungoverned, unhampered, uninhibited, unrestrained, unsecured, unshackled, untied, wild

loosen *v* 1 ease, ease off, lax, mellow out, relax, slack, slacken

v 2 discharge, emancipate, free, liberate, release, unbind, unchain, unshackle

v 3 disengage, extricate, open, unbind, unclasp, undo, unfasten, unknot, unloose, unloosen, untie

loosening *n* abatement, diminishing, easing, letup, relaxation, slackening

loot *n* booty, bounty, fortune, kitty, money, plunder, pot, prize, spoils, swag, treasure, trove

v 1 comb, ransack, rifle, scour, search, separate, sift, sort

v 2 see: RAVAGE *v* 2

looter *n* see: CROOK *n* 2

looting *n* burglary, larceny, plagiarism, robbery, theft, thievery

lop *v* clip, crop, cut, pare, prune, shave, shear, snip, trim, whittle

lope *v* bob, bound, hop, jaunt, jump, leap, prance, skip, spring, sprint, trip

lopsided *adj* askew, awry, crooked, off-center

loquacious *adj* bombastic, chatty, diffuse, garrulous, long-winded, redundant, repetitious, superfluous, talkative, verbose, wordy

lord *n* 1 nobleman

n 2 autocrat, chief, commander, despot, dictator, governor, head, king, leader, master, monarch, potentate, ruler

lordly *adj* 1 see: GRAND *adj* 5

adj 2 see: VAIN *adj* 5

lore *n* 1 data, discipline, facts, information, knowledge, news, science, wisdom

n 2 allegory, fable, fantasy, fiction, legend, lesson, myth, mythology, parable, story, tale

lose *v* 1 shake, slip, throw off

v 2 abstain, cast, decline, drop, eschew, forbear, forfeit, forgo, give up, pass, reject, renounce, sacrifice, surrender, turn down, waive

v 3 misplace

v 4 fail, give out, miss, run out

v 5 abscond, bolt, break, depart, elude, escape, flee, fly, hightail it, run, sneak away, split

loss *n* 1 casualty, fatality, victim

n 2 cost, damage, deficit, penalty, suffering

n 3 discipline, dockage, fee, fine, penalty, punishment

n 4 chaos, damage, destruction, devastation, disaster, disorder, harm, havoc, hurt, injury, mayhem, ruin, ruination

lost *adj* 1 forgotten, gone, left behind, once, past, suppressed, unremembered, vague

adj 2 bygone, dead, defunct, departed, extinct, gone, vanished

adj 3 absent-minded, abstracted, bemused, careless, dazed, dizzy, groggy, inattentive, mindless, oblivious, preoccupied, silly, spaced, vapid

lot *n* 1 land, parcel, plot, property, tract

n 2 abundance, glut, great deal, mass, much, ton

n 3 destiny, fate, good fortune, karma, kismet, luck, providence

n 4 array, bale, batch, battery, body, bunch, bundle, clump, cluster, group, pack, parcel, quantity, set

n 5 see: ALLOWANCE *n* 2

n 6 see: CATEGORY *n*

n 7 see: SECTION *n* 4

lots *n* droves, loads, many, multitudes, plenty, scads, slew

loud *adj* 1 belligerent, extroverted, free, intimidating, outspoken, vocal, vociferous

adj 2 acute, annoying, grating, high, piercing, piping, sharp, shrill

adj 3 blatant, boisterous, clamorous, disturbing, loudmouthed, noisy, obstreperous, raucous, rowdy, tumultuous, vociferous

adj 4 see: OSTENTATIOUS *adj* 1

loudmouthed *adj* blatant, boisterous, clamorous, disturbing, loud, noisy, obstreperous, raucous, rowdy, tumultuous, vociferous

lounge *n* 1 bar, barroom, cocktail lounge, den, dive, dump, gin mill, hangout, haunt, joint, pub, rathskeller, saloon, tavern, watering hole

n 2 couch, divan, settee, sofa

v 1 languish, loll, recline, repose

v 2 dally, dawdle, delay, diddle, goof off, idle, lag, linger, loaf, loiter, loll, malinger, poke, put off, putter, shirk, tarry

louse *n* cad, cheat, knave, lecher, rake, rascal, reprobate, rogue, scoundrel

lousy *adj* 1 awful, contemptible, dreadful, mean

adj 2 dirty, disgusting, foul, nasty, putrid, rotten, sordid adj **3** flawed, flimsy, imperfect, inferior, mediocre, miserable, paltry, poor, second-rate, shabby, shoddy, sorry, so-so, tacky, unworthy, worthless

lovable adj affable, amiable, approachable, cordial, friendly, genial, gentle, gracious, likable, peaceful, pleasant, serene

love n **1** commitment, passion, religion

n **2** affection, affinity, attachment, attraction, compassion, concern, devotion, fondness, heart, kinship, warmth

n **3** amorousness, passion

v **1** admire, adore, cherish, dote on, idolize, respect, revere, venerate, worship

v **2** admire, adore, appreciate, cherish, consider, covet, esteem, honor, idolize, prize, regard, respect, treasure, value

v **3** caress, cradle, cuddle, embrace, feel, fondle, fool around, hold, hug, make out, neck, nuzzle, pet, snuggle, stroke

loved adj adored, beloved, cherished, dear, esteemed, precious, respected, revered, treasured, venerable, worshiped

loveliness n attractiveness, aura, beauty, comeliness, pulchritude, radiance

lovely adj alluring, attractive, beautiful, breathtaking, comely, cute, fair, fine, foxy, gorgeous, luscious, magnificent, pretty, shapely, stunning

lover n **1** date, fiancée, girlfriend

n **2** concubine, mistress, trifle

n **3** beau, boyfriend, date, escort, fiancé, mate, paramour, suitor

n **4** buck, Casanova, Don Juan, flirt, gallant, ladies' man, lecher, philanderer, playboy, Romeo, stud

loving adj affectionate, amorous, attached, caring, devoted, enamored, fond, romantic, tender

low adj **1** cheap, economical, inexpensive, low-cost, moderate, reasonable

adj **2** base, common, humble, ignoble, knavish, lowly, mean, plebeian

adj **3** base, beneath, despicable, ignoble, inferior, lowdown, sordid, squalid, unworthy, vile, vulgar, wretched

adj **4** see: TRIVIAL adj **1**

low-cost adj cheap, economical, inexpensive, low, moderate, reasonable

lower adj **1** recessed, sunken, under

adj **2** inferior, lesser, subordinate, under

v **1** bend, bow, droop, duck, slouch, slump, stoop

v **2** clip, cut, cut back, cut down, mark down, reduce, shave, slash

v **3** depress, droop, flop, let down, mire, sag, sink, wallow

v **4** disdain, frown, glare, gloom, glower, grimace, pout, scowl, sulk

v **5** cheapen, depreciate, devalue, diminish, downgrade, dwindle, mark down, reduce, underrate, undervalue

v **6** descend, dive, drop, fall, lapse, leap, plummet, plunge, sink, swoop

v **7** see: BELITTLE v **1**

lowest adj **1** last, least, poorest, worst

adj **2** first, least, minimum, slightest, smallest, tiniest

lowly adj **1** humble, meek, modest, unassuming, unpretentious

adj **2** base, common, humble, ignoble, knavish, low, mean, plebeian

adj **3** see: SERVILE adj **2**

low-set adj short

low-statured adj short

loyal adj **1** blind, conscientious, meticulous, religious, strict, zealous

adj **2** ardent, constant, dedicated, dependable, devoted, faithful, resolute, staunch, steadfast, steady, true, trusty

loyally adv fast, firm, firmly, hard, reliably, solidly, tight, tightly

loyalty n allegiance, ardor, devotion, fidelity

lube n lubrication, moistener, oil, ointment, salve

lubrication n lube, moistener, oil, ointment, salve

lucid adj **1** ethical, moral, rational, responsible, sane, stable

adj **2** clear, clear-cut, crystal, limpid, translucent, transparent, unambiguous, unblurred

adj **3** clear, coherent, direct, easy, elementary, intelligible, logical, simple, understandable

adj **4** beaming, bright, brilliant, burnished, emitting, glistening, glossy, luminous, lustrous, polished, radiant, shining, shiny

adj **5** see: WISE adj **4**

lucidity n **1** mind, rationality, reason, saneness, sanity, sense, soundness, wit

n **2** clarity, clearness, distinctness, exactness, freshness, plainness, purity

luck n **1** chance, coincidence, good fortune, happenstance, serendipity

n **2** destiny, fate, good fortune, karma, kismet, lot, providence

n **3** bet, chance, fortune, gamble, hazard, risk, stake

n **4** blessing, bonanza, boon, fortune, gain, godsend, miracle, serendipity, stroke of luck, windfall *v* chance, discover, encounter, find, happen, hit, meet, stumble

luckless *adj* 1 cursed, damned, doomed, hapless, hopeless, ill-fated, jinxed, unfortunate, unhappy, unlucky, untoward

lucky *adj* 1 auspicious, favorable, fortunate, happy, providential, serendipitous

adj 2 see: ACCIDENTAL *adj* 3

lucrative *adj* beneficial, gainful, profitable, rewarding

lucre *n* see: MONEY *n* 4

ludicrous *adj* absurd, comic, comical, crazy, droll, farcical, foolish, funny, hilarious, humorous, laughable, outrageous, ridiculous, silly

lug *v* 1 carry, cart, drag, draw, haul, pull, tow, truck, tug

v 2 bear, carry, convey, crate, ferry, haul, lift, pack, shoulder, shuttle, tote, traffic, transport, truck

luger *n* automatic, firearm, gun, handgun, heater, iron, piece, pistol, revolver, rod

luggable *adj* carryable, compact, lightweight, movable, pocket-size, portable, small, transportable

luggage *n* bag, baggage, case, equipment, gear, grip, kit, pack, pouch, purse, sack, suitcase, valise, wallet

lukewarm *adj* heated, hot, tepid, warm

lull *n* 1 idle time, interlude, recreation, relaxation, repose, rest, vacation

n 2 calm, hush, peace, peacefulness, quiet, repose, respite, rest, siesta, silence, sleep, stillness, tranquillity

n 3 delay, interval, pause, stay, suspension, wait

n 4 abeyance, dormancy, inaction, inactivity, limbo, pause, suspension

n 5 break, cessation, delay, gap, interim, interval, lapse, pause, stop

v 1 abate, cease, decline, decrease, die down, diminish, drain, dwindle, ease, ebb, fall, lessen, let up, recede, reduce, relax, relent, shrink, slacken, soften, stop, subside, taper off, wane, waste away, weaken

v 2 allay, appease, assuage, balm, becalm, calm, compose, conciliate, ease, mollify, pacify, placate, propitiate, quell, quiet, reconcile, satiate, settle, soften, soothe, still, sweeten, tranquilize

lullaby *n* air, call, carol, cry, melody, note, rhapsody, song, tune

lumber *n* forest, trees, wood

v persevere, persist, plod, plug, toil

lumbering *adj* awkward, bumbling, clumsy, faltering, gauche, gawky, halting, hesitant, inept, maladroit, ungainly, ungraceful

luminary *n* celebrity, dignitary, movie star, name, notable, personality, star

luminescence *n* illumination, lamps, lighting

luminous *adj* 1 beaming, bright, brilliant, burnished, emitting, glistening, glossy, lucid, lustrous, polished, radiant, shining, shiny

adj 2 glowing, incandescent, moonlit, sunlit

lump *n* 1 clot, coagulation, mass

n 2 bulge, jut, projection, protrusion, swelling

n 3 bead, blob, bubble, drib, drop, droplet, globule, sphere

v 1 batch, send, ship together

v 2 see: ASSEMBLE *v* 3

v 3 see: COMBINE *v* 3

lunacy *n* 1 craziness, folly, foolishness, frivolity, insanity, madness, mania, nonsense, senselessness

n 2 aberration, abnormality, craziness, delusion, dementia, derangement, distraction, eccentricity, fugue, hallucination, insanity, irregularity, madness, mania, psychosis, unbalance

lunatic *n* card, character, eccentric, kook, nut, oddball, weirdo

adj see: ABSURD *adj* 2

lunch *n* 1 banquet, buffet, dinner, feast, meal, repast, smorgasbord, supper

n 2 bread, breakfast, brunch, chow, cuisine, diet, dinner, dish, edibles, entree, fare, food, grub, meals, nosh, nutrition, provisions, rations, snack, supper, victuals, vittles

luncheonette *n* automat, cafe, cafeteria, canteen, diner, grill, lunchroom, restaurant, tearoom

lunchroom *n* automat, cafe, cafeteria, canteen, diner, grill, luncheonette, restaurant, tearoom

lunge *v* 1 attack, butt, drive, knock, pass, plunge, ram, sink, stab, stick, thrust

v 2 dive, lurch, pitch, plunge

lurch *v* 1 careen, pitch, reel, stagger, sway, toss, totter, wheel

v 2 fall, skid, skim, slide, slip, stumble, totter, trip, tumble

v 3 dive, lunge, pitch, plunge

lure *n* attraction, bait, come-on, decoy, enticement, magnet, ruse, seduction, snare, temptation, trap, wile

v 1 attract, bait, decoy, entice, entrap, tantalize

v 2 attract, court, encourage, flirt, invite, pursue, romance, solicit, tempt, woo

v 3 appeal, arouse, attract, excite, fascinate, fire, interest, intrigue, lead on, seduce, stir, tantalize

v 4 see: ATTRACT *v* 3, 4, 5, 6

lures *n* bait, gear, tackle

lurid *adj* see: AWFUL *adj* 2

luscious *adj* 1 abundant, elaborate, flamboyant, ornate, replete

  adj 2 appetizing, delectable, delicious, exquisite, palatable, savory, sweet, tasty

  adj 3 see: BEAUTIFUL *adj* 2

  adj 4 see: SENSUAL *adj* 1

lush *adj* 1 abundant, cornucopian, extravagant, exuberant, garish, generous, lavish, luxuriant, opulent, prodigal, profuse, rich, wasteful

  adj 2 see: SENSUAL *adj* 1

lust *n* appetite, craving, desire, eroticism, hankering, hunger, itch, longing, passion, urge, yearning, yen

  v 1 choose, covet, crave, desire, envy, fancy, want, wish

  v 2 ache, covet, crave, desire, hanker, hunger, itch, long, need, pine, thirst, want, yearn

luster *n* 1 coating, gloss, glow, patina, polish, radiance, sheen, shimmer, shine

  n 2 see: PROMINENCE *n*

lusterless *adj* see: DULL *adj* 7

lustful *adj* 1 amorous, ardent, aroused, carnal, earthy, erotic, fervent, fleshly, horny, hot, impassioned, lascivious, lecherous, lewd, licentious, passionate, provocative, randy, raunchy, romantic, sensual, sexual, sexy, sultry, titillated, torrid, turned on, voluptuous, wanton

  adj 2 amorous, aroused, horny, in heat, in the mood, passionate, stimulated

lustiness *n* see: VIGOR *n* 3

lustrous *adj* beaming, bright, brilliant, burnished, emitting, glistening, glossy, lucid, luminous, polished, radiant, shining, shiny

lusty *adj* 1 brave, courageous, macho, male, manlike, manly, masculine, potent, stalwart, virile

  adj 2 concentrated, hearty, heavy-duty, potent, powerful, robust, stalwart, stout, strong, sturdy

  adj 3 coercive, compelling, dynamic, energetic, forceful, hardy, mighty, passionate, powerful, robust, strong, sturdy, vigorous

  adj 4 carnal, delicious, enticing, erotic, hedonistic, luscious, lush, luxurious, pleasure-seeking, sensual, sensualistic, sensuous, sexual, voluptuous

luxuriant *adj* 1 abundant, cornucopian, extravagant, exuberant, garish, generous, lavish, lush, opulent, prodigal, profuse, rich, wasteful

  adj 2 choice, deluxe, elegant, first-class, grand, luxurious, opulent, ornate, palatial, plush, posh, rich, soft, stately, sumptuous, thick

luxuriate *v* bask, delight, enjoy, like, loaf, relax, relish, rest, savor, wallow

luxurious *adj* 1 exclusive, expensive, high-class

  adj 2 choice, deluxe, elegant, first-class, grand, luxuriant, opulent, ornate, palatial, plush, posh, rich, soft, stately, sumptuous, thick

  adj 3 see: SENSUAL *adj* 1

luxury *n* 1 bauble, delicacy, frill, treat

  n 2 abundance, affluence, bounty, comfort, cornucopia, elegance, glut, good fortune, grandeur, opulence, plenty, prosperity, success, wealth

lyceum *n* academy, college, institute, school, seminary, university

lying *adj* see: EVIL *adj* 4

  n see: FRAUD *n* 4

lyric *adj* choral, euphonious, harmonious, mellow, melodic, melodious, musical, orchestral, philharmonic, rhythmical, symphonic, tuneful, vocal

  n ditty, limerick, madrigal, poem, poetry, rhyme, song, sonnet, verse

M

ma *n* mama, mater, matriarch, mom, momma, mommy, mother, mummy, parent

macabre *adj* abnormal, depressing, dismal, funereal, ghastly, gloomy, gruesome, morbid, sepulchral

Machiavellian *adj* bad, corrupt, crooked, deceitful, dishonest, evil, fraudulent, immoral, iniquitous, lying, manipulative, mercenary, reprobate, roguish, scheming, shady, shifty, sinful, unethical, unfair, unprincipled, unscrupulous, untruthful, venal, vile, wicked, wrong

machinate *v* cogitate, collude, connive, conspire, contrive, devise, frame, intrigue, maneuver, orchestrate, plan, plot, scheme

machination *n* cabal, collusion, conspiracy, intrigue, junta, plot, scheme, secret

machine *n* 1 device, engine, generator, motor, turbine

n 2 see: DEVICE *n* 2

machinery *n* 1 action, apparatus, gear, workings, works

n 2 ammo, ammunition, armor, arms, equipment, guns, munitions, ordnance, weapons

macho *adj* brave, courageous, lusty, male, manlike, manly, masculine, potent, stalwart, virile

macrocosm *n* cosmos, creation, firmament, grand scale, nature, solar system, universe, vast, world

mad *adj* 1 agitated, disorderly, excited, fierce, frantic, frenzied, furious, stormy, tumultuous, turbulent, violent, wild

adj 2 aggravated, angry, annoyed, cross, enraged, excited, fuming, furious, hot, incensed, indignant, irate, irritable, provoked, teed off, upset

adj 3 see: ABSURD *adj* 2

madden *v* see: BOTHER *v* 5

madhouse *n* 1 asylum, booby hatch, funny farm, institution

n 2 see: ACTIVITY *n* 3

madness *n* 1 craziness, folly, foolishness, frivolity, insanity, lunacy, mania, nonsense, senselessness

n 2 aberration, abnormality, craziness, delusion, dementia, derangement, distraction, eccentricity, fugue, hallucination, insanity, irregularity, lunacy, mania, psychosis, unbalance

madrigal *n* ditty, limerick, lyric, poem, poetry, rhyme, song, sonnet, verse

magazine *n* booklet, gazette, journal, monthly, periodical, publication, quarterly, weekly

magazines *n* media, newspapers, press, television

magic *n* bewitchment, enchantment, incantation, occultism, sorcery, spell, voodoo, witchcraft, wizardry

magician *n* conjurer, diviner, soothsayer, sorcerer, wizard

magisterial *adj* august, baronial, exalted, grand, grandiose, haughty, imperial, imposing, impressive, lofty, lordly, magnificent, majestic, noble, portly, princely, regal, royal, stately

magistrate *n* court, judge, justice

magnanimous *adj* benevolent, big, chivalrous, considerate, generous, grandiose, lofty, noble

magnate *n* baron, big shot, businessman, businessperson, businesswoman, capitalist, entrepreneur, executive, financier, industrialist, mogul, plutocrat, tycoon, VIP

magnet *n* attraction, bait, come-on, decoy, enticement, lure, ruse, seduction, snare, temptation, trap, wile

magnetic *adj* electric

magnetism *n* 1 charisma, dominance, influence, leadership, personality, power, strength

n 2 affinity, allure, appeal, attraction, attractiveness, aura, beguilement, charisma, charm, enchantment, enticement, fascination, glamour, infatuation, sex appeal, spell

magnetize *v* allure, attract, bedevil, beguile, bewitch, captivate, charm, conjure, delight, draw, enchant, enthrall, fascinate, lure, mesmerize, tempt, wile

magnificent *adj* 1 arousing, awesome, breathtaking, exciting, stimulating, stirring, stunning

adj 2 admirable, beautiful, delightful, glorious, good, peachy, splendid, terrific, wonderful

adj 3 elevated, exalted, excellent, grand, great, heavenly, high, lofty, prominent, sublime, superb

adj 4 best, elegant, finest, gilt-edged, majestic, outstanding, preeminent, sensational, splendid, superb, superior, superlative

adj 5 alluring, attractive, beautiful, breathtaking, comely, cute, fair, fine, foxy, gorgeous, lovely, luscious, pretty, shapely, stunning

adj 6 splendid

adj 7 august, baronial, exalted, grand, grandiose, haughty, imperial, imposing, impressive, lofty, lordly, magisterial, majestic, noble, portly, princely, regal, royal, stately

magnify *v* 1 augment, enhance, maximize, optimize, utilize

v 2 amplify, bloat, dilate, distend, enlarge, expand, fatten, grow, increase, inflate, stretch, swell, widen

v 3 amplify, append, augment, boost, build, enlarge, expand, extend, grow, heighten, increase, intensify, multiply, run up, snowball, supplement, upsurge, wax

magnitude *n* 1 amplitude, caliber, concentration, potency, strength

n 2 consequence, import, importance, moment, significance, substance, weight

n 3 amount, amplitude, dimensions, proportions, quantity, scope, size, volume

mahogany *adj* beige, brown, chestnut, chocolate, tan

maid *n* 1 maiden, single, spinster
n 2 damsel, girl, maiden, wench

maiden *adj* earliest, first, founding, fundamental, initial, original, pioneer, primary, prime
n 1 maid, single, spinster
n 2 damsel, girl, maid, wench

maidenly *adj* abstinent, celibate, chaste, continent, pure, virginal, virtuous

mail *n* delivery, package, parcel
v see: SEND *v* 3

mailer *n* envelope, file, folder, sleeve

maim *v* cripple, dismember, mangle, mutilate

main *adj* 1 central, chief, distinguished, dominant, famed, great, key, leading, major, number one, outstanding, predominant, preeminent, primary, prime, principal, prominent, star, successful, superior, top
adj 2 see: FOREMOST *adj* 3
adj 3 see: UTTER *adj*

mainland *adj* continental

mainly *adv* as a rule, customarily, frequently, generally, most, mostly, most often, normally, ordinarily, primarily, principally, usually

maintain *v* 1 egg on, encourage, lead on, string
v 2 conserve, preserve, protect, save
v 3 allege, assert, avow, claim, say, state
v 4 commit, continue, extend, perpetuate, prolong, pull
v 5 assist, keep up, provide, support, sustain, uphold
v 6 argue, assert, believe, claim, contend, defend, justify, know, state, think, vindicate, warrant
v 7 adapt, adjust, balance, fit, fix, inspect, overhaul, recondition, refurbish, regulate, repair, service, support, tune up

maintenance *n* 1 installation, repair, service, upkeep
n 2 keep, livelihood, living, minimum, subsistence, support, sustenance

majestic *adj* 1 aristocratic, blue-blooded, imperial, kingly, noble, regal, royal, stately, well-bred
adj 2 best, elegant, finest, gilt-edged, magnificent, outstanding, preeminent, sensational, splendid, superb, superior, superlative
adj 3 august, baronial, exalted, grand, grandiose, haughty, imperial, imposing, impressive, lofty, lordly, magisterial, magnificent, noble, portly, princely, regal, royal, stately

major *adj* 1 acute, burning, critical, crucial, desperate, dire, grave, heavy, important, momentous, ponderous, pressing, profound, serious, severe, solemn, somber, urgent, vital
adj 2 central, chief, distinguished, dominant, famed, great, key, leading, main, number one, outstanding, predominant, preeminent, primary, prime, principal, prominent, star, successful, superior, top
adj 3 see: BIG *adj* 4

majority *adj* foremost, maximum, most, optimal, top, unequaled
n 1 most
n 2 quorum
n 3 bulk, greater part, mass, preponderance

make *v* 1 coerce, compel, constrain, force, overpower, propel, push
v 2 craft, define, develop, formulate, list, process, specify, synthesize
v 3 actuate, bring about, cause, create, draw on, effect, execute, invoke, produce, secure
v 4 assemble, build, construct, erect, establish, fabricate, forge, form, manufacture, mold, produce, trailblaze
v 5 begin, coin, conceive, craft, create, define, develop, devise, formulate, innovate, invent, originate, start
v 6 acquire, earn, obtain, procure
v 7 bear, beget, breed, come into, create, effect, engender, father, generate, hatch, impregnate, mate, multiply, originate, parent, procreate, promulgate, propagate, reproduce, sire, spawn

maker *n* 1 builder, manufacturer, producer
n 2 author, creator, founder, initiator, instigator, inventor, originator, parent, pioneer, seed, source

makeshift *adj* impromptu, provisional, stopgap, temporary
n expedient, means, measure, recourse, refuge, replacement, resort, stopgap, substitute, surrogate

makeup *n* 1 character, constitution, fiber, nature, quality, substance
n 2 aptitude, character, complexion, disposition, distinctiveness, heart, humor, identity, inclination, individuality, nature, personality, quality, spirit, state, temperament, tendency

makings *n* ingredients, potential, substance

maladroit *adj* awkward, bumbling, clumsy, faltering, gauche, gawky, halting, hesitant, inept, lumbering, ungainly, ungraceful

malady n affliction, ailment, complaint, condition, disease, disorder, evil, harm, ill, illness, sickness

malaise n apathy, boredom, dreariness, dullness, ennui, monotony, tedium

malapropos adj 1 see: INADEQUATE adj 5

adj 2 see: SUPERFLUOUS adj 3

malarkey n baloney, bilge, bosh, bull, bunk, drivel, fiddlesticks, foolishness, junk, nonsense, nothing, poppycock, rot, rubbish, schlock, silliness, trivia

malcontent n agitator, defector, dissident, heretic, iconoclast, insurgent, maverick, misfit, nonconformist, rebel, renegade, traitor, troublemaker, turncoat

male adj brave, courageous, lusty, macho, manlike, manly, masculine, potent, stalwart, virile

n bachelor, chap, dude, fellow, gent, gentleman, guy, man, mister, widower

malediction n anathema, condemnation, curse, execration, imprecation, voodoo

malevolence n chip, grudge, ill will, malice, maliciousness, malignancy, resentment, spite

malevolent adj 1 catty, hostile, malicious, resentful, spiteful, treacherous

adj 2 bad, baleful, corrupt, cunning, forbidding, harmful, hurtful, malignant, menacing, ominous, sinister, sneaky

malfeasance n error, malpractice, misbehavior, misdeed, mismanagement, offense, transgression, wrong, wrongdoing

malfunctioning adj bad, defective, futile, inadequate, incorrect, inferior, invalid, poor, void

malice n 1 chip, grudge, ill will, malevolence, maliciousness, malignancy, resentment, spite

n 2 acrimony, animosity, antagonism, antipathy, aversion, bitterness, dislike, enmity, gall, hate, hatred, hostility, ill will, rancor, spite, venom, vindictiveness

malicious adj 1 catty, hostile, malevolent, resentful, spiteful, treacherous

adj 2 derogatory, disparaging, insulting, nasty, sarcastic, snide

adj 3 revengeful, spiteful, unforgiving, unmerciful, vengeful, vindictive

adj 4 see: NASTY adj 7

maliciousness n chip, grudge, ill will, malevolence, malice, malignancy, resentment, spite

malign v 1 befoul, besmirch, blacken, darken, defame, disparage, injure, libel, revile, scandalize, slander, slur, smear, soil, tear down, traduce

v 2 abuse, asperse, bad-mouth, belittle, condemn, damage, decry, defame, degrade, denigrate, denounce, deprecate, detract, diminish, discount, disparage, insult, knock, put down, revile, run down, slander, take away, vilify

malignancy n 1 chip, grudge, ill will, malevolence, malice, maliciousness, resentment, spite

n 2 cancer, corruption, decay, evil, infection, poison, rot, toxin, venom

malignant adj bad, baleful, corrupt, cunning, forbidding, harmful, hurtful, malevolent, menacing, ominous, sinister, sneaky

malinger v see: DELAY v 3

mall n business, department store, market, mart, shop, store, supermarket

malleable adj 1 bouncy, elastic, expansive, plastic, resilient

adj 2 alterable, impressionable, inexperienced, naive, sensitive, susceptible

adj 3 adaptable, adjustable, changeable, flexible, limber, maneuverable, moldable, plastic, pliable, pliant, responsive, soft, supple, swayed, versatile, yielding

mallet n bat, blackjack, boomerang, club, cudgel, cue, nightstick, stave, stick

malodorous adj 1 improper, indecent, indelicate, lewd, off-color, offensive, rough, scurrilous, suggestive, unbecoming, unseemly, untoward

adj 2 decaying, fetid, foul, gamy, musty, putrid, rancid, rank, reeking, rotten, smelly, sour, spoiled, stale, stinking, tainted

malpractice n error, malfeasance, misbehavior, misdeed, mismanagement, offense, transgression, wrong, wrongdoing

maltreat v see: HARM v 1

mama n ma, mater, matriarch, mom, momma, mommy, mother, mummy, parent

mammoth adj colossal, enormous, fantastic, Gargantuan, giant, gigantic, Goliath, great, huge, immense, jumbo, leviathan, massive, mighty, monstrous, monumental, overwhelming, phenomenal, prodigious, Promethean, stupendous, Titanic, towering, tremendous, unfathomed, untold, vast, walloping, whopping

man n 1 being, citizen, creature, entity, Homo sapiens, human, human being, individual, person

n 2 bachelor, chap, dude, fellow, gent, gentleman, guy, male, mister, widower *n* 3 bridegroom, groom, hubby, husband, master, mate, mister, spouse

v appoint, arm, equip, fortify, furnish, gear, outfit, rig, set up, supply, turn out

manacle *n* bond, chain, fetter, handcuff, iron, shackle, tie

manage *v* 1 oversee, supervise

v 2 behave, handle, treat

v 3 accomplish, behave, contend, cope, make do, persevere

v 4 do, fare, get along, get by, get on, make out, muddle through, shift, stagger

v 5 carry on, conduct, direct, keep, operate, ordain, oversee, pilot, run

v 6 administer, boss, command, direct, guide, oversee, regulate, steer, supervise

v 7 boss, command, control, direct, dominate, govern, handle, influence, lead, manipulate, order, supervise, sway

manageable *adj* controllable, docile, maneuverable, pliable, yielding

management *n* 1 authority, brass, leaders, officers

n 2 administration, care, charge, conduct, handling, intendance, overseeing, running, supervision

n 3 authority, command, commission, control, direction, domination, jurisdiction, mastery, might, power, rule

n 4 administration, administrators, authorities, bureaucracy, civil service, commission, department, direction, forces, government, ministry, officials, power, powers, rule, rulers

manager *n* 1 architect, designer, draftsperson, engineer, inventor, operator, plotter, schemer, surveyor

n 2 director

n 3 agent, custodian, steward

mandate *n* 1 claim, demand, requirement, ultimatum

n 2 behest, bidding, canon, charge, command, criterion, decree, dictate, direction, edict, fiat, guideline, injunction, institution, law, order, ordinance, precept, prescript, prescription, regulation, rite, rule, ruling, statute, word

v advise, authorize, command, decree, designate, dictate, direct, ordain, order, rule

mandated *adj* see: FIXED *adj* 9

mandatory *adj* 1 compulsory, imperative, must do, necessary, obligatory, prerequisite, required

adj 2 critical, essential, imperative, indispensable, necessary, needed, prerequisite, required, vital

maneuver *n* 1 action, measure, method, step

n 2 antic, device, diversion, gambit, gimmick, mischief, move, plan, plot, ploy, prank, ruse, scheme, stratagem, strategy, tactic, trick, wile

v 1 control, deploy, direct, manipulate, use

v 2 dispense, handle, manipulate, ply, swing, wield

v 3 see: PLOT *v* 1

maneuverable *adj* 1 controllable, docile, manageable, pliable, yielding

adj 2 see: PLASTIC *adj* 2

mangle *v* 1 cripple, maim, mutilate

v 2 bruise, hurt, injure, wound

v 3 see: CUT *v* 7

mania *n* 1 craziness, folly, foolishness, frivolity, insanity, lunacy, madness, nonsense, senselessness

n 2 aberration, abnormality, craziness, delusion, dementia, derangement, distraction, eccentricity, fugue, hallucination, insanity, irregularity, lunacy, madness, psychosis, unbalance

maniac *n* bug, crusader, enthusiast, fanatic, fiend, freak, hobbyist, monomaniac, nut, radical, zealot

maniacal *adj* 1 delirious, deranged, fantasizing, frenzied, hallucinating, raving

adj 2 amok, berserk, crazy, frenzied, out of control, rushed about, violent

manifest *v* 1 display, exhibit, flaunt, parade, promenade

v 2 disclose, display, evince, express, imply, indicate, reflect, reveal, show

v 3 appear, arise, befall, break, come, come about, develop, do, ensue, evolve, fall out, happen, materialize, occur, pass, rise, take place, transpire, turn up

adj see: OBVIOUS *adj* 3

manifestation *n* clue, example, illustration, indication, proof, sign

manifold *adj* complex, diverse, multifarious, multifold

manipulate *v* 1 exploit, misuse, take advantage

v 2 control, deploy, direct, maneuver, use

v 3 dispense, handle, maneuver, ply, swing, wield

v 4 examine, feel, finger, fondle, grope, handle, maul, palpate, paw, probe, touch

v 5 boss, command, control, direct, dominate, govern, handle, influence, lead, manage, order, supervise, sway

manipulative *adj* 1 bad, corrupt, crooked, deceitful, dishonest, evil, fraudulent, immoral, iniquitous, lying, Machiavellian, mercenary, reprobate, roguish, scheming, shady, shifty, sinful, unethical, unfair, unprincipled, unscrupulous, untruthful, venal, vile, wicked, wrong

adj 2 see: TREACHEROUS *adj* 2

mankind *n* humanity, humankind, human race, world

manlike *adj* brave, courageous, lusty, macho, male, manly, masculine, potent, stalwart, virile

manly *adj* brave, courageous, lusty, macho, male, manlike, masculine, potent, stalwart, virile

man-made *adj* artificial, counterfeit, fake, false, manufactured, plastic, synthetic

mannequin *n* doll, dummy, effigy, replica

manner *n* 1 accent, elocution, enunciation, inflection, intonation, pronunciation

n 2 fashion, flavor, mode, style, tone, vein

n 3 custom, fashion, formality, habit, mores, observance, practice, routine, tradition, usage, use, way, wont

n 4 angle, approach, code, delivery, execution, expression, fashion, method, mode, organization, process, program, style, system, technique, way

mannerism *n* affectation, airs, peculiarity, pose, posturing, pretense, trait

mannerly *adj* chivalrous, civil, civilized, cordial, courteous, courtly, decent, dignified, gallant, genteel, gentlemanly, gracious, noble, polite, well-mannered

manners *n* 1 action, bearing, behavior, conduct, demeanor

n 2 convention, custom, decorum, etiquette, formality, good form, propriety, protocol, rites

n 3 see: UTILITY *n*

mansion *n* abode, castle, domicile, dwelling, estate, home, house, palace, residence

manslaughter *n* assassination, foul play, homicide, murder

mantilla *n* bandanna, muffler, scarf, shawl

mantle *n* 1 ledge, shelf, sill

n 2 cape, cloak, coat, shawl, wrap

manual *adj* menial, physical

n 1 atlas, compendium, directory, guide, guidebook, handbook, list, listing, phone book, textbook, Yellow Pages

n 2 Bible, scripture

manufacture *v* assemble, build, construct, erect, establish, fabricate, forge, form, make, mold, produce, trailblaze

manufactured *adj* artificial, counterfeit, fake, false, man-made, plastic, synthetic

manufacturer *n* builder, maker, producer

manure *n* dirt, dung, filth, garbage, muck, mud, slime, sludge

manuscript *n* 1 book, correspondence, edition, folio, issue, monograph, opus, paperback, printing, publication, text, tome, volume, work, writing

n 2 see: ESSAY *n*

many *adj* 1 countless, immeasurable, incalculable, infinite, innumerable, innumerous, legion, numberless, uncountable, unlimited, untold

adj 2 abundant, assorted, copious, diverse, extensive, legion, multifarious, multitudinous, myriad, numerous, plentiful, populous, prolific, sundry, various, voluminous

n 1 droves, loads, lots, multitudes, plenty, scads, slew

n 2 crush, dozens, horde, host, legion, multitude, numerousness, oodles, press, push, scores, squash, swarm

map *n* blueprint, chart, diagram, draft, outline, plan, sketch

v see: DESIGN *v* 4

mar *v* abuse, blemish, damage, hamper, harm, hurt, injure, impair, obstruct, ruin, sabotage, scuttle, spoil, tarnish, vandalize

marathon *n* see: COMPETITION *n* 2

maraud *v* see: RAVAGE *v* 2

marble *n* ball, balloon, globe, orb, sphere

march *n* 1 hike, stroll, tramp, trek, walk

n 2 gait, pace, shuffle, step, stride, walk

v 1 amble, hike, journey, pace, parade, plod, saunter, step, stride, stroll, strut, tramp, tread, trek, walk

v 2 advance, begin again, continue, cycle, depart, get along, get on, go, leave, move, move forward, overture, part, proceed, progress, push on, recommence, reembark, restart, wend

mare *n* colt, equine, filly, foal, gelding, horse, mount, nag, pony, steed, yearling

margin *n* 1 excess, give, leeway, play, slack, stretch

n 2 border, boundary, bounds, brim, brink, curb, edge, fringe, limits, lip, outskirt, perimeter, periphery, rim, side, skirt, verge

marginal *adj* borderline, casual, frivolous, insignificant, light, lightweight, little, meager, minor, minute, negligible, nonessential, off, outside, petty, remote, secondary, slender, slight, slim, small, tenuous, trivial, unimportant

marijuana *n* dope, drug, grass, narcotic, pot

mariner *n* mate, navy man, sailor, salt, seafarer, seaman, yachtsman

marines *n* airborne, army, battalion, brigade, cavalry, company, footmen, guard, horsemen, infantry, legion, militia, minutemen, paratroops, platoon, reserve, storm troopers

mark *n* 1 circle, spot

n 2 bit, chip, dent, fragment, piece

n 3 approval, autograph, endorsement, John Hancock, name, signature

n 4 chump, dupe, pushover, stooge, sucker, victim

n 5 brand, cachet, emblem, imprint, logo, logotype, seal, stamp, trademark

n 6 copy, impression, imprint, indent, indentation, notch, print, stamp, tab

n 7 attribute, character, characteristic, feature, highlight, peculiarity, property, quality, trait, virtue

n 8 class, degree, grade, interval, level, notch, position, rank, rate, step

n 9 character, emblem, example, icon, letter, logo, model, representation, sign, symbol, token

n 10 clue, cue, guide, hint, indication, indicator, inkling, intimation, key, lead, notion, pointer, sign, signal, tip, trace

n 11 attention, awareness, care, carefulness, cognizance, concern, consciousness, consideration, heed, intimacy, knowing, knowledge, note, notice, observance, observation, perception, recognition, regard, remark, sense

v 1 evaluate, grade, rate, score

v 2 drive, hammer, impress, imprint, pound, press, print, stamp, strike, thump, whack

v 3 denote, flag, star

v 4 number, score, tally

v 5 accent, accentuate, amplify, concentrate, emphasize, feature, flag, focus, heighten, highlight, italicize, punctuate, spotlight, stress, underline, underscore

marked *adj* see: PROMINENT *adj* 2

marker *n* brush, chalk, crayon, pen, pencil, quill

market *v* barter, distribute, merchandise, peddle, retail, sell, vend, wholesale

n 1 bazaar, carnival, fair

n 2 business, department store, mall, mart, shop, store, supermarket

marketable *adj* commercial, salable, vendible, wanted

marketer *n* dealer, merchant, monger, purveyor, seller, trader, vendor

marketing *n* allocation, distribution, merchandising, selling, share, sharing

marks *n* grade, score

marl *n* clay, dirt, dry land, dust, earth, ground, land, loam, soil, *terra*, terra firma

marriage *n* coupling, liaison, linking, matrimony, union, wedlock

marrow *n* see: ESSENCE *n* 3

marry *v* 1 associate, blend, bond, coalesce, combine, compound, connect, couple, fasten, fuse, join, link, mate, meet, merge, pair, unite, wed

v 2 interbreed

v 3 attach, bind, bond, cord, fasten, hitch, join, link, tether, tie, tie up

marsh *n* bog, mire, moor, swamp

marshal *v* 1 arrange, array, dispose, order, organize, systemize

v 2 see: ASSEMBLE *v* 3

mart *n* business, department store, mall, market, shop, store, supermarket

martial *adj* military

marvel *n* miracle, phenomenon, sensation, spectacle, wonder

v wonder

marvelous *adj* 1 excellent, fabulous, fantastic, fine, good, great, super, terrific, tremendous, wonderful

adj 2 see: UNUSUAL *adj* 4

masculine *adj* brave, courageous, lusty, macho, male, manlike, manly, potent, stalwart, virile

mash *v* 1 compact, compress, constrain, crowd, crush, jam, pack, press, push, squash, squeeze

v 2 bruise, crush, mush up, pulp, squash

mask *n* 1 camouflage, cloak, costume, cover, curtain, disguise, pretense, shield, shroud, veil

n 2 overlay, pattern, stencil, template

v camouflage, cloak, conceal, cover, darken, disguise, envelop, hide, occult, seclude, shield, shroud, veil

masquerade *v* disguise, pass, pose, posture, pretend

mass *n* 1 clot, coagulation, lump

n 2 bulk, greater part, majority, preponderance

n 3 abundance, glut, great deal, lot, much, ton

n 4 bank, drift, heap, hill, mound, mountain, pile, stack, stockpile

n 5 basis, body, bulk, core, essence, essentials, gist, heart, import, nucleus, object, staple, substance, volume

n 6 band, bunch, crew, crowd, drove, flock, following, gaggle, gang, herd, huddle, mob, pack, rabble, riffraff, swarm, team, throng *n* **7** agglomerate, agglomeration, aggregate, total

v **1** cluster, swarm, teem

v **2** assemble, associate, call, cluster, collect, concentrate, congregate, convene, flock, gather, group, lump, marshal, mingle, mobilize, muster, order, rally, rendezvous, round up, send for, summon

massacre *n* bloodbath, bloodshed, butchery, carnage, extermination, genocide, holocaust, killing, pogrom, shambles, slaughter

v abolish, annihilate, assassinate, bump off, butcher, decimate, destroy, dispatch, execute, exterminate, hang, hit, kill, knock off, liquidate, murder, put away, rub out, slaughter, slay, wipe out

massage *v* **1** knead

v **2** apply, rub, spread

masses *n* citizens, civilization, colony, community, crowd, culture, folks, group, human beings, individuals, laity, men and women, neighbors, people, persons, populace, population, public, settlement, society, staff, tribe

massive *adj* **1** formidable, huge, immense, impressive, intimidating, significant, substantial

adj **2** athletic, brawny, burly, husky, muscular, ponderous, powerful, robust, stocky, stout, strapping, strong

adj **3** colossal, enormous, fantastic, Gargantuan, giant, gigantic, Goliath, great, huge, immense, jumbo, leviathan, mammoth, mighty, monstrous, monumental, overwhelming, phenomenal, prodigious, Promethean, stupendous, Titanic, towering, tremendous, unfathomed, untold, vast, walloping, whopping

master *adj* dominant, overbearing, overwhelming, paramount, predominant, preponderant, prevailing, prevalent, sovereign

n **1** ace, champion, expert, wizard

n **2** authority, expert, guide, guru, leader, mentor, pundit, teacher, wise man

n **3** adviser, artist, authority, expert, guru, official, pro, professional, specialist, veteran, virtuoso, wizard

n **4** advocate, champion, conqueror, hero, heroine, lead, leader, principal, protagonist, star, trailblazer, victor, winner

n **5** bridegroom, groom, hubby, husband, man, mate, mister, spouse

n **6** autocrat, chief, commander, despot, dictator, governor, head, king, leader, lord, monarch, potentate, ruler

v **1** get, learn, pick up, read, realize, study, understand

v **2** best, conquer, defeat, overcome, prevail, succeed, triumph, win

masterful *adj* **1** see: AUTHORITATIVE *adj* 2

adj **2** see: QUALIFIED *adj* 4

masterpiece *n* accomplishment, legacy, monument

mastery *n* **1** authority, command, commission, control, direction, domination, jurisdiction, management, might, power, rule

n **2** ability, adequacy, adroitness, aptitude, art, caliber, calling, capability, capacity, command, competence, craft, dexterity, experience, expertise, familiarity, forte, knack, know-how, knowledge, proficiency, prowess, qualification, savvy, skill, specialty, strength, talent, training, workmanship

masticate *v* consume, devour, digest, eat, ingest, swallow

mat *n* carpet, mattress, pad, rug

match *n* **1** counterpart, double, duplicate, mate, twin

n **2** complement, counterpart, equal, equivalent, like, parallel, peer

n **3** bout, competition, conflict, contest, event, game, marathon, meet, meeting, race, regatta, round robin, run, tournament, tourney

n **4** see: ENEMY *n*

n **5** see: SIMILARITY *n* 2

v **1** equal, measure up, meet, rival, tie, touch

v **2** bracket, collate, compare, contrast, correlate, equate, liken, relate, sort

v **3** combat, compete, contend, contest, counter, dispute, duel, fight, oppose, parry, pit, play, repel, resist, rival, strive, struggle, vie

v **4** amount, approach, correspond to, equal

matching *adj* see: ALIKE *adj*

matchless *adj* alone, incomparable, only, peerless, unequaled, unique, unmatched, unpaired, unparalleled, unrivaled

mate *n* **1** counterpart, double, duplicate, match, twin

n **2** accomplice, acquaintance, adjunct, ally, associate, buddy, chum, cohort, colleague, companion, compatriot, comrade, confidant, confrere, connection, copartner, counterpart, co-worker, crony, equal, fellow, follower, friend, intimate, pal, partner, peer, relative, supporter

n **3** mariner, navy man, sailor, salt, seafarer, seaman, yachtsman *n* 4 bride, cohabitant, consort, fiancée, spouse, squaw, wife, woman

n 5 beau, boyfriend, date, escort, fiancé, lover, paramour, suitor

n 6 bridegroom, groom, hubby, husband, man, master, mister, spouse

v 1 associate, blend, bond, coalesce, combine, compound, connect, couple, fasten, fuse, join, link, marry, meet, merge, pair, unite, wed

v 2 bear, beget, breed, come into, create, effect, engender, father, generate, hatch, impregnate, make, multiply, originate, parent, procreate, promulgate, propagate, reproduce, sire, spawn

mater *n* ma, mama, matriarch, mom, momma, mommy, mother, mummy, parent

material *adj* 1 concrete, corporeal, objective, physical, real, sensible, substantial, tactile, tangible

adj 2 consequential, considerable, critical, crucial, important, meaningful, momentous, prominent, significant, substantial, vital, weighty

adj 3 see: APPLICABLE *adj*

n 1 chemicals, matter, substance

n 2 content, matter, property, stuff, substance

n 3 cloth

materialize *v* 1 come together, crystallize, develop, form, jell, shape up

v 2 appear, arise, befall, break, come, come about, develop, do, ensue, evolve, fall out, happen, manifest, occur, pass, rise, take place, transpire, turn up

materials *n* 1 equipment, fixtures, furnishings, gear, provisions, supplies

n 2 articles, basics, commodities, essentials, goods, inventory, line, merchandise, products, properties, staples, stock, wares

mating *n* coitus, conjugation, copulation, fooling around, foreplay, fornication, intercourse, reproduction, sex, union

matriarch *n* ma, mama, mater, mom, momma, mommy, mother, mummy, parent

matriculate *v* admit, enroll, receive, register

matrimonial *adj* connubial

matrimony *n* coupling, liaison, linking, marriage, union, wedlock

matrix *n* die, form, mold, punch

matron *n* dame, female, gentlewoman, lady, miss, mistress, spinster, widow, woman

matter *n* 1 affair, business, concern

n 2 chemicals, elements, material, substance

n 3 content, material, property, stuff, substance

n 4 boundary, extent, field, range, reach, scope, vicinity

n 5 argument, controversy, issue, item, motif, motive, point, proposition, question, subject, text, theme, topic

matter-of-fact *adj* cold, dry, dull, impassive, laid-back, phlegmatic, poker-faced, reserved, stoic, stolid, unaffected, unemotional, unfeeling, unmoved, untouched

mattress *n* carpet, mat, pad, rug

mature *adj* 1 adult, full-grown, grown, grown-up, matured, ripened

adj 2 experienced, expert, grizzled, hardened, seasoned, trained, weathered

v 1 derive, develop, evolve, progress, unfold

v 2 age, develop, grow, grow up, mellow, progress, ripen

matured *adj* 1 aged, grown old, mellow, ripe, ripened

adj 2 adult, full-grown, grown, grown-up, mature, ripened

maudlin *adj* bittersweet, poignant, sad, sentimental, sorrowful

maul *v* examine, feel, finger, fondle, grope, handle, manipulate, palpate, paw, probe, touch

mausoleum *n* burial, catacomb, cenotaph, crypt, grave, memorial, monument, pit, sepulcher, tomb, vault

mauve *adj* amethyst, lavender, lilac, orchid, plum, purple, violet

maverick *n* 1 freelance, independent, individualist, nonconformist

n 2 agitator, defector, dissident, heretic, iconoclast, insurgent, malcontent, misfit, nonconformist, rebel, renegade, traitor, troublemaker, turncoat

maxim *n* 1 announcement, aphorism, axiom, cliché, declaration, decree, dictum, edict, gospel, homily, moral, precept, pronouncement, rule, saying, teaching, truism, truth, verity

n 2 adage, axiom, byword, cliché, dictum, motto, proverb, saying, slogan, talk

maximize *v* augment, enhance, magnify, optimize, utilize

maximum *adj* 1 forceful, highhanded, important, intense, powerful, utmost

adj 2 foremost, majority, most, optimal, top, unequaled

adj 3 best, biggest, finest, greatest, largest,

most, number one, prime, select, superior, top, top-notch

n 1 majority

n 2 altitude, ceiling, limits, restraint

maybe *adv* conditionally, perchance, perhaps, possibly, tentatively

mayhem *n* 1 chaos, damage, destruction, devastation, disaster, disorder, harm, havoc, hurt, injury, loss, ruin, ruination

n 2 chaos, clutter, confusion, derangement, disarray, disorder, jumble, mess, mix-up, muddle, predicament, snafu, snarl, tangle, tumult, turmoil

n 3 see: CLAMOR *n*

maze *n* 1 complex, infrastructure, network, organization, system

n 2 befuddlement, daze, fog, haze, muddledness, muddleheadedness

meadow *n* field, grassland, lea, pasture, plain, prairie

meager *adj* 1 faint, imperceptible, remote, slight, subtle, vague

adj 2 bare, deficient, few, inadequate, inferior, insufficient, little, paltry, petty, poor, scant, scanty, skimpy, spare, sparse

adj 3 see: THIN *adj* 4

adj 4 see: TRIVIAL *adj* 2

meal *n* banquet, buffet, dinner, feast, lunch, repast, smorgasbord, supper

meals *n* bread, breakfast, brunch, chow, cuisine, diet, dinner, dish, edibles, entree, fare, food, grub, lunch, nosh, nutrition, provisions, rations, snack, supper, victuals, vittles

mean *adj* 1 intermediate, middle

adj 2 awful, contemptible, dreadful

adj 3 ineffectual, limited, little, narrow, paltry, set, small

adj 4 base, common, humble, ignoble, knavish, low, lowly, plebeian

adj 5 balking, balky, contrary, cranky, disagreeable, irascible, obstinate, ornery, perverse, wayward

adj 6 austere, brutal, callous, cold-blooded, compassionless, cruel, ferocious, fierce, hardened, hardhearted, heartless, indifferent, inhuman, inhumane, malicious, merciless, nasty, obdurate, pitiless, ruthless, savage, spiteful, stony, tough, uncaring, unemotional, unfeeling, unkind, unmerciful, unpitying, unrelenting, unsympathetic, vicious

adj 7 bad, rough, tough

adj 8 cheap, close, greedy, miserly, niggardly, parsimonious, penny-pinching, stingy, tight, tightfisted, ungenerous, ungiving

adj 9 annoying, bothersome, glaring, harassing, irksome, irritating, onerous, painful, pesky, troublesome, ugly, unwelcome, vexatious, wicked

n average, median, medium, middle, norm, par, rule, standard

v 1 aim, contemplate, design, intend, plan, propose

v 2 add up to, connote, convey, denote, identify, import, indicate, intend, show, signify, symbolize

v 3 denote, depict, express, illustrate, imply, represent, speak for, symbolize

meander *v* 1 bend, curve, veer, wind, zigzag

v 2 detour, deviate, differ, digress, diverge, swerve

v 3 itinerate, perambulate, promenade, ramble, range, roam, rove, saunter, stray, stroll, traipse, travel, traverse, walk, wander

meandering *adj* crooked, serpentine, sinuous, spiral, turning, twisting, winding, zigzagging

meaner *adj* deficient, inferior, not as good, poorer, worse

meaning *n* 1 content, significance

n 2 clarification, definition, denotation, explanation, translation

n 3 ambition, bent, design, goal, intent, intention, objective, plan, purpose

n 4 import, intent, message, sense, significance, understanding

meaningful *adj* 1 eloquent, expressive, intelligible

adj 2 consequential, considerable, critical, crucial, important, material, momentous, prominent, significant, substantial, vital, weighty

meaningless *adj* 1 empty, hollow, idle, insincere, shallow, vain

adj 2 see: SILLY *adj* 2

adj 3 see: TRIVIAL *adj* 1

means *n* 1 choice, option, recourse, remedy

n 2 assets, capacity, reserves, resources, wherewithal

n 3 agency, agent, channel, conduit, instrument, mechanism, medium, mode, vehicle

n 4 expedient, makeshift, measure, recourse, refuge, replacement, resort, stopgap, substitute, surrogate

n 5 circuit, course, itinerary, journey, line, passage, path, road, route, trip, voyage, way

n 6 see: MONEY *n* 4

meantime *adv* concurrently, in the interim, in the interval, meanwhile

meanwhile *adv* concurrently, in the interim, in the interval, meantime

measly *adj* immaterial, inconsequential, inconsiderable, insignificant, little, low, meaningless, minor, nominal, paltry, petty, picayune, picky, puny, skimpy, slight, small, tiny, trifling, trivial, unessential, unimportant, worthless

measure *n* 1 calibration

n 2 capacity, content, volume

n 3 action, maneuver, method, step

n 4 benchmark, criterion, test

n 5 act, law, legislation, ruling, statute

n 6 degree, extent, intensity, ratio, scope

n 7 air, harmony, medley, melody, music, strain, tune

n 8 benchmark, criterion, gauge, observation, rule, standard, yardstick

n 9 expedient, makeshift, means, recourse, refuge, replacement, resort, stopgap, substitute, surrogate

n 10 moderateness, moderation, temperance

n 11 piece, strip

n 12 dial, disk, display, gauge, indicator, meter, pointer, selector

n 13 allotment, allowance, apportionment, budget, dispensation, dispersion, lot, part, percentage, portion, quota, ration, share, slice

v 1 calibrate, grade, graduate

v 2 gauge, indicate, meter

v 3 calibrate, gauge, range, rank, size

v 4 adapt, conform, convert, cut, fashion, fit, modify, rig, shape, suit, tailor

v 5 allocate, allot, allow, apportion, assign, designate, distribute, divide, divvy, earmark, give, parcel, partition, portion, prorate, quota, ration, section, share, slice

measured *adj* 1 continual, continuing, gradual, increasing, incremental, intensifying, moderate, progressive, successive

adj 2 advised, calculated, careful, considered, contrived, deliberate, forewarned, planned, premeditated, studied, studious

meat *n* beef, guts, substance

meaty *adj* 1 deep, profound, rich, stimulating

adj 2 compact, definitive, pithy, seminal, tight

adj 3 see: FAT *adj* 1

mechanical *adj* 1 automated, automatic, habitual, robotic, routine

adj 2 adept, dexterous, proficient, skilled

mechanism *n* 1 agency, agent, channel, conduit, instrument, means, medium, mode, vehicle

n 2 see: DEVICE *n* 3

mechanization *n* habit, repetition, rote, routine

medal *n* 1 award, honor, prize, trophy

n 2 anklet, band, bangle, bracelet, brooch, earring, jewelry, medallion, necklace, pin, ring

n 3 accolade, award, commendation, credit, decoration, distinction, honor, kudos, laurels, note, praise, recognition, reputation, reward, tribute

medallion *n* anklet, band, bangle, bracelet, brooch, earring, jewelry, medal, necklace, pin, ring

meddle *v* butt in, chisel in, cut in, fiddle, horn in, interfere, interlope, intrude, mess around, peek, peer, poke, pry, snoop, tamper with

meddler *n* busybody, gossip, interloper, intruder, kibitzer, snoop, yenta

meddlesome *adj* busy, impertinent, intrusive, obtrusive, officious

media *n* 1 journalists, press, reporters

n 2 magazines, newspapers, press, television

n 3 bubble memory, diskettes, floppy, hard disk, memory, RAM

median *adj* 1 central

adj 2 center, centermost, equidistant, halfway, mid, middle, middlemost, midmost

n average, mean, medium, middle, norm, par, rule, standard

mediate *v* 1 adjudicate, arbitrate, judge, referee, try, umpire

v 2 arbitrate, intercede, interfere, interpose, intervene, intrude, settle, step in

mediation *n* adjudication, arbitration, facilitation, intercession, intervention

mediator *n* 1 arbiter, arbitrator, judge, moderator, referee, umpire

n 2 advocate, attorney, barrister, counsel, counselor, intercessor, lawyer, solicitor

n 3 absorber, agent, broker, catalyst, distributor, go-between, intermediary, middleman, negotiator

medic *n* attendant, nurse, orderly, therapist

medical *adj* curative, healing, medicinal, therapeutic

medication *n* antidote, cure, medicine, panacea, prescription, remedy, serum, therapy, treatment

medicinal *adj* curative, healing, therapeutic

medicine *n* 1 compound, drug, elixir, formula, narcotic, painkiller, pharmaceutical, prescription

n 2 antidote, cure, medication, panacea, prescription, remedy, serum, therapy, treatment

mediocre *adj* 1 average, common, intermediate, medium, middle, normal, ordinary, regular, standard, unimpressive

adj 2 flawed, flimsy, imperfect, inferior, lousy, miserable, paltry, poor, secondrate, shabby, shoddy, sorry, so-so, tacky, unworthy, worthless

adj 3 see: ADEQUATE *adj* 2

meditate *v* see: PONDER *v*

meditation *n* analysis, cogitation, consideration, contemplation, deliberation, logic, reason, reasoning, reflection, speculation, study, thinking, thought

meditative *adj* 1 melancholy, musing, nostalgic, pensive, wistful

adj 2 pensive, philosophical, pondering, reflective, speculative, thinking, thoughtful

medium *adj* average, common, intermediate, mediocre, middle, normal, ordinary, regular, standard, unimpressive

n 1 average, mean, median, middle, norm, par, rule, standard

n 2 agency, agent, channel, conduit, instrument, means, mechanism, mode, vehicle

n 3 clairvoyant, psychic, soothsayer, spiritualist

mediumistic *adj* clairvoyant, intuitive, prescient, psychic

medley *n* 1 assortment, jumble, mixture

n 2 air, harmony, measure, melody, music, strain, tune

meek *adj* 1 humble, lowly, modest, unassuming, unpretentious

adj 2 acquiescent, compliant, docile, easy, mild, nonresistant, obedient, passive, resigned, submissive, tame, tolerant, unassertive, yielding

meet *n* bout, competition, conflict, contest, event, game, marathon, match, meeting, race, regatta, round robin, run, tournament, tourney

v 1 converge

v 2 confer, discuss, interview

v 3 court, date, entertain

v 4 equal, match, measure up, rival, tie, touch

v 5 encounter, greet, interview, receive, see, visit

v 6 answer, do, fulfill, qualify, satisfy, suffice, work

v 7 chance, discover, encounter, find, happen, hit, luck, stumble

v 8 achieve, answer, execute, fill, finish, fulfill, realize, satisfy

v 9 address, call to, embrace, greet, hail, salute, summon, welcome

v 10 associate, blend, bond, coalesce, combine, compound, connect, couple, fasten, fuse, join, link, marry, mate, merge, pair, unite, wed

adj see: APPLICABLE *adj*

meeting *n* 1 confrontation, encounter

n 2 conference, discourse, discussion, interview, query

n 3 conference, parley, powwow, talk, tête-à-tête

n 4 assembly, clinic, congress, council, court, diet, forum, hearing, parliament, seminar, symposium

n 5 assemblage, assembly, caucus, conference, congregation, convention, council, crowd, gathering, group, rally, symposium

n 6 bout, competition, conflict, contest, event, game, marathon, match, meet, race, regatta, round robin, run, tournament, tourney

n 7 see: DISCUSSION *n* 2, 4

megalopolis *n* borough, city, metropolis, municipality, suburb, town

melancholy *adj* 1 meditative, musing, nostalgic, pensive, wistful

adj 2 black, bleak, blue, cheerless, dejected, depressed, despairing, despondent, discouraging, disheartening, distressing, down, forlorn, gloomy, hopeless, joyless, moody, mournful, oppressive, prostrate, sad, somber, sorry, unhappy

adj 3 dismal, doleful, gloomy, lamentable, mournful, plaintive, regretful, regrettable, rueful, sorrowful, woeful

n distress, grief, sadness, sorrow, suffering

meld *v* amalgamate, band, blend, coalesce, combine, compound, consolidate, fuse, intermingle, league, lump, merge, mingle, mix, unify, unite

melee *n* 1 affray, battle, brawl, brush, clash, conflict, difference, disagreement, dispute, encounter, fight, fracas, quarrel, run-in, scrimmage, skirmish, spat, touch

n 2 see: QUARREL *n* 2

mellow *adj* 1 aged, grown old, matured, ripe, ripened

adj 2 choral, euphonious, harmonious, lyric, melodic, melodious, musical, orchestral, philharmonic, rhythmical, symphonic, tuneful, vocal

adj 3 mild

v 1 soften, tame, temper

v 2 age, develop, grow, grow up, mature, progress, ripen

melodic *adj* choral, euphonious, harmonious, lyric, mellow, melodious, musical, orchestral, philharmonic, rhythmical, symphonic, tuneful, vocal

melodious *adj* choral, euphonious, harmonious, lyric, mellow, melodic, musical, orchestral, philharmonic, rhythmical, symphonic, tuneful, vocal

melodrama *n* 1 drama, mystery, theatrics, tragedy, tragicomedy

n 2 cliff-hanger, soap opera, thriller

melodramatic *adj* 1 emotional, flowery, gushy, sentimental

adj 2 dramatic, sensational, theatrical, thrilling

melody *n* 1 air, harmony, measure, medley, music, strain, tune

n 2 air, call, carol, cry, lullaby, note, rhapsody, song, tune

melt *v* 1 dissolve, flux, fuse, liquefy, run, thaw

v 2 bake, broil, burn, char, cook, parch, roast, scorch, sear, singe, swelter, toast, warm

melted *adj* heated, liquefied, molten

member *n* 1 associate, collaborator, individual, participant, party, person, registrant

n 2 bit, clipping, cut, division, lot, parcel, part, piece, portion, sample, section, segment, slice

n 3 constituent

n 4 appendage, arm, extremity, leg, limb, part

members *n* 1 associates, constituency, constituents, membership, personnel

n 2 congregation, devotees, flock, fold, followers, laity, parishioners

membership *n* associates, constituency, constituents, members, personnel

membrane *n* coating, covering, film, layer, sheet, tissue

memento *n* 1 relic, remnant, shadow, trace, vestige

n 2 antique, gift, heirloom, keepsake, memorial, relic, remembrance, reminder, souvenir, token, trophy

memo *n* chit, letter, memorandum, notandum, notation, note, record, reminder

memoir *n* 1 account, diary, digest, journal, log, minutes, notation, notes, proceedings, record, recording, report

n 2 article, composition, discourse, dissertation, essay, manuscript, monograph, paper, report, study, theme, thesis, tract, treatise, work

memorable *adj* indelible, momentous, unforgettable

memorandum *n* chit, letter, memo, notandum, notation, note, record, reminder

memorial *n* 1 antique, gift, heirloom, keepsake, memento, relic, remembrance, reminder, souvenir, token, trophy

n 2 burial, catacomb, cenotaph, crypt, grave, mausoleum, monument, pit, sepulcher, tomb, vault

n 3 monument, shrine, statue

memorialize *v* celebrate, commemorate, keep, observe, solemnize

memorize *v* learn, remember, retain

memory *n* 1 nostalgia, recall, recollection, remembrance, reminiscence

n 2 bubble memory, diskettes, floppy, hard disk, media, RAM

n 3 engram, recall, remembrance, retention, retentiveness, retrospection

men *n* army, battalion, brigade, company, force, gang, power, soldiers, troops

menace *n* danger, downside, exposure, hazard, jeopardy, liability, peril, risk, threat

v alarm, attack, bully, club, coerce, frighten, harass, intimidate, strong-arm, terrorize, threaten

menacing *adj* 1 bullying, coercive, forceful, strong-arm, threatening

adj 2 foreboding, imminent, impending, ominous, portentous, predictive, prophetic, sinister, threatening

adj 3 bad, baleful, corrupt, cunning, forbidding, harmful, hurtful, malevolent, malignant, ominous, sinister, sneaky

menagerie *n* aquarium, aviary, terrarium, zoo

mend *v* 1 adjust, correct, cure, fix, heal, make well, remedy, repair, restore

v 2 doctor, fix, overhaul, patch, rebuild, recondition, reconstruct, refit, renovate, repair, revamp

v 3 ameliorate, convalesce, gain, heal, improve, loop up, perk, rally, recover, recuperate, rehabilitate, revive

v 4 see: ADJUST *v* 11, 12

mendacity *n* dishonesty, falsehood, untruthfulness

mendicant *n* beggar, bum, derelict, drifter, hobo, loafer, panhandler, pauper, tramp, vagabond, vagrant

menial *adj* 1 blue-collar, manual, physical

adj 2 abject, common, groveling, humble,

ingratiating, lowly, obeisant, obsequious, servile, slavish, subservient

mental *adj* affective, cognitive, emotional, psychic, psychological, subconscious, subjective

mentality *n* confidence, disposition, feeling, frame of mind, mood, morale, outlook, state

mention *n* citation, clipping, excerpt, extract, passage, portion, quotation, quote, reference, section

v allude, denote, indicate, point out, refer to, reveal, show, speak of, specify, suggest, tell

mentor *n* 1 coach, educator, instructor, leader, schoolteacher, teacher, trainer, tutor

n 2 authority, expert, guide, guru, leader, master, pundit, teacher, wise man

mercantile *adj* business, commercial, trade, trading

mercenary *adj* see: EVIL *adj* 4

n soldier, trooper

merchandise *n* 1 acquisition, asset, buy, gain, property, purchase

n 2 articles, basics, commodities, essentials, goods, inventory, line, materials, products, properties, staples, stock, wares

v barter, distribute, market, peddle, retail, sell, vend, wholesale

merchandising *n* allocation, distribution, marketing, selling, share, sharing

merchant *n* dealer, marketer, monger, purveyor, seller, trader, vendor

merciful *adj* 1 accepting, charitable, easy, forbearing, indulgent, lenient, patient, restrained, sympathetic, tolerant

adj 2 altruistic, benevolent, bountiful, caring, charitable, Christian, compassionate, generous, giving, good, humane, humanitarian, kind, lenient, philanthropic, tender

mercifulness *n* clemency, forbearance, indulgence, lenience, leniency, mercy, toleration

merciless *adj* austere, brutal, callous, cold-blooded, compassionless, cruel, ferocious, fierce, hardened, hardhearted, heartless, indifferent, inhuman, inhumane, malicious, mean, nasty, obdurate, pitiless, ruthless, savage, spiteful, stony, tough, uncaring, unemotional, unfeeling, unkind, unmerciful, unpitying, unrelenting, unsympathetic, vicious

mercurial *adj* 1 arbitrary, capricious, changeable, erratic, fickle, flighty, inconsistent, inconstant, uncertain, unstable,

unsteady, variable, volatile, wavering, wayward

adj 2 breakneck, expeditious, explosive, fast, fleet, hasty, impulsive, instant, lightning, meteoric, precipitous, quick, rapid, spectacular, speedy, sudden, swift

mercy *n* 1 altruism, charity, generosity, goodness, good will, grace, kindness

n 2 affinity, compassion, empathy, kindness, pity, rue, sympathy, tenderness, understanding

n 3 clemency, forbearance, indulgence, lenience, leniency, mercifulness, tolerance, toleration

merely *adv* but, except that, further, however, just, nevertheless, only, simply, solely, yet

merge *v* 1 centralize, concentrate, consolidate, focus

v 2 amalgamate, band, blend, coalesce, combine, compound, consolidate, fuse, intermingle, league, lump, meld, mingle, mix, unify, unite

v 3 associate, blend, bond, coalesce, combine, compound, connect, couple, fasten, fuse, join, link, marry, mate, meet, pair, unite, wed

merger *n* 1 coupling, crossing, interchange, joining, juncture, linking

n 2 affiliation, alliance, association, axis, bloc, coalition, concord, confederation, consolidation, faction, federation, joint venture, league, organization, partnership, relationship, treaty, union

merging *n* blend, combination, fusion, intermingling, joining, mixture, union

merit *n* caliber, excellence, goodness, quality, stature, value, worth

v access, accomplish, achieve, attain, derive, earn, fulfill, gain, get, net, obtain, perform, profit, rack up, reach, realize, score, win

merited *adj* appropriate, correct, deserved, due, fitting, just, proper, rightful, suitable, warranted

merriment *n* amusement, elation, excitement, exhilaration, frivolity, gaiety, glee, guffaws, happiness, hilarity, jocularity, jocundity, jollity, joviality, joy, laughter, levity, mirth

merry *adj* 1 blithe, cheerful, cheery, lightsome, sunny

adj 2 bright, cheerful, cheery, content, ebullient, ecstatic, elated, exuberant, festive, gay, glad, happy, jovial, joyful, joyous, mirthful, pleased, radiant, rejoicing

mesh *n* barrier, netting, protection, screen, shield

v connect, engage, hook up, interlock, network

mesmerize *v* 1 captivate, charm, delight, engross, enrapture, enravish, enthrall, entrance, hypnotize, move, ravish, transport

v 2 see: ATTRACT *v* 6

mesmerizing *adj* alluring, beguiling, bewitching, captivating, catchy, charming, dazzling, dynamic, enchanting, engaging, enthralling, enticing, fascinating, glamorous, intriguing, riveting, spectacular, spellbinding

mess *n* 1 chaos, clutter, confusion, derangement, disarray, disorder, jumble, mayhem, mix-up, muddle, predicament, snafu, snarl, tangle, tumult, turmoil

n 2 see: DILEMMA *n* 4

v disarray, dislocate, disorder, disorganize, disrupt, disturb, interfere, interrupt, jumble, mix up, muss, rummage, shuffle, sift through, unsettle

message *n* import, intent, meaning, sense, significance, understanding

messenger *n* 1 carrier, courier, delivery person, envoy, herald, runner

n 2 envoy, foregoer, forerunner, harbinger, herald, outrider, precursor, predictor, prophet

messiah *n* deliverer, liberator, rescuer, salvation, savior

messy *adj* careless, disheveled, scruffy, slatternly, slipshod, sloppy, sloven, slovenly, tacky, uncombed, unkempt, untidy

metamorphose *v* alter, change, commute, convert, evolve, further, improve, modernize, modify, mutate, revolutionize, transfer, transfigure, transform, transmute, vary

metaphor *n* affinity, analogy, approximation, comparison, likeness, match, resemblance, semblance, similarity, simile

metaphysical *adj* 1 bodiless, celestial, disembodied, ethereal, heavenly, incorporeal, insubstantial, intangible, nonmaterial, spiritual, unearthly, unreal, unsubstantial

adj 2 see: WEIRD *adj* 1

meteoric *adj* see: RAPID *adj* 2

meter *n* dial, disk, display, gauge, indicator, measure, pointer, selector

v gauge, measure

method *n* 1 action, maneuver, measure, step

n 2 habit, mores, procedure, routine, system

n 3 arrangement, blueprint, order, orderliness, outline, pattern, plan, system

n 4 appliance, application, employment, form, operation, play, technique, use, utilization

n 5 methodology, practice, procedure, process, routine, science, system, technique, technology

n 6 angle, approach, code, delivery, execution, expression, fashion, manner, mode, organization, process, program, style, system, technique, way

methodic *adj* methodical, orderly, recurring, regular, steady, systematic

methodical *adj* 1 methodic, orderly, recurring, regular, steady, systematic

adj 2 deliberate, dilatory, diligent, leisurely, meticulous, painstaking, patient, procrastinating, slow, thorough, unhasty, unhurried

methodology *n* 1 expression, formula, plan, procedure, recipe, scheme, system, theorem

n 2 method, practice, procedure, process, routine, science, system, technique, technology

meticulous *adj* 1 blind, conscientious, loyal, religious, strict, zealous

adj 2 exacting, fastidious, finicky, picky, precise, rigid, strict

adj 3 careful, cautious, choosy, discriminating, fastidious, finicky, fussy, nitpicking, particular, persnickety, picky, selective

adj 4 careful, carping, cautious, conscientious, ethical, exacting, fussy, heedful, painstaking, punctilious, scrupulous, unrelenting

adj 5 deliberate, dilatory, diligent, leisurely, methodical, painstaking, patient, procrastinating, slow, thorough, unhasty, unhurried

adj 6 neat, orderly, prim, shipshape, tidy, trim, well-groomed

metropolis *n* borough, city, megalopolis, municipality, suburb, town

mezzanine *n* balcony

micro *adj* see: TINY *adj* 1

microcosm *n* miniature, miniaturization, model, scale model

microscope *n* binoculars, eye, field glass, glass, lens, magnifying glass, mirror, periscope, scope, spyglass, telescope

microscopic *adj* see: TINY *adj* 1

mid *adj* center, centermost, equidistant, halfway, median, middle, middlemost, midmost

prep 1 amid, among, inside, inside of, midst, with, within *prep* **2** amidst, among, atwixt, between, betwixt, halfway to, midway, 'twixt

middle *adj* **1** central

adj **2** halfway, intermediate, mean

adj **3** center, centermost, equidistant, halfway, median, mid, middlemost, midmost

adj **4** average, common, intermediate, mediocre, medium, normal, ordinary, regular, standard, unimpressive

n **1** center, core, hub, midpoint, midst

n **2** average, mean, median, medium, norm, par, rule, standard

middleman *n* absorber, agent, broker, catalyst, distributor, go-between, intermediary, mediator, negotiator

middlemost *adj* center, centermost, equidistant, halfway, median, mid, middle, midmost

midget *adj see:* TINY *adj* 1

n dwarf, Lilliputian, mite, pygmy

midmost *adj* center, centermost, equidistant, halfway, median, mid, middle

midpoint *n* center, core, hub, middle, midst

midriff *n* abdomen, belly, gut, paunch, stomach, tummy, tum-tum

midst *n* center, core, hub, middle

prep amid, among, inside, inside of, mid, with, within

midway *prep* amidst, among, atwixt, between, betwixt, halfway to, mid, 'twixt

mien *n* angle, aspect, facet, hand, opinion, perspective, phase, side, slant, view

miff *n* anger, animosity, hostility, huff, indignation, offense, pique, resentment

v see: BOTHER *v* 5

might *n* **1** ardor, beef, brawn, drive, energy, force, intensity, lustiness, muscle, pep, potency, power, punch, steam, strength, verve, vigor, vim, virility, vitality

n **2** *see:* AUTHORITY *n* 5

mightily *adv* awfully, dreadfully, eminently, endlessly, exceedingly, exceptionally, extremely, greatly, highly, notably, quite, remarkably, terribly, thoroughly, very

mighty *adj* **1** invincible, omnipotent, powerful, supreme

adj **2** coercive, compelling, dynamic, energetic, forceful, hardy, lusty, passionate, powerful, robust, strong, sturdy, vigorous

adj **3** aggressive, dominant, durable, firm, forceful, hardy, hearty, powerful, robust, rugged, stalwart, stout, strong, sturdy, tenacious, tough

adj **4** colossal, enormous, fantastic, Gargantuan, giant, gigantic, Goliath, great, huge, immense, jumbo, leviathan, mammoth, massive, monstrous, monumental, overwhelming, phenomenal, prodigious, Promethean, stupendous, Titanic, towering, tremendous, unfathomed, untold, vast, walloping, whopping

migrant *n* drifter, emigrant, itinerant, nomad, transient

migrate *v* coast, cruise, explore, go, journey, proceed, sail, survey, tour, trek, voyage

mild *adj* **1** amiable, benign, genial, kind, kindly, nonmalignant

adj **2** moderate, modest, pleasant, rational, reasonable, temperate

adj **3** amiable, complaisant, easy, good-humored, good-natured, lenient, obliging

adj **4** balmy, bland, faint, gentle, pleasant, smooth, soft, weak

adj **5** benign, harmless, innocent, innocuous, inoffensive, naive, pure, safe, unoffending, unoffensive

adj **6** acquiescent, compliant, docile, easy, meek, nonresistant, obedient, passive, resigned, submissive, tame, tolerant, unassertive, yielding

adj **7** mellow

milepost *n* event, milestone, occasion

milestone *n* **1** event, occasion

n **2** highlight, landmark

militant *adj* **1** angry, bellicose, belligerent, combative, contentious, hostile, pugnacious, quarrelsome, warlike

adj **2** aggressive, ambitious, assertive, assured, compelling, compulsive, confident, decided, dogmatic, driven, emphatic, energetic, insistent, positive, pushing, pushy, self-assertive, sure, urging

militaristic *adj* aristocratic, arrogant, authoritarian, authoritative, autocratic, belligerent, bossy, despotic, dictatorial, dogmatic, domineering, haughty, imperial, imperious, masterful, opinionated, oppressive, overbearing, peremptory, pushy, stubborn

military *adj* martial

militia *n* airborne, army, battalion, brigade, cavalry, company, footmen, guard, horsemen, infantry, legion, marines, minutemen, paratroops, platoon, reserve, storm troopers

milk *v* **1** exploit

v **2** drain, extract, squeeze

milky *adj* chalky, ivory, snowy, white

millennium *n see:* PERIOD *n* 2

mime *v* act, ape, copy, emulate, follow, imitate, lip-synch, mimic, mock, model, mouth, pantomime, parody, pattern, take off

mimic v act, ape, copy, emulate, follow, imitate, lip-synch, mime, mock, model, mouth, pantomime, parody, pattern, take off

mince v chop

mind n 1 comprehension, intellect, reason, understanding

n 2 brain, cerebrum, head, wit

n 3 lucidity, rationality, reason, saneness, sanity, sense, soundness, wit

n 4 ego, id, individuality, persona, personality, psyche, self, soul, spirit

n 5 attitude, disposition, feeling, humor, mood, spirit, temper, timbre, tone, vein

n 6 bent, disposition, fancy, fondness, idea, inclination, liking, notion, pleasure, propensity, yen

n 7 attitude, belief, bias, conviction, feeling, inducement, leaning, opinion, persuasion, sentiment, slant, view

n 8 see: TALENT n 2

v 1 care

v 2 beware, look out for, take caution, watch

v 3 care, consider, heed, listen, review

v 4 accommodate, comply, conform, follow, keep, obey, observe, submit

v 5 behold, glimpse, look, see, sight, spot, watch, witness

mindful adj alert, aware, wise

mindless adj 1 absurd, anile, asinine, brainless, childish, fatuous, foolish, idiotic, inept, meaningless, senseless, silly, simple, thoughtless, unintelligent, witless

adj 2 see: PREOCCUPIED adj 1

mine n 1 bomb, bombshell, explosive, missile, payload, rocket, rocketry, warhead

n 2 dig, excavation, lode, quarry

v burrow, dig, excavate, gouge, scoop, shovel, unearth

mingle v 1 beat, blend, mix, stir, toss, whip

v 2 see: ASSEMBLE v 3

v 3 see: COMBINE v 3

mini-series n cartoons, docudrama, documentary, game shows, movies, news, programs, series, sitcom, soap opera, soaps, talk shows, television, variety shows

mini adj see: TINY adj 1

miniature adj bantam, dainty, diminutive, dwarfish, Lilliputian, little, micro, microscopic, midget, mini, minuscule, minute, petite, pygmy, slight, small, tiny, wee

n microcosm, miniaturization, model, scale model

miniaturization n microcosm, miniature, model, scale model

minimally adv a tad, barely, hardly, just about, least, not much, not quite, scarce, scarcely

minimize v 1 deprecate, play down, pooh-pooh

v 2 see: RELIEVE v 3

minimum n 1 quorum

n 2 base, bottom, floor

n 3 keep, livelihood, living, maintenance, subsistence, support, sustenance

adj first, least, lowest, slightest, smallest, tiniest

minister n chaplain, clergyman, cleric, father, guru, padre, parson, pastor, priest, rabbi, reverend

ministry n see: ADMINISTRATION n 3

minor adj 1 ancillary, auxiliary, incidental, related, secondary, side, subordinate

adj 2 ancillary, assistant, collateral, complementary, dependent, lesser, secondary, sub, subject, subordinate, subsidiary, substitute, supporter, tributary, worker

adj 3 see: TRIVIAL adj 1, 2

n adolescent, boy, child, girl, juvenile, kid, teenager, teeny-bopper, youngster, youth

mint adj new, unused

v coin, stamp, strike

n fortune, heap, loads, scads

minus v deduct, diminish, lessen, reduce, subtract, take away

minuscule adj see: TINY adj 1

minute adj 1 bantam, dainty, diminutive, dwarfish, Lilliputian, little, micro, microscopic, midget, mini, miniature, minuscule, petite, pygmy, slight, small, tiny, wee

adj 2 imperceptible, imponderable, inappreciable, indiscernible, insensible, intangible, invisible, scant, unapparent, unobservable, weak

adj 3 borderline, casual, frivolous, insignificant, light, lightweight, little, marginal, meager, minor, negligible, nonessential, off, outside, petty, remote, secondary, slender, slight, slim, small, tenuous, trivial, unimportant

n blink of an eye, crack, flash, instant, jiffy, moment, second, shake, twinkling, wink

minutemen n airborne, army, battalion, brigade, cavalry, company, footmen, guard, horsemen, infantry, legion, marines, militia, paratroops, platoon, reserve, storm troopers

minutes n see: JOURNAL n 3

minutia n see: FRAGMENT n 3

minutiae n details, nuances, particulars, second level, trivia

miracle n 1 marvel, phenomenon, sensation, spectacle, wonder
n 2 blessing, bonanza, boon, fortune, gain, godsend, luck, serendipity, stroke of luck, windfall

mirage n aberration, apparition, delusion, fantasy, figment, ghost, hallucination, illusion, image, phantasm, specter, vision

mire v 1 depress, droop, flop, let down, lower, sag, sink, wallow
v 2 bog, delay, detain, hang up, impede, retard, set back, slacken, slow
v 3 accuse, associate, blame, confuse, connect, embroil, enmesh, ensnare, entangle, implicate, involve, tangle
n bog, marsh, moor, swamp

mirror n 1 binoculars, eye, field glass, glass, lens, magnifying glass, microscope, periscope, scope, spyglass, telescope
n 2 epitome, example, exemplar, ideal, model, outline, paradigm, pattern, plan, prototype, rule of thumb, standard
v 1 reflect
v 2 clone, copy, duplicate, image, imitate, print, re-create, redo, reduplicate, remake, replicate, reprint, reproduce, simulate

mirth n amusement, elation, excitement, exhilaration, frivolity, gaiety, glee, guffaws, happiness, hilarity, jocularity, jocundity, jollity, joviality, joy, laughter, levity, merriment

mirthful adj bright, cheerful, cheery, content, ebullient, ecstatic, elated, exuberant, festive, gay, glad, happy, jovial, joyful, joyous, merry, pleased, radiant, rejoicing

misapply v abuse, corrupt, ill-use, misemploy, mishandle, misuse, pervert, prostitute

misappropriate v appropriate, burglarize, defraud, embezzle, filch, heist, lift, pilfer, pillage, pinch, plunder, pocket, purloin, rip off, rob, snake, snitch, steal, swindle, swipe, take, thieve

misbegotten adj bastard, fatherless, illegitimate, orphaned, spurious, unauthentic, ungenuine

misbehaving adj bad, disobedient, illbehaved, mischievous, naughty

misbehavior n error, malfeasance, malpractice, misdeed, mismanagement, offense, transgression, wrong, wrongdoing

misbelief n apprehension, distrust, doubt, fear, hesitation, mistrust, suspicion, wariness

miscalculate v err, misconstrue, misinterpret, misjudge, underestimate

miscarry v fail, fizzle, misfire, miss

miscellaneous adj assorted, diverse, mixed, motley, varied

mischance n adversity, affliction, blow, burden, calamity, difficulty, distress, hardship, misfortune, mishap, relapse, reversal, setback, suffering, tragedy, trouble

mischief n 1 adventure, antic, caper, escapade, joke, lark, prank, trick
n 2 see: MANEUVER n 2
n 3 see: TROUBLE n 5

mischievous adj bad, disobedient, illbehaved, naughty

misconstrue v 1 err, miscalculate, misinterpret, misjudge, underestimate
v 2 angle, confuse, deceive, distort, falsify, garble, incline, misinterpret, misquote, misread, misrepresent, misunderstand, mix up, mumble, slant, slope, taint, twist

misdeed n 1 error, malfeasance, malpractice, misbehavior, mismanagement, offense, transgression, wrong, wrongdoing
n 2 see: CRIME n 3

misdemeanor n 1 breach, default, infraction, trespass, violation
n 2 crime, dishonor, disobedience, evil, fault, felony, infamy, infraction, iniquity, injury, lawbreaking, misdeed, offense, outrage, sin, transgression, trespass, vice, violation, wrong, wrongdoing

misdirected adj foolish, ill-advised, indiscreet, misguided, mistaken, unwise

misemploy v abuse, corrupt, ill-use, misapply, mishandle, misuse, pervert, prostitute

miserable adj 1 affecting, deplorable, lamentable, paltry, pathetic, pitiable, pitiful, poor, sad, unfortunate, woeful, wretched
adj 2 see: INFERIOR adj 6

miserly adj 1 cheap, close, greedy, mean, niggardly, parsimonious, penny-pinching, stingy, tight, tightfisted, ungenerous, ungiving
adj 2 acquisitive, avaricious, covetous, craving, desirous, eager, grabby, grasping, greedy, hungry, longing, selfish, wishful, yearning

misery n 1 gloom, grief, pessimism, woe
n 2 agony, anguish, bale, concern, distress, nightmare, pain, sadness, sorrow, suffering, torment, travail, tribulation, trouble, woe, worry

misfire v fail, fizzle, miss

misfit n agitator, defector, dissident, heretic, iconoclast, insurgent, malcontent, maverick, nonconformist, rebel, renegade, traitor, troublemaker, turncoat

misfortune *n* 1 calamity, cataclysm, catastrophe, debacle, disaster, tragedy, upheaval

n 2 adversity, affliction, blow, burden, calamity, difficulty, distress, hardship, mischance, mishap, relapse, reversal, setback, suffering, tragedy, trouble

n 3 bane, curse, disease, evil, plague, pestilence, scourge

misgiving *n* annoyance, anxiety, apprehension, bother, care, concern, disquiet, disquietude, doubt, irritation, reservation, restlessness, restraint, skepticism, trouble, uneasiness, vexation, worry

misguided *adj* foolish, ill-advised, indiscreet, misdirected, mistaken, unwise

mishandle *v* abuse, corrupt, ill-use, misapply, misemploy, misuse, pervert, prostitute

mishap *n* 1 accident, collision, crackup, crash, destruction, pileup, smash, smash-up, wreck, wreckage

n 2 adversity, affliction, blow, burden, calamity, difficulty, distress, hardship, mischance, misfortune, relapse, reversal, setback, suffering, tragedy, trouble

n 3 see: ANGUISH *n* 2

misinterpret *v* 1 err, miscalculate, misconstrue, misjudge, underestimate

v 2 see: MISREPRESENT *v* 2

misjudge *v* err, miscalculate, misconstrue, misinterpret, underestimate

misleading *adj* deceptive, false, illusive, illusory, sham, unreal

mismanagement *n* error, malfeasance, malpractice, misbehavior, misdeed, offense, transgression, wrong, wrongdoing

mismatch *v* clash, conflict, crash, discord, jangle

misplace *v* lose

misquote *v* angle, confuse, deceive, distort, falsify, garble, incline, misconstrue, misinterpret, misread, misrepresent, misunderstand, mix up, mumble, slant, slope, taint, twist

misread *v* see: MISREPRESENT *v* 2

misreading *n* see: MISTAKE *n* 2

misrepresent *v* 1 bias, corrupt, distort, pervert, skew, slant, warp

v 2 angle, confuse, deceive, distort, falsify, garble, incline, misconstrue, misinterpret, misquote, misread, misunderstand, mix up, mumble, slant, slope, taint, twist

miss *n* 1 child, coed, daughter, debutante, girl, lass, young lady, young woman

n 2 dame, female, gentlewoman, lady,

matron, mistress, spinster, widow, woman

v 1 lack

v 2 fail, give out, lose, run out

v 3 fail, fizzle, miscarry, misfire

v 4 defy, discount, disregard, exclude, forget, ignore, neglect, omit, ostracize, overlook, overpass, pass, pass by, pass over, shun, skip, slight, snub

misshape *v* deform, distort, torture, warp

missile *n* 1 bomb, bombshell, explosive, mine, payload, rocket, rocketry, warhead

n 2 lance

n 3 buckshot, bullet, lead, projectile, shell, shot, slug

missing *adj* absent, away, gone, lacking, omitted, truant, wanting

mission *n* 1 commission, delegation

n 2 assignment, chore, duty, effort, job, responsibility, stint, task

n 3 aim, goal, motive, objective, purpose, reason, sake, target, task

missionary *n* crusader, evangelist, proselytizer

misstate *v* concoct, deceive, equivocate, fabricate, falsify, fib, invent, lie, perjure

misstatement *n* 1 bull, falsehood, lie, overstatement, untruth

n 2 exaggeration, fabrication, falsehood, falsity, fib, invention, lie, story, tale

mist *n* cloud, fog, haze, steam, vapor

mistake *n* 1 blunder, folly, impropriety, indiscretion, slip

n 2 accident, blooper, blunder, bungle, confusion, error, faux pas, foul-up, lapse, misreading, misunderstanding, slip, slip-up

mistaken *adj* 1 foolish, ill-advised, indiscreet, misguided, unwise

adj 2 erroneous, false, faulty, imprecise, inaccurate, incorrect, inexact, specious, untrue, wrong

mister *n* 1 bachelor, chap, dude, fellow, gent, gentleman, guy, male, man, widower

n 2 bridegroom, groom, hubby, husband, man, master, mate, spouse

mistreat *v* abuse, brutalize, exploit, harm, ill-treat, injure, maltreat, molest, persecute, victimize, wrong

mistreatment *n* abuse, defamation, scurrility

mistress *n* 1 dame, female, gentlewoman, lady, matron, miss, spinster, widow, woman

n 2 concubine, lover, trifle

mistrust *n* 1 apprehension, distrust, doubt, fear, hesitation, suspicion, wariness *n* 2 concern, doubt, dubiety, incertitude, indecision, query, question, skepticism, suspicion, uncertainty, wonder

v 1 distrust, doubt, suspect

v 2 challenge, dispute, doubt, query, question

misty *adj* 1 damp, dank, drizzly, foggy, humid, moist, wet

adj 2 ambiguous, bleary, confused, fuzzy, hazy, mixed up, nebulous, unclear

adj 3 cloudy, dismal, foggy, gray, hazy, murky, overcast, steamy, vaporous, vapory

misunderstand *v* see: MISREPRESENT *v* 2

misunderstanding *n* 1 break, disagreement, dissension, fight, quarrel, rift, separation, spat

n 2 see: MISTAKE *n* 2

misuse *v* 1 exploit, manipulate, take advantage

v 2 abuse, corrupt, ill-use, misapply, misemploy, mishandle, pervert, prostitute

n exploitation

mite *n* 1 dwarf, Lilliputian, midget, pygmy

n 2 bit, dab, end, fragment, iota, minutia, morsel, particle, piece, pinch, portion, scrap, shred, speck, spot, strip, tidbit, trifle

mitigate *v* 1 absolve, acquit, cover up, exonerate, extenuate, whitewash

v 2 abate, allay, assuage, moderate, quench, satiate, satisfy

v 3 allay, alleviate, assuage, attenuate, diminish, ease, extenuate, lessen, lighten, minimize, moderate, mollify, reduce, relieve

mitigating *adj* excusable, extenuating, justifying, offsetting

mix *n* blend, brew, combination, composite, compound, concoction, mixture

v 1 alter, assort, diversify, modify, vary

v 2 confuse, disorder, jostle, scramble, shuffle

v 3 complicate, confound, confuse, entangle, mix up, snarl

v 4 beat, blend, mingle, stir, toss, whip

v 5 amalgamate, band, blend, coalesce, combine, compound, consolidate, fuse, intermingle, league, lump, meld, merge, mingle, unify, unite

mixed *adj* 1 assorted, diverse, miscellaneous, motley, varied

adj 2 diverse, haphazard, jumbled, promiscuous, random

adj 3 integrated

adj 4 complex, composite, compound

mixed up *adj* bewildered, confused, foggy

mixture *n* 1 assortment, hodgepodge, jumble, medley

n 2 assortment, bunch, collection, selection, spectrum, variety

n 3 blend, combination, fusion, intermingling, joining, merging, union

n 4 blend, brew, combination, composite, compound, concoction, ferment, mix

mix-up *n* see: CHAOS *n* 5

moan *v* 1 brood, crab, grouch, mope, pout, scowl, sulk

v 2 bawl, bemoan, cry, grieve, groan, lament, mourn, sigh, snivel, sob, wail, weep, whimper, whine

n groan, sigh, sob, wail

mob *n* 1 band, cabal, camp, circle, clan, clique, coterie, coven, cult, faction, family, gang, group, ring, school, sect, tribe

n 2 band, bunch, crew, crowd, drove, flock, following, gang, gaggle, herd, huddle, mass, pack, rabble, riffraff, swarm, team, throng

n 3 band, gang, posse, vigilantes

v crowd, herd, jam, press, push, swarm, teem, throng

mobile *adj* ambulatory, locomotive, moving

mobilize *v* 1 activate, actuate, compel, drive, force, goad, impel, induce, motivate, move, persuade, press, propel, push, spur, start, turn on

v 2 see: ASSEMBLE *v* 3

mobster *n* gangster

moccasin *n* boot, brogan, chukka, footwear, sandal, shoe, slipper, thong

mock *adj* 1 fake, feigned, fictitious, sham, simulated

adj 2 artificial, bogus, counterfeit, ersatz, fake, false, imitation, phony, pseudo, sham, simulated, spurious, substitute, unreal

v 1 grimace, leer, ogle, scorn, smirk, sneer

v 2 banter, deride, gibe, jeer, joke, knock, needle, rib, ridicule, roast, tease

v 3 act, ape, copy, emulate, follow, imitate, lip-synch, mime, mimic, model, mouth, pantomime, parody, pattern, take off

v 4 belittle, deride, flaunt, jab, jeer, jest, quip, razz, ridicule, scoff, scorn, sneer, taunt, tease

v 5 see: SCOLD *v* 4

mockery *n* 1 aspersion, contempt, derision, disdain, irony, ridicule, sarcasm, satire, scorn

n 2 buffoonery, burlesque, caricature, comedy, farce, humor, imitation, joke, lampoon, parody, satire, spoof, takeoff, travesty

mocking *adj* contemptuous, cynical, derisive, ironic, sarcastic, sardonic, scornful, skeptical, wry

mode *n* 1 fashion, flavor, manner, style, tone, vein

n 2 chic, craze, fad, fashion, rage, style, thing, trend, vogue

n 3 agency, agent, channel, conduit, instrument, means, mechanism, vehicle

n 4 angle, approach, code, delivery, execution, expression, fashion, manner, method, organization, process, program, style, system, technique, way

n 5 condition, perspective, posture, situation, state, status, update

model *adj* 1 ideal, optimal, perfect, very

adj 2 exemplary, flawless, ideal, perfect, perfected

adj 3 characteristic, classic, exemplary, ideal, representative, typical

n 1 microcosm, miniature, miniaturization, scale model

n 2 angel, idol, prince, saint

n 3 drawing, icon, image, representation, simulation, symbol

n 4 demo, example, first, forerunner, prototype, sample, test

n 5 character, emblem, example, icon, letter, logo, mark, representation, sign, symbol, token

n 6 epitome, example, exemplar, ideal, mirror, outline, paradigm, pattern, plan, prototype, rule of thumb, standard

n 7 clone, copy, counterfeit, duplicate, duplication, image, imitation, likeness, mock up, print, replica, replication, representation, reproduction, resemblance, simulation

v 1 pose, posture, sit

v 2 see: MIMIC *v*

moderate *adj* 1 levelheaded, sober, temperate, unimpassioned

adj 2 cheap, economical, inexpensive, low, low-cost, reasonable

adj 3 mild, modest, pleasant, rational, reasonable, temperate

adj 4 continual, continuing, gradual, increasing, incremental, intensifying, measured, progressive, successive

v 1 chair, head, preside

v 2 inflect, modify, modulate, regulate, restrain, temper

v 3 abate, allay, assuage, mitigate, quench, satiate, satisfy

v 4 see: RELIEVE *v* 3

moderately *adv* 1 fairly, pretty, reasonably, somewhat, so-so

adv 2 adequately, amply, enough, equitably, fairly, justly, passably, rather, satisfactorily, tolerably

moderateness *n* moderation, temperance

moderation *n* 1 economy, frugality, prudence, thrift

n 2 abstinence, continence, restraint, self-restraint, sobriety, temperance

n 3 measure, moderateness, temperance

moderator *n* arbiter, arbitrator, judge, mediator, referee, umpire

modern *adj* bright, contemporary, fresh, high-tech, modernistic, new, novel, recent, up-to-date

modernistic *adj* bright, contemporary, fresh, high-tech, modern, new, novel, recent, up-to-date

modernize *v* 1 freshen, redo, refresh, refurbish, rejuvenate, remodel, renew, renovate, restore, revamp, revitalize, revive, update

v 2 alter, change, commute, convert, evolve, further, improve, metamorphose, modify, mutate, revolutionize, transfer, transfigure, transform, transmute, vary

modest *adj* 1 humble, lowly, meek, unassuming, unpretentious

adj 2 mild, moderate, pleasant, rational, reasonable, temperate

adj 3 discreet, dry, homely, plain, simple, unadorned, undecorated, unembellished, unembroidered, ungarnished, unpretentious

adj 4 backward, bashful, coy, demure, diffident, innocent, quiet, reserved, retiring, shy, staid, timid, unassured

adj 5 celibate, chaste, clean, decent, decorous, immaculate, moral, pristine, proper, pure, spotless, stainless, stuffy, taintless, unadulterated, unblemished, undefiled, upstanding, virginal, wholesome

modesty *n* 1 humility, reserve, shyness

n 2 humility, propriety, virtue

modification *n* 1 adaptation, agreement, compliance

n 2 adjustment, alteration, anomaly, change, deviation, mutation, permutation, shift, variation

modified *adj* diminished, limited, qualified, reduced

modify *v* 1 bring about, carry, change

v 2 adjust, finesse, fine-tune, tweak, vary

v 3 alter, assort, diversify, mix, vary

v 4 alter, effect, impact, influence

v **5** better, correct, improve, reform, rehabilitate

v **6** inflect, moderate, modulate, regulate, restrain, temper

v **7** adjust, alter, catalyze, change, mutate, refashion, vary

v **8** annotate, compile, correct, denote, edit, polish, proofread, revise

v **9** adapt, conform, convert, cut, fashion, fit, measure, rig, shape, suit, tailor

v **10** alter, change, commute, convert, evolve, further, improve, metamorphose, modernize, mutate, revolutionize, transfer, transfigure, transform, transmute, vary

v **11** edit, redraft, redraw, rehash, revamp, revise, rework, rewrite

v **12** adjust, amend, correct, fix, improve, mend, position, rectify, remedy, restore, right, straighten

modulate *v* inflect, moderate, modify, regulate, restrain, temper

module *n* component, part, unit

mogul *n* baron, big shot, businessman, businessperson, businesswoman, capitalist, entrepreneur, executive, financier, industrialist, magnate, plutocrat, tycoon, VIP

moist *adj* **1** juicy, savory, succulent, tender

adj **2** damp, dank, drizzly, foggy, humid, misty, wet

adj **3** damp, fluid, juicy, liquefied, liquid, watery, wet

adj **4** damp, drenched, dripping, humid, mucky, muggy, soaked, soggy, sopping, sticky, sultry, sweaty, wet

moisten *v* lap, lick, tongue

moistener *n* lube, lubrication, oil, ointment, salve

moisture *n* **1** perspiration, sweat, wetness

n **2** dampness, humidity, sogginess, wetness

molar *n* digger, fang, gasher, tooth, tush, tusk

mold *v* **1** carve, chisel, craft, cut, define, design, fashion, form, sculpt, sculpture, shape, steer

v **2** assemble, build, construct, erect, establish, fabricate, forge, form, make, manufacture, produce, trailblaze

v **3** abstain, cast, decline, drop, eschew, forbear, forfeit, forgo, give up, lose, pass, reject, renounce, sacrifice, surrender, turn down, waive

n **1** decay, fungus, germ

n **2** die, form, matrix, punch

n **3** bracket, breed, cast, category, class, division, family, genre, genus, group, grouping, ilk, kind, lot, nature, order, persuasion, section, sector, set, sort, species, style, type, variety

moldable *adj* adaptable, adjustable, changeable, flexible, limber, malleable, maneuverable, plastic, pliable, pliant, responsive, soft, supple, swayed, versatile, yielding

molecule *n* see: DOT *n* **1**

molest *v* **1** condemn, curse, damn, denounce, profane, swear, vex

v **2** abuse, brutalize, exploit, harm, illtreat, injure, maltreat, mistreat, persecute, victimize, wrong

mollify *v* **1** allay, alleviate, assuage, attenuate, diminish, ease, extenuate, lessen, lighten, minimize, mitigate, moderate, reduce, relieve

v **2** allay, appease, assuage, balm, becalm, calm, compose, conciliate, ease, lull, pacify, placate, propitiate, quell, quiet, reconcile, satiate, settle, soften, soothe, still, sweeten, tranquilize

mollusk *n* clam, cockle, crab, crustacean, mussel, prawn, shellfish, shrimp, snail

molt *v* cast off, drop, peel, repel, shed

molten *adj* heated, liquefied, melted

mom *n* ma, mama, mater, matriarch, momma, mommy, mother, mummy, parent

moment *n* **1** instant, occasion, time

n **2** current time, now, nowadays, present, today

n **3** consequence, import, importance, magnitude, significance, substance, weight

n **4** blink of an eye, crack, flash, instant, jiffy, minute, second, shake, twinkling, wink

momentarily *adv* anon, any moment, at once, directly, immediately, instantaneously, instantly, now, presently, promptly, quickly, right now, shortly, soon, straightaway, *tout de suite*

momentary *adj* **1** any second, immediate, imminent, impending, looming, poised, threatening

adj **2** brief, ephemeral, fleeting, impermanent, passing, short, temporary, transient, transitory, volatile

momentous *adj* **1** memorable, unforgettable

adj **2** calamitous, cataclysmic, catastrophic, critical, crucial, devastating, disastrous, fatal, fateful, ruinous, vital

adj **3** consequential, considerable, critical, crucial, important, material, meaningful, prominent, significant, substantial, vital, weighty

adj 4 acute, burning, critical, crucial, desperate, dire, grave, heavy, important, major, ponderous, pressing, profound, serious, severe, solemn, somber, urgent, vital

momma *n* ma, mama, mater, matriarch, mom, mommy, mother, mummy, parent

mommy *n* ma, mama, mater, matriarch, mom, mommy, mother, mummy, parent

monarch *n* autocrat, chief, commander, despot, dictator, governor, head, king, leader, lord, master, potentate, ruler

monarchy *n* administration, dominion, government, power, regime, reign, rule, sovereignty

monastery *n* abbey, cloister, priory

monetary *adj* financial, fiscal, pecuniary

money *n* 1 bread, buck, cash, dollar, dough, moolah

n 2 account, budget, capital, cash, fund, savings, stock

n 3 assets, belongings, equity, estate, fortune, goods, holdings, inheritance, ownership, possessions, property, prosperity, riches, treasure, wealth

n 4 assets, bills, capital, cash, coffers, currency, dinero, dollars, estate, funds, goods, income, lucre, means, notes, pelf, pesos, property, resources, revenue, riches, rubles, shekels, sum, wealth

n 5 see: REWARD *n* 8

n 6 see: TREASURE *n* 3, 5

money-changer *n* banker, cashier, paymaster, purser, teller

moneyed *adj* affluent, copious, leisure class, loaded, opulent, rich, wealthy, well-to-do

monger *n* dealer, marketer, merchant, purveyor, seller, trader, vendor

v deal, hawk, horse-trade, huckster, hustle, peddle, push, sell, swap

mongrel *n* canine, dog, hound, mutt, pooch, pup, puppy

moniker *n* alias, designation, handle, name, nickname, title

monitor *n* console, CRT, display, screen, terminal

v bug, check, eavesdrop, observe, oversee, snoop, spy, wiretap

monk *n* abbé, abbot, ascetic, friar, hermit, recluse

monkey *v* dabble, dally, diddle, fiddle, fool, piddle, play, poke about, putter, tinker, toy, trifle

n ape, gorilla, primate, simian

monograph *n* 1 book, correspondence, edition, folio, issue, manuscript, opus, paperback, printing, publication, text, tome, volume, work, writing

n 2 article, composition, discourse, dissertation, essay, manuscript, memoir, paper, report, study, theme, thesis, tract, treatise, work

monomaniac *n* bug, crusader, enthusiast, fanatic, fiend, freak, hobbyist, maniac, nut, radical, zealot

monopolize *v* control, corner, dominate

monopoly *n* corner, exclusive, lock, restraint

monotonous *adj* 1 blah, boring, commonplace, dim, dreary, dull, flat, humdrum, ordinary, pedestrian, stodgy, tedious, tiresome

adj 2 arid, bland, bleak, boring, colorless, dead, desolate, drab, dreary, dull, flat, lackluster, lifeless, lusterless, muted, somber, trite, unexciting, uninteresting

monotony *n* apathy, boredom, dreariness, dullness, ennui, malaise, tedium

monster *n* 1 animal, beast, being, brute, creature, ogre

n 2 freak

monstrosity *n* monster

monstrous *adj* 1 barbarous, outrageous, uncivilized, unconscionable, unethical, ungodly, unholy, wicked

adj 2 atrocious, awful, crying, desperate, disgraceful, ghastly, grizzly, heinous, notorious, odious, offensive, outrageous, scandalous, shocking, tasteless, wicked

adj 3 see: HUGE *adj* 3

monthly *n* booklet, gazette, journal, magazine, periodical, publication, quarterly, weekly

monument *n* 1 accomplishment, masterpiece

n 2 burial, catacomb, cenotaph, crypt, grave, mausoleum, memorial, pit, sepulcher, tomb, vault

n 3 structure

n 4 memorial, shrine, statue

monumental *adj* see: HUGE *adj* 3

mood *n* 1 atmosphere, climate, condition, temperature, trend

n 2 confidence, disposition, feeling, frame of mind, mentality, morale, outlook, state

n 3 air, ambience, atmosphere, aura, emanation, feel, feeling, semblance, spirit

n 4 attitude, disposition, feeling, humor, mind, spirit, temper, timbre, tone, vein

moody *adj* 1 brooding, crabby, dour, gloomy, glum, morose, sour, sulky, sullen, surly, ugly

adj 2 antsy, edgy, excitable, fidgety, highstrung, irritable, jittery, jumpy, nervous, nervy, restless, shaky, skittish, temperamental

adj 3 black, bleak, blue, cheerless, dejected, depressed, desperate, despondent, discouraging, disheartening, distressing, down, forlorn, gloomy, hopeless, joyless, melancholy, mournful, oppressive, prostrate, sad, somber, sorry, unhappy

adj 4 see: VAIN *adj* 5

moolah *n* bread, buck, cash, dollar, money

moonlighting *n* avocation, distraction, diversion, hobby, pastime, sideline

moonlit *adj* glowing, incandescent, luminous, sunlit

moonshine *n* alcohol, booze, drinks, grog, liquor, spirits, whiskey

moor *v* 1 anchor, establish, plant, root
v 2 anchor, catch, fasten, secure
n bog, marsh, swamp

mooring *n* arrival, debarkation, landing

moot *adj* see: PREPOSTEROUS *adj* 2

mope *v* brood, crab, grouch, moan, pout, scowl, sulk

moral *adj* 1 ethical, lucid, rational, responsible, sane, stable

adj 2 conscientious, ethical, honest, honorable, noble, principled, proper, respectable, right, righteous, scrupulous, sound, true, trustworthy, upright, virtuous

adj 3 elevated, ethical, high-minded, noble

adj 4 celibate, chaste, clean, decent, decorous, immaculate, modest, pristine, proper, pure, spotless, stainless, stuffy, taintless, unadulterated, unblemished, undefiled, upstanding, virginal, wholesome

n announcement, aphorism, axiom, cliché, declaration, decree, dictum, edict, gospel, homily, maxim, precept, pronouncement, rule, saying, teaching, truism, truth, verity

morale *n* confidence, disposition, feeling, frame of mind, mentality, mood, outlook, state

morality *n* goodness, principle, probity, purity, rectitude, righteousness, uprightness, virtue

morals *n* code of conduct, ethics, principles

moratorium *n* 1 abeyance, cessation, halt, impasse, standstill, stay, stop, stopping, suspension

n 2 absolution, amnesty, discharge, disengagement, dispensation, freedom, pardon, release, relief, reprieve, respite, stay, suspension

morbid *adj* abnormal, depressing, dismal, funereal, ghastly, gloomy, gruesome, macabre, sepulchral

more *adv* above, aloft, greater, on top of, over, overhead, superior

adj see: ADDITIONAL *adj* 2

moreover *adv* 1 additionally, also, and, as well, as well as, besides, further, furthermore, in addition, likewise, plus, too

adv 2 at any rate, but, however, nevertheless, nonetheless, notwithstanding, still, though, yet

mores *n* 1 culture, customs, traditions

n 2 habit, method, procedure, routine, system

n 3 belief, custom, doctrine, relic, rite, ritual, throwback, tradition

n 4 custom, fashion, formality, habit, manner, observance, practice, routine, tradition, usage, use, way, wont

morning *n* dawn, daybreak, daylight, first light, sunrise, sunup

moronic *adj* backward, blunt, deficient, dense, dimwitted, dull, dumb, feebleminded, idiotic, obtuse, retarded, simple, simple-minded, slow, stupid, thick, uneducated, unintelligent

morose *adj* brooding, crabby, dour, gloomy, glum, moody, sour, sulky, sullen, surly, ugly

morphologist *n* linguist, phonetician, semanticist

morsel *n* 1 sample, taste, tidbit

n 2 atom, bead, dab, dash, dot, drop, grain, iota, molecule, particle, pea, pellet, smidgen, speck, tad

n 3 bit, dab, end, fragment, iota, minutia, mite, particle, piece, pinch, portion, scrap, shred, speck, spot, strip, tidbit, trifle

n 4 bite, nip, piece, quick meal, snack

mortal *adj* 1 human

adj 2 baneful, deadly, fatal, lethal, noxious, pernicious, pestilent, ruinous

mortality *n* carnage, death, demise, fatality, ruin

mortgage *n* encumbrance, indebtedness, liability, lien, obligation, security
v borrow, hock, pawn

mortified *adj* abashed, ashamed, chagrined, embarrassed, shamed

mortify *v* abase, abash, belittle, cast down, cheapen, debase, defile, deflate, degrade, demean, depreciate, derogate, devalue, dishonor, embarrass, humble, humiliate, lower, put down, shame, sink

mosque *n* basilica, cathedral, chapel, church, house of god, sanctuary, synagogue, tabernacle, temple

most adj 1 foremost, majority, maximum, optimal, top, unequaled

adj 2 best, biggest, finest, greatest, largest, maximum, number one, prime, select, superior, top, top-notch

n majority

adv see: USUALLY adv 2

mostly adv as a rule, customarily, frequently, generally, mainly, most, most often, normally, ordinarily, primarily, principally, usually

mother n 1 custodian, father, guardian, parent, trustee

n 2 housemother, mother superior, superintendent

n 3 ma, mama, mater, matriarch, mom, momma, mommy, mummy, parent

n 4 beginning, conception, cradle, derivation, fountainhead, inception, infancy, origin, root, seed, source, stem

v care, cherish, foster, nourish, nurse, nurture, parent, protect, raise, rear, suckle

motherland n country, fatherland, home, homeland, land, soil

motif n 1 design, device, figure, pattern

n 2 see: SUBJECT n 4

motion n 1 headway, locomotion, movement, progress

n 2 change, current, drift, flow, flux, gush, movement, rush, stream, tide, transition

n 3 bid, expectation, hope, inducement, invitation, offer, proffer, proposal, proposition, recommendation, request, suggestion

v 1 beckon, gesture, nod, signal

v 2 alert, augur, caution, flag, forebode, forewarn, indicate, inform, notify, signal, warn, wave

motionless adj 1 asleep, dormant, idle, immobile, inactive, inanimate, inert, inoperative, laid-back, nodding, passive, quiet, sleepy, slumbering, stable, stagnant, still

adj 2 see: CALM adj 2

adj 3 see: STILL adj 2

motivate v 1 arouse, awaken, excite, induce, instill, move, pique, prime, provoke, quicken, rouse, roust, spark, start, stimulate, titillate, urge

v 2 see: CONVINCE v

v 3 see: INSTIGATE v 1

v 4 see: MOVE v 5

motivation n 1 bonus, consideration, goal, incentive, inducement, motive, reason, reward, stimulus

n 2 encouragement

motive n 1 design, device, figure, motif, pattern

n 2 cause, excuse, purpose, rationale, reason, why

n 3 aim, cause, consideration, goal, purpose, reason

n 4 bonus, consideration, goal, incentive, inducement, motivation, reason, reward, stimulus

n 5 aim, goal, mission, objective, purpose, reason, sake, target, task

n 6 see: SUBJECT n 4

motley adj assorted, diverse, miscellaneous, mixed, varied

motor n device, engine, generator, machine, turbine

v ride

motorcade n caravan, procession

motorcar n auto, automobile, bus, car, carriage, chariot, coach, jeep, omnibus, sedan, truck, van, vehicle, wagon

motto n 1 inscription

n 2 adage, axiom, byword, cliché, dictum, maxim, proverb, saying, slogan, talk

mound n 1 bank, drift, heap, hill, mass, mountain, pile, stack, stockpile

n 2 foothill, hill, hillock, hump, knoll, mount, raise, rise, swelling

v bank, drift, heap, pile, stack

mount v 1 ascend, climb, escalate, intensify, scale, surmount

v 2 climb, crest, increase, jump, rise, surge

v 3 arise, ascend, aspire, go up, lift, rise, soar

n 1 foothill, hill, hillock, hump, knoll, mound, raise, rise, swelling

n 2 colt, equine, filly, foal, gelding, horse, mare, nag, pony, steed, yearling

mountain n bank, drift, heap, hill, mass, mound, pile, stack, stockpile

mountaintop n alp, peak, summit

mourn v 1 brood, grieve, lament, languish, sorrow

v 2 bawl, bemoan, cry, grieve, groan, lament, moan, sigh, snivel, sob, wail, weep, whimper, whine

mournful adj 1 dismal, doleful, gloomy, lamentable, melancholy, plaintive, regretful, regrettable, rueful, sorrowful, woeful

adj 2 black, bleak, blue, cheerless, dejected, depressed, desperate, despondent, discouraging, disheartening, distressing, down, forlorn, gloomy, hopeless, joyless, melancholy, moody, oppressive, prostrate, sad, somber, sorry, unhappy

mousetrap n booby trap, pit, pitfall, snare, trap

mouth *n* **1** access, aperture, approach, entrance, inlet, opening, passage

n **2** expression, face, grimace, pout, scowl, smirk, sneer, visage

n **3** gullet, opening, orifice

v act, ape, copy, emulate, follow, imitate, lip-synch, mime, mimic, mock, model, pantomime, parody, pattern, take off

movable *adj* **1** alterable, elastic, flexible, pliable, resilient, springy, supple

adj **2** carryable, compact, lightweight, luggable, pocket-size, portable, small, transportable

adj **3** ambulatory, gypsy, itinerant, nomadic, perambulatory, roving, transient, vagrant, wandering, wayfaring

move *n* **1** change, reversal, shift, turnabout

n **2** see: MANEUVER *n* **2**

v **1** distress, disturb, rend, sadden, wring

v **2** bring, cause, lead, persuade

v **3** dislocate, dislodge, displace, disturb, oust, remove, shift, ship, transfer

v **4** captivate, charm, delight, engross, enrapture, enravish, enthrall, entrance, hypnotize, mesmerize, ravish, transport

v **5** activate, actuate, compel, drive, force, goad, impel, induce, mobilize, motivate, persuade, press, propel, push, spur, start, turn on

v **6** arouse, awaken, excite, induce, instill, motivate, pique, prime, provoke, quicken, rouse, roust, spark, start, stimulate, titillate, urge

v **7** advance, begin again, continue, cycle, depart, get along, get on, go, leave, march, move forward, overture, part, proceed, progress, push on, recommence, reembark, restart, wend

v **8** abscond, bolt, defect, depart, exit, fall back, flee, get away, give back, go, leave, pull away, pull out, push off, retreat, run along, secede, shove off, take off, vacate, withdraw

v **9** see: CONVINCE *v*

movement *n* **1** headway, locomotion, motion, progress

n **2** action, battle, engagement, fray, gesture, operation, proceeding

n **3** exchange, traffic, travel

n **4** change, current, drift, flow, flux, gush, motion, rush, stream, tide, transition

n **5** action, activity, ado, animation, bedlam, bother, bustle, chaos, commotion, excitement, flurry, fluster, fuss, hum, liveliness, madhouse, stir, to-do, tumult, turmoil, whirlpool, whirlwind

movie *n* cinema, film, flick, motion picture

movies *n* cartoons, docudrama, documentary, game shows, mini-series, news, programs, series, sitcom, soap opera, soaps, talk shows, television, variety shows

moving *adj* **1** ambulatory, locomotive, mobile

adj **2** intimate, romantic, tender, touching

adj **3** affecting, heartbreaking, impressive, poignant, sad, touching

moxie *n* backbone, chutzpah, determination, endurance, fortitude, grit, guts, nerve, persistence, pluck, resilience, spirit, spunk, stamina, strength, tenacity, tolerance, vigor, willpower

much *n* abundance, glut, great deal, lot, mass, ton

muck *n* **1** dirt, dung, filth, garbage, manure, mud, slime, sludge

n **2** deposit, mud, sediment, silt, sludge

mucky *adj* **1** damp, drenched, dripping, humid, moist, muggy, soaked, soggy, sopping, sticky, sultry, sweaty, wet

adj **2** black, dark, dingy, dirty, filthy, foul, grimy, grubby, murky, polluted, seedy, shabby, sooty, squalid, stained, unclean, unlit, unwashed

mud *n* **1** dirt, dung, filth, garbage, manure, muck, slime, sludge

n **2** deposit, muck, sediment, silt, sludge

muddle *v* **1** addle, confuse, daze, foul up, fumble, jumble, mix up, snarl up

v **2** befuddle, bewilder, confuse, daze, distract, dizzy, embarrass, fluster, mix up, rattle, ruffle, trick, unglue, unhinge

n see: CHAOS *n* **5**

muddled *adj* **1** see: ABSURD *adj* **2**

adj **2** see: VAGUE *adj* **6**

muddledness *n* befuddlement, daze, fog, haze, maze, muddle-headedness

muddleheadedness *n* befuddlement, daze, fog, haze, maze

muddy *v* becloud, bedim, befog, blur, cloud, confuse, darken, dim, diminish, dull, eclipse, fade, obscure, overshadow, pale, shade, shadow, tarnish

muffle *v* **1** calm, lessen, quiet, reduce, soften, subdue

v **2** asphyxiate, choke, constrict, gag, garrote, quash, repress, smother, stifle, strangle, suffocate, suppress

v **3** censor, curb, gag, hush, inhibit, mute, quell, quiet, repress, restrain, silence, squelch, stifle, still, subdue, suppress, throttle, tone down

muffled *adj* see: VAGUE *adj* **6**

muffler *n* bandanna, scarf, shawl

mug *n* **1** countenance, face, features

n **2** chalice, container, cup, dish, Dixie

cup, glass, goblet, shot glass, stein, tumbler, vessel, wineglass

mugger *n* bandit, brigand, burglar, cheat, con artist, con man, criminal, crook, embezzler, gyp, highwayman, looter, outlaw, robber, swindler, thief

muggy *adj* 1 hot, humid, steamy, sticky, stifling, sunny, tropical

adj 2 damp, drenched, dripping, humid, moist, mucky, soaked, soggy, sopping, sticky, sultry, sweaty, wet

mulch *v* fertilize

mull *v* see: PONDER *v*

multifarious *adj* 1 complex, diverse, manifold, multifold

adj 2 abundant, assorted, copious, diverse, extensive, legion, many, multitudinous, myriad, numerous, plentiful, populous, prolific, sundry, various, voluminous

multifold *adj* complex, diverse, manifold

multiply *v* 1 abound, increase, overrun, proliferate, propagate, teem

v 2 amplify, append, augment, boost, build, enlarge, expand, extend, grow, heighten, increase, intensify, magnify, run up, snowball, supplement, upsurge, wax

v 3 see: BEGET *v*

multipurpose *adj* see: PRACTICAL *adj* 4

multitude *n* crush, dozens, horde, host, legion, many, numerousness, oodles, press, push, scores, squash, swarm

multitudes *n* droves, loads, lots, many, plenty, scads, slew

multitudinous *adj* abundant, assorted, copious, diverse, extensive, legion, many, multifarious, myriad, numerous, plentiful, populous, prolific, sundry, various, voluminous

mumble *n* murmur, mutter, undertone, whisper

v 1 garble, mutter, slur

v 2 see: MISREPRESENT *v* 2

mummify *v* atrophy, decay, deteriorate, dry up, dwindle, shrink, shrivel, waste away, welter, wilt, wither, wizen

mummy *n* ma, mama, mater, matriarch, mom, momma, mommy, mother, parent

munch *v* bite, chew, crunch, gnaw, gulp, guzzle, nibble, rend, wolf

mundane *adj* 1 universal

adj 2 common, earthly, earthy, pedestrian, terrestrial, uncelestial, worldly

adj 3 average, common, commonplace, daily, everyday, general, natural, normal,

ordinary, plain, prevalent, regular, routine, typical, unexceptional, unremarkable, usual, workaday

municipal *adj* civic, civil, national, public

municipality *n* 1 borough, city, megalopolis, metropolis, suburb, town

n 2 county, district, jurisdiction, parish, precinct, township, ward

munitions *n* ammo, ammunition, armor, arms, equipment, guns, machinery, ordnance, weapons

mural *n* acrylic, art, canvas, depiction, drawing, etching, illustration, landscape, lithograph, oil, painting, pastel, pen and ink, picture, portrait, print, seascape, sketch, still life, watercolor

murder *n* assassination, foul play, homicide, killing, manslaughter

v abolish, annihilate, assassinate, bump off, butcher, decimate, destroy, dispatch, execute, exterminate, hang, hit, kill, knock off, liquidate, massacre, put away, rub out, slaughter, slay, wipe out

murderer *n* assassin, killer

murky *adj* 1 dark, dim, dusky, gloomy, lightless, obscure, shadowy, somber, tenebrous, unilluminated

adj 2 cloudy, dismal, foggy, gray, hazy, misty, overcast, steamy, vaporous, vapory

adj 3 black, dark, dingy, dirty, filthy, foul, grimy, grubby, mucky, polluted, seedy, shabby, sooty, squalid, stained, unclean, unlit, unwashed

adj 4 see: VAGUE *adj* 6

murmur *n* 1 mumble, mutter, undertone, whisper

n 2 gossip, grapevine, hearsay, report, rumble, rumor, scuttlebutt, story, talk, word

n 3 babble, babbling, burble, chatter, gibber, prattle, rattle

v babble, blab, blurt, burble, chatter, gossip, prattle, talk, tattle

muscle *n* ardor, beef, brawn, drive, energy, force, intensity, lustiness, might, pep, potency, power, punch, steam, strength, verve, vigor, vim, virility, vitality

muscular *adj* athletic, brawny, burly, husky, massive, ponderous, powerful, robust, stocky, stout, strapping, strong

muse *n* author, bard, composer, folk singer, narrator, poet, storyteller, troubadour

v 1 dream, fantasize, imagine, suppose

v 2 cerebrate, chew, consider, contemplate, deliberate, digest, meditate, mull, ponder, reason, reflect, ruminate, see, speculate, study, think, weigh

museum *n* archive, gallery, treasury

mushy *adj* 1 sentimental

adj 2 pulpy, soft, spongy, squashy, squelchy, squishy, yielding

music *n* 1 air, harmony, measure, medley, melody, strain, tune

n 2 blues, classical, country, folk, jazz, ragtime, rock-and-roll, soul, swing

musical *adj* choral, euphonious, harmonious, lyric, mellow, melodic, melodious, orchestral, philharmonic, rhythmical, symphonic, tuneful, vocal

n 1 libretto, opera, operetta, score

n 2 follies, review, revue, song and dance, variety show, vaudeville

n 3 Broadway, comedy, drama, extravaganza, production, stage, theater

musician *n* accompanist, artiste, conductor, instrumentalist, performer, virtuoso

musing *adj* meditative, melancholy, nostalgic, pensive, wistful

n daydream, dream, fancy, fantasy, reverie, vision

musket *n* carbine, firearm, flintlock, gun, rifle, shotgun

muss *v* 1 crease, fold, pleat, rumple, wrinkle

v 2 disarray, dislocate, disorder, disorganize, disrupt, disturb, interfere, interrupt, jumble, mess, mix up, rummage, shuffle, sift through, unsettle

mussel *n* clam, cockle, crab, crustacean, mollusk, prawn, shellfish, shrimp, snail

must *n* condition, essential, necessity, precondition, prerequisite, requirement

v should

muster *v* 1 cause, generate, induce, occasion, produce

v 2 engage, enlist, enroll, recruit, register, secure, sign up

v 3 assemble, associate, call, cluster, collect, concentrate, congregate, convene, flock, gather, group, lump, marshal, mass, mingle, mobilize, order, rally, rendezvous, round up, send for, summon

v 4 see: INSTIGATE *v* 1

musty *adj* 1 decaying, fetid, foul, gamy, malodorous, putrid, rancid, rank, reeking, rotten, smelly, sour, spoiled, stale, stinking, tainted

adj 2 see: STALE *adj* 2, 3

mutate *v* 1 adjust, alter, catalyze, change, modify, refashion, vary

v 2 alter, change, commute, convert, evolve, further, improve, metamorphose, modernize, modify, revolutionize, trans-

fer, transfigure, transform, transmute, vary

mutation *n* adjustment, alteration, anomaly, change, deviation, modification, permutation, shift, variation

mute *adj* dumb, inarticulate, reticent, silent, speechless, tacit, voiceless

v censor, curb, gag, hush, inhibit, muffle, quell, quiet, repress, restrain, silence, squelch, stifle, still, subdue, suppress, throttle, tone down

muted *adj* see: DULL *adj* 7

mutilate *v* 1 cripple, dismember, maim, mangle

v 2 see: CUT *v* 7

mutinous *adj* defiant, disobedient, insubordinate, insurgent, rebellious, seditious

mutiny *n* betrayal, insurrection, revolt, sedition, subversion, treason, uprising

v 1 insurrect, rebel, revolt, rise against

v 2 brave, challenge, confront, dare, defy, face, rebel, resist

mutt *n* canine, dog, hound, mongrel, pooch, pup, puppy

mutter *n* mumble, murmur, undertone, whisper

v 1 garble, mumble, slur

v 2 see: COMPLAIN *v* 2

mutual *adj* aggregate, collective, common, communal, joint, public, shared

mutually *adv* as one, collectively, in unison, together

muzzle *n* beak, bill, nib, nose, proboscis, prow, snout, trunk

myopic *adj* 1 careless, foolish, impulsive, irresponsible, not smart, reckless, risky, shortsighted, unthinking, unwise

adj 2 nearsighted

myriad *adj* see: MANY *adj* 2

mysterious *adj* 1 baffling, elusive, frustrating, puzzling, subtle

adj 2 enigmatic, incomprehensible, inexplicable, inscrutable, occult, puzzling

adj 3 complex, complicated, elaborate, enigmatic, intricate, involved, knotty, tangled

adj 4 arcane, hermetic, impenetrable, impervious, mystic, obscure, puzzling, secret, unexaminable, unknown, unseen

adj 5 abstruse, deep, esoteric, heartfelt, heavy, hermetic, insightful, obscure, occult, penetrating, profound, recondite

adj 6 illegible, incomprehensible, inconceivable, unclear, unintelligible, unthinkable

adj 7 curious, exotic, far-out, fascinating, intriguing, kinky, marvelous, new, novel, odd, outlandish, strange, ultra, unaccustomed, unexplored, unfamiliar, unique, unknown, unusual, weird

mystery n 1 confidence, enigma, intrigue, secret

n 2 drama, melodrama, theatrics, tragedy, tragicomedy

n 3 confusion, conundrum, difficulty, dilemma, enigma, obstacle, paradox, perplexity, problem, puzzle, quandary, question, riddle, secret

mystic adj 1 mystical, psychic, transcendental

adj 2 arcane, hermetic, impenetrable, impervious, mysterious, obscure, puzzling, secret, unexaminable, unknown, unseen

mystical adj 1 mystic, psychic, transcendental

adj 2 see: WEIRD adj 1

mystically adv clandestinely, covertly, furtively, hush-hush, secretly, sneakily, stealthily, surreptitiously, under cover

mystifying adj ambiguous, cryptic, enigmatic, occult, puzzling, vague

myth n 1 delusion, fallacy, illusion, old wives' tale, superstition

n 2 allegory, fable, fantasy, fiction, legend, lesson, lore, mythology, parable, story, tale

n 3 anecdote, description, fantasy, fiction, invention, narration, narrative, novel, sketch, story, tale, yarn

mythical adj fabulous, legendary, mythological

mythological adj legendary, mythical

mythology n see: LEGEND n 3

N

nab v 1 catch, clasp, clutch, grab, grapple, grasp, grip, hold, nail, seize, snatch, take

v 2 apprehend, arrest, bag, book, bust, capture, catch, collar, detain, get, grab, lock up, nail, pick up, pinch, pull in, run in, secure, seize, take

nag v 1 complain, crab, criticize, grieve, gripe, grumble, mutter, object, protest, whine

v 2 berate, carp, cavil, criticize, find fault, flay, fuss, henpeck, nit-pick, nudge, peck, quibble, scold

n 1 harpy, shrew

n 2 colt, equine, filly, foal, gelding, horse, mare, mount, pony, steed, yearling

v aggravate, annoy, badger, bait, bedevil, beleaguer, bother, bug, harass, harry, hassle, heckle, hound, hurt, intimidate, jeer, needle, persecute, pester, plague, pro-

voke, ride, spite, taunt, tease, threaten, torment, worry

nagging adj annoying, anxious, bothersome, chafing, crabby, edgy, fretful, galling, impatient, irritating, jittery, on edge, restless, touchy, unsettling

naiad n elf, fairy, nymph, pixie, sprite

nail v 1 connect, join, peg, pin, tack

v 2 attach, clip, fasten, pin, staple, tack

v 3 bat, clout, hit, pop, smite, sock, strike, swat, whack

v 4 catch, clasp, clutch, grab, grapple, grasp, grip, hold, nab, seize, snatch, take

v 5 apprehend, arrest, bag, book, bust, capture, catch, collar, detain, get, grab, lock up, nab, pick up, pinch, pull in, run in, secure, seize, take

naive adj 1 alterable, impressionable, inexperienced, malleable, sensitive, susceptible

adj 2 believing, credulous, easy, gullible, innocent, susceptible, trustful

adj 3 green, immature, inexperienced, new, novice, raw, unsophisticated, virgin

adj 4 benign, harmless, innocent, innocuous, inoffensive, mild, pure, safe, unoffending, unoffensive

adj 5 artless, candid, frank, guileless, ingenuous, innocent, natural, open, plain, simple, simple-hearted, unadorned, unaffected, unsophisticated, unstudied, untutored, unworldly

naked adj 1 plain, stark, unadorned

adj 2 bare, exposed, in the raw, nude, open, peeled, stripped, unclothed, uncovered, visible

name n 1 alias, designation, handle, moniker, nickname, title

n 2 approval, autograph, endorsement, John Hancock, signature

n 3 celebrity, dignitary, luminary, movie star, notable, personality, star

n 4 esteem, fame, good standing, perception, regard, reputation, stature

n 5 expression, idiom, locution, phrase, saying, term, word, wording

v 1 distinguish, identify, know, recognize, specify

v 2 call, define, designate, entitle, label, term

v 3 appoint, declare, designate, nominate, propose, select, specify

v 4 baptize, bestow, call, christen, confer, designate, dub, entitle, nickname, tag, term, title

nameless adj anonymous, obscure, uncelebrated, unfamed, unheard-of, unknown, unnamed, unrenowned

nanny n baby sitter, governess, nursemaid

nap v doze, rest, sleep, snooze

napping adj dozing, drowsy, lethargic, nodding, sleepy, slumberous, snoozy, somnolent, tired

narcissism n airs, arrogance, cockiness, conceit, condescension, disdain, egotism, haughtiness, image, loftiness, pride, self-esteem, self-image, vanity

narcissistic adj arrogant, cocky, conceited, haughty, self-assured, smug, stuck-up, vain

narcotic n 1 compound, drug, elixir, formula, medicine, painkiller, pharmaceutical, prescription
n 2 sedative, tranquilizer, Valium
n 3 dope, drug, grass, marijuana, pot

narrate v 1 analyze, annotate, clarify, define, detail, elucidate, explain, expound, express, interpret, spell out, state, understand
v 2 brief, communicate, convey, declare, describe, disclose, divulge, explain, impart, inform, orate, portray, read, recite, recount, relate, report, retell, reveal, share, state, tattle, tell, transmit

narration n 1 depiction, description, explanation, illustration, report, sketch, story, verbalization
n 2 anecdote, description, fantasy, fiction, invention, myth, narrative, novel, sketch, story, tale, yarn

narrative n anecdote, description, fantasy, fiction, invention, myth, narration, novel, sketch, story, tale, yarn

narrator n author, bard, composer, folk singer, muse, poet, storyteller, troubadour

narrow adj 1 devout, orthodox, strict, unquestioning
adj 2 confined, controlled, ignorant, limited, parochial, provincial, unsophisticated
adj 3 ineffectual, limited, little, mean, paltry, set, small
adj 4 committed, determined, fixed, focused, limited, obsessive, one-track
adj 5 austere, narrow-minded, prim, prudish, puritanical, rigid, severe, strict
adj 6 definite, determinate, exclusive, fixed, limited, precise, restricted, segregated, specific
adj 7 lank, skinny, slender, slight, slim, thin, wiry

narrow-minded adj see: STUBBORN adj 6

narrows n arm, bay, cove, estuary, fiord, gulf, inlet, sound, strait

nascent adj beginning, embryonic, founding, incipient, initial, introductory, rudimentary, starting

nasty adj 1 derogatory, disparaging, insulting, malicious, sarcastic, snide
adj 2 brackish, briny, foul, salty, stagnant, undrinkable
adj 3 abusive, contemptuous, derisive, disrespectful, insulting, offensive, slighting
adj 4 dirty, disgusting, foul, lousy, putrid, rotten, sordid
adj 5 adverse, antagonistic, bellicose, hostile, ill, inimical, spiteful, unfriendly
adj 6 annoying, bad, difficult, disagreeable, displeasing, objectionable, offensive, rotten, sour, unhappy, unpleasant, upsetting
adj 7 austere, brutal, callous, cold-blooded, compassionless, cruel, ferocious, fierce, hardened, hardhearted, heartless, indifferent, inhuman, inhumane, malicious, mean, merciless, obdurate, pitiless, ruthless, savage, spiteful, stony, tough, uncaring, unemotional, unfeeling, unkind, unmerciful, unpitying, unrelenting, unsympathetic, vicious
adj 8 repulsive
adj 9 choppy, rainy, rough, sloppy, wet
adj 10 abrupt, bluff, blunt, brash, brusque, cheeky, crusty, curt, flip, flippant, gruff, harsh, impertinent, impudent, irritable, quick, rude, sarcastic, sassy, short, snippy, snotty, surly, testy, wisenheimer
adj 11 bawdy, coarse, crude, dirty, erotic, filthy, foul, gamy, gross, improper, indecent, lascivious, lewd, licentious, obscene, off-color, pornographic, profane, prurient, racy, rank, raunchy, ribald, risqué, scandalous, smutty, suggestive, tainted, uncouth, vulgar, x-rated

natal adj basic, congenital, genetic, inborn, indigenous, ingrained, inherent, inherited, innate, instinctive, intrinsic, native

nation n area, country, entity, province, state

national adj 1 ethnic, racial, tribal
adj 2 civic, civil, public
n citizen, countryman, indigene, inhabitant, native, subject

native adj 1 aboriginal, endemic, indigenous, primitive
adj 2 domestic, endemic, folk, indigenous, local, traditional
adj 3 see: INSTINCTIVE adj 3

n 1 citizen, countryman, indigene, inhabitant, national, subject

n 2 aborigine, primitive, savage

natty *adj* see: SUAVE *adj* 2

natural *adj* 1 basic, congenital, genetic, inborn, indigenous, ingrained, inherent, inherited, innate, instinctive, intrinsic, natal, native

adj 2 artless, candid, frank, guileless, ingenuous, innocent, naive, open, plain, simple, simple-hearted, unadorned, unaffected, unsophisticated, unstudied, untutored, unworldly

adj 3 average, common, commonplace, daily, everyday, general, mundane, normal, ordinary, plain, prevalent, regular, routine, typical, unexceptional, unremarkable, usual, workaday

adj 4 see: SPONTANEOUS *adj* 2

naturally *adv* easily, effortlessly, lightly, readily, willingly

nature *n* 1 character, constitution, fiber, makeup, quality, substance

n 2 cosmos, creation, firmament, grand scale, macrocosm, solar system, vast, universe, world

n 3 characteristic, flavor, impression, property, quality, ring, sound, tendency, tone, type

n 4 center, core, crux, essence, gist, heart, life, marrow, nucleus, pith, quick, quintessence, root, spirit, substance

n 5 aptitude, character, complexion, disposition, distinctiveness, heart, humor, identity, inclination, individuality, makeup, personality, quality, spirit, state, temperament, tendency

n 6 see: CATEGORY *n*

naught *n* goose egg, nil, none, nonentity, nothing, zero, zilch

naughty *adj* bad, disobedient, ill-behaved, misbehaving, mischievous

nausea *n* aversion, contempt, disgust, distaste, horror, loathing, repugnance, repulsion, revulsion

nauseate *v* abhor, disgust, repel, repulse, revolt, sicken

nauseated *adj* queasy, queer, seasick, sick, squeamish

navigable *adj* seaworthy, staunch, watertight

navy *adj* aqua, azure, blue, cobalt, indigo, Prussian, sapphire, turquoise

n armada, assembly, boats, convoy, fleet, flotilla, grouping, ships, squadron

naysayer *n* 1 adversary, antagonist, obstructionist, schmuck, shnook

n 2 critic, cynic, detractor, hatchet man, pessimist, skeptic

near *adv* 1 adjacently, around, aside, atop, beside, by, nearby, on

adv 2 close, nearby, nigh

adv 3 see: NEARBY *adv* 2

prep see: AT *prep*

adj 1 available, close by, convenient, nearby

adj 2 close, familiar, intimate, personal

adj 3 close, immediate, near at hand, nigh, proximate, virtual

v approach, come

near at hand *adj* 1 close, immediate, near, nigh, proximate, virtual

adj 2 see: ADJOINING *adj*

nearby *adv* 1 around, encircling, enclosing, on all sides, surrounding

adv 2 adjacently, around, aside, atop, beside, by, near, on

adv 3 close, near, nigh

adj 1 available, close by, convenient

adj 2 contiguous, current, direct, immediate, instant, primary, prompt, sudden, timely

adj 3 abutting, adjacent, adjoining, alongside, bordering, close by, connected, contiguous, juxtaposed, local, near at hand, neighboring, outlining, regional, touching, verging on

adj 4 accessible, available, close, convenient, feasible, functional, handy, helpful, multipurpose, open, practical, public, reachable, ready, serviceable, suitable, unrestricted, usable, useful, utilitarian, well-suited, within reach, working

nearest *adj* closest

nearing *adj* advancing, approaching, forthcoming, imminent, looming, oncoming, pending

nearly *adv* about, almost, approximately, around, close to, more or less, not quite

nearness *n* 1 closeness, proximity, vicinity

n 2 association, closeness, proximity

nearsighted *adj* shortsighted

neat *adj* 1 aligned, ordered, proper, straight

adj 2 meticulous, orderly, prim, ship shape, tidy, trim, well-groomed

adj 3 chic, dapper, dashing, debonair, jaunty, natty, rakish, sleek, smart, snazzy, spiffy, suave, trim

neaten *v* arrange, organize, pick up, tidy

nebulous *adj* ambiguous, bleary, confused, fuzzy, hazy, misty, unclear

necessary *adj* 1 critical, essential, integral, significant, strategic

adj 2 compulsory, imperative, mandatory, must do, obligatory, prerequisite, required

adj 3 critical, essential, imperative, indispensable, mandatory, needed, prerequisite, required, vital

adj 4 see: APPLICABLE *adj*

necessitate *v* ask, call, crave, demand, require, take

necessity *n* 1 call, cause, obligation, occasion

n 2 condition, essential, must, precondition, prerequisite, requirement

n 3 demand, exigency, need, pressure, requirement, stress, urgency

neck *n* barrier, breaker, cape, harbor, head, jetty, point, sea wall

v caress, cradle, cuddle, embrace, feel, fondle, fool around, hold, hug, love, make out, nuzzle, pet, snuggle, stroke

necklace *n* anklet, band, bangle, bracelet, brooch, earring, jewelry, medal, medallion, pin, ring

necktie *n* cravat, tie

need *n* 1 demand

n 2 defect, deficiency, demerit, fault, flaw, imperfection, inadequacy, lack, shortcoming, want

n 3 deficiency, deprivation, destitution, inadequacy, indigence, lack, poverty, privation, scarcity, want

n 4 demand, exigency, necessity, pressure, requirement, stress, urgency

v 1 bank on, build on, count on, depend, rely, trust

v 2 call, challenge, claim, demand, exact, postulate, require, requisition, solicit

v 3 ache, covet, crave, desire, hanker, hunger, itch, long, lust, pine, thirst, want, yearn

needed *adj* critical, essential, imperative, indispensable, mandatory, necessary, prerequisite, required, vital

needle *v* 1 banter, deride, gibe, jeer, joke, knock, mock, rib, ridicule, roast, tease

v 2 see: ANNOY *v* 3

needy *adj* broke, destitute, dirt-poor, down and out, impoverished, indigent, penniless, poor, poverty-stricken, strapped, unprosperous

nefarious *adj* base, corrupt, deadly, degenerate, depraved, deviant, evil, immoral, infamous, kinky, perverse, putrid, rotten, ruthless, savage, vicious, villainous, wicked, wild

negate *v* 1 counter, counterbalance, neutralize, nullify, offset, thwart

v 2 contradict, cross, deny, disaffirm, disagree, impugn, rebut, traverse

v 3 cancel, contradict, deny, disallow, forbid, nix, nullify, override, overrule, reject, renege, repeal, revoke, torpedo, veto, void

v 4 abrogate, annul, cancel, contradict, discharge, dismantle, dissolve, dwindle, fade, nullify, quash, recall, repeal, rescind, reverse, revoke, set aside, vacate, void

v 5 see: TERMINATE *v* 8

v 6 see: THWART *v* 4

negative *adj* 1 indifferent

adj 2 cynical, depressed, gloomy, glum, pessimistic

adj 3 adverse, deleterious, detrimental, harmful, unfavorable

neglect *n* absence, disregard, error, omission, oversight, slip-up

v defy, discount, disregard, exclude, forget, ignore, miss, omit, ostracize, overlook, overpass, pass, pass by, pass over, shun, skip, slight, snub

neglectful *adj* careless, defiant, delinquent, derelict, heedless, inattentive, lax, negligent, reckless, sloppy

negligee *n* bathrobe, gown, housecoat, nightgown, robe

negligent *adj* careless, defiant, delinquent, derelict, heedless, inattentive, lax, neglectful, reckless, sloppy

negligible *adj* borderline, casual, frivolous, insignificant, light, lightweight, little, marginal, meager, minor, minute, nonessential, off, outside, petty, remote, secondary, slender, slight, slim, small, tenuous, trivial, unimportant

negotiate *v* 1 clear, hurdle, leap, surmount, vault

v 2 argue, bargain, barter, dicker, haggle, wrangle

negotiations *n* arrangements, business, commerce, dealings, enterprise, industry, intercourse, trade, traffic

negotiator *n* absorber, agent, broker, catalyst, distributor, go-between, intermediary, mediator

neighborhood *n* area, district, domain, environs, jurisdiction, locality, parish, precinct, province, range, region, section, sphere, vicinity, ward, zone

neighboring *adj* abutting, adjacent, adjoining, alongside, bordering, close by, connected, contiguous, juxtaposed, local, near at hand, nearby, outlining, regional, touching, verging on

neighborly *adj* affable, amenable, amiable, amicable, congenial, empathetic, friendly, gregarious, hospitable, outgoing, receptive, sociable, social, sympathetic

neighbors *n* see: SOCIETY *n* 3

neophyte *n* **1** amateur, beginner, dabbler, dilettante, hobbyist, layman, nonprofessional, novice, part-timer

n **2** apprentice, beginner, disciple, freshman, intern, newcomer, novice, novitiate, pupil, recruit, rookie, student, tenderfoot, trainee

nepotism *n* bias, favoritism, patronage

nerd *n* **1** hacker

n **2** blockhead, boor, clod, creep, cretin, dimwit, dolt, dope, dullard, dumbbell, dummy, dunce, fool, goof, idiot, imbecile, jerk, nincompoop, numskull, oaf, pain, schlemiel, schmuck, simpleton, stooge, turkey

nerve *n* **1** aplomb, assurance, confidence, esteem, poise, presence, savoir-faire, self-assurance, self-confidence

n **2** backbone, chutzpah, determination, endurance, fortitude, grit, guts, moxie, persistence, pluck, resilience, spirit, spunk, stamina, strength, tenacity, tolerance, vigor, willpower

n **3** arrogance, assurance, audacity, boldness, brashness, brass, cheek, chutzpah, condescension, confidence, crust, effrontery, face, gall, haughtiness, insolence, patronage, presumption, ridicule, sass, stamina, temerity

nervous *adj* **1** anxious, insecure, precarious, threatened, uncertain, vulnerable

adj **2** afraid, aghast, anxious, apprehensive, concerned, discerning, fearful, frightened, paranoid, scared, scary, terrified, worried

adj **3** antsy, edgy, excitable, fidgety, highstrung, irritable, jittery, jumpy, moody, nervy, restless, shaky, skittish, temperamental

adj **4** anxious, edgy, fidgety, impatient, nervy, queasy, restive, restless, tense, troubled, uncomfortable, uneasy, uptight, worried

nervy *adj* **1** anxious, edgy, fidgety, impatient, nervous, queasy, restive, restless, tense, troubled, uncomfortable, uneasy, uptight, worried

adj **2** antsy, edgy, excitable, fidgety, highstrung, irritable, jittery, jumpy, moody, nervous, restless, shaky, skittish, temperamental

adj **3** audacious, bold, brash, brazen, cheeky, daring, disrespectful, forward,

fresh, impertinent, impudent, insolent, irreverent, pert, rude, sassy, saucy

nest *n* brood

v bivouac, camp, dwell, lodge, quarter, station

nestle *v* ensconce, harbor, settle, shelter, snuggle

net *n* assets, cash, earnings, gain, gross, haul, payback, proceeds, profits, receipts, return, revenue, take, yield

v access, accomplish, achieve, attain, derive, earn, fulfill, gain, get, merit, obtain, perform, profit, rack up, reach, realize, score, win

netting *n* barrier, mesh, protection, screen, shield

nettle *v* see: BOTHER *v* 5

network *n* complex, infrastructure, maze, organization, system

v connect, engage, hook up, interlock

neutral *adj* **1** detached, free, impartial, independent, nonpartisan, unattached, uncommitted, uninvolved

adj **2** candid, dispassionate, equal, equitable, fair, impartial, impersonal, indifferent, just, objective, open-minded, square, unbiased, uncolored, unprejudiced

neutralize *v* counter, counterbalance, negate, nullify, offset, thwart

never-ending *adj* see: PERPETUAL *adj* 2

never-failing *adj* abiding, enduring, firm, steadfast, sure, unfaltering, unshakable, unwavering

nevertheless *adv* **1** but, excepting, further, however, just, merely, only, simply, solely, yet

adv **2** at any rate, but, however, moreover, nonetheless, notwithstanding, still, though, yet

new *adv* afresh, anew, lately, newly, of late, recently

adj **1** fresh, mint, unused

adj **2** tentative, untested, young

adj **3** dawning, frontier, unexplored, unknown

adj **4** innovative, novel, original, pioneering, trailblazing, unprecedented

adj **5** green, immature, inexperienced, naive, novice, raw, unsophisticated, virgin

adj **6** bright, contemporary, fresh, hightech, modern, modernistic, novel, recent, up-to-date

adj **7** curious, exotic, far-out, fascinating, intriguing, kinky, marvelous, mysterious, novel, odd, outlandish, strange, ultra, unaccustomed, unexplored, unfamiliar, unique, unknown, unusual, weird

newborn *n* babe, baby, child, infant, tot, tyke

newcomer *n* 1 alien, outsider, stranger

n 2 apprentice, beginner, disciple, freshman, intern, neophyte, novice, novitiate, pupil, recruit, rookie, student, tenderfoot, trainee

newly *adv* afresh, anew, lately, new, of late, recently

news *n* 1 coverage, press, reporting

n 2 data, discipline, facts, information, knowledge, lore, science, wisdom

n 3 communication, data, disclosure, exchange, expression, facts, information, intelligence, knowledge, notification

n 4 cartoons, docudrama, documentary, game shows, mini-series, movies, programs, series, sitcom, soap opera, soaps, talk shows, television, variety shows

newsletter *n* 1 bulletin, daily, journal, organ, newspaper, publication, review

n 2 article, bulletin, byline, column, communication, dispatch, editorial, feature, headline, item, report, story, vignette

newspaper *n* bulletin, daily, journal, newsletter, organ, publication, review

newspaperman *n* columnist, commentator, correspondent, editor, interviewer, journalist, publicist, writer

newspapers *n* magazines, media, press, television

next *adj* 1 ensuing, following, latter, subsequent, succeeding, successive

adj 2 approaching, eventual, expected, future, imminent, impending, prospective, subsequent

nexus *n* association, connection

nib *n* 1 edge, end, nub, tip

n 2 beak, bill, muzzle, nose, proboscis, prow, snout, trunk

nibble *v* bite, chew, crunch, gnaw, gulp, guzzle, munch, rend, wolf

nice *adj* 1 agreeable, bright, fine, good, pleasant, sunny

adj 2 dainty, delicate, fine, gentle, refined, subtle

adj 3 conventional, correct, decorous, fitting, orthodox, polite, proper, right, suitable, well

adj 4 agreeable, congenial, favorable, good, grateful, gratifying, pleasant, pleasing, pleasurable, welcome

niche *n* atmosphere, climate, conditions, environment, habitat, perimeter, settings, surroundings

nick *n* 1 cut, gash, incision, pierce, prick, puncture, slit, wound

n 2 dent, groove, indentation, notch

nickname *n* alias, designation, handle, moniker, name, title

v baptize, bestow, call, christen, confer, designate, dub, entitle, name, tag, term, title

niggardly *adj* cheap, close, greedy, mean, miserly, parsimonious, penny-pinching, stingy, tight, tightfisted, ungenerous, ungiving

nigh *adj* close, immediate, near, near at hand, nearly, proximate, virtually

adv close, near

night *n* dark, evening, nighttime, wee hours

nightfall *n* dusk, sundown, sunset, twilight

nightgown *n* bathrobe, gown, housecoat, robe

nightmare *n* see: PAIN *n* 4

nightstick *n* bat, blackjack, boomerang, club, cudgel, cue, mallet, stave, stick

nighttime *n* dark, evening, night, wee hours

nil *n* 1 emptiness, nothing, nothingness, oblivion, void

n 2 goose egg, naught, none, nonentity, nothing, zero, zilch

nimble *adj* 1 active, agile, astir, brisk, catty, energetic, lively, quick, sprightly, spry, zippy

adj 2 adroit, apt, canny, clever, cunning, deft, handy, ingenious, skilled, skillful, sly, wily

nincompoop *n* see: IDIOT *n*

nip *v* 1 blast, blight, dash, decompose, wither

v 2 bibulate, booze, consume, drink, gulp, guzzle, imbibe, partake, polish off, put away, put down, sample, savor, sip, suck, swig, swill, taste

n bite, morsel, piece, quick meal, snack

nipple *n* breast, teat, udder

nippy *adj* 1 biting, hot, pungent, seasoned, sharp, spicy, tangy, tart

adj 2 arctic, chilly, cold, cool, freezing, frigid, frosty, glacial, icy, wintry

nirvana *n* bliss, delight, ecstasy, Eden, elation, enchantment, heaven, joy, paradise, pleasure, rapture, rhapsody

nit-picker *n* fusspot, perfectionist, purist, stickler

nit-picking *adj* captious, carping, censorious, critical, cutting, disparaging, faultfinding

nix *v* 1 ban, bar, confine, enjoin, forbid,

inhibit, outlaw, prevent, prohibit, stop, suppress, veto

v 2 cancel, contradict, deny, disallow, forbid, negate, nullify, override, overrule, reject, renege, repeal, revoke, torpedo, veto, void

nobility *n* aristocracy, blue blood, cream, elite, gentry, royalty, upper class

noble *adj* 1 dramatic, epic, grand, heroic, legendary, stirring, vivid

adj 2 benevolent, big, chivalrous, considerate, generous, grandiose, lofty

adj 3 deserving, estimable, excellent, honorable, precious, sterling, valuable, worthy

adj 4 aristocratic, blue-blooded, imperial, kingly, majestic, regal, royal, stately, well-bred

adj 5 conscientious, ethical, honest, honorable, moral, principled, proper, respectable, right, righteous, scrupulous, sound, true, trustworthy, upright, virtuous

adj 6 august, baronial, exalted, grand, grandiose, haughty, imperial, imposing, impressive, lofty, lordly, magisterial, magnificent, majestic, portly, princely, regal, royal, stately

adj 7 elevated, ethical, moral

adj 8 chivalrous, civil, civilized, cordial, courteous, courtly, decent, dignified, gallant, genteel, gentlemanly, gracious, mannerly, polite, well-mannered

nobleman *n* lord

nod *n* 1 address, bow, greeting, honor, recognition, salute

n 2 sign, signal, symbol, symptom, token, trait

n 3 acceptance, accord, agreement, approval, assent, compliance, concurrence, consent, go-ahead, sympathy

n 4 apathy, coma, doze, ennui, grogginess, inertia, languor, lassitude, lethargy, sleep, slumber, stupor

v beckon, gesture, motion, signal

nodding *adj* 1 dozing, drowsy, lethargic, napping, sleepy, slumberous, snoozy, somnolent, tired

adj 2 see: INACTIVE *adj* 2

no-holds-barred *adj* see: SINCERE *adj*

noise *n* 1 bang, blare, blast, boom, discharge, explosion, pop, report, roar

n 2 brouhaha, cacophony, chaos, clamor, confusion, din, discord, disorder, hubbub, mayhem, pandemonium, racket, tumult, uproar

n 3 sound

noiseless *adj* dead, hush, inanimate, inert, lifeless, quiet, silent, still, soundless

noisy *adj* blatant, boisterous, clamorous, disturbing, loud, loudmouthed, obstreperous, raucous, rowdy, tumultuous, vociferous

nomad *n* drifter, emigrant, itinerant, migrant, transient

nomadic *adj* ambulatory, gypsy, itinerant, movable, perambulatory, roving, transient, vagrant, wandering, wayfaring

nom-de-plume *n* alias, anonym, pen name, pseudonym

nomenclature *n* buzzwords, jargon, lexicons, lingo, terminology, terms, vocabulary

nominal *adj* 1 hollow, perfunctory, professed, representative, small, symbolic, token

adj 2 see: TRIVIAL *adj* 1

nominate *v* 1 appoint, declare, designate, name, propose, select, specify

v 2 appoint, ballot, choose, elect, opt, select, vote

nominee *n* aspirant, candidate, contestant, entrant

nonabundant *adj* few, lacking, limited, not many, scant, short, sparse

nonaggressive *adj* calm, coolheaded, nonviolent, pacifist, passive, peaceful

nonattender *n* absentee, hooky player, no-show, truant

nonbeliever *n* agnostic, infidel, skeptic

noncancelable *adj* irrevocable, nonrescindable, permanent, unalterable, uncancelable

nonchalant *adj* 1 accidental, careless, caustic, heedless, inadvertent, inconsiderate, selfish, sharp, short, tactless, thoughtless, uncaring, unceremonious, ungracious, unheeding, unintended, unintentional, unreflective, unthinking

adj 2 aloof, blasé, calm, careless, casual, composed, cool, detached, diffident, disinterested, distant, indifferent, informal, inhibited, numb, remote, reserved, shy, unconcerned, unfriendly, uninterested, withdrawn

adj 3 see: CALM *adj* 2

noncommittal *adj* reserved, restrained

nonconformist *adj* original, unbounded, unconventional

n 1 freelance, independent, individualist, loner, maverick

n 2 agitator, defector, dissident, heretic, iconoclast, insurgent, malcontent, maverick, misfit, rebel, renegade, traitor, troublemaker, turncoat

noncurrent adj see: OBSOLETE adj

nondomestic adj foreign, imported, offshore

none n goose egg, naught, nil, nonentity, nothing, zero, zilch

nonentity n goose egg, naught, nil, none, nothing, zero, zilch

nonessential adj 1 abnormal, extra, extraneous, foreign, illogical, immaterial, insignificant, irregular, irrelevant, malapropos, peripheral, superfluous, surplus, unimportant, unnecessary, unrelated
adj 2 borderline, casual, frivolous, insignificant, light, lightweight, little, marginal, meager, minor, minute, negligible, off, outside, petty, remote, secondary, slender, slight, slim, small, tenuous, trivial, unimportant

nonetheless adv at any rate, but, however, moreover, nevertheless, notwithstanding, still, though, yet

nonexistent adj conceived, conjured, created, fancied, fanciful, fantastic, fictional, fictitious, illusory, imaginary, imagined, invented, make-believe, notional, unreal, whimsical

nonmalignant adj amiable, benign, genial, kind, kindly

nonmaterial adj 1 intangible
adj 2 see: SPIRITUAL adj 2

nonpartisan adj detached, free, impartial, independent, neutral, unattached, uncommitted, uninvolved

nonplus v amaze, astonish, astound, awe, boggle, confound, dazzle, dumbfound, flabbergast, stagger, stun, surprise

nonproductive adj see: FUTILE adj 3

nonprofessional n amateur, beginner, dabbler, dilettante, hobbyist, layman, neophyte, novice, part-timer
adj amateur, inexperienced, lay, unprofessional

nonpublic adj exclusive, private, restricted

nonrescindable adj irrevocable, noncancelable, permanent, unalterable, uncancelable

nonresistant adj acquiescent, compliant, docile, easy, meek, mild, obedient, passive, resigned, submissive, tame, tolerant, unassertive, yielding

nonsense n 1 craziness, folly, foolishness, frivolity, insanity, lunacy, madness, mania, senselessness
n 2 baloney, bilge, bosh, bull, bunk, drivel, fiddlesticks, foolishness, junk, malar-

key, nothing, poppycock, rot, rubbish, schlock, silliness, trivia

nonstop adj express, fast, next-day, quick, rapid, speedy, swift

nonviolent adj calm, coolheaded, nonaggressive, pacifist, passive, peaceful

nook n 1 cabinet, chest, closet, compartment, cubby, locker, wardrobe
n 2 blank, cavity, crack, depression, emptiness, gap, hole, hollow, opening, space, void

noon n see: APEX n

norm n average, mean, median, medium, middle, par, rule, standard

normal adj 1 conventional, customary, habitual
adj 2 established, regular, standard, uniform
adj 3 average, common, intermediate, mediocre, medium, middle, ordinary, regular, standard, unimpressive
adj 4 average, common, commonplace, daily, everyday, general, mundane, natural, ordinary, plain, prevalent, regular, routine, typical, unexceptional, unremarkable, usual, workaday

normally adv as a rule, customarily, frequently, generally, mainly, most, mostly, most often, ordinarily, primarily, principally, usually

northeaster n blast, blizzard, blow, gale, gust, hurricane, snowstorm, squall, storm, tempest, typhoon, wind

nose n 1 bent, brains, brilliance, faculty, flair, genius, gift, head, intelligence, knack, prowess, talent
n 2 beak, bill, muzzle, nib, proboscis, prow, snout, trunk

nosh n bread, breakfast, brunch, chow, cuisine, diet, dinner, dish, edibles, entree, fare, food, grub, lunch, meals, nutrition, provisions, rations, snack, supper, victuals, vittles

no-show n absentee, hooky player, nonattender, truant

nostalgia n memory, recall, recollection, remembrance, reminiscence

nostalgic adj meditative, melancholy, musing, pensive, wistful

nosy adj curious, inquiring, inquisitive, investigative, probing, prying, questioning, snooping

notable adj acclaimed, celebrated, distinguished, eminent, esteemed, excellent, famed, famous, foremost, illustrious, outstanding, prestigious, prominent, renowned, well-known *n* celebrity, dignitary, luminary, movie star, name, personality, star

notably *adv* **1** chiefly, especially, particularly, primarily, specifically

adv **2** awfully, dreadfully, eminently, endlessly, exceedingly, exceptionally, extremely, greatly, highly, mightily, quite, remarkably, terribly, thoroughly, very

notandum *n* chit, letter, memo, memorandum, notation, note, record, reminder

notarize *v* attest, authenticate, certify, confirm, corroborate, justify, prove, ratify, sanction, substantiate, support, validate, verify, vouch, witness

notation *n* **1** chit, letter, memo, memorandum, notandum, note, record, reminder

n **2** allusion, connotation, hint, implication, innuendo, reference, suggestion

n **3** account, diary, digest, journal, log, memoir, minutes, notes, proceedings, record, recording, report

notch *n* **1** groove, opening, slot

n **2** copy, impression, imprint, indent, indentation, mark, print, stamp, tab

n **3** class, degree, grade, interval, level, mark, position, rank, rate, step

n **4** dent, groove, indentation

v ax, carve, chip, chop, cleave, cut, dissect, fell, hack, hew, mangle, mutilate, pulverize, rend, saw, sever, slice, sliver, snip, split, sunder, whittle

note *n* **1** comment, commentary, observation, remark, statement

n **2** bill, charge, check, debt, fee, invoice, tab

n **3** chit, letter, memo, memorandum, notandum, notation, record, reminder

n **4** air, call, carol, cry, lullaby, melody, rhapsody, song, tune

n **5** brilliance, celebrity, distinction, excellence, fame, glory, halo, honor, luster, popularity, prominence, renown, repute, splendor

n **6** attention, awareness, care, carefulness, cognizance, concern, consciousness, consideration, heed, intimacy, knowing, knowledge, mark, notice, observance, observation, perception, recognition, regard, remark, sense

n **7** see: COMMENDATION *n* 2

v **1** commemorate, remember

v **2** add, comment, declare, remark, say, state

v **3** copy, record, summarize, transcribe, type, write

v **4** capture, chart, denote, enter, itemize, jot, list, log, preserve, record, register, take notes, tally, tape, write down

notes *n* **1** assets, bills, capital, cash, coffers, currency, dinero, dollars, estate, funds, goods, income, lucre, means, money, pelf, pesos, property, resources, revenue, riches, rubles, shekels, sum, wealth

n **2** see: JOURNAL *n* 3

noteworthy *adj* **1** excellent, extraordinary, great, impressive, outstanding, shining, smashing, superb, wonderful

adj **2** amazing, brilliant, exceptional, extraordinary, phenomenal, rare, remarkable, significant, singular, stunning, super, uncommon, uncustomary, unique, unusual

nothing *n* **1** emptiness, nil, nothingness, oblivion, void

n **2** goose egg, naught, nil, none, nonentity, zero, zilch

n **3** see: NONSENSE *n* 2

nothingness *n* emptiness, nil, nothing, oblivion, void

notice *n* **1** announcement, placard, poster, proclamation, sign

n **2** attention, awareness, care, carefulness, cognizance, concern, consciousness, consideration, heed, intimacy, knowing, knowledge, mark, note, observance, observation, perception, recognition, regard, remark, sense

v **1** detect, experience, feel, perceive, sense

v **2** bill, charge, debit, dun, invoice, render, solicit

v **3** see: UNDERSTAND *v* 6

noticeable *adj* **1** appreciable, cognizant, concrete, detectable, discernible, observable, palpable, perceptible, sensible, tangible, visible

adj **2** arresting, astonishing, astounding, conspicuous, eye-catching, marked, obvious, pointed, prominent, salient, sensational, striking, stunning

notification *n* **1** citation, subpoena, summons, ticket, warrant, writ

n **2** communication, data, disclosure, exchange, expression, facts, information, intelligence, knowledge

notify *v* **1** cable, radio, telegraph, telex, wire

v **2** acquaint, advise, apprise, fill in, inform, post, tell, update

v **3** communicate, disclose, display, divulge, exhibit, inform, open, reveal, uncover, unveil

v **4** alert, augur, caution, flag, forebode, forewarn, indicate, inform, motion, signal, warn, wave

notion *n* **1** belief, superstition, tradition

n **2** caprice, fancy, humor, impulse, vagary, whim, whimsy

n **3** assumption, conclusion, conjecture, discretion, estimate, guess, judgment, presumption, theorization

n **4** concept, conception, hunch, idea, image, impression, perception, recollection, thought, view

n **5** bent, disposition, fancy, fondness, idea, inclination, liking, mind, pleasure, propensity, yen

n **6** see: CLUE *n* 2

n **7** see: EVALUATION *n* 2

notional *adj* see: FICTITIOUS *adj* 3

notoriety *n* censure, contempt, discredit, disfavor, disgrace, dishonor, disparagement, disrepute, humiliation, infamy, scandal, shame

notorious *adj* **1** despicable, infamous, offensive, scandalous, shady, unsavory, villainous

adj **2** arrant, barefaced, blatant, brassy, brazen, extreme, impudent, obtrusive, shameless, unabashed

adj **3** ill-famed, infamous, opprobrious

adj **4** atrocious, awful, crying, desperate, disgraceful, ghastly, grizzly, heinous, monstrous, odious, offensive, outrageous, scandalous, shocking, tasteless, wicked

notwithstanding *conj* albeit, although, even if, even though, whereas, while, whilst

adv at any rate, but, however, moreover, nevertheless, nonetheless, still, though, yet

nourish *v* **1** feed, fire, fuel, ignite, incite, kindle, light, propel, stoke, sustain

v **2** care, cherish, foster, mother, nurse, nurture, parent, protect, raise, rear, suckle

v **3** see: SERVE *v* 4

v **4** see: STRENGTHEN *v* 5

nourishment *n* **1** energy, provisions, rations, supply

n **2** food, nutriment, support, sustenance

novel *adj* **1** innovative, new, original, pioneering, trailblazing, unprecedented

adj **2** bright, contemporary, fresh, high-tech, modern, modernistic, new, recent, up-to-date

adj **3** see: UNUSUAL *adj* 4

n anecdote, description, fantasy, fiction, invention, myth, narration, narrative, sketch, story, tale, yarn

novelist *n* author, authoress, biographer, creator, dramatist, essayist, journalist, playwright, reporter, screenwriter, writer

novelty *n* antique, bric-a-brac, curio, curiosity, objet d'art, oddity, rarity, treasure, wonder

novice *adj* green, immature, inexperienced, naive, new, raw, unsophisticated, virgin

n **1** amateur, beginner, dabbler, dilettante, hobbyist, layman, neophyte, nonprofessional, part-timer

n **2** apprentice, beginner, disciple, freshman, intern, neophyte, newcomer, novitiate, pupil, recruit, rookie, student, tenderfoot, trainee

novitiate *n* apprentice, beginner, disciple, freshman, intern, neophyte, newcomer, novice, pupil, recruit, rookie, student, tenderfoot, trainee

now *adv* anon, any moment, at once, directly, immediately, instantaneously, instantly, momentarily, presently, promptly, quickly, right now, shortly, soon, straightaway, *tout de suite*

n current time, moment, nowadays, present, today

nowadays *n* current time, moment, now, present, today

noxious *adj* **1** harmful, poisonous, toxic, unhealthy

adj **2** baneful, deadly, fatal, lethal, mortal, pernicious, pestilent, ruinous

nozzle *n* cock, faucet, spigot, spout, tap, valve

nuance *n* degree, distinction, enhancement, shade, subtlety, touch, trace, variation

nuances *n* details, minutiae, particulars, second level, trivia

nub *n* edge, end, tip

nucleus *n* **1** cadre, center, core, framework, infrastructure

n **2** basis, body, bulk, core, essence, essentials, gist, heart, import, mass, object, staple, substance, volume

n **3** see: ESSENCE *n* 2, 3

nude *adj* bare, exposed, in the raw, naked, open, peeled, stripped, unclothed, uncovered, visible

nudge *v* **1** cue, jog, prompt, push, remind, stimulate, stir, suggest

v **2** boost, budge, drive, force, impel, propel, push, shove, thrust

v **3** berate, carp, cavil, criticize, find fault, flay, fuss, henpeck, nag, nit-pick, peck, quibble, scold

nuisance *n* annoyance, bother, conflict, contention, difference, discord, disharmony, dispute, dissension, dissent, dissidence, dissonance, disunity, division, hassle, inconvenience, mischief, strife, trouble, variance

nullify *v* 1 counter, counterbalance, negate, neutralize, offset, thwart

v 2 cancel, contradict, deny, disallow, forbid, negate, nix, override, overrule, reject, renege, repeal, revoke, torpedo, veto, void

v 3 abrogate, annul, cancel, contradict, discharge, dismantle, dissolve, dwindle, fade, negate, quash, recall, repeal, rescind, reverse, revoke, set aside, vacate, void

v 4 see: TERMINATE *v* 8

v 5 see: THWART *v* 4

numb *adj* 1 dazed, insensible, senseless, unconscious

adj 2 dormant, inert, sluggish, torpid

adj 3 see: INDIFFERENT *adj* 4

number *n* 1 calculation, summation

n 2 cipher, digit, integer, numeral

n 3 aggregate, amount, body, budget, bulk, count, quantity, tally, total

v 1 aggregate, paginate, sequence

v 2 aggregate, amount, plus, sum, total

v 3 calculate, cite, count, enumerate, itemize, list, numerate, tally

v 4 score, tally

numberless *adj* countless, immeasurable, incalculable, infinite, innumerable, innumerous, legion, many, uncountable, unlimited, untold

numbers *n* banking, economics, finance, statistics

numeral *n* cipher, digit, number

numerate *v* calculate, cite, count, enumerate, itemize, list, number, tally

numerous *adj* 1 abundant, ample, countless

adj 2 alternate, another, certain, different, discrete, disparate, dissimilar, distinct, diverse, other, separate, several, some, unlike, various, varying

adj 3 abundant, assorted, copious, diverse, extensive, legion, many, multifarious, multitudinous, myriad, plentiful, populous, prolific, sundry, various, voluminous

numerousness *n* see: HORDE *n*

numskull *n* see: IDIOT *n*

nurse *v* 1 aid, baby, care for, help, nurture, pamper, succor

v 2 care, cherish, foster, mother, nourish, nurture, parent, protect, raise, rear, suckle

v 3 suckle

n attendant, medic, orderly, therapist

nursemaid *n* baby sitter, nanny

nurture *n* aid, assistance, benefit, comfort, cure, hand, help, lift, relief, remedy, succor, support

v 1 aid, baby, care for, help, nurse, pamper, succor

v 2 care, cherish, foster, mother, nourish, nurse, parent, protect, raise, rear, suckle

v 3 see: HELP *v* 3, 4

v 4 see: SERVE *v* 4, 5

v 5 see: STRENGTHEN *v* 5

nurturing *adj* female, feminine, gentle, ladylike, tender, womanly

nut *n* 1 card, character, eccentric, kook, lunatic, oddball, weirdo

n 2 bolt, brad, peg, pin, rivet, spike, staple, stud, weld

n 3 bug, crusader, enthusiast, fanatic, fiend, freak, hobbyist, maniac, monomaniac, radical, zealot

nutriment *n* food, nourishment, support, sustenance

nutrition *n* bread, breakfast, brunch, chow, cuisine, diet, dinner, dish, edibles, entree, fare, food, grub, lunch, meals, nosh, provisions, rations, snack, supper, victuals, vittles

nuts *adj* absurd, balmy, bizarre, crazy, emotional, foolish, frivolous, goofy, illogical, impossible, inane, insane, irrational, loony, lunatic, mad, muddled, preposterous, ridiculous, silly, touched, wacky, zany

nuzzle *v* see: CARESS *v* 2

nymph *n* elf, fairy, naiad, pixie, sprite

nymphomaniac *n* coquette, flirt, harlot, seductress, siren, tart, tease, temptress, vamp, wanton woman

O

oaf *n* see: IDIOT *n*

oasis *n* see: SANCTUARY *n* 2

oath *n* assurance, declaration, pledge, promise, vow, word

obdurate *adj* see: NASTY *adj* 7

obedience *n* acquiescence, compliance, dependence, subjection, submission

obedient *adj* 1 amenable, complaisant, compliant, cooperative, submissive, subservient, tractable, willing

adj 2 acquiescent, compliant, docile, easy, meek, mild, nonresistant, passive, resigned, submissive, tame, tolerant, unassertive, yielding

obeisance *n* bow

obeisant *adj* 1 dedicated, deferential, devout, respectful

adj 2 abject, common, groveling, humble,

ingratiating, lowly, menial, obsequious, servile, slavish, subservient

obese *adj* 1 chubby, chunky, corpulent, fat, fleshy, gross, heavy, hefty, meaty, overweight, plump, portly, pudgy, rotund, stocky, stout

adj 2 see: BIG *adj* 3

obey *v* accommodate, comply, conform, follow, keep, mind, observe, submit

object *n* 1 article, element, entity, item, piece, thing

n 2 butt, casualty, prey, subject, sufferer, target, victim

n 3 being, entity, organism, sum, system, thing, totality, whole

n 4 see: SUBSTANCE *n* 9

v 1 mind

v 2 decline, delay, disagree

v 3 except, inveigh, kick, protest, remonstrate

v 4 complain, crab, criticize, grieve, gripe, grumble, mutter, nag, protest, whine

v 5 condemn, decline, disapprove, dismiss, exile, refuse, reject, reprobate, repudiate, spurn, turn down

v 6 belittle, deprecate, disapprove, disfavor, disparage

objection *n* 1 protest

n 2 beef, complaint, criticism, grievance, gripe, protest

n 3 challenge, demur, difficulty, hindrance, hurdle, obstacle, problem, protest, question, snag

objectionable *adj* 1 annoying, bad, difficult, disagreeable, displeasing, nasty, offensive, rotten, sour, unhappy, unpleasant, upsetting

adj 2 ill-favored, inadmissible, unacceptable, undesirable, unwanted, unwelcome

objective *adj* 1 concrete, corporeal, material, physical, real, sensible, substantial, tactile, tangible

adj 2 candid, dispassionate, equal, equitable, fair, impartial, impersonal, indifferent, just, neutral, open-minded, square, unbiased, uncolored, unprejudiced

n 1 ambition, bent, design, goal, intent, intention, meaning, plan, purpose

n 2 aim, goal, mission, motive, purpose, reason, sake, target, task

objectivity *n* equity, fairness, impartiality

objects *n* contents, junk, scrap, stuff, substance, things

oblation *n* alms, assistance, charity, contributions, dole, donations, offering

obligated *adj* 1 bound, committed, liable, required

adj 2 appreciative, grateful, indebted, obliged, thankful

obligation *n* 1 call, cause, occasion

n 2 commitment, guarantee, pledge, promise

n 3 debt, loan, promise, responsibility

n 4 affiliation, allegiance, association, connection, tie

n 5 encumbrance, indebtedness, liability, lien, mortgage, security

n 6 burden, charge, commitment, duty, onus, responsibility

n 7 assurance, bond, commitment, earnest, guarantee, pawn, pledge, security, surety, token, warrant

obligatory *adj* 1 binding, committed, compelling, unalterable

adj 2 compulsory, imperative, mandatory, must do, necessary, prerequisite, required

oblige *v* accommodate, convenience, favor, help, please, provide, serve

obliged *adj* appreciative, grateful, indebted, obligated, thankful

obliging *adj* amiable, complaisant, easy, good-humored, good-natured, lenient

oblique *adj* circuitous, circular, deviate, diagonal, indirect, round, roundabout

obliterate *v* abate, abolish, abrogate, annihilate, annul, call off, cancel, cease, delete, destroy, efface, erase, excise, expunge, invalidate, kill, negate, nullify, omit, quash, remove, stop, terminate, wipe out

oblivion *n* 1 limbo

n 2 emptiness, nil, nothing, void

oblivious *adj* 1 dense, ignorant, obtuse

adj 2 absent-minded, abstracted, bemused, careless, dazed, dizzy, groggy, inattentive, lost, mindless, preoccupied, silly, spaced, vapid

oblong *adj* elongated

obnoxious *adj* abhorrent, base, gross, invidious, offensive, repellent, repugnant, revulsive

obscene *adj* 1 coarse, crass, crude, flagrant, glaring, gross, rough, shocking, uncouth, uncultured, unrefined

adj 2 bawdy, coarse, crude, dirty, erotic, filthy, foul, gamy, gross, improper, indecent, lascivious, lewd, licentious, nasty, off-color, pornographic, profane, prurient, racy, rank, raunchy, ribald, risqué, scandalous, smutty, suggestive, tainted, uncouth, vulgar, x-rated

adj 3 see: SCATHING *adj*

obscenity *n* 1 abomination, blasphemy,

curse word, expletive, imprecation, profanity, swearing

n 2 dirt, filth, grossness, indecency, porn, pornography, ribaldry, smut, trash

obscure *adj* 1 concealed, covert, invisible, unseen, veiled

adj 2 distant, far, faraway, outlying, out-of-the-way, remote, removed

adj 3 anonymous, nameless, uncelebrated, unfamed, unheard-of, unknown, unnamed, unrenowned

adj 4 dark, dim, dusky, gloomy, lightless, murky, shadowy, somber, tenebrous, unilluminated

adj 5 arcane, hermetic, impenetrable, impervious, mysterious, mystic, puzzling, secret, unexaminable, unknown, unseen

adj 6 ambiguous, borderline, clouded, doubtful, dubious, equivocal, garbled, illogical, inarticulate, incalculable, incoherent, inexplicit, muddled, muffled, murky, precarious, questionable, shaky, suspect, suspicious, uncertain, unclear, uneasy, unintelligible, unsure, vague, wary

v becloud, bedim, befog, blur, cloud, confuse, darken, dim, diminish, dull, eclipse, fade, muddy, overshadow, pale, shade, shadow, tarnish

adj see: ESOTERIC *adj*

obsequious *adj* abject, common, groveling, humble, ingratiating, lowly, menial, obeisant, servile, slavish, subservient

observable *adj* appreciable, cognizant, concrete, detectable, discernible, noticeable, palpable, perceptible, sensible, tangible, visible

observance *n* 1 ceremonial, ceremony, formality, liturgy, rite, ritual, service

n 2 celebration, ceremony, commemoration, festival, festivity, fiesta, gala, holiday, party, revelry

n 3 attention, awareness, care, carefulness, cognizance, concern, consciousness, consideration, heed, intimacy, knowing, knowledge, mark, note, notice, observation, perception, recognition, regard, remark, sense

n 4 see: PRACTICE *n* 6

observant *adj* 1 advertent, alert, attentive, careful, heedful

adj 2 dependable, on time, precise, prompt, punctual, reliable, timely

observation *n* 1 espionage, reconnaissance, surveillance

n 2 analysis, assay, examination, experiment, test

n 3 comment, commentary, note, remark, statement

n 4 benchmark, criterion, gauge, measure, rule, standard, yardstick

n 5 attention, awareness, care, carefulness, cognizance, concern, consciousness, consideration, heed, intimacy, knowing, knowledge, mark, note, notice, observance, perception, recognition, regard, remark, sense

observe *v* 1 examine, inspect, peruse, scan

v 2 celebrate, commemorate, keep, memorialize, solemnize

v 3 accommodate, comply, conform, follow, keep, mind, obey, submit

v 4 bug, check, eavesdrop, monitor, oversee, snoop, spy, wiretap

v 5 eye, eyeball, gape, gawk, gaze, goggle, ogle, peer, stare, study

v 6 see: EXAMINE *v* 3, 9, 12

v 7 see: PROBE *v* 5

v 8 see: UNDERSTAND *v* 6

observer *n* lookout, outrider, scout

obsess *v* attend, frequent, hang around, hang out, haunt, patronize, resort to, visit

obsession *n* fetish, fixation, infatuation, passion, preoccupation

obsessive *adj* committed, determined, fixed, focused, narrow, one-track

obsolete *adj* ancient, antiquated, archaic, bygone, dated, dead, extinct, noncurrent, old, outdated, outmoded, passé, past, worn

obstacle *n* 1 bar, barricade, barrier, block, blockade, fence, roadblock, stop, wall

n 2 complication, difficulty, dilemma, plight, predicament, problem, quandary, situation, snag

n 3 blockage, bottleneck, catch, flaw, hitch, impediment, jam, obstruction, snag

n 4 bar, barrier, bottleneck, crimp, dead end, deadlock, difficulty, encumbrance, hurdle, impasse, impediment, obstruction, snag, stumbling block

n 5 challenge, demur, difficulty, hindrance, hurdle, objection, problem, protest, question, snag

n 6 confusion, conundrum, difficulty, dilemma, enigma, mystery, paradox, perplexity, problem, puzzle, quandary, question, riddle, secret

obstinate *adj* 1 balking, balky, contrary, cranky, disagreeable, irascible, mean, ornery, perverse, wayward

adj 2 adamant, ceaseless, dedicated, determined, firm, immovable, inexhaustible, inexorable, inflexible, narrow-minded, relentless, resolute, resolved, rigid, single-minded, steadfast, stubborn, unbendable, unbending, uncompromising, unswayable, unyielding

adj 3 bullheaded, closed-minded, deaf, firm, hardheaded, hard-line, inelastic, inflexible, intractable, intransigent, perverse, pigheaded, refractory, resolute, rigid, stiff, stubborn, tough, unbending, uncompromising, unpliable, unpliant, unwieldy, unyielding, willful

obstreperous *adj* blatant, boisterous, clamorous, disturbing, loud, loudmouthed, noisy, raucous, rowdy, tumultuous, vociferous

obstruct *v* 1 collide, conflict, hinder, impinge, interfere

v 2 block, close, occlude, plug, shut, stop

v 3 block, catch, cut off, detain, hinder, intercept, stop

v 4 defy, disobey, ignore, infringe, oppose, rebel, resist, violate

v 5 burden, check, encumber, hamper, hinder, impede, restrain, restrict, retard

v 6 abuse, blemish, damage, hamper, harm, hurt, impair, injure, mar, ruin, sabotage, scuttle, spoil, tarnish, vandalize

v 7 bar, block, brake, choke, clog, dam, deter, detract, encumber, frustrate, halt, hamper, hesitate, hinder, impair, impede, inhibit, jam, prevent, repress, restrain, retard, slow, stay, stop, stop up, throttle

obstruction *n* 1 blockage, bottleneck, catch, flaw, hitch, impediment, obstacle, snag

n 2 bar, barrier, bottleneck, crimp, dead end, deadlock, difficulty, encumbrance, hurdle, impasse, impediment, obstacle, snag, stumbling block

obstructionist *n* adversary, antagonist, naysayer, schmuck, shnook

obtain *v* 1 acquire, annex, buy, capture, gain, get, have, land, pick up, procure, purchase, requisition, secure, solicit, win

v 2 access, accomplish, achieve, attain, derive, earn, fulfill, gain, get, merit, net, perform, profit, rack up, reach, realize, score, win

v 3 acquire, earn, make, procure

obtrusive *adj* 1 busy, impertinent, intrusive, meddlesome, officious

adj 2 arrant, barefaced, blatant, brassy, brazen, extreme, impudent, notorious, shameless, unabashed

adj 3 see: VAIN *adj* 5

obtuse *adj* 1 ignorant, oblivious

adj 2 see: DUMB *adj* 2

obvious *adj* 1 outright, overt, public, visible

adj 2 arrogant, audacious, conspicuous, flagrant

adj 3 apparent, clear, conspicuous, distinct, evident, given, indisputable, indubitable, manifest, patent, plain, presumed, self-evident, straightforward, true, unambiguous, unequivocal, unmistakable

adj 4 see: PROMINENT *adj* 2

obviously *adv* clearly, evidently, plainly, undoubtedly, unquestionably

occasion *n* 1 event, milepost, milestone

n 2 instant, moment, time

n 3 call, cause, necessity, obligation

n 4 circumstance, episode, event, happening, incident, occurrence, scene, thing

n 5 break, chance, crack, gap, opening, opportunity, shot, show, stroke of luck, time

v cause, generate, induce, muster, produce

occasional *adj* few, infrequent, isolated, rare, scarce, seldom, sporadic, uncommon, unusual

occasionally *adv* every so often, now and then, once in a while, periodically, sometimes

occlude *v* block, close, obstruct, plug, shut, stop

occult *adj* 1 ambiguous, cryptic, enigmatic, mystifying, puzzling, vague

adj 2 enigmatic, incomprehensible, inexplicable, inscrutable, mysterious, puzzling

adj 3 abstruse, deep, esoteric, heartfelt, heavy, hermetic, insightful, mysterious, obscure, penetrating, profound, recondite

v see: DISGUISE *v* 2

occultism *n* bewitchment, enchantment, incantation, magic, sorcery, spell, voodoo, witchcraft, wizardry

occupancy *n* duration, hold, interval, length, tenure, term, time

occupant *n* 1 inhabitant, lessee, renter, resident, squatter, tenant

n 2 addressee, citizen, dweller, inhabitant, owner, resident, tenant

occupation *n* art, avocation, business, calling, career, discipline, employment, field, gig, job, labor, line, livelihood, office, profession, pursuit, role, schtick, situation, specialty, task, thing, trade, vocation, work

occupied *adj* busy, employed, engaged, functional, in use, working

occupy *v* 1 absorb, blot, consume, engross, engulf, soak up *v* 2 domicile, dwell, inhabit, live, reside, room, settle, stay

v 3 fill

occur *v* 1 happen

v 2 appear, arise, befall, break, come, come about, develop, do, ensue, evolve, fall out, happen, manifest, materialize, pass, rise, take place, transpire, turn up

occurrence *n* 1 case, eventuality

n 2 circumstance, episode, event, happening, incident, occasion, scene, thing

ocean *n* sea

ocular *adj* optic, optical, visual

odd *adj* 1 coincidental, curious, ironic, strange, unexpected

adj 2 charming, funny, old-fashioned, peculiar, picturesque, puzzling, quaint, remarkable, special, uncommon, unusual, whimsical

adj 3 exclusive, individual, lone, one, only, particular, separate, single, singular, sole, solitary, unique, unshared

adj 4 bizarre, eerie, ghostly, incredible, metaphysical, mystical, ominous, spooky, strange, supernatural, uncanny, unearthly, weird

adj 5 aberrant, bizarre, eccentric, erratic, oddball, outlandish, peculiar, quaint, queer, singular, strange, uncanny, unconventional, unusual, weird

adj 6 curious, exotic, far-out, fascinating, intriguing, kinky, marvelous, mysterious, new, novel, outlandish, strange, ultra, unaccustomed, unexplored, unfamiliar, unique, unknown, unusual, weird

adj 7 see: ACCIDENTAL *adj* 3

oddball *adj* aberrant, bizarre, eccentric, erratic, odd, outlandish, peculiar, quaint, queer, singular, strange, uncanny, unconventional, unusual, weird

n card, character, eccentric, kook, lunatic, nut, weirdo

oddity *n* 1 abnormality, eccentricity, habit, idiosyncrasy, peculiarity, quirk, trademark

n 2 antique, bric-a-brac, curio, curiosity, novelty, objet d'art, rarity, treasure, wonder

odious *adj* 1 abhorrent, abominable, appalling, detestable, disgusting, dreadful, evil, frightful, ghastly, hateful, horrible, horrid, loathsome, repulsive, revolting, shocking

adj 2 atrocious, awful, crying, desperate, disgraceful, ghastly, grizzly, heinous, monstrous, notorious, offensive, outra-

geous, scandalous, shocking, tasteless, wicked

odor *n* 1 aroma, fragrance, scent, smell

n 2 reek, smell, stench, stink

odorize *v* perfume

off *adj* 1 down, idle, lax, slack, slow, sluggish

adj 2 see: TRIVIAL *adj* 2

offbeat *adj* bizarre, bohemian, unconventional, unorthodox

off-center *adj* crazy, eccentric

off-color *adj* see: VULGAR *adj* 2

offend *v* 1 affront, encounter, face, insult, outrage, slight

v 2 err, fall, sin, transgress, trespass, violate

v 3 amaze, daze, electrify, horrify, outrage, overwhelm, scandalize, shock, stun

offended *adj* alienated, angry, bitter, emotional, hurt, jealous, provoked, resentful

offender *n* accused, con, convict, criminal, crook, culprit, delinquent, felon, guilty party, inmate, lawbreaker, perpetrator, prisoner, scofflaw, suspect, swindler, transgressor, wrongdoer

offense *n* 1 aggression, assault, attack, incursion, inroad, offensive, onset, onslaught

n 2 anger, animosity, hostility, huff, indignation, miff, pique, resentment

n 3 error, malfeasance, malpractice, misbehavior, misdeed, mismanagement, transgression, wrong, wrongdoing

n 4 crime, dishonor, disobedience, evil, fault, felony, infamy, infraction, iniquity, injury, lawbreaking, misdeed, misdemeanor, outrage, sin, transgression, trespass, vice, violation, wrong, wrongdoing

offensive *adj* 1 abusive, contemptuous, derisive, disrespectful, insulting, nasty, slighting

adj 2 despicable, infamous, notorious, scandalous, shady, unsavory, villainous

adj 3 abhorrent, base, gross, invidious, obnoxious, repellent, repugnant, revulsive

adj 4 improper, indecent, indelicate, lewd, malodorous, off-color, rough, scurrilous, suggestive, unbecoming, unseemly, untoward

adj 5 annoying, bad, difficult, disagreeable, displeasing, nasty, objectionable, rotten, sour, unhappy, unpleasant, upsetting

adj 6 atrocious, awful, crying, desperate, disgraceful, ghastly, grizzly, heinous, monstrous, notorious, odious, outrageous, scandalous, shocking, tasteless, wicked *n* 1 attack, attempt, blockade, bout, campaign, siege

n 2 aggression, assault, attack, incursion, inroad, offense, onset, onslaught

adj appalling, awful, dire, dreadful, fearful, formidable, frightening, frightful, ghastly, horrendous, horrible, ominous, portentous, scary, shocking, spooky, terrible, terrifying, unpleasant

offer *n* 1 approach, come-on, overture, proposal, proposition, suggestion

n 2 bid, expectation, hope, inducement, invitation, motion, proffer, proposal, proposition, recommendation, request, suggestion

v 1 connote, hint, implant, imply, infer, insinuate, lead, put forth, seed

v 2 bid, counsel, endorse, pose, present, proffer, propose, proposition, put forth, recommend, suggest, urge

v 3 allude, assume, extend, hypothesize, imagine, pose, present, presume, propose, speculate, suggest, suppose, surmise, theorize

v 4 see: GIVE *v* 8

v 5 see: TRY *v* 4

offering *n* 1 alms, assistance, charity, contributions, dole, donations

n 2 see: FEE *n* 5

offhand *adj* ad-lib, extemporaneous, impromptu, improvised, instantaneous, invented, off the cuff, spontaneous, unrehearsed, unstudied

office *n* 1 branch, department, division, unit

n 2 building, facility, place, service

n 3 appointment, connection, duty, function, job, position, post, situation

n 4 see: STANDING *n* 1

n 5 see: TRADE *n* 3

officers *n* authority, brass, elders, leaders, management

official *adj* basic, established, standard

n 1 bureaucrat, civil servant, clerk, pen pusher

n 2 adviser, artist, authority, expert, guru, master, pro, professional, specialist, veteran, virtuoso, wizard

officialdom *n* bureaucracy, red tape, regulations

officials *n* see: ADMINISTRATION *n* 3

officious *adj* busy, impertinent, intrusive, meddlesome

off-key *adj* see: IRREGULAR *adj* 2

offset *v* 1 counter, counterbalance, negate, neutralize, nullify, thwart

v 2 adjust, balance, compensate, make equal, make up, outweigh, redeem, set off

offsetting *adj* excusable, extenuating, justifying

offshore *adj* foreign, imported

offspring *n* 1 child, descendant, heir, progeny, scion

n 2 brood, children, descendants, posterity, progeny

often *adv* 1 frequently, regularly, repeatedly, typically, usually

adv 2 chronically, commonly, constantly, continually, customarily, daily, every day, familiarly, frequently, habitually, recurringly, regularly, routinely, traditionally, usually

ogle *v* 1 grimace, leer, mock, scorn, smirk, sneer

v 2 eye, eyeball, gape, gawk, gaze, goggle, observe, peer, stare, study

ogre *n* animal, beast, being, brute, monster

oil *n* 1 lube, lubrication, ointment, salve

n 2 acrylic, art, canvas, depiction, drawing, etching, illustration, landscape, lithograph, mural, painting, pastel, pen and ink, picture, portrait, print, seascape, sketch, still life, watercolor

v anoint

oily *adj* greasy, sleek, slick, slippery, smooth, unctuous

ointment *n* lube, lubrication, moistener, oil, salve

old *adj* 1 bygone, erstwhile, former, late, once, onetime, past, sometime

adj 2 aged, age-old, ancient, antique, elderly, gray, grizzled, olden, senior, timeworn, venerable, vintage, worn

adj 3 continuing, enduring, inveterate, lifelong, long-lasting, long-lived, ongoing, perennial

adj 4 ancient, antiquated, archaic, bygone, dated, dead, extinct, noncurrent, obsolete, outdated, outmoded, passé, past, worn

olden *adj* see: OLD *adj* 2

older *adj* elder, first, senior

oldest *adj* elder, first, older, senior

ombudsman *n* advocate, ally, angel, backer, benefactor, booster, champion, cheerleader, donor, friend, guarantor, helper, partner, patron, promoter, proponent, sponsor, supporter

omen *n* apprehension, foreboding, forewarning, harbinger, intuition, premonition, presage, sign, warning

ominous *adj* 1 foreboding, imminent, impending, menacing, portentous, predictive, prophetic, sinister, threatening

adj 2 bad, baleful, corrupt, cunning, forbidding, harmful, hurtful, malevolent, malignant, menacing, sinister, sneaky

adj 3 bizarre, eerie, ghostly, incredible, metaphysical, mystical, odd, spooky, strange, supernatural, uncanny, unearthly, weird

adj 4 appalling, awful, dire, dreadful, fearful, formidable, frightening, frightful, ghastly, horrendous, horrible, offensive, portentous, scary, shocking, spooky, terrible, terrifying, unpleasant

omission *n* absence, disregard, error, neglect, oversight, slip-up

omit *v* 1 banish, bar, blackball, cut, debar, dismiss, eliminate, except, exclude, ignore, leave out, suspend

v 2 defy, discount, disregard, exclude, forget, ignore, miss, neglect, ostracize, overlook, overpass, pass, pass by, pass over, shun, skip, slight, snub

v 3 abate, abolish, abrogate, annihilate, annul, call off, cancel, cease, delete, destroy, efface, erase, excise, expunge, invalidate, kill, negate, nullify, obliterate, quash, remove, stop, terminate, wipe out

omitted *adj* absent, away, gone, lacking, missing, truant, wanting

omnibus *n* auto, automobile, bus, car, carriage, chariot, coach, jeep, motorcar, sedan, truck, van, vehicle, wagon

omnipotent *adj* invincible, mighty, powerful, supreme

omnipresent *adj* ubiquitous, widespread

on *prep* adjacent to, around, at, atop, beside, by, near

once *adj* 1 forgotten, gone, left behind, lost, past, suppressed, unremembered, vague

adj 2 bygone, erstwhile, former, late, old, onetime, past, sometime

adv before, earlier, first, formerly, heretofore, hitherto, previously, prior to

oncoming *adj* advancing, approaching, forthcoming, imminent, looming, nearing, pending

one *adj* 1 a, a few, any, at least one, each, every, individual, several, some

adj 2 exclusive, individual, lone, odd, only, particular, separate, single, singular, sole, solitary, unique, unshared

adj 3 see: UNIQUE *adj* 2, 3

one-fourth *n* quarter

oneness *n* distinctiveness, individuality, singularity, singularness, unity

onerous *adj* 1 arduous, burdensome, demanding, exacting, grievous, oppressive, taxing, tough, trying

adj 2 annoying, bothersome, glaring, harassing, irksome, irritating, mean, painful,

pesky, troublesome, ugly, unwelcome, vexatious, wicked

onerously *adv* arduously, difficultly, laboriously, painfully

onetime *adj* bygone, erstwhile, former, late, old, once, past, sometime

one-track *adj* committed, determined, fixed, focused, limited, narrow, obsessive

ongoing *adj* 1 continuing, current, going

adj 2 constant, continuing, durable, enduring, eternal, lasting, permanent, stable

adj 3 continuing, enduring, inveterate, lifelong, long-lasting, long-lived, old, perennial

adj 4 ageless, boundless, ceaseless, constant, continual, continuous, endless, eternal, everlasting, incessant, infinite, interminable, limitless, never-ending, perpetual, persistent, relentless, timeless, unceasing, unending, uninterrupted, unremitting

only *adv* but, except that, further, however, just, merely, nevertheless, simply, solely, yet

adj 1 alone, incomparable, matchless, peerless, unequaled, unique, unmatched, unpaired, unparalleled, unrivaled

adj 2 exclusive, individual, lone, odd, one, particular, separate, single, singular, sole, solitary, unique, unshared

onset *n* 1 aggression, assault, attack, incursion, inroad, offense, offensive

n 2 beginning, birth, debut, delivery, inception, kindling, outset, start

onslaught *n* 1 assault, attack, blitz, raid, strike

n 2 aggression, assault, attack, incursion, inroad, offense, offensive, onset

onus *n* 1 burden, charge, commitment, duty, responsibility

n 2 accountability, blame, burden, culpability, fault, guilt, responsibility, shame, stigma

onward *adv* ahead, before, beyond, forward

oodles *n* see: HORDE *n*

ooze *v* 1 flow, gurgle, purl, spurt

v 2 dribble, drip, drop, leak, run, seep, trickle

v 3 discharge, drip, emit, exude, leak, secrete, seep, trickle

open *adj* 1 patent, unclosed, unobstructed

adj 2 due, outstanding, owed, payable, unpaid

adj 3 airy, breezy, brisk, drafty, gusty, windy

adj 4 ample, big, capacious, comfortable, commodious, roomy, spacious, vast, wide *adj* 5 bare, exposed, in the raw, naked, nude, peeled, stripped, unclothed, uncovered, visible

adj 6 artless, candid, frank, guileless, ingenuous, innocent, naive, natural, plain, simple, simple-hearted, unadorned, unaffected, unsophisticated, unstudied, untutored, unworldly

adj 7 ajar, cracked, unshut

adj 8 illogical, inconclusive, indecisive, indefinite, unconvincing, unsettled, unverified

adj 9 candid, direct, earnest, forthright, frank, genuine, heartfelt, hearty, honest, no-holds-barred, real, sincere, straightforward, true, trustworthy, truthful, undesigning, unfeigned, unpretentious, wholehearted

adj 10 accessible, available, close, convenient, feasible, functional, handy, helpful, multipurpose, nearby, practical, public, reachable, ready, serviceable, suitable, unrestricted, usable, useful, utilitarian, well-suited, within reach, working

v 1 crack, husk, peel, remove, shell

v 2 broaden, enlarge, spread, widen

v 3 expand, extend, fan, outstretch, spread, unfold

v 4 communicate, disclose, display, divulge, exhibit, inform, notify, reveal, uncover, unveil

v 5 unblock, undo, unlock, unshut

v 6 disengage, extricate, loosen, unbind, unclasp, undo, unfasten, unknot, unloose, unloosen, untie

v 7 air, bring up, broach, communicate, discuss, expose, express, give, introduce, put, reveal, state, tap, tell, vent, ventilate, verbalize

v 8 activate, begin, cause, commence, constitute, create, embark, enter, establish, inaugurate, induct, initiate, install, instigate, instill, institute, introduce, kick off, launch, lead off, originate, precipitate, preface, set up, start, tee off, usher in, venture forth

open-air *adj* alfresco, outdoor, outside

open-eyed *adj* alert, careful, cautious, unsleeping, vigilant, wakeful, wary, watchful, wide-awake

openhanded *adj* bounteous, bountiful, free, generous, handsome, liberal, unsparing

opening *adj* beginning, introductory, preliminary, preparatory, prior

n 1 groove, notch, slot

n 2 crack, hole, leak, puncture

n 3 place, position, slot, vacancy

n 4 crack, cut, gash, rent, slit, trench

n 5 access, aperture, approach, entrance, inlet, mouth, passage

n 6 breach, break, crack, fracture, gap, space, split

n 7 break, chance, crack, gap, occasion, opportunity, shot, show, stroke of luck, time

n 8 blank, cavity, crack, depression, emptiness, gap, hole, hollow, nook, space, void

n 9 gullet, mouth, orifice

n 10 gap, portal, window

open-minded *adj* see: FAIR *adj* 7

opera *n* libretto, musical, operetta, score

operate *v* 1 carry on, conduct, direct, keep, manage, ordain, oversee, pilot, run

v 2 see: GUIDE *v* 3

operation *n* 1 action, battle, engagement, fray, gesture, movement, proceeding

n 2 appliance, application, employment, form, method, play, technique, use, utilization

operative *adj* active, alive, functioning, live, running, working

operator *n* 1 architect, designer, draftsperson, engineer, inventor, manager, plotter, schemer, surveyor

n 2 airman, aviator, barnstormer, pilot

operetta *n* libretto, musical, opera, score

opinion *n* 1 advice, counsel, recommendation, suggestion

n 2 consensus, feeling, flavor, sense

n 3 expression, say, say-so, voice

n 4 assumption, conjecture, deduction, supposition, surmise

n 5 adjudication, award, determination, judgment, ruling, sentence, verdict

n 6 angle, aspect, facet, hand, mien, perspective, phase, side, slant, view

n 7 analysis, assessment, commentary, criticism, critique, evaluation, examination, judgment, notion, review, ruling

n 8 attitude, belief, bias, conviction, feeling, inducement, leaning, mind, persuasion, sentiment, slant, view

n 9 see: PRINCIPLE *n* 5

opinionated *adj* aristocratic, arrogant, authoritarian, authoritative, autocratic, belligerent, bossy, despotic, dictatorial, dogmatic, domineering, haughty, imperial, imperious, masterful, militaristic, oppressive, overbearing, peremptory, pushy, stubborn

opponent *n* adversary, antagonist, anti, challenger, competitor, con, contender, enemy, foe, match, rival

opportune *adj* auspicious, favorable, propitious, seasonable, timely

opportunism *n* see: UTILITY *n*

opportunity *n* 1 chance, freedom, latitude, room

n 2 break, chance, crack, gap, occasion, opening, shot, show, stroke of luck, time

oppose *v* 1 attack, challenge, contradict, deny, impugn, rebut

v 2 attack, battle, combat, contend, fight, struggle, war

v 3 check, resist, stanch, stem, stop, weather, withstand

v 4 defy, disobey, ignore, infringe, obstruct, rebel, resist, violate

v 5 argue, confer, contest, contradict, contrast, debate, dialogue, differ, disagree, discord, discuss, dispute, dissent, divide, vary

v 6 combat, compete, contend, contest, counter, dispute, duel, fight, match, parry, pit, play, repel, resist, rival, strive, struggle, vie

opposed *adj* 1 adverse, against, antagonistic, anti, contrary, opposing

adj 2 conflicting, contradictory, contrary, converse, counter, diametric, inverse, opposing, opposite, polar, reverse

adj 3 afraid, averse, disinclined, hesitant, indisposed, loath, recalcitrant, reluctant, shy, timid, uneager, unwilling

opposing *adj* 1 competing, rival, vying

adj 2 adverse, antagonistic, anti, opposed

adj 3 see: CONFLICTING *adj* 2

opposite *adj* 1 different, disparate, diverse, incongruous, unequal, unlike, unmatched, unrelated

adj 2 conflicting, contradictory, contrary, converse, counter, diametric, inverse, opposed, opposing, polar, reverse

n antithesis, converse, reverse

prep across from, fronting

opposition *n* 1 antagonism, antithesis, con

n 2 contrast, difference, dissimilarity, distinction

n 3 aversion, disfavor, dislike, displeasure, distaste

oppress *v* 1 attack, beat, scourge, smite

v 2 aggrieve, exploit, persecute, torture

v 3 burden, encumber, hamper, load, overdo, overload, saddle, strain, tax

v 4 see: CONCERN *v* 3

oppression *n* austerity, rigidity, severity, tyranny

oppressive *adj* 1 arduous, burdensome, demanding, exacting, grievous, onerous, taxing, tough, trying

adj 2 see: AUTHORITATIVE *adj* 2

adj 3 see: GLOOMY *adj* 5

opprobrious *adj* infamous, notorious

opt *v* appoint, ballot, choose, elect, nominate, select, vote

optic *adj* optical, visual

optical *adj* ocular, optic, visual

optimal *adj* 1 ideal, model, perfect, very

adj 2 foremost, majority, maximum, most, top, unequaled

optimistic *adj* 1 affirmative, positive

adj 2 auspicious, cheerful, confident, encouraging, hopeful, promising, sanguine, upbeat

optimize *v* augment, enhance, magnify, maximize, utilize

optimum *adj* best, prime, select, superior, top

n best, choice, elite, favorite, finest, pick, pride, select

option *n* 1 choice, means, recourse, remedy

n 2 ballot, choice, franchise, preference, say, selection, vote

n 3 alternative, choice, preference, rathers, selection, vote

optional *adj* 1 elective

adj 2 deliberate, free, intentional, unforced, unprescribed, voluntary, willful, willing

options *n* alternatives, possibilities, potential

opulence *n* see: WEALTH *n* 1

opulent *adj* 1 affluent, copious, leisure class, loaded, moneyed, rich, wealthy, well-to-do

adj 2 abundant, cornucopian, extravagant, exuberant, garish, generous, lavish, lush, luxuriant, prodigal, profuse, rich, wasteful

adj 3 choice, deluxe, elegant, first-class, grand, luxuriant, luxurious, ornate, palatial, plush, posh, rich, soft, stately, sumptuous, thick

opus *n* 1 chronicle, epic, legend, saga, story, tale

n 2 book, correspondence, edition, folio, issue, manuscript, monograph, paperback, printing, publication, text, tome, volume, work, writing

oracle *n* 1 astrologer, augur, fortuneteller, predictor, prophet, psychic, seer, soothsayer, visionary

n 2 apocalypse, prophecy, revelation, vision

oral *adj* expressed, spoken, stated, unwritten, verbal, word-of-mouth

n exam, examination, final, inquiry, questionnaire, quiz, test

orange *adj* apricot, coral, salmon, tangerine

orate *v* **1** announce, articulate, assert, couch, describe, dictate, draft, enunciate, express, intonate, phrase, proclaim, pronounce, say, speak, state, stress, talk, utter, verbalize, vocalize, voice, word

v **2** see: INFORM *v* 6

oratory *n* rhetoric

orb *n* ball, balloon, globe, sphere

orbit *n* **1** curve, flight path, trajectory

n **2** see: REACH *n* 3

orchestra *n* band, ensemble, strings

orchestral *adj* choral, euphonious, harmonious, lyric, mellow, melodic, melodious, musical, philharmonic, rhythmical, symphonic, tuneful, vocal

orchestrate *v* **1** arrange, blend, combine, compound, concoct, harmonize, integrate, make one, synthesize, unify

v **2** cogitate, collude, connive, conspire, contrive, devise, frame, intrigue, machinate, maneuver, plan, plot, scheme

orchid *adj* amethyst, lavender, lilac, mauve, plum, purple, violet

ordain *v* **1** approve, authorize, decree, enact, legalize, legislate, pass, ratify, sanction

v **2** carry on, conduct, direct, keep, manage, operate, oversee, pilot, run

v **3** see: MANDATE *v*

ordained *adj* definite, determined, fixed, foregone, inevitable, inexorable, irrevocable, predestined, unalterable, unavoidable, unchangeable

ordeal *n* **1** adventure, encounter, event, experience, hazard, peril, risk

n **2** see: FEAR *n* 3

order *n* **1** line, queue, rank

n **2** contract, purchase order, requisition, sale

n **3** line, priority, procession, sequence, succession, timing

n **4** arrangement, blueprint, method, orderliness, outline, pattern, plan, system

n **5** chain, course, lineup, progression, row, run, sequence, series, string, succession, train

n **6** see: CATEGORY *n*

n **7** see: COMMAND *n* 3

v **1** arrange, array, dispose, marshal, organize, systemize

v **2** bid, charge, claim, command, demand, direct, enjoin, instruct

v **3** advise, authorize, command, decree, designate, dictate, direct, mandate, ordain, rule

v **4** see: ASSEMBLE *v* 3

v **5** see: CLASSIFY *v* 2

v **6** see: GOVERN *v* 4

ordered *adj* aligned, neat, proper, straight

ordering *n* arrangement, disposal, disposition, distribution, grouping, sequence

orderliness *n* arrangement, blueprint, method, order, outline, pattern, plan, system

orderly *adj* **1** methodic, methodical, recurring, regular, steady, systematic

adj **2** meticulous, neat, prim, shipshape, tidy, trim, well-groomed

n attendant, medic, nurse, therapist

ordinance *n* behest, bidding, canon, charge, command, criterion, decree, dictate, direction, edict, fiat, guideline, injunction, institution, law, mandate, order, precept, prescript, prescription, regulation, rite, rule, ruling, statute, word

ordinarily *adv* as a rule, customarily, frequently, generally, mainly, most, mostly, most often, normally, primarily, principally, usually

ordinary *adj* **1** banal, commonplace, conventional, trite, undistinguished

adj **2** common, commonplace, dull, pedestrian, prosaic, uneventful, unexceptional

adj **3** average, common, intermediate, mediocre, medium, middle, normal, regular, standard, unimpressive

adj **4** casual, cavalier, colloquial, familiar, informal, regular, relaxed, unceremonious, unconstrained, unofficial, usual, vernacular

adj **5** average, common, commonplace, daily, everyday, general, mundane, natural, normal, plain, prevalent, regular, routine, typical, unexceptional, unremarkable, usual, workaday

adj **6** see: MONOTONOUS *adj* 1

ordnance *n* ammo, ammunition, armor, arms, equipment, guns, machinery, munitions, weapons

organ *n* **1** bulletin, daily, journal, newsletter, newspaper, publication, review

n **2** genitalia, genitals, gonad

organism *n* being, entity, object, sum, system, thing, totality, whole

organization *n* **1** association, institute, institution, society, union

n **2** complex, infrastructure, network, system

n **3** business, company, concern, corporation, enterprise, establishment, firm, house, partnership

n 4 association, body, club, company, contingent, delegation, fellowship, fraternity, group, guild, society, union

n 5 assembly, association, band, bevy, brood, bunch, camp, clique, cluster, collection, covey, crew, flock, group, party, team, unit

n 6 see: ALLIANCE n

n 7 see: TECHNIQUE n 3

organizational *adj* collective, common, group, public, social, societal

organize *v* 1 arrange, array, dispose, marshal, order, systemize

v 2 arrange, bespeak, book, engage, plan, program, reserve, schedule, slate

v 3 align, arrange, array, assort, catalog, categorize, class, classify, cluster, compile, file, format, grade, group, lay out, line up, list, order, outline, pigeonhole, place, position, prioritize, program, rank, rate, sort, stack, tabulate

v 4 arrange, conceive, conceptualize, structure

v 5 arrange, neaten, pick up, tidy

v 6 arrange, cater, deliver, dish out, dispense, feed, furnish, give, hand, nourish, nurture, provide, purvey, serve, supply, sustain

organizer *n* agitator, initiator, instigator, rabble-rouser, spark plug, troublemaker

orgy *n* bash, bender, binge, do, party, spree

orifice *n* mouth, opening

origin *n* 1 birth, creation, fountain, genesis, parent, root, source

n 2 ancestry, blood, blood line, descent, family, genealogy, heritage, line, lineage, pedigree, stock, strain

n 3 beginning, conception, cradle, derivation, fountainhead, inception, infancy, mother, root, seed, stem, source

original *adj* 1 nonconformist, unbounded, unconventional

adj 2 innovative, new, novel, pioneering, trailblazing, unprecedented

adj 3 earliest, first, founding, fundamental, initial, maiden, pioneer, primary, prime

adj 4 aboriginal, ancient, early, former, prehistoric, primeval, primitive, primordial, rudimentary

adj 5 basic, early, elementary, embryonic, essential, fundamental, initial, intrinsic, rudimentary, underlying

originality *n* 1 innovation

n 2 distinctiveness, individuality, uniqueness

originate *v* 1 arise, come from, derive, emanate, flow, head, issue, spring, stem

v 2 begin, coin, conceive, craft, create, define, develop, devise, formulate, innovate, invent, make, start

v 3 activate, begin, cause, commence, constitute, create, embark, enter, establish, inaugurate, induct, initiate, install, instigate, instill, institute, introduce, kick off, launch, lead off, open, precipitate, preface, set up, start, tee off, usher in, venture forth

v 4 come from

v 5 bear, beget, breed, come into, create, effect, engender, father, generate, hatch, impregnate, make, mate, multiply, parent, procreate, promulgate, propagate, reproduce, sire, spawn

originative *adj* causal, causative, germinal

originator *n* author, creator, founder, initiator, instigator, inventor, maker, parent, pioneer, seed, source

ornament *n* adornment, decoration, embellishment

v adorn, beautify, bedeck, deck, decorate, dress up, embellish, enhance, garnish, glamorize, grace, polish, trim

ornate *adj* 1 abundant, elaborate, flamboyant, luscious, replete

adj 2 see: LUXURIOUS adj 2

ornery *adj* 1 argumentative, cantankerous, contentious, controversial, debatable, disputatious, ill-natured

adj 2 balking, balky, contrary, cranky, disagreeable, irascible, mean, obstinate, perverse, wayward

orphaned *adj* bastard, fatherless, illegitimate, misbegotten, motherless, spurious, unauthentic, ungenuine

orthodox *adj* 1 straight, traditional, unhip

adj 2 devout, narrow, strict, unquestioning

adj 3 conventional, correct, decorous, fitting, nice, polite, proper, right, suitable, well

oscillate *v* 1 alternate, fluctuate, pendulate, sway, swing, vacillate, wave

v 2 alternate, change, cycle, lap, rotate, shift, switch

v 3 dance, flap, flicker, flitter, flutter, prance, sparkle, sway, twinkle, undulate, wave

v 4 fluctuate, pulsate, surge, throb, undulate, vibrate

ostensible *adj* 1 conceivable, likely, plausible, possible, probable

adj 2 apparent, illusive, illusory, quasi, seeming, specious, superficial

ostentatious *adj* 1 blatant, brazen, conspicuous, flagrant, flashy, garish, gaudy, glaring, loud, showy, tacky, tasteless, tawdry, tinsel

adj 2 ambitious, bombastic, flamboyant, garish, grandiose, inflated, jaunty, lofty, pompous, portentous, pretentious, showy, splendid, splashy, utopian, visionary

ostracize *v* 1 differentiate, discriminate, exclude, isolate, segregate, separate, sequester

v 2 banish, cast out, deport, dispel, displace, exile, expatriate, expel, extradite, oust, relegate, remove

v 3 blackball, boycott, cut, ignore, rebuff, snub, spurn

v 4 defy, discount, disregard, exclude, forget, ignore, miss, neglect, omit, overlook, overpass, pass, pass by, pass over, shun, skip, slight, snub

other *adj* 1 alternate, another, certain, different, discrete, disparate, dissimilar, distinct, diverse, numerous, separate, several, some, unlike, various, varying

adj 2 see: ADDITIONAL *adj* 2

ought *v* must

oust *v* 1 depose, discharge, remove, unseat

v 2 dislocate, dislodge, displace, disturb, move, remove, shift, ship, transfer

v 3 see: BANISH *v* 1

ouster *n* dismissal, ejection, expulsion, extraction, firing, impeachment, removal, termination

out *v* douse, extinguish, put out, quench

outback *n* frontier, hinterland, outland, threshold

outbreak *n* 1 fight, incident, scene, spectacle, tantrum

n 2 see: COMMOTION *n* 1

outburst *n* 1 eruption, flare-up

n 2 see: REPRIMAND *n*

outcast *n* derelict, outsider, recluse

outcome *n* 1 consequence, end, issue, result

n 2 climax, payoff, result, return, reward

n 3 conclusion, culmination, denouement, resolution, result, solution

n 4 aftermath, consequence, corollary, effect, eventuality, reaction, repercussion, result, reverberation, reward, upshot

outdated *adj* 1 ancient, antiquated, archaic, bygone, dated, dead, extinct, noncurrent, obsolete, old, outmoded, passé, past, worn

outdo *v* 1 best, defeat, down, outmaneuver, outsmart, outwit

v 2 beat, best, better, cap, dwarf, eclipse, exceed, excel, go beyond, outgo, outshine,

outstrip, overshadow, pass, surpass, top, transcend

outdoor *adj* alfresco, open-air, outside

outermost *adj* extreme, farthest, furthermost, furthest, hindmost, most distant, most remote, utmost

outfit *n* band, body, company, corps, group, party, troop, troupe

v 1 clothe, fit, furnish, provide, supply

v 2 accouter, apparel, array, attire, clad, clothe, dress, garb, gear

v 3 appoint, arm, equip, fortify, furnish, gear, man, rig, set up, supply, turn out

outgo *v* see: SURPASS *v* 2

outgoing *adj* see: FRIENDLY *adj* 3

outgrowth *n* 1 continuation, corollary, epilogue, sequel, supplement

n 2 see: PRODUCT *n* 1

outing *n* 1 drive, excursion, jaunt, journey, ride, spin

n 2 barbecue, cookout, picnic

outland *adj* bucolic, country, garden, pastoral, peaceful, provincial, rural, rustic, suburban, wooded

n frontier, hinterland, outback, threshold

outlandish *adj* 1 outrageous, unbelievable, unheard-of

adj 2 back, frontier, remote, unsettled

adj 3 excessive, exorbitant, expensive, extravagant, extreme, ghastly, lavish, overpriced, profuse, ultimate, unbelievable

adj 4 aberrant, bizarre, eccentric, erratic, odd, oddball, peculiar, quaint, queer, singular, strange, uncanny, unconventional, unusual, weird

adj 5 see: UNUSUAL *adj* 4

outlast *v* 1 outlive, outwear, survive

v 2 see: STAY *v* 4

outlaw *n* 1 escapee, fugitive, runaway

n 2 bandit, brigand, burglar, cheat, con artist, con man, criminal, crook, embezzler, gyp, highwayman, looter, mugger, robber, swindler, thief

v ban, bar, confine, enjoin, forbid, inhibit, nix, prevent, prohibit, stop, suppress, veto

outlay *n* charge, cost, expense, fare, payment, price, rate, value, worth

outlet *n* doorway, exit, gateway, portal

outline *n* 1 contour, form, profile, shape

n 2 definition, design, distinctness, precision, specificity

n 3 boundaries, form, framework, pattern, structure

n 4 arrangement, array, format, layout, plan, style

n 5 direction, directive, guideline, instruction, policy, rule

n 6 blueprint, chart, diagram, draft, map, plan, sketch

n 7 arrangement, blueprint, method, order, orderliness, pattern, plan, system

n 8 bar graph, chart, diagram, distribution, figure, flowchart, graph, histogram, pie chart, plot, table

n 9 abridgement, abstract, brief, compendium, condensation, digest, essence, example, review, sketch, summary, syllabus, synopsis

n 10 draft, skeleton, sketch

n 11 epitome, example, exemplar, ideal, mirror, model, paradigm, pattern, plan, prototype, rule of thumb, standard

v 1 approach, border, bound, define, edge, hem, limit, skirt, verge

v 2 analyze, brief, condense, evaluate, retrace, review, study, summarize, synopsize, update

v 3 arrange, blueprint, cast, chart, design, devise, draft, draw, engineer, fashion, lay out, map, plan, plot, project, set out, sketch

v 4 align, arrange, array, assort, catalog, categorize, class, classify, cluster, compile, file, format, grade, group, lay out, line up, list, order, organize, pigeonhole, place, position, prioritize, program, rank, rate, sort, stack, tabulate

outlining *adj* abutting, adjacent, adjoining, alongside, bordering, close by, connected, contiguous, juxtaposed, local, near at hand, nearby, neighboring, regional, touching, verging on

outlive *v* outlast, survive

outlook *n* 1 horizon, lookout, perspective, prospect, vista

n 2 landscape, scene, scenery, sight, view, vista

n 3 distance, future, horizon, perspective, purview, vision, vista

n 4 beliefs, code, doctrine, ethics, philosophy, rites, values

n 5 confidence, disposition, feeling, frame of mind, mentality, mood, morale, state

n 6 future, posterity, tomorrow

outlying *adj* distant, far, faraway, obscure, out-of-the-way, remote, removed

outmaneuver *v* best, defeat, down, outdo, outsmart, outwit

outmoded *adj* ancient, antiquated, archaic, bygone, dated, dead, extinct, noncurrent, obsolete, old, outdated, passé, past, worn

out-of-order *adj* broken, cracked, damaged

out-of-the-way *adj* distant, far, faraway, obscure, outlying, remote, removed

output *n* by-product, derivative, end product, end result, growth, outgrowth, produce, product, production, productivity, result, yield

outrage *n* 1 corruption, crime, disgrace, scandal

n 2 agitation, craze, excitement, frenzy, furor, fury, fuss, passion, tumult, uproar, wrath

n 3 anger, dander, fit, frenzy, fury, indignation, ire, paroxysm, rage, tantrum, wrath

n 4 see: CRIME *n* 1, 3

v 1 affront, encounter, face, insult, offend, slight

v 2 amaze, daze, electrify, horrify, offend, overwhelm, scandalize, shock, stun

v 3 see: BOTHER *v* 5

outrageous *adj* 1 outlandish, unbelievable, unheard-of

adj 2 barbarous, monstrous, uncivilized, unconscionable, unethical, ungodly, unholy, wicked

adj 3 absurd, comic, comical, crazy, droll, farcical, foolish, funny, hilarious, humorous, laughable, ludicrous, ridiculous, silly

adj 4 atrocious, awful, crying, desperate, disgraceful, ghastly, grizzly, heinous, monstrous, notorious, odious, offensive, scandalous, shocking, tasteless, wicked

outrider *n* 1 envoy, foregoer, forerunner, harbinger, herald, messenger, precursor, predictor, prophet

n 2 observer, scout

outright *adj* 1 forthright, outspoken

adj 2 obvious, overt, public, visible

adj 3 all, all-out, complete, entire, full-blown, gross, integral, integrated, total, unlimited, whole

outset *n* beginning, birth, debut, delivery, inception, kindling, start

outshine *v* 1 eclipse, excel, surpass

v 2 beat, best, better, cap, dwarf, eclipse, exceed, excel, go beyond, outdo, outgo, outstrip, overshadow, pass, surpass, top, transcend

outside *adv* beyond, farther than, past, yonder

adj 1 exterior, external, superficial

adj 2 open-air, outdoor

adj 3 borderline, casual, frivolous, insignificant, light, lightweight, little, marginal, meager, minor, minute, negligible, nonessential, off, petty, remote, secondary, slender, slight, slim, small, tenuous, trivial, unimportant

n exterior, facade, skin, surface

outsider *n* 1 alien, foreigner, newcomer, stranger

n 2 derelict, outcast, recluse

outskirt *n* see: EDGE *n* 4

outsmart *v* best, defeat, down, outdo, outmaneuver, outwit

outspoken *adj* 1 belligerent, forthright, outright

adj 2 belligerent, extroverted, free, intimidating, loud, vocal, vociferous

outstanding *adj* 1 eminent, great, important, superior

adj 2 due, open, owed, payable, unpaid

adj 3 excellent, extraordinary, great, impressive, noteworthy, shining, smashing, superb, wonderful

adj 4 best, elegant, finest, gilt-edged, magnificent, majestic, preeminent, sensational, splendid, superb, superior, superlative

adj 5 central, chief, distinguished, dominant, famed, great, key, leading, main, major, number one, predominant, preeminent, primary, prime, principal, prominent, star, successful, superior, top

adj 6 dynamite, excellent, extraordinary, great, out of sight, phenomenal, premier, super, superb, superlative, tremendous, wonderful

adj 7 acclaimed, celebrated, distinguished, eminent, esteemed, excellent, famed, famous, foremost, renowned, illustrious, notable, prestigious, prominent, well-known

adj 8 basic, dominant, elementary, first, foremost, fundamental, head, highest, leading, main, paramount, preeminent, premier, primary, rudimentary, supreme, top

outstretch *v* expand, extend, fan, open, spread, unfold

outstrip *v* see: SURPASS *v* 2

outweigh *v* adjust, balance, compensate, make equal, make up, offset, redeem, set off

outwit *v* best, defeat, down, outdo, outmaneuver

over *adv* above, aloft, greater, more, on top of, overhead, superior

adj accomplished, complete, concluded, done, ended, finished, performed, terminated, through, wrapped up

overabundance *n* deluge, excess, fat, glut, overflow, overkill, plethora, redundancy, surfeit, surplus

overage *n* asset, excess, inventory, overstock, oversupply, plus, surplus

overbearing *adj* 1 dominant, master, overwhelming, paramount, predominant, preponderant, prevailing, prevalent, sovereign

adj 2 see: AUTHORITATIVE *adj* 2

adj 3 see: VAIN *adj* 5

overcast *adj* 1 cheerless, cloudy, dim, dismal, drab, dull

adj 2 cloudy, dismal, foggy, gray, hazy, misty, murky, steamy, vaporous, vapory

overcome *adj* crushed, defeated, distraught, emotional, subdued

v 1 best, conquer, defeat, master, prevail, succeed, triumph, win

v 2 conquer, crush, defeat, destroy, down, hurdle, lick, overthrow, surmount

overdo *v* burden, encumber, hamper, load, oppress, overload, saddle, strain, tax

overdoer *n* glutton, hog, overeater, pig, swine

overdue *adj* belated, delayed, late, slow, tardy, unpunctual

overeat *v* fill, glut, gorge, pig out, satiate, stuff, surfeit

overeater *n* glutton, hog, overdoer, pig, swine

overflow *n* 1 deluge, flood, submersion, surge, torrent

n 2 deluge, excess, fat, glut, overabundance, overkill, plethora, redundancy, surfeit, surplus

v 1 bury, drown, engulf, flood, inundate, swamp, wash over

v 2 cascade, emit, flood, inundate, plunge, pour, rain, shower, spill, swamp, tumble

overflowing *adj* 1 alive, ample, replete, rife, swarming, teeming

adj 2 abounding, abundant, ample, bounteous, bountiful, copious, enough, galore, generous, liberal, plentiful, plenty, prodigal, profuse, teeming

overhang *v* bulge, jut, overlap, overlay, poke, pop, project, protrude, protuberate, rise, stand out, stick out, swell

overhaul *v* 1 doctor, fix, mend, patch, rebuild, recondition, reconstruct, refit, renovate, repair, revamp

v 2 adapt, adjust, balance, fit, fix, inspect, maintain, recondition, refurbish, regulate, repair, service, support, tune up

overhead *adv* above, aloft, greater, more, on top of, over, superior

n 1 burden, commitments, costs, expenses

n 2 slide, transparency

adj aloft, elevated, high, lofty, soaring, tall

overheat *v* boil, heat, parboil, seethe, simmer, stew

overindulge *v* accommodate, baby, cater, coddle, gratify, humor, indulge, pamper, pander, placate, satisfy, spoil

overindulgence *n* gluttony

overindulgent *adj* excessive, gluttonous, immoderate, inordinate, intemperate, prodigious, unbridled, undue, unrestrained, voracious

overjoyed *adj* 1 ecstatic, entranced, rapturous

adj 2 ecstatic, elated, delighted, enchanted, thrilled

overkill *n* deluge, excess, fat, glut, overabundance, overflow, plethora, redundancy, surfeit, surplus

overlap *v* see: PROJECT *v* 5

overlay *v* 1 cover, fix, patch, repair

v 2 bulge, jut, overhang, overlap, poke, pop, project, protrude, protuberate, rise, stand out, stick out, swell

n mask, pattern, stencil, template

overload *v* flood, glut, oversupply

v 1 burden, encumber, hamper, load, oppress, overdo, saddle, strain, tax

v 2 see: SATURATE *v* 2

overlook *v* see: DISREGARD *v*

overpass *n* bridge, trestle, viaduct

v see: DISREGARD *v*

overpower *v* 1 crush, defeat, drown, overwhelm, stifle

v 2 coerce, compel, constrain, force, make, propel, push

v 3 bear down, beat down, conquer, crush, defeat, dominate, enslave, exploit, quash, reduce, subdue, subjugate, suppress, vanquish

overpowering *adj* 1 crushing, overwhelming

adj 2 alluring, compelling, desirable, irresistible, seductive, tantalizing

overpriced *adj* excessive, exorbitant, expensive, extravagant, extreme, ghastly, lavish, outlandish, profuse, ultimate, unbelievable

override *v* cancel, contradict, deny, disallow, forbid, negate, nix, nullify, overrule, reject, renege, repeal, revoke, torpedo, veto, void

overrule *v* 1 control, govern, reign, rule

v 2 see: REJECT *v* 7

overrun *v* 1 attack, invade, raid

v 2 infest, invade, pervade, plague, swarm

v 3 abound, increase, multiply, proliferate, propagate, teem

v 4 beat, belittle, blast, clobber, conquer, cream, defeat, dust, lambaste, lick, overwhelm, rout, shellac, smear, thrash, wallop, whip

n excess

overseas *adv* abroad

oversee *v* 1 care, manage, supervise

v 2 defend, guard, patrol, police, protect, regulate, safeguard, watch

v 3 bug, check, eavesdrop, monitor, observe, snoop, spy, wiretap

v 4 carry on, conduct, direct, keep, manage, operate, ordain, pilot, run

v 5 administer, boss, command, direct, guide, manage, regulate, steer, supervise

overseeing *n* administration, care, charge, conduct, handling, intendance, management, running, supervision

overseer *n* boss, chief, foreman, head, owner, superior, supervisor

oversell *v* exaggerate, expand, inflate, overstate, stretch

overshadow *v* 1 see: OBSCURE *v*

v 2 see: SURPASS *v* 2

oversight *n* absence, disregard, error, neglect, omission, slip-up

oversize *adj* big, extra-large, fat, grand, great, huge, husky, immense, jumbo, large, obese, tremendous

overstate *v* exaggerate, expand, inflate, stretch

overstatement *n* 1 bull, falsehood, lie, misstatement, untruth

n 2 ballyhoo, embellishment, exaggeration, hoopla, hype, hyperbole, promotion, public relations

overstep *v* cross the line, exceed, transgress, trespass

overstock *n* asset, excess, inventory, overage, oversupply, plus, surplus

oversupply *n* asset, excess, inventory, overage, overstock, plus, surplus

v flood, glut

overt *adj* obvious, outright, public, visible

overthrow *n* 1 collapse, downfall, failure, fall, ruin, upset

n 2 destruction, downfall, infiltration, ruin, subversion, upset

n 3 debacle, defeat, disaster, downfall, rout, ruination, thrashing, trouncing, undoing, vanquishment

v 1 conquer, crush, defeat, destroy, down, hurdle, lick, overcome, surmount

v 2 capsize, collapse, defeat, dislodge, knock over, overturn, tip over, topple, tumble, turn over, upset

overture *n* 1 approach, come-on, offer, proposal, proposition, suggestion *n* 2 beginning, foreword, forward, intro, introduction, preamble, preface, prelude, prologue, start

v see: PROCEED *v* 2

overturn *v* 1 capsize, roll, tip over, upset

v 2 capsize, collapse, defeat, dislodge, knock over, overthrow, tip over, topple, tumble, turn over, upset

v 3 annihilate, decimate, demolish, destroy, destruct, devastate, dismantle, pulverize, raze, rub out, ruin, shatter, smash, tear down, undo, wreck

overweight *adj* chubby, chunky, corpulent, fat, fleshy, gross, heavy, hefty, meaty, obese, plump, portly, pudgy, rotund, stocky, stout

overwhelm *v* 1 bestow, deluge, lavish, shower

v 2 crush, defeat, drown, overpower, stifle

v 3 amaze, astonish, astound, awe, delight, floor, impress, wow

v 4 amaze, daze, electrify, horrify, offend, outrage, scandalize, shock, stun

v 5 see: THRASH *v* 1

overwhelming *adj* 1 crushing, devastating, overpowering

adj 2 dominant, master, overbearing, paramount, predominant, preponderant, prevailing, prevalent, sovereign

adj 3 see: HUGE *adj* 3

ovum *n* bud, egg, embryo, fetus, seed, zygote

owed *adj* due, open, outstanding, payable, unpaid

own *adj* exclusive, individual, intimate, personal, private, secret, special

v 1 possess, have, hold, keep, retain

v 2 acknowledge, admit, allow, avow, concede, confess, fess up, grant, own up

owner *n* 1 landlord, lessor, possessor, proprietor, stockholder

n 2 addressee, citizen, dweller, inhabitant, occupant, resident, tenant

n 3 boss, chief, foreman, head, overseer, superior, supervisor

ownership *n* 1 possession, proprietorship, title

n 2 assets, belongings, equity, estate, fortune, goods, holdings, inheritance, money, possessions, property, prosperity, riches, treasure, wealth

ox *n* bull, calf, cow, heifer, steer

oxidize *v* 1 burn, cremate, incinerate

v 2 corrode, deteriorate, eat, erode, gnaw, rust, wear

P

pa *n* dad, dada, daddy, father, papa, pappy, parent, pater, patriarch, pop, poppa

pace *n* 1 alacrity, cadence, celerity, dispatch, gait, quickness, rapidity, rate, speed, step, stride, swiftness, trot, velocity, walk

n 2 gait, march, shuffle, step, stride, walk

v amble, hike, journey, march, parade, plod, saunter, step, stride, stroll, strut, tramp, tread, trek, walk

pacesetters *n* innovators, leaders, pioneers, trendsetters, vanguard

pacifist *adj* calm, coolheaded, nonaggressive, nonviolent, passive, peaceful

pacify *v* 1 disarm

v 2 allay, appease, assuage, balm, becalm, calm, compose, conciliate, ease, lull, mollify, placate, propitiate, quell, quiet, reconcile, satiate, settle, soften, soothe, still, sweeten, tranquilize

pack *v* 1 box, bundle, crate, stow

v 2 fill, heap, load, place, stack, stuff

v 3 cram, crush, force, gorge, insert, jam, press, ram, stuff

v 4 compact, compress, constrain, crowd, crush, jam, mash, push, press, squash, squeeze

v 5 bear, carry, convey, crate, ferry, haul, lift, lug, shoulder, shuttle, tote, traffic, transport, truck

v 6 clot, clog, coagulate, condense, congeal, curdle, dry, gel, harden, intensify, jell, set, solidify, thicken

n 1 bag, baggage, case, equipment, gear, grip, kit, luggage, pouch, purse, sack, suitcase, valise, wallet

n 2 array, bale, batch, battery, body, bunch, bundle, clump, cluster, group, lot, parcel, quantity, set

n 3 band, bunch, crew, crowd, drove, flock, following, gaggle, gang, herd, huddle, mass, mob, rabble, riffraff, swarm, team, throng

package *n* delivery, mail, parcel

v 1 bundle, cover, enclose, envelop, wrap

v 2 close, seal, tape, wrap

packed *adj* bursting, chock-full, crowded, filled up, full, jammed, jampacked, loaded, rending, replete, stuffed

pact *n* agreement, bargain, bond, compact, contract, convention, covenant, deal, pledge, promise, transaction, treaty, understanding

pad *n* 1 carpet, mat, mattress, rug

n 2 address, apartment, condo, condominium, domicile, dwelling, flat, home, house, location, place, property, residence, site

paddock *n* barn, coop, enclosure, lean-to, pen, pound, shack, shed, shelter, stable, stall, sty

padlock *n* bolt, clamp, clasp, lock

padre *n* chaplain, clergyman, cleric, father, guru, minister, parson, pastor, priest, rabbi, reverend

pagan *n* agnostic, atheist, gentile, heathen, heretic, unbeliever

page *n* letterhead, paper, papyrus, parchment, sheepskin, sheet, stationery, vellum

v announce, call, summon

paginate *v* format, sequence

paid *adj* indemnified, paid off, reimbursed, remunerated, repaid, rewarded

pail *n* bottle, bucket, caddy, can, canister, jar, shell, tin, vessel

pain *n* 1 bruise, hurt, injury, sprain, strain, wound

n 2 ache, affliction, agony, anguish, hurt, injury, punishment, suffering, torture

n 3 ache, agony, angina, burn, cramp, crick, heartache, hurt, pang, soreness, spasm, sting, twinge

n 4 agony, anguish, bale, concern, distress, misery, nightmare, sadness, sorrow, suffering, torment, travail, tribulation, trouble, woe, worry

n 5 see: ANGUISH *n* 1, 2, 3

n 6 see: IDIOT *n*

v 1 ache, despair, grieve, suffer

v 2 afflict, aggrieve, bother, burden, distress, grieve, hurt

v 3 see: ANNOY *v* 1

painful *adj* 1 bruised, irritated, sore, tender

adj 2 excruciating, intolerable, unbearable, unendurable

adj 3 disabling, disturbing, shocking, traumatic, upsetting

adj 4 annoying, difficult, hurt, irksome, irritated, irritating, sensitive, sore

adj 5 annoying, bothersome, glaring, harassing, irksome, irritating, mean, onerous, pesky, troublesome, ugly, unwelcome, vexatious, wicked

painfully *adv* 1 badly, harshly, imperfectly, improperly, inadequately, inappropriately, poorly, unsatisfactorily

adv 2 agonizingly

adv 3 arduously, difficultly, laboriously

painkiller *n* compound, drug, elixir, formula, medicine, narcotic, pharmaceutical, prescription

pains *n* effort, elbow grease, exertion, labor, strain, struggle, toil, trouble, try, work

painstaking *adj* 1 deliberate, dilatory, diligent, leisurely, methodical, meticulous, patient, procrastinating, slow, thorough, unhasty, unhurried

adj 2 see: CONSCIENTIOUS *adj* 3

painstakingly *adv* 1 accurately

adv 2 see: COMPLETELY *adv*

paint *n* color, coloring, dye, pigment, stain, tincture, tint

v 1 dab, pat, tap, touch

v 2 color, dye, stain, tinge, tint

v 3 depict, design, draw, represent, sketch

v 4 brush, sweep

painting *n* acrylic, art, canvas, depiction, drawing, etching, illustration, landscape, lithograph, mural, oil, pastel, pen and ink, picture, portrait, print, seascape, sketch, still life, watercolor

pair *v* associate, blend, bond, coalesce, combine, compound, connect, couple, fasten, fuse, join, link, marry, mate, meet, merge, unite, wed

n couple, duet, duo, set, twins, twosome

pal *n* accomplice, acquaintance, adjunct, ally, associate, buddy, chum, cohort, colleague, companion, compatriot, comrade, confidant, confrere, connection, copartner, counterpart, co-worker, crony, equal, fellow, follower, friend, intimate, mate, partner, peer, relative, supporter

palace *n* 1 heaven, utopia, Zion

n 2 abode, castle, domicile, dwelling, estate, home, house, mansion, residence

palatable *adj* appetizing, delectable, delicious, exquisite, luscious, savory, sweet, tasty

palate *n* flavor, sample, savor, spice, tang, taste

palatial *adj* choice, deluxe, elegant, first-class, grand, luxuriant, luxurious, opulent, ornate, plush, posh, rich, soft, stately, sumptuous, thick

pale *adj* 1 anemic, bloodless, gaunt, haggard, lifeless, pallid, passionless, spiritless, watery, weak

adj 2 ashen, ashy, blanched, colorless, pallid, sallow, sickly, sooty, wan, waxen, yellow

v 1 blanch, fade, whiten

v 2 becloud, bedim, befog, blur, cloud, confuse, darken, dim, diminish, dull, eclipse, fade, muddy, obscure, overshadow, shadow, shade, tarnish

pall *v* bore, tire, weary

pallid *adj* 1 anemic, bloodless, gaunt, haggard, lifeless, pale, passionless, spiritless, watery, weak

adj 2 ashen, ashy, blanched, colorless, pale, sallow, sickly, sooty, wan, waxen, yellow

palm *n* fingers, hand, knuckles

palpable *adj* appreciable, cognizant, concrete, detectable, discernible, noticeable, observable, perceptible, sensible, tangible, visible

palpate *v* examine, feel, finger, fondle, grope, handle, manipulate, maul, paw, probe, touch

palpation *n* exploration, feel, feeling, texture, touch, sensation

palpitate *v* beat, flutter, pulsate, pulse, quiver, throb, tremble, vibrate

paltry *adj* 1 ineffectual, limited, little, mean, narrow, set, small

adj 2 bare, deficient, few, inadequate, inferior, insufficient, little, meager, petty, poor, scant, scanty, skimpy, spare, sparse

adj 3 flawed, flimsy, imperfect, inferior, lousy, mediocre, miserable, poor, second-rate, shabby, shoddy, sorry, so-so, tacky, unworthy, worthless

adj 4 see: PATHETIC *adj* 1

adj 5 see: TRIVIAL *adj* 1

pamper *v* 1 aid, baby, care for, help, nurse, nurture, succor

v 2 accommodate, baby, cater, coddle, gratify, humor, indulge, over-indulge, pander, placate, satisfy, spoil

pamphlet *n* brochure, circular, flier, handbill, handout, leaflet, sheet

panacea *n* antidote, cure, medication, medicine, prescription, remedy, serum, therapy, treatment

pandemonium *n* brouhaha, cacophony, chaos, clamor, confusion, din, discord, disorder, hubbub, mayhem, noise, racket, tumult, uproar

pander *v* see: BABY *v* 2

panel *n* 1 jury

n 2 curtain, divider, partition, wall

pang *n* 1 ache, agony, angina, burn, cramp, crick, heartache, hurt, pain, soreness, spasm, sting, twinge

n 2 compunction, conscience, qualm, regret, restraint, scruple, twinge

panhandler *n* beggar, bum, derelict, drifter, hobo, loafer, mendicant, pauper, tramp, vagabond, vagrant

panic *n* 1 chaos, frenzy, hysteria, riot

n 2 affliction, alarm, anxiety, apprehension, care, consternation, dismay, dread, fear, fright, horror, ordeal, terror, trepidation, trial, trouble, worry

v 1 appall, daunt, discourage, dismay, horrify, petrify, scare, shock, terrify, unnerve

v 2 abash, alarm, awe, cow, daunt, frighten, horrify, intimidate, scare, shock, spook, startle, terrify, terrorize, unnerve

panting *adj* breathless, winded

pantomime *v* see: MIMIC *v*

papa *n* dad, dada, daddy, father, pa, pappy, parent, pater, patriarch, pop, poppa

paper *n* 1 deed, document, title

n 2 letterhead, page, papyrus, parchment, sheepskin, sheet, stationery, vellum

n 3 see: ESSAY *n*

paperback *n* see: BOOK *n* 2

pappy *n* dad, dada, daddy, father, pa, papa, parent, pater, patriarch, pop, poppa

papyrus *n* letterhead, page, paper, parchment, sheepskin, sheet, stationery, vellum

par *n* 1 equality, equilibrium, equity, equivalence, evenness, parity, similarity, symmetry

n 2 average, mean, median, medium, middle, norm, rule, standard

adj equal

parable *n* allegory, fable, fantasy, fiction, legend, lesson, lore, myth, mythology, story, tale

parade *n* array, blare, display, exhibit, exhibition, fanfare, fuss, performance, presentation, procession, publicity, show, showing

v 1 display, exhibit, flaunt, manifest, promenade

v 2 see: WALK *v* 1

paradigm *n* epitome, example, exemplar, ideal, mirror, model, outline, pattern, plan, prototype, rule of thumb, standard

paradise *n* bliss, delight, ecstasy, Eden, elation, enchantment, heaven, joy, nirvana, pleasure, rapture, rhapsody

paradox *n* 1 contradiction, disagreement, discrepancy, hypocrisy, incongruity, inconsistency, variance

n 2 confusion, conundrum, difficulty, dilemma, enigma, mystery, obstacle, perplexity, problem, puzzle, quandary, question, riddle, secret

paradoxical *adj* ambivalent, conflicting, equivocal, uncertain

paragon *n* gem, treasure

paragraph *n* chapter, passage, stanza, verse

parallel *adj* 1 agreeable, compatible, concurrent, congruent

adj 2 affiliated, akin, aligned, allied, associated, fraternal, friendly, kindred, related

adj 3 alike, akin, analogous, comparable, corresponding, equivalent, identical, kindred, like, matching, related, same, similar, such, uniform

n complement, counterpart, equal, equivalent, like, match, peer

v approximate, complement, correspond, equal

paralysis *n* apathy, impotence, inaction, inactivity

paralyze *v* 1 daze, shock, stun, stupefy

v 2 cripple, disable, disarm, encumber, freeze, halt, handcuff, immobilize, incapacitate, prostrate, stop, stun

paramount *adj* 1 dominant, master, overbearing, overwhelming, predominant, preponderant, prevailing, prevalent, sovereign

adj 2 basic, dominant, elementary, first, foremost, fundamental, head, highest, leading, main, outstanding, preeminent, premier, primary, rudimentary, supreme, top

paramour *n* beau, boyfriend, date, escort, fiancé, lover, mate, suitor

paranoid *adj* afraid, aghast, anxious, apprehensive, concerned, discerning, fearful, frightened, nervous, scared, scary, terrified, worried

paraphernalia *n* equipment

paraphrase *n* collection, epitome, recapitulation, summary, summation

v 1 copy, plagiarize, rephrase, reword

v 2 cite, quote, repeat, restate

parasite *n* barnacle, dependent, freeloader, hanger-on, leech, remora, sponge, vine

paratroops *n* airborne, army, battalion, brigade, cavalry, company, footmen, guard, horsemen, infantry, legion, marines, militia, minutemen, platoon, reserve, storm troopers

parboil *v* boil, heat, overheat, seethe, simmer, stew

parcel *n* 1 delivery, package

n 2 land, lot, plot, property, tract

n 3 bit, clipping, cut, division, lot, member, part, piece, portion, sample, section, segment, slice

n 4 array, bale, batch, battery, body, bunch, bundle, clump, cluster, group, lot, pack, quantity, set

v allocate, allot, allow, apportion, assign, designate, distribute, divide, divvy, earmark, give, measure, partition, portion, prorate, quota, ration, section, share, slice

parch *v* bake, broil, burn, char, cook, melt, roast, scorch, sear, singe, swelter, toast, warm

parched *adj* 1 burnt, scorched, shriveled

adj 2 arid, dry, thirsty, waterless

parchment *n* letterhead, page, paper, papyrus, sheepskin, sheet, stationery, vellum

pardon *n* absolution, amnesty, discharge, disengagement, dispensation, freedom, moratorium, release, relief, reprieve, respite, stay, suspension

v absolve, acquit, clear, condone, exculpate, excuse, exempt, exonerate, forgive, free, remit, reprieve, vindicate

pare *v* clip, crop, cut, lop, prune, shave, shear, snip, trim, whittle

parent *n* 1 custodian, father, guardian, mother, trustee

n 2 birth, creation, fountain, genesis, origin, root, source

n 3 author, creator, founder, initiator, instigator, inventor, maker, originator, pioneer, seed, source

n 4 ma, mama, mater, matriarch, mom, momma, mommy, mother

n 5 dad, dada, daddy, father, pa, papa, pappy, pater, patriarch, pop, poppa

n 6 ancestor, antecedent, ascendant, elder, forebear, forefather, forerunner, founder, grandparent, patriarch, predecessor, progenitor

v 1 care, cherish, foster, mother, nourish, nurse, nurture, protect, raise, rear, suckle

v 2 bear, beget, breed, come into, create, effect, engender, father, generate, hatch, impregnate, make, mate, multiply, originate, procreate, promulgate, propagate, reproduce, sire, spawn

parenthesis *n* bracket

parish *n* 1 area, district, domain, environs, jurisdiction, locality, neighborhood, precinct, province, range, region, section, sphere, vicinity, ward, zone

n 2 county, district, jurisdiction, municipality, precinct, township, ward

parishioners *n* congregation, devotees, flock, fold, followers, laity

parity *n* equality, equilibrium, equity, equivalence, evenness, par, similarity, symmetry

park *n* common, green, plaza, square

parlance *n* 1 buzzwords, expression, idiom, jargon, language, lingo, verbiage, vernacular, vocabulary

n 2 cliché, diction, expression, phrase, saying, slogan, style, term, wording

parlay *v* apply, augment, capitalize on, enlarge, increase, use

parley *n* conference, meeting, powwow, talk, tête-à-tête

v 1 chat, chatter, converse, discuss, speak, talk, visit

v 2 advise, communicate, confer, consult, discuss, group, huddle, powwow

parliament *n* assembly, clinic, congress, council, court, diet, forum, hearing, meeting, seminar, symposium

parlor *n* family room, foyer, living room, salon

parochial *adj* confined, controlled, ignorant, limited, narrow, provincial, unsophisticated

parochialism *n* bias, bigotry, chauvinism, discrimination, intolerance, partiality, prejudice, provincialism, racism, sexism

parody *n* 1 act, farce, make-believe, performance, show, sketch, skit

n 2 buffoonery, burlesque, caricature, comedy, farce, humor, imitation, joke, lampoon, mockery, satire, spoof, takeoff, travesty

v act, ape, copy, emulate, follow, imitate, lip-synch, mime, mimic, mock, model, mouth, pantomime, pattern, take off

paroxysm *n* anger, dander, fit, frenzy, fury, indignation, ire, outrage, rage, tantrum, wrath

parry *v* 1 combat, compete, contend, contest, counter, dispute, duel, fight, match, oppose, pit, play, repel, resist, rival, strive, struggle, vie

v 2 see: AVOID *v* 4

parsimonious *adj* cheap, close, greedy, mean, miserly, niggardly, penny-pinching, stingy, tight, tightfisted, ungenerous, ungiving

parson *n* chaplain, clergyman, cleric, father, guru, minister, padre, pastor, priest, rabbi, reverend

part *n* 1 component, module, unit

n 2 component, installment, portion, segment

n 3 detail, feature, item, particular, specific

n 4 adjunct, annex, fitting, fixture, piece, unit

n 5 component, constituent, element, factor, ingredient, item, segment

n 6 bit, clipping, cut, division, lot, member, parcel, piece, portion, sample, section, segment, slice

n 7 allotment, allowance, apportionment, budget, dispensation, dispersion, lot, measure, percentage, portion, quota, ration, share, slice

n 8 character, portrayal, role

n 9 appendage, arm, extremity, leg, limb

v 1 breach, break up, cleave, divide, disjoin, dismember, disrupt, dissect, dissever, disunite, divorce, polarize, rupture, separate, sever, split, sunder

v 2 advance, begin again, continue, cycle, depart, get along, get on, go, leave, march, move, move forward, overture, proceed, progress, push on, reembark, recommence, restart, wend

partake *v* 1 involve, participate, receive, share

v 2 benefit, experience, have, profit, touch, use

v 3 bibulate, booze, consume, drink, gulp, guzzle, imbibe, nip, polish off, put away, put down, sample, savor, sip, suck, swig, swill, taste

partaker *n* participant, partner, party, sharer

partial *adj* 1 fragmentary, incomplete, unfinished

adj 2 biased, emotional, predisposed, prejudiced, subjective

adj 3 apt, inclined, liable, likely, prone

adj 4 better, favored, preferential, select, special

adj 5 feigned, pseudo, quasi, semi, so-called, somewhat, unofficial

adj 6 biased, inequitable, uneven, unfair, unjust, unrighteous, wrongful

partiality *n* 1 bias, bigotry, chauvinism, discrimination, intolerance, parochialism, prejudice, provincialism, racism, sexism

n 2 bent, bias, drift, habit, inclination, leaning, penchant, predilection, preference, priority, proclivity, propensity, talent, taste, tendency

partially *adv* a tad, partly, slightly, somewhat, to a degree

participant *n* 1 competitor, contestant, player, team member

n 2 associate, collaborator, individual, member, party, person, registrant

n 3 partaker, partner, party, sharer

participate *v* involve, partake, receive, share

participation *n* complicity, connivance

participatory *adj* collective, cooperative, helpful, joint, together, unified, united

particle *n* 1 atom, bead, dab, dash, dot, drop, grain, iota, molecule, morsel, pea, pellet, smidgen, speck, tad

n 2 bit, dab, end, fragment, iota, minutia,

mite, morsel, piece, pinch, portion, scrap, shred, speck, spot, strip, tidbit, trifle

particular *adj* 1 individual, personal, special, specific

adj 2 careful, cautious, choosy, discriminating, fastidious, finicky, fussy, meticulous, nit-picking, persnickety, picky, selective

adj 3 characteristic, differentiating, distinctive, lone, one, peculiar, select, single, solitary, special, unique, unusual

adj 4 exclusive, individual, lone, odd, one, only, separate, single, singular, sole, solitary, unique, unshared

n detail, feature, item, part, specific

particularly *adv* chiefly, especially, notably, primarily, specifically

particulars *n* details, minutiae, nuances, second level, trivia

parting *n* departure, exit, farewell, leaving, passing

partition *n* 1 apportionment, division, segmentation, segregation, separation, subdivision

n 2 curtain, divider, panel, wall

v 1 exclude, fence, restrict, separate

v 2 allocate, allot, allow, apportion, assign, designate, distribute, divide, divvy, earmark, give, measure, parcel, portion, prorate, quota, ration, section, share, slice

partly *adv* a tad, partially, slightly, somewhat, to a degree

partner *n* 1 abettor, accessory, accomplice, coconspirator, confederate, conspirator, supporter

n 2 partaker, participant, party, sharer

n 3 advocate, ally, angel, backer, benefactor, booster, champion, cheerleader, donor, friend, guarantor, helper, ombudsman, patron, promoter, proponent, sponsor, supporter

n 4 accomplice, acquaintance, adjunct, ally, associate, buddy, chum, cohort, colleague, companion, compatriot, comrade, confidant, confrere, connection, copartner, counterpart, co-worker, crony, equal, fellow, follower, friend, intimate, mate, pal, peer, relative, supporter

partnership *n* 1 business, company, concern, corporation, enterprise, establishment, firm, house

n 2 cartel, chain, coalition, collaboration, combine, conglomerate, consortium, federation, group, pool, syndicate, trust

n 3 affiliation, alliance, association, axis, bloc, coalition, concord, confederation, consolidation, faction, federation, joint venture, league, merger, organization, relationship, treaty, union

part-timer *n* 1 amateur, beginner, dabbler, dilettante, hobbyist, layman, neophyte, nonprofessional

n 2 agent, alternate, backup, contingency, replacement, representative, standby, substitute, surrogate

party *n* 1 associate, collaborator, individual, member, participant, person, registrant

n 2 bash, bender, binge, do, fling, orgy, spree

n 3 band, body, company, corps, group, outfit, troop, troupe

n 4 celebration, ceremony, commemoration, festival, festivity, fiesta, gala, holiday, observance, revelry

n 5 partaker, participant, sharer

n 6 ball, cotillion, dance, hop, prom

n 7 assembly, association, band, bevy, brood, bunch, camp, clique, cluster, collection, covey, crew, flock, group, organization, team, unit

v carouse, celebrate, drink, frolic, make merry, revel, romp

pass *n* 1 admission, cover charge, entrance fee, fee, ticket

n 2 identification, passport, permit, ticket, visa

n 3 certificate, credential, document, instrument, license, permit

n 4 badge, card, label, tag, ticket, voucher

n 5 abyss, canyon, chasm, cleft, crack, depth, fissure, gorge, gulch, ravine

n 6 access, approach, artery, avenue, boulevard, channel, drag, highway, path, promenade, road, roadway, route, strait, street, thoroughfare, trail, way

v 1 traverse

v 2 disguise, masquerade, pose, posture, pretend

v 3 carry, channel, conduct, convey, funnel, pipe, siphon, transmit

v 4 cease, die, elapse, expire, lapse, pass away, perish, succumb, terminate

v 5 approve, authorize, decree, enact, legalize, legislate, ordain, ratify, sanction

v 6 attack, butt, drive, knock, lunge, plunge, ram, sink, stab, stick, thrust

v 7 accept, approbate, approve, authorize, certify, condone, confirm, countenance, endorse, favor, ratify, sanction, validate

v 8 beat, best, better, cap, dwarf, eclipse, exceed, excel, go beyond, outdo, outgo, outshine, outstrip, overshadow, surpass, top, transcend

v 9 see: DISREGARD v

v 10 see: FORFEIT v

v 11 see: OCCUR v 2

passable adj acceptable, adequate, competent, decent, enough, fair, good, mediocre, reasonable, respectable, satisfactory, sufficient, tolerable

passably adv adequately, amply, enough, equitably, fairly, justly, moderately, rather, satisfactorily, tolerably

passage n 1 chapter, paragraph, stanza, verse

n 2 access, aperture, approach, entrance, inlet, mouth

n 3 approval, confirmation, doctrine, enactment, evidence, proof, testament, testimony, witness

n 4 citation, clipping, excerpt, extract, mention, portion, quotation, quote, reference, section

n 5 circuit, course, itinerary, journey, line, means, path, road, route, trip, voyage, way

n 6 rate

n 7 adventure, air travel, cruise, excursion, expedition, flight, journey, safari, sally, tour, travel, trek, trip, venture, voyage

passageway n 1 corridor

n 2 crossing, intersection

n 3 conduit, pathway, shaft, subway, tube, tunnel

n 4 canal, channel, conduit, crevice, curb, cut, ditch, duct, furrow, gorge, groove, gully, gutter, ravine, rut, trench, trough

passé adj ancient, antiquated, archaic, bygone, dated, dead, extinct, non-current, obsolete, old, outdated, outmoded, past, worn

passenger n commuter, rider, traveler

passing adj 1 brief, ephemeral, fleeting, impermanent, momentary, short, temporary, transient, transitory, volatile

adj 2 brief, fleeting, short, swift, transient

n 1 death, decease, departure

n 2 departure, exit, farewell, leaving

passion n 1 commitment, love, religion

n 2 fit, rage, tantrum, temper

n 3 fetish, fixation, infatuation, obsession, preoccupation

n 4 affection, emotion, feeling, regard, sensation, sense, sensibility, sentiment, tenderness

n 5 agitation, craze, excitement, frenzy, furor, fury, fuss, outrage, tumult, uproar, wrath

n 6 appetite, craving, desire, eroticism, hankering, hunger, itch, longing, lust, urge, yearning, yen

n 7 alacrity, ardor, delight, devotion, diligence, enjoyment, enthusiasm, excitement, fervor, fire, flame, gaiety, gusto, relish, savor, thrill, zeal, zest

n 8 amorousness, amour, love

passionate adj 1 drastic, excessive, extreme, intense, radical, severe, strong

adj 2 ardent, enthusiastic, excitable, fervent, fiery, flaming, hot-blooded, impassioned, intense, stirring, sweaty, torrid, zealous

adj 3 anxious, ardent, avid, breathless, desirous, eager, enthusiastic, excited, fain, impatient, impetuous, keen, raring, zealous

adj 4 amorous, ardent, aroused, carnal, earthy, erotic, fervent, fleshly, horny, hot, impassioned, lascivious, lecherous, lewd, licentious, lustful, provocative, randy, raunchy, romantic, sensual, sexual, sexy, sultry, titillated, torrid, turned on, voluptuous, wanton

adj 5 amorous, aroused, horny, in heat, in the mood, lustful, stimulated

adj 6 coercive, compelling, dynamic, energetic, forceful, hardy, lusty, mighty, powerful, robust, strong, sturdy, vigorous

passionless adj 1 anemic, bloodless, gaunt, haggard, lifeless, pale, pallid, spiritless, watery, weak

adj 2 cold, frigid, inhibited, repressed, restrained, reticent, unresponsive

passive adj 1 apathetic, indifferent, languid, torpid

adj 2 calm, coolheaded, nonaggressive, nonviolent, peaceful

adj 3 acquiescent, compliant, docile, easy, meek, mild, nonresistant, obedient, resigned, submissive, tame, tolerant, unassertive, yielding

adj 4 asleep, dormant, idle, immobile, inactive, inanimate, inert, inoperative, laid-back, motionless, nodding, quiet, sleepy, slumbering, stable, stagnant, still

adj 5 see: DORMANT adj 2, 3

passport n identification, pass, permit, ticket, visa

past adv beyond, farther than, outside, yonder

adj 1 forgotten, gone, left behind, lost, once, suppressed, unremembered, vague

adj 2 bygone, erstwhile, former, late, old, once, onetime, sometime

adj 3 aforementioned, ancient, antecedent, anterior, archaic, earlier, foregoing, former, preceding, previous, prior, recent

adj 4 ancient, antiquated, archaic, bygone, dated, dead, extinct, noncurrent, obsolete, old, outdated, outmoded, passé, worn

n background, breeding, culture, development, education, environment, experience, schooling, training, upbringing

paste *v* affix, bind, bond, cement, fasten, fuse, glue, join, lock, seal, secure, stick, unite

n adhesive, glue

pastel *n* acrylic, art, canvas, depiction, drawing, etching, illustration, landscape, lithograph, mural, oil, painting, picture, pen and ink, portrait, print, seascape, sketch, still life, watercolor

pastime *n* 1 avocation, distraction, diversion, hobby, moonlighting, sideline

n 2 amusement, distraction, diversion, enjoyment, entertainment, frolic, fun, game, hobby, play, recreation, sport

pastor *n* chaplain, clergyman, cleric, father, guru, minister, padre, parson, priest, rabbi, reverend

pastoral *adj* bucolic, country, garden, outland, peaceful, provincial, rural, rustic, suburban, wooded

pasture *n* field, grassland, lea, meadow, plain, prairie

pat *v* dab, paint, tap, touch

patch *n* 1 area, divot, land, sod, space, turf

n 2 end, piece, rag, scrap, shred, tatter

v 1 cover, fix, repair

v 2 doctor, fix, mend, overhaul, rebuild, recondition, reconstruct, refit, renovate, repair, revamp

patent *adj* 1 open, unclosed, unobstructed

adj 2 apparent, clear, conspicuous, distinct, evident, given, indisputable, indubitable, manifest, obvious, plain, presumed, self-evident, straightforward, true, unambiguous, unequivocal, unmistakable

n exemption, grant, permission, right, safeguard

v claim, copyright, protect, register, trademark

pater *n* dad, dada, daddy, father, pa, papa, pappy, parent, patriarch, pop, poppa

path *n* 1 course, direction, drift, strategy, tack, tactic, tendency, tenor, trend

n 2 circuit, course, itinerary, journey, line, means, passage, road, route, trip, voyage, way

n 3 access, approach, artery, avenue, boulevard, channel, drag, highway, pass,

promenade, road, roadway, route, strait, street, thoroughfare, trail, way

pathetic *adj* affecting, deplorable, lamentable, miserable, paltry, pitiable, pitiful, poor, sad, unfortunate, woeful, wretched

pathos *n* poignance

pathway *n* conduit, passageway, shaft, subway, tube, tunnel

patience *n* endurance, forbearance, perseverance, persistence, resignation, resolution, tenacity

patient *adj* 1 accepting, charitable, easy, forbearing, indulgent, lenient, merciful, restrained, sympathetic, tolerant

adj 2 deliberate, dilatory, diligent, leisurely, methodical, meticulous, painstaking, procrastinating, slow, thorough, unhasty, unhurried

n convalescent, invalid, shut-in

patina *n* coating, gloss, glow, luster, polish, radiance, sheen, shimmer, shine

patio *n* lanai, piazza, porch, terrace, veranda

patois *n* accent, brogue, dialect, speech, tongue

patriarch *n* 1 ancestor, antecedent, ascendant, elder, forebear, forefather, forerunner, founder, grandparent, parent, predecessor, progenitor

n 2 dad, dada, daddy, father, pa, papa, pappy, parent, pater, pop, poppa

patrimony *n* birthright, endowment, entitlement, estate, heritage, legacy

patrol *n* exploration, foray, infiltration, invasion, penetration, raid

v defend, guard, oversee, police, protect, regulate, safeguard, watch

patron *n* 1 buyer, client, consumer, customer, end user, purchaser, shopper, user

n 2 see: ADVOCATE *n* 2

patronage *n* 1 bias, favoritism

n 2 auspices, authorization, backing, command, confirmation, endorsement, fiat, sanction, sponsorship, support

n 3 see: AUDACITY *n*

patronize *v* 1 befriend

v 2 condescend, deign, kowtow, stoop

v 3 attend, frequent, hang around, hang out, haunt, obsess, resort to, visit

patronizing *adj* 1 arrogant, condescending, haughty, pretentious, snobbish

adj 2 arrogant, cavalier, conceited, contemptuous, curt, dictatorial, disdainful, grandiose, haughty, huffy, insolent, lofty, lordly, moody, obtrusive, overbearing, proud, scornful, snooty, stuck up, supercilious, superior, vain

patrons *n* audience, spectators, witnesses

pattern n 1 design, device, figure, motif, motive

n 2 boundaries, form, framework, structure

n 3 current, drift, run, series, succession, tendency, trend

n 4 arrangement, blueprint, method, order, orderliness, outline, plan, system

n 5 epitome, example, exemplar, ideal, mirror, model, outline, paradigm, plan, prototype, rule of thumb, standard

n 6 mask, stencil, template

v act, ape, copy, emulate, follow, imitate, lip-synch, mime, mimic, mock, model, mouth, pantomime, parody, take off

paunch n abdomen, belly, gut, midriff, stomach, tummy, tum-tum

pauper n 1 chattel, peasant, peon, serf, slave, vassal

n 2 beggar, bum, derelict, drifter, hobo, loafer, mendicant, panhandler, tramp, vagabond, vagrant

pause n 1 delay, interim, interval

n 2 break, delay, distraction, disturbance, diversion, hold-up, interruption

n 3 break, breath, breather, breathing space, intermission, reprieve, respite, rest

n 4 break, cessation, delay, gap, interim, interval, lapse, lull, stop

n 5 joint, juncture, period

n 6 delay, interval, lull, stay, suspension, wait

n 7 abeyance, dormancy, inactivity, inaction, limbo, lull, suspension

v 1 demur, halt, hold up, interrupt, rest, stop, suspend

v 2 delay, falter, halt, hesitate, stagger, stall, vacillate, waver

pavement n ground, paving, sidewalk, walkway

paving n ground, pavement, sidewalk, walkway

paw v examine, feel, finger, fondle, grope, handle, manipulate, maul, palpate, probe, touch

n extremity, foot, hand

pawn n 1 chessman, front, instrument, peon, puppet, stooge, tool

n 2 see: COMMITMENT n 4

v borrow, mortgage

pay n bill, bonus, charge, commission, compensation, consideration, earnings, fee, gross, income, revenue, salary, stipend, wage

v 1 bring in, profit, return, yield

v 2 avenge, compensate, cover, disburse, indemnify, reciprocate, redress, reimburse, remedy, remunerate, repair, repay, requite, retaliate, revenge, settle, vindicate

payable adj due, open, outstanding, owed, unpaid

payback n see: PROFITS n

payload n 1 bomb, bombshell, explosive, mine, missile, rocket, rocketry, warhead

n 2 burden, cargo, consignment, freight, lading, load, shipment, transportation, truck

paymaster n banker, cashier, money-changer, purser, teller

payment n 1 alimony, allowance, annuity, residual, stipend

n 2 alimony, compensation, fee, honorarium, remuneration, reward, stipend

n 3 cost, charge, expense, fare, outlay, price, rate, value, worth

n 4 bribe, payoff, payola, ransom

payoff n 1 climax, outcome, result, return, reward

n 2 bribe, payment, payola, ransom

payola n bribe, payoff, ransom

pea n see: DOT n 1

peace n 1 accord, calm, harmony, serenity, stillness, tranquillity

n 2 calm, hush, lull, peacefulness, quiet, repose, respite, rest, siesta, silence, sleep, stillness, tranquillity

n 3 utopia

peaceful adj 1 calm, coolheaded, nonaggressive, nonviolent, pacifist, passive

adj 2 bucolic, country, garden, outland, pastoral, provincial, rural, rustic, suburban, wooded

adj 3 see: AMIABLE adj 3

adj 4 see: CALM adj 1, 2

peacefulness n 1 calm, hush, lull, peace, quiet, repose, respite, rest, siesta, silence, sleep, stillness, tranquillity

n 2 calmness, composure, equanimity, harmony, self-possession, serenity, tranquillity

peachy adj admirable, beautiful, delightful, glorious, good, magnificent, splendid, terrific, wonderful

peak v 1 crest, top

v 2 flood, flow, gush, pour, rise, roll, spill, stream, surge, swell

n 1 alp, hill, mountaintop, summit

n 2 acme, apex, apogee, climax, crescendo, crest, crown, culmination, epitome, height, noon, pinnacle, point, prime, summit, tip, top, ultimate, utmost, zenith

peal v boom, chime, clang, resonate, resound, reverberate, ring, sound, toll

peasant n 1 commoner, common man, countryman, plebeian, proletarian *n* 2 chattel, pauper, peon, serf, slave, vassal

pebble *n* boulder, detritus, fragments, rock, stone

peck *v* 1 jab, pick, poke

v 2 see: SCOLD *v* 2

peculiar *adj* 1 charming, funny, odd, old-fashioned, picturesque, puzzling, quaint, remarkable, special, uncommon, unusual, whimsical

adj 2 characteristic, differentiating, distinctive, lone, one, particular, select, single, solitary, special, unique, unusual

adj 3 aberrant, bizarre, eccentric, erratic, odd, oddball, outlandish, quaint, queer, singular, strange, uncanny, unconventional, unusual, weird

peculiarity *n* 1 characteristic, difference, distinction

n 2 abnormality, eccentricity, habit, idiosyncrasy, oddity, quirk, trademark

n 3 affectation, airs, mannerism, posturing, pose, pretense, trait

n 4 attribute, character, characteristic, feature, highlight, mark, property, quality, trait, virtue

pecuniary *adj* financial, monetary

pedal *v* bike, propel, push

n lever

pedantic *adj* academic, educated, educational, erudite, intellectual, learned, literary, literate, scholarly, scholastic, well-read

peddle *v* 1 barter, distribute, market, merchandise, retail, sell, vend, wholesale

v 2 deal, hawk, horse-trade, huckster, hustle, monger, push, sell, swap

pedestrian *adj* 1 common, commonplace, dull, ordinary, prosaic, uneventful, unexceptional

adj 2 common, earthly, earthy, mundane, terrestrial, uncelestial, worldly

adj 3 blah, boring, commonplace, dim, dreary, dull, flat, humdrum, monotonous, ordinary, stodgy, tedious, tiresome

pedigree *n* see: ANCESTRY *n* 1

peek *n* glance, look

v 1 butt in, chisel in, cut in, fiddle, horn in, interfere, interlope, intrude, meddle, mess around, peer, poke, pry, snoop, tamper with

v 2 eye, glance, glimpse

peel *n* bark, case, coating, crust, husk, rind, shell, shuck, skin

v 1 crack, husk, open, remove, shell

v 2 flay, scale, skin, strip

v 3 cast off, drop, molt, repel, shed

peeled *adj* bare, exposed, in the raw, naked, nude, open, stripped, unclothed, uncovered, visible

peer *n* 1 complement, counterpart, equal, equivalent, like, match

n 2 see: FRIEND *n* 1

v 1 eye, eyeball, gape, gawk, gaze, goggle, observe, ogle, stare, study

v 2 see: MEDDLE *v*

v 3 see: PROBE *v* 5

peerless *adj* alone, incomparable, matchless, only, unequaled, unique, unmatched, unpaired, unparalleled, unrivaled

peeve *v* see: BOTHER *v* 5

peg *n* brad, bolt, nut, pin, rivet, spike, staple, stud, weld

v connect, join, nail, pin, tack

pelf *n* see: MONEY *n* 4

pellet *n* atom, bead, dab, dash, dot, drop, grain, iota, molecule, morsel, particle, pea, smidgen, speck, tad

pelt *v* assail, attack, batter, beat, birch, buffet, flagellate, flog, hammer, lambaste, lash, lather, pound, pummel, punish, scourge, thrash, tromp, wallop, whip

n coat, fur, hide, jacket, skin, stole

pen *n* 1 brush, chalk, crayon, marker, pencil, quill

n 2 barn, coop, enclosure, hatch, lean-to, paddock, pound, shack, shed, shelter, stable, stall, sty

n 3 brig, cage, cell, cooler, coop, hoosegow, jail, penitentiary, pokey, prison, reformatory, slammer, stir, stockade, tower

v author, compose, create, draft, prepare, type, write

penalize *v* 1 adjudge, condemn, convict, discipline, imprison, punish, sentence

v 2 chastise, dock, fine, punish, sentence, tariff, tax

penalty *n* 1 cost, damage, deficit, loss, suffering

n 2 assessment, damages, fine, punishment, tax

n 3 discipline, dockage, fee, fine, loss, punishment

n 4 assessment, cost, duty, expense, fee, impost, levy, offering, price, sacrifice, tariff, tax, toll, trade-off

penance *n* atonement, attrition, contrition, penitence, reconciliation, remorse

penchant *n* bent, bias, drift, habit, inclination, leaning, partiality, predilection, preference, priority, proclivity, propensity, talent, taste, tendency

pencil *n* brush, chalk, crayon, marker, pen, quill

pending *adj* 1 awaiting, contingent, impending, unfinished, unsettled

adj 2 advancing, approaching, oncoming, forthcoming, imminent, looming

pendulate *v* alternate, fluctuate, oscillate, sway, swing, vacillate, wave

pendulous *adj* feeble, flabby, flaccid, lax, limp, loose, relaxed, slack

penetrate *v* 1 enter, infiltrate, infuse, permeate, transfuse

v 2 break through, perforate, pierce, poke, prick, punch

v 3 gore, impale, lance, pierce, puncture, spear, stab

v 4 edge in, foist, imbue, infiltrate, insinuate, permeate, sneak in, work in, worm

v 5 analyze, assess, determine, diagnose, estimate, examine, probe, scope, solve, survey, understand, unravel

v 6 imbue, impart, infuse, ingrain, inject, inoculate, instill, invest, pervade, spread, steep, suffuse, teach, train

v 7 register

v 8 cut, gash, incise, pierce, punch, slash, slice, slit

penetrating *adj* 1 inquiring, keen, piercing, probing, searching

adj 2 biting, caustic, cutting, incisive, pointed, trenchant

adj 3 see: ESOTERIC *adj*

adj 4 see: QUICK *adj* 5

penetration *n* exploration, foray, infiltration, invasion, patrol, raid

peninsula *n* cape, isthmus, point, promontory

penitence *n* 1 guilt, regret, remorse, repentance, sorrow

n 2 atonement, attrition, contrition, penance, reconciliation, remorse

penitent *adj* 1 ashamed, guilty, repentant

adj 2 apologetic, contrite, remorseful, repentant, sorry

penitentiary *n* brig, cage, cell, cooler, coop, hoosegow, jail, pen, pokey, prison, reformatory, slammer, stir, stockade, tower

penmanship *n* handwriting, script, writing

pennant *n* flag

penniless *adj* 1 bankrupt, broke, busted, destitute, dissolved, insolvent, out of business, ruined

adj 2 broke, destitute, dirt-poor, down and out, impoverished, indigent, needy, poor, poverty-stricken, strapped, unprosperous

penny-pinching *adj* cheap, close, greedy, mean, miserly, niggardly, parsimonious, stingy, tight, tightfisted, ungenerous, ungiving

pen pusher *n* bureaucrat, clerk, official

pension *v* dismiss, retire, superannuate

pensive *adj* 1 meditative, melancholy, musing, nostalgic, wistful

adj 2 meditative, philosophical, pondering, reflective, speculative, thinking, thoughtful

adj 3 dignified, earnest, grave, sedate, serious, sober, solemn, somber, staid, stoic, unemotional, unflinching

peon *n* chattel, pauper, peasant, serf, slave, vassal

n chessman, front, instrument, pawn, puppet, stooge, tool

people *n* 1 family, kin, relation, relative

n 2 crew, employees, faculty, help, personnel, staff, workers

n 3 breed, clan, class, family, household, race, relatives, stock, tribe

n 4 citizens, civilization, colony, community, crowd, culture, folks, group, human beings, individuals, laity, masses, men and women, neighbors, persons, populace, population, public, settlement, society, staff, tribe

pep *n* 1 effectiveness, flair, kick, pizzazz, potency, punch, sizzle, snap, spark, verve, vigor, wallop

n 2 animation, drive, élan, energy, enthusiasm, esprit de corps, go, gusto, potency, sparkle, spirit, spunk, verve, vigor, vim, vitality, zing, zip

n 3 see: VIGOR *n* 2, 3

peppery *adj* 1 aromatic, lively, piquant, poignant, pungent, racy, snappy, spicy, spirited, vigorous, zesty

adj 2 see: HOT-TEMPERED *adj*

peppy *adj* see: LIVELY *adj* 8

perambulate *v* see: WANDER *v*

perambulatory *adj* ambulatory, gypsy, itinerant, movable, nomadic, roving, transient, vagrant, wandering, wayfaring

perceive *v* 1 detect, experience, feel, notice, sense

v 2 behold, catch, comprehend, conjure, descry, digest, discern, distinguish, espy, fathom, grasp, know, look at, notice, observe, realize, recognize, savvy, see, sight, take in, understand, view

v 3 scent, smell, sniff

percentage *n* 1 proportion, quota, quotient, rate, ratio

n 2 comparison, proportion, ratio, relation, share

n 3 allotment, allowance, apportionment, budget, dispensation, dispersion, lot, measure, part, portion, quota, ration, share, slice

n 4 ante, award, bonus, booty, cash, commission, dividend, donation, fee, gift, gratuity, largess, money, perk, perquisite, premium, prize, profit, purse, reward, sharing, stake, stipend, tip, winnings

perceptible *adj* appreciable, cognizant, concrete, detectable, discernible, noticeable, observable, palpable, sensible, tangible, visible

perception *n* 1 detection, discovery

n 2 sight, vision

n 3 cognition, comprehension, grasp, insight, recognition, understanding

n 4 esteem, fame, good standing, name, regard, reputation, stature

n 5 concept, conception, hunch, idea, image, impression, notion, recollection, thought, view

n 6 acumen, astuteness, awareness, cleverness, discernment, discrimination, insight, intellect, intuition, keenness, sagacity, sensitivity, shrewdness, understanding, wit

n 7 attention, awareness, care, carefulness, cognizance, concern, consciousness, consideration, heed, intimacy, knowing, knowledge, mark, note, notice, observance, observation, recognition, regard, remark, sense

n 8 awareness, emotion, faculty, feel, feeling, intuition, reaction, response, sensation, sense

perceptive *adj* 1 astute, consequent, intelligent, knowing, logical, rational, reasonable, sane, sensible, shrewd, sober, sound, wise

adj 2 acute, alert, astute, cagey, canny, clever, cunning, deft, keen, knowing, penetrating, piercing, quick, quick-sighted, quick-witted, receptive, responsive, sagacious, savvy, sensitive, sharp, sharp-witted, shrewd, slick, smart, street-smart, wise

adj 3 see: INTELLIGENT *adj* 3, 4

peremptory *adj* see: AUTHORITATIVE *adj* 2

perennial *adj* continuing, enduring, inveterate, lifelong, long-lasting, long-lived, ongoing

perfect *adj* 1 ideal, model, optimal, very

adj 2 exemplary, flawless, ideal, model, perfected

adj 3 accurate, certain, distinct, explicit, incontestable, infallible, unerring

adj 4 errorless, excellent, exquisite, fastidious, faultless, flawless, ideal, immaculate, impeccable

adj 5 absolute, complete, flawless, good, intact, sound, unblemished, unbroken, undamaged, unimpaired, uninjured, unmarred, untouched, whole

adj 6 absolute, chief, complete, consummate, dominant, godlike, leading, main, principal, pure, ranking, sheer, supreme, total, unsurpassed, utter, whole

v 1 refine

v 2 drill, learn, practice, prepare, rehearse, repeat, review, study

v 3 see: EDUCATE *v*

v 4 see: FINISH *v* 3

perfected *adj* exemplary, flawless, ideal, perfect

perfection *n* 1 integrity

n 2 correctness, flawlessness, precision

perfectionist *n* fusspot, nit-picker, purist, stickler

perfectly *adv* 1 exactly, precisely

adv 2 adequately, altogether, assiduously, completely, earnestly, entirely, exhaustively, fully, hard, intensely, intensively, painstakingly, quite, sufficiently, thoroughly, totally, unremittingly, utterly, wholly

perfidious *adj* cheating, conniving, deceitful, deceptive, dishonest, disloyal, faithless, false, insidious, manipulative, sneaky, traitorous, treacherous, unfaithful, untrue, untrustworthy

perfidy *n* betrayal, deception, subversion, treachery, trickery

perforate *v* 1 permeate, pierce, riddle, shoot

v 2 break through, penetrate, pierce, poke, prick, punch

perform *v* 1 achieve, do, execute

v 2 act, function, go, run, work

v 3 actuate, commit, do, enact, execute, perpetrate

v 4 accomplish, achieve, attain, consummate, execute, fulfill, produce, pull off, realize, succeed, triumph, win

v 5 access, accomplish, achieve, attain, derive, earn, fulfill, gain, get, merit, net, obtain, profit, rack up, reach, realize, score, win

v 6 accomplish, complete, consummate, execute, fulfill, realize

performance *n* 1 act, farce, make-believe, parody, show, sketch, skit

n 2 accomplishment, action, conduct, deed, delivery, demonstration, execution, talent

n 3 career, diary, events, experience, history, record, résumé, track record, vita

n 4 see: EXHIBITION *n*

performed *adj* accomplished, complete, concluded, done, ended, finished, over, terminated, through, wrapped up

performer *n* 1 achiever

n 2 actor, actress, artist, entertainer, hero, heroine, lead, movie star, player, protagonist, star, thespian, tragedian

n 3 accompanist, artiste, conductor, instrumentalist, musician, virtuoso

perfume *n* aroma, balm, bouquet, fragrance, incense, scent, spice

v scent

perfunctory *adj* hollow, nominal, professed, representative, small, symbolic, token

perhaps *adv* conditionally, maybe, perchance, possibly, tentatively

peril *n* 1 adventure, encounter, event, experience, hazard, ordeal, risk

n 2 danger, downside, exposure, hazard, jeopardy, liability, menace, risk, threat

perilous *adj* breakneck, critical, dangerous, harmful, hazardous, precarious, risky, serious, unsafe, venturesome

perimeter *n* 1 boundary, circuit, circumference, compass, periphery

n 2 atmosphere, climate, conditions, environment, habitat, niche, settings, surroundings

n 3 border, boundary, bounds, brim, brink, curb, edge, fringe, limits, lip, margin, outskirt, periphery, rim, side, skirt, verge

period *n* 1 cycle, duration, interval, season, span, spell, stage, stretch, term, time

n 2 aeon, age, cycle, decade, eon, epoch, era, eternity, forever, long time, millennium, reign, span, stage, time, years

n 3 juncture, pause

periodic *adj* alternate, cyclic, cyclical, intermittent, periodical, recurrent, recurring, repeated, repetitive, sporadic

periodical *n* booklet, gazette, journal, magazine, monthly, publication, quarterly, weekly

adj see: RECURRENT *adj*

periodically *adv* every so often, now and then, occasionally, sometime

peripheral *adj* abnormal, extra, extraneous, foreign, illogical, immaterial, insignificant, irregular, irrelevant, malapropos, nonessential, superfluous, surplus, unimportant, unnecessary, unrelated

periphery *n* 1 borderline, boundary, bounds

n 2 boundary, circuit, circumference, compass, perimeter

n 3 edge, fringe, border, boundary, bounds, brim, brink, curb, limits, lip, margin, outskirt, perimeter, rim, side, skirt, verge

n 4 border, extreme, extremity, limit

periscope *n* binoculars, eye, field glass, glass, lens, magnifying glass, microscope, mirror, scope, spyglass, telescope

perish *v* 1 cease, die, elapse, expire, lapse, pass, pass away, succumb, terminate

v 2 corrupt, crumble, decay, decompose, degenerate, deteriorate, disintegrate, putrefy, rot, smell, spoil, taint, wane, weaken, wither

perjure *v* concoct, deceive, equivocate, fabricate, falsify, fib, invent, lie

perjury *n* deceit, deception, fabrication, falsehood, fraud, fraudulence, hypocrisy, lying, trickery, untruth

perk *v* ameliorate, convalesce, gain, heal, improve, loop up, mend, rally, recover, recuperate, rehabilitate, revive

n see: REWARD *n* 8

permanent *adj* 1 indelible, unalterable, unerasable

adj 2 irrevocable, noncancelable, nonrescindable, unalterable, uncancelable

adj 3 constant, continuing, durable, enduring, eternal, lasting, ongoing, stable

adj 4 fastened, fixed, in position, motionless, set, solid, standing, static, stationary, still

adj 5 hopeless, impossible, incurable, irreparable, irresolvable, irrevocable, terminal, unalterable, uncorrectable, uncurable, unfixable

permeate *v* 1 perforate, pierce, riddle, shoot

v 2 imbue, impregnate, saturate, wet

v 3 enter, infiltrate, infuse, penetrate, transfuse

v 4 diffuse, disseminate, distribute, spread, sprinkle, strew

v 5 edge in, foist, imbue, infiltrate, insinuate, penetrate, sneak in, work in, worm

permissible *adj* allowable, authorized, lawful, legal, legitimate, rightful, valid

permission *n* 1 exemption, grant, patent, right, safeguard

n 2 approval, authorization, consent, leave, license, sanction

permit *n* 1 identification, pass, passport, ticket, visa

n 2 certificate, credential, document, instrument, license

v 1 charter, franchise, hire, lease, let, rent, sublet

v 2 accredit, authorize, certify, commission, empower, enable, entitle, facilitate, invest, license, sanction, validate

v 3 see: TOLERATE *v*

permutation *n* adjustment, alteration, anomaly, change, deviation, modification, mutation, shift, variation

pernicious *adj* baneful, deadly, fatal, lethal, mortal, noxious, pestilent, ruinous

perpendicular *adj* sheer, steep, upright, vertical

perpetrate *v* actuate, commit, do, enact, perform

perpetrator *n* accused, con, convict, criminal, crook, culprit, delinquent, felon, guilty party, inmate, lawbreaker, offender, prisoner, scofflaw, suspect, swindler, transgressor, wrongdoer

perpetual *adj* 1 endless, eternal, immortal, infinite, unceasing, undying

adj 2 ageless, boundless, ceaseless, constant, continual, continuous, endless, eternal, everlasting, incessant, infinite, interminable, limitless, never-ending, ongoing, persistent, relentless, timeless, unceasing, unending, uninterrupted, unremitting

perpetually *adv* ad infinitum, all the time, always, constantly, continually, endlessly, forever, eternally, timelessly, unceasingly

perpetuate *v* 1 attempt, bring about, cultivate, practice, proceed, pursue

v 2 commit, continue, extend, maintain, prolong, pull

perplex *v* 1 baffle, confound, confuse, frustrate, stymie, thwart

v 2 amaze, befog, bewilder, boggle, confound, confuse, daze, puzzle, stumble, stump

v 3 aggravate, baffle, balk, bewilder, circumvent, confuse, dash, elude, foil, frustrate, hamper, impede, negate, thwart

perplexity *n* 1 befuddlement, bewilderment, complication, confusion

n 2 see: ENIGMA *n* 2

perquisite *n* 1 advantage, birthright, claim, edge, enablement, prerogative, privilege, right, title

n 2 ante, award, bonus, booty, cash, commission, dividend, donation, fee, gift, gratuity, largess, money, percentage, perk, premium, prize, profit, purse, reward, sharing, stake, stipend, tip, winnings

persecute *v* 1 aggrieve, exploit, oppress, torture

v 2 abuse, brutalize, exploit, ill-treat, injure, harm, maltreat, mistreat, molest, victimize, wrong

v 3 see: ANNOY *v* 3

perseverance *n* endurance, forbearance, patience, persistence, resignation, resolution, tenacity

persevere *v* 1 lumber, persist, plod, plug, toil

v 2 accomplish, behave, contend, cope, manage

v 3 abide, continue, endure, last, outlast, persist, prevail, remain, stay, stick to, stick with, survive

persevering *adj* ambitious, assiduous, diligent, energetic, hard-working, industrious, persistent, resolute, sedulous, zealous

persist *v* 1 lumber, persevere, plod, plug, toil

v 2 be, endure, exist, last, live, prevail, survive

v 3 assert, demand, emphasize, force, insist, require, urge

v 4 abide, continue, endure, last, outlast, persevere, prevail, remain, stay, stick to, stick with, survive

persistence *n* 1 discipline, self-control, volition, will, willpower

n 2 endurance, forbearance, patience, perseverance, resignation, resolution, tenacity

n 3 backbone, chutzpah, determination, endurance, fortitude, grit, guts, moxie, nerve, pluck, resilience, spirit, spunk, stamina, strength, tenacity, tolerance, vigor, willpower

persistent *adj* 1 adamant, tenacious, unrelenting

adj 2 determined, resolute, stubborn, tenacious

adj 3 chronic, extended, incurable, protracted, refractory, stubborn

adj 4 ambitious, assiduous, energetic, diligent, hard-working, industrious, persevering, resolute, sedulous, zealous

adj 5 see: PERPETUAL *adj* 2

persnickety *adj* careful, cautious, choosy, discriminating, fastidious, finicky, fussy, meticulous, nit-picking, particular, picky, selective

person *n* 1 associate, collaborator, individual, member, participant, party, registrant

n 2 being, citizen, creature, entity, Homo sapiens, human, human being, individual, man, woman

persona n ego, id, individuality, mind, personality, psyche, self, soul, spirit

personal adj **1** close, familiar, intimate

adj **2** individual, particular, special, specific

adj **3** individual, introspective, private, subjective

adj **4** exclusive, individual, intimate, own, private, secret, special

personality n **1** celebrity, dignitary, luminary, movie star, name, notable, star

n **2** charisma, dominance, influence, leadership, magnetism, power, strength

n **3** ego, id, individuality, mind, persona, psyche, self, soul, spirit

n **4** aptitude, character, complexion, disposition, distinctiveness, heart, humor, identity, inclination, individuality, make-up, nature, quality, spirit, state, temperament, tendency

personify v embody, exemplify, express, represent, symbolize, typify

personnel n **1** associates, constituency, constituents, membership

n **2** crew, employees, faculty, help, people, staff, workers

persons n citizens, civilization, colony, community, crowd, culture, folks, group, human beings, individuals, laity, masses, men and women, neighbors, people, populace, population, public, settlement, society, staff, tribe

perspective n **1** horizon, lookout, outlook, prospect, vista

n **2** distance, future, horizon, outlook, purview, vision, vista

n **3** angle, aspect, facet, hand, mien, opinion, phase, side, slant, view

n **4** condition, mode, posture, situation, state, status, update

perspicuous adj articulate, expressive, fluent

perspiration n moisture, sweat, wetness

perspire v sweat

persuade v **1** bring, cause, convert, lead, move

v **2** campaign, canvass, influence, lobby, strive, support

v **3** brainwash, convert, inculcate, indoctrinate, preach, proselytize

v **4** affect, assure, convince, impel, induce, influence, inspire, instigate, motivate, move, pressure, prompt, stir, sway, talk into, touch, win over

v **5** see: MOVE v **2, 3**

v **6** see: URGE v **3**

persuasion n **1** denomination, sect

n **2** affiliation, belief, church, creed, denomination, faith, religion, rite, seat, theology

n **3** attitude, belief, bias, conviction, feeling, inducement, leaning, mind, opinion, sentiment, slant, view

n **4** bracket, breed, cast, category, class, division, family, genre, genus, group, grouping, ilk, kind, lot, mold, nature, order, section, sector, set, sort, species, style, type, variety

persuasive adj **1** articulate, clear, cogent, eloquent, fluent, well-spoken

adj **2** aggressive, coercive, compelling, forceful, hard sell, high-pressure, intensive, pushy

adj **3** see: SOLID adj **4**

pert adj **1** alert, animated, bouncy, bright, brisk, buoyant, chipper, dashing, dynamic, ebullient, energetic, enthusiastic, exuberant, frisky, frolicsome, gay, jumpy, kinetic, lively, peppy, playful, rousing, scintillating, spirited, sprightly, spry, vivacious

adj **2** see: RUDE adj **3**

pertain v apply, bear, concern, refer, regard, relate

pertinence n see: UTILITY n

pertinent adj applicable, appropriate, apropos, apt, befitting, convenient, desirable, felicitous, fit, fitting, germane, good, handy, just, material, meet, necessary, proper, relevant, right, shipshape, suitable, suited, timely, useful

perturb v annoy, antagonize, argue, bother, bug, concern, distress, disturb, goad, harass, hassle, inconvenience, irk, irritate, pain, strain, stress, taunt, trouble, try, upset, worry

peruse v **1** examine, inspect, observe, scan

v **2** browse, glance at, scan, skim

v **3** comprehend, decipher, decode, infer, interpret, read, study, understand

v **4** see: EXAMINE v **3, 9**

pervade v **1** infest, invade, overrun, plague, swarm

v **2** imbue, impart, infuse, ingrain, inject, inoculate, instill, invest, penetrate, spread, steep, suffuse, teach, train

perverse adj **1** balking, balky, contrary, cranky, disagreeable, irascible, mean, obstinate, ornery, wayward

adj **2** base, corrupt, deadly, degenerate, depraved, deviant, evil, immoral, infamous, kinky, nefarious, putrid, rotten, ruthless, savage, vicious, villainous, wicked, wild

adj **3** bullheaded, closed-minded, deaf, firm, hardheaded, hard-line, inelastic, inflexible, intractable, intransigent, obstinate, pigheaded, refractory, resolute, rigid, stiff, stubborn, tough, unbending, uncompromising, unpliable, unpliant, unwieldy, unyielding, willful

pervert n debaucher, deviant, deviate, weirdo

v 1 contaminate, debase, degrade, desecrate, profane

v 2 bias, corrupt, distort, misrepresent, skew, slant, warp

v 3 abuse, corrupt, ill-use, misapply, misemploy, mishandle, misuse, prostitute

v 4 adulterate, corrupt, debase, debauch, defile, demoralize, dishonor, ruin, seduce, taint

pesky adj annoying, bothersome, glaring, harassing, irksome, irritating, mean, onerous, painful, troublesome, ugly, unwelcome, vexatious, wicked

pesos n see: MONEY n 4

pessimism n gloom, misery, woe

pessimist n critic, cynic, detractor, hatchet man, skeptic

pessimistic adj cynical, depressed, gloomy, glum, grim, negative

pester v 1 aggravate, annoy, badger, bait, bedevil, beleaguer, bother, bug, harass, harry, hassle, heckle, hound, hurt, intimidate, jeer, nag, needle, persecute, plague, provoke, ride, spite, taunt, tease, threaten, torment, worry

v 2 see: BOTHER v 5

pestilence n 1 affliction, blight, impediment, scourge

n 2 bane, curse, disease, evil, plague, scourge

pestilent adj baneful, deadly, fatal, lethal, mortal, noxious, pernicious, ruinous

pet adj cherished, special

v caress, cradle, cuddle, embrace, feel, fondle, fool around, hold, hug, love, make out, neck, nuzzle, snuggle, stroke

petite adj bantam, dainty, diminutive, dwarfish, Lilliputian, little, micro, microscopic, midget, mini, miniature, minuscule, minute, pygmy, slight, tiny, small, wee

petition n 1 invocation, plea, prayer, request

n 2 appeal, desire, favor, plea, request, solicitation, wish

v 1 apply, claim, enroll, file, request, sign up

v 2 appeal, apply, attack, file suit, go to court, litigate, plead, prosecute, solicit, sue

petrify v appall, daunt, discourage, dismay, horrify, panic, scare, shock, terrify, unnerve

petrol n energy, fuel, gasoline, propellant

petty adj 1 begrudging, small-minded, spiteful

adj 2 immaterial, inconsequential, inconsiderable, insignificant, little, low, meaningless, measly, minor, nominal, paltry, picayune, picky, puny, skimpy, slight, small, tiny, trifling, trivial, unessential, unimportant, worthless

adj 3 borderline, casual, frivolous, insignificant, light, lightweight, little, marginal, meager, minor, minute, negligible, nonessential, off, outside, remote, secondary, slender, slight, slim, small, tenuous, trivial, unimportant

adj 4 see: MEAGER adj 2

pew n bench, chair, seat, stool

phantasm n aberration, apparition, delusion, fantasy, figment, ghost, hallucination, illusion, image, mirage, specter, vision

pharmaceutical n compound, drug, elixir, formula, medicine, narcotic, painkiller, prescription

phase n 1 condition, level, stage, state, step

n 2 angle, aspect, facet, hand, mien, opinion, perspective, side, slant, view

phenomenal adj 1 amazing, brilliant, exceptional, extraordinary, noteworthy, rare, remarkable, significant, singular, stunning, super, uncommon, uncustomary, unique, unusual

adj 2 dynamite, excellent, extraordinary, great, out of sight, outstanding, premier, super, superlative, superb, tremendous, wonderful

adj 3 colossal, enormous, fantastic, Gargantuan, giant, gigantic, Goliath, great, huge, immense, jumbo, leviathan, mammoth, massive, mighty, monstrous, monumental, overwhelming, prodigious, Promethean, stupendous, Titanic, towering, tremendous, unfathomed, untold, vast, walloping, whopping

phenomenon n marvel, miracle, sensation, spectacle, wonder

philanderer n buck, Casanova, Don Juan, flirt, gallant, ladies' man, lecher, lover, playboy, Romeo, stud

philanthropic adj altruistic, benevolent, bountiful, caring, charitable, Christian, compassionate, generous, giving, good, humane, humanitarian, kind, lenient, merciful, tender

philharmonic adj choral, euphonious, harmonious, lyric, mellow, melodic, melodious, musical, orchestral, rhythmical, symphonic, tuneful, vocal

philosopher n academician, egghead, highbrow, intellectual, pundit, researcher, sage, savant, scholar, thinker, wise man

philosophical adj meditative, pensive, pondering, reflective, speculative, thinking, thoughtful

philosophy n 1 knowledge, laws, principles, thinking, wisdom

n 2 beliefs, code, doctrine, ethics, outlook, rites, values

phlegmatic adj cold, dry, dull, impassive, laid-back, matter-of-fact, poker-faced, reserved, stoic, stolid, unaffected, unemotional, unfeeling, unmoved, untouched

phone v buzz, call, communicate, contact, ring, telephone, touch

phone book n atlas, compendium, directory, guide, guidebook, handbook, list, listing, manual, textbook, Yellow Pages

phonetician n linguist, semanticist

phony adj 1 contrived, fake, seeming

adj 2 affected, effeminate, genteel, pretentious

adj 3 artificial, bogus, counterfeit, ersatz, fake, false, imitation, mock, pseudo, sham, simulated, spurious, substitute, unreal

n charlatan, counterfeit, fake, faker, fraud, hypocrite, impostor, liar, pretender

photo n halftone, photograph, picture, slide, snapshot

photograph n halftone, photo, picture, slide, snapshot

photographic adj detailed, graphic, illustrative, pictorial, picturesque, visual, vivid

phrase n 1 expression, idiom, locution, name, saying, term, word, wording

n 2 cliché, diction, expression, parlance, saying, slogan, style, term, wording

v announce, articulate, assert, couch, describe, dictate, draft, enunciate, express, intonate, orate, proclaim, pronounce, say, speak, state, stress, talk, utter, verbalize, vocalize, voice, word

physic n cleansing, laxative, purge

physical adj 1 carnal, intimate, sexual

adj 2 blue-collar, manual, menial

adj 3 concrete, corporeal, material, objective, real, sensible, substantial, tactile, tangible

physician n diagnostician, doctor, healer, intern, resident, specialist, surgeon

physique n anatomy, body, build, figure, form, frame, shape

piazza n lanai, patio, porch, terrace, veranda

picayune adj immaterial, inconsequential, inconsiderable, insignificant, little, low, meaningless, measly, minor, nominal, paltry, petty, picky, puny, skimpy, slight, small, tiny, trifling, trivial, unessential, unimportant, worthless

pick n 1 best, choice, elite, favorite, finest, optimum, pride, select

n 2 alternative, choice, decision, druthers, election, option, preference, rathers, selection, vote

v 1 jab, poke

v 2 choose, elect, wish, will

v 3 choose, cull, elect, remove, select, separate, sift, single out, sort

picked adj chosen, designated, elected, select, selected

picket n 1 boycott, dispute, strike, walkout

n 2 guard, lookout, sentinel, sentry, ward, warden, watch, watchman

pickup n 1 seduction

n 2 acceleration, achievement, advance, advancement, betterment, breakthrough, furtherance, growth, headway, improvement, increment, proficiency, progress, promotion, strengthening, upgrade

picky adj 1 exacting, fastidious, finicky, meticulous, precise, rigid, strict

adj 2 careful, cautious, choosy, discriminating, fastidious, finicky, fussy, meticulous, nit-picking, particular, selective

adj 3 see: TRIVIAL adj 1

picnic n barbecue, clambake, cookout, outing

pictorial adj detailed, graphic, illustrative, photographic, picturesque, visual, vivid

picture n 1 sight, view

n 2 halftone, photo, photograph, slide, snapshot

n 3 acrylic, art, canvas, depiction, drawing, etching, illustration, landscape, lithograph, mural, oil, painting, pastel, pen and ink, portrait, print, seascape, sketch, still life, watercolor

v 1 delineate, depict, illustrate, portray, represent, sketch

v 2 clarify, clear, clear up, delineate, depict, elucidate, explain, illuminate, illustrate, portray, reveal

picturesque adj 1 detailed, graphic, illustrative, photographic, pictorial, visual, vivid

adj 2 charming, funny, odd, old-fashioned, peculiar, puzzling, quaint, remarkable, special, uncommon, unusual, whimsical

piddle *v* see: TRIFLE *v* 1

piece *n* 1 article, element, entity, item, object, thing

n 2 bit, chip, dent, flake, fragment, mark

n 3 adjunct, annex, fitting, fixture, part, unit

n 4 end, patch, rag, scrap, shred, tatter

n 5 bit, clipping, cut, division, lot, member, parcel, part, portion, sample, section, segment, slice

n 6 bit, dab, end, fragment, iota, minutia, mite, morsel, particle, pinch, portion, scrap, shred, speck, spot, strip, tidbit, trifle

n 7 length, measure, strip

n 8 bite, morsel, nip, quick meal, snack

n 9 automatic, firearm, gun, handgun, heater, iron, luger, pistol, revolver, rod

pier *n* dock, jetty, landing, wharf

pierce *n* cut, gash, incision, nick, prick, puncture, slit, wound

v 1 perforate, permeate, riddle, shoot

v 2 auger, bore, drill, ream, tool

v 3 break through, penetrate, perforate, poke, prick, punch

v 4 gore, impale, lance, penetrate, puncture, spear, stab

v 5 cut, gash, incise, penetrate, punch, slash, slice, slit

piercing *adj* 1 acute, sharp, shooting, stabbing

adj 2 inquiring, keen, penetrating, probing, searching

adj 3 acute, annoying, grating, high, loud, piping, sharp, shrill

adj 4 see: QUICK *adj* 5

pig *n* glutton, hog, overdoer, overeater, swine

pigeonhole *v* see: CLASSIFY *v* 2

pigheaded *adj* bullheaded, closed-minded, deaf, firm, hardheaded, hard-line, inelastic, inflexible, intractable, intransigent, obstinate, perverse, refractory, resolute, rigid, stiff, stubborn, tough, unbending, uncompromising, unpliable, unpliant, unwieldy, unyielding, willful

pigment *n* color, coloring, dye, paint, stain, tincture, tint

pile *n* 1 building, edifice, erection, foundation, house, store, structure, warehouse

n 2 bank, drift, heap, hill, mass, mound, mountain, stack, stockpile

n 3 see: STOCKPILE *n* 1, 2

v 1 bank, drift, heap, mound, stack

v 2 amass, collect, gather, heap, rake, take in

pileup *n* accident, collision, crackup, crash, destruction, mishap, smash, smashup, wreck, wreckage

pilfer *v* appropriate, burglarize, defraud, embezzle, filch, heist, lift, misappropriate, pillage, pinch, plunder, pocket, purloin, rip off, rob, snake, snitch, steal, swindle, swipe, take, thieve

pillage *v* 1 assault, attack, force, rape, ravish, sack, violate

v 2 deflower, desecrate, despoil, devastate, devour, loot, maraud, plunder, ravage, sack, scourge, spoil, strip, violate

v 3 see: STEAL *v* 2

pillar *n* column, pole, post, stake

pilot *adj* experimental, developmental, suggested, tentative, test, trial, untested

v 1 carry on, conduct, direct, keep, manage, operate, ordain, run

v 2 conduct, control, develop, direct, drive, guide, lead, operate, route, shepherd, show, steer

n airman, aviator, barnstormer, flier, operator

Pilsner *n* ale, beer, bock, brew, lager, stout, suds

pimple *n* abscess, boil, carbuncle, ulcer

pin *n* 1 axis, axle, pivot, pole, rod, shaft, spindle

n 2 bolt, brad, nut, peg, rivet, spike, staple, stud, weld

n 3 buckle, catch, clasp, clip, fastener, latch, snap, zipper

n 4 anklet, band, bangle, bracelet, brooch, earring, jewelry, medal, medallion, necklace, ring

v 1 connect, join, nail, peg, tack

v 2 attach, clip, fasten, nail, staple, tack

pinch *v* 1 pull, tweak, twist

v 2 apprehend, arrest, bag, book, bust, capture, catch, collar, detain, get, grab, lock up, nab, nail, pick up, pull in, run in, secure, seize, take

v 3 appropriate, burglarize, defraud, embezzle, filch, heist, lift, misappropriate, pilfer, pillage, plunder, pocket, purloin, rip off, rob, snake, snitch, steal, swindle, swipe, take, thieve

n 1 see: DILEMMA *n* 4

n 2 see: FRAGMENT *n* 3

pinched *adj* see: WEARY *adj* 1

pinch-hitter *n* stand-in, substitute, understudy

pine *v* ache, covet, crave, desire, hanker, hunger, itch, long, lust, need, thirst, want, yearn

pinko *n* Bolshevik, communist, red

pinnacle *n* acme, apex, apogee, climax,

crescendo, crest, crown, culmination, epitome, height, noon, peak, point, prime, summit, tip, top, ultimate, utmost, zenith

pioneer adj earliest, first, founding, fundamental, initial, maiden, original, primary, prime

n 1 forefront, front, head, lead, spearhead, vanguard

n 2 author, creator, founder, initiator, instigator, inventor, maker, originator, parent, seed, source

n 3 cowboy, rustic, yokel

v antedate, come before, forego, precede, preface, spearhead

pioneering adj innovative, new, novel, original, trailblazing, unprecedented

pioneers n innovators, leaders, pacesetters, trendsetters, vanguard

pious adj devout, godly, holy, prayerful, religious, reverent, sanctimonious

pipe n channel, conduit, cylinder, duct, tube

v carry, channel, conduct, convey, funnel, pass, siphon, transmit

piping adj acute, annoying, grating, high, loud, piercing, sharp, shrill

piquant adj aromatic, lively, peppery, poignant, pungent, racy, snappy, spicy, spirited, vigorous, zesty

pique n anger, animosity, hostility, indignation, huff, miff, resentment

v 1 adorn, plume, preen, pride, primp, stroke

v 2 arouse, awaken, excite, induce, instill, motivate, move, prime, provoke, quicken, rouse, roust, spark, start, stimulate, titillate, urge

v 3 see: BOTHER v 5

piracy n sabotage

pirouette v gyrate, purl, reel, spin, swim, turn, twirl, whirl

pistol n automatic, firearm, gun, handgun, heater, iron, luger, piece, revolver, rod

pit n 1 burial, catacomb, cenotaph, crypt, grave, mausoleum, memorial, monument, sepulcher, tomb, vault

n 2 booby trap, mousetrap, snare, trap

v combat, compete, contend, contest, counter, dispute, duel, fight, match, oppose, parry, play, repel, resist, rival, strive, struggle, vie

pitch n 1 frequency, sound, tone

n 2 come-on, line, presentation, spiel, talk

n 3 angle, grade, gradient, incline, ramp, rise, slant, slope, tilt

v 1 incline, bank, bend, lean, slant, slope

v 2 bob, heave, rock, roll, sway, swing, toss

v 3 careen, lurch, reel, stagger, sway, toss, totter, wheel

v 4 cast, flick, fling, flip, heave, hurl, launch, propel, sling, throw, toss

v 5 cave in, collapse, disintegrate, drop, fall, go down, keel over, plunge, slump, spill, topple, tumble

v 6 buck, throw, unseat

v 7 dive, lunge, lurch, plunge

v 8 advertise, air, boom, boost, drum up, endorse, plug, promote, publicize, push, rave, sell, tout

pitch-black adj black, charcoal, dark, shadowy

pitfall n booby trap, mousetrap, pit, snare, trap

pith n see: ESSENCE n 3

pithy adj 1 compact, definitive, meaty, seminal, tight

adj 2 abbreviated, brief, compressed, concise, crisp, curt, laconic, short, succinct, terse, to the point

pitiable adj affecting, deplorable, lamentable, miserable, paltry, pathetic, pitiful, poor, sad, unfortunate, woeful, wretched

pitiful adj 1 dire, disastrous, dreadful, lamentable, sorrowful, tragic

adj 2 affecting, deplorable, lamentable, miserable, paltry, pathetic, pitiable, poor, sad, unfortunate, woeful, wretched

pitiless adj 1 see: NASTY adj 7

adj 2 see: SEVERE adj 8

pity n affinity, compassion, empathy, kindness, mercy, rue, sympathy, understanding, tenderness

v ache, commiserate, empathize, feel for, sympathize with

pivot n axis, axle, pin, pole, rod, shaft, spindle

v see: SKEW v 3

pivotal adj central, crucial, dominant

pixie n elf, fairy, naiad, nymph, sprite

pizzazz n 1 sex appeal, sexiness, sizzle

n 2 effectiveness, flair, kick, pep, potency, punch, sizzle, snap, spark, verve, vigor, wallop

placard n 1 banner, headline, poster, sign

n 2 announcement, notice, post, poster, proclamation, sign

placate v 1 allay, appease, assuage, balm, becalm, calm, compose, conciliate, ease, lull, mollify, pacify, propitiate, quell, quiet, reconcile, satiate, settle, soften, soothe, still, sweeten, tranquilize

v 2 see: BABY *v* 2

place *n* 1 building, facility, office, service

n 2 opening, position, slot, vacancy

n 3 area, locale, location, locus, point, property, scene, site, spot

n 4 capacity, grade, office, position, post, quality, rank, situation, spot, standing, state, station, status

n 5 address, apartment, condo, condominium, domicile, dwelling, flat, home, house, location, pad, property, residence, site

v 1 approximate, call, estimate, judge, put, reckon

v 2 fill, heap, load, pack, stack, stuff

v 3 calibrate, establish, fix, insert, install, lay, locate, plant, position, put, set, settle, situate, station

v 4 see: CLASSIFY *v* 2

placid *adj* see: CALM *adj* 2

plagiarism *n* burglary, larceny, looting, robbery, theft, thievery

plagiarize *v* 1 copy, paraphrase, rephrase, reword

v 2 cheat, copy, crib

plague *v* 1 infest, invade, overrun, pervade, swarm

v 2 aggravate, annoy, badger, bait, bedevil, beleaguer, bother, bug, harass, harry, hassle, heckle, hound, hurt, intimidate, jeer, nag, needle, persecute, pester, provoke, ride, spite, taunt, tease, threaten, torment, worry

n bane, curse, disease, evil, misfortune, pestilence, scourge

plain *adj* 1 naked, stark, unadorned

adj 2 hideous, homely, repulsive, ugly, unattractive

adj 3 basic, crude, primitive, rough, simple, undeveloped

adj 4 consistent, homogeneous, pure, straight, unadulterated, undiluted, unmixed

adj 5 discreet, dry, homely, modest, simple, unadorned, undecorated, unembellished, unembroidered, ungarnished, unpretentious

adj 6 artless, candid, frank, guileless, ingenuous, innocent, naive, natural, open, simple, simple-hearted, unadorned, unaffected, unsophisticated, unstudied, untutored, unworldly

adj 7 apparent, clear, conspicuous, distinct, evident, given, indisputable, indubitable, manifest, obvious, patent, presumed, self-evident, straightforward,

true, unambiguous, unequivocal, unmistakable

adj 8 homely, unalluring, unattractive, unbeauteous, uncomely, unpretty

adj 9 average, common, commonplace, daily, everyday, general, mundane, natural, normal, ordinary, prevalent, regular, routine, typical, unexceptional, unremarkable, usual, workaday

n field, grassland, lea, meadow, pasture, prairie

plainly *adv* clearly, evidently, obviously, undoubtedly, unquestionably

plainness *n* clarity, clearness, distinctness, exactness, freshness, lucidity, purity

plaintive *adj* dismal, doleful, gloomy, lamentable, melancholy, mournful, regretful, regrettable, rueful, sorrowful, woeful

plan *n* 1 course, determination, purpose, resolution, resolve

n 2 agenda, appointments, calendar, itinerary, list, schedule

n 3 arrangement, design, form, prearrangement, preparation, provision

n 4 arrangement, array, format, layout, outline, style

n 5 budget, estimate, forecast, prediction, projection, quota

n 6 blueprint, chart, diagram, draft, map, outline, sketch

n 7 blueprint, design, game plan, project, proposal, scheme, strategy

n 8 arrangement, blueprint, method, order, orderliness, outline, pattern, system

n 9 expression, formula, methodology, procedure, recipe, scheme, system, theorem

n 10 conduct, course, guidelines, policy, procedures, program, rules, scheme

n 11 ambition, bent, design, goal, intent, intention, meaning, objective, purpose

n 12 itinerary

n 13 epitome, example, exemplar, ideal, mirror, model, outline, paradigm, pattern, prototype, rule of thumb, standard

n 14 antic, device, diversion, gambit, gimmick, maneuver, mischief, move, plot, ploy, prank, ruse, scheme, stratagem, strategy, tactic, trick, wile

v 1 allocate, budget

v 2 aim, contemplate, design, intend, mean, propose

v 3 administer, construct, dispense, move along, prepare, process, treat

v 4 arrange, bespeak, book, engage, organize, program, reserve, schedule, slate

v 5 arrange, blueprint, cast, chart, design, devise, draft, draw, engineer, fashion, lay out, map, outline, plot, project, set out, sketch

v 6 cogitate, collude, connive, conspire, contrive, devise, frame, intrigue, machinate, maneuver, orchestrate, plot, scheme

v 7 anticipate, augur, bode, budget, call, divine, estimate, forecast, foresee, foreshadow, foretell, guess, harbinger, herald, judge, portend, preannounce, predict, presage, proclaim, prognosticate, project, prophesy, signify, soothsay

plane *adj* even, flat, flush, level, smooth

n 1 horizontal

n 2 aircraft, airliner, airplane, glider

v even, flatten, flush, grade, lay, level, smooth, tamp

planetary *adj* broad, general, global, universal, urban, widespread, worldwide

plank *n* 1 block, slab

n 2 beam, board, boom, girder, log, rafter, spar, support, timber

planned *adj* 1 anticipated, contingent, hoped for, iffy, probable, proposed, tentative

adj 2 calculated, conscious, contrived, deliberate, intentional, plotted, premeditated

adj 3 advised, calculated, careful, considered, contrived, deliberate, forewarned, measured, premeditated, studious, studied

planning *n* timing

plant *n* 1 bush, grass, hedge, sapling, shrub, tree, vegetation, vine, weed

n 2 flora, foliage, herb, vegetable

v 1 anchor, establish, moor, root

v 2 implant, root, seed, sow, strew

v 3 cultivate, farm, grow, harvest, plow, produce, raise, till

v 4 bury, cache, cloister, conceal, cover, ditch, ensconce, hide, secrete, sequester, stash

v 5 calibrate, establish, fix, insert, install, lay, locate, place, position, put, set, settle, situate, station

plasma *n* blood, sap, serum

plastered *adj* bombed, crocked, doped up, drunk, drunken, high, inebriated, intoxicated, juiced, loaded, looped, messed up, polluted, sloshed, smashed, stoned, tight, tipsy, turned on, wasted, wired

plastic *adj* 1 bouncy, elastic, expansive, malleable, resilient

adj 2 adaptable, adjustable, changeable, flexible, limber, malleable, maneuverable, moldable, pliable, pliant, responsive, soft, supple, swayed, versatile, yielding

adj 3 artificial, counterfeit, fake, false, man-made, synthetic

plate *n* 1 dish, platter, saucer

n 2 armor, covering, protection, shell, shield

n 3 cap, cork, cover, lid, plug, top

v coat, electroplate, laminate

platform *n* deck, forecastle, quarterdeck

platitude *n* cliché, banality, triteness

platoon *n* airborne, army, battalion, brigade, cavalry, company, footmen, guard, horsemen, infantry, legion, marines, militia, minutemen, paratroops, reserve, storm troopers

platter *n* dish, plate, saucer

plaudit *n* see: COMMENDATION *n* 1

plaudits *n* applause, cheers, compliments, congratulations, kudos, praise

plausible *adj* conceivable, likely, ostensible, possible, probable

play *n* 1 excess, give, leeway, margin, slack, stretch

n 2 appliance, application, employment, form, method, operation, technique, use, utilization

n 3 see: RECREATION

v 1 sport

v 2 caper, cavort, frisk, frolic, gambol, prance, rollick, romp, skip

v 3 see: ACT *v* 3

v 4 see: BET *v*

v 5 see: COMPETE *v*

v 6 see: TRIFLE *v* 1

playboy *n* buck, Casanova, Don Juan, flirt, gallant, ladies' man, lecher, lover, philanderer, Romeo, stud

player *n* 1 athlete, jock, sportsman

n 2 competitor, contestant, participant, team member

n 3 see: ACTOR *n*

playful *adj* 1 fun-loving, gamesome, lively

adj 2 amusing, entertaining, diverting, enjoyable, fun, humorous

adj 3 see: LIVELY

playhouse *n* assembly hall, auditorium, theater

plaything *n* amusement, game, knickknack, toy, trinket

playwright *n* author, authoress, biographer, creator, dramatist, essayist, journalist, novelist, reporter, screenwriter, writer

plaza *n* common, green, park, square

plea *n* 1 invocation, petition, prayer, request

n 2 alibi, defense, excuse, explanation, justification, pretext, rationalization, reason, ruse *n* 3 appeal, desire, favor, petition, request, solicitation, wish

plead *v* 1 appeal, apply, attack, file suit, go to court, litigate, petition, prosecute, solicit, sue

v 2 appeal, ask, beg, beseech, conjure, crave, desire, entreat, grovel, implore, indicate, invoke, pray, request, seek, solicit, supplicate, whine

pleasant *adj* 1 agreeable, gratifying, pleasing, satisfying

adj 2 balmy, bright, clear, fair, serene

adj 3 clear, cloudless, fair, sunny, unclouded

adj 4 mild, moderate, modest, rational, reasonable, temperate

adj 5 agreeable, bright, fine, good, nice, sunny

adj 6 balmy, bland, faint, gentle, mild, smooth, soft, weak

adj 7 agreeable, congenial, favorable, good, grateful, gratifying, nice, pleasing, pleasurable, welcome

adj 8 affable, amiable, approachable, cordial, friendly, genial, gentle, gracious, likable, lovable, peaceful, serene

please *v* 1 amuse, delight, tickle

v 2 amuse, charm, divert, entertain, interest, recreate, stimulate

v 3 accommodate, convenience, favor, help, oblige, provide, serve

v 4 appease, comfort, comply, content, delight, elate, gratify, relieve, satisfy, suit

v 5 delight, encourage, enjoy, gladden, hearten, inspire

pleased *adj* 1 delighted, glad, honored, proud

adj 2 accommodating, agreeing, amenable, disposed, eager, glad, inclined, pliant, responsive, willing

adj 3 see: MERRY *adj* 2

pleasing *adj* 1 agreeable, gratifying, pleasant, satisfying

adj 2 beneficial, fulfilling, rewarding, worthwhile

adj 3 agreeable, congenial, favorable, good, grateful, gratifying, nice, pleasant, pleasurable, welcome

adj 4 alluring, attractive, becoming, coy, cute, enchanting, enticing, fascinating, foxy, inviting, ravishing, seductive, sexy

adj 5 attractive, becoming, comely, exquisite, fair, good-looking, gorgeous, handsome, radiant, stately

pleasurable *adj* agreeable, congenial, favorable, good, grateful, gratifying, nice, pleasant, pleasing, welcome

pleasure *n* 1 delight, enjoyment, joy, satisfaction

n 2 enjoyment, excitement, kicks, stimulation, thrills

n 3 fondness, liking, bent, disposition, fancy, idea, inclination, mind, notion, propensity, yen

n 4 see: DELIGHT *n* 1, 2

pleat *v* crease, fold, muss, rumple, wrinkle

n crease, fold, rumple, wrinkle

plebeian *adj* base, common, humble, ignoble, knavish, low, lowly

n commoner, common man, countryman, peasant, proletarian

pledge *n* 1 commitment, guarantee, obligation, promise

n 2 assurance, declaration, oath, promise, vow, word

n 3 covenant, coverage, guarantee, indemnity, insurance, policy, promise, warranty

n 4 assurance, bond, commitment, earnest, guarantee, obligation, pawn, security, surety, token, warrant

n 5 see: PACT *n*

v 1 bind, commit, contract

v 2 agree, contract, covenant, promise

v 3 assure, certify, contract, endorse, guarantee, sanction, underwrite, vouch, warrant

v 4 advocate, affirm, assure, avouch, avow, commit, devote, guarantee, promise, ratify, swear, vow

pledged *adj* betrothed, committed, engaged, promised

plentiful *adj* 1 abounding, abundant, ample, bounteous, bountiful, copious, enough, galore, generous, liberal, overflowing, plenty, prodigal, profuse, teeming

adj 2 see: MANY *adj* 2

plenty *adj* abounding, abundant, ample, bounteous, bountiful, copious, enough, galore, generous, liberal, overflowing, plentiful, prodigal, profuse, teeming

n 1 booty, bounty, gifts, largess, plunder, presents, reward

n 2 abundance, affluence, bounty, comfort, cornucopia, elegance, glut, good fortune, grandeur, luxury, opulence, prosperity, success, wealth

n 3 droves, loads, lots, many, multitudes, scads, slew

plethora *n* deluge, excess, fat, glut, overabundance, overflow, overkill, redundancy, surfeit, surplus

pliable *adj* 1 controllable, docile, manageable, maneuverable, yielding *adj* 2 alterable, elastic, flexible, movable, resilient, springy, supple

adj 3 adaptable, adjustable, changeable, flexible, limber, malleable, maneuverable, moldable, plastic, pliant, responsive, soft, supple, swayed, versatile, yielding

pliant *adj* 1 adaptable, adjustable, changeable, flexible, limber, malleable, maneuverable, moldable, plastic, pliable, responsive, soft, supple, swayed, versatile, yielding

adj 2 see: WILLING *adj* 4

plight *n* 1 complication, difficulty, dilemma, obstacle, predicament, problem, quandary, situation, snag

n 2 see: DILEMMA *n* 2, 4

plod *v* 1 lumber, persevere, persist, plug, toil

v 2 see: WALK *v* 1

plot *n* 1 land, lot, parcel, property, tract

n 2 field, grass, green, grounds, lawn, yard

n 3 cabal, collusion, conspiracy, intrigue, junta, machination, scheme, secret

n 4 bar graph, chart, diagram, distribution, figure, flow chart, graph, histogram, outline, pie chart, table

n 5 see: MANEUVER *n* 5

v 1 cogitate, collude, connive, conspire, contrive, devise, frame, intrigue, machinate, maneuver, orchestrate, plan, scheme

v 2 see: DESIGN *v* 4

v 3 see: FORMULATE *v* 2

plotted *adj* calculated, conscious, contrived, deliberate, intentional, planned, premeditated

plotter *n* architect, designer, draftsperson, engineer inventor, manager, operator, schemer, surveyor

plotting *n* intrigue, strategy, tactics

plow *v* cultivate, farm, grow, harvest, plant, produce, raise, till

ploy *n* antic, device, diversion, gambit, gimmick, maneuver, mischief, move, plan, plot, prank, ruse, scheme, stratagem, strategy, tactic, trick, wile

pluck *n* 1 drag, jerk, pull, tug, yank

n 2 see: PERSISTENCE *n* 3

plug *n* 1 ad, advertisement, commercial, promo, promotion, sponsorship, spot

n 2 cap, cork, cover, lid, plate, top

v 1 lumber, persevere, persist, toil

v 2 block, close, obstruct, occlude, shut, stop

v 3 advertise, air, boom, boost, drum up, endorse, pitch, promote, publicize, push, rave, sell, tout

plum *adj* amethyst, lavender, lilac, mauve, purple, violet

plumb *v* explore, fathom, probe, sound

adj full

plume *v* adorn, pique, preen, pride, primp, stroke

n feather

plummet *v* descend, dive, drop, fall, lapse, leap, lower, plunge, sink, swoop

plump *adj* chubby, chunky, corpulent, fat, fleshy, gross, heavy, hefty, meaty, obese, overweight, portly, pudgy, rotund, stocky, stout

plunder *n* 1 booty, bounty, gifts, largess, plenty, presents, reward

n 2 booty, bounty, fortune, kitty, loot, money, pot, prize, spoils, swag, treasure, trove

v 1 deflower, desecrate, despoil, devastate, devour, loot, maraud, pillage, ravage, sack, scourge, spoil, strip, violate

v 2 see: STEAL *v* 2

v 3 see: TAKE *v* 5

plunge *n* 1 comedown, decline, decrease, descent, dive, drop, failure, fall, regression, setback, slide, tumble

n 2 see: FALL *n* 2, 3

v 1 commit

v 2 descend, dive, drop, fall, lapse, leap, lower, plummet, sink, swoop

v 3 attack, butt, drive, knock, lunge, pass, ram, sink, stab, stick, thrust

v 4 cave in, collapse, disintegrate, drop, fall, go down, keel over, pitch, slump, spill, topple, tumble

v 5 cascade, decant, emit, flood, inundate, overflow, pour, rain, shower, spill, swamp, tumble

v 6 dive, lunge, lurch

plus *n* 1 asset, excess, inventory, overage, overstock, surplus

n 2 addition, advancement, advantage, betterment, enhancement, gain, growth

v aggregate, amount, number, sum, total

adv see: ALSO *adv*

plush *adj* choice, deluxe, elegant, first class, grand, luxuriant, luxurious, opulent, ornate, palatial, posh, rich, soft, stately, sumptuous, thick

plutocrat *n* baron, big shot, businessman, businessperson, businesswoman, capitalist, entrepreneur, executive, financier, industrialist, magnate, mogul, tycoon, VIP

ply *n* caste, layer, rank, row, stratum, tier

v 1 dispense, handle, maneuver, manipulate, swing, wield

v 2 angle, arch, bend, bow, curve, flex, round, tilt, tip, turn, twist, vault

pocket v appropriate, burglarize, defraud, embezzle, filch, heist, lift, misappropriate, pilfer, pillage, pinch, purloin, rip off, rob, snake, snitch, steal, swindle, swipe, take, thieve

pocketknife n blade, cutlass, dagger, knife, rapier, saber, scimitar, switchblade, sword

pocket-size adj carryable, compact, lightweight, luggable, movable, portable, small, transportable

podium n dais, desk, lectern, pulpit, rostrum, soapbox, stage, stand

poem n ditty, limerick, lyric, madrigal, poetry, rhyme, song, sonnet, verse

poet n author, bard, composer, folk singer, muse, narrator, storyteller, troubadour

poetry n ditty, limerick, lyric, madrigal, poem, rhyme, song, sonnet, verse

pogrom n bloodbath, bloodshed, butchery, carnage, extermination, genocide, holocaust, killing, massacre, shambles, slaughter

poignance n poignancy

poignancy n poignance

poignant adj 1 bittersweet, maudlin, sad, sentimental, sorrowful

adj 2 affecting, heartbreaking, impressive, moving, sad, touching

adj 3 aromatic, lively, peppery, piquant, pungent, racy, snappy, spicy, spirited, vigorous, zesty

point n 1 climax, crisis, crux, dilemma, emergency, juncture, predicament

n 2 area, locale, location, locus, place, property, scene, site, spot

n 3 argument, controversy, issue, item, matter, motif, motive, proposition, question, subject, text, theme, topic

n 4 dot

n 5 cape, isthmus, peninsula, promontory

n 6 barrier, breaker, harbor, cape, head, jetty, neck, sea wall

n 7 acme, apex, apogee, climax, crescendo, crest, crown, culmination, epitome, height, noon, peak, pinnacle, prime, summit, tip, top, ultimate, utmost, zenith

v 1 aim, establish, focus, set, shoot at, target

v 2 address, aim, cast, direct, level, train, zero in

pointed adj 1 biting, caustic, cutting, incisive, penetrating, trenchant

adj 2 honed, keen, razor sharp, sharp, unblunted, whetted

adj 3 see: PROMINENT adj 2

pointer n 1 dial, disk, display, gauge, indicator, measure, meter, selector

n 2 see: CLUE n 2

pointless adj foolish, futile, ill-advised, profitless, stupid, vain

poise n 1 balance, equilibrium, stability

n 2 consideration, diplomacy, discretion, regard, savoir-faire, tact, tactfulness, thoughtfulness

n 3 aplomb, assurance, confidence, esteem, nerve, presence, savoir-faire, self-assurance, self-confidence

n 4 see: STANCE n 3

poised adj 1 aloof, reserved

adj 2 assured, confident, sanguine, secure, self-assured, self-confident

adj 3 any second, immediate, imminent, impending, looming, threatening

adj 4 civilized, cosmopolitan, cultivated, cultured, elegant, genteel, ingratiating, polished, refined, smooth, sophisticated, suave, urbane, well-bred

adj 5 calm, collected, composed, cool, demure, dormant, easy, gentle, hushed, idle, imperturbable, motionless, nonchalant, peaceful, placid, quiet, relaxed, restful, sedate, self-composed, self-possessed, serene, soft, steady, still, tranquil, unflappable, unruffled, untroubled

poison n 1 contamination, corruption, decay, taint

n 2 cancer, corruption, decay, evil, infection, malignancy, rot, toxin, venom

v contaminate, dirty, foul, pollute

poisonous adj harmful, noxious, toxic, unhealthy

poke v 1 jab, peck, pick

v 2 break through, penetrate, perforate, pierce, prick, punch

v 3 bulge, jut, overhang, overlap, overlay, pop, project, protrude, protuberate, rise, stand out, stick out, swell

v 4 butt in, chisel in, cut in, fiddle, horn in, interfere, interlope, intrude, meddle, mess around, peer, peek, pry, snoop, tamper with

v 5 dally, dawdle, delay, diddle, goof off, idle, lag, linger, loaf, loiter, loll, lounge, malinger, put off, putter, shirk, tarry

poker-faced adj see: IMPASSIVE adj

pokey n see: JAIL n

polar adj conflicting, contradictory, contrary, converse, counter, diametric, inverse, opposed, opposite, opposing, reverse

polarization n split

polarize v breach, break up, cleave, disjoin, dismember, disrupt, dissect, dissever, disunite, divide, divorce, part, rupture, separate, sever, split, sunder

pole n 1 column, pillar, post, stake

n 2 bar, ingot, rod, stick, strip

n 3 axis, axle, pin, pivot, rod, shaft, spindle

n 4 birch, cane, club, rod, shaft, staff, stake, stave, stick

police v defend, guard, oversee, patrol, protect, regulate, safeguard, watch

n authorities, bobbies, constabulary, cops, gendarmes, highway patrol, military police, troopers

policy n 1 direction, directive, guideline, instruction, rule

n 2 covenant, coverage, guarantee, indemnity, insurance, pledge, promise, warranty

n 3 conduct, course, guidelines, plan, procedures, program, rules, scheme

polish n 1 elegance, finesse, refinement, style

n 2 finish, glaze, gloss, shine

n 3 coating, gloss, glow, luster, patina, radiance, sheen, shimmer, shine

v 1 perfect

v 2 edge, file, grind, hone, sharpen, whet

v 3 annotate, compile, correct, denote, edit, modify, proofread, revise

v 4 buff, burnish, furbish, glaze, glimmer, gloss, renovate, rub, shine

v 5 brush, clean, rub, wipe

v 6 adorn, beautify, bedeck, deck, decorate, dress up, embellish, enhance, garnish, glamorize, grace, ornament, trim

polished adj 1 beaming, bright, shiny, brilliant, burnished, emitting, glistening, glossy, lucid, luminous, lustrous, radiant, shining

adj 2 civilized, cosmopolitan, cultivated, cultured, elegant, genteel, ingratiating, poised, refined, smooth, sophisticated, suave, urbane, well-bred

polite adj 1 conventional, correct, decorous, fitting, nice, orthodox, proper, right, suitable, well

adj 2 chivalrous, civil, civilized, cordial, courteous, courtly, decent, dignified, gallant, genteel, gentlemanly, gracious, mannerly, noble, well-mannered

politic adj advisable, expedient, prudent, recommended, suggested, wise

polka n ballet, cha-cha, dance, fox trot, hula, jitterbug, tap, twist, waltz

poll v campaign, canvass, drum, drum up, prospect, seek, solicit

pollutant n contaminant, defect, impurity

pollute v contaminate, dirty, foul, infect, poison

polluted adj 1 bombed, crocked, doped up, drunk, drunken, high, inebriated, intoxicated, juiced, loaded, looped, messed up, plastered, sloshed, smashed, stoned, tight, tipsy, turned on, wasted, wired

adj 2 see: DIRTY adj 2

pompous adj 1 boring, dull, formal, stodgy, stuffy

adj 2 ambitious, bombastic, flamboyant, garish, grandiose, inflated, jaunty, lofty, ostentatious, portentous, pretentious, showy, splendid, splashy, utopian, visionary

pond n 1 pool, puddle, swimming hole

n 2 basin, lagoon, lake, loch, pool, spring

ponder v cerebrate, chew, consider, contemplate, deliberate, digest, meditate, mull, muse, reason, reflect, ruminate, see, speculate, study, think, weigh

pondering adj meditative, pensive, philosophical, reflective, speculative, thinking, thoughtful

ponderous adj 1 clumsy, heavy-handed, slow

adj 2 athletic, brawny, burly, husky, massive, muscular, powerful, robust, stocky, stout, strapping, strong

adj 3 acute, burning, critical, crucial, desperate, dire, grave, heavy, important, major, momentous, pressing, profound, serious, severe, solemn, somber, urgent, vital

pony n colt, equine, filly, foal, gelding, horse, mare, mount, nag, steed, yearling

pooch n canine, dog, hound, mongrel, mutt, pup, puppy

pooh-pooh v deprecate, minimize

pool v accompany, band, coincide, collaborate, collude, combine, cooperate, unite

n 1 pond, puddle, swimming hole

n 2 basin, lagoon, lake, loch, pond, spring

n 3 cartel, chain, coalition, collaboration, combine, conglomerate, consortium, federation, group, partnership, syndicate, trust

pooped adj see: WEARY adj 1

poor adj 1 faded, frayed, run-down, shabby, tattered, threadbare, worn

adj 2 bad, defective, futile, inadequate, incorrect, inferior, invalid, malfunctioning, void

adj 3 afoul, amiss, awry, bad, bum, improper, out of kilter, rotten, unsatisfactory, wrong

adj 4 broke, destitute, dirt-poor, down and out, impoverished, indigent, needy, penniless, poverty-stricken, strapped, unprosperous

adj **5** affecting, deplorable, lamentable, miserable, paltry, pathetic, pitiable, pitiful, sad, unfortunate, woeful, wretched

adj **6** bare, deficient, few, inadequate, inferior, insufficient, little, meager, paltry, petty, scant, scanty, skimpy, spare, sparse

adj **7** flawed, flimsy, imperfect, inferior, lousy, mediocre, miserable, paltry, second-rate, shabby, shoddy, sorry, so-so, tacky, unworthy, worthless

poorer *adj* deficient, inferior, meaner, worse

poorest *adj* last, least, worst

poorly *adv* badly, harshly, imperfectly, improperly, inadequately, inappropriately, painfully, unsatisfactorily

pop *n* **1** bang, blare, blast, boom, discharge, explosion, noise, report, roar

n **2** attempt, chance, effort, fling, go, guess, heave, lob, shot, slap, sling, stab, throw, toss, try, whirl

n **3** dad, dada, daddy, father, pa, papa, pappy, parent, pater, patriarch

v **1** bat, clout, hit, nail, smite, sock, strike, swat, whack

v **2** bang, crack, snap, thump

v **3** bulge, jut, overhang, overlap, overlay, poke, project, protrude, protuberate, rise, stand out, stick out, swell

poppa *n* dad, dada, daddy, father, pa, papa, pappy, parent, pater, patriarch, pop

poppycock *n* see: NONSENSE *n* 2

populace *n* citizens, civilization, colony, community, crowd, culture, folks, group, human beings, individuals, laity, masses, men and women, neighbors, people, persons, population, public, settlement, staff, society, tribe

popular *adj* **1** best-selling, favorite, hot

adj **2** current, democratic, dominant, extensive, fashionable, general, in vogue, prevailing, prevalent, rampant, rife, sought after, well-liked, widespread

popularity *n* brilliance, celebrity, distinction, excellence, fame, glory, halo, honor, luster, note, prominence, renown, repute, splendor

population *n* citizens, civilization, colony, community, crowd, culture, folks, group, human beings, individuals, laity, masses, men and women, neighbors, people, persons, populace, public, settlement, society, staff, tribe

populous *adj* **1** concentrated, crowded, teeming

adj **2** see: MANY *adj* 2

porch *n* lanai, patio, piazza, terrace, veranda

porn *n* dirt, filth, grossness, indecency, obscenity, pornography, ribaldry, smut, trash

pornographic *adj* bawdy, coarse, crude, dirty, erotic, filthy, foul, gamy, gross, improper, indecent, lascivious, lewd, licentious, nasty, obscene, off-color, profane, prurient, racy, rank, raunchy, ribald, risqué, scandalous, smutty, suggestive, tainted, uncouth, vulgar, x-rated

pornography *n* dirt, filth, grossness, indecency, obscenity, porn, ribaldry, smut, trash

porous *adj* absorbent

port *n* **1** asylum, cover, harbor, haven, oasis, preserve, protection, refuge, reserve, retreat, safety, sanctuary, seaport, security, shelter

n **2** burgundy, chablis, champagne, chianti, claret, sauterne, sherry, wine

portable *adj* carryable, compact, lightweight, luggable, movable, pocket-size, small, transportable

portal *n* **1** doorway, exit, gateway

n **2** anteroom, approach, atrium, court, doorway, entrance hall, entry, foyer, hall, hallway, lobby, vestibule

n **3** gap, opening, window

portend *v* **1** appear, indicate, look, seem, sound

v **2** anticipate, augur, bode, budget, call, divine, estimate, forecast, foresee, foreshadow, foretell, guess, harbinger, herald, judge, plan, preannounce, predict, presage, proclaim, prognosticate, project, prophesy, signify, soothsay

portentous *adj* **1** foreboding, imminent, impending, menacing, ominous, predictive, prophetic, sinister, threatening

adj **2** appalling, awful, dire, dreadful, fearful, formidable, frightening, frightful, ghastly, horrendous, horrible, offensive, ominous, scary, shocking, spooky, terrible, terrifying, unpleasant

adj **3** see: FLAMBOYANT *adj* 2

portfolio *n* binder, file, record

portion *n* **1** amount, dose, prescription

n **2** component, installment, part, segment

n **3** citation, clipping, excerpt, extract, mention, passage, quotation, quote, reference, section

n **4** bit, clipping, cut, division, lot, member, parcel, part, piece, sample, section, segment, slice

n 5 allotment, allowance, apportionment, budget, dispensation, dispersion, lot, measure, part, percentage, quota, ration, share, slice

n 6 see: FRAGMENT *n* 3

v allocate, allot, allow, apportion, assign, designate, distribute, divide, divvy, earmark, give, measure, parcel, partition, prorate, quota, ration, section, share, slice

portly *adj* 1 see: FAT *adj* 1

adj 2 see: GRAND *adj* 5

portrait *n* acrylic, art, canvas, depiction, drawing, etching, illustration, landscape, lithograph, mural, oil, painting, pastel, pen and ink, picture, print, seascape, sketch, still life, watercolor

portray *v* 1 delineate, depict, illustrate, picture, represent, sketch

v 2 brief, communicate, convey, declare, describe, disclose, divulge, explain, impart, inform, narrate, orate, read, recite, recount, relate, report, retell, reveal, share, state, tattle, tell, transmit

v 3 clarify, clear, clear up, delineate, depict, elucidate, explain, illuminate, illustrate, picture, reveal

portrayal *n* 1 characterization, delineation, depiction, expression, representation

n 2 part, role

pose *n* 1 affectation, airs, mannerism, peculiarity, posturing, pretense, trait

n 2 air, attitude, bearing, calmness, carriage, demeanor, disposition, poise, posture, presence, set, stance

v 1 model, posture, sit

v 2 disguise, masquerade, pass, pretend

v 3 bid, counsel, endorse, offer, present, proffer, propose, proposition, put forth, recommend, suggest, urge

v 4 see: GIVE *v* 8

v 5 see: SUGGEST *v* 5, 6

posh *adj* choice, deluxe, elegant, first-class, grand, luxuriant, luxurious, opulent, ornate, palatial, plush, rich, soft, stately, sumptuous, thick

posit *v* assume, expect, postulate, premise, presume, presuppose, propose

position *n* 1 opening, place, slot, vacancy

n 2 bearings, course, direction, heading

n 3 attitude, belief, point of view, stance, stand

n 4 angle, bearing, degree, heading, setting

n 5 fame, prestige, prosperity, station, status, success

n 6 appointment, connection, duty, function, job, office, post, situation

n 7 caste, class, degree, echelon, estate, hierarchy, level, rank, status

n 8 class, degree, grade, interval, level, mark, notch, rank, rate, step

n 9 capacity, grade, office, place, post, quality, rank, situation, spot, standing, state, station, status

v 1 adjust, amend, correct, fix, improve, mend, modify, rectify, remedy, restore, right, straighten

v 2 calibrate, establish, fix, insert, install, lay, locate, place, plant, put, set, settle, situate, station

v 3 see: CLASSIFY *v* 2

positive *adj* 1 affirmative, agreeing, optimistic

adj 2 brazen, certain, cocksure, convinced, sure

adj 3 buoyant, cheerful, ecstatic, elated, exuberant

adj 4 constructive, favorable, fruitful, helpful, productive, useful, worthwhile

adj 5 absolute, agreed, bounded, categorical, clear, decided, definite, emphatic, established, exact, finite, fixed, guaranteed, limited, specific, unequivocal, unmistakable, vested

adj 6 aggressive, ambitious, assertive, assured, compelling, compulsive, confident, decided, dogmatic, driven, emphatic, energetic, insistent, militant, pushing, pushy, self-assertive, sure, urging

adj 7 absolute, actual, authentic, bona fide, certain, definite, existent, factual, genuine, hard, inarguable, incontestable, incontrovertible, indisputable, indubitable, irrefutable, real, sure, true, undeniable, undisputable, undoubtable, undoubted, unequivocal, unquestionable, veritable, viable

positively *adv* 1 absolutely, certainly, decidedly, definitely, entirely, incontrovertibly, indeed, indubitably, surely, truly, unequivocally, unquestionably, verily, well, without doubt

adv 2 favorably, fortunately, successfully, well

posse *n* band, gang, mob, vigilantes

possess *v* 1 bear, carry

v 2 have, hold, keep, own, retain

possession *n* 1 custody

n 2 ownership, proprietorship, title

possessions *n* assets, belongings, equity, estate, fortune, goods, holdings, inheritance, money, ownership, property, prosperity, riches, treasure, wealth

possessor *n* landlord, lessor, owner, proprietor, stockholder

possibilities *n* alternatives, options, potential

possibility *n* 1 prospect

n 2 chance, expectation, likelihood, prospect, probability

possible *adj* 1 conceivable, likely, ostensible, probable

adj 2 inherent, latent, potential, promising, realizable

adj 3 achievable, capable, doable, feasible, practical, viable, workable

possibly *adv* 1 most likely, predictably, probably

adv 2 conditionally, maybe, perchance, perhaps, tentatively

post *adv* after, anon, behind, in pursuit, later, subsequently

n 1 column, pillar, pole, stake

n 2 appointment, connection, duty, function, job, office, position, situation

n 3 see: STANDING *n* 1

v 1 display, exhibit, proclaim

v 2 acquaint, advise, apprise, fill in, inform, notify, tell, update

v 3 see: SEND *v* 3

poster *n* 1 banner, headline, sign

n 2 announcement, notice, placard, proclamation, sign

posterior *adj* aft, back, backward, dorsal, rear, tail

n ass, backside, base, behind, bottom, bucket, buns, butt, buttocks, derrière, end, fanny, hindquarters, rump, seat, stub, stump, tip, tush

posterity *n* 1 future, tomorrow

n 2 brood, children, descendants, offspring, progeny

posthaste *adv* expeditiously, explosively, fast, fleetly, hastily, impulsively, instantly, mercurially, meteorially, precipitously, quickly, rapidly, spectacularly, speedily, suddenly, swiftly, with breakneck speed

postpone *v* adjourn, avoid, defer, delay, hold, hold up, interrupt, lay over, procrastinate, prolong, put off, remit, reschedule, set aside, shelve, stay, suspend, table, wait, waive

postponement *n* delay, interruption, reprieve, stay, stop, suspension

postulate *n* 1 assumption, foundation, ground rule, premise, proposition, supposition, theorem

n 2 see: THEORY *n* 2

v 1 assume, expect, posit, premise, presume, presuppose, propose

v 2 call, challenge, claim, demand, exact, need, require, requisition, solicit

posture *n* 1 air, attitude, bearing, calmness, carriage, demeanor, disposition, poise, pose, presence, set, stance

n 2 condition, mode, perspective, situation, state, status, update

v 1 model, pose, sit

v 2 disguise, masquerade, pass, pose, pretend

posturing *n* affectation, airs, mannerism, peculiarity, pose, pretense, trait

pot *n* 1 amphora, urn, vase, vessel

n 2 dope, drug, grass narcotic

n 3 booty, bounty, fortune, kitty, loot, money, plunder, prize, spoils, swag, treasure, trove

potency *n* 1 amplitude, caliber, magnitude, strength

n 2 effectiveness, flair, kick, pep, pizzazz, punch, sizzle, snap, spark, verve, vigor, wallop

n 3 animation, drive, élan, energy, enthusiasm, esprit de corps, go, gusto, pep, sparkle, spirit, spunk, verve, vigor, vim, vitality, zing, zip

n 4 ardor, beef, brawn, drive, energy, force, intensity, lustiness, might, muscle, pep, power, punch, steam, strength, verve, vigor, vim, virility, vitality

potent *adj* 1 effective, lively, punchy, snappy, strong

adj 2 ardent, decisive, determined, emphatic, extreme, forceful, intense, powerful, severe, strong

adj 3 brave, courageous, lusty, macho, male, manlike, manly, masculine, stalwart, virile

adj 4 concentrated, hearty, heavy-duty, lusty, powerful, robust, stalwart, stout, strong, sturdy

adj 5 colorful, expressive, graphic, impressive, intense, powerful, striking, strong, unforgettable, vivid

potentate *n* see: LEADER *n* 4

potential *adj* 1 inherent, latent, possible, promising, realizable

adj 2 dormant, inactive, inert, latent, on hold, passive, quiet, suspended, unused

n 1 alternatives, options

n 2 capacity

n 3 ingredients, substance

potty *n* bathroom, can, head, john, latrine, lavatory, loo, powder room, toilet, water closet, wc

pouch *n* bag, baggage, case, equipment, gear, grip, kit, luggage, pack, purse, sack, suitcase, valise, wallet

pounce v assault, jump, leap, strike, surprise, swoop

pound n barn, coop, enclosure, lean-to, paddock, pen, shack, shelter, shed, stable, stall, sty

v 1 crush, grind, powder, pulverize

v 2 bang, beat, bludgeon, clobber, club, hit, strike, whack

v 3 see: BATTER v

v 4 see: STAMP v 2

pour v 1 flood, flow, gush, peak, rise, roll, spill, stream, surge, swell

v 2 cascade, decant, emit, flood, inundate, overflow, plunge, rain, shower, spill, swamp, tumble

v 3 deluge, drizzle, fall, rain, shower, sprinkle

pout n expression, face, grimace, mouth, scowl, smirk, sneer, visage

v 1 brood, crab, grouch, moan, mope, scowl, sulk

v 2 disdain, frown, glare, gloom, glower, grimace, lower, scowl, sulk

poverty n 1 insolvency

n 2 deficiency, deprivation, destitution, inadequacy, indigence, lack, need, privation, scarcity, want

powder v 1 crush, grind, pulverize

v 2 chalk, dust, sprinkle

powdery adj 1 coarse, grainy, granular, gritty, sandy

adj 2 fine, ground, pulverized

power n 1 intensity, severity, tumult, turbulence, violence

n 2 charisma, dominance, influence, leadership, magnetism, personality, strength

n 3 administration, dominion, government, monarchy, regime, reign, rule, sovereignty

n 4 army, battalion, brigade, company, force, gang, men, soldiers, troops

n 5 authority, clout, control, in, influence, leverage, prestige, pull, weight

n 6 administration, administrators, authorities, bureaucracy, civil service, commission, department, direction, forces, government, management, ministry, officials, powers, rule, rulers

n 7 ardor, beef, brawn, drive, energy, force, intensity, lustiness, might, muscle, pep, potency, punch, steam, strength, verve, vigor, vim, virility, vitality

n 8 capacity

n 9 current, electricity, juice

n 10 agent, catalyst, force

n 11 authority, command, commission, control, direction, domination, jurisdiction, management, mastery, might, rule

powerful adj 1 invincible, mighty, omnipotent, supreme

adj 2 commanding, compelling, forceful, influential, important

adj 3 brisk, heavy, intense, stiff, strong

adj 4 forceful, highhanded, important, intense, maximum, utmost

adj 5 concentrated, hearty, heavy-duty, lusty, potent, robust, stalwart, stout, strong, sturdy

adj 6 colorful, expressive, graphic, impressive, intense, potent, striking, strong, unforgettable, vivid

adj 7 athletic, brawny, burly, husky, massive, muscular, ponderous, robust, stocky, stout, strapping, strong

adj 8 coercive, compelling, dynamic, energetic, forceful, hardy, lusty, mighty, passionate, robust, strong, sturdy, vigorous

adj 9 aggressive, dominant, durable, firm, forceful, hardy, hearty, mighty, robust, rugged, stalwart, stout, strong, sturdy, tenacious, tough

adj 10 see: EXTREME adj 4

powerless adj 1 feeble, helpless, impotent, weak

adj 2 defenseless, dependent, disarmed, exposed, helpless, susceptible, unprotected, vulnerable, weak

powers n see: ADMINISTRATION n 3

powwow n conference, meeting, parley, talk, tête-à-tête

v advise, communicate, confer, consult, discuss, group, huddle

practical adj 1 doable, justifiable, realistic, tenable

adj 2 achievable, capable, doable, feasible, possible, viable, workable

adj 3 basic, businesslike, down-to-earth, efficient, pragmatic, sensible

adj 4 accessible, available, close, convenient, feasible, functional, handy, helpful, multipurpose, nearby, open, public, reachable, ready, serviceable, suitable, unrestricted, usable, useful, utilitarian, well-suited, within reach, working

practically adv by itself, effectively, essentially, intrinsically, virtually

practice n 1 activity, discipline, drill

n 2 execution, exercise, implementation, training

n 3 drill, exercise, rehearsal, training, workout

n 4 education, experience, exposure, skill

n 5 method, methodology, procedure, process, routine, science, system, technique, technology *n* 6 custom, fashion, formality, habit, manner, mores, observance, routine, tradition, usage, use, way, wont

v 1 attempt, bring about, cultivate, perpetuate, proceed, pursue

v 2 drill, learn, perfect, prepare, rehearse, repeat, review, study

v 3 see: EDUCATE *v*

practiced *adj* adept, experienced, proficient, seasoned, versed, veteran

pragmatic *adj* basic, businesslike, down-to-earth, efficient, hardheaded, practical, sensible

prairie *n* field, grassland, lea, meadow, pasture

praise *n* 1 admiration, adoration, glory, worship

n 2 advertisement, championship, promotion, publicity, salesmanship

n 3 applause, cheers, compliments, congratulations, kudos

n 4 accolade, award, commendation, credit, decoration, distinction, honor, kudos, laurels, medal, note, recognition, reputation, reward, tribute

n 5 see: COMMENDATION *n* 1, 2

v 1 acclaim, applaud, charm, cheer, commend, compliment, flatter, greet, hail, laud, recognize, salute, stroke

v 2 acclaim, applaud, celebrate, commend, eulogize, exalt, extol, glorify, hail, honor, lauds, resound, salute, toast, tout, worship

praised *adj* admired, honored, prized, respected, valued

praiseworthy *adj* admirable, commendable, excellent, fine, laudable, worthwhile

praising *adj* approving, commending, complimentary, congratulatory, flattering

prance *v* 1 amble, flaunt, stride, strut, swagger

v 2 caper, cavort, frisk, frolic, gambol, play, rollick, romp, skip

v 3 dance, flap, flicker, flitter, flutter, oscillate, sparkle, sway, twinkle, undulate, wave

v 4 bob, bound, hop, jaunt, jump, leap, lope, skip, spring, sprint, trip

prank *n* 1 adventure, antic, caper, escapade, joke, lark, mischief, trick

n 2 see: MANEUVER *n* 2

prattle *v* babble, blab, blurt, burble, chatter, gossip, murmur, talk, tattle

n babble, babbling, burble, chatter, gibber, murmur, rattle

prawn *n* clam, cockle, crab, crustacean, mollusk, mussel, shellfish, shrimp, snail

pray *v* appeal, ask, beg, beseech, conjure, crave, desire, entreat, grovel, implore, indicate, invoke, plead, request, seek, solicit, supplicate, whine

prayer *n* invocation, petition, plea, request

prayerful *adj* devout, godly, holy, pious, religious, reverent, sanctimonious

preannounce *v* see: PREDICT *v* 2

preach *v* 1 address, deliver, lecture, proclaim, speak, talk

v 2 brainwash, convert, inculcate, indoctrinate, persuade, proselytize

preaching *n* assignment, diatribe, discourse, exercise, homily, lecture, lesson, sermon

preamble *n* beginning, foreword, intro, introduction, overture, preface, prelude, prologue, start

prearrangement *n* arrangement, design, form, plan, preparation, provision

precarious *adj* 1 anxious, insecure, nervous, threatened, uncertain, vulnerable

adj 2 breakneck, critical, dangerous, harmful, hazardous, perilous, risky, serious, unsafe, venturesome

adj 3 dangerous, delicate, fluctuating, hazardous, rickety, risky, rocky, sensitive, shaky, tender, ticklish, touchy, tricky, unpredictable, unstable, wobbly

adj 4 ambiguous, borderline, clouded, doubtful, dubious, equivocal, garbled, illogical, inarticulate, incalculable, incoherent, inexplicit, muddled, muffled, murky, obscure, questionable, shaky, suspect, suspicious, uncertain, unclear, uneasy, unintelligible, unsure, vague, wary

precaution *n* 1 caution, defense, protection, safeguard

n 2 anticipation, caution, deterrent, preclusion, preparation, prevention, safeguard

precede *v* antedate, come before, forego, pioneer, preface, spearhead

precedence *n* advantage, prerogative, priority, privilege, rank, seniority

preceding *adj* 1 aforementioned, ancient, antecedent, anterior, archaic, earlier, foregoing, former, past, previous, prior, recent

adj 2 earlier, first, former, once, previous, prior

precept *n* 1 see: CLICHÉ *n* 3

n 2 see: COMMAND *n* 3

precinct *n* 1 area, district, domain, environs, jurisdiction, locality, neighborhood, parish, province, range, region, section, sphere, vicinity, ward, zone *n* **2** county, district, jurisdiction, municipality, parish, township, ward

precious *adj* **1** costly, dear, expensive, valuable

adj **2** invaluable, irreplaceable, priceless, rare, unparalleled

adj **3** blessed, glorious, golden, great, splendid, superb

adj **4** deserving, estimable, excellent, honorable, noble, sterling, valuable, worthy

adj **5** adored, beloved, cherished, dear, esteemed, loved, respected, revered, treasured, venerable, worshiped

precipitance *n* alacrity, dispatch, expedition, haste, hastiness, hurry, hustle, precipitation, quickness, rush, rustle, speed, swiftness

precipitant *adj* abrupt, hasty, headlong, hurried, impetuous, impulsive, precipitate, quick, rapid, rash, reckless, rushing, sudden

precipitate *adj* abrupt, hasty, headlong, hurried, impetuous, impulsive, precipitant, quick, rapid, rash, reckless, rushing, sudden

v see: INITIATE *v* 2

precipitation *n* **1** cloudburst, deluge, downpour, drizzle, hail, rain, shower, sprinkle

n **2** alacrity, dispatch, expedition, haste, hastiness, hurry, hustle, precipitance, quickness, rush, rustle, speed, swiftness

precipitous *adj* see: RAPID *adj* 2

precise *adj* **1** clear, descriptive, effective

adj **2** exact, identical, same, very

adj **3** accurate, correct, exact, proper, right, valid

adj **4** exact, faithful, literal, strict, true, verbatim, word for word

adj **5** exacting, fastidious, finicky, meticulous, picky, rigid, strict

adj **6** dependable, observant, on time, prompt, punctual, reliable, timely

adj **7** definite, determinate, exclusive, fixed, limited, narrow, restricted, segregated, specific

adj **8** blunt, clear, clear-cut, concise, decisive, definite, definitive, distinct, exact, explicit, specific, unambiguous

precisely *adv* **1** exactly, just, perfectly

adv **2** accurately, exactly, just so, right, sharp, smack, square, squarely

adv **3** actually, exactly, genuinely, really, sincerely, truly, verifiably, veritably, very

precision *n* **1** thoroughness

n **2** definition, design, distinctness, outline, specificity

n **3** correctness, flawlessness, perfection

preclude *v* avert, bar, deter, eliminate, foil,

forestall, hinder, hold off, inhibit, prevent, stave off, thwart, turn back, ward off

preclusion *n* anticipation, caution, deterrent, precaution, preparation, prevention, safeguard

precocious *adj* **1** advanced, bright, gifted, intelligent, promising, talented

adj **2** adolescent, fresh, green, immature, juvenile, undeveloped, unfledged, unready, young, youthful

precondition *n* condition, essential, must, necessity, prerequisite, requirement

precursor *n* **1** warning

n **2** envoy, foregoer, forerunner, harbinger, herald, messenger, outrider, predictor, prophet

predecessor *n* ancestor, antecedent, ascendant, elder, forebear, forefather, forerunner, founder, grandparent, parent, patriarch, progenitor

predestined *adj* definite, determined, fixed, foregone, inevitable, inexorable, irrevocable, ordained, unalterable, unavoidable, unchangeable

predetermine *v* diagnose, estimate, forecast, gauge, predict, project

predicament *n* **1** climax, crisis, crux, dilemma, emergency, juncture

n **2** complication, difficulty, dilemma, obstacle, plight, problem, quandary, situation, snag

n **3** bind, box, corner, difficulty, dilemma, fix, impasse, jam, mess, pinch, plight, quandary, scrape, spot, trap, trouble

n **4** see: CHAOS *n* 5

predicate *v* **1** affirm, assert, attest, avow, confirm, declare, depose, profess, protest

v **2** establish

predict *v* **1** diagnose, estimate, forecast, gauge, predetermine, project

v **2** anticipate, augur, bode, budget, call, divine, estimate, forecast, foresee, foreshadow, foretell, guess, harbinger, herald, judge, plan, portend, preannounce, presage, proclaim, prognosticate, project, prophesy, prophetize, signify, soothsay

predictably *adv* most likely, possibly, probably

prediction *n* **1** forecast, prophecy, revelation, warning

n **2** forecast, budget, estimate, plan, projection, quota

predictive *adj* foreboding, imminent, impending, menacing, ominous, portentous, prophetic, sinister, threatening

predictor *n* **1** envoy, foregoer, recursor, harbinger, herald, messenger, outrider, prophet *n* 2 astrologer, augur, fortuneteller, oracle, prophet, psychic, seer, soothsayer, visionary

predilection *n* bent, bias, drift, habit, inclination, leaning, partiality, penchant, preference, priority, proclivity, propensity, talent, taste, tendency

predispose *v* bend, bias, brainwash, compel, convert, indoctrinate, influence, prejudice, proselytize, slant

predisposed *adj* biased, emotional, partial, prejudiced, subjective

predominance *n* control, influence, preponderance, supremacy

predominant *adj* 1 dominant, master, overbearing, overwhelming, paramount, preponderant, prevailing, prevalent, sovereign

adj 2 central, chief, distinguished, dominant, famed, great, key, leading, main, major, number one, outstanding, preeminent, primary, prime, principal, prominent, star, successful, superior, top

preeminent *adj* 1 central, chief, distinguished, dominant, famed, great, key, leading, main, major, number one, outstanding, predominant, primary, prime, principal, prominent, star, successful, superior, top

adj 2 see: SUPERB *adj* 4

adj 3 see: FOREMOST *adj* 3

preempt *v* annex, appropriate, commandeer, confiscate, expropriate, grab, impound, plunder, repossess, seize, sequester, shanghai, take

preen *v* adorn, pique, plume, pride, primp, stroke

preface *n* beginning, foreword, forward, intro, introduction, overture, preamble, prelude, prologue, start

v 1 antedate, come before, forego, pioneer, precede, spearhead

v 2 see: INITIATE *v* 2

prefer *v* 1 choose, desire, elect, favor, select

v 2 see: HELP *v* 4

preferable *adj* advantageous, better, desirable, enjoyable, superior, worthier, worthwhile

preferably *adv* before, desirably, rather

preference *n* 1 ballot, choice, franchise, option, say, selection, vote

n 2 alternative, choice, decision, druthers, election, option, pick, rathers, selection, vote

n 3 bent, bias, drift, habit, inclination, leaning, partiality, penchant, predilection, priority, proclivity, propensity, talent, taste, tendency

preferential *adj* better, favored, partial, select, special

preferred *adj* 1 choice, dainty, delicate, elegant, exquisite, favorite, fine, rare, select

adj 2 choice, favorite, select

prehistoric *adj* aboriginal, ancient, early, former, original, primeval, primitive, primordial, rudimentary

prejudice *n* 1 inequity, injustice, unfairness, wrong

n 2 bias, bigotry, chauvinism, discrimination, intolerance, parochialism, partiality, provincialism, racism, sexism

v bend, bias, brainwash, compel, convert, indoctrinate, influence, predispose, proselytize, slant, sway

prejudiced *adj* biased, emotional, partial, predisposed, subjective

preliminary *adj* beginning, introductory, opening, preparatory, prior

prelude *n* beginning, foreword, forward, intro, introduction, overture, preamble, preface, prologue, start

premature *adj* advanced, early, first, hasty, previous, soon, too soon, untimely

premeditated *adj* 1 calculated, conscious, contrived, deliberate, intentional, planned

adj 2 advised, calculated, careful, considered, contrived, deliberate, forewarned, measured, planned, studied, studious

premier *adj* 1 chief, first, foremost, head, inaugural, initial, lead, leading, prime

adj 2 basic, dominant, elementary, first, foremost, fundamental, head, highest, leading, main, outstanding, paramount, preeminent, primary, rudimentary, supreme, top

adj 3 dynamite, excellent, extraordinary, great, out of sight, outstanding, phenomenal, super, superb, superlative, tremendous, wonderful

premise *n* assumption, foundation, ground rule, postulate, proposition, supposition, theorem

v assume, expect, posit, postulate, presume, presuppose, propose

premium *n* see: REWARD *n* 8

premonition *n* 1 feeling, foreboding, guess, hunch, instinct, intuition, sense, suspicion

n 2 apprehension, foreboding, forewarning, harbinger, intuition, omen, presage, sign, warning

n 3 anticipation, expectation

preoccupation n 1 aloofness, detachment, indifference, separation

n 2 fetish, fixation, infatuation, obsession

preoccupied adj 1 absent-minded, abstracted, bemused, careless, dazed, dizzy, groggy, inattentive, lost, mindless, oblivious, silly, spaced, vapid

adj 2 absorbed, agog, concentrated, deep, determined, distracted, engaged, engrossed, enraptured, entranced, fascinated, immersed, intent, rapt, wrapped up

preparation n 1 arrangement, design, form, plan, prearrangement, provision

n 2 anticipation, caution, deterrent, precaution, preclusion, prevention, safeguard

preparatory adj beginning, introductory, opening, preliminary, prior

prepare v 1 adapt, process, ready, treat

v 2 administer, construct, dispense, move along, process, treat

v 3 author, compose, create, draft, pen, type, write

v 4 drill, learn, perfect, practice, rehearse, repeat, review, study

v 5 see: EDUCATE v

prepared adj game, primed, ready, ripe, set

prepayment n advance

preponderance n 1 control, influence, predominance, supremacy

n 2 bulk, greater part, majority

preponderant adj dominant, master, overbearing, overwhelming, paramount, predominant, prevailing, prevalent, sovereign

preposterous adj 1 extravagant, fantastic, wild

adj 2 absurd, chancy, debatable, doubtful, dubious, iffy, implausible, improbable, incredible, moot, questionable, theoretical, unbelievable, uncertain, unlikely

adj 3 absurd, balmy, bizarre, crazy, emotional, foolish, frivolous, goofy, illogical, impossible, inane, insane, irrational, loony, lunatic, mad, muddled, nuts, ridiculous, silly, touched, wacky, zany

prerequisite adj 1 compulsory, imperative, mandatory, must do, necessary, obligatory, required

adj 2 critical, essential, imperative, indispensable, mandatory, necessary, needed, vital, required

n 1 requirement

n 2 condition, essential, must, necessity, requirement

prerogative n 1 advantage, precedence, priority, privilege, rank, seniority

n 2 advantage, birthright, claim, edge, enablement, perquisite, privilege, right, title

presage n apprehension, foreboding, forewarning, harbinger, intuition, omen, premonition, sign, warning

v see: PREDICT v 2

prescient adj clairvoyant, intuitive, psychic

prescribe v burden, demand, force

prescript n see: COMMAND n 3

prescription n 1 dose, portion

n 2 drug, compound, elixir, formula, medicine, narcotic, painkiller

n 3 antidote, cure, medication, medicine, panacea, remedy, serum, therapy, treatment

n 4 see: COMMAND n 3

presence n 1 actuality, being, existence, fact, life, reality, truth, vitality

n 2 aplomb, assurance, confidence, esteem, nerve, poise, savoir-faire, self-assurance, self-confidence

n 3 see: STANCE n 3

present adj contemporary, current, existent, instant, living

n 1 current time, moment, now, today

n 2 benevolence, boon, contribution, donation, favor, gift, grant

v 1 acquaint, announce, delineate, depict, introduce, reflect, represent, show

v 2 administer, administrate, carry out, deliver, do, execute, give, render, submit

v 3 bid, counsel, endorse, offer, pose, proffer, propose, proposition, put forth, recommend, suggest, urge

v 4 allude, assume, extend, hypothesize, imagine, offer, pose, presume, propose, speculate, suggest, suppose, surmise, theorize

v 5 accord, adduce, award, bequeath, bestow, concede, confer, contribute, deliver, devote, donate, endow, extend, fund, give, give away, grant, hand down, hand out, impart, offer, pose, proffer, provide, supply, tender, volunteer

v 6 see: PROVE v 2

presentation n 1 come-on, line, pitch, spiel, talk

n 2 array, blare, display, exhibit, exhibition, fanfare, fuss, parade, performance, procession, publicity, show, showing

presently adv 1 currently, promptly, today

adv 2 anon, any moment, at once, directly, immediately, instantaneously, instantly, momentarily, now, promptly, quickly, right now, shortly, soon, straightaway, tout de suite

presents n booty, bounty, gifts, largess, plenty, reward

preserve v 1 conserve, maintain, protect, save

v 2 capture, chart, denote, enter, itemize, jot, list, log, note, record, register, take notes, tally, tape, write down

n see: SANCTUARY n 2

preside v chair, head, lead, moderate

press n 1 journalists, reporters

n 2 magazines, media, newspapers, television

n 3 coverage, journalism, news, reporting

n 4 see: HORDE n

v 1 bulldoze, elbow, hustle, jostle, push, shoulder, shove

v 2 clasp, clinch, cuddle, embrace, enfold, hold, hug, squeeze

v 3 crowd, herd, jam, mob, push, swarm, teem, throng

v 4 cram, crush, force, gorge, insert, jam, pack, ram, stuff

v 5 compact, compress, constrain, crowd, crush, jam, mash, pack, push, squash, squeeze

v 6 drive, hammer, impress, imprint, mark, pound, print, stamp, strike, thump, whack

v 7 activate, actuate, compel, drive, force, goad, impel, induce, mobilize, motivate, move, persuade, propel, push, spur, start, turn on

pressing adj acute, burning, critical, crucial, desperate, dire, grave, heavy, important, major, momentous, ponderous, profound, serious, severe, solemn, somber, urgent, vital

pressure n 1 anxiety, burden, frustration, strain, stress, tension

n 2 demand, exigency, necessity, need, requirement, stress, urgency

v affect, assure, convince, impel, incent, induce, influence, inspire, instigate, motivate, move, persuade, prompt, stir, sway, talk into, touch, win over

pressured adj burdened, encumbered, fraught, harried, laden, loaded

prestige n 1 fame, position, prosperity, station, status, success

n 2 achievement, distinction, rank, recognition, stance, stature, status

n 3 authority, clout, control, in, influence, leverage, power, pull, weight

prestigious adj acclaimed, celebrated, distinguished, eminent, esteemed, excellent, famed, famous, foremost, illustrious, notable, outstanding, prominent, renowned, well-known

presumably adv apparently, seemingly, supposedly

presume v 1 bother, burden, encroach, impose, intrude, saddle

v 2 assume, expect, posit, postulate, premise, presuppose, propose

v 3 assume, believe, comprehend, conceive, estimate, expect, fathom, gather, grasp, guess, imagine, infer, know, suppose, surmise, suspect, think, trust, understand

v 4 see: DEDUCE v 3

v 5 see: SUGGEST v 6

presumed adj 1 accepted, implied, supposed, tacit, understood

adj 2 see: IMPLIED adj 2

adj 3 see: OBVIOUS adj 3

presumption n 1 assumption, conclusion, conjecture, discretion, estimate, guess, judgment, notion, theorization

n 2 assumption, conjecture, deduction, explanation, guess, hypothesis, inference, postulate, proposition, speculation, supposition, theory

n 3 see: AUDACITY n

presuppose v assume, expect, posit, postulate, premise, presume, propose

pretend v 1 affect, feign, profess, purport

v 2 disguise, masquerade, pass, pose, posture

v 3 act, assume, bluff, counterfeit, fabricate, fake, feign, imitate, invent, make believe, play, put on, sham

pretender n charlatan, counterfeit, fake, faker, fraud, hypocrite, impostor, phony

pretense n 1 make-believe, ruse, sham, show

n 2 affectation, airs, mannerism, peculiarity, pose, posturing, trait

n 3 camouflage, cloak, costume, cover, curtain, disguise, mask, shield, shroud, veil

pretentious adj 1 arrogant, condescending, haughty, patronizing, snobbish

adj 2 artificial, corny, exaggerated, staged, theatrical

adj 3 ambitious, bombastic, flamboyant, garish, grandiose, inflated, jaunty, lofty, ostentatious, pompous, portentous, showy, splendid, splashy, utopian, visionary

adj 4 affected, effeminate, genteel, phony

pretext n 1 alibi, con, deception, lie, ruse, subterfuge, trick

n 2 alibi, defense, excuse, explanation, justification, plea, rationalization, reason, ruse

pretty *adv* **1** fairly, moderately, reasonably, so-so, somewhat

adj alluring, attractive, beautiful, breathtaking, comely, cute, fair, fine, foxy, gorgeous, lovely, luscious, magnificent, shapely, stunning

prevail *v* **1** bully, dominate, domineer, reign, rule

v **2** be, endure, exist, last, live, survive

v **3** defeat, best, conquer, master, overcome, succeed, triumph, win

v **4** abide, continue, endure, last, outlast, persevere, persist, remain, stay, stick to, stick with, survive

prevailing *adj* **1** dominant, master, overbearing, overwhelming, paramount, predominant, preponderant, prevalent, sovereign

adj **2** current, democratic, dominant, extensive, fashionable, general, in vogue, popular, prevalent, rampant, rife, sought after, well-liked, widespread

prevalent *adj* **1** dominant, master, overbearing, overwhelming, paramount, predominant, preponderant, prevailing, sovereign

adj **2** current, democratic, dominant, extensive, fashionable, general, in vogue, popular, prevailing, rampant, rife, sought after, well-liked, widespread

adj **3** average, common, commonplace, daily, everyday, general, mundane, natural, normal, ordinary, plain, regular, routine, typical, unexceptional, unremarkable, usual, workaday

prevent *v* **1** ban, bar, confine, enjoin, forbid, inhibit, nix, outlaw, prohibit, stop, suppress, veto

v **2** avert, bar, deter, eliminate, foil, forestall, hinder, hold off, inhibit, preclude, stave off, thwart, turn back, ward off

v **3** bar, block, brake, choke, clog, dam, deter, detract, encumber, frustrate, halt, hamper, hesitate, hinder, impair, impede, inhibit, jam, obstruct, repress, restrain, retard, slow, stay, stop, stop up, throttle

prevention *n* anticipation, caution, deterrent, precaution, preclusion, safeguard

previous *adj* **1** advanced, early, first, hasty, premature, soon, too soon, untimely

adj **2** aforementioned, ancient, antecedent, anterior, archaic, earlier, foregoing, former, past, preceding, prior, recent

previously *adv* before, earlier, first, formerly, heretofore, hitherto, once, prior to

prey *n* **1** butt, casualty, object, subject, sufferer, target, victim

n **2** catch, game, quarry, target

price *n* **1** charge, cost, expense, fare, outlay, payment, rate, value, worth

n **2** see: FEE *n* **5**

v see: APPRAISE *v*

priceless *adj* invaluable, irreplaceable, precious, rare, unparalleled

prick *n* cut, gash, incision, nick, pierce, puncture, slit, wound

v **1** break through, penetrate, perforate, pierce, poke, punch

v **2** egg, encourage, exhort, goad, incite, persuade, prod, prompt, propel, spur, urge

pride *n* **1** dignity, ego, self-esteem, selfregard, self-respect

n **2** best, choice, elite, favorite, finest, optimum, pick, select

n **3** airs, arrogance, egotism, cockiness, conceit, condescension, disdain, haughtiness, image, loftiness, narcissism, selfesteem, self-image, vanity

v adorn, pique, plume, preen, primp, stroke

priest *n* chaplain, clergyman, cleric, father, guru, minister, padre, parson, pastor, rabbi, reverend

prim *adj* **1** prissy, prudish, straight-laced, stuffy

adj **2** austere, narrow, narrow-minded, prudish, puritanical, rigid, severe, strict

adj **3** meticulous, neat, orderly, shipshape, tidy, trim, well-groomed

primarily *adv* **1** chiefly, especially, notably, specifically

adv **2** as a rule, customarily, frequently, generally, mainly, most, mostly, most often, normally, ordinarily, principally, usually

primary *adj* **1** cardinal, essential, fundamental, prime, principal

adj **2** contiguous, current, direct, immediate, instant, nearby, prompt, sudden, timely

adj **3** earliest, first, founding, fundamental, initial, maiden, original, pioneer, prime

adj **4** basic, dominant, elementary, first, foremost, fundamental, head, highest, leading, main, outstanding, paramount, preeminent, premier, rudimentary, supreme, top

adj **5** central, chief, distinguished, dominant, famed, great, key, leading, main, major, number one, outstanding, predominant, preeminent, prime, principal, prominent, star, successful, superior, top

primate *n* ape, gorilla, monkey, simian

prime *adj* 1 best, optimum, select, superior, top

adj 2 cardinal, essential, fundamental, primary, principal

adj 3 chief, first, foremost, head, inaugural, initial, lead, leading

adj 4 earliest, first, founding, fundamental, initial, maiden, original, pioneer

adj 5 best, biggest, finest, greatest, largest, maximum, most, number one, select, superior, top, top-notch

adj 6 champion, excellent, fine, first-class, first rate, foremost, good, grade A, leading, number one, principal, prominent, quality, select, stellar, superb, superior, top, top-drawer, top-notch, tops

adj 7 see: PRIMARY *adj* 1, 3, 5

n see: APEX *n*

v see: PROVOKE *v* 2

primed *adj* game, prepared, ready, ripe, set

primeval *adj* aboriginal, ancient, early, former, original, prehistoric, primitive, primordial, rudimentary

primitive *adj* 1 aboriginal, indigenous, native

adj 2 basic, crude, plain, rough, simple, undeveloped

adj 3 aboriginal, ancient, early, former, original, prehistoric, primeval, primordial, rudimentary

n aborigine, barbarian, native, savage

primordial *adj* aboriginal, ancient, early, former, original, prehistoric, primeval, primitive, rudimentary

primp *v* adorn, pique, plume, preen, pride, stroke

prince *n* angel, model, saint

princely *adj* see: GRAND *adj* 5

principal *adj* 1 cardinal, essential, fundamental, primary

adj 2 champion, excellent, fine, first-class, first-rate, foremost, good, grade A, leading, number one, prime, prominent, quality, select, stellar, superb, superior, top, top-drawer, top-notch, tops

adj 3 central, chief, distinguished, dominant, famed, great, key, leading, main, major, number one, outstanding, predominant, preeminent, primary, prime, prominent, star, successful, superior, top

adj 4 lead, star, top-billed

adj 5 absolute, chief, complete, consummate, dominant, godlike, leading, main, perfect, pure, ranking, sheer, supreme, total, unsurpassed, utter, whole

n advocate, champion, conqueror, hero, heroine, lead, leader, master, protagonist, star, trailblazer, victor, winner

principally *adv* as a rule, customarily, frequently, generally, mainly, most, mostly, most often, normally, ordinarily, usually

principle *n* 1 flag, guideline, rule, standard

n 2 honesty, honor, integrity, trustworthiness, virtue

n 3 basic, element, essential, foundation, fundamental, rudiment

n 4 arguments, basis, cause, explanation, foundation, grounds, rationale, reason, rudiments, source

n 5 belief, canon, code, conviction, creed, doctrine, dogma, law, opinion, rule, tenet, theory

n 6 goodness, morality, probity, purity, rectitude, righteousness, uprightness, virtue

principled *adj* conscientious, ethical, honest, honorable, moral, noble, proper, respectable, right, righteous, scrupulous, sound, true, trustworthy, upright, virtuous

principles *n* 1 ethics, morals

n 2 knowledge, laws, philosophy, thinking, wisdom

print *n* 1 copy, impression, imprint, indent, indentation, mark, notch, stamp, tab

n 2 acrylic, art, canvas, depiction, drawing, etching, illustration, landscape, lithograph, mural, oil, painting, pastel, pen and ink, picture, portrait, seascape, sketch, still life, watercolor

n 3 see: REPLICA *n* 2

v 1 bring out, distribute, get out, give out, go to press, issue, publish, put out, reissue, reprint, set type

v 2 drive, hammer, impress, imprint, mark, pound, press, stamp, strike, thump, whack

v 3 copy, clone, duplicate, image, imitate, mirror, re-create, redo, reduplicate, remake, replicate, reprint, reproduce, simulate

printing *n* see: BOOK *n* 2

printwheel *n* face, family, font, size, style, type, typeface

prior *adj* 1 beginning, introductory, opening, preliminary

adj 2 aforementioned, ancient, antecedent, anterior, archaic, earlier, foregoing, former, past, preceding, previous, prior

prioritize *v* align, arrange, array, assort, catalog, categorize, class, classify, cluster, compile, file, format, grade, group, lay out, line up, list, order, organize, outline, pigeonhole, place, position, program, rank, rate, sort, stack, tabulate

priority n 1 advantage, precedence, prerogative, privilege, rank, seniority

n 2 line, order, procession, sequence, succession, timing

n 3 accent, emphasis, highlighting, importance, significance, stress, weight

n 4 see: INCLINATION n 2

priory n abbey, monastery

prison n brig, cage, cell, cooler, coop, hoosegow, jail, pen, penitentiary, pokey, reformatory, slammer, stir, stockade, tower

prisoner n 1 captive, hostage, victim

n 2 see: CRIMINAL n 2

prissy adj prim, prudish, straight-laced, stuffy

pristine adj 1 celibate, chaste, clean, decent, decorous, immaculate, modest, moral, proper, pure, spotless, stainless, stuffy, taintless, unadulterated, unblemished, undefiled, upstanding, virginal, wholesome

adj 2 clean, immaculate, pure, spotless, taintless, unsoiled, unspoiled, unsullied, untouched, virgin

privacy n 1 detachment, isolation, quiet, seclusion, solitude

n 2 camouflage, cover, incognito, secrecy, stealth

private adj 1 exclusive, nonpublic, restricted

adj 2 discreet, off the record, quiet, secretive

adj 3 individual, introspective, personal, subjective

adj 4 exclusive, individual, intimate, own, personal, secret, special

adj 5 enclosed, hidden, inner, innermost, interior, internal, secret

adj 6 alienated, alone, apart, detached, hidden, isolated, removed, secluded, separated, sequestered, severed

adj 7 clandestine, classified, concealed, confidential, covert, hidden, off the record, privileged, secret, sensitive, sub rosa

privation n deficiency, destitution, deprivation, inadequacy, indigence, lack, need, poverty, scarcity, want

privilege n 1 advantage, precedence, prerogative, priority, rank, seniority

n 2 advantage, birthright, claim, edge, enablement, perquisite, prerogative, right, title

n 3 consideration, courtesy, dispensation, favor, indulgence, kindness, respect, service

privileged adj see: SECRET adj 5

privy adj see: DECEITFUL adj 1

prize n 1 award, honor, medal, trophy

n 2 bag, booty, catch, spoils

n 3 booty, bounty, fortune, kitty, loot, money, plunder, pot, spoils, swag, treasure, trove

n 4 see: REWARD n 8

v admire, adore, appreciate, cherish, consider, covet, esteem, honor, idolize, love, regard, respect, treasure, value

prized adj admired, honored, praised, respected, valued

pro adj supportive

n adviser, artist, authority, expert, guru, master, official, professional, specialist, veteran, virtuoso, wizard

probability n chance, expectation, likelihood, possibility, prospect

probable adj 1 conceivable, likely, ostensible, plausible, possible

adj 2 anticipated, contingent, hoped for, iffy, planned, proposed, tentative

probably adv possibly, predictably

probate n will

probe v 1 explore, fathom, sound

v 2 examine, feel, finger, fondle, grope, handle, manipulate, maul, palpate, paw, touch

v 3 ask, cross-examine, examine, grill, inquire, interrogate, investigate, pump, query, question, quiz

v 4 analyze, assess, determine, diagnose, estimate, examine, penetrate, scope, solve, survey, understand, unravel

v 5 delve, dig, examine, explore, feel out, grope, hunt, inquire, investigate, look, observe, peer, pursue, research, scan, scrutinize, search, seek, sound, study, test

probing adj 1 analytical, logical, subtle

adj 2 inquiring, keen, penetrating, piercing, searching

adj 3 curious, inquiring, inquisitive, investigative, nosy, prying, questioning, snooping

n examination, inquiry, inspection, scrutiny, search, study, survey

probity n goodness, morality, principle, purity, rectitude, righteousness, uprightness, virtue

problem n 1 complication, difficulty, dilemma, obstacle, plight, predicament, quandary, situation, snag

n 2 confusion, conundrum, difficulty, dilemma, enigma, mystery, obstacle, paradox, perplexity, puzzle, quandary, question, riddle, secret

n 3 challenge, demur, difficulty, hindrance, hurdle, objection, obstacle, protest, question, snag

proboscis n beak, bill, muzzle, nib, nose, prow, snout, trunk

procedure n 1 habit, method, mores, routine, system

n 2 expression, formula, methodology, plan, recipe, scheme, system, theorem

n 3 method, methodology, practice, process, routine, science, system, technique, technology

procedures n conduct, course, guidelines, plan, policy, program, rules, scheme

proceed v 1 attempt, bring about, cultivate, perpetuate, pursue

v 2 advance, begin again, continue, cycle, depart, get along, get on, go, leave, march, move, move forward, overture, part, progress, push on, reembark, recommence, restart, wend

v 3 coast, cruise, explore, go, journey, migrate, sail, survey, tour, travel, trek, voyage

proceeding n 1 action, battle, engagement, fray, gesture, operation

n 2 action, case, indictment, lawsuit, litigation, prosecution, suit

proceedings n see: JOURNAL n 3

proceeds n assets, cash, earnings, gain, gross, haul, net, payback, profits, receipts, return, revenue, take, yield

process n 1 method, methodology, practice, procedure, routine, science, system, technique, technology

n 2 angle, approach, code, delivery, execution, expression, fashion, manner, method, mode, organization, program, style, system, technique, way

v 1 filter, screen, sift

v 2 adapt, prepare, ready, treat

v 3 administer, construct, dispense, move along, plan, prepare, treat

v 4 craft, define, develop, formulate, list, make, specify, synthesize

procession n 1 caravan, convoy, motorcade

n 2 line, order, priority, sequence, succession, timing

n 3 array, blare, display, exhibit, exhibition, fanfare, fuss, parade, performance, presentation, publicity, show, showing

proclaim v 1 display, post

v 2 address, deliver, lecture, preach, speak, talk

v 3 advertise, announce, blaze, broadcast, circulate, declare, disperse, disseminate, promulgate, publish

v 4 see: PREDICT v 2

v 5 see: VERBALIZE v 2

proclamation n announcement, notice, placard, post, sign

proclivity n see: INCLINATION n 2

procrastinate v adjourn, avoid, defer, delay, hold up, hold, interrupt, lay over, postpone, prolong, put off, remit, reschedule, set aside, shelve, stay, suspend, table, wait, waive

procrastinating adj deliberate, dilatory, diligent, leisurely, methodical, meticulous, painstaking, patient, slow, thorough, unhasty, unhurried

procreate v bear, beget, breed, come into, create, effect, engender, father, generate, hatch, impregnate, make, mate, multiply, originate, parent, promulgate, propagate, reproduce, sire, spawn

procreation n 1 birth, conception, creation, formulation

n 2 adultery, congress, copulation, fooling around, fornication, sex

procreative adj carnal, genital, erogenous, erotic, reproductive, sexual

procure v 1 buy, examine, purchase, shop

v 2 acquire, annex, buy, capture, gain, get, have, land, obtain, pick up, purchase, requisition, secure, solicit, win

v 3 acquire, earn, obtain

prod v 1 egg, encourage, exhort, goad, incite, persuade, prick, prompt, propel, spur, urge

v 2 agitate, anger, arouse, encourage, foment, ignite, incite, induce, inflame, inspire, instigate, invoke, motivate, muster, propel, provoke, raise, set, set on, spur, stimulate, stir, urge

prodigal adj 1 abundant, cornucopian, extravagant, exuberant, garish, generous, lavish, lush, luxuriant, opulent, profuse, rich, wasteful

adj 2 see: PLENTIFUL adj 1

prodigious adj 1 excessive, gluttonous, immoderate, inordinate, intemperate, overindulgent, unbridled, undue, unrestrained, voracious

adj 2 colossal, enormous, fantastic, Gargantuan, giant, gigantic, Goliath, great, huge, immense, jumbo, leviathan, mammoth, massive, mighty, monstrous, monumental, overwhelming, phenomenal, Promethean, stupendous, Titanic, towering, tremendous, unfathomed, untold, vast, walloping, whopping

prodigy *n* brain, Einstein, genius, intellect, wizard

produce *n* 1 by-product, derivative, end product, end result, growth, outgrowth, output, product, production, productivity, result, yield

n 2 crop, fruits, grain, harvest, yield

v 1 give

v 2 constitute, form

v 3 bear, turn out, yield

v 4 cause, generate, induce, muster

v 5 cultivate, farm, grow, harvest, plant, plow, raise, till

v 6 actuate, bring about, cause, create, draw on, effect, execute, invoke, make, secure

v 7 assemble, build, construct, erect, establish, fabricate, forge, form, make, manufacture, mold, trailblaze

v 8 accomplish, achieve, attain, consummate, execute, fulfill, perform, pull off, realize, succeed, triumph, win

producer *n* maker, manufacturer

product *n* 1 by-product, derivative, end product, end result, growth, outgrowth, output, produce, production, productivity, result, yield

n 2 fruit, harvest, result, reward

production *n* 1 by-product, derivative, end product, end result, growth, outgrowth, output, produce, product, productivity, result, yield

n 2 Broadway, comedy, drama, extravaganza, musical, stage, theater

productive *adj* 1 basic, creative, formative, fundamental, initiatory, seminal

adj 2 copious, creative, fecund, fertile, fruitful, prolific

adj 3 constructive, favorable, fruitful, helpful, positive, useful, worthwhile

productivity *n* by-product, derivative, end product, end result, growth, outgrowth, output, produce, product, production, result, yield

products *n* articles, basics, commodities, essentials, goods, inventory, line, materials, merchandise, properties, staples, stock, wares

profane *v* 1 contaminate, debase, degrade, desecrate

v 2 condemn, curse, damn, denounce, molest, swear, vex

adj see: VULGAR *adj* 2

profanity *n* abomination, blasphemy, curse word, expletive, imprecation, obscenity, swearing

profess *v* 1 affect, feign, pretend, purport

v 2 affirm, bear witness, declare, depose, swear, testify

v 3 affirm, assert, attest, avow, confirm, declare, depose, predicate, protest

professed *adj* hollow, nominal, perfunctory, representative, small, symbolic, token

profession *n* art, avocation, business, calling, career, discipline, employment, field, gig, job, labor, line, livelihood, occupation, office, pursuit, role, schtick, situation, specialty, task, thing, trade, vocation, work

professional *n* adviser, artist, authority, expert, guru, master, official, pro, specialist, veteran, virtuoso, wizard

adj see: QUALIFIED *adj* 4

professor *n* academician, educator, instructor, teacher

professors *n* department, faculty, instructors, staff, teachers

proffer *n* bid, expectation, hope, inducement, invitation, motion, offer, proposal, proposition, recommendation, request, suggestion

v 1 bid, counsel, endorse, offer, pose, present, propose, proposition, put forth, recommend, suggest, urge

v 2 see: GIVE *v* 8

proficiency *n* 1 ability, adequacy, adroitness, aptitude, art, caliber, calling, capability, capacity, command, competence, craft, dexterity, experience, expertise, familiarity, forte, knack, know-how, knowledge, mastery, prowess, qualification, savvy, skill, specialty, strength, talent, training, workmanship

n 2 acceleration, achievement, advance, advancement, betterment, breakthrough, furtherance, growth, headway, improvement, increment, pickup, progress, promotion, strengthening, upgrade

proficient *adj* 1 accomplished, experienced, schooled, trained, versed

adj 2 adept, dexterous, handy, mechanical, skilled

adj 3 adept, experienced, practiced, seasoned, versed, veteran

adj 4 adequate, capable, competent, effective, efficacious, efficient, successful, sufficient

adj 5 able, accomplished, adept, apt, capable, competent, deft, dexterous, expert, fit, gifted, masterful, professional, proper, qualified, skillful, talented

profile *n* 1 contour, form, outline, shape

n 2 autobiography, biography, compendium, résumé, sketch, vita

profit *n* 1 account, advantage, applicabili-

ty, appropriateness, aptness, avail, benefit, decorum, expediency, fitness, manners, opportunism, pertinence, propriety,
relevance, rightness, service, suitability,
use, usefulness, utility

n 2 see: REWARD *n* 8

v 1 bring in, return, yield

v 2 advance, benefit, gain, improve, reward

v 3 benefit, experience, have, partake,
touch, use

v 4 access, accomplish, achieve, attain,
derive, earn, fulfill, gain, get, merit, net,
obtain, perform, rack up, reach, realize,
score, win

v 5 benefit from, capitalize, gain

profitable *adj* beneficial, gainful, lucrative,
rewarding

profitless *adj* foolish, futile, ill-advised,
pointless, stupid, vain

profits *n* assets, cash, earnings, gain, gross,
haul, net, payback, proceeds, receipts,
return, revenue, take, yield

profound *adj* 1 deep, meaty, rich, stimulating

adj 2 convincing, effective, forcible, impressive, inspiring, striking

adj 3 abstruse, deep, esoteric, heartfelt,
heavy, hermetic, insightful, mysterious,
obscure, occult, penetrating, recondite

adj 4 acute, burning, critical, crucial, desperate, dire, grave, heavy, important, major, momentous, ponderous, pressing,
serious, severe, solemn, somber, urgent,
vital

profundity *n* concentration, depth, energy,
intensity, strength, substance, vigor

profuse *adj* 1 abundant, cornucopian, extravagant, exuberant, garish, generous,
lavish, lush, luxuriant, opulent, prodigal,
rich, wasteful

adj 2 see: EXTRAVAGANT *adj* 3, 4

adj 3 see: PLENTIFUL *adj* 1

profusion *n* abundance

progenitor *n* ancestor, antecedent, ascendant, elder, forebear, forefather, forerunner, founder, grandparent, parent,
predecessor

progeny *n* 1 child, descendant, heir, offspring, scion

n 2 brood, children, descendants, offspring

prognosis *n* forecast

prognosticate *v* anticipate, augur, bode,
budget, call, divine, estimate, forecast,
foresee, foreshadow, foretell, guess, harbinger, herald, judge, plan, portend, pre-

announce, predict, presage, proclaim,
project, prophesy, signify, soothsay

program *n* 1 conduct, course, guidelines,
plan, policy, procedures, rules, scheme

n 2 concert, concerto, étude, fugue, recital, serenade, sonata, symphony

n 3 angle, approach, code, delivery, execution, expression, fashion, manner,
method, mode, organization, process,
style, system, technique, way

v 1 encode

v 2 arrange, bespeak, book, engage, organize, plan, reserve, schedule, slate

v 3 align, arrange, array, assort, catalog,
categorize, class, classify, cluster, compile, file, format, grade, group, lay out,
line up, list, order, organize, outline, pigeonhole, place, position, prioritize,
rank, rate, sort, stack, tabulate

programs *n* cartoons, docudrama, documentary, game shows, mini-series, movies, news, series, sitcom, soap opera,
soaps, talk shows, television, variety
shows

progress *n* 1 headway, locomotion, movement

n 2 correction, reform

n 3 acceleration, achievement, advance,
advancement, betterment, breakthrough,
furtherance, growth, headway, improvement, increment, pickup, proficiency,
promotion, strengthening, upgrade

v 1 derive, develop, evolve, unfold

v 2 age, develop, grow, grow up, mature,
mellow, ripen

v 3 advance, begin again, continue, cycle,
depart, get along, get on, go, leave, march,
move, move forward, overture, part, proceed, push on, recommence, reembark,
restart, wend

v 4 advance, ascend, bloom, climb, develop, do well, excel, expand, flourish, flower, get ahead, grow, improve, prosper,
rise, strive, survive, thrive

progression *n* 1 hierarchy

n 2 consequence, development, ramification, result

n 3 chain, course, lineup, order, row, run,
sequence, series, string, succession, train

progressive *adj* 1 chronological, consecutive, continuous, sequential, serial, successive

adj 2 advanced, broad, broad-minded,
liberal, radical, tolerant, unbiased

adj 3 continual, continuing, gradual, increasing, incremental, intensifying, measured, moderate, successive

prohibit *v* ban, bar, confine, enjoin, forbid,

inhibit, nix, outlaw, prevent, stop, suppress, veto

prohibited adj 1 banned, forbidden, taboo

adj 2 criminal, disgraceful, felonious, illegal, illegitimate, illicit, lawless, unlawful, wrong, wrongful

prohibition n 1 ban, blockage, boycott, curtailment, embargo, restriction, stoppage

n 2 ban, bar, constraint, interdiction, restriction, taboo

prohibitive adj costly, dear, excessive, exorbitant, expensive, high, overpriced, steep, stiff

project n 1 activity, business, endeavor, enterprise, exercise, undertaking, venture

n 2 blueprint, design, game plan, plan, proposal, scheme, strategy

v 1 discharge, emit, fire, hurl, shoot

v 2 diagnose, estimate, forecast, gauge, predict

v 3 discharge, emanate, emit, expel, radiate, release, send

v 4 conceive, conjecture, conjure up, create, envision, fancy, image, imagine, invent, realize, think, visualize

v 5 bulge, jut, overhang, overlap, overlay, poke, pop, protrude, protuberate, rise, stand out, stick out, swell

v 6 arrange, blueprint, cast, chart, design, devise, draft, draw, engineer, fashion, lay out, map, outline, plan, plot, set out, sketch

v 7 anticipate, augur, bode, budget, call, divine, estimate, forecast, foresee, foreshadow, foretell, guess, harbinger, herald, judge, plan, portend, preannounce, predict, presage, proclaim, prognosticate, prophesy, signify, soothsay

projectile n buckshot, bullet, lead, missile, shell, shot, slug

projection n 1 bulge, jut, lump, protrusion, swelling

n 2 budget, estimate, forecast, plan, prediction, quota

proletarian n commoner, common man, countryman, peasant

proliferate v abound, increase, multiply, overrun, propagate, teem

prolific adj 1 copious, creative, fecund, fertile, productive

adj 2 see: MANY adj 2

prologue n beginning, foreword, intro, introduction, overture, preamble, preface, prelude, start

prolong v 1 commit, continue, extend, maintain, perpetuate, pull

v 2 continue, drag out, draw, elongate, extend, lengthen, protract, stretch

v 3 see: DELAY v 4

prolonged adj 1 chronic, incessant, severe

adj 2 drawn-out, elongated, extended, lengthened, lengthy, long, protracted, stretched, sustained

prom n ball, cotillion, dance, party

promenade n access, approach, artery, avenue, boulevard, channel, drag, highway, pass, path, road, roadway, route, strait, street, thoroughfare, trail, way

v 1 display, exhibit, flaunt, manifest

v 2 see: WANDER v

Promethean adj see: HUGE adj 3

prominence n brilliance, celebrity, distinction, excellence, fame, glory, halo, honor, luster, note, popularity, renown, repute, splendor

prominent adj 1 elevated, exalted, excellent, grand, great, heavenly, high, lofty, magnificent, sublime, superb

adj 2 arresting, astonishing, astounding, conspicuous, eye-catching, marked, noticeable, obvious, pointed, salient, sensational, striking, stunning

adj 3 acclaimed, celebrated, distinguished, eminent, esteemed, excellent, famed, famous, foremost, illustrious, notable, outstanding, prestigious, renowned, well-known

adj 4 champion, excellent, fine, first-class, first-rate, foremost, good, grade A, leading, number one, prime, principal, quality, select, stellar, superb, superior, top, top-drawer, top-notch, tops

adj 5 central, chief, distinguished, dominant, famed, great, key, leading, main, major, number one, outstanding, predominant, preeminent, primary, prime, principal, star, successful, superior, top

adj 6 see: SUBSTANTIAL adj 4

promiscuous adj 1 diverse, haphazard, jumbled, mixed, random

adj 2 casual, easy, fast, immoral, incontinent, indiscriminate, lax, lecherous, lewd, licentious, light, loose, unchaste, wanton, whorish

promise n 1 engagement

n 2 commitment, guarantee, obligation

n 3 debt, loan, obligation, responsibility

n 4 assurance, declaration, pledge, oath, vow, word

n 5 covenant, coverage, guarantee, indemnity, insurance, pledge, warranty

n 6 see: PACT n

v 1 agree, contract, covenant, pledge

v 2 affirm, attest, avow, contend, say, swear, vouch, warrant

v 3 affirm, assure, avouch, avow, commit, devote, guarantee, pledge, ratify, swear, vow

promised *adj* betrothed, committed, engaged

promising *adj* 1 inherent, latent, possible, potential, realizable

adj 2 gifted, advanced, bright, intelligent, talented

adj 3 auspicious, bright, confident, favorable, hopeful, rosy, sunny, utopian

adj 4 auspicious, cheerful, confident, encouraging, hopeful, optimistic, sanguine, upbeat

promo *n* ad, advertisement, commercial, plug, promotion, sponsorship, spot

promontory *n* cape, peninsula, point

promote *v* 1 discount, rebate, reduce

v 2 endorse, ratify, second, support

v 3 cultivate, develop, encourage, foster, further, grow

v 4 advocate, back, champion, endorse, guarantee, sanction, side, support, uphold

v 5 advertise, air, boom, boost, drum up, endorse, pitch, plug, publicize, push, rave, sell, tout

v 6 see: HELP *v* 4

promoter *n* advocate, ally, angel, backer, benefactor, booster, champion, cheerleader, donor, friend, guarantor, helper, ombudsman, partner, patron, proponent, sponsor, supporter

promotion *n* 1 publicity

n 2 advertisement, championship, praise, publicity, salesmanship

n 3 ad, advertisement, commercial, plug, promo, sponsorship, spot

n 4 bargain, buy, deal, discount, reduction, sale, special, steal

n 5 ballyhoo, embellishment, exaggeration, hoopla, hype, hyperbole, overstatement, public relations

n 6 certification, commencement, graduation

n 7 acceleration, achievement, advance, advancement, betterment, breakthrough, furtherance, growth, headway, improvement, increment, pickup, proficiency, progress, strengthening, upgrade

prompt *adj* 1 alert, quick, ready

adj 2 dependable, observant, on time, precise, punctual, reliable, timely

adj 3 contiguous, current, direct, immediate, instant, nearby, primary, sudden, timely

v 1 activate, cause, elicit, generate, provoke, spark, trigger

v 2 cue, jog, nudge, push, remind, stimulate, stir, suggest

v 3 egg, encourage, exhort, goad, incite, persuade, prick, prod, propel, spur, urge

v 4 affect, assure, convince, impel, induce, influence, inspire, instigate, motivate, move, persuade, pressure, stir, sway, talk into, touch, win over

promptly *adv* 1 currently, presently, today

adv 2 at once, forthwith, immediately, instantly, right now, this instant, *tout de suite*

adv 3 expeditiously, fast, full-tilt, hastily, in a snap, lickety-split, pronto, quick, quickly, rapidly, right away, soon, speedily, swiftly, urgently

adv 4 anon, any moment, at once, directly, immediately, instantaneously, instantly, momentarily, now, presently, quickly, right now, shortly, soon, straightaway, *tout de suite*

promulgate *v* 1 advertise, announce, blaze, broadcast, circulate, declare, disperse, disseminate, proclaim, publish

v 2 bear, beget, breed, come into, create, effect, engender, father, generate, hatch, impregnate, make, mate, multiply, originate, parent, procreate, propagate, reproduce, sire, spawn

prone *adj* 1 exposed, liable, subject, vulnerable

adj 2 apt, inclined, liable, likely

adj 3 flat, horizontal, lengthwise, longways, prostrate, reclining, recumbent

pronounce *v* announce, articulate, assert, couch, describe, dictate, draft, enunciate, express, intonate, orate, phrase, proclaim, say, speak, state, stress, talk, utter, verbalize, vocalize, voice, word

pronouncement *n* 1 accusation, allegation, assertion, charge, comment, declaration, deposition, statement

n 2 see: CLICHÉ *n* 3

pronto *adv* expeditiously, fast, full-tilt, hastily, in a snap, lickety-split, promptly, quick, quickly, rapidly, right away, soon, speedily, swiftly, urgently

pronunciation *n* accent, elocution, enunciation, inflection, intonation

proof *n* 1 argument, demonstration, representation, thesis

n 2 affirmation, confirmation, documentation, evidence, verification

n 3 argument, grounds, justification, reason, wherefore, why *n* 4 clue, example, illustration, indication, manifestation, sign

n 5 approval, confirmation, doctrine, enactment, evidence, passage, testament, testimony, witness

proofread *v* annotate, compile, correct, denote, edit, modify, revise

prop *n* base, brace, buttress, column, footing, foundation, shore, stay, support, underpinning

v bear up, bolster, brace, build up, buoy, buttress, carry, fortify, harden, nourish, nurture, reinforce, shore, support, sustain, strengthen, toughen, uphold

propagate *v* 1 abound, increase, multiply, overrun, proliferate, teem

v 2 bear, beget, breed, come into, create, effect, engender, father, generate, hatch, impregnate, make, mate, multiply, originate, parent, procreate, promulgate, reproduce, sire, spawn

propagation *n* conception, fertilization, insemination, reproduction, spawning

propel *v* 1 bike, pedal, push

v 2 coerce, compel, constrain, force, make, overpower, push

v 3 boost, budge, drive, force, impel, nudge, push, shove, thrust

v 4 feed, fire, fuel, ignite, incite, kindle, light, nourish, stoke, sustain

v 5 cast, flick, fling, flip, heave, hurl, launch, pitch, sling, throw, toss

v 6 activate, actuate, compel, drive, force, goad, impel, induce, mobilize, motivate, move, persuade, press, push, spur, start, turn on

v 7 see: INSTIGATE *v* 1

v 8 see: URGE *v* 3

propellant *n* fuel, energy, gasoline

propensity *n* 1 bent, disposition, fancy, fondness, idea, inclination, liking, mind, notion, pleasure, yen

n 2 bent, bias, drift, habit, inclination, leaning, partiality, penchant, predilection, preference, priority, proclivity, talent, taste, tendency

proper *adj* 1 aligned, neat, ordered, straight

adj 2 accurate, correct, exact, precise, right, valid

adj 3 acceptable, defensible, justifiable, reasonable, valid

adj 4 conventional, correct, decorous, fitting, nice, orthodox, polite, right, suitable, well

adj 5 appropriate, correct, deserved, due, fitting, just, merited, rightful, suitable, warranted

adj 6 applicable, appropriate, apropos, apt, befitting, convenient, desirable, felicitous, fit, fitting, germane, good, handy, just, material, meet, necessary, pertinent, relevant, right, shipshape, suitable, suited, timely, useful

adj 7 see: ETHICAL *adj* 3

adj 8 see: PURE *adj* 7

adj 9 see: QUALIFIED *adj* 4

properly *adv* acceptably, adequately, amply, appropriately, correctly, right, satisfactorily, suitably, well

properties *n* see: GOODS *n* 2

property *n* 1 land, lot, parcel, plot, tract

n 2 content, material, matter, stuff, substance

n 3 acquisition, asset, buy, gain, purchase

n 4 acreage, domain, estate, grounds, holdings, land, real estate

n 5 area, locale, location, locus, place, point, scene, site, spot

n 6 attribute, character, characteristic, feature, highlight, mark, peculiarity, quality, trait, virtue

n 7 characteristic, flavor, impression, nature, quality, ring, sound, tendency, tone, type

n 8 assets, belongings, equity, estate, fortune, goods, holdings, inheritance, money, ownership, possessions, prosperity, riches, treasure, wealth

n 9 belongings, stuff, things

n 10 address, apartment, condo, condominium, domicile, dwelling, flat, home, house, location, pad, place, residence, site

n 11 assets, bills, capital, cash, coffers, currency, dinero, dollars, estate, funds, goods, income, lucre, means, money, notes, pelf, pesos, resources, revenue, riches, rubles, shekels, sum, wealth

prophecy *n* 1 forecast, prediction, revelation, warning

n 2 apocalypse, oracle, revelation, vision

prophesy *v* see: PREDICT *v* 2

prophet *n* 1 envoy, foregoer, forerunner, harbinger, herald, messenger, outrider, precursor

n 2 astrologer, augur, fortuneteller, oracle, predictor, psychic, seer, soothsayer, visionary

prophetic *adj* foreboding, imminent, impending, menacing, ominous, portentous, predictive, sinister, threatening

propitiate *v* see: APPEASE *v* 2

propitious *adj* 1 auspicious, favorable, opportune, seasonable, timely

adj 2 favorable, fortunate

proponent *n* advocate, ally, angel, backer, benefactor, booster, champion, cheerleader, donor, friend, guarantor, helper, ombudsman, partner, patron, promoter, sponsor, supporter

proportion *n* 1 percentage, quota, quotient, rate, ratio

n 2 comparison, percentage, ratio, relation, share

v see: COORDINATE *v* 2

proportional *adj* balanced, commensurate, equal, symmetrical

proportions *n* amount, amplitude, dimensions, magnitude, quantity, scope, size, volume

proposal *n* 1 approach, come-on, offer, overture, proposition, suggestion

n 2 blueprint, design, game plan, plan, project, scheme, strategy

n 3 bid, expectation, hope, inducement, invitation, motion, offer, proffer, proposition, recommendation, request, suggestion

propose *v* 1 aim, contemplate, design, intend, plan

v 2 appoint, declare, designate, name, nominate, select, specify

v 3 assume, expect, posit, postulate, premise, presume

v 4 bid, counsel, endorse, offer, pose, present, proffer, proposition, put forth, recommend, suggest, urge

v 5 allude, assume, extend, hypothesize, imagine, offer, pose, present, presume, speculate, suggest, suppose, surmise, theorize

proposed *adj* anticipated, contingent, hoped for, iffy, planned, probable, tentative

proposition *n* 1 approach, come on, offer, overture, proposal, suggestion

n 2 assumption, foundation, ground rule, postulate, premise, supposition, theorem

n 3 bid, expectation, hope, inducement, invitation, motion, offer, proffer, proposal, recommendation, request, suggestion

n 4 argument, controversy, issue, item, matter, motif, motive, point, question, subject, text, theme, topic

n 5 see: THEORY *n* 2

v bid, counsel, endorse, offer, pose, present, proffer, propose, put forth, recommend, suggest, urge

proprietor *n* landlord, lessor, owner, possessor, stockholder

proprietorship *n* ownership, possession, title

propriety *n* 1 convention, custom, decorum, etiquette, formality, good form, manners, protocol, rites

n 2 humility, modesty, virtue

n 3 account, advantage, applicability, appropriateness, aptness, avail, benefit, decorum, expediency, fitness, manners, opportunism, pertinence, profit, relevance, rightness, service, suitability, use, usefulness, utility

prorate *v* 1 adjust, convert, regulate, scale

v 2 allocate, allot, allow, apportion, assign, designate, distribute, divide, divvy, earmark, give, measure, parcel, partition, portion, quota, ration, section, share, slice

prosaic *adj* common, commonplace, dull, ordinary, pedestrian, uneventful, unexceptional

prosecute *v* 1 appeal, apply, attack, file suit, go to court, litigate, petition, plead, solicit, sue

v 2 accuse, allege, arraign, assert, charge, cite, impeach, imply, impute, incriminate, indict, litigate, sue, try

prosecution *n* action, case, indictment, lawsuit, litigation, proceeding, suit

proselytize *v* 1 brainwash, convert, inculcate, indoctrinate, persuade

v 2 bend, bias, brainwash, compel, convert, indoctrinate, influence, predispose, prejudice, slant, sway

proselytizer *n* evangelist, missionary

prospect *n* 1 lead

n 2 horizon, lookout, outlook, perspective, vista

n 3 chance, expectation, possibility, probability

v campaign, canvass, drum, drum up, poll, seek, solicit

prospective *adj* approaching, eventual, expected, future, imminent, impending, next, subsequent

prosper *v* 1 arrive, flourish, go, make out, score, succeed, thrive

v 2 advance, ascend, bloom, climb, develop, do well, excel, expand, flourish, flower, get ahead, grow, improve, progress, rise, strive, survive, thrive

prospering *adj* alive, developing, living, viable

prosperity *n* 1 fame, prestige, position, station, status, success

n 2 abundance, affluence, bounty, comfort, cornucopia, elegance, glut, good fortune, grandeur, luxury, opulence, plenty, success, wealth

n 3 account, advantage, behalf, benefit,

betterment, gain, good, happiness, interest, sake, welfare, well-being

n 4 assets, belongings, equity, estate, fortune, goods, holdings, inheritance, money, ownership, possessions, property, riches, treasure, wealth

prosperous *adj* affluent, booming, successful, thriving, wealthy

prostitute *v* abuse, corrupt, ill-use, misapply, misemploy, mishandle, misuse

n call girl, harlot, hooker, hussy, slut, streetwalker, tart, tramp, trollop, wanton woman, wench, whore

prostrate *adj* 1 flat, horizontal, lengthwise, longways, prone, reclining, recumbent

adj 2 see: GLOOMY *adj* 5

v 1 bow, cringe, kneel, genuflect, grovel, kowtow, scrape

v 2 cripple, disable, disarm, encumber, freeze, halt, handcuff, immobilize, incapacitate, paralyze, stop, stun

protagonist *n* 1 actor, actress, artist, entertainer, hero, heroine, lead, movie star, performer, player, star, thespian, tragedian

n 2 advocate, champion, conqueror, hero, heroine, lead, leader, master, principal, star, trailblazer, victor, winner

protect *v* 1 barricade, fortify

v 2 conserve, preserve, save

v 3 hide, screen, shade, shadow

v 4 claim, copyright, patent, register, trademark

v 5 defend, guard, oversee, patrol, police, regulate, safeguard, watch

v 6 conceal, harbor, hide, house, keep, safeguard, shelter, shield

v 7 bulwark, cover, defend, fend, fortify, guard, hide, safeguard, screen, secure, shield

v 8 see: NURTURE *v* 2

protected *adj* 1 exempt, guarded, immune, safe, secure

adj 2 consecrated, intact, inviolable, inviolate, pure, sacred, sacrosanct

adj 3 impregnable, invulnerable, safe, safeguarded, secure

protection *n* 1 buffer, defense, shield

n 2 care, charge, custody, safekeeping

n 3 caution, defense, precaution, safeguard

n 4 barrier, mesh, netting, screen, shield

n 5 assurance, exemption, guarantee, immunity, impunity, release, safety, security

n 6 armor, covering, plate, shell, shield

n 7 asylum, cover, harbor, haven, oasis, port, preserve, refuge, reserve, retreat,

safety, sanctuary, seaport, security, shelter

protest *n* 1 objection

n 2 beef, complaint, criticism, grievance, gripe

n 3 challenge, demur, difficulty, hindrance, hurdle, objection, obstacle, problem, question, snag

v 1 except, inveigh, kick, object, remonstrate

v 2 affirm, assert, attest, avow, confirm, declare, depose, predicate

v 3 complain, crab, criticize, grieve, gripe, grumble, mutter, nag, object, whine

protocol *n* convention, custom, decorum, etiquette, formality, good form, manners, propriety, rites

prototype *n* 1 demo, example, first, forerunner, model, sample, test

n 2 epitome, example, exemplar, ideal, mirror, model, outline, paradigm, pattern, plan, rule of thumb, standard

protract *v* continue, drag out, draw, elongate, extend, lengthen, prolong, stretch

protracted *adj* 1 chronic, extended, incurable, persistent, refractory, stubborn

adj 2 drawn-out, elongated, extended, lengthened, lengthy, long, prolonged, stretched, sustained

protrude *v* bulge, jut, overhang, overlap, overlay, poke, pop, project, protuberate, rise, stand out, stick out, swell

protrusion *n* bulge, jut, lump, projection, swelling

protuberate *v* bulge, jut, overhang, overlap, overlay, poke, pop, project, protrude, rise, stand out, stick out, swell

proud *adj* 1 boastful, smug, triumphant

adj 2 delighted, glad, pleased

adj 3 arrogant, cavalier, conceited, contemptuous, curt, dictatorial, disdainful, grandiose, haughty, huffy, insolent, lofty, lordly, moody, obtrusive, overbearing, patronizing, scornful, snooty, stuck up, superior, supercilious, vain

prove *v* 1 demonstrate, determine, establish, evidence, reveal, show

v 2 demonstrate, describe, display, draw, establish, examine, exhibit, explain, present, show, sketch, tell

v 3 attest, authenticate, certify, confirm, corroborate, justify, notarize, ratify, sanction, substantiate, support, validate, verify, vouch, witness

proved *adj* authentic, certified, confirmed, demonstrated, tested, tried, verified

proven *adj* accepted, established, sound, standard, traditional

proverb *n* adage, axiom, byword, cliché, dictum, maxim, motto, saying, slogan, talk

provide *v* 1 endow, equip, furnish, give

v 2 clothe, fit, outfit, supply

v 3 assist, keep up, maintain, support, sustain, uphold

v 4 accommodate, convenience, favor, help, oblige, please, serve

v 5 arrange, cater, deliver, dish out, dispense, feed, furnish, give, hand, nourish, nurture, organize, purvey, serve, supply, sustain

v 6 see: GIVE *v* 8

providence *n* 1 destiny, fate, good fortune, karma, kismet, lot

n 2 caveat, foresight, forethought, prudence, vigilance, vision, wariness

provident *adj* 1 canny, conservative, economical, frugal, sparing, spartan, stewardly, thrifty, unwasteful

adj 2 see: CAREFUL *adj* 7

providential *adj* auspicious, favorable, fortunate, happy, lucky, serendipitous

province *n* 1 area, country, entity, government, nation, state

n 2 domain, dominion, field, kingdom, realm, sphere, territory

n 3 area, district, domain, environs, jurisdiction, locality, neighborhood, parish, precinct, range, region, section, sphere, vicinity, ward, zone

provincial *adj* 1 confined, controlled, ignorant, limited, narrow, parochial, unsophisticated

adj 2 bucolic, country, garden, outland, pastoral, peaceful, rural, rustic, suburban, wooded

provincialism *n* bias, bigotry, discrimination, chauvinism, intolerance, parochialism, partiality, prejudice, racism, sexism

provision *n* 1 arrangement, design, form, plan, prearrangement

n 2 agreement, clause, condition, proviso, requirement, reservation, specification, stipulation, string, terms

provisional *adj* 1 impromptu, makeshift, stopgap, temporary

adj 2 ancillary, conditional, contingent, dependent, indefinite, relative, reliant, temporary, uncertain

provisions *n* 1 energy, nourishment, rations, supply

n 2 equipment, fixtures, furnishings, materials, supplies

n 3 goods, inventory, reserve, stock, store, supply

n 4 bread, breakfast, brunch, chow, cuisine, diet, dinner, dish, edibles, entree, fare, food, grub, lunch, meals, nosh, nutrition, rations, snack, supper, victuals, vittles

proviso *n* agreement, clause, condition, provision, requirement, reservation, specification, stipulation, string, terms

provocative *adj* 1 provoking, stimulating, suggestive

adj 2 electric, exciting, exhilarating, rousing, stimulating, stirring

adj 3 exciting, exotic, inspiring, interesting, intriguing, stimulating, tingling, titillating

adj 4 arousing, exciting, intriguing, seductive, sexy, stimulating, suggestive, tantalizing

adj 5 amorous, ardent, aroused, carnal, earthy, erotic, fervent, fleshly, horny, hot, impassioned, lascivious, lecherous, lewd, licentious, lustful, passionate, randy, raunchy, romantic, sensual, sexual, sexy, sultry, titillated, torrid, turned on, voluptuous, wanton

provoke *v* 1 activate, cause, elicit, generate, prompt, spark, trigger

v 2 arouse, awaken, excite, induce, instill, motivate, move, pique, prime, quicken, rouse, roust, spark, start, stimulate, titillate, urge

v 3 agitate, anger, arouse, encourage, foment, ignite, incite, induce, inflame, inspire, instigate, invoke, motivate, muster, prod, propel, raise, set, set on, spur, stimulate, stir, urge

v 4 aggravate, anger, annoy, bother, bug, enrage, exasperate, frazzle, gall, grate, hassle, incense, inflame, infuriate, irk, irritate, madden, miff, nettle, outrage, peeve, pester, pique, rile, upset, vex

v 5 aggravate, annoy, badger, bait, bedevil, beleaguer, bother, bug, harass, harry, hassle, heckle, hound, hurt, intimidate, jeer, nag, needle, persecute, pester, plague, ride, spite, taunt, tease, threaten, torment, worry

provoked *adj* 1 alienated, angry, bitter, emotional, hurt, jealous, resentful

adj 2 see: ANGRY *adj* 1, 4

provoking *adj* provocative, stimulating, suggestive

prow *n* 1 bow, crown, fore, front, head, stem, top

n 2 beak, bill, muzzle, nib, nose, proboscis, snout, trunk

prowess *n* 1 bent, brains, brilliance, faculty, flair, genius, gift, head, intelligence, knack, mind, nose, talent

n 2 see: SKILL n 3

prowl v coast, crawl, creep, glide, skate, skim, skulk, slick, slide, slink, slip, slither, snake, sneak, steal, wiggle, wriggle, writhe

proximate adj 1 approximate, crude, estimated, rough, rounded

adj 2 close, immediate, near, nearly, near at hand, nigh, virtually

proximity n 1 closeness, nearness, vicinity

n 2 association, closeness, contact, nearness

proxy n agent, alternate, dummy, representative, substitute

prudence n 1 economy, frugality, moderation, thrift

n 2 caveat, foresight, forethought, providence, vigilance, vision, wariness

prudent adj 1 advisable, expedient, politic, recommended, suggested, wise

adj 2 alert, careful, heedful, leery, suspicious, vigilant, wary, watchful

adj 3 enlightened, judgmatical, judicious, just, lucid, rational, sage, sane, sapient, sensible, wise

adj 4 calculating, careful, cautious, circumspect, considerate, discreet, gingerly, guarded, heedful, judicious, provident, restrained, reticent, safe, shrewd, wary

prudish adj 1 prim, prissy, straight-laced, stuffy

adj 2 austere, narrow, narrow-minded, prim, puritanical, rigid, severe, strict

prune v clip, crop, cut, lop, pare, shave, shear, snip, trim, whittle

prurient adj bawdy, coarse, crude, dirty, erotic, filthy, foul, gamy, gross, improper, indecent, lascivious, lewd, licentious, nasty, obscene, off-color, pornographic, profane, racy, rank, raunchy, ribald, risqué, scandalous, smutty, suggestive, tainted, uncouth, vulgar, x-rated

Prussian adj aqua, azure, blue, cobalt, indigo, navy, sapphire, turquoise

pry v 1 butt in, chisel in, cut in, fiddle, horn in, interfere, interlope, intrude, meddle, mess around, peek, peer, poke, snoop, tamper with

v 2 force

prying adj curious, inquiring, inquisitive, investigative, nosy, probing, questioning, snooping

psalm n hymn

pseudo adj 1 copied, imitated, simulated, unoriginal

adj 2 feigned, partial, quasi, so-called, semi, somewhat, unofficial

adj 3 artificial, bogus, counterfeit, ersatz, fake, false, imitation, mock, phony, sham, simulated, spurious, substitute, unreal

pseudonym n alias, anonym, nom de plume, pen name

psyche n ego, id, individuality, mind, persona, personality, self, soul, spirit

psychic adj 1 mystic, mystical, transcendental

adj 2 clairvoyant, intuitive, mediumistic, prescient

adj 3 affective, cognitive, emotional, mental, psychological, subconscious, subjective

n 1 astrologer, augur, fortuneteller, oracle, predictor, prophet, seer, soothsayer, visionary

n 2 clairvoyant, medium, soothsayer, spiritualist

psychological adj affective, cognitive, emotional, mental, psychic, subconscious, subjective

psychosis n aberration, abnormality, craziness, delusion, dementia, derangement, distraction, eccentricity, fugue, hallucination, insanity, irregularity, lunacy, madness, mania, unbalance

psychotic adj demented, deranged, distraught, insane

pub n bar, barroom, cocktail lounge, den, dive, dump, gin mill, hangout, haunt, joint, lounge, rathskeller, saloon, tavern, watering hole

puberty n adolescence, youth

public adj 1 obvious, overt, visible

adj 2 collective, common, group, organizational, social, societal

adj 3 aggregate, collective, common, communal, joint, shared

adj 4 civic, civil, municipal, national

adj 5 accessible, available, close, convenient, feasible, functional, handy, helpful, multipurpose, nearby, open, practical, reachable, ready, serviceable, suitable, unrestricted, usable, useful, utilitarian, well-suited, within reach, working

n citizens, civilization, colony, community, crowd, culture, folks, group, human beings, individuals, laity, masses, men and women, neighbors, people, persons, populace, population, settlement, society, staff, tribe

publication n 1 bulletin, daily, journal, newsletter, newspaper, organ, review *n* 2 booklet, gazette, journal, magazine, monthly, periodical, quarterly, weekly

n 3 book, correspondence, edition, folio, issue, manuscript, monograph, opus, paperback, printing, text, tome, volume, work, writing

publicist *n* columnist, commentator, correspondent, editor, interviewer, journalist, newspaperman, writer

publicity *n* 1 promotion

n 2 advertisement, championship, praise, promotion, salesmanship

n 3 array, blare, display, exhibit, exhibition, fanfare, fuss, parade, performance, presentation, procession, show, showing

publicize *v* advertise, air, boom, boost, drum up, endorse, pitch, plug, promote, push, rave, sell, tout

publish *v* 1 advertise, announce, blaze, broadcast, circulate, declare, disperse, disseminate, proclaim

v 2 bring out, distribute, get out, give out, go to press, issue, print, put out, reissue, reprint, set type

puddle *n* pond, pool, swimming hole

pudgy *adj* chubby, chunky, corpulent, fat, fleshy, gross, heavy, hefty, meaty, obese, overweight, plump, portly, rotund, stocky, stout

puff *n* air, blow, breath, breeze, current, draft, wind

v drag, inhale, smoke

puffy *adj* bloated, distended, inflated, swollen, tumescent, tumid, turgid

pugnacious *adj* angry, bellicose, belligerent, combative, contentious, hostile, militant, quarrelsome, warlike

pugnacity *n* aggression, aggressiveness, attack, bellicosity, belligerence, combativeness

pulchritude *n* attractiveness, aura, beauty, comeliness, loveliness, radiance

pull *n* 1 drag, jerk, pluck, tug, yank

n 2 authority, clout, control, in, influence, leverage, power, prestige, weight

n 3 removal

v 1 pinch, tweak, twist

v 2 force, seize, turn, twist, wrest

v 3 extract, remove, suck, tear, withdraw, yank

v 4 commit, continue, extend, maintain, perpetuate

v 5 draw, flex, strain, stretch, tense, tighten, twist

v 6 jerk, tear, tug, twist, wrench, wring, yank

v 7 carry, cart, drag, draw, haul, lug, tow, truck, tug

pullback *n* abandon, departure, desertion, evacuation, exit, going, leaving, pullout, removal, retreat, withdrawal

pulling *n* adhesion, friction, tension, traction

pullout *n* 1 abandon, departure, desertion, evacuation, exit, going, leaving, pullback, removal, retreat, withdrawal

n 2 deletion, erasure, removal

pulp *v* bruise, crush, mash, squash

pulpit *n* dais, desk, lectern, podium, rostrum, soapbox, stage, stand

pulpy *adj* mushy, soft, spongy, squashy, squelchy, squishy, yielding

pulsate *v* 1 beat, flutter, palpitate, pulse, quiver, throb, tremble, vibrate

v 2 fluctuate, oscillate, surge, throb, undulate, vibrate

v 3 flinch, flutter, jar, quake, quaver, quiver, shake, shiver, shudder, tremor, tremble, twitter, twitch, vibrate

pulse *n* beat, cadence, cycle, lilt, rate, rhythm, tempo, time

v beat, flutter, palpitate, pulsate, quiver, throb, tremble, vibrate

pulverize *v* 1 crush, grind, pound, powder

v 2 annihilate, decimate, demolish, destroy, destruct, devastate, dismantle, overturn, raze, rub out, ruin, shatter, smash, tear down, undo, wreck

v 3 see: CUT *v* 7

pulverized *adj* fine, powdery

pummel *v* see: BATTER *v*

pump *v* 1 draft, drain, draw, draw off, siphon, suck, tap

v 2 ask, cross-examine, examine, grill, inquire, interrogate, investigate, probe, query, question, quiz

punch *n* 1 effectiveness, flair, kick, pep, pizzazz, potency, sizzle, snap, spark, verve, vigor, wallop

n 2 bang, blow, box, bump, chop, clap, conk, crack, crash, cuff, hit, impact, jar, jolt, knock, lick, rap, slap, slug, smack, smash, swat, swipe, tap, wallop, whack

n 3 jab, swing, thrust

n 4 die, form, mold

n 5 ardor, beef, brawn, drive, energy, force, intensity, lustiness, might, muscle, pep, potency, power, steam, strength, verve, vigor, vim, virility, vitality

v 1 break through, penetrate, perforate, pierce, poke

v 2 box, clap, cuff, knock, slap, smack, spank, strike, tap, whack

v 3 bang, blow, bump, cuff, hit, strike

v 4 cut, gash, incise, penetrate, pierce, slash, slice, slit

punchy *adj* 1 effective, lively, potent, snappy, strong

adj 2 confused, daffy, daft, dazed, dizzy, groggy, stunned

punctilious *adj* careful, carping, cautious, conscientious, ethical, exacting, fussy, heedful, meticulous, painstaking, scrupulous, unrelenting

punctual *adj* dependable, observant, on time, precise, prompt, reliable, timely

punctuate *v* accent, accentuate, amplify, concentrate, emphasize, feature, flag, focus, heighten, highlight, italicize, mark, spotlight, stress, underline, underscore

puncture *n* 1 break, cavity, slot

n 2 crack, hole, opening

n 3 cut, gash, incision, nick, pierce, prick, slit, wound

v gore, impale, lance, penetrate, spear, stab

pundit *n* 1 authority, expert, guide, guru, leader, master, mentor, teacher, wise man

n 2 academician, egghead, highbrow, intellectual, philosopher, researcher, sage, savant, scholar, thinker, wise man

pungent *adj* 1 acerbic, acid, biting, curt, dry, sharp, sour, tart

adj 2 acerbic, acrid, biting, bitter, caustic, corrosive, critical, sarcastic

adj 3 biting, hot, nippy, seasoned, sharp, spicy, tangy, tart

adj 4 aromatic, lively, peppery, piquant, poignant, racy, snappy, spicy, spirited, vigorous, zesty

punish *v* 1 castigate, chasten, chastise, correct, discipline, torment

v 2 convict, adjudge, condemn, discipline, imprison, sentence

v 3 chastise, dock, fine, penalize, sentence, tariff, tax

v 4 admonish, berate, blame, censure, chide, condemn, disapprove, lay into, rebuke, reprimand, reproach, reprove, scold, warn

v 5 assail, attack, batter, beat, birch, buffet, flagellate, flog, hammer, lambaste, lash, lather, pelt, pound, pummel, scourge, thrash, tromp, wallop, whip

punishment *n* 1 retaliation, retribution, vengeance

n 2 assessment, damages, fine, penalty, tax

n 3 discipline, dockage, fee, fine, penalty

n 4 ache, affliction, agony, anguish, hurt, injury, pain, suffering, torture

punk *n* gorilla, hoodlum, hooligan, roughneck, rowdy, ruffian, thug, tough

puny *adj* 1 immaterial, inconsequential, inconsiderable, insignificant, little, low, meaningless, measly, minor, nominal, paltry, petty, picayune, picky, skimpy, slight, small, tiny, trifling, trivial, unessential, unimportant, worthless

adj 2 see: FRAGILE *adj* 3

pup *n* canine, dog, hound, mongrel, mutt, pooch

pupil *n* 1 coed, collegian, scholar, schoolmate, student, undergraduate

n 2 see: BEGINNER *n* 2

puppet *n* chessman, front, instrument, pawn, peon, stooge, tool

puppy *n* canine, dog, hound, mongrel, mutt, pooch, pup

pups *n* brood, litter, young

purchase *n* acquisition, asset, buy, gain, merchandise, property

v 1 buy, examine, procure, shop

v 2 see: OBTAIN *v* 1

purchaser *n* buyer, client, consumer, customer, end user, patron, shopper, user

pure *adj* 1 abstinent, celibate, chaste, continent, maidenly, virginal, virtuous

adj 2 consecrated, intact, inviolate, inviolable, protected, sacred, sacrosanct

adj 3 consistent, homogeneous, plain, straight, unadulterated, undiluted, unmixed

adj 4 blameless, commendable, guiltless, exemplary, exonerated, innocent, irreproachable, righteous, virtuous

adj 5 holy, sacred, blessed, celestial, consecrated, divine, godly, hallowed, sanctified, spiritual

adj 6 benign, harmless, innocent, innocuous, inoffensive, mild, naive, safe, unoffending, unoffensive

adj 7 celibate, chaste, clean, decent, decorous, immaculate, modest, moral, pristine, proper, spotless, stainless, stuffy, taintless, unadulterated, unblemished, undefiled, upstanding, virginal, wholesome

adj 8 clean, immaculate, pristine, spotless, taintless, unsoiled, unspoiled, unsullied, untouched, virgin

adj 9 absolute, chief, complete, consummate, dominant, godlike, leading, main, perfect, principal, ranking, sheer, supreme, total, unsurpassed, utter, whole

purge *v* 1 cleanse, eradicate, erase, eliminate, remove

v 2 dispose of, eliminate, expel, flush, remove, rid, vanquish

n cleansing, enema, laxative, physic

purify *v* 1 absolve, clean, sanctify

v 2 compress, condense, distill, express, refine

v 3 clean, cleanse, filter, refine, sterilize, wash

v 4 anoint, baptize, bless, consecrate, dedicate, devote, enshrine, exalt, hallow, sanctify

v 5 attenuate, dilute, diminish, lessen, rarefy, reduce, refine, shorten, thin out, weaken

purist *n* fusspot, nit-picker, perfectionist, stickler

puritanical *adj* austere, narrow, narrow-minded, prim, prudish, rigid, severe, strict

purity *n* 1 integrity

n 2 clarity, clearness, distinctness, exactness, freshness, lucidity

n 3 goodness, morality, principle, probity, rectitude, righteousness, uprightness, virtue

purl *v* 1 flow, gurgle, ooze, spurt

v 2 gyrate, pirouette, reel, spin, swim, turn, twirl, whirl

purloin *v* 1 extract, remove, take out, withdraw

v 2 see: STEAL *v* 2

purple *adj* amethyst, lavender, lilac, mauve, orchid, plum, violet

purport *n* drift, implication, intent, substance, tenor

v 1 affect, pretend, profess

v 2 convey, express, hint, impart, imply, indicate, say, suggest

purpose *n* 1 duty, function, use

n 2 course, determination, resolution, resolve

n 3 cause, excuse, motive, rationale, reason, why

n 4 aim, cause, consideration, motive, reason

n 5 ambition, bent, design, goal, intent, intention, meaning, objective

n 6 aim, goal, mission, motive, objective, reason, sake, target, task

purposeful *adj* bent, committed, dedicated, determined, fixed, intentional, resolved, resolute, set, tenacious

purse *n* 1 bag, baggage, case, equipment, gear, grip, kit, luggage, pack, pouch, sack, suitcase, valise, wallet

n 2 ante, award, bonus, booty, cash, commission, dividend, donation, fee, gift, gratuity, largess, money, percentage, perk, perquisite, premium, prize, profit, reward, sharing, stake, stipend, tip, winnings

purser *n* banker, cashier, money-changer, teller

pursue *v* 1 conduct, proceed with, undertake, wage

v 2 attempt, bring about, cultivate, perpetuate, practice, proceed

v 3 attract, court, encourage, flirt, invite, lure, romance, solicit, tempt, woo

v 4 chase, follow, hunt, seek, shadow, shoot for, tail, trace, track, trail

v 5 see: PROBE *v* 5

pursuit *n* 1 exploration, quest, search

n 2 chase, exploration, hunt, quest, search, undertaking, venture

n 3 see: TRADE *n* 3

purvey *v* see: SERVE *v* 4

purveyor *n* dealer, marketer, merchant, monger, seller, trader, vendor

purview *n* 1 distance, future, horizon, outlook, perspective, vision, vista

n 2 circle, compass, confines, dimension, distance, extension, extent, length, limit, orbit, range, reach, realm, scope, size, spectrum, sweep, width

push *n* 1 campaign, crusade, drive, effort

n 2 ambition, drive, enterprise, initiative, lead, leadership, thrust, volition

n 3 see: HORDE *n*

v 1 pedal, propel

v 2 coerce, compel, constrain, force, make, overpower

v 3 bulldoze, elbow, hustle, jostle, press, shoulder, shove

v 4 cue, jog, nudge, prompt, remind, stimulate, stir, suggest

v 5 crowd, herd, jam, mob, press, swarm, teem, throng

v 6 deal, hawk, horse-trade, huckster, hustle, monger, peddle, sell, swap

v 7 boost, budge, drive, force, impel, nudge, propel, shove, thrust

v 8 compact, compress, constrain, crowd, crush, jam, mash, pack, press, squash, squeeze

v 9 advertise, air, boom, boost, drum up, endorse, pitch, plug, promote, publicize, rave, sell, tout

v 10 activate, actuate, compel, drive, force, goad, impel, induce, mobilize, motivate, move, persuade, press, propel, spur, start, turn on

pushcart *n* cart, handcart, truck, wagon, wheelbarrow

pushing *adj* see: ASSERTIVE *adj*

pushover *n* chump, dupe, mark, stooge, sucker, victim

pushy *adj* 1 aggressive, coercive, compelling, forceful, hard-sell, high-pressure, intensive

adj 2 aggressive, ambitious, assertive, assured, compelling, compulsive, confident, decided, dogmatic, driven, emphatic, energetic, insistent, militant, positive, pushing, self-assertive, sure, urging

adj 3 see: AUTHORITATIVE *adj* 2

puss *n* cat, feline, kit, kitten, kitty, pussy, tabby, tiger

pussy *n* cat, feline, kit, kitten, kitty, puss, tabby, tiger

put *v* 1 approximate, call, estimate, judge, place, reckon

v 2 calibrate, establish, fix, insert, install, lay, locate, place, plant, position, set, settle, situate, station

v 3 air, bring up, broach, communicate, discuss, expose, express, give, introduce, open, reveal, state, tap, tell, vent, ventilate, verbalize

put-down *n* crack, gibe, jeer, quip, shot, sneer, torment

put-on *n* bastard, deception, fake, hoax, sham

putrefy *v* corrupt, crumble, decay, decompose, degenerate, deteriorate, disintegrate, perish, rot, smell, spoil, taint, wane, weaken, wither

putrid *adj* 1 dirty, disgusting, foul, lousy, nasty, rotten, sordid

adj 2 bad, decayed, rancid, rotten, sharp, sour, spoiled

adj 3 decaying, fetid, foul, gamy, malodorous, musty, rancid, rank, reeking, rotten, smelly, sour, spoiled, stale, stinking, tainted

adj 4 see: VICIOUS *adj* 3

putter *v* 1 dabble, dally, diddle, fiddle, fool, monkey, piddle, play, poke about, tinker, toy, trifle

v 2 dally, dawdle, delay, diddle, goof off, idle, lag, linger, loaf, loiter, loll, lounge, malinger, poke, put off, shirk, tarry

puzzle *n* confusion, conundrum, difficulty, dilemma, enigma, mystery, obstacle, paradox, perplexity, problem, quandary, question, riddle, secret

v amaze, befog, bewilder, boggle, confound, confuse, daze, perplex, stumble, stump

puzzling *adj* 1 baffling, elusive, frustrating, mysterious, subtle

adj 2 ambiguous, cryptic, enigmatic, mystifying, occult, vague

adj 3 enigmatic, incomprehensible, inexplicable, inscrutable, mysterious

adj 4 arcane, hermetic, impenetrable, impervious, mysterious, mystic, obscure, secret, unexaminable, unknown, unseen

adj 5 see: QUAINT *adj* 1

pygmy *adj* see: TINY *adj* 1

n dwarf, Lilliputian, midget

Q

quack *n* charlatan, cheat, fake, fraud

quail *v* cower, cringe, flinch, grovel, recoil, shrink, sneak

quaint *adj* 1 charming, funny, odd, old-fashioned, peculiar, picturesque, puzzling, remarkable, special, uncommon, unusual, whimsical

adj 2 see: STRANGE *adj* 5

quake *v* flinch, flutter, jar, pulsate, quaver, quiver, shake, shiver, shudder, tremble, twitch, twitter, vibrate

n flutter, quiver, shiver, tingle, tremor

qualification *n* 1 caveat, limitation, requisite, restriction, stipulation

n 2 ability, adequacy, adroitness, aptitude, art, caliber, calling, capability, capacity, command, competence, craft, dexterity, experience, expertise, familiarity, forte, knack, know-how, knowledge, mastery, proficiency, prowess, savvy, skill, specialty, strength, talent, training, workmanship

qualifications *n* background, credentials, education, training

qualified *adj* 1 diminished, modified, reduced

adj 2 skilled, specialized, technical, trained

adj 3 acceptable, allowable, eligible, suitable

adj 4 able, accomplished, adept, apt, capable, competent, deft, dexterous, expert, fit, gifted, masterful, professional, proficient, proper, skillful, talented

qualify *v* answer, do, fulfill, meet, satisfy, suffice, work

quality *adj* champion, excellent, fine, first-class, first-rate, foremost, good, grade A, leading, number one, prime, principal, prominent, select, stellar, superb, superior, top, top-drawer, top-notch, tops

n 1 caliber, class, grade, rating

n 2 character, constitution, fiber, make-up, substance

n 3 caliber, excellence, goodness, merit, stature, value, worth

n 4 attribute, character, characteristic, feature, highlight, mark, peculiarity, property, trait, virtue

n 5 characteristic, flavor, impression, nature, property, ring, sound, tendency, tone, type

n 6 capacity, grade, office, place, position, post, rank, situation, spot, standing, state, station, status

n 7 aptitude, character, complexion, disposition, distinctiveness, heart, humor, identity, inclination, individuality, make-up, nature, personality, spirit, state, temperament, tendency

qualm *n* compunction, conscience, pang, regret, reservation, restraint, scruple, twinge

quandary *n* 1 complication, difficulty, dilemma, obstacle, plight, predicament, problem, situation, snag

n 2 confusion, conundrum, difficulty, dilemma, enigma, mystery, obstacle, paradox, perplexity, problem, puzzle, question, riddle, secret

n 3 bind, box, corner, difficulty, dilemma, fix, impasse, jam, mess, pinch, plight, predicament, scrape, spot, trap, trouble

quantity *n* 1 amount, amplitude, dimensions, magnitude, proportions, scope, size, volume

n 2 aggregate, amount, body, budget, bulk, count, number, tally, total

n 3 see: BUNCH *n* 2

quarantine *n* exile, isolation, leisure, relaxation, rest, retirement, retreat, seclusion, solitude, withdrawal

quarrel *n* 1 break, disagreement, dissension, fight, misunderstanding, rift, separation, spat

n 2 altercation, argument, battle, brawl, challenge, combat, controversy, disagreement, discord, dispute, feud, fight, fracas, fray, hassle, melee, rancor, rift, row, ruckus, scrap, scuffle, skirmish, spat, squabble, struggle, tiff, war

n 3 see: CLASH *n* 2

v altercate, argue, battle, bicker, brawl, clash, conflict, dispute, engage, equivocate, feud, fight, fray, haggle, hassle, quibble, row, scrap, spar, squabble, wrangle

quarrelsome *adj* 1 bellicose, brawling, difficult, feisty, scrappy, spirited

adj 2 angry, bellicose, belligerent, combative, contentious, hostile, militant, warlike

quarry *n* 1 dig, excavation, lode, mine

n 2 catch, game, prey, target

quarter *v* bivouac, camp, dwell, lodge, nest, station

n one-fourth

quarterdeck *n* deck, platform

quarterly *n* booklet, gazette, journal, maga-zine, monthly, periodical, publication, weekly

quarters *n* berth, billet, housing, shelter, space

quash *v* 1 bear down, beat down, conquer, crush, defeat, dominate, enslave, exploit, overpower, reduce, subdue, subjugate, suppress, vanquish

v 2 annihilate, crush, demolish, extinguish, put down, quell, quench, repress, squash, stamp out, suppress

v 3 asphyxiate, choke, constrict, gag, garrote, muffle, repress, smother, stifle, strangle, suffocate, suppress

v 4 abrogate, annul, cancel, contradict, discharge, dismantle, dissolve, dwindle, fade, negate, nullify, recall, repeal, rescind, reverse, revoke, set aside, vacate, void

v 5 abate, abolish, abrogate, annihilate, annul, call off, cancel, cease, delete, destroy, efface, erase, excise, expunge, invalidate, kill, negate, nullify, obliterate, omit, remove, stop, terminate, wipe out

quasi *adj* 1 apparent, illusive, illusory, ostensible, seeming, specious, superficial

adj 2 feigned, partial, pseudo, semi, so-called, somewhat, unofficial

quaver *v* 1 trill, vocalize, warble

v 2 flinch, flutter, jar, pulsate, quake, quiver, shake, shiver, shudder, tremble, tremor, twitch, twitter, vibrate

queasy *adj* 1 nauseated, queer, seasick, sick, squeamish

adj 2 anxious, edgy, fidgety, impatient, nervous, nervy, restive, restless, tense, troubled, uncomfortable, uneasy, uptight, worried

queer *adj* 1 nauseated, queasy, seasick, sick, squeamish

adj 2 aberrant, bizarre, eccentric, erratic, odd, oddball, outlandish, peculiar, quaint, singular, strange, uncanny, unconventional, unusual, weird

v see: BLUNDER *v*

quell *v* 1 allay, appease, assuage, balm, becalm, calm, compose, conciliate, ease, lull, mollify, pacify, placate, propitiate, quiet, reconcile, satiate, settle, soften, soothe, still, sweeten, tranquilize

v 2 annihilate, crush, demolish, extinguish, put down, quash, quench, repress, squash, stamp out, suppress

v 3 censor, curb, gag, hush, inhibit, muffle, mute, quiet, repress, restrain, silence, squelch, stifle, still, subdue, suppress, throttle, tone down

quench *v* 1 douse, extinguish, out

v 2 abate, allay, assuage, mitigate, moderate, satiate, satisfy

v 3 annihilate, crush, demolish, extinguish, put down, quash, quell, repress, squash, stamp out, suppress

quenched *adj* filled, full, sated, satisfied, saturated

query *n* 1 conference, discourse, discussion, meeting

n 2 concern, doubt, dubiety, incertitude, indecision, mistrust, question, skepticism, suspicion, uncertainty, wonder

n 3 question

v 1 challenge, dispute, doubt, mistrust

v 2 ask, cross-examine, examine, grill, inquire, interrogate, investigate, probe, pump, question, quiz

quest *n* 1 exploration, hunt, pursuit, search

n 2 chase, exploration, hunt, pursuit, search, undertaking, venture

v see: TRY *v* 4

question *n* 1 argument, controversy, issue, item, matter, motif, motive, point, proposition, subject, text, theme, topic

n 2 confusion, conundrum, difficulty, dilemma, enigma, mystery, obstacle, paradox, perplexity, problem, puzzle, quandary, riddle, secret

n 3 query

n 4 challenge, demur, difficulty, hindrance, hurdle, objection, obstacle, problem, protest, snag

n 5 concern, doubt, dubiety, incertitude, indecision, mistrust, query, skepticism, suspicion, uncertainty, wonder

v 1 challenge, dispute, doubt, mistrust, query

v 2 ask, cross-examine, examine, grill, inquire, interrogate, investigate, probe, pump, query, quiz

questionable *adj* 1 amazing, fabulous

adj 2 distrusted, suspect, suspicious

adj 3 cynical, distrustful, doubtful, dubious, incredulous, leery, shy, skeptical, skittish, suspicious, uncertain, unsure

adj 4 absurd, chancy, debatable, doubtful, dubious, iffy, implausible, improbable, incredible, moot, preposterous, theoretical, unbelievable, uncertain, unlikely

adj 5 ambiguous, borderline, clouded, doubtful, dubious, equivocal, garbled, illogical, inarticulate, incalculable, incoherent, inexplicit, muddled, muffled, murky, obscure, precarious, shaky, suspect, suspicious, uncertain, unclear, uneasy, unintelligible, unsure, vague, wary

adj 6 dubious, insecure, undependable, unreliable, unsure, untrustworthy

questioning *adj* curious, inquiring, inquisitive, investigative, nosy, probing, prying, snooping

questionnaire *n* exam, examination, final, inquiry, oral, quiz, test

queue *n* line, order, rank

v fall in, line up, wait

quibble *v* 1 altercate, argue, battle, bicker, brawl, clash, conflict, dispute, engage, equivocate, feud, fight, fray, haggle, hassle, quarrel, row, scrap, spar, squabble, wrangle

v 2 see: SCOLD *v* 2

quick *adv* 1 abruptly, fast, hastily, immediately, instantaneously, instantly, quickly, short, suddenly, swiftly

adv 2 expeditiously, fast, full-tilt, hastily, in a snap, lickety-split, promptly, pronto, quickly, rapidly, right away, soon, speedily, swiftly, urgently

adj 1 brisk, curt, snappy

adj 2 alert, apt, prompt, ready

adj 3 immediate, instant, instantaneous, rapid, swift, urgent

adj 4 breakneck, expeditious, explosive, fast, fleet, hasty, impulsive, instant, lightning, mercurial, meteoric, precipitous, rapid, spectacular, speedy, sudden, swift

adj 5 acute, alert, astute, cagey, canny, clever, cunning, deft, keen, knowing, penetrating, perceptive, piercing, quick-sighted, quick-witted, receptive, responsive, sagacious, savvy, sensitive, sharp, sharp-witted, shrewd, slick, smart, street-smart, wise

adj 6 express, fast, next-day, nonstop, rapid, speedy, swift

adj 7 active, agile, astir, brisk, catty, energetic, lively, nimble, sprightly, spry, zippy

adj 8 abrupt, hasty, headlong, hurried, impetuous, impulsive, precipitant, precipitate, rapid, rash, reckless, rushing, sudden

adj 9 alert, astute, brainy, bright, brilliant, clever, discerning, discriminating, educated, insightful, intellectual, intelligent, knowing, knowledgeable, perceptive, sagacious, sage, sharp, smart, swift

adj 10 abrupt, bluff, blunt, brash, brusque, cheeky, crusty, curt, flip, flippant, gruff, harsh, impertinent, impudent, irritable, nasty, rude, sarcastic, sassy, short, snippy, snotty, surly, testy, wisenheimer

n center, core, crux, essence, gist, heart, life, marrow, nature, nucleus, pith, quintessence, root, spirit, substance

quicken *v* 1 accelerate, expedite, hasten, hurry, rush, shake up, speed, step up
v 2 animate, brighten, cheer up, enliven, incite, inspire, liven, resuscitate, vivify
v 3 see: PROVOKE *v* 2

quickly *adv* 1 abruptly, fast, hastily, immediately, instantaneously, instantly, quick, short, suddenly, swiftly
adv 2 anon, any moment, at once, directly, immediately, instantaneously, instantly, momentarily, now, presently, promptly, right now, shortly, soon, straightaway, *tout de suite*
adv 3 expeditiously, fast, full-tilt, hastily, in a snap, lickety-split, promptly, pronto, quick, rapidly, right away, soon, speedily, swiftly, urgently

quickness *n* 1 abruptness, brevity, briefness, conciseness, curtness, shortness, transience
n 2 alacrity, dispatch, expedition, haste, hastiness, hurry, hustle, precipitance, precipitation, rush, rustle, speed, swiftness
n 3 alacrity, cadence, celerity, dispatch, gait, pace, rapidity, rate, speed, step, stride, swiftness, trot, velocity, walk

quick-tempered *adj* see: HOT-TEMPERED *adj*

quiet *adj* 1 discreet, off the record, secretive
adj 2 conservative, dim, inconspicuous, restrained, subdued, tasteful, unassuming, unobtrusive
adj 3 dead, hush, inanimate, inert, lifeless, noiseless, silent, soundless, still
adj 4 asleep, dormant, idle, immobile, inactive, inanimate, inert, inoperative, laid-back, motionless, nodding, passive, sleepy, slumbering, stable, stagnant, still
adj 5 see: CALM *adj* 2
adj 6 see: DORMANT *adj* 2, 3
adj 7 see: SHY *adj* 2
n 1 detachment, isolation, seclusion, solitude
n 2 calm, hush, lull, peace, peacefulness, repose, respite, rest, siesta, silence, sleep, stillness, tranquillity
v 1 calm, lessen, muffle, reduce, soften, subdue
v 2 censor, curb, gag, hush, inhibit, muffle, mute, quell, repress, restrain, silence, squelch, stifle, still, subdue, suppress, throttle, tone down
v 3 see: APPEASE *v* 2

quill *n* 1 brush, chalk, crayon, pen, pencil
n 2 feather

quilt *n* blanket, comforter, cover, warmer

quintessence *n* center, core, crux, essence, gist, heart, life, marrow, nature, nucleus, pith, quick, root, spirit, substance

quip *n* 1 crack, gibe, jeer, put-down, shot, sneer, torment
n 2 answer, comeback, put-down, reaction, rejoinder, reply, response, retort, return
n 3 banter, comedy, crack, funniness, gag, humor, jest, joke, small talk, wisecrack, wit, witticism
v belittle, deride, flaunt, jab, jeer, jest, mock, razz, ridicule, scoff, scorn, sneer, taunt, tease

quirk *n* abnormality, eccentricity, habit, idiosyncrasy, oddity, peculiarity, trademark

quit *v* 1 drop, go, leave, resign, retire, terminate
v 2 abdicate, relinquish, renounce, resign, step down, vacate
v 3 abandon, discard, dispose of, dump, eliminate, empty, reject, scrap, unload
v 4 abstain, cease, conclude, desist, discontinue, end, finish, forbear, freeze, halt, knock off, refrain, sever, stop, terminate
v 5 abandon, break up, cast off, chuck, defect, desert, disavow, discard, disenfranchise, disown, ditch, dump, forsake, jilt, junk, leave, reject, renounce, spurn, strand, throw out

quite *adv* 1 considerably, dramatically, far, rather, significantly, very, well
adv 2 awfully, dreadfully, eminently, endlessly, exceedingly, exceptionally, extremely, greatly, highly, mightily, notably, remarkably, terribly, thoroughly, very
adv 3 see: COMPLETELY *adv*

quiver *v* 1 beat, flutter, palpitate, pulsate, pulse, throb, tremble, vibrate
v 2 flinch, flutter, jar, pulsate, quake, quaver, shake, shiver, shudder, tremble, tremor, twitch, twitter, vibrate
n flutter, quake, shiver, tingle, tremor

quiz *n* exam, examination, final, inquiry, oral, test
v ask, cross-examine, examine, grill, inquire, interrogate, investigate, probe, pump, question

quorum *n* minimum

quota *n* 1 percentage, proportion, quotient, rate, ratio
n 2 budget, estimate, forecast, plan, projection
n 3 allotment, allowance, apportionment, budget, dispensation, dispersion, lot,

measure, part, percentage, portion, ration, share, slice

v see: ALLOCATE *v* 3

quotation *n* citation, clipping, excerpt, extract, mention, passage, portion, quote, reference, section

quote *n* citation, clipping, excerpt, extract, mention, passage, portion, quotation, reference, section

v cite, paraphrase, repeat, restate

quotient *n* percentage, proportion, quota, rate, ratio

R

rabbi *n* chaplain, clergyman, cleric, father, guru, minister, padre, parson, pastor, priest, reverend

rabble *n* see: CROWD *n* 1

rabid *adj* 1 savage, untamed, vicious, violent, wild

adj 2 extreme, extremist, fanatic, fanatical, radical, revolutionary, ultra, zealous

race *n* 1 breed, clan, class, family, household, people, relatives, stock, tribe

n 2 bout, competition, conflict, contest, event, game, marathon, match, meet, meeting, regatta, round robin, run, tournament, tourney

v 1 dash, gallop, jog, run, speed, sprint

v 2 flash, speed, zoom

racial *adj* ethnic, national, tribal

racism *n* 1 bias, bigotry, chauvinism, discrimination, intolerance, parochialism, partiality, prejudice, provincialism, sexism

n 2 apartheid, segregation

racist *n* bigot, segregationist, supremacist

racket *n* 1 con, crime, graft, hustle, rip-off, scam, scheme, sting, swindle

n 2 brouhaha, cacophony, chaos, clamor, confusion, din, discord, disorder, hubbub, mayhem, noise, pandemonium, tumult, uproar

racketeer *n* gangster

racy *adj* 1 erotic, improper, indecent, suggestive, unbecoming

adj 2 aromatic, lively, peppery, piquant, poignant, pungent, snappy, spicy, spirited, vigorous, zesty

adj 3 bawdy, coarse, crude, dirty, erotic, filthy, foul, gamy, gross, improper, indecent, lascivious, lewd, licentious, nasty, obscene, off-color, pornographic, profane, prurient, rank, raunchy, ribald, risqué, scandalous, smutty, suggestive, tainted, uncouth, vulgar, x-rated

radiance *n* 1 attractiveness, aura, beauty, comeliness, loveliness

n 2 coating, gloss, glow, luster, patina, polish, sheen, shimmer, shine

radiant *adj* 1 beaming, bright, brilliant, burnished, emitting, glistening, glossy, lucid, luminous, lustrous, polished, shining, shiny

adj 2 bright, cheerful, cheery, content, ebullient, ecstatic, elated, exuberant, festive, gay, glad, happy, jovial, joyful, joyous, merry, mirthful, pleased, rejoicing

adj 3 attractive, becoming, comely, exquisite, fair, good-looking, gorgeous, handsome, pleasing, stately

radiate *v* 1 brighten, glow, illuminate, irradiate, light up, spotlight

v 2 discharge, emanate, emit, expel, project, release, send

v 3 beam, burn, disperse, emit, gleam, glisten, shed, shine, transmit

radical *adj* 1 drastic, excessive, extreme, intense, passionate, severe, strong

adj 2 advanced, broad, broad-minded, liberal, progressive, tolerant, unbiased

adj 3 extreme, extremist, fanatic, fanatical, rabid, revolutionary, ultra, zealous

n bug, crusader, enthusiast, fanatic, fiend, freak, hobbyist, maniac, monomaniac, nut, zealot

radio *v* cable, notify, telegraph, telex, wire

radius *n* bore, caliber, circle, diameter

raft *n* barge, boat, canoe, craft, dory, ferry, float, kayak, scow, skiff, tender

rafter *n* beam, board, boom, girder, log, plank, spar, support, timber

rag *n* end, patch, piece, scrap, shred, tatter

rage *n* 1 ferocity, frenzy, fury

n 2 fit, passion, tantrum, temper

n 3 brutality, destructiveness, ferocity, force, frenzy, fury, violence

n 4 chic, craze, fad, fashion, mode, style, thing, trend, vogue

n 5 anger, dander, fit, frenzy, fury, indignation, ire, outrage, paroxysm, tantrum, wrath

v 1 frenzy, rampage, rebel, revolt, riot, stampede, storm

v 2 anger, blow up, boil, boil over, brew, bristle, burn, flare up, fume, seethe, simmer, smoke, steam, storm

ragged *adj* cheap, chintzy, seedy

ragtime *n* blues, classical, country, folk, jazz, music, rock-and-roll, soul, swing

raid *n* 1 exploration, foray, infiltration, invasion, penetration *n* 2 assault, attack, blitz, bombardment, onslaught, strike

v 1 attack, foray, invade, overrun

v 2 ambush, assail, assault, attack, beset, invade, storm, strike, trap, waylay

rail *v* see: SCOLD *v* 4

railroad *v* force

rain *n* cloudburst, deluge, downpour, drizzle, hail, precipitation, shower, sprinkle

v 1 deluge, drizzle, fall, pour, shower, sprinkle

v 2 cascade, emit, flood, inundate, overflow, plunge, pour, shower, spill, swamp, tumble

rainy *adj* choppy, nasty, rough, sloppy, wet

raise *v* 1 elevate, heave, hoist, lift, pick up, take up

v 2 boost, hike, increase, jack up, jump, put up, up

v 3 cultivate, farm, grow, harvest, plant, plow, produce, till

v 4 care, cherish, foster, mother, nourish, nurse, nurture, parent, protect, rear, suckle

v 5 agitate, anger, arouse, encourage, foment, ignite, incite, induce, inflame, inspire, instigate, invoke, motivate, muster, prod, propel, provoke, set, set on, spur, stimulate, stir, urge

n foothill, hill, hillock, hump, knoll, mound, mount, rise, swelling

rake *n* cad, cheat, knave, lecher, louse, rascal, reprobate, rogue, scoundrel

v amass, collect, gather, heap, pile, take in

rakish *adj* see: SUAVE *adj* 2

rally *n* 1 comeback, improvement, reappearance, recovery, renewal, resurrection, return, revival

n 2 assemblage, assembly, caucus, conference, congregation, convention, council, crowd, gathering, group, meeting, symposium

v 1 bounce back, come' round, rebound, recoup, recover, revitalize, snap back

v 2 arouse, awaken, challenge, excite, kindle, rouse, stir, wake, waken

v 3 ameliorate, convalesce, gain, heal, improve, loop up, mend, perk, recover, recuperate, rehabilitate, revive

v 4 assemble, associate, call, cluster, collect, concentrate, congregate, convene, flock, gather, group, lump, marshal, mass, mingle, mobilize, muster, order, rendezvous, round up, send for, summon

ram *v* 1 cram, crush, force, gorge, insert, jam, pack, stuff

v 2 attack, butt, drive, knock, lunge, pass, plunge, sink, stab, stick, thrust

RAM *n* bubble memory, diskettes, floppy, hard disk, memory

ramble *v* 1 discourse, discuss, elaborate, expatiate, sermonize

v 2 itinerate, meander, perambulate, promenade, range, roam, rove, saunter, stray, stroll, traipse, travel, traverse, walk, wander

rambling *adj* babbling, confused, incoherent, irrational, wild

rambunctious *adj* aggressive, defiant, insubordinate, restless, stubborn, unruly

ramification *n* consequence, development, result

ramp *n* angle, grade, gradient, incline, pitch, rise, slant, slope, tilt

rampage *n* riot, stampede, storm

v frenzy, rage, rebel, revolt, riot, stampede, storm

rampant *adj* 1 current, democratic, dominant, extensive, fashionable, general, in vogue, popular, prevailing, prevalent, rife, sought after, well-liked, widespread

adj 2 audacious, free, liberated, licentious, loose, unbridled, unconfined, uncontrolled, uncurbed, ungoverned, unhampered, uninhibited, unrestrained, unsecured, unshackled, untied, wild

rampart *n* bastion, bulwark, defense, embankment, fortification, wall

ranch *n* farm, range, spread

rancid *adj* 1 bad, decayed, putrid, rotten, sharp, sour, spoiled

adj 2 decaying, fetid, foul, gamy, malodorous, musty, putrid, rank, reeking, rotten, smelly, sour, spoiled, stale, stinking, tainted

rancor *n* 1 acrimony, animosity, antagonism, antipathy, aversion, bitterness, dislike, enmity, gall, hate, hatred, hostility, ill will, malice, spite, venom, vindictiveness

n 2 see: QUARREL *n* 2

random *adj* 1 diverse, haphazard, jumbled, mixed

adj 2 accidental, aimless, arbitrary, casual, chance, chaotic, haphazard, hit-or-miss, indiscriminate, irregular, unaimed, uncontrolled, unplanned

randy *adj* amorous, ardent, aroused, carnal, earthy, erotic, fervent, fleshly, horny, hot, impassioned, lascivious, lecherous, lewd, licentious, lustful, passionate, provocative, raunchy, romantic, sensual, sexual, sexy, sultry, titillated, torrid, turned on, voluptuous, wanton

range *n* 1 breadth, depth, dimensions, scope, span, width *n* 2 boundary, extent, field, matter, reach, scope, vicinity

n 3 circle, compass, confines, dimension, distance, extension, extent, length, limit, orbit, purview, reach, realm, scope, size, spectrum, sweep, width

n 4 farm, ranch, spread

n 5 area, district, domain, environs, jurisdiction, locality, neighborhood, parish, precinct, province, region, section, sphere, vicinity, ward, zone

v 1 calibrate, gauge, measure, rank, size

v 2 extend, go, run, span, vary

v 3 itinerate, meander, perambulate, promenade, ramble, roam, rove, saunter, stray, stroll, traipse, travel, traverse, walk, wander

ranging *adj* ample, broad, expansive, extended, extensive, vast, wide

rank *adj* 1 decaying, fetid, foul, gamy, malodorous, musty, putrid, rancid, reeking, rotten, smelly, sour, spoiled, stale, stinking, tainted

adj 2 see: VULGAR *adj* 2

n 1 line, order

n 2 advantage, precedence, prerogative, priority, privilege, seniority

n 3 caste, layer, ply, row, stratum, tier

n 4 achievement, distinction, prestige, recognition, stance, stature, status

n 5 caste, class, degree, echelon, estate, hierarchy, level, status

n 6 class, degree, grade, interval, level, mark, notch, position, rate, step

n 7 capacity, grade, office, place, position, post, quality, situation, spot, standing, state, station, status

v 1 calibrate, gauge, measure, range, size

v 2 analogize, associate, compare, correlate, relate

v 3 see: APPRAISE *v*

v 4 see: CLASSIFY *v* 2

ranking *adj* absolute, chief, complete, consummate, dominant, godlike, leading, main, perfect, principal, pure, sheer, supreme, total, unsurpassed, utter, whole

ransack *v* comb, loot, rifle, scour, search, separate, sift, sort

ransom *v* buy, convert, reclaim, recover, redeem, save

n bribe, payment, payoff, payola

rant *v* bawl out, bellow, berate, chew out, mock, rail, rave, revile, roar, scold, tell off, tongue-lash, upbraid, yell

rap *n* 1 bull session, discussion, talk

n 2 admonishment, admonition, blast, chewing out, chiding, criticism, denunciation, diatribe, harangue, hassle, libel,

outburst, rebuke, reprimand, reproach, reproof, scolding, slander, tirade

n 3 bang, blow, box, bump, chop, clap, conk, crack, crash, cuff, hit, impact, jar, jolt, knock, lick, punch, slap, slug, smack, smash, swat, swipe, tap, wallop, whack

n 4 chat, chatter, gab, talk

rapacity *n* gluttony

rape *v* assault, attack, force, pillage, ravish, sack, violate

n abuse, assault, attack, sack, violation

rapid *adj* 1 immediate, instant, instantaneous, quick, swift, urgent

adj 2 breakneck, expeditious, explosive, fast, fleet, hasty, impulsive, instant, lightning, mercurial, meteoric, precipitous, quick, spectacular, speedy, sudden, swift

adj 3 express, fast, next-day, nonstop, quick, speedy, swift

adj 4 abrupt, hasty, headlong, hurried, impetuous, impulsive, precipitant, precipitate, quick, rash, reckless, rushing, sudden

rapidity *n* alacrity, cadence, celerity, dispatch, gait, pace, quickness, rate, speed, step, stride, swiftness, trot, velocity, walk

rapidly *adv* expeditiously, fast, full-tilt, hastily, in a snap, lickety-split, promptly, pronto, quick, quickly, right away, soon, speedily, swiftly, urgently

rapier *n* blade, cutlass, dagger, knife, pocketknife, saber, scimitar, switchblade, sword

rapport *n* 1 affair, association, communication, friendship, intimacy, liaison, relationship, union

n 2 accord, affinity, agreement, assent, concert, concord, congruence, cooperation, empathy, harmony, synergy, teamwork, unity

rapscallion *n* rascal, scalawag, scamp

rapt *adj* absorbed, agog, concentrated, deep, determined, distracted, engaged, engrossed, enraptured, entranced, fascinated, immersed, intent, preoccupied, wrapped up

rapture *n* bliss, delight, ecstasy, Eden, elation, enchantment, heaven, joy, nirvana, paradise, pleasure, rhapsody

rapturous *adj* entranced, overjoyed

rare *adj* 1 invaluable, irreplaceable, precious, priceless, unparalleled

adj 2 choice, dainty, delicate, elegant, exquisite, favorite, fine, preferred, select

adj 3 few, infrequent, isolated, occasional, scarce, seldom, sporadic, uncommon, unusual

adj 4 amazing, brilliant, exceptional, extraordinary, noteworthy, phenomenal, remarkable, significant, singular, stunning, super, uncommon, uncustomary, unique, unusual

adj 5 raw, uncooked

rarefied *adj* attenuate, diminished, lessened, subtle, tenuous, thin

rarefy *v* attenuate, dilute, diminish, lessen, purify, reduce, refine, shorten, thin out, weaken

rarely *adv* infrequently, now and then, once in a while, sporadically

raring *adj* see: EAGER *adj 2*

rarity *n 1* antique, bric-a-brac, curio, curiosity, objet d'art, novelty, oddity, treasure, wonder

n 2 dearth, deficiency, deficit, drought, famine, lack, scarcity, shortage, sparseness, undersupply, want

rascal *n 1* cad, cheat, knave, lecher, louse, rake, reprobate, rogue, scoundrel

n 2 rapscallion, scalawag, scamp

rash *adj 1* abrupt, audacious, desperate, headstrong, reckless

adj 2 automatic, impulsive, instinctive, involuntary, natural, reflex, spontaneous, unconscious, unforced, unpremeditated, unprompted

adj 3 see: HURRIED *adj*

n allergy, hay fever, hives, reaction, spots

rasp *v* file, grate, grind, grit, sand

rasping *adj* caustic, grating, guttural, harsh, hoarse, husky, raucous, rough, strident

rat *n* cad, bird, bum, fink, heel, jerk, turkey

v fink, inform, sing, snitch, squeal, stool, tattle, tattletale

rate *n 1* percentage, proportion, quota, quotient

n 2 beat, cadence, cycle, lilt, pulse, rhythm, tempo, time

n 3 charge, cost, expense, fare, outlay, payment, price, value, worth

n 4 class, degree, grade, interval, level, mark, notch, position, rank, step

n 5 passage

n 6 alacrity, cadence, celerity, disnatch, gait, pace, quickness, rapidity, speed, step, stride, swiftness, trot, velocity, walk

v 1 evaluate, grade, score

v 2 appraise, assay, assess, charge, estimate, evaluate, levy, price, rank, set at, survey, tax, valuate, value

v 3 align, arrange, array, assort, catalog, categorize, class, classify, cluster, compile, file, format, grade, group, lay out, line up, list, order, organize, outline, pigeonhole, place, position, prioritize, program, rank, sort, stack, tabulate

rather *adv 1* before, preferably

adv 2 considerably, dramatically, far, quite, significantly, very, well

adv 3 adequately, amply, enough, equitably, fairly, justly, moderately, passably, satisfactorily, tolerably

rathers *n* alternative, choice, decision, druthers, election, option, pick, preference, selection, vote

rathskeller *n* bar, barroom, cocktail lounge, den, dive, dump, gin mill, hangout, haunt, joint, lounge, pub, saloon, tavern, watering hole

ratify *v 1* endorse, promote, second, support

v 2 approve, authorize, decree, enact, legalize, legislate, ordain, pass, sanction

v 3 advocate, affirm, assure, avouch, avow, commit, devote, guarantee, pledge, promise, swear, vow

v 4 accept, approbate, approve, authorize, certify, condone, confirm, countenance, endorse, favor, pass, sanction, validate

v 5 attest, authenticate, certify, confirm, corroborate, justify, notarize, prove, sanction, substantiate, support, validate, verify, vouch, witness

rating *n 1* classification

n 2 caliber, class, grade

ratio *n 1* degree, extent, intensity, measure, scope

n 2 percentage, proportion, quota, quotient, rate

n 3 comparison, percentage, proportion, relation, share

ration *n* allotment, allowance, apportionment, budget, dispensation, dispersion, lot, measure, part, percentage, portion, quota, share, slice

v see: ALLOCATE *v 3*

rational *adj 1* cogent, correct, logical, sound

adj 2 mild, moderate, modest, pleasant, reasonable, temperate

adj 3 ethical, lucid, moral, responsible, sane, stable

adj 4 astute, consequent, intelligent, knowing, logical, perceptive, reasonable, sane, sensible, shrewd, sober, sound, wise

adj 5 see: WISE *adj 4*

rationale *n 1* cause, excuse, motive, purpose, reason, why

n 2 basis, arguments, cause, explanation, foundation, grounds, principle, reason, rudiments, source

rationality *n* lucidity, mind, reason, saneness, sanity, sense, soundness, wit

rationalization *n* alibi, defense, excuse, explanation, justification, plea, pretext, reason, ruse

rationalize *v* account, explain, explain away, justify

rations *n* 1 energy, nourishment, provisions, supply

n 2 bread, breakfast, brunch, chow, cuisine, diet, dinner, dish, edibles, entree, fare, food, grub, lunch, meals, nosh, nutrition, provisions, snack, supper, victuals, vittles

rattle *v* 1 bump, jar, jolt, jostle, shake, shock, startle

v 2 befuddle, bewilder, confuse, daze, distract, dizzy, embarrass, fluster, mix up, muddle, ruffle, trick, unglue, unhinge

n babble, babbling, burble, chatter, gibber, murmur

raucous *adj* 1 caustic, grating, guttural, harsh, hoarse, husky, rasping, rough, strident

adj 2 blatant, boisterous, clamorous, disturbing, loud, loudmouthed, noisy, obstreperous, rowdy, tumultuous, vociferous

raunchy *adj* 1 bawdy, coarse, crude, dirty, erotic, filthy, foul, gamy, gross, improper, indecent, lascivious, lewd, licentious, nasty, obscene, off-color, pornographic, profane, prurient, racy, rank, ribald, risqué, scandalous, smutty, suggestive, tainted, uncouth, vulgar, x-rated

adj 2 see: EROTIC *adj* 3, 6

ravage *v* 1 demolish, destroy

v 2 deflower, desecrate, despoil, devastate, devour, loot, maraud, pillage, plunder, sack, scourge, spoil, strip, violate

rave *n* acclaim, applause, boost, citation, commendation, compliment, eulogy, plaudit, praise, tribute

v 1 advertise, air, boom, boost, drum up, endorse, pitch, plug, promote, publicize, push, sell, tout

v 2 bawl out, bellow, berate, chew out, mock, rail, rant, revile, roar, scold, tell off, tongue-lash, upbraid, yell

ravenous *adj* 1 famished, hungry, starved, starving, voracious

adj 2 avaricious, covetous, endless, insatiable, unquenchable, voracious

ravine *n* 1 abyss, canyon, chasm, cleft, crack, depth, fissure, gorge, gulch

n 2 canal, channel, conduit, crevice, curb, cut, ditch, duct, furrow, gorge, groove, gully, gutter, passageway, rut, trench, trough

raving *adj* delirious, deranged, fantasizing, frenzied, hallucinating

ravish *v* 1 assault, attack, force, pillage, rape, sack, violate

v 2 captivate, charm, delight, engross, enrapture, enravish, enthrall, entrance, hypnotize, mesmerize, move, transport

v 3 debauch, deflower, deprave, seduce

ravishing *adj* see: ATTRACTIVE *adj* 3

raw *adj* 1 green, immature, inexperienced, naive, new, novice, unsophisticated, virgin

adj 2 crude, rough, rude, undressed, unfashioned, unfinished, unhewn, unpolished

adj 3 fresh, rare, uncooked

ray *n* beam, flicker, glimmer, hint, light, sliver, spark, trace

raze *v* 1 annihilate, decimate, demolish, destroy, destruct, devastate, dismantle, overturn, pulverize, rub out, ruin, shatter, smash, tear down, undo, wreck

v 2 ax, fell, cut down, topple

razz *v* belittle, deride, flaunt, jab, jeer, jest, mock, quip, ridicule, scoff, scorn, sneer, taunt, tease

re *prep* about, apropos, as to, concerning, regarding, respecting, with respect to

reach *n* 1 distance, span, stretch

n 2 boundary, extent, field, matter, range, scope, vicinity

n 3 circle, compass, confines, dimension, distance, extension, extent, length, limit, orbit, purview, range, realm, scope, size, spectrum, sweep, width

v 1 arrive

v 2 convey

v 3 contact, extend, get

v 4 see: PERFORM *v* 5

reachable *adj* see: PRACTICAL *adj* 4

react *v* 1 answer, recur, respond, return, revert, turn back

v 2 acknowledge, answer, come back, rejoin, reply, respond, retort, return

reaction *n* 1 condition, habit, impulse, reflex, response

n 2 answer, comeback, put-down, quip, rejoinder, reply, response, retort, return

n 3 allergy, hay fever, hives, rash, spots

n 4 awareness, emotion, faculty, feel, feeling, intuition, perception, response, sensation, sense

n 5 aftermath, consequence, corollary, effect, eventuality, outcome, repercussion, result, reverberation, reward, up-shot

reactive *adj* acidic, caustic, corrosive

read *v* 1 get, learn, master, pick up, realize, study, understand

v 2 comprehend, decipher, decode, infer, interpret, peruse, study, understand

v 3 see: INFORM *v* 6

readable *adj* clear, distinct, legible, understandable

readily *adv* easily, effortlessly, lightly, naturally, willingly

reading *n* assessment, impression, interpretation, understanding

ready *adj* 1 alert, apt, prompt, quick

adj 2 game, prepared, primed, ripe, set

adj 3 see: PRACTICAL *adj* 4

v 1 adapt, prepare, process, treat

v 2 see: EDUCATE *v*

real *adj* 1 concrete, corporeal, material, objective, physical, sensible, substantial, tactile, tangible

adj 2 accurate, authentic, believable, certain, convincing, credible, dependable, faithful, reliable, safe, sure, tenable, true, trustworthy, trusty

adj 3 candid, direct, earnest, forthright, frank, genuine, heartfelt, hearty, honest, no-holds-barred, open, sincere, straightforward, true, trustworthy, truthful, undesigning, unfeigned, unpretentious, wholehearted

adj 4 absolute, actual, authentic, bona fide, certain, definite, existent, factual, genuine, hard, inarguable, incontestable, incontrovertible, indisputable, indubitable, irrefutable, positive, sure, true, undeniable, undisputable, undoubtable, undoubted, unequivocal, unquestionable, veritable, viable

realistic *adj* doable, justifiable, practical, tenable

reality *n* actuality, being, existence, fact, life, presence, truth, vitality

realizable *adj* inherent, latent, possible, potential

realization *n* accomplishment, achievement, arrival, attainment, completion, fruition, fulfillment, satisfaction, success, triumph, victory

realize *v* 1 admit, confront, face

v 2 derive, gain, harvest, reap

v 3 encounter, endure, know, understand

v 4 get, learn, master, pick up, read, study, understand

v 5 achieve, answer, execute, fill, finish, fulfill, satisfy

v 6 accomplish, achieve, attain, consum-

mate, execute, fulfill, perform, produce, pull off, succeed, triumph, win

v 7 conceive, conjecture, conjure up, create, envision, fancy, image, imagine, invent, project, think, visualize

v 8 access, accomplish, achieve, attain, derive, earn, fulfill, gain, get, merit, net, obtain, perform, profit, rack up, reach, score, win

v 9 behold, catch, comprehend, conjure, descry, digest, discern, distinguish, espy, fathom, grasp, know, look at, notice, observe, perceive, recognize, savvy, see, sight, take in, understand, view

v 10 accomplish, complete, consummate, execute, fulfill, implement, perform

really *adv* actually, exactly, genuinely, precisely, sincerely, truly, verifiably, veritably, very

realm *n* 1 domain, dominion, field, kingdom, province, sphere, territory

n 2 area, arena, belt, field, region, section, space, territory, tract, turf, zone

n 3 circle, compass, confines, dimension, distance, extension, extent, length, limit, orbit, purview, range, reach, scope, size, spectrum, sweep, width

realtor *n* agent

ream *v* auger, bore, drill, pierce, tool

reap *v* derive, gain, get, harvest, realize

reappearance *n* 1 comeback, improvement, rally, recovery, renewal, resurrection, return, revival

n 2 encore

rear *adj* aft, back, backward, dorsal, posterior, tail

v 1 cant, careen, heel, incline, list, roll, tilt

v 2 care, cherish, foster, mother, nourish, nurse, nurture, parent, protect, raise, suckle

rearward *adv* aft

reason *n* 1 comprehension, intellect, understanding

n 2 argument, grounds, justification, proof, wherefore, why

n 3 cause, excuse, motive, purpose, rationale, why

n 4 aim, cause, consideration, goal, motive, purpose

n 5 lucidity, mind, rationality, saneness, sanity, sense, soundness, wit

n 6 bonus, consideration, goal, incentive, inducement, motivation, motive, reward, stimulus

n 7 alibi, defense, excuse, explanation, justification, plea, pretext, rationalization, ruse *n* 8 aim, goal, mission, motive, objective, purpose, sake, target, task

n 9 arguments, basis, cause, explanation, foundation, grounds, principle, rationale, rudiments, source

n 10 see: CONSIDERATION *n* 1, 4, 5

v cerebrate, chew, consider, contemplate, deliberate, digest, meditate, mull, muse, ponder, reflect, ruminate, see, speculate, study, think, weigh

reasonable *adj* 1 cheap, economical, inexpensive, low, low-cost

adj 2 mild, moderate, modest, pleasant, rational, temperate

adj 3 acceptable, defensible, justifiable, legitimate, proper, valid

adj 4 acceptable, adequate, competent, decent, enough, fair, good, mediocre, passable, respectable, satisfactory, sufficient, tolerable

adj 5 astute, consequent, intelligent, knowing, logical, perceptive, rational, sane, sensible, shrewd, sober, sound, wise

reasonably *adv* fairly, moderately, pretty, somewhat, so-so

reasoning *n* 1 conclusion, deduction, guess, inference, summation

n 2 analysis, cogitation, consideration, contemplation, deliberation, logic, meditation, reason, reflection, speculation, study, thinking, thought

reassure *v* amplify, bolster, encourage, enhance, enhearten, hearten, increase, inspire, strengthen, support

rebate *v* discount, reduce

rebel *n* agitator, defector, dissident, heretic, iconoclast, insurgent, malcontent, maverick, misfit, nonconformist, renegade, traitor, troublemaker, turncoat

v 1 insurrect, mutiny, revolt, rise against

v 2 brave, challenge, confront, dare, defy, face, mutiny, resist

v 3 defy, disobey, ignore, infringe, obstruct, oppose, resist, violate

v 4 frenzy, rage, rampage, revolt, riot, stampede, storm

rebellion *n* anarchy

rebellious *adj* defiant, disobedient, insubordinate, insurgent, mutinous, seditious

rebirth *n* refurbishment, renaissance, renewal, renovation, repair, restoration

rebound *v* 1 bounce back, come round, rally, recoup, recover, revitalize, snap back

v 2 backfire, boomerang, bounce, brush, glance, graze, ricochet, skim, skip, touch

rebuff *v* 1 reject, renounce, repel

v 2 alienate, estrange, fend off, repel, repulse, snub

v 3 blackball, boycott, cut, ignore, ostracize, snub, spurn

n refusal, rejection, turndown

rebuild *v* 1 recall, reestablish, reinstate, reintroduce, renew, repair, restore, resume, resurrect, revive

v 2 doctor, fix, mend, overhaul, patch, recondition, reconstruct, refit, renovate, repair, revamp

rebuke *n* admonishment, admonition, blast, chewing out, chiding, criticism, denunciation, diatribe, harangue, hassle, libel, outburst, rap, reprimand, reproach, reproof, scolding, slander, tirade

v 1 berate, scold

v 2 admonish, berate, blame, censure, chide, condemn, disapprove, lay into, punish, reprimand, reproach, reprove, scold, warn

rebut *v* 1 attack, challenge, contradict, deny, oppose

v 2 contradict, cross, deny, disaffirm, disagree, impugn, negate, traverse

v 3 break, confound, confute, contend, contradict, deny, disprove, refute

recalcitrant *adj* 1 indomitable, intractable, stubborn, uncontrollable, undisciplined, unmanageable, unruly, untoward, wild

adj 2 afraid, averse, disinclined, hesitant, indisposed, loath, opposed, reluctant, shy, timid, uneager, unwilling

recall *n* 1 cancellation, repeal, reversal, revocation

n 2 memory, nostalgia, recollection, remembrance, reminiscence

n 3 engram, memory, remembrance, retention, retentiveness, retrospection

v 1 look back, recollect, remember, reminisce, retrospect, revoke

v 2 rebuild, reestablish, reinstate, reintroduce, renew, repair, restore, resume, resurrect, revive

v 3 back, disavow, fall back, recant, recede, renege, rescind, retract, retreat, retrograde, take back

v 4 see: CANCEL *v* 3

recant *v* back, disavow, fall back, recall, recede, renege, rescind, retract, retreat, retrograde, take back

recapitulation *n* collection, epitome, paraphrase, summary, summation

recast *v* reconstruct, refashion, remold

recede *v* 1 ebb, go backwards, regress, retrograde, retrogress, return, revert, throw back

v 2 back, disavow, fall back, recall, recant,

renege, rescind, retract, retreat, retrograde, take back

v 2 see: SUBSIDE *v* 2

receipt *n* bill

receipts *n* assets, cash, earnings, gain, gross, haul, net, payback, proceeds, profits, return, revenue, take, yield

receive *v* 1 acquire

v 2 admit, enroll, matriculate, register

v 3 involve, partake, participate, share

v 4 encounter, greet, interview, meet, see, visit

recent *adj* 1 bright, contemporary, fresh, high-tech, modern, modernistic, new, novel, up-to-date

adj 2 aforementioned, ancient, antecedent, anterior, archaic, earlier, foregoing, former, past, preceding, prior

recently *adv* afresh, anew, lately, new, newly, of late

receptacle *n* 1 bank, depository, lender, repository

n 2 box, carton, case, chest, container

receptive *adj* 1 affable, amenable, amiable, amicable, congenial, empathetic, friendly, gregarious, hospitable, neighborly, outgoing, sociable, social, sympathetic

adj 2 see: QUICK *adj* 5

recess *n* burrow, cave, den, grotto, lair, tunnel

recessed *adj* lower, sunken, under

recipe *n* expression, formula, methodology, plan, procedure, scheme, system, theorem

reciprocate *v* avenge, compensate, cover, disburse, indemnify, pay, redress, reimburse, remedy, remunerate, repair, repay, requite, retaliate, revenge, settle, vindicate

reciprocity *n* getting even, reprisal, retaliation, retribution, revenge, vengeance, vindictiveness

recital *n* concert, concerto, étude, fugue, program, serenade, sonata, symphony

recite *v* brief, communicate, convey, declare, describe, disclose, divulge, explain, impart, inform, narrate, orate, portray, read, recount, relate, report, retell, reveal, share, state, tattle, tell, transmit

reckless *adj* 1 abrupt, audacious, desperate, rash

adj 2 hasty, inconsiderate, indiscreet, tactless, thoughtless

adj 3 extravagant, intemperate, loose, unrestrained, wanton, wild

adj 4 careless, foolish, impulsive, irresponsible, myopic, not smart, risky, shortsighted, unthinking, unwise

adj 5 see: HURRIED *adj*

adj 6 see: NEGLIGENT *adj*

reckon *v* 1 calculate, cipher, code, compute, estimate

v 2 approximate, call, estimate, judge, place

v 3 account, calculate, consider, deem, judge, regard, surmise, view

reclaim *v* 1 buy, convert, ransom, recover, redeem, save

v 2 invigorate, recondition, reconstruct, recover, recur, rehabilitate, rejuvenate, restore, resuscitate, retrain, revitalize, revive

recline *v* languish, lounge, repose

reclining *adj* flat, horizontal, lengthwise, longways, prone, prostrate, recumbent

recluse *n* 1 loner

n 2 derelict, outcast

n 3 abbé, abbot, ascetic, hermit, monk

reclusive *adj* antisocial, introverted, standoffish

recognition *n* 1 acknowledgment, answer, credit

n 2 appreciation, gratitude, thankfulness

n 3 address, bow, greeting, honor, salute

n 4 cognition, comprehension, grasp, insight, understanding

n 5 achievement, distinction, prestige, rank, stance, stature, status

n 6 accolade, award, commendation, credit, decoration, distinction, honor, kudos, laurels, medal, note, praise, reputation, reward, tribute

n 7 attention, awareness, care, carefulness, cognizance, concern, consciousness, consideration, heed, intimacy, knowing, knowledge, mark, note, notice, observance, observation, perception, regard, remark, sense

recognize *v* 1 acknowledge, admit

v 2 attribute, credit, honor, reward

v 3 distinguish, identify, know, name, specify

v 4 acknowledge, applaud, appreciate, approve, clap, show gratitude, thank

v 5 acclaim, applaud, charm, cheer, commend, compliment, flatter, greet, hail, laud, praise, salute, stroke

v 6 behold, catch, comprehend, conjure, descry, digest, discern, distinguish, espy, fathom, grasp, know, look at, notice, observe, perceive, realize, savvy, see, sight, take in, understand, view

recoil *v* 1 cower, cringe, flinch, grovel, quail, shrink, sneak *v* 2 avoid, duck, elude, escape, eschew, evade, shun, shy

v 3 blanch, cringe, flinch, jump, shrink, start, startle, wince

recollect *v* look back, recall, remember, reminisce, retrospect, revoke

recollection *n* 1 memory, nostalgia, recall, remembrance, reminiscence

n 2 see: IDEA *n* 1

recommence *v* see: PROCEED *v* 2

recommend *v* 1 advise, caution, counsel, evaluate, reprove

v 2 allude, bring up, hint, refer

v 3 bid, counsel, endorse, offer, pose, present, proffer, propose, proposition, put forth, suggest, urge

recommendation *n* 1 good word, reference, testimonial

n 2 advice, counsel, opinion, suggestion

n 3 bid, expectation, hope, inducement, invitation, motion, offer, proffer, proposal, proposition, request, suggestion

recommended *adj* advisable, expedient, politic, prudent, suggested, wise

reconcile *v* 1 accommodate, adjust, attune, conform, coordinate, harmonize, integrate, proportion, reconciliate, tune

v 2 allay, appease, assuage, balm, becalm, calm, compose, conciliate, ease, lull, mollify, pacify, placate, propitiate, quell, quiet, satiate, settle, soften, soothe, still, sweeten, tranquilize

reconciliate *v* accommodate, adjust, attune, conform, coordinate, harmonize, integrate, proportion, reconcile, tune

reconciliation *n* atonement, attrition, contrition, penance, penitence, remorse

recondite *adj* see: ESOTERIC *adj*

recondition *v* 1 doctor, fix, mend, overhaul, patch, rebuild, reconstruct, refit, renovate, repair, revamp

v 2 invigorate, reclaim, reconstruct, recover, recur, rehabilitate, rejuvenate, restore, resuscitate, retrain, revitalize, revive

v 3 adapt, adjust, balance, fit, fix, inspect, maintain, overhaul, refurbish, regulate, repair, service, support, tune up

reconnaissance *n* observation, surveillance

reconsider *v* reevaluate, rethink, review

reconstruct *v* 1 doctor, fix, mend, overhaul, patch, rebuild, recondition, refit, renovate, repair, revamp

v 2 invigorate, reclaim, recondition, recover, recur, rehabilitate, rejuvenate, re-

store, resuscitate, retrain, revitalize, revive

v 3 recast, refashion, remold

record *n* 1 count, score, tally, total

n 2 chit, letter, memo, memorandum, notandum, notation, note, reminder

n 3 career, diary, events, experience, history, performance, résumé, track record, vita

n 4 account, diary, digest, journal, log, memoir, minutes, notation, notes, proceedings, recording, report

n 5 binder, file, folder, portfolio

v 1 copy, note, summarize, transcribe, type, write

v 2 capture, chart, denote, enter, itemize, jot, list, log, note, preserve, register, take notes, tally, tape, write down

v 3 enter, log, register

recorder *n* aide, assistant, clerk, scribe, secretary, stenographer

recording *n* account, diary, digest, journal, log, memoir, minutes, notation, notes, proceedings, report

recount *v* brief, communicate, convey, declare, describe, disclose, divulge, explain, impart, inform, narrate, orate, portray, read, recite, relate, report, retell, reveal, share, state, tattle, tell, transmit

recoup *v* 1 bounce back, come round, rally, rebound, recover, revitalize, snap back

v 2 get back, recover, recruit, regain, repossess, retrieve, solicit

recourse *n* 1 choice, means, option, remedy

n 2 expedient, makeshift, means, measure, refuge, replacement, resort, stopgap, substitute, surrogate

recover *v* 1 recycle, rescue, restore, salvage, save

v 2 buy, convert, ransom, reclaim, redeem, save

v 3 bounce back, come round, rally, rebound, recoup, revitalize, snap back

v 4 get back, recoup, recruit, regain, repossess, retrieve, solicit

v 5 ameliorate, convalesce, gain, heal, improve, loop up, mend, perk, rally, recuperate, rehabilitate, revive

v 6 invigorate, reclaim, recondition, reconstruct, recur, rehabilitate, rejuvenate, restore, resuscitate, retrain, revitalize, revive

recovery *n* 1 deliverance, extrication, freeing, release, rescue, saving

n 2 comeback, improvement, rally, reappearance, renewal, resurrection, return, revival

recreate *v* 1 play

v 2 amuse, charm, divert, entertain, interest, please, stimulate

re-create *v* clone, copy, duplicate, image, imitate, mirror, print, redo, reduplicate, remake, replicate, reprint, reproduce, simulate

recreation *n* 1 idle time, interlude, lull, relaxation, repose, rest, vacation

n 2 amusement, distraction, diversion, enjoyment, entertainment, frolic, fun, game, hobby, pastime, play, sport

recruit *n* apprentice, beginner, disciple, freshman, intern, neophyte, newcomer, novice, novitiate, pupil, rookie, student, tenderfoot, trainee

v 1 employ, engage, hire, put on, retain, take on

v 2 get back, recoup, recover, regain, repossess, retrieve, solicit

v 3 engage, enlist, enroll, muster, register, secure, sign up

recruitment *n* employment, engagement, hiring

rectangular *adj* elongated

rectify *v* 1 remedy, repair

v 2 see: ADJUST *v* 12

rectitude *n* goodness, morality, principle, probity, purity, righteousness, uprightness, virtue

recumbent *adj* flat, horizontal, lengthwise, longways, prone, reclining

recuperate *v* ameliorate, convalesce, gain, heal, improve, loop up, mend, perk, rally, recover, rehabilitate, revive

recur *v* 1 answer, react, respond, return, revert, turn back

v 2 invigorate, reclaim, recondition, reconstruct, recover, rehabilitate, rejuvenate, restore, resuscitate, retrain, revitalize, revive

recurrent *adj* alternate, cyclic, cyclical, intermittent, periodic, periodical, recurring, repeated, repetitive, sporadic

recurring *adj* 1 methodical, methodical, orderly, regular, steady, systematic

adj 2 accepted, accustomed, chronic, common, constant, continual, customary, daily, everyday, familiar, frequent, habitual, inured, often, regular, routine, traditional, usual

adj 3 see: RECURRENT *adj*

recycle *v* recover, rescue, restore, salvage, save

red *adj* 1 cardinal, crimson, ruby, scarlet, vermilion

adj 2 florid, flush, full-blooded, glowing, ruddy, sanguine

n bolshevik, communist, comrade, pinko

redden *v* 1 blare, blaze, burn, flame, flare, glare, glow

v 2 blush

redeem *v* 1 complete, satisfy

v 2 buy, convert, ransom, reclaim, recover, save

v 3 adjust, balance, compensate, make equal, make up, offset, outweigh, set off

redirect *v* divert, refer, submit

redo *v* 1 freshen, modernize, refresh, refurbish, rejuvenate, remodel, renew, renovate, restore, revamp, revitalize, revive, update

v 2 see: DUPLICATE *v*

redraft *v* edit, modify, redraw, rehash, revamp, revise, rework, rewrite

redraw *v* edit, modify, redraft, rehash, revamp, revise, rework, rewrite

redress *n* amends, compensation, damages, indemnity, reparation, restitution, restoration

v see: PAY *v* 2

reduce *v* 1 discount, promote, rebate

v 2 diet, fast, lose weight, slenderize, slim, trim down

v 3 calm, lessen, muffle, quiet, soften, subdue

v 4 deduct, diminish, lessen, minus, subtract, take away

v 5 break, bump, bust, degrade, demerit, demote, downgrade

v 6 clip, cut, cut back, cut down, lower, mark down, shave, slash

v 7 cheapen, depreciate, devalue, diminish, downgrade, dwindle, lower, mark down, underrate, undervalue

v 8 attenuate, dilute, diminish, lessen, purify, rarefy, refine, shorten, thin out, weaken

v 9 abbreviate, abridge, condense, curtail, cut, cut back, diminish, edit, lessen, restrict, shorten, slash

v 10 compress, concentrate, condense, contract, shrink

v 11 bear down, beat down, conquer, crush, defeat, dominate, enslave, exploit, overpower, quash, subdue, subjugate, suppress, vanquish

v 12 allay, alleviate, assuage, attenuate, diminish, ease, extenuate, lessen, lighten, minimize, mitigate, moderate, relieve

v 13 abate, cease, decline, decrease, die down, diminish, drain, dwindle, ease, ebb, fall, lessen, let up, lull, recede, relax, relent, shrink, slacken, soften, stop, subside, taper off, wane, waste away, weaken

reduced *adj* diminished, limited, modified, qualified

reduction n 1 bargain, buy, deal, discount, promotion, sale, special, steal
n 2 cutback
n 3 decline, decrease, decrement, lessening, weakening
redundancy n deluge, excess, fat, glut, over-abundance, overflow, overkill, plethora, surfeit, surplus
redundant adj 1 bombastic, chatty, diffuse, garrulous, long-winded, loquacious, repetitious, superfluous, talkative, verbose, wordy
adj 2 see: STALE adj 3
reduplicate v see: DUPLICATE v
reef n sandbank, sandbar, shallow, shelf, shoal
reek n odor, smell, stench, stink
reeking adj see: FOUL adj 3
reel v 1 careen, lurch, pitch, stagger, sway, toss, totter, wheel
v 2 gyrate, pirouette, purl, spin, swim, turn, twirl, whirl
reeling adj confused, dizzy, faint, foggy, light-headed
reembark v see: PROCEED v 2
reestablish v rebuild, recall, reinstate, reintroduce, renew, repair, restore, resume, resurrect, revive
reevaluate v reconsider, rethink, review
refashion v 1 adjust, alter, catalyze, change, modify, vary
v 2 reconstruct, remold
refer v 1 allude, bring up, hint, point out, recommend
v 2 apply, bear, concern, pertain, regard, relate
v 3 accredit, apply, ascribe, assign, attribute, charge
v 4 divert, redirect, submit
referee n arbiter, arbitrator, judge, mediator, moderator, umpire
v adjudicate, arbitrate, judge, mediate, try, umpire
reference n 1 good word, recommendation, testimonial
n 2 authority, dictionary, encyclopedia, source
n 3 allusion, connotation, hint, implication, innuendo, insinuation, notation, suggestion
n 4 citation, clipping, excerpt, extract, mention, passage, portion, quotation, quote, section
n 5 assignment, direction, instruction, referral
referral n assignment, direction, instruction

refill v refresh, replace, replenish, restore, stock
refine v 1 perfect
v 2 compress, condense, distill, express, extract, purify
v 3 clean, cleanse, filter, purify, sterilize, wash
v 4 advance, cultivate, elevate, enhance, enrich, improve, upgrade
v 5 amplify, construct, develop, devise, elaborate, enhance, enlarge, expand, expound
v 6 see: WEAKEN v 4
refined adj 1 aesthetic, artistic, classy, elegant, stylish, tasteful, well-chosen
adj 2 dainty, delicate, fine, gentle, nice, subtle
adj 3 civilized, cosmopolitan, cultivated, cultured, elegant, genteel, ingratiating, poised, polished, smooth, sophisticated, suave, urbane, well-bred
refinement n 1 elegance, finesse, polish, style
n 2 attractiveness, charm, decorum, elegance
refit v see: REPAIR v 5
reflect v 1 acquaint, announce, delineate, depict, introduce, present, represent, show
v 2 disclose, display, evince, express, imply, indicate, manifest, reveal, show
v 3 bounce
v 4 cerebrate, chew, consider, contemplate, deliberate, digest, meditate, mull, muse, ponder, reason, ruminate, see, speculate, study, think, weigh
reflection n 1 analysis, cogitation, consideration, contemplation, deliberation, logic, meditation, reason, reasoning, speculation, study, thinking, thought
n 2 see: INSULT n
reflective adj meditative, pensive, philosophical, pondering, speculative, thinking, thoughtful
reflex adj automatic, impulsive, instinctive, involuntary, natural, rash, spontaneous, unconscious, unforced, unpremeditated, unprompted
n condition, habit, reaction, response
reform v better, correct, improve, modify, rehabilitate
n correction, improvement, progress
reformatory n see: JAIL n
refract v bend
refraction n deflection
refractory adj 1 chronic, extended, incurable, persistent, protracted, stubborn
adj 2 bullheaded, closed-minded, deaf,

firm, hardheaded, hard-line, inelastic, inflexible, intractable, intransigent, obstinate, perverse, pigheaded, resolute, rigid, stiff, stubborn, tough, unbending, uncompromising, unpliable, unpliant, unwieldy, unyielding, willful

refrain v 1 abstain, forbear, keep, withhold

v 2 abstain, avoid, constrain, curb, deny, forgo, govern, hold back, resist, restrict, stop, tame

v 3 see: STOP v 8

refresh v 1 refill, replace, replenish, restore, stock

v 2 freshen, modernize, redo, refurbish, rejuvenate, remodel, renew, renovate, restore, revamp, revitalize, revive, update

refreshing adj 1 fresh

adj 2 energizing, exhilarating, fresh, invigorating, stimulating

refrigerate v chill, cool, freeze

refuge n 1 expedient, makeshift, means, measure, recourse, replacement, resort, stopgap, substitute, surrogate

n 2 asylum, cover, harbor, haven, oasis, port, preserve, protection, reserve, retreat, safety, sanctuary, seaport, security, shelter

refugee n castaway, émigré, escapee, evacuee, exile

refund v adjust, reimburse, repay, return

refurbish v 1 freshen, modernize, redo, refresh, rejuvenate, remodel, renew, renovate, restore, revamp, revitalize, revive, update

v 2 see: SERVICE v

refurbishment n rebirth, renaissance, renewal, renovation, repair, restoration

refusal n 1 denial

n 2 ban, disapproval, rejection, thumbs down, turndown, veto

n 3 rebuff, rejection, turndown

refuse n crap, crud, debris, detritus, dirt, garbage, junk, litter, rubbish, rubble, sweepings, trash, waste

v 1 deny, disallow, reject, withhold

v 2 condemn, decline, disapprove, dismiss, exile, object, reject, reprobate, repudiate, spurn, turn down

refute v break, confound, confute, contend, contradict, deny, disprove, dispute, rebut

regain v get back, recoup, recover, recruit, repossess, retrieve, solicit

regal adj 1 aristocratic, blue-blooded, imperial, kingly, majestic, noble, royal, stately, well-bred

adj 2 august, baronial, exalted, grand, grandiose, haughty, imperial, imposing, impressive, lofty, lordly, magisterial,

magnificent, majestic, noble, portly, princely, royal, stately

regard n 1 concern, curiosity, interest

n 2 account, admiration, consideration, esteem, favor, respect

n 3 esteem, fame, good standing, name, reputation, stature

n 4 consideration, diplomacy, discretion, poise, savoir-faire, tact, tactfulness, thoughtfulness

n 5 affection, emotion, feeling, passion, sensation, sense, sensibility, sentiment, tenderness

n 6 attention, awareness, care, carefulness, cognizance, concern, consciousness, consideration, heed, intimacy, knowing, knowledge, mark, note, notice, observance, observation, perception, recognition, remark, sense

n 7 deference, devotion, esteem, homage, honor, just due, respect, reverence

v 1 apply, bear, concern, pertain, refer, relate

v 2 account, calculate, consider, deem, judge, reckon, surmise, view

v 3 canvass, case, check, examine, glance over, inspect, observe, peruse, pore over, scrutinize, study, survey, watch

v 4 admire, adore, appreciate, cherish, consider, covet, esteem, honor, idolize, love, prize, respect, treasure, value

regarding prep about, apropos, as to, concerning, re, respecting, with respect to

regardless adv despite, further, however

regards n greetings, respects, salutations, salvo

regatta n see: COMPETITION n 2

regime n administration, dominion, government, monarchy, power, reign, rule, sovereignty

region n 1 area, arena, belt, field, realm, section, space, territory, tract, turf, zone

n 2 see: WARD n 2

regional adj see: ADJACENT adj

register n catalog, index, list, roster, schedule

v 1 admit, enroll, matriculate

v 2 claim, copyright, patent, protect, trademark

v 3 engage, enlist, enroll, muster, recruit, secure, sign up

v 4 capture, chart, denote, enter, itemize, jot, list, log, note, preserve, record, take notes, tally, tape, write down

v 5 impress

v 6 enter, record

v 7 catalog, enroll, inscribe, list, sign up, write

registrant *n* associate, collaborator, individual, member, participant, party

regress *v* ebb, go backwards, recede, retrograde, retrogress, return, revert, throw back

regression *n* comedown, decline, decrease, descent, dive, drop, failure, fall, plunge, setback, slide, tumble

regret *n* 1 excuse, explanation

n 2 discontent, dissatisfaction, unhappiness, vexation

n 3 guilt, penitence, remorse, repentance, sorrow

n 4 affliction, anguish, care, catastrophe, despair, disaster, dole, grief, heartache, mishap, pain, remorse, rue, sickness, sorrow, woe

n 5 compunction, conscience, pang, qualm, reservation, restraint, scruple, twinge

v 1 apologize, excuse, repent, seek penance

v 2 bemoan, deplore, lament, repent, rue

regretful *adj* dismal, doleful, gloomy, lamentable, melancholy, mournful, plaintive, regrettable, rueful, sorrowful, woeful

regrettable *adj* dismal, doleful, gloomy, lamentable, melancholy, mournful, plaintive, regretful, rueful, sorrowful, woeful

regular *adj* 1 established, normal, standard, uniform

adj 2 methodic, methodical, orderly, recurring, steady, systematic

adj 3 average, common, intermediate, mediocre, medium, middle, normal, ordinary, standard, unimpressive

adj 4 accepted, accustomed, chronic, common, constant, continual, customary, daily, everyday, familiar, frequent, habitual, inured, often, recurring, routine, traditional, usual

adj 5 average, common, commonplace, daily, everyday, general, mundane, natural, normal, ordinary, plain, prevalent, routine, typical, unexceptional, unremarkable, usual, workaday

adj 6 see: INFORMAL *adj* 1

regularly *adv* frequently, often, repeatedly, typically, usually

regulate *v* 1 adjust, convert, prorate, scale

v 2 curb, discipline, govern, limit, restrain, retard

v 3 inflect, moderate, modify, modulate, restrain, temper

v 4 adjust, conform, equalize, level, set policy, standardize

v 5 defend, guard, oversee, patrol, police, protect, safeguard, watch

v 6 administer, boss, command, direct, guide, manage, oversee, steer, supervise

v 7 see: SERVICE *v*

regulation *n* see: COMMAND *n* 3

regulations *n* bureaucracy, officialdom, red tape

rehabilitate *v* 1 better, correct, improve, reform

v 2 ameliorate, convalesce, gain, heal, improve, loop up, mend, perk, rally, recover, recuperate, revive

v 3 invigorate, reclaim, recondition, reconstruct, recover, recur, rejuvenate, restore, resuscitate, retrain, revitalize, revive

rehabilitation *n* cure, therapy, treatment

rehash *v* 1 beat, reiterate, repeat

v 2 edit, modify, redraft, redraw, revamp, revise, rework, rewrite

rehearsal *n* drill, exercise, practice, training, workout

rehearse *v* drill, learn, perfect, practice, prepare, repeat, review, study

reign *n* 1 heyday

n 2 administration, dominion, government, monarchy, power, regime, rule, sovereignty

n 3 aeon, age, cycle, decade, eon, epoch, era, eternity, forever, long time, millennium, period, span, stage, time, years

v 1 control, govern, rule

v 2 bully, dominate, domineer, prevail, rule

reimburse *v* 1 adjust, refund, repay, return

v 2 avenge, compensate, cover, disburse, indemnify, pay, reciprocate, redress, remedy, remunerate, repair, repay, requite, retaliate, revenge, settle, vindicate

reimbursed *adj* indemnified, paid, paid off, remunerated, repaid, rewarded

rein *n* bond, boundary, bridle, check, constraint, control, curb, damper, harness, leash, limit, restraint, restriction

v bridle, check, constrain, control, crimp, curb, hold back, hold down, inhibit, leash, restrain, restrict, withhold

reinforce *v* 1 augment, buttress, fortify, harden, intensify, strengthen

v 2 bear up, bolster, brace, build up, buoy, buttress, carry, fortify, harden, nourish, nurture, prop, shore, strengthen, support, sustain, toughen, uphold

reinstate *v* 1 give back, put back, remit, replace, restore, return, take back

v 2 rebuild, recall, reestablish, reintroduce, renew, repair, restore, resume, resurrect, revive

reintroduce *v* rebuild, recall, reestablish,

reinstate, renew, repair, restore, resume, resurrect, revive

reissue *v* bring out, distribute, get out, give out, go to press, issue, print, publish, put out, reprint, set type

reiterate *v* 1 beat, belabor, rehash, repeat

v 2 emphasize, repeat, reprise, resay, stress

v 3 emphasize, iterate, repeat, restate, stress

reject *v* 1 rebuff, renounce, repel

v 2 deny, disallow, refuse, withhold

v 3 abjure, deny, disavow, disclaim, disown, forswear, renounce, repudiate

v 4 abandon, discard, dispose of, dump, eliminate, empty, quit, scrap, unload

v 5 condemn, decline, disapprove, dismiss, exile, object, refuse, reprobate, repudiate, spurn, turn down

v 6 abhor, abominate, bristle, desecrate, despise, detest, disdain, dislike, hate, loathe, revile, scorn

v 7 cancel, contradict, deny, disallow, forbid, negate, nix, nullify, override, overrule, renege, repeal, revoke, torpedo, veto, void

v 8 abstain, cast, decline, drop, eschew, forbear, forfeit, forgo, give up, lose, pass, renounce, sacrifice, surrender, turn down, waive

v 9 abandon, break up, cast off, chuck, defect, desert, disavow, discard, disenfranchise, disown, ditch, dump, forsake, jilt, junk, leave, quit, renounce, spurn, strand, throw out

n discard, failure, garbage, junk, scrap, second

rejection *n* 1 disapproval, repudiation

n 2 ban, disapproval, refusal, thumbs down, turndown, veto

n 3 rebuff, refusal, turndown

rejoicing *adj* see: MERRY *adj* 2

rejoin *v* acknowledge, answer, come back, react, reply, respond, retort, return

rejoinder *n* answer, comeback, put-down, quip, reaction, reply, response, retort, return

rejuvenate *v* 1 invigorate, reclaim, recondition, reconstruct, recover, recur, rehabilitate, restore, resuscitate, retrain, revitalize, revive

v 2 freshen, modernize, redo, refresh, refurbish, remodel, renew, renovate, restore, revamp, revitalize, revive, update

relapse *n* adversity, affliction, blow, burden, calamity, difficulty, distress, hardship, mischance, misfortune, mishap,

reversal, setback, suffering, tragedy, trouble

relate *v* 1 clarify, disclose, explain, reveal, unfold

v 2 apply, bear, concern, pertain, regard

v 3 analogize, associate, compare, correlate, explain, rank

v 4 bracket, collate, compare, contrast, correlate, equate, liken, sort

v 5 brief, communicate, convey, declare, describe, disclose, divulge, explain, impart, inform, narrate, orate, portray, read, recite, recount, report, retell, reveal, share, state, tattle, tell, transmit

related *adj* 1 ancillary, auxiliary, incidental, minor, secondary, side, subordinate

adj 2 affiliated, akin, aligned, allied, associated, fraternal, friendly, kindred

adj 3 see: ALIKE *adj*

relation *n* 1 family, kin, relative

n 2 comparison, percentage, proportion, share

relationship *n* 1 blood, descent, kinship, lineage, stock

n 2 affair, association, communication, friendship, intimacy, liaison, rapport, union

n 3 see: ALLIANCE *n*

relative *adj* 1 comparative

adj 2 ancillary, conditional, contingent, dependent, indefinite, provisional, reliant, temporary, uncertain

n 1 family, kin, people, relation

n 2 see: FRIEND *n* 1

relatives *n* breed, clan, class, family, household, people, race, stock, tribe

relax *v* 1 rest

v 2 relent, soften, thaw

v 3 ease, ease off, lax, loosen, mellow out, slack, slacken

v 4 bask, delight, enjoy, like, loaf, luxuriate, relish, rest, savor, wallow

v 5 see: SUBSIDE *v* 2

relaxation *n* 1 abandonment

n 2 idle time, interlude, lull, recreation, repose, rest, vacation

n 3 exile, isolation, leisure, quarantine, rest, retirement, retreat, seclusion, solitude, withdrawal

n 4 abatement, diminishing, easing, letup, loosening, slackening

relaxed *adj* 1 feeble, flabby, flaccid, lax, limp, loose, slack

adj 2 casual, cavalier, colloquial, familiar, informal, ordinary, regular, unceremonious, unconstrained, unofficial, usual, vernacular

adj 3 calm, collected, composed, cool,

demure, dormant, easy, gentle, hushed, idle, imperturbable, motionless, nonchalant, peaceful, placid, poised, quiet, restful, sedate, self-composed, self-possessed, serene, soft, steady, still, tranquil, unflappable, unruffled, untroubled

adj 4 see: LAZY *adj*

relay *v* air, broadcast, telecast, televise, transmit

release *n* 1 deliverance, extrication, freeing, recovery, rescue, saving

n 2 assurance, exemption, guarantee, immunity, impunity, protection, safety, security

n 3 absolution, amnesty, discharge, disengagement, dispensation, freedom, moratorium, pardon, relief, reprieve, respite, stay, suspension

n 4 capitulation, compliance, submission, subordination, subservience, surrender

v 1 extricate, free, liberate, remove, rescue

v 2 discharge, emanate, emit, expel, project, radiate, send

v 3 discharge, emancipate, free, liberate, loosen, unbind, unchain, unshackle

v 4 deliver, free, rescue, save

relegate *v* 1 commend, commit, confide, consign, entrust, hand over, turn over

v 2 see: BANISH *v* 1

relent *v* 1 relax, soften, thaw

v 2 accede, acquiesce, bend, bow, buckle, capitulate, cave, comply, concede, cry uncle, defer, give in, give up, submit, succumb, surrender, twist, yield

v 3 abate, cease, decline, decrease, die down, diminish, drain, dwindle, ease, ebb, fall, lessen, let up, lull, recede, reduce, relax, shrink, slacken, soften, stop, subside, taper off, wane, waste away, weaken

relentless *adj* 1 adamant, cold, cruel, fierce, vindictive

adj 2 see: PERPETUAL *adj* 2

adj 3 see: STUBBORN *adj* 6

relevance *n* account, advantage, applicability, appropriateness, aptness, avail, benefit, decorum, expediency, fitness, manners, opportunism, pertinence, profit, propriety, rightness, service, suitability, use, usefulness, utility

relevant *adj* applicable, appropriate, apropos, apt, befitting, convenient, desirable, felicitous, fit, fitting, germane, good, handy, just, material, meet, necessary, pertinent, proper, right, shipshape, suitable, suited, timely, useful

reliable *adj* 1 dependable, fail-safe, infallible, sure, tested, tried

adj 2 dependable, observant, on time, precise, prompt, punctual, timely

adj 3 accountable, answerable, dependable, honorable, honored, liable, reputable, respected, responsible, secure, solid, trusted, trustworthy, trusty, upstanding

adj 4 consistent, constant, continuing, endless, equable, established, even, invariable, routine, same, serene, stable, steady, unchanging, unfailing, unfluctuating, uniform, unvarying

adj 5 see: AUTHENTIC *adj* 2

reliably *adv* fast, firm, firmly, hard, loyally, solidly, tight, tightly

reliant *adj* ancillary, conditional, contingent, dependent, indefinite, provisional, relative, temporary, uncertain

relic *n* 1 memento, remnant, shadow, trace, vestige

n 2 belief, custom, doctrine, mores, rite, ritual, throwback, tradition

n 3 antique, gift, heirloom, keepsake, memento, memorial, remembrance, reminder, souvenir, token, trophy

relief *n* 1 abatement, alleviation, comfort, correction, cure, help, remedy, respite, solace, solution

n 2 aid, assistance, benefit, comfort, cure, hand, help, lift, nurture, remedy, succor, support

n 3 see: RELEASE *n* 3

relieve *v* 1 aid, comfort, cure, soothe, strengthen, support

v 2 appease, comfort, comply, content, delight, elate, gratify, please, satisfy, suit

v 3 allay, alleviate, assuage, attenuate, diminish, ease, extenuate, lessen, lighten, minimize, mitigate, moderate, mollify, reduce

v 4 replace, spell, take over

religion *n* 1 commitment, passion

n 2 affiliation, belief, church, creed, denomination, faith, persuasion, rite, seat, theology

n 3 belief, confidence, contingency, credence, credit, creed, dependence, desire, faith, hope, trust

religious *adj* 1 blind, conscientious, loyal, meticulous, strict, zealous

adj 2 devout, godly, holy, pious, prayerful, reverent, sanctimonious

relinquish *v* 1 abdicate, quit, renounce, resign, step down, vacate

v 2 abandon, acquiesce, cede, give up,

hand over, leave, resign, submit, surrender, waive, yield

relish *n* 1 appetite, enjoyment, liking, taste

n 2 alacrity, ardor, delight, devotion, diligence, enjoyment, enthusiasm, excitement, fervor, fire, flame, gaiety, gusto, passion, savor, thrill, zeal, zest

v 1 crave, like, savor, taste

v 2 admire, appreciate, cherish, delight, enjoy, revel, savor

v 3 bask, delight, enjoy, like, loaf, luxuriate, relax, rest, savor, wallow

reluctant *adj* 1 diffident, faltering, halting, hesitant, indecisive, tentative, unsure, waffling, wavering

adj 2 afraid, averse, disinclined, hesitant, indisposed, loath, opposed, recalcitrant, shy, timid, uneager, unwilling

reluctantly *adv* painfully

rely *v* bank on, build on, count on, depend, need, trust

remain *v* 1 abide, await, bide, linger, loiter, stay, stick around, tarry, wait

v 2 abide, continue, endure, last, outlast, persevere, persist, prevail, stay, stick to, stick with, survive

remainder *n* dregs, leftovers, remains, remnant, residual, residue, rest, scrap, shred, silt

remaining *adj* 1 excess, leftover, residual, superfluous

adj 2 current, extant, surviving, visible

remains *n* 1 body, cadaver, carcass, corpse, shell, stiff

n 2 debris, fragment, hulk, rubbish, rubble, shell, trash, wreck, wreckage

n 3 dregs, leftovers, remainder, remnant, residual, residue, rest, scrap, shred, silt

n 4 bone, fossil, skeleton

remake *v* see: DUPLICATE *v*

remark *n* 1 comment, commentary, note, observation, statement

n 2 accusation, aspersion, defamation, libel, slander, slur, smear

n 3 attention, awareness, care, carefulness, cognizance, concern, consciousness, consideration, heed, intimacy, knowing, knowledge, mark, note, notice, observance, observation, perception, recognition, regard, sense

v 1 cut, insult, taunt

v 2 add, comment, declare, say, state

remarkable *adj* 1 amazing, astounding, bizarre, strange

adj 2 astonishing, exceptional, incredible, uncanny

adj 3 amazing, brilliant, exceptional, extraordinary, noteworthy, phenomenal, rare, significant, singular, stunning, super, uncommon, uncustomary, unique, unusual

adj 4 see: QUAINT *adj* 1

remarkably *adv* awfully, dreadfully, eminently, endlessly, exceedingly, exceptionally, extremely, greatly, highly, mightily, notably, quite, terribly, thoroughly, very

remedy *n* 1 choice, option, recourse

n 2 antidote, cure, medication, medicine, panacea, prescription, serum, therapy, treatment

n 3 abatement, alleviation, comfort, correction, cure, help, relief, respite, solace, solution

n 4 aid, assistance, benefit, comfort, cure, hand, help, lift, nurture, relief, succor, support

v 1 correct, rectify, repair

v 2 adjust, correct, cure, fix, heal, make well, mend, repair, restore

v 3 adjust, amend, correct, fix, improve, mend, modify, position, rectify, restore, right, straighten

v 4 see: PAY *v* 2

remember *v* 1 commemorate, keep in mind, note

v 2 learn, memorize, retain

v 3 bequeath, endow, give, reward, tip

v 4 look back, recall, recollect, reminisce, retrospect, revoke

remembrance *n* 1 memory, nostalgia, recall, reminiscence

n 2 engram, memory, recall, retention, retentiveness, retrospection

n 3 antique, gift, heirloom, keepsake, memento, memorial, relic, reminder, souvenir, token, trophy

remind *v* cue, jog, nudge, prompt, push, stimulate, stir, suggest

reminder *n* 1 chit, letter, memo, memorandum, notandum, notation, note

n 2 antique, gift, heirloom, keepsake, memento, memorial, relic, remembrance, souvenir, token, trophy

reminisce *v* look back, recall, recollect, remember, retrospect, revoke

reminiscence *n* memory, nostalgia, recall, recollection, remembrance

remiss *adj* blameworthy, criminal, culpable, felonious, reprehensible

remit *v* 1 give back, put back, reinstate, replace, restore, return, take back

v 2 absolve, acquit, clear, condone, exculpate, excuse, exempt, exonerate, forgive, free, pardon, reprieve, vindicate

v 3 address, channel, consign, dispatch,

export, forward, mail, post, route, send, ship, transmit, transport

v 4 see: DELAY *v* 4

remnant *n* 1 memento, relic, shadow, trace, vestige

n 2 dregs, leftovers, remainder, remains, residual, residue, rest, scrap, shred, silt

remodel *v* freshen, modernize, redo, refresh, refurbish, rejuvenate, renew, renovate, restore, revamp, revitalize, revive, update

remold *v* recast, reconstruct, refashion

remonstrate *v* except, inveigh, object, protest

remora *n* barnacle, dependent, freeloader, hanger-on, leech, parasite, sponge, vine

remorse *n* 1 guilt, penitence, regret, repentance, sorrow

n 2 atonement, attrition, contrition, penance, penitence

n 3 see: ANGUISH *n* 2

remorseful *adj* apologetic, contrite, penitent, repentant, sorry

remote *adj* 1 alien, foreign, separate, unrelated

adj 2 back, frontier, outlandish, unsettled

adj 3 far-fetched, impractical, unfeasible, unrealistic

adj 4 faint, imperceptible, meager, slight, subtle, vague

adj 5 distant, far, faraway, obscure, outlying, out-of-the-way, removed

adj 6 see: INDIFFERENT *adj* 4

adj 7 see: TRIVIAL *adj* 2

removal *n* 1 abandon, departure, desertion, evacuation, exit, going, leaving, pullback, pullout, retreat, withdrawal

n 2 pull

n 3 deletion, erasure

n 4 dismissal, ejection, expulsion, extraction, firing, impeachment, ouster, termination

remove *v* 1 depose, discharge, oust, unseat

v 2 extract, purloin, take out, withdraw

v 3 cleanse, eliminate, eradicate, erase

v 4 crack, husk, open, peel, shell

v 5 extricate, free, release, rescue

v 6 extract, pull, suck, tear, withdraw, yank

v 7 dispose of, eliminate, expel, flush, purge, rid, vanquish

v 8 dislocate, dislodge, displace, disturb, move, oust, shift, ship, transfer

v 9 choose, cull, elect, pick, select, separate, sift, single out, sort

v 10 bare, denude, discard, disrobe, doff, flash, reveal, shed, strip, take off, unclothe, undress

v 11 abate, abolish, abrogate, annihilate, annul, call off, cancel, cease, delete, destroy, efface, erase, excise, expunge, invalidate, kill, negate, nullify, obliterate, omit, quash, stop, terminate, wipe out

v 12 see: BANISH *v* 1

removed *adj* 1 distant, far, faraway, obscure, out-of-the-way, remote

adj 2 alienated, alone, apart, detached, hidden, isolated, private, secluded, separated, sequestered, severed

remunerate *v* compensate, cover, disburse, indemnify, pay, reciprocate, redress, reimburse, remedy, repair, repay, requite, settle, vindicate

remunerated *adj* indemnified, paid, paid off, reimbursed, repaid, rewarded

remuneration *n* alimony, compensation, fee, honorarium, payment, reward, stipend

renaissance *n* rebirth, refurbishment, renewal, renovation, repair, restoration

rend *v* 1 distress, disturb, move, sadden, wring

v 2 rip, tatter, shred, slice, tear

v 3 bite, chew, crunch, gnaw, gulp, guzzle, munch, nibble, wolf

v 4 claw, cleave, disrupt, divide, rip, rive, scratch, split, tear

v 5 see: CUT *v* 7

render *v* 1 clarify, depict, interpret, rephrase, represent, translate

v 2 bill, charge, debit, dun, invoice, notice, solicit

v 3 administer, administrate, carry out, deliver, do, execute, give, present, submit

rendezvous *n* see: AFFAIR *n* 3

v see: ASSEMBLE *v* 3

rending *adj* see: FULL *adj* 2

renegade *n* agitator, defector, dissident, heretic, iconoclast, insurgent, malcontent, maverick, misfit, nonconformist, rebel, traitor, troublemaker, turncoat

renege *v* 1 back, disavow, fall back, recall, recant, recede, rescind, retract, retreat, retrograde, take back

v 2 welsh

v 3 cancel, contradict, deny, disallow, forbid, negate, nix, nullify, override, overrule, reject, repeal, revoke, torpedo, veto, void

renew *v* 1 rebuild, recall, reestablish, reinstate, reintroduce, repair, restore, resume, resurrect, revive

v 2 freshen, modernize, redo, refresh, refurbish, rejuvenate, remodel, renovate, restore, revamp, revitalize, revive, update

renewal *n* 1 rebirth, refurbishment, renaissance, renovation, repair, restoration

n 2 comeback, improvement, rally, reappearance, recovery, resurrection, return, revival

renounce *v* 1 rebuff, reject, repel

v 2 abdicate, quit, relinquish, resign, step down, vacate

v 3 abjure, deny, disavow, disclaim, disown, forswear, repudiate

v 4 abandon, break up, cast off, chuck, defect, desert, disavow, discard, disenfranchise, disown, ditch, dump, forsake, jilt, junk, leave, quit, reject, spurn, strand, throw out

v 5 see: FORFEIT *v*

renovate *v* 1 buff, burnish, furbish, glaze, glimmer, gloss, polish, rub, shine

v 2 freshen, modernize, redo, refresh, refurbish, rejuvenate, remodel, renew, restore, revamp, revitalize, revive, update

v 3 see: REPAIR *v* 5

renovation *n* rebirth, refurbishment, renaissance, renewal, repair, restoration

renown *n* brilliance, celebrity, distinction, excellence, fame, glory, halo, honor, luster, note, popularity, prominence, repute, splendor

renowned *adj* acclaimed, celebrated, distinguished, eminent, esteemed, excellent, famed, famous, foremost, illustrious, notable, outstanding, prestigious, prominent, well-known

rent *n* 1 crack, cut, gash, opening, slit, trench

n 2 chink, cleft, crack, crevice, division, fissure, rift, rupture, split

v charter, franchise, hire, lease, let, permit, sublet

renter *n* inhabitant, lessee, occupant, resident, squatter, tenant

repaid *adj* indemnified, paid, paid off, reimbursed, remunerated, rewarded

repair *n* 1 case, condition, shape, state

n 2 installation, maintenance, service, upkeep

n 3 rebirth, refurbishment, renewal, renovation, restoration

n 4 condition, fitness, kilter, shape, trim

v 1 correct, rectify, remedy

v 2 cover, fix, overlay, patch

v 3 adjust, correct, cure, fix, heal, make well, mend, remedy, restore

v 4 rebuild, recall, reestablish, reinstate, reintroduce, renew, restore, resume, resurrect, revive

v 5 doctor, fix, mend, overhaul, patch,

rebuild, recondition, reconstruct, refit, renovate, revamp

v 6 adapt, adjust, balance, fit, fix, inspect, maintain, overhaul, recondition, refurbish, regulate, service, support, tune up

v 7 compensate, cover, disburse, indemnify, pay, reciprocate, redress, reimburse, remedy, remunerate, repay, requite, settle, vindicate

reparation *n* amends, compensation, damages, indemnity, redress, restitution, restoration

repast *n* banquet, buffet, dinner, feast, lunch, meal, smorgasbord, supper

repay *v* 1 adjust, refund, reimburse, return

v 2 avenge, compensate, cover, disburse, indemnify, pay, reciprocate, redress, reimburse, remedy, remunerate, repair, requite, retaliate, revenge, settle, vindicate

v 3 clear, clear off, discharge, liquidate, pay up, satisfy, settle, square

repeal *n* cancellation, recall, reversal, revocation

v 1 cancel, contradict, deny, disallow, forbid, negate, nix, nullify, override, overrule, reject, renege, revoke, torpedo, veto, void

v 2 see: CANCEL *v* 2, 3

repeat *v* 1 cite, quote, paraphrase, restate

v 2 beat, belabor, rehash, reiterate

v 3 emphasize, reiterate, reprise, resay, stress

v 4 emphasize, iterate, reiterate, restate, stress

v 5 backfire, echo, resonate, resound, reverberate, vibrate

v 6 drill, learn, perfect, practice, prepare, rehearse, review, study

repeated *adj* see: RECURRENT *adj*

repeatedly *adv* 1 ditto

adv 2 frequently, often, regularly, typically, usually

repel *v* 1 reject, renounce

v 2 alienate, estrange, fend off, rebuff, repulse, snub

v 3 cast off, drop, peel, shed

v 4 abhor, disgust, nauseate, repulse, revolt, sicken

v 5 combat, compete, contend, contest, counter, dispute, duel, fight, match, oppose, parry, pit, play, resist, rival, strive, struggle, vie

repellent *adj* abhorrent, base, gross, invidious, obnoxious, offensive, repugnant, revulsive

repent *v* 1 apologize, excuse, regret, seek penance

v 2 bemoan, deplore, lament, regret, rue

repentance *n* guilt, penitence, regret, remorse, sorrow

repentant *adj* 1 ashamed, penitent

adj 2 apologetic, contrite, penitent, sorry

repercussion *n* aftermath, consequence, corollary, effect, eventuality, outcome, reaction, result, reverberation, reward, upshot

repertoire *n* 1 acts, bag of tricks, résumé, skills, talents

n 2 account, amount, catalog, enumeration, inventory, itemization, list, litany, supply, tally

repetition *n* habit, mechanization, rote, routine

repetitious *adj* 1 bombastic, chatty, diffuse, garrulous, long-winded, loquacious, redundant, superfluous, talkative, verbose, wordy

adj 2 banal, boring, clichéd, commonplace, corny, dull, hackneyed, musty, redundant, repetitive, stale, tedious, threadbare, timeworn, tired, tiresome, trite, worn-out

repetitive *adj* 1 alternate, cyclic, cyclical, intermittent, periodic, periodical, recurrent, recurring, repeated, sporadic

adj 2 see: STALE *adj* 3

rephrase *v* 1 copy, paraphrase, reword

v 2 clarify, depict, interpret, render, represent, translate

replace *v* 1 change

v 2 substitute, supersede, supplant

v 3 refill, refresh, replenish, restore, stock

v 4 exchange, represent, return, substitute, supplant, swap, switch

v 5 give back, put back, reinstate, remit, restore, return, take back

v 6 relieve, spell, take over

replacement *n* 1 alternate, equivalent, exchange, substitute, substitution

n 2 agent, alternate, backup, contingency, part-timer, representative, standby, substitute, surrogate

n 3 expedient, makeshift, means, measure, recourse, refuge, resort, stopgap, substitute, surrogate

replenish *v* 1 refill, refresh, replace, restore, stock

v 2 fill, furnish, stock, store, supply

replete *adj* 1 abundant, elaborate, flamboyant, luscious

adj 2 bursting, chock-full, crowded, filled up, full, jammed, jampacked, loaded, packed, rending, stuffed

adj 3 alive, ample, overflowing, rife, swarming, teeming

replica *n* 1 duplicate, carbon, carbon copy, copy, facsimile, reproduction, telecopy, Xerox copy

n 2 clone, copy, counterfeit, duplicate, duplication, image, imitation, likeness, mock-up, model, print, replication, representation, reproduction, resemblance, simulation

n 3 doll, dummy, effigy

replicate *v* clone, copy, duplicate, image, imitate, mirror, print, re-create, redo, reduplicate, remake, reprint, reproduce, simulate

replication *n* see: REPLICA *n* 2

reply *n* answer, comeback, put-down, quip, reaction, rejoinder, response, retort, return

v acknowledge, answer, come back, react, rejoin, respond, retort, return

report *n* 1 data, details, dope, facts, information, scoop

n 2 depiction, description, explanation, illustration, narration, sketch, story, verbalization

n 3 bang, blare, blast, boom, discharge, explosion, noise, pop, roar

n 4 gossip, grapevine, hearsay, murmur, rumble, rumor, scuttlebutt, story, talk, word

n 5 account, diary, digest, journal, log, memoir, minutes, notation, notes, proceedings, record, recording

n 6 article, bulletin, byline, column, communication, dispatch, editorial, feature, headline, item, newsletter, story, vignette

n 7 see: ESSAY *n*

v 1 account, delineate, specify

v 2 brief, communicate, convey, declare, describe, disclose, divulge, explain, impart, inform, narrate, orate, portray, read, recite, recount, relate, retell, reveal, share, state, tattle, tell, transmit

reporter *n* author, authoress, biographer, creator, dramatist, essayist, journalist, novelist, playwright, screenwriter, writer

reporters *n* journalists, media, press

reporting *n* coverage, journalism, news, press

repose *n* 1 idle time, interlude, lull, recreation, relaxation, rest, vacation

n 2 see: PEACE *n* 2

v languish, loll, lounge, recline

repository *n* 1 storehouse, treasure trove, treasury

n 2 bank, depository, lender

n 3 cache, stockroom, storehouse, warehouse

repossess v 1 get back, recoup, recover, recruit, regain, retrieve, solicit

v 2 see: TAKE v 5

reprehensible adj blameworthy, criminal, culpable, felonious, guilty, remiss

represent v 1 depict, design, draw, paint, sketch

v 2 embody, exemplify, express, personify, symbolize, typify

v 3 delineate, depict, illustrate, picture, portray, sketch

v 4 clarify, depict, interpret, render, rephrase, translate

v 5 exchange, replace, return, substitute, supplant, swap, switch

v 6 acquaint, announce, delineate, depict, introduce, present, show

v 7 denote, depict, express, illustrate, imply, mean, speak for, symbolize

representation n 1 argument, demonstration, proof, thesis

n 2 characterization, delineation, depiction, expression, portrayal

n 3 drawing, icon, image, model, simulation, symbol

n 4 character, emblem, example, icon, letter, logo, mark, model, sign, symbol, token

n 5 see: REPLICA n 2

representative adj 1 characteristic, classic, exemplary, ideal, typical

adj 2 hollow, nominal, perfunctory, professed, small, symbolic, token

n 1 agent, alternate, dummy, proxy, substitute

n 2 assemblyman, congressman, councilman, lawmaker, legislator, senator

n 3 agent, alternate, backup, contingency, part-timer, replacement, standby, substitute, surrogate

n 4 case, case history, clarification, example, explanation, illumination, illustration, instance, sample, sampling, specimen

n 5 clerk, salesman, salesperson, saleswoman, shopkeeper, vendor

repress v 1 diminish, lessen, subject, subordinate, suppress, weaken

v 2 asphyxiate, choke, constrict, gag, garrote, muffle, quash, smother, stifle, strangle, suffocate, suppress

v 3 brake, confine, contain, control, curb, drag, govern, hamper, hem, hold back, impede, restrain, retard

v 4 annihilate, crush, demolish, extinguish, put down, quash, quell, quench, squash, stamp out, suppress

v 5 censor, curb, gag, hush, inhibit, muffle, mute, quell, quiet, restrain, silence, squelch, stifle, still, subdue, suppress, throttle, tone down

v 6 bar, block, brake, choke, clog, dam, deter, detract, encumber, frustrate, halt, hamper, hesitate, hinder, impair, impede, inhibit, jam, obstruct, prevent, restrain, retard, slow, stay, stop, stop up, throttle

repressed adj cold, frigid, inhibited, passionless, restrained, reticent, unresponsive

repression n block, check, curb, hangup, inhibition, restraint, reticence

reprieve n 1 delay, interruption, postponement, stay, stop, suspension

n 2 break, breath, breather, breathing space, intermission, pause, respite, rest

n 3 absolution, amnesty, discharge, disengagement, dispensation, freedom, moratorium, pardon, release, relief, respite, stay, suspension

v absolve, acquit, clear, condone, exculpate, excuse, exempt, exonerate, forgive, free, pardon, remit, vindicate

reprimand n admonishment, admonition, blast, chewing out, chiding, criticism, denunciation, diatribe, harangue, hassle, libel, outburst, rap, rebuke, reproach, reproof, scolding, slander, tirade

v admonish, berate, blame, censure, chide, condemn, disapprove, lay into, punish, rebuke, reproach, reprove, scold, warn

reprint v 1 bring out, distribute, get out, give out, go to press, issue, print, publish, put out, reissue, set type

v 2 clone, copy, duplicate, image, imitate, mirror, print, re-create, redo, reduplicate, remake, replicate, reproduce, simulate

reprisal n getting even, reciprocity, retaliation, retribution, revenge, vengeance, vindictiveness

reprise v emphasize, reiterate, repeat, resay, stress

reproach n admonishment, admonition, blast, chewing out, chiding, criticism, denunciation, diatribe, harangue, hassle, libel, outburst, rap, rebuke, reprimand, reproof, scolding, slander, tirade

v 1 disfavor, disgrace, dishonor, humiliate, shame, stain, tarnish

v 2 accuse, blame, charge, complain, condemn, criticize, fault

v 3 admonish, berate, blame, censure, chide, condemn, disapprove, lay into, punish, rebuke, reprimand, reprove, scold, warn

reprobate adj bad, corrupt, crooked, deceitful, dishonest, evil, fraudulent, immoral, iniquitous, lying, Machiavellian, manipulative, mercenary, roguish, scheming, shady, shifty, sinful, unethical, unfair, unprincipled, unscrupulous, untruthful, venal, vile, wicked, wrong

n cad, cheat, knave, lecher, louse, rake, rogue, scoundrel

v condemn, decline, disapprove, dismiss, exile, object, refuse, reject, repudiate, spurn, turn down

reproduce *v* 1 clone, copy, duplicate, image, imitate, mirror, print, re-create, redo, reduplicate, remake, replicate, reprint, simulate

v 2 see: BEGET *v*

reproduction *n* 1 carbon, carbon copy, copy, duplicate, facsimile, replica, telecopy, Xerox copy

n 2 clone, copy, counterfeit, duplicate, duplication, image, imitation, likeness, mock-up, model, print, replica, replication, representation, resemblance, simulation

n 3 conception, fertilization, insemination, propagation, spawning

n 4 coitus, conjugation, copulation, fooling around, foreplay, fornication, intercourse, mating, sex, union

reproductive *adj* carnal, erogenous, erotic, genital, procreative, sexual

reproof *n* see: REPRIMAND *n*

reprove *v* 1 advise, caution, counsel, recommend

v 2 admonish, berate, blame, censure, chide, condemn, disapprove, lay into, punish, rebuke, reprimand, reproach, scold, warn

reptile *n* accuser, betrayer, double-crosser, fink, informer, snake, sneak, stooge, traitor

repudiate *v* 1 abjure, deny, disavow, disclaim, disown, forswear, reject, renounce

v 2 condemn, decline, disapprove, dismiss, exile, object, refuse, reject, reprobate, spurn, turn down

repudiation *n* censure, disapproval, rejection

repugnance *n* aversion, contempt, disgust, distaste, horror, loathing, nausea, repulsion, revulsion

repugnant *adj* abhorrent, base, gross, invidious, obnoxious, offensive, repellent, revulsive

repulse *v* 1 alienate, estrange, fend off, rebuff, snub

v 2 abhor, disgust, nauseate, repel, revolt, sicken

repulsion *n* aversion, contempt, disgust, distaste, horror, loathing, nausea, repugnance, revulsion

repulsive *adj* 1 abhorrent, despicable, revolting, ugly

adj 2 hideous, homely, ugly, unattractive

adj 3 awful, frightful, grim, grisly, gruesome, hideous, lurid, sensational, shocking, terrible, ugly, violent

adj 4 abhorrent, abominable, appalling, detestable, disgusting, dreadful, evil, frightful, ghastly, hateful, horrible, horrid, loathsome, odious, revolting, shocking

adj 5 nasty

reputable *adj* accountable, answerable, dependable, honorable, honored, liable, reliable, respected, responsible, secure, solid, trusted, trustworthy, trusty, upstanding

reputation *n* 1 esteem, fame, good standing, name, perception, regard, stature

n 2 see: COMMENDATION *n* 2

repute *n* brilliance, celebrity, distinction, excellence, fame, glory, halo, honor, luster, note, popularity, prominence, renown, splendor

request *n* 1 invocation, petition, plea

n 2 bid, expectation, hope, inducement, invitation, motion, offer, proffer, proposal, proposition, recommendation, suggestion

n 3 appeal, desire, favor, petition, plea, solicitation, wish

v 1 ask, bid, encourage, invite, solicit

v 2 apply, claim, enroll, file, petition, sign up

v 3 appeal, ask, beg, beseech, conjure, crave, desire, entreat, grovel, implore, indicate, invoke, plead, pray, seek, solicit, supplicate, whine

require *v* 1 demand, expect, levy, want, wish

v 2 demand, designate, indicate, insist, specify, stipulate

v 3 ask, call, crave, demand, necessitate, take

v 4 assert, demand, emphasize, force, insist, persist, urge

v 5 call, challenge, claim, demand, exact, need, postulate, requisition, solicit

required *adj* 1 bound, committed, obligated

adj 2 compulsory, imperative, mandatory, must do, necessary, obligatory

adj 3 critical, essential, imperative, indispensable, mandatory, necessary, needed, prerequisite, vital

requirement n 1 criterion

n 2 claim, demand, mandate, ultimatum

n 3 condition, essential, must, necessity, precondition, prerequisite

n 4 agreement, clause, condition, provision, proviso, reservation, specification, stipulation, string, terms

n 5 demand, exigency, pressure, necessity, need, stress, urgency

requisite n caveat, limitation, qualification, restriction, stipulation

requisition n contract, order, purchase order, sale

v 1 call, challenge, claim, demand, exact, need, postulate, require, solicit

v 2 acquire, annex, buy, capture, gain, get, have, land, obtain, pick up, procure, purchase, secure, solicit, win

requite v avenge, compensate, cover, disburse, indemnify, pay, reciprocate, redress, reimburse, remedy, remunerate, repair, repay, retaliate, revenge, settle, vindicate

resay v emphasize, reiterate, repeat, reprise, stress

reschedule v adjourn, avoid, defer, delay, hold, hold up, interrupt, lay over, postpone, procrastinate, prolong, put off, remit, set aside, shelve, stay, suspend, table, wait, waive

rescind v 1 back, disavow, fall back, recall, recant, recede, renege, retract, retreat, retrograde, take back

v 2 abrogate, annul, cancel, contradict, discharge, dismantle, dissolve, dwindle, fade, negate, nullify, quash, recall, repeal, reverse, revoke, set aside, vacate, void

rescue n deliverance, extrication, freeing, recovery, release, saving

v 1 extricate, free, liberate, release, remove

v 2 recover, recycle, restore, salvage, save

v 3 deliver, free, liberate, release, save

rescuer n deliverer, liberator, messiah, salvation, savior

research n 1 education, instruction, learning, scholarship, schooling, study

n 2 analysis, digging, experimentation, exploration, inquiry, inquisition, investigation, study, testing, trial

v see: PROBE v 5

researcher n see: INTELLECTUAL n

resemblance n 1 affinity, analogy, approximation, comparison, likeness, match, metaphor, semblance, similarity, simile

n 2 clone, copy, counterfeit, duplicate,

duplication, image, imitation, likeness, mock-up, model, print, replica, replication, representation, reproduction, simulation

resemble v 1 favor, imitate, look like

v 2 imply, savor, smack, smell, suggest, taste

resent v begrudge, covet, envy

resentful adj 1 covetous, distrusting, envious, jealous, suspicious

adj 2 catty, hostile, malevolent, malicious, spiteful, treacherous

adj 3 alienated, angry, bitter, emotional, hurt, jealous, offended, provoked

resentment n 1 anger, animosity, hostility, huff, indignation, miff, offense, pique

n 2 chip, grudge, ill will, malevolence, malice, maliciousness, spite

reservation n 1 appointment, booking, date, engagement, listing, schedule

n 2 agreement, clause, condition, provision, proviso, requirement, specification, stipulation, string, terms

n 3 annoyance, anxiety, apprehension, bother, care, concern, disquiet, disquietude, doubt, irritation, misgiving, restlessness, restraint, skepticism, trouble, uneasiness, vexation, worry

n 4 compunction, conscience, pang, qualm, regret, restraint, scruple, twinge

reserve n 1 humility, modesty, shyness

n 2 goods, inventory, provisions, stock, store, supply n 3 backlog, cache, hoard, holdings, inventory, nest egg, pile, reservoir, stash, stock, stockpile, store, supply

n 4 coolness, distance, restraint, reticence

n 5 asylum, cover, harbor, haven, oasis, port, preserve, protection, refuge, retreat, safety, sanctuary, seaport, security, shelter

n 6 airborne, army, battalion, brigade, cavalry, company, footmen, guard, horsemen, infantry, legion, marines, militia, minutemen, paratroops, platoon, storm troopers

v 1 arrange, bespeak, book, engage, organize, plan, program, schedule, slate

v 2 detain, hold, hold back, keep, keep back, keep out, retain, set aside, withhold

reserved adj 1 aloof, conservative, poised

adj 2 constrained, noncommittal, restrained

adj 3 closed, diffident, introverted, laconic, restrained, reticent, secretive, shy, subdued, taciturn, timid, timorous, uncommunicative, undaring

adj 4 cold, dry, dull, laid-back, impassive, matter-of-fact, phlegmatic, poker-faced, stoic, stolid, unaffected, unemotional, unfeeling, unmoved, untouched

adj 5 see: INDIFFERENT *adj* 4

adj 6 see: SHY *adj* 2

reserves *n* assets, capacity, means, resources, wherewithal

reservoir *n* 1 accumulation, fund, source, store, supply

n 2 backlog, cache, hoard, holdings, inventory, nest egg, pile, reserve, stash, stock, stockpile, store, supply

n 3 cauldron, cistern, container, jug, tank, vat

reside *v* domicile, dwell, inhabit, live, occupy, room, settle, stay

residence *n* 1 address, apartment, condo, condominium, domicile, dwelling, flat, home, house, location, pad, place, property, site

n 2 abode, castle, domicile, dwelling, estate, home, house, mansion

resident *n* 1 inhabitant, lessee, occupant, renter, squatter, tenant

n 2 addressee, citizen, dweller, inhabitant, occupant, owner, tenant

n 3 diagnostician, doctor, healer, intern, physician, specialist, surgeon

n 4 member

residual *adj* excess, leftover, remaining, superfluous

n 1 alimony, allowance, annuity, payment, stipend

n 2 dregs, leftovers, remainder, remains, remnant, residue, rest, scrap, shred, silt

residue *n* dregs, leftovers, remainder, remains, remnant, residual, rest, scrap, shred, silt

resign *v* 1 drop, go, leave, quit, retire, terminate

v 2 abdicate, quit, relinquish, renounce, step down, vacate

v 3 abandon, acquiesce, cede, give up, hand over, leave, relinquish, submit, surrender, waive, yield

resignation *n* 1 endurance, forbearance, patience, perseverance, persistence, resolution, tenacity

n 2 abdication, departure, retirement

resigned *adj* acquiescent, compliant, docile, easy, meek, mild, nonresistant, obedient, passive, submissive, tame, tolerant, unassertive, yielding

resilience *n* 1 elasticity, spring

n 2 see: PERSISTENCE *n* 3

resilient *adj* 1 bouncy, elastic, expansive, malleable

adj 2 alterable, elastic, flexible, movable, pliable, springy, supple

resist *v* 1 check, oppose, stanch, stem, stop, weather, withstand

v 2 brave, challenge, confront, dare, defy, face, mutiny

v 3 defy, disobey, ignore, infringe, obstruct, oppose, rebel, violate

v 4 abstain, avoid, constrain, curb, deny, forgo, govern, hold back, refrain, restrict, stop, tame

v 5 see: COMPETE *v*

resolute *adj* 1 determined, persistent, stubborn, tenacious

adj 2 adamant, firm, steadfast, stern, strict

adj 3 absolute, firm, fixed, steadfast, unconditional, unreserved

adj 4 bent, committed, dedicated, determined, fixed, intentional, purposeful, resolved, set, tenacious

adj 5 ardent, constant, dedicated, dependable, devoted, faithful, loyal, staunch, steadfast, steady, true, trusty

adj 6 constant, determinate, firm, fixed, hard, immutable, inflexible, invariable, ironclad, stable, unalterable, unchangeable, unmovable

adj 7 adamant, ceaseless, dedicated, determined, firm, immovable, inexhaustible, inexorable, inflexible, narrow-minded, obstinate, relentless, resolved, rigid, single-minded, steadfast, stubborn, unbendable, unbending, uncompromising, unswayable, unyielding

adj 8 bullheaded, closed-minded, deaf, firm, hardheaded, hard-line, inelastic, inflexible, intractable, intransigent, obstinate, perverse, pigheaded, refractory, rigid, stiff, stubborn, tough, unbending, uncompromising, unpliable, unpliant, unwieldy, unyielding, willful

adj 9 see: HARD-WORKING *adj*

resolution *n* 1 course, determination, plan, purpose, resolve

n 2 conclusion, culmination, denouement, outcome, result, solution

n 3 endurance, forbearance, patience, perseverance, persistence, resignation, tenacity

resolve *n* course, determination, plan, purpose, resolution

v 1 answer, explain, solve, unravel

v 2 adjust, arrange, calibrate, decide, determine, establish, fix, set

v 3 adjudicate, conclude, decide, determine, establish, rule, settle, will

resolved *adj* 1 bent, committed, dedicated,

determined, fixed, intentional, purposeful, resolute, set, tenacious

adj 2 see: STUBBORN *adj* 6

resonance *n* timbre, tone, vibration

resonate *v* 1 backfire, echo, repeat, resound, reverberate, vibrate

v 2 boom, chime, clang, peal, resound, reverberate, ring, sound, toll

resort *n* 1 expedient, makeshift, means, measure, recourse, refuge, replacement, stopgap, substitute, surrogate

n 2 club, hotel, inn, lodge, spa

v apply, exercise, use, utilize

resound *v* 1 backfire, echo, repeat, resonate, reverberate, vibrate

v 2 boom, chime, clang, peal, resonate, reverberate, ring, sound, toll

v 3 acclaim, applaud, celebrate, commend, eulogize, exalt, extol, glorify, hail, honor, laud, praise, salute, toast, tout, worship

n bang, boom, clang, clap, crash, roar, rumble, shake, thunder

resounding *n* reverberation

resource *n* asset, credit, treasure, valuable

resourceful *adj* 1 adaptive, bold, canny, clever, daring, enterprising, venturesome

adj 2 active, bustling, busy, creative, driving, energetic, enterprising, inventive, lively

adj 3 clever, creative, deft, enterprising, fertile, imaginative, ingenious, inventive, skillful, talented

resourcefulness *n* 1 enterprise, gumption, initiative, spirit, spunk, volition

n 2 creativity, fancy, fantasy, image, imagination, ingenuity, inspiration, invention, whimsy

resources *n* 1 assets, capacity, means, reserves, wherewithal

n 2 assets, bills, capital, cash, coffers, currency, dinero, dollars, estate, funds, goods, income, lucre, money, notes, pelf, pesos, property, revenue, riches, rubles, shekels, sum, wealth

respect *n* 1 account, admiration, consideration, esteem, regard

n 2 amazement, awe, consternation, dread, fear, reverence, wonder

n 3 consideration, courtesy, dispensation, favor, indulgence, kindness, privilege, service

n 4 deference, devotion, esteem, homage, honor, just due, regard, reverence

v 1 admire, adore, cherish, dote on, idolize, love, revere, venerate, worship

v 2 admire, adore, appreciate, cherish,

consider, covet, esteem, honor, idolize, love, prize, regard, treasure, value

respectable *adj* 1 admirable, appreciable, worthy

adj 2 ample, decent, generous, sizable, substantial

adj 3 acceptable, adequate, competent, decent, enough, fair, good, mediocre, passable, reasonable, satisfactory, sufficient, tolerable

adj 4 see: ETHICAL *adj* 3

respected *adj* 1 admired, honored, praised, valued

adj 2 adored, beloved, cherished, dear, esteemed, loved, precious, revered, treasured, venerable, worshiped

adj 3 accountable, answerable, dependable, honorable, honored, liable, reliable, reputable, responsible, secure, solid, trusted, trustworthy, trusty, upstanding

respectful *adj* dedicated, deferential, devout

respecting *prep* about, apropos, as to, concerning, re, regarding, with respect to

respectively *adv* individually

respects *n* greetings, regards, salutations, salvo

respite *n* 1 abeyance, cease-fire, timeout, truce

n 2 day off, furlough, holiday, leave, sabbatical, time off, vacation

n 3 break, breath, breather, breathing space, intermission, pause, rest

n 4 abatement, alleviation, comfort, correction, cure, help, relief, remedy, solace, solution

n 5 absolution, amnesty, discharge, disengagement, dispensation, freedom, moratorium, pardon, release, relief, reprieve, stay, suspension

n 6 see: PEACE *n* 2

respond *v* 1 answer, react, recur, return, revert, turn back

v 2 acknowledge, answer, come back, react, rejoin, reply, retort, return

response *n* 1 condition, habit, impulse, reaction, reflex

n 2 answer, comeback, put-down, quip, reaction, rejoinder, reply, retort, return

n 3 awareness, emotion, faculty, feel, feeling, intuition, perception, reaction, sensation, sense

responsibility *n* 1 debt, loan, obligation

n 2 burden, charge, commitment, duty, obligation, onus

n 3 assignment, chore, duty, effort, job, mission, stint, task *n* 4 accountability, blame, burden, culpability, fault, guilt, onus, shame, stigma

responsible *adj* 1 blamable, condemned, convicted, culpable, guilty

adj 2 ethical, lucid, moral, rational, sane, stable

adj 3 see: REPUTABLE *adj*

responsive *adj* 1 alive, attentive, awake, aware, cognizant, conscious, conversant, knowing, sentient, thinking

adj 2 accommodating, agreeing, amenable, disposed, eager, glad, inclined, pleased, willing

adj 3 affectionate, compassionate, considerate, empathetic, empathic, gentle, humane, kind, kindhearted, softhearted, sympathetic, tender, warm, warmhearted

adj 4 see: PLASTIC *adj* 2

adj 5 see: QUICK *adj* 5

rest *n* 1 idle time, interlude, lull, recreation, relaxation, repose, vacation

n 2 break, breath, breather, breathing space, intermission, pause, reprieve, respite

n 3 dregs, leftovers, remainder, remains, remnant, residual, residue, scrap, shred, silt

n 4 exile, isolation, leisure, quarantine, relaxation, retirement, retreat, seclusion, solitude, withdrawal

n 5 calm, hush, lull, peace, peacefulness, quiet, repose, respite, siesta, silence, sleep, stillness, tranquillity

v 1 relax

v 2 doze, nap, sleep, snooze

v 3 demur, halt, hold up, interrupt, pause, stop, suspend

v 4 bask, delight, enjoy, like, loaf, luxuriate, relax, relish, savor, wallow

restart *v* see: PROCEED *v* 2

restate *v* 1 cite, paraphrase, quote

v 2 emphasize, iterate, reiterate, repeat, stress

restaurant *n* automat, cafe, cafeteria, canteen, diner, grill, luncheonette, lunchroom, tearoom

restful *adj* see: CALM *adj* 2

restitution *n* amends, compensation, damages, indemnity, redress, reparation, restoration

restive *adj* anxious, edgy, fidgety, impatient, nervous, nervy, queasy, restless, tense, troubled, uncomfortable, uneasy, uptight, worried

restless *adj* 1 awake, fitful, fretful, sleepless

adj 2 aggressive, defiant, insubordinate, rambunctious, stubborn, unruly

adj 3 annoying, anxious, bothersome, chafing, crabby, edgy, fretful, galling, impatient, irritating, jittery, nagging, on edge, touchy, unsettling

adj 4 anxious, edgy, fidgety, impatient, nervous, nervy, queasy, restive, tense, troubled, uncomfortable, uneasy, uptight, worried

adj 5 antsy, edgy, excitable, fidgety, highstrung, irritable, jittery, jumpy, moody, nervous, nervy, shaky, skittish, temperamental

restlessness *n* annoyance, anxiety, apprehension, bother, care, concern, disquiet, disquietude, doubt, irritation, misgiving, reservation, restraint, skepticism, trouble, uneasiness, vexation, worry

restoration *n* 1 rebirth, refurbishment, renaissance, renewal, renovation, repair

n 2 amends, compensation, damages, indemnity, reparation, restitution

restore *v* 1 refill, refresh, replace, replenish, stock

v 2 recover, recycle, rescue, salvage, save

v 3 give back, put back, reinstate, remit, replace, return, take back

v 4 adjust, correct, cure, fix, heal, make well, mend, remedy

v 5 rebuild, recall, reestablish, reinstate, reintroduce, renew, repair, resume, resurrect, revive

v 6 adjust, amend, correct, fix, improve, mend, modify, position, rectify, remedy, right, straighten

v 7 invigorate, reclaim, recondition, reconstruct, recover, recur, rehabilitate, rejuvenate, resuscitate, retrain, revitalize, revive

v 8 freshen, modernize, redo, refresh, refurbish, rejuvenate, remodel, renew, renovate, revamp, revitalize, revive, update

restrain *v* 1 curb, discipline, govern, limit, regulate, retard

v 2 inflect, moderate, modify, modulate, regulate, temper

v 3 burden, check, encumber, hamper, hinder, impede, obstruct, restrict, retard

v 4 bridle, check, constrain, control, crimp, curb, hold back, hold down, inhibit, leash, rein, restrict, withhold

v 5 brake, confine, contain, control, curb, drag, govern, hamper, hem, hold back, impede, repress, retard

v 6 bind, clog, confine, curb, fetter, hamper, handcuff, hold, leash, limit, restrict, shackle, tie, tie up

v 7 see: HINDER *v* 3, 5

v 8 see: IMPRISON *v* 2

v 9 see: STIFLE *v* 3

restrained *adj* 1 constrained, noncommittal, reserved

adj 2 conservative, dim, inconspicuous, quiet, subdued, tasteful, unassuming, unobtrusive

adj 3 accepting, charitable, easy, forbearing, indulgent, lenient, merciful, patient, sympathetic, tolerant

adj 4 cold, frigid, inhibited, passionless, repressed, reticent, unresponsive

adj 5 closed, diffident, introverted, laconic, reserved, reticent, secretive, shy, subdued, taciturn, timid, timorous, uncommunicative, undaring

adj 6 calculating, careful, cautious, circumspect, considerate, discreet, gingerly, guarded, heedful, judicious, provident, prudent, reticent, safe, shrewd, wary

restraint *n* 1 altitude, ceiling, maximum

n 2 abstinence, continence, moderation, self-restraint, sobriety, temperance

n 3 bridle, check, cord, rope, tether

n 4 block, check, curb, hangup, inhibition, repression, reticence

n 5 bond, boundary, bridle, check, constraint, control, curb, damper, harness, leash, limit, restriction

n 6 annoyance, anxiety, apprehension, bother, care, concern, disquiet, disquietude, doubt, irritation, misgiving, reservation, restlessness, skepticism, trouble, uneasiness, vexation, worry

n 7 corner, exclusive, monopoly

n 8 coolness, reserve, reticence

n 9 compunction, conscience, pang, qualm, regret, reservation, scruple, twinge

restrict *v* 1 exclude, fence, partition, separate

v 2 bound, confine, cramp, demarcate, limit

v 3 bound, limit, scrimp, short, skimp, spare, stint

v 4 burden, check, encumber, hamper, hinder, impede, obstruct, restrain, retard

v 5 abstain, avoid, constrain, curb, deny, forgo, govern, hold back, refrain, resist, stop, tame

v 6 bridle, check, constrain, control, crimp, curb, hold back, hold down, inhibit, leash, rein, restrain, withhold

v 7 bind, clog, confine, curb, fetter, hamper, handcuff, hold, leash, limit, restrain, shackle, tie, tie up

v 8 see: ABRIDGE *v*

restricted *adj* 1 exclusive, private

adj 2 close, cramped, uncomfortable

adj 3 definite, determinate, exclusive, fixed, limited, narrow, precise, segregated, specific

restriction *n* 1 caveat, limitation, qualification, requisite, stipulation

n 2 ban, blockage, boycott, curtailment, embargo, prohibition, stoppage

n 3 bond, boundary, bridle, check, constraint, control, curb, damper, harness, leash, limit, rein, restraint

n 4 ban, bar, constraint, interdiction, prohibition, taboo

restrictive *adj* authoritarian, authoritative, autocratic, controlled, despotic, disciplined, firm, harsh, inflexible, iron-handed, rigid, rigorous, ruthless, severe, solid, stern, strict, stringent, strong, tough, tyrannical

result *n* 1 consequence, development, progression, ramification

n 2 consequence, end, outcome

n 3 answer, explanation, key, secret, solution

n 4 climax, outcome, payoff, return, reward

n 5 amount, balance, sum, total

n 6 conclusion, culmination, denouement, outcome, resolution, solution

n 7 aftermath, consequence, corollary, effect, eventuality, outcome, reaction, repercussion, reverberation, reward, upshot

n 8 by-product, derivative, end product, end result, growth, outgrowth, output, produce, product, production, productivity, yield

n 9 fruit, harvest, product, reward

v 1 emanate, ensue, follow, succeed

v 2 develop, emerge, ensue, follow, happen

resume *v* rebuild, recall, reestablish, reinstate, reintroduce, renew, repair, restore, revive

résumé *n* 1 autobiography, biography, compendium, profile, sketch, vita

n 2 career, diary, events, experience, history, performance, record, track record, vita

n 3 acts, bag of tricks, repertoire, skills, talents

resurrect *v* rebuild, recall, reestablish, reinstate, reintroduce, renew, repair, restore, resume, revive

resurrection n comeback, improvement, rally, reappearance, recovery, renewal, return, revival

resuscitate v 1 animate, brighten, cheer up, enliven, incite, inspire, liven, quicken, vivify

v 2 invigorate, reclaim, recondition, reconstruct, recover, recur, rehabilitate, rejuvenate, restore, retrain, revitalize, revive

retail v barter, distribute, market, merchandise, peddle, sell, vend, wholesale

retain v 1 learn, memorize

v 2 have, hold, keep, possess

v 3 employ, engage, hire, put on, recruit, take on

v 4 detain, hold, hold back, keep, keep back, keep out, reserve, set aside, withhold

retaliate v see: PAY v 2

retaliation n 1 punishment, retribution, vengeance

n 2 getting even, reciprocity, reprisal, retribution, revenge, vengeance, vindictiveness

retard v 1 curb, discipline, govern, limit, regulate

v 2 burden, check, encumber, hamper, hinder, impede, obstruct, restrain

v 3 bog, delay, detain, hang up, impede, mire, set back, slacken, slow

v 4 brake, confine, contain, control, curb, drag, govern, hamper, hem, hold back, impede, restrain

v 5 see: HINDER v 3, 5

retarded adj backward, blunt, deficient, dense, dimwitted, dull, dumb, feebleminded, idiotic, moronic, obtuse, simple, simple-minded, slow, stupid, thick, uneducated, unintelligent

retell v see: INFORM v 6

retention n 1 possession

n 2 engram, memory, recall, remembrance, retentiveness, retrospection

retentiveness n engram, memory, recall, remembrance, retention, retrospection

rethink v reconsider, reevaluate, review

reticence n 1 block, check, curb, hangup, inhibition, repression

n 2 coolness, distance, reserve, restraint

reticent adj 1 dumb, inarticulate, mute, silent, speechless, tacit, voiceless

adj 2 closed, diffident, introverted, laconic, reserved, restrained, secretive, shy, subdued, taciturn, timid, timorous, uncommunicative, undaring

adj 3 cold, frigid, inhibited, passionless, repressed, unresponsive

adj 4 calculating, careful, cautious, circumspect, considerate, discreet, gingerly, guarded, heedful, judicious, provident, prudent, restrained, safe, shrewd, wary

retinue n bodyguard, chaperon, companion, escort, guide, scout

retire v 1 dismiss, pension, superannuate

v 2 drop, go, leave, quit, resign, terminate

v 3 turn in

retirement n 1 exile, isolation, leisure, quarantine, relaxation, rest, retreat, seclusion, solitude, withdrawal

n 2 abdication, resignation

retiring adj backward, bashful, coy, demure, diffident, innocent, modest, quiet, reserved, shy, staid, timid, unassured

retort n answer, comeback, put-down, quip, reaction, rejoinder, reply, response, return

v acknowledge, answer, come back, react, rejoin, reply, respond, return

retrace v analyze, brief, condense, evaluate, outline, review, study, summarize, synopsize, update

retract v back, disavow, fall back, recall, recant, recede, renege, rescind, retreat, retrograde, take back

retrain v invigorate, reclaim, recondition, reconstruct, recover, recur, rehabilitate, rejuvenate, restore, resuscitate, revitalize, revive

retreat n 1 exile, isolation, leisure, quarantine, relaxation, rest, retirement, seclusion, solitude, withdrawal

n 2 abandon, departure, desertion, evacuation, exit, going, leaving, pullback, pullout, withdrawal

n 3 asylum, cover, harbor, haven, oasis, port, preserve, protection, refuge, reserve, safety, sanctuary, seaport, security, shelter

v 1 back, disavow, fall back, recall, recant, recede, renege, rescind, retract, retrograde, take back

v 2 see: LEAVE v 4

retrenchment n reduction

retribution n 1 punishment, retaliation, vengeance

n 2 getting even, reciprocity, reprisal, retaliation, revenge, vengeance, vindictiveness

retrieve v get back, recoup, recover, recruit, regain, repossess, solicit

retrograde v 1 ebb, go backwards, recede, regress, retrogress, return, revert, throw back

v 2 back, disavow, fall back, recall, recant,

recede, renege, rescind, retract, retreat, take back

retrogress v ebb, go backwards, recede, regress, retrograde, return, revert, throw back

retrospect v look back, recall, recollect, remember, reminisce, revoke

retrospection n engram, memory, recall, remembrance, retentiveness

return n 1 climax, outcome, payoff, result, reward

n 2 comeback, improvement, rally, reappearance, recovery, renewal, resurrection, revival

n 3 answer, comeback, put-down, quip, reaction, rejoinder, reply, response

n 4 assets, cash, earnings, gain, gross, haul, net, payback, proceeds, profits, receipts, revenue, take, yield

v 1 adjust, reimburse, repay

v 2 bring in, pay, profit, yield

v 3 answer, react, recur, respond, revert, turn back

v 4 exchange, replace, represent, substitute, supplant, swap, switch

v 5 give back, put back, reinstate, remit, replace, restore, take back

v 6 ebb, go backwards, recede, regress, retrograde, retrogress, revert, throw back

v 7 acknowledge, answer, come back, react, rejoin, reply, respond

rev v 1 speed, throttle

v 2 abet, advance, aid, ameliorate, amend, assist, avail, benefit, better, boost, cultivate, do for, ease, egg on, encourage, enhance, forward, foster, further, help, improve, nurture, prefer, promote, serve, spur on, support

revamp v 1 doctor, fix, mend, overhaul, patch, rebuild, recondition, reconstruct, refit, repair

v 2 edit, modify, redraft, redraw, rehash, revise, rework, rewrite

v 3 freshen, modernize, redo, refresh, refurbish, rejuvenate, remodel, renew, renovate, restore, revitalize, revive, update

reveal v 1 divulge, hint, leak

v 2 betray, cross, divulge, double-cross, sell out

v 3 clarify, disclose, explain, relate, unfold

v 4 blab, divulge, gossip, inform, tell

v 5 demonstrate, determine, establish, evidence, prove, show

v 6 disclose, display, evince, express, imply, indicate, manifest, reflect, show

v 7 communicate, disclose, display, divulge, exhibit, inform, notify, open, uncover, unveil

v 8 allude, denote, indicate, mention, point out, refer to, show, speak of, specify, suggest, tell

v 9 bare, denude, discard, disrobe, doff, flash, remove, shed, strip, take off, unclothe, undress

v 10 air, bring up, broach, communicate, discuss, expose, express, give, introduce, open, put, state, tap, tell, vent, ventilate, verbalize

v 11 brief, communicate, convey, declare, describe, disclose, divulge, explain, impart, inform, narrate, orate, portray, read, recite, recount, relate, report, retell, share, state, tattle, tell, transmit

v 12 clarify, clear, clear up, delineate, depict, elucidate, explain, illuminate, illustrate, picture

revealing adj 1 academic, educational, enlightening, eye-opening, illuminating, informative, instructive, scholastic

adj 2 see: SOLID adj 4

revel v 1 admire, appreciate, cherish, delight, enjoy, relish, savor

v 2 carouse, celebrate, drink, frolic, make merry, party, romp

v 3 boast, brag, crow, exult, flaunt, gloat, show off, strut, vaunt

revelation n 1 admission

n 2 breach, disclosure, leak

n 3 forecast, prophecy, warning

n 4 breakthrough, discovery, disclosure, exposition, find, unearthing

n 5 solution

n 6 apocalypse, oracle, prophecy, vision

revelry n celebration, ceremony, commemoration, festival, festivity, fiesta, gala, holiday, observance

revenge n getting even, reciprocity, reprisal, retaliation, retribution, vengeance, vindictiveness

v see: PAY v 2

revengeful adj malicious, spiteful, unforgiving, unmerciful, vengeful, vindictive

revenue n 1 assets, cash, earnings, gain, gross, haul, net, payback, proceeds, profits, receipts, return, take, yield

n 2 bill, bonus, charge, commission, compensation, consideration, earnings, fee, gross, income, pay, salary, stipend, wage

n 3 see: MONEY n 4

n 4 see: SUM n 3

reverberant adj cavernous, echo-filled, gaping, hollow, spacious, vast

reverberate v 1 backfire, echo, repeat, resonate, resound, vibrate *v* 2 boom, chime, clang, peal, resonate, resound, ring, sound, toll

reverberation *n* 1 resounding

n 2 aftermath, consequence, corollary, effect, eventuality, outcome, reaction, repercussion, result, reward, upshot

revere *v* admire, adore, cherish, dote on, idolize, love, respect, venerate, worship

revered *adj* adored, beloved, cherished, dear, esteemed, loved, precious, respected, treasured, venerable, worshiped

reverence *n* 1 devotion, sanctity, worship

n 2 amazement, awe, consternation, dread, fear, respect, wonder

n 3 deference, devotion, esteem, homage, honor, regard, respect

reverend *n* chaplain, clergyman, cleric, father, guru, minister, padre, parson, pastor, priest

reverent *adj* devout, godly, holy, pious, prayerful, religious, sanctimonious

reverie *n* daydream, dream, fancy, fantasy, musing, vision

reversal *n* 1 cancellation, recall, revocation

n 2 change, move, shift, turnabout

n 3 adversity, affliction, blow, burden, calamity, difficulty, distress, hardship, mischance, misfortune, mishap, relapse, setback, suffering, tragedy, trouble

reverse *adj* 1 backward, converse, counter

adj 2 conflicting, contradictory, contrary, converse, counter, diametric, inverse, opposed, opposing, opposite

n antithesis, converse, opposite

v 1 change, invert, revert, transpose, turn

v 2 abrogate, annul, cancel, contradict, discharge, dismantle, dissolve, dwindle, fade, negate, nullify, quash, recall, repeal, rescind, revoke, set aside, vacate, void

revert *v* 1 change, invert, reverse, transpose, turn

v 2 answer, react, recur, respond, return, turn back

v 3 ebb, go backwards, recede, regress, retrograde, retrogress, return, throw back

review *n* 1 bulletin, daily, journal, newsletter, newspaper, organ

n 2 assessment, examination, inquiry, scope, search, study, survey

n 3 analysis, assessment, commentary, criticism, critique, evaluation, examination, judgment, notion, opinion, ruling

n 4 abridgement, abstract, brief, compendium, condensation, digest, essence, example, outline, sketch, summary, syllabus, synopsis

n 5 follies, musical, revue, song and dance, variety show, vaudeville

v 1 study

v 2 reconsider, reevaluate

v 3 care, consider, heed, listen

v 4 drill, learn, perfect, practice, prepare, rehearse, repeat, study

v 5 analyze, brief, condense, evaluate, outline, retrace, study, summarize, synopsize, update

reviewer *n* commentator, critic, evaluator, judge

revile *v* 1 bawl out, bellow, berate, chew out, mock, rail, rant, rave, roar, scold, tell off, tongue-lash, upbraid, yell

v 2 abuse, asperse, bad-mouth, belittle, condemn, damage, decry, defame, degrade, denigrate, denounce, deprecate, detract, diminish, discount, disparage, insult, knock, malign, put down, run down, slander, take away, vilify

v 3 see: DEFAME *v* 1, 2

v 4 see: HATE *v*

revise *v* 1 annotate, compile, correct, denote, edit, modify, polish, proofread

v 2 edit, modify, redraft, redraw, rehash, revamp, rework, rewrite

revision *n* alchemy, alteration, changeover, transformation

revitalize *v* 1 bounce back, come round, rally, rebound, recoup, recover, snap back

v 2 invigorate, reclaim, recondition, reconstruct, recover, recur, rehabilitate, rejuvenate, restore, resuscitate, retrain, revive

v 3 see: REJUVENATE *v* 1, 2

revival *n* comeback, improvement, rally, reappearance, recovery, renewal, return

revive *v* 1 rebuild, recall, reestablish, reinstate, reintroduce, renew, repair, restore, resume, resurrect

v 2 invigorate, reclaim, recondition, reconstruct, recover, recur, rehabilitate, rejuvenate, restore, resuscitate, retrain

v 3 see: RECOVER *v* 5, 6

v 4 see: REJUVENATE *v* 1, 2

revocation *n* cancellation, recall, repeal, reversal

revoke *v* 1 look back, recall, recollect, remember, reminisce

v 2 abrogate, annul, cancel, contradict, discharge, dismantle, dissolve, dwindle, fade, negate, nullify, quash, recall, repeal, rescind, reverse, set aside, vacate, void

v 3 see: REJECT *v* 7

revolt n betrayal, insurrection, mutiny, sedition, subversion, treason, uprising

v 1 insurrect, mutiny, rebel, rise against

v 2 abhor, disgust, nauseate, repel, sicken

v 3 frenzy, rage, rampage, rebel, riot, stampede, storm

revolting adj 1 abhorrent, despicable, repulsive, ugly

adj 2 abhorrent, abominable, appalling, detestable, disgusting, dreadful, evil, frightful, ghastly, hateful, horrible, horrid, loathsome, odious, repulsive, shocking

revolution n 1 curl, loop, ring, roll, rotation, spin, spiral, turn, twirl, twist

n 2 alternation, circuit, circulation, gyration, rotation, round, sequence, spinning, succession, turn, whirl

revolutionary adj extreme, extremist, fanatic, fanatical, rabid, radical, ultra, zealous

revolutionize v alter, change, commute, convert, evolve, further, improve, metamorphose, modernize, modify, mutate, transfer, transfigure, transform, transmute, vary

revolve v 1 circulate, pass around, route, travel

v 2 circle, gyrate, roll, rotate, spin, turn

revolver n automatic, firearm, gun, handgun, heater, iron, luger, piece, pistol, rod

revue n follies, musical, review, song and dance, variety show, vaudeville

revulsion n aversion, contempt, disgust, distaste, horror, loathing, nausea, repulsion

revulsive adj abhorrent, base, gross, invidious, obnoxious, repellent, repugnant

reward n 1 compensation, earnings, wages

n 2 climax, outcome, payoff, result

n 3 award, bequest, endowment, gift, grant, scholarship

n 4 booty, bounty, gifts, largess, plenty, plunder, presents

n 5 alimony, compensation, fee, honorarium, payment, remuneration, stipend

n 6 bonus, consideration, goal, incentive, inducement, motivation, motive, reason, stimulus

n 7 aftermath, consequence, corollary, effect, eventuality, outcome, reaction, repercussion, result, reverberation, upshot

n 8 ante, award, bonus, booty, cash, commission, dividend, donation, fee, gift, gratuity, largess, money, percentage, perk, perquisite, premium, prize, profit,

purse, sharing, stake, stipend, tip, winnings

n 9 fruit, harvest, result

n 10 accolade, award, commendation, credit, decoration, distinction, honor, kudos, laurels, medal, note, praise, recognition, reputation, tribute

v 1 attribute, credit, honor

v 2 advance, benefit, gain, improve

v 3 bequeath, endow, give, remember, tip

rewarded adj indemnified, paid, paid off, reimbursed, remunerated

rewarding adj 1 beneficial, gainful, lucrative

adj 2 beneficial, fulfilling, gratifying, pleasing, worthwhile

reword v copy, paraphrase, plagiarize, rephrase

rework v edit, modify, redraft, redraw, rehash, revamp, revise, rewrite

rewrite v edit, modify, redraft, redraw, rehash, revamp, revise

rhapsody n 1 air, call, carol, cry, lullaby, melody, note, song, tune

n 2 bliss, delight, ecstasy, Eden, elation, enchantment, heaven, joy, nirvana, paradise, pleasure

rhetoric n elocution

rhyme n ditty, limerick, lyric, madrigal, poem, poetry, song, sonnet, verse

rhythm n beat, cadence, cycle, lilt, pulse, rate, tempo, time

rhythmical adj choral, euphonious, harmonious, lyric, mellow, melodic, melodious, musical, orchestral, philharmonic, symphonic, tuneful, vocal

rib v banter, deride, gibe, jeer, joke, knock, mock, needle, ridicule, roast, tease

ribald adj bawdy, coarse, crude, dirty, erotic, filthy, foul, gamy, gross, improper, indecent, lascivious, lewd, licentious, nasty, obscene, off-color, pornographic, profane, prurient, racy, rank, raunchy, risqué, scandalous, smutty, suggestive, tainted, uncouth, vulgar, x-rated

ribaldry n dirt, filth, grossness, indecency, obscenity, porn, pornography, smut, trash

ribbon n band, strip

rich adj 1 deep, meaty, profound, stimulating

adj 2 affluent, comfortable, excessive, superfluous

adj 3 abundant, fattening, heavy, sweet, thick

adj 4 affluent, copious, leisure-class, loaded, moneyed, opulent, wealthy, well-to-do *adj* 5 abundant, cornucopian, extravagant, exuberant, garish, generous, lavish, lush, luxuriant, opulent, prodigal, profuse, wasteful

adj 6 see: LUXURIOUS *adj* 2

riches *n* 1 abundance

n 2 assets, belongings, equity, estate, fortune, goods, holdings, inheritance, money, ownership, possessions, property, prosperity, treasure, wealth

n 3 assets, bills, capital, cash, coffers, currency, dinero, dollars, estate, funds, goods, income, lucre, means, money, notes, pelf, pesos, property, resources, revenue, rubles, shekels, sum, wealth

rickety *adj* 1 flimsy, insecure, jiggly, shaky, teetering, unstable, unsure, vacillating, wavering, weak, wobbly

adj 2 see: DELICATE *adj* 7

rickshaw *n* cab, hack, jitney, taxi, taxicab

ricochet *v* backfire, boomerang, bounce, brush, glance, graze, rebound, skim, skip, touch

rid *v* dispose of, eliminate, expel, flush, purge, remove, vanquish

riddle *n* confusion, conundrum, difficulty, dilemma, enigma, mystery, obstacle, paradox, perplexity, problem, puzzle, quandary, question, secret

v perforate, permeate, pierce, shoot

ride *n* drive, excursion, jaunt, journey, outing, spin

v 1 come through, get by, succeed, survive

v 2 aggravate, annoy, badger, bait, bedevil, beleaguer, bother, bug, harass, harry, hassle, heckle, hound, hurt, intimidate, jeer, nag, needle, persecute, pester, plague, provoke, spite, taunt, tease, threaten, torment, worry

v 3 motor

v 4 drift, float, wash

v 5 drive, travel

rider *n* 1 commuter, passenger, traveler

n 2 addendum, addition, appendix, supplement

ridicule *n* 1 aspersion, contempt, derision, disdain, irony, mockery, sarcasm, satire, scorn

n 2 arrogance, assurance, audacity, boldness, brashness, brass, cheek, chutzpah, condescension, confidence, crust, effrontery, face, gall, haughtiness, insolence, nerve, patronage, presumption, sass, stamina, temerity

v 1 banter, deride, gibe, jeer, joke, knock, mock, needle, rib, roast, tease

v 2 belittle, deride, flaunt, jab, jeer, jest,

mock, quip, razz, scoff, scorn, sneer, taunt, tease

ridiculous *adj* 1 absurd, comic, comical, crazy, droll, farcical, foolish, funny, hilarious, humorous, laughable, ludicrous, outrageous, silly

adj 2 see: ABSURD *adj* 2

rife *adj* 1 current, democratic, dominant, extensive, fashionable, general, in vogue, prevailing, prevalent, popular, rampant, sought after, well-liked, widespread

adj 2 alive, ample, overflowing, swarming, teeming

riffraff *n* see: CROWD *n* 1

rifle *v* comb, loot, ransack, scour, search, separate, sift, sort

n carbine, firearm, flintlock, gun, musket, shotgun

rift *n* 1 break, disagreement, dissension, fight, misunderstanding, quarrel, separation, spat

n 2 chink, cleft, crack, crevice, division, fissure, rent, rupture, split

n 3 see: QUARREL *n* 1, 2

rig *n* buggy, carriage, coach, surrey, vehicle

v 1 appoint, arm, equip, fortify, furnish, gear, man, outfit, set up, supply, turn out

v 2 see: ADAPT *v* 2

rigging *n* cable, wire

right *adv* 1 accurately, exactly, just so, precisely, sharp, smack, square, squarely

adv 2 acceptably, adequately, amply, appropriately, correctly, properly, satisfactorily, suitably, well

adj 1 accurate, correct, exact, precise, proper, valid

adj 2 conventional, correct, decorous, fitting, nice, orthodox, polite, proper, suitable, well

adj 3 applicable, appropriate, apropos, apt, befitting, convenient, desirable, felicitous, fit, fitting, germane, good, handy, just, material, meet, necessary, pertinent, proper, relevant, shipshape, suitable, suited, timely, useful

adj 4 see: ETHICAL *adj* 3

n 1 exemption, grant, patent, permission, safeguard

n 2 advantage, birthright, claim, edge, enablement, perquisite, prerogative, privilege, title

v adjust, amend, correct, fix, improve, mend, modify, position, rectify, remedy, restore, straighten

righteous *adj* 1 blameless, commendable, exemplary, exonerated, guiltless, innocent, irreproachable, virtuous

adj 2 conscientious, ethical, honest, honorable, moral, noble, principled, proper, respectable, right, scrupulous, sound, true, trustworthy, upright, virtuous

righteousness *n* goodness, morality, principle, probity, purity, rectitude, uprightness, virtue

rightful *adj* 1 allowable, authorized, lawful, legal, legitimate, permissible, valid

adj 2 authoritative, dependable, due, faithful, legitimate, strict, true, trustworthy, undistorted, veracious

adj 3 appropriate, correct, deserved, due, fitting, just, merited, proper, suitable, warranted

rightness *n* see: UTILITY *n*

rigid *adj* 1 exacting, fastidious, finicky, meticulous, picky, precise, strict

adj 2 ascetic, astringent, austere, chaste, simple, spartan, stern, stoic

adj 3 austere, narrow, narrow-minded, prim, prudish, puritanical, severe, strict

adj 4 compact, firm, hard, hardened, secure, solid, sound, specific, stable, stiff, tight

adj 5 authoritarian, authoritative, autocratic, controlled, despotic, disciplined, firm, harsh, inflexible, ironhanded, restrictive, rigorous, ruthless, severe, solid, stern, strict, stringent, strong, tough, tyrannical

adj 6 bullheaded, closed-minded, deaf, firm, hardheaded, hard-line, inelastic, inflexible, intractable, intransigent, obstinate, perverse, pigheaded, refractory, resolute, stiff, stubborn, tough, unbending, uncompromising, unpliable, unpliant, unwieldy, unyielding, willful

adj 7 see: SECURE *adj* 5, 6

adj 8 see: STUBBORN *adj* 6

rigidity *n* austerity, oppression, severity, tyranny

rigor *n* 1 thoroughness

n 2 adversity, difficulty, discipline, discomfort, hardness, severity, strictness, stringency, uneasiness

rigorous *adj* 1 careful, diligent, studious, thorough

adj 2 see: RESTRICTIVE *adj* 6, 7

adj 3 see: SEVERE *adj* 8

rile *v* see: BOTHER *v* 5

rim *n* border, boundary, bounds, brim, brink, curb, edge, fringe, limits, lip, margin, outskirt, perimeter, periphery, side, skirt, verge

rind *n* bark, case, coating, crust, husk, peel, shell, shuck, skin

ring *n* 1 band, coil, crown, garland, loop, spiral, wreath

n 2 characteristic, flavor, impression, nature, property, quality, sound, tendency, tone, type

n 3 curl, loop, revolution, roll, rotation, spin, spiral, turn, twirl, twist

n 4 band, cabal, camp, circle, clan, clique, coterie, coven, cult, faction, family, gang, group, mob, school, sect, tribe

n 5 anklet, band, bangle, bracelet, brooch, earring, jewelry, medal, medallion, necklace

v 1 buzz, call, communicate, contact, phone, telephone, touch

v 2 boom, chime, clang, peal, resonate, resound, reverberate, sound, toll

rinse *v* bathe, clean, cleanse, clean up, dip, flush, immerse, launder, rub, scour, scrape, scrub, shower, wash

riot *n* 1 rampage, stampede, storm

n 2 chaos, hysteria, panic

n 3 anarchy, chaos, commotion, confusion, disorder, disturbance, fracas, fray, outbreak, ruckus, storm, tempest

v frenzy, rage, rampage, rebel, revolt, stampede, storm

rip *v* 1 rend, shred, slice, tatter, tear

v 2 claw, cleave, disrupt, divide, rend, rive, scratch, split, tear

n slash, slit, split, tear

ripe *adj* 1 game, prepared, primed, ready, set

adj 2 aged, grown old, matured, ripened

ripen *v* age, develop, grow, grow up, mature, mellow

ripened *adj* 1 aged, grown old, matured, mellow, ripe

adj 2 adult, full-grown, grown, grown-up, mature

rip-off *n* con, crime, graft, hustle, racket, scam, scheme, sting, swindle

ripple *n* breaker, roller, swell, wave, whitecap

rise *n* 1 ascent, climb, escalation

n 2 angle, grade, gradient, incline, pitch, ramp, slant, slope, tilt

n 3 increase, enlargement, growth, swell

n 4 foothill, hill, hillock, hump, knoll, mound, mount, raise, swelling

v 1 ascend, climb, increase, soar, speed, zoom

v 2 climb, crest, increase, jump, mount, surge

v 3 arise, ascend, aspire, go up, lift, mount, soar

v 4 stand up

v 5 ascend, come up, surface

v 6 flood, flow, gush, peak, pour, roll, spill, stream, surge, swell *v* 7 bulge, jut, overhang, overlap, overlay, poke, pop, project, protrude, protuberate, stand out, stick out, swell

v 8 advance, ascend, bloom, climb, develop, do well, excel, expand, flourish, flower, get ahead, grow, improve, progress, prosper, strive, survive, thrive

v 9 appear, arise, befall, break, come, come about, develop, do, ensue, evolve, fall out, happen, manifest, materialize, occur, pass, take place, transpire, turn up

rising *adj* ambitious, aspiring, striving

risk *n* 1 adventure, encounter, event, experience, hazard, ordeal

n 2 bet, chance, fortune, gamble, hazard, luck, stake

n 3 danger, downside, exposure, hazard, jeopardy, liability, menace, threat

v attempt, bet, chance, dare, gamble, hazard, play, speculate, stake, venture, wager

risky *adj* 1 breakneck, critical, dangerous, harmful, hazardous, perilous, precarious, serious, unsafe, venturesome

adj 2 careless, foolish, impulsive, irresponsible, myopic, not smart, reckless, shortsighted, unthinking, unwise

adj 3 see: DELICATE *adj* 7

risqué *adj* bawdy, coarse, crude, dirty, erotic, filthy, foul, gamy, gross, improper, indecent, lascivious, lewd, licentious, nasty, obscene, off-color, pornographic, profane, prurient, racy, rank, raunchy, ribald, scandalous, smutty, suggestive, tainted, uncouth, vulgar, x-rated

rite *n* 1 ceremonial, ceremony, formality, liturgy, observance, ritual, service

n 2 belief, custom, doctrine, mores, relic, ritual, throwback, tradition

n 3 see: COMMAND *n* 3

n 4 see: RELIGION *n* 2

rites *n* 1 beliefs, code, doctrine, ethics, outlook, philosophy, values

n 2 convention, custom, decorum, etiquette, formality, good form, manners, protocol

ritual *n* 1 ceremonial, ceremony, formality, liturgy, observance, rite, service

n 2 belief, custom, doctrine, mores, relic, rite, throwback, tradition

rival *adj* competing, opposing, vying

n adversary, antagonist, anti, challenger, competitor, con, contender, enemy, foe, opponent

v 1 equal, match, measure up, meet, tie, touch

v 2 see: COMPETE *v*

rivalry *n* 1 envy, jealousy

n 2 battle, clash, competition, conflict, contest, discord, duel, fight, fighting, strife, struggle, war, warfare

rive *v* claw, cleave, disrupt, divide, rend, rip, scratch, split, tear

river *n* bayou, brook, creek, stream, tributary

rivet *n* bolt, brad, nut, peg, pin, spike, staple, stud, weld

v 1 concentrate, fix, fixate

v 2 affix, attach, bind, clip, connect, fasten, fix, weld

riveting *adj* see: FASCINATING *adj* 2

road *n* 1 circuit, course, itinerary, journey, line, means, passage, path, route, trip, voyage, way

n 2 access, approach, artery, avenue, boulevard, channel, drag, highway, pass, path, promenade, roadway, route, strait, street, thoroughfare, trail, way

roadblock *n* bar, barricade, barrier, block, blockade, fence, obstacle, stop, wall

roadway *n* access, approach, artery, avenue, boulevard, channel, drag, highway, pass, path, promenade, road, route, strait, street, thoroughfare, trail, way

roam *v* itinerate, meander, perambulate, promenade, ramble, range, rove, saunter, stray, stroll, traipse, travel, traverse, walk, wander

roar *n* 1 bang, blare, blast, boom, discharge, explosion, noise, pop

n 2 bark, bellow, blare, holler, scream, shout, shriek, thunder, yell

n 3 bang, boom, clang, clap, crash, resound, rumble, shake, thunder

v 1 chortle, chuckle, giggle, guffaw, laugh, smile, snicker, snigger

v 2 bawl out, bellow, berate, chew out, mock, rail, rant, rave, revile, scold, tell off, tongue-lash, upbraid, yell

v 3 bark, bellow, blare, call, cry, holler, howl, scream, screech, shout, shriek, shrill, squeal, thunder, wail, yell

roast *v* 1 banter, deride, gibe, jeer, joke, knock, mock, needle, rib, tease

v 2 bake, broil, burn, char, cook, melt, parch, scorch, sear, singe, swelter, toast, warm

v 3 see: SEETHE *v* 2

rob *v* 1 defraud, deprive, swindle, take, usurp

v 2 appropriate, burglarize, defraud, embezzle, filch, heist, lift, misappropriate, pilfer, pillage, pinch, plunder, pocket, purloin, rip off, snake, snitch, steal, swindle, swipe, take, thieve

robber *n* see: CROOK *n* 2

robbery *n* 1 burglary, larceny, looting, theft, thievery

n 2 heist, holdup, theft

robe *n* bathrobe, gown, housecoat, negligee, nightgown

robot *n* android, automaton, droid

robotic *adj* 1 auto, automatic, cybernetic, self-steering

adj 2 automated, automatic, habitual, mechanical, routine

robust *adj* 1 fit, hardy, healthy, rubicund, ruddy, sound, sturdy, well, wholesome

adj 2 concentrated, hearty, heavy-duty, lusty, potent, powerful, stalwart, stout, strong, sturdy

adj 3 athletic, brawny, burly, husky, massive, muscular, ponderous, powerful, stocky, stout, strapping, strong

adj 4 coercive, compelling, dynamic, energetic, forceful, hardy, lusty, mighty, passionate, powerful, strong, sturdy, vigorous

adj 5 aggressive, dominant, durable, firm, forceful, hardy, hearty, mighty, powerful, rugged, stalwart, stout, strong, sturdy, tenacious, tough

rock *v* 1 bob, heave, pitch, roll, sway, swing, toss

v 2 agitate, derange, disorder, disturb, fluster, ruffle, shake, sicken, unhinge, unsettle, upset

n boulder, detritus, fragments, gravel, pebble, stone

rock-and-roll *n* blues, classical, country, folk, jazz, music, ragtime, soul, swing

rocket *n* bomb, bombshell, explosive, mine, missile, payload, rocketry, warhead

v barrel, bullet, expedite, fly, hasten, hurry, hustle, rush, speed, whisk, zip

rocketry *n* bomb, bombshell, explosive, mine, missile, payload, rocket, warhead

rocky *adj* 1 dangerous, delicate, fluctuating, hazardous, precarious, rickety, risky, sensitive, shaky, tender, ticklish, touchy, tricky, unpredictable, unstable, wobbly

adj 2 see: HARD *adj* 3

rod *n* 1 bar, ingot, pole, stick, strip

n 2 axis, axle, pin, pivot, pole, shaft, spindle

n 3 birch, cane, club, pole, shaft, staff, stake, stave, stick

n 4 baton, scepter, staff, wand

n 5 automatic, firearm, gun, handgun, heater, iron, luger, piece, pistol

rogue *n* 1 brute, demon, devil, fiend, Satan, villain, wretch

n 2 cad, cheat, knave, lecher, louse, rake, rascal, reprobate, scoundrel

roguish *adj* see: EVIL *adj* 4

role *n* 1 character, part, portrayal

n 2 art, avocation, business, calling, career, discipline, employment, field, gig, job, labor, line, livelihood, occupation, office, profession, pursuit, schtick, situation, specialty, task, thing, trade, vocation, work

roll *n* curl, loop, revolution, ring, rotation, spin, spiral, turn, twirl, twist

v 1 capsize, overturn, tip over, upset

v 2 circle, gyrate, revolve, rotate, spin, turn

v 3 bob, heave, pitch, rock, sway, swing, toss

v 4 cant, careen, heel, incline, list, tilt

v 5 see: POUR *v* 1

roller *n* breaker, ripple, swell, wave, whitecap

rollick *v* caper, cavort, frisk, frolic, gambol, play, prance, romp, skip

romance *n* adultery, affair, cheating, dalliance, entanglement, fling, flirtation, fooling around, infatuation, intimacy, intrigue, liaison, love affair, playing around, rendezvous, tryst

v attract, court, encourage, flirt, invite, lure, pursue, solicit, tempt, woo

romantic *adj* 1 intimate, moving, tender, touching

adj 2 affectionate, amorous, attached, caring, devoted, enamored, fond, loving, tender

adj 3 amorous, ardent, aroused, carnal, earthy, erotic, fervent, fleshly, horny, hot, impassioned, lascivious, lecherous, lewd, licentious, lustful, passionate, provocative, randy, raunchy, sensual, sexual, sexy, sultry, titillated, torrid, turned on, voluptuous, wanton

n dreamer, idealist, utopian, visionary

Romeo *n* buck, Casanova, Don Juan, flirt, gallant, ladies' man, lecher, lover, philanderer, playboy, stud

romp *v* 1 carouse, celebrate, drink, frolic, make merry, party

v 2 caper, cavort, frisk, frolic, gambol, play, prance, rollick, skip

roof *n* ceiling

rookie *n* apprentice, beginner, disciple, freshman, intern, neophyte, newcomer, novice, novitiate, pupil, recruit, student, tenderfoot, trainee

room *n* 1 chance, freedom, opportunity

n 2 capacity, elbowroom, leeway, space

n 3 alcove, chamber, ward

n **4** apartment, dorm, housing, lodging, shelter, suite

v domicile, dwell, inhabit, live, occupy, reside, settle, stay

roomy *adj* ample, big, capacious, comfortable, commodious, open, spacious, vast, wide

root *n* **1** base, basis, bedrock, footing, foundation

n **2** birth, creation, fountain, genesis, origin, source

n **3** beginning, conception, cradle, derivation, fountainhead, inception, infancy, mother, origin, seed, source, stem

n **4** see: ESSENCE *n* 3

v **1** anchor, establish, plant

v **2** implant, plant, seed, sow, strew

rope *n* **1** bridle, check, cord, leash, restraint, tether

n **2** cable, cord, fiber, hemp, lanyard, line, strand, string, thread, twine, yarn

n **3** lasso

v clump, fasten, hitch, join, knot, lace, lash, link, loop, secure, tie, unite

roster *n* catalog, index, list, register, schedule

rostrum *n* dais, desk, lectern, podium, pulpit, soapbox, stage, stand

rosy *adj* **1** auspicious, bright, confident, favorable, hopeful, promising, sunny, utopian

adj **2** favorable, healthy

rot *n* **1** cancer, corruption, decay, evil, infection, malignancy, poison, toxin, venom

n **2** baloney, bilge, bosh, bull, bunk, drivel, fiddlesticks, foolishness, junk, malarkey, nonsense, nothing, poppycock, rubbish, schlock, silliness, trivia

v corrupt, crumble, decay, decompose, degenerate, deteriorate, disintegrate, perish, putrefy, smell, spoil, taint, wane, weaken, wither

rota *n* jury

rotate *v* **1** circle, gyrate, revolve, roll, spin, turn

v **2** alternate, change, cycle, lap, oscillate, shift, switch

rotation *n* **1** curl, loop, revolution, ring, roll, spin, spiral, turn, twirl, twist

n **2** alternation, circuit, circulation, gyration, revolution, round, sequence, spinning, succession, turn, whirl

rote *n* habit, mechanization, routine

rotten *adj* **1** dirty, disgusting, foul, lousy, nasty, putrid, sordid

adj **2** bad, decayed, putrid, rancid, sharp, sour, spoiled

adj **3** afoul, amiss, awry, bad, bum, improper, out of kilter, poor, unsatisfactory, wrong

adj **4** annoying, bad, difficult, disagreeable, displeasing, nasty, objectionable, offensive, sour, unhappy, unpleasant, upsetting

adj **5** decaying, fetid, foul, gamy, malodorous, musty, putrid, rancid, rank, reeking, smelly, sour, spoiled, stale, stinking, tainted

adj **6** base, corrupt, deadly, degenerate, depraved, deviant, evil, immoral, infamous, kinky, nefarious, perverse, putrid, ruthless, savage, vicious, villainous, wicked, wild

rotund *adj* **1** circular, global, globular, round, sphere-like, spherical

adj **2** chubby, chunky, corpulent, fat, fleshy, gross, heavy, hefty, meaty, obese, overweight, plump, portly, pudgy, stocky, stout

rough *adj* **1** approximate, crude, estimated, proximate, rounded

adj **2** basic, crude, plain, primitive, simple, undeveloped

adj **3** brief, crude, cursory, hasty, shallow, sketchy, superficial, uncritical

adj **4** crude, raw, rude, undressed, unfashioned, unfinished, unhewn, unpolished

adj **5** caustic, grating, guttural, harsh, hoarse, husky, rasping, raucous, strident

adj **6** bouncy, bumpy, craggy, irregular, jagged, jolting, rugged, scraggy, uneven, unsmooth

adj **7** coarse, crass, crude, flagrant, glaring, gross, obscene, shocking, uncouth, uncultured, unrefined

adj **8** mean, tough

adj **9** choppy, nasty, rainy, sloppy, wet

adj **10** improper, indecent, indelicate, lewd, malodorous, off-color, offensive, scurrilous, suggestive, unbecoming, unseemly, untoward

adj **11** arduous, demanding, difficult, formidable, hard, heavy, labored, laborious, rocky, rugged, serious, severe, strenuous, tough, trying, uphill

adj **12** bitter, brutal, cruel, fierce, hard, harsh, inclement, intemperate, pitiless, rigorous, rugged, severe, stern, strong, unkind, violent

roughneck *n* gorilla, hoodlum, hooligan, punk, rowdy, ruffian, thug, tough

round *adj* **1** circular, global, globular, rotund, sphere-like, spherical *adj* 2 circuitous, circular, deviate, diagonal, indirect, oblique, roundabout

n 1 barrage, burst, fusillade, shot, volley

n 2 arc, arch, bend, bow, coil, crook, curvature, curve, hook, spiral

n 3 alternation, circuit, circulation, gyration, revolution, rotation, sequence, spinning, succession, turn, whirl

v angle, arch, bend, bow, curve, flex, ply, tilt, tip, turn, twist, vault

roundabout *adj* circuitous, circular, deviate, diagonal, indirect, oblique

rounded *adj* 1 approximate, crude, estimated, proximate

adj 2 arched, bent, bowed, curved, curvilinear, flexed, unstraight

rouse *v* 1 arouse, awaken, challenge, excite, kindle, rally, stir, wake, waken

v 2 arouse, electrify, excite, fire, incite, inspire, spark, stimulate, tantalize, thrill, titillate, turn on, whet

v 3 arouse, awaken, excite, induce, instill, motivate, move, pique, prime, provoke, quicken, roust, spark, start, stimulate, titillate, urge

rousing *adj* 1 electric, exciting, exhilarating, provocative, stimulating, stirring

adj 2 see: LIVELY *adj* 8

roust *v* see: PROVOKE *v* 2

rout *n* debacle, defeat, disaster, downfall, overthrow, ruination, thrashing, trouncing, undoing, vanquishment

v see: THRASH *v* 1

route *n* 1 circuit, course, itinerary, journey, line, means, passage, path, road, trip, voyage, way

n 2 access, approach, artery, avenue, boulevard, channel, drag, highway, pass, path, promenade, road, roadway, strait, street, thoroughfare, trail, way

v 1 circulate, pass around, travel

v 2 conduct, control, develop, direct, drive, guide, lead, operate, pilot, shepherd, show, steer

v 3 address, channel, consign, dispatch, export, forward, mail, post, remit, send, ship, transmit, transport

routine *adj* 1 automated, automatic, habitual, mechanical

adj 2 accepted, accustomed, chronic, common, constant, continual, customary, daily, everyday, familiar, frequent, habitual, inured, often, recurring, regular, traditional, usual

adj 3 consistent, constant, continuing, endless, equable, established, even, invariable, reliable, same, serene, stable,

steady, unchanging, unfailing, unfluctuating, uniform, unvarying

adj 4 average, common, commonplace, daily, everyday, general, mundane, natural, normal, ordinary, plain, prevalent, regular, typical, unexceptional, unremarkable, usual, workaday

n 1 habit, mechanization, repetition, rote

n 2 habit, method, mores, procedure, system

n 3 method, methodology, practice, procedure, process, science, system, technique, technology

n 4 custom, fashion, formality, habit, manner, mores, observance, practice, tradition, usage, use, way, wont

rove *v* itinerate, meander, perambulate, promenade, ramble, range, roam, saunter, stray, stroll, traipse, travel, traverse, walk, wander

roving *adj* ambulatory, gypsy, itinerant, movable, nomadic, perambulatory, transient, vagrant, wandering, wayfaring

row *n* 1 caste, layer, ply, rank, stratum, tier

n 2 chain, course, lineup, order, progression, run, sequence, series, string, succession, train

n 3 see: QUARREL *n* 2

v see: QUARREL *v*

rowdy *adj* blatant, boisterous, clamorous, disturbing, loud, loudmouthed, noisy, obstreperous, raucous, tumultuous, vociferous

n gorilla, hoodlum, hooligan, punk, roughneck, ruffian, thug, tough

royal *adj* 1 aristocratic, blue-blooded, imperial, kingly, majestic, noble, regal, stately, well-bred

adj 2 see: GRAND *adj* 5

royalty *n* aristocracy, blue blood, cream, elite, gentry, nobility, upper class

rub *v* 1 chafe, irritate, scrape

v 2 buff, burnish, furbish, glaze, glimmer, gloss, polish, renovate, shine

v 3 bathe, clean, cleanse, clean up, dip, flush, immerse, launder, rinse, scour, scrape, scrub, shower, wash

v 4 apply, massage, spread

v 5 brush, clean, wipe

rubbish *n* 1 debris, fragment, hulk, remains, rubble, shell, trash, wreck, wreckage

n 2 crap, crud, debris, detritus, dirt, garbage, junk, litter, refuse, rubble, sweepings, trash, waste

n 3 baloney, bilge, bosh, bull, bunk, drivel, fiddlesticks, foolishness, junk, malarkey, nonsense, nothing, poppycock, rot, schlock, silliness, trivia

rubble *n* 1 debris, fragment, hulk, remains, rubbish, shell, trash, wreck, wreckage

n 2 crap, crud, debris, detritus, dirt, garbage, junk, litter, refuse, rubbish, sweepings, trash, waste

rubicund *adj* fit, hardy, healthy, robust, ruddy, sound, sturdy, well, wholesome

rubles *n* see: MONEY *n* 4

ruby *adj* cardinal, crimson, red, scarlet, vermilion

ruckus *n* 1 anarchy, chaos, commotion, confusion, disorder, disturbance, fracas, fray, outbreak, riot, storm, tempest

n 2 see: QUARREL *n* 2

ruddy *adj* 1 florid, flush, full-blooded, glowing, red, sanguine

adj 2 fit, hardy, healthy, robust, rubicund, sound, sturdy, well, wholesome

rude *adj* 1 clumsy, gauche, indiscreet, insensitive, tactless, thoughtless

adj 2 crude, raw, rough, undressed, unfashioned, unfinished, unhewn, unpolished

adj 3 audacious, bold, brash, brazen, cheeky, daring, disrespectful, forward, fresh, impertinent, impudent, insolent, irreverent, nervy, pert, sassy, saucy

adj 4 audacious, boorish, discourteous, disrespectful, ill-behaved, ill-bred, ill-mannered, impertinent, impolite, insolent, surly, uncalled for, uncivil, uncivilized, uncouth, uncultured, unpolished, unrefined

adj 5 see: BLUNT *adj* 1

rudeness *n* back talk, impudence, lip, sass

rudiment *n* basic, element, essential, fundamental, principle

rudimentary *adj* 1 aboriginal, ancient, early, former, original, prehistoric, primeval, primitive

adj 2 basic, dominant, elementary, first, foremost, fundamental, head, highest, leading, main, outstanding, paramount, preeminent, premier, primary, supreme, top

adj 3 beginning, embryonic, founding, incipient, initial, introductory, starting

adj 4 basic, early, elementary, embryonic, essential, fundamental, initial, intrinsic, original, underlying

rudiments *n* arguments, basis, cause, explanation, foundation, grounds, principle, rationale, reason, source

rue *n* 1 affinity, compassion, empathy, kindness, mercy, pity, sympathy, tenderness, understanding

n 2 affliction, anguish, care, catastrophe, despair, disaster, dole, grief, heartache, mishap, pain, regret, remorse, sickness, sorrow, woe

v bemoan, deplore, lament, regret

rueful *adj* dismal, doleful, gloomy, lamentable, melancholy, mournful, plaintive, regretful, regrettable, sorrowful, woeful

ruffian *n* gorilla, hoodlum, hooligan, punk, roughneck, rowdy, thug, tough

ruffle *v* 1 agitate, derange, disorder, disturb, fluster, rock, shake, sicken, unhinge, unsettle, upset

v 2 see: BEWILDER *v* 2

rug *n* carpet, mat, pad

rugged *adj* 1 bouncy, bumpy, craggy, irregular, jagged, jolting, rough, scraggy, uneven, unsmooth

adj 2 aggressive, dominant, durable, firm, forceful, hardy, hearty, mighty, powerful, robust, stalwart, stout, strong, sturdy, tenacious, tough

adj 3 bitter, brutal, cruel, fierce, hard, harsh, inclement, intemperate, pitiless, rigorous, rough, severe, stern, strong, unkind, violent

adj 4 see: HARD *adj* 5

ruin *n* 1 carnage, death, demise, fatality

n 2 collapse, downfall, failure, fall, overthrow, upset

n 3 destruction, downfall, infiltration, overthrow, subversion, upset

n 4 breakdown, catastrophe, crash, crisis, death, destruction, doom, failure

n 5 chaos, damage, destruction, devastation, disaster, disorder, harm, havoc, hurt, injury, loss, mayhem, ruination

v 1 bankrupt, break, bust, decay, do in, fold up

v 2 abuse, blemish, damage, hamper, harm, hurt, impair, injure, mar, obstruct, sabotage, scuttle, spoil, tarnish, vandalize

v 3 blow, blunder, botch, bungle, butcher, damage, err, foul up, goof, hash, hurt, jeopardize, jumble, mess up, queer, screw up

v 4 see: DEBASE *v* 2

v 5 see: DEMOLISH *v* 3

ruination *n* 1 chaos, damage, destruction, devastation, disaster, disorder, harm, havoc, hurt, injury, loss, mayhem, ruin

n 2 see: ROUT *n* 2

ruined *adj* bankrupt, broke, busted, destitute, dissolved, insolvent, out of business

ruinous *adj* 1 damaging, dangerous, deleterious, harmful, hurting, injurious, unhealthy *adj* 2 baneful, deadly, fatal, lethal, mortal, noxious, pernicious

adj 3 calamitous, cataclysmic, catastrophic, critical, crucial, devastating, disastrous, fatal, fateful, momentous, vital

rule *n* 1 flag, principle, standard

n 2 direction, directive, guideline, instruction, outline, policy

n 3 benchmark, criterion, gauge, measure, observation, standard, yardstick

n 4 administration, dominion, government, monarchy, power, regime, reign, sovereignty

n 5 average, mean, median, medium, middle, norm, par, standard

n 6 belief, canon, code, conviction, creed, doctrine, dogma, law, opinion, principle, tenet, theory

n 7 administration, administrators, authorities, bureaucracy, civil service, commission, department, direction, forces, government, management, ministry, officials, power, powers, rulers

n 8 announcement, aphorism, axiom, cliché, declaration, decree, dictum, edict, gospel, homily, maxim, moral, precept, pronouncement, saying, teaching, truism, truth, verity

n 9 see: AUTHORITY *n* 5

n 10 see: COMMAND *n* 3

v 1 control, govern, overrule, reign

v 2 bully, dominate, domineer, prevail

v 3 act, bear, behave, carry, comport, conduct

v 4 adjudicate, conclude, decide, determine, establish, resolve, settle, will

v 5 advise, authorize, command, decree, designate, dictate, direct, mandate, ordain

ruler *n* autocrat, chief, commander, despot, dictator, governor, head, king, leader, lord, master, monarch, potentate

rulers *n* administration, administrators, authorities, bureaucracy, civil service, commission, department, direction, forces, government, management, ministry, officials, power, powers

rules *n* conduct, course, guidelines, plan, policy, procedures, program, scheme

ruling *n* 1 act, law, legislation, measure, statute

n 2 adjudication, decision, decree, finding, judgment, sentence, verdict

n 3 adjudication, award, determination, judgment, opinion, sentence, verdict

n 4 see: COMMAND *n* 3

n 5 see: EVALUATION *n* 2

rumble *v* bark, gnarl, growl, snarl

n 1 bang, boom, clang, clap, crash, resound, roar, shake, thunder

n 2 gossip, grapevine, hearsay, murmur, report, rumor, scuttlebutt, story, talk, word

ruminate *v* see: PONDER *v*

rummage *v* 1 grub, search, uncover

v 2 disarray, dislocate, disorder, disorganize, disrupt, disturb, interfere, interrupt, jumble, mess, mix up, muss, shuffle, sift through, unsettle

rumor *n* gossip, grapevine, hearsay, murmur, report, rumble, scuttlebutt, story, talk, word

rump *n* ass, backside, base, behind, bottom, bucket, buns, butt, buttocks, derrière, end, fanny, hindquarters, posterior, seat, stub, stump, tip, tush

rumple *v* crease, fold, muss, wrinkle

n crease, fold, wrinkle

run *n* 1 current, drift, pattern, series, succession, tendency, trend

n 2 bout, competition, conflict, contest, event, game, marathon, match, meet, meeting, race, regatta, round robin, tournament, tourney

n 3 see: SERIES *n* 1, 2

v 1 dart, gallop, jog, trot

v 2 flow, gush, rush, stream

v 3 extend, go, range, span, vary

v 4 act, function, go, work

v 5 dissolve, flux, fuse, melt, thaw

v 6 dash, gallop, jog, race, speed, sprint

v 7 dribble, drip, drop, leak, ooze, seep, trickle

v 8 carry on, conduct, direct, keep, manage, operate, ordain, oversee, pilot

v 9 abscond, bolt, break, depart, elude, escape, flee, fly, hightail it, lose, sneak away, split

runaround *n* avoidance, deceit, diversion, escape, evasion

runaway *n* fugitive, outlaw

run-down *adj* 1 faded, frayed, poor, shabby, tattered, threadbare, worn

adj 2 crumbled, decaying, decrepit, dilapidated

adj 3 see: WEARY *adj* 1

run-in *n* see: CLASH *n* 2

runner *n* carrier, courier, delivery person, envoy, messenger

running *adj* 1 active, alive, functioning, live, operative, working *adj* 2 casual, coming along, developing, easy, effortless, flowing, fluent, smooth

n administration, care, charge, conduct, handling, intendance, management, supervision

rapture *n* chink, cleft, crack, crevice, division, fissure, rent, rift, split

v 1 break, burst, erupt, explode, fragment, shatter, smash, smatter, splinter

v 2 see: SEPARATE *v* 7

rural *adj* bucolic, country, garden, outland, pastoral, peaceful, provincial, rustic, suburban, wooded

ruse *n* 1 make-believe, pretense, sham, show

n 2 alibi, con, deception, lie, pretext, subterfuge, trick

n 3 alibi, defense, excuse, explanation, justification, plea, pretext, rationalization

n 4 attraction, bait, come-on, decoy, enticement, lure, magnet, seduction, snare, temptation, trap, wile

n 5 see: MANEUVER *n* 2

rush *n* 1 ecstasy, euphoria

n 2 gush, surge, swell, wave

n 3 change, current, drift, flow, flux, gush, motion, movement, stream, tide, transition

n 4 alacrity, dispatch, expedition, haste, hastiness, hurry, hustle, precipitance, precipitation, quickness, rustle, speed, swiftness

v 1 flow, gush, stream

v 2 accelerate, expedite, hasten, hurry, quicken, shake up, speed, step up

v 3 barrel, bullet, expedite, fly, hasten, hurry, hustle, rocket, speed, whisk, zip

rushing *adj* abrupt, hasty, headlong, hurried, impetuous, impulsive, precipitant, precipitate, quick, rapid, rash, reckless, sudden

rust *v* corrode, deteriorate, eat, erode, gnaw, oxidize, wear

rustic *adj* bucolic, country, garden, outland, pastoral, peaceful, provincial, rural, suburban, wooded

n cowboy, pioneer, yokel

rustle *n* alacrity, dispatch, expedition, haste, hastiness, hurry, hustle, precipitance, precipitation, quickness, rush, speed, swiftness

rusty *adj* deficient, inept, out of practice, stale, unpracticed, unprepared

rut *n* 1 depression, doldrums

n 2 canal, channel, conduit, crevice, curb, cut, ditch, duct, furrow, gorge, groove, gully, gutter, passageway, ravine, trench, trough

ruthless *adj* 1 base, corrupt, deadly, degenerate, depraved, deviant, evil, immoral, infamous, kinky, nefarious, perverse, putrid, rotten, savage, vicious, villainous, wicked, wild

adj 2 austere, brutal, callous, cold-blooded, compassionless, cruel, ferocious, fierce, hardened, hard-hearted, heartless, indifferent, inhuman, inhumane, malicious, mean, merciless, nasty, obdurate, pitiless, savage, spiteful, stony, tough, uncaring, unemotional, unfeeling, unkind, unmerciful, unpitying, unrelenting, unsympathetic, vicious

adj 3 see: RESTRICTIVE *adj*

S

sabbatical *n* day off, furlough, holiday, leave, respite, time off, vacation

saber *n* blade, cutlass, dagger, knife, pocketknife, rapier, scimitar, switchblade, sword

sable *adj* black, ebony

sabotage *n* vandalism

v abuse, blemish, damage, hamper, harm, hurt, impair, injure, mar, obstruct, ruin, scuttle, spoil, tarnish, vandalize

sack *v* 1 assault, attack, force, pillage, rape, violate

v 2 ax, boot, bounce, can, discharge, dismiss, drop, fire, impeach, let go, terminate

n 1 abuse, assault, attack, violation

n 2 bag, baggage, case, equipment, gear, grip, kit, luggage, pack, pouch, purse, suitcase, valise, wallet

v deflower, desecrate, despoil, devastate, devour, loot, maraud, pillage, plunder, ravage, scourge, spoil, strip, violate

sacred *adj* 1 consecrated, intact, inviolable, inviolate, protected, pure, sacrosanct

adj 2 blessed, celestial, consecrated, divine, godly, hallowed, holy, pure, sanctified, spiritual

adj 3 biblical

sacrifice *n* assessment, cost, duty, expense, fee, impost, levy, offering, penalty, price, tariff, tax, toll, trade-off

v abstain, cast, decline, drop, eschew, forbear, forfeit, forgo, give up, lose, pass, reject, renounce, surrender, turn down, waive

sacrilege *n* blasphemy, desecration, heresy, impiety, irreverence, violation

sacrilegious *adj* blasphemous, disrespectful, heretical, irreverent

sacrosanct *adj* consecrated, intact, inviolable, inviolate, pure, sacred

sad *adj* 1 bittersweet, maudlin, poignant, sentimental, sorrowful

adj 2 affecting, heartbreaking, impressive, moving, poignant, touching

adj 3 dour, firm, forbidding, grim, serious, severe, sour, stern, unpleasant

adj 4 affecting, deplorable, lamentable, miserable, paltry, pathetic, pitiable, pitiful, poor, unfortunate, woeful, wretched

adj 5 black, bleak, blue, cheerless, dejected, depressed, despondent, discouraging, disheartening, distressing, down, forlorn, gloomy, hopeless, joyless, melancholy, moody, mournful, oppressive, prostrate, somber, sorry, unhappy

sadden *v* 1 distress, disturb, move, rend, wring

v 2 burden, deject, depress, dishearten, grieve, hurt, lament, weigh down, wound

saddle *v* 1 bother, burden, encroach, impose, intrude

v 2 burden, encumber, hamper, load, oppress, overdo, overload, strain, tax

sadness *n* 1 distress, grief, melancholy, sorrow, suffering

n 2 see: PAIN *n* 4

safari *n* see: JOURNEY *n* 2

safe *adj* 1 able, solvent, sound

adj 2 exempt, guarded, immune, protected, secure

adj 3 benign, harmless, innocent, innocuous, inoffensive, mild, naive, pure, unoffending, unoffensive

adj 4 calculating, careful, cautious, circumspect, considerate, discreet, gingerly, guarded, heedful, judicious, provident, prudent, restrained, reticent, shrewd, wary

adj 5 sound, undamaged, unharmed, unhurt

adj 6 impregnable, invulnerable, protected, safeguarded, secure

adj 7 accurate, authentic, believable, certain, convincing, credible, dependable, faithful, real, reliable, sure, tenable, true, trustworthy, trusty

n chest, coffer, strongbox, treasury, vault

safeguard *n* 1 caution, precaution, protection

n 2 exemption, grant, patent, permission

n 3 anticipation, caution, deterrent, precaution, preclusion, preparation, prevention

v 1 conserve, economize, husband, store

v 2 defend, guard, oversee, patrol, police, protect, regulate, watch

v 3 conceal, harbor, hide, house, keep, protect, shelter, shield

v 4 bulwark, cover, defend, fend, fortify, guard, hide, protect, screen, secure, shield

safeguarded *adj* impregnable, invulnerable, protected, safe, secure

safekeeping *n* care, charge, custody

safety *n* 1 assurance, exemption, guarantee, immunity, impunity, protection, release, security

n 2 see: SANCTUARY *n* 2

saffron *adj* canary, lemon, yellow

sag *v* 1 droop

v 2 drop off, fall away, slide, slip, slump

v 3 depress, droop, flop, let down, lower, mire, sink, wallow

n see: FALL *n* 3

saga *n* 1 adventure, escapade, story

n 2 chronicle, epic, legend, story, tale

sagacious *adj* 1 alert, astute, brainy, bright, brilliant, clever, discerning, discriminating, educated, insightful, intellectual, intelligent, knowing, knowledgeable, perceptive, quick, sage, sharp, smart, swift

adj 2 acute, alert, astute, cagey, canny, clever, cunning, deft, keen, knowing, penetrating, perceptive, piercing, quick, quick-sighted, quick-witted, receptive, responsive, savvy, sensitive, sharp, sharp-witted, shrewd, slick, smart, street-smart, wise

sagacity *n* acumen, astuteness, awareness, cleverness, discernment, discrimination, insight, intellect, intuition, keenness, perception, sensitivity, shrewdness, understanding, wit

sage *adj* 1 enlightened, judgmatical, judicious, just, lucid, prudent, rational, sane, sapient, sensible, wise

adj 2 see: INTELLIGENT *adj* 4

n academician, egghead, highbrow, intellectual, philosopher, pundit, researcher, savant, scholar, thinker, wise man

sail *v* 1 cross, cruise, fly, traverse, voyage

v 2 coast, drift, float, fly, glide, slide, soar

v 3 ascend, flit, flutter, fly, soar, sweep, wing

v 4 coast, cruise, explore, go, journey, migrate, proceed, survey, tour, travel, trek, voyage

sailboat *n* craft, cruiser, freighter, frigate, ketch, liner, ocean liner, schooner, ship, steamship, vessel, yacht

sailor *n* mariner, mate, navy man, salt, seafarer, seaman, yachtsman

saint *n* angel, idol, model, prince

sake *n* 1 aim, goal, mission, motive, objective, purpose, reason, target, task

n 2 account, advantage, behalf, benefit, betterment, gain, good, happiness, interest, prosperity, welfare, well-being

salable *adj* commercial, marketable, vendible, wanted

salary *n* bill, bonus, charge, commission, compensation, consideration, earnings, fee, gross, income, pay, revenue, stipend, wage

sale *n* 1 contract, order, requisition

n 2 deal, exchange, trade, transaction, transfer

n 3 bargain, buy, deal, discount, promotion, reduction, special, steal

n 4 auction

sales *n* aggregate, all, entirety, gross, revenue, sum, sum total, total, totality, whole

salesman *n* clerk, representative, salesperson, saleswoman, shopkeeper, vendor

salesmanship *n* advertisement, championship, praise, promotion

salesperson *n* clerk, representative, salesman, saleswoman, shopkeeper, vendor

saleswoman *n* clerk, representative, salesman, salesperson, shopkeeper, vendor

salient *adj* 1 chief, crucial, vital

adj 2 arresting, astonishing, astounding, conspicuous, eye-catching, marked, noticeable, obvious, pointed, prominent, sensational, striking, stunning

sallow *adj* ashen, ashy, blanched, colorless, pale, pallid, sickly, sooty, wan, waxen, yellow

sally *n* 1 expedition, foray, sortie

n 2 see: JOURNEY *n* 2

v dash

salmon *adj* apricot, orange, tangerine

salon *n* family room, foyer, parlor

saloon *n* bar, barroom, cocktail lounge, den, dive, dump, gin mill, hangout, haunt, joint, lounge, pub, rathskeller, tavern, watering hole

salt *v* color, enhance, flavor, imbue, infuse, season, spice

n mariner, mate, navy man, sailor, seafarer, seaman, yachtsman

salty *adj* 1 brackish, briny, foul, nasty, stagnant, undrinkable

adj 2 caustic, coarse, cutting, obscene, scathing, scorching, sharp, spicy, trenchant, vulgar, witty

salutary *adj* beneficial, good, helpful, useful

salutation *n* 1 greeting, hospitality, welcome

n 2 commemoration, drink, toast

salutations *n* greetings, regards, respects, salvo

salute *n* address, bow, greeting, honor, nod, recognition

v 1 address, call to, embrace, greet, hail, meet, summon, welcome

v 2 see: LAUD *v* 1, 2

v 3 see: RECOGNIZE *v* 5

salvage *v* recover, recycle, rescue, restore, save

salvation *n* deliverer, liberator, messiah, savior

salve *n* 1 analgesic, balm, emollient

n 2 lube, lubrication, moistener, oil, ointment

v anoint

salvo *n* greetings, regards, respects

same *adj* 1 exact, identical, precise, very

adj 2 duplicate, equal, equivalent, identical, substitute, synonymous, tantamount

adj 3 consistent, constant, continuing, endless, equable, established, even, invariable, reliable, routine, serene, stable, steady, unchanging, unfailing, unfluctuating, uniform, unvarying

adj 4 see: ALIKE *adj*

sample *n* 1 morsel, taste, tidbit

n 2 flavor, palate, savor, spice, tang, taste

n 3 demo, example, first, forerunner, model, prototype, test

n 4 case, case history, clarification, example, explanation, illumination, illustration, instance, representative, sampling, specimen

n 5 see: SECTION *n* 4

v 1 experience, taste

v 2 bibulate, booze, consume, drink, gulp, guzzle, imbibe, nip, partake, polish off, put away, put down, savor, sip, suck, swig, swill, taste

sampling *n* case, case history, clarification, explanation, example, illumination, illustration, instance, representative, sample, specimen

sanctified *adj* blessed, celestial, consecrated, divine, godly, hallowed, holy, pure, sacred, spiritual

sanctify *v* 1 absolve, purify

v 2 anoint, baptize, bless, consecrate, dedicate, devote, enshrine, exalt, hallow

sanctimonious *adj* devout, godly, holy, pious, prayerful, religious

sanction *n* 1 approval, authorization, consent, leave, permission

n 2 auspices, authorization, backing,

command, confirmation, endorsement, fiat, patronage, sponsorship, support

v 1 assure, certify, contract, endorse, guarantee, pledge, underwrite, vouch, warrant

v 2 approve, authorize, decree, enact, legalize, legislate, ordain, pass

v 3 advocate, back, champion, endorse, guarantee, promote, side, support, uphold

v 4 accredit, authorize, certify, commission, empower, enable, entitle, facilitate, invest, license, permit, validate

v 5 accept, approbate, approve, authorize, certify, condone, confirm, countenance, endorse, favor, pass, ratify, validate

v 6 attest, authenticate, certify, confirm, corroborate, justify, notarize, prove, ratify, substantiate, support, validate, verify, vouch, witness

sanctity *n* devotion, reverence, worship

sanctuary *n* 1 basilica, cathedral, chapel, church, house of God, mosque, synagogue, tabernacle, temple

n 2 asylum, cover, harbor, haven, oasis, port, preserve, protection, refuge, reserve, retreat, safety, seaport, security, shelter

sanctum *n* den

sand *v* file, grate, grind, grit

sandal *n* boot, brogan, chukka, footwear, moccasin, shoe, slipper, thong

sandbank *n* reef, sandbar, shallow, shelf, shoal

sandbar *n* reef, sandbank, shallow, shelf, shoal

sandy *adj* coarse, grainy, granular, gritty

sane *adj* 1 ethical, lucid, moral, rational, responsible, stable

adj 2 astute, consequent, intelligent, knowing, logical, perceptive, rational, reasonable, sensible, shrewd, sober, sound, wise

adj 3 see: WISE *adj* 4

saneness *n* lucidity, mind, rationality, reason, sanity, sense, soundness, wit

sanguine *adj* 1 assured, confident, poised, secure, self-assured, self-confident

adj 2 glowing, florid, flush, full-blooded, red

adj 3 auspicious, cheerful, confident, encouraging, hopeful, optimistic, promising, upbeat

sanitary *adj* clean, healthy, hygienic, immaculate, sterile

sanity *n* lucidity, mind, rationality, reason, saneness, sense, soundness, wit

sap *n* 1 blood, plasma, serum

n 2 fluid, juice, liquid, secretion, solution

v cripple, debilitate, disable, drain, enfeeble, exhaust, undermine, weaken

sapient *adj* enlightened, judgmatical, judicious, just, lucid, prudent, rational, sage, sane, sensible, wise

sapling *n* bush, grass, hedge, plant, shrub, tree, vegetation, vine, weed

sapphire *adj* aqua, azure, blue, cobalt, indigo, navy, Prussian, turquoise

sarcasm *n* 1 aspersion, contempt, derision, disdain, irony, mockery, ridicule, satire, scorn

n 2 see: INSULT *n*

sarcastic *adj* 1 derogatory, disparaging, insulting, malicious, nasty, snide

adj 2 acerbic, acrid, biting, bitter, caustic, corrosive, critical

adj 3 comical, facetious, funny, humorous, jesting, jocular, joking, kidding, witty

adj 4 contemptuous, cynical, derisive, ironic, mocking, sardonic, scornful, skeptical, wry

adj 5 abrupt, bluff, blunt, brash, brusque, cheeky, crusty, curt, flip, flippant, gruff, harsh, impertinent, impudent, irritable, nasty, quick, rude, sassy, short, snippy, snotty, surly, testy, wisenheimer

sardonic *adj* contemptuous, cynical, derisive, ironic, mocking, sarcastic, scornful, skeptical, wry

sass *n* 1 back talk, impudence, rudeness

n 2 arrogance, assurance, audacity, boldness, brashness, brass, cheek, chutzpah, condescension, confidence, crust, effrontery, face, gall, haughtiness, insolence, nerve, patronage, presumption, ridicule, stamina, temerity

sassy *adj* 1 audacious, bold, brash, brazen, cheeky, daring, disrespectful, forward, fresh, impertinent, impudent, insolent, irreverent, nervy, pert, rude, saucy

adj 2 see: BLUNT *adj* 1

Satan *n* brute, demon, devil, fiend, rogue, villain, wretch

sated *adj* filled, full, quenched, satisfied, saturated

satellite *n* dependent, follower, sycophant

satiate *v* 1 fill, glut, gorge, overeat, pig out, stuff, surfeit

v 2 abate, allay, assuage, mitigate, moderate, quench

v 3 allay, appease, assuage, balm, becalm, calm, compose, conciliate, ease, lull, mollify, pacify, placate, propitiate, quell, quiet, reconcile, settle, soften, soothe, still, sweeten, tranquilize

satiny *adj* cottony, silky, slippery, smooth, soft, supple, velvety

satire *n* 1 aspersion, contempt, derision, disdain, irony, mockery, ridicule, scorn

n 2 buffoonery, burlesque, caricature, comedy, farce, humor, imitation, joke, lampoon, mockery, parody, spoof, take-off, travesty

satisfaction *n* 1 delight, joy, pleasure

n 2 accomplishment, achievement, arrival, attainment, completion, fruition, fulfillment, realization, success, triumph, victory

satisfactorily *adv* 1 acceptably, adequately, amply, appropriately, correctly, properly, right, suitably, well

adv 2 adequately, amply, enough, equitably, fairly, justly, moderately, passably, rather, tolerably

satisfactory *adj* 1 acceptable, adequate, competent, decent, enough, fair, good, mediocre, passable, reasonable, respectable, sufficient, tolerable

adj 2 cogent, compelling, convincing, effective, forceful, influential, persuasive, revealing, satisfying, solid, sound, telling, valid

satisfied *adj* filled, full, quenched, sated, saturated

satisfy *v* 1 complete, fulfill, redeem

v 2 abate, allay, assuage, mitigate, moderate, quench, satiate

v 3 answer, do, fulfill, meet, qualify, suffice, work

v 4 achieve, answer, execute, fill, finish, fulfill, meet, realize

v 5 appease, comfort, comply, content, delight, elate, gratify, please, relieve, suit

v 6 clear, clear off, discharge, liquidate, pay up, repay, settle, square

v 7 accommodate, baby, cater, coddle, gratify, humor, indulge, overindulge, pamper, pander, spoil

satisfying *adj* 1 agreeable, gratifying, pleasing

adj 2 cogent, compelling, convincing, effective, forceful, influential, persuasive, revealing, satisfactory, solid, sound, telling, valid

saturate *v* 1 imbue, impregnate, permeate, wet

v 2 deluge, douse, drench, drown, dunk, flood, inundate, irrigate, overload, slosh, soak, sop, souse, swamp, swill, tax, wet

saturated *adj* 1 filled, full, quenched, sated

adj 2 drenched, dripping, full, immersed, inundated, soaked, soaking, sodden, sopping, waterlogged, wet

saucer *n* dish, plate

saucy *adj* see: RUDE *adj* 3

saunter *v* 1 amble, hike, journey, march, pace, parade, plod, step, stride, stroll, strut, tramp, tread, trek, walk

v 2 itinerate, meander, perambulate, promenade, ramble, range, roam, rove, stray, stroll, traipse, travel, traverse, walk, wander

sauterne *n* burgundy, chablis, champagne, chianti, claret, port, sherry, wine

savage *adj* 1 rabid, untamed, vicious, violent, wild

adj 2 barbarian, barbaric, uncivil, uncivilized, uncultivated, wild

adj 3 angry, ferocious, fierce, furious, heated, intense, severe, terrible, vehement, vicious, violent

adj 4 austere, brutal, callous, coldblooded, compassionless, cruel, ferocious, fierce, hardened, hardhearted, heartless, indifferent, inhuman, inhumane, malicious, mean, merciless, nasty, obdurate, pitiless, ruthless, spiteful, stony, tough, uncaring, unemotional, unfeeling, unkind, unmerciful, unpitying, unrelenting, unsympathetic, vicious

adj 5 see: VICIOUS *adj* 2, 3, 4

n aborigine, barbarian, native, primitive

savant *n* academician, egghead, highbrow, intellectual, philosopher, pundit, researcher, sage, scholar, thinker, wise man

save *prep* aside from, barring, except, excluding, unless

v 1 economize, scrape, scrimp, skimp

v 2 conserve, maintain, preserve, protect

v 3 recover, recycle, rescue, salvage

v 4 buy, convert, ransom, reclaim, redeem

v 5 accumulate, bank, deposit, hoard, squirrel away, stockpile, store

v 6 deliver, free, liberate, release, rescue

v 7 bank, hoard, lay aside, lay away, lay by, lay in, lay up, put by, salt away, spare

v 8 accrue, accumulate, acquire, amass, assemble, collect, garner, gather, grow, hoard, squirrel, stash, stockpile, store up

saving *n* deliverance, extrication, freeing, recovery, rescue

savings *n* account, budget, capital, cash, fund, money, stock

savior *n* deliverer, liberator, messiah, rescuer, salvation

savoir-faire *n* 1 consideration, diplomacy,

discretion, poise, regard, tact, tactfulness, thoughtfulness

n 2 aplomb, assurance, confidence, esteem, nerve, poise, presence, self-assurance, self-confidence

savor *n* 1 flavor, palate, sample, spice, tang, taste

n 2 see: PASSION *n* 7

v 1 crave, like, relish, taste

v 2 imply, resemble, smack, smell, suggest, taste

v 3 admire, appreciate, cherish, delight, enjoy, relish

v 4 bask, delight, enjoy, like, loaf, luxuriate, relax, relish, rest, wallow

v 5 see: DRINK *v* 2

savory *adj* 1 juicy, moist, succulent, tender

adj 2 appetizing, delectable, delicious, exquisite, luscious, palatable, sweet, tasty

savvy *n* 1 diplomacy, discretion, finesse, skill, subtlety, tact

n 2 see: SKILL *n* 2, 3

adj see: QUICK *adj* 5

v see: UNDERSTAND *v* 6

saw *v* see: CUT *v* 7

say *n* 1 expression, opinion, say-so, voice

n 2 ballot, choice, franchise, option, preference, selection, vote

v 1 allege, assert, avow, claim, maintain, state

v 2 add, comment, declare, note, remark, state

v 3 convey, express, hint, impart, imply, indicate, purport, suggest

v 4 affirm, attest, avow, contend, promise, swear, vouch, warrant

v 5 see: VERBALIZE *v* 2

saying *n* 1 expression, idiom, locution, name, phrase, term, word, wording

n 2 cliché, diction, expression, parlance, phrase, slogan, style, term, wording

n 3 announcement, aphorism, axiom, cliché, declaration, decree, dictum, edict, gospel, homily, maxim, moral, precept, pronouncement, rule, teaching, truism, truth, verity

n 4 adage, axiom, byword, cliché, dictum, maxim, motto, proverb, slogan, talk

sayonara *n* adieu, adios, aloha, *arrivederci*, *auf Wiedersehen*, au revoir, bon voyage, bye, cheerio, *ciao*, farewell, goodbye, good day, *shalom*, so long

say-so *n* expression, opinion, voice

scads *n* 1 fortune, heap, loads

n 2 droves, loads, lots, many, multitudes, slew

scalawag *n* rascal, scamp

scalding *adj* baking, blistering, boiling, broiling, burning, fiery, hot, scorching, sizzling, sultry, sweltering, torrid

scale *n* 1 calibration

n 2 hierarchy

n 3 coating, covering, skin

v 1 adjust, convert, regulate

v 2 ascend, climb, escalate, intensify, mount, surmount

v 3 flay, skin, strip

scam *n* con, crime, graft, hustle, racket, rip-off, scheme, sting, swindle

scamp *n* rapscallion, rascal, scalawag

scamper *v* dart, dash, hasten, scoot, scurry, sprint

scan *v* 1 examine, inspect, observe

v 2 browse, glance at, look through, peruse, skim

v 3 see: PROBE *v* 5

scandal *n* 1 corruption, crime, disgrace, exposé, outrage

n 2 censure, contempt, discredit, disfavor, disgrace, dishonor, disparagement, disrepute, humiliation, infamy, shame

scandalize *v* 1 amaze, daze, electrify, horrify, offend, outrage, overwhelm, shock, stun

v 2 befoul, besmirch, blacken, darken, defame, disparage, injure, libel, malign, revile, slander, slur, smear, soil, tear down, traduce

scandalous *adj* 1 despicable, infamous, notorious, offensive, shady, unsavory, villainous

adj 2 atrocious, awful, crying, desperate, disgraceful, ghastly, grizzly, heinous, monstrous, notorious, odious, offensive, outrageous, shocking, tasteless, wicked

adj 3 see: VULGAR *adj* 2

scant *adj* 1 few, lacking, limited, nonabundant, not many, short, sparse

adj 2 deficient, failing, inadequate, inferior, insufficient, scarce, scrimpy, short, shy, wanting

adj 3 bare, deficient, few, inadequate, inferior, insufficient, little, meager, paltry, petty, poor, scanty, skimpy, spare, sparse

adj 4 imperceptible, imponderable, inappreciable, indiscernible, insensible, intangible, invisible, minute, unapparent, unobservable, weak

scanty *adj* see: MEAGER *adj* 2

scar *n* blemish, defect, failing, fault, flaw, imperfection, shortcoming, weakness

scarce *adv* a tad, barely, hardly, just about, least, minimally, not much, not quite, scarcely

adj 1 few, infrequent, isolated, occasional, rare, seldom, sporadic, uncommon, unusual

adj 2 deficient, failing, inadequate, inferior, insufficient, scant, scrimpy, short, shy, wanting

scarcely *adv* a tad, barely, hardly, just about, least, minimally, not much, not quite, scarce

scarcity *n* 1 deficiency, deprivation, destitution, inadequacy, indigence, lack, need, poverty, privation, want

n 2 dearth, deficiency, deficit, drought, famine, lack, rarity, shortage, sparseness, undersupply, want

scare *v* 1 appall, daunt, discourage, dismay, horrify, panic, petrify, shock, terrify, unnerve

v 2 abash, alarm, awe, cow, daunt, frighten, horrify, intimidate, panic, shock, spook, startle, terrify, terrorize, unnerve

n fright, horror, shock, start, terror

scared *adj* afraid, aghast, anxious, apprehensive, concerned, discerning, fearful, frightened, nervous, paranoid, scary, terrified, worried

scarf *n* bandanna, mantilla, muffler, shawl

scarlet *adj* cardinal, crimson, red, ruby, vermilion

scary *adj* 1 frightening, forbidding, hairy, spooky

adj 2 afraid, aghast, anxious, apprehensive, concerned, discerning, fearful, frightened, nervous, paranoid, scared, terrified, worried

adj 3 appalling, awful, dire, dreadful, fearful, formidable, frightening, frightful, ghastly, horrendous, horrible, offensive, ominous, portentous shocking, spooky, terrible, terrifying, unpleasant

scathing *adj* caustic, coarse, cutting, obscene, salty, scorching, sharp, spicy, trenchant, vulgar, witty

scatter *v* 1 drop, litter

v 2 dispel, disperse, disseminate, dissipate, strew

v 3 disband, disperse, dissipate, dissociate, dissolve, separate

v 4 broadcast, disseminate, dissipate, distribute, sow, spread, strew, transmit

scatterbrained *adj* capricious, dizzy, flighty, frivolous, giddy, irresponsible, silly

scene *n* 1 arena, locale, site, theater

n 2 fight, incident, outbreak, spectacle, tantrum

n 3 landscape, outlook, scenery, sight, view, vista

n 4 amphitheater, arena, bowl, coliseum, dome, stadium

n 5 circumstance, episode, event, happening, incident, occasion, occurrence, thing

n 6 area, locale, location, locus, place, point, property, site, spot

n 7 backdrop, curtain, environment, scenery, set, setting, stage set, stage setting, surroundings

scenery *n* 1 landscape, outlook, scene, sight, view, vista

n 2 backdrop, curtain, environment, scene, set, setting, stage set, stage setting, surroundings

scent *n* 1 aroma, odor, smell

n 2 aroma, balm, bouquet, fragrance, incense, perfume, spice

v 1 perfume

v 2 perceive, smell, sniff

scepter *n* baton, rod, staff, wand

schedule *n* 1 catalog, index, list, roster

n 2 agenda, appointments, calendar, itinerary, plan

n 3 appointment, booking, date, engagement, listing

n 4 itinerary

v arrange, bespeak, book, engage, organize, plan, program, reserve, slate

scheme *n* 1 blueprint, design, game plan, plan, project, strategy

n 2 cabal, collusion, conspiracy, intrigue, junta, machination, plot, secret

n 3 expression, formula, methodology, plan, procedure, recipe, system, theorem

n 4 conduct, course, guidelines, plan, policy, procedures, program

n 5 con, crime, graft, hustle, racket, rip-off, scam, sting, swindle

n 6 see: MANEUVER *n* 2

v 1 brew, concoct, construe, contrive, create, devise, engineer, fabricate, formulate, hatch, invent, make up, plot

v 2 cogitate, collude, connive, conspire, contrive, devise, frame, intrigue, machinate, maneuver, orchestrate, plot

schemer *n* architect, designer, draftsperson, engineer, inventor, manager, operator, plotter, surveyor

scheming *adj* see: EVIL *adj* 4

schlemiel *n* blockhead, boor, clod, creep, cretin, dimwit, dolt, dope, dullard, dumbbell, dummy, dunce, fool, goof, idiot, imbecile, jerk, nerd, nincompoop, numskull, oaf, pain, schmuck, simpleton, stooge, turkey

schlock *n* see: NONSENSE *n* 2

schmuck *n* 1 blockhead, boor, clod, creep, cretin, dimwit, dolt, dope, dullard, dumbbell, dummy, dunce, fool, goof, idiot, imbecile, jerk, nerd, nincompoop, numskull, oaf, pain, schlemiel, simpleton, stooge, turkey

n 2 adversary, antagonist, naysayer, obstructionist, shnook

scholar *n* 1 coed, collegian, pupil, schoolmate, student, undergraduate

n 2 academician, egghead, highbrow, intellectual, philosopher, pundit, researcher, sage, savant, thinker, wise man

scholarly *adj* academic, educated, educational, erudite, intellectual, learned, literary, literate, pedantic, scholastic, well-read

scholarship *n* 1 award, bequest, endowment, gift, grant

n 2 education, instruction, learning, research, schooling, study

scholastic *adj* 1 academic, educational, enlightening, eye-opening, illuminating, informative, instructive

adj 2 academic, educated, educational, erudite, intellectual, learned, literary, literate, pedantic, scholarly, well-read

school *n* 1 academy, college, institute, lyceum, seminary, university

n 2 band, cabal, camp, circle, clan, clique, coterie, coven, cult, faction, family, gang, group, mob, ring, sect, tribe

v coach, communicate, condition, convey, cultivate, develop, discipline, drill, edify, educate, enlighten, exercise, explain, groom, imbue, impart, implant, improve, inculcate, indoctrinate, inform, infuse, inseminate, inspire, instill, instruct, perfect, practice, prepare, ready, teach, train, tutor

schooled *adj* accomplished, experienced, proficient, trained, versed

schooling *n* 1 education, instruction, learning, research, scholarship, study

n 2 see: EXPERIENCE *n* 4

schoolmate *n* coed, collegian, pupil, scholar, student, undergraduate

schooner *n* craft, cruiser, freighter, frigate, ketch, liner, ocean liner, sailboat, ship, steamship, vessel, yacht

schtick *n* see: TRADE *n* 3

science *n* 1 data, discipline, facts, information, knowledge, lore, news, wisdom

n 2 method, methodology, practice, procedure, process, routine, system, technique, technology

scientific *adj* clinical, detached, impersonal, systematic, technical

scimitar *n* blade, cutlass, dagger, knife,

pocketknife, rapier, saber, switchblade, sword

scintillate *v* excite, flash, gleam, glimmer, glint, glisten, glitter, shimmer, shine, sparkle, twinkle

scintillating *adj* 1 brilliant, clever, dazzling, good, irrepressible, smart, sparkling, sprightly, witty

adj 2 see: LIVELY *adj* 8

scion *n* child, descendant, heir, progeny

scoff *v* belittle, deride, flaunt, jab, jeer, jest, mock, quip, razz, ridicule, scorn, sneer, taunt, tease

scofflaw *n* see: CRIMINAL *n* 2

scold *v* 1 berate, lambaste, rebuke

v 2 berate, carp, cavil, criticize, find fault, flay, fuss, henpeck, nag, nit-pick, nudge, peck, quibble

v 3 admonish, berate, blame, censure, chide, condemn, disapprove, lay into, punish, rebuke, reprimand, reproach, reprove, warn

v 4 bawl out, bellow, berate, chew out, mock, rail, rant, rave, revile, roar, tell off, tongue-lash, upbraid, yell

scolding *n* see: REPRIMAND *n*

scoop *n* 1 data, details, dope, facts, information

n 2 cut, gouge

n 3 bucket, ladle, shovel

v burrow, dig, excavate, gouge, mine, shovel, unearth

scoot *v* dart, dash, hasten, scamper, scurry, sprint

scope *n* 1 degree, extent, intensity, measure

n 2 breadth, depth, dimensions, range, span, width

n 3 boundary, extent, field, matter, range, reach, vicinity

n 4 assessment, examination, inquiry, review, search, study, survey

n 5 amount, amplitude, dimensions, magnitude, proportions, quantity, size, volume

n 6 circle, compass, confines, dimension, distance, extension, extent, length, limit, orbit, purview, range, reach, realm, size, spectrum, sweep, width

n 7 binoculars, eye, field glass, glass, lens, magnifying glass, microscope, mirror, periscope, spyglass, telescope

v analyze, assess, determine, diagnose, estimate, examine, penetrate, probe, solve, survey, understand, unravel

scorch *v* bake, broil, burn, char, cook, melt,

parch, roast, sear, singe, swelter, toast, warm

scorched *adj* burnt, parched, shriveled

scorching *adj* 1 see: SCATHING *adj*

adj 2 baking, blistering, boiling, broiling, burning, fiery, hot, scalding, sizzling, sultry, sweltering, torrid

score *n* 1 average, grade, marks

n 2 count, record, tally, total

n 3 account, balance sheet, book, credit, ledger, statement, tab

n 4 libretto, musical, opera

v 1 count, gain, tally, win

v 2 evaluate, grade, mark, rate

v 3 arrive, flourish, go, make out, prosper, succeed, thrive

v 4 mark, number, tally

v 5 access, accomplish, achieve, attain, derive, earn, fulfill, gain, get, merit, net, obtain, perform, profit, rack up, reach, realize, win

scores *n* see: HORDE *n*

scorn *n* 1 aspersion, contempt, derision, disdain, irony, mockery, ridicule, sarcasm, satire

n 2 see: INSULT *n*

v 1 grimace, leer, mock, ogle, smirk, sneer

v 2 belittle, deride, flaunt, jab, jeer, jest, mock, quip, razz, ridicule, scoff, sneer, taunt, tease

v 3 see: HATE *v*

scornful *adj* 1 contemptuous, cynical, derisive, ironic, mocking, sarcastic, sardonic, skeptical, wry

adj 2 see: VAIN *adj* 5

scoundrel *n* cad, cheat, knave, lecher, louse, rake, rascal, reprobate, rogue

scour *v* 1 comb, loot, ransack, rifle, search, separate, sift, sort

v 2 bathe, clean, cleanse, clean up, dip, flush, immerse, launder, rinse, rub, scrape, scrub, shower, wash

scourge *n* 1 affliction, blight, impediment

n 2 bane, curse, disease, evil, misfortune, pestilence, plague

v 1 attack, beat, smite

v 2 assail, attack, batter, beat, birch, buffet, flagellate, flog, hammer, lambaste, lash, lather, pelt, pound, pummel, punish, thrash, tromp, wallop, whip

v 3 deflower, desecrate, despoil, devastate, devour, loot, maraud, pillage, plunder, ravage, sack, spoil, strip, violate

scout *n* 1 bodyguard, chaperon, companion, escort, guide

n 2 lookout, observer, outrider

v examine, explore, investigate, spy, survey

scow *n* barge, boat, canoe, craft, dory, ferry, float, kayak, raft, skiff, tender

scowl *n* expression, face, grimace, mouth, pout, smirk, sneer, visage

v 1 brood, crab, grouch, moan, pout, sulk

v 2 disdain, frown, glare, gloom, glower, grimace, lower, pout, sulk

scowling *adj* frowning

scraggly *adj* see: THIN *adj* 4

scraggy *adj* see: ROUGH *adj* 6

scramble *v* confuse, disorder, jostle, mix, shuffle

n contest, encounter, skirmish, struggle

scrap *n* 1 contents, junk, objects, stuff, substance, things

n 2 end, patch, piece, rag, shred, tatter

n 3 dregs, leftovers, remainder, remains, remnant, residual, residue, rest, shred, silt

n 4 bit, dab, end, fragment, iota, minutia, mite, morsel, particle, piece, pinch, portion, shred, speck, spot, strip, tidbit, trifle

n 5 discard, failure, garbage, junk, reject, second

n 6 altercation, argument, battle, brawl, challenge, combat, controversy, disagreement, discord, dispute, feud, fight, fracas, fray, hassle, melee, quarrel, rancor, rift, row, ruckus, scuffle, skirmish, spat, squabble, struggle, tiff, war

v 1 abandon, discard, dispose of, dump, eliminate, empty, quit, reject, unload

v 2 altercate, argue, battle, bicker, brawl, clash, conflict, dispute, engage, equivocate, feud, fight, fray, haggle, hassle, quarrel, quibble, row, spar, squabble, wrangle

scrape *n* 1 abrasion, cut, hurt, itch, scratch, sore

n 2 see: DILEMMA *n* 4

v 1 chafe, rub

v 2 economize, save, scrimp, skimp

v 3 bow, cringe, genuflect, grovel, kneel, kowtow

v 4 bathe, clean, cleanse, clean up, dip, flush, immerse, launder, rinse, rub, scour, scrub, shower, wash

v 5 brush, graze, scratch, shave, skim, touch

scrappy *adj* bellicose, brawling, difficult, feisty, quarrelsome, spirited

scratch *n* abrasion, cut, hurt, itch, scrape, sore

v 1 doodle, draw, jot, scrawl, scribble, sketch, write

v 2 claw, cleave, disrupt, divide, rend, rip, rive, split, tear

v 3 brush, graze, scrape, shave, skim, touch

scrawl v doodle, draw, jot, scratch, scribble, sketch, write

scrawny adj angular, bony, emaciated, gaunt, lanky, lean, meager, scraggly, skinny, slender, thin

scream n bark, bellow, blare, holler, roar, shout, shriek, thunder, yell

v bark, bellow, blare, call, cry, holler, howl, roar, screech, shout, shriek, shrill, squeal, thunder, wail, yell

screech v bark, bellow, blare, call, cry, holler, howl, roar, scream, shout, shriek, shrill, squeal, thunder, wail, yell

screen n 1 console, CRT, display, monitor, terminal

n 2 barrier, mesh, netting, protection, shield

n 3 shade

v 1 filter, process, sift

v 2 hide, protect, shade, shadow

v 3 bulwark, cover, defend, fend, fortify, guard, hide, protect, safeguard, secure, shield

screenwriter n see: WRITER n 2

screw v bamboozle, beat, beguile, bilk, burn, cajole, cheat, chicane, chisel, con, cross, deceive, defraud, dupe, embezzle, fleece, flimflam, fob, foist, fool, gyp, hoax, hoodwink, hustle, inveigle, shaft, sham, swindle, trick, victimize

scribble v doodle, draw, jot, scratch, scrawl, sketch, write

scribbled adj illegible, unclear, undecipherable, unreadable

scribe n aide, assistant, clerk, recorder, secretary, stenographer

scrimmage n affray, battle, brawl, brush, clash, conflict, difference, disagreement, dispute, encounter, fight, fracas, melee, quarrel, run-in, skirmish, spat, touch

scrimp v 1 economize, save, scrape, skimp

v 2 bound, limit, restrict, short, skimp, spare, stint

scrimpy adj deficient, failing, inadequate, inferior, insufficient, scant, scarce, short, shy, wanting

script n 1 lines

n 2 penmanship, writing

scriptural adj biblical

scripture n Bible, gospel, manual

scrub v bathe, clean, cleanse, clean up, dip, flush, immerse, launder, rinse, rub, scour, scrape, shower, wash

scruffy adj careless, disheveled, messy, slatternly, slipshod, sloppy, sloven, slovenly, tacky, uncombed, unkempt, untidy

scrumptious adj ambrosial, delightful, heavenly

scruple n compunction, conscience, pang, qualm, regret, reservation, restraint, twinge

scrupulous adj 1 careful, carping, cautious, conscientious, ethical, exacting, fussy, heedful, meticulous, painstaking, punctilious, unrelenting

adj 2 conscientious, ethical, honest, honorable, moral, noble, principled, proper, respectable, right, righteous, sound, true, trustworthy, upright, virtuous

scrutinize v 1 canvass, case, check, examine, glance over, inspect, observe, peruse, pore over, regard, study, survey, watch

v 2 see: PROBE v 5

scrutiny n examination, inspection, inquiry, probing, search, study, survey

scuffle v combat, conflict, contend, contest, engage, skirmish, struggle, tussle

n see: QUARREL n 2

sculpt v carve, chisel, craft, cut, define, design, fashion, form, mold, sculpture, shape, steer

sculpture n bust, figure, icon, idol, image, statue, statuette, symbol

v carve, chisel, craft, cut, define, design, fashion, form, mold, sculpt, shape, steer

scurrility n abuse, mistreatment

scurrilous adj improper, indecent, indelicate, lewd, malodorous, off-color, offensive, rough, suggestive, unbecoming, unseemly, untoward

scurry v dart, dash, hasten, scamper, sprint

scuttle v abuse, blemish, damage, hamper, harm, hurt, impair, injure, mar, obstruct, ruin, sabotage, spoil, tarnish, vandalize

scuttlebutt n grapevine, gossip, hearsay, murmur, report, rumble, rumor, story, talk, word

scuttled adj submerged, sunken, underwater

sea n 1 abundance

n 2 ocean

seafarer n mariner, mate, navy man, sailor, salt, seaman, yachtsman

seal n brand, cachet, emblem, imprint, logo, logotype, mark, stamp, trademark

v 1 bolt, close, latch, lock, secure, shut, slam

v 2 affix, bind, bond, cement, fasten, fuse, glue, join, lock, paste, secure, stick, unite

v 3 close, package, tape, wrap

seam n connection, groove, joining, joint, link

seaman n mariner, mate, navy man, sailor, salt, seafarer, yachtsman

seaport n asylum, cover, harbor, haven, oasis, port, preserve, protection, refuge, reserve, retreat, safety, sanctuary, security, shelter

sear v bake, broil, burn, char, cook, melt, parch, roast, scorch, singe, swelter, toast, warm

search n 1 exploration, hunt, pursuit, quest

n 2 examination, inquiry, inspection, probing, scrutiny, study, survey

n 3 chase, exploration, hunt, pursuit, quest, undertaking, venture

n 4 assessment, examination, inquiry, review, study, survey

v 1 explore, frisk, seek

v 2 grub, rummage, uncover

v 3 comb, loot, ransack, rifle, scour, separate, sift, sort

v 4 delve, dig, examine, explore, feel out, grope, hunt, inquire, investigate, look, observe, peer, probe, pursue, research, scan, scrutinize, seek, sound, study, test

searching adj inquiring, keen, penetrating, probing

seascape n acrylic, art, canvas, depiction, drawing, etching, illustration, landscape, lithograph, mural, oil, painting, pastel, pen and ink, picture, portrait, print, sketch, still life, watercolor

seashore n bank, beach, coast, shoal, shore

seasick adj nauseated, queasy, queer, sick, squeamish

season n cycle, duration, interval, period, span, spell, stage, stretch, term, time

v 1 color, enhance, flavor, imbue, infuse, salt, spice

v 2 harden, toughen

seasonable adj auspicious, favorable, opportune, timely

seasoned adj 1 adept, experienced, practiced, proficient, versed, veteran

adj 2 experienced, expert, grizzled, hardened, mature, trained, weathered

adj 3 biting, hot, nippy, pungent, sharp, spicy, tangy, tart

seat n 1 base

n 2 bench, chair, pew, stool

n 3 affiliation, belief, church, creed, denomination, faith, persuasion, religion, rite, theology

n 4 ass, backside, base, behind, bottom, bucket, buns, butt, buttocks, derrière, end, fanny, hindquarters, posterior, rump, stub, stump, tip, tush

seaworthy adj navigable, staunch, watertight

secede v see: LEAVE v 4

seclude v 1 detach, insulate, isolate, separate, sequester

v 2 see: DISGUISE v 2

secluded adj 1 abandoned, depraved, derelict, deserted, desolate, forsaken, solitary, uninhabited

adj 2 alienated, alone, apart, detached, hidden, isolated, private, removed, separated, sequestered, severed

adj 3 buried, secret, sequestered, withdrawn

seclusion n 1 detachment, isolation, privacy, quiet, solitude

n 2 exile, isolation, leisure, quarantine, relaxation, rest, retirement, retreat, solitude, withdrawal

second n 1 blink of an eye, crack, flash, instant, jiffy, minute, moment, shake, twinkling, wink

n 2 discard, failure, garbage, junk, reject

v endorse, promote, support

secondary adj 1 additional, covert, hidden, secret, ulterior, undeclared

adj 2 ancillary, auxiliary, incidental, minor, related, side, subordinate

adj 3 derivative, derived, stemming from

adj 4 ancillary, assistant, collateral, complementary, dependent, lesser, minor, sub, subject, subordinate, subsidiary, substitute, supporter, tributary, worker

adj 5 borderline, casual, frivolous, insignificant, light, lightweight, little, marginal, meager, minor, minute, negligible, nonessential, off, outside, petty, remote, slender, slight, slim, small, tenuous, trivial, unimportant

secondhand adj by proxy, indirect, surrogate, vicarious

second-rate adj flawed, flimsy, imperfect, inferior, lousy, mediocre, miserable, paltry, poor, shabby, shoddy, sorry, so-so, tacky, unworthy, worthless

secrecy n 1 sneakiness, stealth, subterfuge

n 2 camouflage, cover, incognito, privacy, stealth

secret adj 1 additional, covert, hidden, secondary, ulterior, undeclared

adj 2 exclusive, individual, intimate, own, personal, private, special

adj 3 enclosed, hidden, inner, innermost, interior, internal, private

adj 4 arcane, hermetic, impenetrable, impervious, mysterious, mystic, obscure, puzzling, unexaminable, unknown, unseen

adj 5 clandestine, classified, concealed, confidential, covert, hidden, off the record, private, privileged, sensitive, sub rosa

adj 6 clandestine, concealed, covert, crafty, deceitful, devious, evasive, foxy, furtive, guileful, indirect, privy, shifty, sly, sneaky, surreptitious, tricky, underground, underhand, underhanded, wily

adj 7 buried, secluded, sequestered, withdrawn

n 1 confidence, enigma, intrigue, mystery

n 2 answer, explanation, key, solution

n 3 cabal, collusion, conspiracy, intrigue, junta, machination, plot

n 4 confusion, conundrum, difficulty, dilemma, enigma, mystery, obstacle, paradox, perplexity, problem, puzzle, quandary, question

secretary *n* 1 desk, table

n 2 aide, assistant, clerk, recorder, scribe, stenographer

secrete *v* 1 discharge, drip, emit, exude, leak, ooze, seep, trickle

v 2 bury, cache, cloister, conceal, cover, ditch, ensconce, hide, plant, sequester, stash

secretion *n* fluid, juice, liquid, sap, solution

secretive *adj* 1 discreet, off the record, private, quiet

adj 2 closed, diffident, introverted, laconic, reserved, restrained, reticent, shy, subdued, taciturn, timid, timorous, uncommunicative, undaring

secretly *adv* clandestinely, covertly, furtively, hush-hush, mystically, sneakily, stealthily, surreptitiously, under cover

sect *n* 1 group, denomination, persuasion

n 2 band, cabal, camp, circle, clan, clique, coterie, coven, cult, faction, family, gang, group, mob, ring, school, tribe

section *n* 1 addition, adjunct, annex, annexation, branch, extension, wing

n 2 citation, clipping, excerpt, extract, mention, passage, portion, quotation, reference

n 3 area, arena, belt, field, realm, region, space, territory, tract, turf, zone

n 4 bit, clipping, cut, division, lot, member, parcel, part, piece, portion, sample, segment, slice

n 5 see: CATEGORY *n*

n 6 see: WARD *n* 2

v see: ALLOCATE *v* 3

sector *n* see: CATEGORY *n*

secure *adj* 1 stable, staunch, strong, sure

adj 2 exempt, guarded, protected, safe

adj 3 assured, confident, poised, sanguine, self-assured, self-confident

adj 4 comfortable, comfy, contented, cozy, cushy, homey, snug, soft, warm

adj 5 attached, fast, firm, fixed, rigid, set, taut, tense, tight

adj 6 compact, firm, hard, hardened, rigid, solid, sound, specific, stable, stiff, tight

adj 7 impregnable, invulnerable, protected, safe

adj 8 accountable, answerable, dependable, honorable, honored, liable, reliable, reputable, respected, responsible, solid, trusted, trustworthy, trusty, upstanding

v 1 clinch, confirm, fasten

v 2 anchor, catch, fasten, fix, moor

v 3 engage, enlist, enroll, muster, recruit, register, sign up

v 4 bolt, close, latch, lock, seal, shut, slam

v 5 actuate, bring about, cause, create, draw on, effect, execute, invoke, produce

v 6 bulwark, cover, defend, fend, fortify, guard, hide, protect, safeguard, screen, shield

v 7 clump, fasten, hitch, join, knot, lace, lash, link, loop, rope, tie, unite

v 8 acquire, annex, buy, capture, gain, get, have, land, obtain, pick up, procure, purchase, requisition, solicit, win

v 9 affix, bind, bond, cement, fasten, fuse, glue, join, lock, paste, seal, stick, unite

v 10 apprehend, arrest, bag, book, bust, capture, catch, collar, detain, get, grab, lock up, nab, nail, pick up, pinch, pull in, run in, seize, take

securities *n* bonds, holdings, stocks

security *n* 1 encumbrance, indebtedness, liability, lien, obligation

n 2 assurance, exemption, guarantee, immunity, impunity, protection, release

n 3 assurance, bond, commitment, earnest, guarantee, obligation, pawn, pledge, surety, token, warrant

n 4 see: SANCTUARY *n* 2

sedan *n* auto, automobile, bus, car, carriage, chariot, coach, jeep, motorcar, omnibus, truck, van, vehicle, wagon

sedate *adj* 1 dignified, earnest, grave, pensive, serious, sober, solemn, somber, staid, stoic, unemotional, unflinching

adj 2 calm, collected, composed, cool, demure, dormant, easy, gentle, hushed, idle, imperturbable, motionless, nonchalant, peaceful, placid, poised, quiet, relaxed, restful, self-composed, self-possessed, serene, soft, steady, still, tranquil, unflappable, unruffled, untroubled

v calm, drug, tranquilize

sedative *n* narcotic, tranquilizer

sediment *n* deposit, muck, mud, silt, sludge

sedition *n* betrayal, insurrection, mutiny, revolt, subversion, treason, uprising

seditious *adj* defiant, disobedient, insubordinate, insurgent, rebellious

seduce v 1 adulterate, corrupt, debase, debauch, defile, demoralize, dishonor, pervert, ruin, taint

v 2 appeal, arouse, attract, excite, fascinate, fire, interest, intrigue, lead on, lure, stir, tantalize

v 3 debauch, deflower, ravish

seduction n 1 attraction, bait, come-on, decoy, enticement, lure, magnet, ruse, snare, temptation, trap, wile

n 2 pickup

seductive adj 1 alluring, compelling, desirable, irresistible, overpowering, tantalizing

adj 2 arousing, exciting, intriguing, provocative, sexy, stimulating, suggestive, tantalizing

adj 3 alluring, attractive, desirable, erotic, exciting, sexy, tantalizing, tempting

adj 4 alluring, attractive, becoming, coy, cute, enchanting, enticing, fascinating, foxy, inviting, pleasing, ravishing, sexy

adj 5 see: APPEALING adj 2

seductress n coquette, flirt, harlot, nymphomaniac, siren, tart, tease, temptress, vamp, wanton woman

sedulous adj ambitious, assiduous, diligent, energetic, hard-working, industrious, persevering, persistent, resolute, zealous

see v 1 encounter, greet, interview, meet, receive, visit

v 2 behold, glimpse, look, mind, sight, spot, watch, witness

v 3 behold, catch, comprehend, conjure, descry, digest, discern, distinguish, espy, fathom, grasp, know, look at, notice, observe, perceive, realize, recognize, savvy, sight, take in, understand, view

v 4 see: PONDER v

seed n 1 basis, essence, kernel

n 2 bud, egg, embryo, fetus, ovum, zygote

n 3 sperm

n 4 author, creator, founder, initiator, instigator, inventor, maker, originator, parent, pioneer, source

n 5 beginning, conception, cradle, derivation, fountainhead, inception, infancy, mother, origin, root, source, stem

v 1 implant, plant, root, sow, strew

v 2 connote, hint, implant, imply, infer, insinuate, lead, offer

seedy adj 1 cheap, ragged

adj 2 black, dark, dingy, dirty, filthy, foul, grimy, grubby, mucky, murky, polluted, shabby, sooty, squalid, stained, unclean, unlit, unwashed

seek v 1 explore, frisk, search

v 2 campaign, canvass, drum, drum up, poll, solicit

v 3 chase, follow, hunt, pursue, shadow, shoot for, tail, trace, track, trail

v 4 assay, attempt, endeavor, essay, offer, quest, strive, struggle, try, undertake

v 5 delve, dig, examine, explore, feel out, grope, hunt, inquire, investigate, look, observe, peer, probe, pursue, research, scan, scrutinize, search, sound, study, test

v 6 see: PLEAD v 2

seem v appear, indicate, look, portend, sound

seeming adj 1 fake, phony

adj 2 apparent, illusive, illusory, ostensible, quasi, specious, superficial

seemingly adv apparently, supposedly

seep v 1 dribble, drip, drop, leak, ooze, trickle *

v 2 discharge, drip, emit, exude, leak, ooze, secrete, trickle

seer n astrologer, augur, fortuneteller, oracle, predictor, prophet, psychic, soothsayer, visionary

seethe v 1 boil, heat, overheat, parboil, simmer, stew

v 2 agitate, bake, boil, bubble, burn, churn, ferment, foam, fume, roast, simmer, smolder

v 3 anger, blow up, boil, boil over, brew, bristle, burn, flare up, fume, rage, simmer, smoke, steam, storm

segment n 1 component, installment, part

n 2 component, constituent, element, factor, ingredient, item

n 3 bit, clipping, cut, division, lot, member, parcel, part, piece, portion, sample, section, slice

segmentation n apportionment, division, partition, segregation, separation, subdivision

segregate v differentiate, discriminate, exclude, isolate, ostracize, separate, sequester

segregated adj definite, determinate, exclusive, fixed, limited, narrow, precise, specific

segregation n 1 apportionment, division, partition, segmentation, separation, subdivision

n 2 apartheid, discrimination, racism

segregationist n bigot, racist, supremacist

seize v 1 tackle

v 2 force, pull, turn, twist, wrest

v 3 abduct, carry away, grab, kidnap, shanghai, steal

v 4 catch, clasp, clutch, grab, grapple, grasp, grip, hold, nab, nail, snatch, take *v* 5 annex, appropriate, commandeer, confiscate, expropriate, grab, impound, plunder, preempt, repossess, sequester, shanghai, take

v 6 apprehend, arrest, bag, book, bust, capture, catch, collar, detain, get, grab, lock up, nab, nail, pick up, pinch, pull in, run in, secure, take

seizure *n* convulsion, spasm, twitch

seldom *adj* few, infrequent, isolated, occasional, rare, scarce, sporadic, uncommon, unusual

select *adj* 1 best, optimum, prime, superior, top

adj 2 chosen, designated, elected, picked, selected

adj 3 better, favored, partial, preferential, special

adj 4 choice, dainty, delicate, elegant, exquisite, favorite, fine, preferred

adj 5 characteristic, differentiating, distinctive, lone, one, particular, peculiar, single, solitary, special, unique, unusual

adj 6 best, biggest, finest, greater, greatest, larger, largest, maximum, most, number one, prime, superior, top, top notch

adj 7 champion, excellent, superb, fine, first-class, first-rate, foremost, good, grade A, leading, number one, prime, principal, prominent, quality, stellar, superior, top, top-drawer, top-notch, tops

adj 8 choice, preferred

n choice, elite, favorite, optimum, pick

v 1 adjust, dial, tune

v 2 choose, desire, favor, prefer

v 3 appoint, declare, designate, name, nominate, propose, specify

v 4 appoint, ballot, choose, elect, nominate, opt, vote

v 5 call, conscript, draft, enroll, force, impress, induct, shanghai

v 6 choose, cull, elect, pick, remove, separate, sift, single out, sort

selected *adj* chosen, designated, elected, picked

selection *n* 1 assortment, bunch, collection, mixture, spectrum, variety

n 2 ballot, choice, franchise, option, preference, vote

n 3 alternative, choice, decision, druthers, election, option, pick, preference, rathers, vote

selective *adj* careful, cautious, choosy, discriminating, fastidious, finicky, fussy, meticulous, nit-picking, particular, persnickety, picky

selector *n* dial, disk, display, gauge, indicator, measure, meter

self *n* ego, id, individuality, mind, persona, personality, psyche, soul, spirit

self-assertive *adj* aggressive, ambitious, assertive, assured, compelling, compulsive, confident, decided, dogmatic, driven, emphatic, energetic, insistent, militant, positive, pushing, pushy, sure, urging

self-assurance *n* aplomb, assurance, confidence, esteem, nerve, poise, presence, savoir-faire, self-confidence

self-assured *adj* 1 assured, confident, poised, sanguine, self-confident

adj 2 arrogant, cocky, conceited, haughty, narcissistic, smug, stuck-up, vain

self-composed *adj* see: CALM *adj* 2

self-confidence *n* aplomb, assurance, confidence, esteem, nerve, poise, presence, savoir-faire

self-confident *adj* assured, confident, poised, sanguine, secure, self-assured

self-control *n* discipline, persistence, volition, will, willpower

self-esteem *n* 1 dignity, ego, pride, self-regard, self-respect

n 2 airs, arrogance, cockiness, conceit, condescension, disdain, egotism, haughtiness, image, loftiness, narcissism, pride, self-image, vanity

self-evident *adj* see: OBVIOUS *adj* 3

self-governing *adj* autonomous, democratic, independent

self-image *n* airs, arrogance, cockiness, conceit, condescension, disdain, egotism, haughtiness, image, loftiness, narcissism, pride, vanity

selfish *adj* 1 caustic, inconsiderate, sharp, short, tactless, thoughtless, unceremonious, ungracious

adj 2 acquisitive, avaricious, covetous, craving, desirous, eager, grabby, grasping, greedy, hungry, longing, miserly, wishful, yearning

adj 3 accidental, careless, caustic, heedless, inadvertent, inconsiderate, nonchalant, sharp, short, tactless, thoughtless, uncaring, unceremonious, ungracious, unheeding, unintended, unintentional, unreflective, unthinking

selfishness *n* avarice, covetousness, craving, desire, greed, yearning

selfless *adj* generous, giving, unselfish

self-possessed *adj* calm, collected, composed, cool, demure, dormant, easy, gentle, hushed, idle, imperturbable, motionless, nonchalant, peaceful, placid, poised, quiet, relaxed, restful, sedate, self-composed, serene, soft, steady, still, tranquil, unflappable, unruffled, untroubled

self-possession n calmness, composure, equanimity, harmony, peacefulness, serenity, tranquillity

self-regard n dignity, ego, pride, self-respect

self-respect n dignity, ego, pride, self-esteem, self-regard

self-restraint n abstinence, continence, moderation, restraint, sobriety, temperance

self-steering adj auto, automatic, robotic

sell v 1 barter, distribute, market, merchandise, peddle, retail, vend, wholesale
v 2 deal, hawk, horse-trade, huckster, hustle, monger, peddle, push, swap
v 3 advertise, air, boom, boost, drum up, endorse, pitch, plug, promote, publicize, push, rave, tout

seller n dealer, marketer, merchant, monger, purveyor, trader, vendor

selling n allocation, distribution, marketing, merchandising, share, sharing

semanticist n linguist, morphologist, phonetician

semblance n 1 air, ambience, atmosphere, aura, emanation, feel, feeling, mood, spirit
n 2 see: SIMILARITY n 2

semen n sperm

semi adj feigned, partial, pseudo, quasi, so-called, somewhat, unofficial

seminal adj 1 compact, definitive, meaty, pithy, tight
adj 2 basic, creative, formative, fundamental, initiatory

seminar n assembly, clinic, congress, council, court, diet, forum, hearing, meeting, parliament, symposium

seminary n academy, college, institute, lyceum, school, university

senate n capitol, legislature

senator n assemblyman, congressman, councilman, legislator, representative

send v 1 batch, lump, ship together
v 2 discharge, emanate, emit, expel, project, release
v 3 address, channel, consign, dispatch, export, forward, mail, post, remit, route, ship, transmit, transport

sending n consignment, dismissal, dispatch, forwarding

senior adj 1 elderly
adj 2 elder, first, older, oldest
adj 3 aged, age-old, ancient, antique, elderly, gray, grizzled, old, olden, timeworn, venerable, vintage, worn
n chief, higher ranked, superior, veteran

seniority n advantage, precedence, prerogative, priority, privilege

sensation n 1 standout
n 2 marvel, miracle, phenomenon, spectacle, wonder
n 3 exploration, feel, feeling, palpation, texture, touch
n 4 affection, emotion, feeling, passion, regard, sense, sensibility, sentiment, tenderness
n 5 awareness, emotion, faculty, feel, feeling, intuition, perception, reaction, response, sense

sensational adj 1 dramatic, melodramatic, theatrical, thrilling
adj 2 dramatic, extraordinary, shocking, startling
adj 3 exciting, hot, sexy, spectacular, stirring
adj 4 best, elegant, finest, gilt-edged, magnificent, majestic, outstanding, preeminent, splendid, superb, superior, superlative
adj 5 arresting, astonishing, astounding, conspicuous, eye-catching, marked, noticeable, obvious, pointed, prominent, salient, striking, stunning
adj 6 see: AWFUL adj 2

sense n 1 consensus, feeling, opinion
n 2 feeling, foreboding, guess, hunch, instinct, intuition, premonition, suspicion
n 3 lucidity, mind, rationality, reason, saneness, sanity, soundness, wit
n 4 affection, emotion, feeling, passion, regard, sensation, sensibility, sentiment, tenderness
n 5 attention, awareness, care, carefulness, cognizance, concern, consciousness, consideration, heed, intimacy, knowing, knowledge, mark, note, notice, observance, observation, perception, recognition, regard
n 6 import, intent, meaning, message, significance, understanding
n 7 common sense, faculty, good sense, gumption, horse sense, judgment, logic, wisdom
n 8 awareness, emotion, faculty, feel, feeling, intuition, perception, reaction, response
v detect, experience, feel, perceive

senseless adj 1 dazed, insensible, numb, unconscious
adj 2 cold, comatose, unconscious

adj 3 absurd, anile, asinine, brainless, childish, fatuous, foolish, idiotic, inept, meaningless, mindless, silly, simple, thoughtless, unintelligent, witless

senselessness *n* craziness, folly, foolishness, frivolity, insanity, lunacy, madness, mania

sensibility *n* affection, emotion, feeling, passion, regard, sensation, sense, sentiment, tenderness

sensible *adj* 1 basic, businesslike, down-to-earth, efficient, hardheaded, practical, pragmatic

adj 2 concrete, corporeal, material, objective, physical, real, substantial, tactile, tangible

adj 3 appreciable, cognizant, concrete, detectable, discernible, noticeable, observable, palpable, perceptible, tangible, visible

adj 4 enlightened, judgmatical, judicious, just, lucid, prudent, rational, sage, sane, wise

adj 5 astute, consequent, intelligent, knowing, logical, perceptive, rational, reasonable, sane, shrewd, sober, sound, wise

sensitive *adj* 1 aesthetic, empathetic, intuitive

adj 2 tender, ticklish, touchy

adj 3 emotional, feeling, sentient, susceptible, tender

adj 4 alterable, impressionable, inexperienced, malleable, naive, susceptible

adj 5 discerning, discreet, discriminating, keen, subtle, tactful

adj 6 annoying, difficult, hurt, irksome, irritated, irritating, sore

adj 7 dangerous, delicate, fluctuating, hazardous, precarious, rickety, risky, rocky, shaky, tender, ticklish, touchy, tricky, unpredictable, unstable, wobbly

adj 8 see: QUICK *adj* 5

adj 9 see: SECRET *adj* 5

sensitivity *n* acumen, astuteness, awareness, cleverness, discernment, discrimination, insight, intellect, intuition, keenness, perception, sagacity, shrewdness, understanding, wit

sensual *adj* 1 carnal, delicious, enticing, erotic, hedonistic, luscious, lush, lusty, luxurious, pleasure-seeking, sensualistic, sensuous, sexual, voluptuous

adj 2 see: EROTIC *adj* 2, 3

sensualistic *adj* carnal, delicious, enticing, erotic, hedonistic, luscious, lush, lusty, luxurious, pleasure-seeking, sensual, sensuous, sexual, voluptuous

sensuous *adj* carnal, delicious, enticing, erotic, hedonistic, luscious, lush, lusty, luxurious, pleasure-seeking, sensual, sensualistic, sexual, voluptuous

sentence *n* 1 adjudication, decision, decree, finding, judgment, ruling, verdict

n 2 adjudication, award, determination, judgment, opinion, ruling, verdict

v 1 adjudge, condemn, convict, discipline, imprison, penalize, punish

v 2 chastise, dock, fine, penalize, punish, tariff, tax

sentient *adj* 1 emotional, feeling, sensitive, susceptible, tender

adj 2 alive, attentive, awake, aware, cognizant, conscious, conversant, knowing, responsive, thinking

sentiment *n* 1 affection, emotion, feeling, passion, regard, sensation, sense, tenderness

n 2 attitude, belief, bias, conviction, feeling, inducement, leaning, mind, opinion, persuasion, slant, view

sentimental *adj* 1 mushy

adj 2 emotional, flowery, gushy

adj 3 bittersweet, maudlin, poignant, sad, sorrowful

sentinel *n* guard, lookout, picket, sentry, ward, warden, watch, watchman

sentry *n* guard, lookout, picket, sentinel, ward, warden, watch, watchman

separate *adj* 1 alien, foreign, remote, unrelated

adj 2 autonomous, distinct, free, independent, lone, sovereign, unconnected

adj 3 exclusive, individual, lone, odd, one, only, particular, single, singular, sole, solitary, unique, unshared

adj 4 alternate, another, certain, different, discrete, disparate, dissimilar, distinct, diverse, numerous, other, several, some, unlike, various, varying

v 1 exclude, fence, restrict

v 2 detach, insulate, isolate, seclude, sequester

v 3 classify, define, differentiate, discriminate, distinguish

v 4 exclude, differentiate, discriminate, isolate, ostracize, segregate, sequester

v 5 comb, loot, ransack, rifle, scour, sift, sort

v 6 choose, cull, elect, pick, remove, select, sift, single out, sort

v 7 breach, break up, cleave, disjoin, dismember, disrupt, dissect, dissever, disunite, divide, divorce, part, polarize, rupture, sever, split, sunder *v* 8 disband, disperse, dissipate, dissociate, dissolve

v 9 cut, detach, disconnect, disengage, dissociate, sever, uncouple, unfasten, unhook, unyoke

separated *adj* 1 alienated, disaffected, disunited, estranged, weaned

adj 2 alienated, alone, apart, detached, hidden, isolated, private, removed, secluded, sequestered, severed

separately *adv* individually

separation *n* 1 aloofness, detachment, indifference

n 2 apportionment, division, partition, segmentation, segregation, subdivision

n 3 break, disagreement, dissension, fight, misunderstanding, quarrel, rift, spat

n 4 annulment, dissolution, divorce, split

sepulcher *n* burial, catacomb, cenotaph, crypt, grave, mausoleum, memorial, monument, pit, tomb, vault

sepulchral *adj* abnormal, depressing, dismal, funereal, ghastly, gloomy, macabre, morbid

sequel *n* continuation, corollary, epilogue, supplement

sequence *n* 1 line, order, priority, procession, succession, timing

n 2 chain, course, lineup, order, progression, row, run, series, string, succession, train

n 3 alternation, circuit, circulation, gyration, revolution, rotation, round, spinning, succession, turn, whirl

n 4 arrangement, disposal, disposition, distribution, ordering

v format, number, paginate

sequential *adj* chronological, consecutive, continuous, progressive, serial, successive

sequester *v* 1 detach, insulate, isolate, seclude

v 2 differentiate, discriminate, exclude, isolate, ostracize, separate

v 3 annex, appropriate, commandeer, confiscate, expropriate, grab, impound, plunder, preempt, repossess, seize, shanghai, take

v 4 see: HIDE *v* 3

sequestered *adj* alienated, alone, apart, detached, hidden, isolated, private, removed, secluded, separated, severed

adj 2 buried, secluded, withdrawn

serenade *n* concert, concerto, étude, fugue, program, recital, sonata, symphony

serendipitous *adj* 1 auspicious, favorable, fortunate, happy, lucky

adj 2 accidental, casual, chance, chancy, circumstantial, coincidental, contingent, eventful, fluky, fortuitous, freak, incidental, lucky, odd, synchronous

serendipity *n* 1 chance, coincidence, good fortune, luck

n 2 blessing, bonanza, boon, fortune, gain, godsend, luck, miracle, stroke of luck, windfall

serene *adj* 1 balmy, bright, clear, fair

adj 2 calm, collected, composed, cool, demure, dormant, easy, gentle, hushed, idle, imperturbable, motionless, nonchalant, peaceful, placid, poised, quiet, relaxed, restful, sedate, self-composed, self-possessed, soft, steady, still, tranquil, unflappable, unruffled, untroubled

adj 3 consistent, constant, continuing, endless, equable, established, even, invariable, reliable, routine, same, stable, steady, unchanging, unfailing, unfluctuating, uniform, unvarying

adj 4 see: AMIABLE *adj* 3

serenity *n* 1 composure

n 2 accord, calm, harmony, peace, stillness, tranquillity

n 3 calmness, composure, equanimity, harmony, peacefulness, self-possession, tranquillity

serf *n* chattel, pauper, peasant, peon, slave, vassal

serfdom *n* bondage, enslavement, imprisonment, indenture, servility, servitude, slavery

serial *adj* chronological, consecutive, continuous, progressive, sequential, successive

series *n* 1 current, drift, pattern, run, succession, tendency, trend

n 2 chain, course, lineup, order, progression, row, run, sequence, string, succession, train

n 3 cartoons, docudrama, documentary, game shows, mini-series, movies, news, programs, sitcom, soap opera, soaps, talk shows, television, variety shows

serious *adj* 1 dour, firm, forbidding, grim, sad, severe, sour, stern, unpleasant

adj 2 breakneck, critical, dangerous, harmful, hazardous, perilous, precarious, risky, unsafe, venturesome

adj 3 dignified, earnest, grave, pensive, sedate, sober, solemn, somber, staid, stoic, unemotional, unflinching

adj 4 acute, burning, critical, crucial, desperate, dire, grave, heavy, important, major, momentous, ponderous, pressing, profound, severe, solemn, somber, urgent, vital

adj 5 see: HARD *adj* 5

sermon n assignment, diatribe, discourse, exercise, homily, lecture, lesson

sermonize v discourse, discuss, elaborate, ramble

serpentine adj 1 crooked, meandering, sinuous, spiral, turning, twisting, winding, zigzagging

adj 2 adroit, artful, cagey, canny, crafty, cunning, evasive, foxy, sly

serum n 1 blood, plasma

n 2 antidote, cure, medication, medicine, panacea, prescription, remedy, therapy, treatment

n 3 antibody, antidote, antigen, antitoxin, defense, vaccine

servant n aide, aide-de-camp, assistant, attendant, employee, hand, helper, hired hand, laborer, supporter, worker

serve v 1 attend, help, wait

v 2 call, cite, evoke, subpoena, summon

v 3 accommodate, convenience, favor, help, oblige, please

v 4 arrange, cater, deliver, dish out, dispense, feed, furnish, give, hand, nourish, nurture, organize, provide, purvey, supply, sustain

v 5 abet, advance, aid, ameliorate, amend, assist, avail, benefit, better, boost, cultivate, do for, ease, egg on, encourage, enhance, forward, foster, further, help, improve, nurture, prefer, promote, rev, spur on, support

service n 1 building, facility, office

n 2 installation, maintenance, repair, upkeep

n 3 arm, branch, division, limb, subsidiary, tributary

n 4 ceremonial, ceremony, formality, liturgy, observance, ritual

n 5 account, advantage, applicability, appropriateness, aptness, avail, benefit, decorum, expediency, fitness, manners, opportunism, pertinence, profit, propriety, relevance, rightness, suitability, use, usefulness, utility

n 6 consideration, courtesy, dispensation, favor, indulgence, kindness, privilege

v adapt, adjust, balance, fit, fix, inspect, maintain, overhaul, recondition, refurbish, regulate, repair, support, tune up

serviceable adj see: PRACTICAL adj 4

servile adj 1 abject, base, contemptible, debasing, despicable

adj 2 abject, common, groveling, humble, ingratiating, lowly, menial, obeisant, obsequious, slavish, subservient

servility n bondage, enslavement, imprisonment, indenture, serfdom, servitude, slavery

servitude n bondage, enslavement, imprisonment, indenture, serfdom, servility, slavery

set adj 1 authorized, conventional, established

adj 2 game, prepared, primed, ready

adj 3 ineffectual, limited, little, mean, narrow, paltry, small

adj 4 attached, fast, firm, fixed, rigid, secure, taut, tense, tight

adj 5 fastened, fixed, in position, motionless, permanent, solid, standing, static, stationary, still

adj 6 certain, explicit, expressed, firm, fixed, formal, mandated, settled, spoken, stated, stipulated

adj 7 see: DEDICATED adj 3

n 1 backdrop, curtain, environment, scene, scenery, setting, stage set, stage setting, surroundings

n 2 couple, duet, duo, pair, twins, twosome

n 3 air, attitude, bearing, calmness, carriage, demeanor, disposition, poise, pose, posture, stance

n 4 array, bale, batch, battery, body, bunch, bundle, clump, cluster, group, lot, pack, parcel

n 5 bracket, breed, cast, category, class, division, family, genre, genus, group, grouping, ilk, kind, lot, mold, nature, order, persuasion, section, sector, sort, species, style, type, variety

v 1 aim, establish, focus, point, shoot at, target

v 2 allocate, appoint, assign, establish, implement

v 3 adjust, arrange, calibrate, decide, determine, establish, fix

v 4 calibrate, establish, fix, insert, install, lay, locate, place, plant, position, put, settle, situate, station

v 5 clog, clot, coagulate, condense, congeal, curdle, dry, gel, harden, intensify, jell, pack, solidify, thicken

v 6 lay

v 7 agitate, anger, arouse, encourage, foment, ignite, incite, induce, inflame, inspire, instigate, invoke, motivate, muster, prod, propel, provoke, raise, set on, spur, stimulate, stir, urge

setback n 1 comedown, decline, decrease, descent, dive, drop, failure, fall, plunge, regression, slide, tumble

n 2 adversity, affliction, blow, burden, calamity, difficulty, distress, hardship, mischance, misfortune, mishap, relapse, reversal, suffering, tragedy, trouble

settee *n* couch, divan, sofa

setting *n* 1 circumstance, context, situation

n 2 angle, bearing, degree, heading, position

n 3 backdrop, curtain, environment, scene, scenery, set, stage set, stage setting, surroundings

settings *n* atmosphere, climate, conditions, environment, habitat, niche, surroundings

settle *v* 1 adjust, agree, arrange, compromise

v 2 ensconce, harbor, nestle, shelter, snuggle

v 3 alight, come down, descend, dismount, land

v 4 adjudicate, conclude, decide, determine, establish, resolve, rule, will

v 5 arbitrate, intercede, interfere, interpose, intervene, intrude, mediate, step in

v 6 domicile, dwell, inhabit, live, occupy, reside, room, stay

v 7 decline, die down, diminish, dip, sink, slide, slip, subside

v 8 calibrate, establish, fix, insert, install, lay, locate, place, plant, position, put, set, situate, station

v 9 avenge, compensate, cover, disburse, indemnify, pay, reciprocate, redress, reimburse, remedy, remunerate, repair, repay, requite, retaliate, revenge, vindicate

v 10 wind up

v 11 clear, clear off, discharge, liquidate, pay up, repay, satisfy, square

v 12 allay, appease, assuage, balm, becalm, calm, compose, conciliate, ease, lull, mollify, pacify, placate, propitiate, quell, quiet, reconcile, satiate, soften, soothe, still, sweeten, tranquilize

settled *adj* 1 ensconced, entrenched, established, fixed, fundamental, ingrained, intrinsic, inveterate, sworn

adj 2 certain, explicit, expressed, firm, fixed, formal, mandated, set, spoken, stated, stipulated

settlement *n* 1 agreement, arrangement, compromise, concession, decision, determination, franchise

n 2 citizens, civilization, colony, community, crowd, culture, folks, group, human beings, individuals, laity, masses, men and women, neighbors, people, persons, populace, population, public, society, staff, tribe

n 3 borough, burgh, community, hamlet, township, village

sever *v* 1 abort, erase, stop, terminate

v 2 break, chip, crack, fracture, gap, smash, split

v 3 breach, break up, cleave, disjoin, dismember, disrupt, dissect, dissever, disunite, divide, divorce, part, polarize, rupture, separate, split, sunder

v 4 cut, detach, disconnect, disengage, dissociate, separate, uncouple, unfasten, unhook, unyoke

v 5 abstain, cease, conclude, desist, discontinue, end, finish, forbear, freeze, halt, knock off, quit, stop, terminate

v 6 ax, carve, chip, chop, cleave, cut, dissect, fell, hack, hew, mangle, mutilate, notch, pulverize, rend, saw, slice, sliver, snip, split, sunder, whittle

several *adj* 1 a, a few, any, at least one, each, every, individual, one, some

adj 2 alternate, another, certain, different, discrete, disparate, dissimilar, distinct, diverse, numerous, other, separate, some, unlike, various, varying

severe *adj* 1 incessant, prolonged

adj 2 atrocious, dreadful, calamitous, grievous

adj 3 drastic, excessive, extreme, intense, passionate, radical, strong

adj 4 austere, narrow, narrow-minded, prim, prudish, puritanical, strict

adj 5 dour, firm, forbidding, grim, sad, serious, sour, stern, unpleasant

adj 6 abusive, hard, harsh, stern, stiff, strict, tough, uncaring, unsympathetic

adj 7 ardent, decisive, determined, emphatic, extreme, forceful, intense, potent, powerful, strong

adj 8 bitter, brutal, cruel, fierce, hard, harsh, inclement, intemperate, pitiless, rigorous, rough, rugged, stern, strong, unkind, violent

adj 9 acute, burning, critical, crucial, desperate, dire, grave, heavy, important, major, momentous, ponderous, pressing, profound, serious, solemn, somber, urgent, vital

adj 10 see: HARD *adj* 2, 5, 6

adj 11 see: RESTRICTIVE *adj*

adj 12 see: VIOLENT *adj* 3, 5

severed *adj* see: ALONE *adj* 3

severity *n* 1 austerity, oppression, rigidity, tyranny

n 2 intensity, power, tumult, turbulence, violence

n 3 adversity, difficulty, discipline, dis-

comfort, hardness, rigor, strictness, stringency, uneasiness

sex *n* **1** gender

n **2** adultery, congress, copulation, fooling
around, fornication, intimacy, procreation

n **3** coitus, conjugation, copulation, fooling around, foreplay, fornication, intercourse, mating, reproduction, union

sexiness *n* pizzazz, sex appeal, sizzle

sexism *n* bias, bigotry, chauvinism, discrimination, intolerance, parochialism,
partiality, prejudice, provincialism

sexual *adj* **1** intimate, physical

adj **2** carnal, delicious, enticing, erotic,
hedonistic, luscious, lush, lusty, luxurious, pleasure-seeking, sensual, sensualistic, sensuous, voluptuous

adj **3** carnal, erogenous, erotic, genital,
reproductive

adj **4** amorous, ardent, aroused, carnal,
earthy, erotic, fervent, fleshly, horny, hot,
impassioned, lascivious, lecherous, lewd,
licentious, lustful, passionate, provocative, randy, raunchy, romantic, sensual,
sexy, sultry, titillated, torrid, turned on,
voluptuous, wanton

sexy *adj* **1** exciting, hot, sensational, spectacular, stirring

adj **2** sleek, slender, slim, slinky, svelte

adj **3** arousing, exciting, intriguing, provocative, seductive, stimulating, suggestive, tantalizing

adj **4** alluring, attractive, desirable, erotic,
exciting, seductive, tantalizing, tempting

adj **5** alluring, attractive, becoming, coy,
cute, enchanting, enticing, fascinating,
foxy, inviting, pleasing, ravishing

adj **6** amorous, ardent, aroused, carnal,
earthy, erotic, fervent, fleshly, horny, hot,
impassioned, lascivious, lecherous, lewd,
licentious, lustful, passionate, provocative, randy, raunchy, romantic, sensual,
sexual, sultry, titillated, torrid, turned on,
voluptuous, wanton

adj **7** see: APPEALING *adj* **2**

shabby *adj* **1** faded, frayed, poor, run-
down, tattered, threadbare, worn

adj **2** flawed, flimsy, imperfect, inferior,
lousy, mediocre, miserable, paltry, poor,
second-rate, shoddy, sorry, so-so, tacky,
unworthy, worthless

adj **3** see: DIRTY *adj* **2**

shack *n* **1** abode, barn, bungalow, cabin,
coop, cottage, hovel, hut, lodge, shanty

n **2** barn, coop, enclosure, lean-to, paddock, pen, pound, shed, shelter, stable,
stall, sty

shackle *n* bond, chain, fetter, handcuff,
iron, manacle, tie

v **1** bind, chain, fasten, link

v **2** bind, clog, confine, curb, fetter, hamper, handcuff, hold, leash, limit, restrain,
restrict, tie, tie up

shade *n* **1** cast, color, hue, tinge, tint, tone

n **2** degree, distinction, enhancement, nuance, subtlety, touch, trace, variation

n **3** breath, clue, dash, glimmer, hint,
insinuation, lick, smell, smidgen, spice,
sprinkling, suggestion, suspicion, tinge,
tip, touch, trace, trifle, whiff, whisper,
wisp

n **4** screen

v **1** hide, protect, screen, shadow

v **2** blend

v **3** becloud, bedim, befog, blur, cloud,
confuse, darken, dim, diminish, dull,
eclipse, fade, muddy, obscure, overshadow, pale, shadow, tarnish

shadow *n* memento, relic, remnant, trace,
vestige

v **1** hide, screen, shade

v **2** chase, follow, hunt, pursue, seek,
shoot for, tail, trace, track, trail

v **3** becloud, bedim, befog, blur, cloud,
confuse, darken, dim, diminish, dull,
eclipse, fade, muddy, obscure, overshadow, pale, shade, tarnish

shadowy *adj* **1** black, charcoal, dark

adj **2** dark, dim, dusky, gloomy, lightless,
murky, obscure, somber, tenebrous, unilluminated

shady *adj* **1** despicable, infamous, notorious, offensive, scandalous, unsavory, villainous

adj **2** see: EVIL *adj* **4**

shaft *n* **1** axis, axle, pin, pivot, pole, rod,
spindle

n **2** birch, cane, club, pole, rod, stave,
staff, stake, stick

n **3** conduit, passageway, pathway, subway, tube, tunnel

v bamboozle, beat, beguile, bilk, burn,
cajole, cheat, chicane, chisel, con, cross,
deceive, defraud, dupe, embezzle, fleece,
flimflam, fob, foist, fool, gyp, hoax, hoodwink, hustle, inveigle, screw, sham, swindle, trick, victimize

shake *n* **1** blink of an eye, crack, flash,
instant, jiffy, minute, moment, second,
twinkling, wink

n **2** bang, boom, clang, clap, crash, resound, roar, rumble, thunder

v **1** lose, slip, throw off

v **2** bump, jar, jolt, jostle, rattle, shock,
startle

v 3 agitate, derange, disorder, disturb, fluster, rock, ruffle, sicken, unhinge, unsettle, upset

v 4 flinch, flutter, jar, pulsate, quake, quaver, quiver, shiver, shudder, tremble, twitch, twitter, vibrate

v 5 jig, jiggle, joggle, jump, twitch, wiggle

shaky *adj* 1 flimsy, insecure, jiggly, rickety, teetering, unstable, unsure, vacillating, wavering, weak, wobbly

adj 2 dangerous, delicate, fluctuating, hazardous, precarious, rickety, risky, rocky, sensitive, tender, ticklish, touchy, tricky, unpredictable, unstable, wobbly

adj 3 see: TEMPERAMENTAL *adj*

adj 4 see: VAGUE *adj* 6

shallow *adj* 1 empty, hollow, idle, insincere, meaningless, vain

adj 2 brief, crude, cursory, hasty, rough, sketchy, superficial, uncritical

n reef, sandbank, sandbar, shelf, shoal

shalom *n* adieu, adios, aloha, *arrivederci*, *auf Wiedersehen*, au revoir, bon voyage, bye, cheerio, *ciao*, farewell, goodbye, good day, *sayonara*, so long

sham *adj* 1 fake, feigned, fictitious, mock, simulated

adj 2 deceptive, false, illusive, illusory, misleading, unreal

adj 3 artificial, bogus, counterfeit, ersatz, fake, false, imitation, mock, phony, pseudo, simulated, spurious, substitute, unreal

n 1 make-believe, pretense, show

n 2 cheating, deceit, deception, dishonesty, fraud, hoax, lie, subterfuge, trickery

n 3 bastard, deception, fake, fraud, hoax, put-on

v 1 act, assume, bluff, counterfeit, fabricate, fake, feign, imitate, invent, make-believe, play, pretend

v 2 bamboozle, beat, beguile, bilk, burn, cajole, cheat, chicane, chisel, con, cross, deceive, defraud, dupe, embezzle, fleece, flimflam, fob, foist, fool, gyp, hoax, hoodwink, hustle, inveigle, screw, shaft, swindle, trick, victimize

shambles *n* bloodbath, bloodshed, butchery, carnage, extermination, genocide, holocaust, killing, massacre, slaughter

shame *n* 1 accountability, blame, burden, culpability, fault, guilt, onus, responsibility, stigma

n 2 censure, contempt, discredit, disfavor, disgrace, dishonor, disparagement, disrepute, humiliation, infamy, notoriety, scandal

v 1 disfavor, disgrace, dishonor, humiliate, reproach, stain, tarnish

v 2 abase, abash, belittle, cast down, cheapen, debase, defile, deflate, degrade, demean, depreciate, derogate, devalue, dishonor, embarrass, humble, humiliate, lower, mortify, put down, sink

shamed *adj* abashed, ashamed, chagrined, embarrassed, humiliated, mortified

shameless *adj* arrant, barefaced, blatant, brassy, brazen, extreme, impudent, notorious, unabashed

shanghai *v* 1 abduct, carry away, grab, kidnap, seize, steal

v 2 call, conscript, draft, enroll, force, impress, induct

v 3 see: TAKE *v* 5

shanty *n* abode, barn, bungalow, cabin, coop, cottage, hovel, hut, lodge

shape *n* 1 case, condition, state

n 2 contour, form, outline

n 3 border, boundary, casing, frame

n 4 cast, configuration, conformation, figure, form, structure

n 5 anatomy, body, build, figure, form, physique

n 6 condition, fitness, kilter, repair, trim

v 1 build, conceive, construct, devise, frame, surround

v 2 adapt, conform, convert, cut, fashion, fit, measure, modify, rig, suit, tailor

v 3 carve, chisel, craft, cut, define, design, fashion, form, mold, sculpt, sculpture, steer

shapely *adj* see: BEAUTIFUL *adj* 2

share *n* 1 claim, stake

n 2 comparison, percentage, proportion, ratio, relation

n 3 allocation, distribution, marketing, merchandising, selling, sharing

n 4 allotment, allowance, apportionment, budget, dispensation, dispersion, lot, measure, part, percentage, portion, quota, ration, slice

v 1 involve, partake, participate

v 2 breathe, confide, divulge, tell, whisper

v 3 brief, communicate, convey, declare, describe, disclose, divulge, explain, impart, inform, narrate, orate, portray, read, recite, recount, relate, report, retell, reveal, state, tattle, tell, transmit

v 4 see: ALLOCATE *v* 3

shared *adj* aggregate, collective, common, communal, joint, mutual, public

sharer *n* partaker, participant, partner, party

sharing *n* 1 allocation, distribution, marketing, merchandising, selling

n 2 see: REWARD *n* 8

sharp *adv* accurately, exactly, just so, precisely, right, smack, square, squarely

adj 1 acute, piercing, shooting, stabbing

adj 2 honed, keen, pointed, razor sharp, unblunted, whetted

adj 3 bad, decayed, putrid, rancid, rotten, sour, spoiled

adj 4 acerbic, acid, biting, curt, dry, pungent, sour, tart

adj 5 acute, annoying, grating, high, loud, piercing, shrill

adj 6 biting, hot, nippy, pungent, seasoned, spicy, tangy, tart

adj 7 caustic, inconsiderate, selfish, short, tactless, thoughtless, unceremonious, ungracious

adj 8 caustic, coarse, cutting, obscene, salty, scathing, scorching, spicy, trenchant, vulgar, witty

adj 9 accidental, careless, caustic, heedless, inadvertent, inconsiderate, nonchalant, selfish, short, tactless, thoughtless, uncaring, unceremonious, ungracious, unheeding, unintended, unintentional, unreflective, unthinking

adj 10 alert, astute, brainy, bright, brilliant, clever, discerning, discriminating, educated, insightful, intellectual, intelligent, knowing, knowledgeable, perceptive, quick, sagacious, sage, smart, swift

adj 11 acute, alert, astute, cagey, canny, clever, cunning, deft, keen, knowing, penetrating, perceptive, piercing, quick, quick-sighted, quick-witted, receptive, responsive, sagacious, savvy, sensitive, sharp-witted, shrewd, slick, smart, street-smart, wise

adj 12 see: SLY *adj* 3

sharpen *v* edge, file, grind, hone, polish, whet

shatter *v* 1 break, burst, erupt, explode, fragment, rupture, smash, smatter, splinter

v 2 see: DEMOLISH *v* 3

shave *v* 1 clip, cut, cut back, cut down, lower, mark down, reduce, slash

v 2 clip, crop, cut, lop, pare, prune, shear, snip, trim, whittle

v 3 brush, graze, scrape, scratch, skim, touch

shawl *n* 1 bandanna, mantilla, muffler, scarf

n 2 cape, cloak, coat, mantle, wrap

shear *v* clip, crop, cut, lop, pare, prune, shave, snip, trim, whittle

sheath *n* binder, capsule, case, casing, cover, envelope, holder, skin, wrapper

shed *n* barn, coop, enclosure, lean-to, paddock, pen, pound, shack, shelter, stable, stall, sty

v 1 beam, burn, disperse, emit, gleam, glisten, radiate, shine, transmit

v 2 bare, denude, discard, disrobe, doff, flash, remove, reveal, strip, take off, unclothe, undress

v 3 cast off, drop, molt, peel, repel

sheen *n* coating, gloss, glow, luster, patina, polish, radiance, shimmer, shine

sheepskin *n* 1 letterhead, page, paper, papyrus, parchment, sheet, stationery, vellum

n 2 certificate, credential, degree

sheer *adj* 1 perpendicular, steep, upright, vertical

adj 2 delicate, filmy, fine, flimsy, thin, transparent

adj 3 full

adj 4 absolute, chief, complete, consummate, dominant, godlike, leading, main, perfect, principal, pure, ranking, supreme, total, unsurpassed, utter, whole

sheet *n* 1 coating, covering, film, layer, membrane, tissue

n 2 brochure, circular, flier, handbill, handout, pamphlet

n 3 letterhead, page, paper, papyrus, parchment, sheepskin, stationery, vellum

shekels *n* see: MONEY *n* 4

shelf *n* 1 ledge, mantle, sill

n 2 reef, sandbank, sandbar, shallow, shoal

shell *n* 1 body, cadaver, carcass, corpse, remains, stiff

n 2 bark, case, coating, crust, husk, peel, rind, shuck, skin

n 3 bottle, bucket, caddy, can, canister, jar, pail, tin, vessel

n 4 debris, fragment, hulk, remains, rubbish, rubble, trash, wreck, wreckage

n 5 armor, covering, plate, protection, shield

n 6 buckshot, bullet, lead, missile, projectile, shot, slug

v 1 crack, husk, open, peel

v 2 blitz, bomb, bombard

shellac *v* see: THRASH *v* 1

shellfish *n* clam, cockle, crab, crustacean, mollusk, mussel, prawn, shrimp, snail

shelter *n* 1 barn, coop, enclosure, lean-to, paddock, pen, pound, shack, shed, stable, stall, sty

n 2 asylum, cover, harbor, haven, oasis,

port, preserve, protection, refuge, reserve, retreat, safety, sanctuary, seaport

n 3 berth, billet, housing, quarters, space

n 4 apartment, dorm, housing, lodging, room, suite

v 1 board, host, house, put up

v 2 ensconce, harbor, nestle, settle, snuggle

v 3 conceal, harbor, hide, house, keep, protect, safeguard, shield

shelve v adjourn, avoid, defer, delay, hold, hold up, interrupt, lay over, postpone, procrastinate, prolong, put off, remit, reschedule, set aside, stay, suspend, table, wait, waive

shepherd v conduct, control, develop, direct, drive, guide, lead, operate, pilot, route, show, steer

sherry n burgundy, chablis, champagne, chianti, claret, port, wine

shield n 1 defense, protection

n 2 barrier, mesh, netting, screen

n 3 camouflage, cloak, costume, cover, curtain, disguise, mask, pretense, shroud, veil

n 4 armor, covering, plate, protection

v 1 conceal, harbor, hide, house, keep, safeguard, shelter

v 2 bulwark, cover, defend, fend, fortify, guard, hide, protect, safeguard, screen

v 3 camouflage, cloak, conceal, cover, darken, disguise, envelop, hide, mask, occult, seclude, shroud, veil

shift n 1 change, move, reversal, turnabout

n 2 adjustment, alteration, anomaly, change, deviation, modification, mutation, variation

n 3 angle, bend, bow, detour, deviation, double, tack, turn, turning, yaw

v 1 change

v 2 alternate, change, cycle, lap, oscillate, switch

v 3 avoid, dodge, equivocate, evade, fence, hedge, shuffle, sidestep

v 4 dislocate, dislodge, displace, disturb, move, oust, remove, ship, transfer

v 5 do, fare, get along, get by, get on, make out, manage, muddle through, stagger

shifty adj 1 see: DECEITFUL adj 1

adj 2 see: EVIL adj 4

shill n decoy

shimmer n 1 coating, gloss, glow, luster, patina, polish, radiance, sheen, shine

n 2 flash, gleam, glimmer, glitter, shine, sparkle, twinkle

v excite, flash, gleam, glimmer, glint, glisten, glitter, scintillate, shine, sparkle, twinkle

shine n 1 finish, gloss, polish

n 2 coating, gloss, glow, luster, patina, polish, radiance, sheen

n 3 flash, gleam, glimmer, glitter, shimmer, sparkle, twinkle

v 1 buff, burnish, furbish, glaze, glimmer, gloss, polish, renovate

v 2 beam, burn, disperse, emit, gleam, glisten, radiate, shed, transmit

v 3 excite, flash, gleam, glimmer, glint, glisten, glitter, scintillate, shimmer, sparkle, twinkle

shining adj 1 excellent, extraordinary, great, impressive, noteworthy, outstanding, smashing, superb, wonderful

adj 2 see: BRIGHT adj 6

shiny adj 1 glossy, sleek, smooth

adj 2 beaming, bright, brilliant, burnished, emitting, glistening, glossy, lucid, luminous, lustrous, polished, radiant, shining

ship v 1 dislocate, dislodge, displace, disturb, move, oust, remove, shift, transfer

v 2 address, channel, consign, dispatch, export, forward, mail, post, remit, route, send, transmit, transport

n craft, cruiser, freighter, frigate, ketch, liner, ocean liner, sailboat, schooner, steamship, vessel, yacht

shipment n burden, cargo, consignment, freight, lading, load, payload, transportation, truck

ships n armada, assembly, boats, convoy, fleet, flotilla, grouping, navy, squadron

shipshape adj 1 meticulous, neat, orderly, prim, tidy, trim, well-groomed

adj 2 applicable, appropriate, apropos, apt, befitting, convenient, desirable, felicitous, fit, fitting, germane, good, handy, just, material, meet, necessary, pertinent, proper, relevant, right, suitable, suited, timely, useful

shirk v 1 avoid, circumvent, deflect, detour, dodge, duck, evade, hedge, parry, sidestep, skirt, ward off

v 2 see: DELAY v 3

shiver v flinch, flutter, jar, pulsate, quake, quaver, quiver, shake, shudder, tremble, twitch, twitter, vibrate

n quake, quiver, flutter, tingle, tremor

shnook n adversary, antagonist, naysayer, obstructionist

shoal n 1 bank, beach, coast, seashore

n 2 reef, sandbank, sandbar, shallow

shock *n* 1 astonishment, amazement, awe, bewilderment, surprise, wonder

n 2 blow, jerk, jolt, jump, start, surprise

n 3 blow, disturbance, jolt, trauma, upheaval, upset

n 4 fright, horror, scare, start, terror

v 1 daze, paralyze, stun, stupefy

v 2 bump, jar, jolt, jostle, rattle, shake, startle

v 3 amaze, daze, electrify, horrify, offend, outrage, overwhelm, scandalize, stun

v 4 appall, daunt, discourage, dismay, horrify, panic, petrify, scare, terrify, unnerve

v 5 abash, alarm, awe, cow, daunt, frighten, horrify, intimidate, panic, scare, spook, startle, terrify, terrorize, unnerve

shocking *adj* 1 dramatic, sensational, startling

adj 2 disabling, disturbing, painful, traumatic, upsetting

adj 3 awful, frightful, grim, grisly, gruesome, hideous, lurid, repulsive, sensational, terrible, ugly, violent

adj 4 abhorrent, abominable, appalling, detestable, disgusting, dreadful, evil, frightful, ghastly, hateful, horrible, horrid, loathsome, odious, repulsive

adj 5 atrocious, awful, crying, desperate, disgraceful, ghastly, grizzly, heinous, monstrous, notorious, odious, offensive, outrageous, scandalous, tasteless, wicked

adj 6 appalling, awful, dire, dreadful, fearful, formidable, frightening, frightful, ghastly, horrendous, horrible, offensive, ominous, portentous, scary, spooky, terrible, terrifying, unpleasant

adj 7 see: UNCOUTH *adj* 1

shoddy *adj* 1 see: FRAGILE *adj* 3

adj 2 see: INFERIOR *adj* 6

shoe *n* boot, brogan, chukka, footwear, moccasin, sandal, slipper, thong

shoot *v* 1 discharge, spurt

v 2 bombard, detonate, fire

v 3 perforate, permeate, pierce

v 4 discharge, emit, fire, hurl, launch, project

v 5 execute, hit, kill, wound

v 6 jet, spew, spout, spritz, spurt, squirt, surge

n branch, growth, sprout

shooting *adj* acute, piercing, sharp, stabbing

shop *v* buy, examine, purchase

n business, department store, mall, market, mart, store, supermarket

shopkeeper *n* clerk, representative, salesman, salesperson, saleswoman, vendor

shopper *n* buyer, client, consumer, customer, end user, patron, purchaser, user

shore *n* 1 base, brace, buttress, column, footing, foundation, prop, stay, support, underpinning

n 2 bank, beach, coast, seashore, shoal

v bear up, bolster, brace, build up, buoy, buttress, carry, fortify, harden, nourish, nurture, prop, reinforce, support, strengthen, sustain, toughen, uphold

short *adv* abruptly, fast, hastily, immediately, instantaneously, instantly, quick, quickly, suddenly, swiftly

adj 1 few, lacking, limited, nonabundant, not many, scant, sparse

adj 2 amiss, crude, defective, faulty, flawed, imperfect, incomplete, unfulfilled

adj 3 caustic, inconsiderate, selfish, sharp, tactless, thoughtless, unceremonious, ungracious

adj 4 deficient, failing, inadequate, inferior, insufficient, scant, scarce, scrimpy, shy, wanting

adj 5 brief, ephemeral, fleeting, impermanent, momentary, passing, temporary, transient, transitory, volatile

adj 6 abbreviated, brief, compressed, concise, crisp, curt, laconic, pithy, succinct, terse, to the point

adj 7 accidental, careless, caustic, heedless, inadvertent, inconsiderate, nonchalant, selfish, sharp, tactless, thoughtless, uncaring, unceremonious, ungracious, unheeding, unintended, unintentional, unreflective, unthinking

adj 8 low-statured

adj 9 brief, fleeting, passing, swift, transient

adj 10 abrupt, bluff, blunt, brash, brusque, cheeky, crusty, curt, flip, flippant, gruff, harsh, impertinent, impudent, irritable, nasty, quick, rude, sarcastic, sassy, snippy, snotty, surly, testy, wisenheimer

v bound, limit, restrict, scrimp, skimp, spare, stint

shortage *n* dearth, deficiency, deficit, drought, famine, lack, rarity, scarcity, sparseness, undersupply, want

shortcoming *n* 1 failing, fault, foible, frailty, limitation, vice, weakness

n 2 blemish, defect, failing, fault, flaw, imperfection, scar, weakness

n 3 defect, deficiency, demerit, fault, flaw, imperfection, inadequacy, lack, need, want

shorten *v* 1 check, cramp, curtail, impede, stunt, throttle

v 2 attenuate, dilute, diminish, lessen,

purify, rarefy, reduce, refine, thin out, weaken

v 3 abbreviate, abridge, condense, curtail, cut, cut back, diminish, edit, lessen, reduce, restrict, slash

shortly *adv* anon, any moment, at once, directly, immediately, instantaneously, instantly, momentarily, now, presently, promptly, quickly, right now, soon, straightaway, *tout de suite*

shortness *n* abruptness, brevity, briefness, conciseness, curtness, quickness, transience

shortsighted *adj* 1 careless, foolish, impulsive, irresponsible, myopic, not smart, reckless, risky, unthinking, unwise

adj 2 nearsighted

shot *adj* beat, burnt out, bushed, careworn, drawn, emaciated, exhausted, expended, fatigued, frazzled, haggard, jaded, pinched, pooped, run-down, spent, tired, wearied, weary, worn, worn down, worn-out

n 1 barrage, burst, fusillade, round, volley

n 2 crack, gibe, jeer, put-down, quip, sneer, torment

n 3 break, chance, crack, gap, occasion, opening, opportunity, show, stroke of luck, time

n 4 attempt, chance, effort, fling, go, guess, heave, lob, pop, slap, sling, stab, throw, toss, try, whirl

n 5 booster, injection, inoculation

n 6 buckshot, bullet, lead, missile, projectile, shell, slug

shotgun *n* carbine, firearm, flintlock, gun, rifle

should *v* must

shoulder *v* 1 bulldoze, elbow, hustle, jostle, push, shove

v 2 bear, carry, convey, crate, ferry, haul, lift, lug, pack, shuttle, tote, traffic, transport, truck

shout *n* 1 alarm, call, hail, signal, whoop, yell

n 2 bark, bellow, blare, holler, roar, scream, shriek, thunder, yell

v 1 bark, bay, cry, growl, howl, snap, woof, yap, yelp

v 2 blurt, cackle, cry, ejaculate, exclaim, spill, sputter, tattle, utter

v 3 bark, bellow, blare, call, cry, holler, howl, roar, scream, screech, shriek, shrill, squeal, thunder, wail, yell

shove *v* 1 bulldoze, elbow, hustle, jostle, press, push, shoulder

v 2 boost, budge, drive, force, impel, nudge, propel, push, thrust

shovel *v* burrow, dig, excavate, gouge, mine, unearth

n bucket, ladle, scoop

show *n* 1 make-believe, pretense, ruse, sham

n 2 act, farce, make-believe, parody, performance, sketch, skit

n 3 break, chance, crack, gap, occasion, opening, opportunity, shot, stroke of luck, time

n 4 array, blare, display, exhibit, exhibition, fanfare, fuss, parade, performance, presentation, procession, publicity, showing

v 1 demonstrate, determine, establish, evidence, prove

v 2 acquaint, announce, delineate, depict, introduce, present, reflect, represent

v 3 disclose, display, evince, express, imply, indicate, manifest, reflect

v 4 allude, denote, indicate, mention, point out, refer to, reveal, speak of, specify, suggest, tell

v 5 add up to, connote, convey, denote, identify, import, indicate, intend, mean, signify, symbolize

v 6 conduct, control, develop, direct, drive, guide, lead, operate, pilot, route, shepherd, steer

v 7 demonstrate, describe, display, draw, establish, examine, exhibit, explain, present, prove, sketch, tell

shower *n* cloudburst, deluge, downpour, drizzle, hail, precipitation, rain, sprinkle

v 1 bestow, deluge, lavish

v 2 bathe, clean, cleanse, clean up, dip, flush, immerse, launder, rinse, rub, scour, scrape, wash

v 3 deluge, drizzle, fall, pour, rain, sprinkle

v 4 cascade, emit, flood, inundate, overflow, plunge, pour, rain, spill, swamp, tumble

showing *n* see: EXHIBITION *n*

showstopper *n* blip, catch, glitch, gotcha, hangup, hitch, slip, snag

showy *adj* 1 ambitious, bombastic, flamboyant, garish, grandiose, inflated, jaunty, lofty, ostentatious, pompous, portentous, pretentious, splashy, splendid, utopian, visionary

adj 2 see: OSTENTATIOUS *adj* 1, 2

shred *n* 1 end, patch, piece, rag, scrap, tatter

n 2 dregs, leftovers, remainder, remains, remnant, residual, residue, rest, scrap, silt

n 3 fragment, sliver, splinter

n 4 bit, dab, end, fragment, iota, minutia,

mite, morsel, particle, piece, pinch, portion, scrap, speck, spot, strip, tidbit, trifle

v rend, rip, slice, tatter, tear

shrew *n* harpy, nag

shrewd *adj* 1 see: CAREFUL *adj* 7

adj 2 see: QUICK *adj* 5

adj 3 see: SENSIBLE *adj* 5

adj 4 see: SLY *adj* 3

shrewdness *n* acumen, astuteness, awareness, cleverness, discernment, discrimination, insight, intellect, intuition, keenness, perception, sagacity, sensitivity, understanding, wit

shriek *n* bawl, bellow, blare, holler, roar, scream, shout, thunder, yell

v bark, bellow, blare, call, cry, holler, howl, roar, scream, screech, shout, shrill, squeal, thunder, wail, yell

shrill *adj* acute, annoying, grating, high, loud, piercing, piping, sharp

v bark, bellow, blare, call, cry, holler, howl, roar, scream, screech, shout, shriek, squeal, thunder, wail, yell

shrimp *n* clam, cockle, crab, crustacean, mollusk, mussel, prawn, shellfish, snail

shrine *n* memorial, monument, statue

shrink *v* 1 collapse, contract, crumple, deflate

v 2 cower, cringe, flinch, grovel, quail, recoil, sneak

v 3 blanch, cringe, flinch, jump, recoil, start, startle, wince

v 4 atrophy, decay, deteriorate, dry up, dwindle, mummify, shrivel, waste away, welter, wilt, wither, wizen

v 5 compress, concentrate, condense, constrict, contract, reduce

v 6 abate, cease, decline, decrease, die down, diminish, drain, dwindle, ease, ebb, fall, lessen, let up, lull, recede, reduce, relax, relent, slacken, soften, stop, subside, taper off, wane, waste away, weaken

shrinkage *n* atrophy, decay, degeneration, deterioration, wasting

shrivel *v* atrophy, decay, deteriorate, dry up, dwindle, mummify, shrink, waste away, welter, wilt, wither, wizen

shriveled *adj* 1 burnt, scorched

adj 2 shrunken, withered, wrinkled

shroud *n* camouflage, cloak, costume, cover, curtain, disguise, mask, pretense, shield, veil

v camouflage, cloak, conceal, cover, darken, disguise, envelop, hide, mask, occult, seclude, shield, veil

shrub *n* bush, grass, hedge, plant, sapling, tree, vegetation, vine, weed

shrubbery *n* copse, grove, thicket

shrunken *adj* shriveled, withered, wrinkled

shuck *n* bark, case, coating, crust, husk, peel, shell, skin

shudder *v* flinch, flutter, jar, pulsate, quake, quaver, quiver, shake, shiver, tremble, twitch, twitter, vibrate

shuffle *v* 1 confuse, disorder, mix, scramble

v 2 avoid, dodge, equivocate, evade, fence, hedge, shift, sidestep

v 3 disarray, dislocate, disorder, disorganize, disrupt, disturb, interfere, interrupt, jumble, mess, mix up, muss, rummage, sift through, unsettle

n gait, march, pace, step, stride, walk

shun *v* 1 avoid, duck, elude, escape, eschew, evade, recoil, shy

v 2 defy, discount, disregard, exclude, forget, ignore, miss, neglect, omit, ostracize, overlook, overpass, pass, pass by, pass over, skip, slight, snub

shut *v* 1 block, close, obstruct, occlude, plug, stop

v 2 bolt, close, latch, lock, seal, secure, slam

shut-in *n* invalid, patient

shuttle *v* bear, carry, convey, crate, ferry, haul, lift, lug, pack, shoulder, tote, traffic, transport, truck

shy *adj* 1 deficient, failing, inadequate, inferior, insufficient, scant, scarce, scrimpy, short, wanting

adj 2 backward, bashful, coy, demure, diffident, innocent, modest, quiet, reserved, retiring, staid, timid, unassured

adj 3 see: DOUBTFUL *adj* 1

adj 4 see: INDIFFERENT *adj* 4

adj 5 see: RETICENT *adj* 2

adj 6 see: UNWILLING *adj*

v avoid, duck, elude, escape, eschew, evade, recoil

shyness *n* modesty, reserve

sick *adj* 1 nauseated, queasy, queer, seasick, squeamish

adj 2 ailing, delicate, diseased, down, frail, ill, impaired, indisposed, sickly, suffering, unhealthy, unsound, unwell, weak

adj 3 bored, disgusted, tired, weary

sicken *v* 1 agitate, derange, disorder, disturb, fluster, rock, ruffle, shake, unhinge, unsettle, upset

v 2 abhor, disgust, nauseate, repel, repulse, revolt

sickening *adj* disagreeable, distasteful, disturbing, unappetizing, undesirable, unpalatable, unsavory

sickly *adj* 1 ashen, ashy, blanched, colorless, pale, pallid, sallow, sooty, wan, waxen, yellow

adj 2 ailing, delicate, diseased, down, frail, ill, impaired, indisposed, sick, suffering, unhealthy, unsound, unwell, weak

adj 3 breakable, decrepit, delicate, dilapidated, feeble, flimsy, fragile, frail, jerry-built, jury-rigged, puny, Rube Goldberg, shoddy, thin, tinny, unsound, worn-out

sickness *n* 1 affliction, ailment, complaint, condition, disease, disorder, evil, harm, ill, illness, infirmity, malady

n 2 see: ANGUISH *n* 2

side *adj* ancillary, auxiliary, incidental, minor, related, secondary, subordinate

n 1 angle, aspect, facet, hand, mien, opinion, perspective, phase, slant, view

n 2 face, siding, surface, wall

n 3 border, boundary, bounds, brim, brink, curb, edge, fringe, limits, lip, margin, outskirt, perimeter, periphery, rim, skirt, verge

v advocate, back, champion, endorse, guarantee, promote, sanction, support, uphold

sideline *n* avocation, distraction, diversion, hobby, pastime

sidestep *v* 1 avoid, dodge, equivocate, evade, fence, hedge, shift

v 2 avoid, circumvent, deflect, detour, dodge, duck, evade, hedge, parry, shirk, skirt, ward off

sidewalk *n* ground, pavement, paving, walkway

siding *n* face, side, surface, wall

siege *n* attack, attempt, blockade, bout, offensive

siesta *n* see: PEACE *n* 2

sieve *v* filter

n colander, sifter, strainer

sift *v* 1 filter

v 2 filter, screen

v 3 comb, loot, ransack, rifle, scour, search, separate, sort

v 4 choose, cull, elect, pick, remove, select, separate, single out, sort

sifter *n* sieve, strainer

sigh *v* bawl, bemoan, cry, grieve, groan, lament, moan, mourn, snivel, sob, wail, weep, whimper, whine

n groan, moan, sob, wail

sight *n* 1 look, picture, view

n 2 eyesight, perception, vision

n 3 landscape, outlook, scene, view, vista

v 1 behold, glimpse, look, mind, see, spot, watch, witness

v 2 see: UNDERSTAND *v* 6

sightless *adj* blind, unsighted, visionless

sign *n* 1 banner, headline, placard, poster

n 2 clue, example, illustration, indication, manifestation

n 3 announcement, notice, placard, poster, proclamation

n 4 nod, signal, symbol, symptom, token, trait

n 5 apprehension, foreboding, forewarning, harbinger, intuition, omen, premonition, presage, warning

n 6 character, emblem, example, icon, letter, logo, mark, model, representation, symbol, token

n 7 clue, cue, guide, hint, indication, indicator, inkling, intimation, key, lead, mark, notion, pointer, signal, tip, trace

v autograph, ink, subscribe

signal *n* 1 alarm, bell, buzzer, chime, gong, siren

n 2 alarm, call, hail, shout, whoop, yell

n 3 nod, sign, symbol, symptom, token, trait

n 4 clue, cue, guide, hint, indication, indicator, inkling, intimation, key, lead, mark, notion, pointer, sign, tip, trace

v 1 beckon, gesture, motion

v 2 alert, augur, caution, flag, forebode, forewarn, indicate, inform, motion, notify, warn, wave

signature *n* approval, autograph, endorsement, John Hancock, mark, name

significance *n* 1 content, gist, meaning

n 2 accent, emphasis, highlighting, importance, priority, stress, weight

n 3 concern, emphasis, gravity, import, importance, stress, weight

n 4 consequence, import, importance, magnitude, moment, substance, weight

n 5 import, intent, meaning, message, sense, understanding

significant *adj* 1 critical, essential, integral, necessary, strategic

adj 2 formidable, huge, immense, impressive, intimidating, massive, substantial

adj 3 consequential, considerable, critical, crucial, important, material, meaningful, momentous, prominent, substantial, vital, weighty

adj 4 amazing, brilliant, exceptional, extraordinary, noteworthy, phenomenal, rare, remarkable, singular, stunning, super, uncommon, uncustomary, unique, unusual

significantly *adv* considerably, dramatically, far, quite, rather, very, well

signify *v* 1 add up to, connote, convey, denote, identify, import, indicate, intend, mean, show, symbolize

v 2 see: PREDICT *v* 2

sign up *v* catalog, enroll, inscribe, list, register, write

silence *n* calm, hush, lull, peace, peacefulness, quiet, repose, respite, rest, siesta, sleep, stillness, tranquillity

v censor, curb, gag, hush, inhibit, muffle, mute, quell, quiet, repress, restrain, squelch, stifle, still, subdue, suppress, throttle, tone down

silent *adj* 1 dumb, inarticulate, mute, reticent, speechless, tacit, voiceless

adj 2 dead, hush, inanimate, inert, lifeless, noiseless, quiet, soundless, still

silky *adj* cottony, satiny, slippery, smooth, soft, supple, velvety

sill *n* ledge, shelf

silliness *n* see: NONSENSE *n* 2

silly *adj* 1 capricious, dizzy, flighty, frivolous, giddy, irresponsible

adj 2 absurd, anile, asinine, brainless, childish, fatuous, foolish, idiotic, inept, meaningless, mindless, senseless, simple, thoughtless, unintelligent, witless

adj 3 absurd, balmy, bizarre, crazy, emotional, foolish, frivolous, goofy, illogical, impossible, inane, insane, irrational, loony, lunatic, mad, muddled, nuts, preposterous, ridiculous, touched, wacky, zany

adj 4 see: FUNNY *adj* 3

adj 5 see: PREOCCUPIED *adj* 1

silt *n* 1 dregs, leftovers, remainder, remains, remnant, residue, residual, rest, scrap

n 2 deposit, muck, mud, sediment, sludge

simian *n* ape, gorilla, monkey

similar *adj* akin, alike, analogous, comparable, corresponding, equivalent, identical, kindred, like, matching, parallel, related, same, such, uniform

similarity *n* 1 equality, equilibrium, equity, equivalence, evenness, par, parity, symmetry

n 2 affinity, analogy, approximation, comparison, likeness, match, metaphor, resemblance, semblance, simile

simile *n* affinity, analogy, approximation, comparison, likeness, match, metaphor, resemblance, similarity

simmer *v* 1 boil, heat, overheat, parboil, seethe, stew

v 2 agitate, bake, boil, bubble, burn, churn, ferment, foam, fume, roast, seethe, smolder

v 3 anger, blow up, boil, boil over, brew, bristle, burn, flare up, fume, rage, seethe, smoke, steam, storm

simper *n* beam, glow, grin, smile, smirk

simple *adj* 1 facile, smooth

adj 2 basic, crude, plain, primitive, rough, undeveloped

adj 3 ascetic, astringent, austere, chaste, rigid, spartan, stern, stoic

adj 4 clear, coherent, direct, easy, elementary, intelligible, logical, understandable

adj 5 discreet, dry, homely, modest, plain, unadorned, undecorated, unembellished, unembroidered, ungarnished, unpretentious

adj 6 absurd, anile, asinine, brainless, childish, fatuous, foolish, idiotic, inept, meaningless, mindless, senseless, silly, thoughtless, unintelligent, witless

adj 7 artless, candid, frank, guileless, ingenuous, innocent, naive, natural, open, plain, simple-hearted, unadorned, unaffected, unsophisticated, unstudied, untutored, unworldly

adj 8 see: DUMB *adj* 2

simple-hearted *adj* artless, candid, frank, guileless, ingenuous, innocent, naive, natural, open, plain, simple, unadorned, unaffected, unsophisticated, unstudied, untutored, unworldly

simple-minded *adj* backward, blunt, deficient, dense, dimwitted, dull, dumb, feebleminded, idiotic, moronic, obtuse, retarded, simple, slow, stupid, thick, uneducated, unintelligent

simpleton *n* blockhead, boor, clod, creep, cretin, dimwit, dolt, dope, dullard, dumbbell, dummy, dunce, fool, goof, idiot, imbecile, jerk, nerd, nincompoop, numskull, oaf, pain, schlemiel, schmuck, stooge, turkey

simply *adv* but, except that, further, however, just, merely, nevertheless, only, solely, yet

simulate *v* clone, copy, duplicate, image, imitate, mirror, print, re-create, redo, reduplicate, remake, replicate, reprint

simulated *adj* 1 copied, imitated, pseudo, unoriginal

adj 2 fake, feigned, fictitious, mock

adj 3 artificial, bogus, counterfeit, ersatz, fake, false, imitation, mock, phony, pseudo, sham, spurious, substitute, unreal

simulation *n* 1 drawing, icon, image, model, representation, symbol

n 2 clone, copy, counterfeit, duplicate,

duplication, image, imitation, likeness, mock up, model, print, replica, replication, representation, reproduction

simultaneous *adj* coexistent, coexisting, coincident, concurrent, contemporary, synchronous

simultaneously *adv* concurrently, side by side, together

sin *n* crime, dishonor, disobedience, evil, fault, felony, infamy, infraction, iniquity, injury, lawbreaking, misdeed, misdemeanor, offense, outrage, transgression, trespass, vice, violation, wrong, wrongdoing
v err, fall, offend, transgress, trespass, violate

sincere *adj* candid, direct, earnest, forthright, frank, genuine, heartfelt, hearty, honest, no-holds-barred, open, real, straightforward, true, trustworthy, truthful, undesigning, unfeigned, unpretentious, wholehearted

sincerely *adv* actually, exactly, genuinely, precisely, really, truly, verifiably, veritably, very

sincerity *n* candor, frankness, truthfulness

sinful *adj* bad, corrupt, crooked, deceitful, dishonest, evil, fraudulent, immoral, iniquitous, lying, Machiavellian, manipulative, mercenary, reprobate, roguish, scheming, shady, shifty, unethical, unfair, unprincipled, unscrupulous, untruthful, venal, vile, wicked, wrong

sing *v* 1 carol, chant, harmonize, hum, lilt, yodel
v 2 fink, inform, rat, snitch, squeal, stool, tattle, tattletale

singe *v* bake, broil, burn, char, cook, melt, parch, roast, scorch, sear, swelter, toast, warm

single *adj* 1 sole, spouseless, unmarried, unwed
adj 2 alone, lone, lonely, lonesome, singular, solitary, solo, unaccompanied
adj 3 characteristic, differentiating, distinctive, lone, one, particular, peculiar, select, solitary, special, unique, unusual
adj 4 exclusive, individual, lone, odd, one, only, particular, separate, singular, sole, solitary, unique, unshared
n 1 bachelor
n 2 maid, maiden, spinster

single-minded *adj* see: STUBBORN *adj* 6

singular *adj* 1 alone, lone, lonely, lonesome, single, solitary, solo, unaccompanied
adj 2 amazing, brilliant, exceptional, extraordinary, noteworthy, phenomenal,

rare, remarkable, significant, stunning, super, uncommon, uncustomary, unique, unusual
adj 3 see: LONE *adj* 2, 3
adj 4 see: STRANGE *adj* 5

singularity *n* distinctiveness, individuality, oneness, singularness, unity

singularness *n* distinctiveness, individuality, singularity, unity

sinister *adj* 1 foreboding, imminent, impending, menacing, ominous, portentous, predictive, prophetic, threatening
adj 2 bad, baleful, corrupt, cunning, forbidding, harmful, hurtful, malevolent, malignant, menacing, ominous, sneaky

sink *v* 1 fall, lapse, slip
v 2 descend, stoop, submit
v 3 decline, die down, diminish, dip, settle, slide, slip, subside
v 4 depress, droop, flop, let down, lower, mire, sag, wallow
v 5 descend, dive, drop, fall, lapse, leap, lower, plummet, plunge, swoop
v 6 attack, butt, drive, knock, lunge, pass, plunge, ram, stab, stick, thrust
v 7 abase, abash, belittle, cast down, cheapen, debase, defile, deflate, degrade, demean, depreciate, derogate, devalue, dishonor, embarrass, humble, humiliate, lower, mortify, put down
n basin, washbowl, washstand

sinuous *adj* crooked, meandering, serpentine, spiral, turning, twisting, winding, zigzagging

sip *v* bibulate, booze, consume, drink, gulp, guzzle, imbibe, nip, partake, polish off, put away, put down, sample, savor, suck, swig, swill, taste

siphon *v* 1 draft, drain, draw, draw off, pump, suck, tap
v 2 carry, channel, conduct, convey, funnel, pass, pipe, transmit

sire *v* 1 engender, father, fertilize, impregnate
v 2 bear, beget, breed, come into, create, effect, engender, father, generate, hatch, impregnate, make, mate, multiply, originate, parent, procreate, promulgate, propagate, reproduce, spawn

siren *n* 1 alarm, bell, buzzer, chime, gong
n 2 coquette, flirt, harlot, nymphomaniac, seductress, tart, tease, temptress, vamp, wanton woman

sissy *adj* effeminate, effete, swishy, unmanly, wimpy

sit *v* model, pose

sitcom *n* cartoons, docudrama, documentary, game shows, mini-series, movies, news, programs, series, soap opera, soaps, talk shows, television, variety shows

site *n* 1 arena, locale, scene, theater

n 2 area, locale, location, locus, place, point, property, scene, spot

n 3 see: RESIDENCE *n* 1

situate *v* see: INSTALL *v* 1

situation *n* 1 circumstance, context, environment, setting

n 2 appointment, connection, duty, function, job, office, position

n 3 complication, difficulty, dilemma, obstacle, plight, predicament, problem, quandary, snag

n 4 capacity, grade, office, place, position, post, quality, rank, spot, standing, state, station, status

n 5 cause, issue, thing

n 6 condition, mode, perspective, posture, state, status, update

n 7 art, avocation, business, calling, career, discipline, employment, field, gig, job, labor, line, livelihood, occupation, office, profession, pursuit, role, schtick, specialty, task, thing, trade, vocation, work

sizable *adj* 1 ample, decent, generous, substantial

adj 2 see: BIG *adj* 4

size *n* 1 amount, amplitude, dimensions, magnitude, proportions, quantity, scope, volume

n 2 face, family, font, printwheel, style, type, typeface

n 3 circle, compass, confines, dimension, distance, extension, extent, length, limit, orbit, purview, range, reach, realm, scope, spectrum, sweep, width

v calibrate, gauge, measure, range

sizzle *n* 1 pizzazz, sexiness

n 2 effectiveness, flair, kick, pep, pizzazz, potency, punch, snap, spark, verve, vigor, wallop

v bubble, crackle, hiss, spit, sputter

sizzling *adj* baking, blistering, boiling, broiling, burning, fiery, hot, scalding, scorching, sultry, sweltering, torrid

skate *v* see: SNEAK *v* 2

skeleton *n* 1 framework, infrastructure

n 2 draft, outline, sketch

n 3 bone, fossil, remains

skeptic *n* 1 agnostic, nonbeliever

n 2 critic, cynic, detractor, hatchet man, naysayer, pessimist

skeptical *adj* 1 contemptuous, cynical, derisive, ironic, mocking, sarcastic, sardonic, scornful, wry

adj 2 cynical, distrustful, doubtful, dubious, incredulous, leery, questionable, shy, skittish, suspicious, uncertain, unsure

skepticism *n* 1 disbelief, distrust, doubt, incredulity, unbelief

n 2 concern, doubt, dubiety, incertitude, indecision, mistrust, query, question, suspicion, uncertainty, wonder

n 3 annoyance, anxiety, apprehension, bother, care, concern, disquiet, disquietude, doubt, irritation, misgiving, reservation, restlessness, restraint, trouble, uneasiness, vexation, worry

sketch *n* 1 autobiography, biography, compendium, profile, résumé, vita

n 2 act, farce, make-believe, parody, performance, show, skit

n 3 blueprint, chart, diagram, draft, map, outline

n 4 depiction, description, explanation, illustration, narration, report, story, verbalization

n 5 draft, outline

n 6 anecdote, description, fantasy, fiction, invention, myth, narration, narrative, novel, story, tale, yarn

n 7 abridgement, abstract, brief, compendium, condensation, digest, essence, example, outline, review, summary, syllabus, synopsis

n 8 acrylic, art, canvas, depiction, drawing, etching, illustration, landscape, lithograph, mural, oil, painting, pastel, pen and ink, picture, portrait, print, seascape, still life, watercolor

v 1 depict, design, draw, paint

v 2 delineate, depict, illustrate, picture, portray

v 3 doodle, draw, jot, scratch, scrawl, scribble, write

v 4 demonstrate, describe, display, draw, establish, examine, exhibit, explain, present, prove, show, tell

v 5 arrange, blueprint, cast, chart, design, devise, draft, draw, engineer, fashion, lay out, map, outline, plan, plot, project

sketchy *adj* brief, crude, cursory, hasty, rough, shallow, superficial, uncritical

skew *v* 1 descend, decline, incline, slant, slope, veer

v 2 bias, corrupt, distort, misrepresent, pervert, slant, warp

v 3 avert, deflect, deviate, dip, divert, dodge, pivot, swerve, swing, swivel, turn, veer, wheel, whip

skid *v* fall, lurch, skim, slide, slip, stumble, totter, trip, tumble

skiff *n* barge, boat, canoe, craft, dory, ferry, float, kayak, raft, scow, tender skill *n* 1 education, experience, exposure, involvement, practice

n 2 diplomacy, discretion, finesse, savvy, subtlety, tact

n 3 ability, adequacy, adroitness, aptitude, art, caliber, calling, capability, capacity, command, competence, craft, dexterity, experience, expertise, familiarity, forte, knack, know-how, knowledge, mastery, proficiency, prowess, qualification, savvy, specialty, strength, talent, training, workmanship

skilled *adj* 1 artistic, creative, talented

adj 2 qualified, specialized, technical, trained

adj 3 adept, dexterous, handy, mechanical, proficient

adj 4 adroit, apt, canny, clever, cunning, deft, handy, ingenious, nimble, skillful, sly, wily

skillful *adj* 1 artistic, creative, skilled, talented

adj 2 agile, deft, dexterous, subtle

adj 3 adroit, apt, canny, clever, cunning, deft, handy, ingenious, nimble, skilled, sly, wily

adj 4 able, accomplished, adept, apt, capable, competent, deft, dexterous, expert, fit, gifted, masterful, professional, proficient, proper, qualified, talented

adj 5 see: RESOURCEFUL *adj* 3

skills *n* acts, bag of tricks, repertoire, résumé, talents

skim *v* 1 exploit

v 2 browse, glance at, look through, peruse, scan

v 3 fall, lurch, skid, slide, slip, stumble, totter, trip, tumble

v 4 backfire, boomerang, bounce, brush, glance, graze, rebound, ricochet, skip, touch

v 5 dart, fly

v 6 brush, graze, scrape, scratch, shave, touch

v 7 coast, crawl, creep, glide, prowl, skate, skulk, slick, slide, slink, slip, slither, snake, sneak, steal, wiggle, wriggle, writhe

skimp *v* 1 economize, save, scrape

v 2 bound, limit, restrict, scrimp, short, spare, stint

skimpy *adj* 1 bare, deficient, few, inadequate, inferior, insufficient, little, meager, paltry, petty, poor, scant, scanty, spare, sparse

adj 2 see: TRIVIAL *adj* 1

skin *n* 1 exterior, facade, surface

n 2 case, coat, cover, enclosure, folder

n 3 binder, capsule, case, casing, cover, envelope, holder, wrapper

n 4 bark, case, coating, crust, husk, peel, rind, shell, shuck

n 5 coating, covering

n 6 coat, fur, hide, jacket, pelt, stole

v flay, peel, scale, strip

skinny *adj* 1 lank, narrow, slender, slight, slim, tenuous, thin, veiled, wiry

adj 2 angular, bony, emaciated, gaunt, lanky, lean, meager, scraggly, scrawny, slender, thin

skip *v* 1 bypass, jump, pass over

v 2 bounce, bump, jostle, throw, volley

v 3 caper, cavort, frisk, frolic, gambol, play, prance, rollick

v 4 bob, bound, hop, jaunt, jump, leap, lope, prance, spring, sprint, trip

v 5 defy, discount, disregard, exclude, forget, ignore, miss, neglect, omit, ostracize, overlook, overpass, pass, pass by, pass over, shun, slight, snub

v 6 see: REBOUND *v* 2

skirmish *n* 1 affray, battle, brawl, brush, clash, conflict, difference, disagreement, dispute, encounter, fight, fracas, melee, quarrel, run-in, scrimmage, spat, touch

n 2 contest, encounter, struggle

n 3 altercation, argument, battle, brawl, challenge, combat, controversy, disagreement, discord, dispute, feud, fight, fracas, fray, hassle, melee, quarrel, rancor, rift, row, ruckus, scrap, scuffle, spat, squabble, struggle, tiff, war

v combat, conflict, contend, contest, engage, scuffle, struggle, tussle

skirt *n* 1 border, boundary, bounds, brim, brink, curb, edge, fringe, limits, lip, margin, outskirt, perimeter, periphery, rim, side, verge

n 2 costume, dress, gown

v 1 approach, border, bound, define, edge, hem, limit, outline, verge

v 2 avoid, circumvent, deflect, detour, dodge, duck, evade, hedge, parry, shirk, sidestep, ward off

skit *n* act, farce, make-believe, parody, performance, show

skittish *adj* 1 cynical, distrustful, doubtful, dubious, incredulous, leery, questionable, shy, skeptical, suspicious, uncertain, unsure

adj 2 antsy, edgy, excitable, fidgety, highstrung, irritable, jittery, jumpy, moody, nervous, nervy, restless, temperamental

skulk *v* coast, crawl, creep, glide, prowl, skate, skim, slick, slide, slink, slip, slither, snake, sneak, steal, wiggle, wriggle, writhe

skulking *adj* catlike, cattish, catty, furtive, stealthy

slab *n* block, chunk, plank

slack *adj* 1 down, idle, lax, off, slow, sluggish

adj 2 feeble, flabby, flaccid, lax, limp, loose, pendulous, relaxed

n 1 excess, give, leeway, margin, play, stretch

n 2 inactivity

v ease, ease off, lax, loosen, mellow out, relax, slacken

slacken *v* 1 ease, ease off, lax, loosen, mellow out, slack

v 2 bog, delay, detain, hang up, impede, mire, retard, slow

v 3 see: SUBSIDE *v* 2

slackening *n* abatement, diminishing, easing, letup, relaxation

slam *v* bolt, close, latch, lock, seal, shut

n bang, bell ringer, bull's-eye, gong, hit, smash, strike

slammer *n* brig, cage, cell, cooler, coop, hoosegow, jail, pen, penitentiary, pokey, prison, reformatory, stir, stockade, tower

slander *n* 1 accusation, aspersion, defamation, libel, remark, slur, smear

n 2 admonishment, admonition, blast, chewing out, chiding, criticism, denunciation, diatribe, harangue, hassle, libel, outburst, rap, rebuke, reprimand, reproach, reproof, scolding, tirade

v 1 befoul, besmirch, blacken, darken, defame, disparage, injure, libel, malign, revile, scandalize, slur, smear, soil, tear down, traduce

v 2 abuse, asperse, bad-mouth, belittle, condemn, damage, decry, defame, degrade, denigrate, denounce, deprecate, detract, diminish, discount, disparage, insult, knock, malign, put down, revile, run down, take away, vilify

slant *n* 1 angle, grade, gradient, incline, pitch, ramp, rise, slope, tilt

n 2 angle, aspect, facet, hand, mien, opinion, perspective, phase, side, view

n 3 bluff, cliff, hill, incline, slope, steep bank

n 4 attitude, belief, bias, conviction, feeling, inducement, leaning, mind, opinion, persuasion, sentiment, view

v 1 decline, descend, incline, skew, slope, veer

v 2 bias, color, distort, embellish, exaggerate

v 3 bank, bend, incline, lean, slope

v 4 bias, corrupt, distort, misrepresent, pervert, skew, warp

v 5 bend, bias, brainwash, compel, convert, indoctrinate, influence, predispose, prejudice, sway

v 6 angle, confuse, deceive, distort, falsify, garble, incline, misconstrue, misinterpret, misquote, misread, misrepresent, misunderstand, mix up, mumble, slope, taint, twist

slap *n* 1 attempt, chance, effort, fling, go, guess, heave, lob, pop, shot, sling, stab, throw, toss, try, whirl

n 2 bang, blow, box, bump, chop, clap, conk, crack, crash, cuff, hit, impact, jar, jolt, knock, lick, punch, rap, slug, smack, smash, swat, swipe, tap, wallop, whack

n 3 see: INSULT *n*

v box, clap, cuff, knock, punch, smack, spank, strike, tap, whack

slash *v* 1 clip, cut, cut back, cut down, lower, mark down, reduce

v 2 abbreviate, abridge, condense, curtail, cut, cut back, diminish, edit, lessen, reduce, restrict

v 3 cut, gash, incise, penetrate, pierce, punch, slice, slit

n rip, slit, split, tear

slate *v* arrange, bespeak, book, engage, organize, plan, program, schedule

slatternly *adj* careless, disheveled, messy, scruffy, slipshod, sloppy, sloven, slovenly, tacky, uncombed, unkempt, untidy

slaughter *n* bloodbath, bloodshed, butchery, carnage, extermination, genocide, holocaust, killing, massacre, pogrom, shambles

v abolish, annihilate, assassinate, bump off, butcher, decimate, destroy, dispatch, execute, exterminate, hang, hit, kill, knock off, liquidate, massacre, murder, put away, rub out, slay, wipe out

slave *n* chattel, pauper, peasant, peon, serf, vassal

v drudge, grub, hustle, labor, strain, strive, sweat, toil, work

slavery *n* 1 bondage, enslavement, imprisonment, indenture, serfdom, servitude

n 2 chore, drudgery, grind, labor, sweat, tedium, toil, travail, work

slavish *adj* abject, common, groveling, humble, ingratiating, lowly, menial, obeisant, servile, subservient

slay *v* abolish, annihilate, assassinate, bump off, butcher, decimate, destroy, dispatch, execute, exterminate, hang, hit, kill, knock off, liquidate, massacre, murder, put away, rub out, slaughter, wipe out

slaying *n* death penalty, execution, killing

sleazy *adj* base, cheap, trashy

sleek *adj* 1 glossy, smooth

adj 2 sexy, slender, slim, slinky, svelte

adj 3 greasy, oily, slick, slippery, smooth, unctuous

adj 4 chic, dapper, dashing, debonair, jaunty, natty, neat, rakish, smart, snazzy, spiffy, suave, trim

sleep *n* 1 apathy, coma, doze, ennui, grogginess, inertia, languor, lassitude, lethargy, nod, slumber, stupor

n 2 see: PEACE *n* 2

v doze, nap, rest, snooze

sleepless *adj* awake, fretful, restless

sleepy *adj* 1 dozing, drowsy, lethargic, napping, nodding, slumberous, snoozy, somnolent, tired

adj 2 asleep, dormant, idle, immobile, inactive, inanimate, inert, inoperative, laid-back, motionless, nodding, passive, quiet, slumbering, stable, stagnant, still

sleeve *n* envelope, file, folder

slender *adj* 1 sexy, sleek, slim, slinky, svelte

adj 2 lank, narrow, skinny, slight, slim, tenuous, thin, veiled, wiry

adj 3 angular, bony, emaciated, gaunt, lanky, lean, meager, scraggly, scrawny, thin

adj 4 see: TRIVIAL *adj* 2

slenderize *v* diet, fast, lose weight, reduce, slim, trim down

slew *n* droves, loads, lots, many, multitudes, plenty, scads

slice *v* 1 rend, rip, shred, tatter, tear

v 2 cut, gash, incise, penetrate, pierce, punch, slash, slit

v 3 allocate, allot, allow, apportion, assign, designate, distribute, divide, divvy, earmark, give, measure, parcel, partition, portion, prorate, quota, ration, section

v 4 ax, carve, chip, chop, cleave, cut, dissect, fell, hack, hew, mangle, mutilate, notch, pulverize, rend, saw, sever, sliver, snip, split, sunder, whittle

n 1 see: ALLOWANCE *n* 2

n 2 see: SECTION *n* 4

slick *adj* 1 charming, smooth, sophisticated, suave

adj 2 greasy, oily, sleek, slippery, smooth, unctuous

adj 3 see: QUICK *adj* 5

v see: SNEAK *v* 2

slide *n* 1 comedown, decline, decrease, descent, dive, drop, failure, fall, plunge, regression, setback, tumble

n 2 debasement, decline, deterioration, dip, downturn, drop, ebb, erosion, fall, involution, plunge, sag, slip, slump, wane, weakening

n 3 acetate, overhead, transparency

n 4 halftone, photo, photograph, picture, snapshot

v 1 drop off, fall away, slip, slump

v 2 coast, drift, float, fly, glide, sail, soar

v 3 decline, die down, diminish, dip, settle, sink, slip, subside

v 4 fall, lurch, skid, skim, slip, stumble, totter, trip, tumble

v 5 coast, crawl, creep, glide, prowl, skate, skim, skulk, slick, slink, slip, slither, snake, sneak, steal, wiggle, wriggle, writhe

slight *adj* 1 delicate, feeble, flimsy, inadequate

adj 2 faint, imperceptible, meager, remote, subtle, vague

adj 3 feeble, flimsy, frail, insubstantial, tenuous, unsubstantial, weak

adj 4 lank, narrow, skinny, slender, slim, tenuous, thin, veiled, wiry

adj 5 see: TINY *adj* 1

adj 6 see: TRIVIAL *adj* 1, 2

v 1 affront, encounter, face, insult, offend

v 2 see: DISREGARD *v*

n see: INSULT *n*

slightest *adj* first, least, lowest, minimum, smallest, tiniest

slighting *adj* abusive, contemptuous, derisive, disrespectful, insulting, nasty

slightly *adv* a tad, partially, partly, somewhat, to a degree

slim *adj* 1 sexy, sleek, slender, slinky, svelte

adj 2 lank, narrow, skinny, slender, slight, tenuous, thin, veiled, wiry

adj 3 see: TRIVIAL *adj* 2

v diet, fast, lose weight, reduce, slenderize, trim down

slime *n* dirt, dung, filth, garbage, manure, muck, mud, sludge

slimnastics *n* aerobics, bodybuilding, calisthenics, exercise, workout

sling *n* attempt, chance, effort, fling, go, guess, heave, lob, pop, shot, slap, stab, throw, toss, try, whirl

v cast, flick, fling, flip, heave, hurl, launch, pitch, propel, throw, toss

slink *v* coast, crawl, creep, glide, prowl, skate, skim, skulk, slick, slide, slip, slither, snake, sneak, steal, wiggle, wriggle, writhe

slinky *adj* sexy, sleek, slender, slim, svelte

slip *n* 1 breakout, escape, flight, getaway

n 2 blunder, folly, impropriety, mistake

n 3 blip, catch, glitch, gotcha, hangup, hitch, snag

n 4 accident, blooper, blunder, bungle, confusion, error, faux pas, foul-up, lapse, misreading, mistake, misunderstanding, slip-up

n 5 debasement, decline, deterioration, dip, downturn, drop, ebb, erosion, fall, involution, plunge, sag, slide, slump, wane, weakening

v 1 lapse, sink

v 2 lose, shake, throw off

v 3 drop off, fall away, sag, slide, slump

v 4 deflect, deviate, divert, drift, stray, turn

v 5 decline, die down, diminish, dip, settle, sink, slide, subside

v 6 fall, lurch, skid, skim, slide, stumble, totter, trip, tumble

v 7 see: SNEAK *v* 2

slippage *n* lapse

slipper *n* boot, brogan, chukka, footwear, moccasin, sandal, shoe, thong

slippery *adj* 1 elusive, evasive, fleeting

adj 2 greasy, oily, sleek, slick, smooth, unctuous

adj 3 cottony, satiny, silky, smooth, soft, supple, velvety

slipshod *adj* see: MESSY *adj*

slip-up *n* 1 absence, disregard, error, neglect, oversight

n 2 accident, blooper, blunder, bungle, confusion, error, faux pas, foul-up, lapse, misreading, mistake, misunderstanding

slit *n* 1 crack, cut, gash, opening, rent, trench

n 2 cut, gash, incision, nick, pierce, prick, puncture, wound

n 3 rip, slash, split, tear

v cut, gash, incise, penetrate, pierce, punch, slice

slither *v* coast, crawl, creep, glide, prowl, skate, skim, skulk, slick, slide, slink, slip, snake, sneak, steal, wiggle, wriggle, writhe

sliver *n* 1 beam, flicker, glimmer, hint, light, ray, spark, trace

n 2 fragment, splinter

v ax, carve, chip, chop, cleave, cut, dissect, fell, hack, hew, mangle, mutilate, notch, pulverize, rend, saw, sever, slice, snip, split, sunder, whittle

slobber *v* 1 effuse, emotionalize, gush

v 2 dribble, drool

slogan *n* 1 cliché, diction, expression, parlance, phrase, saying, style, term, wording

n 2 adage, axiom, byword, cliché, dictum, maxim, motto, proverb, saying, talk

slope *n* 1 angle, grade, gradient, incline, pitch, ramp, rise, slant, tilt

n 2 bluff, cliff, hill, incline, slant, steep bank

v 1 decline, descend, incline, skew, slant, veer

v 2 bank, bend, incline, lean, pitch, slant

v 3 angle, confuse, deceive, distort, falsify, garble, incline, misconstrue, misinterpret, misquote, misread, misrepresent, misunderstand, mix up, mumble, slant, taint, twist

sloppy *adj* 1 careless, defiant, delinquent, derelict, heedless, inattentive, lax, neglectful, negligent

adj 2 careless, disheveled, messy, scruffy, slatternly, slipshod, sloven, slovenly, tacky, uncombed, unkempt, untidy

adj 3 choppy, nasty, rainy, rough, wet

slosh *v* see: SATURATE *v* 2

sloshed *adj* bombed, crocked, doped up, drunk, drunken, high, inebriated, intoxicated, juiced, loaded, looped, messed up, plastered, polluted, smashed, stoned, tight, tipsy, turned on, wasted, wired

slot *n* 1 break, cavity

n 2 groove, notch

n 3 opening, place, vacancy

sloth *n* slug, snail, turtle

slothful *adj* dilatory, easygoing, idle, indolent, inert, lackadaisical, laid-back, languid, lazy, lethargic, relaxed, sluggish, unconcerned

slouch *n* bungler

v 1 droop, hunch, stoop

v 2 stoop, bend, bow, droop, duck, lower, slump

sloven *adj* see: MESSY *adj*

slovenly *adj* careless, disheveled, messy, scruffy, slatternly, slipshod, sloppy, sloven, tacky, uncombed, unkempt, untidy

slow *adj* 1 clumsy, ponderous

adj 2 laggard, sluggish, tardy

adj 3 endless, long, tedious, tiresome

adj 4 belated, delayed, late, overdue, tardy, unpunctual

adj 5 down, idle, lax, off, slack, sluggish

adj 6 deliberate, dilatory, diligent, leisurely, methodical, meticulous, painstaking, patient, procrastinating, thorough, unhasty, unhurried

adj 7 backward, blunt, deficient, dense, dimwitted, dull, dumb, feebleminded, idiotic, moronic, obtuse, retarded, simple,

simple-minded, stupid, thick, uneducated, unintelligent

v 1 bog, delay, detain, hang up, impede, mire, retard, set back, slacken

v 2 see: HINDER *v* 5

slowpoke *n* dawdler, laggard

sludge *n* 1 dirt, dung, filth, garbage, manure, muck, mud

n 2 deposit, muck, mud, sediment

slug *n* 1 bang, blow, box, bump, chop, clap, conk, crack, crash, cuff, hit, impact, jar, jolt, knock, lick, punch, rap, slap, smack, smash, swat, swipe, tap, wallop, whack

n 2 snail, turtle

n 3 buckshot, bullet, lead, missile, projectile, shell

v hit

sluggish *adj* 1 laggard, slow, tardy

adj 2 dormant, inert, lethargic, numb, torpid

adj 3 down, idle, lax, slack, slow

adj 4 dilatory, easygoing, idle, indolent, inert, lackadaisical, laid-back, languid, lazy, lethargic, relaxed, slothful, unconcerned

slumber *n* apathy, coma, doze, ennui, grogginess, inertia, languor, lassitude, lethargy, nod, sleep, stupor

slumbering *adj* see: INACTIVE *adj* 2

slumberous *adj* dozing, drowsy, lethargic, napping, nodding, sleepy, snoozy, somnolent, tired

slump *n* debasement, decline, deterioration, dip, downturn, drop, ebb, erosion, fall, involution, plunge, sag, slide, slip, wane, weakening

v 1 drop off, fall away, sag, slide, slip

v 2 bend, bow, droop, duck, lower, stoop

v 3 cave in, collapse, disintegrate, drop, fall, go down, keel over, pitch, plunge, spill, topple, tumble

slur *n* 1 accusation, aspersion, defamation, libel, remark, smear

n 2 see: INSULT *n*

v 1 mumble, mutter

v 2 befoul, besmirch, blacken, darken, defame, disparage, injure, libel, malign, revile, scandalize, slander, smear, soil, tear down, traduce

slut *n* call girl, harlot, hooker, hussy, prostitute, streetwalker, tart, tramp, trollop, wanton woman, wench, whore

sly *adj* 1 adroit, artful, cagey, canny, crafty, cunning, evasive, foxy

adj 2 adroit, apt, canny, clever, cunning, deft, handy, ingenious, nimble, skilled, skillful, wily

adj 3 astute, calculating, crafty, cunning,

foxy, guileful, insidious, sharp, shrewd, smart, subtle, tricky, wily, wise

adj 4 clandestine, concealed, covert, crafty, deceitful, devious, evasive, foxy, furtive, guileful, indirect, privy, secret, shifty, sneaky, surreptitious, tricky, underground, underhand, underhanded, wily

smack *adv* accurately, exactly, just so, precisely, right, sharp, square, squarely

n bang, blow, box, bump, chop, clap, conk, crack, crash, cuff, hit, impact, jar, jolt, knock, lick, punch, rap, slap, slug, smash, swat, swipe, tap, wallop, whack

v 1 imply, resemble, savor, smell, suggest, taste

v 2 box, clap, cuff, knock, punch, slap, spank, strike, tap, whack

small *adj* 1 ineffectual, limited, little, mean, narrow, paltry

adj 2 hollow, nominal, perfunctory, professed, symbolic, token

adj 3 carryable, compact, lightweight, luggable, movable, pocket-size, portable, transportable

adj 4 bantam, dainty, diminutive, dwarfish, Lilliputian, little, micro, microscopic, midget, mini, miniature, minuscule, minute, petite, pygmy, slight, tiny, wee

adj 5 immaterial, inconsequential, inconsiderable, insignificant, little, low, meaningless, measly, minor, nominal, paltry, petty, picayune, picky, puny, skimpy, slight, tiny, trifling, trivial, unessential, unimportant, worthless

adj 6 see: TRIVIAL *adj* 1, 2

smallest *adj* first, least, lowest, minimum, slightest, tiniest

smart *adj* 1 chic, current, fashionable, hip, in, stylish, trendy, vogue

adj 2 brilliant, clever, dazzling, good, irrepressible, scintillating, sparkling, sprightly, witty

adj 3 alert, astute, brainy, bright, brilliant, clever, discerning, discriminating, educated, insightful, intellectual, intelligent, knowing, knowledgeable, perceptive, quick, sagacious, sage, sharp, swift

adj 4 acute, alert, astute, cagey, canny, clever, cunning, deft, keen, knowing, penetrating, perceptive, piercing, quick, quick-sighted, quick-witted, receptive, responsive, sagacious, savvy, sensitive, sharp, sharp-witted, shrewd, slick, streetsmart, wise

adj 5 see: SLY *adj* 3

adj 6 see: SUAVE *adj* 2

v bite, sting

smash *n* 1 accident, collision, crackup, crash, destruction, mishap, pileup, smashup, wreck, wreckage

n 2 bang, bell ringer, bull's-eye, gong, hit, strike

n 3 bang, blow, box, bump, chop, clap, conk, crack, crash, cuff, hit, impact, jar, jolt, knock, lick, punch, rap, slap, slug, smack, swat, swipe, tap, wallop, whack

v 1 collide, crash, demolish, wreck

v 2 bang, bump, collide, crash

v 3 break, chip, crack, fracture, gap, sever, split

v 4 break, burst, erupt, explode, fragment, rupture, shatter, smatter, splinter

v 5 annihilate, decimate, demolish, destroy, destruct, devastate, dismantle, overturn, pulverize, raze, rub out, ruin, shatter, tear down, undo, wreck

smashed *adj* bombed, crocked, doped up, drunk, drunken, high, inebriated, intoxicated, juiced, loaded, looped, messed up, plastered, polluted, sloshed, stoned, tight, tipsy, turned on, wasted, wired

smashing *adj* excellent, extraordinary, great, impressive, noteworthy, outstanding, shining, superb, wonderful

smashup *n* accident, collision, crackup, crash, destruction, mishap, pileup, smash, wreck, wreckage

smatter *v* break, burst, erupt, explode, fragment, rupture, shatter, smash, splinter

smear *n* 1 blemish, blot, blur, smudge, spot, stain

n 2 accusation, aspersion, defamation, libel, remark, slander, slur

v 1 blot, smudge, soil, stain, stigmatize

v 2 defile, dirty, discolor, soil, stain, sully, taint, tarnish

v 3 befoul, besmirch, blacken, darken, defame, disparage, injure, libel, malign, revile, scandalize, slander, slur, soil, tear down, traduce

v 4 see: THRASH *v* 1

smell *n* 1 aroma, fragrance, odor, scent

n 2 odor, stench, stink

n 3 breath, clue, dash, glimmer, hint, insinuation, lick, shade, smidgen, spice, sprinkling, suggestion, suspicion, tinge, tip, touch, trace, trifle, whiff, whisper, wisp

v 1 imply, resemble, savor, suggest, taste

v 2 scent, sniff

v 3 corrupt, crumble, decay, decompose, degenerate, deteriorate, disintegrate, perish, putrefy, rot, spoil, taint, wane, weaken, wither

smelly *adj* see: FOUL *adj* 3

smidgen *n* 1 atom, bead, dab, dash, dot, drop, grain, iota, molecule, morsel, particle, pea, pellet, speck, tad

n 2 see: TRACE *n* 4

smile *n* 1 beam, glow, grin, smirk

n 2 chuckle, grin, laugh, laughter, snigger

v 1 chortle, chuckle, giggle, guffaw, laugh, roar, snicker, snigger

v 2 grin

smirk *n* 1 beam, glow, grin, simper, smile

n 2 expression, face, grimace, mouth, pout, scowl, sneer, visage

v grimace, leer, mock, ogle, scorn, sneer

smite *v* 1 attack, beat, oppress, scourge

v 2 bat, clout, hit, nail, pop, sock, strike, swat, whack

smoke *n* exhaust, fume

v 1 drag, draw, inhale, puff

v 2 anger, blow up, boil, boil over, brew, bristle, burn, flare up, fume, rage, seethe, simmer, steam, storm

smolder *v* agitate, bake, boil, bubble, burn, churn, ferment, foam, fume, roast, seethe

smooth *adj* 1 graceful

adj 2 facile, light, simple

adj 3 glossy, shiny, sleek

adj 4 charming, sophisticated, suave

adj 5 even, flat, flush, level

adj 6 greasy, oily, sleek, slick, slippery, unctuous

adj 7 balmy, bland, faint, gentle, mild, pleasant, soft, weak

adj 8 casual, coming along, developing, easy, effortless, flowing, fluent, laid-back, running

adj 9 mild

adj 10 cottony, satiny, silky, slippery, soft, supple, velvety

adj 11 civilized, cosmopolitan, cultivated, cultured, elegant, genteel, ingratiating, poised, polished, refined, sophisticated, suave, urbane, well-bred

v 1 clear, ease, facilitate

v 2 balance, equal, equalize, equate

v 3 even, flatten, flush, grade, lay, level, plane, tamp

smorgasbord *n* banquet, buffet, dinner, feast, lunch, meal, repast, supper

smother *v* asphyxiate, choke, constrict, gag, garrote, muffle, quash, repress, stifle, strangle, suffocate, suppress

smudge *n* blemish, blot, blur, smear, spot, stain

v blot, smear, soil, stain, stigmatize

smug *adj* 1 boastful, proud, triumphant

adj 2 arrogant, cocky, conceited, haughty, narcissistic, self-assured, stuck-up, vain

smut *n* dirt, filth, grossness, indecency,

obscenity, porn, pornography, ribaldry, trash

smutty *adj* see: VULGAR *adj* 2

snack *n* 1 bread, breakfast, brunch, chow, cuisine, diet, dinner, dish, edibles, entree, fare, food, grub, lunch, meals, nosh, nutrition, provisions, rations, supper, victuals, vittles

n 2 bite, morsel, nip, piece, quick meal

snafu *n* chaos, clutter, confusion, derangement, disarray, disorder, jumble, mayhem, mess, mix-up, muddle, predicament, snarl, tangle, tumult, turmoil

snag *n* 1 blip, catch, glitch, gotcha, hangup, hitch, showstopper, slip

n 2 complication, difficulty, dilemma, obstacle, plight, predicament, problem, quandary

n 3 blockage, bottleneck, catch, flaw, hitch, impediment, jam, obstacle, obstruction

n 4 bar, barrier, bottleneck, crimp, dead end, deadlock, difficulty, encumbrance, hurdle, impasse, impediment, obstacle, obstruction, stumbling block

n 5 catch, hook

n 6 challenge, demur, difficulty, hindrance, hurdle, objection, obstacle, problem, protest

v bag, capture, catch, ensnare, entangle, entrap, hook, snare, snarl, tangle, trap, trick

snail *n* 1 sloth, slug, turtle

n 2 clam, cockle, crab, crustacean, mollusk, mussel, shellfish, shrimp

snake *n* accuser, betrayer, double-crosser, fink, informer, reptile, sneak, stooge, traitor

v 1 see: SNEAK *v* 2

v 2 see: STEAL *v* 2

snap *n* 1 breeze, cinch, dash, ease, waltz, zip

n 2 buckle, catch, clasp, clip, fastener, latch, pin, zipper

n 3 effectiveness, flair, kick, pep, pizzazz, potency, punch, sizzle, spark, verve, vigor, wallop

v 1 break, break down, collapse, come apart

v 2 bark, bay, cry, growl, howl, shout, woof, yap, yelp

v 3 click

v 4 bang, crack, pop, thump

snappy *adj* 1 brisk, curt, lively, quick

adj 2 effective, lively, potent, punchy, strong

adj 3 aromatic, lively, peppery, piquant,

poignant, pungent, racy, spicy, spirited, vigorous, zesty

snapshot *n* halftone, photo, photograph, picture

snare *n* 1 attraction, bait, come-on, decoy, enticement, lure, magnet, ruse, seduction, temptation, trap, wile

n 2 booby trap, mousetrap, pit, pitfall, trap

v bag, capture, catch, ensnare, entangle, entrap, hook, snag, snarl, tangle, trap, trick

snarl *n* 1 bend, crimp, kink, tangle, twist

n 2 chaos, clutter, confusion, derangement, disarray, disorder, jumble, mayhem, mess, mix-up, muddle, predicament, snafu, tangle, tumult, turmoil

v 1 bark, gnarl, growl, grumble, rumble

v 2 complicate, confound, confuse, entangle, mix

v 3 see: TRAP *v* 2

snatch *v* catch, clasp, clutch, grab, grapple, grasp, grip, hold, nab, nail, seize, take

snazzy *adj* see: SUAVE *adj* 2

sneak *n* accuser, betrayer, double-crosser, fink, informer, reptile, snake, stooge, traitor

v 1 cower, cringe, flinch, grovel, quail, recoil

v 2 coast, crawl, creep, glide, prowl, skate, skim, skulk, slick, slide, slink, slip, slither, snake, steal, wiggle, wriggle, writhe

sneakily *adv* clandestinely, covertly, furtively, hush-hush, mystically, secretly, stealthily, surreptitiously, under cover

sneakiness *n* stealth, subterfuge

sneaky *adj* 1 see: DECEITFUL *adj* 1

adj 2 see: SINISTER *adj* 2

adj 3 see: TREACHEROUS *adj* 2

sneer *n* 1 crack, gibe, jeer, put-down, quip, shot, torment

n 2 expression, face, grimace, mouth, pout, scowl, smirk, visage

v 1 grimace, leer, mock, ogle, smirk

v 2 belittle, deride, flaunt, jab, jeer, jest, mock, quip, razz, ridicule, scoff, scorn, taunt, tease

snicker *v* chortle, chuckle, giggle, guffaw, laugh, roar, smile

snide *adj* derogatory, disparaging, insulting, malicious, nasty

sniff *v* perceive, scent, smell

snigger *v* chortle, chuckle, giggle, guffaw, laugh, roar, smile, snicker

n chuckle, grin, laugh, laughter

snip v **1** clip, crop, cut, lop, pare, prune, shave, shear, trim, whittle

v **2** see: CUT v **4**

snippy adj see: BLUNT adj **1**

snitch v **1** fink, inform, rat, sing, squeal, stool, tattle, tattletale

v **2** see: STEAL v **2**

snivel v see: CRY v **3**

snobbish adj **1** distant, unfriendly

adj **2** arrogant, condescending, haughty, patronizing

snoop v **1** bug, check, eavesdrop, monitor, observe, oversee, spy, wiretap

v **2** butt in, chisel in, cut in, fiddle, horn in, interfere, interlope, intrude, meddle, mess around, peek, peer, poke, pry, tamper with

n busybody, gossip, interloper, intruder, kibitzer, meddler, yenta

snooping adj curious, inquiring, inquisitive, investigative, nosy, probing, prying

snooty adj see: VAIN adj **5**

snooze v doze, nap, sleep

snoozy adj dozing, drowsy, lethargic, napping, nodding, sleepy, slumberous, somnolent, tired

snotty adj see: BLUNT adj **1**

snout n beak, bill, muzzle, nib, nose, proboscis, prow, trunk

snowball v see: INCREASE v **8**

snowstorm n blast, blizzard, blow, gale, gust, hurricane, northeaster, squall, storm, tempest, typhoon, wind

snowy adj chalky, ivory, white

snub v **1** alienate, estrange, fend off, rebuff, repel, repulse

v **2** defy, discount, disregard, exclude, forget, ignore, miss, neglect, omit, ostracize, overlook, overpass, pass, pass by, pass over, shun, skip

v **3** blackball, boycott, cut, ignore, rebuff, spurn

snug adj comfortable, comfy, contented, cozy, cushy, homey, secure, soft, warm

snuggle v **1** ensconce, harbor, settle, shelter

v **2** caress, cradle, cuddle, embrace, feel, fondle, fool around, hold, hug, love, make out, neck, nuzzle, pet, stroke

soak v deluge, douse, drench, drown, dunk, flood, inundate, irrigate, overload, saturate, slosh, sop, souse, swamp, swill, tax, wet

soaked adj **1** drenched, dripping, full, immersed, inundated, saturated, soaking, sodden, sopping, waterlogged, wet

adj **2** damp, drenched, dripping, humid, moist, mucky, muggy, soggy, sopping, sticky, sultry, sweaty, wet

soaking adj drenched, dripping, full, immersed, inundated, saturated, soaked, sodden, sopping, waterlogged, wet

soap n suds

soapbox n dais, desk, lectern, podium, pulpit, rostrum, stage, stand

soaps n cartoons, docudrama, documentary, game shows, mini-series, movies, news, programs, series, sitcom, soap opera, talk shows, television, variety shows

soar v **1** ascend, climb, increase, rise, speed, zoom

v **2** coast, drift, float, fly, glide, sail

v **3** ascend, flit, flutter, fly, sail, sweep, wing

v **4** arise, ascend, aspire, go up, lift, rise

soaring adj aloft, elevated, high, lofty, overhead, tall

sob v bawl, bemoan, cry, grieve, groan, lament, moan, mourn, sigh, snivel, wail, weep, whimper, whine

n groan, moan, sigh, wail

sober adj **1** levelheaded, moderate, temperate, unimpassioned

adj **2** dignified, earnest, grave, pensive, sedate, serious, solemn, somber, staid, stoic, unemotional, unflinching

adj **3** astute, consequent, intelligent, knowing, logical, perceptive, rational, reasonable, sane, sensible, shrewd, sound, wise

sobriety n abstinence, continence, moderation, restraint, temperance

so-called adj feigned, partial, pseudo, quasi, semi, somewhat, unofficial

sociable adj congenial, affable, amenable, amiable, amicable, empathetic, friendly, gregarious, hospitable, neighborly, outgoing, receptive, social, sympathetic

social adj **1** collective, common, group, organizational, public, societal

adj **2** see: FRIENDLY adj **3**

societal adj collective, common, group, organizational, public

society n **1** association, institute, institution, organization, union

n **2** association, body, club, company, contingent, delegation, fellowship, fraternity, group, guild, organization, union

n **3** citizens, civilization, colony, community, crowd, culture, folks, group, human beings, individuals, laity, masses, men and women, neighbors, people, persons, populace, population, public, settlement, staff, tribe

sock v bat, clout, hit, nail, pop, smite, strike, swat, whack

sod n area, divot, land, patch, space, turf

sodden *adj* drenched, dripping, full, immersed, inundated, saturated, soaked, soaking, sopping, waterlogged, wet

sofa *n* couch, divan, lounge, settee

soft *adj* 1 delicate, fragile, frail, tender

adj 2 balmy, bland, faint, gentle, mild, pleasant, smooth, weak

adj 3 comfortable, comfy, contented, cozy, cushy, homey, secure, snug, warm

adj 4 cottony, satiny, silky, slippery, smooth, supple, velvety

adj 5 mushy, pulpy, spongy, squashy, squelchy, squishy, yielding

adj 6 choice, deluxe, elegant, first-class, grand, luxuriant, luxurious, opulent, ornate, palatial, plush, posh, rich, stately, sumptuous, thick

adj 7 adaptable, adjustable, changeable, flexible, limber, malleable, maneuverable, moldable, plastic, pliable, pliant, responsive, supple, swayed, versatile, yielding

adj 8 calm, collected, composed, cool, demure, dormant, easy, gentle, hushed, idle, imperturbable, motionless, nonchalant, peaceful, placid, poised, quiet, relaxed, restful, sedate, self-composed, self-possessed, serene, steady, still, tranquil, unflappable, unruffled, untroubled

soften *v* 1 mellow, tame, temper

v 2 relax, relent, thaw

v 3 calm, lessen, muffle, quiet, reduce, subdue

v 4 allay, appease, assuage, balm, becalm, calm, compose, conciliate, ease, lull, mollify, pacify, placate, propitiate, quell, quiet, reconcile, satiate, settle, soothe, still, sweeten, tranquilize

v 5 see: SUBSIDE *v* 2

soft-hearted *adj* see: TENDER *adj* 9

sogginess *n* dampness, humidity, moisture, wetness

soggy *adj* damp, drenched, dripping, humid, moist, mucky, muggy, soaked, sopping, sticky, sultry, sweaty, wet

soil *n* 1 clay, dirt, dry land, dust, earth, ground, land, loam, marl, *terra*, terra firma

n 2 country, fatherland, home, homeland, land

v 1 blot, smear, smudge, stain, stigmatize

v 2 defile, dirty, discolor, smear, stain, sully, taint, tarnish

v 3 befoul, besmirch, blacken, darken, defame, disparage, injure, libel, malign, revile, scandalize, slander, slur, smear, tear down, traduce

sojourn *v* stop over, tour, visit

solace *n* abatement, alleviation, comfort, correction, cure, help, relief, remedy, respite, solution

v bolster, buoy, cheer, comfort, console, gladden, soothe, support, uplift, upraise

soldier *n* hired gun, mercenary, trooper

soldiers *n* army, battalion, brigade, company, force, gang, men, power, troops

sole *adj* 1 single, spouseless, unmarried, unwed

adj 2 exclusive, individual, lone, odd, one, only, particular, separate, single, singular, solitary, unique, unshared

solely *adv* see: ONLY *adv*

solemn *adj* 1 dignified, earnest, grave, pensive, sedate, serious, sober, somber, staid, stoic, unemotional, unflinching

adj 2 acute, burning, critical, crucial, desperate, dire, grave, heavy, important, major, momentous, ponderous, pressing, profound, serious, severe, somber, urgent, vital

solemnize *v* celebrate, commemorate, keep, observe

solicit *v* 1 attract, draw, elicit, induce

v 2 ask, bid, invite, request

v 3 bill, charge, debit, dun, invoice, notice

v 4 campaign, canvass, drum, drum up, poll, prospect, seek

v 5 get back, recoup, recover, recruit, regain, repossess

v 6 call, challenge, claim, demand, exact, need, postulate, requisition

v 7 attract, court, encourage, flirt, invite, lure, pursue, romance, tempt, woo

v 8 appeal, apply, attack, file suit, go to court, litigate, petition, prosecute, sue

v 9 see: OBTAIN *v* 1

v 10 see: PLEAD *v* 1, 2

solicitation *n* appeal, desire, favor, petition, plea, request, wish

solicitor *n* advocate, attorney, barrister, counsel, counselor, intercessor, lawyer

solid *adj* 1 close, compact, crowded, dense, thick, tight

adj 2 fastened, fixed, in position, motionless, permanent, set, standing, static, stationary, still

adj 3 compact, firm, hard, hardened, rigid, secure, sound, specific, stable, stiff, tight

adj 4 cogent, compelling, convincing, effective, forceful, influential, persuasive, revealing, satisfactory, satisfying, sound, telling, valid

adj 5 accountable, answerable, dependable, honorable, honored, liable, reliable, reputable, respected, responsible, secure, trusted, trustworthy, trusty, upstanding

adj 6 see: RESTRICTIVE *adj*

solidarity *n* bond, cohesion, connection, fusion, togetherness, union

solidify *v* clog, clot, coagulate, condense, congeal, curdle, dry, gel, harden, intensify, jell, pack, thicken

solidity *n* compactness, density, firmness, hardness, strength, tensile strength

solidly *adv* fast, firm, firmly, hard, loyally, reliably, tight, tightly

solitary *adj* 1 abandoned, depraved, derelict, deserted, desolate, forsaken, secluded, uninhabited

adj 2 alone, lone, lonely, lonesome, single, singular, solo, unaccompanied

adj 3 exclusive, individual, lone, odd, one, only, particular, separate, single, singular, sole, unique, unshared

adj 4 see: UNIQUE *adj* 2, 3

n loner

solitude *n* 1 detachment, isolation, privacy, quiet, seclusion

n 2 exile, isolation, leisure, quarantine, relaxation, rest, retirement, retreat, seclusion, withdrawal

solo *adj* alone, lone, lonely, lonesome, single, singular, solitary, unaccompanied

n aria, arietta, song

solution *n* 1 answer, explanation, key, result, secret

n 2 conclusion, culmination, denouement, outcome, result

n 3 abatement, alleviation, comfort, correction, cure, help, relief, remedy, respite

n 4 explanation

n 5 fluid, juice, liquid, sap

solve *v* 1 answer, explain, resolve, unravel

v 2 see: ANALYZE *v* 2

solvent *adj* safe, sound

somber *adj* 1 dark, dim, dusky, gloomy, lightless, murky, obscure, shadowy, tenebrous, unilluminated

adj 2 dignified, earnest, grave, pensive, sedate, serious, sober, solemn, staid, stoic, unemotional, unflinching

adj 3 acute, burning, critical, crucial, desperate, dire, grave, heavy, important, major, momentous, ponderous, pressing, profound, serious, severe, solemn, urgent, vital

adj 4 black, bleak, blue, cheerless, dejected, depressed, desperate, despondent, discouraging, disheartening, distressing, down, forlorn, gloomy, hopeless, joyless,

melancholy, moody, mournful, oppressive, prostrate, sad, sorry, unhappy

adj 5 see: DULL *adj* 7

some *adj* 1 a, a few, any, at least one, each, every, individual, one

adj 2 alternate, another, certain, different, discrete, disparate, dissimilar, distinct, diverse, numerous, other, separate, several, unlike, various, varying

sometime *adj* bygone, erstwhile, former, late, old, once, past

sometimes *adv* every so often, now and then, occasionally, once in a while, periodically

somewhat *adv* 1 fairly, moderately, pretty, reasonably

adv 2 a tad, partially, partly, slightly, to a degree

somnolent *adj* dozing, drowsy, lethargic, napping, nodding, sleepy, slumberous, snoozy, tired

son *n* boy, child, cub, junior, lad, young man

sonata *n* concert, concerto, étude, fugue, program, recital, serenade, symphony

song *n* 1 ditty, limerick, lyric, madrigal, poem, poetry, rhyme, sonnet, verse

n 2 air, call, carol, cry, lullaby, melody, note, rhapsody, tune

n 3 aria, solo

song and dance *n* follies, musical, review, revue, variety show, vaudeville

sonnet *n* ditty, limerick, lyric, madrigal, poem, poetry, rhyme, verse

soon *adv* 1 anon, any moment, at once, directly, immediately, instantaneously, instantly, momentarily, now, presently, promptly, quickly, right now, shortly, straightaway, *tout de suite*

adv 2 expeditiously, fast, full tilt, hastily, in a snap, lickety-split, promptly, pronto, quick, quickly, rapidly, right away, speedily, swiftly, urgently

soothe *v* 1 aid, comfort, cure, relieve, strengthen, support

v 2 bolster, buoy, cheer, comfort, console, gladden, solace, support, uplift, upraise

v 3 allay, appease, assuage, balm, becalm, calm, compose, conciliate, ease, lull, mollify, pacify, placate, propitiate, quell, quiet, reconcile, satiate, settle, soften, still, sweeten, tranquilize

soothsay *v* anticipate, augur, bode, budget, call, divine, estimate, forecast, foresee, foreshadow, foretell, guess, harbinger, herald, judge, plan, portend, preannounce, predict, presage, proclaim, prognosticate, project, prophesy

soothsayer *n* 1 conjurer, diviner, magician, sorcerer, wizard

n 2 astrologer, augur, fortuneteller, oracle, predictor, prophet, seer, visionary

n 3 clairvoyant, medium, psychic, spiritualist

sooty *adj* 1 ashen, ashy, blanched, colorless, pale, pallid, sallow, sickly, wan, waxen, yellow

adj 2 black, dark, dingy, dirty, filthy, foul, grimy, grubby, mucky, murky, polluted, seedy, shabby, squalid, stained, unclean, unlit, unwashed

sop *v* deluge, douse, drench, drown, dunk, flood, inundate, irrigate, overload, saturate, slosh, soak, souse, swamp, swill, tax, wet

sophisticated *adj* 1 charming, slick, smooth, suave

adj 2 civilized, cosmopolitan, cultivated, cultured, elegant, genteel, ingratiating, poised, polished, refined, smooth, suave, urbane, well-bred

sophomoric *adj* babyish, callow, childish, infantile

sopping *adj* 1 drenched, dripping, full, immersed, inundated, saturated, soaked, soaking, sodden, waterlogged, wet

adj 2 damp, drenched, dripping, humid, moist, mucky, muggy, soaked, soggy, sticky, sultry, sweaty, wet

sorcerer *n* conjurer, diviner, magician, wizard

sorcery *n* bewitchment, enchantment, incantation, magic, occultism, spell, voodoo, witchcraft, wizardry

sordid *adj* 1 dirty, disgusting, foul, lousy, nasty, rotten

adj 2 base, beneath, despicable, ignoble, inferior, low, lowdown, squalid, unworthy, vile, vulgar, wretched

sore *adj* 1 bruised, irritated, painful, tender

adj 2 annoying, difficult, hurt, irksome, irritated, irritating, painful, sensitive

n 1 abrasion, cut, hurt, itch, scratch

n 2 blister, fester, inflammation, lesion, swelling, welt

sorehead *n* bellyacher, crank, grouch, grump, sourpuss

soreness *n* see: PAIN *n* 3

sorrow *n* 1 distress, grief, melancholy, sadness, suffering

n 2 guilt, penitence, regret, remorse

n 3 affliction, anguish, care, catastrophe, despair, disaster, dole, grief, heartache, mishap, pain, regret, remorse, rue, woe

n 4 agony, anguish, bale, concern, distress, misery, nightmare, pain, sadness, suffering, torment, travail, tribulation, trouble, woe, worry

v brood, grieve, lament, languish

sorrowful *adj* 1 bittersweet, maudlin, poignant, sentimental

adj 2 dire, disastrous, dreadful, lamentable, pitiful, tragic

adj 3 dismal, doleful, gloomy, lamentable, melancholy, mournful, plaintive, regretful, regrettable, rueful, woeful

sorry *adj* 1 apologetic, contrite, penitent, remorseful, repentant

adj 2 see: GLOOMY *adj* 5

adj 3 see: INFERIOR *adj* 6

sort *v* 1 comb, loot, ransack, rifle, scour, search, separate, sift

v 2 choose, cull, elect, pick, remove, select, separate, sift

v 3 bracket, collate, compare, contrast, correlate, equate, liken, match, relate

v 4 see: CLASSIFY *v* 2

n see: CATEGORY *n*

sortie *n* expedition, foray

SOS *n* alarm, warning

so-so *adv* fairly, moderately, pretty, reasonably, somewhat

adj see: INFERIOR *adj* 6

soul *n* 1 ego, id, individuality, mind, persona, personality, psyche, self, spirit

n 2 blues, classical, country, folk, jazz, music, ragtime, rock-and-roll, swing

sound *adj* 1 able, safe, solvent

adj 2 cogent, logical, rational

adj 3 accepted, established, proven, standard, traditional

adj 4 active, alive, dynamic, energetic, spirited, strong, vibrant, vigorous, vital

adj 5 fit, hardy, healthy, robust, rubicund, ruddy, sturdy, well, wholesome

adj 6 compact, firm, hard, hardened, rigid, secure, solid, specific, stable, stiff, tight

adj 7 astute, consequent, intelligent, knowing, logical, perceptive, rational, reasonable, sane, sensible, shrewd, sober, wise

adj 8 cogent, compelling, convincing, effective, forceful, influential, persuasive, revealing, satisfactory, satisfying, solid, telling, valid

adj 9 absolute, complete, flawless, good, intact, perfect, unblemished, unbroken, undamaged, unimpaired, uninjured, unmarred, untouched, whole

adj 10 safe, undamaged, unharmed, unhurt

adj 11 conscientious, ethical, honest,

honorable, moral, noble, principled, proper, respectable, right, righteous, scrupulous, true, trustworthy, upright, virtuous

n 1 frequency, level, pitch, tone

n 2 characteristic, flavor, impression, nature, property, quality, ring, tendency, tone, type

n 3 noise

n 4 arm, bay, cove, estuary, fiord, gulf, inlet, narrows, strait

v 1 explore, fathom, plumb, probe

v 2 appear, indicate, look, seem

v 3 boom, chime, clang, peal, resonate, resound, reverberate, ring, toll

v 4 delve, dig, examine, explore, feel out, grope, hunt, inquire, investigate, look, observe, peer, probe, pursue, research, scan, scrutinize, search, seek, study, test

soundless *adj* dead, hush, inanimate, inert, lifeless, noiseless, quiet, still

soundness *n* lucidity, mind, rationality, reason, sanity, saneness, sense, wit

sour *adj* 1 bad, decayed, putrid, rancid, rotten, sharp, spoiled

adj 2 acerbic, acid, biting, curt, dry, pungent, sharp, tart

adj 3 dour, firm, forbidding, grim, sad, serious, severe, stern, unpleasant

adj 4 annoying, bad, difficult, disagreeable, displeasing, nasty, objectionable, offensive, rotten, unhappy, unpleasant, upsetting

adj 5 decaying, fetid, foul, gamy, malodorous, musty, putrid, rancid, rank, reeking, rotten, smelly, spoiled, stale, stinking, tainted

adj 6 see: SULLEN *adj* 1

v disillusion

source *n* 1 authority, dictionary, reference

n 2 accumulation, fund, reservoir, store, supply

n 3 birth, creation, fountain, genesis, origin, parent, root

n 4 arguments, basis, cause, explanation, foundation, grounds, principle, rationale, reason

n 5 beginning, conception, cradle, derivation, fountainhead, inception, infancy, mother, origin, root, seed, stem

n 6 see: CREATOR *n* 1

sourpuss *n* crank, bellyacher, grouch, grump

souse *v* deluge, douse, drench, drown, dunk, flood, inundate, irrigate, overload, saturate, slosh, soak, sop, swamp, swill, tax, wet

souvenir *n* antique, gift, heirloom, keepsake, memento, memorial, relic, remembrance, reminder, token, trophy

sovereign *adj* 1 autonomous, distinct, free, independent, lone, separate, unconnected

adj 2 dominant, master, overbearing, overwhelming, paramount, predominant, preponderant, prevalent

sovereignty *n* administration, dominion, government, monarchy, power, regime, reign

sow *v* 1 implant, plant, root, seed, strew

v 2 broadcast, disseminate, dissipate, distribute, scatter, spread, strew, transmit

spa *n* club, hotel, lodge, resort

space *n* 1 capacity, elbowroom, leeway, room

n 2 area, divot, land, patch, sod, turf

n 3 breach, break, crack, fracture, gap, opening, split

n 4 blank, cavity, crack, depression, emptiness, gap, hole, hollow, nook, void

n 5 berth, billet, housing, shelter

n 6 area, arena, belt, field, realm, region, section, territory, tract, turf, zone

spaced *adj* absentminded, abstracted, bemused, careless, dazed, dizzy, groggy, inattentive, lost, mindless, oblivious, preoccupied, silly, vapid

spacious *adj* 1 cavernous, echo-filled, gaping, hollow, reverberant, vast

adj 2 ample, big, capacious, comfortable, commodious, open, roomy, vast, wide

adj 3 ample, big, considerable, enormous, extensive, grand, hefty, huge, jumbo, large, major, sizable, vast

span *n* 1 distance, reach, stretch

n 2 breadth, depth, dimensions, range, scope, width

n 3 continuation, duration, endurance, existence, life, subsistence, survival, term

n 4 cycle, duration, interval, period, season, spell, stage, stretch, term, time

n 5 aeon, age, cycle, decade, eon, epoch, era, eternity, forever, long time, millennium, period, reign, stage, time, years

v extend, go, range, run, vary

spank *v* box, clap, cuff, knock, punch, slap, smack, strike, tap, whack

spar *n* beam, board, boom, girder, log, plank, rafter, support, timber

v 1 combat, contend, duel, fight, grapple, struggle, wrestle

v 2 see: QUARREL *v*

spare *adj* 1 added, additional, another, auxiliary, extra, further, incremental, more, one more, other, supplemental, supplementary, surplus

adj 2 see: MEAGER *adj* 2

v 1 bound, limit, restrict, scrimp, short, skimp, stint

v 2 bank, hoard, lay aside, lay away, lay by, lay in, lay up, put by, save

sparing *adj* canny, conservative, economical, frugal, provident, spartan, stewardly, thrifty, unwasteful

spark *n* 1 beam, flicker, glimmer, hint, light, ray, sliver, trace

n 2 effectiveness, flair, kick, pep, pizzazz, potency, punch, sizzle, snap, verve, vigor, wallop

v 1 activate, cause, elicit, generate, prompt, provoke, trigger

v 2 burn, enkindle, fire, ignite, inflame, light

v 3 arouse, electrify, excite, fire, incite, inspire, rouse, stimulate, tantalize, thrill, titillate, turn on, whet

v 4 arouse, awaken, excite, induce, instill, motivate, move, pique, prime, provoke, quicken, rouse, roust, start, stimulate, titillate, urge

sparked *adj* see: HAPPY *adj* 2

sparkle *v* 1 dance, flap, flicker, flitter, flutter, oscillate, prance, sway, twinkle, undulate, wave

v 2 excite, flash, gleam, glimmer, glint, glisten, glitter, scintillate, shimmer, shine, twinkle

n 1 flash, gleam, glimmer, glitter, shimmer, shine, twinkle

n 2 animation, drive, élan, energy, enthusiasm, esprit de corps, go, gusto, pep, potency, spirit, spunk, verve, vigor, vim, vitality, zing, zip

sparkling *adj* 1 bubbly, effervescent

adj 2 brilliant, clever, dazzling, good, irrepressible, scintillating, smart, sprightly, witty

sparse *adj* 1 austere, economical, spartan, terse

adj 2 few, lacking, limited, nonabundant, not many, scant

adj 3 bare, deficient, few, inadequate, inferior, insufficient, little, meager, paltry, petty, poor, scant, scanty, skimpy, spare

sparseness *n* dearth, deficiency, deficit, drought, famine, lack, rarity, scarcity, shortage, undersupply, want

spartan *adj* 1 austere, economical, sparse, terse

adj 2 ascetic, astringent, austere, chaste, rigid, simple, stern, stoic

adj 3 canny, conservative, economical, frugal, provident, sparing, stewardly, thrifty, unwasteful

spasm *n* 1 convulsion, jerk, seizure, twitch

n 2 ache, agony, angina, burn, cramp, crick, heartache, hurt, pain, pang, soreness, sting, twinge

spat *n* 1 break, disagreement, dissension, fight, misunderstanding, quarrel, rift

n 2 altercation, argument, battle, brawl, challenge, combat, controversy, disagreement, discord, dispute, feud, fight, fracas, fray, hassle, melee, quarrel, rancor, rift, row, ruckus, scrap, scuffle, skirmish, squabble, struggle, tiff, war

n 3 see: CLASH *n* 2

spawn *v* see: BEGET *v*

spawning *n* conception, fertilization, insemination, reproduction

speak *v* 1 address, deliver, lecture, preach, proclaim, talk

v 2 chat, chatter, converse, discuss, parley, talk, visit

v 3 announce, articulate, assert, couch, describe, dictate, draft, enunciate, express, intonate, orate, phrase, proclaim, pronounce, say, state, stress, talk, utter, verbalize, vocalize, voice, word

speaking *n* discourse, expression, speech, statement, talk, utterance, verbalization, word

spear *v* gore, impale, lance, penetrate, pierce, puncture, stab

spearhead *n* forefront, front, head, lead, pioneer, vanguard

v antedate, come before, forego, precede, preface

special *adj* 1 cherished, favorite, pet

adj 2 individual, particular, personal, specific

adj 3 favored, better, partial, preferential

adj 4 exclusive, individual, intimate, own, personal, private

adj 5 characteristic, differentiating, distinctive, lone, one, particular, peculiar, select, single, solitary, unique, unusual

adj 6 see: QUAINT *adj* 1

n bargain, buy, deal, discount, promotion, reduction, sale, steal

specialist *n* 1 diagnostician, doctor, healer, intern, physician, resident, surgeon

n 2 adviser, artist, authority, expert, guru, master, official, pro, professional, veteran, virtuoso, wizard

specialized *adj* qualified, skilled, technical, trained

specialty *n* 1 bag, field, hobby, interest, job

n 2 see: SKILL *n* 3

n 3 see: TRADE *n* 3

species n bracket, breed, cast, category, class, division, family, genre, genus, group, grouping, ilk, kind, lot, mold, nature, order, persuasion, section, sector, set, sort, style, type, variety

specific adj 1 individual, particular, personal

adj 2 definite, determinate, exclusive, fixed, limited, narrow, precise, restricted, segregated

adj 3 blunt, clear, clear-cut, concise, decisive, definite, definitive, distinct, exact, explicit, unambiguous

adj 4 absolute, agreed, bounded, categorical, clear, decided, definite, emphatic, established, exact, finite, fixed, guaranteed, limited, positive, unequivocal, unmistakable, vested

adj 5 see: SOLID adj 3

n 1 detail, feature, item, part

n 2 actuality, fact, given, statistic, truth

specifically adv chiefly, especially, notably, particularly, primarily

specification n agreement, clause, condition, provision, proviso, requirement, reservation, stipulation, string, terms

specificity n definition, design, distinctness, outline

specify v 1 define

v 2 account, report

v 3 describe, detail, itemize

v 4 distinguish, identify, know, recognize

v 5 demand, designate, indicate, insist, stipulate

v 6 appoint, declare, designate, name, nominate, propose

v 7 craft, define, develop, formulate, list, make, process, synthesize

v 8 allude, denote, indicate, mention, point out, refer to, reveal, show, speak of, suggest, tell

specimen n case, case history, clarification, example, explanation, illumination, illustration, instance, representative, sample

specious adj 1 apparent, illusive, illusory, ostensible, quasi, seeming, superficial

adj 2 erroneous, false, faulty, imprecise, inaccurate, incorrect, inexact, mistaken, untrue, wrong

speck n 1 atom, bead, dab, dash, dot, drop, grain, iota, molecule, morsel, particle, pea, pellet, smidgen, tad

n 2 see: FRAGMENT n 3

spectacle n 1 fight, incident, outbreak, scene, tantrum

n 2 marvel, miracle, phenomenon, wonder

spectacular adj 1 exciting, hot, sensational, sexy, stirring

adj 2 alluring, beguiling, bewitching, captivating, catchy, charming, dazzling, dynamic, enchanting, engaging, enthralling, enticing, fascinating, glamorous, intriguing, mesmerizing, riveting, spellbinding

adj 3 see: RAPID adj 2

spectators n audience, patrons, witnesses

specter n aberration, apparition, delusion, fantasy, figment, ghost, hallucination, illusion, image, mirage, phantasm, vision

spectrum n 1 assortment, bunch, collection, mixture, variety

n 2 circle, compass, confines, dimension, distance, extension, extent, length, limit, orbit, purview, range, reach, realm, scope, size, sweep, width

speculate v 1 attempt, bet, chance, dare, gamble, hazard, play, risk, stake, venture, wager

v 2 allude, assume, extend, hypothesize, imagine, offer, pose, present, presume, propose, suggest, suppose, surmise, theorize

v 3 see: PONDER v

speculation n 1 approximation, estimation, extrapolation

n 2 attempt, effort, endeavor, struggle, trial, try, undertaking, venture

n 3 assumption, conjecture, deduction, explanation, guess, hypothesis, inference, postulate, presumption, proposition, supposition, theory

n 4 see: CONSIDERATION n 5

speculative adj 1 meditative, pensive, philosophical, pondering, reflective, thinking, thoughtful

adj 2 abstract, conjectural, general, hypothetical, ideal, illustrative, symbolic, theoretical

speech n 1 accent, brogue, dialect, patois, tongue

n 2 discourse, expression, speaking, statement, talk, utterance, verbalization, word

n 3 address, lecture, talk

speechless adj dumb, inarticulate, mute, reticent, silent, tacit, voiceless

speed n 1 alacrity, dispatch, expedition, haste, hastiness, hurry, hustle, precipitance, precipitation, quickness, rush, rustle, swiftness

n 2 alacrity, cadence, celerity, dispatch, gait, pace, quickness, rapidity, rate, step, stride, swiftness, trot, velocity, walk

v 1 ascend, climb, increase, rise, soar, zoom

v 2 dash, gallop, jog, race, sprint

v **3** accelerate, expedite, hasten, hurry, quicken, rush, shake up, step up

v **4** barrel, bullet, expedite, fly, hasten, hurry, hustle, rocket, rush, whisk, zip

v **5** flash, race, zoom

v **6** gun, rev, throttle

speedily *adv* expeditiously, fast, full tilt, in a snap, hastily, lickety-split, promptly, pronto, quick, quickly, rapidly, right away, soon, swiftly, urgently

speedy *adj* **1** breakneck, expeditious, explosive, fast, fleet, hasty, impulsive, instant, lightning, mercurial, meteoric, precipitous, quick, rapid, spectacular, sudden, swift

adj **2** express, fast, next-day, nonstop, quick, rapid, swift

spell *n* **1** daze, trance

n **2** bewitchment, enchantment, incantation, magic, occultism, sorcery, voodoo, witchcraft, wizardry

n **3** see: CHARISMA *n* **2**

n **4** see: TERM *n* **5**

v relieve, replace, take over

spellbinding *adj* alluring, beguiling, bewitching, captivating, catchy, charming, dazzling, dynamic, enchanting, engaging, enthralling, enticing, fascinating, glamorous, intriguing, mesmerizing, riveting

spend *v* consume, deplete, exhaust, expend, finish, go, lessen, run through, use up, waste, weaken

spent *adj* **1** beat, burnt out, bushed, careworn, drawn, emaciated, exhausted, expended, fatigued, frazzled, haggard, jaded, pinched, pooped, run-down, shot, tired, wearied, weary, worn, worn down, worn-out

adj **2** see: INFERTILE *adj*

sperm *n* semen

spew *v* **1** burst, discharge, erupt, explode, gush, spout

v **2** jet, shoot, spout, spritz, spurt, squirt, surge

sphere *n* **1** ball, balloon, globe, marble, orb

n **2** domain, dominion, field, kingdom, province, realm, territory

n **3** bead, blob, bubble, drib, drop, droplet, globule

n **4** see: WARD *n* **2**

sphere-like *adj* circular, global, globular, rotund, round, spherical

spherical *adj* circular, global, globular, rotund, round

spice *n* **1** flavor, palate, sample, savor, tang, taste

n **2** aroma, balm, bouquet, fragrance, incense, perfume

n **3** see: TRACE *n* **4**

v color, enhance, flavor, imbue, infuse, season

spicy *adj* **1** biting, hot, nippy, pungent, seasoned, sharp, tangy, tart

adj **2** caustic, coarse, cutting, obscene, salty, scathing, scorching, sharp, trenchant, vulgar, witty

adj **3** aromatic, lively, peppery, piquant, poignant, pungent, racy, snappy, spirited, vigorous, zesty

spiel *n* come-on, line, presentation, talk

spiffy *adj* chic, dapper, dashing, debonair, jaunty, natty, neat, rakish, sleek, smart, snazzy, suave, trim

spigot *n* cock, faucet, nozzle, spout, tap, valve

spike *n* **1** brad, bolt, nut, peg, pin, rivet, staple, stud, weld

n **2** see: INSULT *n*

spill *v* **1** blurt, cackle, cry, ejaculate, exclaim, shout, sputter, tattle, utter

v **2** flood, flow, gush, peak, pour, rise, roll, stream, surge, swell

v **3** cave in, collapse, disintegrate, drop, fall, go down, keel over, pitch, plunge, slump, topple, tumble

v **4** cascade, emit, flood, inundate, overflow, plunge, pour, rain, shower, swamp, tumble

spin *n* **1** attempt, chance, try, turn

n **2** drive, excursion, jaunt, journey, ride

n **3** curl, loop, revolution, ring, roll, rotation, spiral, turn, twirl, twist

v **1** circle, gyrate, revolve, roll, rotate, turn

v **2** gyrate, pirouette, purl, reel, swim, turn, twirl, whirl

spindle *n* axis, axle, pin, pivot, pole, shaft

spine *n* backbone, spinal column, vertebrae

spineless *adj* **1** emasculate, impotent, inadequate, ineffective, ineffectual, weak

adj **2** chicken, cowardly, fearful, gutless, timid, yellow

spinning *n* alternation, circuit, circulation, gyration, revolution, rotation, round, sequence, succession, turn, whirl

spinster *n* **1** dame, female, gentlewoman, lady, matron, miss, mistress, widow, woman

n **2** maid, maiden

spiral *adj* crooked, meandering, serpentine, sinuous, turning, twisting, winding, zigzagging

n **1** band, coil, crown, garland, loop, ring, wreath

n 2 arc, arch, bend, bow, coil, crook, curvature, curve, hook

n 3 curl, loop, revolution, ring, roll, rotation, spin, turn, twirl, twist

v coil, corkscrew, curl, distort, entwine, gnarl, twist, wind

spire *n* belfry, steeple, tower, turret

spirit *n* 1 humor, wit

n 2 enterprise, gumption, initiative, resourcefulness, spunk, volition

n 3 courage, boldness, bravery, daring, fortitude, heart, heroism, strength, valor

n 4 ego, id, individuality, mind, persona, personality, psyche, self

n 5 air, ambience, atmosphere, aura, emanation, feel, feeling, mood

n 6 attitude, disposition, feeling, humor, mind, mood, temper, timbre, tone, vein

n 7 center, core, crux, essence, gist, heart, life, marrow, nature, nucleus, pith, quick, quintessence, root, substance

n 8 angel, archangel, cherub

n 9 aptitude, character, complexion, disposition, distinctiveness, heart, humor, identity, inclination, individuality, make-up, nature, personality, quality, state, temperament, tendency

n 10 animation, drive, élan, energy, enthusiasm, esprit de corps, go, gusto, pep, potency, sparkle, spunk, verve, vigor, vim, vitality, zing, zip

n 11 backbone, chutzpah, determination, endurance, fortitude, grit, guts, moxie, nerve, persistence, pluck, resilience, spunk, stamina, strength, tenacity, tolerance, vigor, willpower

spirited *adj* 1 bellicose, brawling, difficult, feisty, quarrelsome

adj 2 active, alive, dynamic, energetic, sound, strong, vibrant, vigorous, vital

adj 3 alert, animated, bouncy, bright, brisk, buoyant, chipper, dashing, dynamic, ebullient, energetic, enthusiastic, exuberant, frisky, frolicsome, gay, jumpy, kinetic, lively, peppy, pert, playful, rousing, scintillating, sprightly, spry, vivacious

adj 4 see ZESTY *adj*

spiritless *adj* 1 cold, dead, deceased, defunct, departed

adj 2 anemic, bloodless, gaunt, haggard, lifeless, pale, pallid, passionless, watery, weak

spirits *n* alcohol, booze, drinks, grog, liquor, moonshine, whiskey

spiritual *adj* 1 blessed, celestial, consecrated, divine, godly, hallowed, holy, pure, sacred

adj 2 bodiless, celestial, disembodied, ethereal, heavenly, incorporeal, insubstantial, intangible, metaphysical, nonmaterial, unearthly, unreal, unsubstantial

spiritualist *n* clairvoyant, medium, psychic

spit *v* bubble, crackle, hiss, sizzle, sputter

spite *n* 1 chip, grudge, ill will, malevolence, malice, maliciousness, malignancy, resentment

n 2 acrimony, animosity, antagonism, antipathy, aversion, bitterness, dislike, enmity, gall, hate, hatred, hostility, ill will, malice, rancor, venom, vindictiveness

v see: ANNOY *v* 3

spiteful *adj* 1 begrudging, petty, small-minded

adj 2 catty, hostile, malevolent, malicious, resentful, treacherous

adj 3 malicious, revengeful, unforgiving, unmerciful, vengeful, vindictive

adj 4 adverse, antagonistic, bellicose, hostile, ill, inimical, nasty, unfriendly

adj 5 see: NASTY *adj* 5, 7

splashy *adj* ambitious, bombastic, flamboyant, garish, grandiose, inflated, jaunty, lofty, ostentatious, pompous, portentous, pretentious, showy, splendid, utopian, visionary

splendid *adj* 1 blessed, glorious, golden, great, precious, superb

adj 2 admirable, beautiful, delightful, glorious, good, magnificent, peachy, terrific, wonderful

adj 3 best, elegant, finest, gilt-edged, magnificent, majestic, outstanding, preeminent, sensational, superb, superior, superlative

adj 4 ambitious, bombastic, flamboyant, garish, grandiose, inflated, jaunty, lofty, ostentatious, pompous, portentous, pretentious, showy, splashy, utopian, visionary

adj 5 magnificent

splendor *n* see: PROMINENCE *n*

splinter *v* break, burst, erupt, explode, fragment, rupture, shatter, smash

n fragment, shred, sliver

split *n* 1 disparity

n 2 breach, break, crack, fracture, gap, opening

n 3 chink, cleft, crack, crevice, division, fissure, rent, rift

n 4 annulment, divorce, separation

n 5 rip, slash, tear

v 1 break, chip, crack, fracture, gap, sever

v 2 claw, cleave, disrupt, divide, rend, rip, rive, scratch, tear *v* 3 breach, break up, cleave, disjoin, dismember, disrupt, dissect, dissever, disunite, divide, divorce, part, polarize, rupture, separate, sever, sunder

v 4 abscond, bolt, break, depart, elude, escape, flee, fly, hightail it, lose, run

v 5 ax, carve, chip, chop, cleave, cut, dissect, fell, hack, hew, mangle, mutilate, notch, pulverize, rend, saw, sever, slice, sliver, snip, sunder, whittle

spoil *v* 1 accommodate, baby, cater, coddle, gratify, humor, indulge, overindulge, pamper, pander, placate, satisfy

v 2 deflower, desecrate, despoil, devastate, devour, loot, maraud, pillage, plunder, ravage, sack, scourge, strip, violate

v 3 abuse, blemish, damage, hamper, harm, hurt, impair, injure, mar, obstruct, ruin, sabotage, scuttle, tarnish, vandalize

v 4 corrupt, crumble, decay, decompose, degenerate, deteriorate, disintegrate, perish, putrefy, rot, smell, taint, wane, weaken, wither

spoiled *adj* 1 bad, decayed, putrid, rancid, rotten, sharp

adj 2 see: FOUL *adj* 3

spoils *n* 1 bag, booty, prize

n 2 booty, bounty, fortune, kitty, loot, money, plunder, pot, prize, swag, treasure, trove

spoken *adj* 1 expressed, stated, oral, unwritten, verbal, word-of-mouth

adj 2 certain, explicit, expressed, firm, fixed, formal, mandated, set, settled, stated, stipulated

sponge *n* barnacle, dependent, freeloader, hanger-on, leech, parasite, remora, vine

spongy *adj* 1 absorbent

adj 2 mushy, pulpy, soft, squashy, squelchy, squishy, yielding

sponsor *n* advocate, ally, angel, backer, benefactor, booster, champion, cheerleader, donor, friend, guarantor, helper, ombudsman, partner, patron, promoter, supporter

sponsorship *n* 1 ad, advertisement, commercial, plug, promo, promotion, spot

n 2 see: SUPPORT *n* 4

spontaneous *adj* 1 ad-lib, extemporaneous, impromptu, improvised, instantaneous, invented, off the cuff, offhand, unrehearsed, unstudied

adj 2 automatic, impulsive, instinctive, involuntary, natural, rash, reflex, unconscious, unforced, unpremeditated, unprompted

spoof *n* buffoonery, burlesque, caricature, comedy, farce, humor, imitation, joke,

lampoon, mockery, parody, satire, takeoff, travesty

spook *v* abash, alarm, awe, cow, daunt, frighten, horrify, intimidate, panic, scare, shock, startle, terrify, terrorize, unnerve

spooky *adj* 1 frightening, forbidding, scary

adj 2 bizarre, eerie, ghostly, incredible, metaphysical, mystical, odd, ominous, strange, supernatural, uncanny, unearthly, weird

adj 3 appalling, awful, dire, dreadful, fearful, formidable, frightening, frightful, ghastly, horrendous, horrible, offensive, ominous, portentous, scary, shocking, terrible, terrifying, unpleasant

sporadic *adj* 1 few, infrequent, isolated, occasional, rare, scarce, seldom, uncommon, unusual

adj 2 alternate, cyclic, cyclical, intermittent, periodic, periodical, recurrent, recurring, repetitive

sporadically *adv* infrequently, now and then, rarely

sport *n* amusement, distraction, diversion, enjoyment, entertainment, frolic, fun, game, hobby, pastime, recreation

v play

sportsman *n* athlete, jock, letterman, player

sportsmanlike *adj* clean, equal, equitable, even, fair, honest, just, straight, upright

spot *n* 1 bead, circle, mark

n 2 blemish, blot, blur, smear, smudge, stain

n 3 ad, advertisement, commercial, plug, promo, promotion

n 4 area, locale, location, locus, place, point, property, scene

n 5 see: DILEMMA *n* 4

n 6 see: FRAGMENT *n* 3

n 7 see: STANDING *n* 1

v 1 behold, glimpse, look, mind, see, sight, watch, witness

v 2 ascertain, catch, descry, detect, discover, encounter, espy, ferret, find, locate, turn up, uncover

spotless *adj* 1 clean, immaculate, pristine, pure, taintless, unsoiled, unspoiled, unsullied, untouched, virgin

adj 2 celibate, chaste, clean, decent, decorous, immaculate, modest, moral, pristine, proper, pure, stainless, stuffy, taintless, unadulterated, unblemished, undefiled, upstanding, virginal, wholesome

spotlight *n* attention, center, crux, feature, focus, key

v 1 examine, focus, highlight, target

v 2 brighten, glow, illuminate, irradiate, light up

v 3 see: ACCENTUATE *v*

spots *n* allergy, hay fever, hives, reaction

spouse *n* 1 bride, cohabitant, consort, mate, squaw, wife, woman

n 2 bridegroom, groom, hubby, husband, man, master, mate

spouseless *adj* single, sole, unmarried, unwed

spout *v* 1 burst, discharge, erupt, explode, gush

v 2 jet, shoot, spew, spritz, spurt, squirt, surge

n cock, faucet, nozzle, spigot, tap, valve

sprain *n* 1 bruise, hurt, injury, pain, strain, wound

n 2 injury, strain

spread *v* 1 broaden, enlarge, flare, open, widen

v 2 expand, extend, fan, open, unfold

v 3 diffuse, disseminate, distribute, permeate, sprinkle, strew

v 4 imbue, impart, infuse, ingrain, inject, inoculate, instill, invest, penetrate, pervade, steep, suffuse, teach, train

v 5 set

v 6 massage, rub

v 7 broadcast, disseminate, dissipate, distribute, scatter, sow, strew, transmit

n farm, ranch

spreading *adj* catching, communicable, contagious, contaminative, epidemic, infectious, transmittable

spree *n* bash, bender, binge, do, fling, orgy, party

sprightliness *n* alacrity, cheerfulness, eagerness

sprightly *adj* 1 brilliant, clever, dazzling, good, irrepressible, scintillating, smart, witty

adj 2 active, agile, astir, brisk, catty, energetic, lively, nimble, quick, spry, zippy

adj 3 see: LIVELY *adj* 7, 8

spring *n* 1 bounce, elasticity, resilience

n 2 basin, lagoon, lake, loch, pond

v 1 arise, come from, derive, emanate, flow, head, issue, originate, stem

v 2 bob, bound, hop, jaunt, jump, leap, lope, prance, skip, sprint, trip

v 3 bolt, start, startle

springy *adj* alterable, elastic, flexible, movable, pliable, resilient, supple

sprinkle *n* cloudburst, deluge, downpour, drizzle, hail, precipitation, rain

v 1 diffuse, disseminate, distribute, permeate, spread, strew

v 2 dust, powder

v 3 deluge, drizzle, fall, rain, shower

sprinkling *n* see: TRACE *n* 4

sprint *v* 1 dart, dash, hasten, scamper, scoot, scurry

v 2 dash, gallop, jog, race, run, speed

v 3 see: HOP *v*

sprite *n* elf, fairy, naiad, pixie

spritz *v* jet, shoot, spew, spout, spurt, squirt, surge

sprout *v* bloom, blossom, bud, develop, ferment, flourish, flower, grow

n branch, growth, shoot

spruce *v* dress, equip, groom

spry *adj* 1 active, agile, astir, brisk, catty, energetic, lively, nimble, quick, sprightly, zippy

adj 2 see: LIVELY *adj* 7, 8

spunk *n* 1 enterprise, gumption, initiative, resourcefulness, spirit, volition

n 2 animation, drive, élan, energy, enthusiasm, esprit de corps, go, gusto, pep, potency, sparkle, spirit, verve, vigor, vim, vitality, zing, zip

n 3 backbone, chutzpah, determination, endurance, fortitude, grit, guts, moxie, nerve, persistence, pluck, resilience, spirit, stamina, strength, tenacity, tolerance, vigor, willpower

spur *v* 1 egg, encourage, exhort, goad, incite, persuade, prick, prod, prompt, urge

v 2 agitate, anger, arouse, encourage, foment, ignite, incite, induce, inflame, inspire, instigate, invoke, motivate, muster, prod, propel, provoke, raise, set, set on, stimulate, stir, urge

v 3 activate, actuate, compel, drive, force, goad, impel, induce, mobilize, motivate, move, persuade, press, propel, push, start, turn on

n claw, talon

spurious *adj* 1 inapplicable, inconsistent, unfitting

adj 2 affected, artificial, assumed, feigned, fictitious

adj 3 bastard, fatherless, illegitimate, misbegotten, orphaned, unauthentic, ungenuine

adj 4 artificial, bogus, counterfeit, ersatz, fake, false, imitation, mock, phony, pseudo, sham, simulated, substitute, unreal

spurn *v* 1 condemn, decline, disapprove, dismiss, exile, object, refuse, reject, reprobate, repudiate, turn down *v* 2 blackball, boycott, cut, ignore, ostracize, rebuff, snub

v 3 abandon, break up, cast off, chuck, defect, desert, disavow, discard, disenfranchise, disown, ditch, dump, forsake, jilt, junk, leave, quit, reject, renounce, strand, throw out

spurt *v* 1 discharge, ejaculate, shoot

v 2 flow, gurgle, ooze

v 3 jet, shoot, spew, spout, spritz, squirt, surge

sputter *v* 1 bubble, crackle, hiss, sizzle

v 2 blurt, cackle, cry, ejaculate, exclaim, shout, spill, tattle, utter

spy *v* 1 examine, explore, investigate, scout, survey

v 2 bug, check, eavesdrop, monitor, observe, oversee, snoop, wiretap

spyglass *n* binoculars, eye, field glass, glass, lens, magnifying glass, microscope, mirror, periscope, scope, telescope

squabble *v* altercate, argue, battle, bicker, brawl, clash, conflict, dispute, engage, equivocate, feud, fight, fray, haggle, hassle, quarrel, quibble, row, scrap, spar, wrangle

n see: QUARREL *n* 2

squadron *n* 1 armada, assembly, boats, convoy, fleet, flotilla, grouping, ships

n 2 aircraft, division, formation, wing

squalid *adj* 1 base, beneath, despicable, ignoble, inferior, low, lowdown, sordid, unworthy, vile, vulgar, wretched

adj 2 black, dark, dingy, dirty, filthy, foul, grimy, grubby, mucky, murky, polluted, seedy, shabby, sooty, stained, unclean, unlit, unwashed

squall *n* blast, blizzard, blow, gale, gust, hurricane, northeaster, snowstorm, storm, tempest, typhoon, wind

squally *adj* blustery, stormy, tempestuous, windy

squander *v* cast away, consume, dissipate, drivel, empty, fritter, lavish, throw away, use up, waste

square *adv* accurately, exactly, just so, precisely, right, sharp, smack, squarely

adj 1 even, exact, tie

adj 2 see: FAIR *adj* 7

n common, park, plaza

v 1 clear, clear off, discharge, liquidate, pay up, repay, settle

v 2 accord, agree, check, coalesce, coincide, comply with, concur, conform, consent, consist, correspond, fit in, harmonize, jibe, suit, tally

squarely *adv* accurately, exactly, just so, precisely, right, sharp, smack

squash *v* 1 crush, stomp, tramp, trample, tread, tromp

v 2 compact, compress, constrain, crowd, crush, jam, mash, pack, press, squeeze

v 3 bruise, crush, mash, mush up, pulp

v 4 annihilate, crush, demolish, extinguish, put down, quash, quell, quench, repress, stamp out, suppress

n see: HORDE *n*

squashy *adj* mushy, pulpy, soft, spongy, squelchy, squishy, yielding

squatter *n* inhabitant, lessee, occupant, renter, resident, tenant

squaw *n* bride, cohabitant, consort, mate, spouse, wife, woman

squeal *v* 1 fink, inform, rat, sing, snitch, stool, tattle, tattletale

v 2 bark, bellow, blare, call, cry, holler, howl, roar, scream, screech, shout, shriek, shrill, thunder, wail, yell

squeamish *adj* nauseated, queasy, queer, seasick

squeeze *n* caress, embrace, fondling, hug, kiss, touch

v 1 drain, extract

v 2 coerce, exact, extort, gouge, shake down, wrench, wrest, wring

v 3 clasp, clinch, cuddle, embrace, enfold, hold, hug

v 4 compact, compress, constrain, crowd, crush, jam, mash, pack, press, push, squash

squelch *v* censor, curb, gag, hush, inhibit, muffle, mute, quell, quiet, repress, restrain, silence, stifle, still, subdue, suppress, throttle, tone down

squelchy *adj* mushy, pulpy, soft, spongy, squashy, squishy, yielding

squirm *v* fidget, twitch, writhe

squirrel *v see:* ACCUMULATE *v* 2

squirt *v* jet, shoot, spew, spout, spritz, spurt, surge

squishy *adj* mushy, pulpy, soft, spongy, squashy, squelchy, yielding

stab *n* attempt, chance, effort, fling, go, guess, heave, lob, pop, shot, slap, sling, throw, toss, try, whirl

v 1 gore, impale, lance, penetrate, pierce, puncture, spear

v 2 attack, butt, drive, knock, lunge, pass, plunge, ram, sink, stick, thrust

stabbing *adj* acute, piercing, sharp

stability *n* balance, equilibrium

stable *adj* 1 secure, staunch, strong, sure

adj 2 ethical, lucid, moral, rational, responsible

adj 3 constant, continuing, durable, enduring, eternal, lasting, permanent *adj* **4** constant, determinate, firm, fixed, hard, immutable, inflexible, invariable, ironclad, resolute, unalterable, unchangeable, unmovable

adj **5** consistent, constant, continuing, endless, equable, established, even, invariable, reliable, routine, same, serene, steady, unchanging, unfailing, unfluctuating, uniform, unvarying

adj **6** see: INACTIVE *adj* 2

adj **7** see: SOLID *adj* 3

n barn, coop, enclosure, lean-to, paddock, pen, pound, shack, shed, shelter, stall, sty

stack *n* bank, drift, heap, hill, mass, mound, mountain, pile, stockpile

v **1** bank, drift, heap, pile

v **2** fill, heap, load, pack, place, stuff

v **3** see: CLASSIFY *v* 2

stadium *n* amphitheater, arena, bowl, coliseum, dome, hippodrome

staff *n* **1** department, faculty, instructors, professors, teachers

n **2** crew, employees, faculty, help, people, personnel, workers

n **3** birch, cane, club, pole, rod, shaft, stake, stave, stick

n **4** baton, rod, scepter, wand

n **5** citizens, civilization, colony, community, crowd, culture, folks, group, human beings, individuals, laity, masses, men and women, neighbors, people, persons, populace, population, public, settlement, society, tribe

stage *n* **1** condition, level, phase, state, step

n **2** dais, desk, lectern, podium, pulpit, rostrum, soapbox, stand

n **3** cycle, duration, interval, period, season, span, spell, stretch, term, time

n **4** Broadway, comedy, drama, extravaganza, musical, theater

n **5** aeon, age, cycle, decade, eon, epoch, era, eternity, forever, long time, millennium, period, reign, span, time, years

staged *adj* artificial, corny, exaggerated, theatrical

stagger *v* **1** careen, lurch, pitch, reel, sway, toss, totter, wheel

v **2** do, fare, get along, get by, get on, make out, manage, muddle through

v **3** bumble, falter, flounder, fumble, get stuck, grope, hesitate, stumble, waffle, waver

v **4** delay, falter, halt, hesitate, pause, stall, vacillate, waver

v **5** amaze, astonish, astound, awe, boggle, confound, dazzle, dumbfound, flabbergast, nonplus, stun, surprise

stagnant *adj* **1** close, humid, stuffy

adj **2** brackish, briny, foul, nasty, undrinkable

adj **3** see: INACTIVE *adj* 2

staid *adj* **1** dignified, earnest, grave, pensive, sedate, serious, sober, solemn, somber, stoic, unemotional, unflinching

adj **2** see: SHY *adj* 2

stain *n* **1** blemish, blot, blur, smear, spot

n **2** color, coloring, dye, paint, pigment, tincture, tint

v **1** color, dye, paint, tinge, tint

v **2** blot, smear, smudge, soil, stigmatize

v **3** disfavor, disgrace, dishonor, humiliate, reproach, shame, tarnish

v **4** defile, dirty, discolor, smear, soil, sully, taint, tarnish

stained *adj* see: DIRTY *adj* 2

stainless *adj* see: PURE *adj* 7

stake *n* **1** claim, interest, share

n **2** column, pole, post

n **3** bet, chance, fortune, gamble, hazard, luck

n **4** birch, cane, club, pole, rod, shaft, stave, stick

n **5** see: REWARD *n* 8

v **1** bankroll, capitalize, finance, subsidize

v **2** attempt, bet, chance, dare, gamble, hazard, play, risk, speculate, venture, wager

stale *adj* **1** deficient, inept, out of practice, rusty, unpracticed, unprepared

adj **2** decaying, fetid, foul, gamy, malodorous, musty, putrid, rancid, rank, reeking, rotten, smelly, sour, spoiled, stinking, tainted

adj **3** banal, boring, clichéd, commonplace, corny, dull, hackneyed, musty, redundant, repetitious, repetitive, tedious, threadbare, timeworn, tired, tiresome, trite, worn-out

stalemate *n* bottleneck, deadlock, draw, hung jury, impasse, standoff, standstill, tie

stall *n* **1** bed, berth, bunk, cot, couch, cradle

n **2** barn, coop, enclosure, lean-to, paddock, pen, pound, shack, shed, shelter, stable, sty

v **1** arrest, block, check, freeze, halt, impede, interrupt, stay, stop

v **2** delay, falter, halt, hesitate, pause, stagger, vacillate, waver

stalwart *adj* **1** brave, courageous, lusty, macho, male, manlike, manly, masculine, virile

adj **2** concentrated, hearty, heavy-duty, lusty, potent, powerful, robust, stout, strong, sturdy *adj* 3 audacious, bold, brave, courageous, daring, dauntless, fearless, gallant, game, gutsy, heroic, intrepid, unafraid, undaunted, valiant, valorous

adj 4 aggressive, dominant, durable, firm, forceful, hardy, hearty, mighty, powerful, robust, rugged, stout, strong, sturdy, tenacious, tough

stamina *n* 1 backbone, chutzpah, determination, endurance, fortitude, grit, guts, moxie, nerve, persistence, pluck, resilience, spirit, spunk, strength, tenacity, tolerance, vigor, willpower

n 2 arrogance, assurance, audacity, boldness, brashness, brass, cheek, chutzpah, condescension, confidence, crust, effrontery, face, gall, haughtiness, insolence, nerve, patronage, presumption, ridicule, sass, temerity

stamp *n* 1 brand, cachet, emblem, imprint, logo, logotype, mark, seal, trademark

n 2 copy, impression, imprint, indent, indentation, mark, notch, print, tab

v 1 coin, mint, strike

v 2 drive, hammer, impress, imprint, mark, pound, press, print, strike, thump, whack

stampede *n* rampage, riot, storm

v frenzy, rage, rampage, rebel, revolt, riot, storm

stance *n* 1 attitude, belief, point of view, position, stand

n 2 achievement, distinction, prestige, rank, stature, status

n 3 air, attitude, bearing, calmness, carriage, demeanor, disposition, poise, pose, posture, presence, set

stanch *v* check, oppose, resist, stem, stop, weather, withstand

stand *n* 1 attitude, belief, point of view, position

n 2 dais, desk, lectern, podium, pulpit, rostrum, soapbox

v abide, accept, acquiesce, allow, authorize, bear, concede, condone, digest, endure, experience, have, let, permit, put up with, stomach, suffer, sustain, swallow, take, tolerate, undergo

standard *adj* 1 established, normal, regular, uniform

adj 2 basic, conventional, established, official

adj 3 accepted, established, proven, sound, traditional

adj 4 average, common, intermediate,

mediocre, medium, middle, normal, ordinary, regular, unimpressive

n 1 flag

n 2 flag, guideline, principle, rule

n 3 benchmark, criterion, gauge, measure, observation, rule, yardstick

n 4 average, mean, median, medium, middle, norm, par

n 5 epitome, example, exemplar, ideal, mirror, model, outline, paradigm, pattern, plan, prototype

standardize *v* adjust, conform, equalize, level, regulate, set policy

standby *n* agent, alternate, backup, contingency, part-timer, replacement, representative, substitute, surrogate

stand-in *n* substitute, understudy

standing *adj* fastened, fixed, in position, motionless, permanent, set, solid, static, stationary, still

n 1 capacity, grade, office, place, position, post, quality, rank, situation, spot, state, station, status

n 2 footing, surface

standoff *n* bottleneck, deadlock, draw, hung jury, impasse, stalemate, standstill, tie

standoffish *adj* antisocial, introverted

standout *n* sensation

standstill *n* 1 bottleneck, deadlock, draw, hung jury, impasse, stalemate, tie

n 2 abeyance, cessation, halt, impasse, moratorium, stay, stop, stopping, suspension

stand-up *n* buffoon, comedian, comedienne, comic, fool, zany

stanza *n* chapter, paragraph, passage, verse

staple *n* 1 bolt, brad, nut, peg, pin, rivet, spike, stud, weld

n 2 see: SUBSTANCE *n* 9

v attach, clip, fasten, nail, pin, tack

staples *n* see: GOODS *n* 2

star *adj* 1 central, chief, distinguished, dominant, famed, great, key, leading, main, major, number one, outstanding, predominant, preeminent, primary, prime, principal, prominent, successful, superior, top

adj 2 lead, principal, top-billed

n 1 celebrity, dignitary, luminary, movie star, name, notable

n 2 actor, actress, artist, entertainer, hero, heroine, lead, movie star, performer, player, protagonist, thespian, tragedian

n 3 advocate, champion, conqueror, hero,

heroine, lead, leader, master, principal, protagonist, trailblazer, victor, winner

stare v 1 wonder

v 2 eye, eyeball, gape, gawk, goggle, observe, ogle, peer, study

stark adj 1 naked, plain, unadorned

adj 2 bare, barren, clear, empty, vacant, vacuous, void

start n 1 blow, jerk, jolt, jump, shock, surprise

n 2 beginning, birth, debut, delivery, inception, kindling, onset, outset

n 3 beginning, foreword, intro, introduction, overture, preamble, preface, prelude

n 4 fright, horror, scare, shock, terror

v 1 blanch, cringe, flinch, jump, recoil, shrink, startle, wince

v 2 activate, charge, electrify, energize, enliven, excite, ignite, turn on, vitalize

v 3 activate, actuate, compel, drive, force, goad, impel, induce, mobilize, motivate, move, persuade, press, propel, push, spur, turn on

v 4 activate, begin, cause, commence, constitute, create, embark, enter, establish, inaugurate, induct, initiate, install, instigate, instill, institute, introduce, kick off, launch, lead off, open, originate, precipitate, preface, set up, tee off, usher in, venture forth

v 5 bolt, jump, spring, startle

v 6 build, constitute, construct, create, erect, establish, found, initiate, institute, launch

v 7 begin, coin, conceive, craft, create, define, develop, devise, formulate, innovate, invent, make

v 8 arouse, awaken, excite, induce, instill, motivate, move, pique, prime, provoke, quicken, rouse, roust, spark, stimulate, titillate, urge

starting adj beginning, embryonic, founding, incipient, initial, introductory, nascent, rudimentary

startle v 1 bump, jar, jolt, jostle, rattle, shake

v 2 blanch, cringe, flinch, jump, recoil, shrink, start, wince

v 3 abash, alarm, awe, cow, daunt, frighten, horrify, intimidate, panic, scare, shock, spook, terrify, terrorize, unnerve

v 4 bolt, jump, spring, start

startling adj 1 dramatic, extraordinary, sensational, shocking

adj 2 sudden, surprising, unexpected, unforeseen

starve v 1 deprive

v 2 famish, fast, wither

starved adj famished, hungry, ravenous, starving, voracious

starving adj famished, hungry, ravenous, starved, voracious

stash n backlog, cache, hoard, holdings, inventory, nest egg, pile, reserve, reservoir, stock, stockpile, store, supply

v 1 bury, cache, cloister, conceal, cover, ditch, ensconce, hide, plant, secrete

v 2 see: ACCUMULATE v 2

state n 1 case, condition, repair, shape

n 2 condition, level, phase, stage, step

n 3 area, country, entity, government, nation, province

n 4 confidence, disposition, feeling, frame of mind, mentality, mood, morale

n 5 capacity, grade, office, place, position, post, quality, rank, situation, spot, standing, station, status

n 6 condition, mode, perspective, posture, situation, status, update

n 7 aptitude, character, complexion, disposition, distinctiveness, heart, humor, identity, inclination, individuality, makeup, nature, personality, quality, spirit, temperament, tendency

v 1 allege, assert, avow, claim, maintain

v 2 add, comment, declare, note, remark, say

v 3 air, bring up, broach, communicate, discuss, expose, express, give, introduce, open, put, reveal, tap, tell, vent, ventilate, verbalize

v 4 argue, assert, believe, claim, contend, defend, justify, know, maintain, think, vindicate, warrant

v 5 analyze, annotate, clarify, define, detail, elucidate, explain, expound, express, interpret, narrate, spell out, understand

v 6 announce, articulate, assert, couch, describe, dictate, draft, enunciate, express, intonate, orate, phrase, proclaim, pronounce, say, speak, stress, talk, utter, verbalize, vocalize, voice, word

v 7 brief, communicate, convey, declare, describe, disclose, divulge, explain, impart, inform, narrate, orate, portray, read, recite, recount, relate, report, retell, reveal, share, tattle, tell, transmit

stated adj 1 expressed, oral, spoken, unwritten, verbal, word-of-mouth

adj 2 certain, explicit, expressed, firm, fixed, formal, mandated, set, settled, spoken, stipulated

stately *adj* 1 aristocratic, blue-blooded, imperial, kingly, majestic, noble, regal, royal, well-bred

adj 2 august, baronial, exalted, grand, grandiose, haughty, imperial, imposing, impressive, lofty, lordly, magisterial, magnificent, majestic, noble, portly, princely, regal

adj 3 attractive, becoming, comely, exquisite, fair, good-looking, gorgeous, handsome, pleasing

adj 4 choice, deluxe, elegant, first-class, grand, luxuriant, luxurious, opulent, ornate, palatial, plush, posh, rich, soft, sumptuous, thick

statement *n* 1 affidavit, attestation, testimony

n 2 comment, commentary, note, remark

n 3 account, balance sheet, book, credit, ledger, score, tab

n 4 accusation, allegation, assertion, charge, comment, declaration, deposition

n 5 discourse, expression, speaking, speech, talk, utterance, verbalization, word

static *adj* fastened, fixed, in position, motionless, permanent, set, solid, stationary, still

station *n* 1 fame, position, prestige, prosperity, status, success

n 2 capacity, grade, office, place, position, post, quality, rank, situation, spot, standing, state, status

n 3 depot, location, stop

n 4 boob tube, cable, channel, teevee, television, tube, TV, video

v 1 bivouac, camp, dwell, lodge, nest

v 2 calibrate, establish, fix, insert, install, lay, locate, place, plant, position, put, set, settle

stationary *adj* fastened, fixed, in position, motionless, permanent, set, solid, standing, static, still

stationery *n* letterhead, page, paper, papyrus, parchment, sheepskin, sheet, vellum

statistic *n* actuality, fact, given, specific, truth

statistics *n* banking, economics, finance

statue *n* 1 bust, figure, icon, idol, image, sculpture, statuette, symbol

n 2 memorial, monument

statuette *n* bust, figure, icon, idol, image, sculpture, statue, symbol

stature *n* 1 caliber, excellence, goodness, merit, quality, value, worth

n 2 esteem, fame, good standing, name, perception, regard, reputation

n 3 achievement, distinction, prestige, rank, recognition, stance, status

status *n* 1 fame, position, prestige, prosperity, station, success

n 2 achievement, distinction, prestige, rank, recognition, stance, stature

n 3 caste, class, degree, echelon, estate, hierarchy, level, position, rank

n 4 capacity, grade, office, place, position, post, quality, rank, situation, spot, standing, state

n 5 condition, mode, perspective, posture, state, situation, update

statute *n* 1 act, law, legislation, measure

n 2 see: COMMAND *n* 3

staunch *adj* 1 secure, stable, strong, sure

adj 2 ardent, constant, dedicated, dependable, devoted, faithful, loyal, resolute, steadfast, steady, true, trusty

adj 3 seaworthy, watertight

stave *n* 1 birch, cane, club, pole, rod, shaft, staff, stick, stake

n 2 bat, blackjack, boomerang, club, cudgel, cue, mallet, stick

stay *n* 1 delay, interruption, postponement, reprieve, stop, suspension

n 2 abeyance, cessation, halt, impasse, moratorium, standstill, stop, stopping, suspension

n 3 base, brace, buttress, column, footing, foundation, prop, shore, support, underpinning

n 4 visit

n 5 delay, interval, lull, pause, suspension, wait

n 6 absolution, amnesty, discharge, disengagement, dispensation, freedom, moratorium, pardon, release, relief, reprieve, respite, suspension

v 1 domicile, dwell, inhabit, live, occupy, reside, room

v 2 arrest, block, check, freeze, halt, impede, interrupt, stop

v 3 abide, await, bide, linger, loiter, remain, stick around, tarry, wait

v 4 abide, continue, endure, last, outlast, persevere, persist, prevail, remain, stick to, stick with, survive

v 5 adjourn, avoid, defer, delay, hold, hold up, interrupt, lay over, postpone, procrastinate, prolong, put off, remit, reschedule, set aside, shelve, suspend, table, wait, waive

v 6 bar, block, brake, choke, clog, dam, deter, detract, encumber, frustrate, halt, hamper, hesitate, hinder, impair, impede, inhibit, jam, obstruct, prevent, repress, restrain, retard, slow, stop, stop up, throttle

steadfast *adj* 1 adamant, firm, resolute, stern, strict

adj 2 absolute, firm, fixed, resolute, unconditional, unreserved

adj 3 abiding, enduring, firm, never-failing, sure, unfaltering, unshakable, unwavering

adj 4 ardent, constant, dedicated, dependable, devoted, faithful, loyal, resolute, staunch, steady, true, trusty

adj 5 see: STUBBORN *adj* 6

steady *adj* 1 methodic, methodical, orderly, recurring, systematic

adj 2 ardent, constant, dedicated, dependable, devoted, faithful, loyal, resolute, staunch, steadfast, true, trusty

adj 3 consistent, constant, continuing, endless, equable, established, even, invariable, reliable, routine, same, serene, stable, unchanging, unfailing, unfluctuating, uniform, unvarying

adj 4 calm, collected, composed, cool, demure, dormant, easy, gentle, hushed, idle, imperturbable, motionless, nonchalant, peaceful, placid, poised, quiet, relaxed, restful, sedate, self-composed, self-possessed, serene, soft, still, tranquil, unflappable, unruffled, untroubled

v balance, brace, calm, fix, still

steal *n* bargain, buy, deal, discount, promotion, reduction, sale

v 1 abduct, carry away, grab, kidnap, seize

v 2 appropriate, burglarize, defraud, embezzle, filch, heist, lift, misappropriate, pilfer, pillage, pinch, plunder, pocket, purloin, rip off, rob, snake, snitch, swindle, swipe, take, thieve

v 3 see: SNEAK *v* 2

stealth *n* 1 secrecy, sneakiness, subterfuge

n 2 camouflage, cover, incognito, privacy

stealthily *adv* clandestinely, covertly, furtively, hush-hush, mystically, secretly, sneakily, surreptitiously, under cover

stealthy *adj* catlike, cattish, catty, feline, furtive, skulking

steam *n* 1 cloud, fog, haze, mist, vapor

n 2 ardor, beef, brawn, drive, energy, force, intensity, lustiness, might, muscle, pep, potency, power, punch, strength, verve, vigor, vim, virility, vitality

v anger, blow up, boil, boil over, brew, bristle, burn, flare up, fume, rage, seethe, simmer, smoke, storm

steamship *n* craft, cruiser, freighter, frigate, ketch, liner, ocean liner, sailboat, schooner, ship, vessel, yacht

steamy *adj* 1 hot, humid, muggy, sticky, stifling, sunny, tropical

adj 2 cloudy, dismal, foggy, gray, hazy, misty, murky, overcast, vaporous, vapory

steed *n* colt, equine, filly, foal, gelding, horse, mare, mount, nag, pony, yearling

steep *adj* 1 perpendicular, sheer, upright, vertical

adj 2 costly, dear, excessive, exorbitant, expensive, high, overpriced, prohibitive, stiff

v imbue, impart, infuse, ingrain, inject, inoculate, instill, invest, penetrate, pervade, spread, suffuse, teach, train

steeple *n* belfry, spire, tower, turret

steer *v* 1 administer, boss, command, direct, guide, manage, oversee, supervise

v 2 conduct, control, develop, direct, drive, guide, lead, operate, pilot, route, shepherd

v 3 carve, chisel, craft, cut, define, design, fashion, form, mold, sculpt, shape

n bull, calf, cow, heifer

stein *n* chalice, container, cup, dish, Dixie cup, glass, goblet, mug, shot glass, tumbler, vessel, wineglass

stellar *adj* 1 celestial, heavenly

adj 2 champion, excellent, fine, first-class, first-rate, foremost, good, grade A, leading, number one, prime, principal, prominent, quality, select, superb, superior, top, top-drawer, top-notch, tops

stem *n* 1 bow, crown, fore, front, head, prow, top

n 2 beginning, conception, cradle, derivation, fountainhead, inception, infancy, mother, origin, root, source

v 1 check, oppose, resist, stanch, stop, weather, withstand

v 2 arise, come from, derive, emanate, flow, head, issue, spring

stench *n* odor, reek, smell, stink

stencil *n* mask, overlay, pattern, template

stenographer *n* aide, assistant, clerk, recorder, secretary

step *n* 1 action, maneuver, measure

n 2 condition, level, phase, stage

n 3 class, degree, grade, interval, level, mark, notch, position, rank

n 4 gait, march, pace, stride, walk

n 5 alacrity, cadence, celerity, dispatch, gait, pace, quickness, rapidity, rate, speed, stride, swiftness, trot, velocity, walk

v amble, hike, journey, march, pace, parade, plod, saunter, stride, stroll, strut, tramp, tread, trek, walk

sterile *adj* 1 clean, healthy, hygienic, sanitary

adj 2 barren, effete, frigid, impotent, infertile, spent, unbearing, unfertile, unfruitful, unproductive

adj 3 dull, flat

sterilize *v* clean, cleanse, filter, purify, wash

sterling *adj* deserving, estimable, excellent, honorable, noble, precious, valuable, worthy

stern *adj* 1 adamant, firm, resolute, steadfast, strict

adj 2 austere, ascetic, astringent, chaste, rigid, simple, stoic

adj 3 dour, firm, forbidding, grim, sad, serious, severe, unpleasant

adj 4 abusive, hard, harsh, severe, stiff, strict, tough, uncaring, unsympathetic

adj 5 authoritarian, authoritative, autocratic, controlled, despotic, disciplined, firm, harsh, inflexible, ironhanded, restrictive, rigid, rigorous, ruthless, severe, solid, strict, stringent, strong, tough, tyrannical

adj 6 see: SEVERE *adj* 5, 6, 8

stew *v* 1 brood, fret, fuss, worry

v 2 boil, heat, overheat, parboil, seethe

steward *n* agent, custodian, janitor, manager

stewardly *adj* canny, conservative, economical, frugal, provident, sparing, spartan, thrifty, unwasteful

stick *n* 1 bar, ingot, pole, rod, strip

n 2 birch, cane, club, pole, rod, shaft, staff, stake, stave

n 3 bat, blackjack, boomerang, club, cudgel, cue, mallet, nightstick, stave

v 1 adhere, bond, cleave, cling, cohere, hold, join

v 2 attack, butt, drive, knock, lunge, pass, plunge, ram, sink, thrust

v 3 affix, bind, bond, cement, fasten, fuse, glue, join, lock, paste, seal, secure, unite

stickler *n* fusspot, perfectionist, purist

sticky *adj* 1 adhesive, cohesive, gluey, gummy, tacky

adj 2 awkward, delicate, difficult, embarrassing, tricky

adj 3 hot, humid, muggy, steamy, stifling, sunny, tropical

adj 4 damp, drenched, dripping, humid, moist, mucky, muggy, soaked, soggy, sopping, sultry, sweaty, wet

adj 5 gooey, tacky, thick

stiff *adj* 1 artificial, awkward, formal, stilted, stuffy

adj 2 brisk, heavy, powerful, strong

adj 3 firm, hard, taut, tense, tight

adj 4 costly, dear, excessive, exorbitant, expensive, high, overpriced, prohibitive

adj 5 abusive, hard, harsh, severe, stern, strict, tough, uncaring, unsympathetic

adj 6 compact, firm, hard, hardened, rigid, secure, solid, sound, specific, stable, tight

adj 7 bullheaded, closed-minded, deaf, firm, hardheaded, hard-line, inelastic, inflexible, intractable, intransigent, obstinate, perverse, pigheaded, refractory, resolute, rigid, stubborn, tough, unbending, uncompromising, unpliable, unpliant, unwieldy, unyielding, willful

n body, cadaver, carcass, corpse, remains

stifle *v* 1 crush, defeat, drown, overpower

v 2 asphyxiate, choke, constrict, gag, garrote, muffle, quash, repress, smother, strangle, suffocate, suppress

v 3 censor, curb, gag, hush, inhibit, muffle, mute, quell, quiet, repress, restrain, silence, squelch, still, subdue, suppress, throttle, tone down

stifling *adj* hot, humid, muggy, steamy, sticky, sunny, tropical

stigma *n* accountability, blame, burden, culpability, fault, guilt, onus, responsibility

stigmatize *v* blot, smear, smudge, soil

still *adj* 1 dead, hush, inanimate, inert, lifeless, noiseless, quiet, silent, soundless

adj 2 fastened, fixed, in position, motionless, permanent, set, solid, standing, static, stationary

adj 3 see: CALM *adj* 2

adj 4 see: INACTIVE *adj* 2

adv at any rate, but, however, moreover, nevertheless, nonetheless, notwithstanding, though, yet

v 1 balance, brace, calm, steady

v 2 censor, curb, gag, hush, inhibit, muffle, mute, quell, quiet, repress, restrain, silence, squelch, stifle, subdue, suppress, throttle, tone down

v 3 see: APPEASE *v* 2

stillness *n* 1 accord, calm, harmony, peace, serenity, tranquillity

n 2 calm, hush, lull, peace, peacefulness, quiet, repose, respite, rest, siesta, silence, tranquillity

stilted *adj* artificial, awkward, formal, stuffy

stimulate *v* 1 amuse, charm, divert, entertain, interest, please *v* 2 cue, jog, nudge, prompt, push, remind, stir, suggest

v 3 arouse, awaken, excite, induce, instill, motivate, move, pique, prime, provoke, quicken, rouse, roust, spark, start, titillate, urge

v 4 arouse, electrify, excite, fire, incite, inspire, rouse, spark, tantalize, thrill, titillate, turn on, whet

v 5 agitate, anger, arouse, encourage, foment, ignite, incite, induce, inflame, inspire, instigate, invoke, motivate, muster, prod, propel, provoke, raise, set, set on, spur, stir, urge

stimulated *adj* 1 aroused, ebullient, elated, euphoric, excited, exhilarated, happy, intoxicated, joyful, sparked, turned on
adj 2 amorous, aroused, horny, in heat, in the mood, lustful

stimulating *adj* 1 provocative, suggestive
adj 2 deep, meaty, profound
adj 3 dynamic, electrifying, exciting, thrilling
adj 4 appealing, colorful, entertaining, interesting, lively, varied
adj 5 electric, exciting, exhilarating, provocative, rousing, stirring
adj 6 arousing, awesome, breathtaking, exciting, magnificent, stirring, stunning
adj 7 exciting, exotic, inspiring, interesting, intriguing, provocative, tingling, titillating
adj 8 arousing, exciting, intriguing, provocative, seductive, sexy, suggestive, tantalizing
adj 9 energizing, exhilarating, invigorating, refreshing

stimulation *n* 1 enjoyment, excitement, kicks, pleasure, thrills
n 2 incitement, infection, infusion, inspiration

stimulus *n* 1 impetus, urge
n 2 bonus, consideration, goal, incentive, inducement, motivation, motive, reason

sting *n* 1 con, crime, graft, hustle, racket, rip-off, scam, swindle
n 2 ache, agony, angina, burn, cramp, crick, heartache, hurt, pain, pang, soreness, spasm, twinge
v bite, burn, smart

stingy *adj* cheap, close, greedy, mean, miserly, niggardly, parsimonious, pennypinching, tight, tightfisted, ungenerous, ungiving

stink *n* odor, reek, smell, stench

stinking *adj* see: FOUL *adj* 3

stint *n* assignment, chore, duty, effort, job, mission, task

v bound, limit, restrict, scrimp, short, skimp

stipend *n* 1 alimony, allowance, annuity, payment
n 2 alimony, compensation, fee, honorarium, payment, remuneration
n 3 bill, bonus, charge, commission, compensation, consideration, earnings, fee, gross, income, pay, salary, wage
n 4 see: REWARD *n* 5, 8

stipulate *v* demand, designate, indicate, insist, require, specify

stipulated *adj* certain, explicit, expressed, firm, fixed, formal, mandated, set, settled, spoken

stipulation *n* 1 caveat, limitation, qualification, restriction
n 2 agreement, clause, condition, provision, proviso, requirement, reservation, specification, string, terms

stir *n* 1 action, activity, ado, animation, bedlam, bother, bustle, chaos, commotion, excitement, flurry, fluster, fuss, hum, liveliness, madhouse, movement, to-do, tumult, turmoil, whirlpool, whirlwind
n 2 see: JAIL *n*
v 1 beat, blend, mingle, mix, toss, whip
v 2 cue, jog, nudge, prompt, push, remind, suggest
v 3 arouse, awaken, challenge, excite, kindle, rally, rouse, wake, waken
v 4 appeal, arouse, attract, excite, fascinate, fire, interest, intrigue, lead on, lure, seduce, tantalize
v 5 affect, assure, convince, impel, induce, influence, inspire, instigate, motivate, move, persuade, pressure, prompt, sway, talk into, touch, win over
v 6 agitate, anger, arouse, encourage, foment, ignite, incite, induce, inflame, inspire, instigate, invoke, motivate, muster, prod, propel, provoke, raise, set, set on, spur, stimulate, urge

stirring *adj* 1 exciting, hot, sensational, spectacular
adj 2 electric, exciting, exhilarating, provocative, stimulating
adj 3 arousing, awesome, breathtaking, exciting, magnificent, stimulating, stunning
adj 4 dramatic, epic, grand, heroic, legendary, noble, vivid
adj 5 see: PASSIONATE *adj* 2

stock *n* 1 blood, descent, kinship, relationship
n 2 goods, inventory, provisions, store, supply

n 3 account, budget, capital, cash, fund, money

n 4 breed, clan, class, family, household, people, race, relatives, tribe

n 5 ancestry, blood, bloodline, descent, family, genealogy, heritage, line, lineage, origin, pedigree, strain

n 6 articles, basics, commodities, essentials, goods, inventory, line, materials, merchandise, products, properties, staples, wares

n 7 backlog, cache, hoard, holdings, inventory, nest egg, pile, reserve, reservoir, stash, stockpile, store, supply

v 1 refill, refresh, replace, replenish

v 2 fill, furnish, replenish, store, supply

stockade *n* see: JAIL *n*

stockholder *n* landlord, lessor, owner, proprietor

stockpile *n* 1 bank, drift, heap, hill, mass, mound, mountain, pile

n 2 backlog, cache, hoard, holdings, inventory, nest egg, pile, reserve, reservoir, stash, stock, store, supply

v 1 accumulate, bank, deposit, hoard, save, squirrel away, store

v 2 accrue, accumulate, acquire, amass, assemble, collect, garner, gather, grow, hoard, save, squirrel, stash, store up

stockroom *n* cache, repository, storehouse, warehouse

stocks *n* bonds, holdings, investments, securities

stocky *adj* 1 athletic, brawny, burly, husky, massive, muscular, ponderous, powerful, robust, stout, strapping, strong

adj 2 see: FAT *adj* 1

stodgy *adj* 1 boring, dull, pompous, stuffy

adj 2 see: MONOTONOUS *adj* 1

stoic *adj* 1 ascetic, astringent, austere, chaste, rigid, simple, spartan, stern

adj 2 dignified, earnest, grave, pensive, sedate, serious, sober, solemn, somber, staid, unemotional, unflinching

adj 3 cold, dry, dull, impassive, laid-back, matter-of-fact, phlegmatic, poker-faced, reserved, stolid, unaffected, unemotional, unfeeling, unmoved, untouched

stoicism *n* apathy, dullness, indifference

stoke *v* feed, fire, fuel, ignite, incite, kindle, light, nourish, sustain

stole *n* coat, fur, hide, jacket, pelt

stolid *adj* see: IMPASSIVE *adj*

stomach *n* abdomen, belly, gut, midriff, paunch, tummy, tum-tum

v abide, accept, acquiesce, allow, authorize, bear, concede, condone, digest, endure, experience, have, let, permit, put up

with, stand, suffer, sustain, swallow, take, tolerate, undergo

stomp *v* crush, squash, tramp, trample, tread, tromp

stone *n* boulder, detritus, fragments, gravel, pebble, rock

stoned *adj* bombed, crocked, doped up, drunk, drunken, high, inebriated, intoxicated, juiced, loaded, looped, messed up, plastered, polluted, sloshed, smashed, tight, tipsy, turned on, wasted, wired

stony *adj* see: NASTY *adj* 7

stooge *n* 1 chump, dupe, mark, pushover, sucker, victim

n 2 pawn, puppet, chessman, front, instrument, peon, tool

n 3 accuser, betrayer, double-crosser, fink, informer, reptile, snake, sneak, traitor

n 4 see: IDIOT *n*

stool *v* fink, inform, rat, sing, snitch, squeal, tattle, tattletale

n 1 chair, bench, seat

n 2 excrement, droppings, feces, waste

stoop *v* 1 hunch, slouch

v 2 condescend, deign, kowtow, patronize

v 3 descend, grovel, sink, submit

v 4 bend, bow, droop, duck, lower, slouch, slump

stop *n* 1 delay, interruption, postponement, reprieve, stay, suspension

n 2 bar, barricade, barrier, block, blockade, fence, obstacle, wall

n 3 break, cessation, delay, gap, interim, interval, lapse, pause

n 4 abeyance, cessation, halt, impasse, moratorium, stay, standstill, stopping, suspension

n 5 ceasing, cessation, close, closure, conclusion, end, finale, finis, finish, termination

n 6 depot, station

v 1 cancel, end, halt

v 2 abort, erase, kill, sever, terminate

v 3 block, close, obstruct, occlude, plug

v 4 block, catch, cut off, detain, hinder, intercept

v 5 check, oppose, resist, stanch, stem, weather, withstand

v 6 demur, halt, hold up, interrupt, pause, suspend

v 7 arrest, block, check, freeze, halt, impede, interrupt, stall, stay

v 8 abstain, avoid, constrain, curb, deny, forgo, govern, hold back, refrain, resist, restrict, tame

v 9 cripple, disable, disarm, encumber, freeze, halt, handcuff, immobilize, incapacitate, paralyze, prostrate, stun *v* **10** abstain, cease, conclude, desist, discontinue, end, finish, forbear, freeze, halt, knock off, quit, refrain, sever, terminate

v **11** ban, bar, confine, enjoin, forbid, inhibit, nix, outlaw, prevent, prohibit, suppress, veto

v **12** abate, abolish, abrogate, annihilate, annul, call off, cancel, cease, delete, destroy, efface, erase, excise, expunge, invalidate, kill, negate, nullify, obliterate, omit, quash, remove, terminate, wipe out

v **13** abate, cease, decline, decrease, die down, diminish, drain, dwindle, ease, ebb, fall, lessen, let up, lull, recede, reduce, relax, relent, shrink, slacken, soften, subside, taper off, wane, waste away, weaken

v **14** bar, block, brake, choke, clog, dam, deter, detract, encumber, frustrate, halt, hamper, hesitate, hinder, impair, impede, inhibit, jam, obstruct, prevent, repress, restrain, retard, slow, stay, stop up, throttle

stopgap *adj* impromptu, makeshift, temporary

n expedient, makeshift, means, measure, recourse, refuge, replacement, resort, substitute, surrogate

stop over *v* tour, visit

stoppage *n* ban, blockage, boycott, curtailment, embargo, prohibition

stopping *n* abeyance, cessation, halt, impasse, moratorium, standstill, stay, stop, suspension

stopwatch *n* chronometer, clock, hourglass, timepiece, timer, watch

store *n* **1** accumulation, fund, reservoir, source, supply

n **2** goods, inventory, provisions, reserve, stock, supply

n **3** building, edifice, erection, foundation, house, pile, structure, warehouse

n **4** business, department store, mall, market, mart, shop, supermarket

n **5** backlog, cache, hoard, holdings, inventory, nest egg, pile, reserve, reservoir, stash, stock, stockpile, supply

v **1** conserve, economize, husband

v **2** fill, furnish, replenish, stock, supply

v **3** accumulate, bank, deposit, hoard, save, squirrel away

storehouse *n* **1** repository, treasure trove, treasury

n **2** cache, repository, stockroom, warehouse

storm *n* **1** rampage, riot

n **2** blast, blizzard, blow, gale, gust, hurricane, northeaster, snowstorm, squall, tempest, typhoon, wind

n **3** see: COMMOTION *n* **1**

v **1** ambush, assail, assault, attack, beset, invade, raid, strike, trap, waylay

v **2** frenzy, rage, rampage, rebel, revolt, riot

v **3** anger, blow up, boil, boil over, brew, bristle, burn, flare up, fume, rage, seethe, simmer, smoke

stormy *adj* **1** blustery, squally, tempestuous, windy

adj **2** agitated, disorderly, excited, fierce, frantic, frenzied, furious, mad, tumultuous, turbulent, violent, wild

story *n* **1** adventure, escapade, fantasy, saga

n **2** chronicle, epic, legend, opus, saga, tale

n **3** depiction, description, explanation, illustration, narration, report, sketch, verbalization

n **4** exaggeration, fabrication, falsehood, falsity, fib, invention, lie, misstatement, tale

n **5** allegory, fable, fantasy, fiction, legend, lesson, lore, myth, mythology, parable, tale

n **6** anecdote, description, fantasy, fiction, invention, myth, narration, narrative, novel, sketch, tale, yarn

n **7** article, bulletin, byline, column, communication, dispatch, editorial, feature, headline, item, newsletter, report, vignette

n **8** floor, ground, level, tier, tile

n **9** gossip, grapevine, hearsay, murmur, report, rumble, rumor, scuttlebutt, talk, word

storyteller *n* author, bard, composer, folk singer, muse, narrator, poet, troubadour

stout *adj* **1** concentrated, hearty, heavy-duty, lusty, potent, powerful, robust, stalwart strong, sturdy

adj **2** athletic, brawny, burly, husky, massive, muscular, ponderous, powerful, robust, stocky, strapping, strong

adj **3** chubby, chunky, corpulent, fat, fleshy, gross, heavy, hefty, meaty, obese, overweight, plump, portly, pudgy, rotund

adj **4** aggressive, dominant, durable, firm, forceful, hardy, hearty, mighty, powerful, robust, rugged, stalwart, strong, sturdy, tenacious, tough *n* ale, beer, bock, brew, lager, Pilsner, suds

stow *v* box, bundle, pack

straight *adj* 1 orthodox, traditional, unhip
adj 2 aligned, neat, ordered
adj 3 direct, linear, straightforward, uninterrupted
adj 4 consistent, homogeneous, plain, pure, unadulterated, undiluted, unmixed
adj 5 clean, equal, equitable, even, fair, honest, just, sportsmanlike, upright
adj 6 aboveboard, candid, equitable, fair, forthright, honest, legitimate, plaindealing, straightforward, trustworthy, upright

straightaway *adv* anon, any moment, at once, directly, immediately, instantaneously, instantly, momentarily, now, presently, promptly, quickly, right now, shortly, soon, *tout de suite*

straighten *v* adjust, amend, correct, fix, improve, mend, modify, position, rectify, remedy, restore

straightforward *adj* 1 direct, linear, straight, uninterrupted
adj 2 aboveboard, candid, equitable, fair, forthright, honest, legitimate, plaindealing, straight, trustworthy, upright
adj 3 see: OBVIOUS *adj* 3
adj 4 see: SINCERE *adj*

strain *n* 1 drift, subject, theme, thread
n 2 anticipation, anxiety, apprehension, stress, suspense, tension
n 3 bruise, hurt, injury, pain, sprain, wound
n 4 anxiety, burden, frustration, pressure, stress, tension
n 5 air, harmony, measure, medley, melody, music, tune
n 6 effort, elbow grease, exertion, labor, pains, struggle, toil, trouble, try, work
n 7 ancestry, blood, bloodline, descent, family, genealogy, heritage, line, lineage, origin, pedigree
n 8 cramp, injury, sprain
v 1 burden, tax
v 2 draw, flex, pull, stretch, tense, tighten, twist
v 3 burden, encumber, hamper, load, oppress, overdo, overload, saddle, tax
v 4 drudge, grub, hustle, labor, slave, strive, sweat, toil, work
v 5 annoy, antagonize, argue, bother, bug, concern, distress, disturb, goad, harass, hassle, inconvenience, irk, irritate, pain, perturb, stress, taunt, trouble, try, upset, worry

strainer *n* colander, sieve, sifter

strait *n* 1 access, approach, artery, avenue, boulevard, channel, drag, highway, pass, path, promenade, road, roadway, route, street, thoroughfare, trail, way
n 2 arm, bay, cove, estuary, fiord, gulf, inlet, narrows

strand *n* cable, cord, fiber, hemp, lanyard, line, rope, string, thread, twine, yarn
v 1 land
v 2 see: ABANDON *v* 3

strange *adj* 1 amazing, astounding, remarkable
adj 2 coincidental, curious, ironic, odd, unexpected
adj 3 impossible, inconceivable, incredible, unachievable, undoable, unthinkable
adj 4 bizarre, eerie, ghostly, incredible, metaphysical, mystical, odd, ominous, spooky, supernatural, uncanny, unearthly, weird
adj 5 aberrant, bizarre, eccentric, erratic, odd, oddball, outlandish, peculiar, quaint, queer, singular, uncanny, unconventional, unusual, weird
adj 6 curious, exotic, far-out, fascinating, intriguing, kinky, marvelous, mysterious, new, novel, odd, outlandish, ultra, unaccustomed, unexplored, unfamiliar, unique, unknown, unusual, weird
adj 7 alien, exotic, foreign, unfamiliar

stranger *n* alien, foreigner, newcomer, outsider

strangle *v* asphyxiate, choke, constrict, gag, garrote, muffle, quash, repress, smother, stifle, suffocate, suppress

strap *v* band, belt, bind, corset, fasten, gird, girdle, tie

strapped *adj* broke, destitute, dirt-poor, down and out, impoverished, indigent, needy, penniless, poor, poverty-stricken, unprosperous

strapping *adj* athletic, brawny, burly, husky, massive, muscular, ponderous, powerful, robust, stocky, stout, strong

stratagem *n* antic, device, diversion, gambit, gimmick, maneuver, mischief, move, plan, plot, ploy, prank, ruse, scheme, strategy, tactic, trick, wile

strategic *adj* critical, essential, integral, necessary

strategy *n* 1 intrigue, logistics, plotting, tactics
n 2 blueprint, design, game plan, plan, project, proposal, scheme
n 3 course, direction, drift, path, tack, tactic, tendency, tenor, trend
n 4 antic, device, diversion, gambit, gimmick, maneuver, mischief, move, plan,

plot, ploy, prank, ruse, scheme, stratagem, tactic, trick, wile

stratum *n* caste, layer, ply, rank, tier

stray *v* 1 deflect, deviate, divert, drift, slip, turn

v 2 itinerate, meander, perambulate, promenade, ramble, range, roam, rove, saunter, stroll, traipse, travel, traverse, walk, wander

stream *n* 1 bayou, brook, creek, river, tributary

n 2 change, current, drift, flow, flux, gush, motion, movement, rush, tide, transition

v 1 flow, gush, run, rush

v 2 flood, flow, gush, peak, pour, rise, roll, spill, surge, swell

street *n* access, approach, artery, avenue, boulevard, channel, drag, highway, pass, path, promenade, road, roadway, route, strait, thoroughfare, trail, way

streetwalker *n* call girl, harlot, hooker, hussy, prostitute, slut, tart, tramp, trollop, wanton woman, wench, whore

strength *n* 1 amplitude, caliber, concentration, magnitude, potency

n 2 concentration, depth, energy, intensity, profundity, substance, vigor

n 3 charisma, dominance, influence, leadership, magnetism, personality

n 4 boldness, bravery, courage, daring, fortitude, heart, heroism, spirit, valor

n 5 ardor, beef, brawn, drive, energy, force, intensity, lustiness, might, muscle, pep, potency, power, punch, steam, verve, vigor, vim, virility, vitality

n 6 compactness, density, firmness, hardness, solidity, tensile strength

n 7 backbone, chutzpah, determination, endurance, fortitude, grit, guts, moxie, nerve, persistence, pluck, resilience, spirit, spunk, stamina, tenacity, tolerance, vigor, willpower

n 8 ability, adequacy, adroitness, aptitude, art, caliber, calling, capability, capacity, command, competence, craft, dexterity, experience, expertise, familiarity, forte, knack, know-how, knowledge, mastery, proficiency, prowess, qualification, savvy, skill, specialty, talent, training, workmanship

strengthen *v* 1 better, elevate, enhance, enrich, fortify

v 2 aid, comfort, cure, relieve, soothe, support

v 3 augment, buttress, fortify, harden, intensify, invigorate, reinforce

v 4 amplify, bolster, encourage, enhance, enhearten, hearten, increase, inspire, support

v 5 bear up, bolster, brace, build up, buoy, buttress, carry, fortify, harden, nourish, nurture, prop, reinforce, shore, support, sustain, toughen, uphold

strengthening *n* acceleration, achievement, advance, advancement, betterment, breakthrough, furtherance, growth, headway, improvement, increment, pickup, proficiency, progress, promotion, upgrade

strenuous *adj* see: HARD *adj* 5

stress *n* 1 apprehension, anxiety, distress, sweat, worry

n 2 anticipation, apprehension, anxiety, strain, suspense, tension

n 3 anxiety, burden, frustration, pressure, strain, tension

n 4 accent, emphasis, highlighting, importance, priority, significance, weight

n 5 concern, emphasis, gravity, import, importance, significance, weight

n 6 demand, exigency, necessity, need, pressure, requirement, urgency

v 1 emphasize, reiterate, repeat, resay

v 2 emphasize, iterate, reiterate, repeat

v 3 accent, accentuate, amplify, concentrate, emphasize, feature, flag, focus, heighten, highlight, italicize, mark, punctuate, spotlight, underline, underscore

v 4 annoy, antagonize, argue, bother, bug, concern, distress, disturb, goad, harass, hassle, inconvenience, irk, irritate, pain, perturb, strain, taunt, trouble, try, upset, worry

v 5 announce, articulate, assert, couch, describe, dictate, draft, enunciate, express, intonate, orate, phrase, proclaim, pronounce, say, speak, state, talk, utter, verbalize, vocalize, voice, word

stretch *n* 1 reach, span

n 2 excess, give, leeway, margin, slack

n 3 cycle, duration, interval, period, season, span, spell, stage, term, time

v 1 exaggerate, expand, inflate, oversell, overstate

v 2 draw, flex, pull, strain, tense, tighten, twist

v 3 continue, drag out, draw, elongate, extend, lengthen, prolong

v 4 amplify, bloat, dilate, distend, enlarge, expand, fatten, grow, increase, inflate, magnify, swell, widen

stretched *adj* drawn-out, elongated, extended, lengthened, lengthy, long, prolonged, protracted, sustained

strew v 1 dispel, disperse, disseminate, scatter

v 2 implant, plant, root, sow

v 3 diffuse, disseminate, distribute, spread, sprinkle

v 4 broadcast, disseminate, dissipate, distribute, scatter, sow, spread, transmit

strict adj 1 devout, narrow, orthodox, unquestioning

adj 2 adamant, firm, resolute, steadfast

adj 3 blind, conscientious, loyal, meticulous, zealous

adj 4 exact, faithful, literal, precise, true, verbatim, word for word

adj 5 exacting, fastidious, finicky, meticulous, picky, precise

adj 6 austere, narrow, narrow-minded, prim, prudish, puritanical, rigid, severe

adj 7 abusive, hard, harsh, severe, stern, stiff, tough, uncaring, unsympathetic

adj 8 authoritative, dependable, due, faithful, legitimate, rightful, true, trustworthy, undistorted, veracious

adj 9 authoritarian, authoritative, autocratic, controlled, despotic, disciplined, firm, harsh, inflexible, ironhanded, restrictive, rigid, rigorous, ruthless, severe, solid, stern, stringent, strong, tough, tyrannical

strictness n adversity, difficulty, discipline, discomfort, hardness, rigor, severity, stringency, uneasiness

stride v 1 amble, flaunt, strut, swagger

v 2 amble, hike, journey, march, pace, parade, plod, saunter, step, stroll, strut, tramp, tread, trek, walk

n 1 gait, march, pace, shuffle, step, walk

n 2 alacrity, cadence, celerity, dispatch, gait, pace, quickness, rapidity, rate, speed, step, swiftness, trot, velocity, walk

strident adj caustic, grating, guttural, harsh, hoarse, husky, rasping, rough

strife n 1 battle, clash, competition, conflict, contest, discord, duel, fight, fighting, rivalry, struggle, war, warfare

n 2 see: TROUBLE n 5

strike n 1 boycott, dispute, picket, walkout

n 2 assault, attack, blitz, bombardment, onslaught, raid

n 3 bang, bell ringer, bull's-eye, gong, hit, slam, smash

v 1 coin, mint

v 2 direct, give, impose, inflict

v 3 assault, jump, leap, pounce, surprise, swoop

v 4 bang, beat, bludgeon, clobber, club, hit, pound, whack

v 5 bat, clout, hit, nail, pop, smite, sock, swat, whack

v 6 ambush, assail, assault, attack, beset, invade, raid, storm, trap, waylay

v 7 box, clap, cuff, knock, punch, slap, smack, spank, tap, whack

v 8 walk out

v 9 bang, blow, bump, cuff, hit, knock, punch

v 10 drive, hammer, impress, imprint, mark, pound, press, print, stamp, thump, whack

striking adj 1 convincing, effective, forcible, impressive, inspiring

adj 2 arresting, astonishing, astounding, conspicuous, eye-catching, marked, noticeable, obvious, pointed, prominent, salient, sensational, stunning

adj 3 see: VIVID adj 3

string n 1 cable, cord, fiber, hemp, lanyard, line, rope, strand, thread, twine, yarn

n 2 chain, course, lineup, order, progression, row, run, sequence, series, succession, train

n 3 see: CONDITION n 6

v egg on, encourage, maintain

stringency n adversity, difficulty, discipline, discomfort, hardness, rigor, severity, strictness, uneasiness

stringent adj see: RESTRICTIVE adj

strings n band, orchestra

strip n 1 bar, ingot, pole, stick

n 2 band, banding, ribbon

n 3 length, measure, piece

n 4 adhesive, band, tape

n 5 bit, dab, end, fragment, iota, minutia, mite, morsel, particle, piece, pinch, portion, scrap, shred, speck, spot, tidbit, trifle

v 1 bare, deprive, dismantle, divest

v 2 bare, expose, lay open, subject, uncover

v 3 bare, denude, discard, disrobe, doff, flash, remove, reveal, shed, take off, unclothe, undress

v 4 deflower, desecrate, despoil, devastate, devour, loot, maraud, pillage, plunder, ravage, sack, scourge, spoil, violate

v 5 flay, peel, scale, skin

stripe n band

stripped adj bare, exposed, in the raw, naked, nude, open, peeled, unclothed, uncovered, visible

strive v 1 aim, aspire, wish

v 2 campaign, canvass, influence, lobby, persuade, support

v 3 assay, attempt, endeavor, essay, offer, quest, seek, struggle, try, undertake *v* 4 drudge, grub, hustle, labor, slave, strain, sweat, toil, work

v 5 combat, compete, contend, contest, counter, dispute, duel, fight, match, oppose, parry, pit, play, repel, resist, rival, struggle, vie

v 6 advance, ascend, bloom, climb, develop, do well, excel, expand, flourish, flower, get ahead, grow, improve, progress, prosper, rise, survive, thrive

striving *adj* ambitious, aspiring

stroke *n* blow, kick

v 1 adorn, pique, plume, preen, primp

v 2 acclaim, applaud, charm, cheer, commend, compliment, flatter, greet, hail, laud, praise, recognize

v 3 caress, cradle, cuddle, embrace, feel, fondle, fool around, hold, hug, love, make out, neck, nuzzle, pet

stroll *n* hike, march, tramp, trek, walk

v 1 amble, hike, journey, march, pace, parade, plod, saunter, step, stride, strut, tramp, tread, trek, walk

v 2 itinerate, meander, perambulate, promenade, ramble, range, roam, rove, saunter, stray, traipse, travel, traverse, walk, wander

strong *adj* 1 secure, stable, staunch, sure

adj 2 effective, lively, potent, punchy

adj 3 brisk, heavy, intense, powerful, stiff

adj 4 clear, effective, explicit, forceful, trenchant, vigorous

adj 5 drastic, excessive, extreme, intense, passionate, severe

adj 6 active, alive, dynamic, energetic, sound, spirited, vibrant, vigorous, vital

adj 7 ardent, decisive, determined, emphatic, extreme, forceful, intense, potent, powerful

adj 8 concentrated, hearty, heavy-duty, lusty, potent, powerful, robust, stalwart, sturdy

adj 9 colorful, expressive, graphic, impressive, intense, potent, powerful, striking, unforgettable, vivid

adj 10 athletic, brawny, burly, husky, massive, muscular, ponderous, powerful, robust, stocky, stout

adj 11 coercive, compelling, dynamic, energetic, forceful, hardy, lusty, mighty, passionate, powerful, robust, sturdy, vigorous

adj 12 aggressive, dominant, durable, firm, forceful, hardy, hearty, mighty, powerful, robust, rugged, stalwart, stout, sturdy, tenacious, tough

adj 13 bitter, brutal, cruel, fierce, hard, harsh, inclement, intemperate, pitiless, rigorous, rough, rugged, severe, stern, unkind, violent

adj 14 authoritarian, authoritative, autocratic, controlled, despotic, disciplined, firm, harsh, inflexible, ironhanded, restrictive, rigid, rigorous, ruthless, severe, solid, stern, strict, stringent, tough, tyrannical

strong-arm *v* alarm, attack, bully, club, coerce, frighten, harass, intimidate, menace, terrorize, threaten

strongbox *n* chest, coffer, safe, treasury, vault

stronghold *n* fortress

structure *n* 1 boundaries, form, framework, outline, pattern

n 2 cast, configuration, conformation, form, shape

n 3 building, edifice, erection, foundation, house, pile, store, warehouse

n 4 monument

v arrange, conceive, organize

struggle *n* 1 battle, combat, conflagration, dispute, encounter, fight, war

n 2 attempt, effort, endeavor, speculation, trial, try, undertaking, venture

n 3 effort, elbow grease, exertion, labor, pains, strain, toil, trouble, try, work

n 4 battle, clash, competition, conflict, contest, discord, duel, fight, fighting, rivalry, strife, war, warfare

n 5 contest, encounter, scramble, skirmish

n 6 altercation, argument, battle, brawl, challenge, combat, controversy, disagreement, discord, dispute, feud, fight, fracas, fray, hassle, melee, quarrel, rancor, rift, row, ruckus, scrap, scuffle, skirmish, spat, squabble, tiff, war

v 1 attack, battle, combat, contend, fight, oppose, war

v 2 combat, contend, duel, fight, grapple, spar, wrestle

v 3 combat, conflict, contend, contest, engage, scuffle, skirmish, tussle

v 4 assay, attempt, endeavor, essay, offer, quest, seek, try, undertake

v 5 combat, compete, contend, contest, counter, dispute, duel, fight, match, oppose, parry, pit, play, repel, resist, rival, strive, vie

strut *v* 1 amble, flaunt, prance, stride, swagger

v 2 boast, brag, crow, exult, flaunt, gloat, revel, show off, vaunt

v 3 amble, hike, journey, march, pace, parade, plod, saunter, step, stride, stroll, tramp, tread, trek, walk

stub *n* ass, backside, base, behind, bottom, bucket, buns, butt, buttocks, derrière, end, fanny, hindquarters, posterior, rump, seat, stump, tip, tush

stubborn *adj* **1** determined, persistent, resolute, tenacious

adj **2** chronic, extended, incurable, persistent, protracted

adj **3** aggressive, defiant, insubordinate, rambunctious, unruly

adj **4** indomitable, intractable, recalcitrant, uncontrollable, undisciplined, unmanageable, unruly, untoward, wild

adj **5** aristocratic, arrogant, authoritarian, authoritative, autocratic, belligerent, bossy, despotic, dictatorial, dogmatic, domineering, haughty, imperial, imperious, masterful, militaristic, opinionated, oppressive, overbearing, peremptory

adj **6** adamant, ceaseless, dedicated, determined, firm, immovable, inexhaustible, inexorable, inflexible, narrowminded, obstinate, relentless, resolute, resolved, rigid, single-minded, steadfast, unbendable, unbending, uncompromising, unswayable, unyielding

adj **7** bullheaded, closed-minded, deaf, firm, hardheaded, hard-line, inelastic, inflexible, intractable, intransigent, obstinate, perverse, pigheaded, refractory, resolute, rigid, stiff, tough, unbending, uncompromising, unpliable, unpliant, unwieldy, unyielding, willful

stud *n* **1** brad, bolt, nut, peg, pin, rivet, spike, staple, weld

n **2** buck, Casanova, Don Juan, flirt, gallant, ladies' man, lecher, lover, philanderer, playboy

student *n* **1** coed, collegian, pupil, scholar, schoolmate, undergraduate

n **2** apprentice, beginner, disciple, freshman, intern, neophyte, newcomer, novice, novitiate, pupil, recruit, rookie, tenderfoot, trainee

studied *adj* advised, calculated, careful, considered, contrived, deliberate, forewarned, measured, planned, premeditated

studious *adj* **1** careful, diligent, thorough

adj **2** advised, calculated, careful, considered, contrived, deliberate, forewarned, measured, planned, premeditated, studied

study *n* **1** education, instruction, learning, research, schooling

n **2** examination, inquiry, inspection, probing, scrutiny, search, survey

n **3** assessment, examination, inquiry, review, scope, search, survey

n **4** analysis, digging, experimentation, exploration, inquiry, inquisition, investigation, research, testing, trial

n **5** article, composition, discourse, dissertation, essay, manuscript, memoir, monograph, paper, report, theme, thesis, tract, treatise, work

n **6** den

n **7** course, discipline, subject

n **8** analysis, cogitation, consideration, contemplation, deliberation, logic, meditation, reason, reasoning, reflection, speculation, thinking, thought

v **1** review

v **2** get, learn, master, pick up, read, understand

v **3** drill, learn, perfect, practice, prepare, rehearse, repeat

v **4** comprehend, decipher, decode, infer, interpret, read, understand

v **5** eye, eyeball, gape, gawk, gaze, goggle, observe, ogle, stare

v **6** analyze, brief, condense, evaluate, outline, retrace, review, summarize, synopsize, update

v **7** canvass, case, check, examine, glance over, inspect, observe, peruse, pore over, regard, scrutinize, survey, watch

v **8** cerebrate, chew, consider, contemplate, deliberate, digest, meditate, mull, muse, ponder, reason, reflect, ruminate, see, speculate, think, weigh

v **9** delve, dig, examine, explore, feel out, grope, hunt, inquire, investigate, look, observe, peer, probe, pursue, research, scan, scrutinize, search, seek, sound, test

stuff *n* **1** content, material, matter, substance

n **2** contents, junk, objects, scrap, substance, things

n **3** belongings, property, things

v **1** fill, heap, load, pack, place

v **2** fill, gorge, glut, overeat, pig out, satiate, surfeit

v **3** cram, crush, force, gorge, insert, jam, pack, press, ram

stuffed *adj* bursting, chock-full, crowded, filled up, full, jammed, jampacked, loaded, packed, rending

stuffy *adj* **1** close, humid, stagnant

adj **2** prim, prissy, prudish

adj **3** artificial, awkward, formal, stiff, stilted

adj 4 boring, dull, formal, pompous, stodgy

adj 5 see: PURE *adj* 7

stumble *v* 1 bomb, fail, flop, trip

v 2 chance, discover, encounter, find, happen, hit, luck

v 3 fall, lurch, skid, skim, slide, slip, totter, trip, tumble

v 4 amaze, befog, bewilder, boggle, confound, confuse, daze, perplex, puzzle, stump

v 5 bumble, falter, flounder, fumble, get stuck, grope, hesitate, stagger, waffle, waver

stump *v* amaze, befog, bewilder, boggle, confound, confuse, daze, perplex, puzzle

n ass, backside, base, behind, bottom, bucket, buns, butt, buttocks, derrière, end, fanny, hindquarters, posterior, rump, seat, stub, tip, tush

stun *v* 1 daze, paralyze, shock, stupefy

v 2 amaze, daze, electrify, horrify, offend, outrage, scandalize, shock

v 3 amaze, astonish, astound, awe, boggle, confound, dazzle, dumbfound, flabbergast, nonplus, surprise

v 4 see: INCAPACITATE *v*

stunned *adj* confused, daffy, daft, dazed, dizzy, groggy

stunning *adj* 1 arousing, awesome, breathtaking, exciting, magnificent, stimulating

adj 2 see: BEAUTIFUL *adj* 2

adj 3 see: EXTRAORDINARY *adj* 4

adj 4 see: PROMINENT *adj* 2

stunt *n* accomplishment, achievement, acquirement, act, action, battle, deed, doing, event, exploit, feat, thing, trick

v check, cramp, curtail, impede, shorten, throttle

stupefy *v* 1 dull, weaken

v 2 daze, paralyze, stun

stupendous *adj* see: HUGE *adj* 3

stupid *adj* 1 foolish, futile, ill-advised, pointless, profitless, vain

adj 2 see: DUMB *adj* 2

stupor *n* apathy, coma, doze, ennui, grogginess, inertia, languor, lassitude, lethargy, nod, sleep

sturdy *adj* 1 fit, hardy, healthy, robust, rubicund, ruddy, sound, well, wholesome

adj 2 concentrated, hearty, heavy-duty, lusty, potent, powerful, robust, stalwart, stout, strong

adj 3 aggressive, dominant, durable, firm, forceful, hardy, hearty, mighty, powerful, robust, rugged, stalwart, stout, strong, tenacious, tough

adj 4 see: VIGOROUS *adj* 3

sty *n* barn, coop, enclosure, lean-to, paddock, pen, pound, shack, shed, shelter, stable

style *n* 1 chic, class, flair

n 2 elegance, finesse, refinement

n 3 arrangement, array, format, layout, outline

n 4 fashion, flavor, manner, mode, tone, vein

n 5 chic, craze, fad, fashion, mode, rage, thing, trend, vogue

n 6 cliché, diction, expression, parlance, phrase, saying, slogan, term, wording

n 7 angle, approach, code, delivery, execution, expression, fashion, manner, method, mode, organization, process, program, system, technique, way

n 8 face, family, font, printwheel, size, type, typeface

n 9 bracket, breed, cast, category, class, division, family, genre, genus, group, grouping, ilk, kind, lot, mold, nature, order, persuasion, section, sector, set, sort, species, type, variety

stylish *adj* 1 aesthetic, artistic, classy, elegant, refined, tasteful, well-chosen

adj 2 chic, current, fashionable, hip, in, smart, trendy, vogue

stymie *v* baffle, confound, confuse, frustrate, perplex, thwart

suave *adj* 1 charming, slick, smooth, sophisticated

adj 2 chic, dapper, dashing, debonair, jaunty, natty, neat, rakish, sleek, smart, snazzy, spiffy, trim

adj 3 civilized, cosmopolitan, cultivated, cultured, elegant, genteel, ingratiating, poised, polished, refined, smooth, sophisticated, urbane, well-bred

sub *adj* see: SUBORDINATE *adj* 4

subconscious *adj* affective, cognitive, emotional, mental, psychic, psychological, subjective

subdivision *n* apportionment, division, partition, segmentation, segregation

subdue *v* 1 calm, lessen, muffle, quiet, reduce

v 2 censor, curb, gag, hush, inhibit, muffle, mute, quell, quiet, repress, restrain, silence, squelch, stifle, still, suppress, throttle, tone down

v 3 see: OVERPOWER *v* 3

subdued *adj* 1 crushed, defeated, distraught, overcome

adj 2 conservative, dim, inconspicuous, quiet, restrained, tasteful, unassuming, unobtrusive

adj 3 closed, diffident, introverted, laconic, reserved, restrained, reticent, secretive, shy, taciturn, timid, timorous, uncommunicative, undaring

subject *adj* 1 exposed, liable, prone, vulnerable

adj 2 see: SUBORDINATE *adj* 4

n 1 drift, strain, theme, thread

n 2 citizen, countryman, indigene, inhabitant, national

n 3 butt, casualty, object, prey, sufferer, target, victim

n 4 argument, controversy, issue, item, matter, motif, motive, point, proposition, question, text, theme, topic

n 5 course, discipline, study

v 1 endure, suffer

v 2 bare, expose, lay open, uncover

v 3 diminish, lessen, repress, subordinate, suppress, weaken

subjection *n* acquiescence, compliance, obedience, submission

subjective *adj* 1 individual, introspective, personal

adj 2 biased, emotional, partial, predisposed

adj 3 affective, cognitive, emotional, mental, psychic, psychological

subjugate *v* bear down, beat down, conquer, crush, defeat, dominate, enslave, exploit, overpower, quash, reduce, subdue, suppress, vanquish

sublet *v* charter, franchise, hire, lease, let, rent

sublime *adj* elevated, exalted, excellent, grand, great, heavenly, high, lofty, magnificent, prominent, superb

submerged *adj* scuttled, sunken, underwater

submersion *n* deluge, flood, overflow, surge, torrent

submission *n* 1 acquiescence, compliance, dependence, obedience, subjection

n 2 capitulation, compliance, release, subordination, subservience, surrender

submissive *adj* 1 amenable, complaisant, compliant, cooperative, obedient, subservient, tractable, willing

adj 2 acquiescent, compliant, docile, easy, meek, mild, nonresistant, obedient, passive, resigned, tame, tolerant, unassertive, yielding

submit *v* 1 descend, grovel, sink, stoop

v 2 accommodate, comply, conform, follow, keep, mind, obey

v 3 administer, administrate, carry out, deliver, do, execute, give, present

v 4 accede, acquiesce, bend, bow, buckle, capitulate, cave, comply, concede, cry

uncle, defer, give in, give up, relent, succumb, surrender, twist, yield

v 5 divert, refer

v 6 fall, give up, go under, succumb, surrender, yield

v 7 abandon, acquiesce, cede, give up, hand over, leave, relinquish, resign, surrender, waive, yield

subordinate *adj* 1 dependent, lesser, subservient

adj 2 inferior, lesser, lower, under

adj 3 ancillary, auxiliary, incidental, minor, related, secondary

adj 4 ancillary, assistant, collateral, complementary, dependent, lesser, minor, secondary, sub, subject, subsidiary, substitute, supporter, tributary, worker

n assistant, dependent, employee, underling

v diminish, lessen, repress, subject, suppress, weaken

subordination *n* capitulation, compliance, release, submission, subservience, surrender

subpoena *n* citation, notification, summons, ticket, warrant, writ

v call, cite, evoke, summon

subscribe *v* 1 autograph, sign

v 2 adopt, borrow, embrace, foster, take on, take up, utilize

v 3 accept, agree, allow, approve, assent, comply, concur, consent, endorse

subsequent *adv* after, anon, behind, following, in pursuit, later

adj 1 ensuing, following, latter, next, succeeding, successive

adj 2 approaching, eventual, expected, future, imminent, impending, next

adj 3 after, beyond, ensuing, following, succeeding, successive

subsequently *adv* after, afterward, anon, later, successively, thereafter

subservience *n* capitulation, compliance, release, submission, subordination, surrender

subservient *adj* 1 lesser, subordinate

adj 2 amenable, complaisant, compliant, cooperative, obedient, submissive, tractable, willing

adj 3 abject, common, groveling, humble, ingratiating, lowly, menial, obeisant, obsequious, servile, slavish

subside *v* 1 decline, die down, diminish, dip, settle, sink, slip

v 2 abate, cease, decline, decrease, die down, diminish, drain, dwindle, ease, ebb, fall, lessen, let up, lull, recede, reduce, relax, relent, shrink, slacken, soften, stop, taper off, wane, waste away, weaken

subsidiary *adj* 1 accessory, adjunct, ancillary, assisting, auxiliary, supporting

adj 2 ancillary, assistant, collateral, complementary, dependent, lesser, minor, secondary, sub, subject, subordinate, substitute, supporter, tributary, worker

n arm, branch, division, limb, service, tributary

subsidize *v* 1 aid, endow, finance, fund, underwrite

v 2 bankroll, capitalize, finance, fund, stake

subsistence *n* 1 continuation, duration, endurance, existence, life, span, survival, term

n 2 keep, livelihood, living, maintenance, minimum, support, sustenance

substance *n* 1 beef, meat

n 2 chemicals, elements, material, matter

n 3 drift, implication, intent, purport, tenor

n 4 content, material, matter, property, stuff

n 5 contents, junk, objects, scrap, things

n 6 character, constitution, fiber, make-up, nature, quality

n 7 concentration, depth, energy, intensity, profundity, strength, vigor

n 8 consequence, import, importance, magnitude, moment, significance, weight

n 9 basis, body, bulk, core, essence, essentials, gist, heart, import, mass, nucleus, object, staple, volume

n 10 center, core, crux, essence, gist, heart, life, marrow, nature, nucleus, pith, quick, quintessence, root

n 11 ingredients, makings, potential

substantial *adj* 1 ample, decent, generous, respectable, sizable

adj 2 formidable, huge, immense, impressive, intimidating, massive

adj 3 concrete, corporeal, material, objective, physical, real, sensible, tactile, tangible

adj 4 consequential, considerable, critical, crucial, important, material, meaningful, momentous, prominent, significant, vital, weighty

substantiate *v* attest, authenticate, certify, confirm, corroborate, justify, notarize, prove, ratify, sanction, support, validate, verify, vouch, witness

substitute *adj* 1 alternate, alternative, equivalent

adj 2 duplicate, equal, equivalent, identical, same, synonymous, tantamount

adj 3 ancillary, assistant, collateral, complementary, dependent, lesser, minor, secondary, sub, subject, subordinate, subsidiary, supporter, tributary, worker

adj 4 see: COUNTERFEIT *adj* 1

n 1 agent, alternate, dummy, representative

n 2 alternate, equivalent, exchange, replacement, substitution

n 3 agent, alternate, backup, contingency, part-timer, replacement, representative, standby, surrogate

n 4 expedient, makeshift, means, measure, recourse, refuge, replacement, resort, stopgap, surrogate

n 5 pinch hitter, stand-in, understudy

v 1 replace, supersede, supplant

v 2 exchange, replace, represent, return, supplant, swap, switch

substitution *n* alternate, equivalent, exchange, substitute

subterfuge *n* 1 secrecy, sneakiness, stealth

n 2 alibi, con, deception, lie, pretext, ruse, trick

n 3 cheating, deceit, deception, dishonesty, fraud, hoax, lie, sham, trickery

subtle *adj* 1 analytical, logical

adj 2 agile, deft, skillful

adj 3 baffling, elusive, frustrating, mysterious

adj 4 discerning, discreet, discriminating, keen, sensitive, tactful

adj 5 faint, imperceptible, meager, remote, slight, vague

adj 6 dainty, delicate, fine, gentle, nice

adj 7 astute, calculating, crafty, cunning, foxy, guileful, insidious, sharp, shrewd, sly, smart, tricky, wily, wise

adj 8 attenuate, diminished, lessened, tenuous, thin

subtlety *n* 1 diplomacy, discretion, finesse, savvy, skill, tact

n 2 degree, distinction, enhancement, nuance, shade, touch, trace, variation

subtract *v* deduct, diminish, lessen, minus, reduce, take away

suburb *n* borough, city, megalopolis, metropolis, town

suburban *adj* bucolic, country, garden, outland, pastoral, peaceful, provincial, rural, rustic, wooded

subversion *n* 1 betrayal, deception, perfidy, treachery, trickery

n 2 destruction, downfall, infiltration, overthrow, ruin, upset

n 3 betrayal, insurrection, mutiny, revolt, sedition, treason, uprising

subway *n* conduit, passageway, pathway, shaft, tube, tunnel

succeed *v* 1 emanate, ensue, follow

v 2 come through, get by, pull through, ride, survive

v 3 arrive, flourish, go, make out, prosper, thrive

v 4 best, conquer, defeat, master, overcome, prevail, triumph, win

v 5 accomplish, achieve, attain, consummate, execute, fulfill, perform, produce, pull off, realize, triumph, win

v 6 click, come off, go, go over, pan out, prove out

succeeding *adj* 1 ensuing, following, latter, next, subsequent, successive

adj 2 after, beyond, ensuing, following, subsequent, successive

success *n* 1 fame, position, prestige, prosperity, station

n 2 accomplishment, achievement, arrival, attainment, completion, fruition, fulfillment, realization, satisfaction, triumph, victory

n 3 abundance, affluence, bounty, comfort, cornucopia, elegance, glut, good fortune, grandeur, luxury, opulence, plenty, wealth

n 4 accomplishment, achievement, conquest, triumph, victory, win, winner

successful *adj* 1 conquering, triumphant, undefeated, victorious, winning

adj 2 affluent, booming, prosperous, thriving, wealthy

adj 3 adequate, capable, competent, effective, efficacious, efficient, proficient, sufficient

adj 4 central, chief, distinguished, dominant, famed, great, key, leading, main, major, number one, outstanding, predominant, preeminent, primary, prime, principal, prominent, star, superior, top

successfully *adv* favorably, fortunately, happily, positively, well

succession *n* 1 line, order, priority, procession, sequence, timing

n 2 current, drift, pattern, run, series, tendency, trend

n 3 chain, course, lineup, order, progression, row, run, sequence, series, string, train

n 4 alternation, circuit, circulation, gyration, revolution, rotation, round, sequence, spinning, turn, whirl

successive *adj* 1 ensuing, following, latter, next, succeeding

adj 2 chronological, consecutive, continuous, progressive, sequential

adj 3 continual, continuing, gradual, increasing, incremental, intensifying, measured, progressive

adj 4 after, beyond, ensuing, following, subsequent

successively *adv* afterward, later, subsequently, thereafter

succinct *adj* abbreviated, brief, compressed, concise, crisp, curt, laconic, pithy, short, terse, to the point

succor *n* aid, assistance, benefit, comfort, cure, hand, help, lift, nurture, relief, support

v aid, baby, care for, help, nurse, pamper

succulent *adj* juicy, moist, savory, tender

succumb *v* 1 cease, die, elapse, expire, lapse, pass, pass away, perish, terminate

v 2 accede, acquiesce, bend, bow, buckle, capitulate, cave, comply, concede, cry uncle, defer, give in, give up, relent, submit, surrender, twist, yield

v 3 fall, give up, go under, submit, surrender, yield

such *adj* see: ALIKE *adj*

suck *v* 1 extract, pull, remove, tear, withdraw, yank

v 2 draft, drain, draw, draw off, pump, siphon, tap

v 3 see: DRINK *v* 2

sucker *n* 1 chump, dupe, mark, pushover, victim

n 2 bloodsucker, leech, vampire

suckle *v* 1 nurse

v 2 care, cherish, foster, mother, nourish, nurse, nurture, parent, protect, raise

sudden *adj* 1 startling, surprising, unexpected, unforeseen

adj 2 accidental, surprising, unanticipated, unexpected, unforeseen

adj 3 contiguous, current, direct, immediate, instant, nearby, primary, prompt, timely

adj 4 abrupt, hasty, headlong, hurried, impetuous, impulsive, precipitant, precipitate, quick, rapid, rash, rushing

adj 5 see: RAPID *adj* 2, 4

suddenly *adv* abruptly, fast, hastily, immediately, instantaneously, instantly, quick, quickly, short, swiftly

suds *n* 1 soap

n 2 ale, beer, bock, brew, lager, Pilsner

sue *v* 1 appeal, apply, attack, file suit, go to court, litigate, petition, plead, prosecute, solicit

v 2 accuse, allege, arraign, assert, charge,

cite, impeach, imply, impute, incriminate, indict, litigate, prosecute, try

suffer *v* 1 endure, experience, subject

v 2 ache, despair, grieve, hurt, pain

v 3 abide, accept, acquiesce, allow, authorize, bear, concede, condone, digest, endure, experience, have, let, permit, put up with, stand, stomach, sustain, swallow, take, tolerate, undergo

sufferer *n* butt, casualty, object, prey, subject, target, victim

suffering *n* 1 cost, damage, deficit, loss

n 2 distress, grief, melancholy, sorrow

n 3 ache, affliction, agony, anguish, hurt, injury, pain, punishment, torture

n 4 adversity, affliction, blow, burden, calamity, difficulty, distress, hardship, mischance, misfortune, mishap, relapse, reversal, setback, tragedy, trouble

n 5 agony, anguish, bale, concern, distress, misery, nightmare, pain, sadness, sorrow, torment, travail, tribulation, trouble, woe, worry

adj see: ILL *adj* 3

suffice *v* answer, do, fulfill, meet, qualify, satisfy, work

sufficiency *n* acceptability, adequacy, competency

sufficient *adj* 1 adequate, capable, competent, effective, efficacious, efficient, proficient

adj 2 acceptable, adequate, competent, decent, enough, fair, good, mediocre, passable, reasonable, respectable, satisfactory, tolerable

sufficiently *adv* see: COMPLETELY *adv*

suffocate *v* asphyxiate, choke, constrict, gag, garrote, muffle, quash, repress, smother, stifle, strangle, suppress

suffuse *v* imbue, impart, infuse, ingrain, inject, inoculate, instill, invest, penetrate, pervade, spread, steep, teach, train

suggest *v* 1 imply, resemble, savor, smack, smell, taste

v 2 convey, express, hint, impart, imply, indicate, purport

v 3 cue, jog, nudge, prompt, push, remind, stimulate, stir

v 4 allude, denote, indicate, mention, point out, refer to, reveal, show, speak of, specify, tell

v 5 bid, counsel, endorse, offer, pose, present, proffer, propose, proposition, put forth, recommend, urge

v 6 allude, assume, extend, hypothesize, imagine, offer, pose, present, presume, propose, speculate, suppose, surmise, theorize

suggested *adj* 1 advisable, expedient, politic, prudent, wise

adj 2 developmental, experimental, pilot, tentative, test, trial, untested

adj 3 implicit, implied, indicated, inferred, inherent, insinuated, intuitive, presumed, tacit, understood, unexpressed, unsaid, unspoken, wordless

suggestion *n* 1 advice, counsel, opinion

n 2 approach, come-on, offer, proposal, proposition

n 3 allusion, connotation, hint, implication, innuendo, insinuation, notation, reference

n 4 bid, expectation, hope, inducement, invitation, motion, offer, proffer, proposal, proposition, recommendation

n 5 see: TRACE *n* 4

suggestive *adj* 1 provocative, provoking, stimulating

adj 2 arousing, exciting, intriguing, provocative, seductive, sexy, stimulating, tantalizing

adj 3 improper, indecent, indelicate, lewd, malodorous, off-color, offensive, rough, scurrilous, unbecoming, unseemly, untoward

adj 4 erotic, improper, indecent, racy, unbecoming

adj 5 bawdy, coarse, crude, dirty, erotic, filthy, foul, gamy, gross, improper, indecent, lascivious, lewd, licentious, nasty, obscene, off-color, pornographic, profane, prurient, racy, rank, raunchy, ribald, risqué, scandalous, smutty, tainted, uncouth, vulgar, x-rated

suit *n* action, case, indictment, lawsuit, litigation, prosecution

v 1 adapt, conform, convert, cut, fashion, fit, measure, modify, rig, shape, tailor

v 2 accord, agree, check, coalesce, coincide, comply with, concur, conform, consent, consist, correspond, fit in, harmonize, jibe, square, tally

v 3 see: SATISFY *v* 5

suitability *n* see: UTILITY *n*

suitable *adj* 1 acceptable, allowable, eligible, fitting, qualified

adj 2 compatible, congenial, congruous, kindred

adj 3 conventional, correct, decorous, fitting, nice, orthodox, polite, proper, right, well

adj 4 appropriate, correct, deserved, due, fitting, just, merited, proper, rightful, warranted

adj 5 applicable, appropriate, apropos, apt, befitting, convenient, desirable, felicitous, fit, fitting, germane, good, handy, just, material, meet, necessary, pertinent, proper, relevant, right, shipshape, suited, timely, useful

adj 6 see: PRACTICAL *adj* 4

suitably *adv* acceptably, adequately, amply, appropriately, correctly, properly, right, satisfactorily, well

suitcase *n* bag, baggage, case, equipment, gear, grip, kit, luggage, pack, pouch, purse, sack, valise, wallet

suite *n* apartment, dorm, housing, lodging, room

suited *adj* see: APPLICABLE *adj*

suitor *n* beau, boyfriend, date, escort, fiancé, lover, mate

sulk *v* 1 brood, crab, grouch, moan, mope, pout, scowl

v 2 disdain, frown, glare, gloom, glower, grimace, lower, scowl

sulky *adj* brooding, crabby, dour, gloomy, glum, moody, morose, sour, sullen, surly, ugly

sullen *adj* 1 brooding, crabby, dour, gloomy, glum, moody, morose, sour, sulky, ugly

adj 2 angry, cranky, cross, feisty, grouchy, hot-tempered, irascible, ireful, peppery, quick-tempered, short-fused, testy, touchy

sully *v* defile, dirty, discolor, smear, soil, taint, tarnish

sultry *adj* 1 damp, drenched, dripping, humid, moist, mucky, muggy, soaked, soggy, sopping, sticky, sweaty, wet

adj 2 amorous, ardent, aroused, carnal, earthy, erotic, fervent, fleshly, horny, hot, impassioned, lascivious, lecherous, lewd, licentious, lustful, passionate, provocative, randy, raunchy, romantic, sensual, sexual, sexy, titillated, torrid, turned on, voluptuous, wanton

adj 3 baking, blistering, boiling, broiling, burning, fiery, hot, scalding, scorching, sizzling, sweltering, torrid

sum *n* 1 amount, balance, count, result, total

n 2 being, entity, object, organism, system, thing, totality, whole

n 3 aggregate, all, entirety, gross, revenue, sales, sum total, total, totality, whole

n 4 see: MONEY *n* 4

v aggregate, amount, number, total

summarize *v* 1 copy, note, record, transcribe, type, write

v 2 analyze, brief, condense, evaluate, outline, retrace, review, study, synopsize, update

summary *n* 1 collection, epitome, paraphrase, recapitulation, summation

n 2 abridgement, abstract, brief, compendium, condensation, digest, essence, example, outline, review, sketch, syllabus, synopsis

summation *n* 1 calculation, count, number

n 2 conclusion, deduction, guess, reasoning

n 3 collection, epitome, paraphrase, summary

summit *n* 1 acme, apex, apogee, climax, crescendo, crest, crown, culmination, epitome, height, noon, peak, pinnacle, point, prime, tip, top, ultimate, utmost, zenith

n 2 alp, hill, mountaintop, peak

summon *v* 1 announce, call, hail, page

v 2 call, cite, evoke, serve, subpoena

v 3 address, call to, embrace, greet, hail, meet, welcome

v 4 see: ASSEMBLE *v* 3

summons *n* citation, notification, subpoena, ticket, warrant, writ

sumptuous *adj* choice, deluxe, elegant, first-class, grand, luxuriant, luxurious, opulent, ornate, palatial, plush, posh, rich, soft, stately, thick

sun *v* bask, sunbathe, tan

sunder *v* 1 breach, break up, cleave, disjoin, dismember, disrupt, dissect, dissever, disunite, divide, divorce, part, polarize, rupture, separate, sever

v 2 see: CUT *v* 7

sundown *n* dusk, nightfall, sunset, twilight

sundry *adj* abundant, assorted, copious, diverse, extensive, legion, many, multifarious, multitudinous, myriad, numerous, plentiful, populous, prolific, various, voluminous

sunken *adj* 1 lower, under

adj 2 hollow

adj 3 submerged, underwater

sunlit *adj* glowing, incandescent, luminous

sunny *adj* 1 blithe, cheerful, cheery, merry

adj 2 clear, cloudless, fair, pleasant, unclouded

adj 3 agreeable, bright, fine, nice, pleasant

adj 4 hot, humid, muggy, steamy, sticky, tropical

adj 5 auspicious, bright, confident, favorable, hopeful, promising, rosy, utopian

sunrise *n* dawn, daybreak, daylight, first light, morning, sunup

sunset *n* dusk, nightfall, sundown, twilight

sunup *n* dawn, daybreak, daylight, first light, sunrise

super *adj* 1 excellent, fabulous, fantastic,

fine, good, great, marvelous, terrific, tremendous, wonderful

adj 2 dynamite, excellent, extraordinary, great, out of sight, outstanding, phenomenal, premier, superb, superlative, tremendous, wonderful

adj 3 amazing, brilliant, exceptional, extraordinary, noteworthy, phenomenal, rare, remarkable, significant, singular, stunning, uncommon, uncustomary, unique, unusual

superannuate *v* pension, retire

superb *adj* 1 blessed, glorious, golden, great, splendid

adj 2 excellent, extraordinary, great, impressive, noteworthy, outstanding, shining, smashing, wonderful

adj 3 elevated, exalted, excellent, grand, great, heavenly, high, lofty, magnificent, prominent

adj 4 best, elegant, finest, gilt-edged, magnificent, majestic, outstanding, preeminent, sensational, splendid, superior, superlative

adj 5 champion, excellent, fine, first-class, first-rate, foremost, good, grade A, leading, number one, prime, principal, prominent, quality, select, stellar, superior, top, top-drawer, top-notch, tops

adj 6 dynamite, excellent, extraordinary, great, out of sight, outstanding, phenomenal, premier, super, superlative, tremendous, wonderful

supercilious *adj* arrogant, cavalier, conceited, contemptuous, curt, dictatorial, disdainful, grandiose, haughty, huffy, insolent, lofty, lordly, moody, obtrusive, overbearing, patronizing, proud, scornful, snooty, stuck up, superior, vain

superficial *adj* 1 exterior, outside

adj 2 apparent, illusive, illusory, ostensible, quasi, seeming

adj 3 brief, crude, cursory, hasty, rough, shallow, sketchy, uncritical

superfluous *adj* 1 excess, leftover, remaining

adj 2 affluent, comfortable, rich

adj 3 abnormal, extra, extraneous, foreign, illogical, immaterial, insignificant, irregular, irrelevant, malapropos, nonessential, peripheral, surplus, unimportant, unnecessary, unrelated

adj 4 see: VERBOSE *adj*

superhuman *adj* arduous, formidable, heroic, tremendous

superintendent *n* housemother, mother

superior *adv* above, aloft, greater, more, on top of, over

adj 1 eminent, great, important

adj 2 best, optimum, prime, select, top

adj 3 advantageous, better, desirable, enjoyable, preferable, worthwhile

adj 4 best, elegant, finest, gilt-edged, magnificent, majestic, outstanding, preeminent, sensational, superb, superlative

adj 5 best, biggest, finest, greatest, largest, maximum, most, number one, prime, select, top, top-notch

adj 6 champion, excellent, fine, first-class, first-rate, foremost, good, grade A, leading, number one, prime, principal, prominent, quality, select, stellar, superb, top, top-drawer, top-notch, tops

adj 7 central, chief, distinguished, dominant, famed, great, key, leading, main, major, number one, outstanding, predominant, preeminent, primary, prime, principal, prominent, star, successful, top

adj 8 arrogant, cavalier, conceited, contemptuous, curt, dictatorial, disdainful, grandiose, haughty, huffy, insolent, lofty, lordly, moody, obtrusive, overbearing, patronizing, proud, scornful, snooty, supercilious, vain

n 1 chief, higher ranked, senior, veteran

n 2 boss, chief, foreman, head, overseer, supervisor

superlative *adj* 1 best, elegant, finest, gilt-edged, magnificent, majestic, outstanding, preeminent, sensational, splendid, superb, superior

adj 2 dynamite, excellent, extraordinary, great, out of sight, outstanding, phenomenal, premier, super, superb, tremendous, wonderful

supermarket *n* business, department store, mall, market, mart, shop

supernatural *adj* bizarre, eerie, ghostly, incredible, metaphysical, mystical, odd, ominous, spooky, strange, uncanny, unearthly, weird

supersede *v* replace, substitute, supplant

superstition *n* 1 belief, notion, tradition

n 2 delusion, fallacy, illusion, myth

supervise *v* 1 care, manage, oversee

v 2 administer, boss, command, direct, guide, manage, oversee, regulate, steer

v 3 boss, command, control, direct, dominate, govern, handle, influence, lead, manage, manipulate, order, sway

supervision *n* administration, care, charge, conduct, handling, intendance, management, overseeing, running

supervisor *n* boss, chief, foreman, head, overseer, owner, superior

supper *n* 1 banquet, buffet, dinner, feast, lunch, meal, repast

n 2 bread, breakfast, brunch, chow, cuisine, diet, dinner, dish, edibles, entree, fare, food, grub, lunch, meals, nosh, nutrition, provisions, rations, snack, victuals, vittles

supplant *v* 1 replace, substitute

v 2 displace, usurp

v 3 exchange, replace, represent, return, substitute, swap, switch

supple *adj* 1 willing

adj 2 agile, limber, lissome, lithe, lithesome

adj 3 alterable, elastic, flexible, movable, pliable, resilient

adj 4 adaptable, adjustable, changeable, flexible, limber, malleable, maneuverable, moldable, plastic, pliable, pliant, responsive, soft, swayed, versatile, yielding

adj 5 cottony, satiny, silky, slippery, smooth, soft, velvety

supplement *n* 1 addendum, addition, appendix, insert, rider

n 2 continuation, corollary, epilogue, outgrowth, sequel

v 1 complement, complete, fulfill, round out

v 2 see: INCREASE *v* 8

supplemental *adj* added, additional, another, auxiliary, extra, further, incremental, more, one more, other, spare, supplementary, surplus

supplementary *adj* added, additional, another, auxiliary, extra, further, incremental, more, one more, other, spare, supplemental, surplus

supplicate *v* see: PLEAD *v* 2

supplies *n* equipment, fixtures, furnishings, gear, materials, provisions

supply *n* 1 energy, nourishment, provisions

n 2 accumulation, fund, reservoir, store

n 3 goods, inventory, provisions, reserve, stock, store

n 4 account, amount, catalog, enumeration, inventory, itemization, list, litany, repertoire, tally

n 5 backlog, cache, hoard, holdings, inventory, nest egg, pile, reserve, reservoir, stash, stock, stockpile

v 1 fill, furnish, stock, store

v 2 clothe, fit, furnish, outfit, provide

v 3 appoint, arm, equip, fortify, furnish, gear, man, outfit, rig, set up, turn out

v 4 arrange, cater, deliver, dish out, dispense, feed, furnish, give, hand, nourish, nurture, organize, provide, purvey, serve, sustain

v 5 accord, adduce, award, bequeath, bestow, concede, confer, contribute, deliver, devote, donate, endow, extend, fund, give, give away, grant, hand down, hand out, impart, offer, pose, present, proffer, provide, tender, volunteer

support *n* 1 food, nourishment, nutriment, sustenance

n 2 beam, board, boom, girder, log, plank, rafter, spar, timber

n 3 base, brace, buttress, column, footing, foundation, prop, shore, stay, underpinning

n 4 auspices, authorization, backing, command, confirmation, endorsement, fiat, patronage, sanction, sponsorship

n 5 aid, assistance, benefit, comfort, cure, hand, help, lift, nurture, relief, remedy, succor

n 6 keep, livelihood, living, maintenance, minimum, subsistence, sustenance

v 1 endorse, promote, ratify, second

v 2 assist, keep up, maintain, provide, sustain, uphold

v 3 campaign, canvass, influence, lobby, persuade

v 4 aid, comfort, cure, relieve, soothe

v 5 advocate, back, champion, endorse, guarantee, promote, sanction, side, uphold

v 6 bolster, buoy, cheer, comfort, console, gladden, solace, soothe, uplift, upraise

v 7 amplify, bolster, encourage, enhance, enhearten, hearten, increase, inspire, reassure, strengthen

v 8 adapt, adjust, balance, fit, fix, inspect, maintain, overhaul, recondition, refurbish, regulate, repair, service, tune up

v 9 attest, authenticate, certify, confirm, corroborate, justify, notarize, prove, ratify, sanction, substantiate, validate, verify, vouch, witness

v 10 bear up, bolster, brace, build up, buoy, buttress, carry, fortify, harden, nourish, nurture, prop, reinforce, shore, strengthen, sustain, toughen, uphold

v 11 abet, advance, aid, ameliorate, amend, assist, avail, benefit, better, boost, cultivate, do for, ease, egg on, encourage, enhance, forward, foster, further, help, improve, nurture, prefer, promote, rev, serve

supporter *adj* ancillary, assistant, collateral, complementary, dependent, lesser, minor, secondary, sub, subject, subordinate, subsidiary, substitute, tributary, worker

n 1 abettor, accessory, accomplice, co-conspirator, confederate, conspirator

n 2 advocate, ally, angel, backer, benefactor, booster, champion, cheerleader, donor, friend, guarantor, helper, ombudsman, partner, patron, promoter, proponent, sponsor

n 3 see: FRIEND *n* 1

n 4 see: HELPER *n* 1

supporting *adj* 1 accessory, adjunct, ancillary, assisting, auxiliary

adj 2 approbative, approbatory, approving, favorable, sustaining

supportive *adj* pro

suppose *v* 1 dream, fantasize, imagine

v 2 assume, believe, comprehend, conceive, estimate, expect, fathom, gather, grasp, guess, imagine, infer, know, presume, surmise, suspect, think, trust, understand

v 3 see: SUGGEST *v* 6

supposed *adj* accepted, implied, presumed, tacit, understood

supposedly *adv* apparently, presumably, seemingly

supposition *n* 1 assumption, conjecture, deduction, opinion, surmise

n 2 assumption, foundation, ground rule, postulate, premise, proposition, theorem

n 3 assumption, conjecture, deduction, explanation, guess, hypothesis, inference, postulate, presumption, proposition, theory

suppress *v* 1 diminish, lessen, repress, subject, subordinate, weaken

v 2 ban, bar, confine, enjoin, forbid, inhibit, nix, outlaw, prevent, prohibit, stop, veto

v 3 asphyxiate, choke, constrict, gag, garrote, muffle, quash, repress, smother, stifle, suffocate

v 4 bear down, beat down, conquer, crush, defeat, dominate, enslave, exploit, overpower, quash, reduce, subdue, subjugate, vanquish

v 5 censor, curb, gag, hush, inhibit, muffle, mute, quell, quiet, repress, restrain, silence, squelch, stifle, still, subdue, throttle, tone down

v 6 annihilate, crush, demolish, extinguish, put down, quash, quell, quench, repress, squash

suppressed *adj* forgotten, gone, left behind, lost, once, past, unremembered, vague

supremacist *n* bigot, racist

supremacy *n* control, influence, predominance

supreme *adj* 1 invincible, mighty, powerful

adj 2 absolute, chief, complete, consummate, dominant, godlike, leading, main, perfect, principal, pure, ranking, sheer, total, unsurpassed, utter, whole

adj 3 see: FOREMOST *adj* 3

sure *adj* 1 bound, certain

adj 2 accurate, deadly, effective

adj 3 secure, stable, staunch

adj 4 brazen, certain, cocksure, confident, convinced, positive

adj 5 dependable, fail-safe, infallible, reliable, tested, tried

adj 6 abiding, enduring, firm, never-failing, steadfast, unfaltering, unshakable, unwavering

adj 7 absolute, actual, authentic, bona fide, certain, definite, existent, factual, genuine, hard, inarguable, incontestable, incontrovertible, indisputable, indubitable, irrefutable, positive, real, true, undeniable, undisputable, undoubtable, undoubted, unequivocal, unquestionable, veritable, viable

adj 8 see: ASSERTIVE *adj*

adj 9 see: AUTHENTIC *adj* 2, 3

surely *adv* absolutely, certainly, decidedly, definitely, entirely, incontrovertibly, indeed, indubitably, positively, truly, unequivocally, unquestionably, verily, well, without doubt

surety *n* assurance, bond, commitment, earnest, guarantee, obligation, pawn, pledge, security, token, warrant

surface *n* 1 exterior, facade, outside, skin

n 2 appearance, cover, facade, face, facet, factor, front, look, veneer

n 3 footing, foundation, standing

n 4 face, side, siding, wall

v ascend, rise

surfeit *v* fill, glut, gorge, overeat, pig out, satiate

n deluge, excess, fat, glut, overabundance, overflow, overkill, plethora, redundancy, surplus

surge *n* 1 gush, rush, swell, wave

n 2 deluge, flood, overflow, torrent

v 1 climb, crest, increase, jump, rise

v 2 flood, flow, gush, peak, pour, rise, roll, spill, stream, swell

v 3 fluctuate, oscillate, pulsate, throb, undulate, vibrate

v 4 jet, shoot, spew, spout, spurt, squirt

surgeon *n* diagnostician, doctor, healer, intern, physician, resident

surly *adj* 1 brooding, crabby, dour,

gloomy, glum, moody, morose, sour, sulky, sullen, ugly

adj 2 audacious, boorish, discourteous, disrespectful, ill-behaved, ill-bred, ill-mannered, impertinent, impolite, insolent, rude, uncalled for, uncivil, uncivilized, uncouth, uncultured, unpolished, unrefined

adj 3 see: BLUNT *adj* 1

surmise *n* assumption, conjecture, deduction, supposition

v 1 analyze, conclude, construe, deduce, derive, draw, educe, gather, glean, guess, infer, interpret

v 2 allude, assume, extend, hypothesize, imagine, offer, pose, present, presume, propose, speculate, suggest, suppose, theorize

v 3 assume, believe, comprehend, conceive, estimate, expect, fathom, gather, grasp, guess, imagine, infer, know, presume, suppose, suspect, think, trust, understand

v 4 account, calculate, consider, deem, judge, reckon, regard, view

surmount *v* 1 clear, hurdle, leap, negotiate, vault

v 2 ascend, climb, escalate, intensify, mount

v 3 conquer, crush, defeat, destroy, down, hurdle, lick, overcome

surpass *v* 1 eclipse, excel, outshine

v 2 beat, best, better, cap, dwarf, eclipse, exceed, excel, go beyond, outdo, outgo, outshine, outstrip, overshadow, pass, top, transcend

surplus *n* 1 asset, excess, inventory, overage, overstock, oversupply, plus

n 2 deluge, excess, fat, glut, overabundance, overflow, overkill, plethora, redundancy

adj 1 see: ADDITIONAL *adj* 2

adj 2 see: SUPERFLUOUS *adj* 3

surprise *n* 1 ambush, assault, sneak attack

n 2 amazement, astonishment, awe, bewilderment, shock, wonder

n 3 blow, jerk, jolt, jump, shock

v 1 assault, jump, leap, pounce, strike, swoop

v 2 amaze, astonish, astound, awe, boggle, confound, dazzle, dumbfound, flabbergast, nonplus, stagger, stun

surprising *adj* 1 startling, sudden, unexpected, unforeseen

adj 2 accidental, sudden, unanticipated, unexpected, unforeseen

surrender *v* 1 abandon, acquiesce, cede,

give up, hand over, leave, relinquish, resign, submit, waive, yield

v 2 abstain, cast, decline, drop, eschew, forbear, forfeit, forgo, give up, lose, pass, reject, renounce, sacrifice, turn down, waive

v 3 accede, acquiesce, bend, bow, buckle, capitulate, cave, comply, concede, cry uncle, defer, give in, give up, relent, submit, succumb, twist, yield

v 4 fall, give up, go under, submit, succumb, yield

n capitulation, compliance, release, submission, subordination

surreptitious *adj* clandestine, concealed, covert, crafty, deceitful, devious, evasive, foxy, furtive, guileful, indirect, privy, secret, shifty, sly, sneaky, tricky, underground, underhand, underhanded, wily

surreptitiously *adv* clandestinely, covertly, furtively, hush-hush, mystically, secretly, sneakily, stealthily, under cover

surrey *n* buggy, carriage, coach, vehicle

surrogate *adj* by proxy, indirect, second-hand, vicarious

n 1 agent, alternate, backup, contingency, part-timer, replacement, representative, substitute

n 2 expedient, makeshift, means, measure, recourse, refuge, replacement, resort, stopgap

surround *v* 1 build, conceive, construct, devise, frame

v 2 bound, compass, encircle, enclose, encompass, enfold

v 3 beleaguer, beset, besiege, invest

surroundings *n* 1 atmosphere, climate, conditions, environment, habitat, niche, perimeter, settings

n 2 backdrop, curtain, environment, scene, scenery, set, setting, stage set

surveillance *n* espionage, observation, reconnaissance

survey *n* 1 examination, inquiry, inspection, probing, scrutiny, study

n 2 assessment, examination, inquiry, review, scope, search, study

v 1 examine, explore, investigate, scout

v 2 analyze, assess, determine, diagnose, estimate, examine, penetrate, probe, scope, solve, understand, unravel

v 3 canvass, case, check, examine, glance over, inspect, observe, peruse, pore over, regard, scrutinize, study, watch

v 4 appraise, assay, assess, charge, estimate, evaluate, levy, price, rank, rate, set at, tax, valuate, value

v 5 coast, cruise, explore, go, journey,

migrate, proceed, sail, tour, travel, trek, voyage

surveyor *n* architect, designer, draftsperson, engineer, inventor, manager, operator, plotter

survival *n* continuation, duration, endurance, existence, life, span, subsistence, term

survive *v* 1 outlast, outlive, outwear

v 2 come through, get by, pull through, ride, succeed

v 3 be, endure, exist, last, live, persist, prevail

v 4 abide, continue, endure, last, outlast, persevere, persist, prevail, remain, stay, stick with

v 5 see: FLOURISH *v* 3

surviving *adj* current, extant, remaining, visible

susceptible *adj* 1 vulnerable

adj 2 emotional, feeling, sensitive, tender

adj 3 alterable, impressionable, inexperienced, malleable, naive

adj 4 believing, credulous, easy, gullible, innocent, naive, trustful

adj 5 defenseless, dependent, disarmed, exposed, helpless, powerless, unprotected, vulnerable, weak

suspect *adj* 1 questionable, suspicious

adj 2 see: VAGUE *adj* 6

n accused, con, convict, criminal, crook, culprit, delinquent, felon, guilty party, inmate, lawbreaker, offender, perpetrator, prisoner, scofflaw, swindler, transgressor, wrongdoer

v 1 distrust, doubt, fear, mistrust

v 2 assume, believe, comprehend, conceive, estimate, expect, fathom, gather, grasp, guess, imagine, infer, know, presume, suppose, surmise, think, trust, understand

suspend *v* 1 dangle, hang, swing

v 2 demur, halt, hold up, interrupt, pause, rest, stop

v 3 banish, bar, blackball, cut, debar, dismiss, eliminate, except, exclude, ignore, leave out

v 4 adjourn, avoid, defer, delay, hold, hold up, interrupt, lay over, postpone, procrastinate, prolong, put off, remit, reschedule, set aside, shelve, stay, table, wait, waive

suspended *adj* see: DORMANT *adj* 2

suspense *n* anticipation, anxiety, apprehension, strain, tension

suspension *n* 1 delay, interruption, postponement, reprieve, stay

n 2 abeyance, cessation, halt, impasse, moratorium, standstill, stay, stop

n 3 delay, interval, lull, pause, stay, wait

n 4 abeyance, dormancy, inaction, inactivity, lull, pause

n 5 absolution, amnesty, discharge, disengagement, dispensation, freedom, moratorium, pardon, release, relief, reprieve, respite

suspicion *n* 1 feeling, foreboding, guess, hunch, instinct, intuition, premonition

n 2 apprehension, distrust, doubt, fear, hesitation, misbelief, mistrust, wariness

n 3 concern, doubt, dubiety, incertitude, indecision, mistrust, query, question, skepticism, uncertainty, wonder

n 4 see: TRACE *n* 4

suspicious *adj* 1 distrusted, questionable, suspect

adj 2 covetous, distrusting, envious, resentful

adj 3 alert, careful, heedful, leery, prudent, vigilant, wary, watchful

adj 4 cynical, distrustful, doubtful, dubious, incredulous, leery, questionable, shy, skeptical, skittish, uncertain, unsure

adj 5 see: VAGUE *adj* 6

sustain *v* 1 defend

v 2 assist, keep up, maintain, provide, support, uphold

v 3 feed, fire, fuel, ignite, incite, kindle, light, nourish, propel, stoke

v 4 bear up, bolster, brace, build up, buoy, buttress, carry, fortify, harden, nourish, nurture, prop, reinforce, shore, strengthen, support, toughen, uphold

v 5 abide, accept, acquiesce, allow, authorize, bear, concede, condone, digest, endure, experience, have, let, permit, put up with, stand, stomach, suffer, swallow, take, tolerate, undergo

v 6 see: SERVE *v* 4

sustainable *adj* allowable, bearable, endurable, tolerable

sustained *adj* drawn-out, elongated, extended, lengthened, lengthy, long, prolonged, protracted

sustaining *adj* approbative, approbatory, approving, favorable

sustenance *n* 1 food, nourishment, nutriment

n 2 keep, livelihood, living, maintenance, minimum, subsistence

svelte *adj* sexy, sleek, slender, slim

swag *n* booty, bounty, fortune, kitty, loot, money, plunder, pot, prize, spoils, treasure, trove

swagger v amble, flaunt, prance, stride, strut

swallow v 1 accept, believe

v 2 consume, devour, digest, eat, ingest

v 3 abide, accept, acquiesce, allow, authorize, bear, concede, condone, digest, endure, experience, have, let, permit, put up with, stand, stomach, suffer, sustain, take, tolerate, undergo

swamp v 1 bury, drown, engulf, flood, inundate, overflow, wash over

v 2 cascade, emit, flood, inundate, overflow, plunge, pour, rain, shower, spill, tumble

v 3 deluge, douse, drench, drown, dunk, flood, inundate, irrigate, overload, saturate, slosh, soak, sop, souse, swill, tax, wet

n bog, marsh, mire, moor

swap v 1 barter, exchange, switch, trade

v 2 exchange, replace, represent, return, substitute, supplant, switch

v 3 bargain, barter, convert, deal, exchange, trade, traffic

v 4 deal, hawk, horse-trade, huckster, hustle, monger, peddle, sell

swarm n 1 crush, dozens, horde, host, legion, many, multitude, numerousness, oodles, press, push, scores

n 2 band, bunch, crew, crowd, drove, flock, following, gaggle, gang, herd, huddle, mass, mob, pack, rabble, riffraff, team, throng

v 1 cluster, mass, teem

v 2 infest, invade, overrun, plague

v 3 crowd, herd, jam, mob, press, push, teem, throng

swarming adj alive, ample, overflowing, replete, rife, teeming

swat n bang, blow, box, bump, chop, clap, conk, crack, crash, cuff, hit, impact, jar, jolt, knock, lick, punch, rap, slap, slug, smack, smash, swipe, tap, wallop, whack

v bat, clout, hit, nail, pop, smite, sock, whack

sway v 1 charm, entice

v 2 bob, heave, pitch, rock, roll, swing, toss

v 3 alternate, fluctuate, oscillate, pendulate, swing, vacillate, wave

v 4 careen, lurch, pitch, reel, stagger, toss, totter, wheel

v 5 dance, flap, flicker, flitter, flutter, oscillate, prance, sparkle, twinkle, undulate, wave

v 6 bend, bias, brainwash, compel, convert, indoctrinate, influence, predispose, prejudice, proselytize, slant

v 7 affect, assure, convince, impel, induce, influence, inspire, instigate, motivate, move, persuade, pressure, prompt, stir, talk into, touch, win over

v 8 see: GOVERN v 4

swayed adj see: PLASTIC adj 2

swear v 1 affirm, bear witness, declare, depose, testify

v 2 condemn, curse, damn, denounce, molest, profane, vex

v 3 affirm, attest, avow, contend, promise, say, vouch, warrant

v 4 advocate, affirm, assure, avouch, avow, commit, devote, guarantee, pledge, promise, ratify, vow

swearing n abomination, blasphemy, curse word, expletive, obscenity, profanity

sweat n 1 apprehension, anxiety, distress, worry

n 2 chore, drudgery, grind, labor, slavery, tedium, toil, travail, work

n 3 moisture, perspiration, wetness

v 1 perspire

v 2 drudge, grub, hustle, labor, slave, strain, strive, toil, work

sweaty adj 1 damp, drenched, dripping, humid, moist, mucky, muggy, soaked, soggy, sopping, sticky, sultry, wet

adj 2 see: PASSIONATE adj 2

sweep v 1 ascend, flit, flutter, fly, sail, soar, wing

v 2 brush, comb, paint

n see: REACH n 3

sweeping adj 1 comprehensive, extensive, indiscriminate, large-scale, wholesale

adj 2 blanket, comprehensive, expansive, universal

sweepings n crap, crud, debris, detritus, dirt, garbage, junk, litter, refuse, rubbish, rubble, trash, waste

sweet adj 1 abundant, fattening, heavy, rich, thick

adj 2 appetizing, delectable, delicious, exquisite, luscious, palatable, tasty

sweeten v 1 enrich

v 2 allay, appease, assuage, balm, becalm, calm, compose, conciliate, ease, lull, mollify, pacify, placate, propitiate, quell, quiet, reconcile, satiate, settle, soften, soothe, still, tranquilize

swell n 1 gush, rush, surge, wave

n 2 enlargement, growth, increase

n 3 breaker, ripple, roller, wave, whitecap

v 1 flood, flow, gush, peak, pour, rise, roll, spill, stream

v 2 amplify, bloat, dilate, distend, enlarge, expand, fatten, grow, increase, inflate, magnify, stretch, widen

v 3 bulge, jut, overhang, overlap, overlay,

poke, pop, project, protrude, protuberate, rise, stand out

swelling *n* **1** bulge, jut, lump, projection

n **2** blister, fester, inflammation, sore, welt

n **3** foothill, hill, hillock, hump, knoll, mound, mount, raise

swelter *v* bake, broil, burn, char, cook, melt, parch, roast, scorch, sear, singe, toast, warm

sweltering *adj* baking, blistering, boiling, broiling, burning, fiery, hot, scalding, scorching, sizzling, sultry, torrid

swerve *v* **1** deviate, detour, differ, digress, diverge

v **2** avert, deflect, deviate, dip, divert, dodge, pivot, skew, swing, swivel, turn, veer, wheel, whip

swift *adj* **1** immediate, instant, instantaneous, quick, rapid, urgent

adj **2** breakneck, expeditious, explosive, fast, fleet, hasty, impulsive, instant, lightning, mercurial, meteoric, precipitous, quick, rapid, spectacular, speedy, sudden

adj **3** brief, fleeting, passing, short, transient

adj **4** express, fast, next-day, nonstop, quick, rapid

adj **5** alert, astute, brainy, bright, brilliant, clever, discerning, discriminating, educated, insightful, intellectual, intelligent, knowing, knowledgeable, perceptive, quick, sagacious, sage, sharp

swiftly *adv* **1** abruptly, fast, hastily, immediately, instantaneously, instantly, quick, quickly, suddenly

adv **2** expeditiously, fast, full tilt, hastily, in a snap, lickety-split, promptly, pronto, quick, quickly, rapidly, right away, soon, speedily, urgently

swiftness *n* **1** alacrity, dispatch, expedition, haste, hastiness, hurry, hustle, precipitance, precipitation, quickness, rush, rustle

n **2** alacrity, cadence, celerity, dispatch, gait, pace, quickness, rapidity, rate, speed, step, stride, trot, velocity, walk

swig *v* see: DRINK *v* 2

swill *v* **1** see: DRINK *v* 2

v **2** see: SATURATE *v* 2

swim *v* gyrate, pirouette, purl, reel, spin, turn, twirl, whirl

swindle *n* con, crime, graft, hustle, racket, rip-off, scam, scheme, sting

v **1** defraud, deprive, rob, take, usurp

v **2** see: CHEAT *v* 1

v **3** see: STEAL *v* 2

swindler *n* **1** bandit, brigand, burglar,

cheat, con artist, con man, criminal, crook, embezzler, gyp, highwayman, looter, mugger, outlaw, robber, thief

n **2** see: CRIMINAL *n* 1, 2

swine *n* glutton, hog, overdoer, pig

swing *v* **1** hang, suspend

v **2** dispense, handle, maneuver, manipulate, ply, wield

v **3** bob, heave, pitch, rock, roll, sway, toss

v **4** alternate, fluctuate, oscillate, pendulate, sway, vacillate, wave

v **5** avert, deflect, deviate, dip, divert, dodge, pivot, skew, swerve, swivel, turn, veer, wheel, whip

n **1** punch, thrust

n **2** blues, classical, country, folk, jazz, music, ragtime, rock-and-roll

swipe *n* bang, blow, box, bump, chop, clap, conk, crack, crash, cuff, hit, impact, jar, jolt, knock, lick, punch, rap, slap, slug, smack, smash, swat, tap, wallop, whack

v appropriate, burglarize, defraud, embezzle, filch, heist, lift, misappropriate, pilfer, pillage, pinch, plunder, pocket, purloin, rip off, rob, snake, snitch, steal, swindle, take, thieve

swishy *adj* effeminate, effete, sissy, unmanly, wimpy

switch *v* **1** barter, exchange, trade

v **2** exchange, replace, represent, return, substitute, supplant

v **3** alternate, change, cycle, lap, oscillate, rotate, shift

switchblade *n* blade, cutlass, dagger, knife, pocketknife, rapier, saber, sword

swivel *v* avert, deflect, deviate, dip, divert, dodge, pivot, skew, swerve, swing, turn, veer, wheel, whip

swollen *adj* bloated, distended, inflated, puffy, tumescent, tumid, turgid

swoon *v* collapse, faint, pass out

swoop *v* **1** assault, jump, leap, pounce, strike

v **2** see: DIVE *v* 1

sword *n* blade, cutlass, dagger, knife, pocketknife, rapier, saber, scimitar, switchblade

sworn *adj* ensconced, entrenched, established, fixed, fundamental, ingrained, intrinsic, inveterate

sycophant *n* dependent, follower

syllabus *n* see: SUMMARY *n* 2

symbol *n* **1** drawing, icon, image, model, representation

n **2** nod, sign, signal, symptom, token, trait

n **3** bust, figure, icon, idol, image, sculpture, statue

table **557**

n 4 character, emblem, example, icon, letter, logo, mark, model, representation, sign, token

symbolic *adj* 1 hollow, nominal, perfunctory, professed, representative, small, token

adj 2 abstract, conjectural, general, hypothetical, ideal, illustrative, theoretical

symbolize *v* 1 embody, exemplify, express, personify, represent, typify

v 2 add up to, connote, convey, denote, identify, import, indicate, intend, mean, signify

v 3 denote, depict, express, illustrate, imply, mean, represent

symmetrical *adj* balanced, commensurate, proportional

symmetry *n* 1 balance, harmony, uniformity

n 2 equality, equilibrium, equity, equivalence, evenness, par, parity

sympathetic *adj* 1 accepting, charitable, easy, forbearing, indulgent, lenient, merciful, patient, restrained, tolerant

adj 2 affectionate, compassionate, considerate, empathetic, empathic, gentle, humane, kind, kindhearted, responsive, softhearted, tender, warm, warmhearted

adj 3 see: FRIENDLY *adj* 3

sympathy *n* 1 affinity, compassion, empathy, kindness, mercy, pity, rue, tenderness, understanding

n 2 acceptance, accord, agreement, approval, assent, compliance, concurrence, consent, go-ahead

symphonic *adj* choral, euphonious, harmonious, lyric, mellow, melodic, melodious, musical, orchestral, philharmonic, rhythmical, tuneful, vocal

symphony *n* concert, concerto, étude, fugue, program, recital, serenade

symposium *n* 1 assembly, clinic, congress, council, court, diet, forum, hearing, meeting, parliament

n 2 see: ASSEMBLY *n* 2, 3

symptom *n* nod, sign, signal, symbol, token, trait

synagogue *n* basilica, cathedral, chapel, church, house of god, mosque, sanctuary, tabernacle, temple

synchronize *v* accompany, accord, coexist, coincide, concur, coordinate

synchronous *adj* 1 coexistent, coexisting, coincident, contemporary, simultaneous

adj 2 accidental, casual, chance, chancy, circumstantial, coincidental, contingent, eventful, fluky, fortuitous, freak, incidental, lucky, odd

syndicate *n* cartel, chain, coalition, collab-

oration, combine, conglomerate, consortium, federation, group, partnership, pool, trust

synergy *n* see: AGREEMENT *n* 5

synonymous *adj* duplicate, equal, equivalent, identical, same, substitute, tantamount

synopsis *n* abridgement, abstract, brief, compendium, condensation, digest, essence, example, outline, review, sketch, summary

synopsize *v* see: SUMMARIZE *v* 2

synthesize *v* 1 craft, define, develop, formulate, list, make, process

v 2 arrange, blend, combine, compound, concoct, harmonize, integrate, make one, orchestrate, unify

synthetic *adj* artificial, counterfeit, fake, false, man-made, manufactured, plastic

system *n* 1 habit, method, procedure, routine

n 2 complex, infrastructure, maze, network, organization

n 3 being, entity, object, organism, sum, thing, totality, whole

n 4 arrangement, blueprint, method, order, orderliness, pattern, plan

n 5 expression, formula, methodology, plan, procedure, recipe, scheme, theorem

n 6 method, methodology, practice, procedure, process, routine, science, technique, technology

n 7 angle, approach, code, delivery, execution, expression, fashion, manner, method, mode, organization, process, program, style, technique, way

systematic *adj* 1 clinical, detached, impersonal, scientific, technical

adj 2 methodic, methodical, orderly, recurring, regular, steady

systemize *v* arrange, array, dispose, marshal, organize

T

tab *n* 1 account, balance sheet, book, credit, ledger, statement

n 2 bill, check, charge, debt, fee, invoice

n 3 copy, impression, imprint, indent, indentation, mark, notch, stamp

n 4 earmark, flap, label

tabby *n* cat, feline, kit, kitten, kitty, puss, pussy, tiger

tabernacle *n* basilica, cathedral, chapel, church, house of god, mosque, sanctuary, temple

table *n* 1 list

n 2 bar graph, chart, diagram, distribution, figure, flowchart, graph, histogram, outline, pie chart

n 3 board, desk, secretary

v adjourn, avoid, defer, delay, hold, hold up, interrupt, lay over, postpone, procrastinate, prolong, put off, remit, reschedule, set aside, shelve, stay, suspend, wait, waive

taboo *adj* forbidden, prohibited, verboten

n ban, bar, constraint, interdiction, prohibition

tabulate *v* see: CLASSIFY *v* 2

tacit *adj* 1 accepted, implied, presumed, understood

adj 2 dumb, inarticulate, mute, reticent, silent, speechless, voiceless

adj 3 implicit, implied, indicated, inferred, inherent, insinuated, intuitive, presumed, suggested, understood, unexpressed, unsaid, unspoken, wordless

taciturn *adj* closed, diffident, introverted, laconic, reserved, restrained, reticent, secretive, shy, subdued, timid, timorous, uncommunicative, undaring

tack *n* 1 course, direction, drift, path, strategy, tactic, tendency, tenor, trend

n 2 angle, bend, bow, detour, deviation, double, shift, turn, turning, yaw

v 1 connect, join, nail, peg

v 2 attach, clip, fasten, nail, pin

tackle *v* 1 seize

v 2 assume, attack, attempt, take on, try

n bait, gear, hooks, lures

tacky *adj* 1 adhesive, cohesive, gluey, sticky

adj 2 blatant, brazen, conspicuous, flagrant, flashy, garish, gaudy, glaring, loud, ostentatious, showy, tasteless, tawdry, tinsel

adj 3 flawed, flimsy, imperfect, inferior, lousy, mediocre, miserable, paltry, poor, second-rate, shabby, shoddy, sorry, so-so, unworthy, worthless

adj 4 gooey, sticky, thick

adj 5 careless, disheveled, messy, scruffy, slatternly, slipshod, sloppy, sloven, slovenly, uncombed, unkempt, untidy

tact *n* 1 diplomacy, discretion, finesse, savvy, skill

n 2 consideration, diplomacy, discretion, poise, regard, savoir-faire, tactfulness, thoughtfulness

tactful *adj* discerning, discreet, discriminating, keen, sensitive

tactfulness *n* consideration, diplomacy, discretion, poise, regard, savoir-faire, tact, thoughtfulness

tactic *n* 1 course, direction, drift, path, strategy, tack, tendency, tenor, trend

n 2 antic, device, diversion, gambit, gimmick, maneuver, mischief, move, plan, plot, ploy, prank, ruse, scheme, stratagem, strategy, trick, wile

tactics *n* intrigue, logistics, plotting, strategy

tactile *adj* concrete, corporeal, material, objective, physical, real, sensible, substantial, tangible

tactless *adj* 1 hasty, inconsiderate, indiscreet, reckless, thoughtless

adj 2 clumsy, gauche, indiscreet, insensitive, rude, thoughtless

adj 3 caustic, inconsiderate, selfish, sharp, short, thoughtless, unceremonious, ungracious

adj 4 accidental, careless, caustic, heedless, inadvertent, inconsiderate, nonchalant, selfish, sharp, short, thoughtless, uncaring, unceremonious, ungracious, unheeding, unintended, unintentional, unreflective, unthinking

tad *n* see: DOT *n* 1

tag *n* badge, card, label, pass, ticket, voucher

v baptize, bestow, call, christen, confer, designate, dub, entitle, name, nickname, term, title

tail *adj* aft, back, backward, dorsal, rear

v chase, follow, hunt, pursue, seek, shadow, shoot for, trace, track, trail

n end, last, trailing

tailor *v* adapt, conform, convert, cut, fashion, fit, measure, modify, rig, shape

taint *n* contamination, corruption, decay, impurity, poison

v 1 defile, dirty, discolor, smear, soil, stain, sully, tarnish

v 2 adulterate, corrupt, debase, debauch, defile, demoralize, dishonor, pervert, ruin

v 3 angle, confuse, deceive, distort, falsify, garble, incline, misconstrue, misinterpret, misquote, misread, misrepresent, misunderstand, mix up, mumble, slant, slope, twist

v 4 see: DISINTEGRATE *v* 2

tainted *adj* 1 see: FOUL *adj* 3

adj 2 see: VULGAR *adj* 2

taintless *adj* 1 clean, immaculate, pristine, pure, spotless, unsoiled, unspoiled, unsullied, untouched, virgin

adj 2 celibate, chaste, clean, decent, decorous, immaculate, modest, moral, pristine, proper, pure, spotless, stainless, stuffy, unadulterated, unblemished, undefiled, upstanding, virginal, wholesome

take n 1 batch, catch, collection, heap

n 2 see: PROFITS n

v 1 bring, carry

v 2 defraud, deprive, rob, swindle, usurp

v 3 ask, call, crave, demand, require

v 4 catch, clasp, clutch, grab, grapple, grasp, grip, hold, nab, nail, seize

v 5, annex, appropriate, commandeer, confiscate, expropriate, grab, impound, plunder, preempt, repossess, seize, sequester, shanghai

v 6 see: ARREST v 2

v 7 see: STEAL v 2

v 8 see: TOLERATE v

takeoff n buffoonery, burlesque, caricature, comedy, farce, humor, imitation, joke, lampoon, mockery, parody, satire, spoof, travesty

tale n 1 chronicle, epic, legend, opus, saga, story

n 2 exaggeration, fabrication, falsehood, falsity, fib, invention, lie, misstatement

n 3 allegory, fable, fantasy, fiction, legend, lesson, lore, myth, mythology, parable

n 4 anecdote, description, fantasy, fiction, invention, myth, narration, narrative, novel, sketch, story, yarn

talent n 1 accomplishment, action, conduct, deed, delivery, demonstration, execution

n 2 bent, brains, brilliance, faculty, flair, genius, gift, head, intelligence, knack, mind, nose, prowess

n 3 see: INCLINATION n 2

n 4 see: SKILL n 3

talented adj 1 artistic, creative, skilled, skillful

adj 2 clever, gifted, handy, ingenious, inventive, versatile

adj 3 advanced, bright, gifted, intelligent, precocious, promising

adj 4 able, accomplished, adept, apt, capable, competent, deft, dexterous, expert, fit, gifted, masterful, professional, proficient, proper, qualified

adj 5 see: RESOURCEFUL adj 3

talents n acts, bag of tricks, repertoire, résumé

talisman n amulet, charm

talk n 1 bull session, dialogue, discussion, rap

n 2 conference, meeting, parley, powwow, tête-à-tête

n 3 come-on, line, pitch, presentation, spiel

n 4 discourse, expression, speaking, speech, statement, utterance, verbalization, word

n 5 address, speech

n 6 chat, chatter, gab, gossip, rap

n 7 adage, axiom, byword, cliché, dictum, maxim, motto, proverb, saying

n 8 gossip, grapevine, hearsay, murmur, report, rumble, rumor, scuttlebutt, story, word

n 9 caucus, chat, colloquy, conference, conversation, debate, dialogue, discourse, discussion, exchange, forum, interchange, intercourse, interlocution

v 1 cackle, chat, gab, gossip, yak

v 2 address, deliver, lecture, preach, proclaim

v 3 chat, chatter, converse, discuss, parley, speak, visit

v 4 babble, blab, blurt, burble, chatter, gossip, murmur, prattle, tattle

v 5 announce, articulate, assert, couch, describe, dictate, draft, enunciate, express, intonate, orate, phrase, proclaim, pronounce, say, speak, state, stress, utter, verbalize, vocalize, voice, word

talkative adj 1 articulate, communicative, vocal

adj 2 bombastic, chatty, diffuse, garrulous, long-winded, loquacious, redundant, repetitious, superfluous, verbose, wordy

tall adj aloft, elevated, high, lofty, overhead

tally n 1 count, score, total

n 2 aggregate, amount, body, budget, bulk, count, number, quantity, total

n 3 account, amount, catalog, enumeration, inventory, itemization, list, litany, repertoire

v 1 count, gain, win

v 2 catalog, check, inventory, itemize

v 3 calculate, cite, count, enumerate, itemize, list, number

v 4 mark, number, score

v 5 capture, chart, denote, enter, itemize, jot, list, log, note, preserve, record, register, take notes, tape, write down

v 6 accord, agree, check, coalesce, coincide, comply with, concur, conform, consent, consist, correspond, fit in, harmonize, jibe, square

talon n claw, hook, spur

tame adj acquiescent, compliant, docile, easy, meek, mild, nonresistant, obedient, passive, resigned, submissive, tolerant, unassertive, yielding

v 1 mellow, soften, temper

v 2 abstain, avoid, constrain, curb, deny, forgo, govern, hold back, refrain, resist, restrict

tamp *v* even, flatten, flush, grade, lay, level, smooth

tan *adj* beige, brown, chestnut, chocolate, hazel, mahogany
v bask, sun

tang *n* flavor, palate, sample, savor, taste

tangerine *adj* apricot, coral, orange, salmon

tangible *adj* 1 concrete, corporeal, material, objective, physical, real, sensible, substantial
adj 2 appreciable, cognizant, concrete, detectable, discernible, noticeable, observable, palpable, perceptible, sensible, visible

tangle *n* 1 bend, crimp, kink, twist
n 2 see: CHAOS *n* 5
v 1 accuse, associate, blame, confuse, connect, embroil, enmesh, ensnare, entangle, implicate, involve
v 2 bag, capture, catch, ensnare, entangle, entrap, hook, snag, snare, snarl, trap, trick

tangled *adj* complex, complicated, elaborate, enigmatic, intricate, involved, knotty

tangy *adj* biting, hot, nippy, pungent, seasoned, sharp, spicy, tart

tank *n* cauldron, cistern, container, jug, reservoir, vat

tantalize *v* 1 attract, bait, decoy, entice, lure
v 2 appeal, arouse, attract, excite, fascinate, fire, interest, intrigue, lead on, lure, seduce
v 3 arouse, electrify, excite, fire, incite, inspire, rouse, spark, stimulate, thrill, titillate, turn on, whet

tantalizing *adj* 1 alluring, compelling, desirable, irresistible, seductive
adj 2 arousing, exciting, intriguing, provocative, seductive, sexy, stimulating
adj 3 alluring, attractive, desirable, erotic, enticing, seductive, tempting

tantamount *adj* duplicate, equal, equivalent, identical, same, substitute

tantrum *n* 1 fit, rage, temper
n 2 fight, incident, outbreak, spectacle
n 3 anger, dander, fit, frenzy, fury, indignation, ire, outrage, paroxysm, rage, wrath

tap *v* 1 dab, paint, touch
v 2 draft, drain, draw, draw off, pump, suck

v 3 box, clap, cuff, knock, punch, slap, smack, spank, strike, whack
v 4 air, bring up, broach, communicate, discuss, expose, express, give, introduce, open, put, reveal, state, tell, vent, ventilate, verbalize
n 1 cock, faucet, nozzle, spigot, spout, valve
n 2 ballet, cha-cha, dance, fox trot, hula, jitterbug, polka, twist, waltz
n 3 bang, blow, box, bump, chop, clap, conk, crack, crash, cuff, hit, impact, jar, jolt, knock, lick, punch, rap, slap, slug, smack, smash, swat, swipe, wallop, whack

tape *v* 1 capture, chart, denote, enter, itemize, jot, list, log, note, preserve, record, register, take notes, tally, write down
v 2 close, package, seal, wrap
n adhesive, band, cellophane tape, strip

tardy *adj* 1 laggard, sluggish
adj 2 belated, delayed, late, overdue, slow, unpunctual

target *n* 1 axis, center, focal point, focus, heart, hub
n 2 butt, casualty, object, prey, subject, sufferer, victim
n 3 aim, goal, mission, motive, objective, purpose, reason, sake, task
n 4 catch, game, quarry
v 1 examine, focus, highlight
v 2 aim, establish, focus, point, set, shoot at

tariff *n* assessment, cost, duty, expense, fee, impost, levy, offering, penalty, price, sacrifice, tax, toll, trade off
v chastise, dock, fine, penalize, punish, sentence, tax

tarnish *v* 1 disfavor, disgrace, dishonor, humiliate, reproach, shame
v 2 defile, dirty, discolor, smear, soil, stain, sully, taint
v 3 abuse, blemish, damage, hamper, harm, hurt, impair, injure, mar, obstruct, ruin, sabotage, scuttle, spoil, vandalize
v 4 becloud, bedim, befog, blur, cloud, confuse, darken, dim, diminish, dull, eclipse, fade, muddy, obscure, overshadow, pale, shadow

tarpaulin *n* canvas

tarry *v* 1 abide, await, bide, linger, loiter, remain, stay, wait
v 2 dally, dawdle, delay, diddle, goof off, idle, lag, linger, loaf, loiter, loll, lounge, malinger, poke, put off, putter

tart *adj* 1 acerbic, acid, biting, curt, dry, pungent, sour *adj* 2 biting, hot, nippy, pungent, seasoned, sharp, spicy

n 1 coquette, flirt, harlot, nymphomaniac, seductress, siren, tease, temptress, vamp, wanton woman

n 2 call girl, harlot, hooker, hussy, prostitute, slut, streetwalker, tramp, trollop, wanton woman, wench, whore

task *n* 1 assignment, chore, duty, effort, job, mission, responsibility, stint

n 2 aim, goal, mission, motive, objective, purpose, reason, sake

n 3 see: TRADE *n* 3

v assign, delegate, detail

taste *n* 1 morsel, sample, tidbit

n 2 appetite, enjoyment, relish

n 3 affinity, appreciation, attraction, fondness, liking

n 4 flavor, palate, sample, savor, spice, tang

n 5 see: INCLINATION *n* 2

v 1 experience, feel, sample

v 2 crave, relish, savor

v 3 imply, resemble, savor, smack, smell, suggest

v 4 bibulate, booze, consume, drink, gulp, guzzle, imbibe, nip, partake, polish off, put away, put down, sample, savor, sip, suck, swill

tasteful *adj* 1 aesthetic, artistic, classy, elegant, refined, stylish, well-chosen

adj 2 conservative, dim, inconspicuous, quiet, restrained, subdued, unassuming, unobtrusive

tasteless *adj* 1 banal, bland, dull, flat, innocuous, insipid, unexciting

adj 2 blatant, brazen, conspicuous, flagrant, flashy, garish, gaudy, glaring, loud, ostentatious, showy, tacky, tawdry, tinsel

adj 3 atrocious, awful, crying, desperate, disgraceful, ghastly, grizzly, heinous, monstrous, notorious, odious, offensive, outrageous, scandalous, shocking, wicked

tasty *adj* appetizing, delectable, delicious, exquisite, luscious, palatable, savory, sweet

tatter *n* end, patch, piece, scrap, shred

v rend, rip, shred, slice, tear

tattered *adj* faded, frayed, poor, run-down, shabby, threadbare, worn

tattle *v* 1 fink, inform, rat, sing, snitch, squeal, stool, tattletale

v 2 babble, blab, blurt, burble, chatter, gossip, murmur, prattle

v 3 blurt, cackle, cry, ejaculate, exclaim, shout, spill, sputter, utter

v 4 see: INFORM *v* 3, 6

tattletale *v* fink, inform, rat, sing, snitch, squeal, stool

taunt *v* 1 cut, gibe, insult, remark

v 2 aggravate, annoy, badger, bait, bedevil, beleaguer, bother, bug, harass, harry, hassle, heckle, hound, hurt, intimidate, jeer, nag, needle, persecute, pester, plague, provoke, ride, spite, tease, threaten, torment, worry

v 3 belittle, deride, flaunt, jab, jeer, jest, mock, quip, razz, ridicule, scoff, scorn, sneer, tease

v 4 annoy, antagonize, argue, bother, bug, concern, distress, disturb, goad, harass, hassle, inconvenience, irk, irritate, pain, perturb, strain, stress, trouble, try, upset, worry

taut *adj* 1 firm, hard, stiff, tense, tight

adj 2 see: SECURE *adj* 5

tavern *n* bar, barroom, cocktail lounge, den, dive, dump, gin mill, hangout, haunt, joint, lounge, pub, rathskeller, saloon, watering hole

tawdry *adj* blatant, brazen, conspicuous, flagrant, flashy, garish, gaudy, glaring, loud, ostentatious, showy, tacky, tasteless, tinsel

tax *n* 1 assessment, damages, penalty, punishment

n 2 assessment, cost, duty, expense, fee, impost, levy, offering, penalty, price, sacrifice, tariff, toll, trade off

v 1 burden, impose, strain

v 2 chastise, dock, fine, penalize, punish, sentence

v 3 burden, encumber, hamper, load, oppress, overdo, overload, strain

v 4 see: APPRAISE *v*

v 5 see: SATURATE *v* 2

taxi *n* cab, hack, jitney, rickshaw, taxicab

taxicab *n* cab, hack, jitney, taxi

taxing *adj* arduous, burdensome, demanding, exacting, grievous, onerous, oppressive, tough, trying

teach *v* 1 imbue, impart, infuse, ingrain, inject, inoculate, instill, invest, penetrate, pervade, spread, steep, suffuse, train

v 2 coach, communicate, condition, convey, cultivate, develop, discipline, drill, edify, educate, enlighten, exercise, explain, groom, imbue, impart, implant, improve, inculcate, indoctrinate, inform, infuse, inseminate, inspire, instill, instruct, perfect, practice, prepare, ready, school, train, tutor

teacher *n* 1 academician, educator, instructor, intern, professor *n* 2 coach, educator, instructor, leader, mentor, schoolteacher, trainer, tutor

n 3 authority, expert, guide, guru, leader, master, mentor, pundit, wise man

teachers *n* department, faculty, instructors, staff

teaching *n* see: CLICHÉ *n* 3

team *n* 1 see: CROWD *n* 1

n 2 see: GROUP *n* 5

teamwork *n* accord, affinity, agreement, assent, concert, concord, congruence, cooperation, empathy, harmony, rapport, synergy, unity

tear *v* 1 rend, rip, shred, slice

v 2 extract, pull, remove, suck, withdraw, yank

v 3 jerk, pull, tug, twist, wrench, wring, yank

v 4 claw, cleave, disrupt, divide, rend, rip, rive, scratch

n rip, slash, slit, split

tearoom *n* automat, cafe, cafeteria, canteen, diner, grill, luncheonette, restaurant

tease *v* 1 banter, deride, gibe, jeer, joke, knock, mock, needle, rib, ridicule, roast

v 2 allure, charm, come on to, dally, flirt, fool, jest, kid, lead on, make eyes, make out, pick up, string along, toy, trifle

v 3 belittle, deride, flaunt, jab, jeer, jest, mock, quip, razz, ridicule, scoff, sneer, taunt

v 4 aggravate, annoy, badger, bait, bedevil, beleaguer, bother, bug, harass, harry, hassle, heckle, hound, hurt, intimidate, jeer, nag, needle, persecute, pester, plague, provoke, ride, spite, taunt, threaten, torment, worry

n coquette, flirt, harlot, nymphomaniac, seductress, siren, tart, temptress, vamp, wanton woman

teat *n* breast, nipple, udder

techie *n* hacker

technical *adj* 1 qualified, skilled, specialized, trained

adj 2 clinical, detached, impersonal, systematic

technique *n* 1 appliance, application, employment, form, method, operation, play, use, utilization

n 2 method, methodology, practice, procedure, process, routine, science, system, technology

n 3 angle, approach, code, delivery, execution, expression, fashion, manner, method, mode, organization, process, program, style, system, way

technology *n* method, methodology, practice, procedure, process, routine, science, system

tedious *adj* 1 endless, long, slow, tiresome

adj 2 blah, boring, commonplace, dim, dreary, dull, flat, humdrum, monotonous, ordinary, pedestrian, stodgy, tiresome

adj 3 banal, boring, clichéd, commonplace, corny, dull, hackneyed, musty, redundant, repetitious, repetitive, stale, threadbare, timeworn, tired, tiresome, trite, worn out

tedium *n* 1 apathy, boredom, dreariness, dullness, ennui, monotony

n 2 chore, drudgery, grind, labor, slavery, sweat, toil, travail, work

teed off *adj* see: ANGRY *adj* 4

teem *v* 1 cluster, swarm

v 2 abound, increase, multiply, overrun, proliferate

v 3 crowd, herd, jam, mob, press, swarm, throng

teeming *adj* 1 crowded, populous

adj 2 alive, ample, overflowing, replete, rife, swarming

adj 3 abounding, abundant, ample, bounteous, bountiful, copious, enough, galore, generous, liberal, overflowing, plentiful, plenty, prodigal

teenager *n* adolescent, boy, child, girl, juvenile, kid, minor, teeny-bopper, youngster, youth

teeny-bopper *n* adolescent, boy, child, girl, juvenile, kid, minor, teenager, youngster, youth

teetering *adj* see: UNSTABLE *adj* 1

teevee *n* boob tube, cable, channel, station, television, tube, TV, video

telecast *v* air, broadcast, relay, televise, transmit

telecopy *n* carbon, carbon copy, copy, duplicate, facsimile, replica, reproduction, Xerox copy

telegraph *v* cable, notify, radio, telex, wire

telephone *v* buzz, call, communicate, contact, phone, ring, touch

telescope *n* binoculars, eye, field glass, glass, lens, magnifying glass, microscope, mirror, periscope, scope

televise *v* air, broadcast, relay, telecast, transmit

television *n* 1 magazines, media, press

n 2 boob tube, cable, channel, station, teevee, tube, TV, video

n 3 cartoons, docudrama, documentary, game shows, mini-series, movies, news, programs, series, sitcom, soap opera, soaps, talk shows, variety shows

telex v cable, notify, radio, wire

tell v 1 breathe, confide, divulge, share, whisper

v 2 blab, divulge, gossip, inform, reveal

v 3 acquaint, advise, apprise, fill in, inform, notify, post, update

v 4 allude, denote, indicate, mention, point out, refer to, reveal, show, speak of, specify

v 5 demonstrate, describe, display, draw, establish, examine, exhibit, explain, present, prove, show

v 6 air, bring up, broach, communicate, discuss, expose, express, give, introduce, open, put, reveal, state, tap, vent, ventilate, verbalize

v 7 brief, communicate, convey, declare, describe, disclose, divulge, explain, impart, inform, narrate, orate, portray, read, recite, recount, relate, report, retell, reveal, share, state, tattle, transmit

teller n banker, cashier, money-changer, paymaster, purser

telling adj cogent, compelling, convincing, effective, forceful, influential, persuasive, revealing, satisfactory, satisfying, solid, sound, valid

temerity n arrogance, assurance, audacity, boldness, brashness, brass, cheek, chutzpah, condescension, confidence, crust, effrontery, face, gall, haughtiness, insolence, nerve, patronage, presumption, ridicule, sass

temper n 1 fit, passion, rage, tantrum

n 2 attitude, disposition, feeling, humor, mind, mood, spirit, timbre, tone, vein

v 1 mellow, soften

v 2 inflect, moderate, modify, modulate, regulate

temperament n aptitude, character, complexion, disposition, distinctiveness, heart, humor, identity, inclination, individuality, makeup, nature, personality, quality, spirit, state, tendency

temperamental adj antsy, edgy, excitable, fidgety, high-strung, irritable, jittery, jumpy, moody, nervous, nervy, restless, shaky, skittish

temperance n 1 abstinence, continence, moderation, restraint, self-restraint, sobriety

n 2 measure, moderateness, moderation

temperate adj 1 levelheaded, moderate, sober, unimpassioned

adj 2 mild, moderate, modest, pleasant, reasonable

temperature n 1 heat, warmth

n 2 atmosphere, climate, condition, mood, trend

tempest n 1 blast, blizzard, blow, gale, gust, hurricane, northeaster, snowstorm, squall, storm, typhoon, wind

n 2 see: COMMOTION n 1

tempestuous adj blustery, squally, stormy, windy

template n mask, overlay, pattern, stencil

temple n basilica, cathedral, chapel, church, house of god, mosque, sanctuary, synagogue, tabernacle

tempo n beat, cadence, cycle, lilt, pulse, rate, rhythm, time

temporal adj carnal

temporary adj 1 impromptu, makeshift, provisional, stopgap

adj 2 ancillary, conditional, contingent, dependent, indefinite, provisional, relative, reliant, uncertain

adj 3 brief, ephemeral, fleeting, impermanent, momentary, passing, short, transient, transitory, volatile

tempt v 1 attract, court, encourage, flirt, invite, lure, pursue, romance, woo

v 2 see: ATTRACT v 4, 6

temptation n attraction, bait, come-on, decoy, enticement, lure, magnet, ruse, seduction, snare, trap, wile

tempting adj 1 alluring, attractive, desirable, erotic, exciting, seductive, sexy, tantalizing

adj 2 alluring, appealing, attractive, charming, coquettish, coy, fast, fetching, flirtatious, seductive, sexy, winsome

temptress n coquette, flirt, harlot, nymphomaniac, seductress, siren, tart, tease, vamp, wanton woman

tenable adj 1 doable, justifiable, practical

adj 2 accurate, authentic, believable, certain, convincing, credible, dependable, faithful, real, reliable, safe, sure, true, trustworthy, trusty

tenacious adj 1 adamant, persistent, unrelenting

adj 2 determined, persistent, resolute

adj 3 bent, committed, dedicated, determined, fixed, intentional, purposeful, resolute, resolved

adj 4 aggressive, dominant, durable, firm, forceful, hardy, hearty, mighty, powerful, robust, rugged, stalwart, stout, strong, sturdy, tough

tenacity n 1 endurance, forbearance, patience, perseverance, persistence, resignation

n 2 backbone, chutzpah, determination, endurance, fortitude, grit, guts, moxie, nerve, persistence, pluck, resilience, spirit, spunk, stamina, strength, tolerance, vigor, willpower

tenant *n* 1 inhabitant, lessee, occupant, renter, resident

n 2 addressee, citizen, dweller, inhabitant, occupant, owner

tendency *n* 1 current, drift, pattern, run, series, succession, trend

n 2 course, direction, drift, path, strategy, tack, tactic, tenor, trend

n 3 characteristic, flavor, impression, nature, property, quality, ring, sound, tone, type

n 4 bent, bias, drift, habit, inclination, leaning, partiality, penchant, predilection, preference, priority, proclivity, propensity, talent, taste

n 5 see: PERSONALITY *n* 4

tender *adj* 1 ticklish, touchy

adj 2 delicate, fragile, frail

adj 3 intimate, moving, romantic, touching

adj 4 bruised, irritated, painful

adj 5 juicy, moist, succulent

adj 6 emotional, feeling, sensitive, sentient, susceptible

adj 7 female, feminine, gentle, ladylike, nurturing, womanly

adj 8 affectionate, amorous, attached, caring, devoted, enamored, fond, loving

adj 9 affectionate, compassionate, considerate, empathetic, empathic, gentle, humane, kind, kindhearted, responsive, softhearted, sympathetic, warm, warmhearted

adj 10 dangerous, delicate, fluctuating, hazardous, precarious, rickety, risky, rocky, sensitive, shaky, ticklish, touchy, tricky, unpredictable, unstable, wobbly

adj 11 see: BENEVOLENT *adj* 2

n barge, boat, canoe, craft, dory, ferry, float, kayak, raft, scow

v 1 cash, convert, dissolve, exchange, liquidate

v 2 see: GIVE *v* 8

tenderfoot *n* see: BEGINNER *n* 2

tenderness *n* 1 affection, emotion, feeling, passion, regard, sensation, sense, sensibility, sentiment

n 2 affinity, compassion, empathy, kindness, mercy, pity, rue, understanding

tenebrous *adj* dark, dim, dusky, gloomy,

lightless, murky, obscure, shadowy, somber, unilluminated

tenet *n* belief, canon, code, conviction, creed, doctrine, dogma, law, opinion, principle, rule, theory

tenor *n* 1 drift, implication, intent, purport

n 2 course, direction, drift, path, strategy, tack, tactic, tendency, trend

tense *adj* 1 firm, hard, stiff, taut, tight

adj 2 anxious, edgy, fidgety, impatient, nervous, nervy, queasy, restive, restless, troubled, uncomfortable, uneasy, uptight, worried

adj 3 see: SECURE *adj* 5

v draw, flex, pull, strain, stretch, tighten, twist

tension *n* 1 adhesion, friction, traction

n 2 anticipation, anxiety, apprehension, strain, stress, suspense

n 3 anxiety, burden, frustration, pressure, stress

tent *n* canvas

tentative *adj* 1 new, untested, young

adj 2 anticipated, contingent, hoped for, iffy, planned, probable

adj 3 developmental, experimental, pilot, suggested, test, trial, untested

adj 4 diffident, faltering, halting, hesitant, indecisive, reluctant, unsure, waffling, wavering

tentatively *adv* conditionally, maybe, perchance, perhaps

tenuous *adj* 1 feeble, flimsy, frail, insubstantial, slight, unsubstantial, weak

adj 2 lank, narrow, skinny, slender, slight, slim, thin, veiled, wiry

adj 3 attenuate, diminished, lessened, rarefied, subtle, thin

adj 4 borderline, casual, frivolous, insignificant, light, lightweight, little, marginal, meager, minor, minute, negligible, nonessential, off, outside, petty, remote, secondary, slender, slight, slim, small, trivial, unimportant

tenure *n* duration, hold, interval, length, occupancy, term, time

tepid *adj* heated, hot, lukewarm, warm

term *n* 1 duration, hold, interval, length, occupancy, tenure, time

n 2 continuation, duration, endurance, existence, life, span, survival

n 3 expression, idiom, locution, name, phrase, saying, word, wording

n 4 cliché, diction, expression, parlance, phrase, saying, slogan, style, wording

n 5 cycle, duration, interval, period, season, span, spell, stage, stretch, time

v 1 call, define, designate, entitle, name

v 2 baptize, bestow, call, christen, confer, designate, dub, entitle, name, nickname, tag, title

terminal *adj* 1 concluding, conclusive, final, last, ultimate

adj 2 hopeless, impossible, incurable, irreparable, irresolvable, irrevocable, permanent, unalterable, uncorrectable, uncurable, unfixable

n console, CRT, monitor, screen

terminate *v* 1 abort, erase, kill, sever, stop

v 2 drop, go, leave, quit, resign

v 3 cease, die, elapse, expire, lapse, pass, pass away, perish

v 4 achieve, cease, complete, conclude, consummate, end, finish, halt, perfect, wind up, wrap up

v 5 ax, boot, bounce, can, discharge, dismiss, drop, fire, impeach, let go

v 6 adjourn, cap, climax, complete, conclude, consummate, crown, culminate, dissolve, end, finalize, finish, wind up, wrap up

v 7 abstain, cease, conclude, desist, discontinue, end, finish, forbear, freeze, halt, knock off, quit, refrain, sever, stop

v 8 abate, abolish, abrogate, annihilate, annul, call off, cancel, cease, delete, destroy, efface, erase, excise, expunge, invalidate, kill, negate, nullify, obliterate, omit, quash, remove, stop, wipe out

terminated *adj* accomplished, complete, concluded, done, ended, finished, over, performed, through, wrapped up

termination *n* 1 ceasing, cessation, close, closure, conclusion, end, finale, finis, finish

n 2 dismissal, ejection, expulsion, extraction, firing, impeachment, ouster

terminology *n* buzzwords, jargon, lexicons, lingo, nomenclature, terms, vocabulary

terms *n* 1 buzzwords, jargon, lexicons, lingo, terminology, vocabulary

n 2 agreement, clause, condition, provision, proviso, requirement, reservation, specification, stipulation, string

terra *n* clay, dirt, dry land, dust, earth, ground, land, loam, marl, soil, terra firma

terrace *n* lanai, patio, porch, veranda

terrarium *n* aquarium, menagerie, zoo

terrestrial *adj* common, earthly, earthy, mundane, pedestrian, uncelestial, worldly

terrible *adj* 1 awful, frightful, grim, grisly, gruesome, hideous, lurid, repulsive, sensational, shocking, ugly, violent

adj 2 appalling, awful, dire, dreadful, fearful, formidable, frightening, frightful,

ghastly, horrendous, horrible, offensive, ominous, portentous, scary, shocking, spooky, terrifying, unpleasant

adj 3 see: VIOLENT *adj* 3

terribly *adv* awfully, dreadfully, eminently, endlessly, exceedingly, exceptionally, extremely, greatly, highly, mightily, notably, quite, thoroughly, very

terrific *adj* 1 admirable, beautiful, delightful, glorious, good, magnificent, peachy, wonderful

adj 2 excellent, fabulous, fantastic, fine, good, great, marvelous, super, tremendous, wonderful

terrified *adj* afraid, aghast, anxious, apprehensive, concerned, discerning, fearful, frightened, nervous, paranoid, scared, scary, worried

terrify *v* 1 appall, daunt, discourage, dismay, horrify, panic, petrify, scare, shock, unnerve

v 2 abash, alarm, awe, cow, daunt, frighten, horrify, intimidate, panic, scare, shock, spook, startle, terrorize, unnerve

terrifying *adj* appalling, awful, dire, dreadful, fearful, formidable, frightening, frightful, ghastly, horrendous, horrible, offensive, ominous, portentous, scary, shocking, spooky, terrible, unpleasant

territory *n* 1 domain, dominion, field, kingdom, province, realm

n 2 area, arena, belt, field, realm, region, section, space, tract, turf, zone

terror *n* 1 affliction, alarm, anxiety, apprehension, care, consternation, dismay, dread, fear, fright, horror, ordeal, panic, trepidation, trial, trouble, worry

n 2 fright, horror, scare, shock

terrorism *n* rebellion

terrorize *v* 1 alarm, attack, bully, club, coerce, frighten, harass, intimidate, menace, strong-arm, threaten

v 2 abash, alarm, awe, cow, daunt, frighten, horrify, intimidate, panic, scare, shock, spook, startle, terrify, unnerve

terse *adj* 1 austere, economical, sparse

adj 2 abbreviated, brief, compressed, concise, crisp, curt, laconic, pithy, short, succinct, to the point

test *adj* developmental, experimental, pilot, suggested, tentative, trial, untested

n 1 benchmark, criterion, guideline, measure

n 2 analysis, assay, examination, experiment

n 3 exam, examination, final, inquiry, oral, questionnaire, quiz *n* 4 demo, example, first, forerunner, model, prototype

v 1 determine, evaluate, judge, try, verify

v 2 see: PROBE *v* 5

testament *n* 1 will

n 2 approval, confirmation, doctrine, enactment, evidence, passage, proof, testimony, witness

tested *adj* 1 dependable, fail-safe, infallible, reliable, sure, tried

adj 2 authentic, certified, confirmed, demonstrated, proved, tried, verified

testify *v* affirm, bear witness, declare, depose, profess, swear

testimonial *n* recommendation, reference

testimony *n* 1 affidavit, attestation, deposition, statement

n 2 approval, confirmation, doctrine, enactment, evidence, passage, proof, testament, witness

testing *n* analysis, digging, experimentation, exploration, inquiry, inquisition, investigation, research, study, trial

testy *adj* 1 angry, cranky, cross, feisty, grouchy, hot-tempered, irascible, ireful, peppery, quick-tempered, short-fused, touchy

adj 2 abrupt, bluff, blunt, brash, brusque, cheeky, crusty, curt, flip, flippant, gruff, harsh, impertinent, impudent, irritable, nasty, quick, rude, sarcastic, sassy, short, snippy, snotty, surly, wisenheimer

tête-à-tête *n* conference, meeting, parley, powwow

tether *n* bridle, check, cord, leash, restraint, rope

v attach, bind, bond, cord, fasten, hitch, join, link, marry, tie, tie up

text *n* 1 document

n 2 argument, controversy, issue, item, matter, motif, motive, point, proposition, question, subject, theme, topic

n 3 book, correspondence, edition, folio, issue, manuscript, monograph, opus, paperback, printing, publication, tome, volume, work, writing

textbook *n* atlas, compendium, directory, guide, guidebook, handbook, list, listing, manual, phone book, Yellow Pages

texture *n* exploration, feel, feeling, sensation, touch

thank *v* acknowledge, applaud, appreciate, approve, clap, recognize

thankful *adj* appreciative, grateful, indebted, obligated

thankfulness *n* appreciation, gratitude

thankless *adj* heedless, unappreciative, unaware, ungrateful

thaw *v* 1 relent, soften

v 2 dissolve, flux, fuse, liquefy, melt, run

theater *n* 1 arena, locale, scene

n 2 assembly hall, auditorium, hall, playhouse

n 3 Broadway, comedy, drama, extravaganza, musical, production, stage

theatrical *adj* 1 dramatic, melodramatic, sensational, thrilling

adj 2 artificial, corny, exaggerated, pretentious, staged

theatrics *n* drama, melodrama, mystery, tragedy, tragicomedy

theft *n* 1 burglary, larceny, looting, plagiarism, robbery, thievery

n 2 heist, holdup, robbery

theme *n* 1 drift, strain, subject, thread

n 2 center, core, gist, kernel

n 3 argument, controversy, issue, item, matter, motif, motive, point, proposition, question, subject, text, topic

n 4 see: ESSAY *n*

theology *n* affiliation, belief, church, creed, denomination, faith, persuasion, religion, rite

theorem *n* 1 assumption, foundation, ground rule, postulate, premise, proposition

n 2 expression, formula, methodology, plan, procedure, recipe, system

theoretical *adj* 1 abstract, conjectural, general, hypothetical, ideal, illustrative, speculative, symbolic

adj 2 academic

adj 3 absurd, chancy, debatable, doubtful, dubious, iffy, implausible, improbable, incredible, moot, preposterous, questionable, unbelievable, uncertain, unlikely

theorization *n* assumption, conclusion, conjecture, discretion, estimate, guess, judgment, notion

theorize *v* allude, assume, extend, hypothesize, imagine, offer, pose, present, presume, propose, speculate, suggest, suppose

theory *n* 1 belief, canon, code, conviction, creed, doctrine, dogma, law, opinion, principle, rule

n 2 assumption, conjecture, deduction, explanation, guess, hypothesis, inference, postulate, presumption, proposition, speculation, supposition

therapeutic *adj* curative, healing, medical, medicinal

therapist *n* attendant, medic, nurse

therapy *n* 1 antidote, cure, medication,

medicine, panacea, prescription, remedy, treatment

n 2 cure, treatment

thereafter *adv* afterward, later, subsequently

thesaurus *n* dictionary, glossary, lexicon, list, synonym finder, synonym listing, vocabulary, Word Finder®

thesis *n* 1 argument, demonstration, proof

n 2 article, composition, discourse, dissertation, essay, manuscript, memoir, monograph, paper, report, study, theme, tract, treatise, work

thespian *n* actor, actress, artist, entertainer, hero, heroine, lead, movie star, performer, player, protagonist, star, tragedian

thick *adj* 1 abundant, fattening, heavy, rich

adj 2 close, compact, crowded, dense, solid, tight

adj 3 coagulated

adj 4 sticky, tacky

adj 5 choice, deluxe, elegant, first-class, grand, luxuriant, luxurious, opulent, ornate, palatial, plush, posh, rich, soft, stately

adj 6 backward, blunt, deficient, dense, dimwitted, dull, dumb, feebleminded, idiotic, moronic, obtuse, retarded, simple, simple-minded, slow, stupid, uneducated, unintelligent

thicken *v* clog, clot, coagulate, condense, congeal, curdle, dry, gel, harden, intensify, jell, pack, set, solidify

thicket *n* copse, grove, shrubbery

thief *n* bandit, brigand, burglar, cheat, con artist, con man, criminal, crook, embezzler, gyp, highwayman, looter, mugger, outlaw, robber

thieve *v* see: STEAL *v* 2

thievery *n* burglary, larceny, looting, plagiarism, robbery, theft

thin *adj* 1 watery

adj 2 delicate, filmy, fine, flimsy, sheer, transparent

adj 3 lank, narrow, skinny, slender, slight, slim, tenuous, veiled, wiry

adj 4 angular, bony, emaciated, gaunt, lanky, lean, meager, scraggly, scrawny, skinny, slender

adj 5 attenuate, diminished, lessened, rarefied, subtle, tenuous

adj 6 breakable, decrepit, delicate, dilapidated, feeble, flimsy, fragile, frail, jerry-built, jury-rigged, puny, Rube Goldberg, shoddy, sickly, tinny, unsound, worn-out

thing *n* 1 article, element, entity, item, object

n 2 being, entity, object, organism, sum, system, totality, whole

n 3 circumstance, episode, event, happening, incident, occasion, occurrence

n 4 chic, craze, fad, fashion, mode, rage, style, trend, vogue

n 5 cause, issue

n 6 accomplishment, achievement, acquirement, act, action, battle, deed, doing, event, exploit, feat, stunt, trick

n 7 art, avocation, business, calling, career, discipline, employment, field, gig, job, labor, line, livelihood, occupation, office, profession, pursuit, role, schtick, situation, specialty, task, trade, vocation, work

things *n* 1 contents, junk, objects, scrap, stuff, substance

n 2 belongings, property

thingumajig *n* see: DEVICE *n* 3

think *v* 1 conceive, conjecture, conjure up, create, envision, fancy, image, imagine, invent, project, visualize

v 2 cerebrate, chew, consider, contemplate, deliberate, digest, meditate, mull, muse, ponder, reason, reflect, ruminate, see, speculate, study, weigh

v 3 assume, believe, comprehend, conceive, estimate, expect, fathom, gather, grasp, guess, imagine, infer, know, presume, suppose, surmise, suspect, trust, understand

v 4 see: ARGUE *v* 2

thinker *n* academician, egghead, highbrow, intellectual, philosopher, pundit, researcher, sage, savant, scholar, wise man

thinking *adj* 1 meditative, pensive, philosophical, pondering, reflective, thoughtful

adj 2 see: AWARE *adj* 3

n 1 knowledge, laws, philosophy, principles, wisdom

n 2 analysis, cogitation, consideration, contemplation, deliberation, logic, meditation, reason, reasoning, reflection, speculation, study, thought

thirst *v* see: CRAVE *v* 4

thirsty *adj* arid, dry, parched, waterless

thong *n* boot, brogan, chukka, footwear, moccasin, sandal, shoe

thorough *adj* 1 careful, diligent, rigorous, studious

adj 2 complete, comprehensive, exhaustive, unabridged

adj 3 deliberate, dilatory, diligent, leisurely, methodical, meticulous, painstaking, patient, procrastinating, slow, unhasty, unhurried

thoroughfare *n* access, approach, artery, avenue, boulevard, channel, drag, highway, pass, path, promenade, road, roadway, route, strait, street, trail, way

thoroughly *adv* 1 awfully, dreadfully, eminently, endlessly, exceedingly, exceptionally, extremely, greatly, highly, mightily, notably, quite, remarkably, terribly, very

adv 2 adequately, altogether, assiduously, completely, earnestly, entirely, exhaustively, fully, hard, intensely, intensively, painstakingly, perfectly, quite, sufficiently, totally, unremittingly, utterly, wholly

thoroughness *n* rigor

though *adv* at any rate, but, however, moreover, nevertheless, nonetheless, notwithstanding, yet

thought *n* 1 concept, conception, hunch, idea, image, impression, notion, perception, recollection, view

n 2 analysis, cogitation, consideration, contemplation, deliberation, logic, meditation, reason, reasoning, reflection, speculation, study

thoughtful *adj* 1 attentive, considerate, generous, kind, unselfish

adj 2 meditative, pensive, philosophical, pondering, reflective, speculative, thinking

thoughtfulness *n* consideration, diplomacy, discretion, poise, regard, savoir-faire, tact

thoughtless *adj* 1 hasty, inconsiderate, indiscreet, tactless

adj 2 clumsy, gauche, indiscreet, insensitive, tactless

adj 3 caustic, inconsiderate, selfish, sharp, short, tactless, unceremonious, ungracious

adj 4 accidental, careless, caustic, heedless, inadvertent, inconsiderate, nonchalant, selfish, sharp, short, tactless, uncaring, unceremonious, ungracious, unheeding, unintended, unintentional, unreflective, unthinking

adj 5 see: SILLY *adj* 2

thrash *v* 1 beat, belittle, blast, clobber, conquer, cream, defeat, dust, lambaste, lick, overrun, overwhelm, rout, shellac, smear, wallop, whip

v 2 see: BATTER *v*

thrashing *n* debacle, defeat, disaster, downfall, overthrow, rout, ruination, trouncing, undoing, vanquishment

thread *n* 1 drift, subject, theme

n 2 cable, cord, fiber, hemp, lanyard, line, rope, strand, string, twine, yarn

threadbare *adj* 1 faded, frayed, poor, run-down, shabby, worn

adj 2 banal, boring, clichéd, commonplace, corny, dull, hackneyed, musty, redundant, repetitious, repetitive, stale, tedious, timeworn, tired, tiresome, trite, worn out

threat *n* 1 danger, downside, exposure, hazard, jeopardy, liability, menace, peril, risk

n 2 fulmination, harassment, intimidation, warning

threaten *v* 1 alarm, attack, bully, club, coerce, frighten, harass, intimidate, menace, strong-arm

v 2 see: ANNOY *v* 3

threatened *adj* anxious, insecure, nervous, precarious, uncertain, vulnerable

threatening *adj* 1 bullying, coercive, forceful, menacing, strong-arm

adj 2 any second, immediate, imminent, impending, looming, momentary, poised

adj 3 foreboding, imminent, impending, menacing, ominous, portentous, predictive, prophetic

threesome *n* trilogy, trinity, trio, triplets, triumvirate

threshold *n* frontier, hinterland, outback

thrift *n* economy, frugality, moderation

thrifty *adj* canny, conservative, economical, frugal, provident, sparing, spartan, stewardly, unwasteful

thrill *n* see: PASSION *n* 7

v arouse, electrify, excite, fire, incite, inspire, rouse, spark, stimulate, tantalize, titillate, turn on, whet

thrilled *adj* delighted, ecstatic, elated, enchanted

thriller *n* cliff-hanger, melodrama, soap opera

thrilling *adj* 1 dramatic, melodramatic, sensational

adj 2 dynamic, electrifying, exciting, inspiring, stimulating

thrills *n* enjoyment, excitement, kicks, pleasure

thrive *v* 1 arrive, flourish, go, make out, prosper, score, succeed

v 2 advance, ascend, bloom, climb, develop, do well, excel, expand, flourish, flower, get ahead, grow, improve, progress, prosper, rise, strive, survive

thriving *adj* affluent, booming, prosperous, wealthy

throb *v* 1 beat, flutter, palpitate, pulsate, pulse, quiver, tremble, vibrate

v 2 fluctuate, oscillate, pulsate, surge, undulate, vibrate

throng n band, bunch, crew, crowd, drove, flock, following, gaggle, gang, herd, huddle, mass, mob, pack, rabble, riffraff, swarm

v crowd, herd, jam, mob, press, push, swarm, teem

throttle v 1 check, cramp, curtail, impede, shorten

v 2 bar, block, brake, choke, clog, dam, deter, detract, encumber, frustrate, halt, hamper, hesitate, hinder, impair, impede, inhibit, jam, obstruct, prevent, repress, restrain, retard, slow, stay, stop up

v 3 gun, rev, speed

v 4 censor, curb, gag, hush, inhibit, muffle, mute, quell, quiet, repress, restrain, silence, squelch, stifle, still, subdue, suppress, tone down

n choke

through adj accomplished, complete, concluded, done, ended, finished, over, performed, terminated, wrapped up

throw n attempt, chance, effort, fling, go, guess, heave, lob, pop, shot, slap, sling, stab, toss, try, whirl

v 1 bounce, bump, jostle, skip, volley

v 2 cast, flick, fling, flip, heave, hurl, launch, pitch, propel, sling, toss

v 3 buck, unseat

throwback n belief, custom, doctrine, mores, relic, rite, tradition

thrust n 1 ambition, drive, enterprise, initiative, lead, leadership, push, volition

n 2 jab, punch, swing

v 1 boost, budge, drive, force, impel, nudge, propel, push

v 2 attack, butt, drive, knock, lunge, pass, plunge, ram, sink, stab, stick

thug n gorilla, hoodlum, hooligan, punk, roughneck, rowdy, ruffian, tough

thump v 1 bang, crack, pop

v 2 drive, hammer, impress, imprint, mark, pound, press, print, stamp, strike, whack

thunder n 1 bark, bellow, blare, holler, roar, scream, shout, yell

n 2 bang, boom, clang, clap, crash, resound, roar, rumble

v bark, bellow, blare, call, cry, holler, howl, roar, scream, screech, shout, shriek, shrill, squeal, wail, yell

thunderbolt n bolt, fireball, flash, lightning

thwart v 1 baffle, confound, confuse, frustrate, perplex

v 2 counter, counterbalance, negate, neutralize, nullify

v 3 avert, bar, deter, eliminate, foil, fore-

stall, hinder, hold off, inhibit, preclude, prevent, stave off, turn back, ward off

v 4 aggravate, baffle, balk, bewilder, circumvent, confuse, dash, elude, foil, frustrate, hamper, impede, negate, nullify, perplex

ticket n 1 admission, cover charge, entrance fee, fee

n 2 identification, pass, passport, permit, visa

n 3 citation, notification, subpoena, summons, warrant, writ

n 4 badge, card, label, pass, tag, voucher

tickle v delight, please

ticklish adj 1 sensitive, tender, touchy

adj 2 dangerous, delicate, fluctuating, hazardous, precarious, rickety, risky, rocky, sensitive, shaky, tender, touchy, tricky, unpredictable, unstable, wobbly

tidbit n 1 sample, taste

n 2 bit, dab, end, fragment, iota, minutia, mite, morsel, particle, piece, pinch, portion, scrap, shred, speck, spot, strip, trifle

tide n change, current, drift, flow, flux, gush, motion, movement, rush, stream, transition

tidy adj meticulous, neat, orderly, prim, shipshape, trim, well-groomed

v arrange, neaten, organize, pick up

tie adj even, exact

n 1 affiliation, allegiance, association, connection

n 2 bond, chain, fetter, handcuff, iron, shackle

n 3 bottleneck, deadlock, draw, hung jury, impasse, stalemate, standoff, standstill

n 4 ascot, cravat, necktie

v 1 equal, match, measure up, meet, rival, touch

v 2 band, belt, bind, corset, fasten, gird, girdle, lash, strap

v 3 attach, bind, bond, cord, fasten, hitch, join, link, marry, tether, tie up

v 4 clump, fasten, hitch, join, knot, lace, lash, link, loop, rope, secure, unite

v 5 bind, clog, confine, curb, fetter, hamper, handcuff, hold, leash, limit, restrain, restrict, shackle, tie up

tier n 1 caste, layer, ply, rank, row, stratum

n 2 floor, ground, level, story

tiff n altercation, argument, battle, brawl, challenge, combat, controversy, disagreement, discord, dispute, feud, fight, fracas, fray, hassle, melee, quarrel, rancor, rift, row, ruckus, scrap, scuffle, skirmish, spat, squabble, struggle, war

tiger n cat, feline, kit, kitten, kitty, puss, pussy

tight *adv* fast, firm, firmly, hard, loyally, reliably, solidly, tightly

adj 1 compact, definitive, meaty, pithy

adj 2 firm, hard, taut, tense

adj 3 close, compact, crowded, dense, solid

adj 4 attached, fast, firm, fixed, rigid, secure, set, taut

adj 5 compact, firm, hard, hardened, rigid, secure, solid, sound, specific, stable

adj 6 cheap, close, greedy, mean, miserly, niggardly, parsimonious, penny-pinching, stingy, tightfisted, ungenerous, ungiving

adj 7 bombed, crocked, doped up, drunk, drunken, high, inebriated, intoxicated, juiced, loaded, looped, messed up, plastered, polluted, sloshed, smashed, stoned, tipsy, turned on, wasted, wired

tighten *v* draw, flex, pull, strain, stretch, tense, twist

tightfisted *adj* see: CHEAP *adj* 3

tightly *adv* fast, firm, firmly, hard, loyally, reliably, solidly

till *v* cultivate, farm, grow, harvest, plant, plow, produce

tilt *n* angle, grade, gradient, incline, pitch, ramp, slant, slope

v 1 cant, careen, heel, incline, list, rear, roll

v 2 angle, arch, bend, bow, curve, flex, ply, round, tip, turn, twist, vault

timber *n* beam, board, boom, girder, log, plank, rafter, spar

timbre *n* 1 resonance, tone, vibration

n 2 see: MOOD *n* 4

time *n* 1 instant, occasion

n 2 duration, hold, interval, length, occupancy, term

n 3 beat, cadence, cycle, lilt, pulse, rate, rhythm

n 4 break, chance, crack, gap, occasion, opening, opportunity, shot, show

n 5 cycle, duration, interval, period, season, span, spell, stage, term

n 6 aeon, age, cycle, decade, eon, epoch, era, eternity, forever, long time, millennium, period, reign, span, stage, years

timeless *adj* see: PERPETUAL *adj* 2

timelessly *adv* see: FOREVER *adv*

timely *adj* 1 auspicious, favorable, opportune, propitious, seasonable

adj 2 dependable, observant, on time, precise, prompt, punctual

adj 3 contiguous, current, direct, immediate, instant, nearby, primary, prompt

adj 4 see: APPLICABLE *adj*

timeout *n* abeyance, cease-fire, respite, truce

timepiece *n* chronometer, clock, hourglass, stopwatch, timer, watch

timer *n* chronometer, clock, hourglass, stopwatch, watch

timetable *n* rate

timeworn *adj* 1 banal, boring, clichéd, commonplace, corny, dull, hackneyed, musty, redundant, repetitious, repetitive, stale, tedious, threadbare, tired, tiresome, trite, worn out

adj 2 see: OLD *adj* 2

timid *adj* 1 timorous

adj 2 backward, bashful, coy, demure, diffident, innocent, modest, quiet, reserved, retiring, shy, staid, unassured

adj 3 closed, diffident, introverted, laconic, reserved, restrained, reticent, secretive, shy, subdued, taciturn, timorous, uncommunicative, undaring

adj 4 chicken, cowardly, fearful, gutless, spineless, yellow

adj 5 afraid, averse, disinclined, hesitant, indisposed, loath, opposed, recalcitrant, reluctant, shy, uneager, unwilling

timing *n* 1 execution

n 2 line, order, priority, procession, sequence

timorous *adj* 1 timid

adj 2 see: RETICENT *adj* 2

tin *n* bottle, bucket, caddy, can, canister, jar, pail, vessel

tincture *n* color, coloring, dye, paint, pigment, stain, tint

tinge *n* 1 cast, color, hue, shade, tint, tone

n 2 see: TRACE *n* 4

v color, dye, paint, stain, tint

tingle *n* flutter, quake, quiver, shiver, tremor

tingling *adj* exciting, exotic, inspiring, interesting, intriguing, provocative, stimulating, titillating

tiniest *adj* first, least, lowest, minimum, smallest

tinker *v* dabble, dally, diddle, fiddle, fool, monkey, piddle, play, poke about, putter, toy, trifle

tinny *adj* see: FRAGILE *adj* 3

tinsel *adj* see: OSTENTATIOUS *adj* 1

tint *n* 1 cast, color, hue, shade, tinge, tone

n 2 color, coloring, dye, paint, pigment, stain

v color, dye, paint, stain

tiny *adj* 1 bantam, dainty, diminutive, dwarfish, Lilliputian, little, micro, microscopic, midget, mini, miniature, minuscule, minute, petite, pygmy, slight, small, wee

adj 2 see: TRIVIAL *adj* 1

tip *n* 1 edge, end, nib, nub

n 2 ante, award, bonus, booty, cash, commission, dividend, donation, fee, gift, gratuity, largess, money, percentage, perk, perquisite, premium, prize, profit, purse, reward, sharing, stake, stipend, winnings

n 3 ass, backside, base, behind, bottom, bucket, buns, butt, buttocks, derrière, end, fanny, hindquarters, posterior, rump, seat, stub, stump, tush

n 4 acme, apex, apogee, climax, crescendo, crest, crown, culmination, epitome, height, noon, peak, pinnacle, point, prime, summit, top, ultimate, utmost, zenith

n 5 breath, clue, dash, glimmer, hint, insinuation, lick, shade, smell, smidgen, spice, sprinkling, suggestion, suspicion, tinge, touch, trace, trifle, whiff, whisper, wisp

n 6 see: CLUE *n* 2

v 1 alert, divulge, tip off, warn

v 2 bequeath, endow, give, remember

v 3 angle, arch, bend, bow, curve, flex, ply, round, tilt, turn, twist, vault

tip off *v* alert, divulge, warn

tipsy *adj* bombed, crocked, doped up, drunk, drunken, high, inebriated, intoxicated, juiced, loaded, loose, messed up, plastered, polluted, sloshed, smashed, stoned, tight, turned on, wasted, wired

tirade *n* see: REPRIMAND *n*

tire *v* 1 bore, pall, weary

v 2 drain, exhaust, fatigue, jade, wear down, wear out, weary

tired *adj* 1 dozing, drowsy, lethargic, napping, nodding, sleepy, slumberous, snoozy

adj 2 banal, boring, clichéd, commonplace, corny, dull, hackneyed, musty, redundant, repetitious, repetitive, stale, tedious, threadbare, timeworn, tiresome, trite, worn out

adj 3 beat, burnt out, bushed, careworn, drawn, emaciated, exhausted, expended, fatigued, frazzled, haggard, jaded, pinched, pooped, run-down, shot, spent, wearied, weary, worn, worn down, worn out

adj 4 bored, disgusted, jaded, sick, weary

tiresome *adj* 1 endless, slow, tedious

adj 2 banal, boring, clichéd, commonplace, corny, dull, hackneyed, musty, redundant, repetitious, repetitive, stale,

tedious, threadbare, timeworn, tired, trite, worn out

adj 3 see: MONOTONOUS *adj* 1

tissue *n* coating, covering, film, layer, membrane

Titanic *adj* colossal, enormous, fantastic, Gargantuan, giant, gigantic, Goliath, great, huge, immense, jumbo, leviathan, mammoth, massive, mighty, monstrous, monumental, overwhelming, phenomenal, prodigious, Promethean, stupendous, towering, tremendous, unfathomed, untold, vast, walloping, whopping

titillate *v* 1 arouse, awaken, excite, induce, instill, motivate, move, pique, prime, provoke, quicken, rouse, roust, spark, start, stimulate, urge

v 2 arouse, electrify, excite, fire, incite, inspire, rouse, spark, stimulate, tantalize, thrill, turn on, whet

titillated *adj* see: EROTIC *adj* 3

titillating *adj* exciting, exotic, inspiring, interesting, intriguing, provocative, stimulating

title *n* 1 document, paper

n 2 alias, designation, handle, moniker, name

n 3 advantage, birthright, claim, edge, enablement, perquisite, prerogative, right

n 4 ownership, possession

v baptize, bestow, call, christen, confer, designate, dub, entitle, name, nickname, tag

to *prep* 1 into

prep 2 in the direction of, toward

toast *v* 1 bake, broil, burn, char, cook, melt, parch, roast, scorch, sear, singe, swelter, warm

v 2 acclaim, applaud, celebrate, commend, eulogize, exalt, extol, glorify, hail, honor, laud, praise, resound, salute, tout, worship

n commemoration, drink, salutation

today *adv* currently, presently

n current time, moment, now, nowadays, present

to-do *n* see: ACTIVITY *n* 3

together *adv* 1 concurrently, simultaneously

adv 2 as one, collectively, in unison, jointly, mutually

adv 3 collectively, cooperatively, helpfully, jointly

togetherness *n* bond, cohesion, connection, fusion, solidarity, union

togs *n* accoutrements, apparel, attire, clothes, clothing, dress, garments

toil *n* **1** chore, drudgery, grind, labor, slavery, sweat, tedium, travail, work

   n **2** effort, elbow grease, exertion, labor, pains, strain, struggle, trouble, try, work

   v **1** lumber, persevere, persist, plod, plug

   v **2** drudge, grub, hustle, labor, slave, strain, strive, sweat, work

toilet *n* bathroom, can, head, john, latrine, lavatory, loo, potty, powder room, water closet, wc

token *adj* hollow, nominal, perfunctory, professed, representative, small, symbolic

   n **1** nod, sign, signal, symbol, symptom, trait

   n **2** assurance, bond, commitment, earnest, guarantee, obligation, pawn, pledge, security, surety, warrant

   n **3** antique, gift, heirloom, keepsake, memento, memorial, relic, remembrance, reminder, souvenir, trophy

   n **4** character, emblem, example, icon, letter, logo, mark, model, sign, symbol

tolerable *adj* **1** allowable, bearable, endurable

   adj **2** see: ADEQUATE *adj* 2

tolerably *adv* adequately, amply, enough, equitably, fairly, justly, moderately, passably, rather

tolerance *n* **1** clemency, forbearance, indulgence, lenience, leniency, mercifulness, mercy, toleration

   n **2** backbone, chutzpah, determination, endurance, fortitude, grit, guts, moxie, nerve, persistence, pluck, resilience, spirit, spunk, stamina, strength, tenacity, vigor, willpower

tolerant *adj* **1** advanced, broad, broadminded, liberal, progressive, radical, unbiased

   adj **2** accepting, charitable, easy, forbearing, indulgent, lenient, merciful, patient, restrained

   adj **3** acquiescent, compliant, docile, easy, meek, mild, nonresistant, obedient, passive, resigned, submissive, tame, unassertive, yielding

tolerate *v* abide, accept, acquiesce, allow, authorize, bear, concede, condone, digest, endure, experience, have, let, permit, put up with, stand, stomach, suffer, sustain, swallow, take, undergo

toleration *n* clemency, forbearance, indulgence, lenience, leniency, mercifulness, tolerance

toll *n* assessment, cost, duty, expense, fee, impost, levy, offering, penalty, price, sacrifice, tariff, tax, trade off

v boom, chime, clang, peal, resonate, resound, reverberate, ring

tomahawk *n* ax

tomb *n* burial, catacomb, cenotaph, crypt, grave, mausoleum, memorial, monument, pit, sepulcher, vault

tome *n* book, correspondence, edition, folio, issue, manuscript, monograph, opus, paperback, printing, publication, text, volume, work, writing

tomorrow *adv* henceforth

   n future, outlook, posterity

ton *n* abundance, glut, great deal, lot, much

tone *n* **1** resonance, timbre, vibration

   n **2** frequency, level, pitch, sound

   n **3** cast, color, hue, shade, tinge

   n **4** fashion, flavor, manner, mode, style, vein

   n **5** attitude, disposition, feeling, humor, mind, mood, spirit, temper, timbre, vein

   n **6** characteristic, flavor, impression, nature, property, quality, ring, sound, tendency, type

tongue *n* accent, brogue, dialect, patois

   v lap, lick

too *adv* additionally, also, and, as well, as well as, besides, further, furthermore, in addition, likewise, moreover, plus

tool *n* **1** chessman, front, instrument, pawn, peon, puppet

   n **2** apparatus, appliance, contraption, contrivance, device, doodad, doohickey, gadget, gimmick, gizmo, implement, instrument, invention, machine, mechanism, thingumajig, utensil, widget

   v auger, bore, drill, pierce

tooth *n* digger, fang, gasher, molar, tush, tusk

top *adj* **1** best, optimum, prime, select

   adj **2** foremost, majority, maximum, most, optimal, unequaled

   adj **3** best, biggest, finest, greatest, largest, maximum, most, number one, prime, select, superior, top-notch

   adj **4** champion, excellent, fine, first-class, first-rate, foremost, good, grade A, leading, number one, prime, principal, prominent, quality, select, stellar, superb, superior, top-drawer, top-notch, tops

   adj **5** see: FOREMOST *adj* 3, 4

   adj **6** see: PRIMARY *adj* 4, 5

   n **1** bow, crown, fore, front, head, prow

   n **2** roof

   n **3** cap, cork, cover, lid, plate

   n **4** acme, apex, apogee, climax, crescendo, crest, crown, culmination, epitome, height, noon, peak, pinnacle, point, prime, summit, tip, ultimate, utmost, zenith

v 1 crest, crown, peak

v 2 beat, best, better, cap, dwarf, eclipse, exceed, excel, go beyond, outdo, outgo, outshine, outstrip, overshadow, pass, surpass, transcend

top-drawer adj champion, excellent, fine, first-class, first-rate, foremost, good, grade A, leading, number one, prime, principal, prominent, quality, select, stellar, superb, superior, top, top-notch, tops

topic n argument, controversy, issue, item, matter, motif, motive, point, proposition, question, subject, text

top-notch adj champion, excellent, fine, first-class, first-rate, foremost, good, grade A, leading, number one, prime, principal, prominent, quality, select, stellar, superb, superior, top, top-drawer, tops

topple v 1 cave in, collapse, disintegrate, drop, fall, go down, keel over, pitch, plunge, slump, spill, tumble

v 2 ax, cut down, fell, knock down, raze

v 3 capsize, collapse, defeat, dislodge, knock over, overthrow, overturn, tip over, tumble, turn over, upset

tops adj champion, excellent, fine, first-class, first-rate, foremost, good, grade A, leading, number one, prime, principal, prominent, quality, select, stellar, superb, superior, top, top-drawer

torment n 1 crack, gibe, jeer, put-down, quip, shot

n 2 see: PAIN n 4

v 1 castigate, chasten, chastise, discipline, punish

v 2 see: ANNOY v 3

tormented adj anxious, careworn, distracted, distraught, distressed, frantic, harassed, troubled, upset, worried

torpedo v see: REJECT v 7

torpid adj 1 apathetic, indifferent, languid

adj 2 dormant, inert, lethargic, numb, sluggish

torrent n 1 deluge, flood, overflow, submersion, surge

n 2 abundance

torrid adj 1 amorous, ardent, aroused, carnal, earthy, erotic, fervent, fleshly, horny, hot, impassioned, lascivious, lecherous, lewd, licentious, lustful, passionate, provocative, randy, raunchy, romantic, sensual, sexual, sexy, sultry, titillated, turned on, voluptuous, wanton

adj 2 baking, blistering, boiling, broiling, burning, fiery, hot, scalding, scorching, sizzling, sultry

adj 3 ardent, enthusiastic, excitable, fervent, fiery, flaming, hot-blooded, impassioned, intense, passionate, stirring, sweaty, zealous

torture n ache, affliction, agony, anguish, hurt, injury, pain, punishment

v 1 deform, distort, misshape, warp

v 2 aggrieve, exploit, oppress

toss n attempt, chance, effort, fling, go, guess, heave, lob, pop, shot, slap, sling, stab, throw, try, whirl

v 1 beat, blend, mingle, mix, stir, whip

v 2 bob, heave, pitch, rock, roll, sway

v 3 careen, lurch, pitch, reel, stagger, sway, totter, wheel

v 4 cast, flick, fling, flip, heave, hurl, launch, pitch, propel, throw

tot n babe, baby, child, infant, newborn, tyke

total adj 1 all, all-out, complete, entire, full-blown, gross, integral, integrated, outright, unlimited, whole

adj 2 see: UTTER adj

n 1 count, record, score, tally

n 2 amount, balance, count, result, sum

n 3 aggregate, amount, body, budget, bulk, count, number, quantity

n 4 aggregate, all, entirety, gross, revenue, sales, sum, sum total, totality, whole

n 5 agglomerate, agglomeration, aggregate, conglomerate, mass

v aggregate, amount, number, plus, sum

totality n 1 being, entity, object, organism, sum, system, thing, whole

n 2 aggregate, all, entirety, gross, revenue, sales, sum, sum total, total, whole

totally adv adequately, altogether, assiduously, completely, earnestly, entirely, exhaustively, fully, hard, intensely, intensively, painstakingly, perfectly, quite, sufficiently, thoroughly, unremittingly, utterly, wholly

tote v bear, carry, convey, crate, ferry, haul, lift, lug, pack, shoulder, shuttle, traffic, transport, truck

totter v 1 careen, lurch, pitch, reel, stagger, sway, toss, wheel

v 2 fall, lurch, skid, skim, slide, slip, stumble, trip, tumble

touch n 1 handling

n 2 caress, embrace, fondling, hug, kiss

n 3 exploration, feel, feeling, palpation, sensation, texture *n* 4 degree, distinction, enhancement, nuance, shade, subtlety, trace, variation

n 5 see: CLASH *n* 2

n 6 see: TRACE *n* 4

v 1 dab, paint, pat, tap

v 2 equal, match, measure up, meet, rival

v 3 benefit, experience, have, partake, use

v 4 buzz, call, communicate, contact, phone, ring

v 5 backfire, boomerang, bounce, brush, glance, graze, rebound, ricochet, skim

v 6 examine, feel, finger, fondle, grope, handle, manipulate, maul, palpate, paw

v 7 brush, graze, scrape, scratch, shave

v 8 affect, assure, convince, impel, induce, influence, inspire, instigate, motivate, move, persuade, pressure, prompt, stir, sway, talk into, win over

touched *adj* see: ABSURD *adj* 2

touching *adj* 1 intimate, moving, romantic

adj 2 affecting, heartbreaking, impressive, moving, poignant

adj 3 abutting, adjacent, adjoining, alongside, bordering, close by, connected, contiguous, juxtaposed, local, near at hand, nearby, neighboring, outlining, regional, verging on

touchy *adj* 1 sensitive, tender, ticklish

adj 2 angry, cranky, cross, feisty, grouchy, hot-tempered, irascible, ireful, peppery, quick-tempered, short-fused, sullen, testy

adj 3 annoying, anxious, bothersome, chafing, crabby, edgy, fretful, galling, impatient, irritating, jittery, nagging, on edge, restless, unsettling

adj 4 dangerous, delicate, fluctuating, hazardous, precarious, rickety, risky, rocky, sensitive, shaky, tender, ticklish, tricky, unpredictable, unstable, wobbly

tough *adj* 1 arduous, burdensome, demanding, exacting, grievous, onerous, oppressive, trying

adj 2 abusive, hard, harsh, severe, stern, stiff, strict, uncaring, unsympathetic

adj 3 arduous, demanding, difficult, formidable, hard, heavy, labored, laborious, rocky, rough, rugged, serious, severe, strenuous, trying, uphill

adj 4 bullheaded, closed-minded, deaf, firm, hardheaded, hard-line, inelastic, inflexible, intractable, intransigent, obstinate, perverse, pigheaded, refractory, resolute, rigid, stiff, stubborn, unbending, uncompromising, unpliable, unpliant, unwieldy, unyielding, willful

adj 5 bad, mean, rough

adj 6 aggressive, dominant, durable, firm, forceful, hardy, hearty, mighty, powerful, robust, rugged, stalwart, stout, strong, sturdy

adj 7 authoritarian, authoritative, autocratic, controlled, despotic, disciplined, firm, harsh, inflexible, ironhanded, restrictive, rigid, rigorous, ruthless, severe, solid, stern, strict, stringent, strong, tyrannical

adj 8 austere, brutal, callous, coldblooded, compassionless, cruel, ferocious, fierce, hardened, hardhearted, heartless, indifferent, inhuman, inhumane, malicious, mean, merciless, nasty, obdurate, pitiless, ruthless, savage, spiteful, stony, uncaring, unemotional, unfeeling, unkind, unmerciful, unpitying, unrelenting, unsympathetic, vicious

n gorilla, hoodlum, hooligan, punk, roughneck, rowdy, ruffian

toughen *v* 1 acclimate, harden, season

v 2 bear up, bolster, brace, build up, buoy, buttress, carry, fortify, harden, nourish, nurture, prop, reinforce, shore, strengthen, support, sustain, uphold

tour *n* adventure, air travel, cruise, excursion, expedition, flight, journey, passage, safari, sally, travel, trek, trip, venture, voyage

v 1 sojourn, stop over, visit

v 2 coast, cruise, explore, go, journey, migrate, proceed, sail, survey, travel, trek, voyage

tournament *n* see: COMPETITION *n* 2

tourney *n* see: COMPETITION *n* 2

tout *v* 1 advertise, air, boom, boost, drum up, endorse, pitch, plug, promote, publicize, push, rave

v 2 acclaim, applaud, celebrate, commend, eulogize, exalt, extol, glorify, hail, honor, laud, praise, resound, salute, toast, worship

tow *v* carry, cart, drag, draw, haul, lug, pull, truck, tug

tower *n* 1 belfry, spire, steeple, turret

n 2 brig, cage, cell, cooler, coop, hoosegow, jail, pen, penitentiary, pokey, prison, reformatory, slammer, stir

v dominate

towering *adj* see: HUGE *adj* 3

town *n* borough, city, megalopolis, metropolis, municipality, suburb

township *n* 1 borough, burgh, community, hamlet, village

n 2 county, district, jurisdiction, municipality, parish, precinct, ward

toxic *adj* harmful, noxious, poisonous, unhealthy

toxin *n* cancer, corruption, decay, evil, infection, malignancy, poison, rot, venom

toy *n* amusement, game, knickknack, plaything, trinket

v 1 allure, charm, come onto, dally, flirt, fool, jest, kid, lead on, make eyes, make out, pick up, string along, tease, trifle

v 2 see: TRIFLE *v* 1, 2

trace *n 1* memento, relic, remnant, vestige

n 2 beam, flicker, glimmer, hint, light, ray, sliver

n 3 degree, distinction, enhancement, nuance, shade, subtlety, variation

n 4 breath, clue, dash, glimmer, hint, insinuation, lick, shade, smell, smidgen, spice, sprinkling, suggestion, suspicion, tinge, tip, touch, trifle, whiff, whisper, wisp

n 5 see: CLUE *n* 2

v 1 draw

v 2 chase, follow, hunt, pursue, seek, shadow, shoot for, tail, track, trail

track *v* chase, follow, hunt, pursue, seek, shadow, shoot for, tail, trace, trail

tract *n 1* land, lot, parcel, plot

n 2 area, arena, belt, field, realm, region, section, space, territory, turf, zone

n 3 see: ESSAY *n*

tractable *adj* amenable, complaisant, compliant, cooperative, obedient, submissive, subservient, willing

traction *n* adhesion, friction, pulling, tension

trade *adj* business, commercial, mercantile, trading

n 1 deal, exchange, sale, transaction, transfer

n 2 arrangements, business, commerce, dealings, enterprise, industry, intercourse, negotiations, traffic

n 3 art, avocation, business, calling, career, discipline, employment, field, gig, job, labor, line, livelihood, occupation, office, profession, pursuit, role, schtick, situation, specialty, task, thing, vocation, work

v 1 barter, exchange, swap, switch

v 2 bargain, barter, convert, deal, exchange, swap, traffic

trademark *n 1* abnormality, eccentricity, habit, idiosyncrasy, oddity, peculiarity

n 2 brand, cachet, emblem, imprint, logo, logotype, mark, seal

v claim, copyright, patent, protect

trader *n* dealer, marketer, merchant, monger, purveyor, seller, vendor

trading *adj* business, commercial, mercantile

tradition *n 1* belief, notion

n 2 belief, custom, doctrine, mores, relic, rite, ritual, throwback

n 3 custom, fashion, formality, habit, manner, mores, observance, practice, routine, usage, use, way, wont

traditional *adj 1* orthodox, straight, unhip

adj 2 accepted, established, proven, standard

adj 3 domestic, endemic, folk, indigenous, local

adj 4 accepted, accustomed, chronic, common, constant, continual, customary, daily, everyday, familiar, frequent, habitual, inured, often, recurring, regular, routine, usual

traditions *n* culture, customs, habits, mores

traduce *v* see: DEFAME *v* 1

traffic *n 1* arrangements, business, commerce, dealings, enterprise, industry, intercourse, trade

n 2 exchange, movement, travel

v 1 bargain, barter, convert, deal, exchange, trade

v 2 bear, carry, convey, crate, ferry, haul, lift, lug, pack, shoulder, shuttle, tote, transport, truck

tragedian *n* actor, actress, artist, entertainer, hero, heroine, lead, movie star, performer, player, protagonist, star

tragedy *n 1* drama, melodrama, mystery, theatrics, tragicomedy

n 2 calamity, cataclysm, catastrophe, debacle, disaster, misfortune, upheaval

n 3 adversity, affliction, blow, burden, calamity, difficulty, distress, hardship, mischance, misfortune, mishap, relapse, reversal, setback, suffering, trouble

tragic *adj* dire, disastrous, dreadful, lamentable, pitiful

tragicomedy *n* drama, melodrama, mystery, theatrics

trail *n* access, approach, artery, avenue, boulevard, channel, drag, highway, pass, path, promenade, road, roadway, route, strait, street, thoroughfare, way

v 1 drag, follow, lag, traipse

v 2 chase, follow, hunt, pursue, seek, shadow, shoot for, tail, track

trailblazing *adj* innovative, new, novel, original, pioneering, unprecedented

trailing *adj* end, last

train *n* chain, course, lineup, order, progression, row, run, sequence, series, succession *v* 1 address, aim, cast, direct, level, point, zero in

v 2 imbue, impart, infuse, ingrain, inject, inoculate, instill, invest, penetrate, pervade, spread, steep, suffuse

v 3 coach, communicate, condition, convey, cultivate, develop, discipline, drill, edify, educate, enlighten, exercise, explain, groom, imbue, impart, implant, improve, inculcate, indoctrinate, inform, infuse, inseminate, inspire, instill, instruct, perfect, practice, prepare, ready, school, teach, tutor

trained *adj* 1 qualified, skilled, specialized

adj 2 accomplished, experienced, proficient, schooled, versed

adj 3 experienced, expert, grizzled, hardened, mature, seasoned, weathered

trainee *n* apprentice, beginner, disciple, freshman, intern, neophyte, newcomer, novice, novitiate, pupil, recruit, rookie, student

trainer *n* coach, educator, instructor, leader, mentor, schoolteacher, teacher, tutor

training *n* 1 execution, exercise, implementation

n 2 drill, exercise, practice, rehearsal, workout

n 3 background, breeding, culture, development, education, environment, experience, past, schooling, upbringing

n 4 background, credentials, education

n 5 ability, adequacy, adroitness, aptitude, art, caliber, calling, capability, capacity, command, competence, craft, dexterity, experience, expertise, familiarity, forte, knack, know-how, knowledge, mastery, proficiency, prowess, qualification, savvy, skill, specialty, strength, talent, workmanship

traipse *v* 1 drag, follow, trail

v 2 see: WANDER *v*

trait *n* 1 nod, sign, signal, symbol, symptom

n 2 affectation, airs, mannerism, peculiarity, posturing, pretense

n 3 attribute, character, characteristic, feature, highlight, mark, peculiarity, property, quality, virtue

traitor *n* 1 accuser, betrayer, doublecrosser, fink, informer, reptile, snake, sneak

n 2 see: REBEL *n*

traitorous *adj* cheating, conniving, deceitful, deceptive, dishonest, disloyal, faithless, false, insidious, manipulative,

perfidious, sneaky, treacherous, unfaithful, untrue, untrustworthy

trajectory *n* curve, flight path, orbit

tramp *n* 1 hike, march, stroll, trek, walk

n 2 beggar, bum, derelict, drifter, hobo, loafer, mendicant, panhandler, pauper, vagabond, vagrant

n 3 call girl, harlot, hooker, hussy, prostitute, slut, streetwalker, tart, trollop, wanton woman, wench, whore

v 1 crush, squash, stomp, trample, tread, tromp

v 2 amble, hike, journey, march, pace, parade, plod, saunter, step, stride, stroll, strut, tread, trek, walk

trample *v* crush, squash, stomp, tramp, tread, tromp

trance *n* daydream, daze, spell

tranquil *adj* see: CALM *adj* 2

tranquilize *v* 1 calm, drug, sedate

v 2 see: APPEASE *v* 2

tranquilizer *n* narcotic, sedative

tranquillity *n* 1 accord, calm, harmony, peace, serenity

n 2 calm, hush, lull, peace, peacefulness, quiet, repose, respite, rest, siesta, silence, sleep, stillness

n 3 calmness, composure, equanimity, harmony, peacefulness, self-possession

transaction *n* 1 deal, exchange, sale, trade, transfer

n 2 see: PACT *n*

transcend *v* see: SURPASS *v* 2

transcendental *adj* mystic, psychic

transcribe *v* copy, note, record, summarize, type, write

transfer *n* deal, exchange, sale, transaction

v 1 assign, cede, convey, deed, designate

v 2 dislocate, dislodge, displace, disturb, move, oust, remove, shift

v 3 alter, change, commute, convert, evolve, further, improve, metamorphose, modernize, modify, mutate, revolutionize, transfigure, transform, transmute, vary

transfigure *v* alter, change, commute, convert, evolve, further, improve, metamorphose, modernize, modify, mutate, revolutionize, transfer, transform, transmute, vary

transform *v* alter, change, commute, convert, evolve, further, improve, metamorphose, modernize, modify, mutate, revolutionize, transfer, transfigure, transmute, vary

transformation *n* alchemy, alteration, changeover, conversion, revision

transfuse *v* enter, infiltrate, infuse, permeate

transgress *v* **1** cross the line, exceed, overstep, trespass

v **2** err, fall, offend, trespass, violate

transgression *n* **1** error, malfeasance, malpractice, misbehavior, misdeed, mismanagement, offense, wrong, wrongdoing

n **2** see: CRIME *n* 3

transgressor *n* see: CRIMINAL *n* 2

transience *n* abruptness, brevity, briefness, conciseness, curtness, quickness

transient *adj* **1** brief, ephemeral, fleeting, impermanent, momentary, passing, short, temporary, transitory, volatile

adj **2** ambulatory, gypsy, itinerant, movable, nomadic, perambulatory, roving, vagrant, wandering, wayfaring

adj **3** brief, fleeting, passing, short

n drifter, emigrant, itinerant, migrant

transition *n* see: CURRENT *n* 3

transitory *adj* brief, ephemeral, fleeting, impermanent, momentary, passing, short, temporary, transient, volatile

translate *v* clarify, depict, interpret, render, represent

translation *n* clarification, definition, denotation, meaning

translucent *adj* clear, clear-cut, crystal, limpid, lucid, transparent, unambiguous, unblurred

transmit *v* **1** air, broadcast, relay, telecast

v **2** carry, channel, conduct, convey, funnel, pass, pipe

v **3** beam, burn, disperse, emit, gleam, glisten, radiate, shine

v **4** address, channel, consign, dispatch, export, forward, mail, post, remit, route, send, ship, transport

v **5** brief, communicate, convey, declare, describe, disclose, divulge, explain, impart, inform, narrate, orate, portray, read, recite, recount, relate, report, retell, reveal, share, state, tell

v **6** broadcast, disseminate, dissipate, distribute, scatter, sow, spread

transmittable *adj* catching, communicable, contagious, contaminative, epidemic, infectious

transmute *v* alter, change, commute, convert, evolve, further, improve, metamorphose, modernize, modify, mutate, revolutionize, transfer, transfigure, transform, vary

transparency *n* acetate, overhead, slide

transparent *adj* **1** delicate, filmy, fine, flimsy, thin

adj **2** clear, clear-cut, crystal, limpid, lucid, translucent, unambiguous, unblurred

transpire *v* appear, arise, befall, break, come, come about, develop, do, ensue, evolve, fall out, happen, manifest, materialize, occur, pass, rise, take place, turn up

transport *v* **1** captivate, charm, delight, engross, enrapture, enravish, enthrall, entrance, hypnotize, mesmerize, move

v **2** bear, carry, convey, crate, ferry, haul, lift, lug, pack, shoulder, shuttle, tote, traffic, truck

v **3** see: SEND *v* 3

transportable *adj* carryable, compact, lightweight, luggable, movable, pocketsize, portable

transportation *n* burden, cargo, consignment, freight, lading, load, payload, shipment, truck

transpose *v* change, invert, reverse, turn

trap *n* **1** attraction, bait, come-on, decoy, enticement, lure, magnet, ruse, seduction, snare, temptation, wile

n **2** booby trap, mousetrap, pit, pitfall, snare

n **3** bind, box, corner, difficulty, dilemma, fix, impasse, jam, mess, pinch, plight, predicament, quandary, scrape, spot, trouble

v **1** cage, confine, coop, detain, enclose, impound, imprison, incarcerate, intern, jail, lock up

v **2** bag, capture, catch, ensnare, entangle, entrap, hook, snag, snare, snarl, tangle, trick

v **3** ambush, assail, assault, attack, beset, invade, raid, storm, strike, waylay

trappings *n* paraphernalia

trash *n* **1** debris, fragment, hulk, remains, rubbish, rubble, shell, wreck, wreckage

n **2** crap, crud, debris, detritus, dirt, garbage, junk, litter, refuse, rubbish, rubble, waste

n **3** dirt, filth, grossness, indecency, obscenity, porn, pornography, ribaldry

trashy *adj* base, cheap, common, sleazy

trauma *n* blow, disturbance, jolt, shock, upheaval, upset

traumatic *adj* disabling, disturbing, painful, shocking, upsetting

travail *n* **1** chore, drudgery, grind, labor, slavery, sweat, tedium, toil, work

n **2** see: PAIN *n* 4

travel *n* **1** adventure, air travel, cruise, excursion, expedition, flight, journey, passage, safari, sally, tour, trek, trip, venture, voyage

n 2 movement, traffic

v 1 circulate, pass around, revolve, route

v 2 itinerate, meander, perambulate, promenade, ramble, range, roam, rove, saunter, stray, stroll, traipse, traverse, walk, wander

v 3 commute, drive, ride

v 4 coast, cruise, explore, go, journey, migrate, proceed, sail, survey, tour, trek, voyage

traveler *n* passenger, rider

traverse *v* 1 pass

v 2 cross, cruise, fly, voyage

v 3 contradict, cross, deny, disaffirm, disagree, impugn, negate

v 4 see: WANDER *v*

travesty *n* buffoonery, burlesque, caricature, comedy, farce, humor, imitation, joke, lampoon, mockery, parody, satire, spoof

treacherous *adj* 1 catty, hostile, malevolent, malicious, spiteful

adj 2 cheating, conniving, deceitful, deceptive, dishonest, disloyal, faithless, false, insidious, manipulative, perfidious, sneaky, traitorous, unfaithful, untrue, untrustworthy

treachery *n* betrayal, deception, perfidy, subversion, trickery

tread *v* 1 crush, squash, stomp, tramp, trample, tromp

v 2 amble, hike, journey, march, pace, parade, plod, saunter, step, stride, stroll, strut, tramp, trek, walk

treason *n* betrayal, insurrection, mutiny, revolt, sedition, subversion, uprising

treasure *n* 1 asset, credit, resource, valuable

n 2 antique, bric-a-brac, curio, curiosity, novelty, objet d'art, oddity, rarity, wonder

n 3 booty, bounty, fortune, kitty, loot, money, plunder, pot, prize, spoils, swag, trove

n 4 gem, jewel, paragon

n 5 assets, belongings, equity, estate, fortune, goods, holdings, inheritance, money, ownership, possessions, property, prosperity, riches, wealth

v admire, adore, appreciate, cherish, consider, covet, esteem, honor, idolize, love, prize, regard, respect, value

treasured *adj* adored, beloved, cherished, dear, esteemed, loved, precious, respected, revered, venerable, worshipped

treasury *n* 1 repository, storehouse

n 2 chest, coffer, safe, strongbox, vault

n 3 gallery, museum

treat *n* bauble, delicacy, frill, luxury

v 1 adapt, prepare, ready

v 2 behave, behave towards, handle, manage

v 3 administer, construct, dispense, move along, plan, prepare, process

treatise *n* article, composition, discourse, dissertation, essay, manuscript, memoir, monograph, paper, report, study, theme, thesis, tract, work

treatment *n* 1 behavior, conduct

n 2 antidote, cure, medication, medicine, panacea, prescription, remedy, serum, therapy

n 3 cure, rehabilitation, therapy

treaty *n* 1 agreement, bargain, bond, compact, contract, convention, covenant, deal, pact, pledge, promise, transaction, understanding

n 2 see: ALLIANCE *n*

tree *n* bush, grass, hedge, plant, sapling, shrub, vegetation, vine, weed

v collar, corner

trees *n* forest, wood

trek *n* 1 hike, march, stroll, walk

n 2 adventure, air travel, cruise, excursion, expedition, flight, journey, passage, safari, sally, tour, travel, trip, venture, voyage

v 1 coast, cruise, explore, go, journey, migrate, proceed, sail, survey, tour, travel, voyage

v 2 amble, hike, journey, march, pace, parade, plod, saunter, step, stride, stroll, strut, tramp, walk

tremble *v* 1 beat, flutter, palpitate, pulsate, pulse, quiver, throb, vibrate

v 2 flinch, flutter, jar, pulsate, quake, quaver, quiver, shake, shiver, shudder, twitch, twitter, vibrate

tremendous *adj* 1 arduous, formidable, herculean, heroic, superhuman

adj 2 excellent, fabulous, fantastic, fine, good, great, marvelous, super, wonderful

adj 3 big, extra-large, fat, grand, great, huge, husky, immense, jumbo, large, obese

adj 4 dynamite, excellent, extraordinary, great, out of sight, outstanding, phenomenal, premier, super, superb, superlative, wonderful

adj 5 colossal, enormous, fantastic, Gargantuan, giant, gigantic, Goliath, great, huge, immense, jumbo, leviathan, mammoth, massive, mighty, monstrous, monumental, overwhelming, phenomenal, prodigious, Promethean, stupendous, Titanic, towering, unfathomed, untold, vast, walloping, whopping

tremor *v* flinch, flutter, jar, pulsate, quake, quaver, quiver, shake, shiver, shudder, tremble, twitch, twitter, vibrate
n flutter, quake, quiver, shiver

trench *n* 1 crack, cut, gash, opening, slit
n 2 canal, channel, conduit, crevice, curb, cut, ditch, duct, furrow, gorge, groove, gully, gutter, passageway, ravine, rut, trough

trenchant *adj* 1 biting, caustic, cutting, incisive, pointed
adj 2 clear, effective, explicit, forceful, vigorous
adj 3 caustic, coarse, cutting, obscene, salty, scathing, scorching, sharp, spicy, vulgar, witty

trend *n* 1 atmosphere, climate, condition, mood
n 2 current, drift, pattern, run, series, tendency
n 3 course, direction, drift, path, strategy, tack, tactic, tendency
n 4 chic, craze, fad, fashion, mode, rage, style, thing, vogue

trendsetters *n* innovators, leaders, pacesetters, pioneers, vanguard

trendy *adj* chic, current, fashionable, hip, in, smart, stylish, vogue

trepidation *n* affliction, alarm, anxiety, apprehension, care, consternation, dismay, dread, fear, fright, horror, ordeal, panic, terror, trial, trouble, worry

trespass *n* 1 breach, default, infraction, violation
n 2 attack, conquest, defeat, foray, intrusion, invasion
n 3 see: CRIME *n* 3
v 1 cross the line, exceed, overstep
v 2 err, fall, offend, sin, transgress, violate
v 3 attack, encroach, entrench, infringe, intrude, invade, violate

trestle *n* bridge, overpass, viaduct

trial *adj* developmental, experimental, pilot, suggested, tentative, untested
n 1 attempt, effort, endeavor, speculation, struggle, try, undertaking, venture
n 2 see: FEAR *n* 3
n 3 see: INVESTIGATION *n*

tribal *adj* ethnic, racial

tribe *n* 1 breed, clan, class, family, household, people, race, relatives
n 2 band, cabal, camp, circle, clan, clique,

coterie, coven, cult, faction, family, gang, group, mob, ring, school
n 3 citizens, civilization, colony, community, crowd, culture, folks, group, human beings, individuals, laity, masses, men and women, neighbors, people, persons, populace, population, public, settlement, society

tribulation *n* agony, anguish, bale, concern, distress, misery, nightmare, pain, sadness, sorrow, suffering, torment, travail, trouble, woe, worry

tributary *n* 1 bayou, brook, river, stream
n 2 arm, branch, division, limb, service
adj see: SUBORDINATE *adj* 4

tribute *n* 1 acclaim, applause, boost, citation, commendation, compliment, eulogy, plaudit, praise
n 2 accolade, award, commendation, credit, decoration, distinction, honor, kudos, laurels, medal, note, praise, recognition, reputation

trick *n* 1 alibi, con, deception, lie, pretext, ruse
n 2 adventure, antic, caper, escapade, joke, lark, mischief
n 3 antic, device, diversion, gambit, gimmick, maneuver, mischief, move, plan, plot, ploy, prank, ruse, scheme, stratagem, strategy, tactic, wile
n 4 see: ACCOMPLISHMENT *n* 4
v 1 befuddle, bewilder, confuse, daze, distract, dizzy, embarrass, fluster, mix up, muddle, rattle, ruffle, unglue, unhinge
v 2 see: CHEAT *v* 1
v 3 see: TRAP *v* 2

trickery *n* 1 betrayal, deception, subversion, treachery
n 2 cheating, deceit, deception, dishonesty, fraud, hoax, lie, sham
n 3 deceit, deception, fabrication, falsehood, fraud, fraudulence, hypocrisy, lying, perjury, untruth

trickle *v* 1 dribble, drip, drop, leak, ooze, run, seep
v 2 discharge, drip, emit, exude, leak, ooze, seep

tricky *adj* 1 awkward, delicate, difficult, embarrassing
adj 2 astute, calculating, crafty, cunning, foxy, guileful, insidious, sharp, shrewd, sly, smart, subtle, wily, wise
adj 3 dangerous, delicate, fluctuating, hazardous, precarious, rickety, risky, rocky, sensitive, shaky, tender, ticklish, touchy, unpredictable, unstable, wobbly
adj 4 challenging, difficult

adj **5** clandestine, concealed, covert, crafty, deceitful, devious, evasive, foxy, furtive, guileful, indirect, privy, secret, shifty, sly, sneaky, surreptitious, underground, underhand, underhanded, wily

tried *adj* **1** dependable, fail-safe, infallible, reliable, sure

adj **2** authentic, certified, confirmed, demonstrated, proved, verified

trifle *n* **1** bit, dab, end, fragment, iota, minutia, mite, morsel, particle, piece, pinch, portion, scrap, shred, speck, spot, strip

n **2** breath, clue, dash, glimmer, hint, insinuation, lick, shade, smell, smidgen, spice, sprinkling, suggestion, suspicion, tinge, tip, touch, trace, whiff, whisper, wisp

n **3** lover, mistress

v **1** dabble, dally, diddle, fiddle, fool, monkey, piddle, play, poke about, putter, tinker, toy

v **2** allure, charm, come onto, dally, flirt, fool, jest, kid, lead on, make eyes, make out, pick up, tease, toy

trifling *adj* immaterial, inconsequential, inconsiderable, insignificant, little, low, meaningless, measly, minor, nominal, paltry, petty, picayune, picky, puny, skimpy, slight, small, tiny, trivial, unessential, unimportant, worthless

trigger *v* activate, cause, elicit, generate, prompt, provoke

trill *v* quaver, vocalize, warble

trilogy *n* threesome, trinity, trio, triplets, triumvirate

trim *v* **1** clip, crop, cut, lop, pare, prune, shave, shear, snip, whittle

v **2** adorn, beautify, bedeck, deck, decorate, dress up, embellish, enhance, garnish, glamorize, grace, ornament

adj **1** meticulous, neat, orderly, prim, shipshape, tidy, well-groomed

adj **2** chic, dapper, dashing, debonair, jaunty, natty, neat, rakish, sleek, smart, snazzy, suave

n condition, fitness, kilter, shape

trinity *n* threesome, trilogy, trio, triplets, triumvirate

trinket *n* amusement, game, plaything, toy

trio *n* threesome, trilogy, trinity, triplets, triumvirate

trip *n* **1** adventure, air travel, cruise, excursion, expedition, flight, journey, passage, safari, sally, tour, travel, trek, venture, voyage

n **2** see: PATH *n* 2

v **1** bomb, fail, flop

v **2** fall, lurch, skid, skim, slide, slip, stumble, totter, tumble

v **3** see: HOP *v*

triplets *n* threesome, trilogy, trinity, trio, triumvirate

trite *adj* **1** banal, commonplace, conventional, ordinary, undistinguished

adj **2** banal, boring, clichéd, commonplace, corny, dull, hackneyed, musty, redundant, repetitious, repetitive, stale, tedious, threadbare, timeworn, tired, tiresome, worn out

adj **3** arid, bland, bleak, boring, colorless, dead, desolate, drab, dreary, dull, flat, lackluster, lifeless, lusterless, monotonous, muted, somber, unexciting, uninteresting

triteness *n* banality, cliché, commonplace, platitude

triumph *v* **1** best, conquer, defeat, master, overcome, prevail, succeed, win

v **2** accomplish, achieve, attain, consummate, execute, fulfill, perform, produce, pull off, realize, succeed, win

n **1** accomplishment, achievement, conquest, success, victory, win, winner

n **2** accomplishment, achievement, arrival, attainment, completion, fruition, fulfillment, realization, satisfaction, success, victory

triumphant *adj* **1** boastful, proud

adj **2** conquering, successful, undefeated, victorious, winning

triumvirate *n* threesome, trilogy, trinity, trio

trivia *n* **1** details, minutiae, nuances, particulars

n **2** see: NONSENSE *n* 2

trivial *adj* **1** immaterial, inconsequential, inconsiderable, insignificant, little, low, meaningless, measly, minor, nominal, paltry, petty, picayune, picky, puny, skimpy, slight, small, tiny, trifling, unessential, unimportant, worthless

adj **2** borderline, casual, frivolous, insignificant, light, lightweight, little, marginal, meager, minor, minute, negligible, nonessential, off, outside, petty, remote, secondary, slender, slight, slim, small, tenuous, unimportant

trollop *n* call girl, harlot, hooker, hussy, prostitute, slut, streetwalker, tart, tramp, wanton woman, wench, whore

tromp *v* **1** crush, squash, stomp, trample, tread

v **2** see: BATTER *v*

troop *n* band, body, company, corps, group, outfit, party, troupe

trooper *n* hired gun, mercenary, soldier

troopers *n* authorities, bobbies, constabulary, cops, gendarmes, highway patrol, police

troops *n* army, battalion, brigade, company, force, gang, men, power

trophy *n* 1 award, honor, prize

n 2 antique, gift, heirloom, keepsake, memento, memorial, relic, remembrance, reminder, souvenir

tropical *adj* hot, humid, muggy, steamy, sticky, stifling, sunny

trot *v* dart, gallop, run

n see: SPEED *n* 2

troubadour *n* author, bard, composer, folk singer, muse, narrator, storyteller

trouble *n* 1 effort, elbow grease, exertion, labor, pains, strain, struggle, toil, try, work

n 2 adversity, affliction, blow, burden, calamity, difficulty, distress, hardship, mischance, misfortune, mishap, relapse, reversal, setback, suffering

n 3 agony, anguish, bale, concern, distress, misery, nightmare, pain, sadness, sorrow, suffering, torment, travail, tribulation, woe, worry

n 4 annoyance, anxiety, apprehension, bother, care, concern, disquiet, disquietude, doubt, irritation, misgiving, reservation, restlessness, restraint, skepticism, uneasiness, vexation, worry

n 5 annoyance, bother, conflict, contention, difference, discord, disharmony, dispute, dissension, dissent, dissidence, dissonance, disunity, division, hassle, inconvenience, mischief, nuisance, strife, variance

n 6 see: DILEMMA *n* 4

n 7 see: FEAR *n* 3

v annoy, antagonize, argue, bother, bug, concern, distress, disturb, goad, harass, hassle, inconvenience, irk, irritate, pain, perturb, strain, stress, taunt, try, upset, worry

troubled *adj* 1 anxious, careworn, distracted, distraught, distressed, frantic, harassed, tormented, upset, worried

adj 2 anxious, edgy, fidgety, impatient, nervous, nervy, queasy, restive, restless, tense, uncomfortable, uneasy, uptight, worried

troublemaker *n* 1 agitator, initiator, instigator, organizer, rabble-rouser

n 2 see: REBEL *n*

troublesome *adj* annoying, bothersome, glaring, harassing, irksome, irritating, mean, onerous, painful, pesky, ugly, unwelcome, vexatious, wicked

trough *n* see: CHANNEL *n* 3

trouncing *n* debacle, defeat, disaster, downfall, overthrow, rout, ruination, thrashing, undoing, vanquishment

troupe *n* band, body, company, corps, group, outfit, party

trove *n* booty, bounty, fortune, kitty, loot, money, plunder, pot, prize, spoils, treasure

truant *adj* absent, away, gone, lacking, missing, omitted, wanting

n absentee, hooky player, nonattender

truce *n* abeyance, cease-fire, respite

truck *n* 1 burden, cargo, consignment, freight, lading, load, payload, shipment

n 2 auto, automobile, bus, car, carriage, chariot, coach, jeep, motorcar, omnibus, sedan, van, vehicle, wagon

n 3 cart, handcart, pushcart, wagon, wheelbarrow

v 1 carry, cart, drag, draw, haul, lug, pull, tug

v 2 bear, carry, convey, crate, ferry, haul, lift, lug, pack, shoulder, shuttle, tote, transport

true *adj* 1 exact, faithful, literal, precise, strict, verbatim, word for word

adj 2 authoritative, dependable, due, faithful, legitimate, rightful, strict, trustworthy, undistorted, veracious

adj 3 ardent, constant, dedicated, dependable, devoted, faithful, loyal, resolute, staunch, steadfast, steady

adj 4 accurate, authentic, believable, certain, convincing, credible, dependable, faithful, real, reliable, safe, sure, tenable, trustworthy

adj 5 candid, direct, earnest, forthright, frank, genuine, heartfelt, hearty, honest, no-holds-barred, open, real, sincere, straightforward, trustworthy, truthful, undesigning, unfeigned, unpretentious, wholehearted

adj 6 absolute, actual, authentic, bona fide, certain, definite, existent, factual, genuine, hard, inarguable, incontestable, incontrovertible, indisputable, indubitable, irrefutable, positive, real, sure, undeniable, undisputable, undoubtable, undoubted, unequivocal, unquestionable, veritable, viable

adj 7 see: ETHICAL *adj* 3

adj 8 see: OBVIOUS *adj* 3

truism *n* announcement, aphorism, axiom, cliché, declaration, decree, dictum, edict, gospel, homily, maxim, moral, precept, pronouncement, rule, saying, teaching, truth, verity

truly *adv* **1** actually, exactly, genuinely, precisely, really, sincerely, verifiably, veritably, very

adv **2** absolutely, certainly, decidedly, definitely, entirely, incontrovertibly, indeed, indubitably, positively, surely, unequivocally, unquestionably, verily, well, without doubt

trunk *n* beak, bill, muzzle, nib, nose, proboscis, snout

trust *n* **1** belief, confidence, contingency, credence, credit, creed, dependence, desire, faith, hope

n **2** cartel, chain, coalition, collaboration, combine, conglomerate, consortium, federation, group, partnership, syndicate

v **1** entrust

v **2** bank on, build on, count on, depend, rely

v **3** assume, believe, comprehend, conceive, estimate, expect, fathom, gather, grasp, guess, imagine, infer, know, presume, suppose, surmise, think, understand

trusted *adj* accountable, answerable, dependable, honorable, honored, liable, reliable, reputable, respected, responsible, secure, solid, trustworthy, trusty, upstanding

trustee *n* custodian, father, guardian, parent

trustful *adj* believing, credulous, easy, gullible, innocent, naive

trusting *adj* credulous, gullible, ingenuous, trustworthy

trustworthiness *n* honesty, honor, integrity, virtue

trustworthy *adj* **1** credulous, gullible, trusting

adj **2** factual, honest, truthful, veracious

adj **3** authoritative, dependable, due, faithful, legitimate, rightful, strict, true, undistorted, veracious

adj **4** aboveboard, candid, equitable, fair, forthright, honest, legitimate, plain-dealing, straight, straightforward, upright

adj **5** accurate, authentic, believable, certain, convincing, credible, dependable, faithful, real, reliable, safe, sure, tenable, true, trusty

adj **6** accountable, answerable, dependable, honorable, honored, liable, reliable,

reputable, respected, responsible, secure, solid, trusted, trusty, upstanding

adj **7** see: ETHICAL *adj* 3

adj **8** see: SINCERE *adj*

trusty *adj* **1** see: AUTHENTIC *adj* 2

adj **2** see: FAITHFUL *adj* 3, 4

adj **3** see: REPUTABLE *adj*

truth *n* **1** actuality, fact, given, specific

n **2** candor, honesty, integrity, truthfulness, veracity

n **3** correctness, justice, lawfulness, validity

n **4** actuality, being, existence, fact, life, presence, reality, vitality

n **5** see: CLICHÉ *n* 3

truthful *adj* **1** factual, honest, trustworthy, veracious

adj **2** see: SINCERE *adj*

truthfulness *n* **1** candor, frankness, honesty, sincerity

n **2** candor, honesty, integrity, truth, veracity

try *n* **1** attempt, chance, spin, turn

n **2** attempt, effort, endeavor, speculation, struggle, trial, undertaking, venture

n **3** effort, elbow grease, exertion, labor, pains, strain, struggle, toil, trouble, work

n **4** attempt, chance, effort, fling, go, guess, heave, lob, pop, shot, slap, sling, stab, throw, toss, whirl

v **1** assume, attack, attempt, tackle, take on

v **2** determine, evaluate, judge, test, verify

v **3** adjudicate, arbitrate, judge, mediate, referee, umpire

v **4** assay, attempt, endeavor, essay, offer, quest, seek, strive, struggle, undertake

v **5** accuse, allege, arraign, assert, charge, cite, impeach, imply, impute, incriminate, indict, litigate, prosecute

v **6** see: ANNOY *v* 1

trying *adj* **1** arduous, burdensome, demanding, exacting, grievous, onerous, oppressive, taxing, tough

adj **2** arduous, demanding, difficult, formidable, hard, heavy, labored, laborious, rocky, rough, rugged, serious, severe, strenuous, tough, uphill

tryst *n* adultery, affair, cheating, dalliance, entanglement, fling, flirtation, fooling around, infatuation, intimacy, intrigue, liaison, love affair, meeting, playing around, rendezvous, romance

tsar *n* authoritarian, autocrat, despot, dictator, tyrant

tub *n* **1** barrel, bucket, cask, drum, keg, vat, vessel

n **2** bath

tube *n* 1 channel, conduit, cylinder, duct, pipe

n 2 conduit, passageway, pathway, shaft, tunnel

n 3 boob tube, cable, channel, station, teevee, television, TV, video

tug *n* drag, jerk, pluck, pull, yank

v 1 jerk, pull, tear, twist, wrench, wring, yank

v 2 carry, cart, drag, draw, haul, lug, pull, tow, truck

tumble *n* comedown, decline, decrease, descent, dive, drop, failure, fall, plunge, regression, setback

v 1 fall, lurch, skid, skim, slide, slip, stumble, totter

v 2 cave in, collapse, disintegrate, drop, fall, go down, keel over, pitch, plunge, slump, topple

v 3 cascade, emit, flood, inundate, overflow, plunge, pour, rain, shower, spill

v 4 capsize, collapse, defeat, dislodge, knock over, overthrow, overturn, tip over, topple, turn over, upset

tumbler *n* 1 acrobat

n 2 chalice, container, cup, dish, Dixie cup, glass, goblet, mug, shot glass, stein, vessel, wineglass

tumescent *adj* bloated, distended, inflated, puffy, swollen, tumid, turgid

tumid *adj* bloated, distended, inflated, puffy, swollen, tumescent, turgid

tummy *n* abdomen, belly, gut, midriff, paunch, stomach

tum-tum *n* abdomen, belly, gut, midriff, paunch, stomach, tummy

tumult *n* 1 intensity, power, severity, turbulence, violence

n 2 agitation, craze, excitement, frenzy, furor, fury, fuss, outrage, passion, uproar, wrath

n 3 chaos, clutter, confusion, derangement, disarray, disorder, jumble, mayhem, mess, mix-up, muddle, predicament, snafu, snarl, tangle, turmoil

n 4 see: ACTIVITY *n* 3

n 5 see: CLAMOR *n*

tumultuous *adj* 1 blatant, boisterous, clamorous, disturbing, loud, loudmouthed, noisy, obstreperous, raucous, rowdy, vociferous

adj 2 agitated, disorderly, excited, fierce, frantic, frenzied, furious, mad, stormy, turbulent, violent, wild

tune *n* 1 air, harmony, measure, medley, melody, music

n 2 air, call, carol, cry, lullaby, melody, note, song

v 1 adjust, align, dial, select

v 2 accommodate, adjust, attune, conform, coordinate, harmonize, integrate, proportion, reconciliate

tuneful *adj* choral, euphonious, harmonious, lyric, mellow, melodic, melodious, musical, orchestral, philharmonic, rhythmical, symphonic, vocal

tunnel *n* 1 burrow, cave, den, grotto, lair

n 2 conduit, passageway, pathway, shaft, subway, tube

v burrow, dig, furrow, root out

turbine *n* device, engine, machine, motor

turbulence *n* intensity, power, severity, tumult, violence

turbulent *adj* agitated, disorderly, excited, fierce, frantic, frenzied, furious, mad, stormy, tumultuous, violent, wild

turf *n* 1 area, divot, land, patch, sod

n 2 area, arena, belt, field, realm, region, section, space, territory, tract, zone

turgid *adj* bloated, distended, inflated, puffy, swollen, tumescent

turkey *n* 1 bomb, bust, disaster, dud, failure, fiasco

n 2 bird, bum, cad, fink, heel, jerk

n 3 blockhead, boor, clod, creep, cretin, dimwit, dolt, dope, dullard, dumbbell, dummy, dunce, fool, goof, idiot, imbecile, jerk, nerd, nincompoop, numskull, oaf, pain, schlemiel, schmuck, simpleton, stooge

turmoil *n* 1 chaos, clutter, confusion, derangement, disarray, disorder, jumble, mayhem, mess, mix-up, muddle, predicament, snafu, snarl, tangle

n 2 action, activity, ado, animation, bedlam, bother, bustle, chaos, commotion, excitement, flurry, fluster, fuss, hum, liveliness, madhouse, movement, stir, to-do, tumult, whirlpool, whirlwind

turn *n* 1 attempt, chance, try

n 2 angle, bend, bow, detour, deviation, double, shift, tack, turning, yaw

n 3 curl, loop, revolution, ring, roll, rotation, spin, spiral, twirl, twist

n 4 alternation, circuit, circulation, gyration, revolution, rotation, round, sequence, spinning, succession, whirl

v 1 change, invert, reverse, revert, transpose

v 2 force, pull, seize, twist, wrest

v 3 circle, gyrate, revolve, roll, rotate

v 4 deflect, deviate, divert, drift, stray

v 5 gyrate, pirouette, purl, reel, spin, twirl, whirl

v **6** angle, arch, bend, bow, curve, flex, ply, round, tilt, tip, twist, vault

v **7** avert, deflect, deviate, dip, divert, dodge, pivot, skew, swerve, swing, swivel, veer, wheel, whip

v **8** bend

turnabout *n* change, move, shift

turncoat *n* see: REBEL *n*

turndown *n* **1** ban, disapproval, refusal, rejection, thumbs down, veto

n **2** refusal, rejection

turned on *adj* **1** aroused, ebullient, elated, euphoric, excited, exhilarated, happy, intoxicated, joyful, sparked

adj **2** bombed, crocked, doped up, drunk, drunken, high, inebriated, intoxicated, juiced, loaded, looped, messed up, plastered, polluted, sloshed, smashed, stoned, tight, tipsy, wasted, wired

turning *adj* crooked, meandering, serpentine, sinuous, spiral, twisting, winding, zigzagging

n see: SHIFT *n* **3**

turn on *v* **1** activate, charge, electrify, energize, enliven, excite, ignite, start, vitalize

v **2** arouse, electrify, excite, fire, incite, inspire, rouse, spark, stimulate, tantalize, thrill, titillate, whet

turquoise *adj* aqua, azure, blue, cobalt, indigo, navy, Prussian

turret *n* belfry, steeple, tower

turtle *n* sloth, slug, snail

tush *n* **1** digger, fang, gasher, molar, tooth, tusk

n **2** ass, backside, base, behind, bottom, bucket, buns, butt, buttocks, derrière, end, fanny, hindquarters, posterior, rump, seat, stub, stump

tusk *n* digger, fang, gasher, molar, tooth

tussle *v* combat, conflict, contend, contest, engage, scuffle, struggle

tutor *n* coach, educator, instructor, leader, mentor, schoolteacher, teacher

v coach, communicate, condition, convey, cultivate, develop, discipline, drill, edify, educate, enlighten, exercise, explain, groom, imbue, impart, implant, improve, inculcate, indoctrinate, inform, infuse, inseminate, inspire, instill, instruct, perfect, practice, prepare, ready, school, train

TV *n* boob tube, cable, channel, station, teevee, television, video

tweak *v* **1** pinch, pull, twist

v **2** adjust, finesse, fine-tune, vary

twig *n* bough, branch, limb

twilight *n* dusk, nightfall, sunset

twin *n* counterpart, double, duplicate, match

twine *n* cable, cord, fiber, hemp, lanyard, line, rope, strand, string, thread, yarn

twinge *n* **1** ache, agony, angina, burn, cramp, crick, heartache, hurt, pain, pang, soreness, spasm

n **2** compunction, conscience, pang, qualm, regret, reservation, restraint

twinkle *v* **1** blink, flash, flicker, wink

v **2** dance, flap, flicker, flitter, flutter, oscillate, prance, sparkle, sway, undulate, wave

v **3** excite, flash, gleam, glimmer, glint, glisten, glitter, scintillate, shimmer, sparkle

n flash, gleam, glimmer, glitter, shimmer, shine

twinkling *n* blink of an eye, crack, flash, instant, jiffy, minute, moment, second, shake, wink

twins *n* couple, duet, duo, pair, set, twosome

twirl *n* curl, loop, revolution, ring, roll, rotation, spin, spiral, turn, twist

v gyrate, pirouette, purl, reel, spin, swim, turn, whirl

twist *n* **1** bend, crimp, kink, snarl, tangle

n **2** curl, loop, revolution, ring, roll, rotation, spin, spiral, turn

n **3** ballet, cha-cha, dance, fox trot, hula, jitterbug, polka, waltz

v **1** pinch, tweak

v **2** bend, contort, warp

v **3** bend, connect, encircle, loop

v **4** force, pull, seize, turn, wrest

v **5** draw, flex, pull, strain, stretch, tighten

v **6** jerk, pull, tear, tug, wrench, wring, yank

v **7** coil, corkscrew, curl, distort, entwine, gnarl, spiral, wind

v **8** angle, arch, bend, bow, curve, flex, ply, round, tilt, tip, turn, vault

v **9** angle, confuse, deceive, distort, falsify, garble, incline, misconstrue, misinterpret, misquote, misread, misrepresent, misunderstand, mix up, mumble, slant, slope

v **10** accede, acquiesce, bend, bow, buckle, capitulate, cave, comply, concede, cry uncle, defer, give in, give up, relent, submit, succumb, yield

twisting *adj* crooked, meandering, serpentine, sinuous, spiral, turning, winding, zigzagging

twitch *n* convulsion, jerk, seizure, spasm

v **1** fidget, squirm, writhe

v **2** jig, jiggle, joggle, shake, wiggle

v **3** flinch, flutter, jar, pulsate, quake, quaver, quiver, shake, shiver, shudder, tremble, vibrate

twitter *v* see: QUIVER *v* 2

'twixt *prep* amidst, among, atwixt, between, betwixt, halfway to, midway

twosome *n* couple, duet, duo, pair, set

tycoon *n* baron, big shot, businessman, businessperson, businesswoman, capitalist, entrepreneur, executive, financier, industrialist, magnate, mogul, plutocrat, VIP

tyke *n* babe, baby, child, infant, newborn

type *n* **1** characteristic, flavor, impression, nature, property, quality, ring, sound, tone

n **2** bracket, breed, cast, category, class, division, family, genre, genus, group, grouping, ilk, kind, lot, mold, nature, order, persuasion, section, sector, set, sort, species, style, variety

n **3** face, family, font, printwheel, size, style, typeface

v **1** copy, note, record, summarize, transcribe, write

v **2** author, compose, create, draft, pen, write

typeface *n* face, family, font, printwheel, size, type

typhoon *n* blast, blizzard, blow, gale, gust, hurricane, northeaster, snowstorm, squall, storm, tempest, tornado, wind

typical *adj* **1** characteristic, classic, exemplary, ideal, model, representative

adj **2** average, common, commonplace, daily, everyday, general, mundane, natural, normal, ordinary, plain, prevalent, regular, routine, unexceptional, unremarkable, usual, workaday

typically *adv* frequently, often, regularly, repeatedly, usually

typify *v* embody, exemplify, express, personify, represent

tyrannical *adj* authoritarian, authoritative, autocratic, controlled, despotic, disciplined, firm, harsh, inflexible, ironhanded, restrictive, rigid, rigorous, ruthless, severe, solid, stern, strict, stringent, strong

tyranny *n* **1** autocracy, dictatorship

n **2** austerity, oppression, severity

tyrant *n* authoritarian, autocrat, despot, dictator, fascist, tsar

ubiquitous *adj* common, omnipresent, widespread

udder *n* breast, nipple, teat

ugly *adj* **1** abhorrent, despicable, repulsive

adj **2** hideous, homely, plain, repulsive, unattractive

adj **3** contorted, grotesque, gruesome, hideous, ill-favored, uncomely, unsightly

adj **4** awful, frightful, grim, grisly, gruesome, hideous, lurid, repulsive, sensational, shocking, terrible, violent

adj **5** annoying, bothersome, glaring, harassing, irksome, irritating, mean, onerous, painful, pesky, troublesome, unwelcome, vexatious, wicked

adj **6** see: SULLEN *adj* 1

ulcer *n* abscess, boil, carbuncle

ulcerate *v* blister, fester

ulterior *adj* additional, covert, hidden, secondary, secret, undeclared

ultimate *adj* **1** concluding, conclusive, final, last

adj **2** see: EXTRAVAGANT *adj* 3

n see: APEX *n*

ultimately *adv* at last, eventually, finally, lastly

ultimatum *n* claim, demand, mandate

ultra *adj* **1** extreme, extremist, fanatic, fanatical, rabid, radical, revolutionary, zealous

adj **2** curious, exotic, far-out, fascinating, intriguing, kinky, marvelous, mysterious, new, novel, odd, outlandish, strange, unaccustomed, unexplored, unfamiliar, unique, unknown, unusual, weird

umpire *n* arbiter, arbitrator, judge, mediator, referee

v adjudicate, arbitrate, judge, mediate, referee

unabashed *adj* arrant, barefaced, blatant, brassy, brazen, extreme, impudent, notorious, obtrusive, shameless

unable *adj* see: INADEQUATE *adj* 5

unabridged *adj* complete, comprehensive, thorough

unacceptable *adj* ill-favored, inadmissible, objectionable, undesirable, unwanted, unwelcome

unaccompanied *adj* alone, lone, lonely, lonesome, single, singular, solitary

unaccustomed *adj* curious, exotic, far-out, fascinating, intriguing, kinky, marvelous, mysterious, new, novel, odd, outlandish, strange, ultra, unexplored, unfamiliar, unique, unknown, unusual, weird

unachievable *adj* impossible, inconceivable, incredible, strange, undoable, unthinkable

unacquainted *adj* unaware, unfamiliar, uninformed, unknowing

unadorned *adj* 1 naked, stark

adj 2 discreet, dry, homely, modest, plain, simple, undecorated, unembellished, unembroidered, ungarnished, unpretentious

adj 3 artless, candid, frank, guileless, ingenuous, innocent, naive, natural, open, plain, simple, simple-hearted, unaffected, unsophisticated, unstudied, untutored, unworldly

unadulterated *adj* 1 consistent, homogeneous, plain, pure, straight, undiluted, unmixed

adj 2 see: PURE *adj* 3, 7

unaffected *adj* 1 artless, candid, frank, guileless, ingenuous, innocent, naive, natural, open, plain, simple, simple-hearted, unadorned, unsophisticated, unstudied, untutored, unworldly

adj 2 see: IMPASSIVE *adj*

unafraid *adj* see: BRAVE *adj* 1

unaimed *adj* see: RANDOM *adj* 2

unalluring *adj* homely, plain, unattractive, unbeauteous, uncomely, unpretty

unalterable *adj* 1 permanent, unerasable

adj 2 binding, compelling, obligatory

adj 3 irrevocable, noncancelable, nonrescindable, permanent, uncancelable

adj 4 definite, determined, fixed, foregone, inevitable, inexorable, irrevocable, ordained, predestined, unavoidable, unchangeable

adj 5 hopeless, impossible, incurable, irreparable, irresolvable, irrevocable, permanent, terminal, uncorrectable, uncurable, unfixable

adj 6 see: CONSTANT *adj* 3

unambiguous *adj* 1 clear, clear-cut, crystal, limpid, lucid, translucent, transparent, unblurred

adj 2 blunt, clear, clear-cut, concise, decisive, definite, definitive, distinct, exact, explicit, precise, specific

adj 3 see: OBVIOUS *adj* 3

unanimous *adj* agreeing, concerted, harmonious, uncontested, undivided, unified

unanticipated *adj* accidental, sudden, surprising, unexpected, unforeseen

unapparent *adj* imperceptible, imponderable, inappreciable, indiscernible, insensible, intangible, invisible, minute, scant, unobservable, weak

unappetizing *adj* disagreeable, distasteful, disturbing, sickening, undesirable, unpalatable, unsavory

unappreciative *adj* heedless, thankless, unaware, ungrateful

unassertive *adj* acquiescent, compliant, docile, easy, meek, mild, nonresistant, obedient, passive, resigned, submissive, tame, yielding

unassuming *adj* 1 humble, lowly, meek, modest, unpretentious

adj 2 conservative, dim, inconspicuous, quiet, restrained, subdued, unobtrusive

unassured *adj* backward, bashful, coy, demure, diffident, innocent, modest, quiet, reserved, retiring, shy, timid

unattached *adj* detached, free, impartial, independent, neutral, nonpartisan, uncommitted, uninvolved

unattractive *adj* 1 hideous, homely, plain, repulsive, ugly

adj 2 unflattering

adj 3 homely, plain, unalluring, unbeauteous, uncomely, unpretty

unauthentic *adj* bastard, fatherless, illegitimate, misbegotten, orphaned, spurious, ungenuine

unavailing *adj* abortive, fruitless, futile, ineffective, ineffectual, nonproductive, unproductive, unsuccessful, unyielding, useless, vain, worthless

unavoidable *adj* 1 coercive, compelling, compulsory

adj 2 definite, determined, fixed, foregone, inevitable, inexorable, irrevocable, ordained, predestined, unalterable, unchangeable

unaware *adj* 1 unacquainted, unfamiliar, uninformed, unknowing

adj 2 distracted, heedless, inattentive, unheeding, unnoticing, unobservant, unperceiving, unwatchful

adj 3 heedless, thankless, ungrateful

unbalance *n* aberration, abnormality, craziness, delusion, dementia, derangement, distraction, eccentricity, fugue, hallucination, insanity, irregularity, lunacy, madness, mania

unbalanced *adj* erratic, flaky, unsound

unbearable *adj* excruciating, intolerable, unendurable

unbearing *adj* barren, effete, frigid, impotent, infertile, spent, sterile, unfertile, unfruitful, unproductive

unbeauteous *adj* homely, plain, unalluring, unattractive, uncomely, unpretty

unbecoming *adj* 1 unattractive

adj 2 erotic, improper, indecent, racy

adj 3 improper, indecent, indelicate,

lewd, malodorous, off-color, offensive, rough, scurrilous, suggestive, unseemly, untoward

adj 4 botching, bungling, goofing, helpless, ill-adapted, ill-suited, ill-timed, improper, inadequate, inappropriate, incapable, incongruous, incorrect, ineligible, inept, malapropos, unable, unbefitting, unequipped, unfit, unqualified, unseemly, unskilled, unsuitable, unsuited

unbefitting *adj* see: INADEQUATE *adj* 5

unbelief *n* disbelief, distrust, doubt, incredulity

unbelievable *adj* 1 outlandish, outrageous, unheard-of

adj 2 amazing, extraordinary, fantastic, incredible

adj 3 see: EXTRAVAGANT *adj* 3

adj 4 see: PREPOSTEROUS *adj* 2

unbeliever *n* agnostic, atheist, gentile, heathen, heretic, infidel, pagan

unbendable *adj* see: STUBBORN *adj* 6

unbending *adj* 1 bullheaded, closed-minded, deaf, firm, hardheaded, hard-line, inelastic, inflexible, intractable, intransigent, obstinate, perverse, pigheaded, refractory, resolute, rigid, stiff, stubborn, tough, uncompromising, unpliable, unpliant, unwieldy, unyielding, willful

adj 2 see: STUBBORN *adj* 6, 7

unbiased *adj* 1 advanced, broad, broad-minded, liberal, progressive, radical

adj 2 candid, dispassionate, equal, equitable, fair, impartial, impersonal, indifferent, just, neutral, objective, open-minded, square, uncolored, unprejudiced

unbind *v* 1 discharge, emancipate, free, liberate, loosen, release, unchain, unshackle

v 2 disengage, extricate, loosen, open, unclasp, undo, unfasten, unknot, unloose, unloosen, untie

unblemished *adj* 1 see: INTACT *adj* 2

adj 2 see: PURE *adj* 7

unblock *v* open, undo, unlock, unshut

unblunted *adj* honed, keen, pointed, razor sharp, sharp, whetted

unblurred *adj* clear, clear-cut, crystal, limpid, lucid, translucent, unambiguous

unbounded *adj* original, unconventional

unbridled *adj* 1 excessive, gluttonous, immoderate, inordinate, intemperate, overindulgent, prodigious, undue, unrestrained, voracious

adj 2 audacious, free, liberated, licentious, loose, rampant, unconfined, uncon-

trolled, uncurbed, ungoverned, unhampered, uninhibited, unrestrained, unsecured, unshackled, untied, wild

unbroken *adj* absolute, complete, flawless, good, intact, perfect, sound, unblemished, undamaged, unimpaired, uninjured, unmarred, untouched, whole

uncancelable *adj* irrevocable, noncancelable, nonrescindable, permanent

uncanny *adj* 1 astonishing, exceptional, incredible

adj 2 bizarre, eerie, ghostly, incredible, metaphysical, mystical, odd, ominous, spooky, strange, supernatural, unearthly, weird

adj 3 see: STRANGE *adj* 4, 5

uncaring *adj* 1 abusive, hard, harsh, severe, stern, stiff, strict, tough, unsympathetic

adj 2 accidental, careless, caustic, heedless, inadvertent, inconsiderate, nonchalant, selfish, sharp, short, tactless, thoughtless, unceremonious, ungracious, unheeding, unintended, unintentional, unreflective, unthinking

adj 3 see: NASTY *adj* 7

unceasing *adj* 1 endless, eternal, immortal, infinite, perpetual, undying

adj 2 see: PERPETUAL *adj* 1, 2

unceasingly *adv* see: FOREVER *adv*

uncelebrated *adj* anonymous, nameless, obscure, unfamed, unheard-of, unknown, unnamed, unrenowned

uncelestial *adj* common, earthly, earthy, mundane, pedestrian, worldly

unceremonious *adj* 1 caustic, inconsiderate, selfish, sharp, short, tactless, thoughtless, ungracious

adj 2 casual, cavalier, colloquial, familiar, informal, ordinary, regular, relaxed, unconstrained, unofficial, usual, vernacular

adj 3 accidental, careless, caustic, heedless, inadvertent, inconsiderate, nonchalant, selfish, sharp, short, tactless, thoughtless, uncaring, ungracious, unheeding, unintended, unintentional, unreflective, unthinking

uncertain *adj* 1 ambivalent, conflicting, equivocal

adj 2 circumstantial, contingent, iffy, vague

adj 3 anxious, insecure, nervous, precarious, threatened, vulnerable

adj 4 ancillary, conditional, contingent, dependent, indefinite, provisional, relative, reliant

adj 5 cynical, distrustful, doubtful, dubious, incredulous, leery, questionable, shy, skeptical, skittish, suspicious, unsure

adj 6 see: INCONSISTENT *adj 3*

adj 7 see: PREPOSTEROUS *adj 2*

adj 8 see: VAGUE *adj 6*

uncertainty *n* concern, doubt, dubiety, incertitude, indecision, mistrust, query, question, skepticism, suspicion, wonder

unchain *v* discharge, emancipate, free, liberate, loosen, release, unbind, unshackle

unchangeable *adj 1* definite, determined, fixed, foregone, inevitable, inexorable, irrevocable, ordained, predestined, unavoidable

adj 2 see: CONSTANT *adj 3*

unchanging *adj* consistent, constant, continuing, endless, equable, established, even, invariable, reliable, routine, same, serene, stable, steady, unfailing, unfluctuating, uniform, unvarying

uncharacteristic *adj* aberrant, abnormal, anomalous, artificial, atypical, contrived, deviant, disparate, divergent, incongruous, irregular, off-key, unnatural

unchaste *adj see:* PROMISCUOUS *adj 2*

uncivil *adj 1* barbarian, barbaric, savage, uncivilized, uncultivated, wild

adj 2 audacious, boorish, discourteous, disrespectful, ill-behaved, ill-bred, ill-mannered, impertinent, impolite, insolent, rude, surly, uncalled for, uncivilized, uncouth, uncultured, unpolished, unrefined

uncivilized *adj 1* barbarian, barbaric, savage, uncivil, uncultivated, wild

adj 2 barbarous, monstrous, outrageous, unconscionable, unethical, ungodly, unholy, wicked

adj 3 audacious, boorish, discourteous, disrespectful, ill-behaved, ill-bred, ill-mannered, impertinent, impolite, insolent, rude, surly, uncalled for, uncivil, uncouth, uncultured, unpolished, unrefined

unclasp *v* disengage, extricate, loosen, open, unbind, undo, unfasten, unknot, unloose, unloosen, untie

unclean *adj* black, dark, dingy, dirty, filthy, foul, grimy, grubby, mucky, murky, polluted, seedy, shabby, sooty, squalid, stained, unlit, unwashed

unclear *adj 1* illegible, scribbled, undecipherable, unreadable

adj 2 ambiguous, bleary, confused, fuzzy, hazy, misty, mixed up, nebulous

adj 3 illegible, incomprehensible, inconceivable, mysterious, unintelligible, unthinkable

adj 4 ambiguous, borderline, clouded, doubtful, dubious, equivocal, garbled, illogical, inarticulate, incalculable, incoherent, inexplicit, muddled, muffled, murky, obscure, precarious, questionable, shaky, suspect, suspicious, uncertain, uneasy, unintelligible, unsure, vague, wary

uncloak *v* debunk, discover, expose, show up, unmask, unshroud

unclosed *adj* open, unobstructed

unclothe *v* bare, denude, discard, disrobe, doff, flash, remove, reveal, shed, strip, undress

unclothed *adj* bare, exposed, in the raw, naked, nude, open, peeled, stripped, uncovered, visible

unclouded *adj* clear, cloudless, fair, sunny

uncolored *adj see:* FAIR *adj 7*

uncombed *adj* careless, disheveled, messy, scruffy, slatternly, slipshod, sloppy, sloven, slovenly, tacky, unkempt, untidy

uncomely *adj 1* contorted, grotesque, gruesome, hideous, ill-favored, ugly, unsightly

adj 2 homely, plain, unalluring, unattractive, unbeauteous, unpretty

uncomfortable *adj 1* cramped, restricted

adj 2 anxious, edgy, fidgety, impatient, nervous, nervy, queasy, restive, restless, tense, troubled, uneasy, uptight, worried

uncommitted *adj* detached, free, impartial, independent, neutral, nonpartisan, unattached, uninvolved

uncommon *adj 1* few, infrequent, isolated, occasional, rare, scarce, seldom, sporadic, unusual

adj 2 amazing, brilliant, exceptional, extraordinary, noteworthy, phenomenal, rare, remarkable, significant, singular, stunning, super, uncustomary, unique, unusual

adj 3 see: QUAINT *adj 1*

uncommunicative *adj* closed, diffident, introverted, laconic, reserved, restrained, reticent, secretive, shy, subdued, taciturn, timid, timorous, undaring

uncompromising *adj 1* bullheaded, closedminded, deaf, firm, hardheaded, hardline, inelastic, inflexible, intractable, intransigent, obstinate, perverse, pigheaded, refractory, resolute, rigid, stiff, stubborn, tough, unbending, unpliable, unpliant, unwieldy, unyielding, willful

adj 2 see: STUBBORN *adj*

unconcerned *adj 1 see:* INDIFFERENT *adj 4*

adj 2 see: LAZY *adj*

unconditional *adj* absolute, firm, fixed, resolute, steadfast, unreserved

unconfined *adj* audacious, free, liberated, licentious, loose, rampant, unbridled, uncontrolled, uncurbed, ungoverned, unhampered, uninhibited, unrestrained, unsecured, unshackled, untied, wild

unconnected *adj* autonomous, distinct, free, independent, lone, separate

unconquerable *adj* firm, invincible, unyielding

unconscionable *adj* 1 undue, unjustifiable, unreasonable, unwarranted

adj 2 barbarous, monstrous, outrageous, uncivilized, unethical, ungodly, unholy, wicked

unconscious *adj* 1 dazed, insensible, senseless

adj 2 cold, comatose, insensible, senseless

adj 3 automatic, impulsive, instinctive, involuntary, natural, rash, reflex, spontaneous, unforced, unpremeditated, unprompted

unconstrained *adj* see: INFORMAL *adj* 1

uncontested *adj* agreeing, concerted, harmonious, unanimous, undivided, unified

uncontrollable *adj* indomitable, intractable, recalcitrant, stubborn, undisciplined, unmanageable, unruly, untoward, wild

uncontrolled *adj* 1 accidental, aimless, arbitrary, casual, chance, chaotic, haphazard, hit-or-miss, indiscriminate, irregular, random, unaimed, unplanned

adj 2 audacious, free, liberated, licentious, loose, rampant, unbridled, unconfined, uncurbed, ungoverned, unhampered, uninhibited, unrestrained, unsecured, unshackled, untied, wild

unconventional *adj* 1 nonconformist, original, unbounded

adj 2 bizarre, bohemian, offbeat, unorthodox

adj 3 aberrant, bizarre, eccentric, erratic, odd, oddball, outlandish, peculiar, quaint, queer, singular, strange, uncanny, unusual, weird

unconvincing *adj* illogical, inconclusive, indecisive, indefinite, open, unsettled, unverified

uncooked *adj* fresh, rare, raw

uncorrectable *adj* hopeless, impossible, incurable, irreparable, irresolvable, irrevocable, permanent, terminal, unalterable, uncurable, unfixable

uncountable *adj* countless, immeasurable, incalculable, infinite, innumerable, innumerous, legion, many, numberless, unlimited, untold

uncouple *v* cut, detach, disconnect, disengage, dissociate, separate, sever, unfasten, unhook, unyoke

uncouth *adj* 1 coarse, crass, crude, flagrant, glaring, gross, obscene, rough, shocking, uncultured, unrefined

adj 2 audacious, boorish, discourteous, disrespectful, ill-behaved, ill-bred, ill-mannered, impertinent, impolite, insolent, rude, surly, uncalled for, uncivil, uncivilized, uncultured, unpolished, unrefined

adj 3 bawdy, coarse, crude, dirty, erotic, filthy, foul, gamy, gross, improper, indecent, lascivious, lewd, licentious, nasty, obscene, off-color, pornographic, profane, prurient, racy, rank, raunchy, ribald, risqué, scandalous, smutty, suggestive, tainted, vulgar, x-rated

uncover *v* 1 rummage, search

v 2 bare, expose, lay open, strip, subject

v 3 ascertain, catch on, determine, discover, find out, hear, learn, listen, unearth

v 4 communicate, disclose, display, divulge, exhibit, inform, notify, open, reveal, unveil

v 5 ascertain, catch, descry, detect, discover, encounter, espy, ferret, find, locate, spot

uncovered *adj* 1 discovered, found, located

adj 2 bare, exposed, in the raw, naked, nude, open, peeled, stripped, unclothed, visible

uncreative *adj* uninspired, uninventive, unoriginal

uncritical *adj* brief, crude, cursory, hasty, rough, shallow, sketchy

unctuous *adj* greasy, oily, sleek, slick, slippery

uncultivated *adj* barbarian, barbaric, savage, uncivil, uncivilized, wild

uncultured *adj* 1 coarse, crass, crude, flagrant, glaring, gross, obscene, rough, shocking, uncouth, unrefined

adj 2 audacious, boorish, discourteous, disrespectful, ill-behaved, ill-bred, ill-mannered, impertinent, impolite, insolent, rude, surly, uncalled for, uncivil, uncivilized, uncouth, unpolished, unrefined

uncurable *adj* hopeless, impossible, incurable, irreparable, irresolvable, irrevocable, permanent, terminal, unalterable, uncorrectable, unfixable

uncurbed *adj* audacious, free, liberated, licentious, loose, rampant, unbridled, unconfined, uncontrolled, ungoverned, unhampered, uninhibited, unrestrained, unsecured, unshackled, untied, wild

uncustomary *adj* see: EXTRAORDINARY *adj* 4

undamaged *adj* 1 safe, sound, unharmed, unhurt
adj 2 absolute, complete, flawless, good, intact, perfect, sound, unblemished, unbroken, unimpaired, uninjured, unmarred, untouched, whole

undaring *adj* 1 timid
adj 2 see: RETICENT *adj* 2

undaunted *adj* see: BRAVE *adj* 1

undecipherable *adj* illegible, scribbled, unclear, unreadable

undeclared *adj* additional, covert, hidden, secondary, ulterior

undecorated *adj* discreet, dry, homely, modest, plain, simple, unadorned, unembellished, unembroidered, ungarnished, unpretentious

undefeated *adj* conquering, successful, triumphant, victorious, winning

undefiled *adj* see: PURE *adj* 7

undeniable *adj* absolute, actual, authentic, bona fide, certain, definite, existent, factual, genuine, hard, inarguable, incontestable, incontrovertible, indisputable, indubitable, irrefutable, positive, real, sure, true, undisputable, undoubtable, undoubted, unequivocal, unquestionable, veritable, viable

undependable *adj* 1 capricious, careless, immature, irresponsible, unpredictable, untrustworthy
adj 2 dubious, insecure, questionable, unreliable, unsure, untrustworthy

under *adj* 1 lower, recessed, sunken
adj 2 inferior, lower, subordinate
prep below, beneath, lower than, underneath

under cover *adv* clandestinely, covertly, furtively, hush-hush, mystically, secretly, sneakily, stealthily, surreptitiously

underestimate *v* err, miscalculate, misconstrue, misjudge

undergo *v* see: TOLERATE *v*

undergraduate *n* coed, collegian, pupil, scholar, student

underground *adj* see: DECEITFUL *adj* 1
n basement, cellar, vault

underhand *adj* clandestine, concealed, covert, crafty, deceitful, devious, evasive, foxy, furtive, guileful, indirect, privy, secret, shifty, sly, sneaky, surreptitious, tricky, underground, underhanded, wily

underhanded *adj* see: DECEITFUL *adj* 1

underline *v* see: ACCENTUATE *v*

underling *n* assistant, dependent, employee

underlying *adj* basic, early, elementary, embryonic, essential, fundamental, initial, intrinsic, original

undermine *v* cripple, debilitate, disable, drain, enfeeble, exhaust, weaken

underneath *prep* below, beneath, under

underpinning *n* base, brace, buttress, column, footing, foundation, prop, shore, support

underrate *v* cheapen, depreciate, devalue, diminish, downgrade, dwindle, lower, mark down, reduce

underscore *v* see: ACCENTUATE *v*

understand *v* 1 encounter, endure, experience, know, realize
v 2 get, learn, master, pick up, read, realize, study
v 3 comprehend, decipher, decode, infer, interpret, peruse, read, study
v 4 analyze, assess, determine, diagnose, estimate, examine, penetrate, probe, scope, solve, survey, unravel
v 5 assume, believe, comprehend, conceive, estimate, expect, fathom, gather, grasp, guess, imagine, infer, know, presume, suppose, surmise, suspect, think, trust
v 6 behold, catch, comprehend, conjure, descry, digest, discern, distinguish, espy, fathom, grasp, know, look at, notice, observe, perceive, realize, recognize, savvy, see, sight, take in, view
v 7 see: ELUCIDATE *v* 1

understandable *adj* 1 clear, legible, readable
adj 2 clear, coherent, direct, easy, elementary, intelligible, logical, lucid, simple

understanding *n* 1 comprehension, intellect, mind, reason
n 2 cognition, comprehension, grasp, insight, perception, recognition
n 3 affinity, compassion, empathy, kindness, mercy, pity, rue, sympathy, tenderness
n 4 agreement, bargain, bond, compact, contract, convention, covenant, deal, pact, pledge, promise, transaction
n 5 acumen, astuteness, awareness, cleverness, discernment, discrimination, insight, intellect, intuition, keenness, perception, sagacity, sensitivity, wit
n 6 assessment, interpretation, reading
n 7 import, intent, meaning, message, significance

understood *adj* 1 accepted, implied, presumed, supposed, tacit *adj* 2 implicit, implied, indicated, inferred, inherent, insinuated, intuitive, presumed, suggested, tacit, unexpressed, unsaid, unspoken, wordless

understudy *n* pinch hitter, stand-in, substitute

undersupply *n* dearth, deficiency, deficit, drought, famine, lack, rarity, scarcity, shortage, sparseness, want

undertake *v* 1 conduct, proceed with, pursue, wage

v 2 assay, attempt, endeavor, essay, offer, quest, seek, strive, struggle, try

undertaking *n* 1 activity, business, endeavor, enterprise, exercise, project, venture

n 2 chase, exploration, hunt, pursuit, quest, search, venture

n 3 attempt, effort, endeavor, speculation, struggle, trial, try, venture

undertone *n* mumble, murmur, whisper

undervalue *v* cheapen, depreciate, devalue, diminish, downgrade, dwindle, lower, mark down, reduce, underrate

underwater *adj* scuttled, submerged, sunken

underwrite *v* 1 aid, endow, fund, subsidize

v 2 assure, certify, contract, endorse, guarantee, pledge, sanction, vouch, warrant

undesigning *adj* see: SINCERE *adj*

undesirable *adj* 1 disagreeable, distasteful, disturbing, sickening, unappetizing, unpalatable, unsavory

adj 2 ill-favored, inadmissible, objectionable, unacceptable, unwanted, unwelcome

undeveloped *adj* 1 basic, crude, plain, primitive, rough

adj 2 adolescent, fresh, green, immature, juvenile, precocious, unfledged, unready, young, youthful

undiluted *adj* consistent, homogeneous, plain, pure, straight, unadulterated, unmixed

undisciplined *adj* indomitable, intractable, recalcitrant, stubborn, uncontrollable, unmanageable, unruly, untoward, wild

undisputable *adj* absolute, actual, authentic, bona fide, certain, definite, existent, factual, genuine, hard, inarguable, incontestable, incontrovertible, indisputable, indubitable, irrefutable, positive, real, sure, true, undeniable, undoubtable, undoubted, unequivocal, unquestionable, veritable, viable

undistinguished *adj* banal, commonplace, conventional, ordinary

undistorted *adj* authoritative, dependable,

due, faithful, legitimate, rightful, strict, true, trustworthy, veracious

undistracted *adj* concentrated, exclusive, fixed, undivided, unswerving, whole

undivided *adj* 1 agreeing, concerted, harmonious, unanimous, unified

adj 2 concentrated, exclusive, fixed, undistracted, unswerving, whole

undo *v* 1 disentangle, unravel, untangle, unwind

v 2 open, unblock, unlock, unshut

v 3 disengage, extricate, loosen, open, unbind, unclasp, unfasten, unknot, unloose, unloosen, untie

v 4 annihilate, decimate, demolish, destroy, destruct, devastate, dismantle, overturn, pulverize, raze, rub out, ruin, shatter, smash, tear down, wreck

undoable *adj* 1 impossible, inconceivable, incredible, strange, unachievable, unthinkable

adj 2 impractical, inoperable, unworkable

undoing *n* debacle, defeat, disaster, downfall, overthrow, rout, ruination, thrashing, trouncing, vanquishment

undoubtable *adj* absolute, actual, authentic, bona fide, certain, definite, existent, factual, genuine, hard, inarguable, incontestable, incontrovertible, indisputable, indubitable, irrefutable, positive, real, sure, true, undeniable, undisputable, undoubted, unequivocal, unquestionable, veritable, viable

undoubted *adj* absolute, actual, authentic, bona fide, certain, definite, existent, factual, genuine, hard, inarguable, incontestable, incontrovertible, indisputable, indubitable, irrefutable, positive, real, sure, true, undeniable, undisputable, undoubtable, unequivocal, unquestionable, veritable, viable

undoubtedly *adv* clearly, evidently, obviously, unquestionably

undress *v* bare, denude, discard, disrobe, doff, flash, remove, reveal, shed, strip, take off, unclothe

undressed *adj* crude, raw, rough, rude, unfashioned, unfinished, unhewn, unpolished

undrinkable *adj* brackish, briny, foul, nasty, salty, stagnant

undue *adj* 1 unconscionable, unjustifiable, unreasonable, unwarranted

adj 2 excessive, gluttonous, immoderate, inordinate, intemperate, overindulgent, prodigious, unbridled, unrestrained, voracious

undulate *v* **1** dance, flap, flicker, flitter, flutter, oscillate, prance, sparkle, sway, twinkle, wave

v **2** fluctuate, oscillate, pulsate, surge, throb, vibrate

undying *adj* endless, eternal, immortal, infinite, perpetual

uneager *adj* afraid, averse, disinclined, hesitant, indisposed, loath, opposed, recalcitrant, reluctant, shy, unwilling

unearth *v* **1** burrow, dig, excavate, gouge, mine, scoop, shovel

v **2** ascertain, catch on, determine, discover, find out, hear, learn, listen

unearthing *n* breakthrough, disclosure, discovery, exposition, find

unearthly *adj* **1** bodiless, celestial, disembodied, ethereal, heavenly, incorporeal, insubstantial, intangible, metaphysical, nonmaterial, spiritual, unreal, unsubstantial

adj **2** bizarre, eerie, ghostly, incredible, metaphysical, mystical, odd, ominous, spooky, strange, supernatural, weird

uneasiness *n* **1** adversity, difficulty, discipline, discomfort, hardness, rigor, severity, strictness

n **2** annoyance, anxiety, apprehension, bother, care, concern, disquiet, disquietude, doubt, irritation, misgiving, reservation, restlessness, restraint, skepticism, trouble, vexation, worry

uneasy *adj* **1** anxious, edgy, fidgety, impatient, nervous, nervy, queasy, restive, restless, tense, troubled, uncomfortable, uptight, worried

adj **2** ambiguous, borderline, clouded, doubtful, dubious, equivocal, garbled, illogical, inarticulate, incalculable, incoherent, inexplicit, muddled, muffled, murky, obscure, precarious, questionable, shaky, suspect, suspicious, uncertain, unclear, unintelligible, unsure, vague, wary

uneducated *adj* **1** ignorant, illiterate, uninstructed, unlearned, unlettered, unschooled, untaught, untutored

adj **2** see: DUMB *adj* 2

unembellished *adj* discreet, dry, homely, modest, plain, simple, unadorned, undecorated, unembroidered, ungarnished, unpretentious

unembroidered *adj* discreet, dry, homely, modest, plain, simple, unadorned, undecorated, unembellished, ungarnished, unpretentious

unemotional *adj* **1** apathetic, dispassionate, unresponsive

adj **2** cold, coldhearted, distant, emotionless, frigid, glacial, icy, impersonal, indifferent, unfriendly

adj **3** see: IMPASSIVE *adj*

adj **4** see: NASTY *adj* 7

adj **5** see: SOLEMN *adj* 1

unemployed *adj* idle, jobless

unending *adj* see: PERPETUAL *adj* 2

unendurable *adj* excruciating, intolerable, painful, unbearable

unequal *adj* different, disparate, diverse, incongruous, opposite, unlike, unmatched, unrelated

unequaled *adj* **1** foremost, majority, maximum, most, optimal

adj **2** alone, incomparable, matchless, only, peerless, unique, unmatched, unpaired, unparalleled, unrivaled

unequipped *adj* see: INADEQUATE *adj* 5

unequivocal *adj* **1** apparent, clear, conspicuous, distinct, evident, given, indisputable, indubitable, manifest, obvious, patent, plain, presumed, self-evident, straightforward, true, unmistakable

adj **2** absolute, actual, authentic, bona fide, certain, definite, existent, factual, genuine, hard, inarguable, incontestable, incontrovertible, indisputable, indubitable, irrefutable, positive, real, sure, true, undeniable, undisputable, undoubtable, undoubted, unquestionable, veritable, viable

adj **3** see: EXACT *adj* 6

unequivocally *adv* see: DEFINITELY *adv*

unerasable *adj* indelible, permanent, unalterable

unerring *adj* accurate, certain, distinct, explicit, incontestable, infallible

unessential *adj* see: TRIVIAL *adj* 1

unethical *adj* **1** barbarous, monstrous, outrageous, uncivilized, unconscionable, ungodly, unholy, wicked

adj **2** see: EVIL *adj* 4

uneven *adj* **1** biased, inequitable, partial, unfair, unjust, unrighteous, wrongful

adj **2** bouncy, bumpy, craggy, irregular, jagged, jolting, rough, rugged, scraggy, unsmooth

uneventful *adj* common, commonplace, dull, ordinary, pedestrian, prosaic, unexceptional

unexaminable *adj* see: MYSTIC *adj* 2

unexceptional *adj* **1** common, commonplace, dull, ordinary, pedestrian, prosaic

adj **2** see: TYPICAL *adj* 2

unexciting *adj* **1** banal, bland, dull, flat, innocuous, insipid

adj **2** arid, bland, bleak, boring, colorless,

dead, desolate, drab, dreary, dull, flat, lackluster, lifeless, lusterless, monotonous, muted, somber, trite, uninteresting

unexpected *adj* 1 startling, sudden, surprising, unforeseen

adj 2 coincidental, curious, odd, strange

adj 3 accidental, sudden, surprising, unanticipated, unforeseen

unexplored *adj* 1 dawning, frontier, new, unknown

adj 2 curious, exotic, far-out, fascinating, intriguing, kinky, marvelous, mysterious, new, novel, odd, outlandish, strange, ultra, unaccustomed, unfamiliar, unique, unknown, unusual, weird

unexpressed *adj* see: IMPLIED *adj* 2

unfailing *adj* consistent, constant, continuing, endless, equable, established, even, invariable, reliable, routine, same, serene, stable, steady, unchanging, unfluctuating, uniform, unvarying

unfair *adj* 1 biased, inequitable, partial, uneven, unjust, unrighteous, wrongful

adj 2 see: EVIL *adj* 4

unfairness *n* bias, inequity, injustice, prejudice, wrong

unfaithful *adj* cheating, conniving, deceitful, deceptive, dishonest, disloyal, faithless, false, insidious, manipulative, perfidious, sneaky, traitorous, treacherous, untrue, untrustworthy

unfaltering *adj* abiding, enduring, firm, never-failing, steadfast, sure, unshakable, unwavering

unfamed *adj* anonymous, nameless, obscure, uncelebrated, unheard-of, unknown, unnamed, unrenowned

unfamiliar *adj* 1 unacquainted, unaware, uninformed, unknowing

adj 2 curious, exotic, far-out, fascinating, intriguing, kinky, marvelous, mysterious, new, novel, odd, outlandish, strange, ultra, unaccustomed, unexplored, unique, unknown, unusual, weird

adj 3 alien, exotic, foreign

unfashioned *adj* crude, raw, rough, rude, undressed, unfinished, unhewn, unpolished

unfasten *v* 1 cut, detach, disconnect, disengage, dissociate, separate, sever, uncouple, unhook, unyoke

v 2 disengage, extricate, loosen, open, unbind, unclasp, undo, unknot, unloose, unloosen, untie

unfathomed *adj* see: HUGE *adj* 3

unfavorable *adj* 1 adverse, deleterious, detrimental, harmful, injurious, negative

adj 2 adverse, bad, evil, harmful, ill, unlucky

unfeasible *adj* far-fetched, impractical, remote, unrealistic

unfeeling *adj* 1 see: IMPASSIVE *adj*

adj 2 see: NASTY *adj* 7

unfeigned *adj* see: SINCERE *adj*

unfertile *adj* see: INFERTILE *adj*

unfilled *adj* bare, blank, dull, empty

unfinished *adj* 1 fragmentary, halfway, incomplete, partial

adj 2 awaiting, contingent, impending, pending, unsettled

adj 3 crude, raw, rough, rude, undressed, unfashioned, unhewn, unpolished

unfit *adj* botching, bungling, goofing, helpless, ill-adapted, ill-suited, ill-timed, improper, inadequate, inappropriate, incapable, incongruous, incorrect, ineligible, inept, malapropos, unable, unbecoming, unbefitting, unequipped, unqualified, unseemly, unskilled, unsuitable, unsuited

unfitting *adj* inapplicable, inconsistent, irrelevant, spurious

unfixable *adj* hopeless, impossible, incurable, irreparable, irresolvable, irrevocable, permanent, terminal, unalterable, uncorrectable

unflappable *adj* see: CALM *adj* 2

unflattering *adj* unattractive

unfledged *adj* see: YOUNG *adj* 1

unflinching *adj* see: SOLEMN *adj* 1

unfluctuating *adj* consistent, constant, continuing, endless, equable, established, even, invariable, reliable, routine, same, serene, stable, steady, unchanging, unfailing, uniform, unvarying

unfold *v* 1 derive, develop, evolve, mature, progress

v 2 clarify, disclose, explain, reveal

v 3 expand, extend, fan, open, outstretch, spread

unforced *adj* 1 deliberate, free, intentional, optional, unprescribed, voluntary, willful, willing

adj 2 see: SPONTANEOUS *adj* 2

unforeseen *adj* 1 startling, surprising, unexpected

adj 2 accidental, sudden, surprising, unexpected

unforgettable *adj* 1 indelible, memorable, momentous

adj 2 colorful, expressive, graphic, impressive, intense, potent, powerful, striking, vivid

unforgiving *adj* malicious, revengeful, spiteful, unmerciful, vengeful, vindictive

unfortunate *adj* **1** cursed, damned, doomed, hapless, hopeless, ill-fated, jinxed, luckless, unhappy, unlucky, untoward

adj **2** affecting, deplorable, lamentable, miserable, paltry, pathetic, pitiable, pitiful, poor, sad, woeful, wretched

unfounded *adj* baseless, erroneous, fallacious, groundless, invalid, unsubstantiated

unfriendly *adj* **1** distant, forbidding, snobbish

adj **2** adverse, antagonistic, bellicose, hostile, ill, inimical, nasty

adj **3** cold, coldhearted, distant, emotionless, frigid, glacial, icy, impersonal, indifferent, unemotional

adj **4** aloof, blasé, calm, careless, casual, composed, cool, detached, diffident, disinterested, distant, indifferent, informal, inhibited, nonchalant, numb, remote, reserved, shy, unconcerned, uninterested, withdrawn

unfruitful *adj* barren, effete, frigid, impotent, infertile, spent, sterile, unbearing, unfertile, unproductive

unfulfilled *adj* amiss, crude, defective, dissatisfied, faulty, flawed, imperfect, incomplete

ungainly *adj* awkward, bumbling, clumsy, faltering, gauche, gawky, halting, hesitant, inept, lumbering, maladroit, ungraceful

ungarnished *adj* discreet, dry, homely, modest, plain, simple, unadorned, undecorated, unembellished, unembroidered, unpretentious

ungenerous *adj* see: CHEAP *adj* **3**

ungenuine *adj* bastard, false, fatherless, illegitimate, misbegotten, orphaned, spurious

ungiving *adj* see: CHEAP *adj* **3**

unglue *v* see: BEWILDER *v* **2**

ungodly *adj* barbarous, monstrous, outrageous, uncivilized, unconscionable, unethical, unholy, wicked

ungoverned *adj* audacious, free, liberated, licentious, loose, rampant, unbridled, unconfined, uncontrolled, uncurbed, unhampered, uninhibited, unrestrained, unsecured, unshackled, untied, wild

ungraceful *adj* awkward, bumbling, clumsy, faltering, gauche, gawky, halting, hesitant, inept, lumbering, maladroit

ungracious *adj* **1** caustic, inconsiderate, selfish, sharp, short, tactless, thoughtless

adj **2** accidental, careless, caustic, heedless, inadvertent, inconsiderate, nonchalant, selfish, sharp, short, tactless, thoughtless, uncaring, unceremonious, unheeding, unintended, unintentional, unreflective, unthinking

ungrateful *adj* heedless, thankless, unappreciative, unaware

unhampered *adj* audacious, free, liberated, licentious, loose, rampant, unbridled, unconfined, uncontrolled, uncurbed, ungoverned, uninhibited, unrestrained, unsecured, unshackled, untied, wild

unhappiness *n* discontent, dissatisfaction, regret, vexation

unhappy *adj* **1** cursed, damned, doomed, hapless, hopeless, ill-fated, jinxed, luckless, unfortunate, unlucky, untoward

adj **2** annoying, bad, difficult, disagreeable, displeasing, nasty, objectionable, offensive, rotten, sour, unpleasant, upsetting

adj **3** black, bleak, blue, cheerless, dejected, depressed, desperate, despondent, discouraging, disheartening, distressing, down, forlorn, gloomy, hopeless, joyless, melancholy, moody, mournful, oppressive, prostrate, sad, somber

unharmed *adj* safe, sound, undamaged, unhurt

unhasty *adj* deliberate, dilatory, diligent, leisurely, methodical, meticulous, painstaking, patient, procrastinating, slow, thorough, unhurried

unhealthy *adj* **1** harmful, poisonous, toxic

adj **2** damaging, dangerous, deleterious, harmful, hurting, injurious

adj **3** ailing, delicate, diseased, down, frail, ill, impaired, indisposed, sick, sickly, suffering, unsound, unwell, weak

unheard-of *adj* **1** outrageous, unbelievable

adj **2** anonymous, nameless, obscure, uncelebrated, unfamed, unknown, unnamed, unrenowned

unheeding *adj* **1** distracted, heedless, inattentive, unaware, unnoticing, unobservant, unperceiving, unwatchful

adj **2** accidental, careless, caustic, heedless, inadvertent, inconsiderate, nonchalant, selfish, sharp, short, tactless, thoughtless, uncaring, unceremonious, ungracious, unintended, unintentional, unreflective, unthinking

unhewn *adj* crude, raw, rough, rude, undressed, unfashioned, unfinished, unpolished

unhinge *v* **1** agitate, derange, disorder, disturb, fluster, rock, ruffle, shake, sicken, unsettle, upset

v **2** befuddle, bewilder, confuse, daze,

distract, dizzy, embarrass, fluster, mix up, muddle, rattle, ruffle, trick

unhip *adj* orthodox, traditional

unholy *adj* barbarous, monstrous, outrageous, uncivilized, unconscionable, unethical, ungodly, wicked

unhook *v* cut, detach, disconnect, disengage, dissociate, separate, sever, uncouple, unfasten, unyoke

unhurried *adj* deliberate, dilatory, diligent, leisurely, methodical, meticulous, painstaking, patient, procrastinating, slow, thorough

unhurt *adj* safe, undamaged, unharmed

unified *adj* 1 agreeing, concerted, harmonious, unanimous, uncontested, undivided
adj 2 collective, cooperative, helpful, joint, participatory, united

uniform *adj* 1 established, normal, standard
adj 2 akin, alike, analogous, comparable, corresponding, equivalent, identical, kindred, like, matching, parallel, related, same, similar
adj 3 consistent, constant, continuing, endless, equable, established, even, invariable, reliable, routine, same, serene, stable, steady, unchanging, unfailing, unfluctuating, unvarying

uniformity *n* harmony, symmetry

unify *v* 1 arrange, blend, combine, compound, concoct, harmonize, integrate, make one, orchestrate
v 2 see: COMBINE *v* 2

unilluminated *adj* see: DARK *adj* 2

unimpaired *adj* see: INTACT *adj* 2

unimpassioned *adj* levelheaded, moderate, sober

unimportant *adj* 1 immaterial, inconsequential, inconsiderable, insignificant, little, low, meaningless, measly, minor, nominal, paltry, petty, picayune, picky, puny, skimpy, slight, small, tiny, trifling, trivial, unessential, worthless
adj 2 borderline, casual, frivolous, insignificant, light, lightweight, little, marginal, meager, minor, minute, negligible, nonessential, off, outside, petty, remote, secondary, slender, slight, slim, small, trivial
adj 3 see: SUPERFLUOUS *adj* 3

unimpressive *adj* see: AVERAGE *adj* 1

uninformed *adj* unacquainted, unaware, unfamiliar, unknowing

uninhabited *adj* abandoned, depraved, derelict, deserted, desolate, forsaken, secluded

uninhibited *adj* audacious, free, liberated,

licentious, loose, rampant, unbridled, unconfined, uncontrolled, uncurbed, ungoverned, unhampered, unrestrained, unsecured, unshackled, untied, wild

uninjured *adj* see: INTACT *adj* 2

uninspired *adj* uninventive, unoriginal

uninstructed *adj* ignorant, illiterate, uneducated, unlearned, unlettered, unschooled, untaught, untutored

unintelligent *adj* 1 see: DUMB *adj* 2
adj 2 see: SILLY *adj* 2

unintelligible *adj* 1 illegible, incomprehensible, inconceivable, mysterious, unclear, unthinkable
adj 2 ambiguous, borderline, clouded, doubtful, dubious, equivocal, garbled, illogical, inarticulate, incalculable, incoherent, inexplicit, muddled, muffled, murky, obscure, precarious, questionable, shaky, suspect, suspicious, uncertain, unclear, uneasy, unsure, vague, wary

unintended *adj* accidental, careless, caustic, heedless, inadvertent, inconsiderate, nonchalant, selfish, sharp, short, tactless, thoughtless, uncaring, unceremonious, ungracious, unheeding, unintentional, unreflective, unthinking

unintentional *adj* accidental, careless, caustic, heedless, inadvertent, inconsiderate, nonchalant, selfish, sharp, short, tactless, thoughtless, uncaring, unceremonious, ungracious, unheeding, unintended, unreflective, unthinking

uninterested *adj* see: INDIFFERENT *adj* 4

uninteresting *adj* see: DULL *adj* 7

uninterrupted *adj* 1 direct, linear, straight
adj 2 see: PERPETUAL *adj* 2

uninventive *adj* uncreative, uninspired, unoriginal

uninvolved *adj* detached, free, impartial, independent, neutral, nonpartisan, unattached

union *n* 1 association, institute, institution, organization
n 2 bond, cohesion, connection, fusion, togetherness
n 3 blend, combination, fusion, intermingling, joining, mixture
n 4 association, combination, corporation, establishment, fellowship, foundation, institution
n 5 affair, association, communication, friendship, intimacy, liaison, relationship
n 6 affiliation, alliance, association, axis, bloc, coalition, concord, confederation, consolidation, faction, federation, joint venture, league, merger, organization, partnership, relationship

n 7 coupling, liaison, linking, marriage, matrimony, wedlock

n 8 coitus, conjugation, copulation, fooling around, foreplay, fornication, intercourse, mating, sex

n 9 association, body, club, company, contingent, delegation, fellowship, fraternity, group, organization, society

unique *adj* 1 alone, incomparable, matchless, only, peerless, unequaled, unmatched, unpaired, unparalleled, unrivaled

adj 2 characteristic, differentiating, distinctive, lone, one, particular, peculiar, select, single, solitary, special, unusual

adj 3 exclusive, individual, lone, odd, one, only, particular, separate, single, singular, sole, solitary, unshared

adj 4 amazing, brilliant, exceptional, extraordinary, noteworthy, phenomenal, rare, remarkable, significant, singular, stunning, super, uncommon, uncustomary, unusual

adj 5 curious, exotic, far-out, fascinating, intriguing, kinky, marvelous, mysterious, new, novel, odd, outlandish, strange, ultra, unaccustomed, unexplored, unfamiliar, unknown, unusual, weird

uniqueness *n* individuality, originality

unit *n* 1 component, module

n 2 branch, department, division

n 3 adjunct, annex, fitting, fixture, piece

n 4 see: GROUP *n* 5

unite *v* 1 accompany, band, coincide, collaborate, collude, combine, concur, cooperate, pool

v 2 clump, fasten, hitch, join, knot, lace, lash, link, loop, rope, secure

v 3 associate, blend, bond, coalesce, combine, compound, connect, couple, fasten, fuse, join, link, marry, mate, meet, merge, pair, wed

v 4 see: COMBINE *v* 1, 3, 4

v 5 see: FASTEN *v* 9, 10, 11

united *adj* collective, cooperative, helpful, joint, participatory, unified

unity *n* 1 distinctiveness, individuality, oneness, singularity, singularness

n 2 accord, affinity, agreement, assent, concert, concord, congruence, cooperation, empathy, harmony, rapport, synergy

universal *adj* 1 international

adj 2 common, general, generic

adj 3 blanket, comprehensive, expansive, extensive, sweeping

adj 4 broad, general, global, planetary, urban, widespread, worldwide

universe *n* cosmos, creation, firmament, grand scale, macrocosm, nature, solar system, vastness, world

university *n* academy, college, institute, lyceum, school

unjust *adj* biased, inequitable, partial, uneven, unfair, unrighteous, wrongful

unjustifiable *adj* unconscionable, undue, unreasonable, unwarranted

unkempt *adj* careless, disheveled, messy, scruffy, slatternly, slipshod, sloppy, sloven, slovenly, tacky, uncombed, untidy

unkind *adj* 1 see: NASTY *adj* 7

adj 2 see: SEVERE *adj* 8

unknot *v* disengage, extricate, loosen, open, unbind, unclasp, undo, unfasten, unloose, unloosen, untie

unknowing *adj* unacquainted, unaware, unfamiliar

unknown *adj* 1 dawning, frontier, unexplored

adj 2 anonymous, nameless, obscure, uncelebrated, unfamed, unheard-of, unnamed, unrenowned

adj 3 see: MYSTIC *adj* 2

adj 4 see: UNUSUAL *adj* 4

unlawful *adj* criminal, disgraceful, felonious, illegal, illegitimate, illicit, lawless, prohibited, wrong, wrongful

unlearned *adj* ignorant, illiterate, uneducated, uninstructed, unlettered, unschooled, untaught, untutored

unless *prep* aside from, barring, except, excluding

unlettered *adj* ignorant, illiterate, uneducated, uninstructed, unlearned, unschooled, untaught, untutored

unlike *adj* 1 different, disparate, diverse, incongruous, opposite, unequal, unmatched, unrelated

adj 2 alternate, another, certain, different, discrete, disparate, dissimilar, distinct, diverse, numerous, other, separate, several, some, various, varying

unlikely *adj* absurd, chancy, debatable, doubtful, dubious, iffy, implausible, improbable, incredible, moot, questionable, preposterous, theoretical, unbelievable

unlimited *adj* 1 countless, immeasurable, incalculable, infinite, innumerable, innumerous, legion, many, numberless, uncountable, untold

adj 2 all, all-out, complete, entire, full-blown, gross, integral, integrated, outright, total, whole

unlit *adj* see: DIRTY *adj* 2

unload *v* abandon, discard, dispose of, dump, eliminate, empty, quit, reject

unlock *v* open, unblock, undo, unshut

unloose *v* disengage, extricate, loosen, open, unbind, unclasp, undo, unfasten, unknot, unloosen, untie

unloosen *v* disengage, extricate, loosen, open, unbind, unclasp, undo, unfasten, unknot, unloose, untie

unlucky *adj* 1 adverse, bad, evil, harmful, unfavorable

adj 2 cursed, damned, doomed, hapless, hopeless, ill-fated, jinxed, luckless, unfortunate, unhappy, untoward

unman *v* castrate, debilitate, dismember, emasculate, enervate, geld, unnerve

unmanageable *adj* indomitable, intractable, recalcitrant, stubborn, uncontrollable, undisciplined, unruly, untoward, wild

unmanly *adj* effeminate, effete, sissy, swishy, wimpy

unmarred *adj* see: INTACT *adj* 2

unmarried *adj* single, sole, spouseless, unwed

unmask *v* debunk, discover, expose, show up, uncloak, unshroud

unmatched *adj* 1 different, disparate, diverse, incongruous, opposite, unequal, unlike, unrelated

adj 2 see: UNIQUE *adj* 1

unmerciful *adj* 1 malicious, revengeful, spiteful, unforgiving, vengeful, vindictive

adj 2 see: NASTY *adj* 7

unmistakable *adj* 1 apparent, clear, conspicuous, distinct, evident, given, indisputable, indubitable, manifest, obvious, patent, plain, presumed, self-evident, straightforward, true, unambiguous, unequivocal

adj 2 see: EXACT *adj* 6

unmixed *adj* consistent, homogeneous, plain, pure, straight, undiluted

unmovable *adj* see: CONSTANT *adj* 3

unmoved *adj* cold, dry, dull, impassive, laid-back, matter-of-fact, phlegmatic, poker-faced, reserved, stoic, stolid, unaffected, unemotional, unfeeling, untouched

unnamed *adj* anonymous, nameless, obscure, uncelebrated, unfamed, unheard-of, unknown, unrenowned

unnatural *adj* aberrant, abnormal, anomalous, artificial, atypical, contrived, deviant, disparate, divergent, incongruous, irregular, off-key

unnecessary *adj* abnormal, extra, extraneous, foreign, illogical, immaterial, insig-

nificant, irregular, irrelevant, malapropos, nonessential, peripheral, superfluous, surplus, unimportant, unrelated

unnerve *v* 1 castrate, debilitate, dismember, emasculate, enervate, geld

v 2 appall, daunt, discourage, dismay, horrify, panic, petrify, scare, terrify

v 3 see: FRIGHTEN *v* 2

unnoticing *adj* distracted, heedless, inattentive, unaware, unheeding, unobservant, unperceiving, unwatchful

unobservable *adj* imperceptible, imponderable, inappreciable, indiscernible, insensible, intangible, invisible, minute, scant, unapparent, weak

unobservant *adj* distracted, heedless, inattentive, unaware, unheeding, unnoticing, unperceiving, unwatchful

unobstructed *adj* open, patent, unclosed

unobtrusive *adj* conservative, dim, inconspicuous, quiet, restrained, subdued, tasteful, unassuming

unoffending *adj* see: SAFE *adj* 3

unoffensive *adj* see: SAFE *adj* 3

unofficial *adj* 1 feigned, partial, pseudo, quasi, semi, so-called

adj 2 casual, cavalier, colloquial, familiar, informal, ordinary, regular, relaxed, unceremonious, unconstrained, usual, vernacular

unoriginal *adj* 1 uncreative, uninspired, uninventive

adj 2 copied, imitated, pseudo

unorthodox *adj* bizarre, offbeat, unconventional

unpaid *adj* due, open, outstanding, owed

unpaired *adj* see: UNIQUE *adj* 1

unpalatable *adj* disagreeable, distasteful, disturbing, sickening, unappetizing, undesirable, unsavory

unparalleled *adj* 1 invaluable, irreplaceable, precious, priceless

adj 2 see: UNIQUE *adj* 1

unperceiving *adj* distracted, heedless, inattentive, unaware, unheeding, unnoticing, unobservant, unwatchful

unpitying *adj* see: NASTY *adj* 7

unplanned *adj* see: RANDOM *adj* 2

unpleasant *adj* 1 dour, firm, forbidding, grim, sad, serious, severe, sour, stern

adj 2 annoying, bad, difficult, disagreeable, displeasing, nasty, objectionable, offensive, rotten, sour, unhappy, upsetting

adj 3 appalling, awful, dire, dreadful, fearful, formidable, frightening, frightful, ghastly, horrendous, horrible, offensive, ominous, portentous, scary, shocking, spooky, terrifying

unpliable *adj* bullheaded, closed-minded, deaf, firm, hardheaded, hard-line, inelastic, inflexible, intractable, intransigent, obstinate, perverse, pigheaded, refractory, resolute, rigid, stiff, stubborn, tough, unbending, uncompromising, unpliant, unwieldy, unyielding, willful

unpliant *adj* bullheaded, closed-minded, deaf, firm, hardheaded, hard-line, inelastic, inflexible, intractable, intransigent, obstinate, perverse, pigheaded, refractory, resolute, rigid, stiff, stubborn, tough, unbending, uncompromising, unpliable, unwieldy, unyielding, willful

unpolished *adj 1* crude, raw, rough, rude, undressed, unfashioned, unfinished

adj 2 audacious, boorish, discourteous, disrespectful, ill-behaved, ill-bred, ill-mannered, impertinent, impolite, insolent, rude, surly, uncalled for, uncivil, uncivilized, uncouth, uncultured, unrefined

unpracticed *adj* deficient, inept, out of practice, rusty, unprepared

unprecedented *adj* innovative, new, novel, original, pioneering

unpredictable *adj 1* capricious, careless, immature, irresponsible, undependable, untrustworthy

adj 2 see: DELICATE *adj 7*

unprejudiced *adj see:* FAIR *adj 7*

unpremeditated *adj* automatic, impulsive, instinctive, involuntary, natural, rash, reflex, spontaneous, unconscious, unforced, unprompted

unprepared *adj* deficient, inept, out of practice, rusty, stale, unpracticed

unprescribed *adj* deliberate, free, intentional, optional, unforced, voluntary, willful, willing

unpretentious *adj 1* humble, lowly, meek, modest

adj 2 discreet, dry, homely, modest, plain, simple, unadorned, undecorated, unembellished, unembroidered

adj 3 candid, direct, earnest, forthright, frank, genuine, heartfelt, hearty, honest, no-holds-barred, open, real, sincere, straightforward, true, trustworthy, truthful, undesigning, unfeigned, wholehearted

unpretty *adj* homely, plain, unalluring, unattractive, unbeauteous

unprincipled *adj see:* EVIL *adj 4*

unproductive *adj 1* barren, effete, frigid, impotent, infertile, spent, sterile, unbearing, unfertile

adj 2 abortive, fruitless, futile, ineffective, ineffectual, nonproductive, unavailing, unsuccessful, unyielding, useless, vain, worthless

unprofessional *adj 1* incompetent, inept

adj 2 amateur, inexperienced, nonprofessional

unprompted *adj* automatic, impulsive, instinctive, involuntary, natural, rash, reflex, spontaneous, unconscious, unforced

unprosperous *adj* broke, destitute, dirt-poor, down and out, impoverished, indigent, needy, penniless, poor, poverty-stricken

unprotected *adj* defenseless, dependent, disarmed, exposed, helpless, powerless, susceptible, vulnerable, weak

unpunctual *adj* belated, delayed, late, overdue, tardy

unqualified *adj see:* INADEQUATE *adj 5*

unquenchable *adj* avaricious, covetous, endless, ravenous, voracious

unquestionable *adj* absolute, actual, authentic, bona fide, certain, definite, existent, factual, genuine, hard, inarguable, incontestable, incontrovertible, indisputable, indubitable, irrefutable, positive, real, sure, true, undeniable, undisputable, undoubtable, undoubted, unequivocal, veritable, viable

unquestionably *adv 1* clearly, evidently, obviously, plainly, undoubtedly

adv 2 see: DEFINITELY *adv*

unquestioning *adj* devout, narrow, orthodox

unravel *v 1* answer, explain, solve

v 2 disentangle, undo, untangle, unwind

v 3 see: ANALYZE *v 2*

unreadable *adj* illegible, scribbled, unclear

unready *adj see:* YOUNG *adj 2*

unreal *adj 1* deceptive, false, illusive, illusory, misleading

adj 2 bodiless, celestial, disembodied, ethereal, heavenly, incorporeal, insubstantial, intangible, metaphysical, nonmaterial, spiritual, unearthly, unsubstantial

adj 3 conceived, conjured, created, fancied, fanciful, fantastic, fictional, fictitious, illusory, imaginary, imagined, invented, make-believe, nonexistent, notional, whimsical

adj 4 see: COUNTERFEIT *adj 1*

unrealistic *adj* far-fetched, impractical, unfeasible

unreasonable *adj* unconscionable, undue, unjustifiable, unwarranted

unrefined *adj 1* coarse, crass, crude, flagrant, glaring, gross, obscene, rough, shocking, uncouth

adj 2 audacious, boorish, discourteous, disrespectful, ill-behaved, ill-bred, ill-mannered, impertinent, impolite, insolent, rude, surly, uncalled for, uncivil, uncivilized, uncouth, uncultured

unreflective *adj* accidental, careless, caustic, heedless, inadvertent, inconsiderate, nonchalant, selfish, sharp, short, tactless, thoughtless, uncaring, unceremonious, ungracious, unheeding, unintended, unintentional, unthinking

unrehearsed *adj* ad-lib, extemporaneous, impromptu, improvised, instantaneous, invented, offhand, off the cuff, spontaneous, unstudied

unrelated *adj 1* alien, foreign, separate

adj 2 different, disparate, diverse, incongruous, opposite, unequal, unlike

adj 3 see: SUPERFLUOUS *adj 3*

unrelenting *adj 1* persistent, tenacious

adj 2 see: CONSCIENTIOUS *adj 3*

adj 3 see: NASTY *adj 7*

unreliable *adj* dubious, insecure, questionable, undependable, unsure, untrustworthy

unremarkable *adj* see: TYPICAL *adj 2*

unremembered *adj* forgotten, gone, left behind, lost, once, past, suppressed, vague

unremitting *adj* see: PERPETUAL *adj 2*

unremittingly *adv* see: COMPLETELY *adv*

unrenowned *adj* anonymous, nameless, obscure, uncelebrated, unfamed, unheard-of, unknown

unreserved *adj* absolute, firm, fixed, resolute, steadfast

unresponsive *adj 1* dispassionate, unemotional

adj 2 cold, frigid, inhibited, passionless, repressed, restrained, reticent

unrestrained *adj 1* extravagant, intemperate, loose, reckless, wanton, wild

adj 2 excessive, gluttonous, immoderate, inordinate, intemperate, overindulgent, prodigious, unbridled, undue, voracious

adj 3 audacious, free, liberated, licentious, loose, rampant, unbridled, unconfined, uncontrolled, uncurbed, ungoverned, unhampered, uninhibited, unsecured, unshackled, untied, wild

unrestricted *adj* see: PRACTICAL *adj 4*

unrighteous *adj* biased, inequitable, partial, uneven, unfair, unjust, wrongful

unrivaled *adj* see: UNIQUE *adj 3*

unruffled *adj* see: CALM *adj 2*

unruly *adj 1* aggressive, defiant, insubordinate, rambunctious, restless, stubborn

adj 2 indomitable, intractable, recalcitrant, stubborn, uncontrollable, undisciplined, unmanageable, untoward, wild

unsafe *adj* breakneck, critical, dangerous, harmful, hazardous, perilous, precarious, risky, serious, venturesome

unsaid *adj* see: IMPLIED *adj 2*

unsatisfactorily *adv* badly, harshly, imperfectly, improperly, inadequately, inappropriately, poorly

unsatisfactory *adj* see: WRONG *adj 3*

unsavory *adj 1* disagreeable, distasteful, disturbing, sickening, unappetizing, undesirable

adj 2 despicable, infamous, notorious, offensive, scandalous, villainous

unschooled *adj* ignorant, illiterate, uneducated, uninstructed, unlearned, unlettered, untaught, untutored

unscrupulous *adj* see: EVIL *adj 4*

unseat *v 1* depose, oust, remove

v 2 buck, pitch, throw

unsecured *adj* audacious, free, liberated, licentious, loose, rampant, unbridled, unconfined, uncontrolled, uncurbed, ungoverned, unhampered, uninhibited, unrestrained, unshackled, untied, wild

unseemly *adj 1* see: INADEQUATE *adj 5*

adj 2 see: INDECENT *adj 2*

unseen *adj 1* concealed, covert, invisible, obscure, veiled

adj 2 arcane, hermetic, impenetrable, impervious, mysterious, mystic, obscure, puzzling, secret, unexaminable

unsegregated *adj* integrated

unselfish *adj 1* attentive, considerate, generous, thoughtful

adj 2 generous, giving

unsettle *v 1* agitate, derange, disorder, disturb, fluster, rock, ruffle, shake, sicken, upset

v 2 disarray, dislocate, disorder, disorganize, disrupt, disturb, interfere, interrupt, jumble, mess, mix up, muss, rummage, shuffle

unsettled *adj 1* back, frontier, remote

adj 2 awaiting, contingent, impending, pending

adj 3 illogical, inconclusive, indecisive, indefinite, open, unconvincing, unverified

unsettling *adj* annoying, anxious, bothersome, chafing, crabby, edgy, fretful, galling, impatient, irritating, jittery, nagging, on edge, restless

unshackle *v* discharge, emancipate, free, liberate, loosen, release, unbind

unshackled *adj* audacious, free, liberated,

licentious, loose, rampant, unbridled, un-confined, uncontrolled, uncurbed, ungov-erned, unhampered, uninhibited, unre-strained, unsecured, untied, wild

unshakable *adj* abiding, enduring, firm, never-failing, steadfast, sure, unfaltering, unwavering

unshared *adj* see: LONE *adj* 3

unshroud *v* debunk, discover, expose, show up, uncloak

unshut *adj* ajar, open
  v open, unblock, undo

unsighted *adj* blind, sightless, visionless

unsightly *adj* contorted, grotesque, grue-some, hideous, ill-favored, ugly

unskilled *adj* see: INADEQUATE *adj* 5

unsleeping *adj* alert, careful, cautious, open-eyed, vigilant, wakeful, wary, watchful, wide-awake

unsmooth *adj* bouncy, bumpy, craggy, ir-regular, jagged, jolting, rough, rugged, scraggy

unsoiled *adj* clean, immaculate, pristine, pure, spotless, taintless, unspoiled, unsul-lied, untouched, virgin

unsophisticated *adj* 1 confined, controlled, ignorant, limited, narrow, parochial
  adj 2 green, immature, inexperienced, naive, new, novice, raw, virgin
  adj 3 artless, candid, frank, guileless, in-genuous, innocent, naive, natural, open, plain, simple, simple-hearted, una-dorned, unaffected, unstudied, untu-tored, unworldly

unsound *adj* 1 erratic, unbalanced
  adj 2 see: ILL *adj* 3
  adj 3 see: FRAGILE *adj* 3

unsparing *adj* bounteous, bountiful, free, generous, handsome, liberal

unspoiled *adj* clean, immaculate, pristine, pure, spotless, taintless, unsoiled, unsul-lied, untouched, virgin

unspoken *adj* see: IMPLIED *adj* 2

unstable *adj* 1 flimsy, insecure, jiggly, rick-ety, shaky, teetering, unsure, vacillating, wavering, weak, wobbly
  adj 2 arbitrary, capricious, changeable, erratic, fickle, flighty, inconsistent, incon-stant, mercurial, uncertain, unsteady, variable, volatile, wavering, wayward
  adj 3 see: DELICATE *adj* 7

unsteady *adj* see: INCONSISTENT *adj* 3

unstraight *adj* arched, bent, bowed, curved, curvilinear, flexed

unstudied *adj* 1 ad-lib, extemporaneous, impromptu, improvised, instantaneous, invented, offhand, off the cuff, spontane-ous

adj 2 artless, candid, frank, guileless, in-genuous, innocent, naive, natural, open, plain, simple, simple-hearted, una-dorned, unaffected, unsophisticated, un-tutored, unworldly

unsubstantial *adj* 1 feeble, flimsy, frail, insubstantial, slight, tenuous, weak
  adj 2 see: SPIRITUAL *adj* 2

unsubstantiated *adj* baseless, erroneous, fallacious, groundless, invalid

unsuccessful *adj* abortive, fruitless, futile, ineffective, ineffectual, nonproductive, unavailing, unproductive, unyielding, useless, vain, worthless

unsuitable *adj* botching, bungling, goofing, helpless, ill-adapted, ill-suited, ill-timed, improper, inadequate, inappropriate, in-capable, incongruous, incorrect, ineligi-ble, inept, malapropos, unable, unbe-coming, unbefitting, unequipped, unfit, unqualified, unseemly, unskilled

unsuited *adj* see: INADEQUATE *adj* 5

unsullied *adj* clean, immaculate, pristine, pure, spotless, taintless, unsoiled, un-spoiled, untouched, virgin

unsure *adj* 1 diffident, faltering, halting, hesitant, indecisive, reluctant, tentative, waffling, wavering
  adj 2 flimsy, insecure, jiggly, rickety, shaky, teetering, unstable, vacillating, wavering, weak, wobbly
  adj 3 dubious, insecure, questionable, un-dependable, unreliable, untrustworthy
  adj 4 cynical, distrustful, doubtful, dubi-ous, incredulous, leery, questionable, shy, skeptical, skittish, suspicious
  adj 5 ambiguous, borderline, clouded, doubtful, dubious, equivocal, garbled, il-logical, inarticulate, incalculable, inco-herent, inexplicit, muddled, muffled, murky, obscure, precarious, question-able, shaky, suspect, suspicious, uncer-tain, unclear, uneasy, unintelligible, vague, wary

unsurpassed *adj* see: UTTER *adj*

unswayable *adj* see: STUBBORN *adj* 6

unswerving *adj* concentrated, exclusive, fixed, undivided, whole

unsympathetic *adj* 1 abusive, hard, harsh, severe, stern, stiff, strict, tough
  adj 2 see: NASTY *adj* 7

untamed *adj* rabid, savage, vicious, violent, wild

untangle *v* disentangle, undo, unravel, un-wind

untaught *adj* ignorant, illiterate, uneducated, uninstructed, unlearned, unlettered, unschooled, untutored

untested adj 1 new, tentative, young

adj 2 developmental, experimental, pilot, suggested, tentative, test, trial

unthinkable adj 1 impossible, inconceivable, incredible, strange, unachievable

adj 2 illegible, incomprehensible, inconceivable, mysterious, unintelligible

unthinking adj 1 careless, foolish, impulsive, irresponsible, myopic, not smart, reckless, risky, shortsighted, unwise

adj 2 accidental, careless, caustic, heedless, inadvertent, inconsiderate, nonchalant, selfish, sharp, short, tactless, thoughtless, uncaring, unceremonious, ungracious, unheeding, unintended, unintentional

untidy adj careless, disheveled, messy, scruffy, slatternly, slipshod, sloppy, sloven, slovenly, tacky, uncombed

untie v disengage, extricate, loosen, open, unbind, unclasp, undo, unfasten, unknot, unloosen

untied adj audacious, free, liberated, licentious, loose, rampant, unbridled, unconfined, uncontrolled, uncurbed, ungoverned, unhampered, uninhibited, unrestrained, unsecured, unshackled, wild

untimely adj advanced, early, first, hasty, premature, previous, soon

untold adj 1 countless, immeasurable, incalculable, infinite, innumerable, innumerous, legion, many, numberless, uncountable

adj 2 see: HUGE adj 3

untouched adj 1 clean, immaculate, pristine, pure, spotless, taintless, unsoiled, unspoiled, unsullied, virgin

adj 2 absolute, complete, flawless, good, intact, perfect, sound, unblemished, unbroken, undamaged, unimpaired, uninjured, unmarred, whole

adj 3 cold, dry, dull, impassive, laid-back, matter-of-fact, phlegmatic, poker-faced, reserved, stoic, stolid, unaffected, unemotional, unfeeling

untoward adj 1 indomitable, intractable, recalcitrant, stubborn, uncontrollable, undisciplined, unmanageable, unruly, wild

adj 2 cursed, damned, doomed, hapless, hopeless, ill-fated, jinxed, luckless, unfortunate, unhappy

adj 3 see: INDECENT adj 1

untroubled adj see: CALM adj 2

untrue adj 1 erroneous, false, faulty, imprecise, inaccurate, incorrect, inexact, mistaken, specious, wrong

adj 2 cheating, conniving, deceitful, deceptive, dishonest, disloyal, faithless, false, insidious, manipulative, perfidious, sneaky, traitorous, treacherous, unfaithful

untrustworthy adj 1 capricious, careless, immature, irresponsible, undependable

adj 2 dubious, insecure, questionable, undependable, unreliable

adj 3 cheating, conniving, deceitful, deceptive, dishonest, disloyal, faithless, false, insidious, manipulative, perfidious, sneaky, traitorous, treacherous, unfaithful, untrue

untruth n 1 bull, falsehood, lie, misstatement

n 2 deceit, deception, fabrication, falsehood, fraud, fraudulence, hypocrisy, lying, perjury

untruthful adj see: EVIL adj 4

untruthfulness n dishonesty, falsehood

untutored adj 1 ignorant, illiterate, uneducated, uninstructed, unlearned, unlettered, unschooled

adj 2 artless, candid, frank, guileless, ingenuous, innocent, naive, natural, open, plain, simple, simple-hearted, unadorned, unaffected, unsophisticated, unstudied, unworldly

unused adj 1 fresh, mint, new

adj 2 vacant

adj 3 dormant, inactive, inert, latent, on hold, passive, potential, quiet

unusual adj 1 few, infrequent, isolated, occasional, rare, scarce, seldom, sporadic

adj 2 charming, funny, odd, old-fashioned, peculiar, picturesque, puzzling, quaint, remarkable, special, uncommon, whimsical

adj 3 characteristic, differentiating, distinctive, lone, one, particular, peculiar, select, single, solitary, unique

adj 4 curious, exotic, far-out, fascinating, intriguing, kinky, marvelous, mysterious, new, novel, odd, outlandish, strange, ultra, unaccustomed, unexplored, unfamiliar, unique, unknown, weird

adj 5 see: EXTRAORDINARY adj 4

adj 6 see: STRANGE adj 5

unvarying adj consistent, constant, continuing, endless, equable, established, even, invariable, reliable, routine, same, serene, stable, steady, unchanging, unfailing, unfluctuating

unveil v communicate, disclose, display,

divulge, exhibit, inform, notify, open, uncover

unveiling *n* beginning, briefing, commencement, debut, inauguration, induction

unverified *adj* illogical, inconclusive, indecisive, indefinite, open, unsettled

unwanted *adj* ill-favored, inadmissible, objectionable, unacceptable, undesirable, unwelcome

unwarranted *adj* unconscionable, unjustifiable, unreasonable

unwashed *adj* see: DIRTY *adj* 2

unwasteful *adj* see: FRUGAL *adj*

unwatchful *adj* distracted, heedless, inattentive, unaware, unheeding, unnoticing, unobservant

unwavering *adj* abiding, enduring, firm, never-failing, steadfast, sure, unfaltering

unwed *adj* single, sole, unmarried

unwelcome *adj* 1 ill-favored, inadmissible, objectionable, unacceptable, undesirable
adj 2 annoying, bothersome, glaring, harassing, irksome, irritating, mean, onerous, painful, pesky, troublesome, ugly, vexatious, wicked

unwell *adj* ailing, delicate, diseased, down, frail, ill, impaired, indisposed, sick, sickly, suffering, unhealthy, unsound, weak

unwieldy *adj* bullheaded, closed-minded, deaf, firm, hardheaded, hard-line, inelastic, inflexible, intractable, intransigent, obstinate, perverse, pigheaded, refractory, resolute, rigid, stiff, stubborn, tough, unbending, uncompromising, unpliable, unpliant, unyielding, willful

unwilling *adj* afraid, averse, disinclined, hesitant, indisposed, loath, opposed, recalcitrant, reluctant, shy, timid, uneager

unwind *v* 1 relax
v 2 disentangle, undo, unravel

unwise *adj* 1 careless, foolish, impulsive, irresponsible, myopic, not smart, reckless, risky, shortsighted
adj 2 foolish, ill-advised, indiscreet, misdirected, misguided, mistaken

unworkable *adj* impractical, undoable

unworldly *adj* artless, candid, frank, guileless, ingenuous, innocent, naive, natural, open, plain, simple, simple-hearted, unadorned, unaffected, unsophisticated, unstudied

unworthy *adj* 1 base, beneath, despicable, ignoble, inferior, low, lowdown, sordid, squalid, vile, vulgar, wretched
adj 2 see: INFERIOR *adj* 6

unwritten *adj* expressed, oral, spoken, stated, verbal, word-of-mouth

unyielding *adj* 1 firm, indomitable, invincible, unconquerable
adj 2 bullheaded, closed-minded, deaf, firm, hardheaded, hard-line, inelastic, inflexible, intractable, intransigent, obstinate, perverse, pigheaded, refractory, resolute, rigid, stiff, stubborn, tough, unbending, uncompromising, unpliable, unpliant, unwielding, willful
adj 3 see: FUTILE *adj* 3
adj 4 see: STUBBORN *adj* 6

unyoke *v* cut, detach, disconnect, disengage, dissociate, separate, sever, uncouple, unfasten

up *adj* abreast, acquainted, aware, conversant, familiar, informed, knowledgeable, versed
v boost, hike, increase, jack up, jump, raise

upbeat *adj* auspicious, cheerful, confident, encouraging, hopeful, optimistic, promising

upbraid *v* see: SCOLD *v* 4

upbringing *n* background, breeding, culture, development, education, environment, experience, past, schooling

update *v* 1 acquaint, advise, apprise, fill in, inform, notify, post
v 2 analyze, brief, condense, evaluate, outline, retrace, review, study, summarize
v 3 freshen, modernize, redo, refresh, refurbish, rejuvenate, remodel, renew, renovate, restore, revamp, revitalize
n condition, mode, perspective, posture, situation, status

upgrade *v* advance, cultivate, elevate, enhance, enrich, improve
n acceleration, achievement, advance, advancement, betterment, breakthrough, furtherance, growth, headway, improvement, increment, pickup, proficiency, progress, promotion

upheaval *n* 1 blow, disturbance, jolt, shock, trauma, upset
n 2 calamity, cataclysm, catastrophe, debacle, disaster, misfortune

uphill *adj* arduous, demanding, difficult, formidable, hard, heavy, labored, laborious, rocky, rough, rugged, serious, severe, strenuous, tough

uphold *v* 1 assist, keep up, maintain, provide, support
v 2 advocate, back, champion, endorse, guarantee, promote, sanction, support
v 3 bear up, bolster, brace, build up, buoy, buttress, carry, fortify, harden, nourish,

nurture, prop, reinforce, shore, strengthen, support, sustain

upkeep *n* installation, maintenance, service

uplift *v* see: COMFORT *v* 2

upraise *v* see: COMFORT *v* 2

upright *adj* 1 perpendicular, steep, vertical
adj 2 clean, equal, equitable, even, fair, honest, just, sportsmanlike
adj 3 see: ETHICAL *adj* 3
adj 4 see: HONEST *adj* 2, 3, 4

uprightness *n* goodness, morality, principle, probity, purity, rectitude, virtue

uprising *n* betrayal, insurrection, mutiny, revolt, sedition, subversion

uproar *n* 1 brouhaha, cacophony, chaos, clamor, confusion, din, discord, disorder, hubbub, mayhem, noise, pandemonium, racket, tumult
n 2 see: AGITATION *n*

uproot *v* dig, extract, grub, weed

upset *adj* 1 anxious, careworn, distracted, distraught, distressed, frantic, harassed, tormented, worried
adj 2 see: ANGRY *adj* 4
n 1 collapse, downfall, failure, fall, overthrow
n 2 destruction, downfall, infiltration, ruin, subversion
n 3 blow, disturbance, jolt, shock, trauma
v 1 capsize, overturn, roll
v 2 affect, bother, burden, concern, daunt, disturb, faze, intimidate, oppress, worry
v 3 agitate, derange, disorder, disturb, fluster, rock, ruffle, shake, sicken, unhinge, unsettle
v 4 capsize, collapse, defeat, dislodge, knock over, overthrow, overturn, tip over, topple, tumble, turn over
v 5 annoy, antagonize, argue, bother, bug, concern, distress, disturb, goad, harass, hassle, inconvenience, irk, irritate, pain, perturb, strain, stress, taunt, trouble, try, worry
v 6 aggravate, anger, annoy, bother, bug, enrage, exasperate, frazzle, gall, grate, hassle, incense, inflame, infuriate, irk, irritate, madden, miff, nettle, outrage, peeve, pester, pique, provoke, rile, vex

upsetting *adj* 1 disabling, disturbing, painful, shocking
adj 2 annoying, bad, difficult, disagreeable, displeasing, nasty, objectionable, offensive, rotten, sour, unpleasant

upshot *n* see: CONSEQUENCE *n* 4

upstanding *adj* 1 accountable, answerable, dependable, honorable, honored, liable, reliable, reputable, respected, responsible, secure, solid, trusted, trustworthy
adj 2 see: PURE *adj* 7

upsurge *v* see: INCREASE *v* 8

uptight *adj* anxious, edgy, fidgety, impatient, nervous, nervy, queasy, restive, restless, tense, troubled, uncomfortable, uneasy, worried

up-to-date *adj* bright, contemporary, fresh, high-tech, modern, modernistic, new, novel

urban *adj* broad, general, global, planetary, universal, widespread, worldwide

urbane *adj* civilized, cosmopolitan, cultivated, cultured, elegant, genteel, ingratiating, poised, polished, refined, smooth, sophisticated, suave, well-bred

urge *n* 1 impetus, impulse, stimulus
n 2 appetite, craving, eroticism, desire, hankering, hunger, itch, longing, lust, passion, yearning, yen
v 1 barter, cajole, coax
v 2 assert, demand, emphasize, force, insist, persist
v 3 egg, encourage, exhort, goad, incite, persuade, prick, prod, prompt, propel, spur
v 4 see: INSTIGATE *v* 1
v 5 see: PROPOSE *v* 4
v 6 see: PROVOKE *v* 2, 3

urgency *n* demand, exigency, necessity, need, pressure, requirement

urgent *adj* 1 immediate, instant, instantaneous, quick, rapid
adj 2 acute, burning, critical, crucial, desperate, dire, grave, heavy, important, major, momentous, ponderous, pressing, profound, serious, severe, solemn, somber, vital

urgently *adv* expeditiously, fast, full-tilt, hastily, in a snap, lickety-split, promptly, pronto, quick, quickly, rapidly, right away, soon, swiftly

urging *adj* see: ASSERTIVE *adj*

urn *n* amphora, pot, vase, vessel

usable *adj* see: PRACTICAL *adj* 4

usage *n* 1 convention
n 2 see: PRACTICE *n* 6

use *n* 1 demand
n 2 function, purpose
n 3 appliance, application, employment, form, method, operation, play, technique, utilization
n 4 custom, fashion, formality, habit, manner, mores, observance, practice, routine, tradition, usage, way, wont
n 5 account, advantage, applicability, appropriateness, aptness, avail, benefit, de-

corum, expediency, fitness, manners, opportunism, pertinence, profit, propriety, relevance, rightness, service, suitability, usefulness, utility

v 1 apply, exercise, resort, utilize

v 2 control, deploy, direct, manipulate

v 3 apply, augment, capitalize on, enlarge, increase

v 4 benefit, experience, have, partake, profit, touch

v 5 apply, bestow, employ, exercise, exploit, handle, utilize

useful *adj* 1 beneficial, good, helpful

adj 2 constructive, favorable, fruitful, helpful, positive, worthwhile

adj 3 see: APPLICABLE *adj*

adj 4 see: PRACTICAL *adj* 4

usefulness *n* account, advantage, applicability, appropriateness, aptness, avail, benefit, decorum, expediency, fitness, manners, opportunism, pertinence, profit, propriety, relevance, rightness, service, suitability, utility

useless *adj* abortive, fruitless, futile, ineffective, ineffectual, nonproductive, unavailing, unproductive, unsuccessful, unyielding, vain, worthless

user *n* buyer, client, consumer, customer, end user, patron, purchaser

usher *v* accompany, direct, escort, guide *n* escort, guide

usual *adj* 1 accepted, accustomed, chronic, common, constant, continual, customary, daily, everyday, familiar, frequent, habitual, inured, often, recurring, regular, routine

adj 2 average, common, commonplace, daily, everyday, general, mundane, natural, normal, ordinary, plain, prevalent, regular, routine, typical, unexceptional, unremarkable, workaday

adj 3 see: INFORMAL *adj* 1

usually *adv* 1 frequently, often, regularly, repeatedly

adv 2 as a rule, customarily, frequently, generally, mainly, most, most often, mostly, normally, ordinarily, primarily, principally

usurp *v* 1 cut out, displace, supplant

v 2 defraud, deprive, rob, swindle

utensil *n* see: DEVICE *n* 3

utilitarian *adj* accessible, available, close, convenient, feasible, functional, handy, helpful, multipurpose, nearby, open, practical, public, reachable, ready, serviceable, suitable, unrestricted, usable, useful, well-suited, within reach, working

utility *n* account, advantage, applicability, appropriateness, aptness, avail, benefit, decorum, expediency, fitness, manners, opportunism, pertinence, profit, propriety, relevance, rightness, service, suitability, use, usefulness

utilization *n* appliance, application, employment, form, method, operation, play, technique

utilize *v* 1 apply, exercise, use

v 2 augment, enhance, maximize, optimize

v 3 adopt, borrow, embrace, foster, subscribe, take on

v 4 apply, bestow, employ, exercise, exploit, handle

utmost *adj* 1 forceful, highhanded, important, intense, powerful

adj 2 extreme, farthest, furthermost, furthest, hindmost, most distant, outermost

n acme, apex, apogee, climax, crescendo, crest, crown, culmination, epitome, height, noon, peak, pinnacle, point, prime, summit, tip, top, zenith

utopia *n* 1 heaven, palace, Zion

n 2 peace

utopian *adj* 1 auspicious, bright, confident, favorable, hopeful, promising, rosy

adj 2 see: FLAMBOYANT *adj* 2

n dreamer, idealist, romantic, visionary

utter *adj* absolute, chief, complete, consummate, dominant, godlike, leading, main, perfect, principal, pure, radical, ranking, sheer, supreme, total, unsurpassed, whole

v 1 blurt, cackle, cry, ejaculate, exclaim, shout, spill, sputter

v 2 see: VERBALIZE *v* 2

utterance *n* 1 discourse, expression, speaking, speech, statement, talk, verbalization, word

n 2 airing, expression, venting

utterly *adv* adequately, altogether, assiduously, completely, earnestly, entirely, exhaustively, fully, hard, intensely, intensively, painstakingly, perfectly, quite, sufficiently, thoroughly, totally, unremittingly, wholly

V

vacancy *n* opening, place, position, slot

vacant *adj* 1 bare, barren, clear, empty, stark, vacuous, void

adj 2 unused

vacate *v* 1 clear, deplete, drain, empty, evacuate

v 2 abdicate, quit, relinquish, renounce, resign

v 3 see: CANCEL *v* 3

v 4 see: LEAVE *v* 4

vacation *n* 1 idle time, interlude, lull, recreation, relaxation, repose

n 2 day off, furlough, holiday, leave, respite, sabbatical, time off

vaccinate *v* immunize, inject, inoculate

vaccine *n* antibody, antidote, antigen, antitoxin, defense

vacillate *v* 1 alternate, fluctuate, oscillate, pendulate, sway, swing, wave

v 2 delay, falter, halt, hesitate, pause, stagger, waver

vacillating *adj* see: UNSTABLE *adj* 1

vacuous *adj* bare, barren, clear, empty, stark, vacant, void

vagabond *n* beggar, bum, derelict, drifter, hobo, loafer, mendicant, panhandler, pauper, vagrant

vagary *n* caprice, fancy, humor, impulse, notion, whim, whimsy

vagrant *adj* ambulatory, gypsy, itinerant, movable, nomadic, perambulatory, roving, transient, wandering, wayfaring

n beggar, bum, derelict, drifter, hobo, loafer, mendicant, panhandler, pauper, tramp, vagabond

vague *adj* 1 circumstantial, contingent, uncertain

adj 2 ambiguous, cryptic, enigmatic, mystifying, puzzling

adj 3 faint, imperceptible, meager, remote, slight

adj 4 forgotten, gone, left behind, lost, once, past, suppressed

adj 5 ambiguous, imperceptible, imprecise, indecisive, indefinite, indeterminate, indistinct, inexact, loose, wishy-washy

adj 6 ambiguous, borderline, clouded, doubtful, dubious, equivocal, garbled, illogical, inarticulate, incalculable, incoherent, inexplicit, muddled, muffled, murky, obscure, precarious, questionable, shaky, suspect, suspicious, uncertain, unclear, uneasy, unintelligible, unsure, wary

vain *adj* 1 foolish, futile, ill-advised, pointless, profitless

adj 2 empty, hollow, idle, meaningless, shallow

adj 3 arrogant, cocky, conceited, haughty, narcissistic, self-assured, smug, stuck-up

adj 4 abortive, fruitless, futile, ineffective, ineffectual, nonproductive, unavailing, unproductive, unsuccessful, unyielding, useless, worthless

adj 5 arrogant, cavalier, conceited, contemptuous, curt, dictatorial, disdainful, grandiose, haughty, huffy, insolent, lofty, lordly, moody, obtrusive, overbearing, patronizing, proud, scornful, snooty, stuck-up, supercilious, superior

valiant *adj* audacious, bold, brave, courageous, daring, dauntless, fearless, gallant, game, gutsy, heroic, intrepid, stalwart, unafraid, undaunted, valorous

valid *adj* 1 accurate, correct, exact, precise, proper

adj 2 acceptable, defensible, justifiable, legitimate, proper, reasonable

adj 3 allowable, authorized, lawful, legal, legitimate, permissible

adj 4 cogent, compelling, convincing, effective, forceful, influential, persuasive, revealing, satisfactory, satisfying, solid, sound

validate *v* 1 accredit, authorize, certify, commission, empower, enable, entitle, facilitate, invest, license, permit

v 2 attest, authenticate, certify, confirm, corroborate, justify, notarize, prove, ratify, sanction, substantiate, support, verify, vouch, witness

v 3 see: APPROVE *v* 4

validity *n* correctness, justice, lawfulness, legality, truth

valise *n* bag, baggage, case, equipment, gear, grip, kit, luggage, pack, pouch, purse, sack, suitcase, trunk, wallet

valley *n* basin

valor *n* boldness, bravery, courage, daring, fortitude, heart, heroism, spirit

valorous *adj* audacious, bold, brave, courageous, daring, dauntless, fearless, gallant, game, gutsy, heroic, intrepid, stalwart, unafraid, undaunted

valuable *adj* 1 costly, dear, expensive, precious

adj 2 deserving, estimable, excellent, honorable, noble, precious, worthy

n asset, credit, resource

valuate *v* appraise, assay, assess, charge, estimate, evaluate, levy, price, rank, rate, set at, survey, tax, value

valuation *n* appraisal, assessment, estimate, evaluation

value *n* 1 caliber, excellence, goodness, merit, quality, stature, worth

n 2 charge, cost, expense, fare, outlay, payment, price, rate, worth

v 1 appraise, assay, assess, charge, estimate, evaluate, levy, price, rank, rate, set at, survey, tax

v 2 admire, adore, appreciate, cherish, consider, covet, esteem, honor, idolize, love, prize, regard, respect

valued *adj* admired, honored, praised, prized, respected

values *n* beliefs, code, doctrine, ethics, outlook, philosophy

valve *n* cock, faucet, nozzle, spigot, spout

vamp *n* coquette, flirt, harlot, nymphomaniac, seductress, siren, tart, tease, temptress, wanton woman

vampire *n* leech, sucker

van *n* auto, automobile, bus, car, carriage, chariot, coach, jeep, motorcar, omnibus, sedan, truck, vehicle, wagon

vandalism *n* sabotage

vandalize *v* abuse, blemish, damage, hamper, harm, hurt, impair, injure, mar, obstruct, ruin, sabotage, scuttle, spoil

vanguard *n* **1** innovators, leaders, pacesetters, pioneers

n **2** forefront, front, head, lead, pioneer

vanish *v* clear, depart, disappear, evaporate, fade

vanished *adj* bygone, dead, defunct, departed, extinct, forgotten, gone, lost

vanity *n* airs, arrogance, cockiness, conceit, condescension, disdain, egotism, haughtiness, image, loftiness, narcissism, pride, self-esteem, self-image

vanquish *v* **1** dispose of, eliminate, expel, flush, purge, remove

v **2** see: OVERPOWER *v* **3**

vanquishment *n* debacle, defeat, disaster, downfall, overthrow, rout, ruination, thrashing, trouncing

vapid *adj* absent-minded, abstracted, bemused, careless, dazed, dizzy, groggy, inattentive, lost, mindless, oblivious, preoccupied, silly

vapor *n* cloud, fog, haze, mist

vaporous *adj* cloudy, dismal, foggy, gray, hazy, misty, murky, overcast, steamy, vapory

vapory *adj* cloudy, dismal, foggy, gray, hazy, misty, murky, overcast, steamy

variable *adj* arbitrary, capricious, changeable, erratic, fickle, flighty, inconsistent, inconstant, mercurial, uncertain, unstable, unsteady, volatile, wavering, wayward

variance *n* **1** contradiction, disagreement,

discrepancy, hypocrisy, incongruity, inconsistency

n **2** see: TROUBLE *n* **5**

variation *n* **1** edition

n **2** deviation, difference, distinction

n **3** degree, distinction, enhancement, nuance, shade, subtlety, touch, trace

n **4** adjustment, alteration, anomaly, change, deviation, modification, mutation, permutation, shift

varied *adj* **1** assorted, diverse, miscellaneous, mixed

adj **2** appealing, colorful, entertaining, interesting, lively

variety *n* **1** assortment, bunch, collection, mixture, selection, spectrum

n **2** see: CATEGORY *n*

various *adj* **1** alternate, another, certain, different, discrete, disparate, dissimilar, distinct, diverse, numerous, other, separate, several, some, unlike, varying

adj **2** abundant, assorted, copious, diverse, extensive, legion, many, multifarious, multitudinous, myriad, numerous, plentiful, populous, prolific, sundry, voluminous

vary *v* **1** adjust, finesse, fine-tune, modify, tweak

v **2** alter, assort, diversify, mix

v **3** extend, go, range, span

v **4** adjust, alter, catalyze, change, modify, mutate, refashion

v **5** alter, change, commute, convert, evolve, further, improve, metamorphose, modernize, modify, mutate, revolutionize, transfer, transfigure, transform

v **6** see: DISAGREE *v* **3**

varying *adj* alternate, another, certain, different, discrete, disparate, dissimilar, distinct, diverse, numerous, other, separate, several, some, unlike

vase *n* amphora, pot, urn, vessel

vassal *n* chattel, pauper, peasant, peon, serf

vast *adj* **1** cavernous, echo-filled, gaping, hollow, spacious

adj **2** ample, broad, expansive, extended, extensive, ranging, wide

adj **3** ample, big, capacious, comfortable, commodious, open, roomy, spacious, wide

adj **4** ample, big, considerable, enormous, extensive, grand, hefty, huge, jumbo, large, major, sizable

adj **5** see: HUGE *adj* **3**

n cosmos, creation, firmament, grand scale, macrocosm, nature, solar system, universe, world

vat *n* **1** barrel, bucket, cask, drum, keg, tub, vessel

n **2** cauldron, cistern, container, jug, reservoir

vaudeville *n* follies, musical, review, revue, song-and-dance

vault *n* **1** chest, coffer, safe, strongbox

n **2** burial, catacomb, cenotaph, crypt, grave, mausoleum, memorial, monument, pit, tomb

n **3** basement, cellar

n **4** bound, jump, leap

v **1** clear, hurdle, leap, negotiate

v **2** angle, arch, bend, bow, curve, flex, ply, round, tilt, turn, twist

vaunt *v* boast, brag, crow, exult, flaunt, gloat, revel, show off

veer *v* **1** bend, curve, meander, wind, zigzag

v **2** decline, descend, incline, skew, slope

v **3** avert, deflect, deviate, dip, divert, dodge, pivot, skew, swerve, swing, swivel, turn, wheel, whip

vegetable *n* flora, foliage, plant

vegetation *n* bush, grass, hedge, plant, sapling, shrub, tree, vine, weed

vehement *adj* angry, ferocious, fierce, furious, heated, intense, savage, severe, terrible, vicious, violent

vehicle *n* **1** buggy, carriage, coach, rig, surrey

n **2** agency, agent, channel, conduit, instrument, means, mechanism, medium, mode

n **3** auto, automobile, bus, car, carriage, chariot, coach, jeep, motorcar, omnibus, sedan, truck, van, wagon

veil *n* camouflage, cloak, costume, cover, curtain, disguise, mask, pretense, shield

v camouflage, cloak, conceal, cover, darken, disguise, envelop, hide, mask, occult, seclude, shield

veiled *adj* **1** concealed, covert, invisible, unseen

adj **2** illusory, slight, tenuous

vein *n* **1** fashion, flavor, manner, mode, tone

n **2** attitude, disposition, feeling, humor, mind, mood, spirit, temper, timbre

n **3** artery, blood vessel, capillary, vessel

vellum *n* letterhead, page, paper, papyrus, parchment, sheepskin, stationery

velocity *n* alacrity, cadence, celerity, dispatch, gait, pace, quickness, rapidity, rate, speed, step, stride, swiftness, trot, walk

velvety *adj* cottony, satiny, silky, slippery, smooth, soft

venal *adj* see: EVIL *adj* 4

vend *v* barter, distribute, market, merchandise, peddle, retail, sell, wholesale

vendible *adj* commercial, marketable, salable, wanted

vendor *n* **1** dealer, marketer, merchant, monger, purveyor, trader

n **2** clerk, representative, salesman, salesperson, saleswoman

veneer *n* appearance, cover, facade, face, facet, factor, front, look

venerable *adj* **1** adored, beloved, cherished, dear, esteemed, loved, precious, respected, revered, treasured, worshiped

adj **2** aged, age-old, ancient, antique, elderly, gray, grizzled, old, olden, senior, timeworn, vintage, worn

venerate *v* admire, adore, cherish, dote on, idolize, love, respect, worship

vengeance *n* **1** punishment, retaliation

n **2** getting even, reciprocity, reprisal, retaliation, retribution, revenge, vindictiveness

vengeful *adj* malicious, revengeful, spiteful, unforgiving, unmerciful, vindictive

venom *n* **1** cancer, corruption, decay, evil, infection, malignancy, poison, rot

n **2** see: HATE *n*

vent *v* air, bring up, broach, communicate, discuss, expose, express, give, introduce, open, put, reveal, state, tap, tell, verbalize

ventilate *v* see: COMMUNICATE *v* 4

venting *n* expression, utterance

venture *n* **1** activity, business, endeavor, enterprise, exercise, project

n **2** chase, exploration, hunt, pursuit, quest, undertaking

n **3** attempt, effort, endeavor, speculation, struggle, trial, undertaking

n **4** adventure, air travel, cruise, excursion, expedition, flight, journey, passage, safari, sally, tour, travel, trek, trip, voyage

v attempt, bet, chance, dare, gamble, hazard, play, risk, speculate, stake, wager

venturesome *adj* **1** adaptive, bold, canny, clever, daring, enterprising, resourceful

adj **2** breakneck, critical, dangerous, harmful, hazardous, perilous, precarious, risky, serious

veracious *adj* **1** factual, honest, truthful

adj **2** authoritative, dependable, due, faithful, legitimate, rightful, strict, true, trustworthy

veracity *n* candor, honesty, integrity, truth

veranda *n* lanai, patio, piazza, porch, terrace

verbal *adj* expressed, oral, spoken, stated, unwritten, word-of-mouth

verbalization n 1 depiction, description, explanation, illustration, narration, report, sketch

   n 2 discourse, expression, speaking, speech, statement, talk, utterance, word

verbalize v 1 air, bring up, broach, communicate, discuss, express, give, introduce, open, put, reveal, state, tap, tell, vent

   v 2 announce, articulate, assert, couch, describe, dictate, draft, enunciate, express, intonate, orate, phrase, proclaim, pronounce, say, speak, state, stress, talk, utter, vocalize, voice, word

verbatim adj exact, faithful, literal, precise, strict, word for word

verbiage n see: LANGUAGE n

verbose adj bombastic, chatty, diffuse, garrulous, long-winded, loquacious, redundant, repetitious, superfluous, talkative, wordy

verdict n 1 adjudication, decision, decree, finding, judgment, ruling

   n 2 adjudication, award, determination, judgment, opinion, ruling

verge v approach, border, bound, define, edge, hem, limit, outline

   n see: EDGE n 4

verifiably adv actually, exactly, genuinely, precisely, really, sincerely, truly, veritably, very

verification n affirmation, confirmation, evidence, proof

verified adj authentic, certified, confirmed, demonstrated, proved, tested, tried

verify v 1 audit, balance, check, examine

   v 2 determine, evaluate, judge, test

   v 3 attest, authenticate, certify, confirm, corroborate, justify, notarize, prove, ratify, sanction, substantiate, support, validate, vouch, witness

verily adv absolutely, certainly, decidedly, definitely, entirely, incontrovertibly, indeed, indubitably, positively, surely, truly, unequivocally, unquestionably, well, without doubt

veritable adj absolute, actual, authentic, bona fide, certain, definite, existent, factual, genuine, hard, inarguable, incontestable, incontrovertible, indisputable, indubitable, irrefutable, positive, real, sure, true, undeniable, undisputable, undoubtable, undoubted, unequivocal, unquestionable, viable

veritably adv actually, exactly, genuinely, precisely, really, sincerely, truly, verifiably, very

verity n see: CLICHÉ n 3

vermilion adj cardinal, crimson, red, ruby

vernacular adj casual, cavalier, colloquial, familiar, informal, ordinary, regular, relaxed, unceremonious, unconstrained, unofficial

   n buzz words, expression, idiom, jargon, language, lingo, parlance, vocabulary

versatile adj 1 clever, gifted, handy, ingenious, talented

   adj 2 see: PLASTIC adj 2

verse n 1 chapter, paragraph, passage

   n 2 ditty, limerick, lyric, madrigal, poem, poetry, rhyme, song, sonnet

versed adj 1 accomplished, experienced, proficient, schooled

   adj 2 adept, experienced, practiced, proficient, seasoned, veteran

   adj 3 abreast, acquainted, aware, conversant, familiar, informed, knowledgeable

version n edition

vertebrae n backbone, spine

vertical adj perpendicular, sheer, steep, upright

verve n 1 effectiveness, flair, kick, pep, pizzazz, potency, punch, sizzle, snap, spark, vigor, wallop

   n 2 animation, drive, élan, energy, enthusiasm, esprit de corps, go, gusto, pep, potency, sparkle, spirit, spunk, vigor, vim, vitality, zing, zip

   n 3 see: VIGOR n 2, 3

very adv 1 considerably, dramatically, far, quite, rather, significantly, well

   adv 2 actually, exactly, genuinely, precisely, really, sincerely, truly, verifiably

   adv 3 awfully, dreadfully, eminently, endlessly, exceedingly, exceptionally, extremely, greatly, highly, mightily, notably, quite, remarkably, terribly, thoroughly

   adj 1 exact, identical, same

   adj 2 ideal, model, perfect

vessel n 1 barrel, bucket, cask, drum, keg, tub

   n 2 bottle, bucket, caddy, can, canister, jar, pail, shell, tin

   n 3 artery, blood vessel, vein

   n 4 amphora, pot, vase

   n 5 chalice, container, cup, dish, Dixie cup, glass, goblet, mug, shot glass, stein, tumbler, wineglass

   n 6 craft, cruiser, freighter, frigate, ketch, liner, ocean liner, sailboat, schooner, ship, steamship, yacht

vested adj see: EXACT adj 6

vestibule *n* anteroom, approach, atrium, court, doorway, entrance hall, entry, foyer, hall, hallway, lobby

vestige *n* memento, relic, remnant, shadow, trace

veteran *adj* **1** adept, experienced, practiced, proficient, seasoned
adj **2** chief, higher ranked, senior
n see: EXPERT *n* 4

veto *n* ban, disapproval, refusal, rejection, thumbs down
v **1** ban, bar, confine, enjoin, forbid, inhibit, nix, outlaw, prevent, prohibit, stop
v **2** cancel, contradict, deny, disallow, forbid, negate, nix, nullify, override, overrule, reject, renege, repeal, revoke, torpedo, void

vex *v* **1** condemn, curse, damn, denounce, molest, profane
v **2** see: BOTHER *v* 5

vexation *n* **1** discontent, dissatisfaction, regret
n **2** annoyance, anxiety, apprehension, bother, care, concern, disquiet, disquietude, doubt, irritation, misgiving, reservation, restlessness, restraint, skepticism, trouble, worry

vexatious *adj* annoying, bothersome, glaring, harassing, irksome, irritating, mean, onerous, painful, pesky, troublesome, ugly, unwelcome, wicked

viable *adj* **1** alive, developing, living
adj **2** alive, animate, animated, living, vital
adj **3** achievable, capable, doable, feasible, possible, practical, workable
adj **4** absolute, actual, authentic, bona fide, certain, definite, existent, factual, genuine, hard, inarguable, incontestable, incontrovertible, indisputable, indubitable, irrefutable, positive, real, sure, true, undeniable, undisputable, undoubtable, undoubted, unequivocal, unquestionable

viaduct *n* bridge, overpass

vibrant *adj* active, alive, dynamic, energetic, sound, spirited, strong, vigorous, vital

vibrate *v* **1** backfire, echo, repeat, resonate, reverberate
v **2** beat, flutter, palpitate, pulsate, pulse, quiver, throb
v **3** flinch, flutter, jar, pulsate, quake, quaver, quiver, shake, shiver, shudder, tremble, twitch, twitter
v **4** fluctuate, oscillate, pulsate, surge, throb

vibration *n* resonance, tone

vicarious *adj* by proxy, indirect, surrogate

vice *n* **1** failing, fault, foible, frailty, limitation, shortcoming, weakness
n **2** corruption, depravity, dishonesty, immorality, impurity, wickedness, wrong
n **3** see: CRIME *n* 3

vicinity *n* **1** closeness, nearness
n **2** boundary, extent, field, matter, range, scope
n **3** see: WARD *n* 2

vicious *adj* **1** rabid, savage, untamed, violent, wild
adj **2** angry, fierce, ferocious, furious, heated, intense, savage, severe, terrible, violent
adj **3** base, corrupt, deadly, degenerate, depraved, deviant, evil, immoral, infamous, kinky, nefarious, perverse, putrid, rotten, ruthless, savage, villainous, wicked, wild
adj **4** austere, brutal, callous, cold-blooded, compassionless, cruel, ferocious, fierce, hardened, hardhearted, heartless, indifferent, inhuman, inhumane, malicious, mean, merciless, obdurate, nasty, pitiless, ruthless, savage, spiteful, stony, tough, uncaring, unemotional, unfeeling, unkind, unmerciful, unpitying, unrelenting

victim *n* **1** captive, prisoner
n **2** casualty, fatality, loss
n **3** chump, dupe, mark, pushover, stooge, sucker
n **4** butt, casualty, object, prey, subject, target

victimize *v* **1** abuse, brutalize, exploit, harm, ill-treat, injure, maltreat, mistreat, molest, persecute, wrong
v **2** bamboozle, beat, beguile, bilk, burn, cajole, cheat, chicane, chisel, con, cross, deceive, defraud, dupe, embezzle, fleece, flimflam, fob, foist, fool, gyp, hoax, hoodwink, hustle, inveigle, screw, shaft, sham, swindle

victor *n* advocate, champion, conqueror, hero, heroine, lead, leader, master, principal, protagonist, star, trailblazer, winner

victorious *adj* conquering, successful, triumphant, winning

victory *n* **1** accomplishment, achievement, arrival, attainment, completion, fruition, fulfillment, realization, satisfaction, success
n **2** accomplishment, achievement, conquest, success, triumph, win, winner

victuals *n* bread, breakfast, brunch, chow, cuisine, diet, dinner, dish, edibles, entree, fare, food, grub, lunch, meals, nosh, nutrition, provisions, rations, snack, supper, vittles

video *n* boob tube, cable, channel, station, teevee, television, tube, TV

vie *v* combat, compete, contend, contest, counter, dispute, duel, fight, match, oppose, parry, pit, play, repel, resist, rival, strive

view *n* 1 look, picture, sight

n 2 landscape, outlook, scene, scenery, sight, vista

n 3 concept, conception, hunch, idea, image, impression, notion, perception, recollection

n 4 angle, aspect, facet, hand, mien, opinion, perspective, phase, side

n 5 attitude, belief, bias, conviction, feeling, inducement, leaning, mind, opinion, persuasion, sentiment

v 1 account, calculate, consider, deem, judge, reckon, surmise

v 2 behold, catch, comprehend, conjure, descry, digest, discern, distinguish, espy, fathom, grasp, know, look at, notice, observe, perceive, realize, recognize, savvy, see, sight, understand

vigilance *n* caveat, foresight, forethought, providence, prudence, vision, wariness

vigilant *adj* 1 alert, careful, heedful, leery, prudent, wary, watchful

adj 2 alert, careful, cautious, open-eyed, unsleeping, wakeful, wary, watchful, wide-awake

vigilantes *n* band, gang, mob

vignette *n* see: ARTICLE *n* 2

vigor *n* 1 concentration, depth, energy, intensity, profundity, strength

n 2 animation, drive, élan, energy, enthusiasm, esprit de corps, go, gusto, pep, potency, sparkle, spirit, spunk, verve, vim, vitality, zing, zip

n 3 ardor, beef, brawn, drive, energy, force, intensity, lustiness, might, muscle, pep, potency, power, punch, steam, strength, verve, vim, virility, vitality

n 4 see: PERSISTENCE *n* 3

n 5 see: POTENCY *n* 2, 3, 4

vigorous *adj* 1 clear, effective, explicit, forceful, strong, trenchant

adj 2 active, alive, dynamic, energetic, sound, spirited, strong, vibrant, vital

adj 3 coercive, compelling, dynamic, energetic, forceful, hardy, lusty, mighty, passionate, powerful, robust, strong, sturdy

adj 4 see: ZESTY *adj*

vile *adj* 1 base, beneath, despicable, ignoble, inferior, low, lowdown, sordid, squalid, unworthy, vulgar, wretched

adj 2 bad, corrupt, crooked, deceitful, dishonest, evil, fraudulent, immoral, iniquitous, lying, Machiavellian, manipulative, mercenary, reprobate, roguish, scheming, shady, shifty, sinful, unethical, unfair, unprincipled, unscrupulous, untruthful, venal, wicked, wrong

vilify *v* abuse, asperse, bad-mouth, belittle, condemn, damage, decry, defame, degrade, denigrate, denounce, deprecate, detract, diminish, discount, disparage, insult, knock, malign, put down, revile, run down, slander

village *n* borough, burgh, community, hamlet, settlement, township

villain *n* brute, demon, devil, fiend, rogue, Satan, wretch

villainous *adj* 1 despicable, infamous, notorious, offensive, scandalous, shady, unsavory

adj 2 base, corrupt, deadly, degenerate, depraved, deviant, evil, immoral, infamous, kinky, nefarious, perverse, putrid, rotten, ruthless, savage, vicious, wicked, wild

vim *n* 1 animation, drive, élan, energy, enthusiasm, esprit de corps, go, gusto, pep, potency, sparkle, spirit, spunk, verve, vigor, vitality, zing, zip

n 2 see: VIGOR *n* 2, 3

vindicate *v* 1 argue, assert, believe, claim, contend, defend, justify, know, maintain, state, think, warrant

v 2 absolve, acquit, clear, condone, exculpate, excuse, exempt, exonerate, forgive, free, pardon, remit

v 3 see: PAY *v* 2

vindictive *adj* 1 adamant, cold, cruel, fierce, relentless

adj 2 malicious, revengeful, spiteful, unforgiving, vengeful

vindictiveness *n* 1 getting even, reciprocity, reprisal, retaliation, retribution, vengeance

n 2 see: HATE *n*

vine *n* 1 barnacle, dependent, freeloader, hanger-on, leech, parasite, remora

n 2 bush, grass, hedge, plant, sapling, shrub, tree, vegetation, weed

vintage *adj* aged, age-old, ancient, antique, elderly, gray, grizzled, old, olden, senior, timeworn, venerable, worn

violate *v* 1 err, fall, offend, sin, transgress, trespass

v 2 attack, encroach, entrench, infringe, intrude, trespass *v* 3 assault, attack, force, pillage, rape, ravish, sack

v 4 defy, disobey, ignore, infringe, obstruct, rebel, oppose

v 5 deflower, desecrate, despoil, devastate, devour, loot, maraud, pillage, plunder, ravage, sack, scourge, spoil

violation *n* 1 breach, default, infraction, misdemeanor, trespass

n 2 blasphemy, desecration, heresy, impiety, irreverence

n 3 crime, dishonor, disobedience, evil, fault, felony, infamy, infraction, iniquity, injury, lawbreaking, misdeed, misdemeanor, offense, outrage, sin, transgression, trespass, vice, wrong, wrongdoing

n 4 abuse, assault, attack, rape, sack

violence *n* 1 coercion, compulsion, constraint, force

n 2 intensity, power, severity, tumult

n 3 brutality, destructiveness, ferocity, force, frenzy, fury

violent *adj* 1 rabid, savage, untamed, wild

adj 2 amok, berserk, crazy, frenzied, maniacal, out of control

adj 3 angry, ferocious, fierce, furious, heated, intense, savage, severe, terrible, vehement, vicious

adj 4 agitated, disorderly, excited, fierce, frantic, frenzied, furious, mad, stormy, tumultuous, turbulent, wild

adj 5 bitter, brutal, cruel, fierce, hard, harsh, inclement, intemperate, pitiless, rigorous, rough, rugged, severe, stern, strong

adj 6 see: AWFUL *adj* 2

violet *adj* amethyst, lavender, lilac, mauve, orchid, plum, purple

VIP *n* see: CAPITALIST *n*

virgin *adj* 1 green, immature, inexperienced, naive, new, novice, raw

adj 2 clean, immaculate, pristine, pure, spotless, taintless, unsoiled, unspoiled, unsullied

n innocent

virginal *adj* 1 abstinent, celibate, chaste, continent, maidenly, pure, virtuous

adj 2 celibate, chaste, clean, decent, decorous, immaculate, modest, moral, pristine, proper, pure, spotless, stainless, stuffy, taintless, unadulterated, unblemished, undefiled, upstanding, wholesome

virile *adj* brave, courageous, lusty, macho, male, manlike, manly, masculine, potent, stalwart

virility *n* see: VIGOR *n* 3

virtual *adj* close, immediate, near, near at hand, nigh, proximate

virtually *adv* by itself, effectively, essentially, intrinsically, per se, practically

virtue *n* 1 honesty, honor, integrity, principle, trustworthiness

n 2 attribute, character, characteristic, feature, highlight, mark, peculiarity, property, quality

n 3 humility, modesty

n 4 goodness, morality, principle, probity, purity, rectitude, righteousness, uprightness

virtuoso *n* 1 aesthete, connoisseur, expert

n 2 adviser, artist, authority, expert, guru, master, official, pro, professional, specialist, veteran, wizard

n 3 accompanist, artiste, conductor, musician, performer

virtuous *adj* 1 abstinent, celibate, chaste, continent, maidenly, pure

adj 2 blameless, commendable, exemplary, exonerated, guiltless, innocent, irreproachable, pure, righteous

adj 3 conscientious, ethical, honest, honorable, moral, noble, principled, proper, respectable, right, righteous, scrupulous, sound, true, trustworthy

virus *n* cold, illness

visa *n* identification, pass, passport, permit

visage *n* 1 appearance, aspect, cast, countenance, expression, face

n 2 expression, face, grimace, mouth, pout, scowl, smirk

visceral *adj* automatic, deep, gut, innate, instinctive

visible *adj* 1 obvious, outright, overt, public

adj 2 current, extant, remaining

adj 3 bare, exposed, in the raw, naked, nude, open, peeled, stripped, unclothed

adj 4 appreciable, cognizant, concrete, detectable, discernible, noticeable, observable, palpable, perceptible, sensible

vision *n* 1 eyesight, perception, sight

n 2 daydream, dream, fancy, fantasy, musing

n 3 caveat, foresight, forethought, providence, prudence, vigilance, wariness

n 4 distance, future, horizon, outlook, perspective, purview, vista

n 5 aberration, apparition, delusion, fantasy, figment, ghost, hallucination, illusion, image, mirage, phantasm

n 6 apocalypse, prophecy, revelation

visionary *n* 1 dreamer, idealist, romantic

n 2 astrologer, augur, fortuneteller, oracle, predictor, prophet, psychic, seer, soothsayer

adj see: FLAMBOYANT *adj* 2

visionless *adj* blind, sightless

visit *v* 1 sojourn, stop over, tour

v 2 encounter, greet, interview, meet, receive

v 3 chat, chatter, converse, discuss, parley, talk

v 4 attend, frequent, hang around, hang out, haunt, obsess, patronize

n stay

visitor *n* caller, company, guest

vista *n* 1 horizon, lookout, outlook, perspective

n 2 landscape, outlook, scene, scenery, sight, view

n 3 distance, future, horizon, outlook, perspective, vision

visual *adj* 1 detailed, graphic, illustrative, photographic, pictorial, picturesque, vivid

adj 2 ocular, optic, optical

visualize *v* conceive, conjecture, conjure up, create, envision, fancy, image, imagine, invent, project, realize, think

vita *n* 1 autobiography, biography, compendium, profile, résumé

n 2 career, diary, events, experience, history, performance, record, résumé

vital *adj* 1 chief, crucial, key, salient

adj 2 alive, animate, animated, viable

adj 3 active, alive, dynamic, energetic, sound, spirited, strong, vibrant

adj 4 critical, essential, imperative, indispensable, mandatory, necessary, needed, required

adj 5 acute, burning, critical, crucial, desperate, dire, grave, heavy, important, major, momentous, ponderous, pressing, profound, serious, severe, solemn, urgent

adj 6 see: DISASTROUS *adj* 2

adj 7 see: SUBSTANTIAL *adj* 4

vitality *n* 1 actuality, being, existence, fact, life, presence, reality

n 2 see: VIGOR *n* 2, 3

vitalize *v* activate, charge, electrify, energize, enliven, excite, ignite, start

vittles *n* bread, breakfast, brunch, chow, cuisine, diet, dinner, dish, edibles, entree, fare, food, grub, lunch, meals, nosh, nutrition, provisions, rations, snack, supper

vivacious *adj* alert, animated, bouncy, bright, brisk, buoyant, chipper, dashing, dynamic, ebullient, energetic, enthusiastic, exuberant, frisky, frolicsome, gay, jumpy, kinetic, lively, peppy, pert, playful, rousing, scintillating, spirited, sprightly

vivid *adj* 1 dramatic, epic, grand, heroic, legendary, noble

adj 2 detailed, graphic, illustrative, photographic, pictorial, picturesque

adj 3 colorful, expressive, graphic, impressive, intense, potent, powerful, striking, strong, unforgettable

vivify *v* animate, brighten, cheer up, enliven, incite, inspire, liven, quicken

vocabulary *n* 1 buzzwords, jargon, lexicons, lingo, nomenclature, terminology, terms

n 2 dictionary, glossary, lexicon, list, synonym finder, synonym listing, thesaurus, Word Finder®

n 3 buzzwords, expression, idiom, jargon, language, lingo, parlance, verbiage, vernacular

vocal *adj* 1 articulate, communicative, expressive, talkative

adj 2 belligerent, extroverted, free, intimidating, loud, outspoken, vociferous

adj 3 choral, euphonious, harmonious, lyric, mellow, melodic, melodious, musical, orchestral, philharmonic, rhythmical, symphonic

vocalize *v* 1 trill, warble

v 2 announce, articulate, assert, couch, describe, dictate, draft, enunciate, express, intonate, orate, phrase, proclaim, pronounce, say, speak, state, stress, talk, utter, verbalize, voice, word

vocation *n* art, avocation, business, calling, career, discipline, employment, field, gig, job, labor, line, livelihood, occupation, office, profession, pursuit, role, schtick, situation, specialty, task, thing, trade, work

vociferous *adj* 1 belligerent, extroverted, free, intimidating, outspoken, vocal

adj 2 blatant, boisterous, clamorous, disturbing, loud, loudmouthed, noisy, obstreperous, raucous, rowdy

vogue *adj* chic, current, fashionable, hip, in, smart, stylish

n chic, craze, fad, fashion, mode, rage, style, thing

voice *n* expression, opinion, say, say-so

v see: VERBALIZE *v* 2

voiceless *adj* dumb, inarticulate, mute, reticent, silent, speechless

void *adj* 1 bare, barren, clear, empty, stark, vacant

adj 2 bad, defective, futile, inadequate, incorrect, inferior, invalid, malfunctioning *n* **1** emptiness, nil, nothing, nothingness, oblivion

n **2** blank, cavity, crack, depression, emptiness, gap, hole, hollow, nook, opening, space

v **1** cleanse, discharge, eliminate, empty, evacuate

v **2** abrogate, annul, cancel, contradict, discharge, dismantle, dissolve, dwindle, fade, negate, nullify, quash, recall, repeal, rescind, reverse, revoke, set aside

v **3** see: REJECT *v* 7

volatile *adj* **1** see: FLEETING *adj* 2

adj **2** see: INCONSISTENT *adj* 3

volition *n* **1** discipline, persistence, self-control, will, willpower

n **2** enterprise, gumption, initiative, resourcefulness, spirit

n **3** ambition, drive, enterprise, initiative, lead, leadership, push

volley *n* barrage, burst, fusillade, shot

v bounce, bump, jostle, throw

volume *n* **1** capacity, content

n **2** amount, amplitude, dimensions, magnitude, proportions, quantity, size

n **3** book, correspondence, edition, folio, issue, manuscript, monograph, opus, paperback, printing, publication, text, tome, work, writing

n **4** see: SUBSTANCE *n* 9

voluminous *adj* abundant, assorted, copious, diverse, extensive, legion, many, multifarious, multitudinous, myriad, numerous, plentiful, populous, prolific, sundry

voluntary *adj* deliberate, free, intentional, optional, unforced, unprescribed, willful, willing

volunteer *v* see: GIVE *v* 8

voluptuous *adj* **1** carnal, delicious, enticing, erotic, hedonistic, luscious, lush, lusty, luxurious, pleasure-seeking, sensual, sensualistic, sensuous

adj **2** amorous, ardent, aroused, carnal, earthy, erotic, fervent, fleshly, horny, hot, impassioned, lascivious, lecherous, lewd, licentious, lustful, passionate, provocative, randy, raunchy, romantic, sensual, sexual, sexy, sultry, titillated, torrid, turned on, wanton

vomit *v* choke, cough, disgorge, gag, throw up

voodoo *n* **1** anathema, condemnation, curse, execration, malediction

n **2** bewitchment, enchantment, incantation, magic, occultism, sorcery, spell, witchcraft, wizardry

voracious *adj* **1** famished, hungry, ravenous, starving

adj **2** avaricious, covetous, endless, insatiable, ravenous, unquenchable

adj **3** excessive, gluttonous, immoderate, inordinate, intemperate, overindulgent, prodigious, unbridled, undue

vortex *n* eddy, whirlpool

vote *n* **1** ballot, choice, franchise, option, preference, say, selection

n **2** see: SELECTION *n* 2, 3

v appoint, ballot, choose, elect, nominate, opt

vouch *v* **1** affirm, attest, avow, contend, promise, say, swear, warrant

v **2** assure, certify, contract, endorse, guarantee, pledge, sanction, underwrite, warrant

v **3** attest, authenticate, certify, confirm, corroborate, justify, notarize, prove, ratify, sanction, substantiate, support, validate, verify, witness

voucher *n* **1** receipt

n **2** badge, card, label, pass, ticket

vow *n* assurance, declaration, oath, pledge, promise, word

v advocate, affirm, assure, avouch, avow, commit, devote, guarantee, pledge, promise, ratify

voyage *n* **1** adventure, air travel, cruise, excursion, expedition, flight, journey, passage, safari, sally, tour, travel, trek, trip

n **2** see: PATH *n* 2

v **1** cross, cruise, fly, sail, traverse

v **2** coast, cruise, explore, go, journey, migrate, proceed, sail, survey, tour, travel

vulgar *adj* **1** base, beneath, despicable, ignoble, inferior, low, lowdown, sordid, squalid, vile, wretched

adj **2** bawdy, coarse, crude, dirty, erotic, filthy, foul, gamy, gross, improper, indecent, lascivious, lewd, licentious, nasty, obscene, off-color, pornographic, profane, prurient, racy, rank, raunchy, ribald, risqué, scandalous, smutty, suggestive, tainted, uncouth, x-rated

adj **3** see: SCATHING *adj*

vulnerable *adj* **1** susceptible

adj **2** exposed, liable, prone

adj **3** anxious, insecure, nervous, precarious, threatened

adj **4** defenseless, dependent, disarmed, exposed, helpless, powerless, susceptible, weak

vying *adj* competing, rival

W

wacky *adj* absurd, balmy, bizarre, crazy, emotional, foolish, frivolous, goofy, illogical, impossible, inane, insane, irrational, loony, lunatic, mad, muddled, nuts, preposterous, ridiculous, silly, touched, zany

waffle *v* bumble, falter, flounder, fumble, get stuck, grope, hesitate, stagger, stumble

waffling *adj* diffident, faltering, halting, hesitant, indecisive, reluctant, tentative, unsure

wage *n* bill, bonus, charge, commission, compensation, consideration, earnings, fee, gross, income, pay, revenue, salary, stipend

v conduct, pursue, undertake

wager *v* attempt, bet, chance, dare, gamble, hazard, play, risk, speculate, stake

wages *n* compensation, earnings, gain, reward

wagon *n* 1 auto, automobile, bus, car, carriage, chariot, coach, jeep, motorcar, omnibus, sedan, truck, van

n 2 cart, handcart, pushcart, truck, wheelbarrow

wail *v* 1 bawl, bemoan, cry, grieve, groan, lament, moan, mourn, sigh, snivel, sob, weep, whimper, whine

v 2 bark, bellow, blare, call, cry, holler, howl, roar, scream, screech, shout, shriek, shrill, squeal, thunder, yell

n groan, moan, sigh

wait *v* 1 attend, serve

v 2 line up, queue

v 3 abide, await, bide, linger, loiter, remain, stay, stick around, tarry

v 4 adjourn, avoid, defer, delay, hold, hold up, interrupt, lay over, postpone, procrastinate, prolong, put off, remit, reschedule, set aside, shelve, stay, suspend, table

n delay, interval, lull, pause, stay

waive *v* 1 abandon, acquiesce, cede, give up, hand over, leave, relinquish, resign, submit, surrender, yield

v 2 abstain, cast, decline, drop, eschew, forbear, forfeit, forgo, give up, lose, pass, reject, renounce, sacrifice, surrender

v 3 adjourn, avoid, defer, delay, hold, hold up, interrupt, lay over, postpone, procrastinate, prolong, put off, remit, reschedule, set aside, shelve, stay, suspend, table, wait

wake *v* arouse, awaken, challenge, excite, kindle, rally, rouse, stir, waken

wakeful *adj* alert, careful, cautious, open-eyed, unsleeping, vigilant, wary, watchful, wide-awake

waken *v* arouse, awaken, challenge, excite, kindle, rally, rouse, stir

walk *n* 1 hike, march, stroll, tramp, trek

n 2 gait, march, pace, shuffle, step, stride

n 3 alacrity, cadence, celerity, dispatch, gait, pace, quickness, rapidity, rate, speed, step, stride, swiftness, trot

v 1 amble, hike, journey, march, pace, parade, plod, saunter, step, stride, stroll, strut, tramp, tread, trek

v 2 itinerate, meander, perambulate, promenade, ramble, range, roam, rove, saunter, stray, stroll, traipse, travel, wander

walkout *n* boycott, dispute, strike

walkway *n* ground, pavement, sidewalk

wall *n* 1 bastion, bulwark, defense, embankment, fort, fortification, rampart

n 2 bar, barricade, barrier, block, blockade, fence, obstacle, roadblock, stop

n 3 curtain, divider, partition

n 4 face, side, surface

wallet *n* bag, baggage, case, equipment, gear, grip, kit, luggage, pack, pouch, purse, sack, suitcase

wallop *n* 1 effectiveness, flair, kick, pep, pizzazz, potency, punch, sizzle, snap, spark, verve

n 2 see: HIT *n* 1

v 1 beat, belittle, blast, clobber, conquer, cream, defeat, dust, lambaste, lick, overrun, overwhelm, rout, shellac, smear, thrash, whip

v 2 see: BATTER *v*

walloping *adj* see: HUGE *adj* 3

wallow *v* 1 depress, droop, flop, let down, lower, sag, sink

v 2 bask, delight, enjoy, like, loaf, luxuriate, relax, relish, savor

waltz *n* 1 breeze, cinch, dash, ease, snap, zip

n 2 ballet, cha-cha, dance, fox trot, hula, jitterbug, polka, tap, twist

wan *adj* ashen, ashy, blanched, colorless, pale, pallid, sallow, sickly, sooty, waxen, yellow

wand *n* baton, rod, staff

wander *v* itinerate, meander, perambulate, promenade, ramble, range, roam, rove, saunter, stray, stroll, traipse, travel, traverse, walk

wandering *adj* ambulatory, gypsy, itinerant, movable, nomadic, perambulatory, roving, transient, vagrant, wayfaring

wane *v* 1 abate, decline, deteriorate, fade, fail, flag, impair, languish, weaken, wither, worsen *v* 2 abate, cease, decline, decrease, die down, diminish, drain, dwindle, ease, ebb, fall, lessen, let up, lull, recede, reduce, relax, relent, shrink, slacken, soften, stop, subside, taper off, waste away, weaken

v 3 see: DISINTEGRATE *v* 2

n see: FALL *n* 3

want *n* 1 defect, deficiency, demerit, fault, flaw, imperfection, inadequacy, lack, need

n 2 deficiency, deprivation, destitution, inadequacy, indigence, lack, need, poverty, privation

n 3 see: DEFICIT *n* 2

v 1 demand, expect, levy, require, wish

v 2 choose, covet, crave, desire, envy, fancy, lust, wish

v 3 ache, covet, crave, desire, hanker, hunger, itch, long, lust, need, pine, thirst, yearn

wanted *adj* commercial, marketable, salable

wanting *adj* 1 bereft, deprived, destitute

adj 2 absent, away, gone, lacking, missing, omitted

adj 3 deficient, failing, inadequate, inferior, insufficient, scant, scarce, scrimpy, short

wanton *adj* 1 extravagant, intemperate, loose, reckless, unrestrained, wild

adj 2 casual, easy, fast, immoral, incontinent, indiscriminate, lax, lecherous, lewd, licentious, light, loose, promiscuous, unchaste, whorish

adj 3 amorous, ardent, aroused, carnal, earthy, erotic, fervent, fleshly, horny, hot, impassioned, lascivious, lecherous, lewd, licentious, lustful, passionate, provocative, randy, raunchy, romantic, sensual, sexual, sexy, sultry, titillated, torrid, turned on

war *n* 1 battle, combat, conflagration, dispute, encounter, fight

n 2 battle, clash, competition, conflict, contest, discord, duel, fight, fighting, rivalry, strife, warfare

n 3 see: QUARREL *n* 2

v attack, battle, combat, contend, fight, oppose

warble *v* quaver, trill, vocalize

ward *n* 1 guard, lookout, picket, sentinel, sentry, warden, watch, watchman

n 2 area, district, domain, environs, jurisdiction, locality, neighborhood, parish, precinct, province, range, region, section, sphere, vicinity, zone

n 3 chamber, room

warden *n* guard, lookout, picket, sentinel, sentry, ward, watch, watchman

wardrobe *n* 1 cabinet, chest, closet, compartment, cubby, locker

n 2 clothes, clothing, garb

warehouse *n* 1 cache, stockroom, storehouse

n 2 building, edifice, erection, foundation, house, pile, structure

wares *n* articles, basics, commodities, essentials, goods, inventory, line, materials, merchandise, products, properties, staples

warfare *n* battle, clash, competition, conflict, contest, discord, duel, fight, fighting, rivalry, strife, struggle, war

warhead *n* bomb, bombshell, explosive, mine, missile, payload, rocket

wariness *n* 1 caveat, foresight, forethought, providence, prudence, vigilance

n 2 apprehension, distrust, doubt, fear, hesitation, misbelief, mistrust, suspicion

warlike *adj* 1 military

adj 2 angry, bellicose, belligerent, combative, contentious, hostile, militant, pugnacious, quarrelsome

warm *adj* 1 comfortable, desirable, genial

adj 2 heated, hot, lukewarm, tepid

adj 3 comfortable, comfy, contented, cozy, cushy, homey, secure, snug

adj 4 affectionate, compassionate, considerate, empathetic, empathic, gentle, humane, kind, kindhearted, responsive, softhearted, sympathetic, tender, warmhearted

v bake, broil, burn, char, cook, heat, melt, parch, roast, scorch, sear, singe, swelter

warmer *n* blanket, comforter, quilt

warmhearted *adj* see: TENDER *adj* 9

warmth *n* 1 glow, heat, temperature

n 2 blush, color, fever, flush

n 3 affection, affinity, attachment, attraction, compassion, concern, devotion, fondness, love, heart

warn *v* 1 alert, divulge, tip, tip off

v 2 alert, augur, caution, flag, forebode, forewarn, indicate, inform, motion, notify, signal, wave

v 3 see: BERATE *v* 2

warning *n* 1 caution

n 2 alarm, alert, SOS

n 3 forecast, prediction, prophecy, revelation

n 4 apprehension, foreboding, forewarning, harbinger, intuition, omen, premonition, presage

n 5 fulmination, intimidation, threat

warp *v* 1 contort, twist

v 2 deform, distort, misshape

v 3 bias, corrupt, distort, misrepresent, pervert, skew

warrant *n* 1 authorization, commission

n 2 citation, notification, subpoena, summons, ticket, writ

n 3 assurance, bond, commitment, earnest, guarantee, obligation, pawn, pledge, security, surety

v 1 affirm, attest, avow, contend, promise, say, swear

v 2 assure, certify, contract, endorse, guarantee, pledge, sanction, underwrite

v 3 argue, assert, believe, claim, contend, defend, justify, know, maintain, state, think

warranted *adj* appropriate, correct, deserved, due, fitting, just, merited, proper, suitable

warranty *n* covenant, coverage, guarantee, indemnity, insurance, pledge, policy, promise

wary *adj* 1 alert, careful, heedful, leery, prudent, suspicious, vigilant, watchful

adj 2 alert, careful, cautious, open-eyed, unsleeping, vigilant, wakeful, watchful, wide-awake

adj 3 calculating, careful, cautious, circumspect, considerate, discreet, gingerly, guarded, heedful, judicious, provident, prudent, restrained, reticent, safe

adj 4 ambiguous, borderline, clouded, doubtful, dubious, equivocal, garbled, illogical, inarticulate, incalculable, incoherent, inexplicit, muddled, muffled, murky, obscure, precarious, questionable, shaky, suspect, suspicious, uncertain, unclear, uneasy, unintelligible, vague

wash *v* 1 clean, cleanse, filter, purify, refine, sterilize

v 2 bathe, clean, cleanse, clean up, dip, flush, immerse, launder, rinse, rub, scour, scrape, scrub, shower

v 3 drift, float

washbowl *n* basin, sink, washstand

washing *n* cleansing

washstand *n* sink, washbowl

waste *n* 1 barren, desert, wasteland, wild, wilderness

n 2 crap, crud, debris, detritus, dirt, garbage, junk, litter, refuse, rubbish, rubble, sweepings, trash

n 3 droppings, excrement, feces, stool

v 1 cast away, consume, dissipate, drivel, empty, fritter, lavish, squander, throw away, use up

v 2 consume, deplete, exhaust, expend, finish, go, lessen, run through, spend, use up, weaken

wasted *adj* bombed, crocked, doped up, drunk, drunken, high, inebriated, intoxicated, juiced, loaded, looped, messed up, plastered, polluted, sloshed, smashed, stoned, tight, tipsy, turned on, wired

wasteful *adj* see: EXTRAVAGANT *adj* 4

wasteland *n* barren, desert, wild, wilderness

wasting *n* atrophy, decay, degeneration, deterioration

watch *n* 1 chronometer, clock, hourglass, stopwatch, timepiece, timer

n 2 guard, lookout, picket, sentinel, sentry, ward, watchman

v 1 beware, look out for, mind, take caution

v 2 defend, guard, oversee, patrol, police, protect, regulate

v 3 behold, glimpse, look, mind, see, sight, spot, witness

v 4 see: EXAMINE *v* 9

watchful *adj* 1 alert, careful, heedful, leery, prudent, suspicious, vigilant, wary

adj 2 alert, careful, cautious, open-eyed, unsleeping, vigilant, wakeful, wary, wide-awake

watchman *n* guard, lookout, picket, sentinel, sentry, ward, warden, watch

water *n* fluid, liquid, sea

watercolor *n* acrylic, art, canvas, depiction, drawing, etching, illustration, landscape, lithograph, mural, oil, painting, pastel, pen and ink, picture, portrait, print, seascape, sketch

waterless *adj* arid, dry, parched

waterlogged *adj* drenched, dripping, full, immersed, inundated, saturated, soaked, soaking, sodden, wet

watertight *adj* navigable, seaworthy, staunch

watery *adj* 1 diluted

adj 2 damp, fluid, juicy, liquefied, liquid, moist, wet

adj 3 anemic, bloodless, gaunt, haggard, lifeless, pale, pallid, passionless, spiritless, weak

wave *n* 1 gush, surge, swell

n 2 breaker, ripple, roller, swell, whitecap

v 1 alternate, fluctuate, oscillate, pendulate, sway, swing

v 2 dance, flap, flicker, flitter, flutter, oscillate, prance, sparkle, sway, twinkle *v* 3 alert, augur, caution, flag, forebode, forewarn, indicate, inform, motion, notify, signal

waver *v* 1 bumble, falter, flounder, fumble, get stuck, grope, hesitate, stagger, stumble, waffle

v 2 delay, falter, halt, hesitate, pause, stagger, stall, vacillate

wavering *adj* 1 diffident, faltering, halting, hesitant, indecisive, reluctant, tentative, unsure, waffling

adj 2 flimsy, insecure, jiggly, rickety, shaky, teetering, unstable, unsure, vacillating, weak, wobbly

adj 3 see: INCONSISTENT *adj* 3

wax *v* see: INCREASE *v* 8

waxen *adj* ashen, ashy, blanched, colorless, pale, pallid, sallow, sickly, sooty, wan, yellow

way *n* 1 circuit, course, itinerary, journey, line, means, passage, path, road, route, trip

n 2 custom, fashion, formality, habit, manner, mores, observance, practice, routine, tradition, usage, use, wont

n 3 angle, approach, code, delivery, execution, expression, fashion, manner, method, mode, organization, process, program, style, technique

n 4 access, approach, artery, avenue, boulevard, channel, drag, highway, pass, path, promenade, road, roadway, route, strait, street, thoroughfare

wayfaring *adj* ambulatory, gypsy, itinerant, movable, nomadic, perambulatory, roving, transient, wandering

waylay *v* ambush, assail, assault, attack, beset, invade, raid, storm, strike

wayward *adj* 1 balking, balky, contrary, cranky, disagreeable, irascible, mean, obstinate, ornery

adj 2 see: INCONSISTENT *adj* 3

wc *n* bathroom, can, head, john, latrine, lavatory, loo, potty, powder room, toilet

weak *adj* 1 emasculate, impotent, inadequate, ineffective, ineffectual

adj 2 feeble, flimsy, frail, insubstantial, slight, tenuous

adj 3 balmy, bland, faint, gentle, mild, pleasant, soft

adj 4 flimsy, insecure, jiggly, rickety, shaky, teetering, unstable, unsure, vacillating, wavering, wobbly

adj 5 ailing, delicate, diseased, down, frail, ill, impaired, indisposed, sick, sickly, suffering, unhealthy, unsound

adj 6 feeble, helpless, impotent, inept, powerless

adj 7 defenseless, dependent, disarmed, exposed, helpless, powerless, susceptible, unprotected, vulnerable

adj 8 anemic, bloodless, gaunt, haggard, lifeless, pale, pallid, passionless, spiritless

adj 9 imperceptible, imponderable, inappreciable, indiscernible, insensible, intangible, invisible, minute, scant, unapparent

weaken *v* 1 blunt, dull, stupefy

v 2 diminish, lessen, repress, subject, subordinate

v 3 cripple, debilitate, disable, drain, enfeeble, exhaust, sap, undermine

v 4 attenuate, dilute, diminish, lessen, purify, rarefy, reduce, refine, shorten, thin out

v 5 abate, decline, deteriorate, fade, fail, flag, impair, languish, wane, wither, worsen

v 6 see: DEPLETE *v* 2

v 7 see: DISINTEGRATE *v* 2

v 8 see: SUBSIDE *v* 2

weakening *n* 1 decadence, decline, degeneration

n 2 debasement, decline, deterioration, dip, drop, downturn, ebb, erosion, fall, involution, plunge, sag, slide, slip, slump

n 3 decline, decrease, decrement, reduction

weakness *n* 1 failing, fault, foible, frailty, limitation, shortcoming

n 2 blemish, defect, failing, fault, flaw, imperfection, scar

wealth *n* 1 abundance, affluence, bounty, comfort, cornucopia, elegance, glut, good fortune, grandeur, luxury, opulence, plenty, prosperity, success

n 2 assets, belongings, equity, estate, fortune, goods, holdings, inheritance, money, ownership, possessions, property, prosperity, riches

n 3 see: MONEY *n* 3, 4

wealthy *adj* 1 affluent, booming, prosperous, successful, thriving

adj 2 affluent, copious, leisure-class, loaded, moneyed, opulent, rich, well-to-do

weaned *adj* alienated, disaffected, disunited, separated

weapons *n* ammo, ammunition, armor, arms, equipment, guns, machinery, munitions

wear *v* corrode, deteriorate, eat, erode, gnaw, oxidize

wearied *adj* see: WEARY *adj* 1

weariness *n* exhaustion, fatigue, lassitude

weary *adj* 1 beat, burnt out, bushed, careworn, drawn, emaciated, exhausted, expended, fatigued, frazzled, haggard, jaded, pinched, pooped, run-down, shot, spent, tired, wearied, worn, worn down, worn-out

adj **2** bored, disgusted, jaded, sick, tired

v **1** bore, tire

v **2** drain, exhaust, fatigue, jade, tire, wear out

weather *v* check, oppose, resist, stanch, stem, stop, withstand

weathered *adj* experienced, expert, grizzled, hardened, mature, seasoned

wed *v* associate, blend, bond, coalesce, combine, compound, connect, couple, fasten, fuse, join, link, marry, mate, meet, merge, unite

wedlock *n* coupling, liaison, linking, marriage, matrimony

wee *adj* bantam, dainty, diminutive, dwarfish, Lilliputian, little, micro, microscopic, midget, mini, miniature, minuscule, minute, petite, pygmy, small, tiny

weed *n* bush, grass, hedge, plant, sapling, shrub, tree, vegetation

v dig, extract, uproot

weekly *n* booklet, gazette, journal, magazine, monthly, periodical, publication

weep *v* bawl, bemoan, cry, grieve, groan, lament, moan, mourn, sigh, snivel, sob, wail, whimper, whine

weft *n* fabric, filling, woof

weigh *v* cerebrate, chew, consider, contemplate, deliberate, digest, meditate, mull, muse, ponder, reason, reflect, ruminate, see, speculate, study

weight *n* **1** accent, emphasis, highlighting, importance, priority, significance

n **2** concern, emphasis, gravity, import, importance, significance

n **3** consequence, import, importance, magnitude, moment, significance

n **4** authority, clout, control, in, influence, leverage, power, prestige

weightless *adj* light

weighty *adj* consequential, considerable, critical, crucial, important, material, meaningful, momentous, prominent, significant, substantial

weird *adj* **1** bizarre, eerie, ghostly, incredible, metaphysical, mystical, odd, ominous, spooky, strange, supernatural, uncanny, unearthly

adj **2** aberrant, bizarre, eccentric, erratic, odd, oddball, outlandish, peculiar, quaint, queer, singular, strange, uncanny, unconventional

adj **3** curious, exotic, far-out, fascinating, intriguing, kinky, marvelous, mysterious, new, novel, odd, outlandish, strange, ultra, unaccustomed, unexplored, unfamiliar, unique, unknown, unusual

weirdo *n* **1** debaucher, deviant, deviate

n **2** card, character, eccentric, kook, lunatic, oddball

welcome *adj* agreeable, congenial, favorable, good, grateful, gratifying, nice, pleasant, pleasurable

n greeting, salutation

v address, call to, embrace, greet, hail, meet, salute, summon

weld *n* bolt, brad, nut, peg, pin, rivet, spike, staple

v affix, attach, bind, clip, connect, fasten, fix

welfare *n* account, advantage, behalf, benefit, betterment, gain, good, happiness, interest, prosperity, sake, well-being

well *adv* **1** considerably, dramatically, far, quite, rather, significantly

adv **2** acceptably, adequately, amply, appropriately, correctly, properly, satisfactorily, suitably

adv **3** favorably, fortunately, happily, positively, successfully

adv **4** absolutely, certainly, decidedly, definitely, entirely, incontrovertibly, indeed, indubitably, positively, surely, truly, unequivocally, unquestionably, verily, without doubt

adj **1** fit, hardy, healthy, robust, rubicund, ruddy, sound, sturdy, wholesome

adj **2** conventional, correct, decorous, fitting, nice, orthodox, polite, proper, right

well-bred *adj* **1** aristocratic, blue-blooded, imperial, kingly, majestic, noble, regal, royal

adj **2** civilized, cosmopolitan, cultivated, cultured, elegant, genteel, ingratiating, poised, polished, refined, smooth, sophisticated, suave

well-groomed *adj* meticulous, neat, orderly, prim, shipshape, tidy

well-mannered *adj* see: POLITE *adj* **2**

well-read *adj* academic, educated, educational, erudite, intellectual, learned, literary, literate, pedantic, scholarly

well-spoken *adj* articulate, clear, cogent, eloquent, fluent

well-suited *adj* see: PRACTICAL *adj* **4**

well-to-do *adj* affluent, copious, leisure-class, loaded, moneyed, rich, wealthy

welsh *v* renege

welt *n* blister, fester, inflammation, lesion, sore, swelling

welter *v* see: WITHER *v* 4

wench *n* 1 damsel, girl, maid

n 2 call girl, harlot, hooker, hussy, prostitute, slut, streetwalker, tart, tramp, trollop, whore

wend *v* advance, begin again, continue, cycle, depart, get along, get on, go, leave, march, move, move forward, overture, part, proceed, progress, push on, recommence, reembark

wet *adj* 1 damp, dank, drizzly, foggy, humid, moist

adj 2 damp, fluid, juicy, liquefied, liquid, watery

adj 3 drenched, dripping, full, immersed, inundated, saturated, soaked, soaking, sodden, sopping, waterlogged

adj 4 damp, drenched, dripping, humid, moist, mucky, muggy, soaked, soggy, sopping, sticky, sultry

adj 5 choppy, nasty, rough, sloppy

v 1 imbue, permeate, saturate

v 2 deluge, douse, drench, drown, dunk, flood, inundate, irrigate, overload, saturate, slosh, soak, sop, souse, swamp, swill

wetness *n* 1 perspiration, sweat

n 2 dampness, humidity, moisture

whack *v* 1 bang, beat, bludgeon, clobber, club, hit, pound

v 2 bat, clout, hit, nail, pop, smite, sock, strike, swat

v 3 box, clap, cuff, knock, punch, slap, smack, spank, strike

v 4 see: STAMP *v* 2

n see: HIT *n* 1

wharf *n* dock, jetty, pier

wheel *v* 1 careen, lurch, pitch, reel, stagger, sway, totter

v 2 see: SKEW *v* 3

wheelbarrow *n* cart, handcart, pushcart, wagon

whereas *conj* albeit, although, even if, even though, notwithstanding, while, whilst

wherefore *n* argument, grounds, justification, proof, reason, why

wherewithal *n* assets, capacity, means, resources

whet *v* 1 edge, file, grind, hone, sharpen

v 2 arouse, electrify, excite, fire, incite, inspire, rouse, spark, stimulate, tantalize, thrill, titillate

whetted *adj* honed, keen, pointed, razor sharp, sharp

whiff *n* breath, clue, dash, glimmer, hint, insinuation, lick, shade, smell, smidgen, spice, sprinkling, suggestion, suspicion,

tinge, tip, touch, trace, trifle, whisper, wisp

while *conj* albeit, although, even if, even though, notwithstanding, whereas, whilst

whilst *conj* albeit, although, even if, even though, notwithstanding, whereas, while

whim *n* caprice, fancy, humor, impulse, notion, vagary, whimsy

whimper *v* bawl, bemoan, cry, grieve, groan, lament, moan, mourn, sigh, snivel, sob, wail, weep, whine

whimsical *adj* 1 charming, funny, odd, old-fashioned, peculiar, picturesque, puzzling, quaint, remarkable, special, uncommon

adj 2 conceived, conjured, created, fancied, fanciful, fantastic, fictional, fictitious, illusory, imaginary, imagined, invented, make-believe, nonexistent, notional

whimsy *n* 1 caprice, fancy, humor, impulse, notion, whim

n 2 creativity, fancy, fantasy, image, imagination, ingenuity, inspiration, invention

whine *v* 1 complain, crab, criticize, grieve, gripe, grumble, mutter, nag, object

v 2 see: CRY *v* 3

v 3 see: PLEAD *v* 2

whip *v* 1 beat, blend, mingle, mix, stir

v 2 beat, belittle, blast, clobber, conquer, cream, defeat, dust, lambaste, lick, overrun, overwhelm, rout, shellac, thrash, wallop

v 3 assail, attack, batter, beat, birch, buffet, flagellate, flog, hammer, lambaste, lash, lather, pelt, pound, pummel, punish, scourge, thrash, tromp

v 4 see: SKEW *v* 3

whipped *adj* beaten, clobbered, defeated, dejected, depressed, discouraged

whirl *n* 1 alternation, circuit, circulation, gyration, revolution, rotation, round, sequence, spinning, turn

n 2 attempt, chance, effort, fling, go, guess, heave, lob, pop, shot, slap, sling, stab, throw, try

v gyrate, pirouette, purl, reel, spin, swim, turn, twirl

whirlpool *n* 1 eddy, vortex

n 2 action, activity, ado, animation, bedlam, bother, bustle, chaos, commotion, excitement, flurry, fluster, fuss, hum, liveliness, madhouse, movement, stir, to-do, tumult, turmoil, whirlwind

whirlwind *n* action, activity, ado, animation, bedlam, bother, bustle, chaos, commotion, excitement, flurry, fluster, fuss, hum, liveliness, madhouse, movement, stir, to-do, tumult, turmoil

whisk *v* barrel, bullet, expedite, fly, hasten, hurry, hustle, rocket, rush, speed, zip

whiskey *n* alcohol, booze, drinks, grog, liquor, moonshine

whisper *n* **1** mumble, murmur, mutter, undertone

n **2** breath, clue, dash, glimmer, hint, insinuation, lick, shade, smell, smidgen, spice, sprinkling, suggestion, suspicion, tinge, tip, touch, trace, trifle, whiff, wisp

v breathe, confide, divulge, share

white *adj* chalky, ivory, milky, snowy

whitecap *n* breaker, ripple, roller, wave

whiten *v* blanch, pale

whitewash *v* absolve, acquit, cover up, exonerate, extenuate

n coverup, excuse

whittle *v* **1** ax, carve, chip, chop, cleave, cut, dissect, fell, hack, hew, mangle, mutilate, notch, pulverize, rend, saw, sever, slice, sliver, snip, split

v **2** see: TRIM *v* **1**

whole *adj* **1** concentrated, exclusive, fixed, undistracted, undivided, unswerving

adj **2** all, all-out, complete, entire, fullblown, gross, integral, integrated, outright, total

adj **3** absolute, complete, flawless, good, intact, perfect, sound, unblemished, unbroken, undamaged, unimpaired, uninjured, unmarred

adj **4** see: UTTER *adj*

n **1** being, entity, object, organism, sum, system, thing

n **2** aggregate, all, entirety, gross, revenue, sales, sum, sum total, total

wholehearted *adj* see: SINCERE *adj*

wholesale *adj* comprehensive, extensive, indiscriminate, large-scale

n bargain price, cut rate, discount

v barter, distribute, market, merchandise, peddle, retail, sell

wholesome *adj* **1** fit, hardy, healthy, robust, rubicund, ruddy, sound, sturdy

adj **2** celibate, chaste, clean, decent, decorous, immaculate, modest, moral, pristine, proper, pure, spotless, stainless, stuffy, taintless, unadulterated, unblemished, undefiled, virginal

wholly *adv* adequately, altogether, assiduously, completely, earnestly, entirely, exhaustively, fully, hard, intensely, intensively, painstakingly, perfectly,

quite, sufficiently, thoroughly, totally, unremittingly

whoop *n* alarm, call, hail, shout, yell

whopping *adj* see: HUGE *adj* **3**

whore *n* call girl, harlot, hooker, hussy, prostitute, slut, streetwalker, tart, tramp, trollop, wanton woman, wench

whorish *adj* see: PROMISCUOUS *adj* **2**

why *n* **1** argument, grounds, justification, proof, reason

n **2** cause, excuse, motive, purpose, rationale

wicked *adj* **1** demoniac, devilish, diabolic

adj **2** barbarous, monstrous, outrageous, uncivilized, unconscionable, unethical, ungodly

adj **3** bad, corrupt, crooked, deceitful, dishonest, evil, fraudulent, immoral, iniquitous, lying, Machiavellian, manipulative, mercenary, reprobate, roguish, scheming, shady, shifty, sinful, unethical, unfair, unprincipled, unscrupulous, untruthful, venal, vile, wrong

adj **4** annoying, bothersome, glaring, harassing, irksome, irritating, mean, onerous, painful, pesky, troublesome, ugly, unwelcome

adj **5** atrocious, awful, crying, desperate, disgraceful, ghastly, grizzly, heinous, monstrous, notorious, odious, offensive, outrageous, scandalous, shocking

adj **6** base, corrupt, deadly, degenerate, depraved, deviant, evil, immoral, infamous, kinky, nefarious, perverse, putrid, rotten, ruthless, savage, vicious, villainous, wild

wickedness *n* corruption, depravity, dishonesty, immorality, impurity, vice, wrong

wide *adj* **1** ample, broad, expansive, extended, extensive, ranging

adj **2** ample, big, capacious, comfortable, commodious, open, roomy, spacious

wide-awake *adj* alert, careful, cautious, open-eyed, unsleeping, vigilant, wary, watchful

widen *v* **1** broaden, enlarge, flare, open, spread

v **2** amplify, bloat, dilate, distend, enlarge, expand, fatten, grow, increase, inflate, magnify, stretch

widespread *adj* **1** broad, general, global, planetary, universal, worldwide

adj **2** current, democratic, dominant, extensive, fashionable, general, in vogue, popular, prevailing, prevalent, rampant, rife, sought after

adj **3** common, omnipresent, ubiquitous

widget *n* apparatus, appliance, contraption, contrivance, device, doodad, doohickey, gadget, gimmick, gizmo, implement, instrument, invention, machine, mechanism, thingumajig, tool

widow *n* dame, female, gentlewoman, lady, matron, miss, mistress, woman

widower *n* bachelor, chap, dude, fellow, gent, gentleman, guy, male, man

width *n* **1** breadth, depth, dimensions, range, span

n **2** see: REACH *n* 3

wield *v* dispense, handle, maneuver, manipulate, ply

wife *n* bride, cohabitant, consort, mate, spouse, squaw, woman

wiggle *v* **1** coast, crawl, creep, glide, prowl, skate, skim, skulk, slick, slide, slink, slip, slither, snake, sneak, steal, wriggle, writhe

v **2** jig, jiggle, joggle, jump, shake, twitch

wild *adj* **1** fantastic, preposterous

adj **2** babbling, confused, incoherent, irrational

adj **3** rabid, savage, untamed, vicious, violent

adj **4** extravagant, intemperate, loose, reckless, unrestrained

adj **5** barbarian, barbaric, uncivil, uncivilized, savage

adj **6** indomitable, intractable, recalcitrant, stubborn, uncontrollable, undisciplined, unmanageable, unruly

adj **7** agitated, disorderly, excited, fierce, frantic, frenzied, furious, mad, stormy, tumultuous, turbulent

adj **8** audacious, free, liberated, licentious, loose, rampant, unbridled, unconfined, uncontrolled, uncurbed, ungoverned, unhampered, uninhibited, unrestrained, unsecured, unshackled

adj **9** see: VICIOUS *adj* 1, 3

n barren, desert, waste, wasteland, wilderness

wilderness *n* barren, desert, waste, wasteland, wild

wile *n* **1** attraction, bait, come-on, decoy, enticement, lure, magnet, ruse, seduction, snare, temptation

n **2** antic, device, diversion, gambit, gimmick, maneuver, mischief, move, plan, plot, ploy, prank, ruse, scheme, stratagem, strategy, tactic

v allure, attract, bedevil, beguile, bewitch, captivate, charm, conjure, delight, draw, enchant, enthrall, fascinate, lure, magnetize, mesmerize

will *n* **1** testament

n **2** discipline, persistence, self-control, volition, willpower

n **3** ambition, aspiration, desire, goal, hope, wish

v **1** bequeath, bestow, devise, impart

v **2** choose, elect, like, pick, wish

v **3** adjudicate, conclude, decide, determine, establish, resolve, rule

willful *adj* **1** deliberate, free, intentional, optional, unforced, unprescribed, voluntary

adj **2** bullheaded, closed-minded, deaf, firm, hardheaded, hard-line, inelastic, inflexible, intractable, intransigent, obstinate, perverse, pigheaded, refractory, resolute, rigid, stiff, stubborn, tough, unbending, uncompromising, unpliable, unpliant, unyielding

willing *adj* **1** compliant

adj **2** amenable, complaisant, compliant, cooperative, obedient, submissive, subservient

adj **3** deliberate, free, intentional, optional, unforced, unprescribed, voluntary, willful

adj **4** accommodating, agreeing, amenable, disposed, eager, glad, inclined, pleased, pliant, responsive

willingly *adv* easily, effortlessly, lightly, naturally

willpower *n* **1** discipline, persistence, self-control, will

n **2** backbone, chutzpah, determination, endurance, fortitude, grit, guts, moxie, nerve, persistence, pluck, resilience, spirit, spunk, stamina, strength, tenacity, tolerance

wilt *v* **1** droop

v **2** atrophy, decay, deteriorate, dry up, dwindle, mummify, shrink, shrivel, waste away, welter, wither, wizen

wily *adj* **1** adroit, apt, canny, clever, cunning, deft, handy, ingenious, nimble, skilled, skillful

adj **2** astute, calculating, crafty, cunning, foxy, guileful, insidious, sharp, shrewd, sly, smart, subtle, tricky, wise

adj **3** see: DECEITFUL *adj* 1

wimpy *adj* effeminate, effete, sissy, swishy

win *v* **1** count, gain, score, tally

v **2** best, conquer, defeat, master, overcome, prevail, succeed

v **3** accomplish, achieve, attain, consummate, execute, fulfill, perform, produce, pull off, realize, succeed

v **4** acquire, annex, buy, capture, gain, get, have, land, obtain, pick up, procure, purchase, requisition, secure *v* **5** access, accomplish, achieve, attain, derive, earn, fulfill, gain, get, merit, net, obtain, perform, profit, rack up, reach, realize

n accomplishment, achievement, conquest, success, triumph, victory

wince *v* blanch, cringe, flinch, jump, recoil, shrink, start

wind *n* **1** air, blow, breath, breeze, current, draft, gust, puff

n **2** blast, blizzard, blow, gale, gust, hurricane, northeaster, snowstorm, squall, storm, tempest

v **1** bend, curve, meander, veer, zigzag

v **2** coil, corkscrew, curl, distort, entwine, gnarl, spiral

winded *adj* breathless, gasping, panting

windfall *n* blessing, bonanza, boon, fortune, gain, godsend, luck, miracle, serendipity

winding *adj* crooked, meandering, serpentine, sinuous, spiral, turning, twisting, zigzagging

window *n* gap, opening

windup *n* completion, conclusion, culmination, end, finish

windy *adj* **1** blustery, stormy, tempestuous

adj **2** airy, breezy, brisk, drafty, gusty, lofty, open

wine *n* burgundy, chablis, champagne, chianti, claret, port, sauterne, sherry

wing *n* **1** addition, adjunct, annex, annexation, branch, extension

n **2** aircraft, formation, squadron

v ascend, flit, flutter, fly, sail, soar

wink *n* blink of an eye, crack, flash, jiffy, instant, minute, moment, second, shake

v blink, flash, flicker, glimmer, twinkle

winner *n* **1** advocate, champion, conqueror, hero, heroine, lead, leader, master, principal, protagonist, star, trailblazer

n **2** accomplishment, achievement, conquest, success, triumph, victory, win

winning *adj* conquering, successful, triumphant, undefeated, victorious

winnings *n* see: REWARD *n* 8

winsome *adj* alluring, appealing, attractive, charming, coquettish, coy, fast, fetching, flirtatious, seductive, sexy

wintry *adj* see: COLD *adj* 4

wipe *v* brush, clean, polish, rub

wire *n* cable, hawser, rigging

v cable, notify, radio, telegraph, telex

wired *adj* bombed, crocked, doped up, drunk, drunken, high, inebriated, intoxicated, juiced, loaded, looped, messed up, plastered, polluted, sloshed, smashed, stoned, tight, tipsy, turned on

wiretap *v* bug, check, eavesdrop, monitor, observe, oversee, spy

wiry *adj* lank, narrow, skinny, slender, slight, slim, tenuous, thin

wisdom *n* **1** knowledge, laws, philosophy, thinking

n **2** culture, education, enrichment, erudition, learning

n **3** data, discipline, facts, information, knowledge, lore, news

n **4** common sense, faculty, good sense, gumption, horse sense, judgment, logic, sense

wise *adj* **1** alert, aware

adj **2** advisable, expedient, politic, prudent, recommended, suggested

adj **3** arrogant, cocky, disrespectful, flip, impertinent, impudent

adj **4** enlightened, judgmatical, judicious, just, lucid, prudent, rational, sage, sane, sapient, sensible

adj **5** acute, alert, astute, cagey, canny, clever, cunning, deft, keen, knowing, penetrating, perceptive, piercing, quick, quick-sighted, quick-witted, receptive, responsive, sagacious, savvy, sensitive, sharp, sharp-witted, shrewd, slick, smart

adj **6** see: SENSIBLE *adj* 4, 5

adj **7** see: SLY *adj* 3

wisecrack *n* banter, comedy, crack, funniness, gag, humor, jest, joke, quip, small talk, wit, witticism

wisenheimer *adj* see: BLUNT *adj* 1

wish *n* **1** ambition, aspiration, desire, goal, hope

n **2** appeal, desire, favor, petition, plea, request

v **1** aim, aspire, hope, strive

v **2** demand, expect, require, want

v **3** choose, elect, like, pick, will

v **4** choose, covet, crave, desire, envy, fancy, lust

v **5** anticipate, await, believe, count on, expect, hope, keep the faith, look

wishful *adj* see: GREEDY *adj* 1

wishy-washy *adj* ambiguous, imperceptible, imprecise, indecisive, indefinite, indeterminate, indistinct, inexact, loose

wisp *n* see: TRACE *n* 4

wistful *adj* meditative, melancholy, musing, pensive

wit *n* **1** esprit, humor, spirit

n **2** brain, cerebrum, mind

n **3** lucidity, mind, rationality, reason, saneness, sanity, sense

n **4** banter, comedy, crack, funniness, gag, humor, jest, joke, quip, small talk, wisecrack, witticism *n* **5** acumen, astuteness, awareness, cleverness, discernment, discrimination, insight, intellect, intuition, keenness, perception, sagacity, sensitivity, shrewdness, understanding

witchcraft *n* bewitchment, enchantment, incantation, magic, occultism, sorcery, spell, voodoo, wizardry

with *prep* amid, among, inside, inside of, mid, midst

withdraw *v* **1** extract, purloin, remove, take out

v **2** extract, pull, remove, suck, tear, yank

v **3** abscond, bolt, defect, depart, exit, fall back, flee, get away, give back, go, leave, move, pull away, pull out, push off, retreat, run along, secede, shove off, take off, vacate

withdrawal *n* **1** abandonment

n **2** exile, isolation, leisure, quarantine, relaxation, rest, retirement, retreat, seclusion

n **3** abandon, departure, desertion, evacuation, exit, going, leaving, pullback, pullout, removal, retreat

withdrawn *adj* **1** aloof, blasé, calm, careless, casual, composed, cool, detached, diffident, disinterested, distant, indifferent, informal, inhibited, nonchalant, numb, remote, reserved, shy, unconcerned, unfriendly

adj **2** buried, secluded, secret, sequestered

wither *v* **1** famish, starve

v **2** blast, blight, dash, decompose

v **3** abate, decline, deteriorate, fade, fail, flag, impair, languish, wane, weaken, worsen

v **4** atrophy, decay, deteriorate, dry up, dwindle, mummify, shrink, shrivel, waste away, welter, wilt, wizen

v **5** see: DISINTEGRATE *v* **2**

withered *adj* shriveled, shrunken, wrinkled

withhold *v* **1** abstain, forbear, refrain

v **2** deny, disallow, refuse

v **3** detain, hold, hold back, keep, keep back, keep out, reserve, retain, set aside

v **4** see: CURB *v* **3**

within *prep* amid, among, inside, inside of, mid, midst, with

withstand *v* check, oppose, resist, stanch, stem, stop

witless *adj* see: SILLY *adj* **2**

witness *n* approval, confirmation, doctrine, enactment, evidence, passage, proof, testimony

v **1** behold, glimpse, look, mind, see, sight, spot

v **2** attest, authenticate, certify, confirm, corroborate, justify, notarize, prove, ratify, sanction, substantiate, support, validate, verify

witnesses *n* audience, spectators

witticism *n* banter, comedy, crack, funniness, gag, humor, jest, joke, quip, small talk, wisecrack

witty *adj* **1** comical, facetious, funny, humorous, jesting, jocular, joking, kidding

adj **2** brilliant, clever, dazzling, good, irrepressible, scintillating, smart, sparkling, sprightly

adj **3** caustic, coarse, cutting, obscene, salty, scathing, scorching, sharp, spicy, trenchant

wizard *n* **1** ace, champion, expert

n **2** brain, Einstein, genius, intellect

n **3** conjurer, diviner, magician, soothsayer, sorcerer

n **4** adviser, artist, authority, expert, guru, master, official, pro, professional, specialist, veteran

wizardry *n* bewitchment, enchantment, incantation, magic, occultism, sorcery, spell, witchcraft

wizen *v* see: WITHER *v* **4**

wobbly *adj* **1** flimsy, insecure, jiggly, rickety, shaky, teetering, unstable, unsure, vacillating, weak

adj **2** see: DELICATE *adj* **7**

woe *n* **1** gloom, grief, misery, pessimism

n **2** affliction, anguish, care, catastrophe, despair, disaster, dole, grief, heartache, mishap, pain, regret, remorse, rue, sickness, sorrow

n **3** agony, anguish, bale, concern, distress, misery, nightmare, pain, sadness, sorrow, suffering, torment, travail, tribulation, trouble

woeful *adj* **1** dismal, doleful, gloomy, lamentable, melancholy, mournful, plaintive, regretful, regrettable, rueful

adj **2** affecting, deplorable, lamentable, miserable, paltry, pathetic, pitiable, pitiful, poor, sad, unfortunate, wretched

wolf *v* bite, chew, crunch, gnaw, gulp, guzzle, munch, nibble

woman *n* **1** dame, female, gentlewoman, lady, matron, miss, mistress, spinster, widow

n **2** being, citizen, creature, entity, Homo sapiens, human, human being, individual

n **3** bride, cohabitant, consort, mate, spouse, wife

womanly *adj* female, feminine, gentle, ladylike, nurturing

wonder *n* **1** marvel, miracle, phenomenon, sensation, spectacle *n* 2 amazement, astonishment, awe, bewilderment, shock

n 3 amazement, awe, consternation, dread, fear, respect

n 4 antique, bric-a-brac, curio, curiosity, novelty, objet d'art, oddity, rarity

n 5 concern, doubt, dubiety, incertitude, indecision, mistrust, query, question, skepticism, uncertainty

v marvel

wonderful *adj* 1 excellent, extraordinary, great, impressive, noteworthy, outstanding, shining, smashing

adj 2 admirable, beautiful, delightful, glorious, good, magnificent, peachy, splendid, terrific

adj 3 excellent, fabulous, fantastic, fine, good, great, marvelous, super, terrific, tremendous

adj 4 dynamite, excellent, extraordinary, great, out of sight, outstanding, phenomenal, premier, super, superb, superlative

wont *n* see: PRACTICE *n* 6

woo *v* attract, court, encourage, flirt, invite, lure, pursue, romance, solicit, tempt

wood *n* forest, lumber, trees

wooded *adj* bucolic, country, garden, outland, pastoral, peaceful, provincial, rural, rustic

woodland *n* forest, woods

woods *n* forest, jungle, woodland

woof *v* bark, bay, cry, growl, howl, shout, snap, yap, yelp

n fabric, filling

woolly *adj* furry, hairy

word *n* 1 assurance, declaration, oath, pledge, vow

n 2 expression, idiom, locution, name, phrase, saying, term, wording

n 3 discourse, expression, speaking, speech, statement, talk, utterance

n 4 see: COMMAND *n* 3

n 5 see: RUMOR *n*

v see: VERBALIZE *v* 2

word for word *adj* exact, faithful, literal, precise, strict, true, verbatim

wording *n* 1 expression, idiom, locution, name, phrase, saying, term

n 2 cliché, diction, expression, parlance, phrase, saying, slogan, style

wordless *adj* implicit, implied, indicated, inferred, inherent, insinuated, intuitive, presumed, suggested, tacit, understood, unexpressed, unsaid

word-of-mouth *adj* expressed, oral, spoken, stated, unwritten

words *n* document

wordy *adj* bombastic, chatty, diffuse, garrulous, long-winded, loquacious, redundant, repetitious, talkative, verbose

work *n* 1 chore, drudgery, grind, labor, slavery, sweat, tedium, toil

n 2 effort, elbow grease, exertion, labor, pains, strain, struggle, toil, trouble

n 3 art, avocation, business, calling, career, discipline, employment, field, gig, job, labor, line, livelihood, occupation, office, profession, pursuit, role, schtick, situation, specialty, task, thing, trade

n 4 see: BOOK *n* 2

n 5 see: ESSAY *n*

v 1 act, function, go, perform, run

v 2 answer, do, fulfill, meet, qualify, suffice

v 3 drudge, grub, hustle, labor, slave, strain, strive, toil

workable *adj* achievable, capable, doable, feasible, possible, practical

workaday *adj* see: TYPICAL *adj* 2

worker *adj* ancillary, assistant, collateral, complementary, dependent, lesser, minor, secondary, sub, subject, subordinate, subsidiary, substitute, supporter

n aide, aide-de-camp, assistant, attendant, employee, hand, helper, hired hand, laborer, servant

workers *n* crew, employees, faculty, help, personnel, staff

working *adj* 1 active, alive, functioning, live, operative

adj 2 busy, engaged, employed, functional, in use

adj 3 see: PRACTICAL *adj* 4

workings *n* action, apparatus, gear, machinery, works

workmanship *n* see: SKILL *n* 3

workout *n* aerobics, bodybuilding, calisthenics, exercise, jazzercise, slimnastics

works *n* action, apparatus, gear, machinery

world *n* 1 humanity, human race, mankind

n 2 cosmos, creation, firmament, grand scale, macrocosm, nature, solar system, universe

n 3 earth, globe, home, the planet

worldly *adj* 1 carnal

adj 2 common, earthly, earthy, mundane, pedestrian, terrestrial, uncelestial

worldwide *adj* broad, general, global, planetary, universal, urban, widespread

worm *v* edge in, foist, imbue, infiltrate, insinuate, penetrate, permeate, sneak in

worn *adj* 1 faded, frayed, poor, run-down, shabby, tattered, threadbare

adj 2 aged, age-old, ancient, antique, elderly, gray, grizzled, old, olden, senior, timeworn, venerable

adj 3 see: OBSOLETE *adj*

adj 4 see: WEARY *adj 1*

worried *adj 1* anxious, careworn, distracted, distraught, distressed, frantic, harassed, tormented, troubled, upset

adj 2 anxious, edgy, fidgety, impatient, nervous, nervy, queasy, restive, restless, tense, troubled, uncomfortable, uneasy

adj 3 see: AFRAID *adj 2*

worry *n 1* anxiety, apprehension, distress, stress, sweat

n 2 affliction, alarm, anxiety, apprehension, care, consternation, dismay, dread, fear, fright, horror, ordeal, panic, terror, trepidation, trial

n 3 annoyance, anxiety, apprehension, bother, care, concern, disquiet, disquietude, doubt, irritation, misgiving, reservation, restlessness, restraint, skepticism, trouble, uneasiness, vexation

n 4 see: PAIN *n 4*

v 1 brood, fret, fuss

v 2 affect, bother, burden, concern, daunt, disturb, faze, intimidate, oppress

v 3 see: ANNOY *v 1, 3*

worse *adj* deficient, inferior, meaner, not as good, poorer

worsen *v* abate, decline, deteriorate, fade, fail, flag, impair, languish, wane, weaken

worship *n 1* devotion, reverence

n 2 admiration, adoration, glory

v 1 admire, adore, cherish, dote on, idolize, love, respect, revere, venerate

v 2 acclaim, applaud, celebrate, commend, eulogize, exalt, extol, glorify, hail, honor, laud, praise, resound, salute, toast

worshiped *adj* adored, beloved, cherished, dear, esteemed, loved, precious, respected, revered, venerable

worst *adj* last, least, lowest, poorest

worth *n 1* caliber, excellence, goodness, merit, quality, value

n 2 charge, cost, expense, fare, outlay, payment, price, rate

worthier *adj* advantageous, better, desirable, enjoyable, preferable, superior, worthwhile

worthless *adj 1 see:* FUTILE *adj 3*

adj 2 see: INFERIOR *adj 6*

adj 3 see: TRIVIAL *adj 1*

worthwhile *adj 1* beneficial, fulfilling, gratifying, pleasing, rewarding

adj 2 admirable, commendable, excellent, fine, praiseworthy

adj 3 advantageous, better, desirable, enjoyable, preferable, superior

adj 4 constructive, favorable, fruitful, helpful, positive, productive, useful

worthy *adj 1* admirable, respectable

adj 2 deserving, estimable, excellent, honorable, noble, precious, sterling, valuable

wound *n 1* bruise, hurt, injury, pain, sprain

n 2 cut, gash, incision, nick, pierce, prick, puncture

v 1 bruise, hurt, injure, lacerate, mangle

v 2 execute, hit, shoot

v 3 burden, deject, depress, dishearten, grieve, hurt, lambnt, sadden

wow *v* amaze, astonish, astound, awe, delight, floor, impress

wrangle *v 1* argue, bargain, barter, dicker, negotiate

v 2 see: QUARREL *v*

wrap *v 1* bundle, cover, enclose, envelop, package

v 2 close, package, seal

n cape, cloak, coat, mantle

wrapper *n* binder, capsule, case, casing, cover, envelope, holder, sheath, skin

wrath *n 1* agitation, craze, excitement, frenzy, furor, fury, fuss, outrage, passion, tumult

n 2 see: ANGER *n 2*

wreath *n* band, coil, crown, garland, loop, ring

wreck *n 1* debris, fragment, hulk, remains, rubbish, rubble, shell, wreckage

n 2 accident, collision, crackup, crash, destruction, mishap, pileup, smash, smashup, wreckage

v 1 collide, crash, demolish

v 2 annihilate, decimate, demolish, destroy, destruct, devastate, dismantle, overturn, pulverize, raze, rub out, ruin, shatter, smash, tear down

wreckage *n 1* debris, fragment, hulk, remains, rubbish, rubble, shell, trash, wreck

n 2 accident, collision, crackup, crash, destruction, mishap, pileup, smash, wreck

wrench *v 1* jerk, pull, tear, tug, twist, wring, yank

v 2 coerce, exact, extort, gouge, shake down, squeeze, wrest, wring

wrest *v 1* force, pull, seize, turn

v 2 coerce, exact, extort, gouge, shake down, squeeze, wrench, wring

wrestle *v* combat, contend, duel, fight, grapple, spar

wretch *n* brute, demon, devil, fiend, rogue, villain

wretched *adj 1* affecting, deplorable, lamentable, miserable, paltry, pathetic, pitiable, pitiful, poor, sad, unfortunate

adj 2 base, beneath, despicable, ignoble, inferior, low, lowdown, sordid, squalid, unworthy, vile, vulgar

wriggle *v* coast, crawl, creep, glide, prowl, skate, skim, skulk, slick, slide, slink, slip, slither, snake, sneak, steal, wiggle

wring *v* 1 distress, disturb, move, rend

v 2 jerk, pull, tear, tug, twist, wrench, yank

v 3 coerce, exact, extort, gouge, shake down, squeeze, wrest

wrinkle *v* crease, fold, muss, pleat, rumple

n crease, fold, pleat, rumple

wrinkled *adj* shriveled, withered

writ *n* citation, notification, subpoena, summons, warrant

write *v* 1 copy, note, record, summarize, transcribe

v 2 doodle, draw, jot, scratch, scrawl, scribble

v 3 author, compose, create, draft, pen, prepare, type

v 4 catalog, enroll, inscribe, list, register

writer *n* 1 columnist, commentator, correspondent, editor, interviewer, journalist, newspaperman

n 2 author, authoress, biographer, creator, dramatist, essayist, journalist, novelist, playwright, reporter, screenwriter

writhe *v* 1 fidget, squirm

v 2 coast, crawl, creep, glide, prowl, skate, skim, skulk, slick, slide, slink, slip, slither, snake, sneak, steal, wiggle, wriggle

writing *n* 1 handwriting, penmanship, script

n 2 book, correspondence, edition, folio, issue, manuscript, monograph, opus, paperback, printing, publication, text, tome, volume

wrong *adj* 1 erroneous, false, faulty, imprecise, inaccurate, incorrect, inexact, mistaken, untrue

adj 2 criminal, disgraceful, felonious, illegal, illegitimate, illicit, lawless, prohibited, unlawful, wrongful

adj 3 afoul, amiss, awry, bad, bum, improper, out of kilter, poor, rotten, unsatisfactory

adj 4 see: EVIL *adj* 4

n 1 inequity, injustice, prejudice

n 2 complaint, grievance, hardship, injury, injustice

n 3 corruption, depravity, dishonesty, immorality, impurity, vice

n 4 error, malfeasance, malpractice, mis-

behavior, misdeed, mismanagement, offense, wrongdoing

n 5 see: CRIME *n* 3

v abuse, brutalize, exploit, harm, ill-treat, injure, maltreat, mistreat, molest, persecute

wrongdoer *n* accused, con, convict, criminal, crook, culprit, delinquent, felon, guilty party, inmate, lawbreaker, offender, perpetrator, prisoner, scofflaw, suspect, swindler

wrongdoing *n* 1 error, malfeasance, malpractice, misbehavior, misdeed, mismanagement, offense, transgression, wrong

n 2 crime, dishonor, disobedience, evil, fault, felony, infamy, infraction, injury, iniquity, lawbreaking, misdeed, misdemeanor, offense, outrage, sin, transgression, trespass, vice, violation, wrong

wrongful *adj* 1 biased, inequitable, partial, uneven, unfair, unjust

adj 2 see: ILLICIT *adj*

wry *adj* contemptuous, cynical, derisive, ironic, mocking, sarcastic, sardonic, scornful

X

x-rated *adj* see: VULGAR *adj* 2

Y

yacht *n* craft, cruiser, freighter, frigate, ketch, liner, ocean liner, sailboat, schooner, ship, steamship

yachtsman *n* mariner, mate, navy man, sailor, salt, seaman

yak *v* cackle, chat, gab, talk

yank *n* drag, jerk, pull, tug

v 1 extract, pull, remove, suck, tear

v 2 jerk, pull, tear, tug, twist, wrench

Yank *n* American

Yankee *n* American

yap *v* bark, bay, cry, growl, howl, shout, snap, yelp

yard *n* field, grass, green, grounds, lawn

yardstick *n* benchmark, criterion, gauge, measure, observation, standard

yarn *n* 1 cable, cord, fiber, hemp, lanyard, line, rope, strand, string, thread

n 2 anecdote, description, fantasy, fiction, invention, myth, narration, narrative, novel, sketch, story

yaw *n* angle, bend, bow, detour, deviation, double, shift, tack, turn

yearling *n* colt, equine, filly, foal, gelding, horse, mare, mount, nag, steed

yearn v ache, covet, crave, desire, hanker, hunger, itch, long, lust, need, pine, want

yearning n 1 appetite, craving, desire, eroticism, hankering, hunger, itch, longing, lust, passion, urge, yen

n 2 avarice, covetousness, craving, greed, selfishness

adj see: GREEDY adj 1

years n aeon, age, cycle, decade, eon, epoch, era, eternity, forever, long time, millennium, period, reign, span, stage

yeast n leaven

yell n 1 alarm, call, hail, shout, signal, whoop

n 2 bark, bellow, blare, holler, roar, scream, shout, shriek, thunder

v 1 bawl out, bellow, berate, chew out, mock, rail, rant, rave, revile, roar, scold, tell off, tongue-lash

v 2 bark, bellow, blare, call, cry, holler, howl, roar, scream, screech, shout, shriek, shrill, squeal, thunder

yellow adj 1 canary, jasmine, lemon, saffron

adj 2 chicken, cowardly, fearful, gutless, spineless

adj 3 ashen, ashy, blanched, colorless, pale, pallid, sallow, sickly, sooty, wan

yelp v bark, bay, cry, growl, howl, shout, snap, woof, yap

yen n 1 see: DESIRE n 2

n 2 see: FONDNESS n 2

yenta n busybody, gossip, interloper, intruder, kibitzer, snoop

yet adv 1 but, excepting, further, however, just, merely, nevertheless, only, simply

adv 2 at any rate, but, however, moreover, nevertheless, nonetheless, notwithstanding, still, though

yield n 1 by-product, derivative, end product, end result, growth, outgrowth, output, product, production, productivity, result

n 2 assets, cash, earnings, gain, gross, haul, net, payback, proceeds, profits, receipts, return, revenue

n 3 crop, fruits, grain, harvest

v 1 give

v 2 bear, produce, turn out

v 3 bring in, pay, profit, return

v 4 bring about, conclude, end, generate, result in

v 5 abandon, acquiesce, cede, give up, hand over, leave, relinquish, resign, submit, surrender

v 6 accede, acquiesce, bend, bow, buckle, capitulate, cave, comply, concede, cry

uncle, defer, give in, give up, relent, submit, succumb, surrender, twist

v 7 fall, give up, go under, submit, surrender

yielding adj 1 controllable, docile, manageable, pliable

adj 2 acquiescent, compliant, docile, easy, meek, mild, nonresistant, obedient, passive, resigned, submissive, tame, tolerant, unassertive

adj 3 mushy, pulpy, soft, spongy, squashy, squelchy

adj 4 adaptable, adjustable, changeable, flexible, limber, malleable, maneuverable, moldable, plastic, pliable, pliant, responsive, soft, supple, swayed

yodel v carol, chant, harmonize, hum, sing

yokel n cowboy, rustic

yonder adv beyond, farther than, past

young adj 1 tentative, untested

adj 2 adolescent, fresh, green, immature, juvenile, precocious, undeveloped, unfledged, unready, youthful

n brood, litter

youngster n adolescent, boy, child, girl, juvenile, kid, minor, teenager, youth

youth n 1 adolescence, childhood, puberty

n 2 adolescent, boy, child, girl, juvenile, kid, minor, teenager, teeny-bopper, youngster

youthful adj adolescent, fresh, green, immature, juvenile, precocious, undeveloped, unfledged, young

Z

zany adj see: ABSURD adj 2

n buffoon, comedian, comedienne, comic, fool

zeal n alacrity, ardor, delight, devotion, diligence, enjoyment, enthusiasm, excitement, fervor, fire, flame, gaiety, gusto, passion, relish, savor, zest

zealot n 1 believer, convert, follower

n 2 bug, crusader, enthusiast, fanatic, fiend, freak, hobbyist, maniac, monomaniac, nut

zealous adj 1 blind, conscientious, loyal, meticulous, religious, strict

adj 2 extreme, extremist, fanatic, fanatical, rabid, radical, revolutionary

adj 3 ambitious, assiduous, diligent, energetic, hard-working, industrious, persevering, persistent, resolute

adj 4 ardent, enthusiastic, excitable, fervent, fiery, flaming, hot-blooded, impassioned, intense, passionate, stirring, sweaty *adj* **5** anxious, ardent, avid, breathless, desirous, eager, enthusiastic, excited, fain, impatient, impetuous, keen, passionate

adj **6** emotional, fervent, fiery

zenith *n* acme, apex, apogee, climax, crescendo, crest, crown, culmination, epitome, height, noon, peak, pinnacle, point, prime, summit, tip, top, ultimate, utmost

zero *n* goose egg, naught, nil, none, nonentity, nothing, zilch

zest *n* alacrity, ardor, delight, devotion, diligence, enjoyment, enthusiasm, excitement, fervor, fire, flame, gaiety, gusto, passion, relish, savor, thrill, zeal

zesty *adj* aromatic, lively, peppery, piquant, poignant, pungent, racy, snappy, spicy, spirited, vigorous

zigzag *v* bend, curve, meander, veer

zigzagging *adj* crooked, meandering, serpentine, sinuous, spiral, turning, twisting

zilch *n* goose egg, naught, nil, none, nothing, zero

zing *n* see: VIGOR *n* 2

Zion *n* heaven, utopia

zip *n* **1** breeze, cinch, dash, ease, snap

n **2** see: VIGOR *n* 2

v see: RUSH *v* 3

zipper *n* buckle, catch, clasp, clip, fastener, latch, pin

zippy *adj* active, agile, astir, brisk, catty, energetic, lively, nimble, quick, sprightly

zone *n* **1** address, destination, direction, location

n **2** area, arena, belt, field, realm, region, section, space, territory, tract

n **3** area, district, domain, environs, jurisdiction, locality, neighborhood, parish, precinct, province, range, region, section, sphere, vicinity, ward

zoo *n* aquarium, aviary, menagerie, terrarium

zoom *v* **1** ascend, climb, increase, rise, soar

v **2** focus

v **3** flash, speed

zygote *n* bud, egg, embryo, fetus, seed